TURNER PUBLISHING COMPANY

Pinkney's Tomb ca 1880. Houses the graves of Pinkney Hufstedler, his wife, Louise Jane Randel, daughter, Josephine H. Whitewell, mother-in-law Malinda Mahalia Markham Randel and father-in-law Nathaniel Moses Randel. This structure is on the National Historic Register.

TURNER PUBLISHING COMPANY

Created by Kenny R. Rose, Publishing Consultant
Turner Publishing Company

Copyright © 1994 Perry County Historical Society
Publishing Rights: Turner Publishing Company

This book or any part thereof may not be reproduced without the written consent of the Author and Publisher.

The materials were compiled and produced using available information. Turner Publishing Company and the Perry County Historical Society regret they cannot assume liability for errors or omissions.

Library of Congress Catalog
Card No: 94-61033

ISBN: 978-1-68162-209-5

Limited Edition of which this is number _____.

TABLE OF CONTENTS

Foreword 4	Education in Perry County 23
Publisher's Message 5	Brief History of Black Schools 27
Acknowledgment 6	Perry County Library 28
Perry County History 9	Tribute 31
History of Lobelville 14	Memorials 32
Perry County Newspapers 15	Churches 35
Perry County in the Civil War 16	Photo Album 60
Flatwoods Community 17	Family Histories 63
Grist Mill on Lower Cane Creek 19	Index 311
The Jolly Dozen 20	

A steam driven sawmill on Brush Creek in 1910.

FOREWORD

Billy Tucker

The Perry County Historical Society was formed many years ago by a few individuals with one purpose in mind. That was to bring together those persons interested in the history and genealogy of the county, to preserve and perpetuate the records of our ancestors, to publish public and private genealogical and historical records and to encourage and educate beginning genealogists in their research.

In the beginning, as a rule, we were content to gather bits and pieces of information and to share these with each other. As our interest grew, and the interest of others, the need for space and a place to store materials grew. This led to the creation of an archives area at the Perry County Public Library. Then came the restoration of Pinkney's Tomb and the placing of it on the National Register of Historical Places. Next came our state and federal charters. This led to our charter membership drive that brought 164 new members into our group. Then came the major undertaking of publishing a book. Never did we realize what a major undertaking this was. We set our goal for the book to be in print in time for the 175th anniversary of the forming of the county. This meant moving fast and working hard. We made it!!!!!

To future generations, we believe we are leaving you a rich written legacy, documented to the best of our ability, that shows the wide diversity of people who care about their heritage.

Billy Tucker

Billy Tucker, Coordinator
Perry County History Book

Acknowledgment

Left to right: Billy Tucker, Mary Bowen, Dorotha Hudson and Gus Steele.

When the Perry County Historical Society decided to publish a Perry County History, we knew this was going to be a difficult undertaking. Gus Steele, Billy Tucker, Mary Bowen, and Dorotha Hudson "volunteered" to head up the project and since that day have worked many long hours collecting, organizing, recording, typing, and editing family histories. But they were not alone; many others, too numerous to try to name, helped in many ways. The result of all this work is the 175th Anniversary Perry County History and Families book.

The historical society presents this book to the citizens Perry County of yesterday, today and tomorrow as a symbol of Perry County's spirit that is repeatedly evidenced in the family histories found on its pages.

Old Time Fiddler's Contest in the old high school auditorium.

Logging was a means of earning a living in the early 1900s in many parts of Perry County.

Elected officials in 1893. Front row, l to r: W.R. Thompson, School Superintendent; Eli Duncan, Surveyor; Jimmy Lewis, Circuit Court Clerk; C.L. Pearson, County Court Clerk; Thomas Whitwell, County Judge; Jim Gregory, Magistrate; John Beasley, Trustee. Back row, l to r: J.C. Whitaker, Magistrate; L.R. Owens, Constable; J.H. Nix, Magistrate; E.I. Hinson, Sheriff; Bill Crosby, Deputy Sheriff; Barney Depriest, Assistant Surveyor; John Tatum, Constable.

Perry County History

Perry County History

There is very little to be said about the first settlers as authenticated records are scarce. It is to be assumed that they are of the famous Scotch Irish extraction, which is so prevalent in Tennessee, especially in the hill and mountain districts. From the date of the first settling until now the same families have predominated, indicating that there has been little influx of new blood. The settlements were made in the valleys along the water courses. They, for many years, were confined to these localities. There is no account of settlements prior to 1818; but it is evident that a number of individuals settled in the territory of the county before that date.

These early settlers must have come into the county via the Tennessee River, as the first known settlements were on Tom's Creek. Its proximity to a good landing site would have been a decided advantage for this beginning.

Naturally, the county being wild, they would have encountered numerous obstacles and hardships. First, a crude house of logs had to be raised, which was done next to the land that had to be cleared of its canebrakes and underbrush and growth in preparation for crops.

The settlers of southern Hickman and Humphreys County presented a petition to the state government on September 22, 1819 asking for the creation of a new county in that area. The county was to be named for Commodore Oliver Hazard Perry, a naval officer and hero of the War of 1812.

The county of Perry was created by an act of the General Assembly of the State, passed in November 14, 1819. The act provided "that a new county be established north of Wayne, west of Hickman, by the name of Perry County, beginning at the southeast corner of Humphreys, and to include all the territory lying between Humphreys, Hardin, Wayne and Hickman Counties." The act also provided that, until otherwise directed, the quarterly sessions and circuit court should be held at the house of James Yates, on Tom's Creek, or at such other place in said county as the justices thereof might select. The territory originally included in the county embraced, in addition to what it now contains, nearly all of Decatur County.

The first magistrates (justices) of the county were James Dixon, Joseph Brown, William O. Britt, William Holmes, John L. Houston, Oswald Griffin, Enoch Hooper, Mr. Humm, and Green B. Newson. The house of James Dixon, on Lick Creek, was the place selected by the magistrates for holding their first sessions, and there, on the first Monday of January, 1820, they met and organized the county of Perry. Joseph Brown was elected chairman of the court of quarterly sessions (county court), and the first county officers were elected as follows: William Jarmon, Clerk; West Wood, Sheriff; John A. Rains, Register; Aaron Lewis, Trustee; Jacob Harmon, Ranger; Mark Murphy, Coroner; Joseph Dixon and four others were elected constables. In 1821, the year following the organization, the county seat was established at Perryville, on the west bank of the Tennessee River. At this time and in the days following, Perryville was a political and business center of importance. David Crockett, Andrew Jackson, Sam Houston, James K. Polk

Perry county's first courthouse where Perry County was organized on the first Monday of January in 1820.

Perry County's second courthouse was erected in 1868. It was destroyed by fire on January 1, 1928.

and other dignitaries are said to have visited there. An act of the General Assembly passed in November of 1845 provided that all the territory of Perry County lying west of the Tennessee River be formed into a new county, to be known as the county of Decatur. Accordingly, in 1846, the county of Perry was divided and the county of Decatur established with the Tennessee River as the boundary line between the two counties. The courts of Perry County were then adjourned to Harrisburg, a point 4 miles south of Linden. Here they were held two years. Meanwhile, the location of the new county seat was the absorbing question of the citizens. Harrisburg and Linden were competing points. An election was held and it was decided in favor of Linden by a majority of six votes and in 1848 the county seat was permanently established in Linden where it still remains. The site of Linden, consisting of forty acres, was donated to the county by David R. Harris. He reserved a few lots and named the place Linden at the suggestion of Major Thomas M. Brashear with reference to the poem "Hohenlinden" by Thomas Campbell. The town was surveyed into lots including a public square for county buildings. The lots were sold and the proceeds of the sales thereof were appropriated to defray the expense of erecting public buildings. The county was divided into eleven civil districts.

The following is a copy from *The Linden Times* February 26, 1880:

A correction: In our last issue in a local item we stated that Linden was originally called Harrisburg, after our late citizen David Harris, father of our townsman G. L. Harris, and Mrs. J. M. Dotson, but in this our informant was mistaken.

Harrisburg was at one time the county seat, and the court met there for several terms, but Harrisburg was at what we know as John L. Webb's farm, four miles south of Linden, and was called such in honor of Dr. Wyatt Harris who lived in this county at the time. James Simmons of Cypress Creek was a member of the jury there in 1846 and from what we learn is the only living citizen of the county who served on the jury at the court of Harrisburg.

Linden was first named Milton in honor of Judge Milton Brown who is yet living at Jackson, Tennessee. Judge Brown was then the member of congress from this district and a most popular gentleman with his constituents. The name was selected by commissioners. When the act of legislature came to be enacted Maj. T. M. Brashear gave the name of Linden and established it as a county seat. Mr. David Harris owned the land and gave the county the land for the courthouse, etc. We are informed that the name of the town was not changed from Milton to Linden because of any loss of respect that Maj. Brashear or the people had for Judge Milton Brown, but mainly because there was another place named Milton in the State.

We make this correction and give these facts not because the error of our former statement would injure anyone, but because it is important the present as well as the future generations should not be misinformed as to any historical point of their county, and from the very vague and conflicting ideas already in existence the importance will be seen. There are but few alive now and in a few years there will not be any alive who figured in the early history of our county, so we cannot be too particular in stating any facts relative to our county history, for in future years it will be a matter of no small interest to have full and correct statement of these facts. We are informed by the oldest citizens and the best authority that these facts are correct.

Editor S. L. Neeley

The first courthouse in Perryville was built of logs and the second one of brick. The latter was used until the division of the county in 1846. The first courthouse at Linden was also made of logs. This was replaced in 1849-50 with a frame building. The latter was consumed by fire during the Civil War with all the records therein contained. Some of the public records, however, being in offices outside of the courthouse, were preserved. The next courthouse was a very substantial and quite ornamental brick structure of two stories with the county offices on the first floor and the court rooms on the second. It was erected in 1868 at a cost of $9,500. It was built by a man by the name of A. Gholston of Mt. Pleasant.

The building was destroyed by fire on January 1, 1928. In the years of 1928-29, a modern fire-resistant building was erected and in that time was one of the most attractive courthouses in this section of the state and is presently still in use. (1994)

The topography of this county is beautiful from the regularity and great number of the ridges. Buffalo Ridge, west of Buffalo River, rises to the height of 700 feet above tide water and 300 feet above the adjacent valleys. It traverses the county longitudinally north and south throughout its entire extent, and sends out westward eight subordinate ridges, nearly to the Tennessee River, a distance of nine miles. Between these various ridges streams of pure sparkling water flow in parallel lines and empty into the Tennessee River. On the eastern side of Buffalo River are parallel spurs running down

Present courthouse which was constructed in 1928-29. Photo taken in 1994.

to the banks of Buffalo River. The spurs are seldom over one mile in length and the troughs which they form convey the waters from the eastern slope of the ridge into Buffalo River. The portion of the county east of Buffalo River is also fluted with edges and valleys, similar to the western side and many beautiful streams bordered by fertile lowlands empty into that stream which is the great artery of this county. Beginning at the southern end of the county the tributaries of the Buffalo from the eastern side are: (1) Sinking, (2) Rockhouse, (3) Hurricane, (4) Short Creek, (5) Coon Creek, (6) Brush Creek, (7) Cane Creek, (8) Lagoon, (9) Russell Creek and Lost Creek. Most of these creeks are rapid in their descent and flow alternatively over gravely beds and limestone rock. They have a sufficiency of waterpower to drive mills. The tributaries of the Tennessee beginning at the southern limits of the county are: (1) White Oak, (2) Bee Creek, (3) Cedar Creek, (4) Marsh Creek, (5) Cypress Creek, (6) Spring Creek, (7) Lick Creek, (8)Tom's Creek, (9) Roan's Creek, (10) Crooked Creek and (11) Blue Creek. The average length of these creeks is about nine miles and they usually flow through flat wide bottoms, the channels often changing, the water cutting out the banks on one side or the other and throwing up a wide expanse of rounded pebbles and sand on the other.

In the *Linden News* of December 1924, Mr. B. W. DePriest, a writer of history for the paper states that: White Oak Creek was so called by the vast amount of white oak timber growing there. Marsh Creek was so called because of the wet marshes and slushes near the mouth of the creek. Cedar Creek was so called for the vast amount of cedar timber on that creek. Cypress Creek was so called from the cypress ponds and large trees on that creek. Deer Creek got its name from the large quantity of deer that were there when the county was settled. Roan's Creek from the fact that during the time surveyors were in the area a roan horse got loose and ran away. Lick Creek got its name from the salt licks found there. Buck Fork on Marsh Creek got its name from two large buck deer, both dead with their horns locked together being found there.

The geology of this county, as given by The State Board of Agriculture is as follows: "Blue and gray limestones outcrop in all the valleys excepting a few in the northern part of the county. The limestones belong to the formations known among the geologists as Niagara and Lower Helderberg. Many of the bluffs along the Tennessee River are made up of their strata. There are a number of gladly places in the county formed by the outcrops of the Niagara limestones which have supplied geologists at home and abroad with fine specimens of fossils. Many of the fossils have been taken to Europe. Above the Lower Helderberg limestones, which are generally thin bedded, blue and full of fossils, lay the black shale, a formation which everywhere attracts attention mainly because it is mistaken as an indication of stonecoal. This bed ranges in thickness from a few feet to thirty or more. Above the black shale and constituting the mass of tops of the ridges is the siliceous division of the Lower Carboniferous. The lower strata of this division are often silico-calareous shales, mixed, more or less, with limestones. The upper portion contains more limestone which often shows cherty masses; the latter, being liberated, cover, more or less, the tops of the ridges.

More than one-half of all the land in the county is charged with iron ore. There seems to be an almost inexhaustible supply of the material. It is found, however, in the greatest quantities along Marsh, Cedar and Sinking Creeks. Along the creeks and on the west side of Buffalo Ridge blossoms outcrops in dark, bluish boulders whose great weight shows iron to be the predominant ingredient. The Cedar Creek Iron Furnace was erected on Cedar Creek near its mouth by Wallace Dixon about the year 1834. It was rebuilt about twelve years later by Ewing, McNickle & Co. It was afterward run by different persons and suspended operations in 1862 and has not been run since. It used to make 1,500 tons of pig metal annually.

A rough species of reddish, variegated marble, useful and beautiful for building purposes, is found in great quantities in different parts of the county. There is a mine of wealth in the "bowels of the earth," in Perry County remaining undeveloped. The cheap means of transportation for heavy articles, which the Tennessee River furnishes, will undoubtedly lead capital to this mine and cause it to be developed in some future day.

William Patterson, son of Robert Patterson was born on Tom's Creek in 1818, giving clear indication of permanent settlements at this early date. Rev. Wm. Hodge, Rev. Samuel Atkins, John Stanley, Wm. O. Britt, Enoch Hooper and John Young settled on Tom's Creek about the year 1818. William Patterson, if not the first, was among the first born in the county. The family of Whitwells, Thomas, John, Samuel and James Lomax, Homer Cude, James Salmon, John Anderson, Rev. Joseph Kelley and Jesse DePriest were among the first settlers on Cane Creek. Jacob Hufstedler, born on board a sailing ship en route from Germany to America in 1775, settled with his family on Cane Creek in 1821. John Horner, Elbert Matthews, Jerry Hooligan and James Wilkins and their families settled on Buffalo River near Beardstown about the year 1824. Joseph Tucker, from North Carolina, settled near Linden in 1818. Isaac W. Stanley settled on Buffalo River and was a surveyor of Perry County for many years. James Dixon (at whose house the county of Perry was organized), James Yates, Wiley Tanner, John and Jesse Newton and others settled on Lick Creek as early at least as 1818. Joseph Brown, William and Nathan Ward and Nat Dabbs were among the first settlers on Marsh Creek. Samuel Denton, John Tracy and Jesse Childress settled on Cedar Creek about 1818. Joshua Briley, Thomas Evans, Nicholas Welch and James Scott were the first settlers on White Oak Creek. Jacob Fraley, George Hollabough and John Webb settled on Sinking Creek about 1818 or 1820 and about the same time David Hogan, Hodge Adams and Nancy Randal settled on Rockhouse Creek. Allen Barber and the Jarmons settled on Hurricane Creek; Thomas Dowdy, Joshua Cates, and Abraham Barber on Coon Creek. Other early settlers of the county were Wm. Holmes, John L. Houston, Oswald Griffin, John Weems, Green B. Newsom, West Wood, John A. Rains, Aaron Lewis, Jacob Harmon, Mark Murphy and Joseph Dixon. The first steamboat that passed up the Tennessee River was the "General Green" in 1819. Many of the pioneer settlers visited the river to see the great curiosity.

James Dixon built the first horse mill in the county on Lick Creek about the year 1820 and the first water mill in the county was erected on Cedar Creek in 1821 by John Tracy. The first merchant in the county was James Yates who began business about the year 1819 on Tom's Creek. The first cotton gin was erected on Cedar Creek in 1821 by Samuel Denton. The raising of cotton was not a prominent industry in the county until after the close of the Civil War when the farmers engaged in it extensively for a few years, but, finding it unprofitable, entirely abandoned it.

For some years the leading industry among the farmers was the cultivation of peanuts of which there were from 500,000 to 800,000 bushels produced annually in the county, this being one of the leading counties in the state for that product.

Britt's Landing became the focal point for the peanut industry. William O. Britt, born January 24, 1819 in Humphreys County (which could have been the same area as Tom's Creek since that area was Humphreys County in 1819), used his prior business experience as a sales-

Bridge across Buffalo River going east on Highway 100. It was built in the early 1930s.

Marking off ground for peanuts.

man and merchant to establish Britt's Landing on the east side of the Tennessee River in 1839. Here he erected warehouses and provided docking space for the landing of barges. Cotton was the most prominent product shipped early in the history of this area but peanuts dominated after the 1860s. The post office was established at Britt's Landing in 1850. Britt erected a peanut recleaner and warehouse to consolidate the activities of peanut culture and capture most of the commercial aspect of this business. The cleaner operation burned in the early 1890s and the Britt family ("Billy," his sons Thomas C. and George) headed up a company incorporated as the Southern Peanut Company. In 1895, a second cleaner was erected. Business boomed and a second warehouse was erected at Denson's Landing a few miles south of Britt's. This industry created countless jobs for the citizens of this area. In the cleaning, grading, warehousing, and shipping area, mostly women and blacks were employed but farmers from all across the county were involved in the production of peanuts. One historical account written in 1874 gives the following: "The introduction of the culture of the peanut in the county marked a social revolution. Previous to this time almost all the cloth used in everyday wear was manufactured by the wives and daughters of the farmers. But as the labor required to cultivate the peanut was not so confining, nor so arduous or long continued as the labor of the spinning wheel and loom (the latter were exchanged for the hoe) with which they were able to buy for six months labor in the field what before required twelve to manufacture within doors. It is no uncommon sight to see women of fairest face and comeliest form with hand encased in gloves and their faces screened from the ray of a blazing sun by an old-fashioned sunbonnet, hoeing long rows of peanuts, while the sterner sex drives the plow. And especially when this crop is being harvested are the nimble fingers of the women of peculiar value. It is said that a woman can pick from the vines at least one-third more in a day than a man.

The Southern Peanut Company went bankrupt in the 1920s and the peanut industry was doomed in Perry County.

The number of bushels of cereals raised in Perry County, 1885, was as follows: Indian corn, 423,461; rye, 565; barley, 125; oats, 23,874; wheat, 16,051. The number of animals reported in the county were: horses and mules, 2,462; cattle, 4,806; sheep, 4,799; hogs, 16,764. The number of dogs is not reported but it is declared on good authority that there were more dogs than sheep in the county. Two or three curs and five or six hounds constituted the ordinary pack of dogs owned by many individuals. Owing to the fact that only a small portion of the land were cleared, thus leaving extensive forest, wild animals, such as deer, wildcats, foxes, coons, etc., and wild turkey abounded in considerable numbers. The people enjoy the sport of hunting hence the great number of dogs. When the county was first settled the above enumerated animals as well as bears, wolves and panthers were numerous. There are none of the latter now remaining.

Perry County was somewhat noted for its tanneries. The first yard established in the county was a place on the Tennessee River known as Rat Tail by Charles Gotthardt, a native of Germany. This yard was started about 1843, receiving its peculiar name from the circumstance of its having been infested with rats disembarked from a St. Louis barge loaded with hides. During the ten years succeeding the foregoing date, ten tanyards were established at different points in the county, and the annual product of all then within the county according to the best estimate that can now be made, was $50,000. The war and its consequences compelled all these tanneries, excepting two, to suspend operations. Robert Houssels and James B. Sutton operated the two until the late 1880s. Mousetail Landing, on the Tennessee River, named in contradistinction of the old landing, Rat Tail, was the principal place of shipment for the tanning products. During the early 1960s through the extensive efforts of Dr. James R. Jordan and James O. Tucker, the T.V.A. and the State of Tennessee began the development of a rustic scenic park on the Mousetail Landing site. At the present time, the park consists of 1,197 acres of hiking trails, campgrounds, boat docks, launching ramps, rustic trail shelters and commons area for family outings.

Perry County has not grown in industry and population as many of the counties around it has. The following is a report by the Bureau of Agriculture for the State of Tennessee, published in 1874:

Though Perry County offers some fine inducements for an industrious population few immigrants came to it. This is doubtless owing to a want of railroad facilities and of school advantages. The want of the latter has caused many good citizens to leave the county and seek other locations where their children can enjoy the privilege of attending good schools. This want is scarcely felt by a large portion of the population. Generally with limited education, they do not recognize what a powerful lever it is in building up the prosperity and greatness of a community, in attracting population, in diversifying pursuits, in awakening dormant energies, in multiplying the effectiveness of labor, in softening manners, in nursing manly sentiment, in mitigating ferocity, in harmonizing the different shades of society, and beautifying, adorning, and enabling private life and manners. Schools, without which in this age, there can be no permanent progress, meet with but little favor. A tax for public works is so obnoxious that to advocate it is to render one extremely unpopular. The convenience of the public is made secondary to the convenience of an individual. Money paid for public improvements, in the opinion of the many, is money abstracted to benefit all others except the taxpayer. It is to be regrettable that a county which has so many of the elements of wealth within its limits should be so indifferent or unmindful of the steps necessary for its development. To work up their vast treasures of iron ore there must be skilled labor. To have skilled labor there must be schools. To have schools there must be a public sentiment created which will view the taxes paid for such a purpose in the light of an investment. Were the twenty furnaces in operation in Perry, or twenty cotton factories, the increased revenues which the farmers would derive by reason of the home markets thus created, would pay the tax demanded for the support of a good school system twenty times. The whole community would benefit and the stagnation that now reigns over the county like an incubus would be replaced by activity, zeal, public spirit and awakened enterprise.

In checking population figures over the last 150 years, it is evident that there has not been much change in activities that cause a dramatic growth in population.

Population figures for the 150 years period:
- 1820 - 2,384
- 1830 - 7,094
- 1840 - 7,419
- 1850 - 5,821 (Decatur split)
- 1860 - 6,042
- 1870 - 6,925
- 1880 - 7,174
- 1890 - 7,000
- 1910 - 8,000
- 1920 - 7,765
- 1935 - 7,147
- 1960 - 5,897
- 1970 - 6,025
- 1980 - 6,111
- 1990 - 6,661

As stated earlier, the first term of the Circuit Court was held at the home of James Dixon on Lick Creek in the spring of 1820, Judge Humphreys presiding. The early records of this court have been destroyed so that no sketch of its actions can be compiled.

The following is a partial list of some of the elected officials from that time to 1886:

Register - John A. Rains 1820 - 1828; Thomas Lomax 1846 - 1882; R. A. Kimble 1882 - 1886.

Sheriff - West Woods 1820-1828; John Easley 1828-1832; Larkin Baker 1832-1843; Hugh B. Hand 1843-1846; Thomas Simmons 1846-1847; John L. Webb 1847-1848; James Kelley 1848-1852; Moses Bates 1852-1856; James H. Brown 1856-1858; Moses Bates 1858-1862.

During the Civil War, civil law was replaced by martial law and no elected officials served. The first session of the county court and its officials after the war was held in April 1865 when civil law resumed.

Sheriffs serving after 1865 — James M. Dodson, 1866-1868; Henry H. Long 1868-1870; John L. Webb 1870-1874; William J. Flowers 1874-1876; Edward W. Easley 1876-1878; A. D. Craig 1878-1882; J. M. Hunt 1882-1886.

Prior to the formation of the Chancery Court, the Circuit Court had jurisdiction over the chancery practice. The first term of the Chancery Court of Perry County was begun in Linden on the first Thursday after the third Monday of June, 1854, with the Honorable Stephen C. Pavatt, Chancellor, presiding. This court, as well as the other courts, did not convene during the war period. Chancery Court Clerk and Masters were James H. Kinser 1854-1858; I. N. Hulme 1858-1860; R. N. Thomas 1860-.

After the war, T. M. Brashear 1865-1868; H. J. Young 1868-1871; T. W. Edwards 1871-1877; W. A. Edwards 1877 - 1883; W. C. Webb 1883-1886.

Circuit Court Clerks were F. H. Kimble 1846-1850; T. W. Edwards 1850-1858; B. G. Rickman 1858 to war period; J. P. Ledbetter 1865-1870; Lewis C. Waggoner 1870-1882; J. W. Lewis 1882-1886.

The county was represented during this period of time in the legislature by H. M. Brown, Robert Crudup, Charles Graham, Thomas M. Brashear, Hartwell Barham, F. H. Kimble, William S. Maxwell, William N. Taylor, Jesse Taylor, C. B. Dodson, and J. B. Daniel and in the Senate by H. M. Brown, Thomas M. Brashear and Warren Smith.

Linden, the county seat of justice, is located on the west bank of Buffalo River, about three miles southeast of the geographical center of the county and about ten miles east of Perryville, the former county seat. The first dwelling house in the town was erected in 1847 by Jesse Taylor and Miles Prince. John L. Webb kept the first hotel, commencing in 1849, and Dr. Wm. C. Moore opened the first store in 1847. He was the first physician and also the first postmaster. Linden was incorporated in 1848 and the charter repealed in 1883. For some years prior to 1883, Linden was infested with saloons and intemperance prevailed to an alarming extent. To overcome this evil, the better class of citizens petitioned the legislature to abolish the charter.

The Miles Prince House was the first house built in Linden. It is shown here after it was moved and restored.

This being done, the saloons had to close up in obedience to the "four-mile law," and there is now not a saloon in Perry County where liquors are sold. The town of Linden now consists of the county buildings, two hotels, two schoolhouses (the Linden High School and the colored-free school), one Union Church, three stores, one restaurant, some mechanics' shops and about twenty-five dwelling houses and 200 inhabitants, three doctors and four lawyers.

This account of Linden was written in 1886 and since that time it has continued to be the county seat and at present time (1994) it and Lobelville are the only two towns of any size. Both have a population of about one thousand citizens.

HISTORY OF LOBELVILLE

It is not possible to definitely determine when Lobelville became a settlement of white inhabitants, but there is ample physical evidence in the form of artifacts that much of the area around Lobelville was used as Indian settlement for many, many years. It would be safe to assume that settlers moved into this area, especially after treaties with the Chickasaw Nation in 1816 moved the Indian borders to the Alabama line, about the same time other areas of then southern Hickman and Humphreys County were being occupied. Goodspeed's History of Perry County written in 1880s, says that it was established in 1854 as a Post Village and named after Henry DeLobel, a French immigrant, who remained there seventeen years before returning to France. It is said that he tried to gather French Colonists to return to the area and envisioned a great commercial center based on river traffic on the Buffalo River. It is known that DeLobel did live in the Russell Creek area and his name is carved (in Old English script) in a cave (known as Jaybird Cave) on Russell Creek with the date of 1854. In the same cave, there is an abundance of evidence that the cave was used as a shelter as well as extensive mining of saltpeter. DeLobel later lived in a house overlooking Russell's Creek on the Blackwell farm now belonging to Peggy Easley. The original house stood in this area until sometime in the 1980s when it was torn down and another house built close by.

Goodspeed's History of the 1880s states at that date, Lobelville contained three stores and a combined school and church. As years passed there was minimal growth to the town. The majority of the citizens engaged in agricultural and timber occupations. These products were used locally or shipped through the facilities of Britt's Landing. Some improvements were made over the years in the form of a couple of hotels, churches, a bank and mercantile operations. In the late 1880s, a water mill was built on the Buffalo River by John Leeper that provided a gristmill, sawmill and a limited amount of electrical power. Electricity was furnished by this water mill until sometime between 1932 and 1937. Statements were made by some of the people using electricity from this mill that they could tell every time a log was sawed on the mill because the lights would get dim. It is said that significant improvement was the establishment of an educational center known as "The College." It provided relevant educational activities for all grades. It was located on Main Street in the vicinity of The Flower Basket and McDonald Funeral Home. It is unknown what time it ceased to operate.

Some of the earlier settlers of Lobelville were survivors of the War of 1812. After the war, the soldiers received payment for their services by land grants. Others bought some of the land for one half cent per acre. The military line of this war is located around Lobelville and adjoining communities. The creeks and hollows were usually named after the first settlers.

Like many other southern cities and towns after the Civil War and reconstruction, Lobelville had it's share of desperate and dangerous men, many being survivors of the bloodiest war in history. Some were still holding grudges and there was much bitterness in the aftermath of this war that put friend against friend and in some cases, relative against relative. These were men who were accustomed to handling their own differences, very often violently, especially when the cause was "meddling" in their personal affairs.

One such incident recounted may times by eyewitnesses happened across the street from the old bank building. This notoriously desperate character rode in to town one day with a double barrel shotgun laying across his lap. When asked by one bystander what he was going to do with that gun, he replied quite simply that he was "going to kill the sheriff." Spotting him across the street next to the bank building, he put the gun to his shoulder and pulled the trigger. At this very instant the banker walked out the door of the bank building and was struck by ricocheting pellets. The sheriff began firing back with a pistol, very ineffectively, and decided to cut out. The only unlucky person in this exchange of gunfire was the banker.

Another incident involved an old whiskey maker well known for killing at least two men that had "meddled" in his business when he rode into town one day. The sheriff approached this old gentleman and informed him that he had a warrant in his pocket for his arrest. The old gentleman looked him straight in the eye and replied, "You'd better keep it there." Legend goes that the warrant stayed in the sheriff's pocket.

The bullet holes and lead slugs embedded in the porch of the earlier buildings were grim reminders of the dangerous and reckless conditions that existed in Lobelville up to the early 1900s.

Growing peanuts became a thriving business around Lobelville, replacing cotton, and was considered to be the "cash crop" of this area. But the peanuts also seemed to be responsible for the influx of blackbirds that followed. Many have witnessed what must have been millions of these birds going south in the morning and moving back north in the evening. The movement of these birds would last for hours, with no break in the flights. The blackbirds played havoc with a lot of the peanut crop since they were stacked out in the open fields. As the peanuts faded out as the "cash crop" in this area, so did the black birds.

Another form of business in operation around Lobelville was whiskey making. Prior to and during the Civil War, anyone that wanted to could legally make whatever amount of distilled spirits they so desired, whether for personal use or to sell for profit. Almost every mill around had a whiskey still in operation. Some of the farmers found it more profitable to turn their corn crop into whiskey to ship rather than ship the bulkier grain. After the Civil War a tax of $1.10 was collected for each gallon made. Later the area was voted dry but the practice continued illegally on a broad scale until the late 1950s.

At one time there were four grist mills in Lobelville. One was pulled by a Fordson tractor belonging to Roy Reece and located in the vicinity of the Church of Christ building. Another, belonging to Jim Campbell and pulled by a small gasoline engine was located near Heath's Cee Bee. Bedford Bates operated one in the area of Rudy's TV Service and Abe Lynch's was located at the dam on Buffalo River and pulled by water power.

In 1944, probably the most significant event in the development of Lobelville and other small towns across the southern states was the construction of natural gas pipelines through the area. Over the years four lines were constructed through the Lobelville area and a pumping station was built in Lobelville proper. This wave of construction provided well paying jobs of temporary nature and the permanent facility of the pumping station provided long term higher echelon positions. These activities led to other business being established to provided services to the gas company employees. Over the next few years, other commercial and industrial operations were established. Included in these are Bates Fabricating, Reliable Products, Kolpak, Red Kap, Leatherwood Mfg., Lobelville Garment and Watkins Mfg.

In 1949, nearly 500 people gathered to dedicate their new clinic made possible by the hard work and effort of the people and businesses, in an effort to secure a doctor at Lobelville. Doctors L. B. Murphy and O. A. Harmon, both of whom died several years earlier, were the last local physicians. Perry County's physician at that time was Doctor O. A. Kirk who lived in Linden. The next nearest doctors were thirty to forty miles away at Waverly and Centerville. The efforts were successful and Doctor Carlton was the first doctor to occupy the new clinic at Lobelville. Doctors McPherson, Griffin and Shiefield followed. At this writing, Doctors Earl and Ken Salhany are serving the people in the community.

Other communities that were prominent in prior years were Britt's Landing as mentioned in connecting with the peanut industry. Farmers Valley, on Buffalo River ten miles south of Linden, at one time had a post office, two stores and a warehouse. Theodore was a posthamlet on Hurricane Creek with a wool carding mill and a sawmill. These are no longer in existence. But Beardstown, established in 1830, and named for George Beard, its first merchant, is located on a high bluff on the west side of Buffalo about eight miles north of Linden, had a post office, stores and elementary schools but at present is only a residential area.

Perry County Newspapers

The early history of Perry County newspapers is rather scarce but from bits and pieces of information gathered here and there, the following is a fairly accurate account of that part of Perry County history.

The first newspaper ever printed in Perry County was the *Linden Times*, founded and published by S. L. Neeley and James Martin. The paper began on February 5, 1880 (a reprint of an article is found elsewhere) but was taken over in 1882 by C. L. Pearson. James L. Sloan pur-

Recreational activities of early Perry Countains. Front, l to r: Tom A. Twilla, unidentified, Dock Alexander, Hicks Lancaster, Henry Lancaster and Richard E. Hester.

chased the paper in 1883, changed the name to *The Perry County News* and printed the news until late 1884 and then suspended operation. About 1896, John Turner and Mollie Goblet Turner began publishing a newspaper called *The Linden Mail* (a reprint from this paper is found in the education section). It is known that the *Mail* existed until 1910 (there are copies in existence) but in 1913 there existed a paper by the name of *The Linden News* with J. Kent Sparks as editor. What transpired between 1910 and 1913 is pure conjecture.

The following is a reprint of an editorial by Mr. Sparks printed in 1913:

Our Town Spring

While seated on a rock over the town spring Sunday afternoon, the editor of the *News* listened to a bit of interesting history concerning the spring.

In the antebellum days it was known as the Copeland Spring, near which was located a still where corn juice was freely distributed to the pioneers who frequented the place and many were the days when riotous revelry ran wild.

In these days shooting matches were regularly held nearby and the pioneers with their trusty rifles were on hand from all parts of the county to match their skill with one another, the prize being turkey, beef and John-barley-corn, etc.

At the time we speak of, this spring presented a wonderful appearance. Being a large cavern seven feet high and about sixteen feet wide, a man could walk in it a distance of thirty yards without stooping, at which distance the subterranean way became smaller, so much that a man to go through it, had to go on his hands and knees. Crawling through this small space one entered a large cave with several arms extending in different directions, the main branch running under what is now Linden, and going in southwesterly direction, having a small opening about two feet in diameter in the rear of Mr. Sam Anderson's residence. 'Tis said that parties, when exploring the cavern, always carried a large ball of twine with them, tying one end to an object near the entrance, and as they proceeded, let the ball unwind, thus they were always able to return in safety.

Since the time we speak of, the appearances of this spring have undergone a great change. During one of the mighty floods, the entrance was filled up with dirt and rocks leaving only an outlet for the water.

This spring, from which Old Hickory drank when on his way to Memphis, furnishes a large percent of the water to our citizens; but what a deplorable condition it is in. What appearance does it present to the stranger passing by? Is it a thing of beauty and joy forever? Nay, it is knee-deep in mud, leaves, sticks, tin cans, etc. Nature has done her part. Let us do ours and clean out and beautify it.

We know that *The Linden News* was in existence in 1918 (there are copies). Prior to 1924, Mr. A. W. Wiggs was the owner and publisher of *The Perry Countian* and in July of 1924, Mr. Charles Ary became the editor. The building housing *The Perry Countian* burned in 1930, destroying all the printing equipment. Mr. Wiggs elected not to continue in the publishing business so Mr. Ary became the publisher of the paper.

During the year 1923, there was a paper published by the name of *The Advocate* by Brice Thompson. Nothing else is known about this paper.

The first issue of the *Buffalo River Review* was published on April 15, 1976, by Editor/Publisher and founder Don Dowdle. Volume one, number one was a twelve page, one section tabloid-size newspaper. The paper was produced by Perry County Publishing Company, Inc., with Dowdle as President.

Just over two years later in the September 6, 1978 issue of the *Review*, Dowdle and Mrs. Charles D. Ary, Sr. announced the purchase of *The Perry Countian* by Perry County Publishing, Inc., and the ensuing merger of the two newspapers. *The Perry Countian* had been established in 1924 and Charles D. Ary was publisher until his death in 1971.

In May, 1982, the *Buffalo River Review* ceased its format of tabloid size and became a full broadsheet-sized publication.

Dowdle remained publisher and editor until August 1982 when Randy Mackin was named managing editor of the newspaper. Dowdle, who still held the position of publisher, moved to Somerville, Tennessee and established the *Fayette County Review*, which is still published today by Dowdle (1993).

In August, 1983, one year later, the assets of Perry County Publishing Company, Inc., were purchased by Randy Mackin and David Weatherly. Mackin became the majority stockholder and president; Weatherly served as secretary/treasurer.

This ownership continued until 1988 when Randy and Lynda Mackin became publishers of the *Buffalo River Review* and Weatherly sold his interest to the Mackins. Randy Mackin remains president of the corporation and serves now as editor and publisher of the newspaper which is in its eighteenth year of publication.

Perry County in the Civil War

It was the bloodiest war in American history.

For four long years, 1861 - 1865, this war prevailed, with death and destruction like had never been seen before. The hand to hand combat and sheer courage displayed on the battlefields exemplified both Union and Confederate soldiers above all others. When Tennessee seceded from the Union, Perry County rallied, with the Confederates organizing first, furnishing some 600 men. There was considerable Union sentiment in the county and they tried to be neutral, but were finally forced into organizing, furnishing about 200 men. Various written accounts of the Perry Countians in battle attest to the fact that there were none better. It is highly likely that Perry County, on a per capita comparison, furnished more men in this war than any other county in the state.

The Confederate companies with Perry County men and their respective commanders are as follows:

Company "G," 20th Tennessee Infantry Regiment, Captains Robert D. Anderson, James A. Pettigrew, and J. Lewis Shy were called "The Perry County Guards."

Company "G," formerly 1st Company "D," 23rd Tennessee Infantry Regiment, Captains William H. Harder and John W. Harder.

Company "G," became 2nd "K," 42nd Tennessee Infantry Regiment, Captains Issac N. Hulme and Wiley B. Beard, calling themselves "The Perry Blues."

Company "F," 53rd Tennessee Infantry Regiment, Captains William N. Baker and John R. Coble.

Company "C," 2nd (Biffle's) Tennessee Cavalry Battalion, became Company "I," 6th (Wheeler's) Regiment, Captains Nicholas N. Cox and James H. Lewis.

The 19th (Biffle's) Tennessee Cavalry Bat-

Co. 1 24 Tenn. UNF CSA.

The Methodist Church, built in 1912 in Flatwoods.

A 1986 oil painting by Marie Grimes of the S.T. Sharp General Store and Post Office, 1940

talion, Company "A," Captain J. J. Biffle, Company "H," Captain Thomas S. Beatty, Company "I," Captain J. H. Culp, and Company "K," R. M. Sharp.

Cox's Tennessee Cavlary Battalion, Company "A," Captain W. H. Bass, Company "B," Captain W. H. Lewis, Company "C," Captain Elisha S. Stevens, Company "D," Captain B. G. Rickman, Company "E," Captain J. B. Herron. Consolidated with Napiers Battalion in 1863 to form the 10th Tennessee Cavalry Regiment. Company 1st "A," Captain W. H. Bass, Company "B," Captain William H. Lewis, Company "C," Captain Willis H. Whitwell, Company "H," formerly Company "D," Captain B. G. Rickman, 1st Company "K" formerly Company "E," Captain S. D. H. Whitfield.

Robert D. Anderson's Cavalry Company, Wheeler's Scouts.

The Federal Companies with Perry County men and their respective commanders are as follows:

Company "G," 6th Tennessee Cavalry Regiment, Captains William Chandler and William C. Webb. Company "H," 6th Tennessee Cavalry Regiment, Captains Joseph G. Berry and Drisden DeFord.

Company "E," 2nd Tennessee Mounted Infantry Regiment, Captains Henry D. Hamm and Robert A Guthrie. Company "F," 2nd Tennessee Mounted Infantry Regiment, Captain John W. Taylor.

Colonel Frierson and about 120 Confederate soldiers had possession of and commanded the post of Linden during the Spring of 1863. Early one morning, Colonel Breckenridge of the Sixth Tennessee Federal Cavalry took the place by surprise and captured Colonel Frierson and about 50 of his men and burned the court house in which the Confederates were partially quartered. Only two or three men were killed in this engagement.

Toward the close of the war, a troop of Confederate Cavalry made a raid through Linden, killing and capturing a few Federal soldiers. At this late date in the war, prisoners were generally not taken.

There were isolated skirmishes at Lobelville and Beardstown on September 27, 1864. Local sources seem to think the battle took place somewhere between the Hollis Hinson residence and Buffalo River.

It was clearly a war with brother against brother, cousin against cousin, father against son, and even reached to the highest levels of government. Four of Abraham Lincoln's brothers-in-law wore Confederate uniforms, and one of them, Lieutenant David P. Todd, was charged with brutality to Union prisoners in Richmond. Mary Lincoln's brother, Dr. George R. C. Todd, was a volunteer Confederate surgeon.

Stonewall Jackson was the symbol of Southern resistance, but his sister was a Union sympathizer. She once made the remark that she "could take care of the wounded Federals as fast as brother Thomas could wound them."

Some Confederate soldiers were portrayed brandishing a large knife named the bowie after James Bowie, the Alamo hero who was supposed to have originated the type. The blades ranged from six to more than 18 inches long and some had a D shaped knuckle guard. Although rarely used in battle as weapons, they were regarded as such by Confederate soldiers. A single chop could sever a man's arm. Collectors commonly refer to them as "Rebel Fighting Knives," and even an old rust eaten specimen will bring $500. An original portrait of a soldier holding one of these knives will command the same price.

The accusations by some in the North that Southerners were not well educated seemed to be pretty well founded toward the close of the war. It seems that even simple words like "I give up" were not in their vocabulary. Northern General John N. Schofield summarized the situation when he wrote, "I doubt if any soldiers in the world ever needed so much cumulative evidence to convince them that they were beaten."

Much bitterness existed even after the war, the Reconstruction Period being one of the saddest in our nation's history. Perry County records show there were 10 murders, 8 attempted murders, 63 arrests for illegally carrying guns and 40 cases of trespassing during a period of one year after the war.

Few people in history struggle more fiercely for their homeland and their perception of what was right than did the Confederate soldier. Battle losses were staggering. Barefooted, hungry and outnumbered, their spirit remained unbroken as they marched directly into deadly cannon and musket fire, at times being slaughtered, only to fight again another day as though nothing had happened.

Is it any wonder that we cannot hold back our fascination and awe for men like these? Sir Winston Churchill probably summed it up best when he said, 'It is to the eternal glory of the American nation, that the more hopeless became their cause, the more desperately the Southerner fought."

FLATWOODS COMMUNITY

The scenic community of Flatwoods is believed to have been established around 1844 by

The old Flatwoods Church of Christ, built in 1902.

The new Flatwoods Church of Christ, built around 1954.

Bromley Hotel, home of Dr. & Mrs. R.C. Bromley, built in 1911.

Grimes Canoe Base for Boy Scouts, built in 1976.

several families from Halifax, NC. The earliest name in the area is Whitaker's Bluff, honoring one of the founding fathers. Later in 1871, the community was renamed Flatwoods.

The area became a center of commerce with several stores, a bank, a photography shop and a blacksmith's shop. There were two churches in the community. The oldest is the Methodist church. The new Methodist church was built in 1912. The Church of Christ was organized and established in Flatwoods around 1900. The new building was finished around 1902. Samuel Boyce donated the land and was one of the most prominent leaders in the Church of Christ. The two story building housed an auditorium for worship on the first floor. The Masonic Lodge held their meeting on the second floor. The whole community helped to build the first building. The current Church of Christ was built around 1954. Glenn Grimes, Nesby Kirk and Fount Armstrong were named the trustees. The first school was an academy. Later, a new school building was built around 1884. Students could finish ten grades until the 1930s, when it became only an eight grade school. Students who completed high school had to drive or board in Linden. Later in 1954, a new school was built, but was discontinued in the 1960s.

The largest store in Flatwoods also housed the post office. The store was owned by S. T. "Bud" Sharp, who was also postmaster. Marie Boyce Grimes was the first and only woman every appointed postmaster at Flatwoods. She also owned and operated the general store for six years. Later, when Nesby T. Kirk retired as carrier, she applied for a transfer and she was appointed the first and only woman rural mail carrier there. Ottie Lee Ary was the next and last postmaster. The post office was discontinued and closed permanently January 3, 1985.

The store, owned by Ross Hamm, was formerly owned and operated by Mrs. Izora King for about two years in 1911. Mrs. Audrey Hamm owned and operated it after the death of her husband, Ross Hamm. It has been vacant for several years since. The Charles Bromley store has been torn down. The Bank of Flatwoods was located in the building and the bank president was W. C. Corlew. The A. H. Webster shop and garage has been closed for several years.

The old stores are all closed. Mike Ashton

runs Buffalo River Canoe Rental and the Rogers brothers run the Flatwoods Canoe Rental during the summer months. The Treadwell brothers use the old Sharp store for a wholesale flower business. It is closed except on weekends. There is one restaurant owned by Felix Skelton. The restaurant is open on weekends and gives local residents a place to exchange the news of the week. Most of the time there are no places of business open in Flatwoods.

The old Bromley Hotel was built in 1911 and was owned by Dr. R. C. Bromley. His office was located in a small building nearby. His wife, Dilla, operated the hotel until around the 1920s. Fishermen came to enjoy Buffalo River. Jerry and Dexter Webster live there now after they bought the house from the A. H. Webster's. They plan to open a museum there.

The Grimes Canoe Base is a part of the Middle Tennessee Council of the Boy Scouts. The thirty-two acre tract of land was donated by Glenn "Dick" and Marie Grimes in 1976. Thousands have enjoyed camping and floating the Buffalo River since that time. They come, not only from Tennessee, but several other states, also.

The Dr. W. E. Boyce home, built in the 1920s, had his office in his home, where he saw his patients. He lived in Flatwoods until the 1940s when he opened a clinic and Hospital in Hohenwald. However, he still worked part time at his office in Flatwoods until the late 1950s. His daughter, Marie Grimes, kept his old medical cabinet that holds a display of some of his surgical instruments and other memorabilia. It now stands in the foyer of her home at Flatwoods.

The oldest homes are those of Izora King and Sam Boyce. Mrs. King kept boarders. Her house was built in 1891. The Boyce house was built in 1903. The old way of life at Flatwoods is gone forever. It, too, is Gone With The Wind.

Written and submitted by Marie Boyce Grimes and Glenda James May, 1994, with references from the History of Flatwoods, by Susan M. Carroll, April 1990 and other sources of research.

GRIST MILL ON LOWER CANE CREEK

John Massey built Grist Mill on Cane Creek about 1810 or 1812 a few miles from

Flatwoods old school building, built ca 1890s.

Flatwoods new school building, built in 1949. Left to right: Dr. W.E. Boyce; Jack Stevens, Superintendent; Mrs. Stevens; Claude Dodson; Will Horner; Ethel Kimble; Mrs. A.H. Webster; Dewey Ary, Principal; Glenn Grimes and G. Tillman Stewart. Dedicated June 1949.

Dr. W.E. Boyce home and office, built in 1928.

Mrs. Izora King's home and boarding house, built in 1891.

Grist Mill on Lower Cane Creek, circa 1895.

Beardstown in what was then Humphreys County.

Green D. Leeper apparently bought the mill before 1865. He sold to Harvey Randel in 1865.

Moses Baucom sold land and mills on Cane Creek in 1868 to Josiah Bastian.

In 1879 Josiah Bastian, defendant—J. W. Cooper, claimant. Bought at public auction by Thomas Lomax.

Thomas Lomax, A. O. Barcofcy and wife Mattie Barcofcy sold to W. E. Beard in 1886.

Newton Jasper Hinson bought from W. E. Beard about 1894 or 1895.

Jonathan Harvey Hinson bought the place and mill from his father Newton Jasper Hinson about 1917. Sold to Ab Grinder 1951.

Submitted by Mrs. Fred Duncan.

THE JOLLY DOZEN

The Jolly Dozen Quilting Bee originated in 1957 in a two room house located in the Chestnut Grove Community. It all began when several local ladies discovered their quilt boxes were almost empty. They had grown up piecing quilts and had received quilts as wedding gifts, but during the course of rearing their children and working outside the home, their precious heirlooms were dwindling away.

The art of quilt-making had almost become obsolete, but these ladies believed that quilts like their mothers and grandmothers made were still the most practical and versatile bed covering available. Since quiltmaking is a tediously slow and time consuming process for one person, it was decided to take turns quilting each other a quilt. The ladies began piecing their quilt tops at home. Then on quilting night every one pitched in to help quilt and one lady would carry home the finished product. Within weeks, the quilt boxes began to shape up and more ladies became involved. Soon there was a dozen and since the ladies enjoyed these jolly, weekly get togethers, they named themselves the Jolly Dozen.

The first published photograph taken by Mr. Ary in the mid-fifties for the *Perry Countian* depicted a baker's dozen. This photograph consisted of Ethel Tucker, Norma Hildenbrandt, Grace Tucker, Lou Doyle, Sallie Matt Trull, Vera Tucker, Lillie Gladden, Lolamae Averett, Myrtle Gladden, Lorene Wade, Ellen Qualls, Nona Tucker, and Dovie Qualls.

The two room house belonging to Glenn (Sleepy) Tucker was sold after the quilting bee started. It was then that the ladies moved to Averett's Grocery where for the next 36 years they could be found every Monday applying their trade. It was here that their potluck dinners became almost as popular as their tiny stitches. Judges, doctors, clergymen, truck drivers, farmers, reporters, loggers and hopeful candidates have at one Monday or another found their way to Averett's to take part in the jolly atmosphere and delicious pot luck dinners. At Averett's, there was always an extra plate and you were a stranger there only once.

When arts and crafts fairs became annual events at parks and recreational facilities all over the state, invitations poured in for the Jolly Dozen to demonstrate the vanishing art of quilting. This prompted Mrs. Lolamae Averett to put a camper on her pickup, and the ladies, dressed in their long skirts and bonnets, took to the road. Since most of the ladies were over sixty, they recruited a neighborhood boy, Tony Plunkett, to help with the driving, the loading and the unloading.

Soon orders were pouring in from all over the state for a Jolly Dozen quilt. Articles and pictorial displays were published about the group in major magazines. Before long the ladies were filling orders from Maine to Pago Pago. They were featured on the morning and noon shows in Nashville and entertained conventioneers at the Hyatt Regency with their stitches and salesmanship. The pickup was replaced with a van as the ladies scheduled more appearances. Craft shops in other states carried a line of Jolly Dozen quilts. At one time, a helicopter flew out of state buyers to Averett's front door to make purchases.

The Jolly Dozen donated quilts to needy families and raised money for various fund raising organizations. One of the highlights of their long association was being asked by the neighbors of Lamar and Honey Alexander to quilt a friendship quilt for the newly-elected first family to carry with them to the governor's mansion. During the early years, the Jolly Dozen participated in local Christmas events by designing and building their own Christmas floats. In 1986, Sue Franks and Sharon Tomczak of Houston, TX, published the group's favorite recipes and quilt patterns in a cookbook titled *Cookin' and Quiltin' with The Jolly Dozen*.

Of the original "Baker's Dozen" only Lolamae Averett, Vera Tucker, Lillie Gladden, and Lorene Wade have remained active. Most have passed away or became inactive due to health problems or outside jobs. Other members over the years have included Cletus Richardson, Annie Basin, Jessie Kilpatrick, Betty Barber, Louise Young, Pearl Dotson, Mary Lou Plunkett, Tony Plunkett, Opal Garner, Jean Jackson and Elizabeth Berry. However, there was always an extra needle for anyone that happened by. As this writer knows, they never minded asking you to do a few stitches to pay for your dinner.

Anyone who has ever met these creative craftswomen can appreciate the love they have for their work and for each other. This devotion as a whole, combined with their individual character, has made them a popular, sought-after group for almost four decades. *Submitted by Sue A. Franks.*

Baseball in Perry County. Nearly every community in Perry County had a baseball team during the early and middle 1900s. A number of the local players went on to play organized pro ball.

Top - *Lobelville Baseball Team, 1920-1921.* Standing, left to right: Everette Bates, Carlos (Dutch) Bates, Jack Duff, Paul Buggs, Morris Twomey, John (Jimmy) Barber, Casey (Dommer) Barber, Arthur Batton. Seated: Hicks Bates, Luther Burns, Foster (Humpy) Barber, Frank Easley, Ray Loveless, Boyd Chessor.

Center - *Parnell Baseball Team, September 1936.* Left to right: Lloyd Qualls, Atlas Qualls, Elijah Warren, W.C. Warren, M.H. Warren, Leonard Qualls, Carl Qualls, Ottis Qualls.

Bottom - *Linden Owls Baseball Team, 1942.* Front row: Dan Dudley, Willard Warren, Mouse Marlin, Joe Edney, Morg Conder and Nolan Young. Back row: Jack Stephens, Harley Boss, Hillard Smith, Jack Leeper, Willard Moore, James Paschall, Luke Webb, Wallace Lomax, W.R. Moore and Dick Grimes. The shortstop for the team was Billy Webb, not pictured. The two bat boys are John Inman and Ned Webb.

The College at Lobelville, circa 1910. The building occupied the land which is now occupied by the Flower Basket, the Heath home and the McDonald Funeral Home.

EDUCATION

EDUCATION IN PERRY COUNTY

The education system in Perry County has been one of many different approaches and methods. Goodspeed's History states that Ferney Stanley (not the Stanley that was county surveyor) taught the first school in Perry County on Tom's Creek in 1820. The first known school in what now is Linden was taught by Edwin H. Eldridge in 1848. No doubt these were subscription schools—schools financed by the parents of school children within a given community. The tuition type schools were the only educational activities in the county until the State of Tennessee in 1827 adopted a levy to fund "free schools" throughout the state. Perry County did not contribute any local support to the free school system for many years, thus leaving the schools dependent upon the tax derived from the state levy which was entirely insufficient.

In 1867, the Legislature of the State of Tennessee passed a law providing for "separate but equal" schools for blacks and whites. This was supposed to be accomplished at state expense but in reality it was 1873 before this program gained in credibility and even then phases of it were questionable. The State of Tennessee became more and more involved in the education of its young people during this period. Included in legislation passed during this period was the "Parent Act of Public Education of 1873"; the first State Board of Education in 1875; and the "Four Mile" Liquor Law in 1877.

In later years the county did begin to levy a school tax that supplemented the state levy. Goodspeed's says that in 1886 the county levy was $.10 on each $100 of taxable property and $1.00 on each Poll.

The scholastic population of the county for the year 1885 consisted of 1,418 white males, 1,313 white females, 117 colored males, 121 colored females for a total school age population of 2,969. Of this number 2,610 were enrolled in "free schools." Goodspeed's also states that there were forty-five one teacher's schools in the county in 1885. Forty-one of these were for whites and four for colored. Teachers employed included thirty-six white males, five white females and four colored males.

The average number of days taught this time was seventy days per school year and the average compensation of teachers was $27.50 per month. The total amount expended in the county for school purposes for the year ending June 30, 1886, including teacher's salaries, buildings, superintendent's salary and miscellaneous expenses totaled $5,641.00.

Subscription schools were still in existence at this time, beginning at the end of the "free" school term, enabling some children to further their education.

Modes of transportation and a good road system were not one of the advantages of Perry County and this fact, by a large part, contributed to the establishment of small one or two teacher schools in the communities. This made it possible for students to walk or ride horses to the schools throughout the county. At one time there were as many as forty-five schools in existence at once.

Mt. Olive School in 1912. The teacher is Mollie King.

The first football team of Perry County, 1929. Front row: Curtis Hufstedler, John L. Webb, James Lloyd Sloan, Owen Sharp, Donald Kirk. Center row: Tom Berry, Leonard Culp, Wilson Sharp, Jack Southerland, Jim McGee. Back row: Mark Sanford, Ned Webb, Pinkney Westbrooks, Tom Kent Savage.

In the southern end of the county, elementary schools were, at one time or another, located in the following communities: Upper White Oak, Howard Bottom, Culps, Thompson, Bee Creek, Simmons, Horner, Howell, Cedar Creek, Furnace Hollow and Mayberry. Later Upper White Oak, Culps, Howard Bottom, Thompson and Howell were consolidated to form Lego School.

The following is a reprint of The Linden Mail, July 27, 1907:

TEACHERS ARE EMPLOYED by the County Board of Education.

The Board of Education held its first meeting Saturday. The board is made up as follows: 1st District, J. A. Mayberry; 2nd District, J. H. Nix; 3rd District, J.T. Tinin; 4th District, A. H. Wiggs; County-at-Large, J. K. Hufstedler. Mr. Wiggs was elected chairman. J. W. Seaton, County Superintendent, as ex-officio secretary.

The board employed the teachers named below to teach the schools following their respective names:

1st DISTRICT - Izora Simmons, White Oak; F. W. Harder, Bee Creek; L. G. Bunch, Horner; J. W. Mayberry, Mayberry's; Gussie Gobelet, Marsh Creek; and Emma Hutson, the Hall.

2nd District - Ella Jones, Pope; W. A. Barry, Cypress; Albert Condor, Standing Rock; Lula Patterson, Nathan; W. D. Frazier, Danielsburg; M. O. Cotton, upper Tom's Creek; Laura Bandy, lower Tom's Creek; G. L. O'Guin, Roans Creek; W. L. Curl, Crooked Creek, upper; and W. C. Patterson, Britt's Landing.

3rd District - Lel Whitaker, Mt. Olive; Lillie Fluty, Farmers Valley; Clair Boyce, Sinking Creek; Lockie Graves, Rockhouse; Charlie McLemore, Sugar Hill; Mary Bromley, Theodore; Emma Bromley, Hurricane; and Charlie Watson, Short Creek.

4th District - A. A. Warren, Coon Creek; Hatti Smith, Brush Creek, lower; Bessie Warren, Cane Creek; R. H. Gray, Border Springs; Lizzie Smith, Lagoon; J. W. Seaton and G. W. Long, Lobelville; Anderson Warren, Lost Creek; G. E. White, Bone Spring; L. B. Seaton, Terrapin; Mattie Blackwell, Greer Bend; and Mattie Campbell, Coon Creek, upper.

Most of the schools will open next Monday, July 15th.

No teachers were employed for the following schools: Culp and Simmons in the 1st District; Deer Creek and lower Crooked Creek in the 2nd; Bethel, Frog Pond, and Chestnut Grove in the 3rd; upper Brush Creek and Friendship in the 4th.

The board will meet again in the first Saturday in August.

An examination of colored teachers was held Saturday by Frank J. Hunter. Only two teachers took the examination, Viola Azile Webber and Estella A. Childress. There are seven or eight colored schools in the county, so it will be seen there is a scarcity of teachers.

The schools of Horner, Bee Creek, Furnace Hollow, Mayberry and Simmons were consolidated in 1922 to form the Cedar Creek Elementary school. In this new district, the Simmons Church served as a school for the seventh and eighth grades, taught by Ernest Broadway and the first and second grades taught by Tilda Howell. A cloth partition separated the two groups. Jack Stevens taught the remaining third, fourth, fifth and sixth grades in the old Cedar Creek building. An act of the Legislature in 1924 placed the school in a special district to facilitate the building of a new building and to provide some sort of transportation system for the students. Each taxpayer in the district was assessed three dollars to help defray the costs.

Board members were elected for the special district along with a superintendent. The members selected the teachers and set the salary rate. Board members were Ross Moore, George B. Ward and Marshall Howell. The superintendent was L. G. Bunch.

The new building was completed in 1925 and the teachers for that year were Ernest Broadway, Tilda Howell and Roy Sanders.

The primitive, by modern day standards, transportation system consisted of mule drawn wagons. There were about 135 pupils in the school who either rode the wagons or walked to school. In some instances, one wagon would carry the children for several miles then they would transfer to another wagon for the trip to their homes. Some of the men who drove the wagon-buses were Marshall Howell, Alga Pipkins, Dalton Moore and Bill Inman.

Perhaps this action by the Cedar Creek school triggered the consolidation of many of the one teacher schools throughout the county and this in turn lead to the establishment of Junior High Schools.

Schools on Marsh Creek were Hall, Sutton, and Marsh Creek. There were schools located

One of the first wagon buses used to transport school children during the 1920s.

Lobelville Elementary in the early 1940s.

in the northwestern section of the county known as Upper Lick Creek, Nathan, Standing Rock, Deer Creek, Roans Creek and Crooked Creek. These schools were consolidated in the early 1940s to form Pineview School. In the northern end of the county there were schools located at Red Bank, Pruitt Springs, Lobelville and Lagoon. These were later closed and the students were transported to Lobelville Elementary.

In the eastern section of the county, there were schools located at upper, middle, and lower Brush Creek, upper, middle and lower Coon Creek, Short Creek (which was closed and added to Chestnut Grove School), and Chestnut Grove. These schools closed one by one to form Parnell school located at the intersection of Highways 100 and 20 in 1935.

In the middle of the county, schools were located at Border Springs (below Beardstown), Friendship (on what is the Cotton property above Beardstown), Cane Creek and Craig (sometimes called Frog Pond School). These were consolidated into the new Beardstown school built in 1924.

There were elementary schools located at Cypress Creek (Pope), Upper Cypress (on what is now the Ayer's Farm) and Spring Creek. These along with the two schools on Marsh Creek were consolidated to form what was known as Pope School.

One school was opened on the old Hohenwald ridge to accommodate children of workers at the saw mills in the area. This school

Chestnut Grove School in 1910. The teacher was Dr. W.E. Boyce.

The Sutton and Hall Schools of Marsh Creek. This school was known as the debating school. They paired one boy from each school against another team of the same age to debate against each team. They often had field days and invited speakers to come and make a talk which help train the children who were debating. The Friday evening programs were interesting and brought parents to the school to see the children perform. There were also spelling bees held on Friday evenings. Two leaders would choose the children to be on their teams. Many people who had their first start at this school went on to further training and became teachers, preachers, doctors and lawyers.

Cane Creek School, March 25, 1946. **Front row**, *l to r: James Wilson Curl, Alfred T. Duncan, Hazel Marie Duncan, Shirley Faye Hinson, Bettye Sue Jackson, Betty Jewel Hinson, Bonnie Lou Jackson.* **2nd row**, *l to r: Bobby Riley, Roy Lee Campbell, Alline Hinson, Walter B. (Tip) Black, Lawrence Allen Ledbetter,* **Back row**, *l to r: Miss Montie DePriest, Naomi Ledbetter, Nola Duncan.*

only lasted for a few years. As the mill hands moved from the area, the need for a school no longer existed and it was closed about 1930.

In 1925, a school called Warren Consolidated School was built on lower Rockhouse Creek. Most of the other schools in the area (with the exception of Flatwoods and a one teacher school on upper Sinking Creek) were closed and the students were transported, one way or another, to this new school. This school served grades one through ten. Mrs. Videlle (Warren) Dabbs states in her *History of Rockhouse Creek* that "Al Warren used a covered wagon to cross the hill from his house to Sinking Creek and brought the children from Jack Tatum's on down the Creek." She goes on to say, "Uncle Al later bought a surrey to replace the covered wagon." Grades nine and ten of the school were deleted from the offerings in 1929. Warren Consolidated School was destroyed by fire in 1931, rebuilt and used until the early 50s. The school then was closed and the building torn down. It remained closed for a few years with the students going to either Flatwoods or Linden Elementary. In the late 50s, a new brick building was built and served as a school for students in this area until October 5, 1960 when a tornado hit the building and damaged it so badly it could not be used for education purposes. Since that time the remains have been used as a community building and for a head start program.

The Upper Sinking Creek School was closed in the 40s The Flatwoods school continued to thrive and eventually became a junior high school in 1930. The junior high program continued until the spring of 1939 when it was closed because of the lack of students. Only eight were enrolled during that school term. The elementary school continued to operate there until its closure in the 1960s.

Two elementary schools were in operation at one time on Hurricane Creek. These were known as Upper and Lower Hurricane.

Many thanks go out to Mrs. Helen (Craig) Smith, a teacher at Linden Elementary, for her assistance in preparing an account of educational activities for blacks in Perry County. Her account is as follows:

A Brief History of Black Schools in Perry County

The earliest schools for colored children in Perry County were known as "subscription schools"—schools financed by the parents within a given community. Established soon after Reconstruction, they were supported entirely by black citizens, those convinced of their necessity if the citizenry was to function, independent of its former masters.

In the earliest beginnings, these schools were housed usually in the little community churches—Craig's Chapel on North Lick Creek, Robert's Chapel in Linden, Oak Grove in Flatwoods, and Howard's Chapel in the Pope community on the Tennessee River. Their tenure was determined not only by the availability of finances, but the growing and harvesting of crops; they were, hence, seldom in session for more than three months.

After 1910, tax supported schools became the rule for all, but materials, buildings and even salaries for teachers remained grossly inferior.

In 1914, due to shifts in population, the Craig's Chapel School was discontinued. Young's Chapel, farther down the creek was established the following year, its site near the summit of the Dixon Ridge overlooking the Gotthardt place.

Between 1920 and 1930, two other schools for the accommodation of black children were to endure for a limited time; one of these located on Lower Roans Creek in the area of Britts Landing, the other on Cypress Creek for the children of the "hands" at the Jim Ayers Sawmill.

In 1930, the black neighborhood schools were consolidated, and the pupils from each rural community bussed to Linden. These busses, in actuality, were privately owned automobiles of citizens in the various communities. Driver's salaries averaged between thirty and thirty-five dollars a month.

The first building in Perry County constructed exclusively for the education of black children were erected in the Pope Community in 1942. A one room gray structure, hastily erected from inferior building materials, was an improvement, nonetheless, over the humble churches erected by freed men after the Civil War.

In 1949, funds were appropriated for the building of an elementary school in Linden. The two room brick structure was completed in late winter of 1,950, and dedicated Carver Elementary by Superintendent Jack Stevens on April 1, 1951.

Herein follows a historical sketch of the Linden Elementary Colored School as presented on that day.

"Carver Elementary School in the town of Linden (Perry County), Tennessee, is a public institution for the education of Negro boys and girls.

The first school for Negroes in Linden was known as Linden Negro School, and taught by only one teacher. It was taught in an old discarded building owned by an early Linden pioneer, Mrs. Adeline Brashear Craig. Sometime later it was moved into the Robert's Chapel A. M. E. Church. Here it remained for a period of sixty years.

In the summer of 1950, a site for a new school was secured. By the aid of County Superintendent Jack Stevens, and the Perry County Board of Education, the building was begun.

On December 3, 1950, the new building was completed. It was a modern building, very beautiful constructed of block and brick and reported to be one of the nicest schools in this section of Tennessee. It had two large classrooms, one hot lunch room, two rest rooms and a furnace room.

The boys and girls were very proud of their building and pledged to take care of it.

The P. T. A. members, the faculty and the students decided to name the school for the late, great scientist, Dr. George Washington Carver.

The Negro citizens of Perry County shall always be grateful to the Board of Education and the county superintendent for the beautiful building they have given us."

A gymnasium was added to Carver Elementary in the fall of 1958. This addition was dedicated by Superintendent Homer Long on April 19, 1959.

Due in part to the sparse black population, there was never an attempt to support a high school for coloreds in Perry County. Prior to 1920, few blacks in the county sought learning beyond the elementary grades. Of those who did, a great percentage attended either Tennessee State Norma, Roger Williams or Walden University in Nashville.

By 1930, where even blacks were concerned, high schools had become an integral link between elementary grades and institutions of higher learning. Black students, during this decade to further education, found it necessary to seek boarding places miles from home.

After 1940, a large percentage of black students boarded and attended Montgomery High School in Lexington. During this period the

1939 Team, first coached by Willie Hudson, won District, finished 3rd in the State Tournament. W.R. Moore was selected All State, first ever for Perry County. Back row, l to r: Holly Moore, G.T. Webb, Roy Belsha, Glenn Parnell, Kermit Ary. Front row, l to r: Frank Parnell, Elam Sharp, W.R. Moore, Russell Alexander, Lowell Paschall, Coach Willie Hudson.

Perry County Board of Education provided each student in attendance an allowance of about $10.00 per month toward room and board.

In the early 1950s, bus service was made available to the County Training School in Decaturville for Perry County black high school students wishing to attend. Again, the bus, in actuality, was a privately owned automobile. In 1954, however, following the Supreme Court decision in Brown vs. Board of Education, funds were hastily made available. A driver, having purchased a new, standard school bus was employed by the Board of Education, and the bussing of black Perry County students to high school in Lexington became the accepted way. For eleven school terms, August 23, 1954 until May 21, 1965, this provision continued.

In the fall of 1964, sweeping civil rights legislation doomed the practice of separation of the races and in the fall of 1965, all students of Perry County attended schools of their choice within the county.

An attempt to provide educational activities beyond the elementary grades were made soon after the Civil War but most of these efforts were due to interest of private citizens and for the most part these post elementary activities were conscription type with only the select few attending. Goodspeed's does not mention that there existed a Linden High School in 1886. In about 1885, a school known as The Southern Normal was established in Linden on the property now known as the Johnny Roberts property for the purpose of training of teachers. This school existed for a number of years and was very successful at turning out competent teachers for the schools of the county. It closed in the early 1920s. This building was used again in 1927 as a temporary home after the Linden High School burned in 1926. A portion of the courthouse was also used at this time for classrooms.

In 1914, the State Legislature enacted a law to assist counties in establishing and supporting high schools throughout the state. This law stated that tax of five cents on each $100.00 of taxable property would be collected and used within the community to support a high school system.

During the years of 1880 to 1920, the quality and amount of post elementary (high school) education had its ebbs and flows. When a free school was available, students had to pay for or provide their own transportation and in many cases had to "board" near the school. These conditions did not lend itself to the education of the masses.

A move was made in Perry County in 1923 to improve all aspects of education. This included consolidation of many of the one teacher elementary schools and the beginning of a junior high school system. This, coupled with the improvement of a free transportation system (to most of the schools), made education more readily available for Perry County youth. All schools were stepped up to eight month terms in 1926 and five two year high schools were established in Perry County during these years. These were located at Flatwoods, Cedar Creek, Rockhouse, Toms Creek (Pineview) and Lobelville. This was in addition to the four year school at Linden. These schools accomplished their purpose for a number of years. When the high school in Linden burned in 1926, a larger school (necessitated by the increase in students from the two year schools) was built.

The continuing need for a four year education and the insistence of Mr. J. T. DePriest, who became principal of Lobelville's two year school in 1935, led to the year by year progression of Lobelville into a four year school. Grade eleven began at Lobelville in the fall of 1937; grade twelve in the fall of 1938 with the first graduation in the spring of 1939.

The other four two year schools were gradually closed. Tom's Creek (Pineview) in the early 1940s, Flatwoods in 1939, Cedar Creek in 1945, Rockhouse in 1929.

The two four year high school system continued to operate in Perry County until the spring of 1962 when the Linden High School and the Lobelville High School were consolidated into the new Perry County High School. In the fall of 1965, desegregation of all schools enabled all school age youth in Perry County to attend this school.

With the consolidation of the smaller elementary schools, the building of larger and better school buildings and in some cases the building of gymnasiums, the sport of basketball became the dominant game among the students of the Perry County system.

With the establishment of the four year high school system, the elementary schools provided excellent training grounds and a feeder system to the two high schools. As competition across county lines increased, the schools of Perry County began to emerge as someone to be reckoned with in the game of basketball. Even though the school population was small—not unlike the total county population—the teams of Perry County were able to hold their own against much larger systems.

Over the years the closing of the smaller elementary schools has continued until the present time (1994). There are now elementary schools at Linden and Lobelville.

PERRY COUNTY LIBRARY

On July 7, 1947, the Perry County Quarterly Court voted to create a county free library and provide for its maintenance and operation. A seven-member library board was established with the following persons as charter members: Mrs. Celia Moore, Mrs. Mary Savage, Mrs. Pauline DePriest, Ms. Gussie Gobelet, Mrs. Azilee Smith, Ms. Susan Webb, Ebgert Marvin, Judge L.B. Duncan and Superintendent Tom Kent Savage, Ex-Officios. The first operating budget was $240.00.

The library was located in the basement of the Courthouse with Mrs. Mary Savage serving as librarian. For many years our library operated on a low budget from the basement location. Several other Perry Countains served as librarians after Mrs. Savage. They, along with the patrons, coped with flooded floors and damp books after heavy rains.

In 1981 the library was relocated to a building on Mill Street. Mrs. Dorothy Pevahouse was serving as librarian at this time. The new location was an improvement but library patrons dreamed of having a new modern facility and operated services to meet the needs of the community.

In 1985, County Executive Donnie Qualls helped the county obtain a government grant that provided 95% of needed funds to build a new library building. Perry County citizens would be responsible for raising the other 5%.

The Board of Trustees, Mrs. Pevahouse, and "friends of the library" began a fund-raising effort. Many persons donated money to buy a brick for the library. Mr. B.D. Grayson was instrumental in helping to not only raise money to build the building, but also to help furnish it, once built.

The doors to the new Perry County Library were opened on June 14, 1986. Blue Grass Regional Library has continued to help us expand our facilities, materials and services. Our library is now a resource learning facility we can be proud of.

The Lobelville Branch of the Perry County library started out as a Blue Grass Book Depository site located in the City Hall with Mrs. Mary Francis Leeper serving as librarian. With the help of Lobelville Mayor James Richardson, city commissioners, and the County Court, Lobelville Branch was relocated to a modern facility in 1993 with Mrs. Betty Tucker as the librarian.

People visiting the county libraries and the circulation of books and other materials are ever increasing even doubling in numbers.

Perry Countains should be proud that our present libraries are equipped to fulfill the original intent for establishing a county free library — because the welfare of Perry County requires it.

Judge L. Barney Duncan and Mary Harder Savage.

Perry County Public Library in Linden.

Lobelville Branch of the Perry County Public Library.

Top photo: Horner School on Tom's Creek, early 1900s. Teachers were Jim Bates and Lula Patterson.

Center photo: Perry County Transportation, 1903.

Bottom photo: Gilmer family harvesting sweet potatoes, 1930s.

Tribute to Clinton W. Liverman

Clinton W. Liverman

Clinton W. Liverman was born in New Burn, North Carolina, February 20, 1930. He attended school in North Carolina and Virginia. He was drafted in the U. S. Army in 1951 but found that he liked Army life so well he spent the next twenty-four years working for Uncle Sam. During this period he served at Fort Jackson, South Carolina, Fort Mean, Maryland, Fort Lewis, Washington, Fort Carson, Colorado, Fort Bragg, and Fort Campbell. He also spent almost seven years overseas in Germany, Korea, Japan, and in Vietnam. He was discharged May 1, 1975.

Clint moved to Linden in 1983, became Mayor of Linden in January 1986, was re-elected in January 1990, and became County Executive in September 1990. *Submitted by the Liverman Family.*

Memorial to John Thurman and Mary Bess Suratt DePriest

John Thurman DePriest called "Father of Public Education" in Perry County, was born June 21, 1888 in the Marsh Creek Community, Perry County, TN, son of Henry Houston and Dora Elizabeth Beasley DePriest. His father was a farmer and timber man. His mother was a housewife. Mr. DePriest, Mr. Thurman or Mr. J. T, (as he was called), taught school 39 years within the years 1909 - 1948; served as Superintendent of Perry County Schools, 1923- 1928; served one eight-year term as Judge of Perry County Court, 1950 -1958; and served as superintendent and teacher of Sunday school for 20 years.

He saw the need for public education for the children of Perry County because he had to go out of the county in 1910 to Savannah Institute to pay to get a four-year high school education. The free grammar schools had been only three months in length.

After being principal-teacher of the high school in Rienzi, MS, one year, principal teacher of the high school in Adamsville, TN, two years, and principal-teacher of the high school in Friendship, TN, three years, DePriest returned to Perry County in 1921 to teach at the two-year high school in Lobelville, TN, one year. From Lobelville, he became principal of Perry County High School in Linden. When he went there to be principal and to teach, the enrollment was down. He worked to get many of the older students back into school. He had the first four-year high school of Perry County in 1924. He was able to promote public education by being elected to serve as Superintendent of Schools of Perry County from 1923 - 1928. By special permission from the State Department of Education, he was both superintendent and principal in 1923. During this time, more two-year high schools were built. Some of the many one teacher schools were consolidated. The wooden high school building burned in 1926 which caused a new red brick two story building to be built. It was near the grounds occupied by the former school building. It was finished for the 1928 graduating class. DePriest continued to be principal-teacher in high schools in Perry County as follows: Perry County High School, 1928 - 1930; Tom's Creek two-year high school, 1930 - 1931; Cedar Creek Junior High School (as many two-year schools were called), 1931 - 1933; Perry County High School, 1933 - 1935; and Lobelville High School, 1935 - 1948. While teaching at Cedar Creek High School in 1933, he took a leave of absence and went to the Tennessee State Legislature to sponsor school laws creating new public schools and for public transportation. When he was placed at Lobelville Junior High School in 1935, he saw a need for a four-year high school at Lobelville because many students could not afford to pay for their transportation to go 14 miles to Linden to complete four years of high school. Under his influence, the two-year high school progressed to a four-year high school. Lobelville High School had its first four-year graduating class in 1940. He retired from teaching school while at Lobelville High School in 1948.

He was a good citizen. He was a member of the Democrat Party. He was always active in United States, Tennessee and Perry County government. He looked upon government as a help to improve the lives of the people. He was elected to serve as County Court Judge of Perry County, 1950 - 1958. He used his position to work as a leader for the members of the County Court (now called Commissioners) and the citizens of Perry County for the improvement of the County. During his term of office the following improvements were made: 1954 Department of Public Health Building; 1956, first hospital built in Perry County; a straighter road to Hohenwald from Linden; and Highway 13 built to Flatwoods without crossing the Buffalo River twice between Linden and Bethel.

DePriest was a member of the First Christian Church and was active in any church that needed him. After he retired from teaching, the evangelist, Mr. Dewey Whitwell, asked him to be Sunday school teacher and superintendent of a United Brethern Church he was building on the lower part of Cedar Creek. This church was built and dedication services were held November 2, 1958. Later the church combined with the United Methodist Church.

John Thurman and Mary Bess Suratt DePriest

John Thurman DePriest died in Linden, Perry County, TN, November 29, 1962. He was buried at the Sutton Cemetery, Marsh Creek, Perry County, TN. Dewey Whitwell, who had gone to school with him at Sutton School in elementary school and to high school with him at Rienzi, MS, delivered the funeral message. In the message Whitwell said the following about him: "The field of education was his greatest field. It is impossible to describe the kind of great teacher he was. He taught the textbooks with great efficiency and he also taught a lot of extra curricular subjects, such as public speaking... he was a natural in this great field. He could teach as few teachers can. This was his "God-given" talent. He could inspire pupils to want to study and make good in life. It was impossible to be around him without catching the inspiration of his great life... Also, he was a great disciplinarian... 'Mr. Thurman' (as he was called), was a master in this field. He made something out of students who otherwise would have been a liability to the human race. 'Mr. Thurman' lifted high the torch of education. I have known many teachers on the elementary, high school, college, and university levels, but in MY BOOK I have never met a teacher who was his equal." Statements from many students who went to school to DePriest in more recent years also praise his ability to teach. Some of these statements include: he was a dedicated teacher who wanted his students to learn and was a strict disciplinarian; he taught him to like algebra and Shakespeare; he gave inspirational talks in chapel to help people to have a good character; he wanted to know why his pupils were not in school, and checked on them when they were absent; he is high on his list of those who helped him in his endeavors; and he was the best teacher she ever had. John Thurman DePriest was able to be a good teacher because he had the support of the parents, students, the citizens of the community and his wife and family. His daughters designed a torch and had inscribed under it, "Teacher, Citizen, Father, Friend."

John Thurman DePriest married Mary Bess Suratt July 31, 1915, who was also a teacher. They were wonderful parents of their five daughters who are: Mary Elizabeth, Frances Lorraine, Dora Deane, Jessie Thurman, and Celia Carolyn. Like their parents, they became teachers, and four of them married teachers. Most of their children became teachers. Mary Bess Suratt was born October 21, 1890, McNairy County, TN, daughter of James Anderson and Celia Erwin Suratt. Her father was a teacher, farmer and mail carrier. She finished high school at Savannah Institute in 1914 as the first woman from McNairy County to finish high school. She taught one year at Rienzi, MS before marrying DePriest. She taught private expression lessons and coached plays during the years when her daughters were young. She taught first grade in the public schools, and during World War II, she taught in Lobelville High School. One of her elementary school principals stated that she was the best elementary teacher he ever knew because she had discipline. One of her English students at Lobelville High School said that she could make literature come alive. A student, who had taken private expression lessons under her, said when asked who was the best teacher she ever had, she gave "Mrs. Bess DePriest," (as she was called). She loved to help people. One of her nieces said she was an angel. "Aunt Bess" taught her and her younger sisters to sew.

She was a member of the Methodist Church when she married, but joined the First Christian Church with the remainder of the family in 1926.

Mary Bess Suratt DePriest died December 25, 1952, on Marsh Creek, Perry County, TN. Her husband paid a tribute to her by having written on her tombstone, "A devoted wife and loving mother."

For further information on this DePriest family see "John Thurman DePriest Family" in the *Perry County History Book*. *Submitted by their daughters: Mary DePriest Warren, Lorraine DePriest Hitt, and Dora Deane DePriest.*

CHURCHES

Church of Christ building on Crooked Creek. This building was destroyed by a storm in March 1942.

The old building of the Methodist Church in Linden.

Beardstown Church of Christ

Beardstown Church of Christ

On September 19, 1893, Mr. E. H. Shepard conveyed to J. W. Burns, B. C. Wilkins, W. J. Edwards, W. H. DePriest and J. T. Edwards, Trustees, a one and one-quarter acre lot on which the Beardstown Christian Church house now stands. This deed was recorded May 31, 1898.

In 1956, Mr. George W. Byrd gave an additional strip of land for a road and classrooms at the west end of the building. In 1981, a baptistry, a nursery and a fellowship hall/classroom were added to the building on its north side.

Early record books of this congregation no longer exist, so we do not know exactly when prior to 1893 the congregation started meeting. It has been said that Brown Godwin, who spent part of 1886 in Perry County, preached in Mr. Buddy Shepard's yard in Beardstown. This was probably the beginning of the Beardstown congregation.

Fairly complete written records exist since 1932. It appears that for part of the time in the thirties, services were held as "Sunday School" each Sunday morning, with Mr. L. E. Edwards conducting the lesson. Many times the number present was forty or less, and at several times during this depressed period the contribution was $2.00 or less.

Two of the first preachers mentioned in these records are J. J. Lancaster and John Hill. Some other men preaching once or twice monthly were: F. C. Kimbro, B. B. James, Harold Trimble, C. N. Hudson, Edgar Clark, Bob Riggs, J. B. Austin, W. A. Bradfield, Carmack Skelton, H. W. McClish, M. H. Tucker and Howard Trull. Several of these men were students at David Lipscomb College or Freed-Hardeman College who drove to Beardstown for their Sunday appointments. In 1956, Leonard Johnson preached each Sunday. Later men who preached here each Sunday for a year or so were: James Lee McDonough, Kenneth Holt, Myron Cherry, James Totty, Eugene Johnson, Jerry Mercer and Howard Trull.

Some of the men who have preached in meetings have been D. Ellis Walker, W. C. Hall, Mack Craig, Paul C. Mills, J. A. Thornton, Howard Trull, Bill Rhul, Claude Gardner, Homer Daniel, Martin Ray, Paul Rogers, Ralph Gilmore, Artie Collins, Joe Yarbrough, Ernest Laws, Gordon Turner, Jerrie Barber, Elmer Lusk and Kenny Bass.

Since the early thirties, until a short time before his death in 1993, Brother E. C. (Clay) Hunt was an active leader in the Beardstown congregation. He served as secretary, bookkeeper, caretaker, treasurer, Bible teacher, song leader and in any other capacity needed. Brother Hunt was a great inspiration to us all. His work and influence for good in the church will be greatly missed.

Tom's Creek Missionary Baptist Church

The Tom's Creek Missionary Baptist Church located in the Pineview community off State Route 50 was organized in 1868, just three years after the close of the Civil War. The Church celebrated its 125th Anniversary with special all day services in June 1993.

The first church building was located near the Bible Hill Cemetery. That building was destroyed by fire in 1887. A replacement was erected in approximately the same site. It, too, was destroyed by fire on April 26, 1919. The third building was built and dedicated in 1921. That building was located about a mile north of the previous sites in what has come to be known as "Happy Hollow" on Tom's Creek. The name for that site stems from an indication of the types of services held there.

In 1944, the church was relocated when the Tennessee Valley Authority flooded the area. The building at Happy Hollow was torn down and the materials were used to build the present building which stands on land donated by the late Howell and Nettie Patterson, members of the church. Several additions and improvements have been made to the original building.

Written church records currently in our possession date back to 1884. The present church record book was begun as the "third revision" by John P. Roberts, Jr. in 1917. The earlier two revisions are not in our possession. Records clearly identify Evaline (Simmons) Long, P. M. Roberts, Martha A. (Barnett) Roberts, Eliza (Barnett) Roberts and William Ransom Barnett as Charter Members. Others believed to be Charter Members were: Amanda Barnett; Sarah Ann Barnett; Carline Carrington; Ellen DePriest; Nancy Fitzgarly; several members of the Wm. M. Hill family; Mary M. Nix; Sarah Penix; Martha Quinn; E. E. Tanner; and J. W. York. Present church membership includes many descendants of the Charter Members. The church presently has just over 200 members on roll. Records indicated that over 600 people have been members since the church was organized.

The first Sunday School was organized in 1898. We continue to have an active Sunday School which includes 8 classes, and average attendance of about 70. Records of Sunday School Superintendents are incomplete, but include Howell Patterson, F. M. O'Guin, Elba Parker, William Potts, Larry Acree, and Buster Dabbs.

Additional church services include Discipleship Training on Sunday night. Each fifth Sunday is Youth Sunday, and each fifth Sunday night is gospel singing. The fourth Sunday in July is annual Homecoming Day, with special morning services, "dinner on the ground," and singing in the afternoon.

In 1888, records indicate that church letters were granted to 13 members of this church for the establishment of the Standing Rock Missionary Baptist Church. That church ceased to have services several years ago. At that time several of their members joined the Tom's Creek Church.

Due to proximity to the western edge of Perry County, the church always had ties to the areas across the Tennessee River. It has been a member of both the Beech River and the Southwestern District Associations, both predominantly made up of churches in West Tennessee. One interesting notation in early

Tom's Creek Missionary Baptist Church building as it looked in 1944.

records is the appropriation of 50 cents to pay for ferrying associational delegates over the Tennessee River. The church is now a member of the Alpha Baptist Association, which is affiliated with the Southern Baptist Convention.

Those members who have served as Deacons are: E. C. Nix, D. A. Barnett, W. A. Roberts, Austin Gibson, J. W. Goodman, R. T. Bell, J. Pope Bussell, John P. Roberts, Sr., Elba Parker, F. M. O'Guin, Paul Edwards, Robert Lawrence, Penick Gean, William Potts and Jess W. Warren.

The first church clerk of record was in 1888, Charles W. Hill; 1890, B. W. Medaris; 1891, W. A. Roberts; 1907, John P. Roberts, Jr.; 1918, Bertie Lewis; 1924, John P. Roberts, Jr.; 1929, John P. Roberts, Sr.; 1939, Howell Patterson; and 1957, Rex Patterson, who is clerk at the present time, and also church pianist for the past 46 years.

Some interesting notes about former pastors: Oldtimers said that when Brother E. M.. Franks was pastor, he crossed the Tennessee River on a mule swimming from Decatur to Perry County. J. Pope Bussell was a member of the church when he entered the ministry. He was ordained to the full work of the ministry to become pastor of this church in 1929.

The following is a list of pastors beginning in 1884: J. T. Moore; 1891, Joseph Allen; 1892, N. L. Joyner; 1895, C. C. Bussell; 1899, E. J. Newsome; 1900, John R. Clark; 1902, G. W. Glass; 1903, T. M. Boyd; 1907, L. M. Penkley; 1909, E. M. Franks; 1915, John W. Barnett; 1917, J. G. Cooper; 1918, F. T. Evans; 1919, W. L. King; 1922, J. Y. Butler; 1924, J. Pope Bussell; 1929, Bob Pettigrew; 1935, A. U. Nunnery; 1947, C. L. Haggard; 1949, John Hedges; 1956, Ernest Woods; 1957, A. G. Hayes; 1958, Ernel Broadway; 1959, Elmus Flowers; 1959, M. R. Shouse; 1968, Yancey Wharton; 1970, Osborne Wharton; 1974, C. R. Story; 1974, Jahue McCorkle; and 1978 until present time (1994), Ben Wood, making is pastorate the longest in the history of the church. Over half of the present membership of the church has joined during his pastorate.

A typical mercantile operation of the early 1900s.

The vanishing small town drugstore — Godwin Drugstore, Main Street, Linden.

BUSINESSES

Mill Street Service Station was the first service station in Linden. It caught fire and burned almost the entire block on Mill Street.

Duncan's Store in Linden. Burned in 1930 when the Mill Street Service Station caught fire. Duncan's Store was located across the street.

Bank of Perry County

The Bank of Perry County was organized in 1905 under the name of Bank of Lobelville. The organizers were John H. Twilla, U. J. Lancaster, R. A. Baugus, J. R. Butler and A. P. Poole. J. R. Butler was the president and the remaining organizers made up the first Board of Directors.

The bank opened with a total capitalization of $10,000, and now boasts a total assets account of $37,000,000.

The bank was operated continuously (without closing during the depression) until this date. The bank opened a new branch in Linden in 1974 and then changed the name in 1975 to Bank of Perry County in order to better reflect the entire county in its service area.

Since then, new bank buildings have been built in both Linden and Lobelville.

The bank encountered hard times in the early 1930s and Mr. Ralph Patterson was elected Chief Executive Officer replacing Mr. Butler. Mr. Patterson served until his retirement and was replaced by Jack Daniel. Mr. Daniel was killed in an airplane crash in 1962. John Will Bates was elected cashier at Mr. Daniel's death and was later elevated to president, the position that he holds at this time.

The current directors are: John Will Bates, Bill Bates, Neal H. Ferguson, Tommy Graham, Martin Haggard and Jesse G. Tate.

Top photo: Original Bank of Lobelville (left).
Center photo: Bank of Perry County in Lobelville.
Bottom photo: Branch Bank in Linden 1994.

Dinner Bell Restaurant

The Dinner Bell Restaurant in Linden

The Dinner Bell opened in 1964. Joe and Peggy Plunkett purchased the business in 1985. It continues to be the place to meet and eat! When the people of this area sit back and relax in comfortable friendly surroundings to enjoy a mouth watering, taste tempting meal, they are probably sitting in the pleasant surroundings of the Dinner Bell Restaurant located at Hwy. 13 South in Linden. They have served the Buffalo River area for nine years. This well known restaurant is known in this area as the finest restaurant to obtain a delicious meal prepared exactly the way you want it and served with all the trimmings.

Dinner Bell Restaurant

First State Bank

The earliest documentaries available in the files of First State Bank is dated October 4, 1890. The progressive and foresighted individuals organizing the Linden Bank and Trust Company were: W. W. Meadows, T. W. Simms, J. I. Graves, Thomas P. Whitwell, W. C. Webb and J. B. Beasley. The Charter of Corporation granted by the State of Tennessee authorized the Corporate Group, if the Corporation so chose, to couple with the ordinary business of banking, a Safe Deposit Trust Company.

The signature of W. H. Meadow on the document was witnessed October 4, 1890, by Humphreys County, TN, Clerk of County Court John E. Pullen. The signatures of T. W. Sims, J. I. Graves, Thomas Whitwell, W. C. Webb and J. P. Beasley were witnessed October 7, 1890, by Perry County Clerk of County Court J. M. Hunt.

The witness of the signatures in Humphreys and Perry Counties indicate that there may have been an affiliate relationship with a banking institution in Humphreys County, apparently the Waverly B & T Company. The Charter of Incorporation was received for filing October 11, 1890, at 2:00 p. m. by R. A. Kimbel, Register of Perry County.

The successor to the Linden Bank and Trust Company was organized by Daniel Starbuck, W. J. Richardson, J. E. Smith, H. R. Rushton and W. M. Roberts. The bank, capitalized at $25,000.00, was chartered by the State of Tennessee on October 5, 1901, as Perry County Bank of Linden. The charter was re-

Perry County Bank Building of Linden, Tennessee, 1901.

First National Bank, Linden, Tennessee. Left to right: Mr. Ralph Patterson, Director; Mr. C.B. Zemer, Asst. Cashier; Mr. C.N. Warren, Director; Mr. J.D. Pope, President; Mr. R.H. Godwin, Sr., Director; R.H. Godwin, Jr., Cashier; Bobbie J. Tatum Steele, Bookkeeper, Georgia B. Smith, Bookkeeper.

First State Bank

First State Bank, 1991.

Joy Kilpatrick Gordon operating the 7770 Proof Machine, 1994.

ceived and filed by Register of Perry County R. A. Kimbal October 14, 1901, and was filed with the Secretary of State John W. Norton October 16, 1901. The certificate issued by the Secretary of State was received and filed by R. A. Kimbal, Register of Perry County October 18, 1901.

The bank purchased a parcel of real estate July 27, 1904, known as the Dr. F. A. Cole lots on the southeast corner of the Public Square in Linden. The purchase price was $1,000.00 and was sold to the bank by M. S. Jones and wife R. E. Jones. The deed was witnessed by M. A. Tubbs, Clerk of the County Court, and filed and recorded by County Register R. A. Kimbal on July 27, 1904. Two notes for a total of $350.00 for the balance due after initial payment of $650.00 was signed by J. W. Wiggs, President and J. E. Smith, Cashier of the Bank. The bank building, still standing on the southeast corner of the square, was then erected.

The Directors of Perry County Bank of Linden, Tennessee were authorized by owners of two-thirds of the bank's capital stock to convert the bank into a National Banking Association. The title of the Association was First National Bank of Linden, to be located in Linden, Perry County, Tennessee. Capital stock of the Association was $25,000.00 divided into 250 shares of $100.00 each. Stock owners holding as much as six percent of the stock were: J. E. Smith, H. N. Ledbetter, George W. Pearson, T. D. Patterson, Jesse Sparks, M. B. Kittrell, W. J. Anderson, J. T. Edwards and W. J. Wiggs. The First National Bank of Linden, Perry County, Tennessee, commenced business April 27, 1912, operating with Charter Number 10181.

April 10, 1956, the Directors of The First National Bank of Linden, Tennessee, applied to the State of Tennessee for a Charter of Incorporation for the purpose of organizing a Bank Charter titled First State Bank, Linden, Tennessee, to succeed the First National Bank, those directors were J. D. Pope, C. N. Warren, John L. Webb, R. H. Godwin, Sr., Irvine Shelton and R. H. Godwin, Jr. The application of the State Charter was approved April 11, 1956, by Homer Clark, Superintendent of Banks, with authorization and fully paid up Capital of $40,000.00. The $40,000.00 Capital was divided into 400 shares with the par value of $100.00 each, with the principal place of business at Linden, Tennessee, in Perry County. The Bank has continuously operated under that charter since.

In 1963, the directors saw the need for larger and more modern premises. The building currently occupied by the bank was constructed in 1963 and then expanded in 1971 to its present state.

In 1982 the Perry County Holding Company was chartered and purchased the stock of the banks' shareholders.

The bank has continued to grow and maintain a safe and sound financial position and serve the community well.

The current Directors are: R. H. Godwin, Jr., John L. Webb, Don Pope, Gus Steele, Rosemary Godwin Turnbow and Bruce Cotton.

Graham Lumber Company, Inc.
and
Graham - Hardison Hardwoods Inc.

Three views of Graham Lumber Co., Inc. and Graham-Hardison Hardwoods, Inc.

Tommy Lee Graham serves as President of Graham Lumber Co., Inc. and Graham - Hardison Hardwoods, Inc. with his wife Joan serving as corporate secretary of both companies. Graham Lumber Co., Inc. is owned equally by Tommy and his three children: Lena Graham Heinrich, Ginger Graham Cagle, and Sherry Lee Graham. Graham - Hardison Hardwoods, Inc. is owned solely by Tommy Graham due to a tragic plane crash on November 3, 1993, that took the lives of his partner William L. Hardison and their office manager, Serena Hickerson Young.

Tommy's father, Allen Henry Graham, and Allen's brother, John Wesley Graham, operated a sawmill at the present location in the late 1930s. Allen and Wes, being primarily farmers, sold the sawmill operation to Tommy's brother, Jack Denton Graham, in 1957. They used to move mills around to the timber tracts back then, but Denton brought the mill to its present location in 1958 never to be moved again.

In 1965, Tommy joined his brother, Denton, as an employee at the sawmill after two years attendance at University of Tennessee in Martin, and after graduation from the National Hardwood Lumber Association Inspection School of Memphis, Tennessee. Tommy bought one-half interest in September 1972 and Denton's remaining interest in February 1976. Denton had a stroke April 2, 1975, and died in January 1979.

In July 1980, Graham - Hardison Hardwoods, Inc. was founded. This operation buys lumber from area mills including Graham Lumber Co., Inc. At Graham - Hardison, they remanufacture, dry kiln and dress lumber for sales in the U. S. and Europe.

In 1985, a renovation took place at Graham Lumber Co., Inc, adding a Cooper Scragg Mill beside the head rig already there. The scragg mill dogs the log from each end. The log passes through two saws getting two slabs or two boards on each pass, leaving a tie or cant in the heart. This mill saws 600 to 700 logs per eight hour shift. The head rig saws about 300 logs per shift.

In 1989, a round wood chipper was added at Graham Lumber Co., Inc. This allowed us to use the 30 to 40% of the tree that historically has been left in the woods to rot. Before this we had been leaving the tops under ten inches at the top end. We now can use the top down to three or four inches. This makes our timberlands provide about 30% more jobs, without cutting timber under the 12" across the stump. We now use the tree from the "butt to the bud."

In 1991, Graham Lumber Co., Inc. replaced the circle saw head with a six inch McDonough band mill. This improved the quality of the high grade log production along with an approximate 8% gain in footage.

Gil Cagle, manager at Graham Lumber Co., Inc., and Berry Eastep, manager at Graham - Hardison Hardwoods, Inc., report both companies are running well in 1994. Secretary Peggy Smotherman and Comptroller Ronnie Graves complete the office staff at Graham Lumber Co., Inc. Other office staff at Graham - Hardison Hardwoods, Inc. include Secretary Faye Simmons and Accountant Tommy Rainey. Both companies have about 40 employees each with some 30 or 40 contract loggers and truckers.

Timber cutting was big business in Perry County.

Another phase of the timber business, hauling to transportation points.

HICKERSON'S GROCERY

Long before Fred Lee Hickerson was born, his father, Jake Hickerson had already begun his life in the grocery business. He opened his first store in the Jim Newt Bastin building at the grist mill on Hurricane Creek in 1928. There he provided the staples of the grocery business to the community.

In 1932, he built a small store near his home on Hurricane Creak and continued to provide the necessities of food for his neighbors. The citizens of this area did not have means or the desire to travel any great distances and besides, with the grist mills in the area and the raising of their own food stuffs, their needs were limited.

Changes in lifestyles and easier modes of transportation helped "Mr. Jake" to realize that he needed to change, not only location but in the variety of goods to offer. So in 1948, "Mr. Jake" and Ray Epley became partners and opened a store in Linden, not large in size but with a much greater selection of customer products.

During this time, Fred was born in November 22, 1932, had attended and graduated from school in Linden, and no doubt had developed the same love for the grocery business as his father. After a tour of duty of 2 years in the Army, Fred came home to work with his father in the business in 1955.

In 1955, Fred Lee married Edna Earle Rainey and she immediately became an important part of the family business. Soon after, Fred and Edna purchased the business. "Mr. Jake" remained close by, enjoying the conversations with the many loyal customers he had accumulated over the years and filling-in in the store when necessary.

Fred became known for his ability to find "bargains" and to pass these on to his customers. The trademark of the store was the sale items that were stacked in front of the store, in the aisles and even in back of Fred's pickup. Another fixture was the account books, row after row, of those customers who ran a weekly or monthly account at the store. This was a service that had been a part of the Hickersons since the very beginning and a service that was fast disappearing with the supermarkets and chain stores.

Business, with Fred and Edna Earle working tirelessly, thrived. And after much soul searching in 1978, Fred and Edna moved into a new modern 8,500 square foot facility behind the courthouse. With Edna managing the business and Fred finding the "bargains," business continued to grow. Customers came from surrounding counties to take advantage of items and the bargain prices offered.

Left to right: Ray Epley, Jessie Jackson, and Jake Hickerson, circa 1950s.

Hickerson's Grocery

Edna had taken time out from the business to give birth to a daughter, Dianne Dee born September 24, 1963. In due time, she became a part of the grocery business, also.

In 1988, Hickersons Grocery was recognized as an outstanding independent grocer in the United States.

This led to another expansion, this one increased the space to 17,000 square feet. The ribbon cutting for this event took place September 15, 1988. This was an amazing accomplishment considering the size and population of Perry County.

In 1991, the Hickersons became affiliated with the Piggly Wiggly chain and continue to operate the store under this name. The grocery business is and has been their life and some wonder if they will ever retire.

Epley and Hickerson Market, located in front of the courthouse. Left to right: Ray Epley, Jake Hickerson and Jasper Anderson., 1952

HICKERSON'S GROCERY

Grand opening in 1991.

Perry Farmers Co-op

Perry Farmers Co-op.

Perry Farmers Co-op was established and chartered on July 6, 1948, for the purpose of engaging in any activity in connection with the marketing and selling of agricultural products.

The following persons served as incorporating directors: J. Kent Sparks, J. M. Howell, Thomas Harris, Alf Ashton, Sr., J. W. Rhodes, W. A. Moore, Irvine Shelton, Tom Godwin, Sr., Glenn Grimes, Dick Ayers and John W. Godwin.

Roy P. Wilsdorf served as manager for 25 years, starting in a small building on Mill Street, later moving to a larger facility on Maple Street. He retired shortly before the business moved to its present location on Hwy. 13 South in 1979. Trent DePriest, who was an employee of the Co-op, was promoted to manager in the late 60s, and Roy continued as assistant manager until his death in 1980.

In the early years of the Co-op, Mrs. Elizabeth K. Dodson and Dorothy W. Lawrence served as bookkeeper of the firm and J. C. Beasley did the hauling of goods, until the management decided to purchase their own truck as the business grew larger.

At the present time there are 7 employees: Trent DePriest, manager; Chloe Lacy, bookkeeper; Michael Lawrence; Mike Southall; Tom Culp; Terry Skelton; and Chris Rogers.

The present board of directors include: David Trull, Ronny Southall, Billie Qualls, Wallace Holder, Walton Holder, Keith Ary, Gary Culp and L. B. Smith. *Compiled by Dorothy W. and Michael P. Lawrence.*

Perry County Commissioners and Elected Officials

*Perry County 1994 Commissioners, left to right, **front row:** Ottis Gibson, Natham Mercer, Ray Churchwell, Norma Richardson. **Second row:** Billy R. Dabbs, David Trull, Willard Kennamore, J.R. Warren. **Back row:** Austin Pevahouse, Ray Marshall. Absent Jack Carter, Mary Sam Denton.*

Perry County elected officials, left to right, Hollis Hinson, Trustee; Clovis Parnell, Session Judge; Jane Lewis, County Court Clerk; Robert O'Guin, General Session Clerk; Jean Edwards, Register; Thomas Ward, Sheriff; Clint Liverman, County Executive; Gary Horner, Tax Assessor; Dan Horner, Road Superintendent; Absent David Rhodes, School Superintendent.

Perry County Memorial Hospital

Perry Memorial Hospital

Perry County General Hospital was built in 1956 and located on Mill Street. The Hospital was a 24-bed hospital to serve the citizens of Perry County and surrounding counties. Dr. Gordon H. Turner, Jr. and Dr. Bert Holladay were the first physicians to use the facility. In the early 1980s the hospital was owned and operated by the county until 1981 when the county sold the hospital to Rural Health Care Systems and the new facility was built on Highway 13 South across from Johnson Controls. A new 53-bed facility was constructed in 1983 equipped with modern equipment and the latest technique in health care.

Perry Memorial Hospital serves the people of Perry County and all surrounding counties now with Acute Care Unit, Adult Psychiatry, Adolescent Psychiatry, Outpatient and Surgery Departments. Perry Memorial has a very caring and cooperative staff to serve all the needs of Perry County citizens. We would like to take this opportunity to invite you to visit our facility to review and discuss our services.

Perry County Nursing Home

In 1967, the Quarterly Court of Perry County recognized the need for a modern facility for the care of the sick and disabled in Perry County and commissioned the building of a thirty bed nursing home with an apartment for the administrator. This building was leased to Kenneth and JoAnn Holder. The first patients were admitted in November 1967.

The Perry County Nursing Home was leased to David and Peggy Ramey in 1974, and they continued the same high quality care started by the Holders in 1967.

The demand for additional beds was great and in 1976, the administrator's apartment was converted to patient rooms, increasing bed capacity to thirty-eight.

In 1980, an additional wing was constructed containing thirty beds and a second nurses' station. In 1990, a north wing was added with additional office space and renovation of the kitchen area. This brought the bed capacity to 114.

Since 1991, David Ramey has been the sole lessee of the Perry County Nursing Home. The nursing home employs approximately ninety-two employees with sixteen licensed nurses on staff. The Perry County Nursing Home is known throughout the state for its outstanding care of the elderly and disabled of Perry County.

Perry County Nursing Home, July 1988.

Perry County Nursing Home, May 24, 1974.

Perry County Schools

Perry County High School.

Linden Elementary School.

Lobelville Elementary School.

School Board Members and 1993-94 System-wide Personnel, Principals, and Teacher

School Board Members

Martha R. Sharp, Chairperson
Joseph C. Burns
Jackie C. Duncan
Don Kirk
Michael P. Lawrence
Dewey Mercer

System-wide Personnel

David R. Rhodes, Superintendent
Rickey H. Marshall, Supervisor of Instruction
Rosemary E. Turnbow, Supervisor of Special Education
Linda A. Fesmire, Attendance Supervisor/Vocational Director
Vicky L. Fortner, Food Service Supervisor/Chapter 1 Director
William N. Potts, Adult Education Supervisor
Mary L. Crosby, Early Childhood Special Education
Mary B. Cruse, Speech and Hearing Teacher
Miko C. Goodman, Music Teacher
Patricia A. Qualls, Art Teacher
Lois R. Baker, Materials Clerk
Leslie O. Dabbs, Transportation Director
Billy E. Hinson, System-wide Maintenance
Joyce D. Reeves, Accounting/Payroll
Loretta G. Richardson, Secretary Receptionist

Linden Elementary/Middle School
Janie H. Cotham, Principal (K-4)
Gil Webb, Principal (5-8)
Geneva L. Adkins, Chapter 1
Judith T. Alley, Special Education
Helen L. Ary
Tommy W. Bell
Pamela C. Bishop, Special Education
Denise G. Blackwell
Connie L. Blakemore
Tammy A. Brasher
Roy M.A. Crews, Special Education
Sheila D. Culp
Brenda A. Dabbs, Special Education
Margaret A. Dill, Elementary Guidance Counselor
Sharon D. Doyle, Chapter 1
Donna Q. Erisman
Donna L. Holcomb, Special Education
Lisa A. Howard
Marie M. Howard
Catherine M. Hufstedler
Anita R. Livengood
Jane H. Loggins
Lynda I.M. Mackin
Lisa M. Marlin
Anne E. Mercer
Deborah K. Monroe
Tamra R. Phillips
Terry C. Ritter, Kindergarten
Denise S. Roach
Dana G. Roberts, Kindergarten
Mary K. Smith, Librarian
Donna G. Tucker, Asst. Principal (5-8)
Nancy Warren, Asst. Principal (K-4)
Melinda G. Webb
Steven D. Wilder, P.E.
Traci H. Williams
Billy R. Yarbro

Lobelville Elementary School
Kathy A. Weatherly, Principal
Steven W. Bates
R. Brent Cunningham, Chapter 1 & Asst. Principal
Renee B. Ervin
Patti K. Haston
Nelda C. Hinson
Anna W. Marshall
Clarissa S. McGee, Special Education
Susan R. Pevahouse
Amy J. Sneigr
Carmon S. Trull
Pamela J. Ujcich

Perry County High School
R. Wayne Morris, Principal
Judith A. Bates
Ginger C. Cagle
Larry L. Clifton
Martha R. Edwards, DE
Chester R. Ezell, JTPA
LaDon K. Ezell
Linda K. Gordon, Home Economics
Linda W. Hinson, Librarian
Benjamin R. Howard, IV
Jill E. Lawrence
Cynthia L. Mercer
Barbara L. McGee
Maria V. Rawdon, Spanish
W. Bruce Slatten, Coach
Anita L. Thomison, Special Education
J. David Trull, Vo-Ag
Jon K. Turner
Sherman B. Vaughan, In-School Suspension Program
Rendia H. Ward, Special Education
Larry A. Warren, Asst. Principal
Jacquelyn G. Wilder, Guidance Counselor/Coach
Michele M. Williams
Ben F. Wood, T & I

Cane Creek School in 1937. Mr. Claude DePriest, teacher.

From l to r: Nick Burns, N.J. Hinson, Clem Edwards.

Simmons School on Cedar Creek, 1915.

A mail car of the early 1900s.

Boy's and girl's basketball teams of Cedar Creek Jr. High in 1929. Harley Aldridge, coach.

Warren Boy's Basketball Team, 1956.

Warren Girl's Basketball Team, 1956.

Lobelville High School Girl's Basketball Team, 1952-53.

1927-28 Girl's Basketball Team at Cedar Creek Jr. High School.

Grave marker of David Rice Harris, the man who gave land for Linden.

Pleasant Whitfield DePriest in uniform, CSA.

Early Perry County architecture. The James A. Sutton place, built about 1849, later was the Hufstedler Place.

Clyde A. Daniel General Merchandise in 1911, Beardstown, TN.

Perry County Families

Albert DePriest, Sally Matt Ridings DePriest, Vera Byrd D., Byron Shepard DePriest, Ira DePriest.

A group of people at Lobelville in 1912. Top row, l to r: Clara Dell Dudley Bates Twilla (age 9), Ernie DePriest, Mattie Louise Tate Curry, Albert Gilmer, Nettie Alexander Lancaster. Bottom row: Ada DePriest, Ida Lorina Tate Hester and May DePriest.

MOSES ALBERSON, was born in North Carolina in 1805, came to Tennessee in the early 1800s. He and his wife, Elizabeth, settled on Hurricane Creek in Perry County. Two known children of theirs were Mary and Solomon. Other children are known to have migrated to Missouri.

Solomon Alberson remained with the family home on Hurricane Creek and married Martha Kilpatrick, daughter of Josh Kilpatrick. Solomon and Martha's children were Cora (who died young), Leora who married Henry Hickerson, Laura who married D. Simmons, Albert who married Lou Cindy Hickerson. Leora and Henry Hickerson had one daughter, Jessie, who married Lester Raines.

Laura and D. Simmons had five children: Goldie, Taft, Ralph, Maisies, and Albert. Solomon Alberson was a school teacher and a member of the Perry County quarterly court.

Albert Alberson, born Dec. 23, 1886, married Lou Cindy Hickerson (daughter of William Finley and Rebecca "Becky" Hickerson). Lou Cindy was born May 2, 1890, and died in 1981. Of their seven children, five died in infancy. Irene Clovis was born Feb. 28, 1916, and died in 1932. Dorothy Locky was born to Albert and Lou Cindy on Jan. 25, 1925. She married William Crittendon Deavers on Jan. 3, 1948. He was the son of Benjamin Orion and Kate Jane Deavers.

Dorothy and "W.C." had three children: Joyce Janet who married Franklin Morris, Lounelle who married Phillip Chapman and Albert Benjamin who married Maria Monterio.

Joyce and Franklin Morris have three children: Larry Wayne, Terry Allen who married Annette Gordon and Gregory Scott.

Lounelle and Phillip Chapman had one daughter, Selenia Michelle who attended TN Tech. University.

Albert and Maria have three children: Jotonene Christopher, Doreen Susanne and Colene Jessica. They are building a new house on the Alberson farm.

Moses, Solomon and Albert Alberson are all buried in the Alberson Cemetery on Hurricane Creek. *Submitted by Dorothy Alberson Deavers.*

JAMES ALLEN ALDRIDGE - LEW ELLEN BATES, James Aldridge (1874 - 1931) was the son of William Nelson Aldridge and Nancy Land. Lew Ellen Bates (1874 - 1944) was the daughter of Dillard Hunt Bates (1848 - 1910) and Martha Emmaline Chandler (1855 - 1940), married 1870. James and Ellen and other members of the Land and Aldridge families are buried in the Brush Creek Cemetery. Dillard and Emmaline Bates are buried in Gilmer Cemetery, Lobelville.

The Aldridge children are: Ilene Crosby (1899 - 1970), married Howard Crosby; Nancy Lee (1902 - 1942), married Grady Jones, 1920 (he died 1924), she married Fred Halbrooks, 1928, children - Arthur Jones, Helen Greeson, Rosa Lee Johnson, Ruby Hodges; Faye Malone (1903 - 1924), married Charlie Barber, daughter - Dorothy Click; James Harley (1906 - 1979), married Quanita Webb (lives in Linden). He married Willie Wilson (1938), son - Larry, Larry's daughter - Ashley; Clarice (1908), married Clayton Bates, one daughter - Claydean Cantrell; Geneva (1910), married Lewis Sanders, Hohen-

An Aldridge - Bates Family Reunion in 1950

wald, two children - Gary, Mt. Juliet and Rita, Marysville; Bates (1916), married Mildred Garner, lives Trenton, TN, three children - Robert Allen, Greensboro, NC, Joan Vaughan, KY, Judith Harris, Lexington, KY; Ruth (1918), married W.G. Mullican, lives at McMinnville, no children.

See references: Aldridge, Bates, Fred and Nancy Halbrooks. There is a Chandler history in Hickman County Library.

FLOSSIE ESTHER ALLEN AND TAVY RODGER RHODES, Flossie Allen was the daughter of James David Allen and Leora Myracle Allen, the granddaughter of Joseph Henry Allen. Flossie was born Aug. 20, 1897, in Perry County.

Herman B. and Joy Rhodes

Tavy Rodger Rhodes was the son of William Rhodes and Martha Jane Tanner. Tavy was born January 5, 1895, in Decatur County.

Flossie and Tavy were married Jan. 15, 1922. They had two children James William, born Dec. 25, 1922 and Herman Bliss, born Aug. 13, 1924. They lived in Nashville, TN, where Tavy was Chief Railway Clerk with the U.S. Post Office until he became disabled. They moved back to Perry County and bought the Jim Allen Farm on Marsh Creek in 1936. Tavy died May 10, 1936, and Flossie died June 29, 1984.

James William married Lessie Arness Richardson of Cypress Creek on Oct. 1945. They have two children, Rodger W. and Susan Arness. Rodger was born Jan. 22, 1961 and Susan was born Aug. 11, 1964. James W. worked as a Law Enforcement Officer with the Game and Fish Commission for over 25 years. Lessie was an employee of Washington Manufacturing Company. Lessie died April 8, 1994.

Herman Bliss married Joyzell Adkins of Benton, Kentucky on June 17, 1950. Joyzell was born Aug. 3, 1928, daughter of Ivan Arlyn Adkins and Chloe Frances Bartlett of Arkansas. After they were married in Hartford, Connecticut, they stayed there for the summer of 1950, where he played professional baseball. Then after two years with Monsanto Chemical Company, they moved back to Perry County in Marsh Creek Community where he was employed as a Rural Letter Carrier with the U.S. Postal Service for thirty years. He served 3 years with the U.S. Army with the 78th Division in Germany. Joyzell is a cosmetologist with over 40 years experience.

Herman and Joy have three children, David Rodger born June 4, 1951, Jan born Jan. 10, 1954 and Mike Adkins, born April 4, 1959.

David married Stella Jo Sweeney of Lobelville, TN May 26, 1973. They have two children, David Bryant born May 23, 1977, and Mitchell Bartlett born May 28, 1980. Dave graduated from the University of Mississippi in 1973 and is presently the Superintendent of Perry County Schools. Stella is U.S. Postmaster of Lobelville, TN. They now live in the Beardstown Community.

Jan Rhodes married Thomas Walter Eberly of Westfield, Pennsylvania on July 3, 1987. They have two children, Joseph Frank, born July 3, 1989, and Anna Bliss, born Dec. 26, 1992. Jan is a graduate of Middle Tennessee State University in 1975 with a Fashion Merchandise Degree. Thomas is president of Wickett and Craig of America Tannery in Pennsylvania. They live in the Temple Hills Complex in Williamson County.

Mike married Kristie Lee Jones of Memphis, TN on Feb. 8, 1982. They have three children, Andrew Michael born Oct. 7, 1984, Paige Katlin born June 3, 1988, and Richard Cannon born Aug. 3, 1993. Mike is an engineer with the T.G.T. Division of Tenneco, after graduating from Vanderbilt University in 1981. Kristie is a Certified Dance Instructor. They live in Williamson County in the Thompson Station Area.

JOSEPH HENRY ALLEN AND FRANCES ELIZABETH BYRD, Joseph Henry Allen, born 1843 - died 1896. He came to Tennessee from North Carolina during the Civil War 1861-1865. He served in the Battle of Franklin at Franklin, Tenn. and the Battle of Nashville at Shy Hill.

Carroll Allen

At the end of the war he came to Perry County and traded his shotgun for land on Marsh Creek. He married Frances Byrd. Frances B. died in 1921. Joseph H. Allen continued to buy and clear the land. They built a log home on the Marsh Creek Road and it was known as the Allen Hollow.

To this union six children were born: William Peeler Allen, 1865-1942; Grant Allen, 1866-

1890; James D. Allen, 1868-1932, married Lenora Myracle, 1878-1941; Lou Ella Allen, 1873-1928, married John Ledbetter, died 1948; Alonza Cliton Allen, 1875-1950, married Cora Marshall, 1883-1974; George Carroll Allen, 1877-1950, married Bertha L. Middleton, 1893-1969.

The Allen brothers owned and operated a business on the Tennessee River at Jennings Bluff Landing that was a warehouse and store of peanuts, cotton, grains, groceries and cross ties. They operated a grist mill and sorghum mill near their home on Marsh Creek. All of the Allen Brothers were farmers.

George Carroll was a farmer; he taught school in Perry County early in life. He served as School Board member of Perry County School in the 2nd District. He married Bertha L. Middleton Aug. 17, 1911.

To this union four children were born.

Jessie Maurine Allen born 1914. An educator in the Perry County school system from 1936-1977. She received her bachelor of science degree from Middle Tenn. State Teachers College at Murfreesboro, Tenn. A certificate for Supervision of Instruction grades K-12. She taught school for thirty-five years in the class room and was supervisor of Perry County Schools from 1971-1977.

Joseph Elgia, born 1919, died 1972, married Bonnye White in 1945. He served with the 28th Division of the United States Army during World War II in the European Theater. He was a Salesman. Daisy L. Allen, born 1922, married Thomas Shofner in 1940. Thomas Shofner was born in 1910 and died in 1987. To this union, two sons were born.

Thomas Allen McGee born 1946. He received his Bachelor of Science Degree in Engineering from Tennessee Tech University at Cookeville, Tenn. in 1972. He received his Master Degree in Business Administration from Brenau University at Gainesville, Ga. in 1987.

Patrick Mitchell McGee born 1949. He received his bachelor of Science Degree in Engineering from Tennessee Tech University at Cookeville, Tenn. in 1973. He received his Master Degree in Engineering Administration from the University of Tennessee at Knoxville, Tenn. in 1979. He married Marilyn Elizabeth Arnold in 1973. Marilyn received her Bachelor of Science Degree in Education from Tennessee Tech University at Cookeville, Tenn. in 1971. She is a teacher.

To this union two daughters were born.- Meredith Anne McGee, born 1978 and Lauren Elizabeth McGee, born 1980.

Sally F. Allen born 1929, married Giles T. Webb in 1971. She attended Union University at Jackson, Tenn. She majored in Business Administration.

MAURINE ALLEN, of Perry County, Linden, Tenn., was born on Marsh Creek June 13, 1914. Her parents were George Caroll Allen and Bertha Middleton Allen.

She attended Perry County schools and received her Bachelor of Science Degree from Middle Tennessee State Teachers College, Murfreesboro, Tennessee, including a certification for Supervision of Instruction Grades K-12.

She received a certificate of Merit outstand

Maurine Allen

ing contribution to the Right to Read Program Oct. 12, 1976.

She built an Electric View Classroom Projector and Number Board that won 1st place in a Mid-State Unique use of Electricity show. Her educational aids helped to promote learning.

She was initiated by Alpha Rho Chapter Oct. 31,1959 to become a Delta Kappa Gamma member. She served as President of Alpha Rho 1970-1972.

She received a certificate for Patriotic Service Rendered, from the State of Tennessee on Registration Day Oct. 16, 1940 from Gov. Prentice Cooper.

Her interest was in people, home, church, school, community, and heart and cancer drives. She was also a member of First Baptist Church in Linden, Tenn., and a Sunday School teacher, order of Eastern Star, Chapter no. 127, Parsons, Tennessee.

The letters she wrote to the Tennessee Dept. of Conservation in order to get the construction of the Mousetail Landing State Park were acknowledged by B.R. Allison, Commissioner June 23, 1977 in the final designs for the Mousetail State Park. Maurine Allen's Great Grandfather, Robert Thorton McDonald, owned and operated the General Store located on the site from 1865-1877.

ANDERSON, The earlier eighteen hundreds found four Anderson brothers, David, Robert, Richard and William James moving to Tennessee from North Carolina where they were born. Parents of the men are unknown. Over twenty years of research have failed to turn up anything on them.

David, born Dec. 29, 1772, married Isabelle W. Rogers on Jan. 11, 1803 in Cabarrus County, North Carolina. They were parents of seven children, the first four born in North Carolina.

Robert, born 1774 in North Carolina, and wife, Jane Ross Shinn, along with three children, was the first of the four to move to Tennessee. They settled in Hickman County, while brother David settled in Bedford County.

Richard, born March 28, 1777, married Margaret Craig of York County, South Carolina. They went to Hickman County with four children and settled in the kettle-shaped bend of Duck River. Richard was known as "Kettle Dick". Two more children were born in Tennessee.

The youngest of the four was William James born about 1780. Little is known about him other than he settled on Swan Creek in Hickman County and we know of one son.

There was intermarriage among descendants of Richard and David, the first being when Nancy, the daughter of David, married her cousin David, the son of Richard. In time to come Margarette, the daughter of Nancy and David married her cousin Williamson Anderson, son of Joseph Anderson, Joseph being a brother to her mother. This brings us to the subject of Nancy Crencher Anderson Paschall, a resident of Perry County. After the death of John W. Paschall in 1907, Nancy married Lon Sisco.

Nancy Crencher Anderson was the daughter, and third child of William and Margarette Anderson. Nancy Crencher Anderson Paschall died 17 July 1940 in Perry County. She was born November 16, 1857, in Hickman County Tennessee. She married John W. Paschall on Dec. 19, 1876 Hickman County. They evidently soon moved to Perry County as all five of their children were born in Perry County.

Sarah Margaret, born Oct. 3, 1882, married May 5, 1898, to Wade H. Flowers. After his death, she married to Joe Ward and third to Robert Lee Bell. She died Jan. 5, 1968, in Obion County Tennessee. She and Wade H. Flowers had four children.

Grover, born Dec. 16, 1884, died Nov. 19, 1898, in Perry County.

Mary Docus, born Oct. 15, 1888, married John B. Denton. She died June 29, 1969, in Perry County and was the mother of five children.

William Thomas was born Oct. 25, 1891, and married Jan. 21, 1911, to Ora Lee Walls. He died Aug. 22, 1973, in Lake County Tennessee. They were the parents of seven children.

Alma was born Dec. 17, 1898, and died Feb. 18, 1901, in Perry County, Tennessee at the age of two years.

The descendants of John W. and Nancy Paschall married into the Perry County families of Tomlin and Rainey. Other names that are associated with the family are Hickerson and Patterson, which are believed to be Perry County names and perhaps there are others.

Both John W. and Nancy are buried in the Craig Cemetery. Also buried here are John B. and Mary Dorcus Denton and perhaps others of this family.

ANDY CARROLL ANDERSON, (1882 - 1939), and wife Tennessee Kathryn "Kate" Haynes Anderson (1882 - 1955) lived in the Bethel Community in Perry County, Tennessee. Andy was the youngest son of Solomon Anderson and Nancy Ann Randall Anderson. Andy was a farmer and enjoyed hunting, fishing, and playing dominoes. Kate was a housewife whose love of crocheting left many beautiful crocheted pieces for family to enjoy. Andy and Kate were

Andrew Carroll Anderson and family

active in community and church affairs. Children of Andy and Kate were Solomon Pete (1904 - 1979), Bessie Louise (1907 - 1991), Woodrow Carrol (1913 - 1960), and Cora Alice (1916 -).

Andy Anderson's ancestors migrated from Scotland to Northern Ireland in the early 1600s because of religious persecution; and thence to the colony of Virginia in the person of four brothers whose names were John, George, William and James Anderson in the early 1700s. These brothers settled in the neighborhood of the famous old stone church in Augusta County, Virginia.

William Anderson married Mary Reid and in 1750 a son, Captain John Anderson was born.

In 1773, Captain John Anderson (1750 - 1817) moved from Augusta County, Virginia, to the "Block House", an old fort at the head of Carter's Valley in Southwest Virginia. He took an active part in the affairs of the frontier and was frequently engaged in conflicts with the Indians. In 1775, John and Rebecca Maxwell (1753 - 1824) were married and settled on a large tract of land he purchased in Clinch river area. Later he extended his possessions to include the "Block House" tract, where they made their home and spent the remainder of their days. Their children were William II, John Jr., Mary, Elizabeth, Audley, Sarah, Isaac and Jane.

William Anderson II (b. 1776), oldest son of Captain John Anderson, married Rebecca Skillern in 1799. In the early 1800s, William, Rebecca, and their five children, John W., James, Elkanah, Sarah and William P. migrated from Washington County, Virginia to Perry County, Tennessee. Their family was among the first settlers of Perry County.

John W. Anderson (b. 1805), oldest son of William Anderson II, married Sarah Whitwell (b. 1807) and to this union three sons were born, Elkanah Jr., Solomon and Henry. His wife Sarah died in the early 1840s. He then married Sarah's sister, Elizabeth Whitwell (b. 1816). John W. and Elizabeth had four children, Sarah, Caroline, Sam and Margarette. About 1854, John, Elizabeth, and all his children except Solomon moved to S.W. Missouri. Shortly after moving Elizabeth died. John then married Miss Newton and they had one child, Martha Jane. Shortly after the Civil War, John returned to Perry County with his wife and all his children from second and third wives. He remained in Perry County the remainder of his life.

Solomon Anderson (1830 - 1912), youngest son of John W. Anderson, married Nancy Ann Randell (1838 - 1890). Solomon lived, reared his children, and died in Perry County. He and Nancy lived on a farm near Linden in the Bethel Community. Solomon served in the Confederate Army during the Civil War and was at home on leave of absence when his regiment was in the Battle of Shilo. He is buried in the Sugar Hill Cemetery. Solomon and Nancy had eight children of which Andy Anderson was the youngest: John W. Jr. (1858 - 1900), William H. (1860 - 1888), Louise Frances (1863 - 1923), James Clayborne (1866 - 1900), Mary Alice (1868 - 1888), Martha Marline (1872 - 1938), Newton Jasper (1878 - 1912) and Andy Carroll.

BESSIE LOUISE ANDERSON,

(1907 - 1991), was the second child born to Andy Carroll (1882 - 1939) and Tennessee Kathryn "Kate" Haynes (1882 - 1955) Anderson. Bessie married Horace Greely Dunn (1903 - 1969) and they had three children, Jack Thomas (1928 - 1987), Billy Andrew (1933 - 1984) and Lilly Kathryn (1940 - 1987). After a divorce, Bessie married Ezra McDonald (1909 -). They had no children.

Bessie Louise Anderson Dunn McDonald

Bessie spent most of her life in Perry County. She bought her father's farm in the Bethel Community approximately one mile from the Anderson Family farm. Bessie and Horace moved to Detroit, Michigan, for a few years when the children were small. She returned for a few years later after marrying her second husband, Ezra. After returning to Perry County, Bessie and Ezra farmed for a few years in the Warren Community. She always came back to her beloved home in Bethel where she remained until her death.

Bessie was employed for a number of years in the 1940s and early 1950s in the Linden School Cafeteria. Bessie and Ezra were active in community and church affairs. They attended Bethel Methodist Church. After their retirement, Bessie and Ezra spent most of their time visiting and helping the sick in the community.

Jack Dunn, the oldest son of Bessie and Horace, married Julia Ann Ricci (1930 -) of Shickshinny, PA, and they had two children, Dennis Michael (1950 -) and Diane Sherry (1953 -). Jack spent twenty years in the U.S. Army, serving in Italy, Germany, Korea, and Vietnam. After retiring from the Army, Jack settled next to his mother's farm in the Bethel Community where he was self-employed servicing electrical appliances. Dennis, oldest child of Jack and Julia, married Arden Mary Sharpe (1949 -)and they had three children, Sara (1975 -), Bryan (1983 -), and Elyse (1987 -). Dennis and Arden settled in Shickshinny, PA, close to his mother. Diane married Bob Merick and they settled in New Jersey. They had no children.

Billy Dunn, the second child of Bessie and Horace, moved to Detroit, Michigan, in 1952. Billy had three marriages. The first was to Phyllis Ann Fletcher (1934 -) of Detroit, Michigan, and they had two children, Sherry Lynn (1956 -) and Brenda Darlene (1957 -). His second marriage was to Jean ?, of Detroit and they had one son, Billy II (1959 -). His third wife was Sharon ?, with whom he was living at his death. Billy was employed with the Railroad Station in Detroit.

Lilly Kathryn married James Edgar Turnbow (1936 -) and they had no children. Lilly and James divorced and she married Arthur Ralph Elsey (1933 -). Lilly and Arthur had one daughter, Betty Ann (1962 -). Lilly and Art settled in Detroit, Michigan, and Lilly never worked outside her home. Betty Ann married and she had two children, Samatha (1981 -) and Jimmy III (1991 -). Betty Ann lives with her husband, Jimmy McKuhen in upper Michigan.

BONNIE HALBROOKS ANDERSON,

was born Dec. 25, 1906, daughter of Robert (Bob) Marshall Halbrooks, born Dec. 8, 1871, died Sept. 11, 1960, married March 22, 1896 to Mollie Mac DePriest, born July 29, 1874, died Aug. 10, 1957. Both are buried in Bethel Cemetery near Linden. Bonnie married Nov. 21, 1923 to Jasper Albert Anderson, born Feb. 29, 1892, died Dec. 25, 1974, is buried in Bethel Cemetery. Jasper, son of James Clayburn (J.C.) Anderson, born March 11, 1866, died July 24, 1900, married Dora Alice Holt, born March 27, 1869, died Feb. 3, 1929. James Clayburn is buried in Sugar Hill Cemetery. Dora Alice is buried in Bethel Cemetery. Jasper and Bonnie were life long residents of Perry County.

Jasper Albert Anderson

Their four children and grandchildren:

(1) Mary Lucille, born Feb. 23, 1925, married Oct. 22, 1943 to Jack Milford DePriest, born Jan 31, 1922 - died Dec. 25, 1947 and buried in Horner Cemetery Toms Creek. One child: Milford Trent, born Nov. 9, 1944, married July 2, 1966 to Nell Kathyrn Grimes, born June 30, 1949. Child: Kristy Renae, born June 24, 1972. Mary Lucille married Oct. 28, 1948 to Sammy Douglas Sewell, born May 31, 1925. Four children: Kerry Douglas, born March 4, 1950, married March 18, 1971 to Vickie Elaine Bufford, born July 17, 1952. Child: Matthew Douglas, born Jan 25, 1976. Rickey Kirk, born Nov. 28, 1953, married Sept. 22, 1972. to Deborah Finnell. Child: Jennifer Doran, born Aug. 25, 1974. Rickey Kirk married Feb. 17, 1989 to Melanie Leigh Austin, born Dec. 11, 1967. Linda Doran, born Dec. 27, 1954, married Apr. 21, 1977 to James Payton Mays, born Apr. 23, 1953. Two children: Jimmie Leann, born July 20, 1981 and Kelsey Beth, born Sept. 13, 1984. Kenneth Earl, born July 5, 1957, married April 25, 1982 to Brenda Gail Willhite, born June 29, 1957. Three children: John Brent, born Nov. 16, 1983, Jesse Bryan, born Oct. 25, 1985, and Laura Beth, born Jan. 11, 1988. Mary Lucille, married Aug. 25, 1983 to Bernice E. Hinson, born Nov. 17, 1918, died Aug. 9, 1993 and buried Dr. Kirk Cemetery in Linden.

(2) James (J.B.) Black, born May 7, 1927, married Dec. 22, 1950 to Dorothy Dean Cotham, born Aug. 21, 1929.

(3) Martha Jo, born Dec. 19, 1933, married

Dec. 1, 1954 to Chesley Newton Hudson Jr., born Oct. 4, 1930, died June 24, 1973 and buried Dr. Kirk Cemetery. One child: Rebecca Gail, born Nov. 9, 1959, married May 30, 1980 to William Lane Cude, born Feb. 21, 1959. One child: William Gaylon, born Jan. 27, 1988. Martha Jo, married Sept. 24, 1979 to Daniel Wilson Wallace, born Sept. 24, 1944.

(4) Willie Ray, born Sept. 18, 1937, married May 31, 1958 to Linda Gail Smith, born Nov. 25, 1938. Two children: Deborah Denise, born Oct. 8, 1962, married Dec. 20, 1980 to Timothy Ray Johnson, born Jan. 24, 1960. Three children: Joshua Clay, born Sept. 25, 1987, Amanda Michelle, born June 28, 1989 and Benjamin Andrew, born May 7, 1991. Brian Clark, born Aug. 28, 1965, married July 26, 1986 to Tammy Annette Blaylock, born May 15, 1967. One child: John Cameron, born May 28, 1990.

JAMES M. ANDERSON JR., born Jan. 9, 1961, and Cynthia Sue Tucker, born July 6, 1961, married Nov. 18, 1983. Cindy began life in Nashville, TN but spent most of her childhood in Perry County, played basketball, softball and was Valedictorian of her graduating class at Perry County High School. She played Varsity basketball at Freed-Hardeman College, majored in accounting and graduated with a BBA from Freed-Hardeman. She also met James Marshal Anderson Jr. at Freed-Hardeman where he was majoring in Pre-Pharmacy. He received a BS from Freed-Hardeman and a Doctor of Pharmacy from the University of Tennessee at Memphis. Cindy is a C.P.A. and employed by Kraft CPA's in Nashville. James is a Pharmacist with Krogers, Inc. at Franklin, TN.

Connor, Tucker, James and Cindy Anderson

They have three children, Tucker Wesley Anderson (born May 16, 1987), Connor Presley Anderson (born Jan. 18, 1991), and McKenzie Brooke Anderson (born Apr. 25, 1994).

Cindy is the daughter of Billy and Sue Tucker, the granddaughter of Frank and Vera Tucker and Douglas and Earlie Riley Gilbert.

James is the son of James Marshal Anderson (born July 1, 1937) and Dezmere Marie Clark (born Sept. 24, 1942). James Sr. is the son of Lewis Monroe Anderson (born Sept. 23, 1885) and Mozelle Katherine Massey (born Apr. 29, 1910). Dezmere is the daughter of Elden Wayne Clark (born Nov. 7, 1921) and Pearl Ellen Jennings (born Mar. 18, 1924).

JAMES BLACK (J.B.) & DOROTHY DEAN ANDERSON, live in Linden. J.B. is a veteran of WW II, both are retired. Dorothy Dean's grandparents are Isaac Jesse Cotham, born May 29, 1879, died July 17, 1956, married Sept. 16, 1900 to Annie Alice Hufstedler, born Nov. 4, 1881, died July 23, 1973; both are buried in Bethel Cemetery near Linden and George Dibbrell Whitwell, born Dec. 25, 1868, died Oct. 10, 1953, married Feb. 24, 1894 to Henry Agnes Warren, born Oct. 19, 1879, died Sept. 11, 1953; both are buried in Roberts Cemetery, Marsh Creek. Dorothy Dean's parents: Bynum Trenton Cotham, born May 5, 1903, died June 15, 1975, buried in Dr. Kirk Cemetery, married Dec. 25, 1925 to Byron Mable Whitwell, born Jan. 26, 1905, died May 4, 1948, buried in Roberts Cemetery, Marsh Creek. Bynum married March 3, 1950 to Mary Ethel Kimble, born March 29, 1908, died June 4, 1986.

Bynum Trenton Cotham

Bynum and Byron's four children are:

(1) Margaret Jean, born Oct. 5, 1927, married July 4, 1948 to Albert Gaines Landers, born July 30, 1923. Their four children: Douglas Albert, born Apr. 14, 1951, married Aug. 12, 1972 to Cynthia Cathrine Cox, born March 13, 1955. Children: Douglas Chadwick, born March 12, 1975 and Kansas Kristen, born March 10, 1979. Mark Andrew, born July 24, 1957, married March 12, 1989 to Vanessa Graves, born July 9, 1961. Peter Eric, born Sept. 3, 1959, married June 15, 1985 to Valeria Jean Conners. Child: Courtney Layne, born July 4, 1986. Julia Deanne, born Apr. 22, 1964, married June 7, 1985 to Tony Eugene Clabough. Two Children: Emily Nicole, born March 18, 1986 and Madeline Rebekkah, born Sept. 7, 1990. Julian Deanne, married Nov. 1992 to Randy Wallace Edwards. Child: Randy Wallace Jr., born Sept. 9, 1993.

(2) Dorothy Dean, born Aug. 21, 1929, married Dec. 22, 1950 to James Black Anderson, born May 7, 1927.

(3) Dorris Ann, born Jan. 21, 1934, married Apr. 23, 1952 to Don Parnell, born Apr. 2, 1935. Two Children: Barry Don, born Nov. 15, 1952 and Daryl Roy, born June 1, 1957, died Sept. 26, 1988, buried in Dr. Kirk Cemetery.

(4) James Franklin, born May 30, 1936, married Dec. 17, 1960 to Linda Gay Edwards, born July 26, 1943. Two children: Kimberly Antionette, born Aug. 2, 1961, married Dec. 17, 1982 to Millard Ward Smith, born Oct. 31, 1953, and Robin Gay, born Nov. 21, 1965, married June 2, 1990 to Albert David Clanton, born Oct. 9, 1966. Child: Blair Nicole, born Apr. 2, 1991.

JAMES ROBERT "BOB" ANDERSON, son of Robert Drake Anderson and second wife Sarah Adeline Womark, was born in Perry County on March 8, 1883, died April 18, 1915, age 32.

James Robert Anderson and Anna Plummer Anderson

James Robert married Anna Plummer in Linden Nov. 8, 1905. She was born in Lewis County Sept. 21, 1883. Her parents were Dr. Hugh Kirk Plummer and wife Mary Narcissus Loggins. They were parents of five children; Jim, Bob, Madden, Anna, and Lavina. Anna died Dec. 20, 1970, sister and brothers deceased.

James Robert, known as Bob, and Anna were the parents of four girls all born in Perry County.

Marie married Thomas Harris, attorney in Linden. They had three children, Doris Armentrout, Bob Harris, and Rose Paschall and ten grandchildren. Marie, Thomas and son, Bob, deceased.

Elise married Walton Whitwell in Perry County. He was an attorney and at the time of his death, was General Counsel for N.C. and St. L. Railroad in Nashville. Elise served as Clerk and Master, Chancery Court, Perry County from 1942 to 1975. Their only child, Peggy Ann Mabry, is now living in Linden in the old Anderson house, which is the oldest house in Linden. She has two children living out of the county. Elise died Jan. 30, 1993.

Sue married George Wilson Sharp of Flatwoods, Perry County. He was a school teacher and served as Superintendent of Perry County Schools prior to his death on Jan. 26, 1976. Sue taught school and worked with the County and State Welfare Department from 1939 until retirement in 1975. Two daughters, Suzanne, Judy, Elise and one grandson, Courtney, survive. Sue is now living in Linden.

Lily Hugh married Henry Eikel Jr. of Biloxi, Mississippi. He was a civil engineer. Lily Hugh served for 25 years as Assistant, Mortuary Office, Keesler Air Force Base, Biloxi. They had one child, Henry III, and six grandchildren. Lily Hugh and husband are deceased.

This has been a close related family, interested in education, economic, and political needs of Perry County.

SAMUEL T. ANDERSON, was living in Perry County in 1880. He was born in 1834 and married on Oct. 22, 1859 in Lewis County to Sarah Ann Morris. They lived in Lewis County until moving to Perry County. Sarah Ann was born in 1833, daughter of Joseph Morris. She had several brothers and sisters, Anderson, Samuel, Aaron and Edward Thomas Morris. Sisters were Rebecca Campbell, Betsy Burchard, Jane Berry, Nancy Rosson and Polly Brown. Samuel and Sarah Ann had at least three daughters, Mary, Sarah and Tennessee and perhaps one named Rachel.

SOLOMON PETE ANDERSON,

(1904 - 1979), was the oldest son of Andy Anderson (1882 - 1939) and Tennessee Kathryn "Kate" Haynes (1882 - 1955) Anderson. In 1928, Pete married Donnie V. Canada (1912 -). Donnie was the youngest daughter of John and Martha Jane "Mattie" Reeves Canada of Gibson County, Tennessee.

Solomon Pete Anderson and Donnie V. Canada Anderson

In the mid 1920s, Pete left Perry County to go to Gibson County, Tennessee to grow tomatoes. He earned enough money to buy his first T-Model Ford. It was here that he met his future wife, Donnie.

After a couple of years in Gibson County, Pete returned to Perry County. He worked for the State Highway Department, then the County Highway Department for a number of years.

Pete and Donnie moved to the Anderson family farm in 1942 where they farmed. They also raised tomato and potato plants to sell, employing all neighborhood children who wanted to work.

When electricity became available, Pete sold and installed electric water pumps, which he continued to service until his death, always servicing widow's pumps at no charge.

In the early 1950s, Pete was employed by the Perry County School System as Maintenance Supervisor and continued in this position until his retirement in the mid 1970s.

Pete enjoyed music and could play the banjo, ukulele, fiddle, and piano. He was song leader at his church, Bethel Methodist. Pete was an avid reader and historian. Together with a cousin, Andy Anderson of Oklahoma, traced his ancestors to the 1600s in Scotland.

Pete and Donnie were very family and community oriented. Their house was the gathering place for neighbors and friends.

Donnie did not work outside the home until 1954, when she was employed at Linden School Cafeteria. She became Linden Elementary School Cafeteria Supervisor, a job she continued until her retirement in 1983. Donnie enjoyed all crafts especially piecing and quilting quilts, but her most enjoyable activity was cooking and inviting family, neighbors, and friends in.

Pete and Donnie had one child, Martha Kathryn (1936 -). Martha married William Eddie Ellison (1932 -), the oldest son of Albert Ellison Sr. and Elsie Carrie Harder Ellison. Martha was employed at the Perry County Health Department as Secretary in 1961 and in 1990 became District Clerical Supervisor for Hickman, Lewis, Perry, and Wayne County Health Departments. Martha served as Secretary to the American Red Cross and was Red Cross Service to Military Families contact person, organized the first Girl Scouts in Perry County, was active in the Order of the Eastern Star, and took an active part in Bethel Methodist church activities.

Martha and Eddie had three daughters, Donna Anne (1957 -), Julia Mae (1961 -), and Kathy V (1964 -), Anne married Glyn Mercer, son of Ray Mercer and Marie Trull Mercer, and they had four children, Amy Lyn (1979 -), Benjamin Ryan (1980 -), Craig Matthew (1982 -), and Dray William (1993 -). Both Ann and Glyn were school teachers. Julia married David Edney, son of Joe Edney and Betty Qualls Edney, and they had two daughters, Katrina Renea (1981 -) and Kristal Lenea (1988 -). Both Julia and David were employed by local industries. Kathy had two children, Brian Jack Joseph (1986 -) and Brianette Christine (1989 -) Shannon. Kathy contracted with the State of Tennessee to transport Medicaid patients to medical providers.

Pete and Donnie's family, Martha, Anne, Julia, Kathy, and their families all settled on the Anderson family farm in Bethel Community with them.

WILLIAM EARL (BILL) ANDERSON,

born Oct. 16, 1942, on his Father's birthday at home at Iron Hill near Parsons in Decatur County Tennessee, the oldest of three children of Earl Charles and Dorothy Lois Groom Anderson. Bill's Grandfather, Luther Thomas Groom, Great Grandfather, Sam Denton Groom, Great Great Grandfather, Henry Groom were all born in Perry County and lived there as well. His Great Great Great Grandfather, Billy Groom, came over from Germany to North Carolina and then moved to Perry County to live. Although Bill never lived in Perry County, his ancestors go back five generations and he visits his mother and sister regularly.

William Earl "Bill" Anderson

Bill lived in Lawrenceburg during the school years. He attended Highland Park Baptist Church and professed his faith in Jesus Christ at the age of 12. Bill graduated from Lawrence County High School in 1960 and attended the University of Tennessee at Knoxville in 1961. He then moved to Nashville and in 1964, he joined the United States Army Air National Guard at Berry Field in Nashville. He took basic training at Fort Jackson, South Carolina and received his "On Job Training" with the 50th Signal Battalion of the 18th Airborne Corps in Fort Bragg, North Carolina. Active reserve duty was served with Company E, 30th Maintenance Battalion at Berry Field.

Bill secured a job within a week of his return from active duty and then set the date for his marriage for Dec. 24, 1964. This was the same date that his mother and father were married in 1938. Bill married Miss Linda Faye Walling of Nashville at Hillhurst Baptist Church by Reverend James Lee. Bill and Linda have one son, William (Tim) Timothy Anderson, born August 12, 1966 at Baptist Hospital in Nashville. Tim graduated from Hendersonville High School in 1984, attended a vocational school and got his Journeyman Electrician Certificate in 1991. Tim married Tonya Cramer of Hendersonville, Tennessee and they now have two children, Tamra Lyn, born May 16, 1988 and Kelsie Louise, born Aug. 6, 1991. Tim, Tonya, Tamra, and Kelsie moved to Columbus, Indiana in January 1993 where they now reside.

Bill took a job with Nixon Detroit Diesel in 1970 and now has changed its name to Nixon Power Services Company. They are the distributor for Kohler Generator Sets. Bill has had continuous employment with Nixon since 1970. Bill and Linda were divorced in the Spring of 1987.

Bill married for the second time in 1989 to Virginia Dianne Reese of Dover. Dianne has three children from a previous marriage, Charlotte Michele Allen, Carmen Melissa (Missy) DeWeese, and Richard Edwin Reese. Dianne has four grandchildren, Matthew Kyle Allen, Jay Taylor DeWeese, Corey Michael Allen, and Katelyn Dianne DeWeese. Dianne works in customer service for Francis Lusky Company in Nashville. Bill and Dianne currently live in Hendersonville, Tennessee and attend the First Assembly of God church in Hendersonville.

WILLIAM THOMAS ANDERSON,

a son of Robert Drake and Sarah Adaline Womack Anderson, was born in 1873 in Madison County, Tennessee. The family moved to Perry County when he was young. While in his teens, he became a clerk in the store of Tom Sutton. When Tom Sutton died in 1896, William bought the store from the heirs. While the Suttons were living in Linden, Jennette (Nettie) Sutton, a niece of Tom Sutton, came for a visit. She was born in Hickman County to Joseph Martin and Caroline Stephens Sutton, who were living in Gibson County at that time. Nettie and William were married there in 1899.

Five children were born to Nettie and William: Mary married Robert Cawthon; Jack married Florra Parks Wheeler; Frances married William Moss Gibbs; Tommie married Malcolm Moss Gibbs, a brother of William; Joseph Drake married Anne Woodard. A total of six grandchildren were born to the Anderson children.

While still operating the store, William bought the Rise Mill, that had a flour mill and a lumber mill where a great number of trees were turned into timber. In 1918, William sold both the store and mill and moved to Williamson County where he died in 1938 and Nettie died in 1961. They were both buried in Mt. Hope Cemetery located in Franklin, Tennessee.

William had one sister, Anna, who married William Jordan Milan and to them were born ten children. The children were living in different parts of the country and William and Anna moved to Maury County where he died. She later moved to Texas where she died and their children lived in many states.

The one brother of William Thomas Anderson was James Robert who married Anna Plummer and to them were born four daughters. James Robert and Anna have been dead many years and most of their children are no longer living.

During William's lifetime, he was deeply interested in the education of his children and many of the out-of-town teachers in the Linden school boarded in his home. In addition, he was very active in the Methodist church and was also a Mason. During World War I, he served on the Draft Board, which was an unhappy time for him when many of his friend's sons had to report for Army duty. His sons were too young at that time to serve.

KEITH & HELEN ARY, live on Sinking Creek in Perry County. Helen is the daughter of Whitfield and Melinda Eugenia Holt Lamar. Keith is the grandson of Henry Elijah and Mary (Sis) Tharp. Henry Elijah was the grandson of Henry and Sophia Ary. (See biography of Henry and Sophia Ary.)

Eugenia, Keith and Elbert Ary

Henry Elijah, born 1870, died 1953, married Mary Tharp, born 1870, died 1910. They had eight children: Elbert, Edna, Alma, Elmer, Maurice, Sally, Macie, and Georgia. All of the above children, except Elbert, left Perry County and settled in West Tennessee around Sharon, Tennessee.

Elbert, born 1889, died 1977, and Eugenia Harder, born 1892, died 1987, were married in 1913. They had five children: Mavis Era, born 1914, married Joe Borthick from Robertson County. They had two daughters: Joary and Faye. Melba Lois, born 1917, married Maurice Tollison from Robertson County. They had two sons: Sam and Bert. Kermit Rosevelt, born 1919, married Mildred Chapman from Georgia. They had two sons: Kermit Rosevelt Jr. (Teddy) and Ashley. Kenneth Hammond, born 1921, married Dean Sharp from Perry County. They had three children: Johnnie, Paul, and Linda. Keith Cleamon, born 1934, married Mary Helen Lamar from Perry County. They had one son, Bryan Keith. All of the above children left Perry County except Keith.

Elbert and Eugenia lived all their life either on Rockhouse or Sinking Creek in Perry County. Elbert made a living farming and running a timber business.

ARY - WARREN, William (Bill) Ary, a farmer, the last of 17 children, was born Aug. 7, 1840, died Apr. 20, 1924. On May 24, 1866, he married Mary Jane Warren, born Dec. 18, 1846, died Jan. 14, 1922, buried at Ary Family Cemetery on Sinking Creek, Perry County. Information came from a Tennessee Civil War Veterans Questionnaire belonging to William Ary. His father was Henry Ary, from Salisbury, Roan County, North Carolina, where he lived for 30 years before coming to Perry County. William's mother was Sophia Fraley. Sophia's father was Jacob Fraley. The name of Sophia's mother was unknown. Sophia was born in 1795. Sophia and Henry left North Carolina (probably leaving grown children behind), coming to Tennessee, settling on the head of Sinking Creek. The Ary farm, consisting of 360 acres, was worth about $300.00. Here they built a bark house. Henry died between 1840 and 1850. The 1850 census lists Sophia Ary, 52, as head of household: Daniel, 19, Nancy, 17, Millie, 14, and William 10.

William (Bill) Ary and family

William and Mary Jane Warren Ary had 11 Children:

George Anderson Ary, born Aug. 17, 1868, died Nov. 23, 1960, married Anner Dowdy. Children are: Inus, Trester, Ranzy, and Dewey.

Henry Elige Ary, born Aug. 28, 1870, died Feb. 1953, married Mary Roseann Tharp. Children are: Elbert, Edna, Elmer, Ozarchie, Alma, William, Morrison, Sally, Macy, and Georgia.

William Franklin, born Sept. 14, 1872, died Nov. 3, 1898, died young (single).

Daniel Felix, born Oct. 29, 1874, died Aug. 4, 1953, married Emma Graves. Children are: Annie, Jessie, Ottie Lee, and Frank.

Hubert died in the Army.

Nancy Matilda, born Oct. 25, 1876, died ____, married Newt Hickerson. Children are: Kate, Whitney, Junior, Odis, Winford, and Ruth. Buried in Lewis county.

Mary Jane, born Jan. 10, 1881, died Nov. 19, 1954, married Noah Theodore Grinder. Thirteen children: Izorah, Mollie, Sadie, Zellnah, Abbner, Loyd, Emma, Osburn, Wesson, Opal, Sue, Cletus, Clint, (see Grinder-Ary). Buried Ary Cemetery.

Riley Burdict, born Dec. 13, 1882, married Emma Sharp. Children are: LaVander, Ova, Hazel, Kyle, Arlie, and Victoria. Most of these are close to Martin, Sharon, and Greenfield, Tennessee, Weakley County. Riley and wife are buried in West Tennessee.

Lula Can Sadie, born Feb. 14, 1885, died 1970, married Ezra O'Guin, one son, Willie Taylor. Lula is buried at Ary Cemetery.

Emmanuel Stinson, born Aug. 31, 1887, married Ava Fight, one son, Buford.

Prince Albert, born Oct. 1, 1889, died Aug. 1902, died young, never married.

Zula Namona, born Jan. 20, 1892, died Aug. 24, 1968, married Newt Treadwell. Children are: Katherine, France, Ann, and Jasper. Zula is buried in Ary Cemetery.

William (Bill) enlisted into Masonry, Feb. 27, 1869, went to Fellow Craft, Jan. 19, 1869, and was raised to Master Mason, July 17, 1869. William's Army record revealed that in 1862, he was a Confederate in the 9th Mounted Cavalry at Jackson, Tennessee. William states on his Tennessee Civil War Veterans questionnaire that his ancestors were from Germany. The family later found out that his ancestors went from Germany to Holland, then to England, and from England on to North Carolina. Compiled by Great granddaughter, Joy Gordon, and Grandson, LaVander Ary.

ASHTON-BATES, Bernice Bates, born Apr. 5, 1909, was a granddaughter of John Redner Bates. Her father was William James Bates, born Feb. 7, 1870, died Apr. 17, 1925. William James, known as "Will", married Flora Twomey, born Feb. 9, 1885, died Aug. 12, 1976. They were married Dec. 24, 1907.

Five generations of the Ashton-Bates family

John Redner Bates married Mary Ann Dean in Perry County in 1862. He enlisted in the C.S.A. in Davidson County in 1862 and served in the 53rd Tennessee Infantry. Mary Ann was the daughter of Wade N. "Dick" Dean. After John Redner and Mary Ann married, they came to Perry County (where Dick's mother and several brothers lived). They had ten children of which William James "Will" was number four in line.

William James "Will" was a business man (timber), a Democrat, and a Methodist. He moved his mill from place to place sawing lumber and cross ties. He owned the homeplace that is now occupied in Lobelville by F.M. Horner. He was married to Nettie Murray. They had nine children. Nettie died in 1906. He then married Flora Twomey in 1907. They had eight children, of which Bernice was the eldest. Earline followed, then Georgia, Ruth, Mildred, Tommye, and Willie J. John Andrew was stillborn on Oct. 20, 1915. Out of these two marriages came seven school teachers. Ferd, from the first marriage, was Superintendent of Schools in Georgia when he died in 1959.

Flora Twomey, daughter of Andrew Johnson Twomey and Nancy Jane Daniel, was married to "Will" Bates for only eighteen years. He died in April 1925 at an early age of only fifty-five years, leaving Flora with the girls; Willie J. having not been born. Willie J. was born in July the same year. Luckily she acquired the office of Perry County Register in September

1934 (where she served until August 1942). This means of financial support helped greatly in the rearing of her family. As one daughter would finish high school, they would become employed to help with the finances for the others to remain in school. Three of them became school teachers. When Willie J. died at the age of 47, she was employed in the Pentagon in Washington, D.C.

During this time, they lived in Linden. When they all had left home, Flora moved back to Lobelville, finishing out her remaining days, being a widow for 51 years. She was a stalwart lady, firmly believing and practicing disciplinary measures with her children and grandchildren.

Bernice married Alf Ashton Sr., June 12, 1926, in Waverly. She was employed at Dupont in Old Hickory. Alf was working for the Ford Motor Company in Detroit, Michigan where they went to live. Their oldest son, John Will, was born May 7, 1927. Emma Jean was born June 13, 1928. In 1929, Alf and Bernice already having been back to Lobelville, purchased a house from Russell Gray. He traded Mr. Gray an auto for the house on Leeper Drive. Alf was a truck driver and traded back in the 30s, mostly in mules and horses. He would make occasional trips to Detroit, bringing automobiles back for Authur Batton, who was the automobile dealer in Lobelville at the time. Alf Ashton Jr. was born in Lobelville, Oct. 23, 1930, Flora Joy was born July 27, 1941, Roy Edward, May 17, 1947, and Russell Patterson was born March 1, 1949. John Will married Elizabeth Loggins. They have two sons, Steve and Robert.

Emma Jean married Calvin O'Bryan. They have three sons, John, Mark, and Bobby. Alf Jr. married Videlle Coleman. They have four children, Judy, Mike, Don, and Jane. Flora Joy married Loyd Blair having three children, Brad, Kenny, and Valerie. Roy Edward married Linda Bain having two sons, Jeff and Chad. Russell married Brenda Howell.

Emma Jean's son, John O'Bryan, married Jane Burcham, June 14, 1968. They have two children, Johnnia and Chris. Johnnia married Michael Scott Henderson in 1992. They now have a daughter, Michaela Camille, born in 1993 (shown in the picture above making five generations in the family). *Submitted by Emma Jean Ashton O'Bryan.*

ASHTON-BROWN, Alf Ashton Sr., born Jan. 30, 1903, died Oct. 5, 1993, was a great grandson of Valentine and Isabelle Moreau Wiss. Valentine was a Bavarian tailor and musician whose U.S. citizenship was granted in 1854 in Hickman County. He served from 1861-1864 as a bugler with the 9th Battalion of the Tennessee Cavalry Volunteers.

Valentine and Isabelle's daughter, Tabitha Clagett Wiss, married Walter Walker Brown Jr. in 1880. Walter was a son of Walter W. and Fredonia L. A. Johnson. Fredonia's father, Isham Johnson, had purchased three hundred acres of land in Hickman County for a muzzle loading rifle and $2.00 hard cash. In Perry County land records, he is listed as being administrator of 5,000 acres of land, previously occupied by Indians who had cleared out in the "Trail of Tears Movement." This land was later taken in by Lewis County when lines were changed.

Alf Ashton Sr.

Walter helped build Bethel Methodist Church and was a charter member. Later, he gave land and helped build Goshen Baptist Church.

During the Civil War, when bushwhackers were confiscating livestock, Walter held them off by refusing to relinquish his stock necessary for his livelihood. After the war, Walter and Fredonia were attending church at Goshen and the preacher was one of the bushwhackers. Walter, with Fredonia tugging at his coattails, approached the preacher declaring that he would not listen to a horse stealer preach the Lord's Word in a church for which he gave the land and helped build. With that, he threw the preacher out and the congregation applauded.

Walter Jr. and Tabitha's daughter, Emma Brown, married John Thomas Ashton. John Thomas Ashton was the son of James Thomas Ashton and Mary Downing of Lewis County. He and Emma moved to Lobelville in the early 1900s. They had five children, Annie Maude, Lela, Hazel, Mary Lou, and Alf Sr., the only son. Emma died at the early age of thirty having tuberculosis. John then married Nora Byrd. They had two children, Jim and Catherine. He was in the mercantile business and had a truck, going out and peddling merchandise. The store was located at the corner of Main Street and 7th Avenue near the Duff house. They lived in a house behind the store on 7th Avenue. *Submitted by Emma Jean Ashton O'Bryan.*

AYERS-WYATT, Dick Donald Ayers, born Dec. 30, 1912 to Ernest James and Ethel Starbuck Ayers in Perry County. The youngest of five children, he attended local schools and graduated with a BS degree from Milligan College. While in East Tennessee, he met and married Mary Frank Roberts, who died suddenly at Parsons, Tennessee in 1940. He taught school in various places, coached both football and basketball, was a referee for basketball games, as well as being a teacher for over 20 years before retiring.

Kathleen and Dick Ayers

Mary Kathleen Wyatt Ayers was born to David Chesley and Mary Magdalene Britt Wyatt in Decatur County. After high school, she took a business course and worked at Decaturville Department of Public Welfare, where she met Dick. They were married Jan. 17, 1941. In 1942, they moved to Perry County to the Ayers farm to be near Dick's parents. In 1943, Kathleen went to work at Linden for Conder Chevrolet Company. She rode a Greyhound bus to and from work. Due to the war, no one could buy a car. She remained employed there for 37 years before retiring. During this time, Dick farmed, operated a sawmill with his brother, Paul Ayers. Then in 1963, he returned to the teaching profession and taught until age 65 forced his retirement by law in Perry County. He was chairman of the republican party for several years, was appointed to Election Comm. where he served until his death. He also served on the U.S. Soil Conservation commission for 37 years and was still serving at his death.

Kathleen retired from General Motors Accounting at the Chevrolet Dealership in Linden in 1982. They built a home on the property known as Ayers Farm and lived there 51 years before Dick's death on Dec. 25, 1993. Kathleen remains in the home at the same address.

DANIEL BAARS, born in 1854, died in 1927, buried in Beardstown cemetery. Daniel was the son of George and Lena Baars. He married Ruth A. Clayton on Dec. 9, 1872 in Perry County. Ruth, born in 1854, died in 1940, buried in Beardstown cemetery. Ruth was the daughter of Morris Clayton and Harriet Sharp.

Daniel and Ruth had several children, but only four lived to adulthood. 1) Lena Baars, married or was engaged to marry William Smith in Perry County, 1897. 2) J. Comer Baars, born 1880, married July 5, 1899 in Perry County to C.L. Johnson and lived in Ohio. 3) Ida Baars, born 1882, married June 10, 1900, in Perry County to R. T. Young. 4) Stanley Baars, born Oct. 8, 1899, died Apr. 13, 1977, buried in Beardstown cemetery.

BAARS-MAYER, George Baars, born 1814, married Lena Mayer, born 1811. George and Lena were born in Holland; their families farmed. In 1845, George and Lena, with their infant child, Ann, started their journey for the new world in a sail boat with friends. Five days on their way, a storm raged from several hours, damaging the boat. It was necessary to return to home port. George Baars, a carpenter, repaired the boat. After several days work, they were on their way again to make their home in America. For 47 days, they sailed before landing on the shore of America. George told the story many times. When they stepped on shore, his wife, Lena, said, "Thank God, crossed the ocean once, but never no more."

Traveling west, they first settled in Paducah, Kentucky, for a short time. Moving south into Tennessee, they bought a farm in Perry County on Kings Branch, built a log home and farmed the land.

Their second child, Martha Jane, born Nov. 20, 1848, died July 26, 1936, married J.B. (Pony) King in March 1872. Their children: George 1874-1956, Denna 1876-1943, Rebecca 1878-

1957, William (Billy) 1881-1960, Abner 1884-1969, Norma 1885-1893, Mattie 1889-1970.

Jane and Pony owned a 420 acre farm on upper Kings Branch. George and Billy lived on or near the farm all their lives.

Their third child, Nathaniel (Natt) 1853-1922, married Ellen Cude. Their children: Martha 1875- , Oscar, 1882-1916, Albert 1887-1951. Oscar and one of his girls were drowned in Buffalo River when it was flooded in 1916. Natt married his second wife, Dora Sharp O'Guin, 1876-1924. Their children: Velera 1905- , Sue 1907-1987, Nathaniel, infant death, Mollie 1910-,Willie 1912-1977, Lena 1915- . They owned and lived on a farm on Toms Creek until their death.

George and Lena's fourth child, Daniel, 1854-1927, married in 1872 to Rutha Ann Clayton, 1854-1940. Their children were: Lena, Comer, Ida, and Stanley. Bob and Bessie died as infants. Dan built his home near his parents on Kings Branch where he farmed. They planted an apple orchard that their children and grandchildren enjoyed. Stanley lived most of his life in the home. In later years, he built a new home near the old home place.

The grandchildren of Pony and Jane Baars King living are: Norma Hildenbrandt, Alex King, Johnny Lomax, Louise Curl, and Myrtle Gladden.

The memories are of seeing the old log home where Grandmother Jane was born and grew up, the home place built by Grandmother and Granddaddy King where their children were born and grew up, the big spring and yard, the old apple orchard, and the reunions we all enjoyed in our younger days.

BAKER, William David (Will) and Victoria Harper Baker's second son, William E. (Billy) Baker, was born in Perry County on Feb. 27, 1894.

William D. Baker Family. Top row, L to R: Leeona E. Baker, William David Baker, Victoria Harper Baker, John Rufus Baker. Bottom row, L to R: James D. Baker, Jesse A. Baker, William Edward Baker.

Victoria Harper was born May 15, 1865, to Marcus and Nancy Chandler Harper in Hickman County. Marcus L. Harper was born March 15, 1826, in Hickman County to Wiley and Sarah Harper. Wiley V. Harper, a veteran of the War of 1812, came to Hickman County with his wife, Sarah Green, from Halifax, North Carolina in 1822. They moved to Lobelville in 1857, where Wiley died in 1858. Sarah lived until 1880.

Will Baker was born August 1, 1866, to Rufus and Joannah Wright Baker. Rufus K. Baker was born January 1827, to John W. and Mary Baker of Hickman County. John W. Baker was born about 1793 in Tennessee. Joannah Wright was born about 1832, the daughter of Joseph Wright.

Will and Victoria were married July 10, 1887, in Hickman County by Jackson Blackwell. A daughter, Leeona (Lee) was born Aug. 15, 1888, followed two years later by John Rufus on Jan. 29, 1891. Will's young family had moved to the Cunningham place north of Lobelville by 1894 when Billy was born. A third son, James Dee was born Jan. 6, 1896.

In March of 1897, Will Baker helped build log rafts. When the Duck River rose following a rain, the men rode the rafts downstream to sell the timber. Returning home through slush and drizzle, they rested and ate in Bakerville. Another son, Jesse, was born March 13, 1898.

By 1903, Will had returned to Perry County, living near the John Gilmer house on Russell's Creek where Edd was born on November 22. Leeona and Jim Bates of Hickman County were married by A.B. Gunter on Oct. 13, 1907, and moved west to Obion County. In 1909, John, Billy, Jim, and Jesse Baker were four of 92 students in the Cedar Grove School near Only. The term ended on December 23.

The Great War in Europe took boys from the country. John Baker left home first. He was to die in France. Billy landed in France just after the Armistice. After the war, Will and Victoria sold the Blackwell Hollow farm to Doug Shanes and left Hickman County. They bought the Curry farm on Lost Creek, Oct. 20, 1919, and moved to the old log house. Except for Billy, the boys had moved away, attracted by jobs in St. Louis and Detroit. Jim and Edd later returned to Lobelville.

Victoria had one of the first radios in the area. She regularly listened to Bro. Calhoun of the Central Church of Christ in Nashville, on the new radio station, WSM. Will Baker died Sept. 21, 1930. Billy took over the farming and bought the other children's interests. He married Lela Lafferty of Peter's Landing on May 19, 1940. He completed a new house late in 1943. Victoria died Nov. 9, 1943 (three weeks before Billy and Lela's son Samuel was born on Dec. 1, 1943. *Submitted by Samuel T. Baker.*

DR. JIMISON BANDY, 1788-1872, was born in Virginia. He was educated to be a Presbyterian Minister. He later became a doctor. He was also in the War of 1812 and served in Captain George Smith's Company Tennessee Mil. as 1st Lt. Secret Service, 2nd Lt. under Col. Thomas Williamson, in Capt. Robert Moore, Vol. Mtd. Gunman. 2nd Lt. under Maj. John Cocke, TVM Gunman.

His parents came from Ireland and England. From Virginia, they moved to Sumner County, Tennessee. There he married Elizabeth Wright in 1822. They had four children. Elizabeth probably died somewhere on their way to Hickman County where they were found in 1830. Then Jimison, along with his children, made the move to Perry County on Tom's Creek 4th Dist. In 1842, he married a young widow, Nancy Denson Wilson. They had four children.

Children by Jimison and Elizabeth are:

Mary Hudson, 1814-1893, married Caswell Cotham, 1814-1879. Children: William E., 1833-, Jamison Bandy, 1836-1911, George W.-, 1838-, John Wright, 1842-1906, Mary Jane (Mollie), 1844-, Elizabeth, 1847-, Harwell, 1849-1879, Robert C., 1854-1927, Nancy Ann Frances, 1855-1944, Julia Ann, 1858-, Sarah Dena, 1858-, Mary C., 1859-.

Sallie Ann, 1826-1913, married Harvey Nixon Cotham, 1825-1902. Children: William James, 1847-1927, Elizabeth, 1851-, Richard E., 1856-1919, George B., 1862-1896, Samuel Harvey, 1873-1956.

Jane C., 1830-1910, married William B. Denson, 1822-1865. Children: Sarah Ann (Sis), 1845-1919, Mary Elizabeth (Puss), 1850-1916, Maria Jane, 1853-1918, Nancy M. (Ett), 1850-.

James J., 1828-1890, married Matilda, 1836-. Children: John V., 1856-, Mollie E. James and his family were not found in the 1880 census. By then they had probably moved to another county or state.

Children by Jimison and Nancy. Nancy had a son by her first marriage, Thomas N. Wilson, 1836-. Her husband is not known at this time.

Richard, 1843-, believed to have died in 1861 at the age of 18 of pneumonia. He was thought to be attending college in Bedford County, Tennessee.

William J., 1845-1916, married Melinda E. Terry 1859-1921. Children: Julia, 1876-1964, Jamie May (Jennie), 1878-1926, Anna M., 1880- , Laura, 1884-, Augustus Pat, 1887-, Robert J., 1892-1950, Elmer Lee, 1894-1934.

Amanda, 1850-, nothing else is known about her. In the 1860 census, she is 10 and in the 1870 census, she cannot be found.

Joe W., 1852-1937, married Martha C. Crowell, 1856-1928. Children: Jimison H., 1875-1960, Fannie H., 1881-1964, Edgar S., 1885-1912, Augusta L., 1888-.

Most of the Bandy family is buried at Denson's and Crooked Creek Cemetery. *Submitted by David and Diane Walker.*

ALLEN BARBER, came to the Hickman County area, it's believed, before 1820 and settled on Hurricane Creek, now Perry County. Allen, born 1795 in Anson County, NC, died 1889 in Tennessee, married Martha Kilpatrick, born 1801, died 1869 in Tennessee, daughter of Andrew and Martha Kilpatrick. Allen's parents were Rev. War soldier, John Barber (1738-1802 NC) and Mary Allen (1739-1807 NC).

Allen and Martha Barber's children: Andrew (1820) married Tilitha Smith; Mary "Polly" (1821) married first to Jorden Dowdy, then to Alvin Warren; Gatsey (1824) married Eli Warren; John (1826) married Rhoda Beckham; Charlotte (1830); Nancy Ann (1833) married Ruffin S. Stephens; Joseph (1839); Daniel (1844) married first to Sarah Kilpatrick, then to Mary A. Kilpatrick; and Martha (1856).

Andrew D.J. Barber (b. Oct. 2, 1820 Perry County - died 1870s AR) married Tilitha Smith (b.1822 TN - died 1890s AR) around 1840, probably in Perry County. Their children (most born in TN): Nancy J. (1841), John (1843), Amanda (1844) married W.W. Nuckolls, Mary (1847), Louisa (1849), James (1852), Martha (1854), and Gatsey (1859 AR). They moved to Newton County, AR by 1860. Andrew's brother, John, and his family moved to Madison County, AR by 1880. (Tilitha Smith's parents unknown - need information.)

Amanda Barber (b. Nov. 28, 1844 Perry County - died March 27, 1915 Newton County, AR) married Oct. 5, 1862 in Newton County, AR. to William Washington Nuckolls (b. Oct. 29, 1845 Hardeman County, TN - died Nov. 26, 1927 Johnson County, AR). He was a minister and soldier in Union Army Co. "E" 2nd Ark. Inf.

William W. Nuckolls' parents were John Nuckolls and Dolly Vaughn. John (b. 1798 Robertson County, TN - died June 18, 1880 Madison County, AR) was the son of Rev. War soldier Richard Nuckolls (1762-1835) and Temperance Walton (1764-1834). Richard and Temperance were both born in Louisa County, VA and died in Robertson County, TN. Dolly (b. 1817 SC - died unknown) was the daughter of John Vaughn (1780 NC - died 1860s TN) and Jane _____ (b. 1784 SC - 1850s TN) both are believed to have died in Hardeman County or McNairy County, TN. John and Dolly Vaughn Nuckolls moved from Hardeman County, TN to Madison County, AR by 1860. One of their daughters, Elizabeth Nuckolls (b. 1843 TN) married in Perry County on Dec. 2, 1868 to David Wilson Barber (b. 1852 TN), son of John and Rhoda Barber. Elizabeth and David also moved to Madison County, AR by 1880 along with David's brother, Allen Barber (b. 1847 TN), who is also believed to have married a daughter of John and Dolly, Amanda Nuckolls (b. 1854 TN) around 1869, but no marriage record was found for them in Perry County.

Rev. William W. and Amanda Barber Nuckolls children were: Tilitha (1864-1954 AR) married James R. Patterson; Mandy Adaline (1866) married W.H. Wages; Mary Ln Creasy (1869) married Monroe Wages; Gatsey (1876) married Will Balkin; Margaret Melvina "Mellie" (1878) married Mose Wages; John William (1881-1967 AR) married Ida Bell Marshall; Delaney E. (1884) married first to _____Pruitt, then to Frank Wages; and Dorey E. (1889) married Logan Lyon. *Submitted by Zelma Bowman Smith and Thelma Bowman Woods.*

KENNETH H. BARBER, born July 9, 1929, in Perry County is the great great grandson of Elida and Jane "Dowdy" Barber. Jane was the daughter of Thomas Dowdy Jr. and Francis Hinson Dowdy. Her two brothers were Joseph, born about 1801, Jordan B., born in 1811, and a sister, Jane B., born in 1906. Elida Barber was a farmer. They came to Perry County from North Carolina around 1818 or 1819. They settled on Racoon Creek and Poplin Hollow. Abraham and Allen Barber, John Hinson, and Elijah Warren (born in N.C., Feb. 22, 1799) all came around the same time and also settled up and down Racoon Creek. Allen Barber went over the head of Hurricane Creek about the same time.

Elida and Jane "Dowdy" Barber had three children: Frances B. (1825) married Roberson Warren, Nancy B. (1830) married E.A. Land, William Thomas Barber, born in 1835.

William is the father of Anderson Levie "Jake" Barber. "Jake" is the father of Floyd Barber (born in 1905). W.T. Barber was a farmer. His main cash crop was peanuts. Floyd Barber worked in logging. He helped with road work on the "W.P.A". He trucked general, hauling lumber and scrap iron during World War II. He hauled stock and many loads of peanuts to Nashville, Tennessee. He sawmilled and farmed when he was young and old, too. "Jake" Barber was a carpenter and a furniture maker. He made handles and chairs. He also made white oak split baskets for shucks and eggs. He married Sarah "Elizabeth" Morgan Barber. Their children are: Claggett, born Dec. 31, 1900, married Gertie Qualls. Eva, born Nov. 19, 1902, married William Barber. Floyd, born Sept. 29, 1905, married Lillian "Rodgers". James, born Sept. 4, 1911, married Geneva Qualls. Earlene, born Dec. 4, 1913, married Kent Warren.

Kenneth H. and Martha Sue Barber and children.

The children of William Thomas Barber and Ellender B. McCallister Barber were: James "Jim", born 1853, married Mariah Ann Fuller, her first marriage. Sarah Jane, born 1856, married George Thomas Rodgers. Robert, born 1858, married Martha Warren. Martha "Mollie", married Allen Trull. Joseph "Joe", born 1865, married Mariah Ann "Fuller" Barber, which was her second marriage. Mary, born 1868, married Pete Beasley. Fannie, born 1870, married Ruford Gibbons. Anderson "Jake" Levi, born Jan. 5, 1873, married his first wife Sarah Elizabeth Morgan Barber; his second marriage was to Ruby Pratt.

The family history of Kenneth H. Barber continues under Lewis family history, of Martha Sue "Lewis" Barber.

The above information came from Perry County census reports and other sources. *Submitted by Kenneth H. Barber.*

NANCY CAROLINE BARBER, daughter of Zibe and Sarah (Dobbs) Barber, who resided in Perry County, Tennessee from before 1850 until the Civil War. Prior to coming to Perry County, the Barber family had farmed in Hickman County. Zibe, born about 1784, was a native of North Carolina and Sarah Dobbs was born about 1814 in Tennessee. Based on 1830 Hickman County census data, it appears that Sarah was the second wife of Zibe. Many inconsistencies in the census data cloud the picture concerning the ages of both Zibe and Sarah. Their known children are John, born 1833, Sarah L., born 1835, Martha, born 1838, Jane, born 1841, James C., born 1843, Nancy C., born 1846, Alsie, born 1848.

By 1870, most members of this family had moved to Newton County, Arkansas. The 1870 census lists Sarah, John, Nancy, and Alsie. James was listed on the 1880 census. James is buried in the cemetery at Deer, Newton County with a monument inscribed "Co. B 10 Regt. TN Cav CSA 1843 - 1920." Near him is a monument inscribed "Mary Barber sister of James C. Barber - At Rest." It is believed that this grave is Jane Barber. Also buried in this cemetery is Mary Barber, 1855-1882, wife of James C. Barber. No record of the burial of Zibe, Sarah, or John has been found.

Nancy Barber Clayborn

Nancy Caroline Barber married, Jan. 28, 1871, Frederick J. Clayborn, the son of her neighbors, George and Elizabeth (Phillips) Clayborn. George was a Baptist minister and farmer. The Clayborn family had migrated from South Carolina to Hickman County, Tennessee and on to Newton County, Arkansas.

Frederick and Nancy were the parents of George Zibe Clayborn, born May 8, 1874, died Apr. 5, 1946, Martha, born 1874, James, born 1876, and William Amos, born 1879. Frederick died before the 1880 census and Nancy did not remarry. Her father-in-law and mother-in-law helped her raise the children. She died, June 19, 1927, while living near her son, George Z., at Stonehill, Johnson County, Arkansas and is buried at Woodland Cemetery, Clarksville, Arkansas. Relatives have told that Nancy lived in a one room log cabin with a fire ring in the center of the dirt floor.

George Z. Clayborn married Mary Susan Curtis, daughter of Amos Ferguson Curtis Sr. and Celia Danials. The Curtis family was from Wayne County, Tennessee. Amos reportedly was married five times and the father of over 20 children. During the Civil War, Amos served in Company "E" 2nd Arkansas Infantry.

George Z., like his grandfather, was a Freewill Baptist minister and farmer. George and Susan were the parents of twelve children: James Horce, born 1896, Walter, born 1899, Bertha, born 1901, Amos, born 1903, Celia Nancy, born 1905, Claude C., born 1907, Grace, born 1909, Herman Ratus, born 1912, Ula, born 1915, Eugene, born 1918, and Troy, born 1920.

On Nov. 25, 1917, Bertha Clayborn married Roy Clinton Warren, son of Braxton Edgmon and Ruth Margaret (Smith) Warren. Braxton was the youngest son of William A.J. Warren and Prudance Elizabeth (Wharton) Warren of Newton and Johnson Counties, Arkansas. *Submitted by Cecil James Warren Jr.*

RODGER I. & BROWNIE SUE BARBER, live on Rodger's old homeplace on Short Creek. They are descendants of the Coon Creek Barbers and Brush Creek Qualls. They have two sons, Rodger Daniel and Timothy Waco. Rodger Daniel is married to Lisa Carter and Timothy to Mia Shelton, two more old Perry County names.

Timothy Barber, Hazel Barber Chandler Spencer, Rodge, Brownie Sue and Rodger Daniel

Brownie Sue's parents were James and Geneva Qualls Barber. Their children were Harold Dean (deceased), Brownie and Jerry. Rodger's parents were Elkanah Waco and Emma Qualls Barber. Their children were Hester (deceased), Hazel Barber Chandler Spencer, and Rodger I.

Elidia Barber settled on upper Coon Creek in 1818 from North Carolina and married Jane Dowdy. Their children were William Thomas, Frances and Nancy. Nancy married Elkanah (Cain) Land and William Thomas married Finetta McAlister. Their children were Jim, Sara Jane, Robert, Lewis, Martha, Joseph, Mary, Fannie and Anderson Levi (Brownie's grandfather). Anderson Levi married Sarah Morgan, the daughter of James Walton Morgan and Mary Walls. They had Clagget, Eva, Floyd, Earline and James (Brownie's father).

Isham Qualls was born in Ireland in 1785, came to North Carolina in 1805, entered the army to fight in the War of 1812. On his way back from New Orleans, he stopped in Tennessee, met and married Elizabeth Baucom. She was born on Brush Creek, April 5, 1794, before Perry County was formed and two years before Tennessee became a State. Their children were Moses, Sally Q. Bryson, Tom Matt, Mary Q. Murry, Lucindia A. Baucom, Riley, Hubbard, Patsy Q. Etheridge, and Ishman Jr.

Hubbard Qualls married Poppie Dowdy and their children were Jordan, Joe, Teedie (Rodger's granddad), Nancy Q. Warren, Smithy Q. Westbrooks, Parolee Q. Carroll, Riley and Richard. Joe Qualls married Martha Qualls and their children were America Q. Qualls, Minnie Q. Williams, Herc, Graydon, Dayton, and C.N. (Bud) Qualls. C.N. (Bud) Qualls was married to Annise Barber and they had one child, Geneva.

Being descended from some of the people who pioneered on Brush Creek and Coon Creek and being exposed to sawmilling in the hills and hollows has put the love for this unique and wonderful place we call Perry County deep in the blood of the Barber descendants.

BARHAM, The Barham family trace their ancestors to English Royalty, beginning in Kent where the town of Barham surrounds Sissinghurst Castle, the ancestral home of the Barhams, members of the House of Lords. In addition, the Barhams became part of the Filmer and Argall families when Sir Robert Barham married Kathryn Filmer, the daughter of Sir Edward Filmer and wife, Elizabeth Argall Filmer. Robert Filmer, a brother of Kathryn, came to the Jamestown Colony very early, as did his uncle, Sir Samuel Argall, a brother of Elizabeth Argall Filmer. Sir Samuel Argall was the second Governor of Jamestown, following Sir Walter Raleigh. With the group, was the first known Barham to come to America, Sir Captain Charles Barham, the son of Robert Barham and Kathryn Filmer. Charles Barham's wife was Elizabeth, but her maiden name is unknown. They settled near Williamsburg, then Stokes and Gulliford Counties, North Carolina.

Hartwell Barham in the 1860s.

Charles and Elizabeth Barham had one son, Robert, who married Elizabeth Clarke. Their son, Thomas Barham, married Sarah Newsome. The son of Thomas and Sarah Barham, Hartwell, married, first, Cecelia Freeman, and second, Elizabeth McKillip, the widow of Josiah Stokes. Hartwell and Cecelia had 14 children, only six of whom lived past childhood: Balaam, Edmond, Josiah, Thomas, Littleton, and George. Hartwell and his second wife, Elizabeth McKillip, had no children. Hartwell Barham was in the Revolutionary War from 1776 until 1779.

Josiah Barham, the son of Hartwell and Cecelia Barham, married, first, Rachel Holbrook, Aug. 19, 1806, in Stokes County, North Carolina. Josiah and Sarah Barham had three children: Hartwell, William, and a daughter, name unknown, who married a Doherty. Josiah married, second, Lydia Linville, July 30, 1812, and they had at least 13 children. The names of only seven are known: Thomas, John, George, Lydia, Allen, Josiah Jr., and Balaam. Josiah and family moved to Maury County, Tennessee, on to Gallatin County, Illinois, and, in 1837, to Perry County, Tennessee. The Barham family home was built on the west side of Buffalo River, about five miles north of Linden. Josiah died in 1860 and is buried in the Barham Cemetery near his home.

A son of Josiah and Rachel Barham, Hartwell Barham, was born in Guilford County, North Carolina in 1807 and moved with his parents to Perry County, Tennessee. He married Nancy Coble about 1825. Nancy, born 1811, was the daughter of Paul Coble and Sara Wilson Coble. They had at least 12 children: William C., Thomas N., Major George W., Captain Hartwell, John, Agnes, Nancy, Neil, Milton, Elizabeth, and Mary.

Hartwell Barham was settled on Bush Creek, 8th District, Perry County, by 1822. Hartwell served two terms in the Tennessee State Legislature. He was an extremely wealthy man when the Civil War started, but lost practically everything during the war. He moved to Dunklin County, Missouri in 1867 and died there in 1869.

GEORGE THOMAS "TOMMY" BARHAM AND ETHEL LOU DELLA PARNELL, were married Nov. 9, 1916. Tommy was the son of George Wesley Barham and Josephine Sanders Barham. Ethel was the daughter of E.H. and Meda Vick Parnell.

Ethel and G.T. (Tommy) Barham

They began housekeeping in the Sharp Hollow across the Buffalo river from Beardstown. Tommy's daddy provided the house for them to live and land for the young couple to farm. On Aug. 31, 1918, a daughter, Virginia Pauline was born. They continued to live there for three more years. When they became concerned about how Pauline would be able to attend school, as there was no transportation provided where they lived, Tommy and Ethel bought a farm on Highway 13 so Pauline could ride a bus to the new school just built in Beardstown.

Pauline had Elementary School at Beardstown, went to Linden High School and attended college at MTSU university for two years. She decided to come home and was assigned a school to teach 1st and 2nd grade in Beardstown school with two other teachers, Louise Tate Baker and Claude DePriest, in 1939. On Dec. 26, 1940, Pauline and her school Principal, Claude Raymond DePriest, were married.

They had two daughters; Virginia Dianne DePriest, born Dec. 31, 1941, and Ethel Sharon DePriest, born Feb. 1, 1945. They continued to teach at Beardstown where Claude taught every year and Pauline was out a few years. Claude and Pauline taught in Lobelville Elementary two years in the early 1950s, but came back to Beardstown school. Claude suffered a heart attack in 1971 and had to retire from teaching, but lived until June 1982, when he passed away with his third heart attack. He is buried in DePriest Bend cemetery. Pauline continued to teach until 1979. She retired to help care for her mother, father, and husband. Claude taught 37 years and Pauline taught 34 years. Pauline accepted a part time position as a paralegal with senior citizens in Perry, Wayne and Lewis counties. She retired from that position in 1988. Claude, Pauline and their daughters were members of Beardstown Church of Christ and attended regularly. Ethel Barham passed away Feb. 7, 1981, and is buried in the Barham Family cemetery. Tommy Barham died July 30, 1982. They were both faithful members of Beardstown Church of Christ.

Dianne married Thomas S. Godwin and they have two children; Thomas S. Godwin, III and Tricia Danielle Godwin. Tommy Godwin married Joy Hinson Oliver. They had two children, Brandon Oliver and Jenifer Dyan Godwin. They live in Mobile, Alabama where they own a

Costal Bail Bond Company. Dianne and her second husband, Paul J. Sanford, live in Mobile, Alabama. They manage several offices of Aarco Inc. Company. Danielle lives and works in Nashville, Tennessee.

Sharon married Tommy E. Doyle and they have three children, Amy Colleen Doyle, Ashley Nicole Doyle, and Joshua Ethen Doyle. They live near Linden where Sharon teaches in Elementary School and Tommy Doyle is an attorney.

GEORGE WESLEY BARHAM,

1864-1949, son of Balaam and Henritta Barber Barham, married Mary Ann Josephine Sanders, 1866-1923, daughter of Berryman and Naomi Williams Sanders, Dec. 30, 1885.

George and Josephine Sanders Barham Family

In December, their family started with the birth of their oldest son, Hartie B.L., 1886-1946, married Izora Simmons, Sept. 29, 1911, and had nine children; Wesley Owen, 1888-1889; Annie, 1890-1978, married C.N. Hudson, Feb. 16, 1927, and had two children; Mattie Augusta "Gussie", June 21, 1892 - June 2, 1970, married Arthur Parnell, Aug. 27, 1911, and had two daughters; George Thomas, April 15, 1894 - July 30, 1982, married Ethel Parnell, Nov. 9, 1916, and had one daughter; Ritta Ruth, Jan. 30, 1896 - 1993, married Riley N. Cotton, Dec. 25, 1915, had a daughter and two sons; James Joe Davis, April 30, 1898 - Oct. 31, 1979, married Charlotte Doyle and had four daughters; Oma Udora, May 3 - Dec. 13, 1986, married Herbert Horner, Jan. 10, 1920, and had a daughter and two sons; Bobby, Sept. 15, 1901 - Sept. 14, 1957, married Edna Bell, Dec. 11, 1923, and had two daughters; Bail, Feb. 14, 1904 - Jan. 19, 1966, married Marie Warren, Aug. 26, 1926, and had one son. The last child was a stillborn boy, but no dates are known.

Bob and Edna Bell Barham

Out of all these children and spouses, only one, Marie Warren Barham, is still living.

JOSIAH AND BALAAM BARHAM,

On an October day in 1917, on top of a hill above Buffalo River and across the hollow from where his log house stood, Balaam Barham was buried beside his wife, "Ritta" or Henritta (1827-1891), daughter of Enoch and Susan Hinson Barber.

Balaam Barham 1838-1917

Balaam and Henritta had moved to this farm southeast of Beardstown when their children were small. Balaam's early life was spent on Brush Creek where his father, Josiah, had lived since he was deeded land by Hartwell Barham in 1837. Family members are convinced that Josiah was the son of a Revolutionary War soldier, Hartwell, and Cecilia Freeman Barham. This Hartwell was a proved descendant of Captain Charles Barham, who came to Surry County, Virginia, by 1654, from England.

Balaam was heard to say that he was the youngest of his father's sixteen children. Records exist that show Josiah was married three times; his wives were Lydda Linville, Rachel Holbrook, and Phoebe Stokes. Josiah's children included sons: Hartwell, William, John S., Thomas N., Allen, Josiah Thomas, George Washington and Balaam, and daughters: Jane, Lydia, Lucinda and Peggy. Of this large family, only Allen and Balaam stayed in Perry County.

Josiah died in 1861, and is thought to be buried on "Church House Hill" on Brush Creek. Later his son, Allen, and Allen's wife, Margaret Shepard Barham, were buried in this cemetery. WPA records list this cemetery as Barham Cemetery.

Balaam enlisted in the 10th Tennessee Cavalry, CSA, at Linden, Dec. 11, 1862.

Balaam and Henritta's children were: Martha Jane, born 1858, married James Haywood Lane; William Thomas, born 1861, married Harriet Sharp; George Wesley, born 1864, married Josephine Sanders; Joe S., born 1867, married Della Johnson; Ziba A., born 1870, married Mollie Harrison. All stayed in Tennessee, except Ziba, who moved to Texas around 1902, and died there in 1929.

Evidence of some of Balaam's hard work may be seen in the long rock walls built to protect his farmland along Buffalo River. Among the happy memories related by his grandchildren were those of watching him mold bullets for his muzzle loading gun, then going hunting with him as his good aim brought down squirrels from the tall trees.

Although there are no young men in Perry County with the name Barham to carry on Balaam's family name, several of his great grandchildren live in this area.

THOMAS N. BARHAM,

born in Perry County in 1834, the son of Hartwell and Nancy Barham, married Zerviah "Zerrie" Roberts in 1854. She was the daughter of Thomas Roberts, married, first name unknown, Reeves. Thomas and Zerrie Barham had six children: Nancy Caroline, married William Robert Beakley; Martha Ann, married Robert Elkins; Louisa J., married Moses Little; William Hartwell, moved to McLennan County, Texas; Susan Elizabeth, married William Russell; and Sarah, married Andrew Davis.

Thomas N. Barham was killed March 19, 1863, while fighting in Company C, 10th Tennessee Cavalry Regiment, C.S.A. Zerrie Roberts was remarried in Perry County on Aug. 31, 1871, to James Wesley Beakley. In 1872, they left in a wagon train led by Andrew Whitwell, moving to Ripley County, Missouri.

Nancy Caroline Barham, the daughter of Thomas and Zerrie Barham, married William Robert Beakley in Perry County on Jan. 19, 1872, and left soon after in the wagon train for Ripley County. William Robert was the son of James Wesley Beakley, second husband of Zerrie Roberts Barham, married Rebecca Wade. William Robert and Nancy Beakley had seven children: Eugenia Rebecca, Novella Zerviah, Sarah Ardena, Elnora Girtrude, Robert Hartwell, Martha Elizabeth, and Nannye Barham. William Robert Beakley died in 1908. After his death, Nancy Barham Beakley married Phebus John Ponder, born in Hickman County, the son of Amos Ponder and Nancy Dudley. Nannye Barham Beakley, born 1888, the youngest child of William and Nancy Beakley, married, first, John William Keel on Nov. 23, 1902 in Ripley County, Missouri. They had one daughter, Hazel B. Keel. John W. Keel died Dec. 4, 1904, and in 1905, Nannye married Joseph Laurence Ponder. Nannye died in 1906.

Hazel B. Keel married Leonard Ponder in Ripley County in 1925. There were five children: Paul, Nancy Elaine, Ramona, Jerry, and Larry.

Members of the Barham family still live in Perry County, but the family has also spread out over much of the United States. All are proud of their Perry County roots.

WILLIAM THOMAS BARHAM,

born April 4, 1861, son of Balaam Barham and Henrietta Barber, buried in Sharp Cemetery, Sharp Hollow.

Harriett Sharp Barham

Jim wasorn Nov. 11, 1880, died Oct. 3, 1908, buried Hunt Hill Cemetery, in Perry County. He married, June 16, 1901, Perry County, Minnie Dial, born 1882, daughter of

Martin and Maggie Dial. Their two children, Emery E., born Oct. 30, 1904, died Dec. 22, 1906, buried Hunt Hill Cemetery, and Iline Barham, born 1908. (2) Anna L. Barham, born March 1883, Beardstown, died June 8, 1911, Beardstown, buried in Cook Cemetery. She married May 8, 1901, Perry County, Isaac Franklin Little. He was born 1873, died June 6, 1941, had married first to Lula Johnson, and married third after Anna died. Isaac and Anna had Ilean, died Nov. 5, 1902, Leitha, born 1903, married Cecil Hinson, Lloyd, born 1906, married Sophia Garner, and Isaac Cloyd, born 1909, died May 10, 1911, Beardstown. (3) Johnny B., born Feb. 1886, died Feb. 21, 1902, buried Sharp Cemetery. (4) Maggie Euroth Barham, born March 3, 1888, died May 16, 1946, Beardstown, buried Sharp Cemetery. She married June 24, 1904, Andrew Jackson Russell. Jack, born July 19, 1880, died June 1, 1923, son of John Russell and Josie Little, buried Sharp Cemetery. Their four children - Thomas Floyd, born Oct. 9, 1905, died Dec. 5, 1972; Beulah Mae, born Dec. 11, 1909, married Lee Fernie Aldridge; Arthur John, born Nov. 13, 1914, died June 27, 1990, and Josie Delila, born Oct. 17, 1922, married Jesse Byrd. (5) Isaac Haudie Barham, born 1892, died Nashville, married April 3, 1910, Carrie Spence. Isaac Haudie was a World War I veteran. Their children were Willie Mae, Lorine, and Roy Thomas.

JEREMIAH BARNETT SR., was a descendent of John Barnett of Londonderry, Ireland, born 1678, died September 1734. He and his brother, William, emigrated to Pennsylvania prior to 1730, locating in Hanover Township, then Lancaster County. They were among the earliest settlers in that township. They each had several children. They later began to move to Virginia and North Carolina as territories began to open up.

David Alexander Barnett and family

Jeremiah Barnett Sr. married Sarah Bird, Jan. 3, 1798, in Pittsylvania County, Virginia. They moved on to east Tennessee and were in Clairborne County, Tennessee by 1800. In 1812, they were in Hickman County, Tennessee. They moved to Perry County by 1820. He had a land grant (#29053) or seventy acres on Buffalo River near Beardstown. He sold this land to Peter Roberts, Sept. 20, 1856. Jeremiah Sr. and family moved to Toms Creek. The 1830 census showed they had three sons and three daughters. The TVA map shows a Barnett Hollow settlement. One of the sons, moved to Alabama, one moved to the West during the gold rush, and the other son, Jeremiah Jr., stayed in Perry County and married a Miss Chesser. They had three girls: Sarah, born 1835, Elizabeth, born 1836, Rachel, born 1839. Their mother died and Jeremiah Jr. married in 1841 to Amanda Hogwood, born April 25, 1823. She was part Indian. They had ten children: James D., Ramson, Martha Ann, Agnes, Nancy, David Alexander, Mary, Eliza, Margaret, and Amanda.

David Alexander Barnett, born Jan. 22, 1853, died June 14, 1922, was their sixth child. He married Virginia Haynes of Wayne County on April 12, 1876. She was born March 26, 1861, died July 9, 1930. Both are buried in New Prospect cemetery near Parsons, Tennessee. They had eight children: Roxie, John, Jerry, David A. Jr., Elire, Elizabeth, Lee Elbert, and Lawson.

Jerry, their third child, born May 6, 1882, died Nov. 15, 1955. He married Nancy Morris, July 15, 1906 in Wayne County. She died, Aug. 17, 1971, and both are buried in Parsons, Tennessee. They had four children: Walter, 1907, Marjorie, 1911, Loraine, 1913, and Edith, 1918, all born in Wayne County. Walter died in 1910, Marjorie married Feb. 27, 1941, James M. Brasher Jr. and had a son, James M. Brasher III, July 19, 1943. Loraine married Millard Evans June 14, 1930, and had one daughter, Nancy, born Oct. 22, 1934. She married Virgil McCormic Jr., Nov. 6, 1950. They had three children: Keith, Kim, and Kerry; Five grand children: Kristy, Crystal, Elliott, Ashley, and Christopher.

Jeremiah Barnett Sr. and Jeremiah Barnett Jr. signed the petition, Dec. 12, 1835, to divide Perry County, because it was so large and they had bad roads and a long way to go to pay taxes. *Submitted by Edith V. Barnette.*

ANDREW JACKSON BATES, born Feb. 22, 1859, died Dec. 2, 1914, married Mary Mitchell, born Jan. 6, 1849, died Dec. 2, 1914. Their children were Marvin, Melvin, Austin, and Myrtle.

Melvin and Mattie Bates

Melvin Bates, born Mar. 22, 1880, died Dec. 10, 1961, married Mattie Dyer, born May 17, 1884, died 1959. Their children were: Edna, born March 22, 1903; Jack, born July 22, 1906, died June 21, 1983: Howard, who died in infancy; Wallace, born April 30, 1918, died Sept. 8, 1989; Willie Louise, born Jan. 24, 1911; Leon, born Nov. 2, 1920, died May 8, 1989; Loudene, born May 19, 1923, died Aug. 7, 1961.

Edna married Raymond Chandler and was a homemaker.

Jack Bates married Juanita Webb, Sept. 20, 1943. Jack had different occupations, including being Sheriff of Perry County. In 1955, he went to work as an Inspector for the State Highway Department in Davidson County. Juanita continued her teaching career in the Metro Education System in Nashville, Tennessee. They were in Nashville for 16 years. After retirement, in 1971, they moved back to Perry County.

Wallace enrolled as a member of the Civilian Conservation Core in Lewisburg, Tennessee. He finished with an Honorable Discharge. He then enlisted in World War II, Aug. 13, 1941, in Oglethorpe, Georgia as a Pump Operator, Battles and Campaigns, India and Burma. Date of Separation, Oct. 23. 1945. Honorable discharge with Asiatic-Pacific Theater Ribbon with one Bronze Star, American Theater Ribbon, American Defense Service Medal, Good Conduct Ribbon. He than went to Michigan and worked in the Crucial Steel office until he retired.

Leon enrolled in Civilian Conservation Corps, finished with Honorable Discharge, enlisted in World War II, May 27, 1943. Battles and campaigns, Normandy Air Offensive Europe, Rhineland Ardemes G040WD95. Northern France, Central Europe, Distinguished Unit Badge G0 10 Hg, 9th AF45. With one Oak Leaf cluster. European African Middle Eastern Service Medal, One Silver Star, One Bronze Star. Honorable Discharge, Aug. 30, 1945. He lived in Detroit, Michigan and was employed by General Motors until he retired.

Loudene married Joe Lunn and lived in Valparaiso, Florida. She was a homemaker and beautician until she retired.

Willie married Emery King. They had one daughter, Patricia. Emery was a carpenter until he retired. Willie was a beautician, who owned and operated her own beauty shop from 1937 to 1994. She is also a homemaker and continues to live in Linden.

Patsy came to Nashville in 1962, where she attended David Lipscomb College and graduated with a BS degree in Business in 1966. She continued to make her home in Nashville. In late summer of 1972, she met Fred Michon, who is originally from Michigan. In March of 1973, they were married at West End Church of Christ Chapel, and in April of 1976, they became the proud parents of a daughter, Stephanie Rene Michon.

Stephanie has been a student at David Lipscomb Campus Schools since she was in the Second Grade. In May of 1994, Stephanie graduated from High School and will further her education by going to college.

Patsy has been a part-time secretary and receptionist with Kurzynske & Associates, a mechanical and electrical engineering company for the past sixteen years. Fred has been a Sales Engineer for the past ten years with the Maynard/Fixturcraft Company, which specializes in the design of supermarkets and convenience stores. Their family resides in Nashville at 3909 Valley Road.

ANDREW JACKSON BATES & DORA CALDONIA ARMADA JAMES LILY HUNT (MADIE), Andrew Jackson Bates, born in 1860, died in 1896. Armada Hunt Bates, born Sept. 29, 1870, died June 4, 1951.

Andrew's parents were Andrew Jackson Bates (called Jackson), born 1832 and Polly Loveless Bates. Jackson died in the Civil War. His parents were Isaiah Josiah, born 1799 in South Carolina, and Loucinda Lynn Bates, born

1800 in South Carolina. Isaiah Josiah's parents were James, 1765, and Elizabeth Tubbs Bates. Isaiah was among the early settlers of Cane Creek in Perry County.

Andrew Jackson Bates and wife Dora Caldonia Hunt Bates.

Armada's parents were James Monroe Hunt, born Aug. 11, 1832, died 1868 in Pulaski, Illinois (near Cairo) of typhoid fever, and Rebecca Bates Hunt, born Feb. 1839 or 1840. Other children were Sarah Lucinda (Cindi), 1863-1947; Martha Josephine (Jossie), March 11, 1865-April 2, 1946; and Joel Monroe, Sept. 23, 1867-July 30, 1960. Rebecca was also the daughter of Isaiah Josiah and Lucinda Bates. James' parents were John Hunt, May 9, 1802-Oct. 6, 1854, buried near Mousetail Landing Hunt Cemetery, and Mary McKemie, May 7, 1807-May 22, 1870. John's father was Joel Hunt.

Andrew and Madie had two children, Mattie Ina, born July 31, 1892, died Jan. 5, 1946 and Andrew Bismark Bates, born June 4, 1894, died Sept. 4, 1954.

Ina married Elbert Lynch; four children: Jimmie Pearl, Edna Elva, Andrew Simpson, Bobbie Nell.

Bismark married Dellar Fadillia (Dillie) Doyle in June 1918. They had one daughter, Myrtle Anlee, born March 4, 1919, died July 21, 1981.

After Andrew died, Madie married James Alexander Small. Mr. Small served in the Spanish American War in Cuba and was discharged on May 6, 1899. He and Madie had two daughters, Lillian Adelia (Dee), born Nov. 14, 1904, died April 29, 1976 in Houston, Texas and Ellen Francis Small, born Oct. 13, 1906, lives in Jackson, Tennessee.

Myrtle Bates married William Robert Jackson, Sept. 21, 1936. William was born, Dec. 15, 1915, died Aug. 1, 1985. They had five children: Bonnie Lou and Bettye Sue (Twins), born Oct. 26, 1939; Lena Anne, born Aug. 3, 1944; William Randal, born Nov. 3, 1946; and Andrew Bates, born Sept. 6, 1951.

Dee Small married Nicholas Zane Semander, born in Patmos, Greece, on Apr. 12, 1896, died May 12, 1961. Both are buried in Houston, Texas. They had two sons: Zane Edwin, born April 12, 1926, died March 8, 1958, and John Allan, born June 1, 1932.

John married Nancy Ruth Wallbraun. They had two children: John Allan Jr., born April 16, 1957, and Sherry Lynn, born April 18, 1959. John Jr. has one son, Nicholas Allan, born Aug. 13, 1984.

Ellen Small married William M. Butler.

Divorced. Married Red Beaty. Divorced. Married R.L. Hailey. No Children.

Bismark Bates served in the U.S. Army during World War I and was on the front line when the war ended.

Madie Hunt Bates Small is buried in Jackson, Tennessee.

Bismark and Dillie Bates and William and Myrtle Jackson are buried in the Doyle Cemetery on lower Cane Creek. *Submitted by Bonnie DePriest.*

DILLARD HUNT BATES, son of James Bates and Catherine Black, was born Nov. 29, 1848, in Hickman County, Tennessee. He was the grandson of John and Elizabeth Bates, as well as Marcus Black and Mary A. Sanders, all of Beaverdam. He had been named Dillahunty at birth, probably in honor of the judge by that name, but chose to change his name when he was old enough.

Dillard Hunt Bates family, circa 1905 in Perry County.

Dillard H. Bates was married on Nov. 23, 1870 to Martha Emmaline Chandler, daughter of Rosanah Harper and Tyre Chandler. She was born on Jan. 23, 1855, in Perry County, Tennessee.

Five children were born to this union: Alice Dee, born Dec. 1871, married Billy Brooks, and died April 1945, in Lewis County, Tennessee; Lew Ellen, born Aug. 3, 1874, married to James Aldridge, and died Jan. 15, 1944, in Perry County, Tennessee; James Edward, born Sept. 28, 1875, married to Maggie Fay Wood, and died June 8, 1930, in Sparta, Tennessee; Minnie Bell, born July 12, 1879, married to Thomas L. Horner, and died, May 15, 1924, in Perry County, Tennessee; and Albert L., born ca 1880, married to Margaret Roberts, and died in 1911, in Perry County, Tennessee.

The Bates family made at least two trips to Texas by covered wagon. One of the trips took place in 1879. Minnie Bell was born in Hill County, Texas that year. They were still in Texas for the birth of Albert in 1880.

On the Texas trip of 1879 were Catherine Black Bates and her sons, Whitfield, Gabriel, and Dillard, and her daughters, Adeline, Nancy, and Octavo. It is likely that Ruth Ann, who had married in Hickman County, accompanied them on the trip. The daughters married and remained in Texas, along with their mother, Catherine. Dillard and his family, as well as Gabriel and Whitfield Bates, chose to return to Perry County, Tennessee.

Dillard Bates, a farmer, died on July 26, 1910, in Perry County, Tennessee. His wife, "Emmy", died on June 23, 1940. They were laid to rest at Gilmer Cemetery. Three of their children, Albert Bates, Dee Bates Brooks, and Minnie Bates Horner are buried beside them. *Submitted by Betty Horner Lala.*

JOHN R. BATES, born 1835, and first wife, Nancy, born 1836, lived on lower Cane Creek, near Beardstown and Lobelville. Their sons were David, born 1852, Jesse Wells, born April 14, 1853, died Sept. 18, 1925, James B., born 1856, and John S., born 1858.

Rebecca Bates Hunt

On Sept. 28, 1884, Jesse W. Bates married Martha Josephine "Josie" Hunt, born March 11, 1865, died April 2, 1946. "Josie" was the daughter of James Monroe Hunt and Rebecca Bates. It is believed that Jesse had some children prior to or during this marriage who lived around Lobelville at that time, and a son, John Bates, moved to and lived in New York.

Jesse and "Josie" had ten children: 1. Oscar Monroe (Osco) Bates, born Dec. 28, 1885, died March 15, 1957, married Mable Hunt, born March 12, 1887, died Oct. 3, 1927, five children; 2. Everett Bates, born July 2, 1888, died March 22, 1943, married Clara in Cincinnati, Ohio, no children; 3. Orville Turney Bates, born Aug. 10, 1891, died June 16, 1978, married Melissia "Lissie" Hinson, born Feb. 10, 1901, died April 9, 1972, five children; 4. Nellie Brown Bates, born Dec. 14, 1894, died July 12, 1931, married Dennis Jones Hinson, born Feb. 3, 1888, died Dec. 21, 1963, four children; 5. John M. Bates, born Feb. 29, 1897, died Dec. 17, 1918 in World War I, in France, never married; 6. Paul Eve Bates, born Sept. 24, 1898, died Oct. 8, 1981, married Hattie Harrett Riley, born Aug. 23, 1905; 7. James Grady Bates, born Sept. 3, 1901, died Sept. 6, 1991, married Mary Lewis, born Sept. 3, 1904, died June 28, 1984, one child; 8. Heartie Temple "Buster" Bates, born Jan. 20, 1906, died June 24, 1990, married first to Sarah Harris, one child - second marriage to Melvinia Morgan, born Jan. 17, 1916, one child; 9. Jessie Mae Bates, born July 21, 1909, who is now living in a nursing home in Arkansas, married Joe Reddner Wilburn, born Oct. 20, 1907, died April 4, 1961, one child; 10. Regen Jones Bates, born Nov. 21, 1912, died 1952, married Grace Marie Bates (maiden name), born 1914, died 1979, no children.

John Bate's second marriage, after Nancy's death, was to Rebecca Bates Hunt. No children were born to this union. She was the widow of James Monroe Hunt, who died in Illinois in 1868. John's family and Rebecca's father and brother are shown in the 1860 Perry County census as living next door to each other. Rebecca Bates

Hunt Bates was the daughter of Isiah/Josiah and Lucinda Bates, the granddaughter of James and Elizabeth Tubbs Bates, and the great-granddaughter of William and Elizabeth Tubbs. NOTE: Earlier, John's son, Jesse Wells Bates, married the daughter of Rebecca. Andrew Jackson Bates, born 1832, was one of Rebecca's brothers. John R. Bates and Andrew Jackson Bates, who were next door neighbors, went to Nashville and enlisted in the Confederate Army together on Jan. 1, 1862. They served in Co. "F" 53rd Tennessee Infantry. John was captured on Feb. 16, 1862 at Ft. Donelson, and arrived at Camp Morton Prison, Indiana on March 15, 1862. He was released Aug. 1862 and rejoined his regiment and served until Oct. 5, 1865 as an Orderly Sergeant.

John R. was a magistrate or Justice of the Peace (JP) in Perry County in the later 1800s. He was murdered in the Beardstown Park. John had gone to the park to serve a warrant. A father had issued this warrant on his son for forging the father's name on bad checks. John had arranged for the son to pay back the money and not go to jail. While John sat on a bench working on the papers, the subject slipped behind John and split his head open with a chopping ax. This senseless act ended the life of a man who was greatly admired and appreciated, not only by his family, but the community as well. *Submitted by Charles L. Bates.*

JOHN REDNER BATES, The Bates name has been associated with the middle Tennessee area since the early eighteen hundreds. The first record of our branch of the family is Nov. 29, 1839, the birth of John Redner Bates. His birthplace and the identity of his parents are unknown. He married Mary Ann Dean and to this union nine children were born. They were: G.E., Solloman, William James, Patty, Mary Ellen, Andrew J., Dona, Sophie C., and Samuel Lee.

John Redner joined the Confederate army on Dec. 11, 1862, and was a private in Company H, 10th TN Calvary. A story handed down from generation to generation has it that he came home during his tour of duty (with or without leave) to see his family and help plant crops. While he was plowing, a group or raiders (outlaws) came upon him and demanded his horses. He refused and in the ensuing debate he killed one of them and ran the rest off his property. The shotgun he used is still in the family.

Samuel Lee Bates married Rebecca Harris and they lived in or around Lobelville all their lives. Their children were Amelia, Blount, Kitty, and William Howard. William Howard was a local politician, storekeeper, and farmer. He was the foreman of the W.P.A. Program in Perry County after the depression and helped build Highway Thirteen with mules and "slipscoops". "Daddy Bates", as he was known to all the grandchildren, owned one of the first cars in the area and helped pay for it by giving rides to the Tate Spring in DePriest Bend for twenty-five cents. William Howard married Hallie Jo Peters and to them were born seven children: John Redner, Henry Wallace, Kitty, Sammie, Doris, Laverne, and William Howard Jr.

William Howard Jr. married Audrey Lee Perry and they have spent most of their life in Lobelville, Tennessee. William Howard Jr. (Dave or Howard Jr.) was a farmer and heavy equipment operator of Tennaco and retired after thirty-five years of service. Howard and Audrey currently reside in Lobelville. They have two children, Michael Lynn and Howard Wayne. Both sons are employed by Bates Fabricating, Inc. Michael lives in Lobelville and has two children, Tabitha Lee and Rebecca Boyd, and a stepdaughter, Shayna. He is married to Carol Trull. Wayne also lives in Lobelville and has two children, Adriane Leigh and Jason Elisha, a stepdaughter, Shelli and a stepson, Roger. Adriane is married to Van Medlock and they reside in Lobelville, Tennessee. Wayne is married to Maragaret Bither.

Our branch of the Bates family is rather large. The current family tree of descendants of John Redner and Mary Ann Bates contains over three hundred names and not complete by any means.

BATES-HINSON, Orville Turney Bates was born Aug. 10, 1891, in the Cane Creek area of Perry County, Tennessee. He was one of ten children born to Jesse W. Bates and Martha Josephine Hunt. Turney was drafted into the Army from Perry County, Tennessee for World War I, receiving a medical discharge in 1917. In 1919, Turney Bates married Melissa Hinson, who was born Feb. 10, 1901. She was the daughter of Robert "Rob" and Isabel Hinson of Cane Creek.

Orville and Melissa Bates on their 50th wedding anniversary.

In 1943, after years of farming and operating a Country Store, Turney and Melissa moved the family to Centerville in Hickman County, Tennessee. He worked for General Shoe Company for a few years, then as Night Policeman for the town of Centerville. He was elected and served as Constable for the district of Centerville, from 1957-1969.

They had five daughters; Lorene, Ora Bell, Mildred, Helen, and Laverne.

Lorene Bates, born Feb. 2, 1920, was the oldest child. She married Bert Cowen. They had one daughter, Linda, born April 21, 1945, and Linda has a daughter, Julie Lynn, born July 4, 1965.

Ora Bell Bates, born Aug. 24, 1921, married James B. Baxter and they had two boys: James Michael, born June 13, 1952. He has one son, Christopher Michael, born Sept. 22, 1972; Jerry Randle Baxter, born Dec. 3, 1953. He has one daughter, Lauren Melissa, born July 17, 1980.

Mildred Sue Bates, born Sept. 28, 1925, married William W. Rodgers in 1954.

Helen Pearl Bates, born Dec. 18, 1929, married Jones Cotham. They had three daughters - Tana Cotham, born July 22, 1959, and she has two daughters, Lachelle Caroll and Shaina Lacple Parkinson; Tina Faye Cotham, born Oct. 14, 1960, died in 1962; Melony Jo Cotham, born Feb. 12, 1963, and has one daughter, Kala Tidwell, born March 14, 1990.

Laverne Bates, born Jan. 12, 1935, married J.C. "Sonny" Goodman and had six children: Teresia Goodman, born Dec. 12, 1954, was the oldest and she had four children - Troy Darrell, June 8, 1974, Jason, born Dec. 16, 1977, a daughter, Christy Lynn, who died at birth, Jan. 5, 1977, and Clint, born Feb. 23, 1981; Jesse Goodman Jr., born Dec. 26, 1955; Duane Gerry Goodman, born Aug. 12, 1958; Kirk Goodman, born Dec. 23, 1959. He had a son Joshua, born Sept. 28, 1982; Brian Goodman, born March 15, 1962; Denise Goodman, born Feb. 13, 1964 and she had a son, Brandon Lee Hill, born April 4, 1984.

Turney and Melissa Bates are buried in the Milan Cemetery in Hickman County, Tennessee. *Submitted by Mildred Rodgers.*

BATES-HUNT, Osco Monroe Bates, born Dec. 28, 1885, in Perry County, Tennessee, was the eldest son of Jesse and Josie Bates. He had seven brothers, Everett, John, Turney, Grady, Paul, Heartie, and Regen. He also had two sisters, Nellie and Jessie.

Everett settled in Ohio. John died in World War I. The others, with the exception of Osco, settled in Tennessee. Osco married Mable Hunt in about 1906 and moved to Oklahoma about 1909. There, he sharecropped for Henry and Mamie Dean in Davenport. The Deans were also originally from Perry County.

Osco and Mable had five children. Carter Temple Bates was born Jan. 10, 1908, in Perry County. Edgar Lynn Bates was born June 30, 1911, in Davenport, Oklahoma. Lois Margaret Bates was born Nov. 17, 1913, also in Davenport. Doris Pauline Bates was born Feb. 23, 1920, in Kendrick, Oklahoma and Mildred Reva Bates was born June 17, 1921, in Beggs, Oklahoma.

Osco sharecropped until the oil boom hit Oklahoma, at which time he moved to Beggs and began work for an oil company as a tank builder. The family moved to Okmulgee, Oklahoma in 1920. Osco continued working in the oil patch, sometimes traveling to the Seminole fields and even into some of the Texas fields.

Mable Hunt Bates died in 1927, in Okmulgee, Oklahoma. Osco never remarried and raised the family in Okmulgee. He worked at the Ball Brothers Glass Plant in Okmulgee until he retired. He died in 1957.

Carter Temple Bates died in 1940. Doris Bates Ray died in 1981, and Edgar Lynn Bates died in 1987. Lois Bates Regulski and Mildred Bates Raley still reside in Okmulgee. Carter, Lynn, and Doris's families also still live in the area. *Submitted by Lois Bates Regulski.*

BATES-RILEY, Paul E. Bates, born Sept. 24, 1898, died Oct. 8, 1981, was the sixth child of Jesse W. and Martha Josephine Hunt Bates. He was born in Perry County and lived on Cane Creek until he was 36 years old. On Dec. 24, 1922, he married Hattie Harrett Riley, born Aug. 23, 1905. She was the daughter of Albert Lee and Selma Riley and the granddaughter of John

V. and Sarah Lucinda Hunt Patton. Paul and Hattie moved to Gibson County, Tennessee with their children in 1934. Three of Paul's brothers, James Grady, Heartie Temple, and Regen Jones, also moved to Gibson County, Tennessee.

50th wedding anniversary of Paul and Hattie Bates. Seated left to right: Mary Fairless, Hattie Bates, Opal Wood. Standing left to right: Charles Bates, Paul Bates, James Bates

Paul and Hattie's six children are: Opal Lee, born April 8, 1924; Mary Nell, born Oct. 18, 1925; Frank Paul, born 1927; James Donald, born Oct. 25, 1928; Charles Leslie, born Feb. 1, 1931; and Stella Mae, born Nov. 26, 1935.

I. Opal Lee married Feb. 7, 1947, James Coffman Wood, born Dec. 11, 1923, died 1975. They had four children: (1) James Stephen, born Nov. 12, 1951, married June 5, 1976, Connie Lynn Moore, born Oct. 20, 1953. Their children - Justin Forrest, born June 18, 1978 and Kimberly Lynn, born July 6, 1981; (2) Eddie Wayne, born June 18, 1953, died June 18, 1953; (3) Lawanta Kay, born June 28, 1955, married June 15, 1973, Rev. Randy Preston Latch, born Oct. 28, 1954. Their children - Jennifer Michelle, born June 1, 1977, Melinda Kay, born March 10, 1980, and Jeremy Preston, born Nov. 26, 1984; (4) Patricia Ann, born Aug. 15, 1957, died Aug. 15, 1957.

II. Mary Nell married Sept. 30, 1950, David Marvin Fairless, born July 19, 1927. They had two children: (1) David Michael, born Nov. 25, 1951, married Aug. 28, 1976, Patricia Darlene Williams, born Dec. 29, 1955, and (2) Nancy Rose, born June 19, 1955, married Sept. 1, 1978, Roger Dale Orgain, born Dec. 19, 1953. Their children - Jeff Wayne, born Aug. 23, 1985 and Janet Lynn, born July 9, 1988.

III. Frank Paul was born 1927 and only lived one to two weeks.

IV. James Donald married Dec. 25, 1948, Dorothy Mae Gentry, born Feb. 6, 1928. Their children - Steven Ray, born March 30, 1950, died March 30, 1950, and Richard Lee, born March 2, 1964, died March 2, 1964.

V. Charles Leslie married 1960, Shirley Travis Lollar, born March 1, 1938. Divorced 1973. One child, Barry Jonathan Travis Bates, born Nov. 28, 1968, married 1989, Alecia Renea Hunley, born Dec. 15, 1971. Their children - Chelsea Renea, born April 24, 1990, and Christina Ashley, born March 25, 1992.

Shirley's children: Gary Mack Lollar, born July 17, 1956 and Barbianne Norman Morris, born April 24, 1972. Barbi has one child, Megan Michelle Morris, born March 15, 1990.

Charles Leslie married April 20, 1984, Amy K. Moore Hunt, born Oct. 7, 1951. No children.

Amy's child, Gerald Wayne Hunt Jr., born Sept. 7, 1971, married June 6, 1992, Tracy Williford Riley, born Jan., 15, 1973, divorced 1993. No children.

VI. Stella Mae was born Nov. 26, 1935 and died July 14, 1937. *Submitted by Opal Lee Bates Wood.*

BATES-WARREN The Linden Herald, Fay Hazen, Publisher, Lobelville, quote: "We had a wedding in our town Thursday eve 4-18-1889. Mr. Bedford Bates and Miss Tabbie Warren were the happy couple. A splendid supper was given and a fine time was had at night by the young folks who were engaged in an old fashion country dance. The music was made by Mr. Sam Warren, the bride's father and W.I. Davidson, both of which are excellent performers on the violin."

Nicholas Bedford Bates, Sept. 4, 1864-July 25, 1947, son of William B. and Sarah Bates, married Tabetha Jane Warren, Jan. 19, 1868-Oct. 17, 1934. Tabbie's father was Samuel M. Warren, Oct. 30, 1840-Feb. 11, 1916. Her mother was Leona Louisa Deaumanette, born 1844. Leona's father was Louis Charlemaine Deaumanette, became a U.S. citizen in 1852. Leona's mother was Clara Adele Patri. The family emigrated to the U.S. in 1847 from France, landed in New Orleans and came up the Mississippi River to the Tennessee River to Denson Landing, Tennessee, where they settled in what is known as De Priest Bend.

Descendants of Bedford and Tabbie are:

Henry Arthur Bates Sr., Feb. 10, 1890-Dec. 15, 1946, married Nora Kelly, Sept. 15, 1900-Jan. 23, 1964. They had three children- Montez, born May 15, 1926, married Lum Anderson Jenkins, born Aug. 23, 1928. They had one child, Andra Tez, born April 16, 1949; Henry Arthur Bates Jr., May 13, 1927-Aug. 8, 1982, married Eleanor Warner. Their five children are - Dolores Jean, born July 19, 1951, Judy Lenore, born July 13, 1953, Larry Arthur, born Sept. 24, 1954, Deborah Ann, born Dec. 12, 1955, and Beverly, born April 13, 1957; Billy, Jan. 24, 1930-Dec. 28, 1987, married Jewel Chandler. They had three children - Sherry, born July 2, 1949, Billie Ann, born Feb. 25, 1956, and Stephen Dale, born Oct. 30, 1957. Second marriage, to Ruby McSurley produced two children, Gwendolyn, born Aug. 11, 1960 and Billy Jr., born Nov. 25, 1961.

Lloyd Cleveland, Oct. 7, 1892-Sept. 26, 1950, married Lucy Tankersley, born March 13, 1897. They had one child, Elizabeth Jayne, born Dec. 21, 1923.

Argy May, Dec. 30, 1894-Oct. 18, 1951, married Cecil L. Twomey, Feb. 14, 1887-July 8, 1957.

Hix Charley, May 28, 1900-Aug. 9, 1965, married Lorene Bell. They had one child, Charles Shield.

Walker Ray, May 21, 1903-March 29, 1974, married Mary May Ledbetter, Nov. 30, 1910-March 14, 1993. They had two children, Shelia La Ray, born Nov. 26, 1942, and Carroll Blane, born Sept. 13, 1945.

Lucy Lee, March 20, 1906-Feb. 1, 1973, married John Paul Nickell, Nov. 24, 1906-May 27, 1974. Second marriage to Leonard Wade, May 16, 1905-Nov. 26, 1970.

Fred Carter, July 20, 1908-Oct. 22, 1969, married Kitty Bates. They had one child, Jimmy Ray, March 29, 1934-May 28, 1953. Fred's second marriage was to Willie Hester Ogle. They had two children, Kathy, Aug. 14, 1953-May 17, 1986, and Patsy, born Aug. 15, 1954.

Bedford and Tabbie were devoted parents and highly respected citizens of Perry County. *Submitted by Montez Bates Jenkins, Denver, Colorado (granddaughter).*

ARTHUR BATTON FAMILY, July 25, 1934, the "Nashville Tennessean" carried an obituary from Lobelville. It stated funeral services for Arthur Batton, 48, prominent Perry County citizen and leader, were held Tuesday at the Church of Christ at Coble by Brother John Lancaster, one of his best friends. Burial was at Chessor Cemetery near Coble.

Arthur and May Batton in the year of their marriage in 1905.

Mr. Batton was born July 12, 1886, at Buffalo. He was the son of the late Dr. and Mrs. James Abraham Batton. He died in Dr. Kirk's office at Linden Monday, July 23, of a heart attack. He was on his way home from a business trip to west Tennessee when he was stricken.

Mr. Batton spent his childhood days near Buffalo and then moved with his parents to Coble where he followed the art of blacksmithing and continued that business in Lobelville where he moved in 1915. In 1919, he acquired a dealership from the Ford Motor Company and that business became "Perry County Auto Company." He later received the Chevrolet agency, also, which operated in Linden a few years before his death.

Mr. Batton was member of the Perry County Democratic Committee; also the committee in charge of planning the new Highway 13 between Beardstown and Linden; served several years on the school board; and sponsored a baseball team in Lobelville. He loved Perry County!

Jesse Arthur Batton and his father, Dr. James Abraham Batton (1857-1919) had the same initials. To keep their mail separate, A. Batton dropped "Jesse" from his name. Dr. Batton was named for his father, James, and his uncle, Abraham. James and Abraham were sons of Jacob and Eda Huff Batton who lived on Crooked Creek in Perry County on what was later the Andrew Daniel Place. Dr. Batton was prominent in Cuba Ldg-Buffalo area. His farm along the Tennessee River extended nearly to I-40 bridge. He is remembered as making a worth while contribution to the practice of medicine.

Dr. Batton and Martha Miller (1862-1979) became the parents of Cora Batton (1877-1949), who married Dave Smith (1871-1940). The second wife was Catherine Miller (1869-1897), a sister to the first wife. They were the parents of Jesse Arthur Batton (1886-1934), who married May Rushton (1888-1969) in 1905. She became the bookkeeper for his businesses. They were the parents of Agnes Miller Batton (1912-) and Mildred Rushton Batton (1920-). Agnes married Neil O. Warren (1911-), of Waverly, Dec. 25, 1931. They have a daughter, Beverly Joy, who married Murray Stokely and they are parents of three boys. Mildred married James C. Kennon (1919-), of Nashville, April 20, 1943. They have a son, Carl Batton Kennon and two daughters, Carol Askew and Mildred Rogers, who have given them seven grandchildren.

Agnes taught school in Beardstown and Lobelville five years before moving to Old Hickory where she taught 27 years at DuPont School. Mildred taught school 23 years in Memphis before retiring.

AARON BAUCOM-LUCINDA QUALLS, Aaron Baucom married Lucinda Qualls in 1845. Lucinda was born on Coon Creek in Perry County, Tennessee, May 2, 1826, to Isham and Elizabeth Qualls. They soon moved to Missouri where they spent most of their lives together, and where most of their children were born.

Aaron served with Co. G 12th Regiment Missouri Val. Calvary of the U.S. Army during the Civil War. During the war, the family had small pox and two or three of the children died. They lived and farmed on the St. Francis River and in Wayne County, Missouri until 1875 when they decided to go to Texas. Nearly all of her people from Tennessee had moved there. They crossed Arkansas in two wagons, entered Texas near Texarkana. They stopped there for a while to work picking cotton to make money for provisions for the rest of their journey. Aaron became sick and died and they had to bury him there. They decided to return to Missouri. In 1885, they moved back to Tennessee. They lived on the Cain Land Farm on lower Brush Creek. They later moved to her brother's, Riley Qualls, farm (now Donnie Qualls place). She died in 1901. The children of Aaron and Lucinda number twelve or thirteen. Several died in infancy. Some of the names are, William Baucom, Eli, Levi, Moses, Isaac, Louis, Mary Baucom Qualls, and Susanne.

Mary Adeline Qualls was born in Missouri, Oct. 2, 1871. They came to Tennessee in 1885, where she spent the rest of her life that spanned ninety-four years.

BOB AND FLORA BEASLEY, live on Highway 50 near Mousetail State Park. They had three children: Myra, born 1977, married Matthew McKnight (they had one son, Kavin); Mark, born 1979; and Micah, born 1981, both attend school at Linden. Flora, born 1954, daughter of Perry and Mavis Morgan Moore of Decatur County. Bob, born 1948, son of J. C. and Martha Starbuck Beasley. Bob had one brother, J.M.

Two of Bob's grandparents came from big families all born in Perry County. His grandmother, Annie, born 1889, was one of ten children born to George and Mary Porter Evans on lower Marsh Creek. Jesse was a World War I Veteran. He never married. Will married Mittie Ward. Alford married Lilly Ward. Bob married Flora Craig. Bob and Alf were twins. Annie married Mack Beasley and stayed in Perry County when the rest of the family moved to West Tennessee. The other children married after moving. Mark married Celia Adams. Ethel married Othol Dunahoo. Jim married Florence Applewhite, later married Morene ?. Ollie Lee married Otis West. Ola married Howard Adams.

Bob and Flora Beasley with children Myra (standing), Mark and Micah.

Bob's grandfather, Mack Beasley, born 1887, was one of nine children born to Pete and Mary Barber Beasley. Mack married Annie Evans. Grover married Gerthie Polan. Sims married Vera Polan. Atlas died as a small boy. Kirk married Bessie Ledbetter. Ollie Mae married Albert Tracy. Alma married Bea Trull. Dixie married Fred Lewis, later married John Meadows. Mable married Jim Coleman, later married Taylor Gregory.

Bob's grandfather, Jim Starbuck, born 1895, was one of five children born to Monroe and Emma J. Ament Starbuck in Perry County. Jim married Pearl Hildenbrandt. Clifford married Elizabeth Clifton, later married Bessie Hensley. Reuben married Hessie Ledbetter. Gussie married Charles Grove. John married Pauline Moore of Kentucky. Later Monroe married Lillian Choate. They had two children: Ollie married Claudine Kilpatrick and Mary married Halford Rhodes. Bob's grandmother, Pearl, was one of four children born to Hermon and Tennie Flowers Hildenbrandt. Pearl married Jim Starbuck. Harry married Eulah Hobbs. Ruby married Claude Bell. John married Norma Hildenbrandt. Their father came from Germany. He was killed in a sawmill accident while the children were small.

Bob attended school at Pope on lower Cypress Creek and high school in Linden. In 1968, Bob was inducted into the Army. He served two years, one in Vietnam. He was awarded the purple heart after being wounded by a bomb that struck the truck he was driving. After coming home, he worked with his father until 1976, when he was employed at Graham Lumber Company in Linden where he still works. Bob's wife, Flora, has worked at Smith's Pharmacy in Linden since 1984, where she has met many Perry County people.

DORA ELIZABETH BEASLEY, daughter of Beverly Bates and Carolyn P. Miller Beasley, was born in Hickman County, Tennessee, Feb. 5, 1860, and died on Marsh Creek, Perry County, Tennessee, June 3, 1915. She was married to Henry Houston DePriest, Dec. 6, 1881.

Dora Deane DePriest in 1951

The ancestors of Dora Elizabeth Beasley DePriest, as researched by Raleigh W. Robertson, Nashville, Tennessee, with the help of others, was published in 1992. Most of the information about this Beasley family comes from this source, and it follows.

John Pitts Beasley II, born 1776, died 1848, married Lucy Ellis, born 1781, died 1851. Their children were: Nancy P., born 1801, married Ellis Peach; Wiley Ellis, born 1803, died 1872, married Polly Johnston; John Pitts III, born 1805, died 1892, married Mary T. (Polly) Bates; Mary Ann, born 1809, died 1878, married Reddisk Godwin; Barnabas, born 1812; Littleberry, born 1817, died 1895; and William, born 1825, died 1897.

John Pitts Beasley III, born 1805, Warren County, North Carolina, died 1892, Hickman County, Tennessee, married Mary T. (Polly) Bates, born 1809, died 1894, Hickman County, Tennessee. Their children were: Narcissa, born 1826, died 1899, married Joseph Beasley; Elizabeth, born 1827, Hickman County, Tennessee, married William Burl McCord; Lucy Jane; Mary; Parilee; Beverly Bates Beasley, born 1833, Hickman County, Tennessee, died 1920, Perry County, Tennessee, married Caroline P. Miller; and Sarah Francis.

Beverly Bates Beasley, born 1833, Hickman County, Tennessee, died 1920, Perry County, Tennessee, married Caroline P. Miller, born 1832, Hickman County, Tennessee, died 1932, Perry County, Tennessee. Their children were: William Berry, born 1855, Hickman County, Tennessee, died Perry County, Tennessee, married 1880, Nancy A. Shelton; M.A.F. (Fannie), born 1857, Hickman County, Tennessee, married Pleasant W. Whitwell; Louisa J., born 1859, Hickman County, Tennessee, 1877, married Dr. William B. Tucker; Dora Elizabeth, born 1860, Hickman County, Tennessee, died 1915, Perry County, Tennessee, married 1881, Henry Houston DePriest; John Miller, born 1864, Hickman County, Tennessee, died Perry County, Tennessee, married Nannie Webb; Sarah Caroline, born 1867, Hickman County, Tennessee, died 1941, Perry County, Tennessee, married Sim Allen Kimble; Prudence Roberta Margaret, born 1870, Hickman County, Tennessee, died 1932, Gibson County, Tennessee, married 1886, William Thomas DePriest; Paul Thomas, born 1874, Hickman County, Tennessee, died Perry County, Tennessee, never married.

The children of Dora Elizabeth Beasley and Henry Houston DePriest are: Laura Ethel, married A.W. DePriest; Ida Elizabeth, married R.C. Smith; Addie Lee, married Ruben J. Smith; John Thurman, married Mary Bess Suratt; William

Henry, married Eunice Hodge; Homer Bates, married Leota Dabbs; Thomas Brown, married Ima Fields; Deanna, died at the age of four; and Nora, married Henry Shelton.

Elena Smith Swafford and Beulah Smith Duncan, granddaughters of Dora Beasley DePriest, remembered their grandmother as a good wife, mother and homemaker. Her son, William Henry, remembered that his mother, Dora DePriest, was known as a champion horse back rider. Her son, John Thurman, said that his mother encouraged him to pursue an education. This led him to become a teacher.

John Thurman DePriest had five daughters. Dora Deane DePriest, the third daughter, was named for her grandmother, Dora Elizabeth Beasley DePriest. She, like her parents and sister, chose a teaching career. She retired from teaching in 1975 with 35 years of teaching. Her sisters, Mary DePriest Warren (Mrs. W. O.), Lorraine DePriest Hitt (Mrs. Jas. E.), and Celia DePriest Coley (Mrs. Wm. H.), also had full teaching careers. Jessie DePriest Nunley (Mrs. Joe E.) did teach, but with five children, she devoted most of her time to homemaking. For further information about the Henry Houston DePriest family, see the "John Thurman DePriest Family History" in the *Perry County History Book. Submitted by Dora Deane DePriest.*

J.C. AND MARTHA BEASLEY, live on the Spring Creek road 1 1/2 miles north of Highway 412. Martha is the daughter of Jim and Pearl Hildenbrandt Starbuck. J.C. is the son of Mack and Annie Evans Beasley. J.C. and Martha live in the house where J.C. was born in 1918. Martha was born on Cypress Creek in 1922. She remembers that as a small child, her grandfather, Monroe Starbuck, let her go into the darkroom where he developed his own pictures. Also going to his gristmill on lower Cypress Creek and watching corn being ground into meal. Martha's father, Jim, born 1895, was a farmer. He owned a peanut picker and picked peanuts for the other farmers. Jim served in the Army during World War I in France. The war was over before his unit was called into combat.

J.C. and Martha Beasley

Pearl, born 1898, was a homemaker and Martha was the only child. In 1971, Jim married Birdie Grove Berry. She died in 1988.

J.C.'s father, Mack, born 1887, son of Peter and Mary Barber Beasley was a farmer, raising hay, corn, peanuts, cows, hogs, and a big garden. J.C.'s mother, Annie, born 1889, was a homemaker and was always helping others. J.C. had two sisters, Bonnie Mae died as a small child and Hazel married Zeb Nix. They had one son, Johnny, who was killed in a car wreck at the age of 26.

J.C. and Martha had two sons, J.M. and Bob, both born at the homeplace where J.C. and Martha now live.

Martha taught school one year during the war of 1945. In 1954, she worked at the Pope School cafeteria on Cypress Creek. She worked there for 20 years.

The first few years the Beasleys were married, J.C. worked with his father on the farm. Later he was employed at Perry Farmers Co-op. In 1968, J.C. bought and operated his own sawmill before going into the trucking business. In 1983, he was in a car wreck that broke his neck and forced his retirement. He still enjoys life.

J.M. AND BETTY BEASLEY, live in Philadelphia, Mississippi. J.M. was born in 1943 in Perry County, son of J.C. and Martha Starbuck Beasley. J.M. married Ann Weems in 1963. They had two children, Clarke, born 1965, works with Sarasota County in Florida. Laura, born 1969, married Mark Simmons who trains whales and Laura works with birds and fish at Sea World in Florida. After a divorce, J.M. married Betty Smith Shelton, born 1951, daughter of L.E. and Leona Conner Smith of Alabama. J.M. and Betty have one daughter, Kara, born 1982, who attends school in Philadelphia, Mississippi. J.M. works with Yates Construction Company in Mississippi.

J.M. and Betty Beasley and daughter, Laura

J.M. is a descendent of Edward Starbuck, tenth great grandfather, born 1604, in England. Danial Starbuck, fourth great grandfather, born 1779, came to Perry County from North Carolina in the 1820s. Erastus Starbuck, third great grandfather, born 1824, no record of birthplace. William Monroe Starbuck Sr., second great grandfather, born 1848 in Perry County. He married Nancy J. Simmons. William Monroe Starbuck Jr., great grandfather, born 1872. James M. Starbuck, grandfather, born 1895. The last four people named above were buried in the Starbuck Cemetery on Cypress Creek, on land given to be used for a public cemetery by William Monroe Starbuck Sr.

J.M. has been gone from Perry County for several years, but still has fond memories of his childhood in Perry County. In 1948, J.M. started to school on Spring Creek in a one room building that was used as a school and as churches of different denominations. The land was given by J.M.'s great-great uncle, Marion Starbuck. It was used several years before it was deeded to the County for a school in the 1920s. The building was repaired and was still used for school and church services. This building burned after Spring Creek, lower Cypress Creek and Marsh Creek schools were consolidated into one school on lower Cypress Creek, approximately 1950, and was named Pope School. J.M. went seven years at Pope, and high school in Linden.

J.M. and his brother, Bob, attended church services with their parents at Howard's Methodist Church in a building that was built in 1895, on land donated by R.J. Howard. When this house needed repairing, Ben Howard III, donated land 1/4 mile south of the old church. A new church was built and opened for worship services in 1960. J.M. attends church services whenever he visits his parents.

JEFFREY T. AND GLORIA GHAYLE BEASLEY, were married, Aug. 24, 1973, in Nashville, Tennessee. They have three children: Rachel Abyghayle, born Aug. 12, 1974; Rebekah Elisabeth, born Jan. 14, 1976; and Benjamin Bolivar, born July 9, 1977.

Jeffrey T. and Gloria Beasley with children (from left): Rachel, Rebekah and Benjamin in February 1993.

Jeffrey was born on May 11, 1951, at the United States Naval Base in Guatanamo Bay, Cuba, to Tom and Mary Jo Beasley. After Tom's retirement in 1959, the family moved back to their home in Linden, Tennessee. They built a house on their farm on Brush Creek, about six miles east of Linden on Highway 100. Jeffrey attended Perry County High School, graduating in 1969. He attended Freed Hardeman College from 1969-1971, and graduated from Tennessee Technological University, Cookeville, Tennessee in Mechanical Engineering in 1973. Jeffrey and Gloria met at Freed-Hardeman College in the fall of 1969. Gloria had grown up in California, and had moved with her family to Nashville during the summer of 1969. She is the daughter of Jack and Wilma Rudd.

Rachel, Rebekah, and Benjamin all attended David Lipscomb Elementary, Middle, and High School in Nashville, Tennessee. Rachel is presently a sophomore at Freed-Hardeman University, and Rebekah will enroll as a freshman there this fall. Benjamin is a sophomore at David Lipscomb High School. Rachel, Rebekah, and Benjamin still enjoy holidays and special occasions with their grandparents, Tom and Mary Jo Beasley, at their farm on Brush Creek.

Jeff, Gloria, Rachel, Rebekah, and Ben now live on a farm in McEwen, Tennessee where they continue to enjoy the quiet, rural life, that has been so much a part of Jeffrey's life. They are members of the Crieve Hall Church of Christ in Nashville, Tennessee.

JOEL GOOCH BEASLEY AND MARTHA ELIZABETH CRAIG BEASLEY, were married in 1881. He was born in Williamson County, January 1857, the son of Littleberry Beasley and his third wife, Margaret Etta Pugh. Betty, as she was called, was born December 1864, the daughter of Eleazer Hardeman and Harriet Greer Craig.

Before 1870, Littleberry and his family moved to Perry County. He probably farmed and did carpenter work. When the rest of the family moved to Hickman County, Joe stayed in Perry County.

After Joe and Betty were married, they bought and lived on what is known as the Baker Vaughn place, which is near the Buffalo River. Joe worked as a carpenter for many years, his son, Jack, helping when he got older.

Joe and Betty had four children: Margaret Etta, married Mitchell McGee; Sallie Harriet, married Bernard Warren; William died young; John Allen (Jack) married Augusta Land.

Joe Beasley with his children: Jack, Sally Warren and Etta McGee

Betty died in 1912. In 1914, he married Emma Richardson. They were later divorced. Several years later, Joe married Izora Lewis of Coon Creek.

The last few years of Joe's life were spent at the home of his son, Jack. He died in February of 1944 at the home of his daughter, Etta McGee. He and Betty are buried at the Vaughn Cemetery, near where they had lived.

JOHN ALLEN (JACK) BEASLEY, was born in Perry County, May 23, 1896. He was the son of Joel Gooch and Martha Elizabeth Craig Beasley, born in Perry County, 1864, the daughter of Eleazer Hardeman Craig and his first wife, Margaret Greer.

John Allen (Jack) Beasley and his wife, Augusta Pearl Land Beasley.

Augusta Pearl Land was born in Perry County, March 27, 1898, the daughter of George T. and Leanna E. Warren Land.

They were married in 1912 in Lewis County and lived their lives in Perry County, except for a few years in Trenton, Tennessee, where Jack worked in a cotton mill, as a fireman for a furnace. They went to and from Perry County on a train, probably from Hohenwald to Nashville, then on to Trenton.

They returned to Brush Creek where Jack farmed and worked as a carpenter. He has built and worked on many houses in Perry County. His father and grandfather were also carpenters. Gus was a homemaker and seamstress.

They were the parents of four children: Land, married Minnie Riley; Tom Alva, married Mary Jo King; Joe George, married Marion Rodgers; Betty Lee, married James King.

Gus died June 1, 1948, and Jack died, May 12, 1952. They are buried in the Warren Cemetery on Brush Creek.

LITTLEBERRY BEASLEY, was born Jan. 27, 1817, on Bear Creek, Williamson County. He was the son of John Pitts and Lucy Ellis Beasley, both from Warren County, North Carolina. His first wife was Rebecca Thompson, who died, leaving him with one son, John Pitts Beasley. John married Sarah Sparkman and they came to Perry County before the Civil War. He served as trustee of Perry County in the late 1800s. He and Sarah built the house at the junction of Highways 100 and 412. Littleberry was a chairmaker in Williamson County in the 1850s.

Littleberry and Margaret Beasley

His third wife was Margaret Etta Pugh, born Oct. 11, 1827, at Dunlap, near Shady Grove, in Hickman County. She was the daughter of Joel and Prudence Nicks Pugh. In 1830, Joel, who was a miller, went down the Natchez Trace to see about a mill wheel. He fell ill with yellow fever near Raymond, Mississippi, and was buried there. The family did not know what happened to him for a long time. His wife, Prudence, came from North Carolina with her family.

The date of their marriage is unknown. They were in Williamson County in 1860, and later came to Coon Creek to live on the farm of his brother, Barnabas Beasley. He had another brother here, William, who later went back to Williamson County, two sisters, Nancy Peach and Mary Ann, who married Reddick Godwin. The Godwins are buried in the Vaughn Cemetery. A nephew, Fielding W. Beasley, and his wife, Sarah Mayberry, lived at the mouth of Brush Creek. Fielding fought in the Civil War and came home sick or wounded and died soon after. His burial place is unknown.

Berry may have made chairs on Coon Creek and worked as a carpenter. Most of his sons were carpenters and worked with wood. He and Margaret were members of the Church of Christ.

They had seven children: William Wiley, went to Texas; Joel Gooch, stayed in Perry County; George Wiley, settled in Lyles, Tennessee; James Alexander, married Sarah Lomax and stayed in Perry County; Prudence Etta; Samuel Moore; and Robert Truman, who went to Hickman County.

Berry and Margaret later moved to Beaverdam, Hickman County, then to Lyles, where they died: Berry, June 7, 1895 and Margaret, Sept. 23, 1898. They are buried in Lyles Cemetery.

TOM ALVA BEASLEY AND MARY JO KING, are both Perry Countians. Tom was born Dec. 4, 1919, on Brush Creek, the son of John Allen (Jack) and Augusta Pearl Land Beasley. Mary Jo was born on Coon creek, Oct. 28, 1926, the daughter of Byron Clyde and Mary Lee Bromley King.

Tom and Mary Jo King Beasley

Tom's childhood was spent on Brush Creek, Trenton, Tennessee and Linden. After completion of high school at Linden, he joined the U.S. Navy, Dec. 12, 1938. After Boot Camp at Norfolk, Virginia, he was sent to Pearl Harbor, TH, where he was stationed aboard the USS Oglala, a cruiser minelayer. The ship was sunk during the Japanese attack on Pearl Harbor. He then went to the Mine Assembly Base at West Loch of Pearl Harbor, and was sent to Tarawa and Apemama, in December 1943, then back to West Loch in March. He came home in April, 1944, when he met Mary Jo. He went back and was sent to Boston where he helped put the minelayer DM Robert H. Smith in commission.

When Mary Jo was three, her family moved to Centerville. She attended grade school there. The family moved back to Perry County in 1941, and settled on Brush Creek on Highway 100. She finished high school in 1945 in Linden.

Tom and Mary Jo were married Oct. 9, 1946, in Reno, Nevada, with Tom's sister, Betty Lee, in attendance. Their first home was in San Francisco. Other homes were Berkeley, California, Charleston, South Carolina, Nashville, and Jackson, on recruiting duty, Yorktown, VA twice, and Guantanamo Bay, Cuba. Tom was on an LST at Sasebo, Japan from January 1954 to November 1956, and retired from the Navy at Yorktown, Virginia, June 22, 1959, as a Master Chief.

They have two children: Barbara Jo, born Aug. 19, 1948, Nashville, Tennessee, and Jeffrey Thomas, born May 11, 1951, Guantanamo Bay, Cuba.

After retirement, the family came back to

Perry County and built a house on Brush Creek, Highway 100. Tom sold insurance for two years, then was a substitute mail carrier until 1982. He also raised registered Hampshire hogs.

Barbara and Jeffrey both attended school at Linden, graduating in 1966 and 1969. They both attended Freed Hardeman College. Jeffrey went on to Tennessee Technological University, where he graduated with a degree in Mechanical Engineering. Barbara married Dean Heady of Gallitan, Tennessee. They live in Linden and have three children. Jeffrey married Gloria Rudd of Nashville. They live in McEwen, Tennessee and have three children. All this family are members of the Church of Christ.

BELL - PATTERSON, Thomas Foster Bell, a Perry Countian, born Aug. 20, 1897, died Sept. 2, 1984, was the son of James Thomas, born June 12, 1863, died Aug. 30, 1919, and Molly Ayers Bell, born April 2, 1869, died April 3, 1946.

Foster and Lerlon Bell

Foster was a very handsome young man. He soon took the eye of Lerlon Patterson, born Oct. 22, 1889, died March 5, 1993. She was the daughter of William and Mattie Smith Patterson.

A few horse drawn buggy rides, community picnics, church revivals, all proved they were madly in love. The marriage date was July 14, 1918. They moved into a small house located near the banks of the beautiful Tennessee river. A general merchandise store and post office, named "Daniel's Landing", Mr. Clint Daniel, the owner, served as a trading center for the community. The river provided employment, transportation for merchandise, livestock, mail, etc.

The Foster and Lerlon Bell Family

The river also furnished entertainment in the form of yearly showboats, namely: Cotton Blossom, America, Majestic would perform one night, presenting plays, music and vaudeville. The steam musical calliope attracted people miles away before showtime.

The Bells began growing peanuts, corn and hay. Mules and hand drawn plows were used. The eight children born in the home helped with all the chores. The children attended one or two teacher schools in the community. Children of the union were:

Ramelle, born 1919, married Orby Daniel, born 1919, died June 18, 1986. Children: Brenda married Charles Smith, and Peggy married Jimmy Stacy.

Montie, born 1921, married Cartis Westbrooks, born 1917, died Aug. 16, 1972. Children: Wesley married Doris Crowell; Mary Joe married Gene Warren; Billy married Beverly Barnes; Sandra married Gerald Warren; and Jackie married Darrell Hinson.

Thomas, born 1924, married Ruth Campbell. Children: Ronnie, not married; Ricky married Debbie Edney, divorced, then married Tresia Dickson; Tommie married Bobby Warren; and Donna married Darrel Luna.

Bessie, born 1926, married Roy Bell. One child, Thomas, married Penny Goff.

Tulious, born 1929, married Faye Franklin, divorced. Children: Randel married Tamela Hooper, and Tammy married Barry King.

Bertran, born 1931, married Marie Hicks, divorced. One child, Darlene married Ronny Moran. Then Bertran married Betty Jackson.

Martha, born 1935, married Alton Allison. Children: Robert, married Sheila Alley, and Michelle married Jimmy Frazee.

Janice, born 1938, single.

Foster and Lerlon reared a family during the depression of 1930-?. The 89 days drought ruined the crops. Despite hardships, the family didn't give up. They were determined that each future day would be a better tomorrow.

The Tennessee Valley Authority forced the family to move, due to flooding the area. Soon electricity replaced the kerosene lamps, refrigerators, etc.

The Bells, not happy, moved over the hill to Humphreys County, Blue Creek, near Cuba Landing and bought the old Patterson home place owned by Lerlon's parents, William and Mattie Smith Patterson. They continued farming, raising hogs, horses and cattle.

Foster and Lerlon Bells' life ended, thankful for eight living children, seventeen grandchildren, twenty-six great grandchildren and six great great grandchildren.

Their life was filled with love and understanding of others, by taking two homeless boys in their home. Giving their love and guidance as their own to manhood. All this and more will never be forgotten by the family and friends throughout the days, months, and years of tomorrow.

BELL-ROBERTSON, George Washington Bell, named after our first President, was the son of Eldridge Newson and Caroline J. Pegram. The grandson of John Bell and Ester McDonald. His father served in the Union Army.

George was blessed with a large family, ten brothers and sisters as follows: John married Mary Robertson; William married Mary Coble; Mary married Dock Cagle; E.N. Bell married Sarah O'Guin; Anna married John Clayborn; James married Molly Ayers; Elizabeth married William Cantrell; Charles married Hibernia Coble; Henry married Ida Fuller; Montgomery married Minnie Pirtle, second marriage to Daisy Ashton.

The Bell and Robertson family were neighbors. George fell in love with Manerva Robertson. A short courtship ended with the vows of marriage.

George and Manerva Robertson Bell

George and Manerva were a friendly, peace loving couple. Always helping neighbors, relatives and friends. They were blessed with three sons:

William Nuse, 1879-1943, married Daisy Patterson (deceased). They had two children, Pauline married John Horner (both deceased) and Roy married Bessie Bell; they had one son, Tommy, married Penny Goff. Sons were Chaymus and Drake.

R. Thomas, 1880-1958, married Docia Strickland. They had two children, Fred (deceased) and Alma, married Paul Edwards (both deceased). They had three children; Wallace, married Clara Long - Children are Deborah, married Randall Harris - Children - Chelsey and Chad Qualls; Teresa married David Garrison - Children- Cassie, Nichols, and David; Rodney, married Jill Henley - Step Children - Leslie Dabbs, married Brenda Moore, daughter, Autumn. Terrie married Randall Gray - Children - Lindsey and James. Linda married Franklin DePriest, divorced. Daughters: Sandra, married Wayne Doss - Children - Angie and Laren. Cindy, married Wendell Stone - Children - Kevin and Kyle. Laverne, married John Curl - Children - Glenda, married Bruce Colton. James, married Lois Pennington, divorced. Daughter: Kimberly. Second marriage Elizabeth Quinn, son, James Jr.

Elmer, 1889-1961, married Myrtle Cotton (deceased). Daughter, Gladys, married Lloyd Marress, a school teacher from Humphreys County. Deceased, no children.

George enjoyed hunting wildlife, especially turkeys. It was his desire to furnish each of his sons and family with a turkey for Thanksgiving dinner.

The Bells, a hard working, honest, dependable family enjoyed a horse drawn buggy ride down the road to visit relatives or friends.

Will this quiet, peaceful time return again? The family holds sweet memories of yesterday that will never be forgotten by those that lived and experienced the "Good 'Ole Days".

CHARLES H. AND WILLIE GREEN BELL, sons of Eldridge and Caroline Bell. Charles was born March 1867, died 1941, married to Hiburina (Winnie) Coble (1871-1942), lived at Pine View. Charles and Winnie had nine children: Fernie E., July 1888-1950. For many years, he ran a small store in Pine View; George Royce, Feb. 28, 1893-Sept. 6, 1910; Grady Leonard, March 1, 1896-March 25, 1896; Brown, married Grace Crowell, April 26, 1913; Annie Vera, Feb. 24, 1899-June 5, 1973, was a school teacher, never married; Byron, Jan. 6, 1910, married Kelly ?; Bernard, born and died Jan. 6, 1910; Louise, Nov. 1901-Aug. 7, 1986, married George Matthew Jones; and Mary Love, 1901-Dec. 1, 1983, married Herbert Patterson, Nov. 29, 1983.

Charles and Winnie Coble Bell

William Green, brother to Charles, born March 10, 1853, died Oct. 13, 1933, married Mary Jane Coble, Sept. 29, 1881. Their children were: Minnie Odell, Aug. 26, 1882-1958, married George Porter; William Oscar, Jan. 7, 1884-Oct. 4, 1954, married first to Bessie Harder, Dec. 29, 1906. After her death, he married Rhue Duff in 1944; George A.W., Feb. 12, 1886-Dec. 4, 1972, married Zodie Cox; Ida Virginia, May 29, 1890-1971, married Rex Bates; Bess, Jan. 26, 1892-Feb. 4, 1892; Perry Leslie, April 9, 1894-July 28, 1976, married first to Ann Overby. After her death, he married Mary Helen Armstrong, June 9, 1930; Ray, April 9, 1897-Aug. 26, 1898; Grady, Sept. 17, 1899-Oct. 6, 1925; twins, Grady and Gracie, born Sept. 17, 1899. Grady died Oct. 6, 1925, and Gracie died Sept. 20, 1899.

Ida Virginia (Jennie) and Rex Bates lived in Hohenwald, Tennessee for many years and sister, Minnie, made her home with them after the death of her husband. Minnie did not have children and Jennie was the mother of four, however no one lived to be fifteen years old.

ELDRIDGE NEWSOM BELL, This Civil War gentleman was the oldest son of John and Esther McDanials Bell, born in Davidson County about 1828, died after 1888 in Perry County. He married Caroline J. Pegram, 1831-1882, about 1851. Caroline was the daughter of George W. and Sarah Pegram. The 1850 census of Davidson County listed him being 22 years of age, single and a blacksmith, living with his parents. The 1870 census listed him married with the following children: John, 19; William G. 16; Mary, 17; E.N. Jr., 14; George, 10; James T., 8; Elizabeth, 6; Charles, 5; Henry H., 1; then, Montgomery G. was born in 1873.

We have been told that "Nuse" and Caroline are buried in the Bell-Robertson Cemetery with no marker. Oldest son, John 1852-1880, married Mary ?. William Green, March 10, 1853-Oct. 13, 1933, married Mary J. Coble. Mary, no dates, married Dock Cagle in 1855. E.N. Jr., 1856-?, married Sarah O'Guinn, July 29, 1878. George Washington, 1860-Nov. 22, 1940, married Minerva Robertson, Oct. 10, 1877. Anna Jane, Feb. 6, 1861-Oct. 11, 1908, married John W. Clayborn, July 18, 1877. James Thomas, 1863-1919, married Mollie Ayers, Jan. 15, 1896. Elizabeth Louisa, Dec. 10, 1865-March 6, 1956, married Hibernia Coble. Henry Harrison, May 31, 1867-March 11, 1945, married Ida L. Fuller. Montgomery G., 1873-, married Minnie Pirtle, Dec. 4, 1892.

Eldridge Newsom Bell

Nuse served in Co. F Gantts 9th Tennessee Cavalry, as a blacksmith. He enlisted Nov. 1861 and was taken prisoner at Fr. Donelson. By 1862, he was back home. He re-enlisted and served in Louisiana and Mississippi, where he deserted and was home again by Sept. 1862. Looking at the dates on his children, it is hard to tell when he was in service and when he was home.

JOHN BELL, About 1801, John Bell was born in North Carolina and was in Davidson County before 1827, when he married Esther McDaniels, born about 1805. John died before 1880 and is buried on the hill in what is known as the Horner School House Place, at the corner of Wilsdorf Hollow and Toms Creek Road. Ester died between 1854 and 1860, as her last child was born in 1854 and she was not on the 1860 Perry County census with John and the children. We know of nine children. They had, Eldridge Newson, born 1828, who served as a blacksmith in the Civil War and married Caroline Pegram before 1877. They are buried in the Bell-Robertson cemetery. Sarah (Aunt Mitt), 1833, married George Pegram, Aug. 2, 1846 in Davidson County. George was the father of Caroline, who married Newsom. Nancy, 1835, married to Bart Walker. This is all we know about her. He died young, and she more than likely remarried. John W., 1838, married Georgianna Pegram, and died before 1870. Lucinda, 1840, may have married a Short, not sure of this. Elizabeth, 1844, married Miles L. Lawarnce, Jan. 1, 1871, and died, Nov. 30, 1930. James S., 1846, married Josephine Skaggs, Oct. 14, 1888, died in Arkansas and is buried there. Joseph A., 1848, married Matilda C. Robertson, Sept. 23, 1869, died March 1, 1901. Charles H., May 15, 1854, married Sarah Adeline Robertson, Sept. 6, 1872, died Jan. 4, 1913. Charles and Sarah are the parents of the following children: Samual Morton, June 12, 1873-Oct. 27, 1933, married Laura Patterson, Dec. 26, 1902; Mary Jane, Aug. 18, 1874-July 12, 1909, married to Francis M. Thornnton, Feb. 11, 1900, twin Martha Jean died Dec. 22, 1874; Edward E., March 20, 1879-Sept. 8, 1964, married Vera Elise Shephard, Dec. 26, 1908; Ida Rue, July 19, 1891-July 25, 1980, married to Emmett Lafayette Cotham, Jan. 1, 1914.

Charles and Sarah Robertson Bell

Samual M. and Laura Patterson Bell were the parents of Edna Mae, Nov. 12, 1903-May 27, 1993, married to Bob Barham, Dec. 11, 1923; Laura Lorane, Aug. 14, 1908-Nov. 1990, married Joe M. Starbuck, March 10, 1928.

Edna and Bob had two daughters, Melvis Virginia, Dec. 18, 1929, married Leroy Staggs and Marjorie Ann, Sept. 23, 1935, married Naymond D. Graves, Aug. 22, 1958.

Melvis and Leroy have three children, Sandra Kay, June 9, 1960, Gary Lee, Oct. 9, 1963, and Stephen Barham Staggs, Feb. 16, 1964. Sandra Kay married Jeff Cameron, May 25, 1984 and they have a son, Bret, Dec. 9, 1986. Gary has a daughter, Jerica, Jan. 13, 1986.

CLAUDE TEANEY BERRY, was born in western South Dakota, Oct. 1921, to Emile and Echo (Teaney) Berry. His maternal grandparents were Eri and Jennie Teaney. They came to South Dakota from southern Illinois in 1906. His paternal grandparents were Carl and Thilda Borgstrom, who came to the United States from Sweden. At that time, his name was changed to Charles Berry.

Claude and Mary Berry

In 1944, Claude married Mary Elizabeth Quinn. She was the daughter of Peter and Charlotte (Phalen) Quinn, born in 1923 in western South Dakota. Her father, Peter, came from Ireland and her mother, Charlotte, came from Wisconsin; settling in Haakon County, South Dakota in the early 1900s.

After marriage, Claude and Elizabeth lived and worked on a ranch in Haakon County, South Dakota for 21 years. They raised a family of five children: Rex, Claudia, Barbara, Eli, and Carmel.

In 1965, the family moved to a farm near Mora, Minnesota. They did general farming, with beef cattle, hogs, and dairying for 23 years.

Upon retirement, they decided to move south. While traveling through Tennessee, they found the area in Perry County of interest and moved here Oct. 22, 1988, after buying Mary Lou Plunketts home on Route 3 east of Linden.

They find the numerous historical places of great interest, especially those pertaining to the Civil War. Elizabeth's grandfather, John Phalen, from Wisconsin, spent the majority of his time in the service in this area of Tennessee.

BIRD/BYRD AND JOURNEY, Hugh L. Bird was born, ca 1813, in Green County, Georgia, according to his wife's Mexican War pension application. The spelling of his last name changes from document to document. Sometimes with an I and sometimes with a Y. On October 13, 1829, a marriage bond was issued in Williamson County, Tennessee for the marriage between Hugh and Susan Crane. Susan Crane was the daughter of Thomas and Mattie Crane. Susan was born Sept. 10, 1814. The children of Hugh and Susan were: James Jordan, Martha A., William, Elizabeth, Francis M., Louisa, Susan J., Mary, and Rufus G.

Hugh was a carpenter by trade. He was 5' 8" tall with blue eyes, light hair and a dark complexion. On May 15, 1847, he enlisted in Athens, Alabama and was a private of Company F, 13th Regiment, Alabama Infantry during the Mexican War. Hugh apparently roamed throughout Alabama and middle Tennessee after his discharge, before making his home in Perry County, Tennessee, near Beardstown, about 1882. Hugh also served in the Civil War as a private in the 54th Alabama Regiment, Company B. Hugh died Feb. 13, 1883, near Beardstown, but his burial site is unknown. Susan continued living in Perry County until her death on April 24, 1902. Her burial site also remains a mystery.

James Jordan Bird was the second oldest son of Hugh Bird and Susan Crane. He was born on May 14, 1839, in Williamson County, Tennessee. He married Sarah Elizabeth (Betty) Snellins, April 3, 1864, place unknown. James served in B.W. Alexander's Battalion of Marshall Rangers and in Company B of the 54th Alabama Infantry during the Civil War.

James Jordan Byrd died 1913-1929 in Perry County, Tennessee and is buried in the Chestnut Grove Cemetery in Perry County. Sarah Elizabeth (Betty) Snellins Byrd died March 3, 1929, in Columbia, Tennessee. Her death certificate says she was buried in the Lynden Cemetery in Perry County on March 4, 1929, but no tombstone is found for her in that county.

The two children of James Jordan Byrd and Sarah Elizabeth (Betty) Snellins are: Henry Buford Byrd, born July 20, 1867, in Williamson County and A.M. Byrd (male), born Jan. 9, 1865, died July 10, 1887.

Henry Buford Byrd married Fannie Cornelia Journey, Oct. 13, 1892, in Perry County, Tennessee. Fannie was the daughter of Joe Journey and Elize Ann Foster. Henry and Fannie were the parents of: William Garrett, Bessie Mae, Henry Earl, Paul Eldridge, Addie Lou, and Herman L.

Even though all of the above children were born in Perry County, Henry and Fannie made their home soon afterwards in Columbia, Tennessee. Henry Buford Byrd died April 22, 1949, in Columbia. Fannie Journey Byrd died Jan. 8, 1947, also in Columbia.

Joe Journey is listed on various documents as S.J., Joseph, Joe C., Josephus S. and Flavius J. Journey. Joseph Journey was born March 22, 1827. He married Eliza Ann Foster, Feb. 11, 1852, in Maury County, Tennessee.

Eliza Ann Foster was the daughter of Allen Foster and Elizabeth McMean of Maury County. She was born May 7, 1835.

Joe Journey died Feb. 1, 1905, in Perry County, Tennessee and Eliza Ann, on April 11, 1914. They are both buried at the Tucker cemetery on Short Creek in Perry County along with several of their children.

The children of Joe Journey and Eliza Ann Foster were: Mary E. Journey, Joe Thomas Journey, James Maloy Journey, Charles Washington Journey, Victoria Journey, Lee Journey, Cora Olivia Journey, Fannie Cornelia Journey, William Journey, Ophelia Journey. *Submitted by Wanda Killgore.*

BIRDSONG-WILLIAMS, Richard Cates (Dickie) Craig, born 1861, in Perry County, Tennessee, died 1939, Benton County, Tennessee was first married to Abbie Lynch, Perry County, prior to 1885. Their children were Nettie Mae, born Nov. 17, 1885, died May 21, 1969, and Lockard, dates unknown. The Craigs were divorced in Perry County, Tennessee.

Dickie's second marriage was to Laura Owens in Perry County, Tennessee, April 6, 1892. Laura was born 1871 and died 1951. Soon after their marriage, they, along with their little daughter, Nettie, moved to Benton County, near his brother, Henry L. Craig and family. The little sister, Lockard, remained in Perry County to be raised by her mother.

Daughter, Nettie, first married Wilson Ashby, Feb. 5, 1903; and second, on Nov. 27, 1904, in Benton County, Tennessee to Robert E. Lee Birdsong, born Feb. 23, 1888, died May 5, 1915. They lived near the Craig families in "Craig Hollow", located in District 1. Their children were, Richard Birdsong, Stella Mae Birdsong, Gertrude Hazel Birdsong, Robert Birdsong, Louise Birdsong, and LEneace Birdsong. Lee Birdsong, died May 5, 1915, a few months before the birth of LEneace. He was buried in a cemetery near where the family lived at Green Hills, possibly the Green Hatley cemetery. Five years later, the little LEneace was playing near a fireplace, caught fire and badly burned, causing her death the following day. She is buried next to her father and the graves are unmarked.

Soon after, Nettie Craig Birdsong, married for the third time to Augusta Danvile Markham, born Nov. 19, 1888, and moved to St. Louis, Missouri for employment. They lived there, raising the Birdsong children. Augusta Markham died Jan. 11, 1944. They both died in St. Louis and are buried there.

Further information of their children: (1) Richard, born April 10, 1905, first married Lilla Findley, then married Markie, later married Jewel.

(2) Stella Mae, born July 30, 1907, and on Oct. 30, 1926, married James Williams, born 1905, died 1978. Children: (A) Mabel Mae Williams, born Feb. 27, 1927, married Mr. Pipitone. Their children - (a) Jacqueline Mae Pipitone, born Oct. 13, 1947, (b) Vickie Sue, born July 16, 1952, (c) Sandi, born Nov. 11, 19__. (B) Evelyn Aline Williams, born Dec. 19, 1931, married David Mauer. Their children - (a) Susan Dale Mauer, born Dec. 17, 1952, (b) Diane Lynn, born Jan. 17, 1957, and (c) Cynthia Ann Mauer, born July 4, 1960.

(3) Gertrude Hazel Birdsong, born 1909, married Fred Williams. Children: Blondell; Maxine, born March 6, 1930; Nadine, born Dec. 14, 1933; Donald Fred, born June 19, 1937.

(4) Robert Birdsong, born 1911, married Merle Kedrikid. Children: Robert, born Oct. 12, 1936; Berneta, born May 13, 1934; Stella Pearl, born Nov. 29, 1942; Charles, born June 28, 1940; and Delores Birdsong, born Aug.. 25, 1944.

(5) Louise Birdsong, born 1913, married Joseph N. Williams.

(6) LEneace Birdsong, born 1915, died Nov. 8, 1922.

Stella Mae Birdsong Williams, along with her cousin, C.O. Craig, is attempting to locate the graves of Robert and LEneace Birdsong. If anyone has information on Birdsong family burials, please contact the Benton County, Tennessee library. Stella Mae Birdsong Williams lives in Montgomery City, Missouri. *Submitted by Mae Birdsong Williams.*

DAVID JACKSON AND MARY (RICE) BLACKWELL, According to Spence's History of Hickman County, Tennessee and a Family History Chart prepared in 1943 by Jackson Blackwell's granddaughters, Edna Grimmitt, daughter of Susan Emmaline (Blackwell) Grimmitt, and Eva (Blackwell) Boney, daughter of Samuel Decker Blackwell, the Wilkins and Blackwell families moved from Franklin County, Georgia to middle Tennessee the latter part of the 1700s and early 1800s.

Family of William Jesse and Susan Malinda (Wilkins) Blackwell. Seated: Susan Malinda, Arles B., William Jesse and Lloyd. Standing: Cuba O., B. Varden and Donna S.

The families of John and Sarah (Wells) Blackwell secured land grants in Hickman, Perry and Humphreys Counties.

Jesse Blackwell, the son of John and Sarah (Wells) Blackwell, married Sarah Wilkins, the daughter of John and Mary (Anthony) Wilkins, in Franklin County, Georgia, 1810. Their family moved to Hickman County in 1818. Their children were David Jackson, Joe, Polly, William, Elizabeth, Robert, Wilkins, Seaborn, and Johnnie Blackwell.

Jackson Blackwell married Mary Rice, the daughter of William and Sarah (Daily) Rice, and the granddaughter of Thomas and Biddie (Decker) Rice, and Wesley and Sucky (Mitchell) Daily, Jan. 20, 1842, at Lobelville (Perry County), Tennessee. Mary Rice was born Feb. 8, 1822, near Lobelville, and died Feb. 8, 1909, in Hickman County. Jackson Blackwell, born Jan. 8, 1816, near Only, Hickman County, and died April 15, 1891.

They had eleven children, according to the 1860 Census, all of them were born in Perry County with maybe the exception of the two younger boys who appear in the Hickman County 1870 Census. Susan Emmaline was eight months old on 1860 in the Perry County Census.

Their children were: Dr. James Wells Blackwell, born April 11, 1843, died Dec. 22, 1910; Zebedee Blackwell, born Nov. 2, 1844, died March 13, 1916; Margaret Elizabeth, born Oct.. 2, 1846, died Oct. 11, 1930; William Jesse, born Jan. 15, 1851, died Dec. 27, 1924; Sara Blackwell, born Nov. 15, 1848, died March 22, 1932; Elijah Robert, born March 9, 1853, died June 25, 1928; Seaborn Anthony Blackwell, born Jan. 17, 1855, died March 7, 1928; John Mitchell Blackwell, born May 16, 1857, died Oct. 29, 1915; Susan Emmaline, born Nov. 2, 1859, died May 23, 1943; Andrew Jackson Blackwell, born Oct. 11, 1861, died Jan. 27, 1891, Randall County, Texas; and Samuel Decker Blackwell, born Sept. 6, 1864, died Oct. 30, 1921, Potter County, Texas.

William Jesse, son of Jackson and Mary, married Susan Malinda Wilkins at Only, Hickman County, 1872. She was the daughter of Clement and Jomimma "Jan" (Baugus) Wilkins, the granddaughter of Clement and Clarissa (Decker) Wilkins and Jeremiah and Nancy Baugus. Their children were: B. Varden, J. Memol, Donna S., Cuba O., Lloyd B., and Arles B. They moved to the Texas Panhandle (Hardeman, Randall, Donley, and Potter Counties) around 1888. Arles was three years old. They are both buried in Odd Fellow cemetery, Clarendon Donley County, Texas.

In 1885, Andrew Jackson owned a mercantile business at Lobelville. He carried a general stock of hardware, queensware and glassware, groceries, dry goods, etc. He and his brother, William Jesse, came into possession of the home where the store building was located. This fifty acre track of land contained iron ore. Submitted by Donna Clyde Arms, granddaughter of William Jesse and Susan Malinda (Wilkins) Blackwell, daughter of James Clyde and Arles (Blackwell) Wright.

MICHAEL SCOTT AND DENISE BLACKWELL,

live on Coon Creek in Perry County, Tennessee. Denise is the daughter of Billy and Joy Kilpatrick Gordon of Perry County. Denise Gordon Blackwell was born in Maury County on April 10, 1965. Scott is the great-grandson of the late Sidney Douglas and Eve Tucker Dowdy of Linden, Tennessee. Also the great-grandson of the late Elmer Sanders and Verna Sanders of Lobelville, Tennessee. Scott is the grandson of Jess and Evelyn Dowdy Sanders of Linden, Tennessee. Scott Blackwell is the son of Michael G. and Linda Sanders Blackwell, of Davidson County, Tennessee. Scott was born Sept. 1, 1963, in Davidson County, Tennessee.

Michael Scott, Denise and daughter, Kristin

In 1978, Scott and his mother, Linda Terrell, and sister, Kim Terrell, moved to Linden, Tennessee, to be closer to family that live in Perry County. Scott and Denise were married Aug. 1, 1986, in Linden. They have one child, Kristin Eve, born Oct. 7, 1988.

BOWEN, Moses and Rebecca Reece Bowen emigrated from Wales to Philadelphia about 1682. Their son, John and his wife, Lilly McIlhaney, migrated to Augusta County, Virginia, where they had eight sons and five daughters; Nancy, Agnes, Reece, Robert, William, Arthur, Mary, Henry, Moses, Jane, Rebecca, Charles, and John. All of the sons fought in the Revolution, as well as all their brothers-in-law. Four of them were at the Battle of King's Mountain and one was killed there.

Clint O. Bowen and family

After the war, three of the children settled in Tennessee, near Nashville. The seventh child, Captain Robert Bowen and his wife, Mary Gillespie, moved in the 1770s to George's Creek, South Carolina, where they had nine children: John, Mary, William, Nancy, Reece, Robert Gillespie, Charles, and Rebecca. In 1805, when he was 65, Captain Robert Bowen and his fifth child, Mary Bowen Barr, with her husband, Rev. James Barr; his seventh child, Robert G. Bowen, age, 16; and his ninth child, Charles Bowen, age 14; moved to a square mile of land in Tennessee where the Piney River flows into the Duck river. Captain Robert established the town of Vernon.

About 1815, Robert Gillespie Bowen, 1789-1846, married Mary "Polly" Wilson. They had a large family, three sons and six daughters: Louise, Amanda J., Polly Ann, Eleanor, Rebecca, Robert R., William Reece, Adam R., and Mary Jane. One of these sons, Robert Reese Bowen, 1825-1849, married Lou Emma Polk, about 1845, when he was 20, and she was 16. He died in 1849, leaving her with two small sons, Robert Polk and William. She remarried, leaving her sons to be reared by guardians.

Robert Polk Bowen, 1846-1917, married Mary Myrtle Elizabeth Briggs, in 1864. They lived all their lives in the Pinewood area of Hickman County and raised a family of four sons and three daughters: Ben, Wilson, Mitch, Carrie Myrtle, Ora Allen, Laura, and Will. The youngest child, William Russell Hiram Bowen, 1865-1948, married first Minnie Russell in 1924 and moved from Hickman County to Humphreys County, settling near the Perry County line, where they reared four sons. The youngest, Arthur D. Bowen, 1900-1974, married Mildred Owens in 1924 and had two sons, Clint Owens and William Levi "Billy".

The oldest son, Clint Owens Bowen, born 1925, served twenty years in the US Air Force. Since retirement in 1965, he has lived in Perry County, near the Humphreys County line. He married Mary Nell Stewart and reared two sons and one daughter: John Stewart, Mary Elizabeth (Luna), and Robert Lee.

The oldest son, John Stewart Bowen, graduated from the University of Tennessee at Martin, serves in the Tennessee National Guard, and is the present Park Ranger of Mousetail Landing State Park. Mary Elizabeth "Sissie" graduated from the Methodist Hospital School of Nursing and specialized in Critical Care. Robert Lee "Bob" graduated from the University of Tennessee at Martin and is a Quality Control Engineer. *Submitted by Mary Stewart Bowen.*

JAMES NEWTON BOWMAN,

1826-1871, was born in Perryville, Perry County, on Jan. 7, 1826, to Sarah Graham and William C. Bowman (maybe William Campbell Bowman). He married in Cass County, Texas on Nov. 4, 1851, to Tennessee Texas Graham, first cousin and daughter Mahaly Caughron and Robert Crawford Graham.

He arrived in Texas in time to enlist in Col. Young's 3rd Texas Reg. in the Mexican War, Captain Rice's Company, Texas Mounted Volunteers. Later he was in the Quartermaster's Dept. of Col. Folsom's Reg. of the Confederacy.

Shortly after their 1851 marriage, they moved to Sulphur Springs, Hopkins County, Texas, where James engaged in the mercantile business. In 1863, they moved to Old Pine Bluff, a trading post of the Red River in Red River County, about 15 miles north of (now) Detroit, Texas. Bowman Hill was located on the road that connected Paris (Lamar County, Texas) with Indian Territory. They built a house of hand-hewn logs with puncheon floors and wall cracks large enough for dogs to squeeze through. They went into Indian Territory to find logs. Stories refer to the black walnut trees and wooded area around Bowman Hill. Steamboat demands probably had denuded the Red River banks. Later in 1869, they moved the house to make room for a "lumber" house, but in 1926 the old house was still in use as a corn bin.

Choctaws from the Choctaw Nation, just across the Red River, were a common sight along the highway to Paris. Men would ride horses with guns across their laps followed by their women carrying babies and baskets to sell.

James built the first cotton gin in that part of Texas. It was cranked by hand, so only three or four bales could be ginned per day. The mar-

85

keting custom was that steamboat owners would buy cotton from farmers paying only a small percent of the cotton's actual value, then pay the farmer the balance on a return trip, sometimes six months later.

Constant hardships. James' widow said, "For salt, we would go as far as Grand Saline, Van Zandt County, Texas (100 miles). To mill corn, we would go to Cass County (100 miles). (But, they could travel by water to Cass County, whereas, they had to travel by land to Grand Saline.) For soda, we'd boil ashes down."

Slaves were an important part of the Bowman's lives; all remained close friends the rest of their lives. Manda McCameron, yellow in color, was a wedding gift from father-in-law, R.C., and is recorded in Cass County. Manda married and left their farm. Uncle Jim and Aunt Emma Humphreys had their own farm by the 1920s. Emma was the daughter of Lit Lipscomb: four generations of Lipscombs worked for the Bowmans. Ann McCarty was still alive in the 1920s. Mitch and Joanna Record helped make 19 crops; Joanna received an Indian allotment of land, since she was part Indian. "Aunt Julie's" real name was Julie Ann, Rebecca Jane, Pagy, Angy, Pongy, Lahoe, Tahoe, Yankee Doodle, Liza Hearn. "Toose's" name was Melia, Delia, Celia, Relia, God-in-hand, Lugenia, Alice Jane, Toosy Littleton Johnson, Fleeks. Zill and Tebe Lipscomb had children Sweat Meat and Cuby Spain (not Cuba, born during Spanish-American War.)

While on a business trip in Paris, James became sick and died on Oct. 14, 1871, of "swamp fever" or "hemorrhage of the kidneys" or malaria; buried in Evergreen Cemetery, Lamar County, Texas. His son, James Newton Jr., had died in 1870 of malaria also. Mosquitoes were rampant on the Red River. *Submitted by Patricia Adkins Rochette.*

ALBERT ERASMUS BOYCE, son of Samuel Miles Boyce and Harriett Elzada Sisco, married Margaret Louise Pitts, born 1879, probably in Wayne County. They moved to Oklahoma in the later years.

Members of the Boyce and Rickett families

Children by 1920 were: Alberta Boyce, born June 21, 1910, Perry County, died Aug. 31, 1910, buried Flatwoods Cemetery; Mary Lizzie Boyce, born Jan. 12, 1912, Perry County; Hassell Pitts Boyce, born Aug. 31, 1914, died Sept. 25, 1914, Perry County, buried Flatwoods Cemetery; Etta Louise Boyce, born March 4, 1916, died Sept. 23, 1918, buried Flatwoods Cemetery; and Sam Boyce, born 1919. *Submitted by Merle Stevens.*

ROBERT CLAIR BOYCE, and his twin **Samuel Claud Boyce**, sons of Samuel Miles Boyce and Harriett Elzada Sisco, lived in Nashville. Not sure of all their children. Robert Clair had a son, Robert Clair Boyce II and Samuel Claud had a son, Eugene Boyce. *Submitted by Merle Stevens.*

Top: Mary, Lizzie, Etta, Harriett (Sisco) and Samuel M. Bottom: Claud, Clair, Earl, Herbert and Albert Boyce

SAMUEL MILES BOYCE was born Oct. 23, 1848, in Palestine in Maury County, Tennessee. Harriet Elzada Sisco was born Oct. 18, 1854, in Lewis County in the Swan Creek Community. Samuel and Harriet Boyce were married Oct. 20, 1870, in Lewis County.

Samuel Miles Boyce Family in 1905

Sam's parents were William Hardy Boyce, born 1810, in North Carolina, and Mary Mayfield, born 1810, in Maury County. They were married Sept. 22, 1834, in Maury County, Tennessee.

Harriet's parents were William Walker Sisco, born Sept. 18, 1829, in Lewis County and Mary Ann Campbell, born Jan. 11, 1831. They were married Nov. 5, 1846, on Cane Creek in Lewis County.

Sam and Harriet moved to Farmer's Valley, Perry County, Tennessee, from Lewis County soon after they married. All of their children were born there.

Their children were: Mary Caroline, Dec. 7, 1872-Oct. 6, 1957; Lizzie Boyce Edwards, July 3, 1875-Oct. 21, 1958; Henrietta Boyce Ricketts, June 29, 1879-Jan. 24, 1915; Albert Boyce, Oct. 4, 1883-June 21, 1942; Herbert Boyce, Jan. 8, 1886-Aug. 8, 1948; William Earl Boyce, March 19, 1888-April 9,1968; Samuel Claud Boyce, twin, June 8, 1890-July 13, 1954; and Robert Clair Boyce, twin, June 8, 1890-April 14, 1951.

Sam and Harriet were devout members of the Church of Christ (called the Christian Church until a division later).

Sam's goal was to organize and build a church building as soon as possible after they moved to Flatwoods, around 1900. However, Harriet had a different dream, to build a house first, (for their large family of 10). Sam was determined, so Harriet gave in, and they moved into a small house on the farm down under a steep hill.

Sam worked diligently toward getting the small number of members organized to build. He donated the land for the building. Soon most of the men in Flatwoods were going to the woods to cut and saw the timber. The large frame, two story building was finished around 1902. The Church of Christ met on the first floor. The Masons, who had helped with the building, met on the second floor. A huge bell was lifted to the belfry.

Sam started building a larger house. When they moved, Harriet was happy, because she did not have to climb the steep hill to go to the store and post office, and she had enough room for the family.

Sam and the older boys worked hard on the 150 acre farm and raised most of their food.

Sam and Harriet's sons were ambitious. Earl, Claud, and Clair went to Nashville to attend college. Mary, the oldest daughter, went with them to cook and keep house for them. (She was grown when they were born and she had helped to raise them and keep them disciplined.) Earl attended and graduated from Medical School in Nashville, and Claud went to Peabody College. Earl graduated from the University of Tennessee at Memphis and became a successful medical doctor in Perry and Lewis Counties. Obe Kirk, Dr. O.A. Kirk) boarded with them and graduated with Dr. Boyce in 1912. Both of them returned to Perry County to practice medicine and to devote their lives to relieving and caring for suffering humanity. Clair became a prominent lawyer in Nashville, and Claud became a professor of History and Political Science and Bible, at David Lipscomb College; he was also a Church of Christ preacher. Herbert and Albert went to Oklahoma where they became successful farmers.

Mary returned to the farm to help her parents. She never married. She became a Bible scholar and was known for her sense of humor and wisdom. She was an avid reader.

Lizzie married Jim Edwards and they had nine children. She spent her life raising them, devoted to her family. Henrietta (Etta) married Roper Rickets. She died at age 35, the mother of seven children.

Sam was a kind, humble man. He and Harriet lived long, useful lives, helping others who needed them. They were both buried in Flatwoods Cemetery. *Submitted by Marie B. Grimes.*

WILLIAM EARL BOYCE, son of Samuel Miles Boyce and Harriett Elzada Sisco, married Virginia Ann Bromley. She was born Jan. 22, 1891, Flatwoods, died May 4, 1942, buried Flatwoods. Her parents were William E. Bromley and Minerva Jane Goodman. They had four children: Wilton Louise Boyce, born Jan. 31, 1914, Laman, Oklahoma, married Andrew Hardeman Craig; Mildred Lucille Boyce, born Jan. 6, 1917, Port Arthur, Texas, died Nov. 11, 1988, wife of

James A. Burns; William Earl Boyce Jr., born Nov. 18, 1918, Flatwoods, died June 15, 1944, World War II. He married Vera Jane Anderson; and Etta Marie Boyce, born Nov. 26, 1920, Flatwoods, married Glenn Springer Grimes. *Submitted by Merle Stevens.*

Top: Earl, Herbert, Albert, Etta, Lizzie and Mary. Bottom: Claud, Harriett (Sisco), Samuel Miles and Clair Boyce

LT. WILLIAM EARL BOYCE JR.,
was killed in a plane crash in service to his country, on June 15, 1944.

William Earl was born in Flatwoods, Tennessee on Nov. 18, 1918. He was the only son of Dr. and Mrs. W.E. Boyce of Flatwoods and Hohenwald.

Lt. William Earl Boyce Jr.

He attended school at Flatwoods and graduated from Linden High School in 1935. He attended David Lipscomb College for two years. He took the Civil Service examination for Postal Clerk at the Nashville Post Office and made the highest grade of over a thousand applicants. He was hired as a clerk, where he worked until he enlisted in the U.S. Air Force. He reported for active duty, Feb. 1943. He received his wings and commission as Second Lieutenant at Marfa, Texas A.A.F. pilot school on Dec. 5, 1943.

Lt. Boyce was Co-Pilot of a B-24 Liberator Bomber, enroute to join the 14th Air Service in the Far East when the accident occurred. There was a sand storm at the U.S. Air Base at Abadan, Iran, where they had to land. They were circling the airport, when they ran out of fuel. They were waiting for the storm to clear, so they could see the runway. They had to land and their plane crashed in a date palm grove nearby.

Lt. Boyce and all of the crew members, except one, were killed. Prior to his enlistment, William Earl Jr. married Vera Jane Anderson, of Lewis County, on June 26, 1941. William Earl had three sisters: Wilton Craig, Mildred Burns, and Marie Grimes of Flatwoods.

Lt. William Earl Boyce Jr. was buried in Iran at the National Cemetery. Later, his body was moved to the National Cemetery at Tunis, Tunisia, North Africa, where he rests among thousands of other World War II servicemen. He made the supreme sacrifice so that we could keep our freedom in America. Let us never forget William Earl and the other servicemen, who died for their country. *Submitted by Marie Grimes.*

WILLIAM EARL AND VIRGINIA BROMLEY BOYCE,
William Earl was born March 19, 1888, at Farmer's Valley in Perry County, Tennessee. He moved to Flatwoods around 1900. His parents were Samuel Miles and Harriet Sisco Boyce from Lewis County.

Dr. William Earl Boyce. The photo on the right was taken when Major Boyce was in the U.S. Army Medical Corps in 1919.

Dr. Boyce attended and graduated from Medical School in Nashville, and graduated from the University of Tennessee, School of Medicine, Memphis in 1912. He graduated at the head of his class. Dr. Boyce and Virginia Bromley were married Feb. 7, 1911, in Nashville, Tennessee. Her parents were William Ewing, born Aug. 18, 1867, of Perry and Wayne Counties, and Minerva Goodman Bromley, born Aug. 18, 186_.

Dr. Boyce served in the Army Medical Corps in World War I and was promoted to the rank of Major. He was awarded two U.S. Army Silver Stars for gallantry and bravery on the battlefields of Germany and France. Major Boyce was also awarded the French Medal, Croix de Guerre for bravery in France. After the war, he had no lucrative work to support his family of six, so he returned to Perry County and set up an office in his home in Flatwoods. His wife, "Virgie" helped him with his patients, until her death on May 4, 1942. During the Depression years, he accepted livestock, corn, and hay from his patients, who could not pay him in cash. Most of his cattle and feed were destroyed in a fire when his barn burned on his farm. Dr. Boyce made house calls at all hours of the day or night, and in all kinds of weather, good or bad. When mealtime came, he often ate with the family, especially when he was attending his obstetrics patients, for hours. In the late 1930s, Dr. Boyce opened Boyce Clinic and Hospital at Hohenwald, Tennessee. He became widely known in that area for his abilities in diagnosis and general surgery. His patients no longer needed to travel long distances for most of their medical care. His obstetrics cases came, not only from Lewis County, but also the surrounding counties. Dr. Boyce initiated the use of his hospital facilities for the first time in this area, instead of the doctor home delivery, before this time. Dr. Boyce delivered over 5,000 babies in his forty-five years of medical practice. He did post graduate studies at Vanderbilt University, so that he could keep up with the latest medical and surgical procedures, treatments, and drugs. The Lewis County Civic Club sponsored a "Dr. Boyce Day" to honor him, on Sept. 14, 1957. Governor Frank Clement was the principal speaker for this occasion. Dr. Boyce was recognized for his unselfish devotion to his profession. He had won the respect and admiration of fellow physicians, as well as the gratitude of thousands of his patients and their families. The celebration was held in the Lewis County High School Gymnasium, where a large crowd attended. Dr. Boyce was a member of the Church of Christ, since 1908. He was Democrat and was the chairman of the Perry County Election Committee.

Dr. and Mrs. William Earl Boyce in 1918.

Dr. Boyce did not have time for hobbies, except he did enjoy driving over his farms with his son-in-law, Dick Grimes, to see their pure bred, registered Hereford cattle. He enjoyed reading and having morning coffee with his friends at the restaurant. He enjoyed spending time with his children. His grandchildren were a special joy to him. Dr. Boyce retired in 1958. He died April 9, 1968. He was buried in the Flatwoods cemetery. After his death, he was honored in the 1969 edition of the book, *Personalities of the South*. He was recognized, with over 3,000 other outstanding and distinguished Southern citizens, for his contributions to the community and country.

Dr. Boyce was known as a great humanitarian. He will be remembered for his kindness, unpretentious generosity and his sense of humor.

His children are Mr. A.H. (Wilton) Craig, born Jan. 30, 1914, Mrs. J.A. (Mildred) Burns, born Jan. 6, 1917, died Nov. 1988, and Mrs. Glenn (Marie) Grimes, born Nov. 26, 1920.

His grandchildren are Glenda Grimes James, Joyce Pevahouse Grimes-Safley, Keith Boyce Grimes, died March 13, 1977, Kathryn Craig Wall, Dr. Boyce Craig, and Dr. Barbara Burns Snell-Evans.

He has 15 great grandchildren and one great-great grandchild. *Submitted by Marie B. Grimes.*

WILLIAM H. BOYCE,
born 1811, North Carolina, son of Hardy Boyce and, from two difference sources, either Mary Hubbard or Nancy Sholar. He died May 1, 1878, Perry County, buried Farmers Valley. On Sept. 25, 1834, Maury County, he married Mary Mayfield, daughter of Samuel Mayfield and Zuridice Rhoades. She was born 1810, died Dec. 25, 1880, Perry County,

buried Farmers Valley. Eight children were known to be born: James M. Boyce, born 1835, died Feb. 10, 1863, Douglas, St. Clair County, Illinois, as a prisoner of war, Civil War; Caroline M. Boyce, born Nov. 2, 1836, Hickman County, probably present day Lewis County, died July 27, 1910, Hanson, Oklahoma. She married Nov. 21, 1854, John Newton McKeel; Dicy Boyce, no doubt Zuridice, born 1839, married George W. Hickerson; Elizabeth Armanta Boyce, born March 3, 1841, married first to John J. Garner, second to Samuel Miles Sharp; Minerva E. Boyce, born 1844, married Feb. 16, 1879, Perry County, W. Jack Weaver; George W. Boyce, born March 1846, Palestine, Lewis County, died March 24, 1927. He married March 5, 1867, Mary L. Hovey; John D. Boyce, born Oct. 23, 1848, Palestine, died Feb. 18, 1927, buried Flatwoods, unmarried; Samuel Miles Boyce, twin to John, died April 7, 1928, Flatwoods, buried Flatwoods cemetery. He married Oct. 20, 1870, Swan Creek, Lewis County, Harriett Elzada Sisco.

William H. and Mary (Mayfield) Boyce

John N. McKeel, born May 5, 1834, died April 17, 1910, son of James McKeel and Dorcas Walker. Eight of their ten children were born in Perry County: Mary Edna, married J.L. Cotton; Thomas L. and Billy died young; George Newton; John Francis; Minerva Alvina Josephine, married William Hatfield; Samuel Andrew; Albert Walker; Alice Imogene, married Henry Clay Crim Jr.; and Alonza Allen McKeel.

George W. Hickerson, husband of Dicy Boyce, born 1837, son of John D. Hickerson and Nancy Treece. Their children include at least Sarah C., John D., Mary J., Nancy E., Minerva L., Josephine, William H., and Lawrence Hickerson. This family may have lived in Wayne County. Elizabeth Boyce first married John Garner. He was born 1837, died Feb. 26, 1864, Rock Island, Illinois as a Civil War prisoner. They had three children: John Will Garner, born June 23, 1858, died Aug. 26, 1926, buried Flatwoods cemetery. He married, Nov. 30, 1884, Perry County, Cordelia Grinder. She was born Nov. 23, 1857, died Sept. 28, 1925. Some of their children were Mozella, Robert, Sallie, Samuel Thomas, Rolly, Douglas, Ina Belle, and Anna May; Mary T. Garner, born 1862, married Dec. 27, 1877, Perry County, Elizon Taylor Graves, born Sept. 12, 1859, Perry County, died 1902, buried Graves cemetery, Sinking Creek. His parents were Isaac Lee Graves and Parthena Ledbetter. Their children were Parthena, Martha Ann, John Isaac, George, Andrew, and Sallie; and Martha Elizabeth Garner, born Jan. 20, 1863, Perry County, died Oct. 7, 1936, Missouri, wife of William Edmond Harder.

George W. Boyce's wife, Mary Hovey, born Feb. 13, 1849, died March 24, 1937, buried Hohenwald. Their four children were: William Hovey Boyce, born Nov. 7, 1871, died April 25, 1964, married Margaret E. Galloway in Perry County; John Douglas Boyce, born April 16, 1874, married Ruth Stone in Perry County; Mary Ellen Boyce, born Oct. 19, 1880, died April 8, 1965, married Thomas D. Tatum in Perry County; Lula Pearl Boyce, born Nov. 7, 1882, died 1968, married C. Alfred Yaggie, Perry County.

ELSIE CARRIE HARDER ELLISON BOYD was born Oct. 4, 1910, in Perry County, Cedar Creek Community. She was the daughter of Prince William Harder, 1881-1945, and Ollie Belle Magee Harder, 1886-1975. She had two brothers, Earl Elvis, 1909, and Kelsie Brown, 1922.

The Elsie Boyd Family

Her maternal grandparents and great grandparents were Elijah Bailey Magee, 1859-1930, and Martha Ann Bunch Magee, 1866-1929, John Bunch, 1827-1884, and Sally Denton Bunch, 1832-1906, also, Lewis Magee, 1830-1853, and Mary Brooke of Wayne County, Tennessee.

Her paternal grandparents were William Henry Harder, 1830-1871, and Sarah Atlantic Anderson Harder, 1848-1923. Great grandparents were Jeremiah Harder, 1810-1872, and Harriet Young Harder, 1813-1893, also John M. Anderson, 1805-1880, and Elizabeth Whitwell, 1816-1856.

Elsie Harder and Albert Ellison were married Sept. 14, 1930, by Esq. I.B. Moore. Four children were born to this union: Ollie Mae, 1931, married Roger Oneil Moore; William Eddie, 1932, married Martha Kathrine Anderson; Eula Belle, 1935, married Richard Langford Stockard; and Albert Ellison Jr., 1937, married Martha Jo Millard.

Elsie and Albert moved from lower Cedar Creek to Flowers Prong on upper Cedar Creek. They lived on a farm owned by her parents until they divorced in 1939. She continued living on the farm with her four young children. She worked very hard at farm-related jobs. She found time for fun, disciplining with words of wisdom. She continually stressed the need for an education. Three of the four children graduated with college degrees and became teachers.

She became a member of Cedar Valley Methodist Church in 1940. Her belief in the Christian faith was a great influence in her life.

Her second marriage to Melvin Boyd was in 1948, They had a child, Nancy Boyd, born in 1952. She also helped her husband, Melvin, rear his two sons, Buford William Boyd, 1934, and Loral Chessley Boyd, 1939.

Nancy, their daughter, graduated from UT, Knoxville. She married Joe Barnett, 1976, and they have one daughter, Carrie Lee, born in 1984.

Elsie Harder Boyd has shown much courage, determination and love for her family and friends. Her family, large in number, respects and greatly admires her great qualities. She is known on Cedar Creek and Perry County as "Mama Elsie".

STANLEY AND FRANCES BOYD, live on Cedar Creek in Perry County. Stanley is the son of Douglas and Dorothy Boyd of Wayne County, Tennessee. Frances is the daughter of Fred and Estelle Robbins of Wayne County, Tennessee.

Stanley and Frances Boyd with children, Sabrina Renae holding her sister Erica Rebecca.

Sabrina Renae Boyd is the daughter of Stanley and Frances Boyd. She was born June 28, 1981, in Florence, Alabama.

Erica Rebecca Boyd, also the daughter of Stanley and Frances Boyd, was born March 25, 1992, in Maury County, Tennessee.

Stanley and Frances were married in Clifton, Tennessee on Jan. 23, 1976. In 1987, they moved to Perry County from Wayne County, Tennessee.

They like the peaceful countryside and the wonderful people of Perry County.

JILL DEPRIEST BRADLEY, was born Sept. 27, 1950, in Nashville, Davidson County, Tennessee. She is the daughter of James Edward DePriest and Carrie Nell Shepard DePriest who formerly lived in Perry County.

Emily Bradley, Haylee Bradley, Jill DePriest Bradley

Jill's paternal grandparents were Samuel Rudolph DePriest and Mattie Lucille Hughes DePriest of Perry County. Her maternal grandparents were William Haygood Shepard and Byron Mae DePriest Shepard, also of Perry County.

Jill attended school in Perry County until she moved with her parents to Waverly, Humphreys County, Tennessee, when she became a freshman at Waverly Central High

School. She attended the University of Tennessee at Knoxville where she graduated with a B.S. Degree. She received her M.A. Degree at Austin Peay University. She is presently a teacher in the Humphrey's County School System at Waverly Junior High School.

Jill was married on Dec. 21, 1967, to Danny Ray Bradley, now divorced, an attorney in Waverly. They have two children, Haylee Ann and Emily Jill.

Haylee Ann was born March 24, 1975, and Emily Jill was born Aug. 20, 1979. Haylee is presently attending the University of Tennessee at Knoxville, 1994, where she is a freshman, and Emily is a freshman at Waverly Central High School.

Jill and her daughters attend the Waverly Church of Christ. *Submitted by Jill DePriest Bradley.*

LONNIE AND ELSIE BRAKE,

Lonnie Dalton Brake was born in Hickman County, Tennessee, May 15, 1923, the ninth of ten children born to Albert and Elizabeth Crowell Brake. Albert's Grandfather Brake came from Germany to Ohio where he married a Seneca Indian before he moved his family to Tennessee. Elizabeth was of Irish ancestry.

The Brake Family. Front Row: Joan, Janie. Back Row: June, Lonnie, Elsie and Jean.

Elsie Louise Warner was born Oct. 28, 1925, in Perry County, the seventh child of Johnny and Florence Edwards Warner. Elsie's Grandfather Edwards was thought to be Cherokee and was born in North Carolina, but moved to Tennessee as a young man. Grandfather Warner was born near Jackson, Tennessee.

On April 19, 1944, Lonnie married Elsie Warner. Lonnie and Elsie lived in the Lobelville area for many years. Lonnie worked for Tennessee Gas Pipeline for 31 years. Both were members and very active supporters of Lobelville First Baptist Church. To this marriage, four daughters were born.

Janie Louise was born Feb. 4, 1945. She is married to Roger Betty and they live at Hurricane Mills, Tennessee. She has two children, Jana Denise Duncan, born Dec. 4, 1973 and James Daryl Duncan, born March 14, 1980.

Lonie Jean was born May 16, 1949. She is married to Lee Aldridge Jr. and they live at New Johnsonville, Tennessee. They have three daughters: Regina Leigh, born July 24, 1969, married to Jeff Martin and they now live in Tallahassee, Florida; Nicole Lynn, born Nov. 2, 1972; and Andrea Lauren, born July 25, 1978.

Joan Elizabeth was born June 29, 1951. She is married to Hilton Thompson and they live in Burton, Texas. They have one son, Juston Coleman, born May 24, 1982.

Linda June was born July 5, 1955. She is married to Keith Nix and they live in Hurricane Mills, Tennessee. They have two children, Joshua Lonnie born July 22, 1981, and Robin Danielle, born Jan. 30, 1984.

Lonnie Brake died Sept. 18, 1982, at their home in Hurricane Mills where Elsie still resides.

EDWARD AND SARA BREEDING,

In late 1948, Sara moved from Knoxville to Linden, after living in Knoxville two years. She met Ed while in graduate school and he had just gotten out of the Army. Kentucky Lake lured Ed because he is an avid fisherman. They started Wood-Breeding Hardware Lumber Company and it is still in operation. They have three children, Sara Ann, born Feb. 27, 1948, Scott Wood, born May 18, 1954, and Nancy Leigh, born April 4, 1955. Ed was born and reared in Overton County.

Edward and Sara Breeding

Sara's maiden name was Brison and she had no brothers or sisters. Her grandfather was Rufus Brison and he was a blacksmith. His shop was located where Touch of Elegance is today. He was a widower a long time and had two sons and two daughters. Clarence Brison died in World War I; Luella was never married and died when twenty-seven years old; Rose Brison married Hugh Bowden from Union City. She had three children; Sara's father, Leonard Brison, met her mother when he went to Flatwoods to teach school. Leonard Brison served in World War I and returned from the war a very sick person, dying when Sara was only nine months old. When she was three years old, her mother married Glenn Wood and he became a transplanted Northerner.

Sara's mother was one of eight children born to Sara Amanda and Burton Fluty. She was born in Flatwoods. There is little known about the Flutys. Three brothers walked into the Fluty Hollow. No one knows where they came from. One had a rifle and swapped it to someone for the Fluty Hollow. The other brothers decided to go on, but Sara's great grandfather wanted to start a tannery and there was a good supply of water available. He fought in the Civil War. He married Nancy Ann Dabbs and they had five boys.

Sara's great grandparents were Abrahm Mayberry and Caroline Bunch. The Flutys are buried in the Fluty cemetery, located in Fluty Hollow across from where Calvin Allen lives, but the Brisons are buried in the Bethel cemetery.

Several years ago, Sara visited Mr. Wilburn Qualls (Hayes Parnell's grandfather). He told her that her great grandfather, Columbus Brison, is buried in the Stephens cemetery on Brush Creek. His wife went to live with their son George after he died. When she died, the river and creek were out of banks, so they could not get back to the cemetery on Brush Creek. She was buried in the Tole Hollow on top of a hill. The Tole Hollow is behind where Bill and Bliss Garcia live on Sinking Creek.

JOSEPH BROWN BRIDGES,

was an early, and largely forgotten, settler of Wayne county, who appears to have moved to the area in the late 1830s. The 1840 Wayne census lists Joseph, his wife, and four daughters. Where the family moved from to Wayne County could not be determined absolutely, but the data suggests that it was most likely from Smith County, which had a large number of Bridges families. This county was settled after the Revolutionary War, with some men obtaining land grants for their military service during the war. Several Bridges families emigrated to this area from counties in the central part of North Carolina. Joseph Brown Bridges was born about 1813, probably one of the sons of the large family of the Joseph Bridges, who is listed in the 1820 Smith County census. There is some evidence that this is the same Joseph Bridges who married Mary Tyre in Carter County, on July 18, 1798, and moved to Smith County, about 1813-1815. Joseph Brown Bridges married around 1830, but no record of the marriage was found, since the Smith County marriage records begin in 1838.

Alec F. Bridges

In 1850, the census showed that Joseph's wife's name was Malinda and their children were daughters: Nancy, born 1832; Elizabeth, born 1833; Rachial, born 1834; Elender, born 1839, Mahalia, born 1843; and sons: George, born 1847; and Joseph B. (Junior), born 1849. Joseph was a farmer and tilled the fertile land of the Buffalo River Valley all his life, beginning at Ashwood and slowly moving westward. In 1860, he was living in the Whitaker's Bluff district, probably south of the village of Flatwoods, and had three more children: James, born 1852; Walter, born 1855; and Mary, born 1856. By 1870, Joseph and family had moved to Perry County and he was a tenant farmer on the old plantation of Squire Daniel Henderson McDonald, which was located at the intersection of Buffalo River and Possum Creek. Joseph remained in this area for the rest of his life, and three of his children married into the McDonald families, who were early settlers in this area. Malinda died July, 1879 at age 62, and in May,

1880, Joseph married the widow, Winnie Lineberry, age 57. Joseph outlived many of his children and died in late 1885, at the age of 72. He is likely buried, along with some of his children, in the numerous unmarked graves in the Mt. Olive cemetery, which overlooks the Buffalo River that Joseph had known for so much of his life. Very few descendants of Joseph Brown Bridges can be found today in Perry County. Many died very early, and many others moved to western Tennessee and other states in a wave of emigration that occurred in 1910 to 1920.

Alec F. Bridges, the author of this article, is the grandson of Walter B. Bridges, the youngest son of Joseph and Malinda Bridges. The author has spent the last two years researching and reconstructing the lost history of the Bridges family.

JOSHUA AND NANCY (HOWELL) BRILEY were in Wayne County until the county line was moved, some time after 1850, and are believed to be buried in the White Oak Creek or Briley & Waters cemetery. They had land on the White Oak Creek from about 1832, known deeds.

Andrew Briley, son of Joshua and Nancy, and first wife Sarah Susan James had three children: Caroline Briley, born ca 1840; William Briley, born Oct. 31, 1846 in Perry County, married Nancy Elizabeth Holder, born in Perry County, Dec. 5, 1844. They both died in Grayson County, Texas. Their children were all born in Perry County. 1) Andrew Johnson Briley, born July 22, 1867, married first to Ella Waters, April 5, 1891. When she died, he married Nancy Thompson. 2) L.C. Briley, born Nov. 21, 1868, married Rosa Liles, Nov. 25, 1888. 3) Jesse Lee Briley, born Dec. 25, 1870, married Lula P. Harlson. 4) William Parrish Briley, born Nov. 30, 1872, married Maggie F. Hinkle. 5) Joseph M. Briley, born March 10, 1876, married Manervia Hickerson, May 9, 1894. 6) John Issac Briley, born April 4, 1882, married Lavina Pitt. 7) Sarah Belle Briley, born Aug. 4, 1879, married James Chesley Denton, March 27, 1898. 8) Hester Esther Cleveland Briley, born Sept. 12, 1884, married Jake Badgett; and third child of Andrew was Jack Briley, died infancy.

After Andrew's first wife died, he married Sarah Sewell. Children of this marriage were: Irvin (Doke) Briley, born 1855, married Elizabeth Whit ?, family said her name was Carter, Jan. 28, 1881; Amanda Bell Briley, born Sept. 25, 1856, married William N. Horner, June 6, 1874; James W. Briley, born 1859.

Andrew's third marriage was to Elizabeth Starnes. Their children: Sarah Briley, born Feb. 26, 1861, married Henry A. Sewell; Nora Lee Briley, born Dec. 6, 1866, married W.J. Culp; Jack Briley, born 1865, married Sallie J. Stalling, Dec. 7, 1890; Lewis Briley, went to Arkansas; John Briley, went to Arkansas. Andrew had 16 children all together. In addition were: Armitta Briley, married Harrison Culp; Betty Elizabeth Briley, married Dr. R.H. Strickland. She died and her sister married Dr. R.H. Strickland.

Sarah Briley, daughter of Joshua and Nancy, born 1820, married Murry Sewell. Known children: Samuel Sewell; Henry Sewell; Irvin Sewell; Nancy Sewell; Margaret Sewell; Bebe Sewell. There may have been more children.

Abraham Briley, son of Joshua and Nancy, born 1822, married Alviry James, born March 30, 1826, died Sept. 22, 1867. Children were: Henry Clay Briley, died young; James Briley; Samuel Briley; William Briley; Benjamin Briley, born ca 1840; Martha E. Briley, married Huthin Magee; Mary J. Briley and Nancy Briley (twins), born 1866, Nancy died infancy.

After Abraham's first wife died, he married Nancy Martin, Aug. 18, 1869. Children of this marriage are Robert Briley, Sarah Briley, and Bathsheba Briley.

John Briley, son of Joshua and Nancy, born July 1, 1833, died Aug. 13, 1918 in Oklahoma, married Jennie James, born Oct. 28, 1826, died Feb. 8, 1876. She was a sister to Andrew and Abraham Briley's first wives. Children: James Wesley Briley, born 1853, married Josie Wesson; John Simpson, born June 16, 1856, married Martha Frances Patton; William Henry Briley, born July 12, 1857, married Mary Ann Morton; Malachia (Dood) Briley, born 1858, married Caroline C. Ingle.

After his first wife died, John married Amanda M. Gammill, July 10, 1876, in Hardin County, moved to Texas about 1900 and to Oklahoma in 1904.

Other children of Joshua and Nancy Briley were: Bathsheba Briley, born 1812, died 1886, married Benjamin Steel of Wayne County; Fanny Briley, born 1823, married a man named Aydellott; Jesse Briley, born June 10, 1819, died March 8, 1885 in Texas; Elizabeth Briley, born 1825, died 1891, first married Benjamin Crossno, then married Henry Culp of Wayne County; Rebecca Briley, born 1832, Perry County, married Francis M. Thompson in 1851. They moved to Arkansas. *Submitted by Mr. and Mrs. O.A. Briley.*

BROADAWAY, Little is known about Paschal Broadaway and his wife, Sallie, until they moved to Perry County. They had lived in Stewart County and just over the line in Calloway County, Kentucky.

Ernest and Beulos Broadaway and Mary Caroline Denton holding Roscoe Broadaway

When William Bradley was operating the Cedar Creek Furnace, he needed more carpenters. He had operated a furnace in Stewart County and knew a good carpenter, Paschal Broadaway. So, in the 1850s, Paschal moved his family to the Furnace Hollow so he could be one of Bradley's carpenters. He lived and worked there until his death. In his spare time, he made iron utensils.

Paschal, 1810-1861, and Sallie, 1816-1884, had seven children. They were: Henry W., married Martha C. Wiley; Paschal II; Melissa, married George Turner; Martha, married Columbus Turner; Susie, married Calvin Inman; W.; and Alexander.

Alexander (Alex), 1841-1896, married, 1862, first Sarah Lomax, 1844-1890, daughter of Andrew and Annie Richardson Lomax. Their eleven children were: Melissa Catherine, married Jacob Richardson, one son; Thomas Andrew; Henry Wilburn, married Mary (Polly) Ward, three children; Henry Jefferson, married Ella Thompson, two sons; John Madison, married Melinda Ella Thompson, nine children; James Ulysses, married Delilah (Lila) Harder, three children; Mary Ludy, married Bill Ward, five children; Sarah Ann (Sallie), married Bill Richardson, one daughter; Samuel Alexander, married first, Martha Ward, one daughter, second, Martha Scroggins, seven children, third, Mary Kirk, two daughters; Robert Tecumseh, married Nancy (Nannie) Ward, five children; Bertha Elizabeth, married Spencer Hinson, five children.

Alex buried Sarah on a hill across from their home. That was the beginning of the Broadaway Cemetery.

After Sarah's death, Alex married, 1890, a young widow, Nancy Jane Lomax Hamm, 1854-1891, daughter of William and Mourning Denton Horner Lomax. She and her baby died in childbirth.

Alex's third marriage was in 1893 to Mary Caroline Denton, 1859-1935, daughter of Samuel and Louanna Wiley Denton. Their son, Ernest Roscoe, 1895-1958, was born a year before Alex died of pneumonia.

Alex had been a teacher, a magistrate, and a carpenter. He also made furniture that is highly prized by some of his descendants today. He served in the Union Army during the Civil War and became a staunch Republican. His brother, Henry W., served with the Confederate Army and became a Democrat.

Ernest Rosco married, 1917, Beulos Rebecca Ann Melinda Thompson, 1900, daughter of Joseph Yarbro and Martha Elizabeth Murphy Thompson. They had two children, Roscoe McNally, 1918-1922, and Kathleen Pauline, 1922. Kathleen married, 1941, Hollis Harder. Their children are: Jerry Hollis, 1945, one son, Matthew Allen, 1980; Linda Ann, 1947, married, 1970, James Anthony Ramirez, 1951, one son, Marc Anthony, 1973.

Ernest taught school, clerked in a general store, and was a Rural Letter Carrier from the Pope Post Office.

PASCHAL BROADAWAY, was born April 10, 1810, maybe in Virginia. He married a Sallie C., in 1829. He and Sallie moved to Perry County from Stewart County, Tennessee in 1850. He worked in the iron ore furnaces at Ceder Creek. His wife, Sallie C., built fires for the furnace. Sallie was born in 1807, and she was thought to have been born in Virginia. Paschal died on Feb. 17, 1861, and Sallie died on Jan. 27, 1882. Not much is known about Paschal and Sallie. We do not know who their fathers were. Paschal and Sallie had seven children.

Henry W. was born in 1830, and married Martha Ann Wiley in 1856.

Paschal Jr. died young.

Mellissa was born on March 1, 1838; she married George Turner and she died in 1910.

Martha was born on Aug. 14, 1839; she married Columbus Turner.

Samuel Alexander Broadaway and Martha Scroggins Broadaway with their child, Claude Broadaway.

Alexander was born on April 30, 1842; he married Sarah Lomax on May 25, 1862, and died on Dec. 19, 1896.

W. was born in 1840.

Susie was born in 1857 or 1858, and married on March 31, 1886, Calvin Inman.

Alexander Broadaway was born on April 30, 1842. He married Sarah Lomax on May 25, 1862. Alexander served in the Civil War for the Union Army. According to military records, Alexander deserted at Clifton, Tennessee, on April 1, 1864. He also worked at Ceder Creek and made furniture. He was a teacher and a magistrate. Alexander and Sarah had eleven children.

Melissa Catherine was born on July 28, 1864, and married Jacob Richardson, on Oct. 11, 1885. Melissa died March 12, 1897.

Thomas Andrew was born Nov. 30, 1865, and died on Dec. 12, 1865.

Henry Wilburn was born May 18, 1867, and married Mary Polly Ward on July 20, 1892. Henry died Feb. 27, 1940.

William Jefferson was born on Jan. 20, 1869, and married Ella Thompson on Feb. 13, 1895. He died Feb. 27, 1911.

John Madison was born on Oct. 28, 1870, and married Melinda Ella Thompson on April 16, 1891. John died Dec. 15, 1944.

James Ulysses was born on Sept. 4, 1872, and married Margaret Deliha Harder on Dec. 19, 1894. James died Nov. 11, 1959.

Mary Ludy was born on Oct. 7, 1875, and she married William T. Ward in May 1898. Mary died Aug. 12, 1951.

Sarah Ann was born on Nov. 7, 1876, and she married John W. Richardson on May 10, 1891. Sarah died Jan. 7, 1947.

Samuel Alexander was born on Feb. 14, 1880.

Robert Tecumseh was born on Dec. 8, 1881, and he married Nancy June Ward on Sept. 17, 1905. Robert died May 9, 1926.

Bertha Elizabeth was born on Dec. 18, 1883, and she married Spencer Hinson on July 29, 1903. Bertha died in 1971.

All of Alexander and Sarah's children were born in Perry County, Tennessee. Sarah died on Feb. 27, 1890, and was buried in the Broadaway Cemetery in Perry County, Tennessee.

After the death of Sarah, Alexander married Nancy Jane Lomax Hamm on Sept. 17, 1890. Alexander and Nancy had one daughter, Linda. Mother and daughter died in childbirth.

Alexander then married Mary Caroline Denton on Feb. 2, 1893. Mary was born on Oct. 23, 1859. They had one son. Ernest Rosco was born on Dec. 9, 1895; he married Beulos Rebecca Ann Thompson on May 27, 1917. Ernest died on Dec. 12, 1958. Beulos was born on May 21, 1902, and is still living.

Samuel Alexander Broadaway was born on Feb. 14, 1880. He married Martha Ward on June 20, 1901, and had only one daughter, Ila, born in 1902. She married Dewey Richardson. Martha died on Nov. 11, 1902.

Samuel remarried to Martha Scroggins on Sept. 23, 1906. Martha was born on Dec. 15, 1888. They had five boys.

Wesley Claude was born Nov. 12, 1908, and he married Hazel Luckey.

Hershel Taylor was born Dec. 29, 1909, and he married Mary Anna Sowell.

Buford Leblone was born March 12, 1911, and he married Edna Mays.

Robert Hurbert was born Sept. 22, 1914, and he married Hallie Louise Scroggins. He died July 16, 1991.

Samuel Garland was born May 15, 1925, and he married Annia Mae Ussery.

Martha Scroggins Broadaway died June 19, 1925. Samuel then married Mary Kirk and they had two daughters, Pauline and Irene. Samuel was born in Perry County and made his home there until 1911 when he moved to Madison County. He lived in the Friendship Community and was a farmer.

Hershel Taylor Broadaway was born Dec. 28, 1909, in the city of Linden in Perry County, Tennessee, where he lived part of his childhood. He worked the farm with his father. Hershel joined the Navy on Jan. 1, 1931, and served during peacetime as a seaman. He was injured in a motorcycle accident in April of 1935. Because of this accident, he was given a medical discharge from the Navy. Hershel married Mary Anna Sowell on March 7, 1937, in Madison County, Tennessee. Mary Anna was born May 27, 1915, in Jackson, Tennessee.

Hershel worked in several states as an ironworker during World War II, and he worked at Oak Ridge Ammunition Plant. He had two children. Joyce Labella, born Jan. 22, 1938 and Malvin Alex, born Feb. 22, 1943 in Johnson City, Tennessee. Hershel moved his family to Alabama in 1950. Here, he began working for TVA as an ironworker for the construction branch, where he retired in 1975 as a foreman. Mary Anna died on April 15, 1988. Hershel remarried to Mary Lindsey and now resides in Sheffield.

Hershel is a very talented man. He had only an elementary education, but is very intelligent. He is a kind and gentle person who is loved very much by his children and even more so by his seven grandchildren. Hershel has lived to see four great-grandchildren. *Submitted by Kathleen Pauline Harder, Madison, Tennessee and Sandra Broadway, Leighton, Alabama.*

BROADWAY, The Broadway family was first in Stewart County Tennessee in 1820. There were two listed, "J" and John. Another set of Broadways was in Lincoln County Tennessee. These were from North Carolina. The ones in Stewart County were from Virginia. The connection has not been found, but somewhere in the 1700s, they were related to a Nicholass, who was in North Carolina, then moved to Virginia and in 1783, he had five sons. This branch of the Broadway family begins with Paschall Broadway, born April 10, 1810, in Virginia or Tennessee.

Paschall Broadway was in Stewart County Tennessee until the 1850s. He married a Sallie C. there and had seven children. Children known are: Henry W., born 1830, died May 31, 1879, married Martha A. Uisley. His family moved to Decatur County, Tennessee; Paschall II, died young; Martha, born 1830s, married Columbus W. Turner; Melissa, born March 1, 1838, died in 1916, married George Turner. They moved to Kentucky, then to Arkansas, where he published the Nashville news; Alexander, born April 30, 1841, died Dec. 19, 1896; W., born 1840s, no information; and Susiee, born 1858, married Calvin Inman.

Ernest Broadway did most of the research on the family several years ago. He got the old family Bibles and copied them. Also, his daughter has helped in their search. She was kind enough to share information to help write this history. Thanks to Kathleen Harder.

In the 1840 census of Tennessee, there were only John, Paschall and William Broadway listed in Stewart County. They were probably brothers. In 1829, Paschall worked on the roads with Squire Reynolds.

In 1836, Paschall and John A. were listed in the tax lists. In 1843, Paschall and Thomas, another brother, were listed together in the tax lists. In 1850, John A. Paschall and Thomas were together on the tax lists. In 1852, Henry, William and Paschall were together on the tax lists.

Paschall was not on the 1850 census. He moved to Perry County, Tennessee in the 1850s to work for William Bradley on the furnace, as a carpenter. Paschall died Feb. 1861.

Alexander B. Broadway, born 1841, married Sarah Lomax, born 1844. She was the daughter of Andrew and Anna Lomax. They were the descendants of Samuel Lomax, the Englishman who come from Georgia to Tennessee. Their children were; Melissa C., married Jacob Richardson; Thomas A., born 1865, died same year; Henry W., born 1867; William J., born 1869; John M., born 1869; James Ulysses, born Sept. 4, 1872, married Margaret Delila Harder; Mary L., born 1874; Sally A., born 1876; Samuel A., born 1880; Robert T., born 1881; Bertha E., born 1883.

Alexander married a second time to Nancy Jane Hamm. She had one child and died in child birth 1891.

Alexander married the third time to Mary Caroline Denton. They had one child, Ernest Roscoe, born 1895, who married Beulos Thompson. Their daughter, Kathleen, has kept up the family history.

Alexander fought in the Civil War for the North in 1863, 1864, and was at Franklin and Clifton, Tennessee. He is buried on Cedar Creek in Broadway Cemetery with his three wives beside him.

James Ulysses Broadway, son of Alex, married Margaret Delia Harder. They had three children, Elbert Evins, born Jan. 1897, Adda M. and Flora, who married Lonnie Peace.

Elbert married Lexie Tomblin, the daughter of Tom Tomblin and Dora Kelly. They had four children, Gladys, born 1918, Anna Lou, Margaret, and Thomas Kola.

Gladys Evans, born 1918, married Mark Strickland. Gladys died Jan. 29, 1979, having raised her four children and seeing five grandchildren. She left her love and memory that will always be with us. *Submitted by Robert L. Strickland.*

DIXIE BROADWAY, was one of nine children born to John Madison and Melinda Ella Thompson Broadway. He was born Jan. 24, 1895, on Cedar Creek in Perry County, Tennessee. Dixie farmed, drove a school bus, worked in timber, owned a grocery store and worked as a pipefitter.

Mallie and Dixie Broadway

Around 1912 or 1913, Dixie was hauling crossties to Cedar Creek Landing and saw John Duncan and his children getting off a boat. The Duncans were moving to Cedar Creek from Lyon County, Kentucky. When Dixie saw John's daughter, Mallie, he said "she's the prettiest girl I've ever seen and I'm going to marry her", and that he did. On Oct. 4, 1914, Dixie and Mallie were united in marriage. Mallie was born Jan. 21, 1899, the daughter of John and Mattie Travis Duncan. Mattie died when Mallie was about one year old. Dixie and Mallie were very devoted parents, grandparents, great-grandparents and even great-great grandparents for many years. Their home was always open to anyone and they were loved by all who knew them. Dixie and Mallie had five children: Ida, Ira, Wilburn, Syble, and John Robert.

Ida, born Sept. 3, 1915, married Willie Richardson, born Jan. 7, 1909, on Aug. 29, 1932. Willie died Oct. 16, 1974. They have three children: Don, born April 9, 1933, Frances, born April 11, 1935, and Lyle, born Jan. 14, 1940. Don married Dorothy Ray, Jan. 17, 1959. Frances married Jack Dunkle, April 6, 1976. They have two sons, Caleb, Dec. 28, 1979, and Tyler, March 16, 1984. After Jack died, Frances married R.T. Grooms on Jan. 14, 1961. They have three children: Debbie, Feb. 6, 1962 and twins, Randy and Sandy, Oct. 27, 1964. Debbie married Lynn Monroe and they have two daughters, Kalyn, May 19, 1989, and Sara, June 6, 1993. Randy married Sherry Boyd and they have one daughter, Ashley, March 29, 1991. Sandy married Jacky Richardson and they have two sons, Daniel, March 3, 1989 and Alec, Feb. 1, 1994. Lyle married Dixie Burcham Tucker, Sept. 18, 1981. They have one daughter, Brandi Lee, July 26, 1982.

Ira was born Feb. 10, 1917, and died Sept. 19, 1917.

Wilburn was born Sept. 2, 1919, and died Sept. 8, 1986. In 1943, he served in the armed services for nine months. Wilburn married Mildred LaRue, born July 3, 1918, on Dec. 24, 1943. They have one daughter, Carolyn, born Nov. 20, 1944, who married Jerry Moore, March 26, 1960. They have two sons, Scott, Nov. 6, 1961, and Shannon, July 11, 1966. Scott married Susan Bevill, May 26, 1984, and they have three children: Cassidy, Nov. 11, 1986, Zachery, May 13, 1988, and Haley, March 23, 1993. Shannon married Jamie Lewis, born Jan. 23, 1970, and they have one son, Jonathan Logan, March 31, 1993.

Syble, born Aug. 27, 1924, married Osco Brown Moore, born Jan. 9, 1923, on Aug. 16, 1941. They have three children: Joyce, April 4, 1943, Billy, Jan. 25, 1948, and Tommy, Jan. 29, 1956. Osco served in the Army and was stationed in Ft. Louis, Washington, from Dec. 29, 1944 until Dec. 7, 1946, when he was honorably discharged. Joyce married Kenneth Garrison, Sept. 28, 1962, and they have two children: Sharon Lynn, Feb. 11, 1964, and Brent Ryan, Aug. 12, 1972. Sharon married Tim Bastin, Nov. 24, 1982, and they have three daughters: Ciji Nicole, Jan. 3, 1984, Jena Paige, Jan. 23, 1989, and Macy Brooke, March 6, 1991. Brent is continuing his education at Columbia State Community College. Billy married Melissa Conder, Sept. 1, 1992. Tommy married Becky Patterson, June 4, 1988, and they have two children: Rachel, Feb. 6, 1982, and Mason, Jan. 28, 1991.

John Robert, born, May 22, 1934, married Christine Ward, born Nov. 15, 1935, on May 10, 1952. They have two children: Kaye, May 14, 1953, and Jeffery, March 2, 1957. Kaye married Alex Crowell, Oct. 28, 1979. He had a son, Alex Crowell. Jeff married Debbie Tate, born Sept. 16, 1958, on March 18, 1978. They have three sons: Jason, July 5, 1980, Jordan, Jan. 24, 1984, and Jake, Jan. 27, 1993. *Submitted by Syble Moore.*

JEFF AND NORMA BROADWAY, live on Cypress Creek in Perry County. Norma is the daughter of Leroy F. Barden III of Richmond, Virginia, and Eva Barden of El Paso, Texas.

The Broadway and Ward families in September 1900.

Jeff is the great, great, great, grandson of Paschal Broadway. He was born April 10, 1810, in Stewart County, died Feb. 17, 1861. His wife, Sally, was born 1807, in Virginia, died Jan. 27, 1882. Paschal's family came to Perry County from Stewart County, Tennessee in the mid 1850s to work as a carpenter for William Bradley, who owned the Iron Furnace on Cedar Creek. The Broadways lived in the Furnace Hollow on Cedar Creek.

Paschal's children were Henry W., Paschal II, Melissa, Martha, W., Susie, and Alexander Broadway, who is Jeff's great, great grandfather. Alexander was born April 30, 1841/1842, died Dec. 25, 1896. For many years, he was the Justice of the Peace and after retiring from that office, was generally called "Squire". He was recognized as a leader among the Republicans of his section. He was married three times. First to Sally (Sarah) Lomax. Their children were: Melissa, Thomas, Henry, William, John, James, Mary, Sally, Samuel, Robert, and Bertha. His second wife was Jane Lomax Hamm, both mother and child died during childbirth. His third wife was Mary Caroline Denton. Ernest Roscoe was their child. Alexander's son, Henry W., was Jeff's great grandfather. He was born May 18, 1867, died Feb. 27, 1940. His wife was Polly Ward. They had three children: James Colonel, Maude Myrtle, and M. Pearl.

Jeff's grandfather, James Colonel Broadway, was born Sept. 15, 1893, and died July 31, 1975. He married Addie Hickerson on Dec. 24, 1913. They had three children: Juanita, wife of Willard Westbrooks, Louise, wife of Harl Turnbow, and Jeff's father, James Ross Broadway. Ross was born Aug. 10, 1920. He married Hessie Trull, Feb. 28, 1948. Hessie was born Dec. 6, 1924. Ross and Hessie are still living.

Ross and Hessie have four children: Billy Joe Hunnicutt, Jerry Wayne Broadway, Mary June Hamm, and Jeff Broadway.

JOYCE LABELLE BROADWAY, was born on Jan. 22, 1938, in Columbia, Tennessee. She grew up in several towns in Tennessee. In 1950, her father moved her and her family to Florence, Alabama. There she graduated from Coffee High School in 1956. On June 3, 1956, she married Jimmy Ray Stanfield.

Pauline Eubank with her father, Samuel Alexander Broadway.

Joyce and Jimmy Ray have four sons. Edward Taylor was born June 3, 1958. He married Rebecca Hunt on Sept. 8, 1978, and they have two sons. Zachariah Taylor, born Feb. 2, 1987 and Seth Warren, born Aug. 21, 1989. Eddie is employed with the Florence Electrical Department and lives in Florence, Alabama with his family.

Kevin Ray was born April 21, 1960. He married Karen Allen, Dec. 21, 1984. Karen died Dec. 30, 1992. Kevin is employed with Robert Orr Food supply and he lives in Colbert County.

James Brian was born Oct. 9, 1962. He married Vicki Carter, June 30, 1984, and they have a daughter, Lindsey Joanna, born May 16, 1989. Brian is employed with Robert Orr Food

Supply and lives in Colbert County with his family.

David Wallace was born June 10, 1968. He married Alison Martin on June 2, 1990. David is employed with the Florence Gas Department. He and Alison live in Florence.

After the birth of David, Joyce received her teaching degree from Florence State, which is now University of North Alabama. She went on to teach at Weeden Elementary in the Florence school system for ten years. Joyce also owned and operated a beauty shop and clothing store in Florence, called Reflections, from 1974-1977.

Joyce divorced Jimmy Ray in the late 70s and remarried Tommy Mulligan in late 1987. Tommy died in 1994, and Joyce now resides in Florence.

Joyce has three grandchildren, Zach, Seth, and Lindsey.

Malvin Alex Broadway was born Feb. 22, 1943, in Johnson City, Tennessee. Most of his childhood, he lived in several towns in Tennessee. His father moved him and his family to Florence, Alabama in 1950, where he went to elementary school. They moved again to Ford City, Alabama in 1958, where he went to Colbert County High School. Malvin played football and he graduated in 1964. After graduation, he joined the Alabama National Guard and served six years. Malvin met Sandra Kay McCormack in high school and they were married on Jan. 16, 1965, and have made their home in Leighton, Alabama. He joined Ironworkers Local 477 and worked several construction jobs in Alabama and Tennessee. He worked on the construction of the Browns Ferry Nuclear Plant in Athens, Alabama and at Little Bear Creek. Malvin went to work in 1976 for TVA at Power Service in Muscle Shoals, Alabama. He has several outside interests, such as he is a mason at the Leighton Lodge and a softball umpire, calling girls high school softball. He is also a member of the Leighton Baptist church.

Malvin and Sandra have three children. Tracey Ann was born on July 15, 1966. She married Tim Mitchell, on Aug. 23, 1986. They have one daughter, Hallie Erin, born Oct. 9, 1992. Tracy is self-employed.

Malvin Alex II (Butch) was born March 13, 1970. Butch is a pipefitter's apprentice and employed in Muscle Shoals, Alabama.

Jennifer Jo was born Oct. 7, 1972. Jennifer is a student of Special Education at Athens State College in Athens, Alabama and is employed in Muscle Shoals, Alabama. *Submitted by Tracey Ann Mitchell.*

PASCHAL AND SARAH BROADWAY's

family moved to Perry County in 1850 to help rebuild the Cedar Grove Iron Works on Cedar Creek. Paschal, 1810-1861, was a carpenter, stone mason, and owned a gristmill. He had worked on the Rough and Ready Furnace in Stewart County before coming with William Bradley to Perry County. In the Perry County Court Minutes of 1867, these heirs are listed: Sarah, his widow, Henry, Alexander, Isabella and Susan Broadway, George and Melissa Turner, Columbus and Martha Turner, Joseph and Emily Owens.

Twenty-one year old Alexander married Sarah Lomax, daughter of Andrew and Anna Richardson Lomax, in 1862. He served in the Civil War, Co. F 2nd Tenn. Mounted Inf. He was a farmer, carpenter, owned a gristmill, and served as Justice of the Peace for many years. Their farm included the land where the Cedar Grove Methodist Church is located on Cedar Creek.

John and Ella Broadway

Alexander and Sarah had eleven children: Melissa (Lis), T.A., lived 12 days, Henry Wilburn, Willie, John Madison, Jim, Ludy, Sarah (Sally), Samuel, Robert, and Bertha. Sarah died in 1890 and in 1893, Alexander married Mary Denton and they had one child, Ernest. Alexander died in 1896.

John Madison, 1870, married Malinda Ella Thompson, 1877, daughter of Wiley and Rebecca Randel Thompson, in 1891, at her home near Cedar Creek Landing. John was a carpenter, a farmer and magistrate of Perry County. He served a term in 1895 and again from 1936 until his death in 1944. They were members of Simmons Primitive Baptist Church of Cedar Creek, where he served as deacon.

John used his carpentry skills to make caskets for persons in the community. His caskets were unique for that period because he lined the inside with white fabric and covered the outside with black fabric. He also made the box (vault) to hold the casket. It was said that his caskets were of such fine quality and craftsmanship that they were in great demand.

John and Ella had nine children: Riley, Dixie, Gertie, Guss, Andrew, Mattie, Billy Pope (Preacher), Maggie, Maudie, and raised a grandson, James, son of Riley and Cora Hufstedler Broadway. Cora died and Riley married Ella Ward. Perry County was home to seven of the children. The two surviving children still reside in Perry County, Mrs. Roy (Maggie) Howell and Mrs. Leslie (Maudie) LaRue. There were twenty-seven grandchildren to carry on the Broadway traditions and customs. Only one of whom resides in Perry County with the Broadway name, John Robert, son of Dixie and Mallie Duncan Broadway. Gertie married Ross Moore, who managed a grocery store on Cedar Creek. Andrew married Grace Daniel and they moved to Madison, Tennessee, where they owned Broadway's Grocery. Mattie married Hillard Moore and their son, James, lives at the old homeplace. Preacher married Celia Moore and moved to Hohenwald.

Guss, 1902-1983, was a journeyman pipe fitter and an ordained Primitive Baptist minister, who served the Simmons Primitive Baptist Church and other pastorates. He and Loudean Clifton Broadway had two children, Naomi and Garland. Garland is continuing the tradition of being an ordained Primitive Baptist minister at the Simmons Primitive Baptist Church on Cedar Creek.

BROMLEY-DESANTIS,

Edith Bromley DeSantis' parents were Albert Patterson and Lillian Baston Bromley. His grandfather was John Jefferson Bromley, who fought with the Confederate forces during the Civil War. He was a sergeant with the 9th Tennessee Cavalry Battalion. His brother, Williams, was a captain with the same unit.

Bottom row: Vernon Bromley, Edith DeSantis, Evelyn Nell Bromley Stocks and Joe Bromley. Top row: Albert Bromley, Lillian Bromley, John Lewis Bromley and Dorothea Jones

Albert and Lillian Bromley were parents of seven children. The oldest, John Louis, was followed by Dorothea, Edith, Evelyn, Margey, Vernon, and Joe. These children all attended school in Perry County. Edith and Dorothea graduated from Perry County High in 1937.

Four of the Bromley children still survive today. Dorothea married Sylvester Jones in 1939. She has three living children, Philip, Paul, and Carolyn. Edith married Joseph DeSantis, from New Jersey, in 1943, and had three children, Judith, Peter, and Diane. Vernon, deceased, had two children, Verna Bastin and Lillian Jane Bromley. Joe Bromley had three children, Michael, Vicki, and Cynthia.

Edith is the proud grandmother of three children, Kevin, Mark, and Denise DeFlo.

Edith has resided in New Jersey for 45 years, but looks forward to moving back to Tennessee, the state she loves.

EVELYN NELL BROMLEY,

John Jefferson Bromley was born Oct. 31, 1838, in Bromley Hollow, near Flatwoods, Tennessee. He was the son of John and Editha (Hurst) Bromley. John J. married Mary Belsha, on Oct. 25, 1860. John Jefferson Bromley served in the Confederate Army during the War for Southern Independence, attaining the rank of sergeant.

John Lewis Bromley, the son of John J. and Mary B., was born on Sept. 20, 1868. On Oct. 17, 1889, he married Melissa Emmaline Goodman of Beech Creek in Wayne County. Their son, Albert Patterson Bromley, was born in Bromley Hollow on Jan. 7, 1893. John Lewis died Jan. 7, 1898, on Albert's fourth birthday. On Feb. 8, 1914, Albert married Lillian Dorothea Bastin.

Lillian Dorothea's father was John E. Bastin, the son of A.O. and Phoebe Jane (Sisco) Bastin of Perry County. Lillian Dorothea's mother was Mattie Blanche (Kittrell) Bastin, born Nov. 29, 1879, the eighth child of Confederate veteran, Benjamin Caesar and Martha Jane (Dowdy) Kittrell, of Farmer's Valley in Perry County. John Bastin and Mattie Blanche Kittrell were married on April 19, 1896. They had seven children, the firstborn being Lillian Dorothea, born April 3, 1897.

Albert Patterson Bromley and Lillian Dorothea (Bastin) Bromley lived in Flatwoods. They had seven children: John Lewis, Dorothea, Edith, Evelyn, Margie, Vernon (Bub), and Joe. Margie died in 1927 at the age of four with diphtheria. Lillian died March 21, 1963, and Albert died Oct. 23, 1967. They are buried in the family cemetery near their home in Flatwoods.

Albert and Lillian's fourth child, Evelyn Nell, was born on May 14, 1921. Evelyn and her sisters, Dorothea and Edith, played basketball for Linden High School in the 1930s. Their framed team pictures were proudly displayed in Albert and Lillian's Flatwoods home. Evelyn graduated as salutatorian of her class at Linden High on May 13, 1939. During WW II, she worked at a munitions plant in Milan, Tennessee, where she met a soldier, William Raymond Stocks, born Feb. 20, 1915, Barnesville, Georgia. Bill Stocks left for Europe, participated in the Normandy invasion and served in Europe until the end of the war. He returned to Flatwoods and, on March 16, 1946, he and Evelyn were married.

Bill and Evelyn had four children: Lenore Jean, Steven Raymond, Robin Lillian, and Lois Amanda Stocks. Bill worked as a glazier for Pittsburgh Glass in Memphis. The family often returned to visit in Flatwoods. Their daughter, Lenore Jean, wife of Steven Gary Johnson, is the mother of Bill and Evelyn's three grandchildren, Valentine Bromley, Stephanie Lake, and William Ivor Johnson.

JAMES AKIN BROMLEY,

was born May 19, 1866, in the Bromley Hollow, Wayne County. He was the son of John Jefferson Bromley and his first wife Mary Belsha. J.J. was a veteran of the Civil War, serving with the 9th Cavalry Battalion. He served under Major James Akin, and named his first son, after the war, after him.

The James Akin Bromley family. Eliza (holding Delphia), Mary and James (holding Bessie)

Eliza Elmira Goodman was born Feb. 14, 1873, on Beech Creek, Wayne County, the daughter of Daniel L. and Mary Ann Graham Goodman. Daniel also served in the Civil War, with the TN 9th Cavalry. He was at the Battle of Franklin, lost his horse and never got back with the command. He took the oath of allegiance in Nashville.

James and Eliza were married Jan. 13, 1889, in Wayne County. They had four daughters: Mary Lee, Ada Bessie, Baby girl who lived two days, and Delphia Louise. Ada Bessie lived to be four years old and is buried in the Bromley Cemetery, Bromley Hollow.

They moved to Flatwoods sometime in the 1890s and James hauled freight by wagon between Flatwoods and Clifton, which was then a river port. In February 1899, he drove in sleet and freezing rain, unloaded the freight in Flatwoods and went home with a high fever. He had pneumonia and died Feb. 23, 1899, and is buried in the Bromley Cemetery.

Eliza later married Dr. James T. Cook. After his death, she operated the telephone switchboard at Flatwoods.

Mary married Clyde King and Delphia married Loyd Tatum.

In 1921, Eliza married Alvin Ross Warren of Coon Creek. He was the son of Alvin and Mary Barber Dowdy Warren. Ross and Eliza lived at the family farm. He was a large man, at one time weighing over 300 pounds. He died Aug., 1941, and was buried in the Warren Cemetery. His first wife, Margaret Westbrooks was also buried there.

Eliza lived with her daughters after his death until her death on May 3, 1951. She is buried in the Warren Cemetery. She was a lifelong member of the Church of Christ.

WILLIAM EWING AND MINERVA GOODMAN BROMLEY,

William Ewing Bromley was the oldest son of John Jefferson Bromley, born Oct. 31, 1838, and Mary Belsha Bromley, born Dec. 25, 1839.

William E. Bromley family in 1939. Seated: William and second wife, Ellen Weaver Bromley. Standing: (children of Williams' first wife) Alice Tharp, Virginia Boyce, Jeff Bromley, Bertha Holt and Birdie King

The six children born to John J. and Mary Bromley were: William Ewing, Editha, James, John, (Dr.) Richard, and Thomas Bromley.

After Mary's death, John J. Bromley married Sallie Terry and seven children were born to them: Charles, Samuel, Joseph, Amos, Mary, Emma, and Sallie Bromley (Pitts).

William Ewing Bromley married Minerva Goodman, born Aug. 18, 1867, on Dec. 23, 1888, in Wayne County.

Minerva Jane Goodman's parents were Daniel Goodman, born Oct. 24, 1846, and Mary Jane Graham, born Aug. 6, 1846.

William Ewing and Minerva Goodman Bromley had five children: Virgina (Boyce), Birdie (King), Jeff Bromley, Bertha (Holt), and Alice (Tharp).

Virgina "Virgie" was married to Dr. William Earl Boyce, Feb. 7, 1911, in Nashville, Tennessee. They had four children: Wilton (Craig), Mildred (Burns), William Earl Boyce Jr., and Marie (Grimes).

Minerva Bromley died Aug. 11, 1904, and was buried in the Bromley cemetery in Wayne County.

William E. Bromley married Ellen Weaver after Minerva died. She was born on Oct. 9, 1861, and died June 4, 1949. She is buried in the Flatwoods cemetery.

Will provided for his children with a good living from his farm. In his early marriage to Minerva, they lived in Flatwoods, where his children were born. Later, he sold his house to his brother, Charles, and moved back to his farm at the home place across Buffalo River, in Wayne County. Will and his second wife, Ellen Weaver Bromley, lived there until a few years before he died. They moved back to Flatwoods. It had become too difficult at his age to make his weekly trips across the Buffalo River, often in a boat, to buy groceries and necessary goods.

He was a member of the Methodist Church and a kind and honest man with a good sense of humor. William Ewing Bromley died May 7, 1943. He will be remembered with affection and respect by those who knew him. He was buried in the Bromley Cemetery near his homeplace in Wayne County. *Submitted by Marie B. Grimes.*

HOWARD BUNCH FAMILY,

Anderson Bunch was born in 1809, in Monroe County, Tennessee. He and his wife, Sally, had twelve children. They made their way west and settled in Perry County on Cedar Creek.

Lee Gran and Ada Bunch, Dewey Lee and Cloia Bunch

The youngest of their children was Howard, who was born in 1838 and died in 1913. He was married to Ann Phillips, who was born in 1848 and died in 1898. They farmed on Cedar Creek and inherited the "home place" from Anderson and Sally Bunch. Howard and Ann were buried in the Bunch Cemetery on Cedar Creek.

Their only child was Lee Gran, who was born in 1868 and died in 1947. In 1893, he married Ada Steele, who was born in 1875 and died in 1965. Howard recognized his son's interest in books and reading, so he bought him a book every time the traveling salesman came around. Lee Gran became interested in becoming a school teacher and attended George Peabody College in Nashville to become a teacher. In those days, the parents made up money to have "subscription schools" that lasted three months in the fall and winter. Lee Gran taught several of these on Cedar Creek, White Oak, and other places around the county. He later became County Superintendent of Perry County Schools in which he served for some fourteen years.

A son, Dewey Lee, was born in 1898, and died in 1988.

Lee Gran decided to leave Perry County and move to West Tennessee where opportunities in farming were better for Dewey Lee. About 1925, they bought and moved to a farm in Gibson County near Trenton. Lee Gran continued his teaching at McRee, near Trenton, and Wellsview, near Frog Jump. Lee Gran eventually retired from teaching. He and his wife, Ada, were buried at Follis Chapel, near Trenton.

Dewey Lee married Cloia Graham, who was born in 1904, and is still living. She is the daughter of Jack and Ella Graham. Dewey Lee farmed and worked with a cotton gin in Trenton. He was buried at Follis Chapel Cemetery.

Dewey Lee and Cloia had a son, Dewey Lee Jr., who was born in 1932, and is still living. He farmed for a while and later served in the Navy. Upon discharge from the Navy, he attended college and became a Vocational Agriculture teacher. He taught two years in Crockett County, but returned to farming where he is at the present time. Dewey Lee Jr. is unmarried.

JOSEPH BUNCH, born 1749, son of David and Mary Bunch of Virginia, married Mary (Molly) Woodson Anderson in 1778, and migrated to Perry County, Tennessee with their children in the early 1800s. He died after 1830 and was buried in the old David Bunch Cemetery on Cedar Creek, Perry County. Their children were: David, born 1780, died 1838, buried Perry County; Tarleton, born 1783, died 1852, buried Perry County; Elizabeth, born 1785; Nancy, born 1792, died 1872, Dickson County; and Joseph Anderson Bunch, born 1788.

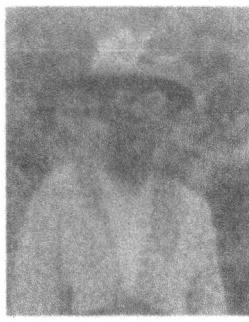

Alice Permelia Bunch

Joseph Anderson Bunch married Sally Bunch in 1809. Their children were: Thomas, Caroline, Mary Jane, Elizabeth, David, John, Amanda, Nelson, Calvin, Howard, George Dabney, and Joseph Anderson Bunch Jr., born 1815, Perry County.

Joseph Anderson Bunch Jr., a Perry County farmer, married Nancy Denton, born 1822. Their children were: Argent, born 1843, Samuel, born 1845, John T., born 1847, Sarah Elizabeth, born 1851, Milly C., born 1853, William R., born 1855, Nancy Jane, born 1857, Martha C., born 1858, Mary Bell, born 1861, Francis A., born 1865, Ophelia J. and Amanda, twins, born 1867, Joseph, and David Tilden Bunch, born 1848, Perry County, died 1921, Gibson County.

In 1871, David Tilden Bunch and Harriet Lavenia Harder, born 1850, died 1933, Gibson County, were married in Perry County. Their children, all born in Perry County, were: Albert Henry, born 1871, died 1922, Oklahoma, married 1903 to Cora Dickson; Carl D., born Aug. 1875, died Oct. 1875; Dona Belle, born 1877, died 1916 Perry County, married 1899 to William Oliver Roberts; Arthur, born 1879, died 1900, never married; Francis Elizabeth, born 1881, died 1917 Perry County, married 1906 to Elisha Alexander Richardson; Ida L, born 1884, died 1909 Perry County. married 1907 to Cleveland Paschal; John Allen, born 1887, died 1968 Illinois, married 1907 to Ethel; Laura M., born 1890, died 1979 Shelby County, married 1906 to Lonnie Hinson; and Alice Permelia Bunch, born 1873, died 1955 Gibson County.

Alice Permelia Bunch and James Alexander Wiley, born 1871 Perry County, died 1940 Gibson County, were married 1893 in Perry County. Their children were; Thomas Kay (1894-1968); Lillie Mable (1897-1974); and James Ross Wiley, born 1904 Perry County, died 1992 Gibson County.

In 1923, James Ross Wiley married Rausy Somers, born 1905 Dyer County, died 1982 Gibson County. Their children, all born in Gibson County, were: James Ewin (1924-1984); Beulah Mae, born 1926; Harold Edward, born 1927; William Robert, born 1930; Martha Jean, born 1935; and Shirley Ann Wiley, born 1937.

In 1955, Shirley Ann Wiley married George Edward Parish, born 1935, and had one child, Jerry Lynn Parish, born 1957.

In 1976, Jerry Lynn Parish married Lita Gay Poet, born 1956, and had one child, Sarah Lynn Parish, born 1989.

Many of the Bunchs are buried in the old David Bunch Cemetery on Cedar Creek and Harder Cemetery, both in Perry County, as well as Salem Methodist Church Cemetery in Gibson County. *Submitted by Shirley Ann Wiley Parish of Antioch, Tennessee.*

SARAH BUNTEN-BENTON-BRUTON-NEWTON, Sarah Graham's maiden name was possibly Buntin, Benton, Bruton, or maybe Newton. John Graham married Sarah Bunton in Rowan County, North Carolina on Jan. 25, 1785. When John Graham died, his obituary appeared in the Rowan, the Anson, and the Randolph County, North Carolina newspapers. In 1785, Sarah would have been 18 years old.

Sarah was definitely married to the John Graham that died in 1827 in Nashville, Davidson County, Tennessee, while serving in the 17th Tennessee State Assembly. Sarah died on Dec. 15, 1856, at age 88, probably while living with her daughter, Jane Graham Houston.

Proven children of Sarah and John Graham were: Charles, 1792-1875, Cass County, Texas, married Jane Rayburn; Elizabeth, c1793-1860, Panola County, Mississippi, married John King Rayburn; Jane, 1802-1860/70, Decatur County, Tennessee, married John Luckey Houston; Sarah, 1803-1875, Red River County, married William C. Bowman, then Wiley Graves; Hiram H., 1804-after 1850, Decatur County, married Melinda Houston; Lydia, 1806-1853, Cass County, Texas, married Bennett Story; Robert Crawford, 1809-1873, Camp County, Texas, married Mahaly Caughron, then Nancy Hill Story; Mary, 1810-1895, Cass County, Texas, married Jeremiah Preston Wood.

Some of the Graham children found in the Perry County area in the 1840s may belong to another Graham: Richard, 1799-after 1860, Decatur County census, married Nancy, with Duncan Canada and Nancy Canada in their home; Samuel, born 1808, married Jane, found 1850 Wayne County and 1860 Perry County censuses; David in 1830 Perry County census; Daniel, born 1816, married Nancy, found 1850 Wayne County, Tennessee census; John Jr., found in 1828 Perry County Circuit Court Docket with William Graham and Charles Graham, found in Oct. 5, 1831 Perry County Court Minutes, with Charles Graham and John Luckey Houston, for deceased McClure, found in Panola County, Mississippi 1841 Tax Assessment was one, Jno Graham and W. Rainey with John King Rayburn.

In an Oct. 13, 1840 Perry County Circuit Court instrument, Sarah Graham swore that she had known Nancy Rains in Randolph County, North Carolina, where she married on March 2, 1787, to Anthony Rains and that Anthony died March 25, 1837, in Randolph County. Sarah stated that she was the widow of Nancy Rain's brother, John Graham. *Submitted by Patricia Adkins Rochette.*

LEVI BURCHAM, came from Wales to Virginia and later, migrated to Tishomingo County, Mississippi, where he died and was buried. His son, Henry, had a son, William Burcham. William's second son, B.F., had a son, John Arden Burcham.

The Burcham's. Left to Right: William Tommy, Benjamin Franklin, John Henry, Hezikiah, Levy, Elijah and Ann

John Arden, born 1882 in Alcorn County, Mississippi, married Dora Etta Jones, 1886, in Prentice County, Mississippi, in 1905. Their children were: Ida (1905-1938), Giffie (1907-1970), Viola (1909-1978), Norma Mae (1913), Marvin Odell (1913-1987), Hattie (1915-1936), Joseph "Joe" Franklin (1917), Marron Dee (1919), Benjaman "Ben" Arden (1921), Gilbert Amos (1922), Maggie Etta (1925), Julia Asbie (1928-1949), Cecil Earl (1931). They also raised their grandson, James Richard "Silver" Morgan (1924-1947). Richard had one son, Johnny Richard Morgan (1945).

Ida Burcham first married Walt Morgan and had one son, Richard. Following her divorce, she married Woodro Bivins and they had Charline and Billy Bivins.

Giffie Burcham married Logan Creasy and had children: J.D., Harvey, Arden, Joel, Donny, Edith, and Jocie Creasy.

Viola Burcham married Ack Creasy and had two children, Atha and Ilean Creasy.

Odell Burcham married Mary Loise (Mozell) Rushing who had a daughter, Shirley Woods, by a previous marriage. Odell and Mozell had nine children: Thomas, Johnny, Jimmy, Wayne, Naoma, Dora, Etta, Linda, Mary Lou, and Lilly Mae Burcham.

Nora Mae married Raymond Robison. They had no children.

Joe Burcham married Jinnie Pearl Gilbert and had four children: Gilbert, Paul, Sylvia, and Collean Burcham.

Dee Burcham married Hazel Richardson and they had seven children: Dixie Lee, Patsy, Jane, Carol, Brenda, Tammy, and Franklin D. Burcham.

Ben Burcham married Lorene Broadway and had four children: James Allen, Neal, Bobby, and Teddy Hoyt Burcham. Following a divorce, Ben married Sybil and had Bruce and Terry Burcham.

Hattie Burcham married George C. Napper and had one son, G.C. Napper.

Amos Burcham married Newell Culp and had Donnie and Karon.

Maggie Etta married Loyd Ward and had Peggie Ann and Johnny Wayne Ward.

Earl Burcham married Betty Pope and had 3 sons, Robert, Danny, and Ricky.

Julia Burcham married Elbert "Jimmy" Peterson and had Anthony Jackson "Tony" and Lynn Peterson.

John Arden Burcham (1882-1950) began his ministry in 1911 and was ordained to the full work of the Gospel Ministry on May 23, 1915, in Decatur County, Tennessee, at Turmins Creek Primitive Baptist Church of Christ. He was called to preach, baptize, marry, and conduct funerals in different states and was called to pastor different churches in Tennessee.

John Arden was called to pastor Cedar Creek Primitive Baptist Church of Christ in the late 1930s. He moved to Bee Creek, Perry County, Tennessee in 1940.

John Arden died Jan. 22, 1950, and Dora Etta died Jan. 24, 1954. They are buried in the Simmons Cemetery, on Cypress Creek, in the Pope Community of Perry County. Buried near them is a daughter, Julie Asbie Peterson (1928-1949) and her infant son, Lynn Peterson (1949). Another daughter, Giffie (1907-1970) and her husband, Albert Logan Creasy (1888-1970) are buried beside them.

BURCHAM-WARD, Maggie Burcham married Loyd W. Ward, son of James Arthur "Boss" and Clara Richardson Ward, in 1941. They had two children, Peggie Ann and Johnny Wayne Ward, and a foster son, Anthony Jackson "Tony" Peterson.

Peggie Ann married David Ward Ramey, son of Louie and Pearl Ward Ramey, in 1963. They had two children, Ginger Ann and Nicholas "Nick" Ward Ramey.

Ginger Ramey married Timithy Hill, son of William "Cooter" and Scarlet Walker Hill, in 1983. Their children are Brandon Seth, 1986, Sarah Nicole, 1988, and Rachel Caitlin, 1989, Hill.

Nicholas Ward Ramey "Nick" married Shannon Potts, daughter of William "Bill" and Glenda Cotham Potts in 1990. They have one son, William David "Will" Ramey, born March 7, 1994.

Left to Right: Peggie, Loyd, Maggie, Tony and Johnnie

Johnny Wayne Ward married Glenda Gail Fraley, daughter of Julius Farris and Jewell Dean Lineberry Fraley, in 1968. The were married by his father, Loyd W. Ward, who was and is a deacon in the Primitive Baptist Church and was also a County Commissioner at that time. Johnny and Glenda have two sons, twins, John Adrian and Gregory Wayne, born Oct. 14, 1977. In 1994, Johnny was elected Commissioner of the First District, Perry County.

Anthony Jackson "Tony" Peterson married Peggy Westbrooks, daughter of John William and Mary Tom Garner Westbrooks. They have a daughter, Amy Tynerra Peterson, 1966, who married Tom Howell, son of Ima Nell and Clarence Howell, in 1991. Tony's second daughter, Jessica Danial Peterson, was born June 14, 1991.

DAVID EDWARD BURNS, was born in 1967 at Westover Air Force Base, near Chicopee Falls, Massachusetts. His parents are Joe and Mattie Burns of Lobelville. He is married to Anissa Cheryl Cotham, and they have one son, Jordan Isaac Burns, born in 1993.

David, Anissa and Jordan Burns in 1994.

David moved to Perry County with his family in 1973 when he was six years old. Prior to that time, he had lived two years at Clark Air Base in the Philippines, where his father was stationed with the U.S. Air Force, and had lived in Kansas City, Missouri three years.

His paternal grandparents are Eldred Burns, born 1905 in Perry County, and Neva Wade Burns, born 1911 in Hickman County. They lived most of their lives in Lewis County, where Eldred was a farmer and carpenter.

His maternal grandparents are George Dewey Robinson and Myrtle Leger Robinson, both born in 1900 in Rockcastle County, Kentucky. Dewey worked in the coal mines in his youth, worked in a steel mill in northern Kentucky during World War II, and then spent the rest of his life farming in Rockcastle County.

Anissa is the daughter of Charles and Carolyn Roberts Cotham. Her grandparents are Isaac Jackson "Ike" Cotham and Reida Brown Dabbs Cotham, and John Presley Roberts and Lela Ann Warren Roberts.

David is the great-great-great grandson of George Burns, born 1818, and Nancy Wilkey Burns, born 1822, who came to Perry County from Williamson County in 1859. They lived in the Lost Creek area, north of Lobelville. George was a farmer until his death in 1878. He is buried in the Beardstown Cemetery, and his wife, Nancy, who died in 1900, is buried in the Burns Hill Cemetery. According to some of the older members of the family, the Buffalo River was "up" when she died, and they could not get her body across the river.

David's great-great grandfather, John Wilkey Burns, born 1842, in Williamson County, came to Perry County with his parents in 1859. At the outset of the Civil War, John enlisted in the 42nd Tennessee Infantry, C.S.A., and served two years. According to Goodspeed's History, he was at Fort Donelson, Jackson, and "several battles of minor note". In 1867, he married Tabitha Greer, the daughter of Henry and Harriet Greer, who came to Perry County from Davidson County, about 1847. In 1880, John purchased a 400 acre farm between Beardstown and Lobelville, and lived out the rest of his life at his home on what is now known as Burns Ridge.

GEORGE BURNS, born 1818, died 1878, and Nancy Wilkey, born May 30, 1822, died Feb. 27, 1900, were married in Williamson County, Tennessee. They had nine children: William B., born 1840; John W., born March 10, 1842, married Tabitha Greer; Margaret A., born 1844; Mary J., born 1846; James L., born 1848, died as a child; Nicholas Terrell, born June 21, 1850, married Julia A. Duncan; Joe C., born Jan. 1855, married Sally Murray; Sarah, born 1856; Carrol P., born 1858, married Betty Alexander.

In 1859, George moved to Perry County with his family, where he purchased a large tract of land and farmed.

At the breaking out of the Civil War, John W. Burns, son of George, enlisted in the 42nd TN Infantry CSA and served two years. He was at Fort Donaldson, Jackson and several battles of minor note. After he returned home, he married Tabitha Greer of Perry County. They had twelve children, not all known: Betty (Ledbetter), Ellen (Bone), Henry, Boss, Johnny, Ada (Cude), Dora (Loveless), infant son, infant son, Joe C., married Leora DePriest.

Nicholas Terrell Burns, son of George and Tabitha Burns, married Julia A. Duncan. They had five children: Nancy Ethel, married William Samuel DePriest; Nellie Alma, married Jessie Frank Gray; Mollie, married Randolph DePriest; Mattie Lou, married Porter Bates; Willie, married Florence Baker.

George and Tabitha lived in Perry County outside of Lobelville, along Cane Creek, in the area known as "Burns Hill". They were buried at Burns Hill Cemetery, as well as most of their children. They also lived in the Beardstown Community.

GEORGE SIMPSON BURNS FAMILY,

Sylvia Dudley Leeper was born in Perry County, and has lived in Beardstown and Lobelville almost all her life. She is the only child of George Simpson Burns and Ola Mae Shepard, and the granddaughter of Joseph Clinton "J.C." Burns, who was born in Williamson County in 1853, and moved to Perry County in 1859, with his parents George and Nancy Wilkey Burns. Her Grandmother Burns was the former Sally Elizabeth Craig, born in 1857, the only child of Mary Wilburn and Simpson Craig. Mr. Craig died of yellow fever in the Civil War and Mary later married Billy Murray.

Simpson and Ola Burns

J.C. Burns came from a large family. Several of his brothers and sisters owned farms in and around the Beardstown-Lobelville area during the late 1800s and early 1900s. One of his older brothers was John W. Burns, who married Tabitha Greer and lived on Burns Ridge from 1880 until his death in 1914. Another brother, Nicholas Terrel "Nick" Burns, born in 1850, married Julia Daniel, and lived in what is now the DePriest Bend. His brother, Carroll P. Burns, born in 1858, married Bettie Black, and was a farmer in this neighborhood. Three of his sisters, who also lived in this area were Mary Jane Burns, born 1846, married Thomas C. "Clem" Edwards; Savannah Burns, born 1857, married Jess Twoomey; and Sally Burns, married to Robert E. Murray Jr.

The first child of J.C. and Sally Burns, Maude Estella, born 1876, only lived a few months.

Their second child, Minnie Bell, born 1879, first married Andrew Bates, and they had one child, Carter Bates, born 1898. Her second marriage was to William Samuel "Sam" Depriest, and they had one child, Minnie Bell Depriest. Sam Depriest had previously been married to Ethel Burns, the daughter of Nicholas Burns and a first cousin of his second wife, and they had six children, Myrtle, Paul, Graden, Rudolph, Ben, and Claude Depriest.

William Arthur "Willie" Burns, born 1881, married Fannie Shepard and they had five children: Thelma, Malcolm, Willie Ray, Randall, and Mary Frances.

Myrtle Mae Burns, the fourth child of J.C. and Sally, was born in 1883 and died in 1894.

Mattie Antonetta Burns, born 1886, married David Rudolph Goodman, and they had three children: Joe Lowell, James Wilbur, and David Rudolph Goodman Jr.

George Simpson, the youngest child born to J.C. and Sally Burns, was born in 1889. His wife, Ola Mae, was born in 1887. Her parents were Joseph B. "Buddy" Shepard and Nancy Jane Edwards. Their daughter, Sylvia, was born in 1914, and was first married to Guy Dudley, the son of Will and Annie Tate Dudley. After Guy passed away in 1952, she later married John T. Leeper, the son of George and Genevive Alexander Leeper. Her second husband died in 1972.

Three children were born to Sylvia and Guy Dudley. A son, Guy Burns Dudley, born in 1934, died as an infant. Their other son, Bobby Burns Dudley, born 1935, married Julia Kay Clark, and has two children, Julie Bobette Dudley and Michael Burns Dudley. Their daughter, Sylvia Joyce Dudley, married Jack F. Osborne, and they have two daughters, Jacquelyn Joyce Osborne and Jodi Lynn Osborne. Jack Osborne passed away in 1970, and Joyce married Robert T. Sircy Jr. in 1978.

JOSEPH CAYCE "JOE" BURNS, and his

wife Mattie have lived near Beardstown since 1973. He was born in 1931 in Nashville, the only child of Eldred and Neva Wade Burns. He grew up in Lewis County.

The Joseph Burns Family. Front: Mattie and Joseph. Standing left to right: David, Wanda Burns Litle, Deborah Burns Qualls, Barbara Burns Hinson and Joseph Burns Jr.

After graduating from high school in 1949, Joe enlisted in the United States Air Force and served over 22 years before his retirement in 1972. His overseas service included assignments in Alaska, Japan, Morocco, the Azores, and the Philippines. He has served as a member of the Perry County Board of Education since 1976.

Mattie, born in 1937 in Rockcastle County, Kentucky, is the youngest of eleven children born to George Dewey Robinson and Myrtle Leger Robinson.

Joe and Mattie have five children and eleven grandchildren. Wanda Sue, born 1953 at Lackland AFB, San Antonio, Texas, is married to Tony Litle, and has three children: Tony Allen Jr., Troy Albert, and Christopher Hubert Litle; Barbara Jo, born 1956, also at Lackland AFB, is married to Timmie Hinson and they have two children, Amanda Dawn and Timmie Jo "T.J." Hinson; Joseph Cayce Jr. "Joey", born 1960 at Columbia, Tennessee, married Linda Rau, and has three children: Justin Michael, Ethan Patrick and Aaron Christopher Burns; Deborah Kay "Debbie", born 1962 at Shaw AFB, Sumter, South Carolina, married Garry Qualls, and has two children, Sabrina Kay and Dakota Duncan Qualls; David Edward, born 1967 at Westover AFB, Massachusetts, is married to Anissa Cotham and has one son, Jordan Isaac Burns.

Joe's grandfather, George Henry Burns, born 1867 in Perry County, was the oldest of twelve children born to John Wilkey Burns and Tabitha Greer. Henry grew up in Perry County and married Lula Sweeney, the daughter of Milton Abercromby Sweeney and Mary Juan Burns Sweeney. He lived near his parents on Burns Ridge and helped farm the family farm until his father's death in 1914. Soon thereafter, he moved to Lewis County and lived near Hohenwald until his death in 1952.

John Wilkey Burns and his wife, Tabitha, had two children who died as infants and another child died young. Henry's other brothers and sisters were: James Edward "Boss", married Mae Daniel; Joe C., born 1873, married Leora Depriest; Johnny Hercules, born 1879, never married; Bettie, born 1876, married Henry Ledbetter; Ellen, born 1871, married William Bone; Dora, born 1870, married F.C. Loveless; Ida, born 1878, married Henry Lancaster; and, Ada, married John Cude.

Henry and Lula Burns were the parents of six children, all born in Perry County. Effie Emma, born 1893, married Charlie Parnell and had two sons, Frank and Fred Parnell. Two of Henry and Lula's children, Jesse Augusta "Gusta", born 1895, and Boyd Sweeney Burns, born 1911, never married. Hollye Marie, born 1903, married Hilman "Red" Mears and never had children. George Ashley, born 1898, and his wife, Naomi Peery, had two children, George Thomas Burns and Sarah Burns Wright. Eldred Cayce, born 1905, married Neva Wade, and had one son, Joe Burns.

CANTRELL-BELL, William D. Cantrell,

1862-1936, was born in Weakley County, the youngest son of William Carroll, 1821-?, and Moriah Ann Claiborne, 1827-1900. His paternal grandparents were Abraham Pitter and Rebecca Cantrell, who came to Weakley County from Warren County and Spartanburg, South Carolina. William had three brothers: Richard Willie (Polie), Franklin Pierce, and James Buchana. He had two sisters: Mary Paralee Daniel and Virginia (Jenny) Claiborne.

William David Cantrell family - Front row: Gertrude Cantrell Henry, William David, Madeline Cantrell Fagon, Elizabeth Bell, Edward Carmock, Ray; Back row: Minnie Ethel Cantrell Wilson, Clint Carroll, Lillie Cantrell Ward, Ida Cantrell Bell, Alice Cantrell Farlow

William moved with his widowed mother and the Claiborne family to Perry County after his father failed to return from the Civil War. He was never located. William grew up in Perry County and married Elizabeth Bell, 1865-1956, daughter of Eldriege Newsom and Caroline Pegram Bell. Caroline was a descendant of George Scott Pegram, who came from Virginia and purchased a farm in Davidson County, now a part of Cheatham County. This settlement became Pegram, Tennessee, seventeen miles west of Nashville.

In 1904, William sold his farm in Perry County to B.F. Brevard and purchased Mr. Brevard's farm in 13th District of Benton County. These farms were directly across the Tennessee River from each other. He moved his family of several children across the river on barges or homemade ferry boats, using mules and wagons.

To this family eleven children were born, nine reared to adulthood: Ida Leota, married Oscar Bell. Children: Lottie, Selmer, John, LeRoy, Byrd, Harrity, Ben, and Lavern; Clint Carroll, married Nettie Cherry. Children: Tilford, Ruth, and Vera Mae; Lillie Bell, married Thurman Ward. Children: William, Willard, Mary, Sudie, Virginia Ann, and J.W.; Minnie Ethel, married Sam Wilson. Children: Elizabeth, Valera, and Mary Frances; Jasper, 1894-1898; Alice Mae, married Joe Farlow. Children: Jack, Mavis, Christine, and Billy; Gertrude, married Clifford Henry. Children: Naomi, Troy, Ralph, and Ann; William Ray, married Flossie Odle. Children: Arthur David, Martha, Sue, Betty, and Bobby; Madeline, married Bruce Spence. One daughter, Marion. She later married Ray Fagan. Madeline is the sole survivor of this family at the present time; Edward Carmack, married Evonne Little. Children: Edward, Elaine, William, and Carl.

William and Elizabeth (Lizzie) lived the remainder of their lives on the farm, a few miles from Sugar Tree. There they reared their children and worked on the farm. The principal crop at that time was peanuts, which they picked by hand before the pea-picker came along.

William was Tax-Assessor in Perry County at one time and was a member of County Court in Benton County. He was called Squire Cantrell. He was one of the three men who were instrumental in organizing Cantrell's Chapel Church of Christ, around 1915. He, along with George Newson and M.F. Henry, built the building and organized the church, which continued to meet until a few years ago. His son, Carmack, kept the church active as long as he lived.

William and Lizzie both died at home and are buried in Manley's Chapel Cemetery nearby.

JIMMY TERRY CARMICAL, was born Feb. 26, 1944, in Perry County, Tennessee. He is the son of Joseph Byrd Carmical and Virginia Janice Shepard Carmical. He was married on June 18, 1965, to Ethel McCoy. She was born March 30, 1946, the daughter of James I. McCoy and Betty Sue Goodman McCoy, also of Perry County. Ethel's paternal grandparents are Ernest Loyd McCoy and Lula Mae McCoy. Her maternal grandparents are Jesse and Ethel Goodman of Perry County.

Terry's paternal grandparents are Robert Walter Carmical and Nina Dolores Mathis Carmical. His maternal grandparents were William Haywood Shepard and Byron Mae DePriest Shepard.

Terry and Ethel attended the Perry County schools, and he later went to Freed Hardeman College.

They moved to Waverly, Tennessee in 1965. Terry's employment is with DuPont Company at New Johnsonville, and Ethel is librarian at the Humphreys County Public Library.

Terry, Joe, Virginia and Rodney Carmical. Christmas 1987.

They have two children, Christopher Todd and Gina Kathleen. Christopher was born April 29, 1966, in Waverly, Tennessee. His wife is Terri Denis Reeves, daughter of J.T. and Patricia Reeves. They have one son, Justin Todd Carmical, born March 7, 1991. Chris is employed at DuPont.

Gina was born Aug. 22, 1969. She married Mark Wanamaker, son of Floyd and Carolyn Wanamaker. They have one son, Marcus Hunter Wanamaker, born June 9, 1991.

Terry has one brother, Joseph Rodney Carmical, who lives in Nashville, Tennessee. Ethel has two brothers, Jesse Lloyd and Howard McCoy, who live in Perry County.

Terry, Ethel, their children and grandchildren presently reside in Humphreys County, Tennessee. They are members of the Church of Christ.

Joseph Rodney Carmical was born Aug. 17, 1946, in Oak Ridge, Tennessee. He is the son of Joseph Byrd Carmical and Virginia Janice Shepard Carmical of Perry County. His paternal grandparents were Robert Walter Carmical and Nina Dolores Mathis Carmical. Maternal grandparents were William Haygood Shepard and Byron Mae DePriest Shepard.

On Dec. 22, 1968, Rodney married Barbara Ann Morrison. She was born June 14, 1945, the daughter of Fred Alford Morrison and Lucille Campbell Morrison, also of Perry County.

Rodney and Barbara have one child, Kelli Jo Carmical, born Feb. 1, 1972, in Nashville, Tennessee.

Rodney graduated from Austin Peay University in 1968. He is presently Executive Director of the University of Tennessee, County Technical Services Association, Nashville, Tennessee.

Barbara has a degree in nursing, and is employed at Dickson, Tennessee. Rodney, Barbara, and Kelli Jo live in Lobelville. Kelli will graduate in May 1994, with a degree in Medical Records. She is engaged to Dirk Beasley of Linden. They plan a wedding June 11, 1994.

JOSEPH BYRD CARMICAL, was born May 11, 1914, in Norman, Oklahoma. He was the son of Robert Walker Carmical and Nina Delores Mathis Carmical.

On Jan. 5, 1943, in Rossville, Georgia, Joseph married Virginia Janice Shepard. She was born June 28, 1924, in Perry County, Tennessee, the daughter of William Haywood Shepard and Byron Mae DePriest Shepard.

Joseph was a retiree from the Tennessee Gas Company at Lobelville, and Virginia is a retired employee of the United States Postal Service there. Joseph is also a veteran of Word War II.

This family has many close ties with Lobelville and Perry County, where they have been active in community affairs, and are members of the Lobelville Church of Christ.

Children born to Joseph and Virginia are Jimmy Terry and Joseph Rodney Carmical. Jimmy Terry was born Feb. 26, 1944, in Perry County, and Joseph Rodney was born Aug. 17, 1946, at Oak Ridge, Tennessee.

Jimmy Terry married Ethel May McCoy of Perry County, daughter of James McCoy and Betty Sue Goodman McCoy.

Rodney married Barbara Ann Morrison of Perry County, daughter of Fred and Lucille Campbell Morrison.

Joseph Byrd Carmical died March 23, 1994, in Goodlark Hospital, Dickson, Tennessee. He is buried in Richlawn Cemetery, Waverly, Tennessee. *Submitted by Virginia Shepard Carmical.*

WILLIAM EDWARD "EDD" CARROLL, born Jan. 5, 1897, in Perry County, Tennessee, died Aug. 17, 1965. He was the son of William T. "Will" and Parlee (Qualls) Carroll.

He married Gladys Thelma Horner, Aug. 4, 1918, in Perry County, Tennessee. Gladys was born Feb. 24, 1902, in Hickman County, Tennessee, died Oct. 23, 1982. She was the daughter of Joseph "Joe" Pleas and Elizabeth A. (Robertson) Horner.

They had four children: Eula Mae Carroll, born June 22, 1919, Perry County, Tennessee, died Dec. 14, 1982. She married Roy Garner Belsha, Nov. 20, 1939. Roy was born March 18, 1920. He was the son of William Newt and Sallie Elizabeth (Garner) Belsha. They had two daughters: Mary Frank Belsha, born Oct. 6, 1940, and Dorothy Mae Belsha, born Jan. 10, 1943;

Edward Hubert Carroll, born Aug. 12, 1921, Perry County, Tennessee, married, June 29, 1951, to Martha Mae Pevahouse. She was born Nov. 21, 1931, the daughter of Lee Roy and Margaret Izore (Bryson) Pevahouse. They have one son, John Hue Carroll, born Jan. 5, 1971. Hubert served in the U.S. Army, from Nov. 2, 1942 - Nov. 9, 1945;

Lee Elizabeth Carroll, born Aug. 4, 1925, Perry County, Tennessee, died Jan. 28, 1993, married Feb. 17, 1947, to Winfred Hickerson Jr. Jr. was born July 18, 1926, the son of Winfred Sr. and Rebecca Emaline (Mercer) Hickerson. They had two sons, Thomas "Tommy" Wayne Hickerson, June 26, 1948, and Edward "Eddie" Lee Hickerson, Nov. 19, 1949;

William Earl Carroll, born July 5, 1932, in Perry County, Tennessee, married May 8, 1953, to Betty June Grinder. She was born July 2, 1934, the daughter of Abb Warren and Alma Lillian (Ward) Grinder. They had two children, Danny Earl Carroll, June 19, 1954, and Deana Ann Carroll, June 21, 1962.

WILLIAM (WILL) T. CARROLL, born Jan. 6, 1866, died Dec. 21, 1929 in Perry County, Tennessee. His parents were William E. and Margaret M. (Dickey) Carroll. He grew up in Lawrence County, Tennessee on a farm. He came to Perry County to work at a sawmill on Coon Creek.

He married Parlee Qualls, May 20, 1894, in Perry County. Parlee was born in 1874, died Jan. 24, 1930 in Perry County. She was the daughter of Hubbard and Poppy (Dowdy) Qualls.

They had eight children: (1) George Hubbard Carroll, Sept. 22, 1895-Jan. 19, 1969. He married Osie Ola Walker, Dec. 19, 1920, in Perry County. Osie was born Sept. 1, 1904 in Wayne County, Tennessee, died Aug. 14, 1987. She was the daughter of Jessie James and Flora Ellen (Coffman) Walker. They had eight children, James Wilton, March 22, 1922, Ralph Don, July 12, 1927, Charles Leamon, Dec. 30, 1929, Bonnie Ruth, Aug. 21, 1933, Ollie Willard, May 22, 1936, Betty Mae, Jan. 20, 1939, twin, Billy Ray, Jan. 20, 1939, twin, Jack Denbey, Nov. 10, 1941.

(2) William Edward (Edd) Carroll, Jan. 5, 1897-Aug. 17, 1965. Married Gladys Thelma Horner, Aug. 4, 1918 in Perry County. They had four children, Eula Mae, June 22, 1919, Edward Hubert, Aug. 12, 1921, Lee Elizabeth, Aug. 4, 1925, and William Earl, July 5, 1932.

(3) Marshall Ross, Aug. 11, 1902-Nov. 9, 1970, married Loraine Hickerson, Feb. 19, 1921 in Perry County. Lorene was born Feb. 11, 1908, died Jan. 2, 1981. She was the daughter of John Mac and Sophia Ann (Bulla) Hickerson. They had six children, Thelma Dean, Oct. 21, 1924, Eunice Duey, Oct. 15, 1927, Cletus Kyle, May 30, 1930, Eva Faye, June 11, 1935, Edward Eugene, July 10, 1941, Peggy Ann, Oct. 8, 1950.

(4) Charlie Franklin Carroll, born April 1904, died June 17, 1968, married Gussie Mae Turner on Sept. 16, 1928. Gussie was born April 17, 1904, died June 17, 1968. Frank and Gussie died the same day at Perry Memorial Hospital, Linden, Tennessee. She was the daughter of John and Sally Mary (MaGee) Turner. They had six children, daughter, Carroll, born and died, Sept. 29, 1929, J.W. Carroll, March 20, 1931, Clovis Franklin, May 31, 1933, Paul DeWayne, Dec. 24, 1935, James Kyle, Sept. 28, 1939, and Charlie Faye, Nov. 16, 1945.

(5) Poppy Gussie Bessie Mae Carroll, June 6, 1906-Nov. 23, 1976, married Edward Gregory Jr. "Dollie", Dec. 1935. Edward was born March 22, 1913, died Jan. 3, 1986. He was the son of William Edward and Stella Mae (Voss) Gregory. They had two children, Ralph Gregory, born Sept. 16, 1939 and Martha Carolyn, born April 1, 1941.

(6) Green Black Newton Carroll, born Aug. 10, 1907, died Sept. 13, 1987, married Vennie Ila Hickerson in Perry County, Oct. 6, 1935. Vennie Ila was born Nov. 13, 1914, daughter of Jake and Martha Jane (Pevahouse) Hickerson. They had two children, Nella Jean, Oct. 31, 1936, and Sarah Dean, Jan. 24, 1940.

(7) Cas Samuel Carroll, born Oct. 6, 1909, died June 26, 1986, married Mary Lillian Grooms, Oct. 18, 1933. Mary Lillian was born May 28, 1920, died Jan. 1, 1938, daughter of Grady and Loua (Hensley) Grooms. They had one daughter, Mary Sue Carroll, April 14, 1935.

(8) Jessie Ruby Lucile Carroll, born July 6, 1912, married Lonnie Allen Pevahouse, Dec. 24, 1932 in Perry County, Tennessee. Son of Eliga and Margaret (Williams) Pevahouse. They had two children, Freda Mae, Dec. 24, 1935, and James Allen, May 29, 1943.

ROBERT CATES, of Person County North Carolina, in 1816, willed his granddaughter, Elizabeth Cates, daughter of John Cates, deceased, a one-fourth interest in one hundred acres of land located in Person County, North Carolina.

Descendants of John Cates

In 1991, while doing research, Hazel Craig of Benton County, Tennessee, ran across a deed recorded in Perry County, Tennessee in 1853, showing Elizabeth Cragg (granddaughter of Robert Cates of Person County, North Carolina, her maiden name having been Cates) conveying all her right, title, claim and interest in and to a certain tract of land being in the State of North Carolina, Person County, it being one-fourth of one hundred acres willed to his daughter Bashebia Cates. Should Bashebia Cates die without children, then one-fourth of the hundred acres was to go to Elizabeth Cates, one-fourth to her brother, Ransom Cates, (children of John Cates, deceased) and one-half to Robert's son, Robert Cates.

This deed of 1853, in Perry County, Tennessee, was made to John Watkins of Maury County, Tennessee. There had been Craigs and Cates marrying Watkins in North Carolina. It is supposed John Watkins was a relative who purchased her land in North Carolina after she buried her husband, Richard William Cragg/Craig, in Perry County, Tennessee, in 1850, keeping it in the family. A sister-in-law, Elizabeth Craig, married Claibourne Watkins in Washington County, Virginia, on May 15, 1794.

Elizabeth Cates married Charles Wilson in Person County, North Carolina, April 1817, and had several children. They, along with several other families and relatives, Ransom Cates family, moved to Williamson County, Tennessee in 1814. Charles Wilson died leaving five known children. Elizabeth (Cates) Cragg/Craig married Richard Cragg and moved to Hickman County where they lived several years. Maury County deed book shows Richard purchasing 311 acres from P.S. Williamson, dated 1818.

Richard Cragg sells to Elijah Cragg, deed book M, p. 54, 60 acres for $400.00. Military line, 61 poles east of Richard Cragg's southwest corner and Enoch Galloway's northeast corner. Witness: John Jameson, M.J. Galloway and Thomas Taylor.

Richard Cragg sells to Enoch Galloway, 217 acres, deed book K, p. 3.

Richard Cragg sells to E.M. Campbell, brother to Robert Jr., 132 acres, deed book P, p. 72, dated Oct. 6, 1830, proved Dec. 1830, by Richard Cragg. Sold for $1,012.00, W. side of Little Carter's Creek, military line. Elijah Craig's northeast corner. Witness: M.C. Campbell and Thomas Mahon. From land sales, it appears Richard Cragg and Elizabeth (Cates) Cragg were getting ready to leave Maury Hickman territory in 1830.

Richard and some of his family went to Perry County where he died. So, Hickman and Perry are intertwined here. In Hickman County Court records, there shows a William B. Cragg who is a witness to various deeds in the 1825 era on Beaverdam Creek. That was probably the William B. Cragg in Perry County, Tennessee, 1847-1849, who is a commissioner in the town of Milton, whose name was later changed to Linden, Tennessee.

Richard Cragg died in Perry County and died within the perimeters of the 1850 Mortality census. It said Richard Cragg died, June 1850 of gravel (which is something to do with the kidneys) at age 78, born in North Carolina, was a farmer.

Elizabeth (Cates) Cragg/Craig continued on Perry County census records for 1860 and 1870. Date of death unknown. Composed by Ann Burton, Craig Links of Michigan. Submitted by Hazel W. Craig.

TYRE CHANDLER, son of Benjamin Chandler and Loucinda Anderson, was born Sept. 20, 1834, at Sulphur Fork in Hickman County, Tennessee. He was the grandson of William Chandler Sr. and Mary "Polly" Bates and the great grandson of James Bates and Elizabeth Tubb.

Tyre Chandler was married April 13, 1854, to Rosanah Harper, born Aug. 27, 1827, in Hickman County, Tennessee, to Wiley V. Harper and Sarah Green.

Four children were born to this union: Martha Emmaline, born Jan. 23, 1855, died June 23, 1940, married to Dillard Hunt Bates; John Whitmore, born Dec. 27, 1856, died March 13, 1922, married to Mary A. Rushton; Loucinda Margaret, born Aug. 16, 1859, died Feb. 20, 1936, married first to a Walters and second to Liberty H. Dudley; and William Banteau, born Dec. 29, 1861, died Feb. 26, 1926, married first to S. Mattie Gilmer and second to Emma Katherine Owens.

Rosanah Harper Chandler, died Jan. 5, 1862, of childbirth complications. Around that time, Tyre Chandler enlisted in Company K, 42nd Tennessee. Regiment of the CSA. Tyre Chandler returned to Sulphur Fork before the end of the Civil War. It has been said that he escaped the Union troops by swimming the Tennessee River.

Tyre Chandler had at least four brothers to die in the Civil War. They were: Joel M., John, Isaac N., and James C. Chandler. It was their patriotic mother, Loucinda, who said that she only wished she had more sons to give to the cause.

All of the children of Rosanah and Tyre Chandler were born in Perry County. Rosanah is believed to be buried at Dudley Cemetery.

Tyre Chandler remarried on Aug. 3, 1864, to Eleanor Jane Pinkerton, daughter of Hugh Pinkerton and Jane Cooper. They were the parents of five children: Mary Jane, 1865-1948; Doctor Samuel, 1867-1944; Sarah Elizabeth, 1869-1926; David Thomas, 1871-1899; and Stephen Lafayette, 1876-1938. All of the children of this second family were born and reared in Dickson County, Tennessee.

Tyre Chandler died July 12, 1881, in Dickson County, Tennessee. He was buried at Fowlke's Cemetery. Submitted by Betty Horner Lala.

CLOVIS GILLHAM CHAPPELL, was born in Perry County, Tennessee, Flatwoods Community, Jan. 8, 1877. He was the youngest son of William B. and Mary C. Chappell. W.B. (known as Squire Chappell) and Mollie Chappell had six children and were owners of a large farm near the Buffalo River.

Clovis married Cecil Hart from Waverly, Tennessee, on April 15, 1908. They had two children, Clovis Gillham and Bob Hart.

Clovis attended Webb School at Bell Buckle, Tennessee, Duke University, and Harvard. He had highly successful pastorates in Washington, D.C., Birmingham, Memphis, Dallas, Houston, Oklahoma City, Jackson, Mississippi, and Charlotte, North Carolina. He retired from active pastoral work in 1949, after serving 41 years in the pulpit. He was the author of more that thirty books and continued to preach until the last year of his life. Dr. Clovis G. Chappell died Aug. 18, 1972, at the age of 95. Soon after his death, Flatwoods Methodist Church at Flatwoods, Tennessee, was named Chappell Memorial United Methodist Church, in his honor. His nephew, Wallace Davis Chappell continues the honorable tradition of ministry work at this time.

JOHN CHILDRESS, born 1839, a private, Co. K, 42nd Tennessee. Reg., C.S.A., married Cynthia Tucker, born 1838. John was possibly a descendant of Jesse Childress, early settler on Cedar Creek.

John and Cynthia became the parents of Andrew (1862-1929), married Emily Jane Shelton (1862-1900); Crockett (1865-1947), married Mary Jane Flippo (1871-1908); Asberry (Berry) (1870-1917), married first to Martha Jane Huffstedder (1873-1898), second to Sallie Morgan (1888-1965); Grange, married Maggie Featherston; Amos (Doc) (1877-1953), married first to Sula Milliken, second to Lida Bell Turner (1890-1966); and two sons who died in infancy.

John and Cynthia Tucker Childress

About 1893, John and Cynthia moved from Perry County to Gibson County, Tennessee. John died in the late 1890s and Cynthia in the early 1900s. They are buried in the Olive Branch United Methodist Church Cemetery.

Children of Crockett, second child of John and Cynthia, and Mary Jane Flippo, daughter of Hezikiah and Nellie Newbern Flippo, were: Carrie (1891-1982), married Fred Culp (1885-1954); Clara (Jack) (1892-1968), married Will Wheat; Sally (1895-1898); Earnest (1901-1959), married first to Alma Strong, and second to Daisy Harris; and Jessie Paul (1906-1936), married Velma Taylor.

Crockett and Mary Jane are buried in Mayfield Cemetery, Gibson County.

The five children of Carrie, the oldest child of Crockett and Mary Jane, and Fred Culp, of Wayne County, Tennessee, are: Mary Estelle (1912), married Joe W. Barker. Children: Alfred Marion (1938) and Joe Maurice (1940); Osborne, born and died 1915; Ben, born and died 1917; Geneva Aileen (1919), married first to Frank M. Ragan. Children: Jack Culp (1941) and Mary Elizabeth (1943), married second to Ralph King; and Frederick Malcolm (1927).

Fred, Carrie, and Estelle moved to Gibson County, Tennessee from Wayne County, Tennessee in 1918, residing near Frog Jump, where Aileen was born. December 1920, the family moved to the Edison Community where Frederick M. was born. The Culps owned and operated a general store at this location until 1949. Fred and Carrie are buried in the Oak Grove United Methodist Church Cemetery, in the Edison Community. *Submitted by Frederick M. Culp.*

CLIFTON-CROSSNO, Jesse Brown Clifton and Mary Frances Crossno were married in Corinth, Mississippi, on Dec. 24, 1954. They now reside in Linden, Tennessee. They have two daughters, Demetra and Coretta. They also have one adopted son, Nathan Scott. They have two granddaughters, Veronica Irene Smith and Rachel Nicole Beasley. Demetra was born Oct. 11, 1955. Coretta was born Nov. 16, 1962. Scott was born April 3, 1973. Veronica was born Sept. 20, 1978. Rachel was born Sept. 2, 1988.

Mary and Jesse Clifton

Jesse was born Feb. 11, 1931, in Linden, Tennessee, to the late James and Ann (LaRue) Clifton. He is grandson to the late Richard and Rose Ann (Haper) LaRue, and the late Ira and Mary Jane Clifton, all of Linden, Tennessee. Both of Jesse's great-great grandfathers fought in the Civil War. Jesse had 11 brothers and sisters, which are all deceased, except Lue Dean (Clifton) Broadway, of Linden, Tennessee, and Toby Clifton, of Camden, Tennessee. Jesse also had 10 half brothers and sisters, which are all deceased except Addie (Clifton) LaRue of Linden, Tennessee.

After the death of his parents in the mid 30s, he lived with his sister, Lue Dean and Gus Johnson Broadway until he went to serve in the United States Army from 1949 to 1952. He was honorably discharged. He then went to Camden, Tennessee to live with his sister and brother-in-law, Lue Dean and Gus Broadway, to finish his senior year of high school at Camden Central High. There, he met, and married Mary Frances Crossno. Jesse and Mary lived in Camden while he taught school and attended/graduated from Bethel College in 1960. He taught until his retirement in 1992.

Demetra and John La Roe were married Jan. 30, 1991; they live in Texas. Coretta and Michael (Mike) were married Sept. 12, 1981, and they have one daughter, Rachel Nicole Beasley. They live in Camden. Scott works in Bruston; he also lives in Camden and Linden. Veronica lives in Linden with Jesse and Mary.

Mary, born April 4, 1935, to the late Lemuel Crossno and to Lounett (Bain) Crossno. Lounett has lived in Camden since Lemuel's death in 1954. Mary is the granddaughter of the late Henery and Cora (Stepp) Crossno. Also the late Benjamin (Ben) and Anna (Williams) Bain, all of Camden. Mary has two sisters, Genola M. Jones and Loretta N. Powers, who live in Camden. The family attends the First United Pentecostal Church of Camden.

TOBE CLIFTON FAMILY, James and Cynthia Garner Clifton married in Lawrence County, Tennessee in 1826. They had ten children, one named Ira, born about 1844. When the Civil War reached Tennessee, Ira enlisted as a Private, K Co. 8th Cavalry and served in the Union Army. After the war, he married Mary Jane LaRue in 1868. They had one child, James Madison (Tobe) Clifton, born in 1871.

Back row: Addie, Jim, Bessie. Front row: James Madison (Tobe), Arthur Lee and Tobe's second wife, Ann Katherine

Tobe married Nancy Hensley in Lewis County, Tennessee in 1888. They moved to Perry County, Tennessee before 1899. Tobe was a horse trader and a farmer, who owned a farm on Cypress Creek. Their children were: Coleman, Ethel, Lizzie, Bessie, Vestle, Addie, Jim, Ernest, and Arthur Lee. Nancy died in 1912, and Tobe married Ann Catherine LaRue, daughter of Dick and Rose Anna Harper LaRue. Their children were: Loudean, Luther, Johnny, Eula (Susie), Ida

Mae, Ila, Jesse and Toby. Tobe died in 1932, leaving Ann with a big family to raise. As a single parent, it was a struggle to feed and clothe the eight children. Ann died in 1941, leaving young children to be raised by older siblings.

Tobe had seven sons who served in three wars. Vestle and Coleman served in World War I. Arthur Lee, Johnny and Luther served in World War II. Jesse and Toby served during the Korean War. Johnny spent twenty-eight months in a German Prison Camp. Luther was a surgical technician who was wounded in action and received the purple heart, oak leaf cluster and silver star. Jesse served in Germany and Toby served on the Korean Front for 17 months, receiving the bronze star and silver star for bravery.

Coleman and Ethel Butler Clifton lived in Paducah, Kentucky before they retired in Michigan. Vestle died at the age of 23, while in the service. Jim married Mary LaRue. After her death, he married Mary Jane Plunkett. Arthur Lee married Jettie Ward and called Perry County home. Johnny married Eileen Shea of Massachusetts; they divorced and he married Cleonius Clifton.

Ernest (1906-1991) was an auto mechanic who worked for Morg Condors many years before opening his own garage, Clifton's Garage on Cypress Creek. Ernest loved cycling on his motorcycles and continued to ride until he was 75 years old. Ernest and Myrtle Broadway Clifton lived on Cypress Creek where Jesse and Frances Crossno Clifton now live.

Only two of Tobe's eight daughters learned to drive and got their driver's license, Mrs. L.B. (Ida) Green, at age 50, and Mrs. Guss (Loudean) Broadway, at age 62. Two of Tobe's daughters moved to West Tennessee; Mrs. Wiley (Ethel) Kimble and Mrs. Jim (Bessie) Byrd. Three of the daughters lived on Cypress Creek; Mrs. Clifford (Lizzie) Starbuck, Mrs. Harold (Susie) Weems, and Ila Clifton.

Of Tobe's four surviving children, three live in Perry County: Addie LaRue, Loudean Broadway, and Jesse Clifton. Toby Clifton lives in Camden, Tennessee, but visits Perry County often. Many of Tobe's grandchildren live in Perry County. Only three have the Clifton name: Jim and Mary's son George and Barry and Gary, sons of Arthur Lee and Jettie Clifton.

COBLE, The name "Coble" originates from the German word "Kobel" of Southwest Germany and Central Switzerland. The early family history has been recorded by John L. Coble Jr. in *Cobles of North Carolina*. A brief synopsis was submitted to *History of Hickman County, Tennessee (1993),* by Anne Taylor Powell, from which the early Coble data was taken for this article.

During the early 1800s, Adam Coble and William Henry Coble migrated to Tennessee with Peter and John Coble. Peter and John are believed to have been half brothers of Adam and William Henry.

Adam Coble, the eldest, erected a pottery near the present-day Coble in Hickman County, in 1823. The pottery produced jars, crocks, churns, jugs, and lamps that were distributed locally and in surrounding counties.

The pottery flourished until 1861 when operations were suspended and Adam Coble joined the Confederate Army. A Tennessee State Historical marker marks the site of the pottery.

Adam Coble married Mary "Polly" Chessor, the daughter of James William (1783-1879) Chessor and his wife, Bessie Cavender. Polly Chessor's father was a soldier in the War of 1812, and fought with Andrew Jackson in the Battle of New Orleans.

Adam Coble and Polly Chessor were the parents of seven children: George C. Coble, Wm. H. Coble, Mary Ellen Coble (Brown), David C. Coble, Jesse Coble, Mary Anne Coble (Rumsey), and Samuel P. Coble.

Adam Coble (1787-1878) is buried in the Chessor Cemetery, Coble, Tennessee.

COBLE-ESTES, James Darrell Coble was born May 17, 1933, in Depriest Bend, Tennessee, the son of William Robert and Obera Howell Coble. He attended Beardstown Elementary School and graduated from Lobelville High School in 1951. He served in the U.S. Army from 1953 to 1955.

On April 3, 1954, James married Sarah Patricia Estes, the youngest daughter of Frank and Lillian Potter Estes.

After his army years, James and Patsy moved to Clarksville, Tennessee, where he graduated from Austin Peay State College in 1957.

In 1960, the young couple moved to Florence, Alabama and James worked as a boilermaker with TVA until he started Coble's Ornamental Iron, Inc. in 1962.

James and Patsy are the parents of four children:

James Ronald Coble, born March 27, 1956, is a graduate of University of North Alabama. He is a CPA, employed with the National Chamber of Commerce.

Rosemary Coble, born Sept. 8, 1958, is a graduate of Belmont College. She married first to Jim Cummings, then to Thomas Estes. She lives in Hendersonville, Tennessee, and is employed by W.F. Corroon Corp. Nashville. Her four children are Caron Cummings, Christopher, Cathryn, and Cody Estes.

John Phillip Coble, born Feb. 17, 1966, is a graduate of University of Alabama, Tuscaloosa, and will graduate from Cumberland School of Law, Samford University in the Spring of 1994.

Robert Franklin Coble, born Oct. 21, 1970, married Marjorie Burnett on April 11, 1988. They have two sons, Darrell Wayne Coble and Robert Brock Coble. Robert joined his parents in the family business.

COBLE-HOWELL, William Robert Coble was born Jan. 17, 1896, in Coble, Tennessee, the son of Adam and Magnolia Burch Coble. He attended the public schools in Lobelville, Tennessee.

He married Manie Obera Howell, born in Perry County, Tennessee, July 25, 1898, the daughter of George Washington and Lora Josephine Madden Howell.

The Cobles were merchants with stores in Depriest Bend and Lobelville. During the depression years, they ran peddler's trucks (rolling stores that traveled to rural areas selling groceries and domestic items). Obera Coble operated a restaurant in Lobelville.

In 1940, Mr. Coble began work as a boilermaker with TVA, an occupation that he continued until his retirement in 1961.

Robert and Obera Howell Coble

The Cobles were the parents of four children: Edith Marie, born June 30, 1919, married Hoover Wilson Kennedy; Raymond Howell, born June 10, 1921, died Oct. 21, 1961, married Sara Sue Rogers; William Robert Jr., married Carlene Cogdill; James Darrell, born May 17, 1933, married Sarah Patricia Estes.

Mr. Coble died May 23, 1966. Mrs. Coble died May 15, 1965. They are buried in Leeper Cemetery, Lobelville, Tennessee.

ADAM COBLE, the son of Jesse and Margaret Chandler Coble, and the grandson of Adam and Polly Chessor Coble, was born Jan. 26, 1867, in Coble, Tennessee. He married first to Magnolia T. Burch, born Feb. 8, 1874, died Feb. 2, 1903, the daughter of James Monroe and Julia Hazeltine Rushton Burch. Their children were: Maude, married Abe Lynch, James "Little Jim" (1892-1895), William Robert Coble (1896-1966), married Manie Obera Howell, and Ora (1899-1935), married Stacker Wright.

Left to Right: Maude, Lucille, Adam (holding Paul), Ada (holding Bertie), Clint and Ora Coble

Second, Adam Coble married Ada Edwards and their children were Clint, died 1955, married Annie Arnold; Lucille, died 1966, married first to Farris, then to Theodore Hudson; Paul; Bertie, married Arthur Lewis; Ray (Pete); Thelma M. Cagle Bates; Roy (Bub); and Ellen, married Carnell Dorton.

Adam was a well-respected merchant in Lobelville for many years. Adam Coble died Sept. 7, 1926, and is buried beside his first wife, Magnolia Burch Coble, in the Chandler Cemetery on Sulphur in Hickman County.

HENRY COBLE, migrated from North Carolina and settled along Brush Creek in the mid 1820s. David Coble also settled on Brush Creek, but his relationship to Henry is not known at this time. Henry's brother, Adam and a half brother, Peter, lived in Hickman County. Adam was famous as a potter. Some feel that John Coble, of Hickman County, was another half brother.

James Laxon and Elizabeth Daniels Coble

Henry married Winnie Laxon (Laxton), daughter of James Laxon, about 1827. They were the parents of five children.

Their first born, James Laxon Coble, was born Sept. 10, 1828. James married Elizabeth Ann Daniel, daughter of Woodson and Mary Daniel. James and Elizabeth were the parents of Elizabeth Ann, John Wiley, Mary Elizabeth, Nancy Jane, Texanaha, William Henry, Sara Camile, George Thomas, James Otto, Lilly Lee, Andrew Jackson, and Edwin Woodson. James Laxon Coble owned and operated a mercantile store in Sugar Tree, Tennessee. His sons, Wiley and William Henry "Bill", worked with him in the store. He was ordained a deacon in the Morgan Creek Baptist Church. From 1889 until his death on Oct. 9, 1902, he was a member of the Flatwoods Baptist Church. Elizabeth Ann died March 10, 1920. Both are buried in Manley's Chapel Cemetery near Sugar Tree.

Second son, George Washington Coble, was born Feb. 27, 1832. He married, orphan, Mary Ann Lloyd (Loyd), Oct. 22, 1852. George and Mary Ann were the parents of Melissa Ann, William Henry, James Perry, Mary Jane, Nancy E., Bettie O., Winnie Hiburnie, and Ida J. Coble. George died in 1908.

Henry and Winnie's only daughter, Elizabeth Ann, was born Sept. 27, 1836. She married William J. Ridings (Ridens), who was the son of Absolum and Sarah. William and "Betsy" were the parents of George H., James W., Viola, John H., William F., Emonia J., and Elizabeth Ridings. Elizabeth Coble Ridings died Oct. 10, 1880, and is buried in Humphreys County.

Son, John R. Coble, born 1838, served in the Confederate Army with the 53rd Tennessee Regiment. He died during the war without issue.

The youngest child in this family was born March 3, 1839, and was named William Henry Coble. He married Sarah Ann Denson. William and Sarah were the parents of John, James Cass, Nellie Jones, Mollie, Fannie, Jennie, George R., Hattie, and Jesse. William died in 1914, and is buried in Denson Cemetery in Perry County.

Henry Coble died between 1847 and 1849. It is thought that he is buried in Hickman County, but his grave has not been located. Winnie married widower, Slathiel Haney, by 1850. Slathiel was a constable and farmer. They were the parents of one son, Thomas Jefferson Haney, born in 1852. It is probable that Slathiel preceded Winnie in death, as Thomas Haney was appointed administrator of his mother's estate in 1879. The location of the graves and the exact death dates of Slathiel and Winnie are not known. *Submitted by Connie Copeland Young, Irving, Texas, great-great granddaughter of James Laxon Coble.*

JAMES JOHN WILLIAM COBLE,

(March 12, 1893-July 5, 1957) was born on Russels Creek near Lobelville, Tennessee. He was the great grandson of Peter Coble (Oct. 20, 1802-Sept. 21, 1860), who migrated to Tennessee from Buncombe County, North Carolina in 1810. Peter, along with three brothers, Adam, William Henry, and John, settled at the mouth of Hurricane Branch in Hickman County, Tennessee.

James John William Coble and wife, Altha E. Autry Coble

Peter Coble married Jemima (Gemina) Brown, (Feb. 20, 1806-Oct. 14, 1856) on March 22, 1822, in Hickman County, Tennessee. They had twelve children. Their son, Samuel Henry Hartwell Coble, was born in 1850 in Williamson County, Illinois where the family had migrated. Their stay in Illinois was short lived for they soon returned to Tennessee.

Samuel Henry Hartwell Coble (1850) and Mary Gunter (1855) married in Hickman County, Tennessee on Aug. 13, 1868. They had four children, one of whom was William Francis Coble (June 5, 1869-Dec. 16, 1908).

William Francis Coble married Sarah Louise Martha "Izora" Anette Gilmer (Jan. 5, 1873-Feb. 19, 1960), on Oct. 16, 1890, in Dyer County, Tennessee. They had a total of eleven children. James John William was their second child. At the time of their marriage, the families of William Francis Coble and Izora Gilmer lived near each other on Russels Creek in Lobelville, Tennessee.

Izora Gilmer Coble was the daughter of James Robert Gilmer (June 30, 1851-Jan. 24, 1928) and Martha Rebecca Flowers Gilmer, born ca 1853. They were married Feb. 19, 1871.

James Robert Gilmer was the son of James Alexander Scott Gilmer (Sept. 9, 1823-May 17, 1906) and Martha Ann Bratton Gilmer (1830-1897). They are both buried in Ledbetter Cemetery located on Lost Creek, three miles from Lobelville, Tennessee.

In the spring of 1899, when James John William Coble was six years old, his family, along with the James Robert Gilmer family, left Lobelville, Tennessee and moved to Newbern, Tennessee, in Dyer County. James John William's family consisted of his father and mother, William Francis and Izora Coble, his brothers, Clifford Cornelius, three, and Elmer, three months.

The James Robert Gilmer family consisted of his second wife, Annie, and their children Arthur, Elbert, Sally, and six month old, Bessie; and the children of James Robert Gilmer and his first wife, Martha Rebecca Flowers Gilmer, i.e., James Robert Littlebury Gilmer (Feb. 27, 1872), David Lonzo Gilmer (1880), and Samuel Newton Gilmer (May 21, 1882).

James John William Coble married Altha E. Autry (Aug. 20, 1899-July 27, 1976), on Oct. 25, 1915, in Blytheville, Arkansas. They had eleven children: Vera "Polly" Coble (March 4, 1917), William Edward Coble (Feb. 27, 1919), Melvin Lee "Joe" Coble (Feb. 8, 1921), Russell Lowell Coble (April 4, 1923-May 8, 1923), Dorothy Christine Coble (April 16, 1924), Arvelle Coble (June 5, 1927-June 30, 1928), Gerald Glen Coble (June 17, 1929-Feb. 13, 1988), Roy Reynolds Coble (Nov. 17, 1931), Elvis Ray Coble (May 14, 1933), Arvis Jannine Coble (Dec. 25, 1936), and Autry Lucille Coble (Sept. 25, 1940). *Submitted by Jannine Coble Gregory and Elvis Ray Coble.*

JESSE COBLE, was born June 2, 1837, in Hickman County, Tennessee, the son of Adam and Polly Chessor Coble. He married Margaret Chandler, who was born Jan. 29, 1837. Their children were: Adam Coble, Jan. 26, 1867-Sept. 7, 1926, married first Magnolia T. Burch, then Ada Edwards; George; Ben; Liz; and Livvie;

Jesse Coble died March 14, 1917. Margaret died July 24, 1903. They are buried in the Chandler Cemetery on Sulphur in Hickman County.

WILLIAM HENRY COBLE, According to the Coble Family research, the William Henry Coble Family began with Albrecht Kobel's birth in Wenger, Switzerland, in 1385. He located in Ulm, Germany. His son, Bartholomaus, born 1415, married. Their son, Hans, born 1436, married Margaretha. They had Michael in 1460, married, wife unknown. They had Leonard, born 1510, married Anna Reyschleg. Their son, Claus, born 1540, married Magdalena. They had Nicholas in 1575, married Brigitta Braun in 1602. A son, Johann Georg, born 1604, married Sybilla Schweickner in 1627. Nicholas, born 1628, married. One of his children, Johann Georg, born 1655, was married second time to Maria E. Gilbert, born 1657. One of twelve children, Johann Georg, born 1690, married Maria Geisler, came to Pennsylvania, then North Carolina. George Adam Coble, born 1727, married Margaret Loffel. (Note: German spelling of Kobel to English spelling Coble.) Their son, Adam, born 1768 in North Carolina, married Maria. A son, William Henry Coble, born in North Carolina, 1801, died in Tennessee, 1844, married Louise Laxon, born 1810. His siblings were; Adam, born North Carolina, 1799, died, Tennessee, 1885, and one half-brother, Peter Coble, born North Carolina, 1802, died Tennessee, 1860.

Their son, William Henry "Billy" Coble, Homer Long's grandfather, (1839-1914) married Sarah Ann "Sis" Denson, (1845-1919). He was born on Hog Creek, later lived on Roans Creek, served in Co. A, 10 Demoss TN Cavalry, CSA. His trade was farming. His siblings were: James L. (1828-1908), George W. (1832-1908), Elizabeth A., John, born 1838, and one half-brother, Thomas Haney (1851-1920).

William Henry Coble Family. Left to Right: William, Sarah Ann Denson Coble, Hattie Haney Coble and Jess Coble.

"Sis" Denson Coble, born at Denson's Ldg., daughter of William B. "Bill" Denson, born 1823, and Jane C. Bandy Denson, born 1825. Her maternal grandparents were: Dr. Jamison Bandy (1788-1872) and first wife, Elizabeth Wright, married 1822 (stated as such in War of 1812 Pensioners). Dr. Bandy lived in Virginia and Perry County, Tennessee. He served in the War of 1812 as an enlisted man, later as a Lieut. in a Co. of Spies.

Paternal grandparents, James "Jimmie" Denson, born about 1790, wife, thought to be a Ms. Churchwell. James also served in the War of 1812, as a private in a Mil. Inf. Co. He probably started Denson's Ldg., and is said to the first man buried in Denson's Ldg. Cemetery. One set of Sis D. Coble's great grandparents was said to be a Bandy from Liverpool, England and a Comens from Dublin, Ireland.

"Sis" Coble's siblings were: Janie, married Gus Walker; Elizabeth, married William Lancaster, and Nancy "Ett", married George Ridings.

Billy and "Sis" Coble's children: John (1864-1936), married Mollie Warren (1876-1928); Cass, born 1867, married Mattie Daniel, born 1874; Nellie (1870-1941), married Andrew Daniel (1869-1965); Mollie, born 1871, married William French; Fannie, born 1874, married Hugh Shannon; Jennie (1879-1942), married George Dukes (1875-1956); George (1881-1951), married Lillie Edwards, born 1891; Hattie Haney (1884-1967), married Henry Hugh Long (1884-1946); and Jess (1887-1951), married Bertha Curtis.

Hattie and Henry H. Long's children: Mabel (1908-1993), married Homer H. Duncan (1897-1961), had children; Van F. (1928-1991), married Jean Loggins, born 1927. Children: Sherry, Bill, Vangela, Leigh, and Tanya; Martha Gayle, born 1943, married J. Wayne Gilmer, born 1937. Children: Scott Wayne and Shelby Gayle; Homer Long, born 1910, married Theda Aline Edwards, born 1917, one daughter, Linda Ann, born 1943, married Travis Milam, born 1943, one daughter, Melody Lynne; Lexie (1912-1962), married Mary Sam Alexander, born 1918, one daughter, Meda Nell, born 1939, married William B. Falls Jr. (1939-1986), one son, William B. Falls III; Clyde (1917-1982), finished at PCHS, served in US Army twenty-one years; and Elsie, born 1921, finished at PCHS, attended David Lipscomb College. She was the bookkeeper for Baker Construction Company and Baker Building, and retired with thirty-four years of experience.

In conclusion, Homer Long writes that his mother, Hattie Coble Long, was an excellent mother, homemaker, and flower gardener. His father, Henry Hugh Long, was a good provider as a farmer, sawmill operator, and an excellent salesman. Submitted by Homer Long.

BENJAMIN COLEMAN, came from England and located in Hickman County (year and location unknown). Benjamin had a son, Abner Coleman, who married Polly Jane Sparks. Their children are believed to be James Sparks Coleman, Elizabeth Betsy Coleman, who married James Dickson Lewis, and Susan Jane Coleman who married William K. Lewis. Other children are unknown. The Colemans moved to the lower end of Cypress Creek in Perry County, around the 1830s.

The old homestead of William Samuel Coleman.

James Sparks Coleman was born Dec. 1828, died Dec. 1902. He is a veteran of the Civil War. He married Margaret Angeline Stanley in Jan., 1852. She died 1880. His second wife was Ruth (Pingleton) Patterson, married Aug. 3, 1884. She died Aug. 17, 1885. He then married his third wife, Martha (Richardson) Lomax in July, 1897. She died in 1922.

James Sparks Coleman and Margaret Angeline had 10 children: Ann Jane Coleman (1853-1920), married William Sparks Horner. They had seven children; Abner Henry Coleman (1856-1915). Also had seven children; Albert Banana Coleman (1859-?), married Martha Hunt. They moved from Tennessee to Colorado with the Mormons. They never returned to Tennessee. They had two children, Albert Jr. and Mildred. After Martha died, he married Arena Brady and had one daughter, Ethel. She and her husband, Heber Boice visited her Coleman relatives in 1948 and 1954. Ethel and Heber, Mormons, lived in California; James Patrick Coleman (1863-1884); William Samuel Coleman (March 27, 1865-Jan. 1, 1950); Joseph A. Harrison Coleman (1867-1950), married Vinnie Horner. Children were Richard Coleman and Leatha Ella (Coleman) Hicks; Margaret Josephine Coleman (1870-1949), married James (Jim) Cooper. They had one daughter, Bertha (Cooper) Shepard; Benjamin Franklin Coleman (1872-1956), married Ida Churchwell. Six children: Albert, Eva, Egbert, Reuben, Elvie, and Ora; Edger Oscar Coleman (1875-1943), married Susan H. (Susie) Lewis. Three sons: Herbert, Grady and Edward; Betsy (Bettie) Philicia Coleman (1877-1948), married Neal Horner in 1894. One daughter, Leland (Horner) Warner.

James Sparks Coleman and family moved from Cypress Creek to Little Spring Creek in a very small house just above the spring where they later moved the old log house from the Hunt Hill, that sat near the Hunt Cemetery. The house is believed to be over one hundred years old. The Hunt Cemetery still remains in the Coleman heirs names.

William Samuel (Will) married Sallie Nannie Lomax, April 13, 1902. Will lived in the old house and raised seven children. He farmed and worked in timber. As a young man, he ran 21 rafts of logs, down the Tennessee River from Mousetail to Paducah, Kentucky. He died at the age of 84, Jan. 1, 1950. His wife lived at the old Coleman place until she died Oct. 13, 1973, with daughter Ruth (Coleman) Ward, Ruth's husband, Fred E. Ward, and their daughter, Melinda. The Wards moved to Parsons, Sept., 1974. The old homeplace was sold to Herbert Volner in March, 1976, and has sold to others since then. The old Coleman house burned around 1978.

Will and Sallie's children were: Leon Coleman, born Nov. 1903, married Marie Horner, 1936; Irma, born July 23, 1906, married Enos Churchwell, 1927; Clyce, born Jan. 29, 1909, married Ina Rhodes, 1932; Wilma, born Oct. 3, 1911, married Hobert Moore in 1933. After being widowed, she married Johnny Stephens; William Hershell, born May 21, 1915, married Norma Lee Churchwell, 1944; Mildred, born Nov. 24, 1918, married Reuben Ledbetter, 1941; and Martha Ruth, born June 27, 1924, married Fred Ward, 1948. Submitted by Martha Ruth (Coleman) Ward.

WILLIAM MORGAN CONDER, oldest of four children, was born Feb. 1, 1897, to John "Buck" and Ella Eugena Weems Conder. They owned and operated a huge warehouse (general store) on the Tennessee River. Large boats and barges would enter Mousetail Landing, trading furs, boots, tobacco, lumber, farm implements, and livestock. The general store sold and traded everything from "piece goods" and hard candy to black skillets and mousetraps.

"Morg" Conder was raised near the Tennessee River. Enjoying the life of the river so much, it was befitting that his first job was that of a riverboat pilot.

Morg attended Oakmont Boarding School in Dickson. While there, he developed a keen interest in the game of baseball and played on the high school team. Due to his love of baseball, he formed the Linden Owls Club. With much hard work and help from interested people, the team was organized in 1938, and played until the late fifties. The Linden Owls traveled throughout the area and in neighboring states. The team won three state championships. During these years, Morg's abundant energy was also seen during the annual July 4th picnics. He and others would do the barbecuing with all the trimmings. A Linden Owl doubleheader would be the highlight of the day.

After his marriage to Alma Mae Starbuck, Dec. 12, 1898-Sept. 1, 1943, Morg opened a sawmill in the Pope Community. Within a short time, they moved to Linden and he negotiated a contract with General Motors for the Chevrolet dealership. Conder Chevrolet Company was located on Main Street. For a short while, he was in partnership with Alan Graham. In 1941, Morg constructed a larger building for his dealership; part of the building was leased to Greyhound Lines for use as a bus terminal. He acquired the Pan Am Oil Distributing Company franchise for this area about 1942.

Morg and Mae had three daughters: Lorene, born Nov. 5, 1918; Hazel, born Nov. 10, 1920; and Dimple, born Nov. 7, 1926, Lorene and Hazel live in Linden. Dimple resides in Waynesboro. Two years after the death of Mae, Morg married Eva Owens. A daughter was born, Marla Kay Conder. She lives in Houston, Texas.

Morg was elected Trustee of Perry County for a period of eight years. Mae served and acted as trustee a good portion of the time, due to Morg's involvement in the car dealership and state politics. In 1946, Morg was elected to the State House of Representatives for Perry and Humphries Counties. He co-authored a bill to remove the toll from all bridges in Tennessee. This bill passed on Feb. 4, 1947. Due to Morg's untimely death at the early age of fifty, Feb. 8, 1947, he traveled only once over his toll free bridge, locally referred to as the Tennessee River Bridge. Morg was also serving as Mayor of Linden at the time of his death.

ELIZABETH ANN COOPER AND WILLIAM H. RANDEL,
Elizabeth Ann Cooper was born March 12, 1856, in Tennessee, probably in Perry County on Upper Sinking Creek. She was the daughter of John M. Cooper and Mary Ann Parker. She married William H. Randel on Aug. 28, 1873, in Perry County. William was born May 1, 1854, and was a son of Nacy M. and Mahala Randel.

William H. Randel and Elizabeth Ann Cooper moved with their infant daughter, Lellah E., born May 7, 1875, to Ripley County, Missouri in the mid 1870s and settled in the Buffalo Creek area. Their son, Egbert E., was born there in 1877. The family moved on to Wright County, Missouri, arriving there before 1900. Lellah E. Randel married John Thomas Lutrell, Jan. 3, 1894, in Howell County, Missouri.

The Randels lived at Mountain Grove in Wright County. William H. Randel died March 6, 1922; Elizabeth Ann Cooper Randel died March 21, 1938. Both are buried in Hillcrest Cemetery at Mountain Grove, as are Lellah E. Randel Lutrell (1875-1921), John Thomas Lutrell (1873-1952), and Egbert E. Randel (1877-1961).

Elizabeth Ann Cooper Randel's brothers were Robert Cross Cooper (1852-1934), Jacob Daniel Cooper (1853-1915), John Moses Cooper Jr. (1858-1951), and Thomas Spencer Cooper (1866-1948). *Submitted by Paul E. Cooper.*

JACOB DANIEL COOPER,
(1853-1915) was born in Tennessee, a son of John M. Cooper and Mary Ann Parker. He lived in Perry County until leaving to go to medical school at Vanderbilt in the 1870s. He graduated from there in 1880 and began practicing medicine in Hickman County (Swan Creek area). He lived on Copperas Branch. He first married Alice Jane Sharp, a daughter of Green G. Sharp and Mary Mathis, in 1881. They had three children: Mayhugh Briggs (1883-1968), married Claudia Lee Peery (a daughter of Robert Gilmore Peery and Barbara Ann Smith); Carl (1885-1965), married Nellie Jane Peery (a daughter of Robert Gilmore Peery and Cordovia Ellen George); Esther, married Ernest Beakley. Alice Sharp Cooper died in the late 1880s.

Jacob then married second wife, Armelia McClannahan (1872-1956) in 1894. She was a daughter of W.W. McClannahan and Jennie Beakley. They had two daughters: Bessie Tom, married Spencer Douglass and Kate, married George Washington Wright.

Dr. Cooper moved his family, all his children and grandchildren, except for Esther's family, to Pemiscot County, Missouri in the winter of 1911/12. He had purchased 80 acres in the Douglass/Oak Ridge community. He lived in and practiced medicine in and around Cooter, where his brother Thomas Spencer Cooper was also a Doctor.

Jacob Daniel Cooper died in 1915, and was buried in Mt. Zion Cemetery, north of Cooter. His widow, Armelia, eventually moved back to Tennessee, where she died in 1956. She is buried beside her parents in Campground Cemetery on Swan Creek in Hickman County. *Submitted by Paul E. Cooper.*

JOHN M. COOPER,
was born Feb. 3, 1811, in Virginia. He married Mary Ann Parker about 1851. She was born Aug. 22, 1827, in Tennessee, probably southeastern Dickson County. She was a daughter of Daniel Parker, who was a son of Moses Parker (1773-1852) of Dickson County. The Parkers came to Dickson County from Georgia in the early 1800s and settled on Big Turnbull Creek. Daniel Parker and family were living in northeastern Hickman County in 1850. The whereabouts of John M. Cooper in 1850 are unknown to this writer. He first appears, to this writer, in 1856, when he buys land on Upper Sinking Creek in Perry County. He would eventually own about 800 acres before his death in the mid 1880s. John M. Cooper was a farmer and tanner, and operated a bonded distillery.

John M. Cooper and Mary Ann Parker had five children: Robert Cross (1852-1934), married Sarah Francis Lewis. Moved to Oregon County, Missouri in 1870s and later (after 1900) to Greer County, Oklahoma; Jacob Daniel (1853-1915), married first to Alice Jane Sharp, daughter of Green G. Sharp and Mary Mathis. Practiced medicine in Hickman County (Swan Creek area) for about 30 years and then moved to Pemiscot County, Missouri. Married second to Armelia McClannahan, daughter of William W. McClannahan and Jennie Beakley; Elizabeth Ann (1856-1938), married William H. Randel, son of Nacy M. and Mahala Randel. Moved to Ripley County, Missouri in 1870s and later to Wright County, Missouri; John Moses Jr. (1858-1951), married first to Savilla Angeline Sharp, daughter of John Sharp and Margaret Whitesides. Married second to Mollie Tolle. Moved to Oklahoma Territory and later to New Mexico; Thomas Spencer (1866-1948), married first to Almeda Brooks. Had moved to Pemiscot County, Missouri in 1891. Was a Doctor of Medicine.

When John M. Cooper died in the mid 1880s, he left a widow, Mary Ann Parker and five children: Robert Cross, who lived in Oregon County, Missouri; Jacob Daniel, who was practicing medicine in Hickman County, Tennessee; Elizabeth Ann Randel, who was living in Missouri; John Moses Jr. of Perry County; and Thomas Spencer, who was probably in medical school at Vanderbilt. John M. Cooper owned approximately 800 acres of land on Upper Sinking Creek in Perry County at the time of his death. The land is located between Sharp Cemetery and Ary Cemetery. Through buying out his brothers and sisters, Jacob Daniel Cooper came into possession of the land around 1900. He sold 200 acres to W.W. Whiteside in 1902. At his death in 1915, his children inherited 550 acres, which they sold in 1923. By that time, all of John M. Cooper's descendants had left Perry County. *Submitted by Paul E. Cooper.*

JOHN MOSES COOPER JR.,
was born Jan. 17, 1858, on Upper Sinking Creek in Perry County, Tennessee. He was a son of John M. Cooper and Mary Ann Parker. He married Savilla Angeline Sharp on Dec. 14, 1876, in Perry County. She was a daughter of John Sharp and Margaret Jane Whitesides.

John Moses Cooper Jr. and Savilla Angeline Sharp had at least four children: Thomas S. and Savilla A. who both died young; James Robert (1881-1963), married Ella Narcissis Mayfield; and Sarah Elizabeth (1883-1972), married Samuel M. Tolle. Savilla Angeline Sharp Cooper died in the mid 1880s.

John Moses Cooper Jr.'s second wife was Molly Evangeline Tolle, a daughter of William A. Tolle. They were married about 1885 in Perry County. They had three children: Anna J., Zelma, and Albert Cecil, who was born Dec. 6, 1900.

John Moses Cooper Jr. and his family moved from Tennessee to Grayson County, Texas, in the late 1800s, and then to the Oklahoma Territory about 1899, where Albert Cecil Cooper was born. In 1901, they moved to Cooke County, Texas, where John Moses Cooper Jr.'s wife, Molly, died in 1902. In 1906, the family moved to New Mexico, near Elida. John Moses Cooper Jr. moved to Portales, New Mexico, where he died Nov. 16, 1951.

John Moses Cooper Jr. was a brother of Robert Cross Cooper (1852-1934), Jacob Daniel Cooper (1853-1915), Elizabeth Ann Cooper Randel (1856-1938), and Thomas Spencer Cooper (1866-1948). *Submitted by Paul E. Cooper.*

ROBERT CROSS COOPER,
was born Feb. 4, 1852, in Tennessee, a son of John M. Cooper and Mary Ann Parker. He lived most of his early years on Upper Sinking Creek in Perry County. He married Sarah Francis Lewis, a daughter of John W. and Levona Lewis, Feb. 4, 1872, in Perry County. Robert and his family moved to Oregon County, Missouri about 1875, living in the Thayer area for the next 25 to 30 years. A son, John Hunter Cooper, died there March 28, 1892. After the turn of the century, Robert and his family moved to Greer County, Oklahoma, settling close to Granite. Sarah Francis Lewis Cooper died in 1933; Robert Cross Cooper died May 29, 1934, at Thayer, Missouri. Both are buried in the cemetery at Granite.

Robert Cross Cooper and Sarah Francis

Lewis had at least eight children: Lewis Gentry (1873-1963); John Hunter, died 1892; Alma J.; Jacob W.; Charles F.; Fredrick; Ada (1889-1918); and Preston Robert.

Robert Cross Cooper was a brother of Jacob Daniel Cooper (1853-1915), Elizabeth Ann Cooper Randel (1856-1938), John Moses Cooper Jr. (1858-1951), and Thomas Spencer Cooper (1866-1948). *Submitted by Paul E. Cooper.*

THOMAS SPENCER COOPER, was born Aug. 21, 1866, on Upper Sinking Creek in Perry County, Tennessee. He was the youngest child of John M. Cooper and Mary Ann Parker. He went to Vanderbilt College and graduated in 1891 with a Doctor of Medicine degree. Shortly thereafter, he moved to Pemiscot County, Missouri where he married Almeda Brooks (1874-1899) in 1891. They had two sons, Lawrence Egbert (1893-1973), who became a doctor, and Paul Hugh (1898-1992), who was a pharmacist.

Lawrence E. Cooper married Ethel McCann in 1917. They had a son, Lawrence E. Cooper Jr. (1918-1945), who was also a doctor. He died in World War II.

Paul Hugh Cooper married Vera Coleman in 1922. They had two daughters, Peggy Marie and Almeda Jane.

Thomas Spencer Cooper practiced medicine in the area around Cooter for many years, as did his son Lawrence. Thomas Spencer Cooper died Jan. 13, 1948, and was buried in Mt. Zion Cemetery, north of Cooter, Missouri.

Although an M.D., Thomas Spencer Cooper had many other interests. He was a farmer, owning several hundred acres of excellent farmland around Cooter and Douglass, as did both of his sons. He was the first postmaster at Douglass, and was instrumental in establishing a telephone company in the area.

Thomas Spencer Cooper was a brother to Robert Cross Cooper (1852-1934), Jacob Daniel Cooper (1853-1915), Elizabeth Ann Cooper Randel (1856-1938), and John Moses Cooper Jr. (1858-1951). *Submitted by Paul E. Cooper.*

COTHAM-SMITH, Isacc Jess Cotham and Annie Alice Hufstedler were married Sept. 16, 1900, at Linden, Tennessee. They had eight children: Richard Fane (Dick) and James Henry, twins, born March 28, 1909. James Henry died, May 5, 1909. Richard Fane married Mahala Louise Smith, daughter of Robert Carroll and Ida Elizabeth (Depriest) Smith, July 9, 1933. Richard worked several years with the State Highway Department and some years as a farmer. Mahala worked over thirty years with Washington Manufacturing Company. Richard died June 27, 1988. Richard and Mahala have five children: Joe Carroll, Shirley June, Elizabeth Ann, Richard Fane Jr., and James Larry.

Joe was born Sept. 27, 1934. He married Shelby Jean Bryson, Oct. 2, 1961. They have three children, Randal, Gretta, and Keith Cotham. Randal and Keith still live at home where Joe and Shelby live in Linden. Gretta married Tim Morgan of Michigan, Aug. 22, 1986, where they now live.

Shirley was born Dec. 19, 1936. She married Troy Wesson Kilpatrick, May 7, 1955. They have two children, Mark Wesson, born March 23, 1960, and Paula Elaine, born Nov. 30, 1965. Mark married Dawn Hill, July 9, 1988. They have one son, Ryan Wesson Kilpatrick, born Dec. 18, 1991. They live at Old Hickory, Tennessee. Paula married Rex Miller, May 25, 1991. They live in Hermitage, Tennessee.

Elizabeth Ann, born July 6, 1941, married George Brown King of Pleasantville, Tennessee, Oct. 11, 1961. Elizabeth and Brown live at Old Hickory, Tennessee. They have one daughter, Kimberly Beth King, born June 16, 1964. Kim married Michael Rolman of Huntsville, Alabama. They now live in Madison, Tennessee.

Richard Fane Cotham Jr., born Dec. 16, 1944, married Sue Ann Smothers of Linden, Tennessee, Sept. 18, 1965. Jr. and Sue have one daughter, Michelle, who is a student at the University of Tennessee. Jr. and Sue live in Crofton, Maryland.

James Larry, born Aug. 31, 1948, married Betty J. Hyder, March 23, 1979. They live in Greenbrier, Tennessee.

COTTON FAMILY, The members of the original Cotton family came from Ireland and settled with their families in New Madrid County, Missouri. In 1811, an earthquake came and Reelfoot Lake was formed near the Mississippi River. This caused the land to sink in several places and the families became afraid that more earthquakes would come and decided to leave the area.

The family of Patrick L. Cotton Sr., along with other families, decided to move to Tennessee. Two of the brothers and their families moved to Wisconsin, crossing the Mississippi above St. Louis with their teams and wagons on the ice. Two other brothers stayed on for a while. It was thought one later moved on to Texas and the other to Arkansas. Contact with the families could not be made and they were never sure where they settled. The families who moved to Wisconsin stayed only for a short time. The weather and cold winds were so bad they made their way back to Tennessee where some of their other relatives lived.

The Reverend P.L. Cotton Jr., a Baptist minister was married to Nellie Langster. They had three sons, Pleas, who was killed in the Civil War, Patrick Lionel Jr., and Irvin; and two daughters, Mary Whitwell and Rachel Ledbetter.

The Cotton family settled on Rockhouse Creek in Perry County and were first listed in the 1860 census of Perry County.

The Cotton family, of Rockhouse Creek, was the issue of the marriage of Irvin Robert Cotton to Savannah Parthenia Graves. She was the sixteenth child of eighteen children born to Isaac Lee Graves and Parthenia Ledbetter Graves.

To the marriage of Savannah Graves Cotton and Irvin Robert Cotton were born ten children: Mary Estalee (Dec. 27, 1892); Willie Lee (Nov. 2, 1894); Claudia Martha Jane (April 10, 1896); Whitney Ambrilla (Oct. 8, 1898); Lloyd Bedford (Nov. 19, 1900); Violet May (Aug. 14, 1902); Marvin Eunice (Jan. 29, 1905); Paris Richard (April 19, 1909); Charlotte Irene (Dec. 28, 1911); and Shelby Lee Cotton (Oct. 5, 1914).

ALVIN M. COTTON, March 8, 1862-July 23, 1928, was the son of King Marion Cotton, who was a teacher who served in the Civil War. Alvin married Addie Sharp, March 28, 1869-Oct. 1952. Their four children were:

Left to Right: Mamie Cotton, baby Mae Cotton, Alvin, Roger, Addie Cotton and Myrtle Cotton.

Mamie Cotton, Oct. 25, 1889-Sept. 24, 1974, married John E. Patterson in Nov. 1913. Children: Mabel Patterson, born Aug. 7, 1914, and Ruberta Patterson, born Jan. 22, 1919;

Myrtle Cotton, April 24, 1891-Aug. 10, 1969, married Elmer Bell. He died in 1961. Children: Gladys Bell Marress, April 27, 1916-Dec. 9, 1989;

Roger Cotton, June 6, 1898-April 3, 1979, married Mary Lee Bates, Oct. 10, 1902-June 21, 1967. Children: Van O. Cotton, Nov. 17, 1926-July 31, 1972, married Anna Lou Broadway, no children, James A. Cotton, born Feb. 12, 1928, married Nova Horner in Aug. 1954. They had two children, Al Cotton, born May 10, 1957, Brent Cotton, born May 22, 1961, married Kathy Gibson of Opp, Alabama, in Dec. 1986, one child, Kelsey Cotton, born Nov. 4, 1993;

Mae Cotton, Sept. 29, 1901-June 4, 1983, married Willie Lane, Feb. 17, 1893-Feb. 7, 1966. Children: Dimple Lane, born Aug. 18, 1924, Loudean Lane, born Aug. 28, 1927. Dimple Lane married Clint Coble in 1950. He died March 21, 1982. Their children were Marlene, Nelda, Emily, and Angela. Loudean Lane married Hale Vick in May 1951. Their children were Carolyn, Sandra, and Kathy. *Compiled by Mabel Patterson.*

DONALD BRUCE COTTON, born Sept. 2, 1948, is the only son of Garvis L. Cotton, March 31, 1926-Jan. 30, 1986, and Virginia Myrick Cotton, May 8, 1928. Garvis and Virginia were married, May 6, 1947, and resided in the Pineview community across the road from where Garvis was raised, the home of his parents, Oda O'Guin Cotton, March 8, 1896-Sept. 23, 1985, and Marion Osby Cotton, Jan. 4, 1889-Oct. 23, 1960.

M.O. Cotton Store

Oda and Osby were married in 1921. In the early 1900s, Osby opened the M.O. Cotton General Store in Pineview and operated it until 1947, when he turned it over to Garvis and Virginia, who continued to run it until they sold it in 1977. During the Depression, many community residents benefitted from the generous credit policies extended to them until they were able to pay.

Garvis and Virginia Cotton

Marion Osby Cotton is one of the four children of Jared N. Cotton, 1857-1948, and Frances Lunn, 1861-1938. Other children are: Arco Sr., unknown dates; Riley N., Feb. 14, 1894-Nov. 20, 1990; Mattie Jane, 1881-1976.

Jared was the son of King Marion Cotton who was born in Hickman County about 1832 and died Sept. 10, 1914. He was married to Melinda Jane Robertson, born 1834. The marriage date is not known, but it is believed to have taken place in Perry County.

Wedding day of Bruce and Glenda Cotton, Jan. 23, 1993. Left to Right: Tracy Lee Cotton, Crystal Rose Cotton (front), Glenda, Bruce and Jeffrey Bruce Cotton.

Bruce married Cynthia Lee Jones, June 9, 1952, in Jan. 1973. They have three children, Tracy Lee, April 10, 1975, Jeffrey Bruce, March 31, 1977, and Crystal Rose, March 18, 1982. They were divorced in 1988, and in 1993, he married Glenda Kay Curl, April 23, 1949.

Bruce has been a banker in Perry County since 1975 and at this writing is employed by First State Bank in Linden.

IRVIN ROBERT COTTON, April 12, 1865-June 16, 1941, son of Lt. John Irvin and Mary Jane (Dabbs) Cotton. Lt. Cotton was killed in Atlanta, Georgia, in April 1865. He is buried in the National Cemetery, Waynesboro, Georgia.

Children of Lt. John Irvin and Mary Jane Cotton were Mary, Benny, and Irvin. Their home was at the mouth of Mill Creek, on Buffalo River in Wayne County.

Mary Jane married for the second time to Patrick Dowdy. He served in the Confederate Army. Children of Patrick and Mary Jane Dowdy were Martha Brown, Lou Grinder, Admira Tharp, Ana Ary, and Evan Dowdy.

The Irvin Cotton Family. Left to Right: Willie Cotton, Estalee, Claudia, Whitney. Bottom Row: Violet, Irvin, Marvin, Savannah, Paris.

Irvin attended school at Hampshire and taught school in the Perry County and Wayne County school system. He was married to Virginia Crowell, who died at an early age. He then married Savannah Graves in March 1891. They lived on Rockhouse Creek where all their children were reared. Their children were: Estalee Cotton, Dec. 27, 1892-Feb. 3, 1978, married Robert Epley; Willie Cotton, Nov. 2, 1894-Dec. 19, 1913, married Sally Hickerson; Claudia Cotton, April 10, 1896, married Charlie Anderson; Whitney Cotton, Oct. 8, 1898-Aug. 1991, married Aaron Duncan; Bedford Cotton, Nov. 19, 1900-Aug. 14, 1901; Violet Cotton, Aug. 14, 1902, married Paul O. Thompson; Marvin Cotton, Jan. 29, 1905-Nov. 25, 1986, married first, April 20, 1930, to Ethel Turnbow, and second, Dec. 9, 1950, to Martha Dunn; Paris Cotton, April 19, 1909-Jan. 19, 1979, married Sue Warren; Charlotte Cotton, Dec. 28, 1911, married Arthur Ray; and Shelby Cotton, Oct. 5, 1914-Nov. 23, 1914.

JARAD COTTON, born in 1800, came to Hickman with his wife, Dorcas, born about 1801. Both were born in North Carolina, and Dorcas could have been Cherokee. They came to Perry County about 1835, with three children. Three children were born in Tennessee. Jarad Cotton's family was like all others in this time. They farmed, raised their food, and made their tools and clothes at home. Their children listed in the 1850 Census of Hickman County were Luguema 23 female, Sir Winfred 20 male, King 18 male, Louisa 17 female, Jesse 12 male, and Jorat 10 male.

King Marion, born in North Carolina, about 1832, and died in Perry County in 1914, is buried in the Bell Robertson Cemetery. His wife, Melinda Jane Robertson Cotton, born 1834, died prior to him. They were the parents of: John L., who went to Tipton County, Jared N. 1857-1948, married Frances Lunn, 1861-1938; Alvin M., 1862-1928, married Addie Sharp. Children: Cora Mae, married Willie Lane, Roger, married Mary Lee Bates, Mamie, married John Patterson, and Della, married Ed Cothan; W. Ed lived in West Tennessee; Mosella Jane, March 8, 1866-Dec. 5, 1946, married O.L. DePriest, March 23, 1959-1918.

Jarad and Francis were the parents of Arco Sr., who married Sadie DePriest. They are the parents of Arco Jr., who married Edna Parnell, daughter of Arthur and Augusta "Gussie" Barham. Arco and Edna were the parents of Margaret Juanita, who has two children Dennis Freeland and Evonne Williams; Alton Barham Cotton, who has Alva Juanita and Alton B. Jr.; William Archo III "Billy", his children William Wayne, Greg and Phamella.

Riley N., Feb. 14, 1894-Nov. 20, 1990, married Ritta Ruth Barham, their children are Melba, married Buddy McNabb, no children; George, married Dorotha Gilmer, daughter, Fay has two children; Lofton, married Joyce, no children. Marion Osby Cotton, married first to Venus Horner, then Oda Barrs, son, Garvis L. married Virginia Myracle, son Bruce: Mattie Jane Cotton married Albert Clayborn. They had several children, one being Harlyn, Jan. 18, 1913-March 25, 1967, married Sara Lou Bell and they had three girls. In Mr. K.M. Cotton's death notice, he is referred to "as a gentleman in the truest sense, that is to say he was honest, kindhearted, industrious man." He and his wife neither have a stone at the cemetery, but this notice refers to him being buried in the cemetery above the George Bell house on Toms Creek, on Sept. 11, 1914.

MARVIN EUNICE COTTON, born Jan. 29, 1905, died Nov. 24, 1986, in Perry County, married Ethel Effie Turnbow, on April 20, 1930, in Perry County, on Rockhouse Creek. She died Aug. 8, 1947.

Marvin Eunice and Martha Cotton

Children of Marvin and Ethel were:
Robert William Cotton, born May 7, 1932, in Lewis County, married, Nov. 4, 1950, in Corinth, Mississippi, to Charlotte Horner. Children: Sherrie Lynn Cotton, born Jan. 17, 1953, in Nashville, married, Aug. 29, 1975, in Pasadena, Texas, to Jimmy L. Davenport. Divorced. No children; Randall William Cotton, born Aug. 31, 1955, in Nashville, married July 4, 1974, in Pasadena, Texas, to Judy Carruth. Divorced. One child, Jason Cotton. Then married Jeanette (?) Cotton. Divorced. Two children, Luke and Emily Cotton; and Rick Wayne Cotton, born March 17, 1961, in Nashville, married Diane (?) Cotton. Their children, Zachary Cotton and Ethan Christopher Cotton.

Eunice Bernice Cotton, born Sept. 5, 1936, in Lewis County, married Dec. 22, 1956, in LaFayette, Georgia, to Annie Ruth Goodman. She was born March 12, 1935, in Lewis County. Their children: Rachel Elaine Cotton, born Aug. 7, 1958, in Nashville, married Peter Van Gregory in Dalton, Georgia. Children: Jerry Keith Gregory, born Feb. 6, 1975, Andrew Scott Gregory, born Jan. 23, 1981, and Steven Christopher Gregory, born Nov. 19, 1986; and Kathy Ann Cotton, born Aug. 27, 1961, in Winchester, Tennessee, married David West, in July 1981, in Murfreesboro, Tennessee. Children: Sara Ann West, born Sept. 5, 1983, died Feb. 21, 1986, Ryan David West, born July 3, 1986, and Emily Ann West, born March 2, 1991.

Marvin Eunice Cotton, married Martha Vera Dunn, Dec. 9, 1950, in Corinth, Mississippi. She was born May 27, 1923. They had one child, Julia Linda Cotton, born March 13, 1952, in Lewis County. She married Larry Wayne Dabbs, June 5, 1970, in Lewis County. He was born May 25, 1948, in Lewis County. Their children: Jennifer Lezlee Dabbs, born Nov. 6, 1973, in Nashville; Lincoln Wayne Dabbs, born April 7, 1976, in Nashville; and Lantz Walker Dabbs, born Aug. 28, 1978, in Nashville. *Submitted by Linda Dabbs, daughter of Marvin and Martha Cotton.*

PARIS COTTON, son of Irvin and Savannah (Graves) Cotton was born April 19, 1909, in Perry County and died Jan. 19, 1979, in Perry County Memorial Hospital. He was buried in the Graves Cemetery.

Paris and Sue Cotton

Paris was married May 8, 1932, in Lobelville, to Minnie Sue Warren, daughter of Carol and Minnie Jane (Hufstedler) Warren. Sue was born April 22, 1910, in Perry County. They have no children. After high school, Paris was employed by South Central Bell T and T Company.

He served in the United States Army, 1942-1946. Paris was affiliated several years with Godwin Drug Company in Linden. Paris and Sue were loyal members of the First United Methodist Church.

WHITNEY COTTON, 1898-1991, daughter of Irvin and Savannah (Graves) Cotton, was born Oct. 8, 1898. She was married April 12, 1925, to Aaron Clarence Duncan, son of Eli and Drucila (Bruce) Duncan. Aaron was born in Perry County on Dec. 11, 1892. Aaron is a veteran of World War I. The family are Methodist. Whitney died July 28, 1991. She and Aaron are buried in the Graves Cemetery in Perry County. Their children are Gene Douglas and Patricia June Duncan.

Gene Douglas Duncan, born June 29, 1929, married Sara Elizabeth "Betty" Starbuck, daughter of Joe and Lorene (Bell) Starbuck. They live in Nashville and are affiliated with the Church of Christ. Their children are Deborah Elizabeth and Susan Jean Duncan.

Deborah Elizabeth, born July 4, 1952, had two teeth at birth. She married Aug. 19, 1972, to Daniel Anderson Gower, son of William Gower. Their children are Whitney Gower, March 22, 1981, and Joey Gower, Nov. 26, 1983.

Valerie Kay Stringer

Susan Jean Duncan, born June 8, 1956, married Jim Kendall Darby of Nashville. Their children are Kendal Alexandria Darby, born July 31, 1986, and Noel Darby, born Dec. 15, 1990. Patricia June Duncan, born Nov. 13, 1933, married J.T. Craig, son of John and Edna (Ledbetter) Craig, May 9, 1953. They live in Nashville. Their child, Valerie Kay Craig, was born March 27, 1955, at Lobelville. She married, July 27, 1974, to Michael Lewis Stringer of Nashville, son of B.E. Stringer. Valerie Kay is divorced. She is a graduate of Metro Fire Dept. curriculum in Nashville, Tennessee, of which she has been employed the past eleven years.

WILLIE LEE COTTON, Nov. 2, 1894-Dec. 19, 1913, was born in Perry County, son of Irvin and Savannah (Graves) Cotton. He was buried in the Graves Cemetery. He was married Jan. 14, 1912, to Sally Ann Hickerson, daughter of Finley and Rebecca (Anderson) Hickerson. Sally was born 1892, died May 29, 1975, and was buried in Graves Cemetery. She married second to Plummer Bryson.

Katherine and Willie Cotton

Children of Willie Lee and Sally Cotton: Infant son, born and died, Sept. 1912, and James Willie Cotton, born Dec. 12, 1913, married Jan. 1936, to Katherine Warren.

Children of Willie and Katherine Warren Cotton: Willie Sue, deceased, and James Harold Cotton, born July 5, 1940, married Sue Smithson, Feb. 11, 1958.

Children of James H. and Sue Cotton: Todd Cotton, born Sept. 4, 1960, married 1981, to Cindi Stuart, daughter of Frank Stuart of Pormona, Missouri, one child, Amy Sue, born March 9, 1986; Tregg Cotton, born Sept. 4, 1964, married Sherry Cole, one daughter, Jamie, born July 3, 1986; and Albert Trevor Cotton who married Donna Blake.

Peggy Jean, third child of Willie Lee and Sally Cotton, married Mac McClearen in 1962. They had three children: Lana, who has one child, Meleah McClearen (1987); Trina, who married Dwayne Kilpatrick and has one daughter, Kacy Kilpatrick (1988); and Lisa (1967), who married Ronnie Brewer and has one son, Miles Brewer (1991).

Katherine Nell, fourth child of Willie Lee and Sally Cotton, married Wade Seiber in 1965. Their children are Donna (1965) and Chad (1975).

Jimmy Don, fifth child, was born July 4, 1944.

CRAIG/CRAGG-CATES, Richard Cragg/Craig, from Orange County, North Carolina (Jan. 5, 1773-June 1850, Perry County, Tennessee), married Frances Glamp (Jan. 20, 1776-Nov. 5, 1824) on Dec. 28, 1795, in Granville County, North Carolina.

Laura (Owens) Craig with great grandchildren.

Known children of Richard and Frances are: Elijah, who died in Humphreys County Tennessee, 1853, according to his estate being settled there at that time; John, born Sept. 15, 1810, Orange County, North Carolina, died in Humphreys County, Tennessee, April 15, 1893. (Much has been written on John Cragg/Craig); Solomon; and possibly Martha, who married Nathaniel Crowder.

In 1814, the Richard Cragg/Craig family moved from North Carolina to Williamson County, Tennessee. Then, about 1830, after selling several tracts of land in Williamson County, moved to Hickman County and on page 255 of Spencer's History of Hickman County Tennessee, reads "Richard Craig, early settler of the 7th Dist. (Bird's Creek), father of John, Solomon and Elijah".

Richard Cragg/Craig married second to Elizabeth (Cates) Wilson, born 1798 in North Carolina, ca. 1825 or 1826. Elizabeth had these minor children by Charles Wilson whom she had married in Person County, North Carolina, on April 21, 1817; Sophia, Thomas, Patsy, Andrew, and Susan Jane Wilson. Richard Cragg was appointed Guardian of minors. Prior to Richard's marriage to widow Wilson, Ransom Cates, brother of Elizabeth (Cates) Wilson Craig was guardian of these children. Ransom Cates sued Thomas Cragg, (believed to be brother or son of Richard) John Jamison, and Robert Campbell to recover the money he had spent on the children. Charles Wilson's estate was being settled in Maury County, Tennessee in "1824" and this was when the minor children were placed under guardianship of Ransom Cates.

The child, Thomas Wilson, was bound out to Martha and Nathaniel Crowder in January 1827. Crowder's wife was Martha Cragg/Craig. It is believed Martha was another child of Richard Cragg, however, there is no proof. The Cragg/Craigs, Cates and Crowders all lived near each other in Granville and Person Counties of North Carolina.

Richard Cragg/Craig and family moved to Perry County, Tennessee where he died in June 1850. He appears on the mortality list for 1850 and Elizabeth and children, and possibly a couple of grandchildren living with her, appear as follows: Elias, Sarah, Simpson, Solomon, Elizabeth, William, and Anderson.

The 1840 Tennessee census, shows the families of Elijah Cragg, John Cragg, Richard Cragg and Joseph L. Cragg all living in Hickman County, Tennessee. The family of William B. Cragg already being residents of Perry County. It is thought that all the Craggs of Hickman County followed William B. Cragg to Perry County as some show on later census. John and Elijah families moved on to Humphreys County. William Craig and family moved to Alabama where William died, May 10, 1851, in Perry County, Alabama. A Joseph L. Cragg descendant has Query in Craig-Links Publication at this time (Feb. 1994) requesting information on him. Anyone with information, please write Ann Burton, Editor of Craig Links Publications, 43779 Valley Road, Decatur, Michigan, who will see information is passed along.

It is believed Irvin/Erwin Craig, born ca 1830, living in Perry County, Tennessee in 1860, in same household as Simpson Craig, each married with one small child, was the son of Richard and Elizabeth (Cates) Craig, in as much as one of his sons was named Richard Cates Craig and one of his sons named Amason Cates Craig. *Submitted by Hazel W. Craig.*

CRAIG-CRAFTON-HARDEMAN, Andrew Craig II, born March 9, 1787, believed in Williamson County, Tennessee, was the son of Andrew David Craig (mainly known as David) of Washington County, Virginia.

Andrew Craig II, first married, Oct. 23, 1810, to Jemima Crafton, born ca 1790/1800, birthplace unknown. Jemima died Aug. 30, 1834. She was the daughter of John Crafton. Andrew II and Jemima's children were: Nancy (Craig) Wade, no dates known; Mary Melissa, born ca 1818, Williamson County, married March 20, 1832, to William Vaughn, who was born 1812 in Tennessee, died 1864, in Perry County, Tennessee.

Andrew II, second married Martha Dupuy Hardeman, daughter of Eleazar Hardeman, April 21, 1835. Martha D. was born March 16, 1803, and died March 12, 1864, in Williamson County, Tennessee.

Children of Andrew Craig II and Martha Dupuy (Hardeman) Craig, all believed born in Williamson County, Tennessee, are:

Eleazar Hardeman Craig, born Feb. 21, 1836, first married Jan. 29, 1857, to Margaret Greer. They had fourteen children. Second, he married March 13, 1886, to Nancy Elizabeth Trull. (See Craig-Greer-Trull history.)

Sarah Elizabeth, born Sept. 4, 1847, other data unknown.

Andrew D. III, born Dec. 15, 1838, first married America Greer, sister of Margaret Greer, on Dec. 22, 1859. Second, he married Adelia Carroll, Jan. 24, 1875.

Martha D. Craig, born Oct. 17, 1840, other data unknown.

Andrew II, died May 27, 1863. Martha Dupuy (Hardeman) Craig died March 12, 1864, in Williamson County. Most of their children moved on to Perry County, Tennessee. *Submitted by Hazel W. Craig.*

CRAIG-DENTON, Brown Craig lived on White Oak in Perry County. He had two children, Andrew Polk and Sophfronia. Polk married Mollie McDonald Jan. 1, 1879, at Farmers Valley. They lived in Linden and Polk was a great worker in the church. He served as Superintendent and song leader of the Christian Church. In 1884, he bought some land from his father and later sold part of it to his sister Sophfronia. Polk and Mollie had six children: Ruby, Julia, Bess, Freddie, Lola, and Leslie. They were all very well educated. Leslie was a dentist and had a practice in Linden and also one in Hohenwald. He attended school at Vanderbilt University and played baseball on their team.

Sophfronia Denton Rainey in 1992.

Sophfronia Craig married Sam Denton and had four boys: Polk, John, Dolph, and Walker. Polk married Delia Stevens and they had seven children: Lissie, Yula, Arkie, Mattie Vivian, Jeanetta, Joe, and Mary. Dolph married Jessie Tomlin and they had four children: Mahalia, Earnest, Brown, and Novilla. Dolph and Jessie lived together over 70 years. Walker married Captola Ramey and they had no children. John Brown married Mary Darcus Paschall and they had five children: Nannie, Bessie, Wade, Sophfronia, and Thetus. Nannie married Ralph Tomlin and had four children: Ray, Charline, Geneva, and Paul. Bessie married Jimmy Rodgers and they had no children. Wade married May Gooch and they had five children: Nancy, Johnnie, Jerry, Sue, and David. Sophfronia married Earl Rainey and had six children: Dorothy, Denton, Edna, Joe, Jimmy, and Dale. Thetus married Anna Lou Broadway and had no children.

Polk Craig and family owned a lot of land in Linden. They owned the property now owned by the Baptist Church, City Hall, Leon Dailey, Christian Church, Factory, and Estelle Jordan. They lived in a very large home on the property between the Baptist Church and the Christian Church. As time passed, the family members all passed away, except Freddie and Leslie. In 1925, Leslie got John Brown and Darcus Denton to move into the Craig home in Linden to take care of Freddie. Leslie died of a heart attack soon after they moved. John was in bad health when they moved and he did not live long. He died in 1931, and left Darcus to take care of Freddie and the children. Darcus kept boarders to provide for the children and send them to school. The people that built the Court House and the Tennessee River Bridge boarded with her. Thetus played football and the team often practiced in the large front yard of the Craig home. Fronia was on the basketball team. Thetus and Wade had to go to the Army in World War II. Thetus drove a tank and served under Gen. Patton in Germany. Darcus later had a small restaurant in Linden, which she operated until her health no longer permitted. She died of a heart attack in 1969. After Darcus passed away, her daughter, Bessie, and husband, Jimmy Rodgers, moved from Memphis to Linden to take care of Freddie. Jimmy did a lot of fishing. Bessie worked in the Methodist Church that she loved. Freddie died in 1991. She was 98 years old. The old Craig home was in a run down condition and in the Spring of 1993 was being torn down and accidentally caught fire and burned down. In Nov. 1993, Bessie died of a heart attack. The property where the old Craig home was, is still in the family, owned by Dorothy Patterson and family, daughter of Sophfronia Denton Rainey.

CRAIG-FARRAR, Edward Harris Craig, born June 22, 1915, died April 21, 1988, was the son of Lillie Evelyn Craig, born Nov. 4, 1893, died May 7, 1988, the daughter of Richard Cates (Dickie) Craig, born 1861, in Perry County, Tennessee, died 1939, in Benton County, and Laura Owens, born 1871, died 1951, married April 6, 1892. They are buried in Morris Chapel Cemetery near Camden, Tennessee.

Edward Harris Craig and his mother, Lillie Evelyn Craig

Family tradition says Richard Cates Craig's father, Erwin or Irvin, (Erwin on 1860 Perry County census) was taken from his home by guerrillas some years after the Civil War and was never heard from again. It is presumed he was killed as no trace was ever found. Erwin was married to Sarah Elizabeth Horner of Perry County. Sarah was born May 25, 1834, died Oct. 15, 1898. She was a descendant of Amos Randell, born in Indiana, and an early pioneer of Perry County. Sarah is buried in Beardstown Cemetery on Duncan Circle, Perry County, next to the grave of her son, George W. Craig, born 1868, died 1903, married to Jane Byrd.

One of Dickie's brothers, Henry Louis Craig, born 1857, died 1947, married April 18, 1880, to Tennessee Matlock, born 1861, died 1939 in Benton County. He went to Benton County from Perry County as a young man. It is believed his father's brothers moved there from Humphreys County as they appear on the mid 1800s census. Henry L. and Tennessee Craig are buried in Eastview Cemetery, Benton County.

A sister, Mary Elizabeth Craig, born 1858, in Perry County, married Edward Williams there on May 24, 1873, and they, also, soon moved to Benton County to make their home. Their children: Sallie, Ella, Henry, Sarah Elizabeth (Lizzie Craig Hedge), Mollie, Infant that died young, James, Irvin, Geraldine, and Robert Lee Craig.

Robert Edward Craig, son of Edward Harris Craig and Oleta Farrar, born Aug. 14, 1914, in Benton County, died March 20, 1975, was born in Dearborn, Michigan, Jan. 4, 1945. He was married to Delores Gainer in Michigan in 1957. She was the mother of three little boys, Patrick, Timothy and Kevin Gainer. Delores and Robert have one daughter, Dianne, born Dec. 1956. Robert's sister, Peggy Dell Craig, born May 30, 1936, in Benton County, Tennessee, died April 7, 1988. Three members of the family died within five weeks time. Peggy, then two weeks later, Edward Harris Craig, then three weeks later, 86 year old, Lillie Evelyn Craig. All are buried in Benton County. Peggy, married Allen Cote of Michigan, in 1954. Their children are: Tab Allen Cote, born March 10, 1955, and Tracy, born Sept. 1957. They reside in Michigan. Peggy married second to Thomas E. Parker III of Huntington, West Virginia and had one child, Trisca, born Feb. 11, 1971, lives in Ohio.

Edward Harris Craig, March 10, 1962, in Dearborn, Michigan, married second to Hazel (Welch) Clark, born Aug. 2, 1923, in Union Parish Louisiana. Hazel resides on the family farm near Holladay, Tennessee. She is very active in the Benton County Genealogical Society, having served several years as the Editor of their Quarterly. She has worked very hard researching the Craig family history. Hazel also has been active in the Nashville Chihuahua Club, having two long-coat Chihuahua bitches of Champion Stoe's Fudge Ripple and Dickerson's Theodores Last. Also sharing the home is one Special Angel, a Hairless Chinese Crested, weighing 2 1/2 pounds and two cats, both named Chessie (this is logo for Chesapeake and Ohio Railway where she was employed twenty-five years. Composed by Hazel W. Craig. *Submitted by Robert E. Craig.*

CRAIG-GREER-TRULL, Eleazar Hardeman Craig, born Feb. 21, 1836, married Jan. 29, 1857, to Margaret Greer and had fourteen children:

Andrew Henry (Sept. 15, 1858-Feb. 18,1859); William Thomas (Dec. 23, 1859-Aug. 25, 1878); James Foster (Oct. 23, 1861-Sept. 1900); Martha Elizabeth (Dec. 27, 1864-ca 1900), married Joe G. Beasley; Joseph Eleazar (Jan. 20, 1867-Nov. 7, 1937), lived Erath County, Texas, never married; John Allen (Dec. 20, 1868), lived Erath County, Texas, never married; Harriet Matilda (Nov. 11, 1870), marred Doss O'Guinn; Nicholas Hardeman (Oct. 1, 1872), moved to Vernon, Texas in 1891 and married Mary Winston Wafer, unverified; George Washington (Jan. 25, 1874), reported married to Bessie O'Rear; Benjamin Franklin (Jan. 30, 1876), reported married to Kate Wilburn; Wiley Black (July 13, 1878-Jan. 1936), first married Lou Thornton, second married to Ida Marshall. Wiley Black Craig and Ida (Marshall) Craig are buried in Obion County, Tennessee, near Troy; Mary Susan (May 26, 1880) reported married to Obe Taylor, unverified; Claburn (Nov. 6, 1881), died in infancy; and O.T. Craig (March 16, 1884), reported married first to Norma Taylor and married second to Lula Lee Paschall.

Margaret (Greer) Craig's monument shows her born 1836, died in 1884. Many of this family are buried in Chestnut Grove Cemetery, Linden, Perry County, Tennessee.

Eleazar Hardeman Craig, married second, March 13, 1886, to Nancy Elizabeth Trull, born March 17, 1857, died May 13, 1922. Their children:

Maggie Eva (Jan. 2, 1887-1956), married Robert Leo Averett; Jessie (Jan. 24, 1889-June 4, 1984), married Clabe B. Dodson; Charlie (Oct. 31, 1890-April 2, 1961), married Laura Viola Chessor (1893-1963); Lelia Jane (June 16, 1893-March 20, 1973, Scott County, Missouri), married Escar Lee Hinson, Dec. 18, 1911; Zula Mae (July 12, 1895-1965).

Eleazar Hardeman Craig died Feb. 16, 1896, at the age of 59 years, 11 months and 25 days.

Much of this information was furnished by Lucille Britton of San Antonio, Texas, whose husband, Calvin John Britton, son of Willie Mae (Craig) Britton, daughter of Andrew D. Craig III. Also Harold Hinson of Webster Groves, Missouri, a descendant of Lelia Jane (Craig) Hinson, daughter of Eleazar Hardeman and Nancy Elizabeth (Trull) Craig furnished considerable information. *Composed and submitted by Hazel W. Craig.*

CRAIG-HORNER, Irvin Craig, born ca 1830, (Perry County 1860 census shows him 30 years old, married to Sarah Horner, born ca 1836, census shows her being 24 years old, along with one son, Henry L., age 3) Known children of Irvin (some records show spelling Ervin) and Sarah are:

Richard and Laura Craig and daughters, Pearl and Lillie.

Richard (Dickie) Cates Craig, born 1871, died 1939, married first in Perry County, to Abbey Lynch. Children: Lockard and Mynetta. Married second to Laura Lee Owens of Perry County, on April 6, 1892. Children: Pearl, Lillie, Hazel, Amason, Ramon (Ray), and Claudine. The last survivor of the children was Lillie, who died May 7, 1988. Dickie and Laura are buried in the Morris Chapel Cemetery in Benton County.

John Calhoun Craig, first married Sarah Patton, on Dec. 23, 1871, then second to Paralee Patton (Sarah's sister), on Oct. 22, 1874, after Sarah's death. Children: William Anderson Craig, John A. Craig, O.L. Craig, Addie Craig, and Tom Craig.

Thomas Craig married Alice Burns. (1900 Perry County census shows Thomas, born March 1860 and Alice, born Jan. 1871.)

Mary E. Craig, born 1858, married Ed Williams. Children: Sallie, Ella, Henry, Sarah Elizabeth (Lizzy Hedge), Mollie, Infant died, James, Irvin, Geraldine, and Robert Lee Craig (Bobbie).

Henry Louis Craig, born 1857, died 1947, married, April 18, 1880, to Tennessee West Matlock, born 1861, died 1939. Both are buried in the Eastview Cemetery, Benton County. Children: Ida Craig, Elmer Craig, born 1883, Lillie, born Nov. 1885, Montie, born Dec. 1887, John, born March 1890, Jean, born Jan. 1893, Albert, born Jan. 1896, Allice, born Jan. 12, 1900, died Dec. 4, 1928, Dolly, born 1901, Ollie, born 1905, and Infant, died at birth.

George W. Craig, born 1868, died 1903, married Jane Byrd. The Perry County census shows children as: Etta, born Sept. 1893; Claude, born March 1897; and J.P., born May 1899. Census also shows Jane's mother, Eliza Byrd, born Oct. 1850, as living in their household.

Census records show son, William Alonzo Craig, born 1878. He married Sissy Stringer in Benton County. Children: Leslie Craig (May 19, 1906-May 27, 1934), married Bettie Marie Flowers. Leslie is buried in the Flowers Cemetery near Holladay, Tennessee. This record furnished by Mrs. Bettie Marie Flowers Craig Hicks of Holladay.

The monument of the mother, Sarah Elizabeth Horner Craig, shows her born May 25, 1834, and died Oct. 15, 1898. The monument also shows mother of Henry L. Craig and it is believed he erected this stone. A new one is being erected, summer of 1994, by Benton County Craigs through the line of Richard Cates (Dickie) Craig as her stone is broken into many pieces. Further Craig history may be found under Craig families. *Submitted by H.W. Craig.*

BROWN CRAIG, married Emma McDonald. The Craigs lived on Cedar Creek on a large farm near Tennessee River at Cedar Creek landing where the boats docked, also a shipping port.

Brown and Emma had two children, Frona and Polk Craig. Polk Craig and his wife moved to Linden on the property he inherited from his father.

Frona married Sam Denton, and stayed on the farm she inherited from her father.

Polk Craig and wife, owned several acres of land in Linden, Tennessee that is known today as the Freddie Craig place. The children were Dr. Leslie Craig, who was a dentist in Linden, Bessie, Julie, Freddie and Ruby. Dr. Craig had some dear friends who cooked for him. He depended on Leonard Catron and Minnie, also Uncle Bud Catron. The Craig Cemetery is on the Craig property where Freddie Craig was buried in May of 1992.

Polk was a member of the Christian Church

and the song leader. His favorite song was Peace in the Valley. One of Frona and Sam Denton's sons was named for Polk Craig (Andrew Polk Denton). Their other children were John Brown, Walker R., and Dolph Denton. The Craig Cemetery is on the lower end of Cedar Creek. This is very helpful to the younger relatives when trying to find the birth dates of the ancestors. *Submitted by Vivian Denton Hickerson.*

HELEN CRAIG, (Smith) is the daughter of Newt Craig and Conna McDonald Craig. Her paternal grandparents were W.R. Craig and Elizabeth Wilburn Craig. Her great-grandparents were Tapp Craig and Amy Gutherie Craig, all of Perry County, Tennessee.

W.R. Craig Family Home: North Prong Lick Creek, around 1910.

Tapp Craig, of Black, Anglo, and American Indian ancestry, was born a slave on Feb. 6, 1829. It is unclear whether his place of birth was Perry or Williamson County, since Andrew Craig II, his first known master, did not arrive in Perry County from Williamson, until the year 1843. Throughout his young adult life, certainly, he worked and resided on the Craig Estate, on the Buffalo River, in the area of Chestnut Grove.

After Andrew II's daughter, Sarah Elizabeth, was married to Benjamin Berry, Tapp, according to oral history, was transferred to the Berry Place. After some time, however, he returned to the Craig Estate, where he continued his indenture with Andrew Craig III.

Several years prior to the onset of the War, Tapp was married to Amy Gutherie, a mulatto servant and housemaid on the Andrew H. Gutherie estate. According to the 1870 Census, five children were born to Tapp and Amy. They are listed as William (1855), Susan (1858), Brown (1861), Tennessee (1863), and Mary Jane (1866). William, Tennessee, and Mary Jane lived until adulthood.

After the War, Tapp and Amy continued to work and resided on Buffalo, until 1871, when they purchased a farm on North Prong Lick Creek. The near one hundred acre tract, purchased from Samuel Young, on Dec. 25, 1871, is reportedly the first, ever in the County, owned by a Person of color.

On Oct. 16, 1884, Tapp and Amy's son, William, was married to Elizabeth Wilburn, of the Wilburn Estate, on the Buffalo River, near Beardstown. Elizabeth's father was Joe Wilburn, master of the estate. Her mother, Agnes (Wilburn), the Colored housemaid. Her date of birth was June 4, 1865.

On Nov. 2, 1889, Will Craig and Elizabeth, purchased a farm on North Lick Creek from Henry Gutherie, Will's half brother. The near three hundred acre tract is located two miles east of that settled by his father, Tapp, eighteen years before. They lived, and all of their children were born, in a log cabin on the place, until around 1906, when they completed the Craig Family Home.

Fifteen children, twelve of whom survived, were born to Will and Elizabeth. Ashley (April 3, 1887-Aug. 18, 1924), Isaac Black (Dec. 4, 1888-Oct. 31, 1918), Amy (Aug. 13, 1891-May 20, 1973), Clarence (May 9, 1893-Oct. 1, 1969), X.L. (Nov. 30, 1894-Oct. 27, 1970), Clint (Aug. 18, 1896-Aug. 4, 1980), Newt (Sept 17, 1898-Dec. 5, 1961), Bernice (1900), Irvin and Walter, identical twins (April 3, 1903), Irvin died Jan. 7, 1977. Walter died Jan. 7, 1979, Elizabeth (June 16, 1905-Sept. 4, 1933), Ercel (Ocie) (May 13, 1908-Sept. 1, 1930).

In 1914, the Craigs purchased additional land on the Tennessee River, and the family moved from Lick Creek to the Perryville Bottoms. Farmland was more fertile on the river, but they continued to return to the Home Place, where they raised and marketed large crops of peanuts, and in off-seasons, worked the timber.

Lamentably, soon after moving, Will Craig died in 1916. Elizabeth Craig survived her husband until 1953.

Ashley Craig married Gretchen Yarbro in 1921. Their only child was a daughter, Jewel (March 6, 1922).

Black Craig married Josie Stegall in 1917. Their only child was a son, Ernest Black (Nov. 6, 1918).

Amy Craig never married.

Clarence Craig married Bernice Montgomery in Feb. 1920. Their children are Dorothy Mae (Dec. 9, 1921), John (Nov. 30, 1922), and Herbert (May 16, 1926).

X.L. Craig married Alma Montgomery in 1921. Their children are George Harding (July 4, 1922) and Roxie Mae (May 13, 1925).

Clint Craig married Susie Randle in 1919. Their children were William Paul (April 14, 1921-Feb. 1, 1940), Wilma Emma (July 8, 1925-July 1933), Ashley B. (April 19, 1929), and Thelma (Nov. 7, 1931).

Clint Craig married Rosie Harbor Whitson in December 1936.

Newt Craig married Conna McDonald in June 1926. Their children are: Helen (May 20, 1927), Newt Jr. (May 3, 1929), McDonald (April 11, 1931), Ray (Nov. 23, 1933), Carolyn (Doll) (Jan. 25, 1936), Roy (March 30, 1938), and Reba (July 4, 1941).

Bernice Craig married Clarence Hicks in June 1929.

Irvin Craig married Cordie Holt in August 1937. Their only child is a daughter, Alma (Dec. 5, 1942).

Walter Craig married Mattie Herring in January 1945.

Elizabeth Craig never married.

Ocie Craig never married.

The Newt Craig line continues:

Helen Craig married Ivory Nuby of Nashville, in September 1945. In 1951, this marriage ended in divorce. She then married Hugh Smith of Linden, August 1952.

Newt Craig Jr. never married.

McDonald Craig married Rosetta Smith of Lexington, in June 1958. Their children are Reginald and Ervin McDonald.

Ray Craig's son is Daniel. Daniel Craig's mother is Marie Kullman, originally of Offenbach, Germany, and of Baltimore, Maryland, since 1972.

Carolyn Craig (Doll) married William Briggs of Fayetteville in April 1959. Their children are William Briggs Jr. and identical twins, John and Roy. Carolyn, today, is Dr. Carolyn Briggs, Educational Specialist, and instructor in the Public Schools of Metro, Nashville.

Roy Craig never married. Roy drowned while serving with the U.S. Navy in 1961.

Reba Craig married Perry Hart of Henderson, in June 1959. Their children are Alan, Jerry and Gary Lynn. Reba is an Administrative Assistant with Jet Propulsion Laboratories, Los Angeles.

Clarence, X.L., and Clint Craig served in World War I. Ernest Black Craig and John Craig served in World War II. Ashley Craig and McDonald Craig served during the Korean Conflict. Ray Craig, retired Captain, served in both Korea and Viet Nam. Ashley Craig was awarded the Purple Heart. McDonald was awarded the Bronze Star. Ray was wounded and cited for valor, in the Republic of Viet Nam, was awarded the Purple Heart and the Bronze Star.

The Old Craigs, Will's sons by tradition, were farmers, loggers, and independent teamsters. Their farm and wood lands, both on Lick Creek and along the Tennessee River, remain in the possession of the fourth generation Craig descendants today.

The dates and facts herein, are supported by the Andrew Craig Family History, the family records of W.R. Craig, and the 1870 Perry County Census. Copies of deeds dating from 1871, document the transfer of properties, and an old letter from Tapp Craig's granddaughter, Ethel Randle, authenticates Tapp's date of birth. It is with pride and appreciation that it becomes a part of the annals of Perry County History. *Researched, written, and submitted by Helen Craig Smith.*

MCDONALD CRAIG, was born April 11, 1931, in Perry County, Tennessee, in the 2nd Civil District North Lick Creek Community. He was the third child of seven, with a sister, Helen, and a brother, Newt Jr., preceding in birth. Following McDonald were Ray, Carolyn, Roy, and Reba. McDonald attended elementary school in the Lower Lick Creek Community just above the scene that almost became the seat of Perry County.

McDonald and Rosetta Craig with their two sons, Reginald and Ervin, in 1967.

After going to school only to the sixth grade, McDonald quit and took a job, along with his older brother, to help with family expenses. With very little time in elementary school again, McDonald was occupied in working timber and doing farm work until age twenty. At this time, he was drafted into military service for two years of duty during the Korean Conflict. He took his basic training at Fort Riley, Kansas. After completing basic training, he was sent to Okinawa for eight months of advanced training. After touring Okinawa, McDonald went to Korea to finish the rest of his time as a draftee. He was assigned to Company D 2nd Bn. 5th Regiment Combat Team that spearheaded for different divisions in time - the 40th, the 45th, and the 3rd. McDonald became gunner on the 75mm recoiless rifle. From front line service, he received the Combat Infantry Badge, three Battle Stars, and the Bronze Star. After being discharged, McDonald returned to timber work and farming for one year before deciding to go to school again. At first, he tried a GI farming school program until deciding it was not what it should be. After talking with a cousin of his about going to high school, he decided to give it a try. The black people of Perry County had never had a high school or transportation to a high school, but much talk was being done about the need of a bus to transport black students to high school. After discussing the thought with eligible students, their parents and school board officials, everyone thought it was a good idea to purchase a bus for the need. McDonald did and included himself as a student passenger and carried all to Montgomery High School in Lexington, Tennessee. McDonald conveyed students to Lexington for ten years. It was in high school that he met his wife, a classmate, Rosetta Smith. Their class graduated in May of 1958, and they married in June of 1958. Continuing to haul students after graduation, he took a part-time job at Bailey's Sawmill. While waiting to pick up the students at the end of the day, he enjoyed this sawmill work with Bailey's very much. The bussing of students and sawmilling continued until May of 1965, when the government order came that schools would integrate the next school season.

McDonald continued to do timber work, mostly until taking a job with the Highway Department in 1975, where he worked until retiring in December of 1993. He and his wife have two sons, Reginald and Ervin, both of whom live and work in Nashville. McDonald developed a special love for music from listening to the music his father and mother played for the many different people who visited their home during his childhood and the depression years. He also remembers the records that were played on his near-by neighbor's Victrola of the original country music artists and became involved in Country Music performances through showing his love and respect to the originals of the art. He took top honors in Meridian, Mississippi, in 1978, at the Jimmie Rodgers Memorial Festival Talent Contest where he competed against 71 other contestants who were all white. McDonald is the only black to ever win this prize. After taking first place in Meridian, it put him in contact with many people and caused him to go places and see things he may have not had if it had not been for music. One of his largest performances each year is at the Ellington Agricultural Center in Nashville each Spring for the Rural Life Festival.

O.T. CRAIG, was the fourteenth son of Eleazor Hardeman Craig, born March 16, 1884. Eleazor was a direct descendant of Andrew D. Craig, who came to the United States from Ireland and settled in North Carolina. Andrew D. Craig I, had five children, one of which was Andrew II, who married Martha Hardeman and they had five children, one of which was O.T.'s father Eleazor Hardeman (E.H.) Craig, born Feb. 21, 1836. Eleazor married Margaret Greer, Jan. 29, 1857, and they had 14 children. E.H. was a farmer. O.T.'s mother died when he was six months old. March 13, 1886, E.H. married Nancy Trull and they had five children. E.H. died at his home, Feb. 16, 1896.

O.T. and Lula Craig

O.T., at the age of 16, moved to Texas and worked on the railroad. After returning to Tennessee, he married Norma Taylor, who died in childbirth. He later married Lula Paschall, born April 25, 1889, the daughter of Michael Henry Paschall and Caldonia Elizabeth Kirk Paschall. M.H. Paschall, her father, was sheriff of Perry County for two terms and served as magistrate and other offices of the County.

O.T. and Lula were married March 7, 1907, and lived in the Chestnut Grove community on the Godwin Farm that once belonged to his ancestor Anderew D. Craig II. In 1927, they bought a farm of their own and moved into the town of Linden where he continued farming. They were members of the Church of Christ. They had two children, Nola Lorine, born Aug. 31, 1911, and Nell, born Oct. 1914. Nell died at age two years in 1916.

Nola Lorine finished high school at Perry County High School in 1930. She went to Freed Hardeman College in 1930 and then taught school various places in Perry County. Nola married George Godwin, June 15, 1935 and their children were: George Craig Godwin (March 12, 1936), infant son who died, Gail Godwin (Nov. 1, 1944). George Craig received his degree from Tennessee Tech in Cookeville and was an officer in the Navy. He moved to San Francisco and married his wife, Gloria, who had one daughter named Susan. He is Vice President of BW/IP International Inc., a company that manufactures nuclear pumps. Gail married Royce Denton from Cedar Creek community. She works at Linden Elementary School as a school secretary/bookkeeper and at Perry Memorial Hospital in the adolescent New Hope Unit as a counselor. They had two children, Patrick (March 14, 1968), who received his degree from Freed Hardeman in Business Administration, Banking, and Finance, and Derrick (Oct. 10, 1972, married Paula Cotham, and works at Linden Automatic Tool Company. They reside in Lobelville.

O.T. Craig died Sept. 28, 1964 at the age of 80. His wife, Lula, died Aug. 19, 1991 at the age of 102.

ROBERT HARDEMAN CRAIG, and wife Betty live on Coon Creek in Perry County, Tennessee. She is the daughter of Monroe B. and Bessie Roberts. Robert, born April 16, 1922, is the son of Charlie Craig and Laura Viola Chessor. Robert is the brother of Hilda Louise, born Oct. 17, 1915, Verna May, born April 9, 1918, Mattie Lorene, born April 26, 1920, Willie Sue, born Sept. 13, 1926, Kenneth Hue, born Dec. 20,1929, Jo Ann, born Feb. 20, 1935, died Feb. 22, 1935, and Wanda June, born June 21, 1936.

*Eleazar Hardeman Craig   Margaret Greer Craig
(Eleazar's first wife)*

Charlie, born Oct. 31, 1890, died April 2, 1961, farmed and lived on Coon Creek all his life. His grandfather was Andrew Craig, born March 9, 1787, and reputed to have been co-founder of the Church of Christ, Williamson County, Tennessee. Goodspeed's History of Tennessee mentions an Andrew Craig and Martha Dupuy Hardeman as having been married, April 20, 1835, in Williamson County, Tennessee.

Nancy Elizabeth Trull Craig (Eleazar's second wife)

Andrew's father and mother were David Craig and Mary Duncan. David was born in or before 1775, and died in Williamson County. He helped form Blount County, Tennessee, one of the eleven counties that chose five delegates each to the constitutional convention held at Knoxville, Tennessee. Another noteworthy delegate to the convention was a Tennessean named Andrew Jackson, later to be elected United States President. On June 1, 1796, President George Washington signed into law the Congressional Act creating Tennessee as the nation's sixteenth state.

Eleazar Hardeman Craig and Margaret Greer, first wife, had fourteen children. He came to Perry County with his father, Andrew, when he was five years old. The children were the following: Andrew Henry, William Thomas, James Foster, Margaret Elizabeth, Joseph Eleazar, John Allen, Harriet Matilda, Nicholas Hardeman, George Washington, Benjamin Franklin, Wiley Black, Mary Susan, Claborn, and O.T.

Children of Eleazar Craig and Nancy Elizabeth Trull, his second wife, all born in Perry County on Coon Creek, are the following: Maggie Eva, married Robert Leo Averett; Jesse, married Clabe Dodson; Charlie, married Laura Viola Chessor; Lelia Jane, married Escar Lee Hinson of Coon Creek; and Zula Mae, married and divorced in Missouri and had no children. Maggie Eva, known as "E", Lelia Jane, and Zula all migrated to Missouri in the early nineteen hundreds where the Averetts and Hinsons both reared large families.

Kenneth Hue Craig grew up in Perry County and married Martha Lou Culp, reared their family in Lewis County. Children were Connie, married Jerry Blakemore, and Garry R. Craig, married Terri Giffin. Kenneth worked for and became District Manager of the power company in Hohenwald. He retired from the power company after serving 43 years, 30 of those as District Manager, and is currently living and farming near Hohenwald.

The Robert and Kenneth Craig brothers can trace their ancestry back to the Revolutionary War Battle of Kings Mt., South Carolina. Also, ancestors include a John Craig, for which early Fort Craig, Tennessee was named.

TAPP CRAIG, father of W.R. Craig; W.R. Craig, father of Newt Craig; Newt Craig, father of McDonald Craig.

Tapp and Amy (Guthrie) Craig and their daughters, Tennie and Mary Jane.

History of Tapp Craig, black American slave, born around 1821, and became the property of Andrew D. Craig II, the year of possession is unknown. Andrew D. Craig died in 1863, but Tapp Craig remained with the farm in the Chestnut Grove community until the end of the Civil War, except for a short period of time he was traded to some Berry, who he was unable to agree with on anything. After a fight, he was repossessed by the Craig farm for the remainder of his servant life or until the end of the war, which ended in 1865. At this period of time, the Craig farm was under the authority of Andrew D. Craig III. Now that the war was over, Tapp Craig was told he would have to go someplace else in order to comply with regulations. Reluctantly Tapp left.

Tapp was married to Amy Guthrie, who was owned by A.H. Guthrie, who owned a farm in the Bethel community, which is known as the Pierson Farm, that includes the area of Perry Farmers Co-op, Perry Memorial Hospital, Johnson Control and all. Tapp and Amy were married during the mid 1850s. At the time of marriage, Amy was already the mother of two children, sons, Henry Guthrie and Frank Guthrie. From their marriage, three children were born, W.R. (Will) Craig, born Feb. 16, 1855, Tennie, oldest daughter, and Mary Jane, the youngest.

Tapp Craig worked the Guthrie farm about six years after the Civil War or until 1871 when he bought his home in the northern Lick Creek community. He purchased the home from Samuel Young, on Dec. 25, 1871, for the sum of $400.00 (taken from courthouse records), $150.00, Dec. 25, 1871 for a down payment and a promissory note for $150.00, Dec. 15, 1872, and a promissory note for $100.00, Dec. 25, 1873, but managed to pay it off Oct. 14, 1873. He was the first black man to buy and own his own home in Perry County.

Tapp, Amy, and all the family were well liked by both black and white, but Amy is believed to have been the favorite of the family, because after moving to Lick Creek, her former master and his wife would drive their team down and visit with her for two and three days at a time. She had a special room fixed for them.

Tapp Craig's skills were farming, blacksmithing and herb doctoring. He and his family remained on Lick Creek until the children were grown and married with children. By this time, Tapp and Amy had become old and were not as active in work as they once were. Both of the stepsons, who were older, were gone by now. Will and Tennie, the oldest children, were seeking better places of their own, so they gave their share of the old homeplace to Mary Jane to take care of Tapp and Amy, under a certain agreement that the place could never be sold out of the family by a two-thirds majority rule, so no one would ever have to say they do not have a place to call home. Later, the youngest daughter, Mary Jane, married a man by the name of Alec Randle, who was a highly skilled carpenter, who still has one beautiful structure on Lick Creek, that he built for Tom Young around 1900. Shortly after this time, Mary Jane and her husband, Alec, took Tapp and Amy with them to Grayville, Illinois where Alec would have a greater demand for building. They lived near a large freight yard, even though Tapp was old by now, he still liked to work a little. He would pick up scrap wood and build a kind of pioneer furniture. His wife preceded him in death.

Tapp made two trips back from Illinois by boat. Between the two trips, he had a stroke. The stroke never stopped him completely, but he didn't live very long after. He died around 1907 or 1908.

McDonald Craig, Tapp's great grandson, was very privileged to buy Tapp and Amy's place in 1958 from Mary Jane's children, Robert Randle and Ida Randle, with all the rights of Mary Jane. The place is nothing fine by no means, but it is a way of saying "thanks for my heritage and to a family of people I love very much." *Submitted by McDonald Craig.*

CROSBY, Jimmy Wayne and Joyce Morehead Crosby. Their son and his wife, Terry Lee and Melanie Breckenridge Crosby and sons, Vincent Michael and Spencer James live on the old homeplace. Shawn Crosby Alfonsetti and Michael Alfonsetti and son, Nicholas, are trying hard to return to the homeplace from Miami, Florida.

William "Bill" Crosby, circa 1897.

Approximately 1847, James Crosby came through Perry County on his way to Arkansas. He was here long enough to meet, fall in love, and marry the daughter of William O. Britt, owner of Britts Landing. He and his new bride left Tennessee and settled in Stutgart, Arkansas, circa 1848. A son was born, William O. Crosby, named after his grandfather.

After the Civil War, W.O. Crosby was sent to live with his grandparents at Britts Landing. There were shady rumors concerning the reasons, but nothing confirmed. Also, there is no evidence that he ever lived with his grandparents. The first record that we have of him is in the 1870 census where he records that he is a carpenter, has property worth $100.00, and that he can read and write.

In 1878, he married Martha Ann Taylor, the daughter of Andrew Jackson Taylor and Temperance Lomax Taylor, prominent persons of Perry County. They had thirteen children and lived in several different locations in Perry County: Lick Creek, Cypress Creek, and Linden.

There is no record of him ever doing carpentry work, but he was a delinquent tax collector in 1880. Sometime between 1880 and 1900, he was the Sheriff of Perry County. One of his children was born at the jail. There is a picture of him in the Perry County Court House when he was Deputy Sheriff in 1893. Now 100 years later, his great-grandson, Jimmy Wayne Crosby, is Deputy Sheriff.

W.O. Crosby died in 1903 of a stroke, and his wife followed on Christmas day 1905 of pneumonia leaving nine of the thirteen children in need of care. They were "farmed out" to relatives and friends in Perry, Dickson, and Decatur Counties. The twelfth, Howard Lomax Crosby, came to live with his Uncle Joe and Aunt Rye Taylor at the age of six. They lived on 60 acres. This was all that was left of 5,000 acres that Uncle Joe's father, Andrew Jackson Taylor, had received in a land grant from President Andrew Jackson in 1854.

In 1917, Howard married Ova Ilene Aldridge, the daughter of James and Ellen Bates Aldridge. They had two children, James Howard and William Andrew "Buddy" Crosby. In 1941, James married Mattie Lou Heath, the daughter of Jesse and Louise Duncan Heath. They had one son, J. Wayne Crosby. His wife, Joyce, was born in Oak Ridge, Tennessee, of Ovid and Alta Flowers Morehead. One of Joyce's sisters, Sandra, and husband, Johnny Messina, moved to Perry County and live on Lick Creek.

Other related names are, Shannon, Halbrooks, Ledbetter, Godwin, Horner, Johnson, Pirtle, and Crockett.

ANDREW C. CUDE, born Jan. 29, 1823, either Hickman or Perry County, died June 28, 1895, Perry County, buried Cude Cemetery. He was a Confederate soldier, member of the Methodist Episcopal Church and son of Horner Cude and Temperance Lomax. His first two wives were sisters, Martha and Caroline Crudup. Martha died soon after their marriage and he married Caroline, who died in 1863. He had several children by Caroline. One was Martha Hughes Cude, born June 1, 1851, died March 15, 1921, Texas. She married Alonzo M. Clayton, Jan. 25, 1871, Perry County. He was the son of William Clayton and Winnie Peyton. Alonzo's half-sister, Martha Clayton, married May 3,1872, Perry County, to Benjamin Rufus Wiggs and they also went to Texas. Martha's mother was Nancy J. Campbell.

Andrew and Indiana King had eight children: Ida Cude, born July 1, 1864, Beardstown, married Lafayette Bates, died in Texas; Ada Cude, twin to Ida, died Oct. 10, 1936, Texas, married, Dec. 22, 1885, Perry County, to Clinton J. Cotham; A. Rebecca Cude, born May 1868, buried in Missouri, married Newt or Charlie McClanahan; Almedia "Meda" Cude, born Nov. 19, 1870, Perry County, died Feb. 22, 1923, Lobelville, buried Leeper Cemetery. She married Samuel John Leeper, July 9, 1893, in Perry County; Temperance A. Cude, known as "Andie", born Aug. 12, 1873, Perry County, died Oct. 21, 1929, buried Leeper Cemetery. She married Charles Cole, 1897, Perry County; John Andrew Cude, born June 1875, married Ada Burns, lived in Nashville; female infant Cude; Byron Cude, born Nov. 30, 1882, Perry County, died Oct. 12, 1964, Kentucky, buried Leeper Cemetery. She married Hurshel R. Loveless, July 9, 1910, Perry County.

JOHN BELL CUDE, grew up on Cane Creek and married Mary Elizabeth Shepard (1865-1925). He ran a grocery in the Cane Creek Community for many years and upon the death of his wife moved to Linden to live with his son Carlos.

John Bell and Mary Elizabeth Shepard Cude and their youngest daughter, Ina Pearl around 1910.

It should be noted here that Mary Elizabeth's uncle Samuel G. Shepard of Wilson County, Tennessee was the Lt. Colonel of the 7th Tennessee Infantry in Archer's Brigade, A.P. Hill's Light Division, Stonewall Jackson's Corps in the Army of Northern Virginia. He fought in all the battles of that army, including reaching the stone wall during Pickett's Charge. He was still with the colors and was the defacto brigade commander at Appomattox when only 43 of the original 1,000 men of the 7th surrendered.

John Bell and Mary Elizabeth's children were Alta Hortense, Era Eva, Ira, Carlos Rushin and Ina Pearl.

Alta (1886-1923) married Thomas Leslie Curl (1883-1963). Their children were Leslie Bell (1906-1967), John Vaughn (1908-1925), Mary Virginia (1910-1980), Ruth (1912-), Thomas Leslie (1917-), Robert Cude (1919-1990) and Mildred Louise (1923-).

Eva (1889-1964) married first Ed Bastin. Their child was Lorene (1915-1983). Second she married John Anderson Land (1869-1949). Their children are Charlotte (1920-) and William Bell (1923-).

Ira married Esther Pace. Their children were Wallace, Elizabeth and twins, Charles and Charlotte.

Carlos (1894-1966) married Martha Berthalee Lane (1895-1979). Their children are Eva Pauline (1919-1994), Lila Pearl (1922-), twins, Ralph Lane (1924-1978) and Ruby Lee (1924-) and Dorothy Ann (1931-).

Here again is an interesting story of Perry County. Carlos was a big, strapping fellow who was the harness maker and cobbler for Linden. He had a small store front in the downtown area. The main piece of machinery for a cobbler was his massive, cast-iron framed sewing machine. It took several men to move Carlos' machine into his shop and bolt it to the floor. In about 1932 a big chunk of downtown Linden burned to the ground. As his shop burned around him, Carlos and a black man who helped him literally pulled the machine free of the bolts holding it to the floor and carried it out into the street. He was back in business almost immediately (in another location).

Ina Pearl (1902-1925) married Claude Warren (1897-1925). Their children were Irene (1918-1925), Mary Bell (1921-1925) and J.W. (1923-). This whole family with the exception of J.W. were gruesomely killed along with Ina's mother Mary Elizabeth and her grandson, John Vaughn Curl when their old, wood-bodied touring car was hit broadside by a freight train doing over sixty miles per hour. They were returning from a visit to other family in the Union City area when their car stalled on the tracks.

The only survivor was baby J.W. who was found still in his dead father's arms atop the cowcatcher of the engine. The baby was only scratched and bruised and had a broken leg in spite of the fact that the train had carried him that way for more than a mile as it came to a stop.

As would be expected, the bodies of the victims were terribly mutilated but the worst aspect of the crash came when the head of 17 year old John Curl was found several hundred yards from his body. This story is documented in a graphic and sensational story in the Sept. 10, 1925 edition of the *Hickman County News*.

WILLIAM HODGE CUDE, (1829-1864) also rode with N.B. Forrest and the 10th Cavalry, Dibrell's Brigade. The 10th was reassigned to Joe Wheeler's command after Chickamauga. Forrest was so angry at losing these units that he confronted General Bragg, and in a now famous incident, in part said "If you were any part of a man, I would slap your face and force you to resent it!"

William Hodge was wounded and had to be left behind during a cavalry raid on the Federal trains at Cassville, Georgia. Cassville was the site of a Union held Confederate hospital where William Hodge was undoubtedly taken. He died as a result of an arm amputation and is believed to be buried among the many unmarked in the small Confederate Cemetery in Cassville.

William Hodge was the son of Horner (1795, Grainger County, Tennessee-1858) and Temperance Lomax Cude (1799 in Georgia-1863). They were married in 1817 in Perry County.

William Hodge married Mary Jane Hufstedler. Two children are on record: John Bell (1859-1949) and Samuel Felix (1864-?). Samuel Felix was born just weeks before his father was killed in Georgia.

CULP/GILMER, Mary Elizabeth Culp, who had moved to Lobelville with her son and his family in 1926, had twelve children: Argent, Tilda, Fred, Tom, Ada, Ben, Elvis, Ed, Nina, Delia, Carrie, and Clarence.

Maggie Evelyn Reeves Culp

Rudolph's mother's family may be traced back to Peter Reeves, born around 1775. Various records who Peter and his wife, Mary sold a farm in Virginia. They later owned land in Pitt County, North Carolina. On July 16, 1802, they were administrators over John E. Judkins estate in Pitt County, in 1827, surveyed and entered 25 acres of land in what is now Lewis County, Tennessee.

Peter was the father of at least nine children, according to the 1830 Wayne County census.

Reddin Fain, one of Peter's sons, was born Feb. 8, 1807, in North Carolina, and was married to Jane Burkett, Sept 1, 1829, in Lawrence County, Tennessee. The couple had ten children, among whom was Jonathon Jones Reeves, born July 25, 1834, in Lewis County.

Jonathon J. was married to Mary (Polly) Churchwell, Jan. 18, 1870. The couple had five children: Betty, Babe, Emma, J.A., and Jonathon Brown.

Jonathon B. Reeves was married to Lucinda Katharine (Kate) Helton. Their children were: Nora, Anna, Jennie, Barney, and Maggie Evelyn.

Maggie's first child was born down the river from Clifton at Grandview Landing, Olive Hill, Tennessee. She named him Rudolph and that is where this story began. *Submitted by Mark Culp.*

CULP-GILMER, Rudolph Nelson Culp and Jessie Gilmer were married June 15, 1946. Rudolph had just finished two years service in the Navy, serving aboard the U.S.S. Enterprise in the Pacific. Jessie had just graduated from Lobelville High School.

George, Mark and Jennie Culp

When he was four years old, Rudolph, born April 13, 1925, moved to Lobelville from Hardin County, with his parents, Herschel Clarence, born Sept. 16, 1899, and Maggie Evelyn Reeves Culp, born Oct. 27, 1899, grandmother, Mary Elizabeth Culp, and his sister, Vada Alvilda, born Sept. 1926. They had bought Bates General Merchandise which became Culp's General Merchandise and home to the family group. Another child, Ruby Jean, was born Dec. 22, 1932.

Jessie was born at the forks of Lost Creek and Russells Creek in Gilmer Hollow on July 25, 1929. She had a sister, Dorothea, born July 20, 1927. Their parents, Roy and Lucille Bates Gilmer, born Oct. 4, and Sept. 9, 1904, respectively, had married in Dec. 1925 and were farmers.

Soon after their marriage (in Corinth, Mississippi), Jessie and Rudolph turned Culp's General Merchandise into The Lobelville Theater and showed nightly movies for the next four years.

A son, George Nelson, was born June 21, 1949. The next year they sold the theater and moved to Chattanooga, where Rudolph worked at the Dupont Nylon plant and for the National Life Insurance Company during the next four years. Another son, Mark Allen Culp, was born on July 26, 1952.

The Culps returned to Lobelville in 1954 to make their home. A daughter, Jennifer Anne, was born Oct. 13, 1954.

Rudolph continued as a business person. He first purchased the Lobelville Pan-Am service station. Selling that later, he built the Four-way Mobil station. Selling this in 1965, they operated the Lobelville Market grocery. They then built the Gulf Kwik-Stop station on Main Street.

The new interstate highway, I-40, opened in 1966, ten miles north of Lobelville on Highway 13. The Culps purchased land on which they built and operated The Country Kitchen restaurant for the next nine years. After selling the restaurant, they retired for a short while.

Jessie entered Columbia State Community College in 1977. She graduated from Austin Peay State University, with a degree in Education in 1984. She taught school at Lobelville Elementary for nine years, retiring in 1993.

A toy and hardware route business kept Rudolph occupied for several years. In 1982, he began a Satellite T.V. business that he still operates.

Descendants of the Culps include: George Nelson and daughters, Kristi Jean and Misti Dawn; Mark Allen, wife, Karen, daughters, Shonda and Jessica Lynn, and son, Matthew Aaron; Jennifer Anne and husband David O. Warren. All three families, except for Kristi and Misti, live in Lobelville. *Submitted by Jessie Culp.*

CULP-GILMER, Aunts, uncles, and cousins abound in the Culps family life. Jessie's maternal grandparents, William James and Emma Murray Bates, with Will's second wife, Flora Twomey, had sixteen children: Everett, Ferd, Otis, Myrtle Coleman, Hazel Depriest, Mary Lee Cotton, Lucille Gilmer, Bernice Ashton, Earline Wright, Ruth Kirk, Mildred Klein, Tommye Rambo, Georgia Smith, Willie J. Bates, and two who died in infancy.

Jessie and Rudolph Culp

Paternal grandparents of Jessie, Samuel Newton and Martha Anne Ledbetter Gilmer, had eleven children: Robert, Albert, Jack, John, Roy, Clayton, Wylie, Myrtle Gilmer, Flora Baker, Florence Burns, and Lizzie Barber.

Samuel Newton Gilmer, born July 8, 1856, had moved to Perry County from Hickman County. His parents, James Alexander Scott (Sept. 9, 1823-Nov. 9, 1906) and Martha Anne Bratton (1830-1897) are buried in the Ledbetter Cemetery on Lost Creek.

James A.S. Gilmer's parents were William H. Gilmer and wife, Sarah, who had moved to Tennessee from North Carolina.

Martha Anne Ledbetter Gilmer was the daughter of John N. and Millie Elizabeth Tate Ledbetter (Aug. 28, 1842-Dec. 16, 1866). John N. (1825, Marshall County-1899) was buried in Young Cemetery on Lick Creek.

John N. was the son of Henry L. (d. May 14, 1859) and Annie Phillips Ledbetter (d. Aug. 27, 1870), who had moved to Tennessee from North Carolina. They are buried in the Young Cemetery, Lick Creek.

Millie E. Tate Ledbetter was the daughter of Lemuel and Polly Ann Strickland Tate. Lemuel was born, Sept. 13, 1822. His wife, Polly Ann, was born to Stephen and Sarah Matlock Strickland, Feb. 25, 1825. Lemuel and Polly Ann are buried in Ledbetter Cemetery on Lost Creek. *Submitted by George Culp.*

CULP-LEE, John Thomas Culp was born Dec. 23, 1941. His parents were Roy Linell Culp and Julia Iris Moore. He was born on Cedar Creek, in Perry County, Tennessee and attended school on Cedar Creek and Linden High School, where he graduated in May 1960. He joined the US Army, in Sept. 1961, and served his country until Jan. 1966. He was stationed aboard the USS Independence on the Mediterranean Sea for several months of his time.

John Thomas Culp and Betty Joyce Culp on their wedding day on December 22, 1967

Tom married Betty Lee, Dec. 22, 1967, at the home of his aunt and uncle, Howard and Sue Trull. Tom and his dad farmed several years together. Tom now drives the truck for Perry Farmer Coop.

Betty was born on Brush Creek at the Uncle Dick Rogers homeplace, in Perry County, Linden, Tennessee, Sept. 11, 1949. She was born to Morris D. Lee and Mary Rue Rogers. Betty attended Lobelville Elementary and Perry County High School, graduating May 12, 1967. Besides being a homemaker, she has worked at factories, area stores and now is a note teller for First State Bank in Linden.

Tom and Betty have three children together: Tammy Lynette C. Cunningham, Sept. 19, 1969; Trudy Gail C. Hinson, Oct. 28, 1972; and Corey Lee Culp, June 4, 1978.

Tammy married Brent Cunningham from Lobelville, March 23, 1989. He is the son of Joe and Frances Long Cunningham. They have one son, Joshua Evan Cunningham, born Dec. 11, 1990. They are expecting a daughter in July 1994. Tammy works as a nurse technician for Tennessee Valley Home Health. Brent is a school teacher and teaches at Lobelville Elementary.

Trudy married Bobby Dwain Hinson of Hohenwald, Tennessee, on Dec. 19, 1992. Bobby is the son of Gary and Wanda Odle Hinson. Bobby works at the Saturn plant in Springhill, Tennessee. Trudy works as a nurse technician for Golden Butterfly Home Health Agency. They live in Hohenwald, Tennessee.

Corey attends Perry County High School, where he will be a junior in 1994.

CULP-SMITH, Rebecca Ann Culp was born Aug. 1, 1942, in Clifton, Tennessee, the daughter of Woodrow Willis and Cornie DeBerry Culp. She attended the Linden Schools and graduated from Linden High School, May 13, 1960. Rebecca graduated from the University of Tennessee, in June 1964, with a B.S. degree in Home Economics. She was a charter member and officer of the Delta Upsilon Chapter of Alpha Delta Pi Sorority. Rebecca's first job (Sept. 1964) was with the U.T. Agricultural Extension Service as an Assistant Home Agent in Waverly, Humphreys County, Tennessee. In July 1966, she was promoted to Home Agent and worked in Erin, Houston County, Tennessee until July 1967.

Rebecca married John Edward Smith, of Waverly, Tennessee, on July 16, 1967, at the First Christian Church in Linden. John's parents were, Ray Lester Smith (April 21, 1906-Feb. 15, 1972) and Sarah Louise Hooper Smith (May 18, 1909-April 21, 1989). Rebecca and John are both members of the Church of Christ. After their marriage, Rebecca taught at the Waverly Central High School until Jan. 1972.

John attended the Waverly schools and graduated from high school in 1956. John attended the University of Tennessee and Middle Tennessee State University. After serving in the Army (1st Missle Br., 80th Artillery) for 18 months, in Vicenza, Italy, he joined his father's insurance business in 1964, and at present owns and operates the John E. Smith Insurance Agency, South Court Square, Waverly, Tennessee. Rebecca and John live in the home they built on Powers Blvd. in Waverly.

Rebecca and John have three daughters: Rae Ann, born April 21, 1972; Martha Jane, born June 25, 1973; and Sarah Jean, born April 12, 1976. All three girls were educated in the Waverly Schools. Rae Ann is a graduate of David Lipscomb University and is presently a student at the University of Tennessee in Memphis, studying for her Doctor of Pharmacy degree. Martha Jane attended David Lipscomb for two years and is presently a student at the University of Tennessee in Memphis, a student of the College of Nursing. Sarah Jean is presently enrolled in college night classes through the University of Tennessee at the Humphreys County Vocational School and will graduate from Waverly Central High School, on May 17, 1994.

Rebecca returned to work for the Humphreys County Board of Education in Jan. 1986, as Supervisor of the School Nutrition Program, until May 1994. She is presently working for the State Department of Education as an Educational Consultant in the School Nutrition Program in Nashville, Tennessee.

ALLEN CULP, (March 22, 1832-June 18,1918) married his step-sister, Eliza Jane Crossno (Sept. 4, 1843-Oct. 13, 1926), on Feb. 8, 1957. Allen was a Pvt. Co. I 19th Tennessee Cav. C.S.A. He joined Forrest's command in Clifton, Wayne County, Tennessee, on Dec. 10,1862. Allen was a furniture and coffin maker. In his old age, when he visited a sick neighbor, he would go up to the bed and with his hands he measured the length of the patient. Then he would make their coffin. Allen and Eliza Jane Culp are buried in the Wm. B. Culp Cemetery, Beech Creek, Wayne County, Tennessee.

Children of Allen and Eliza Jane Crossno Culp were: Amos Jackson (1863-1936); Milley Ann (1865-1865); Thomas Whitfield (1867-1900); Mary Elizabeth (1870-1952); Eli Jones (1873-1960); Nancy May (1876-1917); Ida Jane (1878-1977); John Franklin (1881-1881); Mattie (1883-?); and Charlie (1886-1918).

Allen was the son of Henry Culp Jr. (Aug. 2, 1802-March 23, 1887) and Sarah Robinson (b. ?, d. 1850). Henry Culp Jr. was the oldest son of Henry Culp Sr. (1776-1853) and his wife, Mary. Their other children were: Hartwell (1807-1882); Timothy (1805-1881); William (1808-1860); Benjamin; Ann A. (b.?, d. 1868) Adam; Sarah M.; and Amos B.

Henry Culp Jr. came from North Carolina to Tennessee and settled in the South Western part of Perry County. Family tradition says he came by ox cart. Henry Culp Jr. and his wife, Sarah, were married around 1850 and were the parents of: Anderson R.; Mary Ann (Polly) (1829-1896); Maranda; Allen (1832-1918); Elizabeth (Betty) (1835-1879); John Henry (1837-1911); Franklin (Frank) (1839-1870); and Amos, who was a Pvt., Co. C 2nd Cav. Bat. C.S.A. and was killed in the Civil War in Kentucky.

Henry Culp Jr.'s second marriage, about 1853, was to Elizabeth Betsy Briley Crossno (Sept. 2, 1825-Oct. 10, 1894). Children from Elizabeth's first marriage were: Eliza Jane Crossno, married Allen Culp, 1857; William Whitfield Crossno; Thomas Benton Crossno; and Frances Elizabeth Crossno. These children are step-brothers and sisters of the children of the first marriage of Henry Culp Jr. and the half brothers and sisters of the children of the second marriage of Henry.

Henry Culp Jr. and Elizabeth Briley Crossno Culp were the parents of: Tennessee (Ten); James M. (1856-1925); Sally Mai; William Buchanan (Buck) (1859-1913); Matilda (1863-1906); Amos (1865-1870); and Masa Dona (1869-1924).

Henry and Elizabeth are buried in the Henry Culp Cemetery, Little Beech Creek, Wayne County, Tennessee near their residence that stood until the early 1960s.

FRANK BROWN (PETE) CULP, was born in Wayne County, Tennessee, on July 13, 1885, the second son of Amos Jackson (Jack) Culp (March 28, 1863-March 23, 1936) and Sallie Katherine Parker (May 20, 1862-Oct. 17, 1920), Amos Jackson and Sallie Culp's other children were: Samuel Parker; Maymie Lillian; and Katie Tommie. Sam Culp (Nov. 25, 1883-Feb. 23, 1914) was injured in an oil well accident in Indiana. He was returned to his parents home in Collinwood, Tennessee where Amos owned and operated a large lumber manufacturing establishment. Sam never recovered from this accident and is buried at McGlamery Stand Cemetery, Wayne County, Tennessee.

Maymie (May 10, 1887-1960) married Walter Parnell. Their children are: James Palmer (Dec. 17, 1911); Lucretia (Jan. 10, 1917); and Clovis (April 29, 1926).

Katie (April 6, 1889-July 17, 1962) married Johnie W. Hutson (d. Aug. 31, 1929). They had one son, Reese W. Hutson (1915-1955). Katie's second marriage, Feb. 17, 1937, was to E.H. Cunningham (1879-1952).

Frank Brown (Pete) Culp was in the timber business. He owned and operated sawmills in Hardin, Wayne, and Perry Counties. His first marriage was to Jenny Fraley in the early nineteen hundreds (about 1906 or 1907). She was a daughter of Willis Samuel Fraley and Josephine Weaver Fraley. They had two more daughters, Nannie and Molly Fraley. Molly married Thomas Hurt McLemore and they were the parents of Alton Laban and Millard Fraley.

Pete and Jenny Culp had one son, Leonard Oakley Culp (Jan. 4, 1908-Dec. 6, 1974). Jenny died of tuberculosis soon after Leonard's birth. Leonard was educated in the Perry County Schools and was a member of the First Christian Church. Leonard married Martha Alice Savage, Dec. 25, 1936. He was in the sawmill business until crippling arthritis prevented him from working. Leonard was in an automobile accident in Hickman County and died at Goodlark Hospital in Dickson County, Dec. 6, 1974. He is buried in the Kirk Cemetery in Linden. Pete Culp then married Jenny's younger sister, Nannie (Dec. 25, 1895-Dec. 18, 1984), who was about 15 years old. Pete and Nannie had one son, Woodrow Willis Culp Sr. (Jan. 13, 1913-Oct. 27, 1989).

Pete continued in the sawmill business for nearly thirty years. He served as an Alderman for the city of Linden and was a member of the First Christian Church. Pete died at home, May 18, 1959, and is buried in the Kirk Cemetery, Linden, TN.

Nannie Fraley Culp was born in Perry Co. in the Flatwoods area. Nannie and Pete built their home on Polk Street in Linden, about 1950. Nannie was always a homemaker, being an excellent cook, gardener, and seamstress. She made and designed clothes for the family and many Perry County ladies. Nannie was a member of the First Christian Church. After Pete's death, she married John Lewis, about 1966. John Lewis died, Aug. 8, 1974. Nannie continued to live at her home and died on Dec. 18, 1984. She is buried in the Kirk Cemetery in Linden.

WOODROW WILLIS CULP SR., was born Jan. 13, 1913, in Flatwoods, TN. He was the son of Frank Brown (Pete) and Nannie Fraley Culp. Woodrow was educated in the Perry County Schools and graduated in 1932. After completing his high school education, he entered the sawmill business, working with his father, Pete and brother, Leonard. Woodrow began working in Hardin and Wayne County area. Woodrow and Pete were boarding in the Rex Cole home when Woodrow met and married Cornie Beatrice DeBerry.

Cornie was born at Grandview, Hardin Co., TN, on Sept. 6, 1917, to Luther Oscar DeBerry (July 31, 1874-Dec. 20, 1960) and Regina Ann Reynolds DeBerry (June 8, 1884-March 11, 1982). Cornie had one sister, Roberta Rebecca DeBerry, born March 12, 1913. On June 2, 1929, she married Rex Johnson Cole, born Nov. 17, 1909. Rex and Roberta have one daughter, Dorothy Imogene Cole (Darbo) Carroll born Feb. 23, 1931.

Cornie was educated in the Wayne Co. Schools and graduated from Frank Hughes High School in 1936. Cornie was the Salutatorian and a Superlative of her graduating class. She was also a good basketball player.

After Woodrow and Cornie married, Woodrow continued in the sawmill and timber business. They made their first home in Clifton, TN. Aug. 1, 1942, their daughter, Rebecca Ann was born at the home of her grandparents Papa and Mama DeBerry. About 1946, they moved to Linden. Woodrow was still operating sawmills in Perry Co., TN, Benton, Fredonia and Crofton, KY. Cornie was a homemaker and very active in PTA, school functions and the church. Woodrow and Cornie built their home on Polk Street about 1951, next to his parents Pete and Nannie Culp.

April 27, 1953, a son, Woodrow Willis Culp Jr. (Woody), was born at St. Thomas Hospital in Nashville, TN.

Cornie worked as a cook at Linden Elementary School (1960-1965) and then worked as a nurse at the Perry County Hospital until about 1980. Woodrow sold his sawmill business in the early sixties and began working for the State Highway Department until his retirement in the early eighties.

Rebecca, Cornie, Woodrow, and Pete Culp were all baptized in Coon Creek by Dave Rose, in June 1950, and became members of the First Christian Church in Linden.

Cornie died of cancer at St. Thomas Hospital, Aug. 4, 1988, and is buried in the Kirk Cemetery in Linden. Woodrow continued to live at their home on Polk Street until his health required him to move to the Perry County Nursing Home. He died Oct. 27, 1989, and is buried in the Kirk Cemetery.

WOODROW (WOODY) WILLIS CULP JR., was born April 27, 1953, at St. Thomas Hospital, Nashville, TN to Woodrow Willis Culp Sr. and Cornie Beatrice DeBerry Culp. He attended Perry County Schools in Linden, TN and graduated from Perry County High School, May 14, 1971. On May 15, 1971, he married Wanda Lou Daniel in Collinwood at the Freewill Baptist Church, Collinwood, TN. She is the daughter of Elmer Wade Daniel and the late Jessie Ann Lancaster Daniel of Collinwood. He was employed by Linden Apparel Corp., Linden, TN, from May 1971 until Jan. 1972, and by the State of Tennessee, from Feb. 1972 until Jan. 30, 1973. Jan. 30, 1973 through the present time, he is employed by E. I. DuPont de Nemours Inc., New Johnsonville, TN as a Mechanical Technician. They have two children: Jonathan Daniel Culp, born May 4, 1975, and Jennifer Diane Culp, born Nov. 5, 1978. They are members of the First United Methodist Church, New Johnsonville, TN.

His wife, Wanda Lou Daniel Culp, was born April 14, 1951, at Eliza Coffee Memorial Hospital, Florence, AL. She lived in Collinwood, TN and attended the Collinwood schools and graduated from Collinwood High School, May 12, 1969. She was employed by Dr. Gordon H. Turner, Linden, TN, from Oct. 1969 until Feb. 1972, as a secretary and receptionist. She was employed by Three Rivers Hospital, from Feb. 1972 until 1987, as an Accredited Record Technician in the Medical Records Dept. In 1987, she went to work for Dr. Subhi Ali at the Waverly Clinic, Waverly, TN as an Accredited Record Technician until 1988. She was employed by Three Rivers Hospital, Waverly, TN, from Aug. 1988 until Nov. 1989, at which time she was employed by John E. Smith Insurance Agency, Waverly, TN as a secretary and continues to be employed there at the present time.

Their son, Jonathan Daniel Culp was born May 4, 1975, at Vanderbilt University Hospital, Nashville, TN. He attended the Humphreys County Schools, grades K-8 at Lakeview Elementary, New Johnsonville, TN and grades 9-12 at Waverly Central High School in Waverly, TN. After graduation, May 28, 1993, he attended Nashville State Technical College and at the present time is employed by Raytheon Engineering and Constructors at Cumberland Fossil Plant (TVA) in Cumberland City, TN. Jonathan resides with his parents and sister in New Johnsonville, TN.

Their daughter, Jennifer Diane Culp was born Nov. 5, 1978, at Baptist Hospital, Nashville, TN. She attended grades K-8 at Lakeview Elementary in New Johnsonville and is currently a Freshman at Waverly Central High School. Jennifer lives with her parents and brother in New Johnsonville, TN.

CURL-WARREN, Thomas Curl Jr., born Aug. 31, 1917, son of Thomas Leslie Curl (1883-1963), and Alta Hortence Cude (1886-1923), married Louise Warren, born May 15, 1917, on June 28, 1941. Louise is the daughter of Hugh Warren (1887-1966) and Mattie King (1887-1970), who married in 1914. Thomas worked on the family farm until Jan. 1941, when he volunteered for the service. Serving in the 30 Div. 117th Infantry until July 1943. Thomas transferred into Army Air Force. After graduation from school, he was commissioned as bombardier on B29. He was discharged in June 1947 and returned to Perry Co. where he worked for Tennessee Gas Transmission. He worked in Ashland and Winchester, KY before moving to Franklin, KY in 1950. He retired from TGT in 1982, after 35 years of service.

The Thomas Curl Jr. Family

Thomas Eugene was born Feb. 16, 1949, in Nashville, TN. He grew up in Franklin, KY, graduated from Franklin Simpson Co. High School in 1967. He attended Columbia Military Academy, 1968-1969, graduated from Tennessee Tech, Cookeville, TN in 1972. He was commissioned Second Lt. upon graduation and served three years in the Army. He was stationed at Aberdeen Proving Grounds and at Fort Carson, CO. Thomas Eugene married Ruby Turner, March 29, 1948, in Simpson Co., KY. Eugene and Ruby have two children. Maria Louise, born May 15, 1974 at Fort Carson. First Lieutenant Curl was discharged in 1976 and returned to Simpson Co. in April 1976. Eugene and family moved to Jackson, TN, where he was trained as a dispatcher for Roadway Express Inc. He was then transferred to Forrest City, AR. Tommye Leanne arrived May 8, 1977. Maria graduated from Forrest City High School in 1992. She is now attending the University of Central Arkansas in Conway. Tommye Leanne is in Forrest City High School; she will graduate in 1995. Maria and Leanne have been very active in Girl Scouts; both have received their Silver and Gold awards. The family is very active members of Forrest City First United Methodist.

CURL-WATSON, Abisha Curl (1809-1863), whose parents William Jr. (1767-1862) and Keziah Gamblin Curl (1771-1879), came to Hickman County, Tennessee from North Carolina in 1808. Abisha married in 1836 to Ann Maria Watson (1813-1894), daughter of William and Sara Mathews Watson. Abisha and their three sons, William (1837-186?), Thomas (1842-186?), and John Burton (1845-1931) all served in the Civil War. Abisha died in a POW camp in 1863. John Burton was the only one of the four to survive the war.

John Burton (June 1845-July 1931) married Addie Virginia Vaughn (May 1857-June 1932) in Aug. 1877. She was the daughter of William and Elizabeth Vaughn. John Burton Curl came to Perry County after the war. He farmed on Marsh Creek before buying a farm on Cane Creek in Perry County, where they lived until their deaths.

Their children were John Daniel (1881-1957) who married Verda Oguin and had one child, John Andrew. Thomas Leslie (1883-1963) married Alta Hortence Cude (1886-1923), daughter of John Bell and Mary Elizabeth Shepard Cude, in 1904. Their children are Leslie Bell (1906-1967), a John Vaughn (1908-1925). The untimely death of John Vaughn came in a car/train accident near Union City, TN. Mary Virginia (1910-1980), Ruth, Thomas Jr., Robert Cude (1919-1990), and Mildred Louise.

Thomas Leslie married Elizabeth Edwards (1888-1930) in 1926. He married Minnie Coble (1897-1972) in 1931. Their child is James Wilson. William Lee (1888-1967) married Mary Lane (1888-1949) in 1914. Their children are Grace, Mattie, Myrtle, Mary Lee, William, Ray, and May (twins), and Sue. Allena Anna (1889-1923) married Monroe Mitchell (1879-1966). Their children are Fred, Charles and Carl. Matie May (1892-1961) married Osco Chandler. Their children are Ora, Burton and Pope.

JOHN P. DABBS, M.D., Among the immigrants to Tennessee from the state of North Carolina was Vincent S. Dabbs, who was born in the latter state in 1815. He came to Tennessee with his brothers and sisters at an early date. They settled in Perry, Wayne and Lewis counties. Vincent S. Dabbs was a successful farmer and stock dealer. He was married twice. His first wife was a Miss Grinder. They had two sons and two daughters. After her death, he married Ellen Elizabeth Lancaster, who bore him eight children, four of whom are still living, Dr. John P. Dabbs being the fourth in order of birth. Vincent S. Dabbs died in 1880, and his second wife, who was born in Missouri in 1835, passed away in 1911. He was a Wig until after that party was disbanded, and from that time until his death, he affiliated with the Democratic party. He was a member of the Presbyterian church and his wife was a Primitive Baptist.

Dr. John P. Dabbs was born in Farmers' Valley, Perry County, Tennessee, April 21, 1856. He received his early educational training in the public schools of his native county, after which he took a course in the Bryant & Stratton Business College at Nashville. He then taught in the public schools of Perry County for two years, at the end of which time he began the study of medicine. After suitable preparation, he entered the medical department of the University of Nashville, where he received the degree of M.D. in 1878. He took another course of lectures in 1882. He began practice at Farmers' Valley, but in 1890 moved to Linden and was actively engaged in practice until he relocated to Hohenwald in 1909. He is a member of the Tennessee State Medical Society and the Perry County Medical Society, and although more than a third of a century has elapsed since he first received his degree, he has not permitted himself to fall behind in the march of medical progress. In keeping up with the procession, however, he knows how to be conservative without being non-progressive, and is never in a hurry to abandon a remedy that has been tried for the realm of experiment or empiricism. In addition to his professional work, he has been extensively interested in farming in Perry County, and has dealt in real estate to some extent.

For many years, Dr. Dabbs has been recognized as one of the leaders of the Democratic party in his county and district. In 1896, he was elected to the state senate from the Twentieth senatorial district, composed of Maury, Perry and Lewis counties, and served two years. He served as chairman of the Democratic executive committee of Perry County for some time, and is now the secretary of the executive committee of Lewis County. In 1904, he was appointed by Judge Woods to fill out an unexpired term as clerk of the circuit court of Perry County, and in whatever official position he has been called to serve, he has given a good account of his stewardship.

Fraternally, Dr. Dabbs is a member of the camp of Woodmen of the World at Linden, the Masonic Lodge, No. 256, at Linden, and the Royal Arch chapter at Jackson, Tennessee. He and his wife are members of the Christian Church.

On August 21, 1877, Dr. Dabbs was united in marriage with Miss Sarah L. Randel, daughter of Dr. A. P. Randel, of Oregon County, Missouri. To this union were born seven children, five of whom are still living, viz: Mollie May, Commodore Olna, Ethel, Cleveland R. Sadie Matt. Mollie married Samuel Lomax of Linden, Tennessee; Ethel is the wife of Joseph Tucker, a well known resident of Perry County; Sadie married C. H. Cude and lives in Texas; and the two sons are engaged in the conduct of a large mercantile concern at Hohenwald, under the firm name of J. P. Dabbs & Sons.

OTTIS JAMES DABBS, born Dec. 27, 1915, and Videlle Warren, born July 14, 1913, were married, March 23, 1945. They were married after Ottis served three years in the Air Force during World War II. After the first year of service, he left, March 30, 1943, for two years in the South Pacific area.

Ottis and Videlle were born in Perry County. Both attended one and two-teacher schools on Rockhouse Creek. Videlle attended her first school on Sugar Hill. The house was built to be used for both church and school. Dr. and Mrs. I.W. Black, owners of the land, were responsible for the house being built. They felt the need of a church and a school for the families, who lived and worked for them on the farm. Videlle's first teacher was Jim Denton.

Ottis and Videlle Dabbs

Ottis and Videlle have always been concerned for the youth in Perry County. For this reason, they devoted many years in the field of education. In 1932, Videlle graduated from Perry County High School, and entered State Teachers College at Murfreesboro that fall. At that time, a year in college certified a person to teach four years, and two years, a permanent elementary certificate. Videlle taught six years, 1933-1939, at Warren Consolidated School. The year 1939-1940, she went back to college at Murfreesboro, staying until she received a BS Degree in the fall, Aug. 28, 1940. Tom Kent Savage, who was teaching English at Perry County High School, was elected Superintendent of Schools. Videlle was called to fill his vacancy. The year 1940-1941 was the beginning of Videlle's teaching in High School. She continued to teach in High School until 1950. She took a leave of absence to give birth to their child, James Warren Dabbs, who died May 5, 1950. Videlle taught at Lobelville High School, 1950-1951. She returned to Perry County High School and taught from 1951-1975. She retired in 1975, having taught 41 years. During her teaching years, she attended Austin Peay State College on Saturdays and received a MA Degree, Aug. 17, 1956.

Ottis Dabbs attended Austin Peay State College after finishing High School in 1936. He taught three years, 1939-1942, at Linden Elementary and Warren Consolidated School before leaving for Military Service, May 21, 1942.

After Ottis was discharged from Military Service in the Fall of 1945, he continued his teaching and going to college in the summers. He received his BS Degree, Aug. 17, 1962 from Austin Peay. He taught one year at Bethel, 1945-1946; three years, 1948-1951, in the Veterans Farm Program; 1951-1953 at Flatwoods; 1954-1955 at Linden Elementary; 1955-1956 at Lobelville; 1956-1958 at Warren School; 1958-1963 Principal at Lobelville; 1963-1965 Linden Elementary; 1965-1975 Principal, Perry County High School. Ottis retired in 1975 with a total of 31 years.

Ottis Dabbs' parents were Olan Dabbs (born July 30, 1884; died Dec. 24, 1973) and Lillian Sharp Dabbs (born Sept. 25, 1895; died Sept. 5, 1985). They were married Nov. 16, 1913 and spent most of their married life on Rockhouse Creek. Ottis has two brothers, Orvil Walker Dabbs, born March 15, 1920, and Willis Ollie Dabbs, born Dec. 22, 1922.

Orvie (Cat) Dabbs married Mary Dixie Godwin, April 29, 1946. They had one child, Barbara Joyce, born Sept. 5, 1947. Orvie's second marriage was to Ann Rector, Aug. 1, 1950. They had two children, Pat Walker Dabbs, born May 16, 1952, and Kathy Ann Dabbs, born May 1, 1964.

Ollie Dabbs married Dimple Conder, April 1943. They had one child, Ronald, born March 15, 1945. Ollie's second marriage was to Neely Grooms, March 23, 1953. They had four children: Donna, born Dec. 26, 1953; Devonne, born April 22, 1956; Donald Terry, born/died Nov. 12, 1957; and Tena, born July 25, 1961.

Orvie (Cat) Dabbs died Oct. 21, 1985. Ollie (Shorty) Dabbs died Feb. 27, 1976.

Videlle Warren Dabbs' parents were Carroll Nix Warren (born Oct. 22, 1881; died Nov. 16, 1962) and Minnie Jane Hufstedler Warren (born April 29, 1898; died July 4, 1976). They married Sept. 9, 1900, at Bethel in the home of John M. Dodson.

Carroll and Minnie Warren lived near the mouth of Rockhouse Creek on Buffalo River. They lived in an old log house which was a landmark for many of the early families who settled there. The Warrens lived in the log house many years before building a house across the road. Videlle has one brother, James Gola Warren, born Feb. 14, 1905, and two sisters, Lela Anne Warren, born May 6, 1903, and Minnie Sue Warren, born April 22, 1910. Sue and Videlle were born in the new house, and Videlle still lives in this house.

Lela Warren married Johnny Presley Roberts (born Jan. 7, 1889) on May 21, 1922. They have ten children: Garry P. Roberts (born Feb. 16, 1923; died Feb. 4, 1994); James Gola Roberts, born May 9, 1925 (killed in a car wreck Aug. 22, 1946); Lela June Roberts, born Nov. 28, 1926; Dorothy Jane Roberts, born Feb. 1, 1928; Harris Carroll Roberts, born June 30, 1933; Bobby Clark Roberts, born May 20, 1935; Sue Ann Roberts, born April 16, 1938; Billy Frank Roberts, born May 30, 1939; Carolyn Videlle Roberts, April 22, 1943; Sammy Kirk Roberts, born April 6, 1946.

James Gola Warren married Loy Elizabeth Jowers (born Sept. 18, 1916) on April 17, 1938. They have three children: James Carrol Warren, born March 2, 1940; Richard Warren, born May 2; and Sandra Loy Warren, born Feb. 28, 1948.

Minnie Sue Warren married Paris R. Cotton (born April 19, 1909) on May 8, 1932. They have no children. Paris R. Cotton died Jan. 18, 1979; Johnny P. Roberts died Aug. 29, 1979; James Gola (Jack) Warren died March 7, 1988; Ottis J. Dabbs died April 30, 1989; and Lela Ann Roberts died April 15, 1991.

DANIEL FAMILY, George Washington Daniel, better known as "Uncle Dan", was born on Crooked Creek, Perry County, Aug. 2, 1844. He married Parlee Wootson Daniel, born Oct. 28, 1847. They had two children: William Andrew and Mollie. Andrew was born Feb. 16, 1869. He died May 28, 1965. He married Nellie Jones Coble on March 23, 1887; she was born Aug. 24, 1870 and died Feb. 10, 1941. They had ten children. Three died in infancy: Ida (1888), Annie Parlee (1894) and Paul, a twin, (1903).

John Robert Daniel was born Oct. 16, 1889. He died May 22, 1934, after being gassed in World War I. He was never married.

Sallie Mae Daniel was born Jan. 28, 1893.

She died April 8, 1980. She married Clint Adkins Daniel, born April 2, 1886 and died Jan. 29, 1961. They had one son, Homer Adkins Daniel, born Sept. 4, 1915. He married Margaret Gregory of Chattanooga, born Sept. 30, 1922. They had three children, two daughters and a son.

Charles William Daniel was born Nov. 25, 1897 and died Oct. 27, 1979. He married Myrtle Sweeney, born Nov. 13, 1903. They had three daughters: Hazel, born July 25, 1922, was never married. Nell Catherine, born April 7, 1926, married Robert Barnes Cron, born May 31, 1929. They had one son. Bettie Fay was born Nov. 24, 1930 and died Aug. 9, 1970. She married Harold Womack, born June 29, 1928.

George Dewey Daniel was born March 20, 1900. He died April 21, 1988. He married Ruth Pace, born Oct. 18, 1906. She died Aug. 12, 1993. They had a son and a daughter. Howard, born Dec. 9, 1925, married Velera Hunter, born Dec. 30, 1925. They married Jan. 12, 1951, and had two sons. Audrey, born Oct. 30, 1929, married Will Henry (Pete) McGee. He was born Sept. 17, 1929. They married Oct. 14, 1955. They had one daughter.

Porter Lee Daniel (a twin) was born Feb. 28, 1903 and died April 2, 1994. He married Willie Burrow of Shelbyville, Tennessee. She was born Jan. 10, 1907. They married Jan. 14, 1930. They had no children.

Grace Belle Daniel was born Jan. 20, 1908. She married James Andrew Broadway on March 23, 1934. He was born June 2, 1905 and died June 9, 1972. They had a daughter and a son. Danye Sue, born June 26, 1940, married John Winston Phifer of Spencer, Tennessee on March 23, 1967. He was born Sept. 17, 1937. They have two daughters. John Daniel, born Sept. 24, 1946, married Barbara Jean Newby of McMinnville, born Feb. 26, 1947, on March 23, 1968. They have two sons and a daughter.

Billie Randolph Daniel was born Sept. 11, 1910. He died Oct. 22, 1992. He married Hester Rozelle Whitfield. She was born Dec. 4, 1916 and died June 24, 1983. They married Dec. 8, 1934. They had no children.

Mollie Daniel, second child of George Washington Daniel, married Crockett Daniel. Both died long ago. They had the following children: J. Clint, Clyde, Walter, Pete, Porter, Paul, Grady and Orby. Nellie married Wiley Dudley. Minnie married Henry Loggins. Louise married Walter Westbrook (deceased) and then married Leonard Robinette.

ROBERT DANIEL (R.D.) AND CASSIE SAVAGE LEWIS,

The ancestors of Robert Daniel Lewis came from Wales, of Great Britain. They settled on the North Carolina Shores and followed the trails made by the explorer, James Robertson. The trails led through the Great Smoky Mountains, the Cumberland Gap, and on to Fort Nashboro (Nashville). Aaron Lewis (great-grandfather of Robert Daniel) settled in Perry County, Tennessee in the 1700's. Robert Daniel was born Aug. 20, 1886 in Perry County, Tennessee. He was the son of William Russell and Melvira Patterson Lewis, and grandson of John Tipton Lewis. Robert Daniel's occupation was farmer and active county leader. He married Josephine Catherine (Cassie) Savage of Linden, Jan. 29, 1918. Cassie was born, July 26, 1898, in Maury County, Tennessee. She was the daughter of James Cathey and Alice Kennedy Savage of Linden. Cassie was a member of the first graduating class of Perry County High School. Before her marriage, she taught school.

Seated: R.D. Lewis and wife, Cassie Savage Lewis
Standing: Jack Lewis, Ollin Lewis, Russell Lewis

In 1944, R.D., his wife and a sister, Bertia, moved to a 347 acre farm on U.S. 68, one mile west of Gracey, KY. The family chose Trigg County as their home after TVA bought their property and they were advised to move. The building of KY Dam had flooded their bottom farm land and there was also the dread of mosquitoes transmitting yellow fever.

To this union, three sons were born:

George Ollin Lewis, born Dec. 21, 1918, Denson's Landing, TN; died Feb. 14, 1982; buried McMinnville, TN; June 25, 1948 married Edith Goines, born Nov. 1, 1921. They had one daughter, Lisa Ann Lewis, born Sept. 23, 1961, married Jackie Edward Terrell on Sept. 19, 1987.

James Russell Lewis, born Aug. 15, 1920, Denson's Landing, TN; died July 4, 1985; buried in Trigg Memory Gardens, Cadiz. He married July 21, 1944, to Audrey Cotham, born Dec. 30, 1924, the daughter of Grover Cleveland and Edna Cook Cotham. They had one daughter, Betty Mae Lewis, born June 16, 1945, Cadiz, KY, married Sept. 5, 1964, to Donnie Ray Lancaster, born Sept. 27, 1944. Children: Carey Don Lancaster, born Feb. 5, 1966, married Sherri Decker, Sept. 22, 1990. Judy Leigh Lancaster, born March 17, 1969, married James Keith Sidebottom, Aug. 7, 1988. Trudy Lynn Lancaster, born March 17, 1969, married Kevin Blane Carr, Dec. 21, 1991.

Jack Ross Lewis, born Dec. 9, 1923, Denson's Landing, TN; died May 15, 1974; buried Trigg Memory Gardens, Cadiz, KY. Jack married Sara Lou Young, born Oct. 15, 1930, on May 31, 1948. She was the daughter of Robert and Kyle French Young. They had two sons: William Jerry Lewis born March 3, 1949; died May 10, 1990; buried Trigg Memory Gardens, Cadiz, KY. Randall Thomas Lewis, born April 15, 1956, married Linda Anderson on Sept. 24, 1983, divorced 1989. One son, Patrick Anderson Lewis, born Aug. 17, 1984.

Robert Daniel died of a heart attack Dec. 4, 1959. His wife died on Oct. 29, 1970. She was an active member of the Cadiz Christian Church. Miss Bertia Lewis who lived with them was born Nov. 3, 1888 and died Feb. 21, 1974. She was a charter member of Montgomery Homemakers and a member of Cadiz Baptist Church. They are buried in the Pace Cemetery (Pineview), Tom's Creek.

MARY SMITH AND WOODSON DANIEL,

According to his tombstone in the Northern Cemetery on Crooked Creek, Perry County, TN, Woodson Daniel was born Dec. 30, 1800, and died Aug. 5, 1847. He was a native of North Carolina but came to Tennessee at an early age.

Woodson Daniel was married to Mary (Polly) Smith, born May 7, 1806, in South Carolina and died Dec. 2, 1888. After Woodson Daniel died, Polly Smith Daniel married John T. Scott, a widower who was born in 1794 in Virginia.

Woodson Daniel lived most of his life in Dickson County, TN, where he was a neighbor of and probably kin of James Daniel who married Elizabeth Ragan and of John Daniel who married Elizabeth Taylor. The three families lived on Yellow Creek in Dickson County. John Daniel moved to Perry County in the 1820s. Woodson Daniel came to Perry County about 1844 and purchased a farm on Crooked Creek where his children were raised.

Woodson and Polly Smith Daniel had nine children about whom we have information: (1) Nancy Glenn Daniel (1823-1891), married David W. Daniel (1819-1887). Their children were Mary E. Daniel married G. W. Townsend, Wm. C. Daniel, James W. Daniel married Martha McKeel, Martha Jane Daniel married John James Smith, Julia Daniel, John Daniel, and Commodore Newton Daniel married Julia Bandy. (2) James Wesley Daniel (1825-1849), a deputy sheriff who died of cholera. (3) Wiley J. Daniel (1829-1853). (4) Elizabeth Ann Daniel (1832-1920) married James L. Coble (1828-1902). This family moved to Benton County, TN, near the Decatur County line. Their children were Eliza Ann Coble married David Richard Odle, John Wyly Coble married Ann Mary Rice, Mary Elizabeth Coble; married Richard Cantrell, Nancy Jane Augusta Coble married Jimmy Wilson, Texana Parilee Coble married John D. Rice, William Henry Coble married Josie Adelaide Morris, Sarah Camille Coble, George Thomas Coble married Nuggie Brevard, Josephine Chairsell and Maggie Anderson, James Otto Coble married Emma Zimmerman, Lilly Lee Coble married Enos Cain, Andrew Jackson Coble married Sallie Spence, and Edwin Woodson Coble married Maude Rice and Laura Alexander. (5) Allen F. Daniel (1835-?) married Mrs. Francis E. Thompson. Their child was Samuel T. Daniel. (6) John Nuton Daniel (1837-1925) married Martha A. Young (1845-1923). Among their children were John Beauregard Daniel married Theresa Pendleton and May Ledbetter, Emma Daniel married M. G. Hensley and Dr. Allen Daniel, Sarah Mozella Daniel married James W. Patterson, Mollie Daniel, Jennie Daniel, Robert H. Daniel married Oda Hensley, Samuel Woodson Daniel married Mamie Cotham, Charles H. Daniel, Willie D. Daniel, C. W. Daniel, Dorsey B. Daniel, Albert Daniel, Clint Atkins Daniel married Sally May Daniel, and Walter Lee Daniel married Mae Gibbons. (7) Mary M. Daniel (1840-1907) married Henry R. Putman (1837-) Among their children was Jossie C. Putman. (8) Sarah Daniel (1844/5-?). (9) Paralee Wootson Daniel (1847-1930) married George W. Daniel. Among their children were William Andrew Daniel married Nellie Jones Coble and Mollie Daniel married J.

Crockett Daniel. *Submitted by Carolyn Odle Smotherman*

DAVIDSON-ALEXANDER, William Ira Davidson (W.I.), son of Sarah Davidson, was born Dec. 25, 1829, in Hickman County, TN. His father is unknown, although, he was the grandson of Daniel Davidson (ca 1778-1837) from North Carolina, who moved to Beaverdam in Hickman County about 1820. In 1850, W.I. was single and living with his mother and siblings, James Monroe, Minerva Jane and Esther. Other sisters, Eveline, Nancy E. and Elizabeth were already married by this time.

W.I. married Susannah (Sooky) Alexander, ca 1851, and moved to Lobelville. Sooky already had a son, William Edward, ca 1847, before they married. His birthplace was Missouri. It is uncertain if Alexander was her maiden or her married name. In 1850, she was living in the Nancy Alexander household in Hickman County.

On Oct. 8, 1862, W.I. enlisted in the Co. C. 10th Reg. Tn. Calvary in Linden. Besides Sooky's son, William Edward, he left behind five children. Hester Ann, ca 1852-1904, married first to A. Jackson, and later to John W. Bates. Nancy, ca 1854, married J.M. McCan. Nora Evaline, ca 1855, married W.E. Spencer. Josephine, ca 1860, married Robin Hester. William has no record after 1870. After the war, three other daughters were born. Sarah Anna, ca 1864-1882, married Richard Hester. Polly, ca 1866, has no record after 1870. Mary J. Magdaline, ca 1868-1937, married Richard Hester in 1884 and has descendants now living in Lobelville.

Sooky Alexander Davidson died between 1870-1872. On April 29, 1872, W.I. married Melvina Bugg, daughter of Stiles and Mary Bugg. W.I. was known locally to be a good hearted man. Every Spring, he planted extra crops to be given to widows and poor people. It was well known that he loved to gamble. Tradition says that his last home cost him very little to build in 1880. Each time he paid his carpenter, he won it back in a card game! W.I. Davidson died on Dec. 17, 1894, and is buried in the Davidson cemetery at Qualls Bend near Lobelville.

William Edward, Sooky's son, married, ca 1872, to a neighbor widow, Elizabeth Qualls Rodgers. She was the daughter of David and Mary Wood Qualls. She and her first husband, John Rodgers, had two children, Tennie Byrd, who married Isiah Rosson, and Henry, who married Jennie Roux. Edward and Elizabeth had William Rudolph (1873-1949) and Mary M. (Molly) (1875-1962). Will carried the Davidson name, which is present in today's generation. Molly carried Alexander as her maiden name. William Edward died before 1880.

In 1895, Will Davidson married May Johnson. She was from Humphreys Co. and a sister to Molly's husband, Oscar Johnson. May died prior to 1900 in childbirth. It was said that he loved her so much that a large picture of her hung on his dining room wall until his death.

In 1901, Will married Ada Gentry, daughter of Wiley and Lodocia Whitwell Gentry. Will and Ada were parents of four children, of which, only two survived to adulthood, Claude C. (1901-1952) and Jesse (1911-1965). On Nov. 17, 1911, Ada died after giving birth to Jesse.

Later in 1914, Will married Ada's cousin, Laura Etta Bates. After their fifth child was born, they moved to the Dyersburg area. Both Will and Laura are buried in the Fairview Cemetery there.

Claude C. Davidson, married Oct. 11, 1922, to Daisy Olevia Horner (1905-1992), daughter of Benjiman and Dora O' Neal Horner. They were parents of nine children. They are both interred in the family cemetery at Beechgrove in Hickman Co. *Submitted by Jo Ann Lawson and Marsha Essary.*

DAVIDSON-HESTER, Nicholas Davidson was born in 1580 in Dingwell, Scotland. Nicholas Davidson Jr., born 1611, married Joan Hodges and had two children, Daniel and Sarah.

Gus Hester and sons, John, Leslie, Roy, Bill and Jack

Daniel Davidson (1630) was exiled to Mass. Bay Colony in 1651 as a prisoner of war. His father emigrated to America in 1654 and settled near Charleston, Mass. Daniel married Margaret Low (1657) and had twelve children.

Daniel Davidson Jr. (1662-1703), fourth child of Daniel and Margaret, married Sarah Dodge and had four children.

John Davidson (1694-1754), fourth child of Daniel and Sarah, married a woman named Ann and had eight children.

Daniel Davidson (1753), son of John and Ann, married and had eleven children.

Sarah Davidson, daughter of Daniel, was born in North Carolina in 1801. Sarah had five children: Evaline, James Monroe, William I., Minerva and Esther. Sarah raised her family in Hickman Co.

William I. Davidson, son of Sarah, moved to Arkansas and Missouri with his brother, but was dissatisfied with both areas, returned to Perry County to later become a prosperous man. W.I. married Susannah (Sookey) Alexander and had eight children. Each year, W.I. would plant a field to be harvested for the widows and orphans in the area.

Mary Magdaline Davidson (Feb. 26, 1868), youngest child of W.I. and Susannah, married Richard E. Hester (March 30, 1858) and had three children.

Gus Enlow Hester (May 29, 1891), second child of Mary and Richard, married Ida Lorina Tate in May 1912. Gus and Ida lived and raised their nine children on a farm just north of Lobelville. This land was part of the property owned by William I. Davidson, Gus's maternal grandfather. Their children were Mary Flowers (Ms. Garfield E. Qualls), Foy Wadell, John Tate, Gussie Estelle (Ms. Earl Chandler), Leslie Lemuel, Roy Edward, Bill Davidson, Martha Sue (Ms. James E. Lannom) and Jack Wilson.

John Tate Hester (March 1, 1916), married Sophia Jewell Peercy (1915). John T. was serving in the U.S. Army and Sophia taught at Lobelville High when they met and married Feb. 1, 1943. John T. joined the Army, Jan. 22, 1941 and served until Oct. 14, 1945. John T., a member of the 30th division, 117 Infantry Anti Tank Company, served in the European Theater and was on the English Channel D-Day. From the ship, the soldiers watched the Battle at Cherbourg, France. Their landing gear repaired, they unloaded and went ashore and joined the battles in France. John T. received a purple heart for suffering a gunshot wound in the right arm July 8, 1944.

After his discharge, John T. and Sophia moved to Lost Creek, north of Lobelville, with their three children: Betty Jewell, Johnnia Ruth and William Thomas. In 1950, the Hesters bought the farm near Lobelville. This land was once the home of William I. Davidson.

William Thomas Hester (March 6, 1948), the youngest of three, is the only son of John T. and Sophia. He is married to Elizabeth Eugenia Hittinger (June 17, 1948), daughter of William Smithcors Hittinger and Tennie Mae Stewart of Nashville, TN. Thomas and Betty have three children: Peggy Jean (Ms. Michael Hanna), born April 16, 1971, Connie Marie (Ms. Robert Alberson), born Aug. 4, 1972, and William Thomas Jr., born June 23, 1973.

DEAVER, Claude B. and Irene Deaver moved to Perry County in 1983 to live on property (The Willie Hendrix place on Mud Spring, west of Lobelville) purchased five years before. They moved from Neptune, New Jersey. Claude was born and lived in Long Branch, New Jersey till age one. The family moved in 1937, two miles to West Long Branch, where the parents stayed their remaining years. The members of the family were Claude Benjamin Deaver Jr. (father), Gladys May (Thain) Deaver (mother), Claude Benjamin Deaver 3rd (oldest son), Richard Robert Deaver (second son), and Jack Dale Deaver (youngest son). Irene was born and raised in Accoville, West Virginia. She moved to Long Branch, NJ in 1959 and married Claude in 1973. She has a daughter, Linda Sue. Irene's parents were Joseph Graboski and Genevia Victoria (Hager) Graboski.

Richard Deaver moved to Perry County in 1986 from Florida. In 1988, Richard married Alma Lindgren, then of Perry County. Alma had moved to Lobelville from Long Island in 1985. She has two children, Christina and Paul. Alma's parents were Charles Edward Lindgren and Alma (Nilsen) Lindgren.

Claude's father and grandfather were grocers. His great-grandfather, John, was a physician and pioneer in surgery. Many of the tools and techniques John Deaver developed are still in use today. John was in the military during the Civil War, but the family does not know if he served with the Union or Confederation. Since he owned orange groves in Florida and property in Ohio, he could have served on either side. It is a safe assumption that John, as a doctor, saved lives rather than taking them in that grotesque war. Claude did find one volume of his great-grandfather's multivolume set "Surgical Anatomy" at the University of New Mexico library as late as 1962.

Claude and Richard live one half mile apart as the crow flies, but two miles by road. They all expect to continue living in Perry County. *Submitted by Claude Deaver.*

DEDRICK, The Dedrick family in Perry County can be traced back over 130 years.

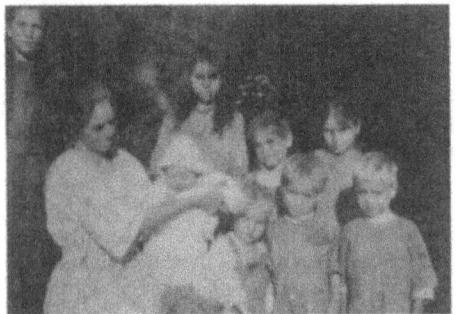

Back Row: Pauline, Mary, Robert and Fannie. Front Row: Roxy, baby Ivy, Marvin and twins, Ashley & Andrew

Charles Herman Dedrich was born in the Saxony province of eastern Germany and came to the U.S. with his brother, Frederick, in Sept. 1852. The trip was funded by their grandmother. The brothers apparently settled in the Pittsburgh area, where they applied for citizenship. Herman was a tanner by trade; further information about Frederick is unavailable.

Between 1852 and 1860, Herman moved to Perry County. He appears on the 1860 Perry County census with his wife, Jane. By that time the surname was modified to "Dedrick", replacing the ending "h" with a "k", probably to match the sound of the pronunciation. It is unknown whether Jane was from this area or came with him from Pennsylvania, or from Germany. Records do indicate, however, that Herman was 37 years of age and Jane was 28 in 1860.

Herman and Jane had three sons: James (b. 1852), Herman (b. 1851 or 1855) and Franklin (b. 1857). It is unknown what happened to James. Franklin went west to become a sheep herder and settled in Utah. A number of his traceable descendants live in Utah and Colorado. Herman, believed to be the middle son, remained in Perry County and married Elizabeth "Betty" Forshe, Dec. 26, 1876.

Herman and Betty had six children: James F. (b. 1881), John Thomas (b. 1883), Mary Jane (b. 1885), Robert Chessly (b. 1886), Florence Ellen (b. 1886) and Cora (b. 1892).

James remained in Perry County and married Ophelia McDonald. They had three children, Bill, Arnie and Emmie.

John married Sally Briley and moved to Adamsville, McNairy County, TN, where their descendants live today. They had six children: Elmer, Earl, Eula, Ardele, Evelyn and Charley.

Herman and Betty's three girls all married and had children. The oldest daughter, Mary Jane, married Rob Gallyon and had two children, Clara and Tom; Florence Ellen married Samuel Ellison and had two children, Albert and Mary Ann; and Cora married Clay Staggs and had three children, Obie, Willie and Hillard.

Robert Chessly Dedrick, the fourth of Herman and Betty's six children, was married to Roxy Ross Westbrooks in 1909. They lived in the Cedar Creek area of Perry County and had nine children: Pauline, married Clarence Holt; Mary, married Ottis Riley; Fanny, married Nelly Lomax; Robert, married Ruby Richardson and had four children, Mary, Paula, Gail and Robert; Andrew, married Lockie Howell and had three children, John, Lannie and Melissa; Ashley, the twin brother of Andrew, had a total of six marriages and 17 children; Marvin, married Mamie Richardson and had two children, Katie and Martha; Ivy, remained a bachelor; and Joe, married Ethel Markin and had two children, Joyce and Tommy.

Many of the Dedrick descendants still live in the Cedar Creek area, especially those of Herman and Betty. Several fourth, fifth, and sixth generation family members, with the Dedrick surname and a number of others (descendants of the Dedrick daughters) live in Perry and surrounding counties.

DEDRICK, The Dedrick family in Perry County, TN can be traced back over 130 years, to the days before the Civil War.

Robert Chessly Dedrick

Charles Herman Dedrich entered the Americas in Sept. 1852. According to ship passenger lists, he was accompanied by his brother Frederick. The trip from their home in the Saxony province of eastern Germany, was funded by their grandmother. After arriving in this country, they apparently first settled in the Pittsburgh, Pennsylvania area, where they applied for citizenship. Herman was a tanner by trade.

Sometime between 1852 and 1860, Herman migrated to Perry County, TN. He appears on the 1860 Perry County census with his wife, Jane. By that time, the surname was modified to Dedrick, replacing the ending "h" with a "k", undoubtedly to match the sound of the pronunciation, a common practice of the time. It is unknown whether Jane was from this area, Pennsylvania, or possibly even from Germany. Records do indicate, however, that Herman was 37 years of age and Jane was 28 in 1860.

Herman and Jane had three sons, all born in Perry County: James (b. 1852), Herman (b. 1851 or 1855-records unclear) and Franklin (b. 1857). It is unknown what happened to the eldest son, James. The youngest son, Franklin, went west to become a sheep herder, reportedly traveling there with Mormons on their westward migration. The middle son, Herman, remained in Perry County and married Elizabeth "Betty" Forshe, on Dec. 26, 1876.

Herman and Betty had six children: James F. (b. 1881), John Thomas (b. 1883), Mary Jane (b. 1885), Robert Chessly (b. 1886), Florence Ellen Voleen (b. 1886) and Cora (b. 1892).

The oldest son, James remained in Perry County and married Ophelia McDonald. They had three children, Bill, Arnie and Emmie.

John married Sally Maude Briley and, at some point, they moved to Adamsville, McNairy County, TN, where their descendants still live today. They had six children: Elmer, Earl, Eula, Ardele, Evelyn and Charley.

Herman and Betty's three girls all married and had children. Herman and Betty's oldest daughter, Mary Jane, married Rob Gallyon and they were the parents of two children, Clara and Tom; Florence Ellen married Samuel Ellison and they had two children, Albert and Mary Ann; and Cora married Clay Staggs and they were the parents of three, Obie, Willie and Hillard.

Robert Chessly Dedrick, the fourth of Herman and Betty's six children, was married to Roxy Ross Westbrooks in 1909. They lived in the Cedar Creek area of Perry County and had nine children: Pauline, married Clarence Holt; Mary, married Ottis Riley; Fanny, married Nelly Lomax; Robert, married Ruby Richardson and had four children, Mary, Paula, Gail and Robert; Andrew, married Lockie Howell and had three children, John, Lannie and Melissa; Ashley, who is Andrew's twin brother, had a total of six marriages and 17 children; Marvin, married Mamie Richardson and had two children, Katie and Martha; Ivy, remained a bachelor; and Joe, married Ethel Markin and had two children, Joyce and Tommy.

A large number of the Dedrick descendants still live in the Cedar Creek area of Perry County, TN, especially those of Herman and Betty. Many of the fourth, fifth and sixth generation family members, with the Dedrick surname and a number of others (descendants of the Dedrick daughters) live in Perry and surrounding counties. One interesting side note: The second generation son, Franklin (b. 1857), who left Perry County and went to Utah to become a sheep herder, now has a number of descendants in both Utah and Colorado.

JAMES YUTHER DEERE (JIM), was born on Lick Creek, Perry County, TN, Feb. 27, 1888. His father was John Calvin Deere and his mother was Frances "Mitt" Azbil from Henderson County. They had three children: Bradie, Jim and Howard. "Mitt" and baby Howard died during childbirth. John, remarried Catherine Arnold from Decatur County and had five children: Johnnie, Audie, Dorothy, Mary and Jack. Soon, they followed the westward movement and took the family to Texas. Bradie married Robert Patterson and farmed in the Pineview community on Tom's Creek.

Dollie Anderson was born in Woodbury, TN, Sept. 28, 1896. Her parents were William Anderson and Betty Hipp. They had ten children: Helen, Marshall, Mary and Martha (twins), Altie, Della, Valter, Dollie, Lillie and Laura. They also moved west to Texas.

Jim and Dollie met, courted and in 1913, married in a buggy in Texas. They had four girls: Vera, Aliene, Louise and Martha Nelle. Aliene died at four years of age during the 1917-1918 flu epidemic. Vera died from pneumonia during her senior year of school. Both girls were buried in the Black Hill Cemetery, Corsicana, Texas.

James & Dollie Deere on wedding day in February 1913.

In 1936, Jim and Dollie Deere moved back to Perry County with Louise and Martha Nelle. They lived in the foreman's home of Ayers and Lord Company, located on Cedar Creek in Furnace Hollow. The company name later changed to Wood Preserving Company and then to Koppers Company. Jim was foreman over several thousand acres of timberland. He collected $0.25 to $1.00 per year rent from those living on the land to stop homesteading. They moved to Linden in 1940 and Jim became well known as a cross-tie buyer and for loading and shipping cross-ties by barges on the Tennessee River.

Dollie Deere was well known as a strong willed, independent woman who picked cotton, raised livestock, gardened and sewed hand-me-downs into new wardrobes during the depression. She was a good electrician, plumber and carpenter, visited the sick, and even played doctor to community people. She was a liberated woman who drove a car in the 20s, 30s, and 40s when most women didn't and even had her hair "bobbed" early.

Jim Deere was a Mason and was secretary for years. Both were officers in the Eastern Star. He served as city alderman for Linden and both were active in all community affairs. They lived in Linden until their deaths and were buried at Kirk's Memorial Cemetery.

Louise became a beautician and ran Deere's Beauty Shop in Lobelville (1939). She moved it to Linden in 1941. She married Benjamin (Ben) Howard III (now deceased). They ran Howard's Cloth Shop on Cypress Creek. They had two children: Benjamin (Benny) Howard IV and James (Jimmy) Howard (deceased). Benny had one child, Mitchell; Jimmy had two, Kelly and Heath.

Martha Nelle was a beautician and owned Modern Beauty Shop and Martha Nelle's Beauty Shop in Linden. She married William (Bill) Gobelet (deceased) and had two children, Dianne Butcher and Robert (Bob) Gobelet. Dianne had three children, Tina Davis and twin sons who died at birth. Bob had two sons, Robert and William.

Louise is now retired and Martha Nelle works at Linden Elementary School. They both plan to enjoy living in Perry County the rest of their lives.

JAMES DENSON, The Densons came to Perry County before 1820. They settled on Tom's Creek, 4th Dist. From the court and census records, it is safe to assume the following.

James Denson was in Captain Peter Searcy, Millita Inf. War of 1812. He was given a land grant on Tom's Creek, now known as Denson's Landing. He owned and operated Denson's Lodge. It has been said he was the first man buried at Denson's Cemetery. He was married to a Churchwell. In the 1830 census, there is a Sarah Denson listed as head of the house, 20-30. James had probably died by then and Sarah is not found in 1840. Children of James Denson were:

Nancy D. Denson, (1816-1888) married in 1842 to Jimison Bandy (1788-1872) (See Bandy). This was a second marriage for both. Nancy had married a Wilson and had one son, Thomas N., (ca 1836-?) Children of Nancy and Jimison: William J. (1845-1916) married Melinda E. Terry (1859-1921); Amanda (ca 1850-1860+); Joe W. (1852-1937) married Martha C. Crowell (1856-1928); Richard (1843-1861+).

William B. Denson (ca 1822-1865+) married Jane C. Bandy (1825-1910) (See Bandy). Children: Sarah Ann (Sis) (1845-1919) married William Henry Coble (1834-1914). They had nine children. (See Coble and Long); Mary Elizabeth (Puss) (1850-1916) married in 1872 to William Henry Lancaster (1844-1914). Children: George Andrew (1874-1942) married Fannie H. Bandy (1881-1964), John Henry (1877-1937) married Martha Ida Burns (1878-?), married second to Gussie Mae Clark (1895-?), Emma Jane (1880-1966) married Thomas Allen Twilla (1871-1920), Flora M. (1882-1882), Annie (1892-1903), Twins, Ada and Ida (1884-?), William Hicks (1888-1938) married Nettie (1893-1954); Maria Jane (1853-1918) married Gus A. Walker (1849-1896) (See Gus A. Walker); Nancy M. (Ett) (ca 1858-?) married in 1874 to G.H. Ridens (ca 1856). Children: William (ca 1876-?), Jane (ca 1878-?), James (ca 1879-?). It is believed that this family may have moved to Dyer County.

Mary (ca 1827-?) lived with different family members and never married. She was listed in the census as being deaf and mute. *Submitted by David and Diane Walker.*

DENTON, The Denton family of Cedar Creek has its early origin in White County, TN, and later in Hickman County.

Andrew Polk and Mary Denton with granddaughter

Sam Denton came to Cedar Creek at about the age of 11, in 1817. He was born in 1801 in White County. Sam's father was Ben Denton. After leaving White County, Ben moved to Hickman County before settling in Perry County.

Sam Denton married Argent Coleman and they had nine children: Abner, John, Ben F., Isaac, Nancy, Jane, Milley, Sallie and Mary.

Ben F. married Sara Helms. Sallie married John Bunch. Mary married George Bunch. Milley married David Bunch. John married Jane (Jinsey) Richardson.

John and Jinsey's children were Argie, who married Dick Tole, Mary, who married Jim Peace and Sam, who married Sophornia Craig.

Sam and Sophornia's four boys were: John Brown Denton, married Dycras Paschall; Dolph Denton, married Jessie Thomlin; Andrew Polk Denton; and Walker Denton, married Tolla Ramey.

Andrew Polk Denton married Mary Cordelia Stephens. They had seven children: Eula Mae, born 1905, married Elsie Allen; Melissa Ann, born 1909, married Will Edwards; Sophornia Arkiedelphia (Arkie), born 1910, married Ira Doyle; Joe Vernard (1912-1916); Mary Love (1922-1925); Mattie Vivian, born 1925, married Thirl Hickerson; and Jeanetta, married Curgus Rainey.

Andrew Polk and Mary Denton are buried in the Cedar Creek Cemetery.

The family still has many ties in Perry County. Papa Dent's (Andrew) favorite pastime was listening to preaching on the radio and smoking his pipe. Mama Dent (Mary) was a loving person and a good cook. Submitted by William Bruce Hickerson, son of W.T. and M. Vivian Hickerson, Waverly, TN.

DENTON-WILEY-WARD, Abraham Denton was born about 1730 in Shenandoah County, Virginia and died late 1820s in Obion County, Tennessee. He was the great-great grandson of the Reverend Richard Denton, who came from England and established a Presbyterian church at Hempstead, Long Island about 1650. By 1774, Abraham was living in western North Carolina. He seemed to be a man of considerable influence in his North Carolina District and later in Washington County, North Carolina which is now Tennessee. By early 1821, he was in Hickman County, Tennessee. This section later became Perry County. About 1827, he moved to Obion County where he died.

From left to right: Ruth and Marion. Back: Bessie, Tom, and Ethel Dabbs.

About 1776, Abraham married Mourning Hogg. They had twelve children. Some of the children and their families moved to Perry County with him, including his son, Samuel Denton (1777-1856) and his family. Samuel married Eunice Conner (1783-1850s). They had nine children. Their eldest son, Elisha Tipton (1808-1882), married Cynthia Burns (1810-1880s). They raised ten children and several grandchildren on their 1,200 acre farm on Cedar

Creek. Their oldest son, Samuel (1833-1861) married in 1854 to Mary Louanna Wiley (1832-1883), the daughter of Alexander and Sarah Ferris Wiley. In July of 1861, Samuel joined Captain Harder's 23rd Tennessee Confederate Infantry, left to fight in the Civil War and never returned. He died October 1861 at Camp Trousdale, TN of complications from measles. He left two small children and an infant for Mary Louanna to rear. Their children were John Thomas (1853-1907), who married Martha Bunch, twelve children. Mary Caroline (1859-1935), married Alex Broadaway and had one son Ernest. Another son, Samuel (1861-1890s) married Sallie Graves and had two children.

Wesley L. Ward (1833-1910), from the Ward Bend, married Evaline DePriest and had two sons. He was the son of Wesley and Ruth Ward. Ruth, known as Granny Ward, had many stories to tell her grandchildren and step grandchildren about her life in the early days of Perry County. Her husband was an officer of the law. After Wesley L.'s wife died, he married Mary Louanna Wiley Denton. They had two children: a son, George Erving (1867-1910) married first to Martha Greene and had three daughters. Second he married Sallie Tomlin and had eight children; and a daughter, Ruth (1871-1932) married first to Joe Dabbs and had three children. Second she married Marion Wilson. Wesley L. married for a third time to Julia Furgerson and had one son.

Mary Louanna Wiley Denton Ward was the granddaughter of Robert and Sarah Wiley. They had moved to Maury County, TN from South Carolina in the early 1800s with their ten children. Their son, Alexander, wife Sarah (daughter of Caleb Ferris) and family moved to Perry County in the 1840s and settled on a farm on Swindle Creek. Alexander had been a soldier in the War of 1812.

There are many descendants of the Denton, Wiley and Ward families in Perry County today, including the present sheriff, Thomas Ward. He is the grandson of George Erving and Sallie Tomlin Ward.

The Denton, Wiley and Ward family histories have been combined here because there are many marriages connecting these families in Perry County down to the present day.

SAMUEL DENTON, moved to Cedar Creek in 1818. He was one of the first settlers on the creek. Samuel had the first cotton gin in Perry County, also a water mill. He was killed during the Civil War by someone trying to rob him of his gold. Samuel's daughter, Nancy Denton, married Joseph Bunch, son of Anderson Bunch. Anderson Bunch moved to Perry County on Cedar Creek about 1836. He sold his farm products to the people that worked the iron furnace.

Joseph Bunch and Nancy Denton Bunch had nine children. The third child, Mary Belle Bunch (Nov. 3, 1861-1952) married on Feb. 12, 1880, to John Edward Howell (Nov. 3, 1858-March 24, 1952). John and Mary had seven children: Newt Howell, Etta Howell Horner, Robert Wesley Howell, Cora Lee Howell, Marshall Howell, Myrtle Howell Smith and Fred Howell.

Robert Wesley Howell (July 24, 1886) married July 1, 1906, to Emma Roxie Mayberry (Jan. 25, 1886). Emma was the daughter of Thomas Anderson Mayberry (1851-1928) and Frances "Fannie" Crossnoe (1852-1933). Thomas and Fannie lived on Mayberry Prong on Cedar Creek. Robert and Emma had three sons: Morris Winfred Howell, Thomas "Tom" Edward Howell and Roy Robert Howell.

DEPRIEST, The DePriest family started in Virginia. The earliest record is of Robert DePriest, who died about 1710. His son, William, born 1689, married Judith ?. They had William, Robert, John and Randolph DePriest.

The above William, died in 1738, was the son or grandson of Robert "Robin" from New Kent Co., VA. They moved to Henrico County and William died about 1738; his widow Judith married John Hodges.

William must have had at least two sisters, one married George Southerland and one to John Salmon.

William and Judith's children were: Randolph married Mary Mimms 1751; William married Tabitha Tony; Robert married Martha Bailey; and John married Elizabeth Rice.

Randolph and Mary's children were: Robert married Patsy Taylor; Turpin married a Patsy; Francis married ?; Randolph II married Amy Mimms in Goochland Co., VA 1751. In 1778, Randolph was on the tax list of Henry Co., VA. In the 1780s, they were in South Carolina where Randolph fought in the Revolutionary War. They moved on to Georgia in 1790s. In 1793, Randolph was on the muster rolls of Elbert Co., VA for the war there. In 1810, the family moved to Hickman Co., TN. Randolph died there about 1828, his will naming his children. His wife, Amy, lived till 1853. She applied for a pension from the Revolutionary War, but was denied. Their children were: Mary, born 1778; Elizabeth, born 1779; Annis, born 1782; Sarah, born 1783, married Issac Cotham; Naomy, born 1785; Catherine, born 1787, married Hiram Casey; Randolph, born 1789, married Mary Bynum; Margaret, born 1791; James, born 1793; Amy, born 1795; Jesse, born 1797; Hugh, born 1801; and John, born 1804.

The above Jesse married first Nancy Andrews and second to Sarah Davidson. With Nancy, he had five sons and one daughter. With Sarah, he had three daughters.

One son was Hugh DePriest, who married Mary Amanda Vanlandingham from Dickson County, 1843. They had three boys and two girls. Hugh married the second time and had one daughter, who married Elisha Gean.

Hugh's son, Barney W. DePriest, married Rebecca Jane Westbrooks, the daughter of Benjamin and Mary E. Tucker Westbrooks. Barney was born in 1848 and in 1925, he wrote a family history in the Perry County newspaper. Barney was the surveyor for Perry County for about forty years. Their children are Sallie, Nannie, John W., Alex W., Fannie and Molly M.

Molly married Robert Halbrooks, the son of Ethelbert and Martha Edwards Halbrooks. Thelbert's mother was the same Mary Tucker who was the widow of William Halbrooks. She married Ben S. Westbrooks second.

Robert and Molly's daughter, Jessie Virginia Halbrooks (1897-1945), married Neal Strickland.

The DePriest family came from France to America. A. Randol DePriest was in North Carolina and came to Tennessee in the 1780s. He is not the same one as Randolph, who came from Virginia. *Submitted by Janis Clark.*

DEPRIEST, The DePriest family records date back to 1571 when Robert DePriest was listed as living in London, England, born in Holland and came to England as a servant. The DePriest were a close family, land owners, highly respected, had many professions, and lines of work. They came from England, Holland and France to America.

Sam DePriest Family

Rich DePriest was the first found in the records of the colony of Virginia.

Randolph DePriest, great-great grandfather, born in 1755, served in the Revolutionary War. He fought Indian Tories and served as a spy. He married Amy Mims. They had 14 children. He died, 1830, in Hickman County, TN.

Randell DePriest, great grandfather, came from North Carolina to Tennessee. He was the first known DePriest to settle in Perry County, with three brothers, John, Hugh and Jesse. They cleared and homesteaded a large tract of land, built a home and raised a big family in a community known as DePriest Bend on the Buffalo River. He married Mary Bynum, born 1795. He had 15 children and lived from 1789 to 1873. Randell DePriest is buried in DePriest Cemetery in DePriest Bend.

Grandfather, Pleasant DePriest grew up in the old home place that now belongs to Henry Loggins family in DePriest Bend. He had slaves. When the slaves were freed, one didn't want to leave. When he left to be with his people he was called Henry DePriest. Pleasant (1837-1914), married Sarah Jane Fuller, (1850-1913). They had six children: Viera, Henrietta, Lee, Robert, Henry and William Samuel.

Father, William Samuel, was known by most people in Perry County as Sam, a landowner, respected, honest, always jolly. He was born, 1875, married Ethel Burns (1880-1914). They had seven children. They were Myrtle Lorene, Paul Edward, Graydon Carrol, Samuel Rudolph, Julia Ruth, Benjamin Burns and Claude Raymond.

Myrtle Lorene (1898-1967) married Fred Burns (1897-1967), a World War I Navy veteran. They had one son, Fred Jr. (1920-1923).

Paul Edward, a farmer and carpenter (1900-1978), married Hazel Bates (1900-1989). They had four children: Juanita, Margaret, Joe and Mary Jane. Joe served in World War II.

Graydon Carrol (1901-1981), owner and

operator of DePriest Bend Grocery, married Dera Loveless (1899-1927). They had one daughter, Helen Sue, born 1922. Graydon married second to Lillie Baars, born 1901. They had a son, Carrol, who served in World War II.

Samuel Rudolph (1903-1979) was a carpenter. He married Lucille Hughes, died 1985. They had four children: William Samuel, James, Clay and Mary Ethel (1929-1932). William (Bill) Samuel, James and Clay were veterans of World War II.

Julia Ruth born 1906, died 1907.

Benjamin Burns (1908-1977) retired from Tennessee Gas. He married Lorene Bowen, born in 1909. They had two children, Kenneth and Catherine. Kenneth served in the Korean War.

Claude Raymond (1910-1982) was a school teacher. He married Pauline Barham, born 1918. Pauline was a teacher. Their children were Dianne and Sharon.

Sam married again in 1916, to Minnie Belle Burns born 1879. She died in 1918, leaving an infant daughter, eight days old, that was given her mother's name, Minnie Belle DePriest.

Minnie Bell, born 1918, married Brady Mathis (1908-1988), a landowner. They had one daughter, Zelta Faye Mathis (1940-1991).

Sam died in 1951. He took a mother's place, caring for his children and an infant daughter, Minnie Belle Mathis. She is the only living member of the Sam DePriest family, age 76.

DEPRIEST, The first known DePriest to be born in Perry County was Octavus LeGrand DePriest in 1859. He was the son of William Harrison DePriest, who served with the Confederate Army during the Civil War in Williamson County, TN.

Jack Milford DePriest during World War II

William married Delilah Emmaline Harder and they had five sons: Rayette, Joe, Gus, LeGrand and Lonnie. Octavus LeGrand was born March 23, 1859, and lived in DePriest Bend near Lobelville, TN. He married Mozella Cotton from Tom's Creek, near Pineview, TN, and they had four sons: Scoby Ross, Andy Harrison, Harvey Loyd and Earl Hicks, and two daughters: Oda Idella and Etta Mozella. Octavus LeGrand was a farmer and left land for each child in DePriest Bend. Harvey Loyd DePriest (April 1, 1881-Jan. 9, 1958) lived and farmed in DePriest Bend on the land his father left him. He married Eunice Harriet Horner in 1914, and after her death in 1927, he married Ruby Pratt. Loyd had eight children with Eunice: Glenn Edward, William Dennis, Jack Milford, Davis Horner, Ralph Daniel (died at four months old), Sybil, Oneta, Floydie Mildred and Sara Elizabeth. He had only one child with Ruby, named Judy. Loyd died in 1958 and was buried at DePriest Bend Cemetery. His son, Jack Milford, was born Jan. 21, 1922, at DePriest Bend and moved to Linden in January of 1946. He was an auto parts salesman in Hohenwald and Linden, TN. He served in the army in World War II and was given an Honorable Discharge. He played an active part in the American Legion Post in Linden. Jack married Lucille Anderson in 1942, the daughter of Jasper and Bonnie Halbrooks Anderson of Linden. They had one son, Milford Trent. Jack died Jan. 25, 1947, and was buried in the Pineview Cemetery. Milford Trent DePriest was born in Linden, Nov. 9, 1944. He graduated from Perry County High School in 1962. He has been the manager of the Perry County Farmers Co-op since 1966 and has served as an Alderman for the City of Linden for over 20 years. He married Nell Kathryn Grimes on July 2, 1966, the daughter of Jack Raymond and Jessie Mae Coble Grimes of Waverly, TN. She was a 1967 graduate from Perry County High School. She has been employed at Perry County Farm Bureau since 1979. They had one daughter, Kristy Renae, born June 24, 1972, in Linden. She graduated from Perry County High School in 1990 and is presently attending the University of Tennessee at Martin.

BEULAH DEPRIEST, was born April 4, 1905, near Linden, Perry Co., TN, a great-great-great granddaughter of Randolph DePriest and wife, Amy. Randolph, born 1755, in Goochland Co., VA, was a son of Randolph DePriest and Mary Mimms. Randolph married Amy in June of 1775, moving soon after to live along the border of Georgia and South Carolina. Randolph served in the Rev. War from South Carolina. They moved their family from Georgia to Hickman Co., TN in 1812. Randolph and Amy had 14 children: William, born 1778, married Rebecca Casey; Mary & Elizabeth, born 1779; Annis, born 1782, married Isaac Skelton; Sarah, born 1783, married Isaac Cotham; Naomy, born 1785; Catherine, born 1787, married Hiram Casey; Randolph "Randoll", born 1789, married Mary Bynum (lived on Cane Creek, Perry Co.); Margaret, born 1791; James, born 1793; Amey, born 1795; Jesse, born 1797, married first to Nancy Andrews, second to Sarah Davidson; Hugh, born 1801, married Sarah Goodman (living in Perry Co. by 1838); and John, born 1804, married Nancy.

Beulah DePriest Bizzell

Hugh DePriest, born 1801, in Elbert Co., GA, married Sarah Goodman in 1828. They had seven children: Green Alexander, born 1829, served in the Confederate 10th Cav.; Nancy, born 1833; John Rober, born 1834, also served in Confederate Army; Henry, born 1838; Thomas, born 1839; Elizabeth, born 1841; and Mahola, born 1844.

Green A. DePriest, born 1829, in Hickman Co., TN, married Louisa Jane Ward, born 1830 (probably in Perry County) a daughter of Nathan Ward and Mary. Green and Louisa were the parents of six children: Sarah, born 1848; Nathan, born 1850; John, born 1854; Legarand, born 1856; Julia Calendonia, born 1859; and William Thomas, born 1863.

Nathan W. DePriest, born 1850 in Perry County, TN, married Anne Lomax, a daughter of William Lomax and Mourning Isabell Denton. William Lomax was a son of John Lomax and Elizabeth Horner. Elizabeth Horner was a daughter of John Horner and Elizabeth Russell and the granddaughter of George Russell and Elizabeth Bean of the Wataugh Settlement. Nathan and Anne were the parents of six children: William Green, born 1870; John, born 1873; Mary Jane, born 1875; Viny, born 1878; Carroll, born 1880; and Nathan, born 1881.

John "Lee" DePriest, born Dec. 7, 1873 in Perry County, TN, married Harriett Harder, a daughter of William Henry Harder and Sarah Atlantic Anderson. Lee and Harriett were the parents of 12 children: William Nathan, born 1892; Robert, born 1894; Lilly Florence, born 1896; Frank Leslie, born 1897; Dewey Bryan, born 1898; infant, born 1900; Fred, born 1902; Bertie Delphia, born 1903; Beulah May, born 1905; Flora Atlantic, born 1909; Ruby Lee, born 1912; and Claude, born 1914.

Beulah's family moved from Perry County, TN to Pemiscott County, MO in 1913. She married Junius Bizzell on June 8, 1924, and they had three children: Jessie, born 1926; Louise, born 1929; and Dolores, born 1935. Jessie married Betty Allen and they have two children: Jerry, born 1947, and Sharon Kay, born 1949. Louise married Jerry Taylor and they have three children: Judy, born 1948; Debra, born 1953; and Michael, born 1961.

Beulah moved from Pemiscott County, MO with her husband and daughter, Dolores, to Memphis, TN in 1953, where she resides with her daughter, Dolores. In addition to five grandchildren, Beulah has eight great-grandchildren, and two great-great grandchildren.

DANNY SHEPARD DEPRIEST, was born April 21, 1947 in Nashville, TN, son of James Edward DePriest and Carrie Nell Shepard DePriest of Perry County.

Amy, Britt, Dan and Kathy DePriest

Danny spent his young life in Perry County, but moved, with his parents, to Waverly, Humphreys County, TN when he was a senior in high school. He graduated from Waverly Central High School in 1965. He attended Austin Peay University, but on Dec. 28, 1966, he enlisted in the U.S. Navy, during the Viet Nam War, being Radar Man III Class, Mine Sweeper, USS Energy. He received his discharge from the Navy on Sept. 1, 1970.

He returned to Austin Peay, where he received his B.S. and M.S. Degrees, graduating in 1973. He is currently a teacher at North-West High School in Clarksville, TN.

On Dec. 23, 1977, Danny married Martha Katherine Anderson, born June 4, 1954, of Williamsport, TN. She is the daughter of Kenneth Gardner Anderson (Feb. 29, 1920-July 2, 1987) and Elizabeth Lee Woodmore Anderson (Jan. 20, 1920-Dec. 13, 1982).

Katherine "Kathy" was the granddaughter of Henry Osgood Anderson and Ethel Claire Gardner Anderson. Her maternal grandparents were Thomas Britton Woodmore and Corrine Gill Harris Woodmore.

Kathy graduated from Austin Peay University, receiving her B.A. Degree in 1977, and the M.A. Degree in 1978. She is a teacher at Fort Campbell High School

Children born to Danny and Kathy were: Daniel Britton, born Aug. 25, 1979, and Amy Elizabeth, born Feb. 21, 1983.

Danny has one sister, Jill DePriest Bradley and Kathy has one sister, Nancy Beyer. Her brother is David Anderson.

JAMES EDWARD DEPRIEST, was born Nov. 27, 1925, in Lobelville, Perry County, TN, the son of Samuel Rudolph "Dock" DePriest (1903-1979) and Mattie Lucille Hughes DePriest (1906-1985).

James Edward and Carrie DePriest

The early DePriests came from France to Virginia and North Carolina, migrating to Georgia, then to Smith County, TN, and on to Hickman and Perry Counties.

James' great-great-great grandfather, Randolph (1755-1830) was born in Goochland County, VA. He lived in South Carolina during the American Revolution and volunteered for service in 1777. His great grandfather, Pleasant W. DePriest (1837-1914) served in the Confederate Army, 42nd Tennessee Infantry, and was captured at Vicksburg, Mississippi. He was later sent to Chicago.

James spent his young life in Lobelville, graduating from the Perry County High School. He served in the U.S. Navy during World War II (1944-1946).

On July 13, 1946, in Corinth, Mississippi, he married Carrie Nell Shepard, born Feb. 11, 1927, in Beardstown, the daughter of William Haywood Shepard (1893-1947) and Byron May DePriest Shepard (1905-1963) of Perry County (See Shepard history).

After World War II, James and Carrie made their home in Perry County where he was a merchant, carpenter, and an employee of the U.S. Postal Service. In 1965, he and his family moved to Waverly, TN, when he accepted employment with Consolidated Aluminum Company at New Johnsonville, TN, from which he is now retired.

James and Carrie have two children, Danny and Jill DePriest.

Danny Shepard DePriest, born April 21, 1947, married Martha Katherine (Kathy) Anderson on Dec. 23, 1977. Kathy was the daughter of Kenneth Gordan Anderson and Elizabeth Lee Woodmore Anderson of Williamsport, TN. They have two children, Daniel Britton, born Aug. 25, 1979, and Amy Elizabeth, born Feb. 21, 1983. Both Danny and Kathy are teachers in the Montgomery County School system and Fort Campbell School.

The second child born to James and Carrie was Phyllis Jill DePriest, born Sept. 27, 1950. She graduated from Waverly Central High School and received her BS degree from University of Tennessee at Knoxville, and her MA from Austin Peay University. She is a teacher in the Waverly Junior High School. Jill married Dan Bradley, divorced in 1987, and they were the parents of two daughters, Haylee Ann and Emily Jill Bradley.

Haylee Ann, born March 24, 1975, is a freshman (1993-1994) at the University of Tennessee, Knoxville, TN. Emily Jill, born Aug. 20, 1979, is a freshman at Waverly Central High School.

James and Carrie, with their children, are members of the Waverly Church of Christ. They have been active in church as well as many other civic organizations in Humphreys County. *Submitted by James Edward DePriest.*

JOHN THURMAN DEPRIEST, son of Henry Houston and Dora Beasley DePriest, was born on Marsh Creek, Perry Co., TN, June 21, 1888, and died on Marsh Creek, Nov. 29, 1962. He taught school 39 years, served as Superintendent of Perry County Schools two terms, served in the Tennessee State Legislature in 1933, and served as Judge of Perry County Court one eight-year term. He was married July 31, 1915, to Mary Bess Suratt, who was born in McNairy Co., TN, Oct. 21, 1890, and died on Marsh Creek, Perry Co., TN, Dec. 25, 1952. She was a teacher. They had five daughters who also became teachers, and four of them married teachers. Most of their children became teachers.

The five daughters are: Mary Elizabeth, b. McNairy Co., TN, Sept. 21, 1916; Frances Lorraine, b. McNairy Co., March 2, 1918; Dora Deane, b. Crockett Co., TN, July 3, 1920; Jessie Thurman, b. Perry Co., TN, March 5, 1923, d. Rutherford Co., TN, Feb. 12, 1991; Celia Carolyn, b. Perry Co., Oct. 8, 1925, d. Wilson Co., TN, June 19, 1991. Mary Elizabeth married Walton O. Warren, June 6, 1937; Frances Lorraine married James E. Hitt, June 25, 1944, and they had one daughter, Margaret Lorraine, b. Hamilton Co., TN, June 26, 1950. Jessie Thurman married Joe E. Nunley, Feb. 13, 1944, and they had five children: Joe Edwin Nunley Jr., b. Duke, NC, Jan. 30, 1946; Nancy Carolyn, b. Warren Co., TN, April 26, 1951; Jeana Elizabeth, b. Warren Co., June 10, 1954; Mary Ann, b. Warren Co., Oct. 31, 1958; and John Thurman DePriest, b. Rutherford Co., TN, May 7, 1963. Celia Carolyn married William H. Coley, June 28, 1953 and had two children: Celia Catherine, b. Wilson Co., TN, May 28, 1956; and John William, b. Wilson Co., Oct. 19, 1958.

John Thurman DePriest in 1954

The John Thurman DePriest Family was researched by Eleanor D. McSwain for William Thomas DePriest, son of Thomas Brown DePriest, a younger brother of John Thurman DePriest. This genealogy will be placed in the Genealogy Department of the Perry County Public Library in Linden, TN.

The following information was from the above genealogy. "No doubt the family came from France; so far, no information has been found to show if Robert DePriest of New Kent County, VA, came directly from France or if he left France, went to England and then came to the colony."... Robert DePress (DePriest) b. ca. (about) 1665-1668, d. New Kent Co., VA, ca. 1708-1711, married Elizabeth, d. New Kent Co., VA, Sept. 27, 1689. Their son, William DePriest, b. New Kent Co., 1689, d. Goochland Co., VA, 1738, married Judith. Their son, Randolph DePriest, b. ca. 1727-1729, married 1751 to Mary Mims. Their son, Randolph DePriest, b. Goochland Co., VA, ca. 1753-1755, d. Hickman Co., TN, Sept. 2, 1830, married Bedford Co., VA, June 1775, to Anne (Amy) Mims, b. ca. 1758-59, d. Hickman Co., TN. Their son, Hugh DePriest, b. Elbert Co., GA, 1801, d. Perry Co., TN, married Sarah Goodman, b. ca. 1810. Their son, John Randolph DePriest, b. Hickman Co., TN, June 23, 1834, d. Gibson Co., TN, March 13, 1912, married Elizabeth Ward (1825-1868). Their son, Henry Houston DePriest, b. Perry Co., TN, March 22, 1858, d. Perry Co., TN, April 21, 1928, married Dec. 6, 1881, to Dora Elizabeth Beasley, b. Hickman Co., TN, Feb. 5, 1860, d. Perry Co., TN, June 3, 1915. They had the following children: Laura Ethel, d. Sept. 19, 1883; Ida Elizabeth, b. Nov. 19, 1885; Addie Lee, b. Nov. 19, 1885 (twins); John Thurman, b. June 21, 1888; William Henry, b. Sept. 29, 1890; Homer Bates, b. June 15, 1894; Thomas Brown, b. Feb. 24, 1896; Deanna, b. Aug. 24, 1899; and Nora, b. Jan. 9, 1903.

John Thurman DePriest's father, Henry

Houston DePriest, was a farmer and timberman. He bought a farm on Marsh Creek in 1889. John Thurman lived on this farm and the farm continues to be in his family. Records show that farming seemed to be the main occupation of the early generations of this DePriest family.

Education was important to Judith of the second generation as she hired tutors to educate her children. It is noted that both her sons, Randolph and William, could sign their name to a deed, whereas, her two sons-in-law had to make their mark.

Randolph DePriest of the fourth generation, served in the Revolutionary War. John Randolph DePriest of the sixth generation, served in the Confederate Army.

JOHN VERNON AND IONE ELIZABETH DEPRIEST,
currently reside in Robertson County. However, they have both lived in Perry County and are landowners in the DePriest Bend community. They often visit for family, business and recreational purposes.

John's 4th great grandfather, Randolph (bc 1755-1830) married Amy Mims (c. 1760-1853) and received a land grant in what is now DePriest Branch, Hickman Co., for service in the Revolutionary War. Randolph is referenced in *Soldiers of the American Revolution Buried in Tennessee*, Tennessee Society, NSDAR, 1979, and *Roster of South Carolina Patriots in the American Revolution* Genealogical Pub. Co., Inc. 1983. He served as a spy among the Indians and Tories. He was in numerous spying missions and is believed to have participated in the battle at Blackstock's Plantation. Both Amy and Randall are believed to be buried in Cotham Cemetery in Hickman County.

His son, Randolph (Randall) Jr. (1789-unk), married Mary (Polly) Bynum (1795-unk), lived in Hickman Co., but eventually moved to the DePriest Bend area of Perry Co. Both are believed to be buried in DePriest Cemetery in DePriest Bend.

One of his many sons, William Harrison (1831-1917), married Delilah Emeline Harder (1833-1917). During the War Between the States, William was wounded at a skirmish at Thompson's Station while serving as a SGT with H Company, 10th Cavalry, C.S.A. William's brother, Pleasant W. (1837-1914), served as a CPL with K Company, 42nd Infantry, C.S.A. Pleasant was captured at the Battle of Vicksburg and taken to a POW camp in Chicago. Both are referenced in *Tennesseans in the Civil War, Part 2*, pub. by Civil War Centennial Commission, 1965, page 127. William and Delilah are buried in Westside Cemetery in DePriest Bend.

The children of William and Delilah are: Millington DeLafayette (1850-1922); Drewery B. (1853-1859); Pleasant Josiah (1854-1935); Gustavas (1856-1919); Octavus Legrand (1859-1916); and Leonidas Alonzo (1861-1936), married Geraldine Emma Dickerson (1861-1930). Leonidas built the house in DePriest Bend where his descendant Willodean (Chandler) and husband, Jimmy Kilpatrick now live. Leonidas and Geraldine are buried in Westside Cemetery.

Leonidas and Geraldine's children are: Ada A. (1880-1961); Nettie I. (1882-1955); William Randolph (1884-1961), married Mollie Burns (1888-1956); Ernie W. (1886-1957); O. May (1889-1954); Obey Davis (1891-1892); Montie Laurie (1884-1967); Lottie O. (1886-1984); Vivian Nola (1899-1950); and Joe A. (1903-1949). Obey is buried in DePriest Cemetery and all others are in Westside Cemetery.

William Randolph and Mollie's children are: Bonnie Laura (1909-1992); Julia May (1914-); and Charles V. (1919-1989), married Mildred Irene Johnson (1923-1992). Bonnie is buried in Duncan Cemetery, near Linden. Charles and Mildred are buried in Westside.

Charles was reared in DePriest Bend and near Coble. He graduated Valedictorian of the Class of 1937, from Hickman County High School. Charles obtained his B.S. Degree in Agriculture from the University of Tennessee at Knoxville in 1941. During WW II, Charles served in the Veterinary Corps of the U.S. Army at Walter Reed Army Medical Center. He once treated President Franklin D. Roosevelt's dog. In 1965, he obtained a Masters Degree in Natural Science from Middle Tennessee State University. His Masters theses was "The Declining Population of Perry County". Charles taught Vocational Agriculture and was the F.F.A. advisor for many years at Lobelville High School. After the closing of the high school at Lobelville, Charles taught for a few years at Franklin Jr. High School in Williamson County. Mildred was reared in Knoxville and met Charles while he was attending UT. Mildred enjoyed art and sewing as hobbies. She worked in several of the local factories and had also worked as a beauty consultant at both Castner-Knott and Cain-Sloan in Nashville. Both Charles and Mildred were active members of the Beardstown Church of Christ.

The children of Charles and Mildred are: John Vernon (1945), married Ione Elizabeth Stayrook (1945); unnamed infant son (1948); and Stephen Randall (1951). The infant son is buried in Westside.

Stephen attended Lobelville Elementary, Franklin Jr. High School, and graduated from Franklin High School. He also attended Columbia Community College and has worked for numerous years at Kolpac Industries, Inc. in Parsons. Stephen lives in DePriest Bend in the house formerly owned by his grandparents.

John Vernon was born June 19, 1945, at Walter Reed Army Medical Center. This was the day that General Eisenhower returned from the European Theater and the ensuing parades made for an eventful trip to the hospital for his parents. After the war, his parents moved to Perry County and built a house in DePriest Bend. (This house is now owned by John's 3rd cousin, twice removed, Edward E. DePriest and his wife, Heidi.) John attended Beardstown and Lobelville Elementaries. Both his future wife and himself were members of the last senior class to graduate from Lobelville High School in May 1963. (See also Stayrook, Jacob Theodore.) John obtained a B.S. Degree and a Second Lieutenant's commission in the U.S. Army from M.T.S.U. in 1967. He served as an Infantry Platoon Leader with the 5th Inf. Div (M) and also as an Infantry Advisor with the South Vietnamese during his tour in Vietnam. In West Germany, as a Capt., he served with the 1st BN, 39th Inf (M) for over three years. He has been employed in the Nashville area since 1972, working primarily in bulk cement distribution with National Cement Co. of Alabama, Inc. and Signal Mountain Cement Co., Inc.

John's daughter, Michelle Renee (1968) was born at Ft. Carson, Colorado, and lived in Perry County her first year of life. Renee graduated with honors from Greenbrier High School and attended Vanderbilt University. She currently attends Ohio State University at Columbus, Ohio. Renee married John David Dillard (1966) from Carthage, TN. David is a graduate of Tennessee Technological University and is employed by Honda of Ohio.

John and Ione's son, William Byron (1970) was born at Neubruke, West Germany. He graduated with honors from Greenbrier High School. William obtained his B.S. Degree and a Second Lieutenant's commission in the U.S. Air Force from UT - Knoxville in 1993. He is currently stationed at Sembach A.F.B., Germany.

John's children's first cousin, eight times removed, was Martha DePriest (1743-unk), who was a good friend of Dolly Madison, wife of President James Madison. Because of their friendship, Dolly had once given Martha a pair of dress gloves and a dress.

His children's third cousin, five times removed, was William DePriest Sutherland (1819-March 6, 1836), who was killed at the siege of the Alamo. He was named for his great-grandmother, Mary DePriest (1735-unk), married George Sutherland, III (1728-1804). Both William and his uncle, Dr. John Sutherland are mentioned in numerous books that have been written about the Alamo. John had been sent as a messenger from the Alamo to Gonzoles just prior to the siege. William's father, Dr. George Sutherland, a few weeks later, fought under Sam Houston at the Battle of San Jacinto. William was a medical student when he went from Alabama to Texas to live with his uncle in order to study the Spanish language. William's name has been handed down through five future generations since 1836.

John's great Aunt Lottie DePriest was a member of the Daughters of the Confederacy. She thus resided in Confederate Hall, free of charge while obtaining her Masters Degree from George Peabody College. The iris that now grow along the stone wall at her house in DePriest Bend came from Peabody. She could recall having known William Harrison and his brother, Pleasant, when she was a young woman. Lottie taught first grade at Lobelville Elementary School for numerous years until her retirement.

MILLINGTON E. DEPRIEST,
born Aug. 29, 1829, Lobelville area, died 1874, Lobelville, buried in DePriest Bend Cemetery, no marker. "Milton" was the son of Randolph DePriest Jr. and Mary Bynum. He married Mary Sharp in Flatwoods. Mary was born 1834, in Perry County, the daughter of James Sharp and Eliza Mayfield. She died 1895, in Lobelville and is buried in DePriest Bend Cemetery, no marker. Milton and Mary had at least eight children: John DePriest, born 1853, may be the John who married 1872, Perry County, to Catherine Lewelling; James DePriest, born 1854, may be the one who married Susan Horner, 1875, Perry County; Martha A. DePriest, born Jan. 16, 1857, Perry County, died Feb. 11, 1923, near Lobelville, bur-

ied DePriest Bend Cemetery. She married James S. Sanders on Dec. 5, 1878, in Perry County; Pleasant Whitfield DePriest, born Jan. 22, 1860, near Flatwoods, died Jan. 22, 1928, Denson Landing, buried DePriest Bend Cemetery. He married Margaret Anna Scott on Jan. 2, 1887; Mary E. DePriest "Paralee", born Dec. 1861, near Flatwoods, married Hugh A. Goodman, born Oct. 1860, on Oct. 20, 1878, Perry County. It is told, she died in the early 1950s around Jackson. Children: Claudius Walker, Claud, Otto, Clifford, Ulessys, Myrtle, Guy, and Nellie Goodman; Elizabeth E. DePriest, born 1866, Lobelville, died around Newburn, married Feb. 15, 1883, Perry County, to James L. Lancaster, born 1860, Perry County. Known children: Robert Lancaster and a daughter, who married a Mr. Pope; Thomas DePriest, born 1871, Flatwoods, died Sept. 1941. At one time he lived in Hayti, Missouri. He married Sophrona A. Warren, Aug. 15, 1899, Perry County. They had at least three children, Milton, Nola and another girl; Oscar Leonida DePriest, born June 1876, Lobelville, died May 1905. He also lived in Hayti, Missouri at one time. Oscar married Dec. 23, 1894, Perry County, to Sally Coble, born Sept. 1876. Some of their children were, Howard, Holly and Willie.

James S. Sanders (May 11, 1849-Feb. 12, 1897), buried DePriest Bend Cemetery. He and Martha DePriest had four children: John Albert Sanders, born July 24, 1881, Beardstown, died March/April 30, 1911, Lobelville, buried DePriest Bend Cemetery. He married, Perry County, 1900, to Jennie M. DePriest (March 16, 1882-May 4, 1928), buried DePriest Bend Cemetery. They had one daughter, Ora Mae Sanders (1900-June 8, 1981), buried DePriest Bend Cemetery. Jennie DePriest Sanders married second to George Albert Baars, Sept. 14, 1914, Perry County; James Elmer Sanders, born Aug. 24, 1883, Beardstown, died Aug. 19, 1946, buried DePriest Bend Cemetery. His first wife, M. Ellen Bates, born June 6, 1875, Lobelville, daughter of John Redner Bates and Mary Ann Dean. Ellen died April 2, 1916, Lobelville, in childbirth. At least four children were born to them: Arthur Ray (Feb. 18, 1902-May 1, 1935), buried DePriest Bend Cemetery, married Vera Mitchell; Roy; M.E., a girl, (June 7, 1906-July 17, 1907), buried DePriest Bend Cemetery; Ruby may be the child born 1912, Lobelville, she married a Coble and a male infant born and died April 2, 1916. James Elmer Sanders married second and had twins that did not live, buried in DePriest Bend Cemetery.

MILLINGTON EASLEY DEPRIEST, was born in Perry County near the community of Beardstown at DePriest Bend on the homestead his parents carved from the wilderness. Millington was born Aug. 29, 1829 to Randolph DePriest III and Mary Bynum DePriest. He was the twelfth child born of 15 children. The children are: Simpson Alexander (1810), William (1813), Barsheba (1814), Isaac (1815), Calvin (1817), Betty (1819), Hetty (1819), Martha (1821), John A. (1823), Drewery (1825), Catherine (1827), Millington E. (1829), Harrison W. (1831), Mary (1834), and Pleasant W. (1837). His parents moved to Perry County summer of 1810 from Georgia. Mary and Randolph were newlyweds and were following the cry of the time (go west young man, go west). They wanted to make a home for themselves and their family to be and Perry County Tennessee was their choice until the day they died in 1873 & 1875.

Millington's forefather came to this country before 1689, for this was the year the first DePriest child was born in America, in the colony of Virginia. Millington's own grandfather, Randolph DePriest II, was a Revolutionary soldier that fought to free us from England. He received a large land grant for his patriotism and he too came to Tennessee, where he lived in Hickman Co. till his death in 1830.

Millington married Marry Sharp, the daughter of James and Elizabeth Mayfield Sharp, in 1851. They lived on their farm near Linden. From this union, eight children were born. They were: John (1853), James (1854), Martha (1857), Pleasant (1860), Mary (1863), Elizabeth (1866), Thomas (1871) and Oscar (1874). Millington died shortly after Oscar was born. Marry died in 1895. They both are buried in the DePriest Cemetery, along with his father and mother and most all of his brothers and sisters.

Thomas Newton DePriest, born Dec. 10, 1871, Linden, TN. Thomas lived in Linden for twenty-one years, when he married Sofronia Adaline Warren of Hickman County. They then moved to Wardell, Missouri, owned a cotton farm and raised three children, Nola May (1901), Milton Easley (1903) and Leah May (1905). Thomas died in July 1941 and Sofronia died Jan. 1963.

Milton Easley DePriest, the only male child born to Thomas and Sofronia, married Rose Bess Turner in 1923 and had three children, Dorothy Allene (1924), Almeta Jewel (1927) and Robert Harold (1930). After Rose died in 1937, Milton married Dorothy Lee Cheek. They had four children, Thomas Milton (1939), Lee Allen (1941), Audrey Janice (1943) and Kenneth Warren (1947). The family moved to Michigan in 1942, where Dorothy still lives.

Thomas Milton DePriest lives in Indiana with his wife, Edeltraud Maria Reinhart. They have two children, Silvia Karin (1959), not married, and Thomas Michael (1963), married Elaine Michelle Jones, one child, Sandy Linn DePriest.

Thomas returns to Perry County every year for the family reunion. He hopes to retire in Perry County some day soon and build a log cabin in DePriest Bend, like his great-great grandfather did in the early years when Tennessee was a new state, of the United States. *Submitted by Thomas Milton DePriest.*

PLEASANT WHITFIELD DEPRIEST, son of Millington DePriest and Mary Sharp, married Margaret Anna Scott. She was born April 21, 1869, Beardstown, daughter of Mack Scott and Margaret Anna Murray. She died Feb. 1, 1925, Denson Landing and is buried DePriest Bend Cemetery. They had ten children: Leonard Easley DePriest, born Jan. 11, 1888, Lobelville, died July 15, 1968, buried Bible Hill Cemetery. He married first, 1912, Perry County, Annie McClanahan, born Sept. 1891. They had two sons, Glenn P. and Charles Edward. His children by the second wife, Vera E. Morris, were: Robert, Louise, Thomas, Betty, Peggy and Paulette; Nellie Fay DePriest, born Sept. 23, 1889, Lobelville, died Sept. 20, 1895, buried DePriest Bend Cemetery; Obed Bray DePriest, born Nov. 7, 1891, Camden, TN, died Sept. 12, 1957, Linden, buried DePriest Bend Cemetery. He married in Lobelville, Dec. 25, 1924, to Mary Alice Patterson, born Oct. 31, 1896; Fernie J. DePriest, born Dec. 24, 1893, Lobelville, died Dec. 8, 1915, Perry County, buried DePriest Bend Cemetery; Fred Bates DePriest, born Nov. 23, 1895, died June 23, 1974, buried Bible Hill Cemetery. He and Elnora Long (1899-1981) were married July 15, 1916, Perry County. Elnora is buried Bible Hill Cemetery; Grady Jones DePriest (Sept. 12, 1898-March 28, 1978), buried Pineview Cemetery. In 1922, he married Minnie Woodford (1905-1963); Mattie Ida DePriest, born June 1900, Lobelville, died 1975, married Feb. 15, 1916, Perry County, to Everett Belisle; Annie Mavis DePriest, born Sept. 13, 1903, Beardstown, died Oct. 3, 1975, buried Denson Cemetery on Tom's Creek. She and Elmer Lee Bandy (Dec. 18, 1894-July 27, 1934) married March 20, 1920; Andrew Jackson DePriest (March 14, 1905-April 28, 1972), buried Indiana. He married Annie Grimes in 1927; and Pleasant Scott DePriest, born June 6, 1909, Beardstown, died Sept. 29, 1915, Perry County, buried DePriest Bend Cemetery.

RANDOLPH DEPRIEST, (1755-1834 or 1838) came to the U.S. with the Haguenots, settled on Cane Creek in Hickman Co. in 1810. His wife, Amy Mimms (1760-unk). They had eight children: Oma; Sally; Randel (Randolph Jr.) born 1789, first DePriest settler in Perry County; Hugh, born 1801, settled on Marsh Creek in Perry County; Jesse, born 1797, settled on Cane Creek in Hickman County, first wife Nancy Andrews, second Sarah K. Davidson; John; James; and Gracey.

Randel (Randolph Jr.) (1789-1873), first DePriest settler in Perry Co., settled on Buffalo River. His wife was Mary Pollie Bynum (1795-unk). They are buried in DePriest Bend Cemetery. They had 18 children (only 14 listed): William (1813); Barsheba (1814); Isaac (1815) (Ike Hollow named for him.); Calvin (1817); Bettie (1819); Hettie (1819); Martha (1821); John H. (1823); Drewry (Drury) (1825); Catherine S. (1827), married Bill Sharp; Millington (Milton) (1829), married Mary Sharp. (Sharps came from Virginia or North Carolina); William Harrison (1831), married Emmaline Harder; Mary (1834); and Pleas (P.W.) (1837), married Sarah Jane Fuller (Redner DePriest family line).

Millington DePriest (1829-1874), married Mary Sharp (1833-1895). They married before the Civil War, in which he fought as a Confederate. Both are buried in DePriest Bend Cemetery. They had six children: Martha, married J.S. Sanders, 187?; Pleasant Whitfield (1860-1928), married Anna Scott; Mary (nickname Paralee), born 1878, married H.A. Goodman; John, married Sophronia Warren; Oscar L. (Boss) (1859-1919), married Sally Coble; and Bettie, born 1891, married J.L. Lancaster.

Pleasant Whitfield DePriest (1860-1928) was born in Flatwoods in Perry County, and died at Densons Landing. He married Anna Scott, daughter of Mack and Margaret Murray Scott. They had 10 children: Leonard (1888-1968), married Annie McClanahan, 1912, second wife,

Vera Marris, 1924; Nellie (1889-1895); Obed (1891-1957), married Alice Patterson, 1924; Fernie J. (1893-1915); Fred B. (1895-1974), married Elnora Long, 1916; Grady J. (1898-unk), married Minnie Woodford, 1922; Mattie (1900-1975), married Everett Belisle; Mavis (1903-1975), married Elmer Bandy, 1920; Andrew J. (Jack) (1905-1972), married Annie Grimes, 1927; and Pleasant Scott (1909-1915).

The Fred and Elnora Long DePriest family is written in the John W. Long history.

RANDOLPH DEPRIEST, The earliest record on the DePriest family dates back to the 1600's, where we find Robert DePriest living in France. He died about 1708. His wife was Elizabeth (maiden name unknown), born about 1665, and died Sept. 27, 1689. His second marriage was to Mary (maiden name unknown, as well as birthdate.) She died in 1711.

Robert DePriest had at least one son, William (Sept. 25, 1689-March 2, 1738). His wife was Judith Austin, and they had at least one son, Randolph, born 1740, who married Mary Mims.

Randolph and Mary's one son, Randolph Jr., born 1755 in Goochland County, VA., died in Hickman County, TN on Sept. 29, 1830.

Randolph Jr. enlisted for service during the American Revolution from South Carolina, serving as a private in Capt. William Young's company; also serving under Col. Sumpter, Col. Nesbett, and Major or Capt. Lewis. He was married to Amy Mims, born about 1760, died Aug. 1853. Amy made application for widow's pension on Dec. 24, 1851, when she was ninety-one years old, in which she stated that she married Randolph DePriest in Bedord County, VA, in June 1775. This application for pension #R2987 can be found on microfilm #804, Roll 799 in National Archives, Washington, D.C. Amy was never granted the pension although she presented much proof that she was his widow.

Family records indicate that Randolph and Amy were living in Franklin County, GA in 1793, that they moved to Smith County, TN, then on to Hickman County about 1812, getting a grant for some land on the head of Cane Creek.

Children born to Randolph Jr. and Amy DePriest were: Jane, born Jan. 24, 1778; William, born 1779; twins, Mary and Elizabeth, born Dec. 12, 1779; Annis, born May 29, 1782, married Isaac Skelton; Sarah (Sallie), born Nov. 20, 1783, married Isaac Cotham; Naomi, born Dec. 6, 1785; Catherine, born April 20, 1787, married Hiram Casey; Randolph (Randal), born March 24, 1789, married in 1810 to Mary Polly Bynum of Virginia. He died in 1873 and is buried in Beardstown Cemetery; Margaret, born March 12, 1791; James, born Sept. 6, 1793; Amy, born June 29, 1795; Jesse, born June 24, 1797, married first Nancy Andrews, second to Sarah Davidson; Hugh, born Sept. 1801, married Sarah Goodman; and John, born May 8, 1804, married Nancy (maiden name unknown). *Submitted by James Edward DePriest.*

RANDOLPH (RANDAL) DEPRIEST, was born March 24, 1789 in North Carolina, son of Randolph Jr. and Amy Mims DePriest. His wife was Mary Polly Bynum, whom he married in 1810. She was born April 19, 1795 in Virginia. According to family Bible Record, they had at least the following children: Simpson (1810-1886) married first Malinda Roberts (1815-1850), second to Percilla Lenard Tarpy (1821); William (1813); Bersheba (1814); Isaac (1815) married Pheobe Sisco (1818); Calvin (1817-1885) married first Louisa, second Ruth Pace; Betty and Hetty (1819), twins; Martha (1821) married George Hollabough; John A. (1823) married Delilah Catherine Lancaster (1828); Drewery (1825); Catherine (1827) married Bill Sharp; Millington (1829-1874) married Mary Sharp (1834-1895); William Harrison (May 29, 1831-March 1, 1917) married Delilah Emmaline Harder (1833-1917); Mary (1834); Pleasant W. (Jan. 17, 1837-April 4, 1914) married Sarah Jane Fuller (May 18, 1850-Sept. 2, 1913), sister of Emmaline Harder.

Randolph Randal died in 1873 and is buried in the Beardstown Cemetery, and probably his wife, Mary Polly, is buried there, but in an unmarked grave. There are many members of the DePriest family buried there.

Jesse DePriest, born in North Carolina on June 24, 1797, was the son of Randolph (1755-1830) and Amy Mims DePriest (1760-1853). Jesse died Jan. 14, 1873. He married Nancy Andrews (May 14, 1792-June 18, 1840). His second wife was Sarah K. Davidson (May 26, 1805-July 11, 1891). They had eight children: Hugh (Jan. 4, 1820-1901) married Mary A. Van Landingham; Mary Ann (March 24, 1823-1897) married a Miss Davidson; John A. (Dec. 9, 1826-1826); James R. (Aug. 5, 1827-1844), twin; Pleasant W. (Aug. 5, 1827-Aug. 15, 1827), twin; Barnet B. (July 13, 1829-Feb. 28, 1848); Martha J. (Feb. 14, 1831); William Andrew (May 30, 1835-May 16, 1862) married Nancy Harder, sister of Emmaline Harder. Children born to second marriage to Sarah K. Davidson were: Nancy (Oct. 15, 1842-1923); Martha E. (Dec. 25, 1843-1923) and Melvina C. (May 15, 1845-July 26, 1885).

SAMUEL RUDOLPH DEPRIEST, (Nov. 1, 1903-April 13, 1979) was born in Perry County, TN, the son of William Samuel DePriest (1875-1951) and Nancy Ethel Burns DePriest (1880-1914). He married on April 7, 1923 to Mattie Lucille Hughes (April 14, 1906-May 13, 1985), daughter of Will and Coffia Baston Hughes, also of Perry County.

Clay, James, Bill, Lucille and Rudolph DePriest at Lucille and Rudolph's 50th wedding anniversary.

Samuel and Mattie are buried in the DePriest Bend Cemetery. He was a farmer. They were members of the Church of Christ and had four children:

William "Bill" Samuel, born Sept. 3, 1924, married Helen Fay Marlin, born Sept. 23, 1931, of Perry County. She is the daughter of Andrew Jackson Marlin and Sally Wilma Lomax Marlin. William is retired from the Tennessee Gas Company in New Albany, Mississippi. Their children include: Steve Marlin, born Sept. 5, 1953, who married Jane Parker Conger, born April 16, 1954. They are the parents of Claire Conger, born May 11, 1983, and William Parker, born June 5, 1989. They live in Oxford, Mississippi. The second child is Patricia Alice, born Jan. 4, 1958, married June 10, 1979, to Joseph Ray Kennedy, born Aug. 3, 1955. Their only child is Kathryn Fay "Kate" Kennedy, born Feb. 19, 1984. They reside in New Albany, Mississippi. Bill served in the Navy during World War II (1943-1946). They are members of the Church of Christ.

James Edward, born Nov. 27, 1925, married Carrie Nell Shepard, daughter of William Haywood Shepard and Byron May DePriest Shepard. (See his history in this book.)

Robert Clay was born Dec. 3, 1927. On Nov. 18, 1960, he married Sylvia Jean Fraley, born Oct. 29, 1942 in Melvin, KY. Robert Clay served in the Korean War. Their children are Jeffrey, born Oct. 23, 1961, married Karen Yuvonne Enesey. They have three children: Joshua Aaron, born Nov. 14, 1982; Christy Lynn, born May 24, 1985; and Benjamin James, born Dec. 28, 1989. The second child, Robin Lucille, was born Feb. 14, 1964, married John Joseph Nederlander, now divorced, and their only child is John Joseph Nederlander Jr. All of Clay's family live in Michigan. They attend the Free Methodist Church.

Mary Ethel was born Dec. 1, 1929 and died June 2, 1933.

THOMAS NEWTON DEPRIEST, (Dec. 10, 1871-July 10, 1941) was born in Flatwoods, Perry County, Tennessee to Millington Easley and Mary Sharp DePriest. His grandparents on his mother's side are James and Elizabeth Mayfield Sharp. On his father's side of the family, Thomas is the fourth generation to live in Tennessee. His great grandfather, Randolph II, lived in Hickman County. His grandfather, Randolph III, lived near Lobelville, and his father, Millington, was born at DePriest Bend, a small community on now Hwy. 13, a couple miles north of Linden.

Thomas's father died three years after he was born, leaving eight children to be cared for by their mother. She did a great job raising the children on her own. This was no small feat in the late 1800's. Mary lived to the year 1895. She and her husband are buried in the family cemetery at DePriest Bend.

Thomas was born at the south end of Perry County, a place he loved dearly with its steep hills, deep valleys, lush forest, and fast running creeks and streams. Thomas, being young and full of adventure had heard of flat, rich land, just three days ride west of Flatwoods, so, in the summer of 1897, after the crops were laid by, he and a younger brother, Oscar, struck out to seek their future across the Mississippi River to the state of Missouri. Two years later, Thomas married his long time sweetheart, Sophrona Adoline Warren, from Hickman County. Then with his new bride and brother, Oscar, and his wife, Sally Coble, he moved to Wardell Missouri. Once settled on new land, they purchased from the state, they built new homes on large cotton farms.

Thomas Newton DePriest and Sophrona Adoline Warren DePriest.

Thomas and Sophrona had three children, Nola May, Leah May and Milton Easley. Milton was born in 1903 and he had seven children: Dorothy, 1924; Almeta, 1927; Robert, 1930; Thomas, 1939; Allen, 1941; Audrey, 1943; and Kenneth, 1947. Milton's first wife, Rose Turner, died Jan. 1937. He then married Dorothy Lee Cheek in 1938 and had four children by her. These seven children and their offspring now live in many different states. They all keep in touch with each other and get back to Tennessee when they can, especially the fourth Saturday in September, when hundreds of them show up for the DePriest family Reunion. *Submitted by Thomas Milton DePriest.*

WILLIAM HARRISON DEPRIEST, was born May 29, 1831, son of Randolph Randel DePriest (1789) and Mary Polly Bynum (1795). He died March 1, 1917. His wife was Delilah Emmaline Harder (Nov. 16, 1833-April 4, 1917).

Children born to this marriage were: Lafayette (Dec. 1, 1850-March 1, 1922), married Eugenia Sutton (Oct. 7, 1863-Feb. 3, 1929); Pleasant Josiah "Joe" (Sept. 8, 1854-Dec. 1935), married Victoria Dickerson (Oct. 31, 1857-?); Gus (Sept. 16, 1856), married Jane Horner (Aug. 20, 1856-1915); Octavus LeGrand (March 23, 1859-March 2, 1916), married Mosella Cotton (March 8, 1866-Dec. 5, 1946); Leonatus "Lonnie" (June 9, 1861-Nov. 17, 1936), married Geraldine Dickerson (July 12, 1861-May 3, 1930).

William Harrison and Delilah are buried in the Westside DePriest Cemetery on Hwy. 50. He served in the Confederate Army during the Civil War and was wounded in the leg at the Battle of Thompson's Station in Williamson County.

Pleasant W. was born Jan. 17, 1837, son of Randolph (1789) and Mary Bynum DePriest (1795), married Sarah Jane Fuller (May 18, 1850-Sept. 2, 1913).

He enlisted in the Confederate Army on Dec. 9, 1861 as Private at Camp Ela Fork for one year. His name is listed on the Company Muster Roll of January, February, March and April 1863. He was taken prisoner at Vicksburg, Mississippi and sent to Chicago. He died April 4, 1914.

Children born to Pleasant and Sarah Jane were: Vera, married first John Lynch, and second Newt Johnson; Henrietta (July 31, 1872-July 7, 1952), married John Byrd (Nov. 10, 1880-Jan. 21, 1925); William Samuel (Sept. 25, 1875-Dec. 14, 1951) married first to Nancy Ethel Burns (May 11, 1880-1914) and second to Minnie Bell Burns (1879-Jan. 14, 1918); Jesse Lee (March 17, 1878-Aug. 2, 1944), married Geneva Aldridge (Sept. 1885-Sept. 1916); Henry, never married; and Robert, married Donna Bates.

Many members of the DePriest family lived, at one time, in a hollow near where the Buffalo River makes a bend between Linden and Lobelville. This is where DePriest Bend gets its name.

WILLIAM HENRY DEPRIEST, son of Henry Houston and Dora Beasley DePriest, was born Sept. 29, 1890, in the Buckfork community of Marsh Creek, Perry County, TN. He attended elementary school in Perry County and high school at Savannah Institute in Hardin County. He completed college at West Tennessee State Teachers College (now Memphis State University), and did graduate work at Peabody College in Nashville. His first teaching jobs were at Frog Pond School in Perry County and Friendship High School at Savannah.

After college, he taught at Eads and Jeter elementary schools in Shelby County. He credited his brother, Thurman DePriest, with encouraging him to complete his education. While teaching at Eads School, Mr. DePriest took a Smith-Hughes course at the University of Tennessee and learned the advantages of using commercial fertilizer. Eads School had a small farm which was used to teach agriculture. A Squire Houston, with whom he boarded, offered to pay $50.00 to the student producing the highest yield of cotton on his plot of ground. One of the boys using commercial fertilizer, was the top producer and won the prize. Henry was proud that he was able to use that event to demonstrate the superior results that could be achieved by using commercial fertilizer.

Mr. DePriest moved to Nashville in 1928 and spent the remainder of his teaching career in Davidson County. He served as Principal of Joelton, Woodbine, John Early and Turner elementary schools, retiring in 1956. Mr. DePriest loved children and wanted each one to develop to his or her highest potential. In his early teaching years, he coached both boys and girls basketball and encouraged others to participate in athletics. He encouraged his students to engage in debates, forensic contests, and school plays. In 1940, two students at Woodbine School in Nashville debated a presidential election before fellow students. One of the students, as President Roosevelt, spoke for the Democrats, while another, as Wendell Wilkie, presented the Republican arguments. He felt these experiences helped students to develop public speaking abilities, self-confidence, leadership and social skills.

During World War I, Mr. DePriest served in the U.S. Navy on the Battleship New Jersey. While on the ship, he had the opportunity to apply skills he had learned as a young man cutting and moving crossties in the woods of Perry County. A big gun needed to be moved on the ship and he volunteered to rig up block and tackle that enabled the gun to be moved much quicker than planned. He was commended by the ship's captain for his help.

Henry was married to Eunice Hodges, July 17, 1925, at Knoxville, Tennessee. Their children are: Robert, Nashville, Tennessee; Frank, Hartford, Alabama; Vera Akin, Killen, Alabama; and Carolyn Lehning, Nashville, Tennessee. There are nine grandchildren and 16 great grandchildren.

Mr. DePriest was a long-time member of the Inglewood Methodist Church in Nashville and was teacher of the Men's Bible Class for many years. He died in June, 1977. *Submitted by Robert O. DePriest.*

WILLIAM JESSE (JESS) DEPRIEST AND BETTY JANE BATES DEPRIEST, lived on Cane Creek near Beardstown, then moved to Lagoon near Lobelville in Perry County. Jess (Aug. 3, 1900-Dec. 2, 1957) was the son of Jesse Lee and Geneva Aldridge DePriest. Betty Jane Bates, born May 3, 1904, daughter of Solomon and Etta Addie Warren Bates. Jess and Betty had 17 children:

Milton Jesse (Oct. 10, 1920-March 8, 1976), married Thelma Hawkins, Oct. 5, 1940. They had eleven children: Linda Joyce, Jessie

The William Jesse DePriest Family around 1950. Front, L to R: W.J. (Jess) holding Carolyn Fay (Blackwell), Betty Jane holding Clifford Gordon, Ralph R. William Bryan (Hoot); Lowell Arden (Buck) holding Lorene Joyce (Boone); Clarence Anderson (Soup) holding Elva Jeanne (Warren) (French); Back, L to R: Dorothy Alline (Warren), Martha Irene (Shepard), Lee Edward (Spider), Annie Mae (French), Fulton Ray (Jim), Mary Agnes (Kimbel) and Cecil Farris. Not pictured: Milton Jesse the oldest son and Bettie Ruth who died at age 11 of lockjaw.

Ray, Roger Wayne, Edward Lewis, Carolyn Ann, Earl Franklin, Gary Lee, Eddie Joe, Ronnie Dale, Michael Lynn and Darryl Glen.

Ralph R. (Nov. 15, 1923-Dec. 8, 1973), married Margaret Sue Dyer, Sept. 18, 1948. They had two children, Kathy Jean and Richard (Ricky) Howard.

William Bryan (Hoot), born July 21, 1925, married Annie Margaret Wright, Dec. 22, 1956. Four children: William Bryan Jr., Deanna Lea, Dwayne Jay and James Michael.

Lowell Arden (Buck), born May 16, 1927, married Loudean DePriest in 1971. One son, Jeffrey Lowell.

Bettie Ruth (Aug. 8, 1928-1939), died of lockjaw.

Clarence Anderson (Soupbeans), born Aug. 3, 1930, married Betty Shelton, Aug. 5, 1950. Three children: Clarence Wesley, Terry Michael and Debra Kay. Divorced and married Jo Ann Marrs, July 3, 1970.

Dorothy Alline (May 19, 1932-Feb. 7, 1992), married Ned Warren, Aug. 1, 1949. Seven children: Jimmy Dale (deceased), Frances Dianne, Pamela Jane, Eddy Gene, Teresa Elaine, Shelia Kay and Timothy Dwight. Alline died from smoke inhalation in a home fire.

Martha Irene (Piney), born March 30, 1933, married Billy Joe Shepard Jr., Dec. 30, 1949. Two children: Lesa Ann and Billy Joe, III.

Lee Edward (Spider), born March 16, 1934, married Bonnie Lou Jackson, Jan. 7, 1956. Two sons: Scotty Edward and Timothy Lee.

Annie Mae, born Feb. 21, 1937, married Edgar Turner French, Oct. 31, 1953. Three sons: Jackie Lynn, Richard Edward and Ronald Dwight.

Fulton Ray (Jim), born March 4, 1938, married Mamie Sue Stephens, July 4, 1958. Two children: Nancy Lynne and David Ray.

Mary Agnes, born July 25, 1939, married Billy Joe Kimbel, March 9, 1957. Four children: Shelia Elaine, Donna Jean, Rickey Joe and Glenda Sue.

Cecil Farris, born Jan. 20, 1941, married Kay Holman, June 1963. Three children: Stephen Farris, Darrin Lee and Jessica Jo.

Elva Jean (Jeanie), born March 24, 1942, married Donald Warren. Four children: Donald Wayne, Cynthia Ann (deceased), Regina Dawn and Deborah Kaye (deceased). Cindy and Debbie were both killed in separate car accidents. Donald died Nov. 19, 1990. Jeanie married Verlo French, Aug. 16, 1991.

Lorene Joyce, born May 30, 1945, married Joe Boone. Two sons: William (Bill) and Daniel (Danny).

Carolyn Fay, born Aug. 10, 1946, married Michael W. Blackwell. Three daughters: Tracey Lynn, Stacia Gwen and Ginger.

Clifford Gordon, born Feb. 25, 1948, married Brenda Louise Epley, May 17, 1969. Two daughters: Shannon Lee and Jennifer Frances. *Submitted by Lee Ed DePriest.*

WILLIAM SAMUEL DEPRIEST, (Sept. 25, 1875-Dec. 14, 1951) was born in Perry County, TN, the son of Pleasant W. DePriest (1837) and Sarah Jane Fuller DePriest (1850). He married Nancy Ethel Burns (May 11, 1880-1914). His second marriage in 1917, was to Minnie Bell Burns (1879-Jan. 14, 1918).

Children born to the first marriage were:
Myrtle Lorene (Aug. 1, 1898-March 11, 1967), married Fred Carter Burns (Aug. 22, 1897-Dec. 16,1967).

Paul Edward, born Jan. 5, 1900, married Hazel Bates, born 1900.

Graydon Carrol, born July 11, 1901, married Dera Loveless. His second wife was Lillie Baars.

Samuel Rudolph, born Nov. 1, 1903, married Mattie Lucille Hughes, born April 14, 1906, the daughter of Will and Coffia Baston Hughes.

Julia Ruth, born Jan. 14, 1906.

Benjamin Barns, born March 27, 1908, married Lorene Brown.

Claude Raymond, born Nov. 19, 1910, married Pauline Barham, born Aug. 31, 1916.

One child, Minnie Bell, was born Jan. 6, 1918, to William Samuel and second wife, Minnie Bell Burns DePriest. She married Brady Mathis, born Jan. 25, 1908. *Submitted by James Edward DePriest.*

DICKSON, The James Dickson family was among the early settlers of Perry County. James Dickson (1770-1846), and two of his sons, Joseph and Hugh, are listed on the 1819 Perry County Petition. It was in his home on Lick Creek that the Perry County government was organized, January 1820, and according to oldtimers, this two story log house also served as the first County Court. The James Dickson house has been placed on the National Register of Historic Places. James Dickson was entry taker and magistrate; son, Joseph was constable.

It is not known how James Dickson made his living. From early deeds, it is known the family members were involved with a tan yard. Perry County's first water transportation was a flat boat to New Orleans run by Mr. Dickson of Lick Creek.

James and Margrett (surname possibly Wilson) had nine children: James, who married Abigail Latimer, Elizabeth, married Fernifore Stanley, and Hannah, married Oscar Gray, all moved to Red River County, Texas. Hugh, married Nancy, and Matilda, married John Boyers, moved to Tishomingo County, Mississippi. Living in Perry County were William Kenedy, son who inherited the home place and married Sarah McGage; Mary, married Aaron Lewis; and Jane who married Henry Stanley.

Son, Joseph (1795-1888), married Rachal Boyers (1792-1867), about 1816. Rachal was born in South Carolina and belonged to the Boyers family in Sumner County. Joseph and Rachal had eight children: sons, Mathew James and Alexander Boyd; Daughter, Margaret Ann (1817-1864), married Jesse Garrett; Mary Elizabeth (1827-1889), the only child to leave Tennessee, married first Lemuel Brakefield, who was killed in the Civil War and second Thomas Kilpatrick; Harriet Ester (1829-1873), married W.G. Mays; nothing known about daughter, Hannah, born in 1832.

Mathew James Dickson (1820-1901), son of Joseph and Rachal, was married to Lenora Jane Mays (1823-1908). Both are buried in the Sutton Cemetery in Linden. Children were: Joseph (1848-1921), who married Martha Jame Blackburn; Mary Elizabeth (1849-1937), who married first William Porter Dickson and second James R. Sutton; Julia Paralee, who married James B. Dickson; and Sally Harriet, who married Reuben H. Ward. Daughter, Martha Caroline (1852-1892), married Herman Gotthardt and they moved to Louisville, KY.

Martha Caroline Dickson married Herman Gotthardt Jan. 1, 1868, at her parents' home on Lick Creek. Herman, born in Germany, was the son of Charles Gotthard, who established Rat Tail Tan Yard on the bank of the Tennessee River. Martha Caroline's children were Lenora, Josephine, Julia, Moritz, Joseph Henry, Agnes and Frederick.

Although it is believed that James Dickson came from North Carolina and is related to the Dickson family of Dickson County, no proof has been found. His son, Joseph's, place of birth is listed as Tennessee on the 1880 Perry County Census. According to this census, Joseph's parents, James and Margrett, were both born in Tennessee.

Not only are many descendants of James Dickson living in Perry County, but they are also scattered throughout the United States. All share a common pride in their ancestor, James Dickson.

DICKSON-KIMBLE, Leander Dickson (1877-1953) was the son of James B. Dickson (1840) and Julia Dickson. Four children were born to this union: Leander Dickson, M.K. Dickson, Baxter Dickson and Lizzie Dickson, died in infancy.

Bessie Kimble Dickson (1893-1936), daughter of Sarah Beasley Kimble (1867-1941) and Simms A. Kimble (1850-1886). Their children: Myrtle Kimble Moore, Nobel Kimble, Bessie Kimble Dickson, Mary Kimble Thompson, Simms Kimble, Sarah Kimble Paschall and Donald Kimble. Donald Kimble is the only surviving child. He married Ruth DePriest Kimble.

Leander and Bessie married, living on Cypress Creek in Perry County, where they farmed. They had 10 children:

Magruder Dickson Whitson, married Joe Whitson (deceased). They live in Tiptonville, TN and operate a farm. Children: Jo Ann Ervin and Winston Whitson.

Carmon Dickson Lomax married Tom Lomax (deceased). They operated a Grocery Store in Linden for several years. Children: Tom Eddy Lomax and Betty Lomax Byrd.

Roy Dickson (deceased) married Grace Dickson. They live in Baltimore, MD. Children: Kira Dickson Lewis, husband Bruce Lewis, and Sharon Dickson Lees, husband Bob Lees.

Jewel Dickson married Jetty Whitson Dickson (deceased). They live in Paducah, KY. He was an electrician. Children: Terry Dan Dickson, Susan Weitlauf, Gary Dickson and Tim Dickson.

Nora Dickson Marcum (deceased) married Bill Marcum. Nora was an R.N. and was employed by the V.A. Hospital prior to retirement. Bill is retired from the military and presently teaches at Middle Tennessee State University in Murfreesboro, TN. Children: Kaye Marcum Tucker, R.N., employed by V.A. Hospital, Barbara Marcum Tolliver, and Jimmy Marcum, wife Rebecca.

Ora Dickson Churchwell married George Churchwell. They live in Paducah, KY, where he is a Home Builder. Children: Linda

Churchwell, D.M.D., F.A.G.D., she owns her own business in Paducah, KY, and Laura Churchwell Alexander, husband Wade Alexander.

Betty Sue Dickson died in infancy.

Thelma Dickson (deceased) was employed by Linden Apparel Corporation until she retired due to illness.

Kira Dickson Godwin married R.H. (Holly) Godwin Jr. They are bankers in Linden, TN. Children: Julia Ann Godwin and Rosemary Elaine Godwin Turnbow, husband Bob Turnbow, one child, Holly Elizabeth Turnbow.

Oneal Dickson married Dorothy Halbrooks Dickson. The reside in Waverly, TN where Oneal owns and operates a Machine and Metal Shop. He served in the Navy during World War II. They have one child, Andrea Dickson Arndt, a school teacher, husband John Arndt; they have a daughter, Mary Kathryn (Katy) Arndt. *Submitted by Kira Dickson Godwin.*

DODSON, The Dodson's earliest known American ancestors were of Scotch Irish blood and came to Virginia in the 17th century from England. However, the Dodsons were originally an English family, and the name had the meaning of "Dods son", which two words became combined into Dodson. John Dodson came to America in 1607 with Captain John Smith to settle in Jamestown, the first colony in America.

Ralph & Nina Dodson . *Addie Ferguson Dodson (right)*

Ralph Dodson, born Oct. 19, 1895, and died in Perry County, TN, Aug. 9, 1980, was married to Nina Godwin, born in Perry County, Jan. 19, 1897, died April 15, 1981. They were married in Nashville, TN, May 30, 1918. They had three children: Lucille, born April 1, 1919 in Crowder, OK; John M., born Feb. 1921, deceased; and Ralph Eugene Dodson, born Aug. 22, 1923 in Perry County.

Ralph Dodson was sheriff of Perry County from 1937-1944. Lucille married to Ernest Sharp on Jan. 19, 1946. They have two children, born in Nashville, TN, Jean Elizabeth and John Franklin. Ralph E. Dodson was married to Dorothy Archer of Henderson, TN, now deceased. He is now married to Tina Robertson of Jackson, MS. He has two children, Holly and Leslie, and three grandchildren.

Ralph Dodson was the son of John Marshall Dodson, born in Perry County, April 29, 1866, died March 18, 1918, and Addie Ferguson, born in Perry County, December 1865, died Oct. 27, 1931. They had four other children: Clarence; Claude, married to Bess Wilsdorf, one son, Dan; Kyle; and Van married to Elizabeth Kembro, one son, Edwin. All are deceased except Elizabeth and she is 92 and the two sons.

John Marshall was the son of Allen William Dodson, born in Tennessee in 1833, and his first wife, Nancy Webb, died July 15, 1869. They married in 1867.

Allen William Dodson was the son of Claiborne Dodson (May 5, 1818-Aug. 3, 1879) and his first wife Miss Eason.

Claiborne was the son of Elias Dodson, born in Halifax County, VA, March 22, 1786. Elias was the son of Joshua Dodson, born in Virginia in 1757 and died there in 1850. He was married to Ann Shelton, who died in 1831. Joshua was the son of Joseph Dodson, born in Richmond County, VA, Feb. 21, 1725, died in 1773 in Virginia. His father was Thomas Dodson Jr., born in Virginia and died in 1783. His mother was Elizabeth Rose. They were married in Virginia in 1723. Among land grants in Accomack County in the 17th Century, was one dated 1798 to Thomas Dodson who obtained 47 acres.

This is nine generations of the Dodson family. The Dodsons of early days were represented in the military establishment of the colony and the State of Virginia.

Joshua Dodson lived to be about 93 years old and his wife, 92. He was a Lieutenant in the Revolutionary War. They had 10 children.

Thomas Dodson, in his last will and testament, left his son, Joshua one Negro woman named Sue and one Negro boy, named Dick, and one feather bed and furniture.

Thomas Dodson was the great-great-great-great-great-great grandfather of Lucille Dodson Sharp of Linden, TN and Ralph Dodson of Henderson, TN.

FANNIE DODSON, was born in Linden, TN, Dec. 16, 1871, to James Elias Dodson and Mary Byron Thomas. Her parents were married in Linden, Aug. 2, 1868. Fannie Dodson was the second oldest of seven children, all born in Linden. Her brothers and sisters were: Robert Elias, born Dec. 17, 1869; Mary Byron, born Feb. 9, 1874; James Eli, born Sept. 21, 1876; Jessie Mattie Lou, born Jan. 16, 1879; Joel Meeks, born March 7, 1882; and Claiborn Allen, born April 8, 1885. Fannie's father fought in the Civil War. In his later years, Dr. Dodson wrote: "Myself and Will Baker, one of my chums, were going to run away and join the army. I wasn't quite 15. Our mothers found it out and fitted us up to go. We joined the infantry. They discharged us because we were too young. We then joined the cavalry and stayed with it." James Elias Dodson served in Company G, Waller's Battalion, Green's Brigade of the Confederate Army. After his return from the war, he enrolled at Vanderbilt University and was graduated from Vanderbilt Medical College in 1875. Upon graduation, Dr. Dodson practiced medicine in Linden, and Bakerville. Fannie wrote: "While we were living in Bakerville, father got blood poison in his index finger. He had to practically give up his practice, the Tennessee winters are so severe. He decided to apply for a government position." In 1885, President Grover Cleveland appointed Dr. Dodson physician and surgeon for the Osage Indian Agency, and the family moved to Pawhuska, Indian Territory. Fannie later recalled: "We went part of the way on a boat - it had a big wheel in the back. I had a plaid flannel dress, polonaise, and did I think I was grown up. The Cap would let me go up in the pilot's cabin. I can just see myself now, feeling so important. My oldest brother stayed in Nashville in school." Fannie's mother died, July 1, 1886, and Fannie, as the oldest daughter at fourteen assumed the responsibility of raising her brothers and sisters.

Fannie Dodson

In November of 1889, the family moved to Vernon, Texas, where Fannie met Thornton G. Lomax. They were married April 25, 1894 in Vernon. Fannie and Thornton had five children. Thornton G. Jr. and James Wellford, were born in Vernon. Fannie and Thornton then moved to Beaumont, Texas, where Mary Frances and Virginia were born. They moved later to Portales, New Mexico, where Presley Byron was born. Finally, the family moved to Wichita Falls, Texas. Thornton Sr. died there on Jan 10, 1930, at the age of 58. Around 1934, Fannie moved to Houston, Texas with her son Presley. They resided there for a short time, and then moved to Dallas, Texas in about 1936, where they resided until Fannie's death on May 8, 1948. At the present time, Fannie's living descendants number six grandchildren, 16 great grandchildren, and 18 great-great grandchildren. Fannie was a member of the Daughters of the American Revolution, the United Daughters of the Confederacy, and the Methodist Church.

IRA W. DOYLE, (Feb. 22, 1908-May 25, 1979) married Arkie Denton (March 22, 1910) on April 29, 1927. They had three daughters: Boneda L. (Feb. 22, 1928) married Ralph C. Hicks from El Darado, AR. They now live in Abilene, TX and have daughters Carolyn June (Edge) and Julia Anna and granddaughter, Jessica Edge and Wendy Hicks Bramblett; Sue Ann (April 8, 1931) married Titus R. Durden, from Metter, GA, now lives in the Metro Atlanta, GA area; Mary C. (April 29, 1938) married Al Thomas from Bowling Green, KY, now lives in the Metro Atlanta, GA area. They have sons Mark A. and Kerry Doyle Thomas.

Ira and Arkie Doyle lived on a farm in the Bethel Community at the old Doyle home place, which is still owned and occupied by the Ira Doyle family members. They were active in the Bethel United Methodist Church, farmed, worked for the state, also worked for the Greyhound Bus Co. and served as a county magistrate until his death. His term was finished out by his wife, Arkie Doyle.

Ira W. Doyle was the seventh son of Commodore J. and Docia Ann Westbrooks Doyle. Their children were: Otis, Lawrence, Ezra, Pleas,

Pete, Ike, Ira and Bill. Commodore's parents were John and Phebe (Joyce) Doyle, his brothers; John, Jeff, Fate, Jim and George, and his sisters; Molly, Anna and Donia. Docia A. Westbrook's parents were John and Ginny (Childress) Westbrooks and her brothers; Newt, Clyde, Jim, Walt, Auth and Tray.

Ira W. and Arkie Doyle

Commodore and Docia Doyle were old settlers of the Bethel Community, very active in the Bethel United Methodist Church and raised eight sons as farmers.

Arkie (Denton) Doyle's parents were Andrew Polk Denton and Cordelia Stephens. Her sisters were: Eula, Melissa, Jeanetta and Mary Love, and her brother was Joe. Arkie's grandparents were: Sam Denton and Franie (Craig) Denton and John Stephens and Melissa (Coleman) Stephens.

Andrew Polk Denton's brothers were John, Dolph and Walker.

Cordelia Stephen's brothers were Will, Charles and Tom.

Andrew Polk and Cordelia Denton lived and farmed on Cedar Creek for years, moved to Linden and ran a boarding house, later farmed and managed the County Farm.

JOHNSON E. DOYLE AND EFFIE RODGERS, life-long residents of Perry County, married Feb. 3, 1929, by Rev. C.N. Hudson on Cane Creek, near Enon Church, were the parents of: Helen Katherine (1931-1993), married James R. Tate; Norma Sue, born 1933, married James Edward Richardson; Dorothy Ruth, born 1935, married James Alfred Warren; Harlon Frank, born 1939, first married Carolyn Gregory, second married Irene Mayhair; Mary Joe, born 1941, married Reuben W. Smith; and Glenda Kay, born 1945, married Jimmy Lewis Tatum.

Johnson E. Doyle and his wife, Effie Rodgers Doyle, in 1979 on their 50th wedding anniversary.

Johnson Doyle was born Dec. 10, 1905, at Mill Hollow, near Linden, Perry County, to William Jefferson Doyle (1875-1958) and Jennie Bessie Lee Johnson (1874-1947), the daughter of Stephen Burton Johnson (1816-1891) and Nancy Jane Barber (1842-1904). Stephen Burton Johnson had six children in a marriage prior to his marriage to Nancy Jane. They were: Harriet (1868-1891), married Z.R. "Buddy" Qualls; Charlie B. (1872-1890); Jennie, married W.J. "Jeff" Doyle; Delia "Eller" (1874-1947), married J.S. Barham.

Nancy Jane was the daughter of Enoch Barber and Susan Hinson. Enoch, born about 1804, was the son of Abraham Jr., grandson of Abraham Sr., and great grandson of John Barber, born in 1735 in North Carolina and a Captain in the Revolutionary War. Susan Hinson was the daughter of George Hinson, born 1786, and Elizabeth (Betsy) Upton who came from North Carolina about 1811, and settled on Short Creek, Perry County.

William Jefferson Doyle was one of 14 children born to Jacob W. "Jake" Doyle (1844-1919) and Pheby Caroline Joyce (1846-1894). They were married Aug. 31, 1863 and lived in Linden, Perry County. Other Doyle siblings were: Mary Elizabeth (1865-1943); John Elacandrew (1867-1935); Nancy Freedony (1868-?); Commodore Jackson (1871-1953); Lafayette "Fate" Ashberry Newton (1873-1940); Martha Anna (1877-?); James Woodall (1880-?); George "Doodler" Thomas (1881-?); Cassie Elonzo (1884-1885); Danah (1915-?); Bentley Albert (1887-?); R. Beadie (1901); Sylvia Almer (1891-1993); Homer Victory (1896-?); and Bennie Albert Doyle.

The marriage of William Jefferson Doyle and Jennie Johnson on Nov. 7, 1892, by Justice of the Peace, M.S. Jones, produced 11 children: Dellar Fa Dillia (1893-1975); Charlie, died in infancy; Troy (1897-1898); Nancy Addongia (1899-1939); Prentice (1900-1901); Charlotte (1902-1988); Johnson (1905-1994); Noalon (1907-1930); J.B. Hardy (1909-1974); Myra Prue (1911); and Mary Elizabeth (1913).

Jacob W. "Jake" Doyle was the son of John W. and Mary Polly (last name unknown) Doyle. John W. was born Aug. 10, 1807, and Mary Polly was born Aug. 2, 1811 (their dates of death cannot be verified). Their 11 children were: Philip B., born 1831; James Asberry (1833-1868); Eliza, born 1835; Samuel J., born 1837; William Pless, born 1838; Mary Ann, born 1843; Jacob W., born 1844; Sarah I., born 1846; Nancy J., born 1848; John Russell (1850-1916); and Issac Jefferson, born 1853.

Not much is known about John W. and Mary Polly, but it is believed that he came from Ireland and settled in Decatur County, TN. His son, Jacob Woodruff, fought in the Civil War, and was at the Battle of Shiloh. They first owned the Duncan Place on Cane Creek, Perry County.

WILLIAM JEFFERSON DOYLE AND JENNIE BESSIE LEE JOHNSON DOYLE, William Jefferson Doyle (Dec. 1, 1875-Jan. 22, 1958) and Jennie Bessie Lee Johnson (Dec. 5, 1874-Feb. 3, 1947) were married Nov. 7, 1892.

Jeff was the son of J.W. (Jacob or Jake) Doyle (Jan. 1, 1844-June 4, 1919) and Pheby C. Joyce Doyle (Aug. 23, 1846-Dec. 1, 1922). Jake and Pheby also were the parents of: Mary E. (Molly) (July 1, 1865-June 15, 1943); J.A. (John) (Feb. 18, 1867-May 22, 1935); Nancy F. (Donna) (Oct. 30, 1868-Sept. 30, 1915); C.J. (Commadore) (May 19, 1871-Feb. 13, 1953); L.A.N. (Fate) (Feb. 15, 1873-Jan. 27, 1940); Martha Anna (April 20, 1877-June 12, 1946); James W. (Jim) (March 4, 1880-May 11, 1959); George F. (Doodler) (Dec. 27, 1881-?); Cassie E. (Feb. 20, 1884-April 8, 1885); Benny A. (Dec. 30, 1887-Oct. 20, 1888). These are the brothers and sisters of Jeff W.J. Doyle.

William Jefferson Doyle Family

Jake (Jacob) Doyle's father was Joseph Doyle, who was among the first settlers on Cane Creek in Perry County. He came over from either Scotland or Ireland.

Jennie was the daughter of Steven Burton Johnson (1816-Oct. 28, 1891) and Nancy Jane Barber Johnson (July 2, 1842-July 1908).

Nancy Jane Barber was the daughter of Enoch Barber (1804) and Susan Hinson Barber (1806). Susan's parents were George Hinson (1786) and Elizabeth (Betsy) Upton.

Jeff and Jennie had 11 children:

Dellar Fadillia (called Dillie) (Oct. 8, 1893-July 6, 1975, married Andrew Bismark Bates, June 1918. Had one daughter, Myrtle.

Charlie Doyle (Jan. 7, 1896-Dec. 8, 1896).

Troy Doyle (July 11, 1898-Jan. 8, 1899).

Nancy Addongia Doyle (called Addie) (Feb. 28, 1899-June 26, 1939), married Robert Osby Chandler. Children: Robert Osby, Elva, Dee, William (Bill), Charles, Obie, Nolan, Mack, Ted and Nancy.

Prentice Doyle (Dec. 14, 1900-Sept. 9, 1901).

Charlotte Doyle (called Lottie) (June 4, 1902-Nov. 27, 1988), married Joe D. Barham. Had four daughters: Mary Josephine, Geneva Pearl, Lottie Irene and Ruby Jo.

Johnson E. Doyle, born Dec. 10, 1905, married Effie Rogers. Children: Helen, Norma Sue, Dorothy, Harlon, Mary Jo and Glenda.

Nolan Doyle, (April 24, 1907-Nov. 6, 1930).

J.B. Hardy Doyle (April 24, 1907-April 16, 1973), married Holly DePriest. No children.

Myra Prue Doyle, born Oct. 13, 1911, married Robert Edward Duncan. Children: Mary Ruth, Myra Lucille, James Robert, Ann, Lavenia Louise and Linda Jane.

Mary Elizabeth Doyle, born Nov. 3, 1913, married Hugh Thornton. Two daughters: Betty Joyce and Sarah Elizabeth.

Jeff and Jennie are buried in the Doyle Cemetery on Cane Creek in Perry County. *Submitted by Bettye J. Westbrook.*

DUFF-LEEPER, Jack Regen Duff (Nov. 11, 1904-Jan. 6, 1987) and Pearl Evelyn Leeper (Aug. 18, 1904-March 1, 1990) were married on Feb. 6, 1927 and were lifetime residents of Lobelville. Both are buried in Leeper Cemetery. Their only child, Irene, is married to Harry Womack of Nashville and still maintains the homeplace. The original part was built in 1894 and was also the home of her great grandfather, John Henry Duff.

Jack Regen Duff and Pearl Leeper Duff

Jack was the son of Etta Duff Ferguson (1883-1970) and the grandson of John Henry Duff (1860-1944) and Ida Williams Duff (1867-1901). A half-brother and sister, Hooper and Ida Ferguson Barton reside in Nashville.

Pearl was one of 11 children born to William (Bill) Thomas Leeper (1867-1939) and Dena Wilburn Leeper (1873-1956). Bill's parents were John Henry Leeper (1840-1923) and Betty Greer Leeper (1845-1886). Dena's parents were Josiah Wilburn and Mary Hollins Wilburn. The other children of Bill and Dena Leeper were: Amsel (1888-1960), married to Willie Matt Twomey; Betty (Mrs. Robert) Goblet (1890-1957); Joe (1893-1937), married to Ona; Oda (Mrs. Boyd) Chessor (1895-1966); Seth (1898-1983), married to Mary Sowell; Mary (Mrs. Wiley) Gilmer (1901-1988); Sallie (Mrs. Charlie) Burns (1903-1984); Willie (Mrs. Mark) Ledbetter (1906); Jack (1910-1994), married Kathryn Edwards; and Glyn (1913-1957), married Mary Frances Burns.

Their father, Bill, served a six-year term as sheriff of Perry County. "It's been said the most daring deed he did, was to catch a dog by the nape of his neck with one hand and the hind feet with the other and pitched it out the courthouse window and did not try to shoot the dog."

Pearl's grandfather, John Henry Leeper, built the old Leeper Mill on the Buffalo River about 1880, when he was about 40 years of age.

Jack will be remembered by many as a very good athlete, excelling especially in baseball, where he received the nickname "Sleepy". During his baseball career, he played professional ball with the Boston Red Sox chain in North Platte, Nebraska during the late 20s and early 30's. He became homesick and left that organization and continued to play for several years with semi-pro teams in different places. After baseball, he farmed for several years and then worked for T.G.T. until his retirement in 1965.

DUNCAN, Willie and Doris Duncan Harlow live in Flatwoods. Willie is the son of Jack D. and Lizzie Gilmer Harlow of Hickman County. Willie and Doris were married in the home of Frank and Hessie Parnell on Sept. 3, 1976. They lived in Wyandotte, MI for six years. On Sept. 3, 1982, they came back to Perry County to live in Flatwoods. Doris worked for Linden Apprl. for 28 years before her move to MI. She is the daughter of Hobson and Nola Dories Duncan. They were married in the Court House in Linden in Dec. 1926. Nola and Hobson lived in and out of Perry County following the sawmill that he operated with his father, Barney.

Hobson & Nola Duncan

Barney and Sarah Barber Duncan had four children: Hobson (Nov. 11, 1903-March 16, 1981); Hester (July 11, 1909-March 2, 1924); Joe (April 21, 1904-June 1, 1906); Hershel (Sept. 12, 1907-March 22, 1908). Jack Ruby was born to Hester, Feb. 17, 1924 and died Oct. 26, 1955.

Barney and family lived in Perry and Lewis Counties. He was in partnership with Walter Grover in the timber business in his early married life, then he bought a farm on Beech Creek. His family and Hobsons family left Lewis County and went to the farm in Wayne County for six years. They continued to run the sawmill, along with the farming.

Hobson and Nola had five children: Vernon, born Sept. 21, 1927; Doris, born July 17, 1930; Virginia, born Jan. 26, 1932; Hershel, born Nov. 9, 1934 (he was in the last part of World War II); and Joe, born Nov. 18, 1939 (he drowned in Buckeye Lake, Ohio, April 11, 1967 and was buried in Dover, Ohio).

Barney bought the Joe Barber farm on Coon Creek in 1942. Hobson and family moved there. Barney and family bought a farm on Marsh Creek, moved there for a few years, then moved to the farm on Coon Creek to live out the rest of their lives. Barney died at the sawmill in 1951. He was born in 1883, son of Pleasant and Victoria Hinson Duncan. They had another son, Webster Calvin (Nov. 29, 1885-1956).

Pleasant was born in 1844 and fought in the Civil War. Victoria died and Pleasant married Anna Warren. They had two children, Edward and Amy. Pleasant was the son of Elijah, born 1807, in Indiana. He then went to North Carolina and married Nancy Morgan. They came to Brush Creek in the early 1800s, bought land, lived with the Indians, while he built a house, went back to North Carolina, brought his wife to Brush Creek and raised nine children: William, Mary, Willis, Elijah, Solomon, Pleasant, Sally, Eli and Nancy. They were the first white settlers there. He died in 1888. *Submitted by Doris Harlow.*

DUNCAN-DEPRIEST, Bernard Ray Duncan (1906-1950), the son of Solomon and Ida Hinson Duncan, married Bonnie Laura DePriest, the daughter of Mollie Mae Burns and William Randolph DePriest, in 1927

Bernard's siblings were: Mattie Rogers, Effie Johnston, Barney, Wesley and Ollie Duncan.

Bonnie's siblings were: Julia Mae DePriest Coble (Mrs. James Jefferson Coble Jr.) and Charles Vernon DePriest.

The children of Bernard and Bonnie were: Thomas Ray Duncan, born 1934, and Mary Alice Duncan, born 1935.

In 1964, Thomas married Judith Buchanan, the daughter of Andrew and Ruth Thomas Buchanan of Nashville. Their children were: Jeffrey Ray, 1965; Darrell Wesley, 1970; and Kevin Andrew, 1977.

Thomas, a graduate of Vanderbilt University and the University of Tennessee Medical School, is a Fellow of the American College of Radiology, a former Chief of Staff of Maury Regional Hospital, a Clinical Professor of Radiology at Vanderbilt University, a member of the Board of Directors of Lipscomb University, and an American Contract Bridge League Life Master.

Alice attended Lipscomb University, and is a graduate of the University of Tennessee School of Pharmacy. She is Director of Pharmaceutical Services at Metro Nashville General Hospital.

DUNCAN-SHANNON Martha Cheryl Duncan, born 1945 in Nashville, daughter of James Fred and Willard Marie Hinson Duncan, married Stanley Tinin Jr., son of S.L. and Elizabeth Arnold Tinin. He was born 1943. Children: Carol Ann (1963), married Michael Wayne Trull, son of Earl and Johnnie Ruth Trull, children - Michael Lynn (1983), Kenneth Wayne (1985), Jessica Ann (1987); and Kevin Wayne Tinin (1975), student at U.T. Martin. Carol is employed by Bates Fabricating. Michael is employed by Johnson Controls. Stanley is employed at General Products and Services.

Mattie Shannon Duncan and her three youngest children

Cheryl's grandparents were Edgar and Mattie Shannon Duncan, Jonathan Harvey and Martha Hickerson Hinson. Her great grandparents were John and Mary Oliphant Duncan, and Joseph James and Nancy Young Shannon.

Joseph Shannon came from Humphreys County to teach school, where he met Nancy Young. She was the daughter of Thomas and Elizabeth Horner Young. Mattie Shannon Duncan was the eleventh child of thirteen children. Robert Shannon, the oldest, attended Vanderbilt University, received a law degree from Cumberland University, and spent most of 30 years revising and upgrading Tennessee laws. He wrote the first edition of Shannon's Annotated Code in 1896. Robert and Anna Johnson Shannon were parents of Joseph. Anna was said to be a cousin to Andrew Johnson. James came to Humphreys County in 1809, along with John Crockett, bought several hundred acres of land. Indian troubles caused him to return to Robertson County. Came back in 1813 and built a log home near Hurricane Mills. His second wife was Jane Crockett. He enlisted in militia in 1813. Parents were Robert, born in Ireland 1739, and Florannah Bowles of Bowen. They came to America as children. He died in Wilson County 1815. First settled in Pennsylvania, later Virginia, before coming to Tennessee. Son, John, served in the Revolutionary War. Joseph James Shannon, born 1830, served in Co. F 53rd Tennessee Infantry. He was captured twice, once at Fort Donelson, exchanged after eight months, made 2nd Lieutenant. He is buried in Britts Chapel Cemetery, along with Nancy, several of their children, and her brother, William Young, who was killed at Shiloh.

Nancy, granddaughter of John Jr. and Sarah Sparks Horner and John Miller Young, great grandparents, John Sr. and Elizabeth Russell Horner, and Jesse and Elizabeth Jones Sparks. William Young, great-great grandparents, William Horner Sr., George and Elizabeth Bean Russell, and Matthew and Sarah Thompson Sparks. Matthew, original land owner, road builder, Jury service, etc.

Sparks can be traced back to the British Isles as early as 800. Matthew came from Maryland to North Carolina, later to Georgia. The family built Sparks Fort as protection from Creek Indians. He was killed by Indians while hunting in 1809. Sarah and children later came to Hickman County.

William and John Young, among earliest settlers on Toms Creek. William, born 1744, came from South Carolina to Tennessee, son of Thomas, whose parents, Hugh and Agnes Young, came to America, 1741. Hugh's parents were Andrew Lamont and Ann Hurton Young of Scotland.

Thomas Young built the first brick house in Perry County. *Submitted by Cheryl Duncan Tinin.*

EDGAR JAMES DUNCAN, son of John C. and Mary Oliphant Duncan (1872-1925) married Mattie Shannon (1881-1930). Their children were: Grace, married Jeff Greenway. Children: Mary Jane, Helen and Douglas; Robert Chester, married Clara Baugus. Children: Robert and Marie; Will Edgar, married Sadie Spencer. Children: Mildred, Mavis (Pat) and Linda; Dorothy Alma, married Dewey Marrs. Daughter: Gladys. Married second to Harry Greve; Taval Louise, married Jesse Heath. Children: Vernon, Robert Van and Mattie Lou; Velma, married Joe DePriest. Son: Danny Wayne; Opal, married Roy Mayhugh. Children: Mary Lee (Polly) and Terry; James Fred, married Willard Marie Hinson. Daughter: Cheryl; Lillian, married John Christian Beebe. Daughter: Jacqueline Diane. She married Samuel Warren Kates, director of Wiregrass Museum of Art, Dothan, AL. Children: Shawn Christian and Heather Christine; Joseph Shannon Duncan, married Ruth Myers. Children: Jean, Susan and Tommy.

John C. and Mary Duncan

John C. Duncan, born 1826, was the son of William and Margaret Kutch Duncan. His wife, Mary, was the daughter of Thomas and Mary Malone Oliphant. John was a member of John Whitfield's Hickory Guards, Co. A 1st Tenn. Reg. from Spence's History of Hickman County. The deeds of this Regiment have gone into the brightest pages of Tennessee history. After its baptism of blood at Montery, the Reg. was known as the bloody first. Later joined General Scott's army and participated in the capture of Santa Cruz. George Duncan, John's brother, died on board ship and was buried at sea. They were in the Mexican War.

Children of John and Mary Duncan were: Elizabeth, married Simmons; William Thomas, married Josephine Daniel, second to Lora Brown; Viola, married F.M. York; Mary (Mollie), married William Shannon; Margaret (Maggie), married John Shannon; Edgar, married Mattie Shannon; and Pearl, married Len Stanfield.

John Duncan was practicing law in Centerville in 1870 and also worked as a surveyor. He helped survey boundaries of states out west.

His father, William Duncan, born in Kentucky, was killed by Indians. According to family tradition, his mother, Mary Crockett was a first cousin of David Crockett. Daniel and Harriet Minerva Whitley Kutch were parents of Margaret Duncan. William was discharged from the Army in 1814. He and his wife were on their way back to Kentucky, and stopped to spend the night at the mouth of Falls Branch, where they spent the rest of their lives. Both are buried at Camp Ground Cemetery on Swan Creek.

He was the first Postmaster on Swan Creek and maintained the Post Office in his home. He was elected as a member of County Court, 1836, reelected in 1842, served again in 1854.

Their children: William Hamilton, married Elizabeth Peery; James, who was the first mail carrier in the area; Permetta; David Melton, married Mary Ann Whitesides; Margaret, married Richard Meece; Marcenus, married Eliza Duran; Mary, married Theodrice Miller; Sarah Elizabeth, married Jesse Briggs; John C., married Mary Oliphant; Crockett; George; Luther; and Leonidas. *Submitted by Lillian Duncan Beebe.*

ELIJAH DUNCAN, Arvell E. and Mary M. Ezell live on Brush Creek in Perry County. Arvell is the son of John D. and Bertha Williams Ezell of Lawrence County, TN. Mary is the great-granddaughter of Elijah and Nancy Morgan Duncan. Elijah Duncan came to Perry County in the 1820s and settled the land on the head waters of Brush Creek. He lived with the Indians until he could clear a field and build a log home for his wife. He raised hogs and to sell the hogs, he drove them down the Natchez Trace to New Orleans. It took approximately six months to make the round trip.

Arvell & Mary Ezell in 1993

Elijah Duncan, born 1807, died 1890, was married to Nancy Morgan, born 1808, died 1888, and had the following children: William, Mary (Polly), Willis, Elijah T., Soloman, Eli and Nancy. Eli and Nancy were twins.

Eli Duncan, born March 9, 1851, died Nov. 10, 1926, was married to Rosanna Allison, born May 22, 1852, died March 9, 1889, and had the following children: Edgar, Frank and Mary Elizabeth. Second marriage, Eli married Frances Drucilla Bruce, born May 20, 1862, died Feb. 16, 1934 and had the following children: Ella Kaziah, Aaron Clarence, Eli Bruce, Paul Eric, Eva Rose and Clyde. Eli was a County Surveyor and school teacher at different times. Also, he had a grocery store on Brush Creek.

Paul E. Duncan, born Nov. 23, 1895, died Jan. 21, 1972, was married to Olive Augusta (Ollie) Harper, born Oct. 17, 1898, died Oct. 20, 1980, and had the following children: Lance and Mary Moody.

Lance Duncan, born March 16, 1917, married Martha Frances Counce, born July 13, 1917, died May 10, 1978, and had the following children: George Raymond and Jimmy Lance.

Mary Moody Duncan, born Oct. 20, 1925, married Arvell E. Ezell, born Jan. 15, 1926, and had the following children: Chester Ray, Andrew William and Dolores Jean.

Chester Ray Ezell, born Aug. 9, 1949, married LaDon Kupfur, born March 18, 1950, and have a girl: Raygan Nicole.

Andrew William Ezell, born Sept. 7, 1950, married Kevier Luedecke, born July 14, 1960, and have the following children: John Eric and Avery Lee.

Dolores Jean Ezell, born Nov. 15, 1954, married Albert Douglas Mathis, born Sept. 21, 1944, died Nov. 23, 1983, and have a girl: Crystal Marie.

ELIJAH DUNCAN, (1807-1888), research can not trace back to why Elijah settled in Perry County, or the exact date he arrived. But, the research can describe the legacy that takes place. Elijah and his wife, Nancy (Morgan 1808-1888), had 10 children: William (1828, killed at Shiloh), Mary (1831), Willis (1836), Elijah (1840), Solomon (1843), James Pleasant (1845-1923), Sara (1847), Eli and Nancy (1851) and Sally (1852).

John C. and Ann Duncan Edwards

The tales of Elijah living with the Indians, and homesteading are fascinating. One can only wonder about the hardships they must have endured. The roads we so easily travel today, must have been devastating to them. The man who will be followed to trace these roots is James Pleasant Duncan. It is with him the legacy of kinship starts.

James Pleasant was a Private First Class, Fifth Cavalry, in the Civil War. He married Victoria Hinson, and they had two children, Barney (1883) and Webster Calvin (1885-1956).

In 1883, a man named McClinahan built a home for James and Victoria, in the Brush Creek Community. They farmed their lands and worked the sawmills. James became widowed, and married Anna Warren. They had two children, Ed and Amy.

Webster Calvin Duncan married Jeanette Ann Norman on May 17, 1903. Jeanette was the daughter of Jim and Zelphia Burns Norman. They had 14 children. Birdie Victoria (1904-1966), Zelpha Genevieve (1905-1991), Robert Edward (1908-1993), James Pleasant (1910-1979), Rose (1911-1911), Ola Reams (1913), Nellie Ann (1915), Barnie Lee (1917), Nedda Ruth (1919), Fredia Edna (1921-1980), Annette (1923), Jeanette (1923-1992), Ina Webb (1925), Webster Calvin (1928).

Webster Calvin and Jeanette's home still stands, and is owned by their grandson, Jimmy Duncan.

Robert E. Duncan married Myra Prue Doyle, daughter of William Jefferson Doyle and Jennie Bessie Lee Johnson, in 1927. They lived on Brush Creek and had six children. Mary Ruth (1928), Myra Lucille (1929), James Robert (1931), Ann (1933), Lavenia Louise (1936), Linda Jane (1945).

Robert and Myra were members of Primitive Baptist Church on Cane Creek for approximately 45 years. In 1993, the Church relocated to Linden, and has been in existence for 150 years.

In 1948, Robert and his family moved to the John Myatt farm in the Lick Creek Community. There they continued to log, farm, raise cattle and hogs. In 1953, Robert and Myra purchased the John Myatt farm from William Jones. In 1962, they purchased the John Simmons farm, which was adjacent to their existing farm. Robert served on the beer board from 1972 until his death in 1993.

Ann Duncan married John C. Edwards in 1949. John is the son of Robert and Mary Bessie (DePriest) Edwards. Ann and John moved to Michigan in 1950. John was employed by Ford Motor, and retired in 1982. Ann worked for United Airlines. They have three children, Wanda Ann, Janice Lynne and Timothy Clay. Wanda Ann married Gary Malyszek and had a daughter named Tracy Ann. Following a divorce, she married Kenneth A. Lee, and they had two sons, Kenneth and Matthew. Janice Lynne married Gary Pace, and they had a daughter named Jessie Ann. Following a divorce, Janice and Jessie moved to Perry County. Timothy Clay is Co-Owner with Keith Hayes of O-Bryan's Flowers in Linden.

In 1982, John and Ann returned to Perry County, and live in the Pineview Community. They are members of the Tom's Creek Baptist Church.

Elijah had no idea he would be the start of hundreds of generations to come.

ELIJAH THOMAS DUNCAN SR., (1807-1890) was born in Indiana and came to the Brush Creek area of Perry County in the early 1800's. He married Nancy Morgan (1808-1888), daughter of James and Tabitha Morgan. They had eight children: Mary (1832), Willis (1835), Elijah T. Jr. (1838), Solomon (1843), Pleasant (1844), Sarah (1847), Eli (1851) and Nancy (1851). Eli and Nancy were twins. Elijah and Nancy were buried in the Eli Duncan Cemetery on Upper Brush Creek.

Lurah Mae and L.B. "Barney" Duncan

Elijah Thomas "Toad" Duncan Jr. (1838-1907) married Smithie Catherine McDonald (1843-1894), daughter of George and Mary Yearn McDonald, and had five children: Solomon, Jim, William B., Mary and Nancy. Elijah and Smithy Catherine were buried in the Qualls Cemetery.

James Solomon Duncan (1868-1931) married Ida Marze Hinson (1871-1950). She was the daughter of Larkin and Mollie Jackson Hinson. They had six children: Mattie, Barney, Wesley Thomas, Ollie, Effie and Bernard.

L.B. "Barney" Duncan (1889-1968) married Lurah Mae McDonald (1895-1969) on Oct. 27, 1912. They had two girls: Elsie Ida Duncan (1913) and Lena Larere Duncan (1917-1919). Lena was buried in Qualls Cemetery on Coon Creek.

Elsie married Fred Tucker (1909-1964) on April 23, 1931. He was the son of Robert and Michael Jane Campbell Tucker. They had three children: Helen May Tucker (1933), Clara Winifred Tucker (1938) and James Roland Tucker (1949).

Helen married William Southall, son of Shaddon and Mary Southall, and they had two sons: William Ronald (1956) and Michael Albert (1960). Ronnie married Genia Coston and had two sons: Tucker Glen and William Duncan.

Clara Tucker Lynn had one son, Mitchell Bradford Tucker Sr. and he had a son, Mitchell Bradford Tucker Jr.

James Ronald Tucker was born and died Dec. 30, 1949.

L.B. "Barney" Duncan served as Magistrate/Commissioner from October 1936 until August 1942. He served as County Judge/Executive, and Juvenile Judge from September 1942 until September 1950. He started the first Perry County Public Library, and was instrumental in setting up the first garment factory in Linden; this was Linden Apparel, plant #1, opened in 1947.

L.B. helped set up the first Health Care Unit in Perry County, which worked from the courthouse. He also helped get the present Health Center which was built in 1945 and served as a board member of Merriwether Lewis Electric Cooperative for a number of years. *Submitted by Elsie Tucker.*

JAMES PLEASANT "PETE" DUNCAN, son of Webster Calvin Duncan and Jeanette Ann "Nettie" Norman, was born Dec. 29, 1910 in Perry County, TN. On Sept. 22, 1931, he married Florence Florine Skelton, born May 22, 1916 to Albert Harrison Skelton and Bessie Ann Fain in Lewis County, TN.

In 1952, they moved to Fulton, KY, then in 1966 returned to the old family home on upper Brush Creek, remaining there until their deaths. Mr. Duncan died at home Aug. 4, 1979, the result of a self-inflicted gunshot. Mrs. Duncan died at home Sept. 14, 1971 of a heart attack, the result of Emphysema from which she suffered for many years. They were preceded in death by a daughter, Mary Francis, born June 30, 1939. She

Webb Duncan and his children

died March 6, 1948 at Vanderbilt Hospital from complications caused by TB of the spine. All three were buried in Qualls Cemetery on Brush Creek.

Back: Lon, Barney, Larry and Joe. Front: Jimmy and Pete

Mr. Duncan was a farmer, service station attendant, general laborer and a lay preacher for the Primitive Baptist Church. Mrs. Duncan was a home-maker and sometimes worked in garment factories. Both were members of the Primitive Baptist Church.

Listed are the descendants of James Pleasant and Florence Florine: Nellie Joan "Ann" Rodriguez, born June 13, 1934; Florence Charmayne Cooke, born Nov. 30, 1953; Gloria Genevieve Sandone, born Dec. 11, 1958; Alan Valdze Rodriguez, born March 9, 1961; David Joe Rodriguez, born Dec. 1, 1962; Lori Sue Ann Payne, born May 17, 1974; Ronald David Payne Jr., born Aug. 29, 1976; Thomas Blair Morris, born March 20, 1980; April Michelle Sandone, born April 6, 1981; Michael Joseph Sandone, born Nov. 14, 1982.

Front: Heather, Bess, Ann and Pat

Virginia Genevieve "Pat" Rushton Kline, born Feb. 11, 1938; Clint Jermone Rushton, born Oct. 27, 1956; Ruthann Westerfield, born Dec. 9, 1957; Robert Scott Rushton, born March 20, 1961; Nichole Annette Rushton, born March 9, 1981; Jessica Nichole Rushton, born Sept. 28, 1992; Jennifer Maiann Rice, born Aug. 15, 1976; Misty Lu Rushton, born Aug. 27, 1981; Kristy Lauran Rushton, born Nov. 25, 1984; Cassy Leigh Rushton, born March 28, 1990.

James Webster, born March 25, 1941; James Webster Duncan Jr., born and died March 11, 1961, buried in Wingo, Graves County, KY; Deirdre Dawn, born Oct. 3, 1963; James Derrick Duncan, born Nov. 6, 1970; Donald Lee Joergens Duncan, born June 8, 1967; David Wendell Joergens Duncan, born June 18, 1969; Jessica Renee Duncan, born May 20, 1988; Tara Caitlin Duncan, born Dec. 23, 1992.

Prince Albert "P.A", born March 27, 1944; Reginna Carole Blaser, born July 6, 1963; Lisa Michelle Boehm, born March 21, 1974; Stefani Michelle Blaser, born March 10, 1990.

Joe David, born April 23, 1946; Gordon Scott Mitchell Duncan, born Aug. 10, 1966; Joe David Duncan II, born March 16, 1972; Adam Scott Duncan, born Aug. 7, 1988; Hannah Jo Duncan, born July 28, 1993.

Larry Don, born Dec. 13, 1947; James Pleasant Duncan II, born Jan. 31, 1978; Jason Don Duncan, born Jan. 18, 1980; Jacob Daniel Duncan, born Feb. 19, 1983; Ramond Jackson Duncan King, born July 22, 1967.

Lonzo Dan, born Feb. 11, 1950; Media Lynn Duncan, born May 27, 1971; Jackie Dan Duncan, born Oct. 14, 1975.

Heather Nettie Florine Young, born June 4, 1951.

Barney Webb, born Aug. 30, 1952; Larry Allen Duncan, born May 11, 1974; Travis Webster Duncan, born Aug. 8, 1976; Jo Ann Virginia Duncan, born Aug. 4, 1977.

Bessie Sue Wilkin, born April 29, 1958; Sarah Jean Wilkin, born July 4, 1991.

Listed are Mr. Duncan's brothers and sisters: Birdie Victoria Qualls, born March 29, 1904, died Sept. 5, 1966; Zelpha Genevieve Qualls, born Dec. 1, 1905, died Jan. 3, 1991; Robert Edward Duncan, born Feb. 6, 1908, died Nov. 9, 1993; Ola Reams Chandler, born Feb. 7, 1913; Nellie Ann Westbrooks, born March 29, 1915; Barnie Lee Duncan, born March 30, 1917; Nedda Ruth Adkins, born Feb. 16, 1919; Fredia Edna Inman, born March 3, 1921, died April 22, 1980; Annette Barber, born Nov. 14, 1923; Jeanette O'Guin, born Nov. 14, 1923, died Feb. 10, 1992; Ina Webb Qualls, born Dec. 11, 1925; Webster Calvin Duncan II, born Oct. 29, 1928.

VERNON AND EDITH DUNCAN, were married on Sept. 25, 1948 and lived in various places in Perry and Hickman Counties. In 1956, they moved to Nashville, TN and lived and worked in the Nashville area until July of 1990. They now live in the Flatwoods Community on the beautiful Buffalo River, having bought the house built by the late Dr. W.E. Boyce.

Edith and Vernon Duncan

One son was born to this union, Steve Randell Duncan, born Aug. 27, 1949. Steve has two children: Christopher and Jenipher Duncan, who live in Nashville. Steve and his wife, Shirleen, live in Murfreesboro, TN.

Vernon was the first of five children, born Sept. 24, 1927 to Hobson and Nola Davis Duncan, the others being Doris D. Harlow, Virginia D. Butler, Hershel Duncan and the late Joe Duncan.

Hobson was the son of C. Barney and Sarah Barber Duncan. Barney was known to many people through the sawmill that he moved from place to place in Perry and surrounding counties. Nola was the daughter of Grover and Rebecca Manning Davis.

Edith was the fourth of five children, born May 4, 1930 to Waco and Lillie Hinson Qualls. Her brothers and sister are Estill Q. Hinson, Melvin, Ernest and Joe Robert Qualls.

Waco was one of nine children born to Joe B. and Ezora Warren Qualls. Joe B. Qualls ran a small country grocery store at the intersection of Highway 100 and Upper Brush Creek Road. He is a descendant of Isham Qualls, who was born in Ireland about 1785. Isham came to North Carolina about 1805. He fought in the War of 1812 and in about 1814, he came to Tennessee where he met and married Elizabeth Baucom of Brush Creek.

Lillie Hinson Qualls was one of nine children born to Robert Thomas and Sarah Isabelle Lomax Hinson. Robert was a Primitive Baptist Preacher and traveled throughout the area on his preaching duties.

EDWARDS, The Edwards family of Cotton Branch on Rockhouse Creek can trace its ancestry back to the distinguished family of Thomas Edwards of Edwards Hall in Wales. Thomas Edwards (Oct. 14, 1690) married Isabel Downing in 1714. Their children were Robert (Feb. 4, 1716), Joshua (1718), William (April 8, 1720), Thomas Jr. (July 7, 1723), Leonard (1725), John (1727), Jacob (1729) and Martha (1731).

Left to Right: Robert Andrew Harder, Dr. Susan Harder Morris and William Lee Harder

Thomas Jr. married Elizabeth Nichol in 1743. Their marriage produced children who were born in Virginia. They were Robert (1743), William (1745), Thomas (1747), Sarah (1750) and Andrew (1752).

Andrew served during the Revolutionary War. According to the War Department Records and to *Revolutionary Soldiers of Virginia*, Vol. 9, Andrew served as a private in Captain Charles Flemming's Company, 7 Virginia Regiment, under the command of Colonel Alexander McClannahan. He enlisted February 2. Andrew's name first appears on the Company's muster for June, 1777 and was discharged Feb. 7, 1778. Daughters of the American Revolution in Centreville, TN have an Andrew Edwards Chapter named in honor of this man. Andrew married Phebe Medows (1744), in 1773. Their children were Sarah (1774), May (1775), James (1777) and David L. (1778). Andrew Edwards died in Cumberland County, VA after 1782.

David L. married Eva Lazenie. They moved from Virginia to North Carolina to Kentucky, to Lincoln County, TN. David L. served in the War of 1812. The children of his marriage were Aaron Burr Anderson (1799), Jacob Simon (killed by a falling tree), Jessee, Caleb and Amos. David L. died Aug. 28, 1817 in Hickman County after drinking cold spring water immediately after eating wild honey. He was buried about one mile from the old Edwards' homeplace.

Aaron Burr Anderson Edwards married Nancy Moody in 1817. This was the first wedding on Cane Creek. Nancy was born in Kentucky (Jan. 28, 1801). Eleven children who resulted from this marriage were Andrew Jackson (Jan. 28, 1819, his mother's 18th birthday), Thomas Wayne (March 20, 1820), David L. (Feb. 4, 1822), John Anderson (March 9, 1824), William H. (Dec. 26, 1825), Elizabeth A. (Dec. 20, 1828), Nicholas H. (May 30, 1830), Martha J. (Aug. 11, 1833), Belinda (April 6, 1836), Margaret (Dec. 21, 1838) and Mary Amanda (Dec. 21, 1841). Aaron Burr lived just above the mouth of Ivy Branch which flows from the north into Cane Creek.

John Anderson Edwards married Mary Ann Wilburn (Dec. 20, 1822). John was a prominent Preacher of the Primitive Baptist Church. Their children were John, who became a magistrate, Thomas and Dr. James A. Edwards, who was an ophthalmologist who did post-graduate training in Heidelberg, Germany. John Anderson Edwards died Jan. 9, 1878.

Nicholas H. Edwards married Casse Skelton. Their children were Amos Raymond (July 18, 1853), Charity who married Allen Barber, John Aaron; who married Rinda Hinson, Ardella who married S.A. Turnbow and Sarah who married Zibe L. Barber. Nicholas later married Virginia Briggins. They had two daughters: Addie who married E.L. Chumney and Mag who married Thomas Ferguson.

Amos Raymond was a boy of nine years of age when he heard the Battle of Shiloh beginning on Sunday morning. He was attending church on Cane Creek which was over 60 miles from Shiloh. The sounds of the guns carried clearly over this distance. Amos married Celestine Higgins on July 20, 1879. Celestine was born in 1863 in Water Valley, MS during the War Between the States. The children of this marriage were John H. (April 11, 1880 and died in infancy), Annie (July 8, 1881), William James (April 13, 1889), Amanda Ardella Victoria (Aug. 21, 1892) and David Lloyd (Dec. 24, 1897). Amos and Celestine moved from Cane Creek to Cotton Branch in the early 1880's where they had a farm with a large farmhouse, pastures, an orchard and a blacksmith's shop. Amos died in June 1930.

Annie attended Scott's Hill Academy to study to be a teacher. She later married Will Francis of Marion, VA. The children of this marriage were Albert Wesley, William Samuel, Walter Edwards, David Lloyd and Annie Edwards.

Albert Wesley married Louise Snodgrass. Their children were Susan and Ann. Albert was the co-founder of Francis Brothers Hardware and Plumbing.

William Samuel was a physician of internal medicine who served on submarines, aircraft carriers and ships during World War II. He had sons Bill and Phil who had a PhD in metallurgical engineering and worked for the space program.

Walter Edwards married Lutie Catron. Their children were Joe and Janet. Walter was Chairman of the Board of the Bank of Marion, Director of United Inter-Mountain Telephone Company, Mayor of Marion, co-founder of Francis Brother's Hardware and Plumbing and Trustee of the First United Methodist Church.

David L. married Virginia Duncan. Their children were Jimmy, Robert and Donald. David was a well-loved dentist in Marion and was followed into this profession by his son, Donald.

Annie E. worked at Appalachian Power Company until retirement.

William James Edwards was principal of Hickman County High School and was president of the Bank of Hohenwald. Sarah Ophelia Colley, alias "Minnie Pearl", taught dramatics at Hickman County High prior to entering show business while William was principal.

David L. Edwards was a pharmacist for 53 years, beginning his career in Memphis and concluding in Virginia. David L. was also a world traveler. He visited 77 countries and went around the world twice, once from east to west and then from west to east.

Victoria was a student and a teacher at the Baptist Church School. Victoria married James Andrew Harder of Rockhouse Creek. Victoria made a home for her brother-in-law and her two sisters-in-law when she was first married as they were orphans. The family lived at the Harder homeplace in Bulley Hollow. According to *A Brief History of Rockhouse Creek* by Videlle Dabbs, the union of Jim and Victoria added greatly to the Rockhouse Community. They were instrumental in moving the road out of the creekbed, Jim helped install the telephone system. They were intelligent, hardworking, religious and visionary.

See the Rockhouse Creek Harders to find out more about Jim, Victoria, their children, their grandchildren and great grandchildren.

Compiled from notes of Professor William James Edwards and David L. Edwards by W. Albert Harder and Dr. Susan Lou Harder Morris. Also from *Spences History of Hickman County.*

EDWARDS-TUCKER, Thomas Edwards was born in Wales in 1680 and married Isabelle Downing in 1714. Their son, Thomas Edwards Jr. (1723) married Elizabeth Nicholus in 1743. Their son, Andrew Edwards (1752) served in the Revolutionary War in 7th Virginia Regiment in Cumberland County, VA. He married Phoebia Meadows.

David L. Edwards (1778) married Eve Lazenia, moved from North Carolina to Kentucky, then to Lincoln County, TN, and later to Cane Creek in Hickman County. He served in the War of 1812. His death in 1817 was said to be caused by eating wild honey and drinking cold spring water. Aaron Burr Edwards (1799-1850) married Nancy Moody in 1818 in the first wedding on Cane Creek.

Andrew Jackson "Jacky" Edwards (1819) was born on his mother's birthday. He married three times, first to Anne Sanders. He was a Primitive Baptist preacher in Hickman and Perry County. Their daughter, Mary Elizabeth, (1848-1920) married Dickson Tucker and had the following children: Lura Craig, Jennie, Dixie King, Joseph, Andrew, William and Thomas Blain.

Thomas Blain Tucker (1884) married Ada Florence Paschall. He was a mail carrier, and one of the first school bus drivers. He carried mail to Lobelville and Perryville, where he once walked across the frozen Tennessee River. She was active in church and community. The Pentecostal Church in Linden was dedicated to her memory. Both were church members, he was a Mason, and she was an Eastern Star. Their children were: Fred, Clara Emogene, Gladys Onedia, Lula Rubena, Thomas Paschall, Verne Elmore, Willie Ray, Linda Ruth, Michael Henry and Loretta Jane. The first child, Fred, died six years after birth.

Clara Emogene (1905) married Ray O'Guin, owner of a truck line. Their children were: Ray Dean McEwing and Delores Jean Mitchell.

Gladys Onedia (1907-1986) married Jack Young, a barber, and had a son, Paul, and a daughter, Helen M. Richardson.

Lula Rubena (1910) married Joe S. Dabbs who was killed by a fallen power line in 1949. She was Perry County Court Clerk for 20 years. Their daughters were Glenda Ann Jacobs and Billie Faye Rutledge.

Thomas Paschall (1914) married Mary Evelyn Orr and was a mechanic/tool & die man, defense work during World War II at Vultee in Nashville. They have two daughters, Barbara Whittle and Lynda Smith.

Willie Ray (1920) married Cloe Warren and had three sons: David, Joel and Patrick. Willie Ray served in the Army in World War II and later performed excavation work and owned his own business.

Linda Ruth (1922) married John Elliott. She was an RN, served in the Air Force in World War II and retired from the City of Memphis Public Health Department. They had two daughters, Shelly Ruth Thompson and Vickie Joe.

Michael Henry (1928) married Betty Faye O'Guin. He became a minister and spent much time in missions in India and Hong Kong. Their children are Beth Jinkerson, Mike and Bruce.

Loretta Jane (1932) married George Osborn. She was an RN and supervisor of school health department in Arkansas. Their children are Portia Routon, Amy Lee Hufstedler and Tony Osborn.

Verna Elmore Tucker (1917) married Thomas Elvin Stutts in 1938. He was born in Wayne County (1911-1970) and served in the Marines during World War II. He was an automotive repair man all his life, living in Anderson, IN many years before returning to Perry County in 1955, where he operated his own business from 1955 until his retirement in 1965.

Their son, Thomas Wayne Stutts (1939) married Jane Moore in 1958 and divorced in 1978. He married Alice Curtis in 1986 and they reside in Nashville where Wayne operates his company, Forms & More, and Alice is employed at Southwestern Co. Wayne and Jane had two children: Karen Elaine (1960) married Frank Ittel and Todd Wayne (1963) who married Gwen

Bowman in 1988. They have one daughter, Nicole Marie (1991). Both Karen and Todd live in the Atlanta area and are both in business management.

AARON BURR (BURRELL) EDWARDS, was born in North Carolina in 1799, son of David L. and Eva Lazenie Edwards. His wife was Nancy Moody, born Jan. 28, 1801 in Kentucky. Nancy's mother was Ruth Pique. Aaron Burr and Nancy were married July 1818 and had 11 children: Andrew Jackson (Jan. 28, 1819) married Anne Sharp; Thomas Wayne (March 20, 1820-Feb. 8, 1880) married Jennie Watson, was one time Circuit Court Clerk of Perry County, buried in Kirk Cemetery at Linden, TN; David L. (Feb. 4, 1822) married Amanda Goodwin; John Anderson (March 9, 1824) married Mary Wilburn; William Hodge (Dec. 26, 1825) married first, Nancy Wilburn, second, Mary Agnes Woolard; Elizabeth A. (Dec. 20, 1828) never married; Nicholas M. (May 30, 1830) married Cassie Skelton; Martha J. (Aug. 11, 1833); Belinda (Malinda) (April 6, 1836); Margaret (Dec. 21, 1838); Mary Amanda (Dec. 21, 1841).

William Hodge Edwards was born Dec. 26, 1825, the son of Aaron Burrell Edwards and Nancy Moody Edwards. He died October 1871. He married Nancy Wilburn. Their children are as follows: Sarah Elizabeth (1849-1887), married G.S. Stephens; Nancy Jane, married Josiah Baker Shepard (called Buddy); John Thomas, married Sallie Shepard, sister to Josiah Shepard; William Joseph, married Alice Daniel; Robert Lee, married Nettye Rebecca Rice. Elbert Wilson died at three years of age, and Gustavus Henry died at one year of age. They are buried in Beardstown Cemetery by the side of their mother.

William Hodge Edward's second wife was Mary Agnes Woolard, born March 18, 1833, daughter of William Woolard and Harriett Lancaster Woolard. Their children were: Mary Malinda (1866-1960) married Joel Monroe Hunt; Samuel David (1868-1906) married Eula Beard; Jackson Hodge (1871-1912) married Lelia Estelle DePriest. Mary Agnes Woolard Edwards died July 18, 1925.

CLAUDE CLEMENT EDWARDS, the family ancestry began with the birth of Thomas Edwards at Edwards Hall, Wales, about 1690, married Isabel Downing in 1714. Thomas Jr. (born 1723), married Elizabeth Nichol in 1743. His son, Andrew (born 1752, Virginia) served in the Revolutionary War.

David L. Edwards (1778-1817), Andrew's son, married Evie Lazenie and lived on Cane Creek in Hickman County. He served in the War of 1812. Aaron B. Edwards (1799-1878), David L's son, married Nancy Moody 1817. One of their sons, William Hodge (1826-1871) married Nancy Wilburn, 1848, Hickman County. Their fourth child, John Thomas (1857-1919) married his first cousin Sarah "Sallie" Shepard in 1879, daughter of Egbert H. Shepard (1825-1904), sister of "Buddy" Shepard, who married his first cousin, Jane Edwards, sister of John Thomas. John Thomas and Sallie had eight children: Lora born 1880, Mabel born 1882, Edith born 1885, William "Will" born 1887, Egbert born 1889, Elbert born 1892, Claude born 1895 and Pearl born 1899. Grandchildren: Lilah "Patsy" and John Blackwell; Thomas d. and James Edwards; Harold, Cleo d. and J.T. Edwards; Theda, Tommye, Kathryn and Claude Edwards Jr.

First Row: Claude, Claude Jr. and wife, Lottye. Back Row: Kathryn, Tommye and Theda

Claude C. Edwards (1895-1989) was born at Beardstown in the house that stands today and later occupied by "Buddy" and Jane Shepard. He attended school at Cane Creek, Border Springs, Friendship and Hohenwald. Some of his teachers were: Mabel, his sister, Egbert, his brother, John Harder, Russell Gray, Leonard DePriest, Obe DePriest and Emma McAfee. He married his schoolmate, Lottye Warren (1896-1987), daughter of "Billy" and "Cathy" Warren. She was an excellent homemaker and businesswoman. They lived at Beardstown and Linden where he was a farmer and merchant. Their children: Theda, Tommye, Kathryn and Claude Edwards Jr.

Theda, born 1917, finished high school at P.C.H.S., and attended two years at MTSU to receive a P.P. certificate to teach. She married Homer Long, born 1910, who was also a teacher. Both attended Peabody College. Theda received a BA degree and retired with 38 years of experience. Homer received a MA degree plus 45. He served as a teacher, Sergeant in the U.S. Army in World War II, administrator and Specialist I ETV for the Tennessee State Dept. of Education. He retired with 41 years of experience. Their daughter, Linda, born 1943, received a BA degree at Peabody, Master of Business Ed. and MA plus 45 at MTSU and TSU. She is now teaching VOE at Fairview High School.

Tommye (1919-1990) finished high school at P.C.H.S. and took a business course. She then became a secretary and bookkeeper for the Supt. of P.C. schools and later for the P.C. Highway Department; retired with 38 years of experience.

Kathryn attended high school at P.C.H.S. and finished at Bakerville. She married Jack Leeper, who attended Freed Hardeman College. He taught and coached in P.C. schools, then started working for TGT; operator and plant foreman for 31 years. After retirement, he and Kathryn moved to Tupelo, MS. She taught in a church kindergarten, instructor of Singer Sewing Classes and aerobics. Now she is teaching at Wellness Center, N.E. Medical Center. Both daughters attended MUW College at Columbus, MS. Jackie is sales representative for Viva Optical Company; Jan is Vice-President of Peoples Bank and Trust Company, in the loan department in Tupelo, MS.

Claude Jr. (1931-1962) attended high school at P.C.H.S. He operated a service station for his parents at Linden. Father of three daughters: Yolanda, mother, Nellie Y. Edwards: Ruth Ann and Claudette d., mother, Dorothy H. Edwards. Yolanda operates a restaurant in Perryville, TN. Ruth Ann received a MA degree in Early Childhood Ed. at MUW MS and taught five years. Claudette was tragically killed while attending N.E. MS Junior College.

Claude C. Edwards' story concludes by listing his great grandchildren: Melody Milam, Stephen and Laura Moore, Brent Carnathan, Tiffany and Dusty Hayes.

JAMES D. EDWARDS, born 1858, married May 26, 1878, Perry County to Dorcas Marcella Sharp. She was born 1857, daughter of William Anderson Sharp and Agnes Hensley. Per 1880 Perry County census, they had one daughter, Elizabeth L. Edwards, born June 1880. This is the last record known of the family.

JAMES MORTON EDWARDS, born Aug. 22, 1868, Maury County, son of William Harvey Edwards and Mary Rebecca Roach, died March 25, 1949.

The old Samuel Miles Boyce home on Sinking Creek.

He married Lizzie Boyce, daughter of Samuel Miles Boyce and Harriett Elzada Sisco. They had nine children. (1) Whitney Harvey Edwards, born Sept. 5, 1893, Hampshire, Maury County, died April 11, 1978, Memphis. She married Nov. 2, 1914, Flatwoods, to Harrison Richardson. (2) Connie Minton Edwards, born Feb. 5, 1895, Flatwoods, died Aug. 10, 1904, Oklahoma. (3) Emma Louise Edwards, born Feb. 10, 1898, Texas, died Jan. 10, 1915, Flatwoods, buried Flatwoods cemetery. (4) Harriett Rebecca Edwards, born Feb. 2, 1900, Texas, married March 14, 1920, Flatwoods, to Arthur Lee Bryson. (5) Willie Ann "Billie" Edwards, born Oct. 20, 1902, Flatwoods, married Frank H. Allen. (6) Samuel Boyce Edwards, born Sept. 17, 1905, Oklahoma, married Rose Ann Barnes. (7) Mattie Clare Edwards, born 1909 Flatwoods, married March 20, 1926, Linden, Lexie Elmer Kirk. (8) Hassell Inez Edwards, born March 3, 1914, Flatwoods, married Glen Whitley. (9) Leo Christine "Pete" Edwards, born Aug. 22, 1916, Flatwoods, wife of Edward Byron Dotson. *Submitted by Merle Stevens.*

JOHN T. EDWARDS AND ADDA MAE WESTBROOKS EDWARDS, moved to Dover, Ohio in 1926 from Nashville, Arkansas, with their two small sons, John Jr., born Oct. 4, 1923, and James W., born Jan. 18, 1925. A daughter, Virginia, born March 1, 1928, and a son, David, born April 17, 1930, added to their family in Dover.

Golden Wedding Anniversary of John T. and Adda Mae Edwards. Back Row: Virginia Edwards Wilcox, James W. Edwards, John T. Edwards Jr., David L. Edwards. Seated: John T. and Adda Mae Edwards

Adda Mae, born Aug. 15, 1902, was the daughter of Andrew and Artie Edwards Westbrooks who were married Jan. 24, 1897 in Perry County, TN. Artie was the daughter of John A. and Marinda Hinson Edwards, married Dec. 23, 1877. John A. Edwards' family had lived in the Cane Creek area. Andrew was the son of Joseph and Melinda Sisco Edwards whose marriage is recorded Nov. 2, 1872 in the early book of marriages in Perry County, TN.

John T. Edwards Sr. was born in Sugar Tree, TN, Oct. 20, 1901, the son of James and Mary Etta Spense Edwards, who married Feb. 5, 1893 in Benton County, TN.

The families of John and Adda Mae moved from Tennessee to Arkansas where they met and were married, Dec. 16, 1922. After coming to Ohio, John worked in a steel mill, owned and operated gasoline stations, and drove a truck. John and Adda Mae, along with their children, owned and operated a trucking company, Edwards Sales & Service, Inc., until their death. The company is still being run by John Edwards Jr.

John Jr. married Dorothy Plotts, Nov. 1, 1941, and has five children: Carole, Nancy, Richard, Susan and Michael. James W. married Mary Ella Diefenbacher, Sept. 8, 1946 and has four children: James, Linda, Daniel and Sandra. Virginia married Dean Wilcoxon March 6, 1949. David married Carol Lauber and has three children: Steven, Robert and Rick. All the families still reside in this area.

THOMAS EDWARDS, the first Edwards on record, was born Oct. 14, 1690 of Edwards Hall, Wales, England. He married Isabel Downing in 1714. Their children were: Robert (1716), Joshua (1718), William (1720), Thomas Jr. (1723), Leonard (1726), John (1727), Jacob (1729), and Martha (1731).

Thomas Edwards Jr. was born July 7, 1723, and married Elizabeth Nichols in 1743. Their children were: Robert (1743), William (1745), Thomas III (1747), Sarah (1750) and Andrew (1752).

Andrew Edwards was born in Virginia in 1752, served in the American Revolution in Captain Charles Blemming's Company, 7th Virginia Regiment, commanded by Col. Alexandra McClannahan. His name first appeared in the Company's muster roll dated June 1777, showing date of enlistment as February 2nd; discharged Feb. 7, 1778. Andrew married Phebe Meadow, born 1744, in 1773. Their children were: Sarah (1774), May (1776), James (1777) and David L. (1778). Andrew died in Cumberland County, VA after 1782.

David L. Edwards was born 1778 and married Eva Lazenie. He moved from North Carolina to Kentucky, hence to Lincoln County, TN. Later, he and his wife located on Cane Creek in Hickman County. He died Aug. 28, 1817. His grave is located about one mile from the old Edwards home owned in 1927 by J.A. Pace. David served in the War of 1812. Children born to this marriage were: Aaron Burr (Burrell), born 1799, married Nancy Moody in 1817; Simon was killed as a young man by a falling tree; Jesse married Mary Ann Moody, sister to Nancy Moody; Jacob; Caleb; and Amos A., born 1814.

Amos Anderson was born Oct. 27, 1814 in North Carolina. His first wife was Blenda Anderson. His second wife was Elizabeth (Betsy) Wilborn, born May 12, 1826, of Perry County. Amos Anderson died Aug. 9, 1895, and Betsy died Aug. 9, 1895. They are buried in Beach Grove Cemetery. Children born, perhaps all by last marriage, are as follows: Emily (1843), John T. (1845), Samuel W. (1847), William F. (1849), Nancy C. (1850), Mary A. (1855); and Burrell Wilburn (1859).

Burrell Wilburn Edwards married Viola Permilia Morrison Dec. 3, 1879. She was born Sept. 8, 1861, daughter of Thomas B. Morrison (1841) and Sarah Rice Morrison (1842-1909). Thomas B. was son of Elias D. Morrison (born 1795 in Mecklenburg County, NC and died 1852 in Hickman or Perry County) and Jane (Jennie) Kimmons Morrison, born 1799 in Tennessee. Sarah Rice Morrison was the daughter of William Rice, born about 1822 and was deceased by 1845, and Mary Minerva (Polly) Spurlock Rice, born Aug. 17, 1822, died Nov. 4, 1900. Sarah Rice Morrison later married Robert Franklin Green of Hickman County.

Burrell and Viola were the parents of Dr. William K. Edwards, Estelle Edwards and Carl F. Edwards of Hickman County, TN.

Burrell died July 11, 1918, and Viola died June 10, 1943. They are buried in the Centerville Cemetery, Hickman County, TN.

JAMES LEE ELLIOTT, born Oct. 16, 1967, Boulder, CO, married Jodie Lynn Jackson, on Jan. 23, 1993, Denver, CO. They have one son, Brandon Scott Elliott, born Nov. 6, 1993, Yokouska, Japan, Naval Hospital.

James and Jodie Elliott on their wedding day

James Lee Elliott is the grandson of John Wilburn Moore. He lived in Colorado all of his life and graduated from Douglas County High School in 1986. He loves his family, being with friends, playing video games, riding motorcycles, weight lifting, foosball and snow skiing. He had the honor of being in the first Colorado Winter Olympics even though he missed a gate in the skiing competition. His mother says he is also a comedian. When he was 12, he walked up to Russ and said, "You know today is moms birthday." Russ answered, "Ya, I remembered." So that night Russ brought home a dozen red roses and a card with $50.00 inside. He said "Happy Birthday Honey." His mother said thanks for the roses and took the card and as she opened it she said, "Gee honey, this is really nice, but now what do I get for my birthday, next month?"

James Lee Elliott with son, Brandon Scott Elliott

James joined the Navy and was sent to the Great Lakes Naval Base near Chicago. While there, he attended several schools and graduated top of his class. He was then sent to San Diego for more schooling. He graduated from his last class in July 1991 with his mother and father present. He had his choice of stations and passed up Florida and Hawaii for Japan. He has enjoyed his time in Japan and all the trips to Australia, Saudia Arabia, United Arib Emmeritz, Guam, Korea, Singapore, Africa, Hong Kong, China, all of Japan and others. While at home on leave in 1992, he met the love of his life at a baseball game he went to with an old friend. They wrote and called each other for a year and then decided to marry. He flew home January 1993, two days before his wedding to Jodie Lynn Jackson. Between Jodie, her parents, and his mother and father, the wedding fell into place and was very beautiful. He picked the church and tails for his tux, the rest was left up to Jodie, even picking the best man from three of his high school friends. They spent the next week visiting old friends that they would not see for two years. The day they were to leave for Japan, his mother and father took them skiing, home to pack their bags and to the airport for a midnight flight. They lived in the Navy lodge in Yokouska for two months before finding a house to rent.

He called home in March and invited his parents to come to Japan for a few weeks so they would be there for his birthday in October. His mother was very excited. He then hit her with the punch line, you're gonna be a grandma. Nine months and two weeks after the wedding, a beautiful boy, Brandon Scott Elliott, was born Saturday, Nov. 6, 1993 in Yokouska, Japan, Naval Base Hospital, weighing in at 7 lbs. 3 oz., 20 3/4" long. Very proud grandparents were there and got to spend two beautiful weeks with the new family.

James' ship, the USS *Thach*, FFG43 was scheduled to pull out 8 Monday 1993 for a month and a half, but the baby was right on time, as he went on a 30 day maternity leave the morning the ship left port. So he had time to spend with his parents and the next two weeks with Jodie and Brandon, before he had to report for shore duty until the ship returned to port, Dec. 22, 1993.

James is a Fire Controller 2nd Class and was named the onboard weapons specialist. He operates and maintains the computers that operate the onboard missile weapons systems.

ROBERT EPLEY, born Dec. 27, 1887, died Sept. 11, 1973, married Estalee Cotton, born Dec. 27, 1891, died Feb. 3, 1978. They were farmers on Sinking Creek and members of the United Pentecost Church. Their children were:

The Epley Family. Left to Right: (front): Adele and Imogene. Back: Bernice, Robert, Ernest, Estalee, Maizel and Mary Helen

Ernest, born Nov. 11, 1912, died May 1, 1983, married Louise Justice. Their children: Joe Epley, born Nov. 12, 1942, married Gale Ashburn. Children: Ginger, Ty and Jody; Brenda Epley, married Clifford DePriest. Their children: Shannon and Jennifer; and Robert Epley, married Lisa. Child: Brittany.

Bernice, born Dec. 3, 1913, married Pauline Davis, born July 18, 1917. Their children: Joan, born March 30, 1947, married William Lynch; Jean, born March 30, 1947, married Tony Hinson. Their child: Amanda, born Oct. 10, 1970; and Aileen, born March 30, 1950, married Van Schwendimann. Their children: Alan, born June 28, 1970, Michael, born March 14, 1974, Jacob and Chelsea.

Fielder, born June 15, 1915, died Oct. 3, 1917.

Maizel, born Oct. 3, 1916, died Sept. 1, 1979, married Vance Tilley. Their children: Barbara, born Jan. 23, 1950, married Jim Volner; and Jane, born June 29, 1951, married Thomas Tarver. Their child: Sloane, born Oct. 28, 1983.

Adele, born Aug. 7, 1918, married Pruitt Ragan. Their children: Ronald, born July 13, 1942; Phillip, born July 24, 1949, married Karen Young. Their children: Robert, born Jan. 16, 1973, Wayne, born June 5, 1977, Matt and Brent; and Melinda, born June 7, 1956, married Larry Huckabee. Their children: Michael, born Aug. 11, 1984, James and David.

Mary Helen, born Nov. 29, 1919, married Willie Riley, born April 10, 1920, died Sept. 15, 1976. Their children: David, born April 4, 1947, married Patricia Potts. Their children: Michelle, born Sept. 24, 1974, died Jan. 28, 1975, Jennifer, born March 30, 1976 and Christopher, born Oct. 4, 1977; Danny, born June 11, 1949, married Theresa McCauley. Their children: James, born July 27, 1977, and Raymond, born Aug. 11, 1978; Jeanette, born July 9, 1951, married Jim Schweitzer. Their children: Brandon, born Oct. 23, 1982, Jacob, born Jan. 1, 1993, Elizabeth and Barbara; and Elizabeth, born Feb. 23, 1955, married Buford Raymer. Their child: Scotty, born Aug. 3, 1980.

Imogene, born Aug. 28, 1922, married Frank Brown, born Nov. 22, 1921, died Sept. 23, 1968. Their child: Frank, born Dec. 12, 1948, married Raylene Lindsey. Their children: Kristyn, born Oct. 12, 1972, died Dec. 20, 1993, Ryan, born Oct. 24, 1988, and Jeff, born Aug. 29, 1971. Imogene married second to Elbert Tatum.

Robert and Estalee lived on their farm on Sinking Creek from 1916 to 1970. While living there, they planted seven maple trees, one for each of their children. This is how the farm became known as Seven Maples. After retiring in 1970, they moved to Hohenwald.

The heirs are now owners of the farm and enjoy spending time there.

ABRAHAM ESTES, In 1471, "the illustrious Marquis Francesco d'Este of Ferrera, son of Marquis Leonello, left Ferrera to live in Burgundy" wrote an historian. Later, a portrait of Francesco was discovered in a villa near Ferrera, and on the back was inscribed, "Francesco, natural son of Leonello d'Este-to Burgundy-then to England".

Neil Gunson, an Estes descendant and a history professor at the Australian National University in Canberra, Australia, writes "a good deal of speculation and incorrect data has been circulated over the past 100 years, both in England and in America." While many Estes researchers contend that Francesco is the progenitor of the Deal, County Kent, England Estes family, Mr. Gunson argues that no record of Francesco appears to survive in the English State Papers. It is the belief of this writer that the Deal, England family is descended from the Germanic branch of the family. The uncommon given names of Otho and Mansfield used in Germany were also used by the Virginia and Kentucky branches of the Estes family in America.

The County Kent Estes families were described as "maritime" or sea-faring people. This may explain why the earliest appearances of the name in England are found scattered along the southeast coast of the English Channel.

Nicholas Estes, born about 1495 (birthplace unknown), lived in Deal, England and died there in 1533. He married Anny in 1520, and they were the parents of Sylvester Estes, born 1522, Deal. His wife was Jone, and they were the parents of three children: Jone, Henry and Robert. Sylvester died in 1579 and is buried in Ringwould, County Kent.

Robert Estes (1575-1616) married Ann Woodward in 1591. His wife survived him by 15 years and she left a will naming their children. Their second son, Sylvester, was baptized at Ringwould, Sept. 26, 1596. He married Ellen Martin of Waldershire on Nov. 24, 1626. They were the parents of six sons and seven daughters. Both Sylvester and Ellen were dead by 1667 when their daughter, Ellen, married her third cousin, Moses Estes. Their eldest son, Robert, settled in Waldershire. Two of his sons, Richard and Matthew, came to America and settled in Lynn, MA.

Abraham Estes, the youngest son of Sylvester and Ellen Martin Estes was born in 1647, and named in his mother's will of 1649. He was a linen weaver in the old Walloon town of Sandwich, when he, at age 25, married Ann Burton, widow of John Burton. Presumably, Ann died and Abraham left England for America. In Nugent's *Cavaliers and Pioneers*, Vol. II, Abraham Easter (sic) is shown transported to America by Lucy Keeling, daughter of Thorowgood Keeling, deceased on April 20, 1682. In 1683, Abraham Estes signed a Petition at St. Stephen's Parish Church in New Kent County, VA. In 1704, he paid taxes on 2000 acres of land in King & Queen County, VA. He died there Nov. 21, 1720, leaving nine sons: Robert, Thomas, Sylvester, Samuel, John, Moses, Elisha, Richard and Abraham. His four daughters were: Barbara, Sara, Susanna and Mary. It is not known if any of these children belonged to his first wife, Ann Burton, or if all of them belonged to his wife, Barbara (?Brock) who survived him. *Submitted by Kitty E. Savage.*

ESTES, Albert Azo II, Margrave of Italy, Count of Este, Rovigo and Lunigiana, was born ca 997, and lived one hundred years, dying in 1097. He was the common ancestor of the two great branches of the family known to later history. At the age of 40, he married for the first time, the only daughter of his kinsman Guelph, the Fourth Duke of Altdorf and the Duke of Bavaria. Cunigunda's only brother, Guelph, inherited his father's titles, and was also invested with the dutchy of Carintha and the marquesate of Verona in the Italian confines. Albert Azo II and Cunigundi were the parents of one son, Guelph. Cunigundi died at a young age, and her brother died without issue, so Guelph, as the last male heir of the House of Altdorf, became in 1055, the head not only of the Italian but also of the German branch of the Guelphic family. From him descended the Dukes of Bavaria, Saxony and Brunswick, the Elector of the House of Hanover, and the reigning royal lines of Europe, including the present day Queen Elizabeth of Great Britain.

Albert Azo II married a second time to the widow Garsende, daughter and heiress of the counts of Maine. By her he had two sons, Hugo and Folco. The younger son, Hugo, succeeded his grandfather as Count of Maine. He died in 1092 without issue. The family heritage in Italy fell to Folco, and from him, through his son, Obizzo, sprang the line that built up the rich and important principality of Ferrera, Modena and Reggio. Ferrera owes to the House of Este her peculiar place in history; she is remembered as the scene of its brilliant and long-lasting tyranny, of its domination over the social and intellectual life of the area, of the turbulent and intriguing events of the next several centuries. In 1597, the last Duke of Ferrera died, and in 1875, the Archduke Francis Ferdinand, heir to the Austro-Hungarian throne, inherited all titles and estates of the Estes family of Ferrera. In the summer of 1914, as Archduke Francis Ferdinand and his wife were leaving the senate house in Sarajevo, they were assassinated by a Bosnian student. This shooting touched off World War I. *Submitted by Kitty E. Savage.*

CHESTER FRANKLIN (FRANK) ESTES,

was born Dec. 2, 1891, Caneyville, Grayson County, KY, the son of Henry Daviess and Sarah Nancy Bozarth Estes. In 1902, he came with his parents to Humphreys County where his father was engaged in the lumber business. He attended the public schools of Humphreys County and Draughons Business College. In 1909, he entered the lumber business with his father. In 1911, he bought his first sawmill and continued in this business until after his 80th birthday. His last years in the business were in partnership with Mr. Will Edwards of Linden. He was considered one of the best sawmill men in the country.

Frank and Lillian Potter Estes on Easter Sunday 1921.

On June 24, 1911, Frank Estes married Lillian Lee Potter, born July 30, 1897, Hickman County, the daughter of Will Allen and Catherine Pruett Potter. Frank and Lillian celebrated their 62nd wedding anniversary four months before his death.

The nature of his work required frequent moves for the family, and over the years, they lived in Perry, Hickman, Lewis, Wayne, Humphreys and Obion Counties in Tennessee. In 1943, the Estes family moved to Linden where Frank Estes spent the rest of his life. He died Oct. 31, 1973 and is buried in the Rice cemetery near Hurricane Mills. Mrs. Estes remained in Linden until 1989 when she went to Florence, AL to live with her youngest daughter, Patsy Estes Coble. After a series of strokes, Mrs. Estes was moved to the Mitchell-Hollingsworth Nursing Home. She will be 97 years old in July 1994.

Mr. and Mrs. Estes were Charter Members of the First Baptist Church in Linden where Mr. Estes served as deacon. Mrs. Estes taught Sunday School and was active in the WMU. They were the parents of 10 children:

Edith Marie Estes, born May 7, 1914, Only, TN, married May 10, 1935 to Herman Earl Devers (1916-1979), the son of John and Georgia Woods Devers of Clifton, TN. They had three children.

Edgar Estes, born June 27, 1917, Cuba Landing, TN, died Dec. 23, 1990, buried Memphis, TN, married March 29, 1942 to Mildred Louise King (1918-1974), the daughter of William Abner and Addie Harris King. They had two sons.

Elsie Catherine Estes, born Jan. 7, 1920, Coon Creek, Perry County, died Dec. 27, 1968, buried Obion County, married July 7, 1940 to Woodrow Wilson Fleming (1918-1991), son of Hugh B. and Lula White Fleming of Obion County. They had one son.

Paul Franklin Estes, born Feb. 2, 1922, died Dec. 4, 1923, buried Rice Cemetery.

Margaret Lucille (Madge) Estes, born May 16, 1924, Humphreys County, TN, married July 10, 1943 to Elroy Huey Allen, born March 28, 1923, son of G.B. and Ada Huey Allen, Obion, TN. They live in Birmingham, AL and have five daughters.

William Robert Estes, born Oct. 3, 1926, Humphreys County, TN, died April 19, 1980. (See William Robert Estes.)

Mary Elizabeth (Kitty) Estes, born Aug. 5, 1928, Waverly, TN. (See James Cathey Savage Jr.)

Lillian Oneita Estes, born Nov. 17, 1931, Waynesboro, TN, died May 14, 1981, Dickson, TN, buried Hohenwald, married April 23, 1949 to Fentress Reed Epley (1923-1976), son of Tom and Dora Epley. They had three sons.

Anna Sue Estes, born April 23, 1935, Clifton, TN, married April 4, 1953 to James Dale Riley (1922-1976), son of Percy Haywood and Nettie Whitwell Riley. They had three children. Anna married second to Alton Wood.

Sarah Patricia (Patsy) Estes, born Feb. 19, 1938, Obion, TN. (See James D. Coble.)

FRANK ESTES,

The ancestral history of Frank Estes (1891-1973) goes back to the early dawn of written history. From Edico, king of the Baltic Sea Heruli tribe in the fourth century and a general in the army of Atilla, the Hun, to the present day royal families of Europe, the chronicles of the family have been recorded. From the pages of British historian Andrew Halliday's *History of the House of Guelph* (1821) and *The House of Hanover* (1826); and the eleventh edition of *Encyclopedia Britannica* (1910), plus countless hours in libraries, this writer has perused many records in an attempt to trace the intricate ramifications of the Gelph (German *Welf*) and Estes families for more than 1600 years.

Two sons of Edico were prominent in the development of modern Europe. Odoacer, who heired his father's title as King of the Heruli, invaded Rome in 476 A.D., extinguishing the Roman Empire in Italy and the West. He reigned as king of Italy for 13 years before he was assassinated. Some historians claim that his brother, Anulphus (Guelph) was also killed, but in truth, Guelph had been left in command of the Baltic Sea island of Rugen, homeland of the Heruli. He was on his way to Rome when he learned of his brother's death. With his troops, he declared the country of Tyrol (in the Bavarian Alps) as his own, and he spent the rest of his life establishing his new homeland. In 530 A.D., Guelph was succeeded by his son who also held a high position in the Roman army.

Three generations later, about 600 A.D., a great-grandson, in the service of the King of the Lombards was rewarded with the duchy of Este on the southern slopes of the Euganean hills in North-central Italy. About 670, a descendant, also Guelph, married a daughter of the Duke of Fruili. Their son, Adalbert, Duke of Fruili, was the grandfather of Bonifacius, County of Lucca, a charge conferred on him by Charlemagne. Bonifacius II not only inherited the states of his father, but acquired the marquisate of Tuscany, and was appointed Protector of the seacoast of Italy and the island of Corsica, where a city today on the southern tip of the island bears his name, Bonifaceio. He actively engaged in expelling the Saracens from their plundering and piracy in the Mediterranean, and he was also victorious in his attack on the Moors and Arabs of North Africa. Bonifacius, the margrave of Tuscany and prefect of Corsica, died after 834, and his line continued with Adalbert I, Adalbert II, Guido, Lambert, Boniface III, Adalbert III, Obizo I, Obizo II, to Albert Azo I, margrave of Italy, and the first of the family to reside at Este, the village that the family had possessed for about 400 years. His wife was Waltfada, daughter of the Duke of Venice. His only son was Albert Azo II. Albert Azo I gave up the family name of Obertenghi and took as the surname Este or d'Este after the town. *Submitted by Kitty E. Savage.*

JOHN ESTES,

They came from England, Germany, The Netherlands and France. All of the Frank Estes' ancestors were in America before the Revolutionary War, most of them before 1700. To New Amsterdam (New York) came the Deckers and Van Meters from The Netherlands, the Dubois (descendants of the House of Este and of Charlemagne) from Germany. The Bruners came from their homeland, Schifferstadt, Germany, and the Bozarths from the Lorainne Province of France, to Pennsylvania. Other ancestors settled in Virginia and North Carolina.

Six ancestors served in the Revolutionary War. They were Jonathan Bozarth, Allen Davies, William Decker, David Glover, Jacob Van Meter and Edward Templeman. After the war, they or their sons went to Kentucky.

Abraham Estes (1649-1720) was the first generation of this branch of the Estes family in America. Thomas Estes, his son, was the second generation. Second Thomas Estes (birthplace and date of birth unknown) lived in St. Margaret's Parish, Caroline County, VA. He married Anne (Rogers?) and they were the parents of two sons: Thomas and John, and three daughters. Thomas died in 1744; Anne in 1745.

Third John Estes was born, Caroline County, VA, Dec. 27, 1725. He married in 1746 to Mary Marshall, daughter of William and Elizabeth Williams Marshall. They were the parents of six sons: Thomas, Marshall, John, William Marshall, Lyttleton and Peter. Their daughters were: Elizabeth, Ann and Mary. Mary Marshall Estes died in 1772, and John Estes married a widow, Elizabeth Coleman Pollard. John Estes died April 18, 1778, four days before his wife died in childbirth. Coleman Estes was born April 22, 1778. All of John's children were born in Caroline County.

Fourth Frank Estes is descended from two sons of John and Mary Marshall Estes. William Marshall Estes, born Dec. 1, 1765, died 1810,

Bourbon County, KY. He married Frances Lewis, daughter of Joel and Sarah Chiles Gordon Lewis. They moved with their nine children to Kentucky about 1800. Their daughter, Mariah Estes, married Henson Boswell in 1808, and they were the parents of Frances Boswell.

Lyttleton Estes, born June 27, 1768, Caroline County, VA, died 1836, Hancock County, KY. He married Anne Fortson, daughter of William and Mildred Johnston Fortson of Spotsylvania County. Lyttleton and Anne moved to Kentucky before 1810; lived in Henry County before settling in Hancock County. They were the parents of twelve children: William Fortson, Ann, Mary, Abraham Ferguson, Frances, John M., Lucy, James L., Elizabeth, Richard Coleman, America and Mildred.

JOHN MARSHALL ESTES, Fifth Generation in America: John Marshall Estes, named for his grandmother's cousin, Supreme Court Justice John Marshall, was born in 1804 in Caroline County, VA. He married, Jan. 10, 1829, in Henry County, KY to Frances Boswell, the daughter of Henson and Mariah Estes Boswell. They made their home in Hancock County, KY. They were the parents of Richard F.M. Estes, Ann Eliza Estes and William Marshall Estes. Frances Boswell died and John M. Estes married Elizabeth Driscoll on Jan. 12, 1842. They had the following children: James Greene, Amanda, Nathaniel, Alice Roberts, Mary Calvin and Almeda. John Estes died Dec. 13, 1876, and he is buried in the Estes Cemetery, Hancock County, KY.

Sixth Generation: William Marshall Estes was born in October of 1834 in Hancock County. He married Aug. 21, 1856 to Cynthia Ellen Bruner, the daughter of Peter and Hannah Davis Bruner. She was the granddaughter of two Revolutionary War soldiers, Allen Davis and Captain Jacob Van Meter. The first child of William Marshall and Cynthia was born and died in 1857. The next six children were: Robert B. (1858), Harriet F. (1861), James L. (1864), Mary Anne (1866), Henry Daviess (1868) and Lucretia (1872). The three eldest children died within a five-week period in 1880 of Typhoid Fever. Cynthia Ellen Bruner Estes died of a heart attack on Nov. 9, 1908. She is buried in the Hopewell Cemetery, Grayson County, KY beside her three children. After her death, William Marshall Estes went to Humphreys County, TN to live with his son. He died of dropsy in 1909, and is buried in the Spence Cemetery on Sugar Creek.

Seventh Generation: Henry Daviess Estes was born in Hancock County, KY, Dec. 21, 1868. He married in Grayson County, KY, Nov. 13, 1889, to Sarah Nancy Bozarth, the daughter of Benjamin Franklin and Lucinda Templeman Bozarth. She was the great-granddaughter of three American Revolution soldiers: Jonathan Bozarth, David Glover and William Decker, and the great-great granddaughter of a fourth: Edward Templeman. Henry Daviess and Sarah Nancy Estes were the parents of Chester Franklin Estes (1891-1973) and twins, Lee and Lena Estes, born July 4, 1902 in Grayson County. They moved to Humphreys County, TN shortly after the twins were born. On June 24, 1908, Edith Estes was born in Humphreys County. Henry Daviess Estes died Sept. 21, 1943; Sarah Nancy Bozarth Estes died Sept. 21, 1948. They are buried in the Cannon Cemetery, Hurricane Mills, TN.

Frank Estes is an 8th generation Estes in America. He and Lillian Lee Potter Estes were the parents of 10 children and 31 grandchildren. There are 47 great-grandchildren and nine great-great grandchildren, which brings the number of American generations to 12.

LILLIAN POTTER ESTES, Tennessee became a state in 1796. Revolutionary War veterans or their sons and daughters came to the new state to claim lands granted for military service. In the East, during the war, crops and produce had been confiscated to feed the Continental Army with little or no pay. Devastated plantations lay in waste along the paths of the Tory troops. Times were lean, and tales of lush forests and cheap or free land lured many settlers to the new state.

Back Row: Kitty, Lillian, Ed, Maria, Elsie, Bob. Front: Frank Estes, Patsy, Lillian Potter Estes and Sue in 1944

The ancestors of Lillian Lee Potter Estes were among those who blazed trails to Tennessee. William Totty came from Chesterfield County, VA to Hickman County where he bought land in 1809; land that has remained in the family for 185 years. His son, William, fought in the War of 1812, and after his return home, married Naomi Whitson, whose grandfather, Revolutionary soldier William Whitson, was the first to record a will in Maury County. Her parents, George and Priscilla Vance Whitson, lived in Coffee County. Priscilla Vance Whitson was the daughter of Colonel David Vance, Revolutionary soldier from Buncombe County, NC. Both he and William Whitson fought at the Battle of King's Mountain.

David Spence, a Revolutionary soldier from New Jersey, married Mary Anne McElyea in Surry County, NC. They traveled over the Blue Ridge Mountains, through Kentucky to Robertson County where he died in 1839. He reared a large family, and his youngest son, Dr. John Lycurgus Spence, arrived in Hickman County in 1834. He taught school and practiced medicine there for 50 years. He married Sophia Davis Totty, daughter of William and Naomi W. Totty, in 1835. They were the parents of four children, including Jerome Spence who wrote *The History of Hickman County* (1900), and Cathleen Spence who married first to Webster Gilbert, who was killed during the Civil War, and second to Robert Potter.

Willis Weatherspoon, son of Revolutionary soldier William Weatherspoon, sold his land in Wake County, NC, and with his wife, Sally Beaver, and five children, traveled over the Cumberland Mountains to Hickman County in the mid-1820s. Spence wrote, "The family was one of mechanics; their children being millers, blacksmiths, wheelwrights, coopers, cabinetmakers and cobblers." They brought with them tools, patterns and silver-milled dollars in a pouch to build a new home. Several children were born after their arrival. Calvin Weatherspoon, the eldest son, married as his second wife, Nancy Kirkland, daughter of Levi and Dicey Bruce Kirkland, who migrated from Edgefield County, SC to Humphreys County in the early 1800s. Sarah Luvenia Weatherspoon, their daughter, was born May 5, 1854. She married Henry Pruett, son of David Pruett, who came from South Carolina to Hickman County about 1830. Henry, a Civil War soldier, died in 1888 when a tree fell on him. Three children were born to Henry and Luvenia Pruett: Abe, Nan and Katherine, born Feb. 2, 1877. Luvenia Pruett married Jim Thompson and had seven more children. She died in 1923.

In 1812, Aaron Potter lived on Garners Creek in Hickman County. The names of his parents are not known. He married Ruth Hobbs, and they were the parents of Joel H. Potter, born 1823, Hickman County. Robert S. Potter, born 1848, was the eldest son of Joel H. and Mary Jane Brown Potter. He married in 1863, Cathleen Spence Gilbert, daughter of Dr. John L. and Sophia D. Totty Spence. When their second son, Will Allen Potter, born Dec. 31, 1868, married Kathrine Pruett, the daughter of Henry and Luvenia Weatherspoon Pruett on Feb. 28, 1892, the family lineages of Lillian Lee Potter, born July 30, 1897, all came together. Lillian Potter Estes was the fourth generation Potter born in Hickman County in the 1800s. Her mother died in 1903 and her father, a Primitive Baptist minister, died in 1943.

They helped to carve out of the wilderness a home for future generations. Submitted by Kitty Estes Savage.

WILLIAM ROBERT (BOB) ESTES, was born Oct. 3, 1926 in the Hurricane Creek Community, Humphrey County, TN. He came to Linden in 1943 with his parents, Chester Franklin (Frank) Estes and Lillian Lee Potter. Bob was one of 10 children born to Frank and Lillian.

William Robert Estes Family

Bob Estes joined the Navy on Sept. 27, 1944 and was stationed in Japan during part of his service time. He received the rank of Seaman First Class and served until June 29, 1946. After returning home from service, he met and mar-

141

ried Julia Elizabeth Warren on Nov. 27, 1947. Julia was born Oct. 26, 1927 in Perry County and was one of three daughters born to Gola Ray Warren and Lessie Reed Parnell.

Bob and Julia moved to Shelby County, TN where Bob learned the sheet metal trade. He later started his own company, General Sheet Metal Works which he owned and operated until his death. Although they lived in Shelby County, both Bob and Julia's hearts were in Perry County. They acquired a cabin in the Crooked Creek Community where they spent as much time as possible fishing, hunting and they were seen quite often searching fields for Indian relics.

Bob and Julia had four children born from their marriage. Robert Warren (Buddy) Estes, Jennifer Elizabeth (Ginger) Estes, William Mark (Bill) Estes and Tamera Hope (Tammy) Estes, were all born and currently reside in Memphis.

Robert Warren (Buddy) Estes was born March 27, 1949 and graduated from Perry County High School in 1967. He married Bobbie Jean Bollinger from Bruce, Calhoun County, MS and they have one son, Brian Lee Estes, born Dec. 19, 1970. Buddy is Co-Owner of Parker, Estes & Associates, a Land Surveying, Planning and Civil Engineering Firm.

Jennifer Elizabeth (Ginger) Estes was born May 15, 1950 and married Larry Alan Duncan on July 1, 1972. She is a Cardiac Nurse at Methodist North Hospital and they own and operate Duncan Orchard in Rosemark, TN. Ginger and Larry owned a farm on Russell Creek for several years and sold it in 1993.

William Mark (Bill) Estes was born July 18, 1958 and is a Heating and Air Conditioning Technician. Bill married Shirley Ann Hamblin and they have one daughter, Jennifer Nicole (Nicky), born July 13, 1982. They divorced and Bill married Sharon Hunt Sing on Dec. 30, 1993.

Tamera Hope (Tammy) Estes was born Sept. 25, 1959 and married Jeffery Keith Rochell on April 14, 1978 and are currently divorced. They have two children, Amanda Rae Rochell born July 5, 1979 and Jemery Keith Rochell born May 30, 1982. Tammy works for the University of Tennessee performing autopsies.

William Robert (Bob) Estes died of cancer on April 19, 1980 and is buried in Gola Warren Cemetery. Julia Elizabeth Warren Estes married Charles O. Patterson on Feb. 14, 1989. Julia finally fulfilled a long time dream to move back to Perry County when on May 1, 1992, she and C.O. moved into the house they reconstructed in Lobelville. The children and grandchildren continue to use the family cabin in Crooked Creek as much as possible.

EVANS, It is uncertain when the Evans family first appeared in Tennessee, but David W. and Virginia Jane Evans were living in Perry County (Marsh Creek area) in 1840. David was born in 1803 in Tennessee. It is thought that his father was John, who lived near him in 1840. Virginia Jane Tucker was born in 1804 in North Carolina of parents who were born in Virginia. David and Virginia were the parents of at least eight children which were: Langston/Lankford Gorden, born 1831; Elizabeth, born 1834; Melinda E., born 1835; Martha Sullivan, born 1837; Allen Lenard, born 1840; George W., born 1841; Sarah S., born 1845; and David L., born 1849. The 1840 Federal Census lists one male and two females older than Lankford. David and Virginia were still living in Perry County in 1880. David was a wagon maker.

Front Row: Joseph, Lankford, Roy and Frank (in wagon). Middle Row: Cynthia, Etta, Irene, Grace, Leonard and Harry. Back: Frank and Julia Dunham. Circa 1917

Lankford G. Evans served in the Civil War. He enlisted in Co. K, 42nd Regiment, TN Infantry, Dec. 28, 1861. He suffered a bayonet wound in the "Battle of Fishing Creek last day of January 1862". He returned to duty and was captured at Corinth, MS, August 1863. He took the oath of Allegiance and was paroled home. In his pension application, he states he was surrendered while serving in Florida early 1865. Lankford was married first to Manerva Jane Dabbs in Perry County, 1851. This marriage produced five children: Richard Allen, born 1853, died 1935 AR; Francis Marion, born 1854, died 1938 AR; John L., born 1857, died 1940 AR; Mary L., born 1859, died 1935 AR; and George W., born 1865, died 1925 CA. After Manerva's death, Lankford married Martha Jane Sanford in 1869. She was born in 1842 in Tennessee, died 1916 AR. This union was blessed with four children who were: Savana I., born 1873, died 1970 CA; Joseph, born 1874, died 1948 AR; Benjamin F., born 1877, died 1964 MI; and Lula E., born 1879, died 1922. The family moved to Oregon County, MO in 1883 with Lankford's sister, Martha Sullivan and husband, John Allen Tomlin. Later, these families moved to Fulton County, AR where Lankford lived until Martha's death in 1916. When Martha died, Lankford lived with his various children until his death on Oct. 3, 1923 in Greene County, AR.

Richard Allen Evans married Frances Elnora Little, daughter of Isaac and Elizabeth Roberts Little, in 1874. They were the parents of 12 children. Two died young and three were born in Perry County, TN. The other seven were born in Missouri and Arkansas.

Ella Jane Evans, fifth child of Richard Allen, married James Ira Wood in 1903 in Fulton County, AR. They had two sons; Euin Lee, born 1904, Fulton County, AR, died 1990, and Everett W., born 1906, Fulton County, AR, died 1993. James I. and Ella Jane moved to Greene County, AR along with Richard Allen and two of his brothers early 1900s.

Members of the David Evans family remained in Perry County, other descendants are scattered from Tennessee to California and Michigan to Florida.

JAMES H. EVANS, born Jan. 16, 1857, Perry County, died April 6, 1918, buried Church Grove Cemetery, Newbern, Dyer County. Jim married first to Fredonia DePriest and had children. After her death, he married Josephine Louise Mathis, daughter of James Bluford Mathis and Mary E. Dabbs. Children of Jim and Josie are: Benjamin H. Evans, born June 28, 1888, died June 10, 1966, married Minnie Curry/Holt, April 6, 1913, Perry County; Caroline Victoria Evans, born January 1890, married Edward W. Taylor; Lillie Otis Evans, born Jan. 3, 1893 near Flatwoods, died April 11, 1953, married Leslie Reuben Richardson; Anna G. Evans, born January 1896, died November 1917, married, Jan. 9, 1910, Perry County, to William Levi Sharp; William Brown Evans, born December 1898; Maud Evans, born 1895, married Dec. 31, 1910, Perry County, to Timothy Beaty; Walter Evans, born 1902, married Annie Lee Ladd; Thomas J. Evans, born Dec. 19, 1904, died Feb. 13, 1960, buried Newbern, TN, married Willie Mae Davis; Gussie Mae Evans, born 1906, married George M. Self; Flora Ila Evans, born May 15, 1909, Perry County, married Luther Thompson; Earlene Evans, born April 16, 1912, died July 8, 1918, buried Newbern, TN.

FAGAN-FERGUSON, On April 26, 1917 in Memphis, TN, John Billings Ferguson was born to John Henderson and Aubrey B. Ferguson. He grew up in Memphis, went to school and enjoyed music, singing and playing in Hugh Anderson's band.

John Ernest Fagan and wife, Anna C. Burger

Aubrey E. Billings was reared in Atoka, TN near the Bethel Presbyterian Church and all of her people are buried in the cemetery there. John Henderson grew up in the Rosemark-Millington, TN area. His father was Newton Shafer Ferguson and his mother was Alice Ligon Ferguson. His people are buried in Bethuel Cemetery, Millington, TN.

Jeremiah Fuller Percifull and wife, Josie Tansil Percifull

Aubrey's father was William David Billings and her mother was Margaret Lena Barnes. William David's father was George Billings.

John Billings Ferguson met and married Mary Frances Fagan in 1938. Mary was born in Haywood County, TN, Nov. 26, 1921. She spent her early years in Chattanooga, TN, moved to Haywood County where her father built a store. They later moved to Memphis, TN. They were Baptists. Mary F. was the great granddaughter of John Fagan, born in Virginia and the granddaughter of John Ernest Fagan and Anna C. Burger Fagan of Knoxville, TN. They are buried in Old Grey Cemetery of downtown Knoxville. They were Lutherans.

Their son, Ernest John Fagan, after serving in the Rainbow Division in France in World War I, met and married Lila Pauline Percifull on Nov. 23, 1920. Lila was in Memphis attending what is now University of Memphis. She was born April 18, 1896 in Haywood County, TN and was reared there until she went away to school.

Ernest J. and Lila had one daughter, Mary Frances. John B. and Mary became the parents of three children, Frances Joanne (Josie), Sandra Kaye and John Billings Ferguson II.

John II graduated from Perry County High School and Hohenwald Vo-Tech and attended Columbia State College. He is presently employed by Tokico Inc. in Detroit, MI.

John B. Sr. served in World War II as a marine on Guam in the South Pacific. He retired from the Southern Region of the U.S. Postal Department after 36 years. Although he retired as senior cost analyst, he has served as temporary Post Master in both Hohenwald, TN and in Collinwood, TN for almost two years. During this time, the beautiful countryside of Perry County beckoned and they bought a farm there, called the old Gutherie or old Percy Pierson place. This was originally part of the Catron farm. There is a cemetery there with burial as early as 1849. This is located at the end of Duncans Camp Road. Later they sold all but 13 acres and built a house on Ira Doyle Road.

Mary's grandmother on her mothers side was Juan F. "Miss Josie" Tansil Percifull, daughter of John Baptist Tansil and Nancy Louise Finley Tansil of Finley, TN. Mary's grandfather was Jeremiah Fuller Percifull, born in Madison County, TN, Maple Springs Community, son of William and Elizabeth Baker Percifull. While Jeremiah was still young, William and Elizabeth moved to Haywood County, TN near the Forked Deer and Woodville Communities.

William served in the Civil War on the side of the Confederates. Elizabeth B.'s mother was Rachel Mariah Fuller Baker, daughter of Temperance and Ezekial Fuller originally from North Carolina. The Percifull family came from Wythe County, Virginia. The Fullers were originally Quaker but became Baptist.

FARRAR/PIERCY/HESTER, Nicholas Farrar, born a French Hugenot in 1546, lived in England all of his 74 years. His descendants, however, later made their way to America by way of Virginia and settling in Kentucky. His great-great-great granddaughter, Josephine Williams, was born July 30, 1865. Josephine married an enterprising man named Samuel Smith, born Dec. 29, 1846. Samuel was not a mere landowner, but controlled about 5000 acres in Kentucky. His land began near Bear Creek and covered what is now the city of Burkesville, KY. On his property stood many oil wells, saw mills, stores and a small schoolhouse for his children and those of the workers. Sam Smith also served as a soldier for the Union during the Civil War.

Richard Peercy & Ida Lou Smith Family with Josephine Williams Smith. Circa 1921.

About 1896, a young man named Richard Peercy (Piercy) came to work for Samuel Smith as an oil well digger. Here Richard met and married Samuel Smith's daughter, Ida Lou.

In 1920, Richard and Ida Lou left Kentucky moving to Tennessee. They loaded all their belongings, including furniture, food, cows, goats, horses and 10 children, onto a steamboat named "Joe Horton Falls" and came down the Cumberland River to Nashville, TN. Richard and Ida bought 333 acres in the forks of the Little and Big Harpeth Rivers in Williamson and Davidson Counties.

Throughout the years, Richard remained an oil well digger, finding work by traveling to different counties and offering his services.

Richard and Ida Lou had 10 children: Nettie, Goebel, Beckham, Rollin, Montie, Ruby (R.L.), Ollie, Sophia, Vernie and Roy (Pete).

Sophia Jewell Piercy, (Feb. 9, 1915) returned to her birthplace in Kentucky in 1934 to attend Lindsey Wilson College. After graduation, she attended Scarrett College and Peabody College in Nashville. While doing graduate work at Peabody, she was interviewed by the superintendent of the Perry County School System to teach history, chemistry, and French at Lobelville High School. While teaching, she met an Army man, named John Tate Hester, Feb. 1, 1943. The two traveled to Corinth, MS and were married. John T. and Sophia had three children: Betty Jewell (resides on Marsh Creek in Linden, TN), Johnnia Ruth (a resident of Glendale, CA) and William Thomas (currently living in Nashville, TN).

FERGUSON-COMBS, Frances Joanne Combs Ferguson (Josie) was born July 10, 1939 to Mary Frances Fagan and John Billings Ferguson in Memphis, Shelby County, TN. She attended school in Haywood County, TN and graduated from Central High School in Memphis, TN.

She is married to Edwin Lee Combs (Buddy), who was born to Lelia Clyde Funderburk and Everett Combs, Aug. 24, 1952 at Johns Hopkins Hospital in Baltimore, MD. They have a daughter, Melissa Finley Gray, and a son, David Edwin Combs. David has attended school in Perry County and will graduate in May 1994.

Mary and John B. Ferguson in 1993.

Buddy is a MSgt in the United States Marine Corp and will be retiring in July 1994. Buddy and Josie will be making their home in Perry County upon Buddy's retirement.

DANIEL REED AND NANCY ETHEL CRAIG FERGUSON, Reed was born July 25, 1893 in Lobelville, TN to George Washington "Whale" Ferguson and Sarah Harriet Pocahontas Jane "Dee" McCollum Ferguson. His grandparents came from Virginia to Hampshire, TN in the early 1800s, where his father was born. The family moved to Lobelville around 1860. They were farmers and his father a census taker for Perry County. Some years later, they moved back to Hampshire, also to Nashville for a short time where Reed attended the old Howard School. Eventually they moved back to Lobelville and along with farming, built a two-story building and operated a general mercantile store. Years later the post office was located in the store.

Reed & Ethel Ferguson

Reed's siblings were brothers Walker, Clint, Jim, John, Willie Scott, McKinley and sisters Maggie and Bess. Walker married, moved to Wyoming and practiced law. Clint and Reed married and lived in Lobelville. Willie Scott died at age 18. McKinley was killed in France during World War I. Jim and John never married and lived at the family homeplace. Maggie married and moved to Humphreys County. Bess married and lived several years in Michigan. After the death of her husband, moved back to Lobelville and lived at the family homeplace until her death. Most of the Fergusons are buried in the Brown Cemetery in Hickman County, near Farmers Exchange. The homeplace was torn down in the late 1960s and is now the site of McDonald Funeral Home.

Ethel was born Oct. 21, 1900 near

Beardstown, TN (Skaggs Bluff) to George Washington Craig and Ameila Laura Jane Byrd Craig. Her father was killed by lightning when she was three and is buried in the DePriest Bend Cemetery. Ethel's siblings were, brothers Claude, Jim, Jack and sister Etta Cora. Her mother later married Lewis W. Johnson. In Ethel's late teen years, the family moved to Obion, TN where Jessie Lou, Andrew and Wilson were born. After Mr. Johnson died, her mother married James B. Ladd and they continued to live around Obion. They had no children. Mrs. Ladd is buried in Elbridge, TN. All are now deceased.

Reed and Ethel had met years earlier, but were not married until 1922 in Union City, TN. They settled back in Lobelville and lived in the Ferguson family home. They had one daughter, Agnes Jane, born Sept. 9, 1928. Reed and Agnes were both born in that same house. In 1933, they bought the Richard Hester farm, moved and lived there until 1950 when they built a house on the old orchard grounds of the family homeplace. Reed lived there until his death in 1971. Ethel continued to live there until 1989 when she fell and, unable to live alone, moved to Nashville to live with her daughter. She died in 1991. Reed and Ethel are buried in Woodlawn Cemetery in Nashville, TN. Agnes lives in Nashville, married Ernest M. Harrell Jr. in 1955. He died in 1977. They had one daughter, Nancy Laurice, born on March 11, 1961. She is single. Agnes continues to own the home in Lobelville.

GEORGE FERGUSON, the earliest traceable Ferguson, was born in 1822 in Hampshire, Maury County, TN, but by 1860, he moved to Lobelville where he was a farmer. He had married Jane Kenner (born 1826) in 1846 and they had six children. Neal Scott (1846-1902) married Charity Shelton of Perry County and moved to Cleburne, Texas. George Washington (second son) born in 1849, died 1920. Little is known about the remaining four children: William, Florence, Thomas and B. (son).

George "Whale" Washington Ferguson married Nancy Agnes Brown in 1871. She was the daughter of Walter and Fedona Johnson Brown of Hickman County. Nancy was born in 1849 and died in 1881. George and Agnes lived in Lobelville where he farmed for many years and later ran a general merchandise store in Lobelville. In 1880, he was the Census Enumerator in the 8th Civil District, Lobelville, TN. The Ferguson family home was located on the property now occupied by the McDonald Funeral Home. They had four children: Mary "Maggie" Lavona, 1873-1956, who married Nicholas Duncan and moved to Humphreys County, TN; George Walker, 1875-1964, married to Pearl White of Wyoming and they lived in Wyoming; Thomas Clint, 1879-1961; and, Willie Scott, 1880-1894.

George Washington Ferguson's first wife died in 1881, leaving him with four small children. Later in 1881, he married Pocohantus "Dee" McCollum (1861-1931). They had five children: James Neal, 1883-1944; John Braden, 1886-1953; Bess Blayne, 1890-1963; Daniel Reed, 1893-1971; Clarence McKinley, 1895-1918. George Washington and other members of his family are buried in the Brown Cemetery in Hickman County on the McCord Hollow Road, Southwest of Farmers Exchange, TN.

Thomas Clint Ferguson married Etta Izora Duff (1883-1970) in 1912. She was the daughter of John and Ida Duff who lived in Lobelville. They had two children: Neal Hooper, born Sept. 22, 1914 and Ida Dee, born Nov. 27, 1918. Clint was a carpenter/painter and blacksmith and served as Chairman of the Perry County Republican Party for many years. Clint and Etta are buried in the Leeper Cemetery in Lobelville, TN.

Neal Hooper married Mary Jane Ray of Nashville, TN, Dec. 19, 1942. They have two daughters: Marjorie Elaine, born Sept. 23, 1947, who is married to David Lawrence and they have one daughter, Elizabeth Bransford, born April 16, 1979 and Elizabeth Ray Ferguson, born Nov. 3, 1949.

Ida Dee married Richard W. Barton of Spring City, TN, Aug. 27, 1943. They have two children: Linda Dee, born March 10, 1949, is married to William Curtiss Follmer, Jan. 5, 1974, and they have two daughters, Jamie Anne, Nov. 20, 1977, and Rebecca Dee, Aug. 24, 1981. They live in Nevada; and Richard Ferguson Barton, born May 29, 1957, lives in Maryland.

Neal Hooper and Ida Dee Barton live in Nashville and both own property in Perry County. Neal Hooper has been a director of the Bank of Perry County since November 1961.

HENRY JEFFERSON FERGUSON, was born in the Marsh Creek Community in Perry County on Sept. 26, 1917. His parents were John Thomas Ferguson and Bertha Ham Ferguson. They had three children: Elsie, Thelma and Henry Ferguson.

Lemma Lee Riley Ferguson was born near the Flatwoods Community in Wayne County on Jan. 13, 1924. She was the youngest of two children, Nancy Yuonne Riley Shull being the oldest.

Henry and Lemma married at Waynesboro, TN, Oct. 31, 1939. They had four children. Their first child, Wanda Jeanne Ferguson, was born July 30, 1941 in Flatwoods, TN.

The Ferguson family moved to Greenway, AR early in the year of 1944. Willard Henry Ferguson was born May 3, 1944 in Greenway, AR. Joy Lee Ferguson was born Oct. 26, 1946.

Henry, Lemma, Jeanne and Willard Ferguson moved back to Tennessee Dec. 6, 1949.

Their last child, John Thomas Ferguson, was born Nov. 21, 1955 in Waverly, TN. They have lived in Humphreys County over 44 years. *Submitted by Henry Ferguson.*

FLOWERS/TATE Rafe Flowers, of Ireland, married a girl named Stinnet, settled in Buckingham County, VA and had four sons and three daughters. Rafe Flowers moved to Tennessee and died in Smith County, near Carthage.

Lemuel & Martha Flowers Tate Family

Valentine Flowers, born July 19, 1765, Buckingham County, VA, son of Rafe Flowers, moved to Tennessee in 1810 and settled on the Duck River in Hickman County. He fought through the Revolutionary War and was present at the surrender of Yorktown. In 1931, a marker was placed at his grave in Old Forsee Cemetery, near McEwen, TN, by Daughters of American Revolution.

William Flippin Flowers, Dec. 5, 1786, son of Valentine Flowers, married Martha Hughes and moved to Tennessee to live on the Duck River with his father. Martha feared the Indians south of the river, so they moved to Carthage, TN, returning to the Duck River 14 years later. William F. Flowers served in the War of 1812. He and Martha had 13 children: Elizabeth Ann, Mary Madison, Martha B., Naomi L., Sarah Price, Valentine Flippin, William Carroll, John Littleberry, Robert Dickson, David Douglas, James Morgan, Nancy Adaline and Gideon Bigalow.

Mary Madison Flowers, second child of William F. Flowers (Sept. 30, 1809) married a Roland and lived on Lost Creek, near Lobelville, TN. She had three daughters and two sons.

James Morgan Flowers, eleventh child of William F. Flowers (Oct. 11, 1826) married Sarah Hungerford (Jan. 15, 1833). They had two girls and four boys: Permelia (Sissy) Flowers

(Left-right) Front Row: (standing) Daniel Reed, (seated) James Neal, Thomas Clint, John Braden (standing) Clarence McKinley. Back Row: (seated) George Walker, Mary Lavona, George Washington, Pocohantus, Bess Blayne

Gilmore, Billy, John Matt, Martha Louise Flowers Tate, Adam and Alonzo.

Martha Louise Flowers, born Jan. 24, 1858, in Hickman County near Centerville, TN, spent her early childhood on a farm. She attended public schools, later entered a private school at Franklin, TN and chose teaching as her profession. This career, however, lasted only three years, ending with her marriage to Lemuel Tate. Lemuel and Martha made their home on the Tate farm north of Lobelville where they raised their eight surviving children: John Thomas, Annie (married William H. Dudley, mail carrier in Lobelville for many years), Douglas, Mattie Louise (a school teacher on Lost Creek before marrying Lloyd A. Curry and moving to Memphis), Loudie (married Dr. William David Cagle, a well respected doctor), her twin Lounie (married George A. Leeper, a sheriff in Perry County in the 1930s), Ida Lorina (married Gus Enlow Hester) and Charles Lemuel.

Lemuel Tate (1859), husband of Martha Louise, was born the ninth child of Lemuel Tate (Sept. 13, 1822) and Polly Ann Strickland (Feb. 5, 1827). Polly Ann was the seventh child of Stephen Strickland (1786) and Sarah Medlock. In 1819, Stephen signed the petition to create Perry County where he and Sarah lived with their eight children.

REX A. FLUTY, was born in Flatwoods, TN, the son of Mr. and Mrs. E.B. Fluty. Lily Fluty was born in Centerville, TN, the daughter of Mr. and Mrs. R.H. Hatcher.

In March of 1933, Rex and Lily were married and have recently celebrated their 61st wedding anniversary. They are the parents of two children, Rex Jr. and Jane Elizabeth. They also have two grandsons, Carl Austin and Rex Kendal Wallace.

Rex's work interests have been varied. Along with working as a garage mechanic and a service station manager, he also worked with TVA before joining the Tennessee Gas Transmission Company (TGT) as an operator at the Lobelville, TN station. He, later, was promoted to Assistant Station Superintendent and transferred to another station. He was, again, transferred and also promoted to Station Superintendent. He remained as a Station Superintendent throughout many transfers to different TGT station. The last transfer being to the Nunnelly, TN station from which he worked until retirement.

Lily has had a life-long career as a homemaker. This has been no easy task. With each job transfer, she cheerfully packed and moved. Upon arrival at each new station, she quickly became involved with numerous clubs and civic organizations.

After retirement, Rex and Lily continue to live in Centerville, TN. Rex enjoys playing golf and fishing and Lily remains involved with church-related activities.

Their son, Rex Jr., is an established artist and Professor of Scenic Design at the Florida Atlantic University in Boca Raton, FL. He graduated from the University of Texas in Austin and earned his Masters degree from Florida Atlantic University.

In the earlier years of Rex Jr.'s career, he worked in New York City as a scenic designer for the NBC and CBS television networks. He has designed sets for several television shows, and continues to design scenery and sets for various theatre productions. Among them have been sets for a theatre in Jupiter, FL, formerly owned by actor, Burt Reynolds.

Rex Jr. is single and resides in Boca Raton, Florida.

Rex and Lily's daughter, Jane, is a school teacher. She teaches kindergarten at Oakmont School in Dickson County. She graduated from Austin Peay State University in Clarksville, TN and earned her Masters degree from Tennessee State University in Nashville. She is married to Carl Austin Wallace Jr. from Centerville, TN. Carl works in Nashville as a salesman for a heating and air-conditioning wholesale distributor.

Carl and Jane reside in Dickson, TN, and are the parents of two sons, Carl Austin and Rex Kendal.

Carl Austin graduated from the University of Tennessee in Knoxville. He is single and resides in Ft. Lauderdale, FL where he works for a computer firm.

Kendal graduated from Martin Methodist College in Pulaski, TN, and is currently enrolled at Maryville College in Maryville, TN. He plans to graduate in the spring of 1995. He is single and is pursuing a career in coaching. *Submitted by Jane Fluty Wallace.*

FRALEY-HOLLABAUGH, John Fraley, a Perry County farmer on Buffalo River, was born in North Carolina about 1815. Around 1838, he married Frances Kaisinger, born in Tennessee to Mathias and Mary Kaisinger. John and Frances had fourteen children: Mary Jane married Jack Sharp, George married Eliza Hickerson, John married Matilda ?, Sarah married James Bridges, Jacob married Sarah Tredwell, William married Louise Jane ?, Margaret Caroline married John Harder, Andrew married Susan Hickerson, Susan Elizabeth married Robert Warren, James married Mary Turnbow, Eliza, Charles married S.E. Hickerson, Willis "Bud" married Jocie Weaver and Frances "Fannie" married B.B. "Buck" Hollabaugh, son of Jacob and Rosanna Harvey Hollabaugh of Wayne County.

B.B. "Buck" & Frances (Fraley) Hollabaugh Family. Left to Right: Isham, John, Buck, Zoe, Carl, Lillian, Francis and Delphia

It is believed that John was the son of Margaret Treadwell's brother, John. Margaret was the daughter of George Fraley of Rowan County, NC, and wife of Anos Treadwell who came to Perry County in 1818. She may be a sister of Jacob Fraley who lived on Sinking Creek, or else his first cousin, as he was most likely the son of Jacob (George's brother) and Catherine Charles Fraley.

Soon after her parents died, John in 1872 and Frances in 1875, Fannie (1864-1902) married Buck Hollabaugh (1856-1934) in 1878. They had 12 children: Charles; Grover; Mary and three girls (names unknown) died before 1902; Isham (1891-1905) died in Oklahoma; John (1889-1946) and Lillian (1896-1944) both unmarried, died in Wichita, KS; Carl (1883-1911) who died in Oklahoma, married Lee Dickson and had son, Joe Bailey (1911-1969) and one granddaughter, Olivia Lee; Delphia (1892-1981) married Hershel McConnell in 1911 and lived in Fort Smith, AR with their five children; Zoe (1912-1964) married Louise Craig; Mildred (1916-1990) married J.N. Birkhead in 1936 and had Delphia Gene and Linda Sue, then married Fred McMillan; Hershel (1921-1991) married Pauline Kimes in 1956 and had Hershel III and Paula Kay and lived in Memphis; Willis (1924-1980) married Mary Buford in 1950, one daughter, Lorna; James (1927) married Madalyn Wofford in 1950, they have two sons, Stephen and Scott and live in Baton Rouge, LA; Zoe (1894-1963) married Mary Fisher (1889-1969) in 1916 and lived in Wichita, KS, son Jack (1918) married Lois Burrell in 1951 and lives in Wichita, daughter Mary Louise, (1923) lives in Orange, Texas and is the family historian.

After Fannie died of malaria in 1902, Buck married Mrs. Kate Reeves and moved the family to Crowder, Pittsburg County, OK, then Indian Territory. They had a daughter, Darthula, who died about age 13. In 1915, Buck married Mary Hartline and had another daughter, Bessie, (1915) who married Max Miller in 1930 and had four children: Elizabeth, died young; Bryon; Leona: and Max Jr. Bessie and Max live in Gary, OK.

Since the Fraleys and Hollabaughs lived in both Perry and Wayne Counties, information about them may be found in both counties.

WATT FRENCH, married Sue Nix. Their children are: Kenneth who married Ann Estelle Smith of Nashville. They have one daughter, Lori; Frances who married Russell Lineberry of Clifton. They have two sons, Terry and Kevin; Martha who married Clovis Carroll (divorced). They have three sons, Wally, Gene and Barry; William Thomas who married Ruby Henderson of Hohenwald (divorced). They have two daughters, Tracy and Rhonda; Judy who married Randal Arnold of Lobelville. Their children are Randy and Alana; James who married Sue Ann Wade. They have one daughter, Shonda; Doris who married Stephen Brewer of Leoma. Their children are Richie, Susie and Stephanie; and Bobby who married Patsy Harder of Linden. They have one son, Chris.

The Watt French Family

Sue Nix French died April 5, 1974. She was preceded in death by an infant daughter, Dorothy Sue, 1946. Kenneth H. French died August 1983.

Watt's second wife was Mary Polan of Spring Creek. Her children were Mary Lee Hamm, Raymond Polan Jr. and Faye Marshall.

WILLIAM HART FRENCH,

Lou Richardson (1883-Sept. 18, 1955) and Hart French (1881-1951) had seven children: Clyde died young; Kyle married Robert Young of Cypress Creek; Lyle married Donald Kirk of Cypress Creek; Loudean married Joseph Kennedy of Nashville; Watt married Rebecca Sue Nix of Blounts Landing, married second to Mary Polan of Spring Creek; Boyd married Jane Blubaugh of Waynesboro, PA; and Nell married Marden Prince of Nashville. All are deceased except Watt.

Back Row: Lyle, Kyle, Clyde. Front: Hart, Loudean and Lou French holding baby Watt

Lou was raised on Cedar Creek and Hart was from Jackson, TN. He came to Perry County in the early 1900s and bought property on Cypress Creek from a Mr. Kelly. He served as Sheriff, Deputy Sheriff and Justice of the Peace.

The French family were good singers and enjoyed going to Bethel and other communities to play piano and sing with their many friends. There were many socials, ice cream suppers and other occasions to get together for singing.

GARNER,

Jimmy Willard and Della Mae, being raised in rural areas, had developed a love for nature and the simple things. When the time came for them to settle down, they chose the beautiful area of Perry County.

Jimmy W., Della Garner and Caleb Bigham

Jimmy was born Sept. 29, 1938 to Ben Willard and Opal Orbit (Grinder) Garner at Flatwoods, TN. He was the oldest of eight children. His brothers and sisters are Jerry, Joe, Agnes, Helen, Connie, Roy and Philip.

After graduating from Perry County High School, he went to Freed-Hardeman College at Henderson, TN. After three years of work, he chose the profession as a minister for the Church of Christ, and moved to Jamestown, KY to work for the Jamestown Church of Christ. While at Jamestown, he met his wife, Della Mae Davis. She was born June 24, 1944 to Archie Arvil and Martha Florinda (Bradley) Davis of Windsor, KY. Her sister and brother are Mary Emily and Jefferson T. Davis.

Della moved to Berea, KY to attend Berea College and Jimmy moved to Lancaster, KY to be close to her and to work for the Lancaster Church of Christ. They were married Aug. 18, 1962.

Their oldest child, Aletha Carol, was born Nov. 27, 1964 at Stuttgart, AR. Jimmy was preaching for the Clarendon Church of Christ at Clarendon, AR and doing work as an undergraduate at Harding Graduate School of Memphis, TN.

To get closer to Della's family they moved to Winchester, KY where Jimmy preached for the Fairfax Church of Christ. Their second child, Mark Stephen was born Nov. 9, 1966 at Winchester, KY.

In 1967, they moved to Clarksville, TN where Jimmy was the minister of the Oakland Church of Christ and did work at Austin Peay State University. March of 1970, they moved to New Zealand to do mission work for three years. Their third child, Benjamin Archie, was born May 5, 1971 at Hamilton, New Zealand.

Upon returning to the U.S.A., they moved to Centerville, TN where Jimmy was the minister of the Brushy Church of Christ. In 1978, after 18 years as a full-time minister, Jimmy decided to move back to beautiful Perry County where he and Della would work at public work and he would preach on weekends. Since moving to Perry County, Jimmy has preached for the Chestnut Grove and Lobelville Churches of Christ, the Upper Sinking Church of Christ in Hickman County and the Pineview, Grinder Creek and Sweetwater Churches of Christ in Lewis County.

Jimmy has been a speaker on radio programs at Lancaster, KY, Centerville and Lobelville, TN for a total of 22 years. He also had a column in the *Waikato Times* while he was in Hamilton, New Zealand.

Their children all graduated from Perry County High School. Aletha went to Freed-Hardeman College and after completing work at the Baptist Hospital in Memphis, TN, she received a BS Degree in Medical Technology. She has worked as a Medical Technologist in Phoenix, AZ, Dayton, OH and Oklahoma City, OK. She is married to Leslie Todd Bigham of Portland, OR and they live at Layton, UT. She has three children, Caleb Bradford, Abby Renae and Emilia Grace.

Mark went to Freed-Hardeman College receiving a BS Degree in education and biology. He then went to UT at Martin and received a BS Degree in Wildlife management and is now at UT Knoxville working on a Master Degree in fisheries. Ben went to Freed-Hardeman University and completed three years of pre-engineering. He then transferred to Tennessee Tech at Cookville, TN.

JOHN SAMUEL GILMER AND KATE LEOTA MORRISON GILMER,

were born and raised in the Lobelville area. They were married Sept. 9, 1922, and lived on the Gilmer Farm on Russell's Creek until 1965 when they sold part of their farm and moved into Lobelville.

John and Kate Gilmer on the farm

John Samuel Gilmer was born in 1895 and died in 1970. He was the son of Samuel Newton "Doc" Gilmer and Martha Ann Ledbetter Gilmer. He served his country during World War I in the 117th Infantry, and was wounded in the battle in France on Aug. 8, 1918. After medical treatment, he asked to rejoin his Company M comrades and continued to serve until Armistice Day. After returning home, most of his years were spent farming, a life he dearly loved. His paternal grandparents were James Alexander Scott Gilmer and Martha Ann Bratton Gilmer, who came from Hickman County. His maternal grandparents were John N. Ledbetter and Millie Elizabeth Tate Ledbetter. John was one of 11 children, including: Robert, twin sisters, Florence and Flora, Albert, Elizabeth (Lizzie), Wiley, Myrtle, Jack, Roy and Clayton. The Gilmer children, along with their parents, were buried in the Gilmer Cemetery on Russell's Creek, except Wiley, who was buried in Michigan.

Kate Leota Morrison Gilmer was born in 1902. She died on her 85th birthday in 1987, and was buried in the Gilmer Cemetery. She was the daughter of Jim D. Morrison and Emma Amelia Warren Morrison. In her younger years, she worked for Mr. John R. Butler at the Bank of Lobelville. She also taught school on Roan's Creek and Lost Creek, where she met John, their courtship began and marriage followed. In later years, she taught at Lobelville Elementary School. Her paternal grandparents were Joel Morrison and Jane Harris Morrison, who came from Hickman County. Her maternal grandparents were Sam Warren and Leona Louisa Deaumanette Warren. Leona Louisa Deaumanette came to the United States from France at age four, arriving in New Orleans in 1848. Her family settled in Perry County in the area now referred to as "Dumonie Hill" (Deaumanette Hill). Kate had one brother, Jack Wilson Morrison, who preceded her in death in 1954 and was buried in Cookeville, TN.

John and Kate had five children. Joe, and a twin brother who died shortly after birth were born in 1923. Joe kept home ties in Lobelville, although he worked several years as an industrial X-ray engineer in other states. He died in 1979 and was buried in Gilmer Cemetery where his twin brother had also been buried.

Jean, born in 1926, first married Henry

Wallace Bates, now deceased, and had a son, Jerry Dale Bates. Jean later moved to Old Hickory, TN due to employment opportunities. Her second marriage was to Walter Hayes Greenwood of Cookeville, TN and they currently reside in Old Hickory.

Leta, born in 1930, married Hugh Edward Fisher of Greenbrier, TN. They are parents of four children: Cherry Beth Fisher May, John Hugh Fisher, Leta Michelle Fisher Wenger and Shawn Gilmer Fisher. Hugh's work with Tennessee Gas Pipeline transferred the family to various locations, including Louisiana and Texas. Hugh, Leta and Shawn chose to return to Lobelville following retirement in Houston in 1984.

Johnnia, born in 1938, married Richard Akers Clark of Stuart, VA. They lived in Norfolk, VA and Houston, Texas prior to Richard's death in 1966. Johnnia resides in Lobelville, where she has been employed by the Bank of Perry County for 33 years.

Great grandchildren of John and Kate are: Samuel Clayton (Clay) and Justin Dale Bates, Kingston, AR; Hugh Christopher and Natalee Kate Fisher, Lafayette, LA; Carter Gilmer; twins, Bailey Anne and Morgan Leigh Wenger, Memphis, TN. *Submitted by Leta G. Fisher.*

WILLIAM H. AND SARAH GILMER,

of North Carolina had one son named James Alexander Scott (1823-1906) who married Martha Ann Bratton (1830-1897). One of their sons, Samuel Newton (Doc) Gilmer (1856-1909) married Martha Ann Ledbetter (1868-1931) in 1883. They lived in a house in the hollow behind where Randy and Diane Warren now live on Lost Creek, north of Lobelville.

The Gilmer Homeplace built around 1894.

The farm where the Gilmers live today has been in the family since 1889. John N. Ledbetter bought about 500 acres near Lobelville, between Lost Creek and Russell's Creek. Part of this land was deeded to his son-in-law and daughter, S.N. and Martha Gilmer. About 1890, they moved to a house on the hill where the Gilmer Cemetery is now located. Three or four years later, they moved to a new house in "Gilmer Hollow". This house is still standing today. They had 11 children: Robert, Florence and Flora (twins), Albert, Lizzie, John, James, Myrtle, Jack, Roy and Clayton.

At Mrs. Gilmer's death, Jack (1902-1983) and Myrtle (1899-1973) bought the house and surrounding farm and timberland, where they would spend the remainder of their lives. The survivor was to receive the house. Jack married Inez Byrd (1900-1986) in 1934. Before marrying, Inez was the chief operator of the Lobelville Telephone Company. Spending their time farming, they were also active in the community. Jack hauled logs to build what is now the Lobelville Church of Christ.

Jack and Inez had one son, Jacky Wayne Gilmer, who married Gayle Duncan, the daughter of Homer and Mabel (Long) Duncan, in 1964. They have two children, Scott and Shelby who married to Robert Olds in 1993.

MARIAN ADOLPH GOBELET SR.,

(1812-1890) was born and grew up in France. He married Jeanne Sophia Marquion (1815-1892) and worked as a shoemaker, cobbler and farmer. They had five children: two were born in France, an infant who died at birth and Marion Adolph Jr. In 1847, they came to New York City from Paris, France. They lived in New York for sometime, but began drifting southward. First, to Philadelphia, PA, where Augusta Eugene was born (1852), then to Cincinnati, OH where Emile and Ernest were born (1855 and 1860).

Bill & Martha Nelle Gobelet

In 1861, the family moved to Lobelville, TN. Around 1868, they moved to a farm on Lick Creek. All four brothers married Ledbetter girls from Perry County. Emile, Ernest and wives moved and lived in Rutherford County. Adolph lived and died on Spring Creek.

Augusta Eugene married Susan Ledbetter, Sept. 26, 1872. They lived on Marsh Creek and had nine children who all grew up and stayed in Perry County: Mary (Mollie) married John Turner, John H. died young, Eugenia married Walker Lewis, Ida married H. Clay Young, Docie never married, Robert married Betty Leeper, Gussie taught school all over Tennessee and never married, Jesse (Jep) fought in World War I and never married and Sue married Ike Dabbs.

Robert Eugene and Betty Leeper married 1910 and lived on Marsh Creek. They are both buried in the Gobelet Cemetery on Marsh Creek. Children of Robert and Betty are: Flora, Grace, Johnny (died young), William, Susan (died at birth) and Mack. Flora married Clem Halbrooks in 1927 and had one son, William Pat. Grace married Billy Webb in 1937 and had one son, Ted. They divorced and she later married Nelson Ryder and had one daughter, Judy. Mack never married and died during World War II in Germany.

William (Bill) Augusta married Martha Nelle Deere, Feb. 2, 1946. He was a World War II veteran and worked as a cross-tie buyer and lumber inspector of Moss-American Tie Company and Koppers Company. He died in 1969 and was buried at Kirk Memorial Cemetery in Linden. They had two children: Dianne Butcher and Robert Euther. Dianne had one daughter, Tina and twin sons who died as infants.

Robert Euther (Bob) left Perry County to become a Marine and served twelve years. He married Becky Colbert from North Carolina. She had Mark Henderson from a previous marriage. They had two sons: Robert Euther II and William Jarret (1982 and 1984). These two boys are the only male Gobelets in the USA left to pass on the Gobelet name. They now live in Lick Creek in Perry County.

Some of the family pronounce Gobelet (French) differently. When Marion came to the USA, he wanted to speak his name in English. The best he could do was Gob-let (leaving the E silent), like goblet glass. Many of the others who moved away, use the French pronunciation (Gobe-la). It's still spelled Gobelet as in France. The family of the late Augusta from Perry County still clings to the English pronunciation.

MARION ADOLPH GOBELET SR.,

(May 1, 1812-Dec. 21, 1890) married Jeanne Sophia Marquion (March 5, 1815-Jan. 22, 1892) born, grew up and married in France. Occupation was shoe maker, cobbler and farmer. They were the parents of six children. Two children were born in France, an infant who died at birth and son, Marion Aldolph Jr. was born Sept. 27, 1845, after Adolph Sr. left Paris, France, April 26, 1845, and came to New York City. Jeanne and son left Paris, France Dec. 31, 1846, landing early January 1847. They lived in New York City, drifted southward to Pennsylvania and Ohio, then to Lobelville, TN, where they bought land on Lick Creek, near Linden, in 1867 or 1868.

There children were as follows: Infant, died at birth. Marion Adolph Jr. married Minerva Ledbetter, no children. Daughter, no record.

August Eugene married Susan Melissa Ledbetter, daughter of a Methodist minister and state senator. They had nine children: Mary (Mollie) Sophia married John Wilford Turner. Five children. Glenn Ray married Clara Elizabeth Gleason - four girls, Mark Felts Turner married Erma Alma Wilhoyt - three boys, Mary Melissa married Robert E. Howver - one girl, Ida Gobelet - single, and Nora Ethel married Henry Jackson Flippo - one son; Eugenia Margaret married William Walker Lewis. Nine girls. (see elsewhere under Lewis); John H. M. infant (Oct. 3, 1874-April 16, 1875); Ida Elizabeth married H. Clay Young. Four boys. Ray - no record of wife or baby, Irl M. married Anna, Paul - died at 3 yrs. and Joe Ira - lived only a few days; Docia M., lived only a few days; Robert Eugene married Betty Jane Leeper. Six children. Flora Eugene married Clem Hallbrooks and George Wilkerson Tribble - one son, Grace Ruth married William Cary Webb and Nelson Harding Ryder - two children, Johnny - died at birth, William (Bill) married Martha Nell Deere - two children, Susan - lived a few hours, and Mark Leeper - single; Gussie McKendra, single, school teacher; Jessie Calbert, single, World War I veteran; and Sue Mayme married Ike Thelma Dabbs - two sons. John Eugene married Margaret Lumsdon Averett, Magie Powell, Mary Anne Evans Beasley - one son, and Guss Gobelet married Donnie Joyce LaRue - two children.

Emile Julian married Caldonia Smith. They had five children. Flora Sophia married James Robert Coleman, one child died at birth; Asbury Almeda (Dooly) married Betty Frances Deere, two boys; Matthew Julian married Lola Harris and Ercell Gibbs, no children; Obed Dubart married Grace Harrell and Goldie Shires, one child; and Clarence Smith married Mamie Wallace, one girl.

Ernest (Pone) Alexander married Elizabeth Ledbetter. They had six children. Alta Floyd married John B. Strickland, four children; Walter Scott married Jewell Webb, no children; John Sherman and James Blain, twins; Sophia Elizabeth married L.L. Johnson, no children; and Grace Ruby, single.

August and Susan bought property on Marsh Creek in 1886, five miles a little southwest of Linden, TN. It was built by Pete Sheffield and is still owned and occupied by the third generation.

GODWIN-SHARP, R.H. Godwin Sr. (Holly) (1892-1976). Parents were John Godwin (1860-1936) and Cora Holly Godwin (1866-1932). Cora was from Texas. Six children were born to this union: Percy Godwin, Holly Godwin, Fred Godwin, Nina Godwin Dodson, George Godwin and Maury Godwin, all deceased. Holly was born and reared in the Bethel Community where his parents were farmers. He served his country in World War I.

Holly Elizabeth Turnbow in 1994.

Catherine Sharp Godwin (1897-1983). Her parents were Dr. and Rowena Shelton Sharp. Two children were born to this union: Dr. Thomas H. Sharp and Catherine Sharp Godwin. Catherine was a graduate of Vanderbilt University, Nashville, TN as a Pharmacist.

After Holly and Catherine were married, they owned and operated Linden Drug Store, located on Main Street, Linden, TN where they faithfully served their customers for approximately 50 years. One child was born to this union, Ralph Holly Godwin Jr. (Dec. 26, 1923).

In 1944, he married Kira Dickson Godwin (June 4, 1925) of Linden, TN. She was one of 10 children born to Leander (1877-1953) and Bessie Kimble Dickson (1893-1936). Kira and Holly moved to Nashville, TN where Holly was employed by American Airlines and Kira attended Nashville Business College and played basketball with N.B.C. They later returned to Linden and purchased Stark's Funeral Home and operated as Godwin Funeral Home. In 1947, they sold the Funeral Home to Willie McDonald who is presently operating it as McDonald Funeral Home. After this, Holly was employed by the then First National Bank in Linden, TN, later to become First State Bank where he is presently serving as President and Chief Executive Officer. Kira was employed by Linden Apparel Corporation from 1950 to 1955, Perry County Hospital from 1956 to 1965, then joining Holly at First State Bank until she retired in 1985. They reside on Main Street in Linden, TN. Two daughters were born to this union:

Julia Ann Godwin (Jan. 1, 1947) graduated from Middle Tennessee State University, Murfreesboro, TN and University of Tennessee as a Registered Nurse. She is employed by Baptist Hospital, Nashville, TN where she resides.

Rosemary Elaine Godwin Turnbow (Nov. 28, 1955) graduated from George Peabody University, Nashville, TN. She is in Special Education with the Perry County School System. She is married to Bob Turnbow; they live in Linden, TN. This union blessed the family with a precious little daughter, Holly Elizabeth Turnbow, on Jan. 27, 1985.

THOMAS STUART GODWIN, of Linden, born Sept. 10, 1910, and Mary Elizabeth Sharp, born Jan. 3, 1910, were married April 14, 1933. They lived in Linden and later on Highway 13 on the Andrew Vaughan Farm. Tom died April 16, 1968 and Mary died Sept. 28, 1992. They are buried in the Vaughan-Godwin Cemetery.

Tom, Tom Jr., Mary Anne & Mary Godwin

Tom was a farmer, jointly owning a farm on Coon Creek and the Andrew Vaughan farm on Highway 13 with brother, John William, and sister, Ruth Vaughan Godwin. He was a member of the First Christian Church of Linden, a member of the Perry County Court for 12 years, highway commissioner and with brother, John, owner of "Godwin Hardware".

He was the son of Commodore Perry "Cap" and Minnie Vaughan Godwin. He was the grandson of William G. and Sara Meacham Godwin and John Locke and Martha Ann Stuart Vaughan, of this county and the great grandson of Reddick Godwin, a farmer from North Carolina and Mary Ann Beasley of Williamson County, TN.

Mary was the daughter of Sameul T. "Bud" and Delphia Graves Sharp of Flatwoods. She had six brothers Kenneth, Kola, Walton, Wilson, Ernest and Elam. Mary remained a member of the Flatwoods Church of Christ and was a graduate of Freed Hardeman College and M.T.S.U. at Murfreesboro. She was a teacher at Linden, Flatwoods and Bethel, and retired as an English teacher at Perry County High School. She was the granddaughter of Sameul M. and Betty Boyce Garner Sharp of Flatwoods and Thomas and Mary Elizabeth Cotton Graves of Riverside.

Tom and Mary's children are Mary Anne Godwin Perdue, born Dec. 25, 1933 and Thomas Stuart Godwin Jr., born Aug. 22, 1939, in Flatwoods, TN. They were both members of Linden First Christian Church and graduates of U.T. Knoxville.

Mary Anne married Herchel Earl Perdue, son of William and Sally Stewart Perdue of Sumner County, TN, on June 29, 1957 in Geralton, Ontario, Canada. Herchel has retired from Tennessee Gas Pipeline. They live in Selmer, TN.

Their children are: Melanie Anne Perdue, born Aug. 10, 1958 in New Orleans, LA; Sharon Rene' Perdue, born Sept. 26, 1959 in Owensboro, KY; and Janet Shelaine Perdue, born July 13, 1966 in Lafayette, LA. Melanie is a graduate of U.T. Martin and Memphis State University. Sharon, U.T. Martin, and Shelaine, U.T. Knoxville.

Melanie married Timothy Cowan Pace, son of Harold "Toby" and Anita Allen Pace of Waverly, TN, on Dec. 23, 1983, and they live in Dickson, TN. They have two children, Timothy Carter Pace, born April 15, 1985 and Mary Rachel Pace, born Dec. 8, 1988.

Sharon Rene' married Stan Jordan Whitley of Covington, TN, March 1, 1986. Stan is the son of George and Gladys Hyde Whitley of Covington. Stan and Sharon live in Covington and have two daughters, Anna Elizabeth, born Feb. 8, 1990 and Jordan Rene', born Dec. 16, 1992.

Janet Shelaine, the younger, stayed in Knoxville after graduation.

Thomas Stuart Godwin Jr. married Dianne DePriest, daughter of Claude and Pauline Barham DePriest in 1959. His children are Thomas "Tommy" Stuart Godwin III, born Dec. 18, 1959 and Tricia Danielle, born June 23, 1961. Tom served as General Sessions Judge in Perry County from 1974 to 1982. He is presently employed as an environmental engineer with the Tennessee Department of Environment and Conservation in Knoxville, TN. Tommy is a graduate of U.T. Martin and lives in Mobile, AL. He married Joy Hinson Oliver on Grandmother Godwin's front porch. His children are Brandon Oliver and Jennifer Dyan Godwin, born July 16, 1989.

Danielle is a graduate of U.T. Knoxville and lives in Nashville, TN.

WILLIAM G. GODWIN, Redrick (Redick) (1803-1880) came from North Carolina. He was a farmer who married Mary Ann Beasley (1809-1878) in Williamson County.

William G. & Sarah Meacham Godwin

They were the parents of William G. Godwin (1832-1903) who married Sara H. Meacham (1840-1905). To this union were born eight children: John, William H., Jim, Nora, Dora, Alec, Commodore Perry (Cap) and Beulah.

John Godwin (1860-1936) married Cora Holly (1866-1932) from Texas. John was a farmer in the Bethel Community. Their children were Percy (1890-1981), Holly (1892-1976), Fred (1894-1979), Nina (1897-1981), George (1905-1974) and Maury (1902-1942).

Percy, Holly and Fred were in World War I. William H. Godwin (1863-1940) was a farmer in Perry County. James (Jim) Godwin (1867-1932) was a teacher in Perry County. Nora Godwin (1870-1927) married John Brewer Harris (1859-1932). Nora was a homemaker who had one child, Edna (1894-1945). Dora Godwin (1870-1916) married Sam Wilburn and they had one child, Roger. Alec Godwin (1873-1926) married Laura Dodson (1876-1926). Alec was a mail carrier. He and Laura had four children: Wallace, Virginia, Sarah and Rebecca Sue. Commodore Perry (Cap) (1875-1919) married Minnie Vaughan (1880-1956). He was a farmer on Coon Creek. Their children were John William (1906-1979), Thomas Stuart (1910-1968) and Ruth Vaughan (1914), a retired teacher who still resides in Perry County. Beulah Godwin (1879-1957) married H. Clagett Williams (1880-1943). She was a homemaker who had two children, Frances (1914-1986) and Billy (1920-1987).

William George Godwin fought in the Civil War and was taken prisoner of war. Sara, his wife, rode a horse from Coon Creek to Franklin, TN to take $350.00 for his release.

The great grandchildren of William George and Sarah Meacham Godwin are Holly Godwin Jr., son of Ralph Holly Godwin; Nina Ruth and Patricia, daughters of Fred Godwin; Nina Lucille, John M. (deceased) and Ralph Eugene, children of Nina Dodson; George Craig and Gail Godwin Denton, children of George Godwin; Mary Anne Godwin Perdue and Thomas S. Godwin Jr., children of Thomas S. Godwin; Martha Ruth Godwin Edwards, daughter of John W. Godwin; Edwin Williams, son of Billy Williams.

Some of the great, great grandchildren are: Julia Anne Godwin and Rosemary G. Turnbow; Carla Ruth Godwin; Jean Elizabeth Sharp and John F. Sharp; Hollie D. Speight and Leslie D. Hunt; Patrick Denton and Derrick Denton; Brian T. Edwards; Melanie P. Pace, Sharon P. Whitley and Shelaine Perdue; Thomas S. Godwin III and Patricia Danelle Godwin; Rhonda Williams.

GORDON-KILPATRICK Billy Joe Gordon, born Dec. 7, 1935 at Coble, TN in Hickman County, is the son of James Elbert Gordon, born Dec. 7, 1897, died Jan. 23, 1977 and Willie Lee Poore, born Oct. 3, 1903, died Dec. 9, 1990. Billy was raised on a large farm and helped do sharecropping throughout the community. All the boys that were big enough to farm had a team of mules for working.

The brothers and sisters are: T.J., killed in World War II, Elvin, Myrtle, Dollie, Mayzelle, Francis, deceased, George Walker, deceased, Sammuel, Sue, Louise and Eddie. Billy is employed by Tennessee Department of Transportation.

Billy Joe married Nov. 11, 1961 to Joy Kilpatrick, born Oct. 12, 1942, Perry County. She is a bank employee. The daughter of Allen Brice, born Dec. 31, 1911, died March 18, 1985, and Emma Jane Grinder Kilpatrick, born Jan. 20, 1910, died Oct. 30, 1982. (See related biography on Kilpatrick and Grinder.)

Billy J. Gordon Family

Billy and Joy have two daughters and one granddaughter.

Emily Denise Gordon, a teacher at Linden Elementary, born April 10, 1965 at Maury County, was married Aug. 1, 1986 to Michael Scott Blackwell, born Sept. 1, 1963. One daughter, Kristin Eve Blackwell, born Oct. 7, 1988 at Maury County. They live in the Coon Creek Community.

Dana Jo Gordon, a teacher at Linden Elementary, born Sept. 12, 1966 at Maury County, was married Sept. 5, 1987 to Gregory Allen Robert from Shelby County. He was born July 10, 1967, no children. They live on the old Dr. I.N. Black farm, Perry County. *Submitted by daughters, Denise Gordon-Blackwell and Dana Gordon-Roberts.*

CARL FREDERICK GOTTHARDT, a master tanner and native of Colditz, Saxony, Germany, established the first tanning yard in Perry County, TN about 1843. It was located on Lick Creek, a short distance from the Tennessee River, near Rat-Tail landing. It burned during the Civil War era.

Carl Friedrick Gotthardt

This location is in the non-accessible cultural management reserve area on the northern boundary of Mouse Tail Landing State Park. Nearby is the abandoned Conner's Cemetery where five "Guthartz" are buried.

Carl had four children born in Saxony: Carl Heinrich, a master tinnier; Caroline Agnes, a homemaker; Herman Adolfe, a tanner; and Friedrick Moritz, a saddler, who was a Civil War volunteer in Schwart's Battery A, of Company E, Second Regiment, Illinois Light Artillery. All of these children lived in Perry County in the Linden area. The first three moved to Louisville, KY and Caroline Agnes finally returned to Perry County. Carl Friedrick's wife died and he married Elizabeth Smith of Virginia. She brought with her five Smith children: Sarah, Mary, John, James and Lucy. She had two children, Caroline and Mary Elizabeth, by Mr. Gotthardt.

During the Civil War, Carl Friedrick Gotthardt (known then as Charles Gotthardt) heard that the confederate authorities were intending to confiscate his shoe leather. Being a Union Sympathizer, he sent his son, Hermann Adolfe, to the nearest Union Army post at Jackson, TN to deliver a letter to Lt. Col. William K.M. Breckenridge commanding officer of the U.S. 6th Tennessee Calvary (also known as the 1st West Tennessee Calvary), requesting him to get the leather before the confederates came to get it. In May 1863, Company E, under command of 2nd Lt. William C. Webb with Lt. Col. Breckenridge and 2nd Lt. William F. Boatright, had about 80 men with horses and wagons working the most part of a day removing the leather. They hauled it from the tannery to Rat Tail landing which was said to be about a quarter mile below Mouse Tail Landing. They loaded it onto the U.S.S. Robb Gunboat, commanded by Captain Jacen Gowdy. It was then carried to Paducah, KY.

Since he was not paid for the leather taken and was given only a receipt signed by Lt. Webb and Capt. Gowdy, Mr. Gotthardt put in a claim after the Civil War for payment of $3,178.00 for 454 hides of sole leather at $7.00 per hide, plus $50.00 for feeding 80 men and horses for one day. His claim was approved by the commissioners of Perry County, TN, allowed in full by the Tennessee General Claims Commission and was approved by the governor of Tennessee, William G. Brownlow. Mr. Gotthardt died shortly after filing this claim with the Southern Claims Commission but it was never finally approved.

Since no payment had been made to the descendent or to his estate, some of his heirs appealed the claim to the U.S. Court of Claims but to no avail.

JOHN GOTTHARDT, was the son of Agnes Caroline Gotthardt, and the grandson of Charles Gotthardt, who migrated to Perry County from Saxon, Germany in 1838. His father was John Dixon of the James Dixon estate on Lower Lick Creek.

Born in 1865, John was married in February 1887 to Tennessee Craig, daughter of Tapp and Amy Gutherie Craig of North Prong Lick Creek.

The Gotthardts lived for a time on North Prong Lick Creek, but around the turn of the century, moved to the Lower Prong into what became known as the Gotthardt Hollow, across the Creek from the Blackburn Tipton Spring.

John and Tenny Craig Gotthardt's daughters were: Agnes, born December 1887; Cora, born September 1889; Emma, born November 1891; Lillian, born July 1901; and Ruth, born 1905. An only son, William Obeth, born July 1897, died in 1918, while serving in World War I.

Agnes Gotthardt married Winfield Parson. Their children were Harvey, Sophia, Denver, Ethel and O.T.

Emma Gotthardt married Commandore Randle. Their only child was a son, Chester.

Cora Gotthardt married Edgar Nunnley. Their children were Berness S. and Amanda Alice.

Lillian (Lily) Gotthardt married Aaron Hughes. Their children are Aaron Jr., Cora Tenny and John.

Obeth Gotthardt never married.

Ruth Gotthardt never married.

In 1928, the Gotthardt family moved from Perry to Hardin County. Tenny Gotthardt died in April of 1935. John Gotthardt died in January 1940.

Except for daughters Emma and Cora, the Gotthardt family is buried in the Craig Family Cemetery on North Prong Lick Creek. *This history was written and submitted by Helen Craig Smith, great niece of Tenny Craig Gotthardt.*

GRAHAM-RAYBURN, Elizabeth Graham Rayburn was born c 1793, in Randolph County, NC, to Sarah (Brewton/Burton/Benton or Newton), born 1768, and John Graham, born c 1760. Both of her parents were born in Scotland. John Graham probably came to Anson County, NC, then Rowan County, then Randolph County, NC. He mustered into the Revolutionary War in Randolph County, NC and served under Captain Hynes. He also was elected to the 17th Tennessee General Assembly in 1827, as a representative of Perry, Humphreys and Stewart Counties.

Elizabeth Graham Rayburn had the following brothers and sisters known by this writer:

Charles Graham, born Jan. 29, 1792, Randolph County, NC, died Sept. 8, 1875, Cass County, Texas, married ? Williamson/Jane Rayburn.

Jane Graham, born 1802, Randolph County, NC, died c 1860-1870, Decatur County, TN, married John L. Houston.

Sarah Graham, born April 11, 1803, Randolph County, NC, died April 10, 1875, probably in Red River County, Texas, married Bowman/Graves.

Robert Crawford "R.C.", born June 15, 1809, Randolph County, NC, died Feb. 4, 1873, Camp County, Texas, married Cauthron/Story.

Mary "Polly" Graham, born March 10, 1810, Warren County, TN, died March 10, 1895, Cass County, Texas, married Jeremiah Wood.

There may be several others.

Elizabeth Graham married c 1807, General John King Rayburn probably in Wayne County, TN. General John Rayburn, born Montgomery County, VA, Oct. 11, 1795, was the son of Sarah Jane Shanklin, Botetourt County, VA and Henry Rayburn. (One source says both were born in Ireland.)

Elizabeth Graham and General John Rayburn had the following children:

Aquilla "Angella" Rayburn, born c 1808, probably in Warren County, TN, married Deroy C. Wright.

Louisa N. Rayburn, born May 28, 1818, probably in Warren County, TN, married John Bratton.

Charlotte Ann Rayburn, born April 4, 1820 in Tennessee, died Pleasant Plains, AR, married James Graham Beard.

Samuel Houston Rayburn, born Feb. 15, 1822 in Tennessee, died before 1860, probably in Panola County, MS. Did not marry.

Margaret Maude Rayburn, born Sept. 23, 1824, Wayne County, TN, died Feb. 22, 1903, Panola County, MS, married Leroy Clay Wright.

A son, born 1826/1827, Tennessee, died 1826/1827.

Sarah Jane Rayburn, born Aug. 28, 1838, probably in Wayne County, TN, died after 1880, probably in Panola County, MS, married Pearce W. Perry.

Lucy Ann Rayburn, born March 18, 1832, Wayne County, TN, died March 23, 1915, Panola County, MS, married Mickel Thomas Wright.

Elizabeth's husband, John King Rayburn, was Sheriff of Wayne County, TN in 1822-1836. John was elected to represent Wayne, Hickman, Lawrence, McNairy and Hardin Counties, TN for the 20th Tennessee General Assembly.

Some of Elizabeth's family, her mother, Sarah Graham, John Graham's sister, Nancy Graham Raines and possibly others, were living in Perry County, TN in 1830. In the year 1837, John and Elizabeth Rayburn moved from Tennessee to Panola County, MS where he farmed and was a physician.

Elizabeth's father, father-in-law, husband and brothers were some of the men who carved their names in American History. John Rayburn helped survey northern Mississippi. President Polk appointed him U.S. Marshal of the Northern District of Mississippi. He and his brothers made their fortune carrying cotton to market in New Orleans, LA on their own fleet of boats. They invested much of their money in land in Texas. Because of his influence in keeping the railroad out so his shipping business would not be hurt, John King Rayburn was gunned down as he was leaving the Panola jail. He was ambushed as he crossed the road to the livery stable. He was left paralyzed, dying later, April 10, 1856, leaving Elizabeth a widow.

Elizabeth Graham Rayburn, a genteel, intelligent lady of the old South, as many other southern ladies did, quietly stayed home, bore her husband's children, following him wherever he chose to live. She was loved and respected by her family and neighbors. She was a gentle, kind lady to her servants and generous to her neighbors and friends, always striving to live a Christian life. She was devoted and loyal to her husband and children. She was 66 when she died on March 8, 1860. She is buried in Eureka Cemetery, Panola County, MS beside her husband. There are many descendants of Elizabeth Graham Rayburn living today throughout Tennessee, Mississippi, Arkansas, Texas and the other states of America. *Submitted by Loretta Bowen McCloskey, Mrs. Barry L. McCloskey Sr.*

ALLEN HENRY GRAHAM, was born Oct. 12, 1896 to Jackson (Jack) Mason and Ella Jane (Moore) Graham of Cedar Creek. He died Jan. 24, 1965. Allen married twice. His first wife was Delphia Mae Denton who was born Dec. 26 or 27, 1896 to John A. and Matilda Denton. Delphia died Feb. 21, 1932. Allen married Arby Earline Strickland Aug. 11, 1935 at her home in the Pope Community of Perry County. She was born April 5, 1913 to Thomas and Ada Strickland.

Allen and Delphia had two children. Robert Allen Graham was the first born on March 17, 1923. Their second child, Jack Denton Graham, was born Jan. 11, 1926 and died April 20, 1979.

Allen Henry Graham

Allen and Earline had two children. Allene was the first born to the couple and the only female child born to Allen. She was born Nov. 25, 1936. Tommy Lee Graham was born April 2, 1944.

Allen's first born, Robert Allen, married Shirley Jean Dredge on Sept. 15, 1945. Shirley was born July 17, 1924 in Galesburg, IL to George Earl and Beulah May Dredge. Robert and Shirley have three children. Bonnie Jean, born Aug. 10, 1946, Joel Allen, born Dec. 30, 1947 and Martha Sue, born Dec. 14, 1951. Robert and Shirley live in Galesburg, IL.

Bonnie married Bruce Norman Harmon on June 28, 1969. They have two children. Dion Kane was born Oct. 11, 1977 and Alyssa Dawn was born July 31, 1982.

Joel married Paula Ann Carlson on Sept. 25, 1968. They have two sons. Christopher Joel, born Aug. 15, 1975, and was adopted by the couple Nov. 7, 1975. Michael Allen was born Nov. 3, 1976.

Martha Sue married David Bruce Shafmand on June 1, 1974. They were divorced November 1986. Martha later married John Boro and they have one son, Joey.

Allen's second born child, Jack Denton, married Edna Marie Griggs on Dec. 3, 1955. Edna was born Aug. 17, 1934 to Gilbert Turner and Golden Modest Griggs. They have four children: Deana Rea born Oct. 4, 1956, Rhonda Mae, born May 9, 1959, Brenda Gaye, born Oct. 15, 1961 and Jack Denton Jr., born March 14, 1971. Edna lives in Linden, TN and Denton is buried in Kirk Cemetery in Linden.

Deana married William Ronald Nichols on June 10, 1978. They have three children. Katherine Marie was born March 10, 1982, William Ryan was born April 18, 1985 and Graham Taylor was born July 14, 1990. They live in Franklin, TN.

Rhonda married Timothy Jenkins Friar on July 17, 1982. They have two children: Rebecca Lynn born Sept. 24, 1987 and Rachel Elizabeth born Sept. 25, 1989. They live in Knoxville, TN.

Brenda Gaye married William Shane Webster on March 21, 1981. Tiffany Marie was born to the couple on May 27, 1982. The couple divorced in December 1986. Gaye later married Terry Treadwell Dec. 29, 1988. Courtney Lee was born to Gaye and Terry March 1, 1990. They live in Linden, TN.

Allen's third child, Allene, married James Robert Fitzsimmons on June 3, 1955. Three children were born to the couple: Vicki Lee, born July 29, 1956, Denise, born Oct. 6, 1958, died at birth, and James Robert Jr. born April 27, 1960. The couple lives in Paris, TN.

Vicki married Randell Fitzhugh April 19, 1988 and they have one child, Brittany, born July 13, 1991. They live in Paris, TN.

James Robert married Lisa Kay Wiles on Aug. 27, 1980. They have two children: Kasey Leigh, born May 18, 1985, and Jarred Whiles, born in 1988. Jimmy and Lisa divorced. Jimmy later married Julia Lancaster. They live in Paris, TN.

Allen's last child, Tommy Lee, married Euletta Joan Ashworth on June 11, 1965. Joan was born Oct. 31, 1947 to Eugene and Reatha Ashworth. They have three children. Lena Joan was born May 4, 1966, Ginger Ann was born May 2, 1969 and Sherry Lee was born Nov. 29, 1975. Tommy and Joan live in Linden, TN.

Lena married Scott Bradley Heinrich in 1986. They have two children: Lauren Elizabeth born Aug. 15, 1986 and Scott Lee born Nov. 26, 1990. They live in Nashville, TN.

Ginger married Don Gilbert (Gil) Cagle Aug. 11, 1990. They live in Linden, TN.

Allen worked at various things in his life. He was a farmer, owned a car dealership in the 1930's and began a lumber company with his brother, Wess Graham, in the late 1930s. This lumber company was referred to as Graham Brothers. Allen's son, Denton, bought the company in 1956 and changed the name to Denton Graham Lumber Company. Allen's youngest son, Tommy, bought half of the lumber company in 1972 and bought the other half in 1976. Tommy changed the name of the company to Graham Lumber Company, Inc. and the company continues to operate under this name.

ALVIN JOHN WESLEY GRAHAM,

married Fannie Estalee Webster on Feb. 9, 1919. Mr. Issac Bratt Moore performed the outdoor ceremony on the Perry-Wayne County line. Wesley, son of Jack and Ella Moore Graham, was born May 14, 1898. Esther, daughter of Johnny Leroy and Lily Steele Webster, was born June 14, 1901. They had four children: Roy Mason, born July 9, 1920; Neva Merle, born Sept. 14, 1928; Reba Nell, born March 21, 1932; and Robert Max "Bobby", born Aug. 26, 1936.

Wesley & Esther Graham

Roy Graham married Grace Marie Averett, born June 15, 1921, on Dec. 24, 1950. They lived on the Averett home place; Roy did construction work and Grace worked for Civil Service. They had no children.

Neva Graham married Johnie Bratte Moore, born June 29, 1921, on May 9, 1947. Both John and Neva devoted many years to an educational profession in Perry County; John as a teacher, principal and supervisor and Neva served as substitute teacher, volunteer, educational assistant and school bookkeeper. They spent their married life on Marsh Creek with their two children, Barbara Jean, born Nov. 15, 1948, and Jimmy Neal, born Aug. 16, 1952. Barbara is a graduate of UT-Martin and a teacher in the Clarksville-Montgomery County School System. Jimmy married Cathy Diane Bates, born June 22, 1952, on Sept. 11, 1970. They had one daughter, Camilla Dawn, born Sept. 2, 1971, then later divorced. Jimmy and Camilla own two pizza parlors and live in Clarksville, TN.

Nell Graham married James Howard Jackson, born Jan. 17, 1931, on Sept. 5, 1951. Howard taught school and served as principal in Christian County, KY. They made their home in Clarksville and had three children: James Michael, born May 27, 1952; Kenneth Wayne, born Feb. 23, 1957; and Linda Renee, born July 22, 1958. Mike married Winnie Belle Harp, born Dec. 24, 1953, on April 24, 1980. They had one son, Preston Michael, born June 9, 1981. They own a pizza business and make their home in Clarksville. Ken married Virginia Rose Winters, born Jan. 6, 1959, on June 22, 1978. They had three children: John Wesley, born May 10, 1979; Rebecca Ann, born Jan. 8, 1989; and Elizabeth Diane, born Nov. 25, 1984. Ken is an RN/Nurse Practitioner and they live in Clarksville. Linda married James Howard Crotzer, born July 6, 1952, on April 21, 1979. They had two children: Courtney Lynn, born April 5, 1981, and Brandon Alan, born July 8, 1982. Linda manages a clothing store in Clarksville where they live.

Bobby Graham married first to Betty Sharp, born April 29, 1939, in June, 1957. They had one son, David Wesley, born June 15, 1958, and later divorced. David was a 1976 graduate of Perry County High School and is a policeman on the Miami, Florida police force. Bobby's second marriage was to Joyce Marie Dees, born Jan. 8, 1937, on Oct. 7, 1962. They had three daughters: Carol Denise, born July 23, 1963; Jacquelyn "Jackie" Marie, born Aug. 22, 1965; and Patti Annette, born Sept. 24, 1966. Carol is an RN at Vanderbilt Hospital in Nashville where she lives. Jacquelyn married Steven Douglas Wilder, a native of Cincinnati, Ohio, born June 7, 1963, on May 31, 1987. They had one son, Joseph "Joey" Dalton Wilder, born May 8, 1991. Steve and Jackie are teachers in the Perry County School System. Patti had one son, Wesley Robert Graham, born Jan. 31, 1987, and one daughter, Samantha Carole Graham, born March 8, 1993. Patti is a nurse technician at the Perry County Nursing Home. After an extended illness, Bobby died Oct. 13, 1982. Joyce later married a native of Henderson County, TN, Sam Reeves, and they made their home in Perry County where she is employed by the Board of Education.

Wess and Esther lived near his father on Cedar Creek; he farmed and worked with his father in their "county store" until about 1945. They moved near Linden on old Highway 13; he was self-employed in the family lumber business. During the eve of their lives together, they moved into a new home in the City of Linden and lived there until their deaths; Wess died July 7, 1978, and Esther died Sept. 4, 1992. Both are buried in the Kirk Cemetery.

CHARLES GRAHAM,

General Charles Graham was born Jan. 29, 1792 in North Carolina, Richmond or possibly Randolph County, to Sarah and John Graham. His family moved to Warren County, Tennessee in about 1809. In 1817, Charles was in Nunnelly, Hickman County for the birth of T.W., then in Wayne County, TN for his September 1823 marriage to Jane Rayburn, daughter of Sarah Jane Shandlin and Henry Rayburn of Montgomery County, VA.

Charles Graham, 1792-1875

Charles Graham enlisted in the War of 1812 on Jan. 28, 1814 at Fayetteville, Lincoln County, TN while living in McMinville, Warren County. He served a six-month tour of duty as a lieutenant in Capt. William Douglas' Infantry, Company G; Johnson's Brigade, Copeland's 3rd Reg., West TN Militia. He was in the campaign against the Creek Indians at Horseshoe Pens, serving with General Andrew Jackson, then discharged at Fayetteville on May 10, 1814. Bounty Land Application No. 28847 and Pension No. 21021 (Grimes in some records).

Charles, a Whig, was elected to the 23rd & 24th Tennessee Gen. Assembly representing Perry County, 1839-1843. In 1845, he was one of the Commissioners that located the county seat of Decatur. Charles first appeared in Texas in the Surveyor Records of Cass County dated Dec. 31, 1839, along with Mr. Frazure, Asa Smith, Charles Standing, Whitaker and Storach. Family tradition said that Charles came to Cass County in 1843 and that son, T.W. was in Texas when baby Granville was born in 1843. Charles had definitely moved his family to Texas by 1845. He was a surveyor and a businessman. He recorded the 1850 Cass County Cen.

Charles had 14 children by two wives, three by his first wife, name unknown but thought to be Williams or Williamson, maybe a daughter of Jessee Williamson/Williams of Hickman County. Tillman Williamson "T.W.", born 1817 Nunnelly, TN - 1893 Indian Territory and married Jency Jane Williams, 11 children; and two unknown girls. T.W. bought 77 acres on the Big Harperth River, Davidson County in 1838, then sold one-third undivided interests in 1843 and 1847. Maybe these undivided interests were part of an inheritance from his mother to him and his two sisters.

Children by Jane Rayburn, April 14, 1801

151

- Jan. 26, 1861: Perry Mancel (maybe Manville or McClure), 1823-1881 Marion County, Texas, married Madeline Lester Darby, one child, Kasiah Frances Rogers, one child, & Josephine Edwards, eight children; John H., 1828-1895, married Sarah Elizabeth Epperson, one child; Sarah Ann, 1829-1888 (Graham Graveyard), married Anderson Ferdinand Holcombe, no children; Elizabeth Caroline, 1830-1851, single; Charlotte Jane, 1831-1853, single; Charles Gibbs, 1833-1896 Marion County, married Sarah Texana Harris, seven children; Samuel R., 1836-1863 Ottawa County, OH, single; Mary F., 1837-1898, married Dr. John P. Mills; Anne Elizabeth, 1839-1867, married Dr. Robert Frank Sloan, three children; Emily P., 1842-1900, single; Robert D.M., 1846-1887, married Martha Priscilla "Mattie" Lee, one child.

General Charles Graham was a title Charles adopted about 1855 and was affectionately called until his death on Sept. 8, 1875, buried in Graham Graveyard or Center Grove Cemetery, Cass County.

CHARLES GIBBS GRAHAM,

was born in Perryville, Perry County on April 30, 1833 to Charles Graham and Jane Rayburn, daughter of Sarah Shanklin and Henry Rayburn. Charles died on June 3, 1896 in Jefferson, Marion County, Texas, buried Oakwood Cemetery with most of his children.

Gibbs families near our Grahams were: Stephen O. Gibbs in the 1830 Perry County census; Clayton Gibbs in the 1820-1837 Perry County Deed Book; and an Anson Gibbs is found in the 1836 Tax List of Panola County, MS where John King and Elizabeth Graham Rayburn lived.

Charles Gibbs Graham stated in the 1867 Texas Voter's Registration dated, Jan. 27, 1868, that he was a native of "Tennessee", had been a resident of Texas "21 years", had been a resident of "Marion County" for "7 years" and a resident of "Precinct 1" for "7 years".

Charles Gibbs Graham married in Carrolton, Carroll County, MO on April 30, 1868 to Sarah Texana Harris (1848-1927), daughter of Martha Freeman and Francis Tennelle Harris, born c1810 in Georgia, probably in Talbottom, Talbot County. Martha Freeman, born 1812, probably in Talbot County, and sister of Williamson M. Freeman who came to Texas in 1830 and died in 1866 in Jefferson, Marion County, Texas. This whole Harris family died in Jefferson within two months in 1858 of "purulent sore throat", probably diphtheria.

Graham children of Charles and Sarah Texana were: Charles G., 1873-1873; Vitia Cooper, 1874-1874 Carroll County, MO; Karl Harris, 1876-1959 Shreveport, LA, married Virginia Lovie Chew, no children; Marcia Tennelle, 1881-1881; Francis Tennelle, 1883-1934 Marion County, Texas, single; Pierson Holcombe, 1885-1946 Marion County, Texas, single; Marie Vesta, 1890-1968 Marion County, Texas, married Horace Clifton Brown.

The National Historic Register and the Texas Historic Register have recognized Charles Gibbs Graham's home that he built in 1885 on a hill in Jefferson overlooking the Big Cypress Bayou. His granddaughter, Dorothy Brown Craver, lovingly maintains it.

Dorothy Craver's father was Horace Clifton Brown, born in Jefferson to Daisy Helen Welch and George Washington Brown of 1854 Armstrong County, PA, son of Robert Alexander Brown, born 1816 Huntingdon County, PA. Daisy Welch was born in 1867 in Canton, Free State of Van Zandt County, Texas to Horace Clifton Welch, born 1823 in Eden, Erie County, New York.

GRANVILLE GRAHAM,

"I was here before you came and I'm gonna drive where I darned well please!" Granville barked to the Duncan police who were protesting his defying traffic with his dilapidated buggy and old gray horse. Granville probably first saw the Duncan area of Stephens County, OK during the first days of the Civil War.

Charles Granville Graham was born Aug. 6, 1843 near Perryville, Perry County to Jency Jane Williams, while his father, T.W. Graham, was in northeast Texas (probably Holcombe's Bluff, near later Linden, Cass County). Jane and baby Granville joined T.W. in Texas and lived near Parthenia Williams and Charles until they moved in 1855 to the Crosstimbers near Whitesboro, Grayson County, Texas.

When the ring of the Civil War sounded at Fort Sumter, Federal troops abandoned Fort Washita, near Tishomingo, the capital of the Chickasaw Nation. The Red River area citizens formed the First Indian Regiment to ward off the depredating Plains Indians, which expanded into 20 companies of the Confederate 22nd Texas Cavalry, later called Taylor's, Steven's, Stone's and Merrick's Reg. Dismounted Cavalry (in mid-1864, dismounting this cavalry was a demoralizing demotion). Most of these units helped with the wheat harvest in North Texas during the summer of 1862 when it was so hot and dry that "the wheels were dropping off the wagons". Granville mustered into Co, B, First Indian Reg. at Fort Washita about July 1861 and served 41 months, discharged May 24, 1865 at Millican, Brazos County, Texas by Lt. Col. George Merrick.

Granville married Mary Louise "Molly" Savage on Jan. 9, 1867 in Grayson County, Texas, daughter of Elizabeth Madon, born 1830 in Mississippi, and Sam B. Savage, born 1829 in Tennessee. Molly was born Sept. 8, 1849 and died March 11, 1935. Their only child, Thomas, July 1867 - Sept. 26, 1947 probably in Cleveland County, OK, married a Choctaw, Zula Blake, who died Nov. 25, 1963. Tommie had three children: Freda married Marvin Johnson; Charles Granville; Dixie and an adopted daughter, Mrs. Hersie Weaver.

When Granville's hired hand became sick in 1868, he hired his 14-year-old brother, Thomas Marion Graham, to pilot a wagon to move Granville's stuff from Texas to Indian Territory, probably the Duncan-Velma area. Thomas' son, Bink Graham, said Thomas drove cattle from Perry County, TN to Indian Territory, then worked as his ranch hand for several years. In the 1870s, Granville went back to the Crosstimbers (east Cooke County) where he had an ideal setup for cattle; good grass, flat terrain and plenty of watering holes. For a long time, it seemed that Granville was the only Graham who knew how to make money. Granville helped all his brothers get started in the cattle business. He was a partner with brother, Tip, in a grocery store in Cooke County; Tip went broke. In 1886, Granville was back in Velma, Chickasaw Nation. At one time Granville lived at Spanish Fort, Montgaue County, Texas. In his later years, he worked on the Graham-Chisum Ranch near Velma.

Granville died on April 4, 1930 in the Confederate Veteran's Home, Ardmore, Carter County, OK. He is buried near "cattle heaven" in the Fairview Cemetery, Gainesville, Cooke County, Texas with his family. Granville was held in high-esteem by his Grahams since several children were named "Granville" to honor him.

JACKSON M. GRAHAM,

Jackson "Jack" Mason and Ella Jane Graham lived on Cedar Creek in Perry County. They were married March 28, 1894. Ella, daughter of William Henry and Mary Elizabeth Richardson Moore, was born Dec. 7, 1878 and died Jan. 30, 1924. Jack, grandson of Thomas Graham, was born Dec. 15, 1874 in Perry County and died Feb. 24, 1963. Jack and Ella had six children: Allen Henry, 1896-1965; Alvin John Wesley, 1898-1978; Lydia May, 1902-1929; Cloia Josephine, born 1904; Nora Alma, 1907-1960; and Fred Hooper, 1910-1912.

Jack and Ella (Moore) Graham

Allen Graham married, first, Delphia Mae Denton, 1896-1932, daughter of John Anderson and Matilda Culp Denton. They had two sons: Robert Allen, born 1923, married Shirley Dredge; Jack Denton, 1926-1979, married Edna Griggs. Allen married, second, Earline Strickland, daughter of Thomas Monroe and Ada Clayborne O'Guin Strickland. They had two children: Allene, born 1936, married James Fitzsimmons; Tommy Lee, born 1944, married Joan Ashworth.

Wesley Graham married Fannie Estalee Webster, 1901-1992, daughter of John Leroy and Lillie May Steele Webster. They had four children: Roy Mason, born 1920, married Grace Averett; Neva Merle, born 1928, married John B. Moore; Reba Nell, born 1932, married Howard Jackson; Robert Max, 1936-1982, first married Betty Sharp. Robert married, second, Joyce Dees.

Lydia Graham married Garrett Hobart Moore, 1898-1979, son of Isaac Bradford and Mary Ophelia Richardson Moore. Their son, Rogers Oneil, 1925-1971, married Ollie Mae Ellison.

Cloia Graham married Dewey Lee Bunch, 1898-1988, son of Lee Grand and Ada Fannie Steele Bunch. A son, Dewey Lee "D L" Bunch Jr. was born in 1932. This family are farmers in Gibson County, near Trenton, TN.

Alma Graham married Robert Jefferson Hinson, 1904-1987, son of Spencer Austin and Bertha Elizabeth Broadway Hinson. Robert was a teacher; Alma was a Postmistress for many years. Their adopted son is James Michael, born in 1944.

Jack M. Graham married, second, Bettie Lee Pevahouse, 1903-1971, daughter of John G. and Ophelia Pevahouse. Their son, Oneal Jackson Graham, 1927-1990, married Margie Jane Cotham. Oneal and Margie had three children: Jeffrey Neal, born 1950, married Delaine Culp; Connie Dale, born 1954, married Virgil Wayne Bates; and Jack Edgar, born 1957, married Carol Lineberry.

Jack M. was a farmer and owned a country store on Cedar Creek. He bought the first store from Tom Treadwell. I.B. Moore helped him with the books. A new store was built in 1919 with the thought of a Graham/Moore partnership. But it was named the J.M. Graham Store as Squire Moore decided not to be a partner.

Jack M. had two sisters: Flora, born about 1877, died young; Emma, born 1882, married Lantie Armstrong. They had eight children and lived in Coble, TN.

Thomas Graham, Jack's grandfather, came with his family from Lewis County to Perry County before 1860. He was a native of North Carolina. Known children were: William H., Alexander, Hugh Cain and Susannah Matilda. Others may be: Catherine Robertson, Frances Langham, Thomas John, Sarah C. and Jessie B.

JOHN GRAHAM, was born 1760 in Scotland and immigrated to America at an early age. Records indicate that his family settled in Anson County, and possibly, Randolph County, NC. John Graham purchased 50 acres in Anson County on Joe's Creek in 1778. In 1779 Richmond County was formed from Anson County. In the 1800 Richmond County, NC census, one John Graham with four children appears. Newspapers in Anson, Rowan and Randolph County, NC ran the obituary of John Graham's 1827 death in Nashville. It is believed that the Perry County-Cass County, Texas progenitor lived in Richmond and Anson Counties.

Randolph County, North Carolina Deed Book 11, page 198, dated July 17, 1805, connects several Perry County families. It mentions Mary Rains and C. Ford of Union County, SC; Thomas Graham of Stokes County, NC; John Graham of Buncombe County, NC; Alex' Graham, John Graham, Richard Graham, John Woodward and Joale Rains (maybe Foate Rains) of Randolph County. Nancy Rains of Randolph County, NC and Perry County, TN was John Graham's sister and wife of Rev. War veteran, Anthony Rains.

In about 1809, it is believed that the Grahams moved to Warren County, TN. His oldest child, Charles, enlisted as a Lieutenant in the War of 1812, Company G, 3rd Reg. at Warren County in 1814. His daughter, Elizabeth Graham Rayburn's, obituary mentions living in Warren County, plus daughter, Jane Graham Houston's son was born in 1824 in Warren County, TN. John Graham possibly served in the War of 1812 under Captain Abner Pearce of Stewart County, TN. The John Graham in the 1820 Warren County, TN census may belong to this family. On Nov. 1, 1826, John Graham first appears in Perry County as a juror. In 1827, he was elected as a Legislator representing the counties of Perry, Stewart and Humphrey in the 17th Tennessee General Assembly. On Oct. 6, 1827, 19 days into his first term of office, John Graham died of a fever in Nashville, Davidson County, TN at age 67 years. His wife, Sarah, was voted a pension by the 17th Gen. Assembly. Sarah died, probably in Decatur County, on Dec. 15, 1856 at age 88 years.

John and Sarah Graham had a minimum of eight children: Charles, 1792-1875 Cass County, Texas, married Jane Rayburn; Elizabeth, 1793-1860 Panola County, MS, married John King Rayburn; Jane, 1802-between 1860-70 Decatur County, TN, married John Luckey Houston; Sarah, 1803-1875, maybe, Red River County, Texas or Cass County, Texas, married William C. Bowman, then Wiley Graves; Hiram H., 1804-after 1850 Henderson County, TN, married Malinda Houston; Lydia, 1806-1853, married Bennett Story; Robert Crawford, 1809-1873 Camp County, Texas, married Mahaly Cauthron, then Nancy Hill Story; Mary "Polly" 1810-1895 Cass County, Texas, married Jeremiah Preston. Other children may be John Jr., Richard, Samuel and David Graham.

RICHARD GRAHAM, married Opal Keeling on Aug. 17, 1934. Richard is the great great grandson of Ballard Collins Sr. and Polly Jackson Collins. They had a son, Ballard Collins Jr., born in 1837 in North Carolina. Ballard Sr. and Polly moved to Anna, IL between 1850-1858. On Sept. 7, 1858, Ballard Sr. died. On Sept. 15, 1856, Ballard Collins Jr. married Elezibeth Huff (1842). They had two children: John C. Collins (Jan. 1858/59) and Mary Collins (Sept. 26, 1861-June 19, 1955).

Ballard Collins fought in the Civil War and was killed at Fort Donaldson. Elezibeth, along with her two children, came to Tennessee and settled at New Era Landing on Cedar Creek. Mary Collins never married but had two children: Jenny, who married Sam Garner and Ethel (March 18, 1888-June 14, 1966) who married Joe Graham (July 7, 1876-Jan. 14, 1966) on Aug. 31, 1901.

Ethel and Joe had the following children: Earnest (July 20, 1904-July 21, 1975); Hillard (May 3, 1911-Oct. 30, 1976); Richard (Oct. 16, 1917-April 25, 1993); Gracy (July 7, 1907-Nov. 23, 1981); Lois (Jan. 27, 1930); Verna Mae; Nora.

Richard Graham and Opal Keeling Graham had the following children: Cleamon (Nov. 25, 1935), Evelyn (Sept. 26, 1937), Ann (Sept. 8, 1945) and Danny (Dec. 19, 1951).

Opal Keeling Graham's parents were Westling Keeling (Feb. 17, 1871-Feb. 10, 1946) and Daisy Carter Keeling (July 16, 1882-Feb. 22, 1976). Westling's parents were George Calvin Keeling and Nancy Howell Keeling. George's parents were Maxwell Keeling and Pamela Keeling.

ROBERT CRAWFORD GRAHAM, "Robert never regretted leaving the more cultured environment of his life in Tennessee for a home in the almost unknown Mexico, called Texas." is family tradition. "Both my husband and my father fought in the Mexican War," quipped Robert's daughter, Tennessee Texas, many times.

Robert Crawford "R.C." Graham was born on June 15, 1809 in North Carolina, probably Randolph County, to John Graham and Sarah (? Bunten or maybe Newton). He died on Feb. 4, 1873 and was buried in the Leeburg Cemetery, Camp County, Texas.

R.C. first married Mahaly Caughron on April 14, 1826 in Perry County. Mahaly was the daughter of Susannah, who died April 8, 1830, and Sam Caughron, born about 1745 in Ireland and died April 1, 1831. This was probably the Samuel Coughlin found in the 1830 Perry County census. Mahaly died Aug. 28, 1839, leaving three children: Texas Tennessee, 1831-1928 Red River County, Texas, married James Newton Bowman (cousin); James Matthew, born Oct. 2, 1832, married Lou Reeves, found in Linden, 1870 Davis County, Texas census; and James Franklin, born Jan. 17, 1835.

R.C. remarried in Perry County on Jan. 5, 1841 to Nancy Hill Story, 1821 Tennessee-Sept. 26, 1879, probably daughter of Senith and Samuel Story Sr., and sister to Henry J. Story and Bennett Story. Nancy was held in high esteem by her step-children who adored her. Nancy and R.C. had two sons: Newton C., born 1845; and Robert C., born 1843 (maybe the R.C. Graham, born 1844, enlisted C.S.A. Jan. 22, 1862 Col. Young's Reg. Texas Inf., Capt. W.M. Nunn's Co K., Camp Herbert, Hemstead, Waller County, Texas, 200 miles rendezvous, still active February 1864 in Capt. Nunn's Co K, 8th Reg. Texas Inf. in Hill County, Texas).

Robert sold lot 16 in Perryville on July 6, 1841 to John McKnight, witnessed by Wily Porter and Jos. Essery.

In 1841 R.C. moved his family to Texas, crossed the Mississippi River at Memphis, and settled in an area later called Linden. Due to changing county lines and several moves, records for R.C. can probably be found in the Texas counties of Bowie, Paschal, Red River, Upshur, Davis, Cass, Camp and Marion.

Through the influence of his Tennessee friend, Colonel Frazier, R.C. was made a public surveyor. His brother Charles was also a surveyor. Other Tennessee families that came to Holcombe's Bluff area near Linden were Wood, Story, Epperson, French, Gibbs, Rains, Reeves, Clopton and Graves.

Postal service was very slow in the 1870s in Texas. It was a month before R.C. found out about his son-in-law's 1871 death. As soon as he could, he left Jefferson, Marion County, Texas to live for several months with his beloved daughter, Tennessee Texas, in Red River County.

TENNESSEE TEXAS (MARY) GRAHAM, was born March 31, 1831 in Perryville, TN. The daughter of Robert Crawford Graham and his first wife, Mahaly Cauthron Graham. Maternal grandparents were Samuel Cauthron (died April 1, 1831) and Susannah Cauthron (died April 8, 1830). Her paternal grandmother was Sarah Bruton\Bunton\Newton, born 1768, Scotland, died Dec. 15, 1856, Decatur County, TN and grandfather was John Graham Sr., born 1760 Scotland, and died Oct. 6, 1827 in Davidson County, TN. Robert Crawford Graham, born June 15, 1809 in Randolph County, NC and died

Feb. 4, 1873 Camp County, Texas. When "Tennessee" was 10 years old, her family moved to Jefferson/Linden, Texas. The story of her journey was featured in the Dallas Morning Newspaper April 1927. Her mother and father taught her sound Christian principles to live by. She was highly regarded and admired by all. Her father married second to Nancy Hill Story, born 1821 Tennessee, who was beloved stepmother to Mahaly's children. Probably it was Nancy H. Story's brother, Henry J. Story, J.P., who married James Newton Bowman to T.T. Graham (first cousins) Oct. 4, 1850. T.T. Bowmans pension papers as a widow of a Mexican War Vet. state that Pvt. Newton J. Bowman served under Capt. Rice F. Texas Mounted Volunteers, June 5, 1846 to Aug. 1848. The papers were notarized by T.T. Bowman's son-in-law, John Cassimer Perot. Tennessee Texas Bowman died Feb. 3, 1928 at Bowman's Hill, Pinebluff, Red River County, Texas. She was also known as "Aunt Tennessee" to everyone and was six feet tall.

Tennessee "Aunt Tinsey" Texas Graham Bowman

James Newton Bowman, born Jan. 7, 1826 in Tennessee, and T.T. Graham had a daughter, Sarah Mahaly Hill Bowman, who married John Cassimer Perot. They had seven children: Lillian Texas Perot, married B.S. McCleary; Cora Corine Perot, never married; Marie Hill Perot, married H. Howard Miller. It was from Marie's memoirs that most of this history is from; J.C. Perot; James Perot, married Irene and had three children; Osward B. Perot, married Johnnie Walker; and Omer Earl Perot.

Another loving family member was Tennessee Texas's brother, R.C. Bowman. He was known as "Uncle Campbell". He was married three times. One son, Newton Harrison Bowman, was an Ear, Nose and Throat Doctor and was an early Methodist Missionary in Korea.

Lillian Texas Perot and B.C. McCleary had five children: Ben Sam McCleary who married three times and had a daughter, Dorothey Taylor, Austin, Texas: Marieta Wilhelm, married and had four children; Sarah Elizabeth McCleary N.M.; Lucille McCleary N.M. John McCleary married Lillian Friesen and had two daughters; Frances L. McCleary married C.C. Barber, (no children) Nelda Lee McCleary married Delos E. Pypes Jr. and had four children - William Graham Pypes married Rhonda Sieck, three children; Elizabeth R. Pypes married Allen Hays Adams, divorced, no children; Evelyn L. Pypes N.M.; and David L. Pypes married Deonne Sederberg, one child.
Submitted by Nelda Lee McCleary Pypes.

TILLMAN WILLIAMSON GRAHAM,
Tillman Williamson "T.W" Graham was born May 15, 1817, near Nunnelly, Hickman County, TN to Charles Graham and maybe a daughter of Jesse Williamson/Williams of Hickman County.

Tillman Williamson Graham 1817-1893

T.W. purchased 77 acres in Davidson County, TN in 1838 and served as a Juror in Perry County, 1838, so maybe he was a non-resident owner. He is listed again in May of 1841 as a Juror in Perry County.

T.W. married Jency Jane Williams in Perry County about 1842. She was born May 22, 1823, in Indiana, or possibly Tennessee. They had 11 children: Charles Granville, James Perry, Rosa Abeen Simpson, John Rayburn, Tillman Williamson Jr., Robert D., James Holcombe, Thomas Marion, Mary Charlotta Belle Zora Thompson, Sarah Emma Camilla Crouch and William Benjamin.

Family tradition said that T.W. and Charles went to Texas in 1843 and that Jane came later with baby Granville. Records show that in 1845 Charles helped select the Decatur County seat, so they must have made at least one trip to Texas before they moved their families in 1845. T.W.'s son, John Rayburn Graham, was born Nov. 1844 in Texas. T.W. sold 77 acres in Davidson County, TN in 1845 to James Newton Bowman, was living in Cass County, Texas. In 1845, T.W. and Jane purchased land in Grayson County, Texas, where they moved to in 1855. He owned a 300 acre cotton plantation with seven slaves that he brought from Tennessee. Texas records for T.W. can be found in the Bowie, Cass and Grayson Counties.

T.W. was a charter member of the Odd Fellows Lodge No. 102 in Whitesboro, Grayson County. On March 30, 1861, T.W. became a member of the Whitesboro Masonic Lodge No. 263. He left the lodge by demit on Jan. 12, 1878, and was affiliated with the Burlington Lodge No. 440, at Spanish Fort, Montague County, Texas.

T.W. enlisted in the Confederate Army for six months on Aug. 6, 1863, at Camp Stonewall in Collin County, Texas, where he was assigned to Co. B, 15th Battalion, Texas State Cavalry commanded by Captain John Goode.

T.W.'s son, Granville, was his first of the family to live in Indian Territory, and son, Tom, worked as one of Granville's ranchhands. It is believed that Granville settled around Velma (now Stephens County, OK), but it is known that later Tom rented, then bought, grassland on Rush Creek from Indians (now Bailey). Tom wrote a letter to his parents in Texas explaining how they "could rent lush river bottom grassland excellent for cattle cheaply from the Indians, who didn't appreciate the fertile land."

In 1885, they moved to Bailey, Erin Springs Post Office, Pickens County, Chickasaw Nation, Indian Territory (now Oklahoma). He was a cattleman and farmer. He died April 9, 1893, and his wife, Jency Jane, died May 21, 1901. Both are buried in the Bailey Cemetery, Grady County, OK.

GRAVES, The following Graves family has descendants in Perry, Decatur and surrounding counties.

George Graves, born about 1775, came from Virginia and settled in Decatur County before 1860. He had two known sons, George (born about 1800) and Balem (born about 1804). George's son, Archibald, (born about 1833) married Sofrona Caroline and had twin sons: George Washington (Biv) and James Madison (Pete) born in 1853; M.A., A.J. (Arch) and Frank.

George Washington Graves, (born 1853) married Melvina Catherine Graham (born 1845), daughter of Hiram H. Graham (born 1804 in North Carolina) of Perry County, and Malinda M. Houston (born 1814). Malinda was a sister to John L. Houston (born 1797), who married Jane Graham (born 1802), sister to Hiram. George and Melvina had six children: Lemuel (born 1874), William Carson (born 1876), Altha (born 1877), Sylvester (born 1880), James Franklin (born 1883) and Francis (born 1885).

James Franklin Graves, born 1883 in Perryville, married Bertha Louise Yarbro (born 1896) daughter of Mike Yarbro (born 1873) and Willie Jane Raney (born 1879). Their children were William Franklin (born 1917), Nell (born 1920) and Imogene (born 1926). Mike Yarbro's mother was Mary Elizabeth Fisher (born 1840, daughter of Jacob F. Fisher (born 1815) and Sophia Yarbro (born 1820). Mike's father was Joseph Gallitin Yarbro (born 1829, whose father, Henry, (born 1790 in North Carolina), married Delilah Crawley (born 1808). Henry's father was Edmund Yarbro (born 1766 in Anson County, NC) and his mother was Sophia Gosset, born in Maryland. Delilah Crawley's father was William Mitchell Crawley and her mother was Sarah Lloyd. Willie Jane Raney was the daughter of Granville Raney (born 1848), son of James H. Raney, a native of Stewart County who settled in Decatur County when it was still known as Perry County. He was married to Amanda Bryant from North Carolina. Granville Raney married Lucy Johnson (born 1855), daughter of William Johnson and Jane Fisher.

William Franklin Graves (born 1917) married Wilma Mae Lancaster (born 1920; died 1981). Their daughters were: Yvonne Mae (born 1937) who married Herbert Hoover Crosby, son of Bessie Crowell (daughter of John Crowell and Victoria Simmons) and George Crosby. George's father, William, (born 1860) was a deputy sheriff in Perry County in 1893. Wilda Faye (born 1940) married Rex Patterson, son of Howell and Nettie Patterson of Pineview. Jo Nell (born 1943) married James C. Wyatt, son of Loyce and Jessie Wyatt of Decatur County. Marcia Gayle (born 1951) married Danny Cordle of Decatur County, son of Nora Bell and Rayfel Edison Cordle; second marriage to Greg Burton of Henderson County. Two other children: James Larry (born and died 1946) and Patricia Ann (born 1948 and died 1960).

ANDY COOK GRAVES, (1882-1959), son of Isaac Lee and Parthena (Ledbetter) Graves, was born June 19, 1882 on Sinking Creek in Perry County, died Oct. 20, 1959 in Hohenwald, and is buried in Graves Cemetery. He married twice, first July 21, 1900 to Minnie Jane Cooper, daughter of Clarence and Nancy Armentha (Grinder) Cooper. Minnie was born April 1882, died 1940, and is buried in Graves Cemetery. Second, Andy married Nancy Duncan. Andy was a farmer and a Methodist. His children are:

Fred Kenny Graves, born Feb. 2, 1903 on Sinking Creek, died March 30, 1951, and is buried in Graves Cemetery. He married twice, first in March 1921 to Mamie Hickerson, daughter of William Nathan and Cordelia Freedonia (Duncan) Hickerson. Mamie was born Nov. 4, 1902, died June 8, 1935, and is buried in Graves Cemetery. Second, he married September 1936 to Ruth Epley, daughter of Tom and Dora (Richardson) Epley. Mamie's children were: Ted Graves, born Dec. 28, 1922 in Lewis County, died Sept. 1987 in Lewis County and was buried in Graves Cemetery. He married Oct. 9, 1948 in Angloa, IN to Virginia Ryhan, daughter of William H. and Thelma (DeNoma) Ryhan. Virginia was born May 5, 1930 in Trenton, MI. Their children - Sandra V. Graves, born Feb. 5, 1951 in Lewis County, married Aug. 18, 1968 in Whiteville, TN to Larry T. Evans. Sherrie L. Graves, born June 12, 1955 in South Bend, IN, married April 12, 1974 in Lewis County to Johnny Dunn. Thomas William Graves, born Nov. 12, 1955 in Detroit, MI (adopted). Janice R. Graves, born Feb. 1, 1962 in South Bend, married Oct. 10, 1986 to Seth Edward Rhodes. Ted Russell Graves, born June 16, 1965 in Lewis County, married Christy Hinson; and Helen Graves, married Douglas Queen, son of Briley and Pauline (Edwards) Queen. Douglas was killed in an automobile accident and Helen married second to Louie Brewer. Two children, Paula Queen (1948-1993) and Susan Brewer.

Ruth's children were: Kenny Paul Graves, born Sept. 11, 1937 in Linden, married Dec. 25, 1959 to Cynthia Ann Cook, daughter of K.H. and Ryanza (Hutchinson) Cook. Cynthia was born Jan. 1, 1943. They had one child, Kenny Brian Graves, born 1961 in Centerville.

Clyde Graves, born Oct. 16, 1911, married Dec. 25, 1930 in Hohenwald to James Moore Turnbow, son of Tommy and Carrie (Lindsey) Turnbow. James was born Nov. 7, 1909, died March 7, 1966, and is buried in Graves Cemetery. Their children: Georgia Ruth Turnbow, born Nov. 17, 1931, married Nov. 2 to Freddie Roth, born Dec. 12 and had two children, David Roth, born March 28, 1952 and Sharon Roth, born Jan. 11, 1957; and Jimmy C. Turnbow, born Nov. 30, 1936, married July 12, 1953 to Ruth Helen Jackson and had two children, Chrystal Lynn Turnbow, born Feb. 10, 1958, married Donald Wayne Wood, and Chandra Kay Turnbow married Tommy Powell.

Retha Mae Graves, born June 8, 1920 on Sinking, married July 3, 1937 in Linden to Alton Laban McLemore, son of Hert McLemore and Molly (Fraley) McLemore. Their children: Doris Nell McLemore, married Wayne Clay and had two children, Randall Clay married Nov. 29, 1975 in New Johnsonville to Kathy Louise Roche and had two children, Randall Anthony Clay born Aug. 11, 1976 in Valdosta, GA and James Matthew Clay, born April 4, 1979 in Valdosta, GA, and Charles Todd Clay married Sandy Dreden Oct. 11, 1991; and Alton Laban McLemore Jr., married Patsy Reeves.

Carmie Nell Graves, born Jan. 12, 1922 on Sinking Creek, married Nov. 16, 1940 to Edward Grimes. They live in Michigan and have one child, Larry Grimes.

Janie Miriam Graves, born July 12, 1925 on Sinking Creek, died Dec. 31, 1989, and was buried in Graves Cemetery. She married July 16, 1946 in Corinth, MS to Alton Crowell. They had one child, Wendell Crowell, who had one daughter, Heather Crowell. *Submitted by Mae Graves McLemore.*

ARTHUR ANSON GRAVES, (1894-1941), son of Lawrence and Sally (Tatum) Graves, was born March 4, 1894 in Flatwoods, Perry County, died Dec. 17, 1941 in Cross Bridges, TN, and is buried in Cedar Hill Cemetery, in Maury County. He moved to Wayne County in 1904 and was married Feb. 13, 1916 in Wayne County to Cleo Lafferty, daughter of Dorsie Burns and Maggie (McAnally) Lafferty. Cleo was born May 28, 1898 on Green River, Wayne County, died Feb. 24, 1978 in Columbia, and is also buried in Cedar Hill Cemetery. The family lived in Wayne, Lawrence and Maury Counties in Tennessee. Their children were:

Arthur Anson Graves

Margaret Eugenia Graves, born Nov. 22, 1916 in Topsy, Wayne County, died April 18, 1981 Craven County Hospital, New Bern, NC. She married first to Martin Haar and second to Verdie Rediker. Her children were: Judy Ann Haar, born Sept. 29, 1948 in Little Rock, AR, married William Paul Santag Jr. They are divorced; and Bennie Ray Haar, born Sept. 17, 1952 Columbia, TN, married Malinda Jane Parnell.

Sarah Louise Graves, born July 18, 1918, Wayne Furnace, Wayne County, married 1938 in Lewisburg, TN to Loyd Hansel Witherspoon. Their children were: Loyd Harvell Witherspoon, born Aug. 9, 1939 in Cross Bridges, Maury County, married Frances Gainey; and Peggy Louise Witherspoon, born Aug. 25, 1950 in Columbia, TN, married Danny Pollock, son of James W. and Mattie Louise (Reed) Pollock. Danny was born Aug. 21, 1950 in Hohenwald. They are divorced.

Clara Maxine Graves, born Aug. 8, 1920, Ethridge, Lawrence County, married Oct. 21, 1939 in Athens, AL to James Lester Sanders, son of Conor Lofton and Lena Hullet (Fisher) Sanders. James was born Oct. 12, 1916 in Waverly, TN, died Oct. 30, 1974 in Columbia, and is buried in Polk Memorial Gardens. Their children are: Betty Carolyn Sanders, born Sept. 20, 194?; Jo Ann Sanders, born April 30, 1942 in Columbia; Barbara Sue Sanders (Feb. 8, 1944-March 4, 1944); James Anson "Jimmy" Sanders, born Oct. 9, 1947; and Earl Wayne Sanders, born Dec. 9, 1952.

Gladys Thelma Graves, born Dec. 27, 1922, Cross Bridges, Maury County, died when lightning struck her on March 18, 1927 in Cross Bridges. She is buried in Cedar Hill Cemetery.

Dorsie Burns Anson Graves, born Dec. 9, 1924 in Cross Bridges, married Joyce Cantrell. Their children were: Lera Gail Graves, Brenda Kay Graves, Larry Houston Graves, Mark Allen Graves, Tauline Joyce Graves and Genah Ann Graves.

Willodine Graves, "Deanie", twin, born March 2, 1927 in Cross Bridges, died Oct. 22, 1980 in Huntsville, AL, and is buried in Hillcrest Memorial Gardens, Shelbyville. She married first to Robert Smith and second to Jerry Lee Kelly. One child, Gloria Jean Smith.

Geraldine Graves, twin, born March 2, 1927 Cross Bridges, married Jessie Allen "Jack" Gannon. Their children: Shirley Marie Gannon and Dianne Gannon.

Bobby Graves, twin, born May 15, 1929 in Cross Bridges, died Aug. 7, 1987 Columbia, and is buried in Polk Memorial Garden, Columbia. He married first to Gwen Walker, second to Peggy Sullivan and third to Sue Cannady. Children: Catherine Marie Graves, Debra Ann Graves, Gwen Allen Graves and Robert Anson Graves.

Billy Graves, twin, born May 15, 1929 in Cross Bridges, married Shirley Dixon. Their children: Pamela Graves, Cynthia Graves, Terry Lee Graves, Vanessa Graves and Billy Gaye Graves.

James Eslic Graves, born Feb. 14, 1933 in Cross Bridges, had polio and died March 7, 1937, and is buried in Cedar Hill Cemetery.

Frankeline Graves, born April 21, 1935 in Cross Bridges, married Davis Harwell. Their children: Sharon Sue Harwell, Ramonia Lynn Harwell, Frank Davis Harwell and Sammie Kent Harwell. *Submitted by Clara Graves Sanders, Columbia, Tennessee.*

CHARLIE GRAVES, (1885-1960), Charlie Olenthus Graves, son of Henry Lee and Louizar (Anderson) Graves, was born May 16, 1885 in Perry County, died March 16, 1960 in Houston, Texas; buried Katie Highway Cemetery in Houston. He was married Nov. 14, 1904 in Perry County to Addie Isabelle "Bell" Kincaid, daughter of Mark A. and Elizabeth (Lancaster) Kincaid. Bell was born June 29, 1888 in Perry County, died March 29, 1964 in Houston, Texas; buried Katie Highway Cemetery.

Children of Charlie and Bell (Kincaid) Graves:

Horace Richard Graves, born Feb. 2, 1906 in Hohenwald, was married Nov. 3, 1934 to Louanna Ingram. They had one child, Charles Richard Graves, born Oct. 15, 1944, Memphis.

Cecil Raymond Graves, born Aug. 13, 1907

155

in Hohenwald, TN, died ___, married July 6, 1931 to Ona Mae Turnage. They had two children: Betty Ann Graves, born March 2, 1932 in Blytheville, AR, married July 7, 1953 to James Mosley, born Oct. 6, 1926 in Gosnell, AR. They had three children - Clifford Ray Mosley, born May 26, 1952, married Dec. 28, 1971 to Terri Ann Holbrooks, born Aug. 22, 1953, Jamie Ann Mosley, born Oct. 10, 1954 and Jackie Lynn Mosley, born May 31, 1956, married June 9, 1972 to James Barlow Christian; and Barbara Lee Graves, born Sept. 24, 1939 in Blytheville, AR, married June 1, 1957 to Larry Neill Perrin, born Jan. 26, 1937 in Newport, AR. They had two children - Cynthia Lorraine Perrin, born Dec. 24, 1958 in Rochester, New Hampshire and Larry Neill Perrin, born Jan. 25, 1963 in West Memphis, AR.

Herman Osteen Graves, born Oct. 27, 1909 in Hohenwald, TN, married three times. First on Sept. 22, 1942 to Martha Baker, second to Mabel, they have one daughter, Patty Graves, and third to Elise.

Melista Pearl Graves, born Sept. 27, 1911 in Hohenwald, TN, married Sept. 23, 1942 to Joseph Applebaum. They had two children: Pearl Ann Applebaum, born Sept. 4, 1944, was married Dec. 24, 1966 to Michael Stentz and had one child, Michael Stentz Jr.; and Lana Joe Applebaum, born Aug. 20, 1947, was married June 10, 1967 to Wayne Banks. They were divorced April 1971.

James Roy Graves, born Aug. 14, 1917 in Newbern, TN, married three times. First to Evelyn Campbell and had one son, James Roy Graves Jr., born Sept. 1940. He was married three times: no issue by first wife, three sons by second wife, but no other information, and third wife is Gerlinde Gudrun, one child, Karen Graves. James Sr. married second to Bobby Rhodes, no issue and third to Kathleen Jordan, two children: Hal Graves and Jan Graves.

Geneva Frances Graves, born June 2, 1920 in Newbern, TN, was married March 24, 1940 to Robert Montgomery Graves. They had three children: Judith Graves, born Dec. 31, 1940; Diana Pearl Graves, born March 25, 1943, was married June 26, 1961 to Marvin Lovic Roberts and had two children - Kelly Kay Roberts, born Sept. 27, 1964, and Eric Craig Roberts, born Oct. 14, 1967; and Robert Montgomery Graves Jr., born Feb. 18, 1946, died Feb. 19, 1946.

Phillip Reed Graves, born May 12, 1926 in Blytheville, AR, married twice. First to Norma, no issue, and second to Mary Geneva Bunn, one child, Phyllis Graves.

ELIJAH THOMAS GRAVES SR., (1830-1892),

son of Isaac Lee and Mary D. (Lincoln) Graves, was born Jan. 17, 1830 in Maury County, died May 28, 1892 at Flatwoods, and is buried in Graves Cemetery on Sinking Creek. Marie Rasbury said, "My grandfather was called "Doc". He was a cripple and was not strong enough to fight in the Civil War."

"Doc" married Susan Hickerson, daughter of John and Nancy (Treece) Hickerson. Susie was born Aug. 1, 1831, died May 5, 1895, and is also buried in Graves Cemetery.

The source of Nancy's maiden name comes from her granddaughter, Ida Sharp of Savannah, TN. Susan and E.T. Graves signed the deed to the property of John Hickerson in 1868 (Perry County Deed Book O, 1873-1876, pages 239-241.)

Elijah Thomas Graves Sr.

The following is found in the Christian Advocate on Thursday, March 16, 1893, Page 13, Column 1.

"ELIJAH T. GRAVES was born in Marshall County, Tenn., Jan 17, 1830; and died at Flat Woods, Tenn., May 28, 1892. He was converted in boyhood and joined the M.E. Church, South, when about sixteen years of age. He was married to Miss Susan Hickerson, Aug 8, 1848. Of this happy union his wife and six children survive. He was a member of the Sinking Creek Church for forty-six years; class leader, steward, and subscriber for the Christian Advocate for more than twenty years. He was a kind husband and father, and his house was a lifelong home for Methodist Preachers. After one month of sickness it was plain that God was calling him to "come over and be at rest." And as his loved ones gathered around he hopefully spoke of the faith that had sustained him through life, and calmly pillowing his weary head upon it in a dying hour, left strong consolation to those who lingered by his bedside of the all-sufficiency of God's grace and power to sustain even unto the end. "At evening time it shall be light." Austin L. Prewett Jr."

Their children: Nancy Mary Jane Graves, born Aug. 6, 1853, died July 22, 1928 at the home of her brother, Tom, in Wayne County, and is buried in Graves Cemetery. It is said Jane was always "sorta sickly". Marie says when she dried the dishes, she dried them sitting in a chair. Wherever she went, she carried her feather bed and rode on top of it in the wagon. Marie also said Aunt Jane could speak Dutch. Family tradition says her grandmother was Dutch.

John Isaac Graves "Bud" (Aug. 21, 1855-Feb. 1, 1926) married Lou E. Burns and lived in Big Spring, Texas.

Frank Abraham Lawrence Graves, born July 25, 1857, married Sarah Tatum.

Elijah Thomas Graves Jr., born Feb. 7, 1860, married first to Mary Cotton and second to Elizabeth Churchwell.

Sarah Elizabeth "Betty" Graves, born Oct. 1862, married Thomas Henry Tharp.

Samuel B. Graves, born May 29, 1865, died June 21, 1896 with a fever, and is buried in Graves Cemetery. Unmarried.

Susan Caroline Graves, born April 1871, died May 27, 1935, and is buried in Graves Cemetery. She married Dec. 16, 1912 in Perry County to A.F. Turnbow, sometimes called "Bud" Sanford. No issue. *Submitted by Willodean Rasbury Weldon.*

ELIJAH THOMAS GRAVES JR., (1860-1947),

Elijah Thomas Graves Jr., son of "Doc" and Susie (Hickerson) Graves, was born Feb. 7, 1860 in Perry County, died April 27, 1947 from a heart attack while visiting his daughter, Delphia Sharp, in Flatwoods, and is buried in the Graves Cemetery on Sinking Creek in Perry County. So many people came to his funeral at the Flatwoods Methodist Church that the floor gave way during the service. In later years, he made his home with his daughter, Marie Rasbury.

Tom was married on Feb. 17, 1880 in Perry County to Mary Elizabeth Cotton, daughter of Jonathan/John Irvin and Mary Jane (Dabbs) Cotton. Mary was born July 27, 1862, died Dec. 25, 1894 according to her tombstone, and is buried in Graves Cemetery.

Tom married secondly, on Nov. 27, 1896 in Wayne County to Susan Elizabeth "Lizzie" Churchwell, daughter of Ulysses and Molly (Rochelle) Churchwell. Lizzie was born Nov. 28, 1878 in Riverside, Wayne County, died July 21, 1921 in her home across Buffalo River from Ashland, Wayne County, and is buried in the small Churchwell Cemetery in Lewis County with her two small children, and her parents. Lizzie was named for her grandmother, Susan Elizabeth (Duckworth) Churchwell.

Children of Tom and Mary Graves: Delphia Izora Graves, born March 9, 1881, married S.T. Sharp. They lived in Flatwoods.

Dellar Graves, born June 16, 1883, died young, and is buried in Graves Cemetery.

Lochie Rankin Graves, born Feb. 17, 1886,

Elijah Thomas Graves Jr. Family. Left to right: Sid Rochelle and Agnes and baby, Tom Graves, Marie, Lucille, Grandmother Lizzie holding Moncey, Vinny, Perry, Lockie, Flavey standing behind William.

married Dr. O.A. Kirk. They lived in Flatwoods and Linden.

Walter W. Graves, born June 2, 1888, died young, and is buried in Graves Cemetery.

Thomas Flavy Graves, born June 15, 1890, married Annie Anderson. They lived in Gibson County.

Perry Telford Graves, born June 15, 1892, married Blanche Bastin. They lived in Wayne and Perry Counties.

Ernest Graves, born Nov. 1895?. This is the birth date in the Tom Graves Bible. He died young and is buried in Graves Cemetery.

Children of Tom and Lizzie Graves:

Infant, born and died Oct. 7, 1897 in Buffalo Valley, Lewis County, and is buried in the Churchwell Family Cemetery in Lewis County.

Vinny Leal Graves, born May 12, 1899, married J.B. Harrison. They lived in Cincinnati, OH and had one child, James Thomas "Buddy" Harrison.

William Allen Graves, born Dec. 13, 1900, married Nellie Shann. Three children: Jewel Dean, Walter and Jerry Paul. They lived in Lewis County.

Marie Frances Graves, born Nov. 11, 1902, married Jan. 1, 1922 in Wayne County to Clyde Rasbury. They lived in Wayne County. Their children are Imogene Parsley of Knoxville, Willodean Weldon of Temple Hills, MD, Ed and Tom Rasbury of Hohenwald and Katherine Fancher of Chamblee, GA.

Lucille Elizabeth Graves, born July 10, 1905 in Wayne County married Charlie Bates. Children: J.T., Christene, J.R., Charlene, Lorence, Haskiel and Mary. She lives in Hickman County.

Moncey Graves (Jan. 27, 1909-Oct. 5, 1909) is buried in the Churchwell Family Cemetery.

Mary Tom Graves, born June 19, 1911, married Berry C. Soper. Their children: Dr. Richard Soper, Murfreesboro, and Charles Soper, Spring Hill.

Bascom Waters Graves, born Aug. 7, 1914, married Gertrude Schroder. They lived in Ohio. Children: Jackie and Mary Tom. *Submitted by C.E. Rasbury.*

HENRY LEE (JACK) GRAVES, (1866-1940), son of Isaac Lee and Parthena (Ledbetter) Graves, born April 19, 1866 in Perry County, died Sept. 11, 1940 in Hazel Green, AL; buried in Graves Cemetery. Henry Lee was married twice. First on Jan. 3, 1884 in Perry County to Louizar E. Anderson, daughter of Joseph M. and Martha Ann (Satterfield) Anderson. Louizar was born Nov. 25, 1864, died Sept. 28, 1904, buried in Graves Cemetery. Second, he married on Oct. 5, 1907 in Lewis County to Mary Maude Lancaster. Mary Maude was born June 27, 1880, died Oct. 19, 1949 and is buried in Graves Cemetery.

Children of Henry Lee and Louizar (Anderson) Graves: Charlie Olenthus Graves, born May 16, 1885, married Addie Isabelle Kincaid; Minnie Jane Graves, born Dec. 6, 1887, married Edward Sherman Marshall; Joseph Lee Graves, born May 3, 1891, married Bertha Grover; Mattie Ann Graves, born Jan. 16, 1893, married Rabe Nichols; and Willie Luther Graves, born June 19, 1886, married Estalee Hickerson.

Children of Henry Lee and Mary M. (Lancaster) Graves:

Ila Marie Graves, born Feb. 27, 1909 in Lewis County, married Elzie Browning. Their children: Elzie P. Browning Jr., born and died Sept. 26, 1925 in Lewis County, and is buried Lewis Park Cemetery; Ruth Marie Browning, born Aug. 21, 1927, married first to Dale Gilliam and second to Melvin Brewer; William Parks Browning (July 25, 1930-Sept. 27, 1930) is buried in Hines Cemetery; Doris Wayne Browning, born Oct. 23, 1939, married June Gaffin; James Turner Browning, twin, born Dec. 10, 1941, married Jean Guffey; and Mary Joyce Browning, twin, born Dec. 10, 1941 in Lewis County, married Carl Wilkerson.

The Henry Lee (Jack) Graves Family

Edith Byron Graves, born Nov. 1, 1911 in Lewis County, married twice. First to John C. Grey (1887-1936) and second on Dec. 24, 1942 to Yeiser Trull (1914-1984). Her children: Johnnie Louise Grey, born Nov. 18, 1930 in Perry County, died Sept. 28, 1978 and is buried in Graves Cemetery, married Richard Castleman; and Mary Gladys Grey, born June 3, 1932 in Perry County, married Jan. 11, 1953 in Corinth, MS to James Roden, son of Ab and Bess (Anderson) Roden. James was born Feb. 14, 1927, died March 7, 1980 in an airplane crash near Pine Mountain in Georgia, and is buried in Graves Cemetery.

Edgar Ervin Graves, born April 14, 1915 in Perry County, died Sept. 7, 1971 in Chicago, IL; is buried in Graves Cemetery, married Dec. 24, 1940 in Huntsville, AL to Opal Clara Woosley. Their children: Shirley Ann Graves, born Oct. 26, 1943 in Hohenwald, married Nov. 15, 1961 to Steve Frank Rozwalka; Mary Helen Graves, born Feb. 6, 1952 in Hohenwald, living in Park Forest, IL; and Barbara June Graves, born June 11, 1955 in Blue Island, IL, married Sept. 16, 1972 to Lloyd Schiemann.

Opal Augusta Graves, born July 15, 1917 in Lewis County, died Oct. 25, 1966 in Huntsville, AL; and is buried in Plain View Cemetery, Hazel Green, AL, married Dec. 20, 1941 to Haskel Benjamin DeWeese. Their children: James Lee DeWeese, born Aug. 29, 1946 in Huntsville, AL, married Jan. 22, 1971 to Mary Elizabeth McCollum; and Linda Jo DeWeese, born June 12, 1952 in Huntsville, AL, married June 1971 to Louie Cleveland Burrough.

Rex Elmer Graves, born Aug. 17, 1919 at Dyersburg, TN, died on a Friday in October 1977, and is buried in Arab, AL. He was married twice. First to Ruth Chambers and had two children, Rex Elmer Graves Jr., born Sept. 30, 1944 in Huntsville, AL, married Oct. 29, 1965, and John Chamber Graves, born March 21, 1947 in Huntsville, AL. Second Rex Elmer married on Aug. 29, 1958 to Ellen Palmer, one son, Michael Lynn Graves, born June 5, 1963 in Arab, Marshall County, AL. *Submitted by Lynnell McKeethen.*

IDA MAE GRAVES, (1890-1961), daughter of Lawrence and Sally (Tatum) Graves, was born Jan. 19, 1890 in Flatwoods, Perry County; died April 2, 1961 in her home in Lewis County, and is buried in Dabbs Cemetery, Lewis County. She moved to Wayne County with her parents in 1904. She married Feb. 7, 1915 to Ollie Brown Cothran, a farmer and son of Zeke and Roena Catherine (Fite) Cothran. Ollie was born Oct. 13, 1883, died June 22, 1969 in Lewis County and is buried in Old Dabbs Cemetery. Ida was baptized by Bro. Skelton sometime in August 1909 in Ashland Methodist Church in Wayne County. Ollie was baptized Sept. 12, 1929 in Ashland Methodist Church by Bro. Parks. Their children:

Ordie Brown Cothran, born Dec. 28, 1915 in Lewis County, married July 1938 in Florence, AL to Nadine Robnett, daughter of Dodson and Hessie (Davis) Robnett. Nadine was born Aug. 19, 1921 in Lewis County. The family live in Hohenwald and attend the Methodist Church there. They had one child, Jane Evelyn Cothran, born Dec. 16, 1948, married Michael Santi and had two children, Emily Jane Santi and Mark Michael Santi.

Sarah Rovine Cothran, born April 28, 1917 in Lewis County, married June 18, 1935 in Columbia to Carl Alexander Poore, son of Lonzo and Oxie (Vaughn) Poore. Sarah married second June 20, 1947 to Lawrence Bryant. Their children: Ronald Lee Poore, born Jan. 31, 1938 in Lewis County, married Alva Jo Warren, daughter of Ralph and Melvina (Higgins) Warren. Ronnie and Alva Jo are divorced and Ronnie married Lela Warren. His children are Keith Warren, Ricky Lee and Tracy Lynn Poore; and Jerry Brown Poore, born Aug. 13, 1940 in Decatur County, TN; died Jan. 7, 1960 in Davidson County, and is buried in Swiss Cemetery, Hohenwald.

Robert Gordon Cothran, born April 17, 1918 in Wayne County, married Dec. 22, 1940 in Hohenwald to Hazel Myrtle Bromley, daughter of Fred and Mary (Smyth) Bromley of Wayne County. Hazel was born Sept. 12, 1915 in Searcy County, AR. Rob was baptized Oct. 5, 1933 in the Ashland Methodist Church by Bro. H. McLemore. Hazel and her parents were also members of the Ashland Methodist Church. Their children: Joe Brown Cothran, born Aug. 13, 1945 in Hohenwald, married Sept. 1, 1967 in Jackson, Madison County, TN to Mary Carlice Webb, daughter of James H. and M. Rebecca (Russell) Webb. Joe did a tour of duty in Vietnam while he was in the USMC. The family are Methodists and farmers. Their children are Harold Webb Cothran and Russell Gordon Cothran; Robert Fred "Jackie" Cothran, born July 12, 1947 in Boyce Clinic, Hohenwald, married Sept. 18, 1970 in Corinth, MS to Mary Melinda Hughes, daughter of H.D. and Julia Anna (McKain) Hughes Jr. Jack chose the Army for his career and is presently a Captain. Their children are Tiffany Marie, Mary Elizabeth, Robert Stanley (deceased) and Robert Fred Cothran Jr.; Peggy Ann Cothran, born March 2, 1952 in Lawrenceburg, married Dec. 29, 1973 in the

Buffalo Valley Methodist Church in Lewis County to Thomas William Davis Jr., son of Thomas and Geraldine (Whitney) Davis. Peggy is a RN. The family live in Paris, TN and are Baptists; and Samuel Morris Cothran, born Oct. 21, 1958 in Lawrenceburg, married July 15, 1983, in the home of his parents in Lewis County, to Margaret Ann Rouse, daughter of Charles Rouse. *Submitted by Ordie Cothran, Hohenwald, Tennessee.*

ISAAC GRAVES, (1810-1894), born Nov. 1, 1810, in North Carolina, died 1894 in Perry County. He came to Maury County, TN at a very young age and lived in the part that was cut off into Marshall County. His Land Grant #28680 calls for 190 acres in Perry County, dated April 21, 1847. He married twice and was the father of nine children by each wife.

Isaac Lee Graves 1810-1894

Isaac married first Nov. 19, 1828 in Maury County to Mary D. Lincoln, born Jan. 6, 1807 in North Carolina and died Feb. 9, 1856 on Sinking Creek and is buried there, but not Graves Cemetery.

The parents of neither Isaac nor Mary are known for sure, but the only other Graves family in the 1830 Census of Maury County is Thomas Graves, who died about 1836 and Isaac Lee was administrator of his estate. Thomas and Margaret Graves were received by experience into the Rock Creek Baptist Church in 1823. One Thomas Graves married Peggy Wall on March 9, 1803 in Randolph County, NC. The siblings of Isaac Lee are Silva, Sherwood and John H. Graves. Silva married Leonard Thompson, John married Sallie Williams and Sherwood married Anna Bagley.

Elijah Lincoln and his wife, Jane, are mentioned in early Maury County Court Records. Mary and Isaac Lee named their first born son Elijah Thomas, and the first born daughter Margaret Jane.

Isaac, married secondly Oct. 28, 1858 in Lewis County to Parthena Ledbetter, daughter of Johnson and Jane (Wade) Ledbetter. She was born Feb. 12, 1837, died about April 10, 1912 in Perry County. Both Isaac and Parthena are buried in Graves Cemetery.

Children of Mary Graves: Elijah Thomas Graves, born Jan. 17, 1830 in Maury County, married Susan Hickerson; Margaret Jane Graves, born Feb. 26, 1831; Sherwood James Graves, born June 17, 1832; Isaac Brantley Graves, born Sept. 1, 1835, died 1870-1880 period and was first person buried in Graves Cemetery. The story - He was plowing in the field where the cemetery is now, stopped to rest at the end of a row, and told his brother working with him, "When I die I want to be buried under this tree. There is always a cool breeze blowing here." Within the week, he died and was buried there in an unmarked grave; thus was the beginning of the Graves Cemetery. Brantley married Eliza Ledbetter, daughter of Johnson and Jane Ledbetter; Silva Elizabeth Graves, born June 1836; Mary Ann Graves, born Nov. 3, 1839, married George Rawdon/Roden; Zilpha Caroline Graves, born Sept. 3, 1841, married James Turnbow; Sarah Emmaline Graves, born Feb. 2, 1844, died unmarried; and John A. Leonard Graves, born Feb. 3, 1848, married Drucilla Catherine Dowdy.

Children of Parthena Graves: Elizon Taylor Graves, born Sept. 12, 1859, married Mary Garner; William Johnson Graves (Jan. 31, 1861-Oct. 9, 1861); Martha Adaline Graves, born Aug. 10, 1863, married John Tole; Henry Lee Graves, born April 19, 1866, married first to Louizar Anderson and second to Mary Maude Lancaster; Eliza Malinda Graves, born Aug. 27, 1868, married Commodore Dabbs; Pitts Brazhere Graves, born Aug. 18, 1870, married Margaret Smith; Parthena Savannah Graves, born April 25, 1873, married Irvin Cotton; Emery Parlee Graves, born June 23, 1878, married Daniel Ary; and Andy Cook Graves, born June 19, 1882, married first to Minnie Cooper and second to Nancy Duncan. *Submitted by Katherine Rasbury Fancher.*

JOSEPH LEE GRAVES, (1891-1954), son of Henry Lee and Louizar (Anderson) Graves, was born May 3, 1891 in Perry County, died April 7, 1954 in Dover, OH; and is buried in Maple Grove Cemetery in Dover. He was married Oct. 16, 1910 in Hohenwald to Bertha Catalina Grover, daughter of Aaron Pryne and Susan Adelia (Schubert) Grover. She was born April 22, 1893 in Hohenwald, died June 9, 1945 in Dover and is buried in Maple Grove Cemetery.

Children of Joseph Lee and Bertha (Grover) Graves:

Stella Marie Graves, born Aug. 17, 1911 in Lewis County, was married Dec. 2, 1930 to Alvin Moser. Their children were: Doris Marie Moser, born Sept. 5, 1931, married May 19, 1950 to Merlyn Harold Keener; Carol Ann Moser, born Dec. 15, 1932 in Dover, was married Aug. 19, 1951 to Harry Duane Allison. He was born June 24, 1931 in Dover and is the son of Harry J. and Amanda (Powell) Allison; Alvin Eugene Moser, born Aug. 28, 1934 in Dover, OH, was married June 10, 1956 in Dover to Frances Carolyn Bair, daughter of George W. and Helen D. (Knisley) Bair. Frances was born May 29, 1938 in Dover; Jane Louise Moser, born Feb. 28, 1936, married Oct. 22, 1960 to Leonard Lawrence Liotti. Deceased Aug. 28, 1987, buried in Indianapolis, IN; Bertha Mae "Peggy" Moser, born Oct. 25, 1940, was married Dec. 27, 1960 to Larry Joe Osburn; David Allen Moser, born Nov. 12, 1947, was married June 11, 1971 to Cherry Miller; and Janet Kay Moser, born Dec. 19, 1949, was married March 20, 1976 to Donald Scott Robinson.

Joseph Russell Graves, born Feb. 6, 1914 in Smyrna, Rutherford County, TN, was married Aug. 14, 1937 to Charlotte Rinehart and had two children, Karen Graves, married Thomas Armstrong Jr. and Jill Marie Graves, married James Wallace.

Nellie Lee Graves, born Oct. 20, 1916 in Perry County, was married Feb. 23, 1935 in West Virginia to Harry Albert Dummermuth. He was born Sept. 5, 1917 in New Philadelphia, OH and was the son of Albert W. and Nora (Henney) Dummermuth. Harry and Nellie had four children: Nancy Lee Dummermuth, born Sept. 23, 1935 in New Philadelphia, OH, married Charles A. Wasylik; Barbara Ann Dummermuth, born Nov. 24, 1938, was married Aug. 1, 1964 in Anchorage, Alaska to Lee Friese; Judith Emily Dummermuth, born Feb. 13, 1941, married July 1965 in Arizona to Burley Geane Lane; and Suzanne Dummermuth, born Feb. 2, 1946, was married in Arizona to Michael C. LeGrand.

William Pryne Graves, born Dec. 6, 1918 in Perry County, TN, died Dec. 10, 1985, married Katherine Patterson. They had three children: Joanne Graves, married Robert; Cynthia Graves married Robert Wood; and William H. Graves.

Carl Edward Graves, born May 29, 1921 in Dover, OH, was married Jan. 2, 1943 to Mella Miller, daughter of Frank and Corday (Latham) Miller. Mella was born Oct. 6, 1923, Newcomerstown, OH. Carl and Mella had three children: Bonnie Jo Graves, born Aug. 9, 1946, was married July 27, 1974 to Harry E. Wood, born July 27, 19??. One child, Michelle Lynn Wood, born Feb. 1, 1976; Linda Margaret Graves, born March 4, 1950, was married June 23, 1973 to John Michael Gorrell; and Edward Carl Graves, born March 24, 1956. Source of information: Marie Graves Moser, Dover, OH and Mella Graves, Lynnell McKeethen and Marjorie Graves. *Submitted by Marie Graves Moser.*

LAWRENCE GRAVES, (1857-1930) Franklin Lawrence Abraham Graves, son of Elijah Thomas "Doc" and Susie (Hickerson) Graves, born June 25, 1857 in Perry County, died Nov. 19, 1930 in Maury County, and is buried in Graves Cemetery on Sinking Creek in Perry County. He married Jan. 11, 1885 in Perry County to Sarah Carolyn Tatum, daughter of Sublet Allen and Margaret Ann (Miller) Tatum. Sallie was born Jan. 9, 1866, died Dec. 15, 1916 in Wayne County, and is also buried in Graves Cemetery. Lawrence was a farmer. The family lived in Perry, Wayne, Lawrence and Maury Counties, TN.

The Lawrence Graves Family

Their children: Oscar Ransom Graves, born June 24, 1887, married Roxie Lafferty.

Ida Mae Graves, born Jan. 19, 1890, married Ollie B. Cothran.

Mary Flora Graves (Jan. 15, 1893-Oct. 10, 1893), buried in Graves Cemetery.

Arthur Anson Graves, born March 4, 1894, married Cleo Lafferty.

Franklin Eslic Graves, born June 7, 1896 at Flatwoods, died May 5, 1930 at Cross Bridges, Maury County, as the result of an automobile accident, and is buried in Cedar Hill Cemetery, Highway 412 in Maury County. Unmarried.

Archie G. Graves (June 15, 1898-April 1, 1904), buried in Graves Cemetery.

Leonard Wallace "Joe" Graves, born Sept. 23, 1900 at Flatwoods, died Nov. 28, 1957 in Lawrenceburg, and is buried at Mimosa Cemetery, Lawrence County. He married July 23, 1922 in Lawrenceburg to Laura Smith, daughter of Whitson and Valeria (Beeler) Smith. Their children: Anita Elizabeth Graves, born July 19, 1923, Lawrenceburg, married Robert Fowler Wright; Maxine Laverne Graves, born Aug. 20, 1925, married Dec. 20, 1945 to Harry Hoyd Sadler; and Billy Joe Graves, born Jan. 19, 1934, married Sept. 14, 1952 to Gail Brock Denson.

Lillie Ila Graves, born Feb. 8, 1903 at Flatwoods, died Aug. 9, 1978 at Lawrenceburg, and is buried in Mimosa Cemetery. She married first to Avery Coffey and second on Nov. 1, 1933 to Jess Smith. Her children: Elise Coffey (Feb. 4, 1925-Nov. 25, 1926), buried in Ethridge Cemetery, Lawrence County; Gerald Lawrence Coffey, born Feb. 26, 1926 at Lawrenceburg, married Anita Reed; and Elizabeth Ann Smith, born Dec. 14, 1935, married George Franklin Lanning.

Olney Clyde Graves, born April 24, 1905 in Wayne County, married Dec. 25, 1929 to Charlotte Smith, daughter of Whitson E. and Valeria (Beeler) Smith. Charlotte was born June 23, 1910. She lives in Lawrenceburg. Their children: June Carolyn Graves, born June 2, 1935 at Ethridge, Lawrence County, married April 6, 1955 to Ludon Sandlin; Marilyn Joyce Graves, born April 4, 1937 at Lawrenceburg, married Sept. 7, 1958 to Coy Eugene Belew, son of Jack and Edna (Coleman) Belew; and Shirley Jean Graves, born Sept. 8, 1945, married July 28, 1967 to Guy Eddie Bates Jr., son of Guy Eddie Sr. and Clara Bates.

Jessie Irene Graves, born Nov. 7, 1908 in Wayne County, married Sept. 9, 1927 to Marvin Tilman "Doc" Holt, son of Alex and Lou Visia (Turner) Holt. "Doc" was born Dec. 29, 1904 in Maury County, died May 8, 1969 at Columbia, and is buried at Cross Bridges Baptist Church Cemetery. Their children: Marvin Tilman Holt Jr., born Sept. 6, 1928 at Cross Bridges, married Imogene Bryant; Mildred Glenn Holt, born Feb. 12, 1930, married Garland Locke; Frances Holt, born July 4, 1931, married Oct. 17, 1948 to Kenneth Voss. No issue; Norman Graves Holt, born Nov. 12, 1940, married Joan Ghist; and Shelia Holt, born Jan. 19, 1949 in Maury County, married first to Jimmy Tucker and second to Jerry Walker.

Two infants, no dates, both buried in Graves Cemetery. Submitted by Bill Graves.

MATTIE ANN GRAVES, (1893-1977), daughter of Henry Lee and Louizar (Anderson) Graves, was born Jan. 16, 1893 in Perry County, died Nov. 27, 1977 in Evansville, IN, and is buried in Sunset Memorial Gardens, Evansville. She was married June 11, 1911 in Lewis County to Rabe Daley Nichols, son of Marion Franklin and Martha Jane (Holley) Nichols from Giles County. Rabe was born Sept. 29, 1886 in Giles County, died Nov. 29, 1958 in Evansville, and is also buried in Sunset Memorial Gardens.

Children of Rabe and Mattie (Graves) Nichols:

Arthur Paul Nichols, born May 20, 1912 at Allens Creek in Lawrence County, TN, died Feb. 21, 1980, and is buried in Sunset Memorial Garden, Evansville. He was married twice. First on Sept. 2, 1942 to Juanita Abel and second on Sept. 26, 1953 to Louise Garrett. Louise died in Jan. 1978.

Virgil Ray Nichols, born Jan. 8, 1916 in Hohenwald, died Aug. 7, 1916, and is buried in Grassie Valley Cemetery, Lewis County.

Vera Nell Nichols, born May 18, 1921, Schubert, Lewis County, died Oct. 25, 1986 and is buried in Sunset Memorial Garden, Evansville. She was married twice. First on Nov. 7, 1941 to Lynn Cleveland Volk, son of Joseph Cleveland and Mary (Hufnagel) Volk. He was born July 21, 1920 in Vanderburg County, IN, died March 10, 1968 in Evansville, IN, and is buried in Sunset Memorial Gardens. Vera married second on Nov. 30, 1973 to Harland J. Schnell.

Children of Lynn and Vera (Nichols) Volk:

Lynnell Volk, born Sept. 12, 1942 in Evansville, Vanderburg County, IN. She was married on Aug. 25, 1961 to Jack Doyle McKeethen, son of James David and Hazel Mae (Oxford) McKeethen.

Paula Michele Volk, born March 15, 1948 in Evansville, was married March 25, 1966 to Robert D. Weir, son of Robert and Gloria (Baker) Weir. He was born May 16, 1947.

Children of Jack and Lynnell (Volk) McKeethen:

Shannon Kaye McKeethen, born March 19, 1962, Evansville, was married Dec. 7, 1985 in Spencer County, IN to James Harold Seiler.

Drista Lynn McKeethen, born Dec. 29, 1964, Evansville, married Jan. 26, 1985 to Larry Ray Beeler. They have one child, Dustin Ray Beeler, born Aug. 16, 1985.

Jack Doyle (Jason) McKeethen, born June 3, 1967, Evansville.

Jeremy Kyle McKeethen, born June 25, 1975, Evansville.

Children of Robert and Michele (Volk) Weir:

Lisa Michele Weir, born Nov. 30, 1966 in Evansville, was married Oct. 18, 1986 to Scott Alan Brown.

Cynthia Lynn Weir, born July 24, 1971 in Evansville.

Stories from Lynnell are as follows:

Mattie (Graves) Nichols said, "Grandma Parthena Graves liked to smoke a pipe and she always carried it in her apron pocket. She wouldn't smoke just any pipe, but always smoked ones that Grandpa Isaac would carve from the root of a shrub." Lynnell continues, "When my grandparents, Mattie and Rabe Nichols, moved from Tennessee to Indiana in 1924, they settled in the community of Howell, which was near the railroad yards. Each night, while lying in bed, Mattie would hear the lonesome whistle of the trains as they left the yards. This caused such a longing for her home in Tennessee that she cried herself to sleep each night for weeks." *Source: Lynnell McKeethen and Marjorie Graves.*

OSBIE BROWN (TICK) GRAVES AND DOROTHY LEE PEVAHOUSE, live in Flatwoods in Perry County. Osbie Brown was born on Cedar Creek in Perry County on Feb. 16, 1919, the son of Pleas Brown (1891-1944) and Sally Mae Treadwell Graves (1892-1961) and the grandson of Susan Graves (husband unknown), and Daniel Webster (Webb) Treadwell (1866-1942) and Dilly Inman Treadwell (1869-1933). Osbie had one sister, Myrtle Louise (1912-1977), married Alfred Kelley, they had three children: Melva Dean, Joe and James. Osbie also had four brothers: Clyde Henry (1914-1993), married Weda L. Treadwell, they had three children - Dorothy, Osbie and Reba; James Claude (1916), married Lillie Anderson, they had three sons - Howard, Billy and Eddie Joe; Robert Webster (1922-1967), married Era Nell Woods, they had three children - Dianne, Brenda and Jeff; and Melvin Arnold (1927-1928).

Osbie B. and Dorothy Pevahouse Graves

Dorothy Lee was born in Perry County on Dec. 31, 1924, the daughter of Lee Roy (1901-1985) and Margaret Zora Bryson Pevahouse (1901-1987) and the granddaughter of Elijah and Margaret (Mag) Williams Pevahouse and George Washington Bryson (1869-1944) and Nancy Kilpatrick Bryson (1868-1902) and the step granddaughter of Sarah Elizabeth Graham Bridges Bryson (1883-1974). Dorothy has three sisters: Lottie Loudean (1922), married Luther Galloway; Martha Mae (1931), married Edward Hubert Carroll, they have one son, John; and Nona Faye (1938), married Jimmy Lee Johnston, they have two children, Doug and Andrea.

Osbie served his Country in World War II from March 10, 1942 to Oct. 31, 1945, while on leave he married Dorothy on July 18, 1942 in Corinth, MS. After the war, they moved to Lewis County for three years, then in the late 1940's to Sinking Creek in Perry County. They moved to Flatwoods in the early 1950's where they now reside. They have one daughter, Margaret Elaine Graves, born July 12, 1958, she has lived all her life in Flatwoods. She graduated from Perry County High School in 1977.

Osbie is a retired school bus driver, Dorothy is a retired factory worker. Osbie, Dorothy and Elaine are members of Chappell Memorial United Methodist Church in Flatwoods.

RANSOM GRAVES, (1887-1944), Oscar Ransom Graves, son of Lawrence and Sally (Tatum) Graves, was born June 24, 1887 in Flatwoods, died Feb. 29, 1944 in Shelbyville, with a heart attack, and is buried in Graves Cemetery, Perry County. He married Dec. 25, 1910 in Wayne County to Roxie Lafferty, daughter of

159

Will T. and Lou (McAnally) Lafferty. Roxie was born Feb. 7, 1891 in Wayne County, died July 23, 1947 in Spring Hill, Maury County and is buried in Graves Cemetery. Their children:

Ransom and Roxie (Lafferty) Graves and daughter, Reba.

Ozie Reba Graves, born Jan. 5, 1912 in Topsy, Wayne County, died June 1, 1981 in Columbia, and is buried in Neapolis Cemetery in Maury County. She married Aug. 23, 1930 in Pruitton, AL to Albert Patton. Their children: George Ransom Patton, born Sept. 14, 1932 in Maury County, married first to Shirley Padgett and second to Bethel Jo Crittendon; Miriam Jane Patton, born Aug. 27, 1936, married Russell Eugene Quarles; and Larry Joe Patton, born Dec. 30, 1944, married Deborah Boutwell.

Jewell Ventus Graves, born May 1, 1914 in Topsy, married Charles David Ingram. One child, Charles Marion Ingram, born July 14, 1945 in Maury County, married Susan Lee Sparkman.

Wilson Moore Graves, born Nov. 20, 1916 in Topsy, married March 4, 1939 in Florence, AL to Sarah Anglan Hargrove, daughter of Louis and Cleo (Bridy) Hargrove. Sarah was born Feb. 9, 1919 in Spring Hill, Maury County. Their children: Deanne Moore Graves, born Nov. 13, 1940 in Nashville, married first to Don Taylor and second to Robert Edward Hill; Mackie Marlene Graves, twin, born June 20, 1947 in Duluth, GA, married Steven Scott Fulmer; and Corkie Carlene Graves, twin, born June 20, 1947, married first to Randy Davis and second to Carey Michael Sink.

Thomas Ransom Graves, born Aug. 22, 1919 in Ethridge, Lawrence County, married Aug. 12, 1941 in Tuscumbia, AL to Evelyn Mangrum, daughter of Walter and Lovie (Haywood) Mangrum. Evelyn was born Nov. 16, 1922 in Columbia. Their children: Mary Tom Graves, born June 25, 1942 in Shelbyville, married Gerald Dan Watkins; Timothy Walter Graves, born April 2, 1944, married Frances Oleta Anderson; Rose Anne Graves, born May 13, 1947 in Columbia, married Douglas Wayne Williams; John Thomas Graves, born Aug. 29, 1949 in Columbia, married Regena Lynn. They are divorced; and Judy Lovie Graves, born Nov. 15, 1954, married Mitchell Lynn Johns.

Stella Mai Graves, born April 3, 1922 in Maury County, married Dec. 13, 1945 to Hugh Prince, born April 14, 1921. Their children: Stella Aloa Prince, born Sept. 9, 1946 in Maury County, married Gary Lee; Lola James Prince, born Nov. 27, 1947, married Winston Burnham; Allen Simpson Prince, born March 16, 1949, married Patsy McKenzie; Roxie Maude Prince, born June 11, 1952, married Randell McGilberry; and Tonia Lee Prince, born Nov. 18, 1962, married Frank Jolercic.

Timothy Maxie Graves, born Sept. 30, 1925 in Cross Bridge, Maury County, married Nov. 19, 1955 in Georgia to Mattie Mildred White, daughter of Leonard and Ora (Reed) White. Mattie was born Nov. 19, 1922. He and Mattie reside in Hamlin, KY.

Frankie Juanell Graves, born March 9, 1931, married Nov. 9, 1952 to James Neely, born April 12, 1923, died April 16, 1974, and is buried in Murfreesboro. Their children: Lana Neely, born Aug. 24, 1953, married Danny Russell Preston; Rita Neely, born Dec. 15, 1955; Michell Neely, born June 23, 1958; Anthony Lee Neely, born March 5, 1962; Paul Neely, born Sept. 14, 1964; and Joseph Franklin Neely, born Dec. 13, 1970.

Jimmy Lafferty Graves, born July 21, 1937, married March 23, 1963 to Barbara Critzer. They are divorced. Their children: Larry Joe Graves, born Jan. 6, 1964; Tony Roger Graves, born March 7, 1966; and Windy Graves. Submitted by Tom Graves.

ROBERT WEBSTER (ROB) GRAVES,

was born Sept. 7, 1922. He passed away Oct. 24, 1967 with a massive heart attack at his home in Flatwoods, TN. His parents were Pleas Brown (1891-1944) and Sally Mae Treadwell Graves (1892-1961). Rob was the fifth child of six children. He had one sister and four brothers. His sister, Myrtle (1912-1977) was married to Alfred Kelley. They had three children, two sons and one daughter. His brother, Clyde Henry (1914-1993) was married to Weda Treadwell and they have three children, two daughters and one son. His brother, James Claude was born in 1916 and is married to Lillie Anderson. They have three sons. His brother, Osbie Brown (Tick) was born in 1919 and is married to Dorothy Lee Pevahouse. They have one daughter. His brother, Melvin Arnold was born in 1927 and passed away in 1928. Rob was the grandson of Susan Graves (husband unknown), Daniel Webster (Webb) Treadwell (1866-1942) and Dillie Inman Treadwell (1869-1933). He was named after his Granddaddy (Webb).

Robert (Rob) and Nell Graves

Rob married Era Nell Woods on Dec. 18, 1954 in Corinth, MS. They have three children, two daughters and one son. Patricia Dianne Graves Eakin was born Nov. 29, 1955 and is married to Bruce Terry Eakin. They have two children, a daughter, Bethany Ann, born Jan. 8, 1982, and Nathan Andrew, born Dec. 2, 1990. Brenda Sue Graves King was born Oct. 12, 1957 and is married to Dennis Vernon King. They have two children, Whitney Denell, born Aug. 22, 1989 and Weston Vernon born Nov. 23, 1992. Jeffery Dan Graves was born Nov. 6, 1962 and is married to Rhonda Kay Whitwell. They have two children, James Robert (Robbie), born July 16, 1992 (named after his Granddaddy) and Jessica Nichole, born Sept. 3, 1993.

Rob served his country in World War II from Sept. 29, 1944 to June 8, 1946. He was Seaman first class in the Navy, and served on NRS Chattanooga and R.E.C.T.R.G. USNTADC, Williamsburg, VA, USS Canallaro APD 128. USS Nuthatch AM 60. He was awarded the Victory medal, American Area Ribbon and the Asiatic Pacific Area Medal. He was laid to rest Oct. 27, 1967 in the Woods and Treadwell Cemetery on Cedar Creek in Perry County.

SARAH GRAHAM BOWMAN GRAVES,

(1803-1875), Sarah was born April 11, 1803 in North Carolina, probably Randolph County, to John Graham and Sarah (maybe Bunten, Brewton, or Newton). She died on April 10, 1875, probably in Red River County, Texas. Sarah first married William C. Bowman.

William C. Bowman died Jan. 27, 1828 in Perry County. William's brother was probably H. F. Bowman listed as A.F. Boen in the 1840 Perry County census. An April 2, 1836 letter from James N. Bowman to "Sarrah Bowmen, Perryville,...that (my) brother Campbell...intent to move to Choctaw Purchase (Mississippi)...send mail to Columbia (or Columbus)...your brother with affection." It is believed this letter was from Sarah's brother-in-law who was referring to his deceased brother and her deceased husband, Campbell. Maybe William C. Bowman was William Campbell Bowman. Sarah's oldest grandson was named Robert Campbell Bowman.

William's only known child was James Newton Bowman, born Jan. 7, 1826 and died Oct. 14, 1871 in Lamar County, Texas and married Tennessee Texas Graham, his first cousin, daughter of Mahaly Caughron and Robert Crawford Graham.

Sarah married on Oct. 23, 1839 to Wiley Graves, born May 7, 1808 in North Carolina to George A. Graves, born in Scotland according to family tradition. Wiley's siblings were Hiram, Archibald D., Benjamin H., James C., Martha, wife of Sexton Rains, and Lucy, wife of Marshall Ivy. Wiley and Sarah moved to Texas in 1847 settling in Cass County. Wiley died Dec. 11, 1867.

Wiley and Sarah's six children were: George Washington, born Oct. 14, 1840, died before 1890 in Red River County, Texas leaving a family, married several times (a different George Washington Graves, June 6, 1853-1908 Decatur County, married Malvina Catherine Houston); John C., born Oct. 30, 1842; Robert Crawford, born Sept. 4, 1845 in Perryville and died Nov. 20, 1914, married Amelia Fleming in Red River County on Feb. 14, 1867, daughter of Perry Fleming of Georgia, buried old Clarksville Cemetery, Red River County; Sarah C., born July 26, 1846, died in Franklin County, Texas, and married William H.H. Story, son of Henry J. Story; Katie, born May 26, 1848, died young; M.J. Tennessee, Sept. 13, 1849-Oct. 11, 1890, married in Cass County to Medford G. Story, born Dec. 11, 1847, buried Bethel Cemetery, Red River County.

Sarah's descendants have her formal invitation to a July 4th Ball at Colonel Johnson's at Perryville dated June 25, 1834. Listed on the invitation are: C. Pettigrew, C.W. Brond, P.P. Rains, and J.S. Allen. Also Sarah left bank deposit slip dated Nov. 11, 1829, signed by J.L. Houston.

THOMAS FLAVY GRAVES, (1890-1960), son of Tom and Mary (Cotton) Graves, was born June 15, 1890 in Perry County, died Oct. 2, 1960 in Detroit, MI with a heart attack while visiting his daughter, Mary. He married Annie Emma Lenora Anderson, daughter of Luther Fate and Mary Luther Adeline Saville Zenia (Aydelott) Anderson. Annie was born Feb. 28, 1893, died July 18, 1965. They are both buried in Graves Cemetery in Perry County.

Flavy was named for a character in a book *Judge Leal Sails for America*, so was his sister, Vinny. Flavy and Annie lived at Ashland in Wayne County for a while, then moved to West Tennessee. They lived at Dyer at the time of his death. Their children:

Obie Lee Graves, born Nov. 8, 1912 in Wayne County, married March 9, 1934 in Obion County to Bernice Louise Doran, daughter of Walker Payne and Ona (Garner) Doran. She was born March 16, 1916 in Gibson County. Their children: Glyn Edwin Graves, born Dec. 17, 1936 in Obion County, married Sept. 26, 1956 in Dyer County to Loretta Elizabeth Hooper, daughter of J. L. Hooper. She was born Nov. 1, 1936. Their children - Anthony Glen Graves, born Sept. 6, 1957 in Memphis, married May 16, 1981 to Monica Lynne Scott, daughter of Laddie Arnold Scott. She was born Dec. 20, 1960 and Timothy Edwin Graves, born Oct. 25, 1963 in Memphis, died April 29, 1964; Mickey David Graves, born Oct. 19, 1943 in Humbolt, Gibson County, married Nov. 25, 1966 in Dyer County to Judy Ann Strawn, born Jan. 29, 1949 in Shelby County, daughter of William R. Strawn. Their children - Kimberly Ann Graves, born June 25, 1969 in Obion County and David Scott Graves, born Dec. 16, 1978.

Hillery Elton "Bill" Graves, born Dec. 6, 1914 in Wayne County, married Feb. 1, 1936 to Mary Kathryn Willis, born May 19, 1913 in Gibson County, daughter of Almus and Fronie (Carroll) Willis. One child, Willis Elton Graves, born Sept. 9, 1937 in Gibson County. He married, June 29, 1960, Rose Marie Charles, born Nov. 19, 1935, daughter of Thomas Alvin Charles. Their children: Harold Wade Graves, born June 12, 1965 and James Keith Graves, born March 17, 1972.

Mary Elizabeth Graves, born Dec. 23, 1916 in Wayne County, died March 16, 1987 in Memphis. She married June 7, 1941 to William "Bill" Michael Assallay, son of Charles and Elizabeth Assallay. Bill was born June 7, 1914, died Aug. 18, 1970 in Michigan, and is buried in Grand Lawn Cemetery. One child, Michael Thomas Assallay, born Dec. 11, 1952, died Nov. 13, 1993.

Thomas Walter Graves, born Jan. 12, 1919 in Wayne County, married Jan. 29, 1944 to Liddie Gladys Cryer, daughter of Clarence and Lucy (Anderson) Cryer. She was born March 31, 1922 in Gibson County. One child, Anita Gayle Graves, born May 20, 1950 in Memphis, married Nov. 13, 1978 to William David Strom, born Nov. 12, 1940.

Vinny Juanita Graves, born Dec. 26, 1921 in Wayne County, married Jan. 3, 1942 in Caruthersville, MO to Ira Ewing Halford, son of Ira and Nettie (Norton) Halford. He was born Aug. 25, 1920 in Gibson County, died July 1, 1986. One child, Pamela Joyce Halford, born Oct. 24, 1951 in Memphis.

Shirley Ann Graves, born Dec. 8, 1934 in Gibson County, died Sept. 30, 1983. She married Nov. 12, 1955 to Jewell Dean Hutcherson, son of G.B. and Arbie (Young) Hutcherson. He was born May 25, 1934. Their children: Cheri Dean Hutcherson, born Nov. 24, 1956. She is a nurse in Memphis. She also likes horses and has some; Jackie Ann Hutcherson, born Feb. 20, 1958; and Thomas Wesley Hutcherson, born Oct. 23, 1963. *Submitted by Obie Graves, Kenton, Tennessee.*

GREGORY-VOSS, Edward Gregory married Stella Voss, born Nov. 14, 1873, Perry County, died Oct. 28, 1952, buried Bethel Cemetery, daughter of John Voss and Mary Ricketts. They had 12 children, all born in Perry County: Leslie Gregory, born Aug. 20, 1892, died March 28, 1962, buried Bethel Cemetery, married a Dabbs; Willie Gregory, born Sept. 23, 1893, married twice; Frank Gregory, born Jan. 12, 1895, died about 1912; Brownie Gregory, born Dec. 23, 1896, died as a child; Clara Jane Gregory, born April 3, 1898, died June 13, 1985, buried Kirk Cemetery, wife of Winford Woodley; Johnnie Freddie Gregory, born Feb. 3, 1910, died Sept. 4, 1989, buried Bethel Cemetery, married Stanley Doc Jackson; James Aubrey Gregory, born June 7, 1902, died April 17, 1966, buried Bethel Cemetery. His wife was Lula M. Berry; Andrew "Boots" Gregory, born June 14, 1904, died in Greensburg, IN, July 20, 1977, married Alma Doles; Elmer "Pug" Gregory, born Aug. 7, 1907, died May 2, 1982, buried Kirk Cemetery. He married Maggie Mable Rodgers; Lillie Mae Gregory, born April 28, 1909, died in Georgia, married twice; Marvin Gregory, born Feb. 22, 1911, died July 7, 1968, Parsons, buried Bible Hill Cemetery. His wife was Callie Houston; and Edward Junior Gregory, born March 22, 1913, called "Dollie", died Jan. 3, 1986, buried Dean Cemetery. He married Poppie Carroll.

JAMES B. GREGORY, born Feb. 1834, died early 1900s, Mill Hollow. His first wife and mother of his children, was Martha Cayce. She was born 1840, probably in Hickman County, died by Oct. 30, 1892, when James married second in Perry County, Mrs. Nancy Jane Johnson. Martha's sister, Margaret Cayce, born 1832, lived with the family at times. They were daughters of John and Rebecca Cayce. Rebecca was thought to be a Morris or a Breece. They had another sister, Frances Elizabeth Cayce, wife of Simeon Smith that lived in Perry County from time to time. A brother, Edward Cayce, born 1839, died during the Civil War, Feb. 19, 1864, Union City, TN. He married in Henderson County. Two of his children, John T. and Mary E. Cayce lived in Perry County with relatives.

Children of Jim and Martha Gregory: Gregory, male, born 1858; Margaret Gregory, born 1860, died between her marriage, May 28, 1876, Perry County to John W. Taylor and the 1880 census; Alice E. Gregory, born 1862, married Jan. 30, 1887, Perry County, George W. Ford. It is told they lived near Flatwoods, however in 1900, they were in Hardin County with children Norman, Omega, twins, Chester and Oscar, and twins, Allen and Alma; Annie L. Gregory, born Sept. 5, 1865, died April 5, 1941, buried Taylor Cemetery, Perry County. She married Sept. 16, 1880, Perry County, John W. Taylor, widower of her sister, Margaret; William Edward Gregory, born Aug. 4, 1868, Perry County, died Oct. 25, 1957, Mill Hollow, buried Bethel Cemetery. He married Nov. 8, 1891, Perry County, Estella Mae Voss; John Taylor Gregory, born summer 1879, no doubt named for his brother-in-law. He lived in West Tennessee. He married first July 30, 1898, Perry County, Lenora M. Marlin and second to Dixie Beasley.

John W. Taylor, born Jan. 6, 1842, died Feb. 25, 1920, buried Taylor Cemetery. He was a Union Captain in the Civil War. Before marrying the Gregory sisters, he had married Priscilla Norton in 1869. He and Annie Gregory had five children: Maud Louise Taylor, born July 23, 1881, died Jan. 12, 1941, married Walter Sloan; Edward W. Taylor, born Feb. 7, 1883, died April 29, 1923, buried Taylor Cemetery. He married 1904, Caroline Victoria Evans; Alf A. Taylor, born Nov. 21, 1884, died Oct. 10, 1954, buried Taylor Cemetery. His wife was Ann Oliver; Mollie "Mon" Taylor, born Oct. 28, 1892, died Sept. 10, 1973, married Aug. 2, 1912, Perry County, A.J. Barnett; and John Wilburn Taylor, born Dec. 30, 1896, died Sept. 2, 1946, buried Taylor Cemetery. He married Lorena Bowman.

GLENN SPRINGER AND MARIE BOYCE GRIMES, Glenn "Dick" and Marie were married Jan. 29, 1938. They were active in church and civic work for over 50 years in Flatwoods and Perry County.

Glenn and Marie Grimes in 1988

Glenn was born June 2, 1914 to Ernest "Jake" Grimes and Lutie Downey in Lewis County. He graduated from Lewis County High School at Hohenwald, where he excelled in baseball, basketball and football. He played professional baseball in the minor leagues for several years.

He was a corporal in the U.S. Army Corps of Engineers during World War II and served in this country in 1943 and 1944.

"Dick", as he was known by the people of Perry County, and Marie settled in Flatwoods in 1942. He worked for the Tennessee Highway

Department for 27 years, where he was in charge of building bridges and highways in the Middle Tennessee area as resident engineer.

Left: Cpl. Glenn "Dick" and Marie Grimes. Right: Marie B. Grimes. First and only woman postmaster at Flatwoods.

Dick and Marie donated 32 acres of land on the Buffalo River in 1976 for the use of the Boy Scouts for float trips and camping. It is known as the "Grimes Canoe Base". Thousands of Boy Scouts from Tennessee and other states come every summer, to enjoy outdoor life.

They have been active in promoting a new Church of Christ building, a new school building and a new telephone system in Flatwoods.

Dick and his father-in-law, Dr. Boyce, raised pure bred registered Hereford cattle, some of which won first place prizes at the Perry County and Lewis County fairs. Dr. Boyce owned extensive farm property in Perry County. Dick and Marie continued to raise cattle on the farms until his death.

Glenn "Dick" Grimes. A professional baseball player with Owensboro, Kentucky.

Dick was active in politics. He served as chairman of the Perry County Democratic Election Committee and chairman of the Perry County Election Commission.

Dick was the song leader at Flatwoods Church of Christ for over 45 years and also served as an elder for several years.

He was an avid sports fan all of his life.

Marie attended school at Flatwoods and graduated from Linden High School, where she was an honor student, and played basketball on the team.

When her mother died in 1942, Dick and Marie returned to Flatwoods to keep the family homeplace. Her father, Dr. Boyce, was still maintaining his home and office there. He also had an office in Hohenwald. In 1944, there was another tragedy when Marie's brother, Lt. William Earl Boyce Jr. was killed in a plane crash in World War II. Dick had already gone to the army and she stayed there.

Marie was commissioned the first and only woman appointed to the position of postmaster at Flatwoods. She also operated the general store, where the post office was located. After Nesby Kirk retired, as rural mail carrier, she applied for a transfer and, again, she was appointed the first and only woman for that position. She retired after 30 years of postal service.

However, Marie's main interests were her family, home and church, as she worked for balance in all areas.

Her philosophy was, "whatever your hands find to do, do it with all your might" from Ecclesiastes.

Marie's hobbies after she retired were reading, oil painting, decorating her new house and traveling. She enrolled at Columbia State Community College for courses of special interest to her. She made an extensive study of the Bible and owns a large collection of religious and inspirational books.

In 1976, Marie and her sisters (Wilton Craig, Mildred Burns and her husband, Jim) made a two week tour of Europe. In 1980, they took a trip for six weeks around the world. They saw many famous places and buildings. The most interesting and exciting places they visited were Buckingham Palace and the Tower of London, the Alps in Switzerland, Rome, the Eiffel Tower in Paris and many famous museums. They saw The Great Pyramid in Egypt; The beautiful white marble Taj Mahal in India; The Himalayan Mountains in Nepal; Singapore; Hong Kong; Japan; Pearl Harbor in Honolulu. The most memorable and awesome place was the Holy Land. They walked where Jesus walked, lived and died; They saw the Garden Tomb where he was buried and other places of inspiration.

The children of Glenn and Marie are: Glenda James, born July 13, 1947. She is married to Chris James. They live in Decatur, AL. She graduated from David Lipscomb College and the University of North Alabama, where she earned two B.S. degrees, a Masters degree and a Specialist in Education degree. She teaches English at John C. Calhoun Community College and she is working in a Ph.D. in Education.

Joyce Pevahouse Grimes-Safley, born June 11, 1954. She is married to Michael Safley. She graduated from Vanderbilt University with a masters degree in nursing and later returned to earn a Doctor of Jurisprudence (Law) degree. She is an attorney in Nashville.

Keith was born July 17, 1955. He was employed by the Tennessee Highway Department and raised Hereford cattle on the family farm. He was killed in an accident in his truck on March 13, 1977. This was the greatest tragedy of their lives.

The grandchildren are Christi James Lakey, Jennifer James, Benja James Dixon, Amanda James, Kathryn Pevahouse, Christopher Safley and Lauren Safley.

They have one great grandson, Ethan James Lakey, and one great granddaughter on the way (due in June of 1994), Johnna Elizabeth Dixon.

GRINDER-ARY, Noah Theodore (Thea) Grinder, born Nov. 11, 1875, died Jan. 12, 1924, married Mary Jane Ary in 1896. Mary Jane was born Jan. 10, 1881, died Nov. 19, 1954. Both are buried at Ary Cemetery, Sinking Creek, Perry County. Thea, the son of William (Bill) Grinder, born 1833, died March 2, 1914, and Sarah Jane Ledbetter, born 1837, died Jan. 29, 1904. Buried at Dabbs Cemetery, Rockhouse Creek, Perry County. (see Grinder-Ledbetter). Thea died early in life, his working career was a timberman and farmer. Mary Jane Ary, daughter of William (Bill) Ary, born Aug. 7, 1840, died April 20, 1924, and Mary Jane Warren, born Dec. 18, 1846, died Jan. 14, 1922. (see Ary and Warren).

Theodore and Mary Jane (Ary) Grinder

Theodore and Mary Jane Ary lived on Sinking Creek and had 13 children. Theodore died young leaving small children, this presented a hardship on Mary Jane, but the older boys helped with the living.

Izorah, buried in Flatwoods, born Oct. 13, 1898, died May 2, 1952, married Elvis Riley and had eight children: Willie, James, Wilodean, Iva, Ruth, Addie Sue, Paul and Joe Lee.

Mollie, buried in Dover, OH, born April 18, 1900, died Jan. 30, 1978, married Clifford Harder. Children: Kenneth, Kathleen, twins - Jane and Jean, Ralph and Reba.

Sadie Mae, buried at Ary Cemetery, born Jan. 2, 1902, died Sept. 9, 1961, married George Tatum and had five children: Carl, Samuel Black (S.B.), Elizabeth Jane, deceased, Harold and Bobbie Jane.

William Zellnah, buried at Warren Cemetery, born Oct. 30, 1904, died July 12, 1990, married Thelma Tharp and had two children; Loudean, deceased, and Eugene Grinder.

Abner Warren, born Feb. 28, 1906, married Jan. 3, 1932 to Lillian Ward. Two children: Betty June and Billy Ward Grinder. Second marriage to Carmie Mercer. Two children: Patricia and David Grinder. Abb died March 29, 1994.

Loyd Jessro, buried at Ary Cemetery, born Jan. 6, 1908, died 1986, married Eva Hinson and had 10 children: Noah, deceased, Mildred, Lettie Sue, Ray, deceased, Doris, Eddie, Pat, Edwin, deceased, Glen, deceased, and Ronald Mark, deceased. Doris was killed in an auto accident April 5, 1994.

Emma Jane, buried at O.A. Kirk Cemetery, born Jan. 20, 1910, died Oct. 30, 1982, married Allen Brice Kilpatrick. Four children: Troy, Loy, Roy and Joy (see Kilpatrick-Grinder).

Wesson Ledbetter, born Jan. 17, 1912, married Osie Harder. Four children: Nelson, Brenton, Lucretia (Chris) and Randy.

Ary Osburn, born March 2, 1914, married Nettie Harder. Five children: Sandra, Nolan, Gaylon, John Wayne and Terry.

Orbit Opal, born Aug. 3, 1916, died April 7, 1989, buried at Flatwoods, married Ben Garner. Eight children: Jimmy, Jerry, Joe, Agnes, Helen, Roy, Connie and Phillip.

Virginia Sue, born Nov. 7, 1918, married Ezra Hamm. Children: Delton, Joyce and Larry.

Norma Cletus, born Nov. 28, 1920, married W.J. (Bill) Richardson. Children: Raymond Dee, deceased, Wanda, Judy and Ricky.

Theodore Clint, born Dec. 3, 1922, married Evlyn Page. Two children: Steven and Kathy. Second marriage was to Lee Skelton. *Submitted by Sue Hamm, Cletus Richardson, Bobbie Steele, Joy K. Gordon and Loy K. Qualls.*

GRINDER-LEDBETTER, William (Billy) Grinder was born 1833 and died March 2, 1914, a farmer, buried on Rockhouse Creek, Perry County, Dabbs Cemetery. Everyone called him uncle Billy Grinder. He served his country, a private Confederate soldier on South side, Company A 19th Calvary. He married Sarah Jane Ledbetter. She was a housewife, born 1837 and died Jan. 29, 1904. She is buried at Dabbs Cemetery on Rockhouse Creek, Perry County.

William "Billy" Grinder and Sarah Jane Ledbetter Grinder

To this union were born seven children: Parlee, born 1858, died ___, married Joe Dabbs and had four children: Flora, Cora, Johnny, Monroe; Mary Margaret, born 1860, died ___, married Jim Baker and had six children: Cleve, Lizzie, Grady, General, Bernice, Jim; Sarah L. (Sack), born 1864, died ___, married Jess Dabbs; James Henry (Bud) born 1867, died ___, married Lou Dowdy and had four children: Ester, Lona, Ervin, Mary; Wintsy Anna Belle Thedus, born 1871, died ___, married Albert Jeff Harder and had four children: Bertha, June, Jim and one killed in World War I (Belgium); Noah Theodore, born Nov. 11, 1875, died Jan. 12, 1924, married Mary Jane Ary and had 13 children: Izorah Riley, Mollie Harder, Sadie Mae Tatum, Zellnah, Abb, Loyd, Emma Kilpatrick, Osburn, Wesson, Opal Garner, Sue Hamm, Cletus Richardson and Clint (See Biography of Grinder and Ary); Elvin Johnson, born Nov. 22, 1881, died May 9, 1956, married Margaret Etta Ethel Lee Edwards and had eight children: Blanch Young, Ruby Dale, Pearl, Paul, Raymond, James Coy, Buford and Charles. Most of these children are in Nashville County, AR at present. The family moved from Perry County, TN to Howard County, AR in December 1920 after Margaret Etta's family moved there in 1919. Great granddaughter - Joy Kilpatrick Gordon.

GRINDER-THARP, William Zell Grinder (Oct. 30, 1904-July 12, 1990). Parents Noah Theodore Grinder (Nov. 11, 1875-Jan. 12, 1924) and Mary Jane Ary Grinder (Jan. 10, 1881-Nov. 19, 1954). Zell was one of 13 children born to this union, Brothers: Abner Warren Grinder, Loyd Jessro Grinder, Wesson Ledbetter Grinder, Ary Osburn Grinder and Theodore Clint Grinder. Sisters: Izora Grinder Riley, Mollie Grinder Harder, Sadie Grinder Tatum, Emma Jane Grinder Kilpatrick, Virginia Sue Grinder Hamm, Orbit Opal Grinder Garner and Norma Cletus Grinder Richardson.

Thelma Tennessee Tharp Grinder & William Zell Grinder

Thelma Tennessee Tharp Grinder (May 18, 1909). Parents Elva Dixie Warren Tharp (May 15, 1890-July 3, 1971) and John Thomas Tharp (March 24, 1886-Feb. 27, 1971). Thelma was the only child born to this union. John Thomas Tharp remarried and had seven children: Eunice Tharp, Obie Tharp, Pearl Tharp, Earl Tharp, Tot Tharp, John Tharp and Jean Tharp.

Zell and Thelma married Dec. 24, 1926. A heavy rain had fallen and the creeks were over the roads, they could not reach the Parsonage where the Preacher lived. He met them at the creek and read the vows on one side of the creek and the couple on the other side. After the ceremony, a rock was rolled up in the marriage license and they were thrown across the creek to the Preacher. This wonderful marriage lasted 63 years. Two children were born to this union. Loudean Grinder Tucker (May 24, 1930-Oct. 20, 1991). Loudean worked for 40 years for Bell Telephone Company in Nashville, TN, and was working up to her death. She married Carl Tucker of Nashville, TN on Dec. 21, 1961; they resided in Nashville. No children.

William Eugene Grinder (Aug. 10, 1936). He is married to Linda Dawn Wills Grinder (Nov. 19, 1941 from Dickson, TN. They reside in Hohenwald, TN where Eugene is employed by the Lewis County Board of Education. One daughter was born to this union, Cindy Lou Grinder Scott (July 13, 1963), married to David Scott (Sept. 5, 1963). Their children are David Brandon Scott (July 10, 1983) and Diksie Jean Scott (Feb. 3, 1989). They reside in Hohenwald, TN.

Zell and Thelma lived their married life on Rockhouse and Sinking Creek in Perry County, TN. Early in their marriage, Thelma went with Zell to gather corn and lost her wedding band which was inscribed with their initials. She was heart broken but 40 something years later, her ring was found by her cousin, Floyd Warren, in a large river bottom of the Chess Warren farm. When it was cleaned up, the ring was in the original shape except for one scratch, she is still wearing the ring today. *Submitted by Bobbie Jane Tatum Steele.*

ARY OSBURN GRINDER, or Ob, as he is known to his friends, was born on March 1, 1914 on Sinking Creek in Perry County. His parents were Noah Theodore Grinder and Mary Jane Ary. He was the ninth of 13 children. The other 12 children were Izorah, Mollie, Sadie, Zell, Abner, Loyd, Emma, Wesson, Opal, Sue, Cletus and Clint.

Life was very hard for this family. Noah Theodore Grinder died in 1924, leaving Mary Jane Ary to rear her children alone. All the children had to work. There was very little time for attending school because they were too busy scrambling to make a living. They grew food on their small farm; they dug May Apple and Ginseng; they worked in the woods, they hunted; and they worked for other people when they could. By the time Ob was 10 he was sawing down trees with his older brother, Wesson.

Ob and Wesson married sisters from Cedar Creek. Ob married Nettie Harder, and Wesson married Ocie Harder. Unfortunately, Nettie died in 1989. Ocie and Wesson live in Wayne County. They have four children, Nelson, (Dot), Brenton, (Sondra), Lucretia, (Tony) and Randall, unmarried.

Ob's five children are Sandra, (Murray), Nolan, (Barbara), Gailand, (Patsy), John Wayne, (Sharon) and Terry, (Sue). His grandchildren are Meredith, Christopher, Kimberly, Kevin, Angela, Brian, Amelia and Alexandrea. He has one great grandson, Victor.

Perhaps Mary Jane Ary learned some of her toughness from her father, William Henry Ary, and her mother, Mary Jane Warren. William spent the Civil War in a cavalry unit fighting for the South. Ob remembers him as a kind man, always ready with sweet potatoes as a treat for him and Wesson. He died in 1924. Ob's other grandfather, William Henry Grinder, died the night Ob was born. William Henry Ary's parents were Henry Ary and Sophia Fraley. Sophia's father was Jacob Fraley. Family tradition also holds there is a connection to Robert Grinder and Priscilla Knight, the couple that owned the inn on the Natchez Trace where Meriwether Lewis died.

When Ob was a teenager he learned to play a fiddle and formed a country music band with some other boys. They played at dances, fiddler's contests and at any other gathering that would let them play. Roy Acuff was just starting out then, and Ob remembers playing at a dance when Roy wanted a break. When he married, he gave up music and concentrated on making a living. He has farmed, worked in the woods and dug ditches. He did whatever he had to do to earn a living.

Ob now lives in Lewis County, near Hohenwald. He enjoys visiting his brothers, Ab, Wesson and Clint and his sisters Sue and Cletus. His children and grandchildren visit often. He now has a brand new great grandson to enjoy, also. He feels he has accomplished the greatest thing a man can achieve. He fed and clothed his children and is surrounded by a family that loves him. *Submitted by Sandra Swanson.*

GROOM-ANDERSON, Dorothy Groom Anderson and Earl C. Anderson moved to Linden, TN in the fall of 1964. They had two daughters, Patsy Kay and Dorothy Elaine, and enrolled them in the ninth and fifth grades. Their oldest child, William Earl (Bill) remained in Nashville where he was working.

Dorothy Groom Anderson & Earl C. Anderson

Earl spent three years in the Navy during World War II. Soon after, he started going to college at Knoxville, and finished four years in three with no summers off. After getting his B.A. degree at the University of Tennessee, he began work for the Extension Service in Lawrence County where he was 4-H agent for 12 years. Then he went to Nashville for three and a half years.

He came to Perry County and served as 4-H agent for several years. During this time, he got his Masters degree Aug. 24, 1968. Then he became U.T. Resource Management Agent, working in five counties.

He retired Jan. 1, 1984 and died of a massive heart attack June 20, 1984.

Their son, Bill, resides in Hendersonville, TN. He has one son, Tim, and two granddaughters, Tamra and Kelsie. Patsy married Andrew Ezell in 1970 and divorced in 1976. Her legal name remains Patsy Anderson Ezell. The youngest Anderson daughter, Elaine, married Ricky Allen Jones in 1972. They have a son, Jeffery Allen, born Nov. 3, 1983. They reside in Linden, TN.

ALFRED WINTRY AND MADIE GROOM, live in Linden. They spent most of their 44 year marriage on Madie's home place, the ridge between Bee Creek and Short Creek. They were married April 22, 1950 and had two children, Wanda, born May 19, 1951, and Donna, born Dec. 31, 1953. They lived at various places in the county and even went north for work on at least a couple of occasions, before buying the homesite from Madie's grandfather, Bob Hickerson. They settled in to rear their girls and renovate the house on the property at that time. Before completion, the house burned to the ground and the young Groom family had to start over. A new house was built in the same place and life went on. Wintry did construction work until he became disabled in April of 1964. He was not able to do physical work after that, but has always been a positive influence on his daughters and sons-in-law. He taught the girls to cook and the guys to build and repair things by talking them through the procedures.

Madie has worked at Johnson Control for more than 20 years. She has been the caretaker of their home and yard in the country for all these years. They moved to town in January of 1993 and things are more convenient for her now and they both have adjusted to "city living".

Alfred & Madie Groom

The children have been gone for a number of years, but both girls attended school at Cedar Creek and later graduated from P.C.H.S. Wanda graduated in 1969 and married Michael Warren. They have two girls of their own now, Emily, born Sept. 5, 1973, and Lori, born Jan. 22, 1979. Emily has completed three years of college and is going into nursing. Lori is still in high school. The Warrens live in Waverly, TN.

Donna graduated in 1971 and is married to Max Garretson. They live in Greenville, SC and have two children. Stephanie, born Jan. 27, 1977, and Chad, born July 20, 1979. They are both in high school.

Wintry is the grandson of Henry Clinton Groom (1860-1940) and Milinda Groom (1860-1953). They were both of German descent. They worked the farm, reared their five children, died and were buried on the family farm. Their children were Noah, Albert, Grady, (Wintry's father), Fred and Nitha.

Grady married Lova Mae Hensley March 10, 1918. They also made their home on Swindle Creek. They had 10 children and named them Zula, Lillian, William Ferd, then a baby girl who died early and was never named, Grady Mirl, Joe Clint, Montie Una, Alfred Wintry, R.T. and Jack Garry. They made their living on the farm and spent their entire married life in Perry County surrounded by many children and grandchildren. Lova died Sept. 6, 1967 and Grady followed Dec. 8, 1980. They are buried on the home place on Swindle Creek. *Submitted by Wanda Warren.*

ALTIE BERTHA GROOM, was born April 7, 1907 in Hardin County, TN. She was the third child born to Luther T. Groom and Annie Florence Davis Groom. The first two died at an early age. Their names were Emma and Gracy. Altie was next, then Wallace, Gladys, Ernest, L.T. and the youngest, Dorothy. Ernest died at the age of 10 years. Gladys died in the Perry County Nursing Home, Nov. 19, 1990. Altie died June 15, 1993 in the home of her sister, Dorothy.

Anderson never married, she gave her life taking care of her mother and daddy and grandmother Lola Davis. Then, later, her aunt came to live with them. She lived a long time after her mother and daddy died. She wrote many poems about her loved ones. Here is one from a book of poems she had published in 1981:

Altie Bertha Groom & Family

Perry County Hills

Down among the Perry County Hills
There is a plot of ground
Where the corn is planted
And they plow all around.

There my great great grandparents are buried
If they could have only known
That in just a few short years
How the Groom family would have grown.

Of all the sorrow and heartache
And the joys we have known, too
Of that great number, Dear Lord
I hope many learned to love and trust you.

WALLACE GROOM was born Sept. 17, 1909 in Clifton, TN, the son of Luther and Florence Davis Groom. He married Alice Hoskins Dec. 24, 1933. He farmed rented land, raising mostly cotton and corn. In 1951, he moved to Peoria, IL and worked with Caterpillar Tractor Co., as inspector until he retired in 1972. He now lives in Lawrenceburg, TN.

Alice & Wallace Groom on their 50th wedding anniversary in December 1983.

Wallace and Alice had four children, Charlotte Ann, born 1935; Wallace D. Jr., born Aug. 9, 1936; Steve Thomas, born April 14, 1939; Danny Hoskins, born June 13, 1941.

Charlotte Ann married James H. Keeton, born Aug. 25, 1933. They have three children: Kim Aline, born Dec. 29, 1956, married Timothy B. Grinder and has three children, Melissa A., born June 27, 1979, Jessica B., born Sept. 2, 1981 and Bey James, born March 21, 1984.

Wallace D. Jr., married Aug. 26, 1955 Jeri S. Keeton. They have three children: Gala L. born 1956, married Richard Slatton in 1979, and has Cord M. Slatton, born Aug. 10, 1982 and Dain Grover Slatton, born June 22, 1985, secondly married Berry Smith and had Molly, born Aug. 15, 1990.

Steve Thomas married Jo Anne Gosnell (1941-1994). They had three children and live in Columbia. Their children were: Cindy, born March 9, 1959, married David, has two children, Colby J., born Dec. 30, 1982 and Kalie Ann, born March 14, 1986. Thomas S. Jr. (Steve), born Aug. 4, 1964, married Edyth Anderson on Sept. 2, 1988. Their one child, Leah Marie, born Nov. 14, 1991; they live in Nashville, TN. Columbia with their two children, Benjamin born Feb. 9, 1990, and Emily Nicole born March 25, 1991.

Danny Hoskins married Roberta L. Sage, Dec. 20, 1969. Their two children are Jana Lorraine, born Sept. 22, 1970 and Brian Scott, born Aug. 30, 1973. They live in Peoria, IL.

WALLACE DENTON GROOM, was born Sept. 17, 1909 off Beech Creek, Wayne County, TN. He married Alice Hoskins, daughter of Thomas Moore and Mary "Ella" Davis Hoskins, Dec. 24, 1933, at Bath Springs, TN. They farmed in Tennessee until 1951 when they moved to Peoria, IL, where Wallace worked at the Caterpillar Tractor Company. After his retirement in 1972, they moved several times, finally staying in Columbia, TN, where Alice died Jan. 23, 1989. They had four children: Charlotte, born 1935, married James Keeton; Wallace Jr., born 1936, married Jeri "Sue" Keeton; Thomas "Steve", born 1939, first married Connie Haines, then JoAnne Gosnell; Danny, born 1941, first married Sharon Bullock, then Roberta Sage.

Samuel Groom & children ca 1940

Wallace's great-great grandfather, William "Billy" Groom, came to Perry County about 1815-1820. Family tradition says that he came from North Carolina and that the family was originally from Germany. Billy and his wife are buried off Swindle Road. Great-great granddaughter, Altie Groom, wrote in her book *Let Not Your Heart Be Troubled:*

Perry County Hills

Down among the Perry County hills
There is a plot of ground
Where the corn is planted
And they plow all around.

There my great great grandparents are buried
If they could have only known
That in just a few short years
How the Groom family would have grown.

Of all the sorrow and heartache
And the joys we have known too
Of that great number, Lord
I hope many learned to love and trust you.

Billy's son, Henry, was a farmer near Linden, TN. Both he and his wife, Lucinda, were born in 1820 in Tennessee. They are buried in the Moore-Groom plots off Swindle Road. They had 10 children: Nancy C., born 1841, married Mr. Inman; William Jaspar, born 1843, married Mahala Dobbs; Martha A., born 1846; Sarah E., born 1848; James R., born 1850; Julina, born 1852, married John G. Moore; Purlina, born 1854; Samuel, born June 7, 1858; Eunice, born 1859; and Henry Clint, born 1860, married Malinda Groom.

Samuel was a farmer who died in 1944 in McNairy County, TN. He first married Martha Campbell, daughter of Willis and Nancy Campbell. She was born in Perry County in 1848, died there in 1890 and is buried in Harder Cemetery. Parts of the Campbell house are still standing off Swindle Fork, near Linden, TN. Samuel later married Sallie Hughes, 1870-1925. They are buried in the Milledgeville Cemetery, Milledgeville, TN. Samuel and Martha had five children: Lula, born 1876, married Wesley Turnbo; Luther, born June 2, 1879; Larry 1881-1883; Ida 1884-1898; and Mary E., born 1886, married Donald Riley. Samuel and Sallie had 10 children: Bertha, born 1893; Emma 1890-1903; Arnold, born 1895, married Jimmie Young; Allen, born 1898; Theodore, born 1908, married Bassie Bishop; Elsie, born 1905, married Mr. Thomas; Hollis; Ben, born 1911; Hillard, born 1913; and Willard, born 1915.

Luther, a farmer, was born in Perry County. He married Annie "Florence" Davis, daughter of John J. and Lola Davis, Oct. 6, 1901. They farmed several years in Wayne County, then moved to Lawrenceburg, TN, where Luther died June 26, 1956 and Florence died Aug. 3, 1960. They are buried in Baucum Cemetery, Wayne County. They had eight children: Emma 1902-1908; Gracie 1904-1905; Altie 1907-1993; Wallace; Gladys 1914-1990, married Roy Phillips; Ernest 1916-1926; L.T., born 1920, first married Wilma Houston, then Mrs. Thelma Schultz Willingham; and Dorothy, born 1921, married Earl Anderson.

GROOMS-PRICE, John David and Janice Grooms Price came to live in Flatwoods April, 1991. She is the daughter of Doris Duncan Grooms Harlow and Mirl Grooms. John David is the son of Flata Skidmore and John J. Price of Union City, IN.

Janice Price, David Price, Betty Duncan & Odie Duncan

Janice grew up and went to school in Flatwoods and Linden. She worked in Decatur, Maury and Davidson Counties at different jobs.

She went to truck driving school, then started driving a tractor trailer for D.T.S. She met and married John David, also a truck driver. They soon started driving as a team for Fred French in Parsons, TN and a Memphis based company.

Their son, Dillon, also trucked with them until he became school age; they quit driving and came to live in Flatwoods to rear and school Dillon.

Janice was born Oct. 10, 1952. Her grandparents are Hobson and Nola Davis Duncan, Grady and Lova Hensley Grooms; great grandparents are Barney and Sarah Barber Duncan, and Clint and Malinda Grooms.

Janice has three children: Travis Grice, born Aug. 4, 1968; Forrest Lumpkins, born Dec. 18, 1980; Dillon Price, born April 1, 1987. She has one granddaughter, Brandy Grice, born March 21, 1992.

Janice has one brother, Odie Duncan, born April 14, 1946. He is married to Betty Shultz. They live in Loretto, TN. Odie has one daughter, Brenda Lee Duncan, born July 26, 1967.

Janice was born and raised in Flatwoods, and wanted to come back wherever she was. She and David decided Flatwoods was the place for Dillon to grow up and and wanted him to go to school in Perry County.

WILLIAM JASPER GROOMS, was born Nov. 14, 1843 on Cedar Creek in Perry County, TN. He was the son of Henry Grooms (June 2, 1820-Nov. 28, 1879). Henry was the son of Billy Grooms from Virginia (1795-March 18, 1849). Henry and his wife are buried on Swindle Creek road in Perry County.

In the late summer of 1877, William Jasper and his wife, Mahala, left Cedar Creek area. They left a small grave and took their young family: Jane, 12; John, 11; Henry, 7 and Mary, 4 months, and traveled west with the wife's family, the Dabbs. This small wagon train traveled west for about six weeks and arrived November 1877 in Oregon County, MO. After crossing the Eleven Point River at Thomasville, they went south to Moten, AR, a small community just south of Mammoth Springs where one of the wife's brothers lived. Moten is located between present day Mammoth Springs and Saddle on English Creek. It had a church and a schoolhouse, that is still standing today and was used as a residence until the early 1970s.

They stayed in Arkansas about two years. In 1879, another son, Jasper Eli, was born. They moved back to Oregon County and settled on Warm Fork River. There were two more additions to the family, Lydia in 1881, and Lee in 1885. William Jasper Grooms and Mahala reared eight children. Of the eight children, there were three of four boys, John, Henry, Eli and Lee settled in the south central part of Oregon County in an area now known as The Norman and Bonds Communities. James, the fourth boy, settled on Kings Point on Warm Fork. Of four girls born to William and Mahala, Lydia and Josephine married and settled close to the four brothers. The older sister, Jane, married and first lived between Thayer and Koshkonong, later moved to Alton.

William Jasper often mentioned that he longed to return to the land of his birth, but the opportunity never came. William Jasper once stated that if he could make one good crop, he would move back to Linden, TN. He never bought any property, but farmed rented land. At one time William, Mahala and their eight children lived in a one room cabin on Warm Fork. William died of a respiratory illness on April 23, 1891, and is buried with his infant child in Childers Cemetery on Cedar Creek, a small tributary of Warm Fork, Oregon County, MO in 1891.

In 1977, the Grooms family held a family reunion celebrating 100 years of living in Oregon County. They made a family tree naming the descendants and their spouses of the eight children of William Jasper and Mahala Dabbs Grooms. They numbered some 600.

FRED HALBROOKS (1901-1954)- Nancy Aldridge Jones (1902-1942). Fred Halbrooks is the second son born to Robert Marshall (1871-1960) and Mary Ann (Mollie) (1874-1957) DePriest Halbrooks. His siblings are: John (Jack), married Myrtle Tucker, children - Dorise, Dean, Robert, Jackie; Clem, married Flora Goblet, son, Pat; Jessie, married Neal Strickland, children - Jewel, Nina, Mack, Paul, and Verna Sue, lives in Perry County; Bonnie, married Jasper Anderson, children - Lucille Hinson, J. B. Anderson, Martha Jo Hudson Wallace, Willie Ray Anderson; Lena Pearson Cunningham, sister, lives in Linden.

Fred Halbrooks with R. D. Hodges, his first grandson.

Family cemeteries are Bethel and Kirk. Paternal grandparents: Ethelbert Anglehart (1843-1914), son of William Halbrooks and Mary Ermaline Tucker, daughter of Joseph Tucker. Thelbert had sisters Mary M. and Virginia, half-siblings Rebecca Jane, Robert J., Lucy, James and Fanny. Their father is Benjamin Westbrooks. Ethelbert married Martha Edwards. Ethelbert joined the army, age 20, and fought for the Confederacy and the Union in the Civil War. He was in the battles of Murfreesboro and Shiloh. Their children are Joseph E., Robert M. (Fred's father), Thelbert, George Andrew, Doshie Marlin, Emilie Anderson, Josephine Kilpatrick and Gee Halbrooks (children-Guy and LeRoy). The Perry County and Hickman County Halbrook, Halbrooks, Holbrooks, originated from a William Holbrook (1738-1806). They lived in Stokes County, NC until late 1700s when they moved to Kentucky. Descendants live in Tennessee, Missouri, Alabama, Texas, Oklahoma. They were descendants of John and Mary Brassie Holbrook (King George Co., VA, John died 1733).

Nancy attended Murfreesboro Normal College. When Grady died, she returned to teaching at "Frog Pond" and Bethel. She and Fred married (1928) at the Linden Town Spring. They rode in a buggy from home, near Frog Pond to Linden.

Fred and Nancy's children are: Arthur Jones (father-Grady Jones), Helen Faye Halbrooks Ashley Greeson, Rosa Lee Halbrooks Johnson, Ruby Fred Halbrooks Hodges, and Mary Ann Halbrooks (died at birth, buried Horner Cemetery, Cypress Creek).

Fred and "Nannie" lived at DePriest Bend, Cypress, and Coon Creeks, Bethel, and Linden. Nannie died of a brain hemorrhage in 1942. Fred died of blood clot in the brain in 1954. Both are buried at Bethel. Fred married Estelle Sparks, Sparta, TN, 1948. After Fred's death, Estelle married Norman Lollar, Sparta. After his death, she moved to Sparta where she still resides at age 88.

Nancy's parents: James and Ellen Bates Aldridge. James and family were committed members of the Beardstown Church of Christ. See references: Aldridge, and above listed children's names.

ROSA LEE HALBROOKS-JAMES EMMETT JOHNSON, JR. James (Nov. 8, 1922, Waverly) and Rosa Lee (July 2, 1931, Lobelville) live in Ithaca, NY. Parents: Fred (1901-1954) and Nancy Aldridge Jones Halbrooks (1902-1942), buried Bethel. Maternal grandparents: James Allen and Lew Ellen Bates Aldridge, "Frog Pond," Lobelville and Lower Sulphur Springs in Hickman County, buried Brush Creek. Maternal great-grandparents: Dillard and Emmaline Chandler Bates, Lobelville and Lower Sulphur Creek, Hickman County, buried Gilmer Cemetery, Lobelville. Emma Chandler's parents: Tyre, buried Fowlkes Cemetery, Dickson County, and Rosanah Harper, buried Chandler Cemetery, Hickman County. Tyre married Eleanor Pinkerton. Paternal grandparents: Robert M. and Mary Ann DePriest Halbrooks, buried Bethel. Great-grandparents: Barney and Rebecca Westbrook DePriest, buried Bethel.

Family of Rosalee Halbrooks Johnson

Rosa Lee's first school was a one room school, Cypress Creek, with Ethel Kimble as her first teacher. Rosa Lee was baptized at age 11. She was graduated Linden High School, class valedictorian, 1948; received scholarships, Lipscomb and Freed-Hardeman Colleges. While at Lipscomb, she studied with Ira North, teacher and preacher. He helped her arrange with the Lawrenceburg Church of Christ to re-establish the Church of Christ in Linden. A tent meeting was held on the present site.

Education: degrees- B.S., M.S., New York Universities; advanced research at Cornell. Career: English teacher, school psychologist, guidance counselor, central office administrator. She retired, 1991, after 30 years in public education work.

While attending Freed-Hardeman, she met James Johnson on Aug. 18, 1951. Both transferred to Lipscomb, 1950. They left November 1952 for a two year missionary stay in Nigeria, West Africa as the first family of missionaries for Churches of Christ. Their first daughter, Pamela Rose, was born (Oct. 21,1953) in Port Harcourt. They were supported by the Lawrence Avenue Church of Christ, Nashville, but helped by many churches including the Linden church. On their return to Nashville, Jimmy graduated from Lipscomb (1955). They became the first minister's family, starting the Ithaca, NY, church. Other children born to them are: Nancy Beth (Sept. 20, 1957), Cynthia Ellen(Mar. 27, 1959), Rebecca Sue (Feb. 9, 1962). Jim and Rosa Lee's grandchildren: To Pamela-Kirstin Leigh (May 29, 1984), Ithaca, NY; to Nancy- Robert Steven (June 14, 1983) and Courtney Lynn (June 21, 1987), Middleburg, FL; to Cynthia- James Quinn and Jared Brooks (twins, Nov. 13, 1991), Jacksonville, FL; to Rebecca- Jordan Rebecca (April 23, 1989) and Chelsea Rose (Aug. 6, 1992), Midland, MI.

Rosa Lee's children graduated from Ithaca High School. Pamela attended Lipscomb, graduated from Ithaca College and Elmira Colleges (B.S., M.S.); teaches in Ithaca, NY. Nancy graduated from Lipscomb (B.S.); teaches sixth grade mathematics and computers, Orange Park, FL. Cynthia attended Michigan Christian College and Lipscomb; Marketing Associate, AT&T, Jacksonville, FL. Rebecca attended Lipscomb, graduated Wayne State University, Detroit, MI (B.A.); Senior Communications Specialist, Dow Chemical, Midland, MI.

See references: Aldridge, Halbrooks, sister and brother, for other family history.

RUBY HALBROOKS - FLOYD HODGES, Ruby Fred Halbrooks (born, September 1932) is the third daughter of Fred and Nancy (Nannie) Aldridge Jones Halbrooks. Her grandparents are James and Lew Ellen Bates Aldridge and Robert and Mollie DePriest Halbrooks. Siblings are Arthur Jones (1922-1979), Ilsley, KY; Helen Halbrooks Greeson, Flat Rock, AL; and Rosa Lee Halbrooks Johnson, Ithaca, NY.

Ruby and Floyd Hodges

Ruby married Floyd Hodges (born 1926) in September, 1948, Linden, TN and moved to Triplett, NC. Children and grandchildren are: Roger Dale 'R.D.' (September 1949) and Elaine Tanner Hodges (married, 1969); son, Tanner (1982), twin daughters, Elizabeth and Katherine

(1991). Deborah Hodges (August 1956) and Roger Jett (married, 1980); son, Jared (1980), daughters, Elizabeth (1984) and Sarah (1989). James (July 1952) and Susan Morris Hodges (married, 1971); son, Jeremy (1986). Audrey Hodges (August 1963) and Jim Watson (married, 1982); sons Jeremy (1986) and _____ (1992). All live in and around the area near Boone, NC (Watauga County).

Ruby attended Perry County Schools. Her children have attended the University of North Carolina. R.D. and Deborah became teachers; James, forestry service; and Audrey, business. Ruby continues to live in Triplett, NC.

Local Linden paternal aunts are Lena Halbrooks Cunningham and Bonnie Halbrooks Anderson; cousins- J.B. Anderson, Lucille A. Hinson and other cousins. Maternal aunts and uncles in Tennessee are Bates Aldridge, Trenton; Geneva Aldridge Sanders, Hohenwald; Clarice A. Bates, Paris; Ruth A. Mullican, McMinnville. A maternal cousin is Jimmy Wayne Crosby.

See notes on Halbrooks, Crosbys, James Aldridge, Rosa Lee Halbrooks Johnson, Helen Halbrooks Greeson, Arthur Jones, Emmaline Chandler Bates, Barney DePriest, Bonnie Anderson, for extended family.

HALBROOK - EDWARDS,
Ethelbert (Thelbert) Halbrook, born 1841 and died Oct. 8, 1913. Married Martha Edwards. She was born July 8, 1844, died Aug. 15, 1908. both are buried at Tucker Cemetery, on Short Creek.

Martha Edwards Halbrook.

Ethelbert's father, William Halbrook (no date) must have died young. 1850 Census states him living with relatives. Benji Westbrook, two girls, Mary M. Westbrook, and Virginia Westbrook in 1850, possible half sisters. Ethelbert's mother had remarried this Benji Westbrook. 1860 census list Benjamin Westbrook, 33, from Illinois. Mary, 30, from Tennessee, Virginia A., 10, Rebecca J., 8, Lucy E., 5, William, 3, Fanny, 10/12, Ethelbert Halbrook, 19, Mary, 15.

Mary Ermaline Tucker Halbrook Westbrook, Ethelbert's mother, died Oct. 22, 1901 and is buried at Tucker Cemetery just off Highway 412 east at the end of Linden Bridge on Bonnie Duncan's land.

Martha Edwards, wife of Ethelbert and daughter of Andrew Jackson Edward, born Jan. 28, 1819, died January 1908. He was a Primitive Baptist preacher and her mother was Ann Sanders.

Martha Edward Halbrook has six brothers and sisters. Mary Elizabeth Edward, b. Oct. 19, 1840, d. Feb. 26, 1920. John Edwards, Isabelle Edwards, Jim Edwards, Emily Edwards, and Willie, who died in childhood.

Ethelbert and Martha's wedding date is unknown. Seven children were born to this union.

George Andrew (Ann) Halbrook, b. 1878, d. 1958, married Lena C. Childress, 1886-1959. Both are buried at Perry Bethel Cemetery.

Joshie Elizabeth Halbrook, b. June 18, 1870, d. June 10, 1944. Married William (Bill) Kilpatrick, b. Feb. 12, 1868, d. June 15, 1952. Both are buried at Rock House Creek, Perry Co., Dabbs Cemetery. (See Kilpatrick-Halbrook)

Robert (Bob) Halbrook, b. Dec. 18, 1871, d. 1960. Married Mollie M. DePriest 1874-1957. Both are buried at Perry Bethel Cemetery.

Emily Jane Halbrook, b. Aug. 13, 1886, d. April 21, 1947. Married Felix Brice Anderson, b. Oct. 26, 1874, d. Dec. 23, 1956. Both are buried at Perry Bethel Cemetery.

Doshie Halbrook, b. May 7, 1894, d. Nov. 9,1952. Married C. W. (Charlie) Martin, b. Mar. 14, 1862, d. Dec. 18, 1945. Both are buried at Chestnut Grove Cemetery.

Gee Halbrook, (dates unknown). Buried in Decatur Co. Had two sons, Leroy, Knoxville and Guy, dead.

Franklin Halbrook?

Ethelbert served his country in Company F, 2nd Mounted Infantry, Union Army. *Submitted by great granddaughter, Joy Kilpatrick Gordon.*

HALBROOKS - GREESON,
Helen Halbrooks-Glenn Greeson (married, 1975). Helen Faye Halbrooks is the first daughter born (April 1930) to Fred (1901-1954) and Nancy (1902-1942) (Nannie) Aldridge Jones Halbrooks at Lobelville, TN. Siblings are Arthur Jones (1922-1979), Ilsley, KY: Rosa Lee Halbrooks Johnson (1931), Ithaca, NY; Ruby Halbrooks Hodges (1932), Triplett, NC. Helen is the granddaughter of Robert and Mollie DePriest Halbrooks (buried Bethel Cemetery) and James and Lew Ellen Bates Aldridge (buried Brush Creek Cemetery); great-grandparents, Barney (B.W.) and Rebecca Westbrook Aldridge (buried Bethel Cemetery) and Dilllard and Emmaline Chandler Bates (buried Gilmer Cemetery), Lobelville), originally of Lower Sulphur Creek, Hickman County. Barney DePriest's parents were Hugh and Mary Amanda VanLandingham DePriest, married June 5, 1843, Dickson County; great-grandfather, Randolph; grandfather, Jesse DePriest. The DePriests and VanLandinghams came from France in the early 1700s via Virginia and North Carolina and settled in DePriest Bend (Beardstown). Helen's great-grandfather, Barney DePriest, was a surveyor of Perry and adjoining counties for more than forty years. He wrote much family history and Perry County History in the *River Counties Quarterly,* Columbia, TN.

Helen was salutatorian of the Linden High School Class of 1947. She married Forrest Ashley, of Hattiesburg, MS (1950). He was in the Air Force. Sheila Faye Ashley Kelso (April 1953) of Pueblo, CO, is her daughter. Sheila is married to Gordon Kelso. Their children and Helen's grandchildren are Erin, Amy and Adam Kelso. Sheila, like her mother, is in medical technology. Helen married Glenn Greeson, Chattanooga, TN (1975). His children are Jimmy Greeson and Gayle Rogers. He also has two grandchildren.

Glenn and Helen (Halbrooks) Greeson

Helen worked in medical technology until her retirement. Her hobbies are flower gardening and quilting.

See references to: Fred and Nancy Aldridge Halbrooks, James Aldridge, Jimmy Crosby, Emmaline Chandler Bates and biographies of her sisters, for additional information.

ROBERT M. HALBROOKS,
(1871-1960), and Mary Anne DePriest, (1874-1957). Robert (Bob) was the son of Ethelbert Anglehart Halbrooks and Martha Edwards. His siblings are George A., Gee, Josephine Kilpatrick, Emilie Anderson and Doshie Marlin.

Robert M. and Mary Ann (Mollie) DePriest Halbrooks.

Ethelbert (went by Thelbert) was the son of William (1819) from Bedford County and Mary Tucker. His sisters were Mary and Virginia and half siblings of B. Westbrooks: Fanny, Thelbert, Rebecca, Lucy, William, Jane.

Robert's grandparents for several generations are William, married in Stokes Co., NC, in 1811 to Judith McGee Reynolds (1783), born in Virginia.

Next generation was John Halbrook (notice name change) (ca 1755-1830 or 35) married Martha (Millie) Ham (Hamm).

Next generation was William (1722) christened at Wybunbury Church, Cheshire, England and died 1806 in

Green County, KY.

Next generation was John Halbrook, in Virginia, 1733; married Mary Brassery; Katherine.

Ralph Holbrook, christened 1657, Hough township, married 1684, Acton, Cheshire, Elizabeth Hodkisson (1699 died). Ralph's will 1725 Walgherton, Cheshire. Second wife, Mary (died 1744).

Randall— christened 1630, Little Budworth; Will—1669; died 1671; wife, Alice.

Randal Holbrook— christened 1586, Little Budworth; died 1642; married 1608, Frances at Dannport, (died 1662).

Randal Holbrook (1560-1638); wife—Ann, died 1608, Little Budworth. Other wives; 1586, a son christened.

(skip generation)

Reverend John Holbrook, near Liverpool, England. John Holbrook went to college in England early 1500. Coat-of-Arms is Suffolk design (Wars-Welsh VS Normans).

The original name was de Holbrook, meaning a place. Further conformation is being researched.

"Mollie" DePriest was daughter of Barney DePriest and Rebecca Westbrook, a half-sister to Ethelbert Halbrooks. See other references for children: Jack, Fred, Jessie Strickland, Bonnie Anderson, Lena Pearson Cunningham and Clem.

The DePriest family came from France in the early 1700's. See Fred Halbrooks and children for other references.

EZRA A. HAMM, born Aug.11, 1912, died Dec. 4, 1980. Ezra was one of nine children. Ezra Hamm's parents were Robert Hill Hamm born Nov. 29, 1884, died Aug. 11, 1965. Maude Emma Baker Oct. 21, 1891 died April 4, 1958. Virginia Sue Grinder Hamm was born Nov. 7, 1918. Sue Grinder Hamm was one of thirteen children. Parents were Noah Theodore Grinder,born Aug. 11, 1875, died Jan. 12, 1924. Ezra A. Hamm and Sue Grinder were married Oct. 20, 1935. Ezra and Sue have three children. Delton Ray Hamm born July 21, 1938. Delton married Alice Faye Churchwell born Sept. 28, 1945. Delton and Faye have two sons, Marty Ray Hamm born Nov. 29, 1974 and Shannon Lee Hamm born July 8, 1980.

Joyce W. Hamm born Nov. 2, 1940. Joyce Hamm married Byron Hankins and had one boy and one girl, Paul Hankins, Jr. born Jan. 28, 1960. Paul Hankins has three children. Brandy Nicole Hankins born Dec. 24, 1979. One son Derrick born May 17, 1986 and one girl Shaina Aug. 16, 1990.

Rhonda Lean Hankins born Sept. 24, 1964. Rhonda Hankins married Frank Wills. Rhonda and Frank have one boy and one girl. Crystal Lynn Wills born Sept. 24, 1983 and Drew Wills born June 12, 1986.

Larry W. Hamm born Oct. 5, 1948 married June Broadway, they have two girls and one boy. Tracy D. Hamm born Nov. 15, 1974, Gina Nicole Hamm born Dec. 22, 1977, and Barton Wade Hamm born June 24, 1980.

HARDER, The Rockhouse and Cedar Creek Harders are all descendants of John Nicholas Harder of Orange County, NC. John Harder was believed to have come to America in 1753 aboard ship "Peggy" from Rotterdam, last from Plymouth, to Pennsylvania. John Nicholas first appeared in state records of North Carolina in 1776. He received a land grant of 400 acres in Orange County on the Haw River in 1780. His will was probated in Williamson County, TN, in January 1819. His property and servants, Lucy and Boss, went to wife, Mary, and to children William, John Sr., James, Jacob, Nancy Barnhill, Elizabeth Campbell, and Mary Coats. Other servants and equipment were sold for cash.

Edmond Harder in Mexican War uniform at age 21 years.

John Harder, Senior received a land grant of 160 acres on Swan Creek, Hickman County in 1819 No. 197 from Governor McMinn after a treaty was resolved with the Indians. *Goodspeed Histories* lists the Harders as being on Swan Creek around 1809. *Spencer's Hickman County History* lists the Harders as settlers from North Carolina. John, Senior married Delilah. They had William (1796), Dillard, Joshiah Powell (Dec. 5,1799), John Junior (Feb. 14, 1801), Rachel (1804), Joel P. (1808), and Jeremian (Sept. 18, 1810).

William Albert and Lucy Lee Harder.

John, Junior was listed in the census of 1820 as living with his parents. He married Rhoda Ramsey. Their children were Sarah, Edmond (Nov. 29, 1824), Willis A. (Mar. 28, 1826) and James B. (Jan. 28, 1827). James B. later moved to Effingham County, IL. John, Junior and his father died before the 1830 census.

Edmond Harder was a member of Wittfield's "Hickory Guards" during the Mexican War 1846. This became Company A of 1st. Tennessee Regiment. Edmond and James B. walked from Centerville to Nashville. They received one day's training in Nashville then they were put on a boat to New Orleans where they received one more day's training. The company was put back on a boat headed for the war. The water supply ran out on the boat. At the mouth of the Rio Grande, the men dug to get water in the sand. The water was clear initially then turned red. This water made the whole company sick. While in Mexico, Edmond encountered Jefferson Davis, who commanded the 1st. Mississippi Rifles. The "Hickory Guards" and the 1st. Mississippi Rifles captured Monterey.

The Harders had arrived in Perry County prior to the War between the States. During the War between the States, Edmond was a member of Company H, 10th Tennessee Cavalry. He fought at the Battle of Chickamauga.

Edmond was married twice. His first wife was Uria Catherine Sharp who died in 1856. Their children were John Franklin, who moved to Missouri, Mary Ann, James Monroe who died in infancy, and William Edmond who moved to Missouri. His second wife was Mary B. Harder, a cousin who was a daughter of William Harder. Their children were Isham Green Harris who moved to Missouri, Albert Jefferson Davis (Mar. 4, 1861), and Robert E. Lee (Jan. 21,1868). Edmond was a member of Perry County Court and a clerk of Providence Primitive Baptist Church from Oct. 1, 1890 to April 29, 1903. Edmond died April 29, 1903.

Mary Ann Harder married Daniel Treadwell. They lived on Rockhouse Creek on Harder land. Their children were George (1871-1952) Sarah, Ellen, Martha (d. 1960), John, and Newt (1888-1975). Newt Treadwell married Zula Ary. Their children were Francis, Ann, Jasper, and Catherine.

During the War between the States, the Harders lived on Cypress Creek, with Edmond fighting with the 10th Cavalry. Albert Jefferson Davis (Jeff) would have to be out chopping firewood for the family. Whenever Federal Troops rode by, he would have to run into the house until they had passed. He was a child under the age of five.

Jeff married Wincie Ann Grinder and lived on Rockhouse Creek at the mouth of Bulley Hollow. This is the Harder home place. James Andrew (Oct. 28, 1892), Noah Lloyd, Bertha Mae (Aug. 20,1896) and Jennie June (June 1, 1900) were their children. Wincie died, leaving Jeff a widower. Jeff died Feb. 4, 1908 of double pneumonia leaving his orphaned children under the care of his brother, Lee.

Robert Lee Harder (Lee) taught school at Farmer's Valley. He married Leora Evelyn Hinson. Their children were Eugenia (April 13, 1892), Wilburn Hillard (May 13, 1894), Edmond Bryan (Mar. 19, 1899), Newton Clifford (Oct. 19, 1900), Robert Leonard (June 20, 1902 d. 1909), Ila Jane (April 19, 1904), Carlus Jones (Jan. 5, 1910), Mary Jewel (June 1, 1914), and Ina Lee (Oct. 17, 1917). Lee and Jeff operated Harder's General Store located across the creek from Lee's house. Lee was appointed Clerk of the Providence Baptist Church September 1913 and in 1918 was appointed Deacon. He held these positions until the church dissolved in 1924.

Eugenia married Elbert Ary. Their children were Era Mavis (Nov. 21, 1914), Lois Melba (Aug. 22, 1917), Kermit R. (May 13, 1919), Kenneth Hammond (April 16, 1921), and Keith Cleman (Jan. 25, 1934).

William Hillard married Inez Ary. Their children were Sherrod (Oct. 27, 1920), Velma Ray (Sept. 12, 1923), Clenna Elane (Feb. 28, 1925), and Leland Douglas (Sept. 23, 1928).

Edmond Bryan married Mary Barber. Their children were Robert Edwin (Feb. 3, 1932), Arlie Douglas (April 17, 1933), Margaret Sue (Oct. 20, 1934), Marian Shirley (Feb. 21, 1936), Shelby Lee (July 7, 1937), James Franklin (Feb. 6, 1940), and Ronnie Wayne (Oct. 6, 1941).

Newton Clifford married Mollie Grinder and moved to Dover, OH.

Carlus Jones married Cyrena Hickerson and lived in Hohenwald.

Ina Lee married Fred Warren (Mar. 9, 1914). Their children were Freddie Joyce (Sept.

18, 1943) who married John White III and lives in Savannah, TN, and Linda Lee who married Johnny Hinson and had children, Brent Edward (Dec. 4, 1973) and Stacie Renae (Dec. 11, 1976).

Albert Jefferson Davis' son, Noah Lloyd, died in action, in Belgium during World War I. Bertha Mae married Isaac Stevens. June married Claude Kirk.

James Andrew (Jim) married Amanda Ardella Victoria Edwards (Aug. 20, 1892). They lived on the home place on Rockhouse Creek and raised children Raymond (Oct. 27, 1916), Ruth (May 7, 1918), Faye (Feb. 24, 1920), William Albert (May 16, 1923), and Lloyd (Dec. 13, 1925). They moved from Bulley Hollow to the present location because Victoria decided the new location would be better situated for raising a family. They built a large two story house. Jim and Victoria also laid out and built the present road in front of the house after deeding the right of way. Like his father and uncle before him, Jim was left a widower with small children to raise and to educate.

Raymond married Esther Holt. They had a son, Steven Edwards (Mar. 16, 1950). The family resides in Nashville.

Ruth married Ward Turnbow (Nov. 12, 1914). They reside at the Harder home place which occupies land that has been in the family for over one hundred years.

Faye married James Franklin Warren. Their children were Patsy Faye (June 23, 1948) and Vicki Ann (June 19, 1955). Patsy married Tex Smith and they have children, Gabriel and Mary Ann. Vicki married Dr. Kent Latham. Their children are Ben and Matthew.

Albert married Lucy Lee Brammer (Aug. 10, 1931). Their children are Robert Andrew (April 12, 1956), Susan Lou (Sept. 9, 1957), and William Lee (June 30, 1962). Susan married Dr. David Lacy Morris from Oxfordshire, England and their children are Gregory Albert Thomas (Jan. 13, 1986) and Simone Lucy Wallace (Sept. 5, 1989). Albert and his family reside in Bassett, VA.

Lloyd married Embree Prater and resides in Blacksburg, VA. Their children are David Lloyd (Mar. 4, 1956) and Michael Andrew (Sept. 15, 1958).

The earlier Harders were tillers of the soil and actively participated in the westward movement from North Carolina all the way to the West Coast. The later generations turned to the professions. There are six pharmacists, one nurse, one physician, one dentist, and one stockbroker. *Compiled from records from Mrs. Helen Young Bishop, from Mary Harder Savage, and from W. Albert Harder.*

HARDER, The first record of John Nicholas Harder, a farmer, is found in Orange County, North Carolina. According to his will in 1819 in Williamson County, TN, he had a wife, Mary, and four sons and three daughters living at that time.

One of his sons John, b. 1765, and his wife Delilah, b. 1770, married in North Carolina in 1793. Their first four children were born in North Carolina. They moved to Williamson County, TN, and the last four children were born there. John, Delilah, and the family settled on Swans Creek, Hickman County, TN, about 1810. They helped to organize the Primitive Baptist Church on Swan Creek in 1825. Their youngest child was Jeremiah Harder.

Henry and Bertha Lomax Harder

Jeremiah Harder, 1810-1872, married 1829, Harriet Young, 1813-1893, (daughter of Henry and Sarah Phipher Young). They had thirteen children but five died very young. Their children were: William Henry; Mary; John Willis; Elizabeth; Pleasant Edmond; Frances Marion; Louise D.; Sarah Phipher; Margaret Delilah; Edmond Zachariah; Harriet Lavina; James Jeremiah; and Permelia Ann. By 1850 Jeremiah had purchased a farm and moved to Cedar Creek, Perry County, TN. The Harder Cemetery where Jeremiah, Harriet and many other Harders are buried is near the old home place.

The oldest son, William Henry, 1830-1897, a Captain in the Confederate Army, organized a company of men at the Primitive Baptist Church on Cedar Creek in 1861. Many served under him for the duration of the war, including two of his brothers. Captain Harder was wounded and taken prisoner during the war. His diary of war experiences is much prized by his descendants. His mother, Harriet, a gifted seamstress made his uniforms and some of his men's uniforms by hand.

William Henry married 1891, Sarah Atlantic Anderson, 1848-1923, (daughter of John M. and Elizabeth Whitwell Anderson). They had eight children: Frank Willis; Harriet Elizabeth; George Leslie; Solomon Henry; John Jeremiah; Laura May; Prince William; and Earl Lamar. William Henry was a farmer and merchant.

Frank Willis, 1872-1941, married 1892, Mary Lee Bates, 1875-1899, (daughter of Greenberry and Julia Whitson Bates). They had three children: John Henry; Edmond Green; and Winnie Davis. Frank Willis was a farmer, school teacher, and very active in the Primitive Baptist Church, as has been many of the Harders. After Mary Lee's death, Frank Willis married 1902, a young widow, Isabelle Lomax Whitehead, 1877-1950. Isabelle had one daughter, Ila. Frank Willis and Isabelle had three daughters; Clora Lessie; Nina Delphia; and Etta Brown.

John Henry Harder, 1893-1959, was a farmer and rural letter carrier from the Pope Post Office. He married 1912, Bertha Lee Lomax, 1898-1988, (daughter of Robert Allen and Mary Adeline Richardson Lomax). Henry and Bertha's five children are; Floyd Allen, 1913, married Norma Jack Morris (daughter of Jack and Lena Bussell Morris); Olaf Hollis, 1920, married Kathleen Pauline Broadaway, two children-Jerry Hollis; Linda Ann; and two grandchildren; Mary Edith, 1923, married John Wesley Hime, three children-Dorothy Helen; Johnnie Lee; William Thomas; and five grandchildren; William Franklin, 1925-1985, married Velma Matilda Dunn (daughter of James and Julia Kilpatrick Dunn), one daughter - Patsy Ann, 1951, married Bobby Joe French, (son of Watt and Rebecca Sue Nix French), one son Christopher Scott; and Sara Helen, 1931-1951, married Hillard Lee Mackin, (son of Jake and Grace Keeling Mackin) one son - Bobby Hillard, 1950, married Beverly Burcham, (daughter of Ira Lincoln and Ona Verla Bates Burcham) three children - Shonda; Tonya; Dustin; and two grandchildren. *Submitted by Linda Harder Ramirez.*

HARDER, The Harder Family have been long time residents of Perry County. The earliest being Captain William Henry Harder, the first son of Jeremiah Harder and Harriet Young from Hickman County. It is through Capt. Harder that I am proud to say, that I am a daughter of the south.

Sam Stockard wrote of his great-great-grandfather, "Capt. Harder, who swore allegiance to his native state of Tennessee, kept a diary throughout the war and wrote a journal afterward on an old store ledger. He served in Company D in the 23rd Regiment, later changed to Company G. He fought in 12 battles, including Shiloh, Stones River, Chickamunga, the Siege of Richmond, and was in a skirmish near Appomattox Courthouse in Virginia when Gen. Robert E. Lee surrendered.

He was wounded in Shiloh, captured and after a prison term, exchanged for Federal prisoners.

Capt. Harder was married to Sarah Atlantic Anderson on Sept. 6, 1871, they were the parents of eight children. Prince William Harder was the seventh child, born Nov. 24, 1881 and died July 5, 1945. He was married to Ollie Belle Magee born Feb. 8, 1886 and died Oct. 23, 1975. Prince was a hard working farmer and member of the Primitive Baptist Church.

They were the parents of Earl Elvis Harder a resident of Linden. He was married to Mary Virginia Dunn. They were the parents of Ronald Lee Harder who lives in Hohenwald. Elvis is a fun loving and kind man who loves to talk on the phone to his kinfolk.

Elsie Carrie is the only daughter of Prince and Ollie Belle. Elsie lives in Linden and has many loving grandchildren, great-grandchildren and relatives. Elsie was married to Albert Ellison and their children were Ollie May, William Eddie, Eula Bell and Albert Ellison. Elsie was also married to Melvin Cidney Boyd and they had a daughter Nancy Zora Boyd.

The last child is Kelsie Brown Harder. He has been at Potsdam College since 1964 and is the Chairman of the English and Drama Department. Kelsie's in-depth work on names has brought him nationwide recognition along with a place in Who's Who. Was the President of the St. Lawrence Historical Association and Member of the American Name Society where he served as past Exec. Secretary-Treasurer and Vice President. Kelsie is the father of Kelsie Terry also an educator and has earned his place in Who's Who. Kelsie's work in drawing and painting has been published in *Look* magazine and *The Saturday Evening Post*. He is currently the

Chairman of the Art Department at Truckee Meadows Community College.

Other children of Kelsie's are Patricia Ann, an avid genealogist and author of genealogical publications living West Valley, UT; Gerald William, an officer in the Navy, living in San Diego, CA, and Dennis Prince who works for Mohawk Electric in Potsdam, NY.

Kelsie is currently living in Potsdam with his wife Louise and their four children Frank Maron, Thomas Brown, Ann Leslie and Marcia Louise. *Submitted by Pat Scherzinger.*

HARDER-RAGSDALL, Caroline Ragsdall was born Jan. 10, 1869 and her brother Robert J. Ragsdall Mar. 10, 1872, in Perry County. On Roberts death certificate his mother is shown Polly Ragsdall. They were raised as Harder. Caroline was my grandmother. She married Richard Milo Standley of Couch, MO. Caroline died 1932 and Milo 1935. They are buried in the New Salem Churchyard at Couch, MO. John Franklin Harder was born Mar. 12, 1848 to Edmund Harder and Uraith Catherine Sharp of Perry County. Jeremiah Harder was his grandfather. Edmund Harder served in the Civil War 10th CV Division. John F. Harder was a Judge 1886-1890 in Oregon County, MO, and in 1891-92 a Justice of Peace. He was called Judge Harder by most of the community and a well-respected man. He died Oct. 11, 1928 and is buried in Lance Cemetery. He resided in Many Springs.

The 1870 Census Perry County shows J. F. Harder and Ruthanne married April in the home of John and Francis Fraley.

Margaret Caroline Fraley and J. F. Harder were married and lived many years in Oregon County. After her death he married Mary Bell Tarlton. *Submitted by Mabel M. Klobnak.*

EDMOND HARDER, born Nov. 29, 1824, possibly Hickman County, died April 29, 1903, Rock House Creek, buried Harder cemetery. He served in both the Civil War and Mexican War. His parents were Edmund Harder and Rhoda Ramsey. Edmond married twice, first to Uraith Catherine Sharp, daughter of Edward Sharp and Tabitha Mayfield. They had five children. (1) John Franklin Harder, born Mar. 12, 1848, Perry County, died Oct. 11, 1923, Oregan County, MO. His first wife, Margaret Caroline Fraley, born Aug. 7, 1849, died Feb. 3, 1908. (2) Mary Ann Harder, born Nov. 9, 1849, Perry County, died July 14, 1923, buried Harder cemetery. She married Dec. 4, 1869, Perry County, Daniel Treadwell. (3) James M. Harder, born Oct. 10, 1851, Perry County, died young. (4) Thomas Gideon Harder, born Dec. 11, 1853, Perry County. (5) William Edmond Harder, born Mar. 7, 1856, Perry County, died Mar. 23, 1914, Oregan County, MO. He married Jan. 1, 1882, Farmers Valley, Martha Elizabeth Garner, daughter of John J. Garner and Elizabeth Boyce. Their children were Mary Elizabeth, Leora, William Spencer, Cora Ella, Harvel Edmond, Oller Elihue, Mattie Rowena, Claude Washington, Douglas Franklin, and Ollie Mae.

Edmond Harder married second, Mary Harder and had children.

Daniel "Dave" Treadwell, born Feb. 5, 1844, died May 6, 1922, Little Rock House Creek, buried Harder cemetery. He was in the Civil War and was son of George and Catherine Treadwell. He and wife, Mary Ann Harder, had 1) George E. Treadwell, born 1871, died 1952, buried Harder cemetery. He married first July 13, 1902, Perry County, Kate James and second, to Lillian Barber. 2) Sarah E. Treadwell, born 1878, died Arkansas. She married Feb. 7, 1897, Perry County, John Kelly Marshall. 3) possibly Mary C. Treadwell, born 1880 or this could be child #4, Ellen. 4) Ellen Treadwell, died between 1903 and 1909, buried Harder cemetery. She married Jan. 17, 1897, Perry County, W.J. "Hy" Campbell. 5) Martha J. Treadwell, born 1883, died Aug. 18, 1960, buried Broadway cemetery. She married Oct. 2, 1907, Perry County, W. Enloe Thompson. 6) John C. Treadwell, born 1886, buried Harder cemetery. He married Aug. 20, 1918, Perry County, Maggie L. Chumney. 7) Newton Jasper Treadwell, born June 20, 1888, died Dec. 19, 1975, buried Ary cemetery. He married Nov. 5, 1916, Perry County, Zula Ary.

EDMUND GREEN HARDER, (1894-1980) and Bonnie Brown Kirk (1901-1979) were married on Dec. 3, 1919 in the Cedar Creek Community of Perry County, TN.

Edmund Green and Bonnie Brown (Kirk) Harder. Circa 1918.

Ed (E.G.) was born at White Oak, the son of Frank Willis Harder (farmer and subscription school teacher) and Mary Lee Bates. His paternal grandparents were William Henry Harder and Sara Atlantic Anderson and his maternal grandparents were Greenberry Walter Bates and Julia Whitson. William Henry Harder was a Captain in the Civil War and the book he wrote of his experiences during the war is in the Perry County Library.

Bonnie was born on Marsh Creek, the daughter of John Issac Newton Black Kirk (veterinarian and farmer) and Emma Maybelle Coleman. Her paternal grandparents were James Akin Kirk and Lucinda Tennessee Grimmett and her maternal grandparents were William Brown Coleman and Martha Caroline Simmons. Her Simmons ancestors originally owned the Marsh Creek Furnace Stack.

After their marriage, Ed and Bonnie lived in the Cedar Creek community for a year, before moving to the Brooklyn section of Linden in 1920. In 1921 they moved to a house on Hill Street, where they lived until their deaths. Ed was a rural letter carrier from 1920 until he became the Linden Postmaster in the late 1940s, a position he held until his retirement, in 1961. He was an ordained minister in the Primitive Baptist Church and was responsible for the building of the Church located in the Bethel community. Ed was involved in local and state civic and service organizations, including the Lion's Club, and the American Legion (local commander). Bonnie was a homemaker and 'adopted' mother for many of her children's friends. She was active in the PTA, serving as treasurer for approximately 12 years. Ed and Bonnie served as the local Red Cross Service Co-Chairmen during World War II.

Known affectionately by many as 'Mama Bonnie' and 'Papa Ed', they had four daughters: Mary Emma (Mrs. Tom K.) Savage (1921-1979), Flora Mavis (Mrs. W.W.) Ragan (1924-1972), Eddie Mildred (Mrs. Claude) Kiser (1927-1990) and Martha Brown (1933-), eight grandchildren, eleven great-grandchildren, and five great-great grandchildren. Their son-in-law, Tom, was Superintendent of Schools in Perry County during the late 1930s and early 1940s and their daughter, Mary, was acting Superintendent while Tom served in World War II. Mary later was an elementary librarian in Clarksville, TN, Mavis a legal secretary and store manager in Huntsville, AL, Martha became a college faculty member and administrator at VPI&SU in Blacksburg, VA and Mildred an elementary teacher in Clarksville, TN.

JOHN NICHOLAS HARDER, History of the Harders of Rock House, John Nicholas Harder born 1752, Columbus County, NY, wife Mary Jane. His will was probated in January 1819 in Williamson County, TN. His son John married Delilah. They were the parents of Edmond II, Willis and James B. After the death of Edmond and Rhoda Jerimeah, his brother raised Edmond II. Edmond II was born Nov. 29, 1824 and died April 29, 1903. He is buried at the Harder Cemetery on Rock House Creek. Edmond II married Uriah Sharp, their children were John, Mary, James M., Gideon and Edmond. Uriah died April 29, 1856. Edmond married Mary B. Harder Feb. 17, 1858. Children, Isom, Albert Jefferson, and Robert E. Lee (1868-1940). He married Leora Hinson. Their children were Jeanie Wilburn, Bryan, Clifford, Leonard, Ila, Jewel, Ina Lee.

Lee and Leora Harder and family.

Albert Jefferson Harder married Wincie Ann (Sis) Grinder the daughter of William Billy Grinder, the son of Robert Grinder, operator of Grinders Stand on the Natchez trace where Lewis was killed. Their children were James Andrew (Jim) (Oct. 28, 1892-Jan. 29, 1976), Mary Jane (Sept. 25, 1894 - Jan. 27, 1895), Noah Lloyd Harder (Nov. 21, 1895 killed in action in Belgium, Aug. 20, 1918). Bertha Mae Dec. 7, 1897 married Ike Stevens, died Mar. 13, 1989, Jenny

June, June 1, 1900 died May 13, 1984. William Edmond Mar. 7, 1903 - Oct. 22, 1904. Infant son 1906. Wincie Harder died May 8, 1906 and Albert died 1908. The children were left orphans age range 4 to 16. They moved up the creek approximately one mile to live with their Uncle Lee and Aunt Leoria Harder. Wilbur and Jim did most of the farm labor. Uncle Lee operated a country store.

James Andrew married Victoria Edwards, the daughter of Amos Raymond and Celestine Higgins. Marriage date is Jan. 5, 1916. children were Raymond Harder, Ruth Harder, Faye Harder, Albert Harder and Lloyd Harder. On March 22, 1943, Raymond (Oct. 27, 1916) married Esther Holt (Oct. 14, at Lawrenceburg, TN. A son Steve Edwards was born Mar. 16, 1950 at Lebanon, TN. Steve graduated from U.T. School of Pharmacy June 2, 1974. Ruth Harder (May 7, 1918) married Ward Turnbow (Nov. 21, 1914) on June 24, 1958 at Corinth, MS.

Faye Harder (Feb. 24, 1920) married James Franklin Warren (Oct. 14, 1914)., Aug. 4, 1935. Daughter Patricia Faye Warren (June 23, 1948), married Tex Smith on June 17, 1968. Children Gabriel Nelson and Mary Ann.

Victoria Ann Warren (Jan. 19, 1955), married Kent Lathem, two children, Mathew Kent and Benjamin.

William Albert Harder (May 16, 1923), married Lucy Lee Bramer (Aug. 10, 1931). Children; Robert Andrew (Andy) April 12, 1956, Susan Lee (Sept. 9, 1957) and William Lee (Bill) (June 30, 1962).

Noah Lloyd Harder born Dec. 13, 1925, married Embree Prater born Mar. 9, 1936. Children David Harder born Mar. 4, 1956 and, Michael Andrew Harder Sept. 5, 1958.

WILEY V. HARPER,

was born Sept. 24, 1785 in Prince George's Co., Md. At some point his family moved to Halifax Co., NC, where he was married in 1806 to Sarah Green.

Wiley Harper, a shopkeeper, enlisted in the U.S. Army on Jan. 5, 1814. He was wounded in his right shoulder during action with the British, near New Orleans, on Dec. 23, 1814. The young corporal was permanently deprived of the use of his right arm. After his discharge in 1815, he became a school teacher, a career which he pursued throughout his life.

Wiley and Sarah Harper began their married life in Halifax, NC, where their first two children were born. Sarah's pension application states that the family moved to Hickman Co., TN, in the fall of 1822.

Hickman Co. records indicate that Wiley Harper taught school at Bird Creek and Little Lot. The family is listed in the Hickman Co. census from 1830 to 1850. It is believed that they became Perry Countians by virtue of a boundary line changed by the State Legislature in 1859.

Wiley V. Harper's tombstone at Dudley Cemetery in Perry County reads: "Wiley V. Harper, Virginia CPL 44 Inf., War of 1812, Sept. 24, 1785-April 14, 1859."

Sarah Green Harper, who was born ca 1788, lived about 31 more years until her obituary appeared in the Linden Times newspaper in April 1880. It said, " Mrs. Harper, 92, of Lost Creek, Perry County, died on Friday, the 2nd; her husband was the educator of Judge Elijah Walker. Judge Walker gave her the farm where she lived at her death."

One wonders if the gift of a farm was necessitated to satisfy the heirs of Wiley Harper, who died intestate. T. W. Lewis and wife began a series of court proceedings in 1879 to be granted permission to sell the land of the deceased. Lemuel Tate's bid of $550.00 was higher than that of Lewis and was accepted by the court. In 1882, the complaints had still not been able to provide a suitable listing of the numerous heirs who were to receive $10.00 each.

The children of Wiley V. Harper and Sarah Green were at least ten in number. They were: Joel, born ca 1815, married Lucretia; Eliza, born July 5, 1818, married William Chandler, Jr.; Margaret, born ca 1824, married Allen Barber; female, born ca 1820/25; Marcus Lafayette, born Mar. 17, 1826, married first to Nancy Chandler and second to Helen E. Fain; Rosanah, born Aug. 27, 1827, married Tyre Chandler; Martha, born ca 1830, married a Lewis; Malinda, born ca 1832, married Pleas Horner; Sarah Jane, born ca 1834, married Thomas W. Lewis; and Elizabeth, born Apr. 18, 1934, never married.

Aunt "Bett" Harper, the youngest child, continued to live on the Harper farm after the death of her mother, Sarah. At some point before her death on Apr. 9, 1916, Aunt Bett gave the farm to Dillard and Emmy Chandler Bates in exchange for taking care of her as long as she lived. "Emmy" was her niece, the daughter of Tyre and Rosanah Harper Chandler. The Harper farm remained in the Bates family until the death of Emmy Chandler Bates on June 23, 1940.

WILLIE PAT AND LUCILLE RODGERS HARPER,

Willie Pat, son of Please Combs and Diana Harper, grandson of Willis and Polly Duncan and grandson of Hansel and Mary Harper; married Lucille A. Rodgers Harper in 1931 in Mill Hollow by Mike Paschall. Willie Pat had three brothers: Chesley, Guy and Olen and six sisters Ollie, Edna, Addie, Annie, Jessie Mae and Nora. Pat and Lucille had four sons: Dewey G. Harper, married to Virginia Aldridge; Leon Harper, married to Mary Rue Walker; Argil Harper, married to Annie Ruth Holt; and Bronie Harper. One daughter Margarette Rachel Ann Harper, married to Sandor Szuliman. Pat and Lucille had 10 grandchildren Jeffery, Vincent, Christopher and John Winston (John married Patricia) - children of Dewey and Virginia Harper. Robert Harper (married Sandra Nelson) - son of Argil and Annie Ruth Harper. Michelle (married Gary Richardson), Patrick, and Lorrie (married Bryant Odem) - children of Margarette and Sandor Szuliman. Elaine and Cindy (married to Dennis Knight) - children of Leon and Mary Rue Harper.

Great grandchildren of Pat and Lucille Harper - Alexandria and Lindsey Richardson, Ashley Nichole Odem, Chole Miranda Carroll, Robbie, Anthony, Britison, Nicole, Morro-Deanna, Ann, Jennipher Harper, Mark Harper, Collin, Jammie and Nathenal Harper. (15 great-grandchildren)

Pat Harper died Sept. 21, 1993 and was buried in Warren Cemetery on Cane Creek, Perry County, TN.

Dewey and Leon Harper served four years in the Korean War. Chris and John Harper served in Desert Storm. Sandor Szuliman served in the Korean War and Viet Nam.

Willie Pat and Lucille Rogers Harper

Dewey Harper served as General Sessions Judge in Wayne County from 1974 through 1984. He is presently a candidate for State Representative in the 74th District (1994).

RALPH HARRIS,

and Jean Scott were married in 1944 in Bowling Green, KY. To this marriage were born two children; Ronald Scott Harris who married Diane Whitworth (they have three children) and Carolyn Harris who married Wayne Fitzgerald (they have two children).

Ralph Harris   *Ralph and Jean Harris*

Jean Scott's mother and father was Edward Scott and Aline Russell from Petersburg, the home of Morgan Prep School.

Ralph was a pitcher in professional baseball, playing in Class D, Kitty League; Class C, Western Association; Class B, Gasden, AL, and in the Southern Association playing for both Chattanooga and New Orleans. An injury to his arm forced retirement from professional ball. He finished his career playing in Industrial leagues.

Ralph is the great-grandson of David Rice Harris, born Aug. 4, 1808 in Prince Edward County, VA. He is the individual mentioned in early Perry County history as giving forty acres of land on which the town of Linden was built in 1848. The early history states "that David retained some lots for himself and these lots are still titled to the Harris heirs".

David R. married first Rebecca Dillard of Maury County, their children were John K., William, Gidean Lewis, Martha Jane and Sarah. After 1860, he married Eliza Roberts. Their children were Giles Tinsley, Martha Safronia, Thomas Blount, Elizabeth and Rebecca Rice Harris,. David Rice Harris died Jan. 30, 1873. He is buried in the Harris Cemetery on Harris branch about six miles north of Linden.

Giles Tinsley Harris, born Nov. 16, 1861 was Ralph's grandfather. He married Sallie C.

Sewell, born May 4, 1861 and they had six children; Alice, who married Fred Godwin; Ruth, who married a Pearson, moved to Georgia and is buried there; Eura, born Feb. 21, 1887, never married; Cecil, born June 30, 1890, who married Ada Twomey, born Aug. 14, 1892. Their children were Sarah, who moved to California, Ralph Twomey and Ruth; David S. Harris born 1893, married Amy Duncan born 1908. They had three children. They are Partarica, David Duncan, who was killed while young in an auto wreck and Maxine. Maude, born July 14, 1888, married Larimore Webb, born April 25, 1885. They had four children, Ned Harris, G.T., Billy and Joe.

HEADY, Silas Dean Heady and Barbara Jo Beasley Heady live in Riverside Drive in Linden, TN. Dean Heady was born in Gallatin, TN, on Jan. 23, 1948 to Silas Enloe Heady, son of William Clayton Heady and Hattie Dudney Heady of Jackson County. TN, and Mattie Louise Vantrease Heady, daughter of George Lee Vantrease and Laura Mae Tittle Vantrease of Nashville, TN.

The Dean Heady Family

Dean has one sister, Ouida Faye Heady Landon of Henderson, TN. Dean grew up in Gallatin and graduated from Gallatin High School in 1966. He went to Freed-Hardeman College in Henderson, TN, where he met Barbara Beasley.

Barbara was born on Aug. 19, 1948 to Tom Alva Beasley, son of John Allen Beasley and Augusta Pearl Land Beasley of Linden, TN, and Mary Jo Beasley, daughter of Byron Clyde King and Mary Lee Bromley King of Linden, TN. Barbara has one brother, Jeffrey Thomas Beasley of McEwen, TN In her younger years Barbara lived in Nashville, TN; Jackson, TN; Yorktown, VA; Guantanamo Bay, Cuba; and Perry County, TN, while her father Tom Beasley was in the U. S. Navy. Barbara moved to Perry County in June 1959 when her farther retired. She graduated from Perry County High School in 1966 and went to Freed-Hardeman College where she met Dean. Barbara and Dean graduated in May of 1968 and were married on July 6, 1968 at Centerville Church of Christ. Their first home was in Nashville, TN, where Dean attended David Lipscomb College. Dean graduated in 1970 with a degree in education. The Heady family moved to Memphis, TN, where Dean was employed by the Memphis City School System and Barbara was a homemaker.

On May 14, 1971 Jason Lee Heady was born in Linden, TN. On Dec. 28, 1973 Vanessa Gayl Heady was born in Linden, TN On April 30, 1976 Joel Thomas Heady was born in Linden, TN In August of 1976 the Heady family moved to Linden and Dean began teaching with the Perry County School System. Dean received his Masters Degree in 1988 and began work with the Lewis County School System. He is principal of the Lewis County Middle School. Barbara worked at the Perry Memorial Hospital part-time from 1977-1979 and began working at the Perry County Medical Center when it opened in November of 1979. In 1981 she became the Executive Director and has served in that capacity since that time.

Jason graduated from Perry County High School in 1989. He studied pre-engineering at Freed Hardeman University for three years and will graduate with a degree in Mechanical Engineering from Tennessee Technological University in December of 1994. Vanessa graduated from Perry County High School in 1992 and is currently studying pre-engineering at Freed Hardeman University in Henderson, TN. Joel finished 8th grade at Linden Elementary and then transferred to Lewis County Schools. He will graduate from Lewis County High School in the spring of 1995. All are members of the Linden Church of Christ where Dean serves as elder and song leader.

HEATH, The Heath name has English origin. This name was first found in America as early as the seventeenth century, when one William Heath went to work on a plantation in New England in 1632. Another Isack Heath, who was an arms maker, was transported to New England on the Hopewell in 1635.

John W. Heath Family

William "Billie" Heath, born in Virginia in 1826, moved to Davidson County and married Jane Bell born 1837. Their children were Alexander, John William, Charles, Lee, Mary, and Samuel.

John William Heath married Arra Justine Godwin and their children were Bessie May, Etter Jane, Albert Henry, Daisy Gertrude, Maud Delia, Claud Dean, Jesse D., Golden Gertrude, and Roy Nixon (my father).

Roy Nixon Heath married Alva Osa Lofton and their four children are; twin sons, age six months and died in 1916, two daughters, Lorene (born 1917), and Fannie Bell (born 1921).

Fannie Bell married James Henry Lee on Feb. 12, 1939 and their children are Roy Sweeney, James Edward, and Linda Carol.

Lorene Heath and Guy Marrs were married June 4, 1933 at Simmons Hollow, Perry County by Brother J. B. Oakley. They made their home in the Seed Tick Community, which was just over the Perry County Line in Humphreys County. This was about the heart of the Great Depression, when jobs were almost non-existent and prices for all farm products were at record low. Times were very trying, since Guy was a farmer, raising peanuts, corn, and hay. They had two children, John L. born Mar. 6, 1935, and Betty Jo, born April 19, 1937.

Guy and Lorene Marrs

At the outbreak of World War II, they moved to Pontiac, MI, to work in the factories. Guy worked at S. & F. Tool Company helping make machine guns and Lorene worked at Yellow Truck & Coach helping make landing craft for the troops. They worked at these jobs until Guy was drafted into military service in 1945. Twelve days before he was scheduled to leave for basic training, the first Atomic Bomb was dropped on Hiroshima. He was never required to go.

After moving back to Perry County in 1948, Lorene went to work with Washington Manufacturing Co. at Linden, and Guy, after working short periods with Tennessee Gas and TVA, purchased a new Frick sawmill. This proved to be a business he liked, and stayed with the rest of his life. Probably the most unusual event with this sawmill happened on a deal made with a company to move this mill to Weldon Springs, MO, just outside St. Louis, in 1956. This was a virgin tract of timber belonging to the University of Missouri. Since sawmill workers were not available around this area, all the help was recruited from around Lobelville. A bunkhouse was built on this Weldon Springs property, complete with a kitchen, and everyone worked for 21 days straight before coming home for a week. Three meals per day were cooked on the job providing the best of food, and at the end of three weeks the cost was divided out per man. Actual cost, including wages for the cook, came to about $1.30 to $1.50 per day per man. This job lasted about fourteen months.

Lorene and Guy bought land on Red Bank in 1963, and built a house there, within a mile of the location they lived at when first married. Guy died in June, 1967, and Lorene still lives at the same location.

HENDRIX-GARRETT, Charles Edward Hendrix and Rebecca Lynn Garrett were married on Aug. 30, 1974 at Dripping Spring Baptist Church in Logan County, Kentucky. They were students at Austin Peay State University when they met. On Nov. 23, 1977, they became the proud parents of a son, Walter Neil Hendrix. They were just as proud of their second child, a daughter who was named Kelly Lynn Hendrix. She was born Jan. 3, 1983. They lived in the Pope Community next to the Pope School until the school was consolidated. They both worked to establish the Pope Volunteer Fire Department near their home on the old school campus.

Charles, Becky with children, Kelly and Walter Hendrix

Charles was the oldest son of Dennis Aaron Hendrix and Mary Lou Mercer, who were both raised in Perry County. He was born May 22, 1948 at the Boyce Clinic in Hohenwald, TN. His two brothers, Jimmy Dan Hendrix and Bobby Joe Hendrix, were also born there later. He worked at Ferro Manufacturing Co. in Linden, which was later bought by Johnson Controls. He worked as a volunteer with M.Y.F. at the Methodist Church and with Explorer and Boy Scouts.

His paternal grandparents were Charlie Neelie Hendrix and Bessie Ann Brooks, who came to Perry County from Houston County by way of Humphreys County.

His maternal grandparents were Edd Walter Mercer and Lillie Young Sharp. Walter came to Perry County as a young child by way of Hickman and Lewis Counties. He and his family, including aunts, uncles, and grandparents came from the area of Leitchfield, KY, shortly before 1900. Lillie's family is traced through Hickman County to Perry County where they lived as she grew up. They lived in the area of Brushy Hollow, Sinking Creek and Flatwoods near the Perry-Wayne County line.

Rebecca was born May 18, 1953, at Muhlenberg County Hospital in Greenville, KY. She was the youngest daughter of Estill Forrest Garrett from Muhlenberg County and Audrey Elizabeth Hudgins of Walter Valley, MS. She has an older sister, Mary Angeline, and two older brothers, James Estill and John Ellis. She worked at Cloverbottom School and Developmental Center in Donelson, TN, as a physical therapist aid until she married. She later worked for Dee Cee Manufacturing Co. then worked at home raising the children. She was active in community volunteer work, including Explorer Scouts, Girl Scouts, Boy Scouts, Cancer Society, Red Cross, Methodist Church and helping out with school activities.

Her paternal grandparents were Adrian Estill Garrett and Arbie Forrest Jackson. They were both raised in the area near Browder in Muhlenberg County, KY. Her maternal grandparents were Jesse Ellis Hudgins and Ester Rampy. They were from Water Valley, MS, but after Ester's death, Jesse moved about while working on the Tennessee Valley Authority dams, including Pickwick and others.

HENDRIX-MERCER, Dennis Aaron Hendrix and Mary Lou Mercer were married on Aug. 24, 1946 in Corinth, Alcorn Co., MS. They first lived in the old Dr. Black house at Sugar Hill area in Perry County. They later moved into a small house on the farm where they lived when their first child was born. His name was Charles Edward Hendrix, and he was born on May 22, 1948. They later bought a farm on the head of Hurricane Creek. Their second son, Jimmy Dan Hendrix was born Sept. 8, 1952 while they lived here. They rented out the farm and went into business partnered with Dennis' brother Elcoe Hendrix in 1954. The grocery store and service station was located at Bear Creek Crossing in Decatur County. They returned to Perry County and lived in a rented house on Mill Hollow Branch until the year end when the farm rent was up. They moved back to the farm and lived there until 1957 when they bought a house and farm in the Bethel Community on the Marsh Creek road. Their third son, Bobby Joe Hendrix was born Sept. 13, 1958 after moving here.

Mary Lou and Dennis Hendrix

Dennis was born Dec. 24, 1918 between the Sugar Hill and Bethel areas of Perry County on the Hunnicut Bluff. He was the fifth of eleven children born to his parents, Charlie Neelie Hendrix and Bessie Ann Brooks who came to Perry County from Humphreys County. His paternal grandparents were John William Hendrix, who died in a mining accident and was buried near Erin, TN and Laney Evelyn Bramlett. His maternal grandparents were Jason Patrick Brooks, a Methodist circuit rider and Mary Elizabeth Sally Jane Little.

Mary Lou was born May 25, 1929 on Hurricane Creek at the mouth of Band Mill Hollow in Perry County. She was the fourth of ten children born to Edd Walter Mercer and Lillie Young Sharp. Walter came to Perry County as an infant from Leitchfield, KY. His family were farmers and in the timber business. He and many of his sons and grandsons followed the same lifestyle. Lillie was raised in the southeastern part of Perry County and possibly the edge of Wayne and Lewis Counties. Her paternal grandparents were John Allen Mercer and Mary Frances Wilson who came to Perry County from Kentucky about 1900 by way of Lewis County. Her maternal grandparents were John Franklin Sharp and Lucinda Junetta Tatum.

HESTER/ELLIOTT, Johnnia Ruth (born Sept. 18, 1945) was the second child born to John and Sophia Hester. She graduated from George Peabody College in June 1966 and married Paul Cherry Elliott (b. Nov. 21, 1941) of Nashville, TN, on July 29, 1966. After one year living and teaching in Nashville, the couple moved to Greensboro, NC, for Paul to pursue a Masters of Fine Arts in Theater at the University of North Carolina. Johnnia worked for the Girl Scouts of America. After completing the degree Paul became Chairman of the Performing Arts Department at Stratford College in Danville, VA. Two daughters, Keats Leigh (b. June 18, 1969) and Kiersten Tate (b. July 12, 1972) were born there.

Pursuing his career as a writer, Paul, Johnnia and the girls moved progressively westward from Virginia. Back in Nashville, TN, he wrote for country recording star, Dolly Parton. While in Provo, UT, he spent two years writing for Donny and Marie Osmond before moving to Glendale, CA, where he wrote and directed for Disneyland and other area theme parks. Johnnia worked for the Glendale Public Library in the Young People's room and managed the Glendale Bookmobile program.

A 1991 graduate of Northwestern University in Evanston, IL, Keats lived in Los Angeles and worked in the entertainment industry. After returning from a year in England, Kiersten finished her senior year at the University of California at Santa Cruz, then continued her education in psychology with a special focus on School Administration and Student Activities.

JOHN AND SOPHIA HESTER, How often does a person get the chance to look back and remember what it was like to be the child of their parents, and to grow up in Lobelville during the fifties and sixties. Our parents were John and Sophia Hester.

John T. and Sophia Hester family

Compared to the forties with its World War and the eighties and nineties with their complexities, the fifties and the sixties were a time for just about everything children needed to know. There was a time for working hard picking strawberries, tending gardens, mowing lawns, canning vegetables and still time to hunt Easter eggs in the buttercups and catch lightning bugs on warm summer evenings. We all had our chores and Mother's philosophy was the more hands that were helping the more pleasant and quicker a task was completed.

TIME....maybe that was the secret.

There was time for both Sunday School and worship at Lobelville United Methodist Church. There was time for Methodist Youth Fellowship on Sunday evening, Vacation Bible School during the summer and church camp, too. There was time for turning the handle on the ice cream freezer and fanning with those hand-held fans; both the temperature and the preaching got hot at a summer revival. There was time for riding the school bus to Lobelville Elementary and having so much fun after you got there that you weren't ready to ride it home at three. Getting a good education was top priority.

There was TIME for 4-H with all its projects and activities that made farm chores, like caring for the cows and chickens, the garden and the house, seem like fun and profitable projects.

There was TIME for big family get-to-gathers. John was one of eight children and Sophia was one of ten. Most of John's brothers and sisters lived near Lobelville so family gatherings were pleasant and happened frequently. Sophia's family lived in the Nashville vicinity so visiting them was a happily anticipated excursion for the whole family.

In our family there always seemed enough time for just about everything three children wanted to do or needed to know to grow up with wonderful childhood memories of their parents and their community. We could not have been guided into adulthood more skillfully or with more love and devotion than was given by our parents, John and Sophia Hester.

HICKERSON-LEDBETTER, Willard

Marie Hinson, daughter of Jonathan Harvey and Martha Hickerson Hinson, born 1917, married James Fred Duncan 1915/1989, buried in Nix Cemetery. Son of Edgar James and Mattie Shannon Duncan. He served four years in the Army. He was at Pearl Harbor Dec. 7th, 1941. Took part in the liberation of the Philippines under General McArthur.

William Finley Hickerson Family

One child, Martha Cheryl Duncan, she married Stanley Tinin Jr. They have two children-Carol Ann and Kevin Wayne.

Grandparents-Newton Jasper and Martha Duncan Hinson 1845/1928 - 1846/1878, and Wm. Finley and Rebecca Ann Anderson Hickerson 1858 / 1919- 1863 / 1944. Buried in Hickerson Cemetery, Hurricane Creek. Children of Wm. Finley and Rebecca - Zine, married Amos Edwards, Jake married Martha Pevahouse, Martha Jane, Susan Minnie married John Galloway, Lucinda married Albert Alberson, Sallie married Willie Cotton, married Plummer Bryson after Willie was killed by a runaway team of mules, Jadie married Oma Dabbs, Joseph Wesley married Mae Hinson, Bessie married Clarence Campell, Willie Martin married Lucille Barber, John married Iva Dell Jackson, Robie Moore married Margaret Swanner, he was killed in an accident in 1945 in Ohio. Parents of William Finley-Nathaniel and Narcissus Ledbetter Hickerson, 1827. His parents were John D. and Mary Hickerson, John born in Kentucky 1804, settled on Sinking Creek. He died before October 1868. Parents of Narcissus - Isaac and Sallie Acuff Ledbetter, he was a Methodist minister, son of Rowland and Sarah Vaughn Ledbetter, Rowland born 1764 in Virginia, died in Marshall County, 1842. From a history by Mary Louise Yeiser Wiley- North Carolina Dept. of Archives, (The said Rowland Ledbetter was granted six pounds, 14 shilling and 10 pence in 1783, for assisting in establishing American Independence. He was drafted at the age of 16 during the Revolution, served as private 1780/81). Sarah, daughter of Steven Vaughn of South Carolina. Ledbetters settled in Virginia about 1635, spread out by 1800.

Rowland's parents were Henry and Winifred Wall Ledbetter, he was born 1728, in Virginia, her parents were Joshua and Martha Wall, he was born before 1687 in Virginia.

His parents were Henry and Edith Williamson Ledbetter, their will in 1765 listed children-Elizabeth married Isaac Rowe Walton, Charles married a Randel, Henry and Drury who married Winifred Lanier.

Parents of Rebecca Hickerson-Joseph and Martha Satterfield Anderson He was a Confederate soldier, son of William (Whig) and Lucinda Berry Anderson, married daughter of George and Jane Berry. Azariah Anderson settler of Fall's Branch, Hickman County, was the father of William, parents of Martha Ann were David and Rebecca Gresham Satterfield. He was born in Kentucky 1820, parents-Ephraim and Ruth Knowles Satterfield, John and Mary Jones Satterfield were Ephraim's parents.

Rebecca was the daughter of George and Ann Nancy Gresham. Her parents were Robert and Amelia Nichols Chaffin, John Nichols was the father of Amelia.

Joseph and Martha Ann are buried in Graves Cemetery on Sinking Creek. William and Lucinda Anderson are buried in Milan Cemetery, Hickman County. *Submitted by Mrs. Fred Duncan.*

HICKERSON, David Leroy Hickerson,

born Dec. 10, 1865, Perry County, possibly Cedar Creek, died Feb. 8, 1931, buried Ary cemetery. He was the son of John Hickerson and Sarah Comelia Treece. David married July 23, 1891, Lewis County, Sarah Landorer (Dora) Pegram. Dora was born Oct. 8, 1874, died Sept. 27, 1944, buried Ary cemetery. Their eight children (1) Ida E. Hickerson, born Oct. 27, 1892, died Aug. 21, 1905, buried Ary cemetery. (2) Andrew Oscar Hickerson, born Sept. 26, 1894, died Oct. 16, 1968, married Audie Brown. (3) William Leroy Hickerson, born Aug. 20, 1896, married Ada Brown. (4) Lawrence M. Hickerson, born Mar. 24, 1898, died May 7, 1970, married Lillie Mai Duncan. (5) Clister Ola Hickerson, born July 4, 1900, died Apr. 15, 1971, buried Graves cemetery, Sinking Creek. She married first Arthur Andrew Goodman and second William Matthew Tatum. (6) George Herbert Hickerson, born Jan. 13, 1902, died Mar. 23, 1970, married Nettie May Duncan. (7) Martha M. Hickerson, born Oct. 19, 1904, died June 19, 1978, married first Ira Alts Riley and second Joel K. Poore. (8) infant Hickerson, born and died July 1, 1906, buried Ary cemetery.

Dora was daughter of William Malibar Pegram and Amanda E. Sharp. They married Feb. 4, 1891, Perry County. Beside Dora, their children were Serenie Almedia Pegram born 1871, married Lee Grant Goodman, moved to Oklahoma. Ida Catherine Pegram, born 1874, married Issac Thomas Skelton, moved to Texas. Mattie Maury Pegram, born Mar. 25, 1879, died Feb. 6, 1949, Texas. Eugene Huse Pegram, born 1882, married and lived in Texas.

William M. and Amanda Sharp Pegram

Amanda Sharp was daughter of James Mountable Sharp and Sarah Clayton. Her grandparents were Edward Sharp and Tabitha Mayfield and John Clayton and Nancy Bridges. *Submitted by Merle Stevens.*

JOHN HICKERSON, (1804-1868),

was born in Kentucky about 1804, died in Perry County, TN, about 1868 and is buried on a hillside on Sinking Creek in the Hickerson Cemetery. He married Nancy Treece, born about 1803 in North Carolina. The maiden name Treece comes from a granddaughter, Ida Sharp. It is not known when they came to Perry County but they appear in the 1840-50-60 Perry County Census.

Some of their children are:

1. Nathaniel Hickerson, born October 1827, died Sept. 10, 1888, married Narcissa Ledbetter, daughter of Isaac Ledbetter. She was born Nov. 29, 1827, died May 19, 1908. They are both buried in the Hickerson Cemetery on Hurricane Creek.

2. William Hickerson, born 1825 in Tennessee, died Apr. 30, 1896, married July 18, 1844, Elizabeth Sharp. She was born Oct. 21, 1823, died October 1875. He was in Co. C, 2nd Arkansas Infantry of the Confederate Army.

3. Susan Hickerson, born Aug. 1, 1831 in Tennessee, died May 5, 1895, married Aug. 8, 1848, Thomas E. Graves, son of Isaac Lee and Mary D. (Lincoln) Graves. They are both buried in Graves Cemetery at the head of Sinking Creek.

4. Catherine Hickerson, "Kate", born 1833 in Tennessee, married Henry Coleman Ledbetter. They went to Arkansas.

5. John Hickerson, born Oct. 10, 1835, died Sept. 9, 1886, married Sarah Cornelia C. Treece (1840-1916). He was in Co. B, 2nd Arkansas Infantry of the Confederate Army. Their children: 1. David Leroy Hickerson, born Dec. 10, 1865, died Feb. 8, 1931, married July 27, 1891, Sarah Landora Pegram. 2. John Samuel Hickerson, born Oct. 3, 1867, died young. 3. Sarah Nancy Elizabeth Hickerson, born Dec. 9, 1869, married Sept. 14, 1890, Bryant Mathis. 4. Henry Newton Hickerson, born Apr. 21, 1872, died Apr. 1, 1948, married July 15, 1894, Nancy Matilda Ary. 5. Ida E. Hickerson, born Sept. 5, 1874, died Mar. 29, 1905, married Apr. 26, 1891 in Lewis

County, John Rakestraw Fain. 6. Andrew Hunt Hickerson, born Sept. 5, 1876, married Oct. 30, 1895, Lou Duncan. 7. Susan C. Hickerson, born May 26, 1878, married Lewis Mathis.

6. George W. Hickerson, born 1838, married Dicy Boyce .

7. David A. Hickerson, born 1840, was in Co. C, 2nd Arkansas Infantry of the Confederate Army.

8. Martha Jane Hickerson, born 1843, married (1) Nehemiah Sharp, son of John and Elizabeth (Vincent) Sharp, married (2) Thomas Flowers. They went to Oregon County, MO about 1880 and stayed.

9. Samuel Hickerson, born April 1845, died Nov. 24, 1919, married Sept. 27, 1870, Sarah E. Dabbs. He was in Co. E, Tennessee Cavalry of the Confederate Army.

10. Sarah Elizabeth Christine Hickerson, born October 1849 in Perry County, died Jan. 4, 1931 in Walkertown, Hardin County, TN, married (1) Sept. 15, 1866 I. G. Roden and (2) James Sharp. There was a James Hickerson born 1823 and Daniel Hickerson born 1829 in the Perry County Census. Were they also children of John and Nancy Hickerson? I would like to hear from anyone researching any of these Hickersons. *Submitted by Imogene Rasbury Parsley, 10908 Melton View Lane, Knoxville, TN 37931.*

MARION D. HICKERSON, Mary Alice Westbrooks, born July 1860 was his first wife. They had several children that did not survive infancy. Those that did, were (1) John Mack Hickerson, born 1882, Perry County, buried in the Alberson cemetery, Hurricane Creek. He married 1903, Perry County, Sophia Bulla, who is also buried Alberson cemetery. (2) Margaret E. Hickerson, born 1886. (3) Mary Jane Hickerson, born Jan. 18, 1890, died Apr. 7, 1973, buried Wayne County. She married Ross Montgomery Pitts. (4) Nora I. Hickerson, born Aug. 27, 1892, Perry County, died Feb. 4, 1938, buried Wayne County. Nora married John F. Edwards.

Marion D. Hickerson, by his second wife, Nan Kirk had at least three children. Nan born 1867, died 1946, buried Bethel cemetery. She married first a Whitwell. (1) Hassell Hickerson, born 1906. (2) Earlene Hickerson, born 1908. (3) Irene Hickerson who died as an infant.

John Mack Hickerson's wife, Sophia Bulla was daughter of James Bulla and Nancy Caroline Rawdon. Sophia had married first John Weems and had a daughter Allie Mae Weems Choate. They had three children (1) Winifred Hickerson, born Jan. 26, 1903, died Jan. 12, 1980, buried Kirk cemetery. He married Rebecca Mercer, born Mar. 26, 1894, died Aug. 10, 1978, daughter of John Allen Mercer and Mary Wilson. (2) Lorene Hickerson, born Feb. 11, 1908, died Jan. 2, 1981, buried Dean cemetery. She married M. Ross Carroll, born Aug. 11, 1902, died Nov. 9, 1970. (3) James Davis Hickerson, born Dec. 6, 1911, died Nov. 20, 1976, buried Kirk cemetery. His wife, Elsie May Rogers, born 1913, died 1990.

THIRL AND VIVIAN HICKERSON, Mattie Vivian Denton was born in the Cedar Creek community of Perry County on Jan. 18, 1925, the youngest of seven children born to Andrew Polk Denton and Mary Cordelia Stephens. Two children, Joe Vernon and Mary Love died at an early age. The other children were Eula Mae, Arkie, Melissa Ann, and Jeanetta.

Thirl and Mattie Denton Hickerson They married on June 25, 1945.

Vivian graduated from Perry County High School in 1943. Her husband, Thirl Hickerson, graduated from Perry County High School in 1936, after transferring from Wayne County High School at Clifton.

Thirl and Vivian met years later and married at Rossville, GA, June 25, 1945.

Thirl served eight years in the Navy. He was aboard the USS West Virginia, in port at Pearl Harbor when it was bombed Dec. 7, 1941. Thirl swam to safety.

Vivian and Thirl have four children: Janis Denton, born Aug. 3, 1946, William Bruce, Dec. 10, 1949, Rita Gail, June 29, 1951, and Trudy Dion, May 27, 1959.

Janis has one son Christopher Patterson. Bruce is married to Kathleen Bradford and has no children. Janis and Bruce live in Humphreys County. Rita Gail is married to Robert Moreland, and has one daughter, Angelia Pratt. Trudy Dion is married to Joe David Satterfield; they have two boys, David William and James Denton.

William Thirl Hickerson was born in the Beech Creek community of Wayne County, on Mar. 9, 1915, to William Jackson Hickerson and Florence Denton Hickerson. Ten of twelve children survived infancy; they were: Grady, Jewele Mae, Lotus, Hershel, Arnez, Paul Stanley, Thirl, Lorene, and Walton.

In 1936 Thirl transferred from Frank Hughes High School in Clifton to Perry County High School in Linden to play football. He boarded in the home of Polk Denton. Vivian was a fourth grader, and Thirl, being a senior, immediately became her hero. After graduation He returned home and worked at odd jobs. On Oct. 5, 1939, he traveled from Wayne County to Nashville and enlisted in the Navy. At the time he had $7.50 in his pocket, and a few clothes in a suitcase. After the bombing of Pearl Harbor, Thirl swam to safety. He lost all his belongings. He had to wear a pair of officer's pants and mismatched shoes he had found at an officer's barracks; one shoe was white and one was brown.

He participated in the Doolittle Raid over Tokyo, Apr. 18-22, 1942.

WILLIAM HICKERSON, born 1825, Tennessee, son of John D. Hickerson and Nancy Treece, died Apr. 30, 1896. He was a Civil War soldier from Perry County and has a Confederate marker in the old Hickerson cemetery, Sinking Creek. On July 18, 1844, probably Perry County, he married Elizabeth Sharp, daughter of James Sharp and Eliza Mayfield. Elizabeth born Oct. 21,1825?, Tennessee, died October 1870s. I assume she is buried in the Old Hickerson cemetery. Eight children were born to them. (1) Eliza Jane Hickerson, born March 1846, believe she died 1909 in Perry County. She married in Perry County, 1866 to George or William Fraley. (2) Nancy E. Hickerson, born 1850, died Oct. 19, 1882, assume Perry County, wife of Joshua Y. Tatum. (3) James Calvin Hickerson, born 1852, died Dec. 5, 1894, buried Ary cemetery on Sinking Creek. He married Mary Rhoden/Rawdon. (4) John Allen Hickerson, born September 1853, died June 11, 1937, Hartley County, TX. He married in Kentucky and moved to Texas. (5) William Jefferson Hickerson, born Aug. 23, 1857, died June 16, 1904, buried Ary cemetery. He married first Feb. 10, 1878, Perry County to Emily Caroline Ary and second, Sept. 15, 1889, Perry County to Sarah H. Grooms. (6) Samuel F. Hickerson, born June 1860, believe he died as a small boy. (7) Marion D. Hickerson, born Dec. 7, 1863, died Oct. 4, 1925, possibly buried in old Hickerson cemetery. He first married, Mar. 27, 1881, Perry County to Mary Alice Westbrooks and second to Mrs. Nancy Kirk Whitwell. (8) George Everett Hickerson, born Feb. 21, 1868, died Dec. 21, 1944, buried old Hickerson cemetery. I am not sure if he married.

Joshua Y. Tatum, husband of Nancy E. Hickerson, born 1848. They had at least six children. (1) Mary Elizabeth Tatum, born June 27, 1868, died Mar. 24, 1936, buried Sharp cemetery, married Willis Sharp. (2) Lucinda J. Tatum, born March 1870 Perry County, died 1964, buried Ary cemetery, wife of John Franklin Sharp. (3) Sarah Jane Tatum, born Feb. 15, 1872, died Dec. 18, 1956, buried Chestnut Grove cemetery, married William Sharp. (4) William M. Tatum, born Mar. 5, 1874, Perry County, died Jan. 28, 1948, buried Ary cemetery. He married first Alice Tolle and second Apr. 22, 1902, Perry County, Ada Sharp. (5) John Tatum, born 1876, may be the one who married Aug. 21, 1895, Perry County, Elizabeth J. Bridges. If so, they were in Dyer County by 1910. (6) Susan A. Hickerson, born August 1879, died 1964, buried Hickerson cemetery on Hurricane Creek. She married 1901, Perry County, John Hickerson, he was born 1883, died 1954.

WILLIAM JEFFERSON HICKERSON, son of William Hickerson and Elizabeth Sharp, married first, Emily Caroline Ary. She was born July 21, 1862, died May 20, 1887, buried Ary cemetery. Three children born to this union (1) Hattie Ella Hickerson, born May 1879, married Dec. 11, 1910, Perry County, Richard Warren. He was born Mar. 11, 1847, died Apr. 26, 1926, Brush Creek. Richard had been married prior to Louise Baucom. (2) Nora Ada Hickerson, born August 1882, died 1955, buried Ary cemetery. She was the wife of John Allen Mercer. He was born 1873, died 1951. (3) Martha Andora Hickerson, born December 1885, died 1972, buried Bethel cemetery, Perry County. Her husband, Lonzo Tate, born 1886, died 1914. At least three children, two are Christine Tate Groom and Cecil William Tate. William Jefferson Hickerson's second wife, Sarah H. Grooms, born

Aug. 11, 1865, died Apr. 20, 1900, buried Ary cemetery. Four children I know of (1) Harvil Hickerson, born June 24, 1891, died Feb. 7, 1942, buried Ary cemetery. (2) male infant Hickerson, born and died Mar. 20, 1893, buried Ary cemetery. (3) Spencer Hickerson, born February 1894, married first Jan. 13, 1911, Perry County to Media Elizabeth Hickerson. Media born June 19, 1895, daughter of Martin Hickerson and Emily J. Inman. (4) Jones Hickerson, born Sept. 19, 1898, Perry County, died Dec. 19, 1911, Brush Creek, buried Barham cemetery. John A. Mercer, husband of Ada Hickerson, had been married before and had children. He and Ada had at least three daughters, Lillian, Thelma, and Carmie, and probably two sons, Hershel and Carl.

HINSON, At Cedar Creek on Apr. 21, 1900, Robert Thomas Hinson and Sarah Isabel Lomax married. His parents were Newton Jasper Hinson and Martha Duncan; her's were Joseph Lomax and Sarah Ann Ricardson.

The Robert and Isabel (Lomax) Hinson family.

Rob and Isabel lived there until they had three children. They then moved to Hinson Hollow on the north side of Cane Creek near the old grist mill where two children were born. While they lived here, a tornado swept the area. None of the family was badly injured but their house lost its roof. Quilts and feather beds were left draped on trees near the house. Two mules in the lot were apparently blown up on the hill nearby, because no tracks went up the hill; only down the hill. The smoke house was totally demolished but a barrel of ash-lye soap that was in it remained where it sat. Half-naked chickens straggled in for several days.

Soon afterward, the family moved one hollow west to Rosson Hollow where Rob and Isabel spent the rest of their lives. Here they had four children.

Rob and Isabel's children were: Melissa Leora, married Turney Bates; Lillie Minerva Jane, married Waco Qualls; Willie Lee, married Addie Wilburn; Della Ann Docia, married first, Fred Chandler, second, William Crouch; Dena Emma, married Carter Campell; Carlos Russ, married Anna Bell Campell; Minnie Delphia Leanna, married Henry Westbrooks; Robert Marable Newt, married Ophelia Ingrum; Christine Isabel, married James Elkins.

Rob and his sons farmed for their living. Other farmers hauled their sorghum cane here for Rob and Willie to cook. They had the know-how and patience to make excellent molasses. They also took their mill, pan, and skimmers to other places and set up where farmers of that area availed themselves of their services.

Isabel and her daughters cooked on a wood stove, washed clothes on rub boards, sewed, pieced and quilted quilts and canned or dried enough fruits and vegetables to feed them through the year.

When they married, each child was given a feather-bed, two pillows and six quilts.

In the mid-1920s, the Hinsons, Edwards, and Sisco steam-powered sawmill sat in the head of this hollow of many springs. Six or eight worker's houses were built around it. There were several tracts of timber in the area for them to harvest.

A Primitive Baptist Church was organized on Brush Creek. on Oct. 17, 1818. It moved over the ridge on Coon Creek by 1830. Rob Hinson, his father, Newton Jasper Hinson; his cousin, David Levi Hinson; his brother, Jonathan Harvey Hinson; and his son, Robert Marable Hinson were all ordained ministers and served Coon Creek Primitive Baptist Church between 1883 and 1994. Rob Hinson's grandparents, his mother, his wife, and six of his children, and the spouses of four were members of this church.

Rob was born Feb. 23, 1874 and died Oct. 5, 1946. Isabel was born Sept. 8, 1882 and died July 5, 1974.. Both were buried in a family cemetery that was part of their farm.

HINSON-INGRUM, Since their marriage in 1946, Robert M. Hinson and Ophelia Ingrum have lived on Cane Creek, most of that time in Rosson Hollow where Robert was born. They have a son, James Thomas, a daughter Tabitha and two grandsons, Robert W. and James K. – Tommy's sons.

Robert and Ophelia Hinson

Robert's parents were Robert T. Hinson and Isabel Lomax, both of Perry County. Ophelia's parents were James F. Ingrum of Maury County and Mary Poore of Hickman County.

Robert served forty-one months in the Army during World War II. Most of this time, he was in the 491st Armored Field Battalion under General George Patton. He was released on Dec. 24, 1945. He went back to farming in the spring and farmed until 1980 when he became unable to continue. He also worked for Tennessee Gas Pipeline Company for seventeen years. He is a Primitive Baptist minister and served as pastor of Coon Creek Primitive Church for twenty-four years, ending Dec. 3, 1993.

Ophelia has lived the typical life of a farmer's wife; animal mid-wife, nurse to various young creatures, and chief "go-fer" (if he needed it, she'd go-for-it).

Ophelia's mother, Mary Poore, was the daughter of Priscillia O. Arnold and Richard P. Poore. Richard's parents were John M. Poore and Martha Harper who was born in Jefferson County, MS, to Joel Harper and his wife, Lucretia.

When Martha was about two years old, her father, Joel, was jarred from sleep by a terrible scream. On investigation, he found a dead man and his killer, apparently a man with authority. This man told Joel, "I wish you had not come here and seen this for I cannot have a witness who can testify against me. You are a good man with a young family. If you want to live, be gone by daylight." Joel loaded his wagon and, with his wife and three small daughters, made a dash for Tennessee where he lived the rest of his life.

This story was told to me by a cousin, Annie Mai Edwards, who taught school in Lewis County for many years.

Joel Harper was the son of Wiley V. Harper, veteran of the War of 1812, and Sarah Green. They are buried in the Dudley Cemetery north of Lobelville. *Submitted by Ophelia Hinson.*

HINSON, Bernice (Red) Hinson and wife Anna Mae Conger were both native Perry Countians and married in 1944. They had two sons, Johnny and Sammy Hinson. Mr. Hinson was the oldest of five children born to John Clifford Hinson and Myrtle Parnell Hinson.

Bernice (Red) and Anna Hinson with grandson, Brent Hinson Photo taken 1973.

Mrs. Hinson was the daughter of Samuel Y. Conger and Minnie Ledbetter Conger. Red was a retired employee of Tennessee Gas Transmission Company (Tenneco), a land owner, and part time farmer. He was a member of the Methodist Church and was a Mason of 46 years at the time of his death. He served in the U. S. Army and was Commander of the Disabled American Veterans (Perry Co. Chapter). Anna Mae was a devoted housewife and worked from time to time for various county government agencies including the Office of Voter Registration and County Court Clerk. She was also very active within the Methodist Church and with various community clubs such as the Ladies Home Demonstration Club.

They were kind and loving parents, excellent providers for the family, good church members, and well respected by others within the community. Anna Mae Hinson died Jan. 12, 1983, and Red died Aug. 9, 1993. *Submitted by son, Johnny E. Hinson.*

GEORGE HINSON, About the year of 1811, there came to Perry County, TN, from North Carolina five brothers; George, Joshua, John, Meredith and Merrill and a sister; Fannie.

Larkin and Molly Hinson

George (Punky) married Betsy Upton in North Carolina in 1811. They settled and built a log cabin in Perry County on the head of Short Creek. To George and Betsy were born Jordan, Elijah I., Larkin I., Samuel I., Susan (Susie), Sallie, Malinda and Lucinda (twins). After the death of Betsy, George married Mary Black and they had one son, George Washington born Apr. 16, 1863.

Jordan Hinson was born Mar. 16, 1812; married Rachel Henry Hufstedler on Dec. 6, 1831. Her grandfather came to America from Germany on the ship Harle in 1736. Her uncle Michael Hufstedler was born on the ship. The Hufstedlers were wealthy, cultured, slave-owning planters. Rachel was born Mar. 25, 1815, in Tennessee. She and Jordan had the following children: Wiliam H. 1832; George W. (Baldy), June 14, 1838; Elizah Meredith, Oct. 22, 1840; Temperence E., Oct. 12, 1841; Eli Larkin, Dec. 28, 1843; Samuel Jefferson, Dec. 8, 1845; Levi David, Apr. 3, 1848; Jacob Franklin, Jan. 2, 1850; Hugh W. (Dr.), Nov. 17, 1851. There were five daughters that all died in infancy.

Rachel died Aug. 10, 1857, and Jordan married Sallie McDonald on Dec. 30, 1858: To this union were born four sons and four daughters. Jordan died Aug. 26, 1881.

Eli Larkin Hinson was married Feb. 25, 1866, to Mary Jane Bob Hunt Martha Ann Virginia Ann Jellico White Jackson but everyone called her "Mollie". She was born Mar. 30, 1853, the only daughter of Willis and Ann Rhandel Jackson. She had a brother, Mitch. "Lark" and "Mollie" had thirteen children. Pleasant Patrick (1867), Annie (Jan. 1, 1869), Ida (Mar. 1, 1871), Ora (June 16, 1873), Arkie (Oct. 12, 1875), Willis (Apr. 23, 1878), Ada (Jan. 6, 1880), Powell (Nov. 29, 1881), Etta (May 21, 1884), Woods H. (Dec. 31, 1886), Belle (Feb. 5, 1890), Egbert (Sept. 1, 1892), and Azalee (Jan. 10, 1895). It is told that the parents never saw all the children at the same time.

E. L. Hinson was a farmer for most of his life. He lived a short time in Lewis and Decatur Counties. He served six years as a revenue commissioner and was a veteran of the Civil War, Co. H. 10th Tennessee Cavalry. He was a minister of the Primitive Baptist Church. *Submitted by Della Hickerson, granddaughter of E. L. Hinson.*

GEORGE HINSON,

was born in North Carolina around 1786 and married Elizabeth (Betsy) Upton around 1811. Elizabeth was born around 1781 in North Carolina. They had many children.

Their first son, Jordan, was born on Mar. 16, 1812 and died Aug. 26, 1881. He married Rachel Hufstedler on Dec. 6, 1831. They had thirteen children before she died Aug. 10, 1857. His second wife, Sarah (Sallie) McDonald, was born Sept. 9, 1858 and married Aug. 26, 1881. Their fifth son, Perry Jones, was born Oct. 24, 1865 and married Minerva Jane Hinson. She was born on Dec. 25, 1869 and died July 26, 1946. Perry died in July of 1937.

Descendents of the John Wesley Barber and Elijah I. Henson families.

Their second son, Elijah I. Hinson, was Minerva Jane's grandfather. He was born May 22, 1815 and died around 1895. He married Evaline M. Davidson around 1837. She was born Sept. 9, 1822 and died around 1911. They raised ten children. Newton Jasper, their second son, was born Jan. 25, 1845 and died Feb. 20, 1928. Newton was married four times. Martha Duncan was his first wife. She was born Jan. 25, 1849 and died July 11, 1878. They had six children. Minerva Jane, the third child, married Perry Jones Hinson, son of Jordan Hinson. Perry and Minerva's second son, Robert William Stanfield was born Feb. 20, 1892 and died June 19, 1967. He was married to Annie Lee Anderson on Mar. 11, 1917. She was born May 7, 1901 and died Mar. 22, 1988. They had six children: Raymond, Edna Chandler, Onis, Mary Dora Vesta Louise Barber, Irene Brison and Marlee Brewer.

Mary Dora Vesta Louise Barber was born Apr. 9, 1924 and married John Wesley Barber on Sept. 19, 1944. He was born Jan. 30, 1921. They had eight children: Rachel Qualls, Reba Reynolds, Cathy Burcham, John, Bruce, Kay Fleming, Roger Barber, and Patti McCann.

Rachel Ann Barber was born Jan. 8, 1947 and married Glenn Webster Qualls on Oct. 20, 1965. He was born Apr. 24, 1945. They have two daughters, Kimberly Renea and Misty Dawn.

Renea was born Oct. 6, 1966 and married Kenneth Paul Barber, Jr. on June 30, 1984. He was born June 10, 1965. They have two sons, Kenneth Paul Barber III born Aug. 24, 1988 and Stephen Mykl born Apr. 23, 1992.

Misty was born Dec. 6, 1973 and lives in Hermitage, TN. She is attending Draughon's Junior College to become a Legal Assistant. *Submitted by Renea Barber.*

JOHNNY AND LINDA HINSON,

were married June 5, 1968. Both are graduates of Perry County High School (1964), and Austin Peay State University in Clarksville, TN (1968). Johnny is the son of Bernice (Red) and Anna Mae Conger Hinson. Linda is the daughter of Fred and Ina Harder Warren. At the time of this writing, their son, Brent is a third year student at Middle State University and their daughter, Stacey is a senior at Perry County High School.

Johnny and Linda Hinson with son Brent and daughter Stacey.

Johnny is an employee of the State of Tennessee Department of Enviorment and Conservation of which his career has spanned 25 years in a management position. Mrs. Hinson is a teacher/librarian at Perry County High School in Linden. Mr. and Mrs. Hinson reside in Linden, but enjoy working on their farm on Rockhouse Creek and the Rise Mill Farm at Linden. Johnny enjoys playing golf and collecting various things, such as baseball cards. He also has an intrest in farm tractors. Linda enjoys outside activities such as gardening and lawn work. She enjoys sports especially fishing. During the time their children were younger, Johnny was a Dixie Youth Baseball League Coach for eight years. Since those years, they spend much time in support of their children as they participated in school and summer athletics. Mr. and Mrs. Hinson are members of the Methodist Church. Johnny is a Mason of the Al Menah Temple of the Shrine. He is also active in the local shriners organization.

JOHNATHAN HARVEY HINSON,

1888/1964, married Callie Barber 1883/1908, daughter of Jordan and Margaret Crowell Barber. Children: Sallie Matt and Myrta Estale 1903/1989. Married second Martha Jane Hickerson, 1888/1983, children: Willard Marie and James Harvey born 1922 in Louisana. He worked as a lumber inspector in Louisana and Mississippi.

Newton Jasper Hinson

James married Zada Ingrum, daughter of James and Mary Poore Ingrum, children - Linda and Laura, Linda married Mike Groves, children - Michael, Melissa, Melinda and Eric. Laura married Wayne Hudgens. James married June O'Dell Crabtree in 1952, daughter of Earl and Sylvia O'Dell Crabtree, children Tonita, Kay, Kiluah and Lucinda Shannon. Tonita married

Mike DePreist, their children are Terry, Angel and Savannah. Kay married Larry Cotham their children are Kanon, Fawn and Kaden, who married second Bobby Hale. Kiluah married first, David Santi, and second Jeffery Brake, one child Sierra.

Johnathan and Martha Hickerson Hinson

Myrta married Lloyd McKinley Warren, son of Hartie and Isabelle Carroll Warren, their children are Elsie, married W. B. Cates, son W. B. III, married second W. B. Hogan, their children are Jonny, Martha and June. Chole married Willie Ray Tucker, children, David, Joel and Pat. Mavos married Harold Hinson, children are Patricia and Kathy, Martha married Ralph Chessor, their children are Carson, Joey, Gerry and Angela, married second John Frank Curry, Claudia married Dean Weatherspoon, their children are Timothy and Judy. Lloyd Orlan married Caroyln Sofge and their children are Tamah, Donna, Lloyd, Connie and Patricia. Jerry married Patricia Brown and their children are Cassie and Corey.

Parents of Johnathan Harvey were Newton Jasper, 1845/1928, and Martha Duncan, 1846/1878, Hinson. Father and son were both Primitive Baptist ministers. Martha's parents were John born in South Carolina 1804 and Mary Duncan. His parents were David, born in South Carolina 1774 and Nancy Duncan. Came to Hickman County early in 1800.

Children of Newton Jasper and Martha are Richard married first Suzanne Barber, second Martha Campbell and third Goldie Simmons. William married Docia Ary, Minerva married Perry Hinson, Leora married Lee Harder. Robert married Isabelle Lomax, Martha married William Hinson, Leanna married Albert Dunn, Harvill married Elta Warren, Jones married Nellie Bates.

Newton Hinson was a member of the County Court when it reconvened after the Civil War.

His parents were Elijah and Evoline Davidson Hinson born 1815 and 1822.

Her mother Sarah, daughter of Daniel Davidson, who settled on Brushy in Hickman County 1825, taught school there. Elijah's parents were George born in North Carolina 1886 and Elizabeth Upton Hinson. They came to this area about 1811, his brothers John, Joshua, Meredith and Merrill and sister Frances and husband Thomas Dowdy also settled in the area.

Other children of Elijah and Evoline are James Harvey, Permelia, Minerva Jane, Rebecca, Robert, Rachel, Amanda, Mirenda and John Harrison Hinson.

Children of George Hinson are Jordan, Elijah, Larkin, Samuel, Susan, Sallie, Malinda, Lucinda and George Washington, child of second wife Mary Black. *Submitted by James H. Hinson.*

HINSON, Larry Haywood and Marion Hinson reside at 230 Cedar Ave. in Linden. Larry was born 1923 at Beardstown to John Clifford (1895-1974) and Myrtle Parnell Hinson (1898-1981). He completed high school at HCHS in Centerville. Higher education was at Austin Peay Normal and later Georgia Tech. Marion was born 1930 at Sidney, NE, to Emanuel and Amelia Weikum Trautman. She completed high school there and went to Denver, CO, to St. Luke's Hospital and Denver University for a career in nursing.

Larry and Marion Hinson in 1991.

They were married in 1951 and moved to Stockbridge, GA, where he was employed with Transcontinental Gas/Pipeline Corp. They have two children, Debbie married to Fred Bradley. They reside in Memphis. Debbie works for the State of Tennessee. Larry, Jr. married Rebecca Duke. They reside in Mobile, AL. Larry, Jr. is an engineer with the Degussa Corp. Larry worked at five locations from Georgia to South Texas. He retired in 1981 and came back to Perry County and spends his time at their farm.

His parents had four other boys, B. E. (Red) (1919-1993) was married to Anna Mae Conger and lived in Linden until his death. They had two boys, Johnny and Sammy. Red served during World War II as a tank driver and gunner. He retired with Tenneco.

Harold V. (1920-1986), married Mavous Warren. They lived much of their married life here and later moved to Humphreys County. They had two girls Patricia and Kathy. Harold served during World War II in the infantry in the Pacific. He retired with the State Highway Dept.

Leland M. (1921-) married Martha Haynes. They lived in Perry County for a short time, before moving to Hickman County. They have two children, Susan Kihlmire and Richard. Leland served during World War II in France in a engineering battalion. He retired with Tenneco.

Charles (1928-) married Helen Dill and they have one son, Mark. They all reside in Harrison, TN. He served in the Army during the Korean War. He retired with DuPont.

John C. Hinson served in the U.S. Army during World War II. After the war they came to Perry County on lower Cane Creek and were farmers until retirement, about 1952. They sold their farm and completed their lives in Linden.

John C.'s parents were John Whitfield Hinson (1861-1937) and Anna Brown (1865-1944). They lived and farmed in Perry County and had ten other children besides John: James Earl, William, Ethel Wiggs, Waymar Johnson, Vealy Cunningham, Beatrice, Cecil. Carl, twins-Paul and Pearl Hunt.

John Whitt Hinson's parents were James Harvey (1835-1930) and Ruth Skelton. James served with the South during the Civil War, dates unknown. Was said to be born in McNairy County and at one point was a Magistrate of Hickman County. He lived on Cane Creek near Enon Church at the time of his death. He had four other children besides John Whitt, they were; Minerva, Amos, Charity Eveline Harbor, and James Nathaniel.

James H. Hinson's parents were Elijah and Evelyn Davidson Hinson. who had nine other children besides James, they were; John Harrison, Newton Jasper, Robert, Marinda Edwards, Mary Buckingham, Rachael Eveline, Stephens, Rebecca Skelton, Minerva Curry and Permelia Skelton.

Elijah's parents were George (Punky) (1786- died approximately 1860 to 1861) and Elizabeth (Betsy) Upton. Both were from North Carolina. It is said that great great great Grandpa George was a hard rider, hard worker and loved corn squeezings more than good food.

George and family immigrated from Ireland to North Carolina. They had seven children besides Elijah, they were; Jordan, Larkin, Samuel, Susie Barber, Sally Barber, and twins, Melinda and Lucinda.

HOLLABAUGH, George and Catherine (Fraley) Hollabaugh were born in North Carolina and came to Tennessee about 1818 locating on Sinking Creek, in what would become Perry County in 1819. These pioneer citizens of Perry County were my great-great-great-grandparents. It is interesting to note that another settler on Sinking Creek at that time was Jacob Fraley. The first child of George and Catherine was Jacob Hollabaugh. He was my great-great-grandfather. George did not live long after locating on Sinking Creek, he died in 1824. His widow lived until 1856 on the home farm in Perry County.

Jacob "Jake" and Rosa Ann (Harvey) Hollabaugh about 1880.

Jacob Hollabaugh, son of George and Catherine was born Nov. 12, 1822. On Jan. 5, 1843 Jacob married Rosanna Harvey, daughter of James and Rachael Harvey. Rosanna was born in Tennessee Jan. 20, 1826. Jacob and Rosanna were my great-great-grandparents.

To the union of Jacob and Rosanna fourteen children were born. All lived to be adults -

which was remarkable at that time. The oldest child, Mary Jane Hollabaugh, married my great-grandfather, Cary Morris Tharp, at Lovic, TN, Dec. 17, 1865.

In 1864 Jacob Hollabaugh sold the pioneer farm of his parents in Perry County and located in Wayne County, TN, on the Buffalo River on what came to be known as the Hollabaugh bend. He was successful in farming, particularly in the bee business. On a high hill on his farm he established the family cemetery known to this day as the Hollabaugh cemetery. In this cemetery are buried many of my Hollabaugh and Tharp ancestors. Here Jacob was buried Jan. 26, 1895, and Rosanna Aug. 31, 1891. *Submitted by William A. Tharp.*

MELINDA EUGENIA (GENIE) HOLT LAMAR

lives with Helen and Keith Ary (her daughter and son-in-law) on Sinking Creek in Perry County. She is the granddaugther of Mitch and Elizabeth Scott Holt, who lived at Sandfield on lower Hurricane Creek. They had five children, three of whom died at an early age. Dora and Albert Lenley lived in Perry County all of their life.

Melinda Eugenia Holt Lamar

Dora's first husband was Clayborn Anderson. They had three children: Jasper, Lula, and Clay. Her second marriage was to Jim Tucker.

Albert Lenley, born 1874, died 1910, married Docia Louise Epley, born 1879, died 1943. They lived in Mill Hollow in 1901 and in 1903 they ran the county farm for the homeless. Albert farmed and carried the mail to Tennessee River. They later bought a farm on lower Hurricane Creek where Albert farmed and sold sewing machines.

Albert and Docia had seven children: Mary Pearl, born 1895, died 1944, married Hart Kilpatrick. They had three children, two died as infants: Vera Elizabeth, born 1913, first married Millard McLemore, second to Elmer Hickerson.

Bessie Alice, born 1899, died 1970, married Grady Whitwell. They had seven children: Ellen Marie, born 1921, first married John Pennington, second Earl Drake; Alton Lee, born 1922, died 1981, first married Mildred Westbrooks, second Jean Hardin; Juanita, born 1924, married Leon Schwendimann; Mildred, born 1927, married Clarence Walker; Willie Dalton, born 1929, died 1977, married Elaine Horner; Mavis Sue, born 1932, married Bobby Gilbert; Patsy Jean, born 1935, first married Curtis Devore, second Randall Lentz.

Clint and Claude (twins), born 1901. Claude died as an infant and Clint died in 1960. Clint married Lillian Mercer. They had seven children: James Dewey, born 1925, died 1944 in World War II; Eunice Carlton, born in 1927, died 1963, first married Betty Garrett, second Jenette Taylor; Clenna Dean, born 1923, married Clyde Clifton; Doris June, born 1936, married Paul Edwin Thompson; Jerry Jean and Joyce Ann (twins), born 1942. Jerry, died 1989, married Darlene Storm. Jerry served in U.S. Navy for 23 years. Joyce married Tommy White.

Melinda Eugenia, born 1903, married Whitfield Lamar. They had one child: Mary Helen, born 1934, first married Charley Thomas Mackin, second Keith Cleamon Ary.

Johnnie Albert, born 1906, died 1980, married Thelma Mercer. They had five children: Walton Eugene, born 1925, died 1982; Edward Lee, born 1928, married Kate Ledbetter; Albert Paul, born 1931, married Evelyn Graham; Velma Rue, born 1935, married Lawrence Ledbetter; James Earl, born 1945, married Helen Sharp.

William (Willie) Lenley, born 1910, died 1979, married Mae Warren. They had one child: Anna Ruth, born 1930, married Argel Harper.

After Albert's death, Docia married Armon Taylor. They had one child: Geneva Gaye, born 1917, married Skelton Adkins. They had four children: James Don, born 1934, married Bettye Sue Warren; Billy Dan, born 1937; Davis Wayne, born 1941, married Marie Jackson; Beverly June, born 1943, died 1992, married first Thomas Laster, second Beryle Moore.

JOHN RILEY HOOTON,

son of Jane and Thomas W. Hooton, was born May 19, 1816 in Perry County. John was a farmer until he died sometime in January 1866 in Lawrence, AR.

John married Nancy Penn sometime in 1840. Nancy Penn, daughter of Kathryn and John Penn, was born July 16, 1819 in Perry County. She died in 1894 in Randolph, AR.

They had nine children (five of which were born in Perry County): Vicey Jane, born 1841; William, born 1844; John J., born 1845; Thomas B., born 1848; Charles, born April 1850; Fairchild B., born 1852 in Arkansas; Richard Jasper, born Mar. 27, 1855 in Strawberry, AR; Amanda C., born 1857 in Arkansas; Susan J., born 1860 in Arkansas.

The Hootons lived in Perry County until 1851 when they migrated to Strawberry, AR, with several other families. They left Perry County with a wagon, horse and dreams. The last record of them in Perry County was the 1850 Federal Census. Thomas B. Hooton, a farmer, married twice and had ten children: Nancy R., born 1868; Joseph, born 1871; Mary I., born 1874; Sam; Leona, born 1882; Lena, born October 1886; Homer, born November 1888; William, born June 1891; Lee, born 1892; Charles, born January 1894.

Fairchild B. Hooton, a farmer, married Panctina in Arkansas. They had three children: Estella, born 1873; Allie, born 1877; Carrie L., born 1879.

Richard Jasper Hooton married Sarah Jane Bearden, daughter of John R. Bearden and Sarah Caroline Wilson, on July 18, 1874 in Arkansas. Richard Jasper died March 1926 in Tipton, OK. They had fourteen children: Joseph Jefferson (Joe), born July 9, 1875, died 1950 in Jonesboro, AR; John Riley, born Feb. 20, 1877, died July 22, 1877 in Arkansas; Nancy Abbie, born June 2, 1878, died 1905; Margaret Catherine, born Sept. 14, 1880, died July 5, 1942; Vicey Jane, born Nov. 2, 1882, died Jan. 1, 1964 in Actus, OK; Thomas A., born Oct. 22, 1884, died 1884 in Arkansas; Richard Bandy, born Dec. 30, 1885, died Mar. 6, 1971 in Brea, CA; Louisa Martha (Ludi), born Mar. 22, 1888, died Feb. 2, 1966; James Franklin (Jim), born Mar. 9, 1890, died May 13, 1956; Cora Uphemico, born Mar. 13, 1893, died Aug. 21, 1893 in Arkansas; William Ross, born March 1894, died Feb. 6, 1976; Bertha Loutishia and Burlie (Doc), born Sept. 22, 1899.

Richard Bandy Hooton married Hattie Mae Pyland, daughter of Britton Alonzo Pyland and Novella Francis Leathers, on Jan. 6, 1913 in Walnut Ridge, AR. They had four children: Nolan Jewel, born June 23, 1914, died 1991; Glenna Earl, born June 12, 1916, died July 28, 1984 in Brea, CA; Constance Bennie, born Oct. 14, 1921; Hilda Jean, born Mar. 4, 1929.

Constance Bennie Hooton married Earl Grant Lambirth on June 6, 1946 in Long Beach, CA. They had two children: Richard Grant, born Oct. 22, 1950, died Jan. 4, 1967; Julia Lynn, born Mar. 26, 1955.

SIR JOHN HORNER,

born 1520 Yorkshire County, England. Knighted by Queen Elizabeth in 1584 and given a Coat of Arms. He had five sons, Thomas, George, John, Edward, Samuel.

George Horner Sr. born 1726 eastern shore of Maryland or Virginia, died Dec. 10, 1811. Married three times. In 1790, moved to Orange County, NC. He became a large land owner and slave owner. William Horner Sr. b. Oct. 30, 1746, died Oct. 12, 1824. First child of George Horner, Sr. He moved to Tennessee and married second wife Elizabeth Alred b. Aug. 17, 1747, North Carolina, died Mar. 11, 1823 lived in Washington County, TN. He bought land from men who served in the Revolutionary War. He was a firm man but always fair in his dealings. They had 14 children: Miriam born Nov. 13, 1768, died June 10, 1845, married Caleb Witt. John Sr. born 1770, died 1816, married Elizabeth. George born 1771, died after 1816, married Jemima Russell. William Jr. born March 1772, died October 1834, married Mary Elizabeth. Mary Polly born 1774, died after 1827, married Thomas Crosby. Ann born 1774, died Apr. 15, 1823 _____. Ester born 1775, died June 17, 1855, married Lewis. Catherine born 1779, died 1822, married Thomas Green. Thomas Nelson, born Mar. 21, 1781, died Dec. 24, 1868, married three times. Cavalier H, Sr. born Jan. 3, 1783, died Apr. 1, 1851, married Jane Crosby. Lavinia born 1785, died before 1837, married Strange Colthrap.

Children of William Horner Sr:
Susannah born November 3, 1786, died June 17, 1855, married John Colthrap III. Elizabeth born 1790, died July 27, 1835, married James Johnson. Isaac born Dec.5, 1791, died May 6, 1857, married Mary Johnson and then Lucy Johnson Lea. Elizabeth Horner twin-born Jefferson County, TN, 1791, died Feb. 14, 1859, daughter of John Horner Sr. married John Lomax-wife #1_____ wife #2 Sarah, William Lomax born 1815 in Perry County married M. Mourning Denton Horner born 1812 first husband Jesse Horner, son of John Horner Sr., uncle to William Lomax.

179

Children of Jesse Horner and Mourning Denton: Jesse Horner Jr. born 1827, married Sarah Davidson, married Hulda P. (Mahulda). Loutitia Horner born 1852 MO. Manda J. Horner born 1853 MO.

Children of Jesse Jr. and Hulda P. (Mahulda) born 1832: John T. Horner born 1856 MO. George R. Horner born 1857 MO. Sarah E. Horner born 1859 MO. Malinda A. Horner born 1860, married Tilman Chambers. Jesse Horner born 1866 MO. Joseph Horner born 1868 MO.

Sarah Horner born 1830 in Perry County, TN married John Lomax born 1825, they had one son and one daughter, born 1876—1877.

Thomas Horner born 1832 in Perry County, TN, married Martha Richardson, they had nine children.

Elizabeth Horner born 1836-37, married John Lomax Jr., they had five children.

William (Buck) Horner born 1834 in Perry County, TN, married Elizabeth(Betty) Kelly Horner born 1832. They had five children:

John Carroll Horner born 1862, died 1919. Nan Horner born 1865. Catherine Horner born 1868. Mourning Horner born 1870. F. E. Horner born 1879. John Carroll Horner married Lissie Richardson Horner around 1898. Exact date not available through research.

HORNER-CURRY, Lewis W. Horner was born ca. 1803 in Dickson County, TN. In about 1827, in Hickman or Perry County, TN, he married Mary A. (Polly) Curry, who was born ca. 1810 in Georgia.

Lewis' parents were: George Horner Sr. and Jemima l. Polly's parents were David Curry Sr. and Elizabeth, last name unknown. Children of Lewis W. Horner and Mary A. Polly Curry Horner were as follows: (1) Elias Horner, born Aug. 25, 1827, in Perry County, TN, married Mariah Adaline Horner ca. 1854, Elias died Oct. 30, 1888; (2) Levi Kirkland Horner, born Dec. 6, 1829, Perry County, TN, first married Malinda E. Dickerson ca. 1852, he married second Matilda R. Dickerson, sister of Malinda, Levi died April 23, 1907; (3) John H. Horner, born 1832 and died 1877. Never married; (4) Sarah E., born May 25, 1834, first married Elias Craig, second married his brother Erwin Craig before 1860. Sarah died Oct. 15, 1898 and was buried in De Priest Bend Cemetery, Beardstown, TN; (5) Elizabeth Horner, born Oct. 4, 1836, died Feb. 16, 1890, first married ca. 1857 to John Wesley Dickerson and second married ca. 1865 to Bursus Warren. Elizabeth and Bursus are buried in De Priest Bend Cemetery, Beardstown, TN; (6) William P. Horner, born 1830 and died before 1868; (7) George W. Horner, born 1844, married ca. 1865 to Nancy, last name unknown.

Of the above men, serving in the Civil War were: E. H. Craig, private, C Co. 10th Cavalry; John W. Dickerson, private, F Co. 53rd Infantry; Bursus Warren, private G Co., 20th Infantry; Elias Horner, private, G Co. 42nd Infantry; Levi Kirkland Horner, sergeant, G Co. 42nd Infantry; John H. Horner, lieutenant C Co. 10th Cavalry; George W. Horner, private, G Co. 20th Infantry; and William P. Horner, private, G Co. 20th Infantry.

This writer's husband, Edward H. Craig, b. June 22, 1915, died April 22, 1988, was the great-grandson of Sarah E. (Horner) Craig. The family is erecting a new, fresh, readable monument as her present stone is broken into several pieces as the stone has been heaved out of the ground by roots of a very large tree near her head.

Submitted by Mrs. Edward H. Craig

HORNER-DANIEL, Emma Suzanne Daniel and Jessie Wilson Horner were married Jan. 6, 1887 at Danielsburg. Jessie Wilson Horner was born Nov. 8, 1869 and died May 6, 1951. Emma S. Daniel Horner died Aug. 4, 1960. Children of this union were: Oscar Floyd born Dec. 13, 1887 and died Dec. 15, 1968. Villa Pearl born Aug. 31, 1889 and died Sept. 13, 1958. Flossie Mae born Aug. 12, 1892 and died Sept. 20, 1967. Eunice Harriet born Feb. 16, 1894 and died Jan. 8, 1927. Herbert Henry born Mar. 8, 1895 and died Sept. 26, 1968. William Nathan born Jan. 10, 1898 and died June 27, 1948. Iva born Sept. 11, 1900 and died in 1902. John Wilson born Sept. 7, 1901 and died in 1980. Ralph Daniel born Feb. 21, 1904 and died in 1988. Eunice Harriet Horner married Lloyd DePriest. Children were: Glen DePriest, Sarah DePriest Edney, Mildred DePriest Coble, Dennis DePriest, Davis DePriest, Jack DePriest, and Syble DePreist. Herbert Henry Horner married Oma Barham. Children of this union were: Sparks Horner, Hope Horner Lashlee and Vonn Horner. John Wilson married Pauline Bell. Ralph Daniel Horner married Opal Marshall.

Wilson and Emma Horner and Syble

Horner, William Nathan and Sue Barrs Horner were married July 11, 1925. They made their home in the Pineview community and resided there all twenty-three years of their married life. William Nathan was a blacksmith by trade, school board member, county road superintendent and worked for the forestry division. At the time of his death in 1948, he owned and operated a service station and worked for the forestry division. Sue Barrs Horner was a homemaker and mother to her children. To this union was born four children: Nova Horner Cotton, Norma Horner Dodson, Dan Horner, and Garry Horner. Nova is married to James Cotton, and they have two sons, Al and Brent. Al lives in Alanta, GA, and Brent along with his wife, Kathy, and daughter Chelsey live in Birmingham, AL. James and Nova make their home in the Pineview community. James is a retired soil scientist and Nova is a homemaker.

The second child born to this union was Norma who died in 1979. Norma married Roger Dodson, and they had one daughter, Pippa Dodson Turner. Pippa, a nurse, is presently married to Jon Turner, who teaches at Perry County High School. They have two children, Tyler and Morgan, and live in the Cypress Creek community on Hwy 412. The third sibling in this marriage is Dan Horner, who presently resides in the Pineview community. Dan is the Road Superintendent for Perry County and has held this position since 1981. The fourth child born into this family is Garry Horner. Garry worked at Johnson Controls, Inc. from 1972 until 1992 at which time he was elected Property Assessor of Perry County and holds this job at the present time. Garry is married to Bonita Davis Horner, who has worked in the educational system in Decatur County since 1971. They have one son, Jeremy.

HORNER-MOORE, The Bob Horner Farm on Cedar Creek in Perry County was recognized as a Century Farm in 1976 by the Department of Agriculture. To be certified the farm had to have been in the same family for 100 years or more. It has been in the same family since 1846. The first owners were Amos Randel and wife Rebecca Finn Randel.

Will Horner and Etta Howell Horner

Nella B. Moore Horner, widow of Bob Horner and their three children live on the farm today (1994).

The children are David Horner (1947) and wife Divonne Dabbs Horner (1956). Their children are Justin Horner (1976), Tessa Horner (1981) and Leigha Horner (1985). Nancy Horner Warren (1950), husband Larry Warren (1948) and their children are Cayce Warren (1975) and Blake Warren (1980). Mark Horner (1957) wife Sharon Tatum Horner (1960), their children are Jared Horner (1989) and Colby Horner (1991).

Bob Horner (1916-1978) was the son of W. A. (Will) Horner and Etta Howell Horner, other children Flavil Horner (deceased), Floyd Horner, Willie Horner Sewell, Mary Horner Bates, Iris Horner Aho Martin and Doris Horner Hamm (deceased).

Nella B. (Nell) Moore Horner (1923) is the daughter of Ab Moore and Cressie Lomax Moore. Sisters are Inez Moore Hamm and Faye Moore Jones.

Submitted by Nella B. Horner

FRANK P. HORNER, In 1936 Frank Porter Horner (b. Apr. 30, 1913) married Zula Lee Smith (b. Aug. 1, 1918). They lived in Perry County when their daughter Mary Ruth was born, July 1, 1938. Soon after she was born, they moved to Hurricane Mills, TN, in Humphreys County. They continued to carry their corn to the mill to be ground into meal as was done in years past. This mill and the property is now known as the Loretta Lynn Ranch. On Aug. 14, 1941 Billy Smith Horner was born.

Frank Porter Horner

Two years later, to seek better employment, they moved to Warren, MI and bought their first home. On Oct. 1, 1944 Frances Joann Horner was born. Seven years later John Frank Horner was born, Mar. 13, 1952. All four of the Horner children graduated from high school in Michigan and all went to college. John met Kathryn Tutor (b. Aug. 7, 1955) and later, Dec. 8, 1973, they were married in Memphis, TN. They have two children, Rebecca Horner born Mar. 8, 1976 and Mark Horner born Jan. 23, 1979. They live in Tyler, TX. John Horner was ordained to Gospel Ministry in the Primitive Bapist church in 1993 in Tyler, TX.

Joann Horner was married to Paul Zider, Jan. 15, 1965. They have one son, Christopher Scott Zider. They now live in Houston, TX. Joann and Chris are artists and Paul an architect.

Bill married Marlene Sands. They have three children and live in Clarkston, MI. Kimberly married Tony Candret, Aug. 11, 1984. They have two sons, Christopher Jacob Candret born Jan. 3, 1987 and Joshua Aaron Candret, born Oct. 2, 1989. They live in White Lake, MI. Todd Alan Horner, born Apr. 14, 1967. Todd is buying his dad's tool and die shop in Pontiac, MI. and is building a new home in Clarkston, MI. Jill Marie Horner, born Sept. 10, 1970 lives in New Baltimore, MI, and is getting married soon.

Mary R. Horner married Curtis L. Owen (b Aug. 21, 1930) on Sept. 5, 1959. They have two sons, Spencer Thomas Owen born Mar. 10, 1968 and Preston Daniel Owen born Aug. 9, 1969. They live in Omaha, NE. Curtis is vice-president and treasurer (also lawyer) for Woodman of World. They plan on moving back to Tyler when he retires.

Frank had a heart attack in 1968 and became disabled. Zula sold real estate until 1979 when she retired and they moved to Lakeland, FL into a new home for retirement.

In 1983 Frank became dissatisfied with Florida and he and Zula moved back to Perry County to a home they had purchased earlier. Frank died on Sept. 5, 1983 at the age of 70.

HOLLIS ROMA HORNER, son of Thomas L. "Boss" Horner and Minnie Bell Bates, was born Apr. 22, 1903 at Kimmins in Lewis County, TN. He was married Sept. 6, 1930 in Gibson County, TN, to Agnes Marie York, daughter of Arthur B. York and Evline Vaughn. Agnes M. York was born June 15, 1911 in Gibson County, TN.

Hollis R. and Agnes Marie York Horner ca 1930

Their married life began in Gibson County where "Boss" Horner and his family had gone in the 1920s to try their hands at farming. It is not known how well they fared, but most of the Horners returned to Perry County in a steady procession.

They became the parents of five children: Elaine Marie, born Mar. 25, 1932 in Gibson County, TN, married June 26, 1950 to Willie Dalton "Kayo" Whitwell; Charles Edward, born July 22, 1935 in Gibson County, married May 29, 1959 to Wanda Mazelle Mercer; Betty, born June 19, 1940 at Tom's Creek, Perry County, TN, married Sept. 29, 1967 to John J. Lala; Berton Thomas, born Oct. 11, 1942 at Sugar Hill in Perry County, TN, married to Brenda Middleton, and died Mar. 7, 1980 in a plane crash in Georgia; and Billy Wayne, born May 9, 1945 in Lewis County, TN, married first to Margie Lemastus and second to Terry Lee Mason.

Perry County had been the primary home of the Horners since the early 1820s, and it was to be the hallowed ground of Tom's Creek that this family returned in the late 1930s.

During this period, Hollis R. Horner, was working with his father in the sawmill business, and the nomadic life of the previous generation continued on into this one. Tom's Creek was followed by a brief residence at Sugar Hill and then to Cane Creek.

Upon the death of "Boss" Horner, the family of Hollis R. Horner moved to Hohenwald in 1944 to the first pernament home the family would know. All five children attended Lewis County Elementary and High Schools. Hollis Horner continued for a time in the sawmill business with Leland Poore, but in 1951 took a job with the State of Tennessee. He worked in the Department of Materials and Tests until his death on May 4, 1965.

Agnes York Horner was a housewife. She died on Aug. 4, 1983 in Lewis County, TN. She and Hollis Horner are buried at Swiss Cemetery in Hohenwald.

It should be noted that Hollis Horner was also a Church of Christ minister who preached and taught Bible classes at many churches. He served at various times at Indian Creek, Little Swan, Kimmins, Napier, Slippery, Beaverdam Springs, and many others. *Submitted by Betty Horner Lala.*

JEMIMA RUSSELL. HORNER, No history of the Horner family would be complete without remembering the life of Jemima Russell Horner.

Jemima Russell was born ca 1770 at historic Wautauga settlement in East Tennessee to Capt. George Russell and Elizabeth Bean. She was the granddaughter of William Russell and William Bean. Her mother, Elizabeth, was born Nov. 21, 1723 in St. Stephen's Parish, Northumberland, VA, and died after January 1800, in Grainger County, TN. Her father, George Russell, was a captain in the battle of King's Mountain. He was born ca 1720 in Virginia and died in the fall of 1796. This Russell family was associated with German Creek in Grainger County, TN.

Andrew Jackson James and his niece Amanda James. (He is the 13 year old school boy who lived with Pleas and Jemima Horner in 1850).

There are varing accounts of the death of Capt. George Russell. Some say that he was killed by Indians while hunting. That version says his skeletal remains were found years later. An article printed in Goodspeed's History of Franklin County, Arkansas says that he was of English birth and was killed in Kentucky by the Indians while on an exploring expedition with Daniel Boone. Most accounts agree with the fall of 1796 as the date.

Jemima Russell and her parents, George and Elizabeth, were charter members of the Bent Creek Baptist Church, which was then in Jefferson County, TN. The church minutes indicate that she was baptized in 1790. Also among the charter members were William Horner, Sr., and his wife, Elizabeth Allred Horner, the parents of George Horner, whom Jemima would marry ca 1799. William Horner, Sr. deeded a parcel of land on May 1, 1810 for the use of Bent Creek Baptist Church of which he was the first deacon.

Bent Creek Baptist Church records show that at least three couples from that church migrated to Dickson County, TN, about 1804. Mentioned are John Horner and his wife, Elizabeth Russell; Ester Horner, and her husband, Lewis Russell; and George Horner, and his wife, Jemima Russell. John, Ester, and George were brothers and sisters, and Lewis, Jemima, and Elizabeth were brothers and sisters. Jemima received her letter of dismissal in good standing with the name of Jemima Russell alias Horner.

The first mention of George Horner in Dickson County records took place in 1805 when he served as a witness. He was appointed in 1806 to lay off a road from the town of Charlotte to come to an encampment on Gardners Creek branch of the Piney River. His last public mention was to serve as member of a Dickson County jury on Mar. 4, 1814 in the county seat of Charlotte.

Jemima Russell Horner was already a widow in the 1820 Hickman County, TN, census. It is believed that George Horner died in Hickman County prior to 1820.

Land grant number 23135, dated Feb. 4, 1825, was issued in the name of Jemima Horner. It consisted of 110 acres on the Buffalo River in Perry County in Range 9. It was a purchase grant and not free land. Subsequent property descriptions indicate that her property adjoined that of W.B. Barfield, William James, Caswell Cotham, and the Stanley heirs. This would probably be Cane Creek.

Jemima Horner appeared as head of household in the 1830 Perry County census. She has not been located in 1840, but in 1850 was living with her son, Pleasant Horner, in Linden. She is believed to have died between 1850 and 1860, but no burial place has been found.

The listing of the children of George and Jemima Russell Horner is a frustrating task. The names of the males are fairly well known and are consistently agreed upon by most researchers. It is the females with whom we have the most trouble.

The male children are: George Horner, Jr., born ca 1799, married Harriet Elizabeth Russell, his double first-cousin; Lewis Horner, born ca 1803, married Mary A. "Polly" Curry; Spencer, born ca 1808, married Permelia Turner, and died Aug. 10, 1864; and Pleasant, born ca 1816, married first to a James, second to Malinda Harper, and third to a Nancy A. Wood.

The daughters are thought to be, although not yet proven, Lydia, born ca 1799/1804; Zilpha, born ca 1807, married Richard Murray; daughter, born ca 1810; daughter, born ca 1813; and daughter, born ca 1815. Circumstantial evidence also points to at least one daughter marrying a James.

It is hoped that this Perry County History project will help us to identify the daughters of Jemima Russell Horner. *Submitted by Betty Horner Lala.*

PLEASANT HORNER, called Pleas, was born ca 1816 in Hickman or Dickson County, TN, to George Horner and Jemima Russell.

Nancy Wood Horner, third wife of Pleas Horner ca 1899.

Family legend tells us that he was first married to a James, thought to be named Lucinda, a daughter of William James. Pleasant Horner did share in the estate of William James who died in Perry County in 1840. We do not know the length of the marriage, but we do know that Pleasant Horner was listed in the 1850 Perry County census as a 37 year old merchant, and he had living in his household his mother, Jemima, and 13 year old Andrew James, a school boy. Andrew James subsequently determined to be Andrew Jackson James, son of William James.

Pleas Horner was married second ca 1852 to Malinda Harper, daughter of Wiley V. Harper and Sarah Green. They were the parents of four children: Elizabeth, born ca 1853, married on Sept. 17, 1870 to A. B. Shelton; George Washington, born August 1854, married to Martha Frances Rumsey on May 12, 1878, and died Apr. 17, 1921; Sarah Jane, born Aug. 20, 1858, married Mar. 27, 1873 to Gustavus DePriest, and died Aug. 20, 1915; and James A., born ca 1859 and died before 1870.

Upon the death of Malinda Harper Horner, in about 1863, Pleas Horner was married for the third and final time to a Nancy A. Wood, who was born in 1844 in Tennessee.

Pleas Horner and Nancy A. Wood were the parents of six children, with one dying in infancy. The remaining five were: Jos. Pleas, born Dec. 27, 1864, married on Jan. 10, 1883 to Eliza A. Robertson, and died Feb. 6, 1940; William Lee, born May 17, 1867, married to Leona A. Robertson, and died Mar. 13, 1950; Mary A., born Aug. 8, 1870, married Nov. 30, 1884 to Alexander Lynch, and later in life to John Nicholson, and died Nov. 20, 1942; Robert Spencer, born Dec. 31, 1872, married briefly to a DePreist, and on Dec. 12, 1896 to Anna Olivia Briscoe, and died Feb. 29, 1928; and Thomas Legrand, born Mar. 24, 1875, married May 29, 1898 to Minnie Bell Bates, and died Feb. 19, 1944.

Pleas Horner very likely lived in several parts of Perry County, probably beginning in Perryville. He bought some lots in Linden 1849 and 1850, which he sold fairly soon afterward. He bought more than 95 acres of the property of Willaim James and went to court in 1867 to prove his ownership. The property adjoined the 110 acre tract of Jemima Horner, and was listed as Range 9, Section 6.

Pleas Horner was no stranger to the court in Perry County, and he generously used it to settle disputes, collect small debts, and obtain clear titles to property.

The family was living on Cane Creek in 1870, and he is thought to have died in that area. Although court records would indicate that he probably died around 1878, his tombstone at Old DePriest Bend Cemetery reads, "P. Horner, June 3, 1879, age 63 years." Still visible in 1993 is the inscription at the bottom of the stone, "Gone But Not Forgotten." His son, Thomas L. Horner is buried beside him. His daughter, Sarah Jane Horner DePriest is buried a few feet away.

Nancy A. Wood Horner died 1912. She is buried at Qualls Cemetery in Perry County. Her son, Robert Spencer Horner and two of his children are buried beside her.

THOMAS L. "BOSS" HORNER, Thomas Legrand Horner, son of Pleas and Nancy Wood Horner, was born Mar. 24, 1875 in Perry County, TN. He was married May 29, 1898 in Perry County to Minnie Bell Bates, daughter of Dillard H. Bates and Martha Emmaline Chandler. Minnie Bell was born in Hill County, TX, on July 12, 1879, and died on May 15, 1924 in Perry County, TN.

Nine children were born to this union:

1. Infant, son, twin to Robert, born Mar. 12, 1899, died in infancy, buried Hornertown.
2. Robert, "Bobby," born Mar. 12, 1899, married first to Molly O'Guin and second to Effie Hinson, and died April 1973. Buried at Chessor Cemetery.

Thomas Legrand Horner and wife, Minnie Bell Bates Horner and infant son Robert (Bobby) ca 1899.

3. Annie U. Dean, born 1901, married Paul Hinson, and died Dec. 22, 1965 in Henry Co., TN. Buried Puryear Cemetery.
4. Hollis Roma, born Apr. 22, 1903, married Sept. 6, 1930 to Agnes Marie York, and died May 2, 1965 in Lewis County, TN. Buried Swiss Cemetery.
5. Sarah Pauline, born Aug. 4, 1905, married Dec. 24, 1924 to Wymer Waco Barber, and died July 15, 1973 in Henry Co., TN. Buried Hillcrest Cemetery.
6. Thomas Oren, born Mar. 5, 1907, married Mattie Pearl King, and died Aug. 24, 1984 in Perry Co., TN. Buried O. A. Kirk Cemetery.
7. Kathryne, born July 29, 1909, married John Quincy Butler, Jr., and died June 1, 1989 in Gibson Co., TN. Buried at Oakland Cemetery.
8. Harvey Carl, born Mar.15, 1911, married to Sept. 9, 1944 to Lucille Byrd, and died July 20, 1976 in Perry Co., TN. Buried Old DePriest Bend Cemetery.
9. Joseph Percy, born June 23, 1914, married May 8, 1943 to Nina Pearline Black, and died Dec, 8, 1978 in Perry Co. TN. Buried Old Depriest Bend Cemetery.

This Horner family led a nomadic life. "Boss" Horner owned and operated sawmills, and they moved where the timber led them. The first six children were born at Kimmins in Lewis Co. TN. The last three were born at Hornertown at Beaverdam Springs in Hickman Co. There was a brief residence in Wayne Co., TN. as well as an attempt at farming in Gibson Co., TN. Around 1920, the family went to Oklahoma in a covered wagon to be with relatives now unknown. It has been said that "Boss" Horner taught school there while the boys worked in the wheat fields. That visit lasted a year before they were back in Perry Co.

In spite of the wandering, Beardstown was the magnet which drew them back, "Boss" Horner died there on Feb. 19, 1944 and was buried at Old DePriest Bend Cemetery. His wife, Minnie who had died in 1924, was buried beside her parents at Gilmer Cemetery.

Upon the death of "Boss" Horner, each of the children received $700.00, and Tom Horner received the sawmill. Daughters, Annie and Pauline and their families moved to Henry Co., TN.. Daughter, Kathryne was already living in

Gibson Co., TN. Son, Hollis and family moved to Hohenwald. Sons, Carl and Percy would spend time in Detroit before returning to Beardstown, while Bob and Tom would spend their lives there on Highway 13. *Submitted by Betty Horner Lala.*

THOMAS OREN HORNER, sixth child and fourth son of Thomas L. (Boss) Horner and Minnie Bell Bates, was born March 5, 1907, at Kimmins in Lewis County, TN. He was married to Mattie Pearl King, daughter of Abner King and Addie Harris. Mattie Pearl King was born in Perry County, TN, in 1914.

Thomas Oren Horner in October 1958.

Tom Horner was never blessed with any children of his own, but he had great affection for his nieces and nephews. He also loved dogs and had a succession of miniature Collies.

It is not known how many years Tom Horner would operate the family's sawmill which he inherited from his father. What is known is that he must have taken his share of the inheritance and bought his own land on Hwy. 13 near Beardstown. He remained there from the 1940s until his death in 1984.

Tom was an excellent mechanic, and he worked until age 75 in a garage at the corner of Hwys. 100 and 13. If you had a noise in your engine, he would listen quietly, not say a word, and go into his shop and select just the right part to take care of the problem.

He was a quiet man, and you could sit with him for long stretches without many words passing through his lips. He was obviously man of few words, but what he did say, you could stake your life on.

In the 1970s he began to compile some records on his Horner ancestors. While he always thirsted for more information, nothing could compare to his obsession with Indian relics. All of his free days were spent poring over his secret places to amass one of the best collections of spear points and arrowheads in the whole state. Before his death, he said that his collection was worth at least $12,000, and he only saved the best.

About a year before his death at age 77, he had one more mission to accomplish. His mother's grave at Gilmer Cemetery had a bought tombstone, but those of his grandparents, Dillard and Emmy Bates, did not. Neither were there stones on the graves of his Aunt Dee and Uncle Albert Bates. He went to Gilmer Cemetery and fashioned some markers for those four relatives and etched their names in the wet cement. And before his death he extracted a promise from his wife Mattie Pearl, that he wanted a stone bought for his brother, Percey, with his money.

He had no trust in doctors and only went one time, for shingles, before the event of his fatal illness. He felt that doctors could make you sick.

He died on Aug. 24, 1984, and was laid to rest at O. A. Kirk Cemetery. His widow, Mattie Pearl, died on Oct. 24, 1986, and was buried beside him. *Submitted by Betty Horner Lala*

WILLIAM HORNER, The Horners who settled in Perry County, TN, were descendants of George Horner (1725 - after 1811) of Orange County, NC, and his first unknown wife through their son William Horner (Oct. 30, 1746 - Oct. 12, 1824). William married Elizabeth Allred (Aug. 17, 1747 - March 11, 1823) and lived in Randolph County, NC, where he furnished supplies for the Revolution for which he was given North Carolina grants in what became Tennessee. He settled for life c. 1783 on Bent Creek of Holston River near Whitesburg in present Hamblen County, TN. He was a surveyor, farmer and charter member of Bent Creek Primitive Baptist Church and gave land for the Bent Creek Cemetery where he and many of his descendants are buried.

William Horner had 14 children and four of them moved to middle Tennessee. John Horner Sr. (1775-1822) and wife Elizabeth Russell (c.1772-after 1820); George Horner (1770s-c.1815) and wife Jemima l (1770-c.1851); Esther Horner (c.1775-June 17, 1855) and husband Lewis Russell (April 5, 1774-Oct. 6, 1846); and Catherine Horner (1779-1822) and husband Thomas Green left East Tennessee in 1804 with their families and traveled by flat boat on Tennessee River to Dickson County, TN, where brother-in-law William Russell had preceded them. These Russells were children of George Russell and Elizabeth Bean. They were pioneers in Dickson, Hickman and Perry counties. John Horner Sr., a surveyor, was a lieutenant in Jefferson County, TN, militia in 1792, captain in Grainger County militia in 1796 and captain in Dickson County militia. He was father of 14 children: (1) Catherine (c.1789-c.1834), married first Tom Ammons and second John Cude; (2) Elizabeth (c.1791-c.1825), married John Lomax; (3) Elijah (c.1791-before 1820), a twin, married Nancy ?. He is believed to be the father of William Horner (March 11, 1815-Sept. 11, 1869), married Nancy Randle; (4) John Jr. (Oct. 3, 1793-July 18-1878), married Sarah (Sally) Sparks (Dec. 23, 1797-July 21, 1856); (5) William Harrison (1795-1850-60), married second to Mary Elizabeth ?; (6) l W. (1797-1850), married unknown born c.1800.; (7) Lewis W. (1799-after 1860), married Anna b.1804; (8) Lydia (c.1801-after 1850), married James Lomax; (9) Mary (Polly) (Sept. 15, 1802-Oct. 20, 1885), married John Richardson; (10) Anne (1804-Nov. 5, 1873), married Thomas Lomax; (11) Thomas (c.1805-after 1850), married Eliza ?; (12) Jesse (c.1807 or 1808-before 1840), married Mourning Denton; (13) Isaac (Feb. 10, 1809-Jan. 24, 1859), married Mary Moore; (14) Jemima (c.1810-March 29, 1853), married Benjamin Richardson.

John Horner Jr. and Sarah (Sally) Sparks, the daughter of Jesse Sparks and Elizabeth Jones, were married Oct. 1, 1814, in Hickman County, TN, and were parents of 10 children. (1) Jesse (March 5, 1816-Oct. 20-1857), married Mary Malinda (Mary B.) Patterson; (2) Elizabeth (Betsy) (March 1, 1818-after 1860), married Thomas Young; (3) Annie (Feb. 20, 1820-March 10, 1889), married John Tipton Lewis; (4) l William (Jan. 7, 1822-Nov. 14-1882), married Martha Ann Patterson and second Mrs. Sarah Patterson Pitts; (5) John Valentine (April 1, 1824-Jan. 18,1913), married Elizabeth Dilworth Patterson and second Mrs. Katie Owens; (6) Nancy Sarah (Nov. 23, 1826-Nov. 7, 1910), married first Daniel A. Whitwell and second Gabriel Lancaster; (7) James Jefferson (July 16, 1829-April 21, 1912), married first Sarah Myra Patterson and second Frances Jane Angel; (8) Nathan Sparks (Feb. 23, 1832-Oct. 4, 1922), married first Mary Harriet Lewis and second Sarah Patterson Pitts Horner; (9) Elijah Egbert (Oct. 9, 1834-c.1865), married Ryanza Nix; (10) Mary Jane (April 28, 1837-Oct. 3, 1905), married William Henry Lancaster (Feb. 7, 1829-Feb. 17, 1875), son of John Lancaster (Feb. 13, 1806-Dec. 19, 1852) and Rachel Harder (Feb. 28, 1806-1870s). Mary Jane was my great-grandmother. Her daughter, Nancy Caroline Lancaster (Dec. 23, 1854-May 9, 1955), married George Washington Young (April 18, 1847-Oct. 12, 1921) on Jan. 16, 1875 in Marion County, AR, and they were grandparents of Helen Young Bishop. *Submitted by Helen Young Bishop*

WILLIAM BUCK HORNER, was to have served in the Civil War with a cousin Andrew (Darby) Lomax. His son John Carroll (nickname Hack) married Lissie Richardson (birth after 1872, death around 1918). They lived on Cedar Creek, Linden, TN. John Carroll Horner died of throat disease after 1919. Lissie Horner died of T.B. of bowel preceding her husband Carroll. Lissie cared for her sick mother, Sarah, who had contracted T.B. She smoked a stone pipe and Lissie would light her pipe. Carroll and Lissie both died leaving two small sons, Taft and Kennie. John and Bertha Smith took into their home Taft at an early age. Grandfather Johnny Richardson cared for Kennie while still a small child until his health was bad and Charlie and Maggie Bunch cared for the young child for a few years.

Carroll and Lissie Horner and son Ollie Horner

John Carroll Horner, b. 1862, d. 1919, married Lissie Richardson Horner, b. 1872?, d. winter of 1918; Olie Horner, b. 1899, d. 1902; Taft Horner, b. July 7, 1911, married first Ocie Carter and second Lucille Waters; Betty M. Horner, b. Feb. 11, 1930, d. Nov. 2, 1932; Tennie (Kennie) Lee Horner, b. July 5, 1917, married Amanda Ruth Ward, b. Nov. 30, 1922, d. Dec. 11, 1969, married second Eva Earl Haynes Wilson, b. Oct. 16, 1916.

Kennie and Ruth Horner married Aug. 24, 1939. Five children were born: (1) Joe Larson Horner, b. March 1, 1941, stillborn; (2) William Parlie Horner, a daughter, b. May 31, 1943, stillborn; (3) Mary Paulette Horner Burcham, b. Aug. 29, 1944, married Sept. 7, 1965, to Franklin Dee Burcham, b. July 1, 1942. Their children were April Burcham (b. July 1, 1942), Franklin Dee Burcham (b. Feb. 12, 1969), and Amanda Lee Burcham (b. June 7, 1974); (4) Freddie Ruth Horner, a daughter, b. July 13, 1947, stillborn; and (5) Patsy June Horner Hinson, b. Jan. 4, 1951, married Willie B. Hinson, b. Dec. 11, 1946, married on March 14, 1969. They had two children Robby B. Hinson, (b. Nov. 13, 1969, married Shirley Flippo on July 3, 1993), and Christopher Lee Hinson (b. Nov. 30, 1974).

WILLIAM LEE (BILLY) HORNER, was the son of Pleas and Nancy Woods Horner, born May 17, 1876, died March 13, 1950, married to Leona Robertson, daughter of W. C. and Adeline Portia Robertson, Sept. 8, 1871-July 4, 1927, and they were the parents of seven children: Elizabeth Myrtle, Feb. 2, 1889-July 17, 1889; A. Nickus, Jan. 6, 1895-June 7, 1973, married Bessie Loveless who was born March 22, 1897. Nickus is buried in the Milam Cemetery in Hickman County; Ollie Nov. 3, 1898-Jan. 30, 1974, married to Homer Johns; Grady E., Oct. 6, 1900-Jan. 30, 1981, married to Dona Warren and buried in Horner Cemetery; Ira Brown, May 2, 1903-Dec. 5, 1989, married to Lucille G. Bastin, second wife Annie Bastin Talley, buried in Horner Cemetery; Fred, Dec. 21, 1906, no other dates, married Feba Lawson; Claude, Dec. 27, 1908-Feb. 14, 1966.

William (Billy) Lee and Leona Robertson Horner and family.

Ira Brown and Lucille Gertrude Bastin Horner were the parents of seven children: Joe Thomas, Nov. 20, 1924, married to Hettie F. Cayce on Oct. 10, 1951, and died Oct. 2, 1961; Edward Brown, Dec. 29, 1926, married on Oct. 27, 1951 to Sarah Travis, buried in the military cemetery in Nashville; Thelma Jewell, Nov. 25, 1928, married Aug. 11, 1945 to Raymond Bingham; Charlotte Ruth, Feb. 16, 1936, married Robert Cotton on Nov. 4, 1950, and died Oct. 12, 1990. Charlotte is buried in the Dabbs Cemetery in Lewis County; David Rex was born Nov. 30, 1931, and died July 20, 1932, buried in the Horner Cemetery; Ruby Fay, July 6, 1940, married on Jan. 17, 1964 to John A. Martin Jr.; Billy Wyatt, Feb. 4, 1942, married Sandra Lee Green on Dec. 24, 1959, second marriage to Sarah Francis Treaghleer on March 22, 1961.

Robert and Charlotte Horner were the parents of three children. The oldest is Sherrie, then Randy and then there is Ricky. They all live in Texas at this time.

HOWARD FAMILY, Matthew Howard, b. 1609, d. before 1659, emigrated from England to Lower Norfolk County, VA, around 1620. He was the son of Sir Thomas Arundel, who was beheaded and his estates confiscated. Matthew took his mother's last name (Howard) and emigrated to Anne Arundel County, MD, in 1649. He never made it to his 4,000 acres granted by Charles I of England, located somewhere in the Carolinas. Two generations prospered in Maryland without claiming their frontier holdings. One-hundred-eleven years later Benjamin Howard, b. Feb. 17, 1742, d. June 6, 1828, took the old Carolina land grant from the attic and moved westward. This move took place after he returned from the American Revolution, serving as a private in the Maryland unit. He settled in Wilkes County, NC, and married Prudence Sater. Prudence Sater was born Nov. 25, 1743, died Sept. 22, 1822. Benjamin served as a weaver for the Sater family and fell in love with Prudence. Mr. Sater refused to allow them to wed so Prudence jumped out of the dining room window and ran away with Benjamin. They bore eight daughters and four sons, one of which was Benjamin Howard II in 1789. Benjamin Howard II married Betsy Walker Howard, born Dec. 12, 1785, in Cerry County, NC, died March 24, 1859. They set out westward across the French Broad and Sequatchie Rivers to settle in the mouth of Cypress Creek, marking the northern boundary of the land grant. They returned to North Carolina with glowing accounts of Cypress Creek. Sadly, Benjamin Howard II died and Betsy packed up her 11 children, and with her brother Robert Walker, toiled five wagons over the mountains to Cypress Creek in 1821. Betsy turned everything over to her older son, James Walker Howard, born July 12, 1805, died Aug. 20, 1863 in Perry County. James Walker Howard married Rachel Davis, born Nov. 18, 1822, and had one son, Richard Johnson Howard, born March 16 and died Oct. 26, 1895.

James Walker Howard and his uncle, Robert Walker, promptly formed the Walker & Howard partnership on the bank of the Tennessee River at Blunts Landing. Faded ledgers plainly document that Davey Crockett failed to disclose an account of $3.50 for whiskey used for election purposes. This document has been handed down and remains intact at the home of Ben and Louise Howard. The Howard and Walker business was passed down through generations. After the Civil War, the Howards settled on the hillside and raised seven barns to house the large produce and livestock. It was then, on April 1, 1868, that the first of four successive generations named Benjamin Richard Howard was born, and the Howard homeplace was built.

On June 13, 1864, Richard Johnson Howard married Frances Sutton Howard, b. Jan. 22, 1844, in Maury County, TN, d. April 14, 1878. They bore five children listed below: James Walker Howard, b. March 28, 1865, d. Aug. 28, 1871, buried at Howard's Family Cemetery; Benjamin Richard Howard, b. April 1, 1868, d. Aug. 24, 1911; Annie Elizabeth Howard, b. Dec. 22, 1870, d. Aug. 4, 1949 in San Juan, NM; Mary Victoria Howard, b. Feb. 29, 1874, d. April 1948 in Chillicathe, TX; and Fannie Dick Howard, b. Sept. 11, 1877, d. Sept. 29, 1895.

Benjamin Richard Howard married on Sept. 2, 1886 to Florence Hester Young, b. March 24, 1870, d. Dec. 26, 1961. They bore six children: Richard Henry Howard, b. Aug. 24, 1889, d. Dec. 12, 1890; Julia Frances Elizabeth Howard, b. April 12, 1892, d. June 19, 1970 in Jacksonville, FL. She married Bob Nicks and had one child, Francis Nicks; James Walker Howard, b. March 23, 1894, d. ?, married Dora Robinson and had two children, Czarina Howard and Nima Jo Howard; Roger Thetus Howard, b. Nov. 18, 1895, d. June 18, 1897; Blanch Roberts Howard, b. Sept. 28, 1897, d. July 20, 1971. Married Leland Carlburg and had no children; Benjamin Richard Howard Jr. (Dick), b. July 23, 1900, d. July 6, 1983.

Benjamin R. Howard Jr. married Ethel Weems Howard, b. Nov. 14, 1902, d. June 12, 1982. They had two sons Benjamin Richard Howard III, b. March 8, 1920, d. March 6, 1979, and George Franklin Howard, b. March 17, 1923, d. Nov. 11, 1989.

On March 27, 1946, Benjamin Richard Howard III married Ellen Louise Deere, b. Sept. 26, 1918. Benjamin R. Howard III served as a sergeant of the U.S. Army during W.W.II. They had two sons, Benjamin Richard Howard IV, b. Feb. 11, 1947, and James Deere Howard, b. March 9, 1949, d. Nov. 7, 1992.

Benjamin Richard Howard IV first married Mary Frances Mitchell Howard, b. Aug. 30, 1950, d. Jan. 2, 1990. They had a son, Benjamin Mitchell Howard, b. March 18, 1980. He later married Constance B. Lowe, b. May 15, 1955. He has one stepson, Gregory Wayne Gee.

James Deere Howard married Alice Marie Moore on Dec. 12, 1970. Marie Moore was born April 1, 1949. They bore two children: Kelly Lynn Howard, b. Jan. 20, 1973, and James Heath Howard, b. Aug. 17, 1978.

The Howards have remained on the land granted to their ancestors over 300 years ago. The Howard homeplace remains relatively the same as the day it was built about 155 years ago.

HOWELL FAMILY, The Howell family was in Perry County, TN, before 1860. Stephen Howell's name is included in the census for that year, however, little is available about his early life except the fact that he was born in Perry County. Stephen served in the Confederate Army during the Civil War in Co. 1, 19th Tennessee Cavalry. He survived the war and returned to Perry County after his military service, taking up residence in the White Oak Creek area of the county. He was married to Martha Holder, apparently after the 1860 census and before he served in the war. Stephen and Martha had four children: Laney Henry (b. 1864-d. 1928), William Jefferson (dates of birth/death unknown), Nannie (dates of birth/death unknown), and Mary Lee (b. 1888-d. 1924). These four children were the second Howell generation in Perry County and the first for which there is fairly complete documentation.

One of Stephen and Martha's sons, William Jefferson Howell, married Melissa Howell (no relation) and they had two children, a daughter, Martha (no doubt named for her grandmother) and a son, Wren. Martha lived and worked in Madison County, TN, and never married. The son, Wren, was killed at an early age. This entire branch of the Howell family is buried in Madison County.

Laney Henry Howell and wife Fannie (Keeling) Howell with children: (front) Laney Clint, Nora (middle) and George and Ruth. Picture made around 1900.

Both of the daughters of Stephen and Martha married, Mary Lee to J. D. (Dave) Lineberry, and they had six children: Nannie to Wes Keeling and they were the parents of three children.

Laney Henry Howell, believed to be the oldest son of Stephen and Martha, was the child through whom this branch of the Howell family name survived. He married Fannie Keeling and they were the parents of four children: Ruth (b. 1888, married name McMahan, d. 1958), George (dates of birth/death unknown), Nora (b. 1891, married name Lineberry, d. 1936) and Laney Clint (b. 1895-d. 1925). Both of the sons, George and Laney Clint, had children and perpetuated the family name.

George Howell married Ann Tune and they had six children: Vesta, Clyde, Clifford, Gladys, Fannie and James. This branch of the family is not traced further here.

Laney Clint Howell married Mary Ellen Landers in 1920 and they had two children, Robert Earl (b. 1923-d. 1991) and Lockie Frances (b. 1924). Laney Clint served in W.W.I, survived to return home, and died of illness at the young age of 30 years in 1925. Robert Earl never married. Lockie married John Andrew Dedrick at Corinth, MS, on Nov. 2, 1944. To this marriage was born three children: John W. (b. 1947), Lannie R. (b. 1949), and Melissa (b. 1967). Coincidentally, all three of these children have two children each, one boy and one girl.

John W. married Judy Woods in 1966 and they have two children, Michael Wayne (b. 1974), and Cheryl Elaine. Michael is presently unmarried; Cheryl married Steve Gammon in 1988 and they have two children, Caleb (b. 1990) and Julia (b. 1994).

Lannie R. married Connie Bates in 1972 and they also have two children, Robert (b. 1976) and Raven (b. 1978). Both Robert and Raven are unmarried, as of this writing.

Melissa G. married Michael Rogers in 1985 and their children are Joshua (b. 1988) and Caitlin (b. 1992).

ROY ROBERT HOWELL, b. Aug. 22, 1911, d. May 8, 1948, married December 24 to Maggie Mae Broadway, b. May 25, 1914. Both were residents of Cedar Creek Community. Roy and Maggie had four children: Roy Frelon, JoNell, Tommie Jean, and John Edward.

Roy Frelon Howell, b. July 7, 1933, married June 24, 1955 to Ima Lois Inman, b. Dec. 15, 1936 (daughter of Brice Matthew Inman and James Addie Myrtle Inman) of the White Oak community. Frelona and Lois live on Cedar Creek and have three children: (1) Rendia Faye Howell, b. July 14, 1956, married Dec. 21, 1979, to Wess Thomas Ward Jr., b. July 14, 1956 (son of Wess Thomas Ward Sr. and Flora Edith Ward) of Marsh Creek. Thomas and Rendia have one son, Wess Frelon Ward, b. June 30, 1981. Rendia taught school at Lobelville, Pineview, Cedar Creek, Pope, and Perry County High School. Thomas was elected sheriff of Perry County in 1986, 1990, and 1994. (2) Jovhina Sue Howell, b. Aug. 24, 1958, lives on Cedar Creek. (3) Robert Matthew Howell, b. July 28, 1963, married June 28, 1986 to Traci LeAnn Alexander, b. Sept. 3, 1966, of Decatur County, TN. Robert and Traci had three children: Hollie LeAnne Howell, b. March 2, 1988, d. March 6, 1988; Bryce Alexander Howell, b. Aug. 8, 1989; Seth Matthew Howell, b. May 13, 1991. Robert and his wife live on Cedar Creek.

JoNell Howell, b., Aug. 6, 1935, married Jan. 18, 1964, to Harold Raine Moore, b. Jan. 21, 1934. JoNell and Harold have a daughter, Valerie Jean Moore, b. Oct. 29, 1965.

Tommie Jean Howell, b. Sept. 16, 1939, d. Sept. 30, 1991, married May 25, 1957, to Donald Ralph (Joe) Inman, b. Jan. 24, 1938 of the White Oak community. Tommie and Joe had two children: Bobby Mitchell Inman, b. June 17, 1958, married May 30, 1979, to Donna Holt, b. June 28, 1954 of Lewis County, TN. Bobby and Donna had three children: Robert Garrett Inman, b. Dec. 27, 1979; Jodi Lynn Inman, b. Oct. 22, 1982; and Chase Brown Inman, b. Feb. 13, 1984. Janet Delores Inman, b. May 26, 1961, d. Sept. 30, 1991, married Terry Paul Walker of Wayne County, TN. Janet and Terry had four children: Memori Shanell Walker, b. April 28, 1978; Jannifer Michelle Walker, b. June 21, 1980; Joshua Paul Walker, b. Jan. 28, 1982; and Te Ja Walker, b. Aug. 15, 1985, d. Sept. 30, 1991.

John Edward Howell, b. Sept. 5, 1946, married Oct. 31, 1964, to Patsy Nell Burcham, b. Feb. 6, 1947. John, Pat and their two sons live on Cedar Creek: Larry Edward Howell, b. July 31, 1965, married March 17, 1989 to Tammy Denise l, b. March 16, 1971 of the Beardstown community. Larry has a daughter, Hayley Nichole, b. June 18, 1988; Darrin Edward Howell, b. March 5, 1976.

HUDSON, During the 1950s, when people talked of high school basketball in Tennessee, the name of Linden High School came to mind. One of the smallest schools in the state accomplished the almost impossible feat of winning the state tournament three consecutive years from 1955-1957. In 1954, the team had an undefeated season, losing in their second game of the state tournament. The coach of these teams was Willie H. Hudson.

Willie, the son of C. N. and Mary Holder Hudson, was born in Perry County in 1914. He played basketball at Linden High and in college at Freed Hardeman College in Henderson, TN, and at Abilene Christian in Abilene, TX. After receiving his college degree, he returned to Perry County to teach. During his career, he was principal, math teacher, and coach of girl's and boy's basketball.

In April 1940, Willie married Elizabeth Sparks, the daughter of Jesse Kent and Bess Edwards Sparks. Elizabeth was born in 1914. She also was a teacher in Perry County, having begun teaching at a time when a four-year college degree was not required. Elizabeth would attend college a year and then teach a year. In these early days of her teaching career, many of her students were older than she.

Like so many men from Perry County, Willie was called to serve in World War II. Part of the time was served in the Pacific, on Okinawa. When he returned home in 1946, he resumed teaching.

After the war, Willie continued his education, receiving his Master's Degree from Peabody College in Nashville. During this time, Elizabeth also continued with her education by attending summer school. She received her degree from Austin Peay in Clarksville, TN.

Willie and Elizabeth had one child, Ann Elizabeth, born in 1945. Ann was married to Reed Westbrook, also of Perry County. They had two sons, Brian Reed and Michael Hudson. Ann and family reside in Memphis. Both boys share their grandfather's love of sports. Brian played football at his high school where Michael is on the football and wrestling teams.

Willie, after having successful high school teams, was offered other coaching jobs, but chose to stay in Perry County. He was selected as one of the coaches in the North-South Game, which was held in Kentucky.

After his death in 1963, Willie was inducted into the Tennessee Secondary Schools Athletic Association Hall of Fame, as well as into the Freed Hardeman Hall of Fame. A memorial was made to the national basketball hall of fame in his honor by the TSSAA.

Elizabeth continued to teach at Linden Elementary School until her retirement in 1977. She had devoted almost 40 years to educating the young people of her home county. Upon retirement, most of her time was spent in Memphis with her daughter and grandsons. Elizabeth died in 1984. She and Willie are buried in Kirk Memorial Cemetery in Linden.

C. N. HUDSON, Chesley Newton Hudson Sr. was born July 30, 1882, on Indian Creek, Hardin County, TN, to John and Nancy Tilley Hudson. He had brothers Henry, Will C., George Riley and sisters Fannie Franks and Clemmie Murphy.

C. N. Hudson family in 1955

As a teenager C. N. came to the Cedar Creek area of Perry County to work with his older brothers. In 1904 C. N. married Mary Elizabeth Holder, daughter of Isaac and Frances Bunch Holder. They had children: Lillie, Fannie, Willie, Pauline and Delphia. Another son and daughter died in early childhood. Mary Elizabeth died in 1922.

In 1927 C. N. married Annie Barham, daughter of George and Josephine Sandra Barham. Their children were Dorotha and Chesley Jr.

As a young man, C.N. was a Bible reader. He told of taking his Testament with him as he farmed with mules. When he stopped to rest he would read a few verses, then meditate on them as he worked. He became a Christian after hearing his second gospel sermon. Soon after, he began preaching, and in 1902 he baptized both his sisters and a sister-in-law.

His early married life was spent in Perry County where he made a living for his family buying and selling cross ties, and running a country store. He preached on weekends and in summer meetings, traveling many miles on horseback or by buggy before he bought a car.

In a report to the *Gospel Advocate*, February 1908, C. N. reported that in the preceding year he had preached 227 sermons, baptized 93 persons, and performed six marriage ceremonies. Another report in 1910 summarized his work as 296 sermons, 93 baptisms and five weddings. In October 1913, he reported that in the last few weeks he had preached five days on Blue Creek in Humphreys County, four days at Mt. View in Hardin County, and two days each at Pleasantville and Beaver Dam Springs in Hickman County.

Most of his preaching was done in rural areas of Perry, Decatur, Hardin and Hickman counties. For about 60 years he returned to Hardin County to the Mt. View Church of Christ to preach in a meeting or some time during the year. His last regular appointments were with the Crooked Creek congregation in Perry County in 1965.

C. N. lived in a time when preachers were called on to defend their beliefs in pubic discussion or debate. He participated in several of these discussions. Following a 1915 debate in Perry County, the moderator for the opposing speaker left that group and became a Christian. Such discussions were effective for causing one to study the Bible more and to examine one's faith.

C. N. died in 1971, shortly before his 89th birthday, and was buried in the Barham family cemetery, near his farm, near Beardstown.

JAMES HENRY HUFSTEDLER,

b. March 3, 1854, Perry County, at a little village known then as Harrisburg, located three miles south of Linden. He died Jan. 20, 1941. His father, Pinckney Hufstedler (b. July 1, 1814-d. March 3, 1895), married Sept. 5, 1847, to Louisa Jane Randel (b. Aug. 30, 1831-d. Jan. 26, 1924), daughter of Nathaniel Moses Randel and Mahalia Markham of Perry County. Both Pinckney and Louisa Jane Hufstedler are buried in a walled-in Hufstedler plot on a hill near their home. The tomb later became known as "Pinckney Tomb." It was built by Pinckney for his own burial. This unique grave site is now on the National Register of Historical Places.

James Henry Hufstedler family

James Henry Hufstedler's grandfather and grandmother are Jacob Hufstedler and Alcey Moore. Jacob was born on a ship coming from Germany.

James Henry Hufstedler's brothers and sisters are as follows: John Kendrick Hufstedler, born June 6, 1848, died April 19, 1919; Amos Eli Hufstedler, born May 6, 1850, died Sept. 17, 1923; Margaret Alice Hufstedler, born March 3, 1857, died 1960; Samuel Nacy Hufstedler, born Aug. 12, 1858, died July 1949; Josephine Hufstedler, born Nov. 11, 1861, died July 15, 1901; Louisa Moore Hufstedler, born June 24, 1864, died June 30, 1864; Robert E. Lee Hufstedler, born June 24, 1864, died May 3, 1865.

James Henry Hufstedler married July 18, 1877, to Eudoxie Anne Rasbury (b. Sept. 8, 1855, died July 27, 1887), daughter of Andrew Caruthers Rasbury (b. 1816) and Jane Voorhies (b. 1820), married 1843; daughter of David and Elizabeth Voorhies. Eudoxie's grandparents are Lovick and Jane (Campbell) Rasbury, who came from North Carolina in 1814 and migrated to Wayne County, TN, in 1816. Lovick died in 1858, and wife died in 1875 at the age of 98. Eudoxie is buried in the Salem Cemetery in Wayne County.

Children of James Henry Hufstedler and Eudoxie A.: Minnie Jane (born April 29, 1878, died July 4, 1976), married Carroll Nix Warren (born Oct. 22, 1881, died Nov. 16, 1962), married Sept. 9, 1900. Children: Lela Anne, born May 6, 1903, died April 15, 1991; James Gola, born Feb. 14, 1905, died March 7, 1988; Minnie Sue, born April 22, 1910; Videlle Eudoxie, born July 14, 1913.

Annie Alice, born Nov. 4, 1881, died July 22, 1973, married Isaac Jesse Cotham (born May 29, 1879, died July 17, 1956), married Sept. 16, 1900. Children: Bynum Trenton, born May 5, 1903, died June 1975; Vera Jane, born Oct. 4, 1906; Richard Fane, born March 28, 1908, died June 27, 1988; John Pinckney, born Aug. 7, 1911, died Jan. 10, 1983; Clofton Thomas, born March 8, 1914, died April 25, 1988; Willie Caruthers, born Feb. 2, 1917, died April 9, 1944; Jesse Glynn, born Feb. 15, 1921.

James Henry Hufstedler's second marriage, June 20, 1889, to Matilda Elizabeth Shelton (born Dec. 3, 1873, died May 23, 1963). Children are as follows: Cora Alma (b. Dec. 25, 1891, died Jan. 11, 1919), married Riley A. Broadway, April 30, 1916. Children: Mildred Larene born April 7, 1918, died June 23, 1987; James Madison, born Nov. 27, 1918, died Aug. 4, 1989.

Mattie Rowena, born Jan. 12, 1895, died Nov. 4, 1976, married Al Warren (born Dec. 1, 1887, died April 2, 1962), married July 23, 1911. Children: Alga Loucille, born Aug. 11, 1912; Fred Olga, born March 19, 1914, died Oct. 13, 1986; Jess Willard, born Dec. 27, 1915, died Aug. 8, 1980; Walton Olenthus, born Sept. 8, 1926; Mattie Ruth, born May 24, 1930.

Jacob Olenthus, born May 12, 1900, died Sept. 29, 1929, married Mabel Sanford (born Oct. 25, 1901), married 1919. Children: Ouida Mae, born Sept. 9, 1920, died Feb. 1, 1984; J.T., born April 14, 1922, died Dec. 12, 1979; Jo Dean, born Feb. 27, 1924; Juanita Ruth, born Jan. 26, 1926.

SAMUEL BOYD HUFSTEDLER, born

1888, died 1962, married Cora Honor Denton, born 1885, died 1949, daughter of Isaac and Fennie McCall Denton, in 1903.

Boyd and Cora Hufstedler

The Perry County Hufstedler family has been traced to the Jacob Hufstedler who came to America from Germany on the ship *Harle*, 1763. Tradition has it that he was born on this ship. He lived in Tyson-Lincoln, NC, and briefly in York County, SC. He then migrated to Anderson County, TN, where he served in the War of 1812 before coming to Perry County, TN, 1821. He settled on what is now known as Cane Creek.

Boyd was the son of Samuel Nacy Hufstedler, born 1858, and married Susan Galloway Polk, born 1862. Their children: Ada Adams, Lula Jane, Willie Kyle, Samuel Boyd, Sadie, Pinckney Claude, and Ralph Sneed. Nacy moved his family, with the exception of Boyd, from Perry County to Arkansas and on to Newbern, TN, where they lived until death.

Boyd told his family many interesting stories about his grandfather, Pinckney Hufstedler, born 1814, and grandmother, Louisa Jane Randel, born 1831, who lived near Buffalo River at Sand Field in Perry County. One story was that Pinckney left strict instructions as to his funeral. He was a mason by trade and had built a walled-in tomb (stands today) on top of a high bluff overlooking the river. He told his family when he died he wanted to be taken to his grave in his farm wagon drawn by his white oxen and not by any mules. He asked that John Kilpatrick drive the oxen and have someone hold the casket while climbing the bluff. He requested his daughter Josephine, who had a good singing voice, sing "How Firm A Foundation." His requests were carried out.

Children of Boyd and Cora Hufstedler: Sidney Curtis, born 1910, died 1972, married Eddie Workman, born 1915, of Hohenwald. Their children: Betty Jane, born 1933 and David, born 1938. Sidney Curtis had a high school education and his occupation was industry.

Hazel Mildred, born 1912, died 1966, married Ervin Warren, born 1911, died 1991, later married Horace Savage. Their children: Merridth Boyd, born 1934; Reed, born 1938; and Sherri, born 1942. Hazel Mildred had a high school education and attended nursing school. Her occupation was as a homemaker and she had a poetry book published.

Reeves Samuel, born 1914, died 1978, married Audra Allen, born 1921. Reeves Samuel had a high school education and a B.S. degree. His occupation was teacher.

Madelyn Loucretia, born 1916, married William Fred Shelton Sr., born 1905, died 1993, from Erin, TN. Their children: William Fred Jr., born 1938, and Samuel Marshall, born 1944. Madelyn Loucretia had a high school education and a B.S. degree. Her occupation was teacher.

Boyd Fielder, born 1917, died 1988. He had a high school education and his occupation was that of farmer, industry and was a World War veteran.

Hershel Clovis, born 1921, died 1984, married Elizabeth Byrd, born 1927. Their children: Joseph Dewitt, born 1946; Fielder Dale, born 1948; Steven, born 1950; John William, born 1951; Dianna Lyn, born 1955. Hershel Clovis had a high school education and attended Austin Peay College. His occupation was as an engineer and he was a World War veteran.

Boyd and Cora lived a simple and happy life. He was a farmer and merchant. Their priorities in life were their family and their fellowman.

JOEL MONROE HUNT, born Dec. 25, 1855, to James and Rebecca (Bates) Hunt. He had three younger sisters: Lucinda, Josephine, and Armada.

Joel Monroe Hunt around 1901

Monroe's father, James, born 1832, was the son of John Hunt. John, born 1802, in Bald Springs, (Franklin County) GA. He was the son of Joel Hunt, born 1766. John left Georgia and came to Tennessee about 1822, where he met and married Mary McKemie. They settled on Spring Creek at Mousetail, where they reared a family of 10 children. John died in 1853 and is buried in Hunt Hill Cemetery on Spring Creek.

Monroe's mother, Rebecca, born 1838, in Hickman County. She was the daughter of Isaiah and Lucinda Bates; both born in South Carolina, but early settlers of Hickman County.

Monroe first married Martha Dudley and had one son, Lando. Monroe and second wife, Kate Trantham, had seven (two died in infancy) daughters: Mamie, Mable, Ester, Lucy and Freda. After the death of his second wife, Monroe married Mary (Mollie) Edwards in 1897. To this union were added six more children; Charlie married Pearl Hinson, Clay married Mollie Wilburn, Sue married James (Jim) Ledbetter, Roy married Ruth Kittrell, Forrest married Vivian Dotson, and Pearl married Wilson DePriest.

Monroe's third wife, Mollie, born Sept. 23, 1866, to William H. and Mary Agnes (Woolard) Edwards. William H. served in the Civil War and died in 1871. He and Mary Agnes are buried in the family cemetery on Cane Creek, along with Mollie and Monroe.

Monroe was a farmer and served in various public offices. He was a democrat and never lost an election. Some of the offices were: Sheriff, County Court Clerk, Trustee, and House Representative (for Perry, Humphreys, and Wayne counties). He had been County Judge many years at the time of his death in 1926.

Pearl Hunt DePriest, born Nov. 9, 1909, is the youngest and only living child of Monroe Hunt. She was reared on Cane Creek and in 1928 married John Wilson DePriest.

Wilson, born Sept. 14, 1903, was the son of Robert E. and Dona (Bates) DePriest. He was the oldest of six children. Sisters were: Wilma Loggins, Janie Ledbetter, and Holly Doyle. Two brothers were: Redner and R. E. DePriest. All were born in Perry County.

Wilson and Pearl had three children, all born in Perry County. They are: Robert, born 1929; Carolyn, born 1933; and Evelyn, born 1938. In 1941, Wilson and Pearl moved to Jackson, TN, where they lived until Wilson's death in 1979. He is buried in Highland Memorial Gardens in Jackson. Pearl was a devoted wife, mother and daughter; helping to care for her mother until her death in 1960.

Robert married Joyce Hillard and has three children living, (one deceased) and six grandchildren. Carolyn married Otha Allen from Louisiana. They have two sons and four grandchildren. Evelyn married James White and has three children and six grandchildren.

Pearl now lives in Humboldt, TN, (in her own apartment) near her daughter, Evelyn.
Submitted by Carolyn DePriest Allen

INMAN, There were three Inman brothers – Shadrack, Meshack, and Abednego of Germany. Meshack was born in Germany about 1760. They traveled to America from England on the Mayflower. Meshack was killed by Indians.

Meshack had a son, Ezekiel Inman. Ezekiel married Catherine Perkins, April 4, 1811. They had a son, Samuel Edward Inman, born Sept. 25, 1818, in Williamson County, TN and died 1884 in CO. Samuel was married in 1838 to Naomi Whitson, born 1819. Their second child, Ezekiel Inman, born July 29, 1841, in Perry County, died April 30, 1933, married Sept. 8, 1870, to Rhoda Jane Keeling. Fourth generation Ezekiel Inman was the first member of the Church of Jesus Christ of Latter Day Saints in Perry County, TN. He was baptized in 1917/18, and helped build the first church in 1928 near the Short Creek Landing on the Tennessee River. Ezekiel and Rhoda had 11 children.

Amos Jackson Inman, first child of Ezekiel and Rhoda, born Feb. 7, 1871, in Tennessee, died April 28, 1952, married April 24, 1892 to Martha Caroline Graham, born July 17, 1873. Amos and Martha had nine children: 1) William Charlie Inman, born April 4, 1893, died July 1894; 2) Mary Laphelia Inman, born May 14, 1895, died March 12, 1983, married April 8, 1916 to Joseph Thomas Bunch; 3) Dora Ardella Inman, born Dec. 26, 1896, died February 1936; 4) James Allen Inman, born Dec. 17, 1898, died Feb. 3, 1966, married Jan. 5, 1921 to Hester Lee Inman; 5) Samuel Dewey Inman, born Oct. 24, 1900, died Oct. 8, 1976, married Dec. 10, 1928 to Mary Pearl Tillie; 6) Brice Matthew Inman, born Oct. 26, 1902, died Sept. 29, 1985, married March 19, 1936 to James Addie Myrtle Inman; 7) Lonnie Carmack Inman, born March 13, 1906, died June 18, 1992; 8) Jessie Inman, born April 15, 1909; 9) Nina Elizabeth Inman, Sept. 4, 1913, died April 28, 1951, married Odis Treadwell on Aug. 15, 1942.

EZEKEIL INMAN, was born July 29, 1840. His father was Samuel Inman and his mother was Neomia Whitson. Samuel and Neomia had the following children: Ezekiel, who married Rhoda Jane Keeling; Allen, who never married; Argee, who married Haymon Dedrick; Cynthia, who married John Pigg; Rebecca, who married John Denton.

(Left to Right): Bertha Inman Richardson, Ezekeil Inman, Rhoda Jane Keeling Inman.

Ezekeil and Allen both served in the military service during the Civil War. One fought for the Confederacy and the other for the Union Army.

Ezekiel and Rhoda Jane Keeling had the following children: Jack, who married Teenie Graham; Sam, who married Alma Shelton; Robert, who married Emma Coffman; Duke, who married Stella Holder; Ophelia, who married Brice Richardson; Catherine, who married Charley Martin; Mary, who married Alvin Richardson; Dora, who married Picard Hickerson and Bertha, who married Robert Richardson.

After Rhoda Jane died, Ezekiel married Permelia Adline Shelton, who had three children by a previous marriage. They were: Ida, who married John Richardson; Alma, who married Sam Inman and Henry, who married Nora DePriest.

Ezekiel and Adaline had three children: Lillie, who married Rube Lineberry; Brown, who married Nora Tillie and Elsie, who married Leonard Ward. *Submitted by a granddaughter, Ida Hickerson*

JOHN INMAN, born 1822, appeared in the census of Perry County in 1850. His wife Lucy was born in 1823 in Kentucky. John and Lucy had five children. The fourth child, Elisha (Tipp) Inman, born 1846, married July 24, 1866 to Easter C. (Puss) Keeling, born 1849. Elisha and Easter had eight children. The first child, John Inman, born 1866, died Dec. 14, 1901, married March 31, 1889 to Sarah Ann Pigg, born April 8, 1873, died Aug. 21, 1942. John and Sarah lived in the Short Creek Community near the Tennessee River. Their children were: 1) Ada Inman, born Jan. 2, 1890, died Dec. 4, 1906; 2) Robert Alvin (Tipp) Inman, born Aug. 22, 1892, died April 27, 1976, married Jimmie Parthena Lineberry; 3) Ida Elizabeth Inman, born March 31, 1896, died July 10, 1964, married Dec. 6, 1909 to Jess Tilly; 4) James Addie Myrtle Inman, born Jan. 12, 1898, died Sept. 2, 1983, married March 17, 1936 to Brice Matthew Inman; 5) Hester Lee Inman, born Nov. 23, 1901, died March 24, 1993, married Jan. 5, 1921 to James Allen Inman.

MARSHALL ALLEN INMAN, born Oct. 29, 1921, died Sept. 3, 1979 (son of James Allen Inman and Hester Lee Inman), married Jan. 4, 1944 to Ruby Lee Kelley, born Aug. 21, 1926 (daughter of John Robert Kelley, born Jan. 25, 1902 and Ida Mae Lomax, born April 3, 1903, died June 15, 1982). Marshall had three children: 1) Rada Evelyn Inman, born and died June 16, 1945; 2) Sandra Gale Inman, born Nov. 22, 1946, married Aug. 3, 1965 to Marshall Travis Spry, born December 1944 of Hardin County, TN. They had one child: Kelvin Allen Spry, born Sept. 16, 1966, married TerriLynn Summers. They had one child – Brittany Leigh Spry, born Aug. 6, 1991. 3) Wanda Jean Inman, born Sept. 15, 1949. Sandra and her family live in Linden, TN.

JESSE RAY JACKSON and Early Mae Barber have lived the last 30 years of their life on Brooklyn Avenue in Linden, TN. They have enjoyed the friends and neighbors of this peaceful community.

Jesse and Early Mae Jackson

Jesse (12-16-24) was the son of the late Will Jackson (1-26-1893) and the late Clara Gregory (4-3-1898), both of the Perry County area.

Early Mae (3-9-32) is the daughter of the late Luther Barber (9-25-09) and the late Irene Trull (4-27-11). The Barber family lived most of their life in Perry County after a few years in Lewis County.

Jesse and Early Mae were lifelong residents of Linden and members of the First Baptist Church of Linden. They enjoyed working with the children at church but Jesse was known best by his love for flowers and gardening.

Jesse and Early Mae had two sons – Ronny Lynn of Texas and Ricky Dale of Linden. They had three grandchildren: Anthony Lynn of Texas, Christopher Scot (deceased) of Texas and Ricky Brian Dale of Linden.

Early Mae still resides on Brooklyn Avenue. Jesse went to be with the Lord on Jan. 30, 1989. He is still deeply missed by his family, friends and all who knew him.

RICKY DALE JACKSON and Barbara Kay Qualls are life long residents of Perry County. They enjoy the surroundings of Perry County. The rivers, creeks, and solitude are the attributes that make Perry County the best place in the world to live.

Ricky Dale and Barbara Kay Qualls Jackson with son Ricky Brian Dale Jackson.

Ricky Dale Jackson (5-5-56) is the son of Jesse Ray Jackson and Early Mae Barber. He is a 1974 graduate of PCHS and is currently employed at Bates Fab. in Lobelville, TN.

Early Mae Jackson, known to most people as Granny Mae (D.O.B. 3-9-32) still lives in Linden. Grandpa or Mr. Jesse (D.O.B. 12-16-25) went to be with the Lord Jan. 30, 1989. They were both employees of Washington Mfg. and Granny Mae is now employed at Robinson Mfg. of Linden.

Barbara is the daughter of Waco Melvin Qualls (10-18-24) and Ina Webb Duncan (12-11-25) of the Brush Creek community of Perry County. Barbara was born Sept. 5, 1959. She was a 1977 graduate of PCHS and is currently employed at The Buffalo River Review office along with doing voluntary work at the church office. Melvin and Ina were both employed at Zemer Eng. of Flatwoods, TN. Now they are both retired and enjoy spending time with all their grandchildren.

Ricky and Barbara were married at the First Baptist Church in Linden on the second day of July 1978. From this union is one son: Ricky Brian Dale, born Sept. 19, 1980. Brian graduated from the eighth grade May 23, 1994. He, along with his parents, loves Perry County's great outdoors – from fishing, camping, hiking, four-wheeler riding to just sitting on their front porch listening to crickets, katy-dids, and frogs.

After their marriage in July, they lived in the Brush Creek Community for a while; then after a short time living in Linden, they returned to Brush Creek. In January 1982 they lost their home by fire; after renting several different places they moved into their new home in November 1986, corner of Hwy. 13S and Hwy. 128 where they still reside.

Ricky is plant manager of Bates Fabricating in Lobelville, TN. He is also a deacon at First Baptist Church Linden, Bro. Mike Adams, pastor; where his wife and son are also members. The Jacksons enjoy attending church and participating in all the church activities.

WILLIAM CODY JACKSON, (Will) and Clara Jane Gregory Jackson. Will Jackson was born Jan. 26, 1893, died Sept. 20, 1951. He married Clara Jane Gregory who was born April 3, 1898, died June 12, 1985.

William Cody (Will) and Clara Jane Gregory Jackson.

Will was the son of Nat Jackson and Ellen Elizabeth Rogers Jackson. Clara was the daughter of William Edward (born Sept. 4, 1868, died Oct 25, 1957) and Stella Mae Gregory (born Nov. 14, 1873, died Oct. 28, 1952).

Will and Clara had two sons and three daughters: William Robert Jackson was born Dec. 15, 1915, died Aug. 1, 1985. He was buried on Cane Creek in Doyle Cemetery. He married Myrtle Anlee Bates, Sept. 21, 1936. They had five children: twins Bonnie Lou and Bettye Sue; a daughter, Lena Anne; a son, William Randal; and a son, Andrew Bates Jackson.

Ellen Elizabeth (Bessie) Jackson, born Dec. 29, 1919. She married Ishmael Aaron Trull on April 29, 1939. They had one son, Teddy Eugene Trull. Marriage ended in divorce. Married Herschel Lewis on Sept. 20, 1947. Divorced. Married Fred Bastin. Divorced. Married Howard Williams. Divorced. Married Clyde (Red) Kilpatrick.

Edward Earl Jackson, born Sept. 24, 1923. Married Phyllis Jean Caudle. They had five children: a daughter, Barbara Jean; a son, Danny Edward; a daughter, Melba Kay; a son, Tommy Kenneth; and a daughter, Marla Lee.

Jesse Ray Jackson, born Dec. 16, 1925, died Jan. 30, 1989. Married Hazel Virginia Matheny, first. They had one son, Ronny Len. Divorced and married Early Mae Barber. They had a son, Ricky Dale.

Thelma Loudean Jackson, born Aug. 5, 1928. Married William David Qualls. They had three children: a son, David Wayne; a daughter, Janice Kay (died at birth); and a son, Jerry Don.

Will had 11 brothers and sisters: Ellen; Atha; Jim A. (1879-1939); Frances Maude (Frankie) (born Feb. 15, 1881, died Oct. 21, 1961); Hattie; Annie; Fred; John; Stanley (Dock); Andrew (Buck); and Leonard (Len).

Clara had 11 brothers and sisters: Leslie, born Sept. 20, 1892, died March 28, 1962; Willie, born Sept. 23, 1893, died Sept. 5, 1925; Frank, born Jan. 12, 1895; Browney, born Dec. 23, 1896, died Oct. 29, 1901; Freddie, born Feb. 3, 1900, died Sept. 4, 1989; James Aubrey, a son, born

June 7, 1902, died April 17, 1966; Andrew (Boots), born June 14, 1904, died July 20, 1977; Elmer (Pug), born Aug. 8, 1907, died May 2, 1982; Lillie, born April 28, 1909, died Jan. 19, 1979; Marvin, born Feb. 22, 1911, died July 7, 1968; Edward Jr. (Dollie), born March 22, 1913.

Will and Nat Jackson are both buried in Bethel Cemetery near Linden in Perry County.

Clara is buried in Dr. O. A. Kirk Cemetery near Linden in Perry County. After Will's death, Clara married Winford Woodley who also preceded her in death. *Submitted by Anne J. Bone*

JACKSON, William Robert and Myrtle Anlee Bates Jackson. William Robert Jackson was born Dec. 15, 1915, died Aug. 1, 1985.

William Robert Jackson Family

Myrtle Anlee Bates Jackson was born March 4, 1919, died July 21, 1981.

William and Myrtle were married in Perry County on Sept. 21, 1936.

William was the son of Will Cody Jackson, born Jan. 26, 1893, died Sept. 20, 1957, and Clara Jane Gregory Jackson, born April 3, 1898, died June 12, 1985.

Myrtle was the daughter of Andrew Bismark Bates, born June 14, 1894, died Sept. 4, 1954, and Della FaDillia (Dillie) Doyle Bates, born Oct. 8, 1893, died July 6, 1975.

William and Myrtle had five children: twin daughters Bonnie Lou and Betty Sue Jackson, born Oct. 26, 1939; a daughter, Lena Anne Jackson, born Aug. 3, 1944; a son, William Randal Jackson, born Nov. 3, 1946; a son, Andrew Bates Jackson, born Sept. 6, 1951.

Bonnie Lou Jackson married Lee Edward DePriest on Jan. 7, 1956. Lee Ed was born March 16, 1934. Two sons were born: Scotty Edward on May 11, 1960; and Timothy Lee on June 4, 1961. Scotty Edward married Donna Darlene Parnell born Jan. 21, 1962. They have two daughters: Ashley Danielle (11-16-86) and Aubrey Leigh (3-19-89). Tim married Janice Kimberly Upchurch, born Nov. 14, 1962. One daughter, Sydney Chantal (1-17-89).

Bettye Sue Jackson married W. C. Thompson on June 22, 1960. W. C. was born Nov. 6, 1941. One son: Jeffrey Alan, born May 30, 1966. Jeff married Rhonda Dee Clinard. Marriage ended in divorce. Married Martie Jean Robison who was born June 15, 1970. Two sons: Justin Derek (12-18-92), and Joshua Cole (1-25-94). Bettye and W. C. divorced and Bettye married Jack Norman Westbrook who was born Sept. 22, 1936.

Lena Anne Jackson married Geral Dean Bone, Feb. 6, 1965. Gerald was born July 19, 1942. No children.

William Randal Jackson married Joan Elizabeth Garner. Joan was born Sept. 22, 1949, died July 3, 1980. Two daughters: Jeanna Lynn, born Sept. 23, 1966, and Andrea Carol, born Aug. 14, 1972. Jeanna married Norman Timothy Barnett; one daughter, Kasy Elizabeth (9-29-83). Divorced. Married Michael McKinney; One son: Joshua Michael (11-30-87). Divorced. Andrea Carol married Jamie Lynn Kilpatrick. Randal then married Kathryn Michelle (Shellie) Mashaw who was born Nov. 3, 1959.

Andrew Bates Jackson married Victoria Mai (Vickie) Murphree on Nov. 2, 1979. Vickie was born Feb. 26, 1951. Two children: a son, Johnny Joseph, born April 1, 1981; a daughter, Tiffany Anne, born Aug. 24, 1982.

William and Myrtle lived most of their lives on Cane Creek in Perry County. Later they moved to Nashville and lived for a few years then moved to Waverly where both were living at the time of their deaths. Both are buried in they Doyle Cemetery on Cane Creek. After Myrtle's death, William married Altie Catherine Cotham Sharpe on Sept. 11, 1982. *Submitted by Timothy Lee DePriest*

WILLIAM JAMES, born in North Carolina ca. 1795, was in Tennessee by 1815. Records show he migrated into Alabama for a short time. Then the family was back in Perry County prior to 1824.

Jeremiah James and his second wife, Mary Polly Campbell.

William, according to circumstantial evidence, married a daughter of George and Jemima (Russell) Horner; however, her first name is yet unknown. Birth dates and birthplaces of their children were: Pleasant L., born in Tennessee ca. 1816; Lucinda, born ca. 1817-1818 in Tennessee; William Russell, born in Alabama in 1819; Jeremiah, born Feb. 10, 1824 in Perry county; Rebecca, born Sept. 23, 1826 in Davidson County; George Washington, born in Perry County ca. 1830; Andrew Jackson James, born in Perry county 1836; Martha is noted in a court document as an heir of William's estate but her birthdate is unknown.

Pleasant stayed in Perry County, and little is known about him except that he died in 1848 leaving two minor children: Mary and Sarah. Peter L. Lovelace became their guardian.

In October 1840, Pleasant James paid Pleasant Horner $100 for his share of the land property of deceased William James indicating that his wife, possibly Lucinda, had already died.

By 1841 William Russell James was in Franklin County, AR, and had married Talitha Campbell from Lincoln County, TN. It is thought that at his father William's death, the mother was already deceased as William R. brought his three younger brothers to Cass, AR, and reared them with his own children, all born in Arkansas except the oldest born in Beardstown, TN: John Wesley, born 1841; Pleasant Horner, born 1847; Jeremiah Alexander, born Aug. 13, 1851; James M., born 1853; Mary J., born 1856; William Russell, died April 4, 1868 at Redding, AR.

Jeremiah married first Nancy Caroline Huggins, born in Tennessee, Feb. 8, 1830. She died soon after the birth of her only child, Nancy Jane, on June 23, 1848. Jeremiah married secondly Mary Polly Campbell, daughter of Billy and Nancy (McCalister) Campbell. They had at least 10 children, five of whom died during the diptheria epidemic of 1885-1886. Surviving children were: William, Andrew, Martha, Emeline, Arabella and Amanda. Jeremiah died Aug. 1, 1903. Mary Polly lived until 1913.

Rebecca married Christopher Swindle in Perry County in 1845. He died in 1865 in Graves County, KY, and Rebecca returned to Tennessee.

George Washington married Sarah Jane Huggins, daughter of John Huggins and Sarah Farris. They had four children: Talitha Jane, born Aug. 15, 1848, married John Childers on Aug. 5, 1867, died in Lakeview, TX, May 18, 1917; William Russell, born Feb. 17, 1850, married Arabel Brown from Paris, TX, in Franklin County, AR, July 14, 1870, died Jan. 8, 1932 (She had died Nov. 9, 1904 in Blue Ridge, TX), he never remarried; Georgianna, born ca. 1852, married Jackson Hood; Sarah Clementine, born Dec. 8, 1854, married John William Anderson on Jan. 16, 1873 (She died at Ozark, AR, on March 29, 1926).

George Washington died at about age 30 from smallpox complications after his trip West to the Gold Rush. Andrew Jackson married Smithy Barham Campbell, (born in 1838 in Perry County, TN) September 1854. Their children, all born in Arkansas, were: John William, born 1856 in Franklin County; Mary E., born in 1858 in Franklin County; Sarah Jane, born April 1, 1865 in Franklin County; Monroe Burnett, born Jan. 4, 1870, died in 1944; Jeremiah Lee, born Jan. 1, 1871 in Johnson County, died in 1943; Mary Rose Della, born Jan. 26, 1875 in Franklin County; Douglas, born in 1877 in Franklin County, died in 1909; Andrew Jackson died before 1900 in Salisaw, Sequoyah County, OK.

ENNIS AND MAIE JOHNSON, Ennis Johnson (1905-1976) and Maie Duncan Johnson (1909) were lifelong residents of Perry County. He was born in Perry County on the Henry Ledbetter farm. He is buried in the Dr. O. A. Kirk Cemetery in Linden. He was a farmer, mechanic and a maintenance man for Tennessee Gas & Transmission Company until he retired in 1968. He married Virginia Maie Duncan in 1924 and had the following four children: (1) Mary Jane, born in 1928, first marriage to Grady Pope of Cedar Creek. They had one child, Norma Jean Pope. A second marriage to John Campbell of Lobelville. They had two daughters, Shirley May and Julia Sue Campbell. (2) Louise was born in 1929, married Charlie William French of Linden. They had one child, Belinda Lou French. (3) Billie Sue was born in 1931 and served in the U.S. Army from 1952-1954. First marriage David Westbrooks. He was killed in the Korean War in 1950; second marriage to James William Spratt of Spokane, WA. He was serving the U.S. Marines when they married in California. They had two children, Susan Marie and James Robert Spratt. Third marriage to Clyde Lloyd. (4) Jimmy Glen was born in 1938 and served in the U.S. Marines from 1956-1959. He was married to Nancy Glass of Nashville. They had three children, Gina Kay, Glen Martin and Anthony Todd Johnson.

Ennis Johnson was the son of Addie (1878-1958) and Liza Jane Johnson (1880-1960). They came to Tennessee from Arkansas in the late 1800s. Uncle Addie, as he was known by friends and relatives, was known for his love of mule trading and his coon dogs. His favorite pasttime was going hunting and listening to his coon dogs run at night. His only occupation was farming. He was a sharecropper for the Henry Ledbetter family for many years. He was born in Arkansas in 1878 and died in 1958 and was buried in the Brush Creek Cemetery on Brush Creek in Perry County. Liza Jane Johnson was born in Arkansas in 1880 and died in 1960 in Perry County. She is also buried in Brush Creek Cemetery. They had the following five children: (1) Willis and (2) Maudie, died at an early age; (3) Maggie, who had three sons, Elmer Howard and Ray Lawrence, living in California, and Paul Edward, killed in a car wreck; (4) Ennis, named above; (5) Elmer, had two sons, Jimmy and Bobby of Florida.

Maie Duncan Johnson was born in 1909 in Wayne County and was the daughter of Scott Duncan (1883-1928) and Lillie Mitchell Duncan (1887-1968). Scott Duncan is buried in the Joe Barber Cemetery on Coon Creek in Perry County. Lillie Duncan is buried in the Woodlawn Cemetery in Nashville. They moved around in Perry County and the surrounding counties because he worked as an estimator of timber. Scott and Lillie Duncan had the following nine children: (1) Katie, (2) Loyce, (3) and an unnamed boy died at an early age; (4) Elva, (5) Maie, (6) Brown, who died at the age of 13, (7) Marie, (8) Nell, and (9) Eva Dell. *Submitted by Louise Johnson French.*

EUGENE E. JOHNSON and Nancy Elise Johnson live in Lobelville, Perry County. Elise, born in Perry County, is the daughter of Eli Thomas and Martha Jane Barber Qualls. Eugene and Elise have three children: Elizabeth Marie, married first Michael Aldridge, children are Jonathan and Adam, married second Kerry McCord; Sarah Ann, married Ricky Clifton, children are Jennifer Marie and Kelly Don; and William, unmarried.

Eli T. Qualls, son of Doctor Wily Qualls and Nancy Duncan, married first Maude Cooper. Children are Doctor Cooper, George, Percy Scott, and Helen. He married second Martha Jane Barber. Their children are Walter Kirk and Nancy Elise.

Martha Jane Barber Qualls was the daughter of Abraham E. (Levi) Barber and Nancy Adiline (Addie) Warren, daughter of Alvin Warren, born 1821, and Mary Barber Dowdy Warren, born 1821, and of this family there was: Izora S., born 1878, married first Joe T. Lewis, and second Joe Beasley; William Kinchen, born 1884, married Edna Hinson; Mary Nancy, born 1886, married J. C. Devore; Calvin D., born 1888, married Jessie Lewis; Martha Jane, born 1890, married Eli Thomas Qualls.

Alvin Warren father of Nancy Adiline Warren Barber was the son of Elijah Warren Jr., wife unknown, and he was the son of Elijah Warren Sr. who first settled in Hickman County which later became part of Perry County. Elijah Warren Sr. was from North Carolina and was a soldier in the Revolutionary War, serving in the North Carolina Line. He removed to Hardiman County, TN, and died there.

Abraham E. (Levi) Barber was the son of Calvin and Nancy Dowdy Barber, daughter of Joseph Dowdy, mother unknown, and of this family there was: Elizabeth Jane, born 1841, married Hiram Campbell; Richard A., born 1843, unmarried; Abraham Levi, born 1849, married Nancy Adiline Warren; Jeramiah Warren, born 1852, married Donna Warren; Joseph H., born 1861, married Parlie Tucker.

Calvin Barber was the son of Abraham (Abram) Jr. and Sarah Edwards Barber and of this family there were: Calvin, born 1817, married Nancy Dowdy; Enoch, born 1804, married Susan Hinson; John E., born 1809, married Sarah Hinson; Susan A., born 1824, married Simon Campbell; Nancy, born 1811, married Tubal Campbell; Fannie, born 1800, married Richard Campbell; James, born 1821, married Jane Hilburn; Ziby, born 1823, married Mary Elizabeth Hilburn; Allen H., born 1826, married Margaret Harper; Abraham, born ?.

Abraham (Abram) Barber Jr., father of Calvin Barber, was born in Anson County, NC, and came to Perry County in the early 1800s, settling on upper Coon Creek. Abram Barber Jr. was the son of Abraham Sr. and Rodah Barber of Anson County, NC, and of this family there were: Elizabeth, married Richard Sasser; John; Noah, married Mary Savannah Moore; Polly, married Uriah Tison; Anna, married Thomas Hemby; Abraham Jr., married Sarah Edwards; James.

Abraham Barber Sr. was the son of Capt. John Barber and Mary Allen. Capt. John Barber, born 1738, was a captain of a troop of militia before the Revolutionary War. When the war began his troops were assigned to the North Carolina Continental Army. Capt. John was a member of the Provincial Congress, 1776, member of the General Assembly, 1777, member of the committee of Safety, Tryon County, NC, 1775.

Capt. John Barber and Mary Ellen had the following children: Abraham, married Rodah; Nicy, married John Davis; Liday, married John Davis; William; Arby; Ziby; James; John; Nancy; Allen; Gatsey; Mary, married John Curlee; and Sidney.

Eugene E. Johnson was born in Richman, IN, Wayne County, and is the son of Lawrence M., born in Hamilton County, TN, and Christina Marie Justice, born in Jefferson County, IN. Lawrence M. was the son of Willis Lester, born in Gilmer County, GA, and Elizabeth Sarah Guthrie Johnson, born in Hamilton County, TN. Willis Lester Johnson was the son of Jesse Jefferson Johnson and Rebecca Jane Woody, daughter of Allen D. and Susan Woddy. Jesse Jefferson Johnson was the son of Jefferson and Pricilla Johnson.

Christina Marie Justice Johnson was the daughter of William T. Justice and Lucinda Hoffman, daughter of Frank and Margaret Ann Severs Hoffman. *Submitted by Elise Qualls Johnson*

JAMES ALBERT JOHNSTON, born Oct. 11, 1858, son of Samuel K. Johnston and Elizabeth A. Sharp, died April 30, 1921, Short Creek, Perry County, buried Chestnut Grove Cemetery, Coon Creek. His paternal grandparents were Andrew Johnston and Elizabeth Nixon and maternal were John M. Sharp and Nancy Hensley. Samuel K. Johnston probably died in the Civil War and his wife, Elizabeth Sharp, also died. James married twice. His first wife, Martha Caroline Carroll, died 1906 and he married Mary Stults. His children were Ninnie, believed married a Hinson; Mary Elizabeth, wife of Eugene Rosson; John A.; Irvin I., born 1892, died 1948, buried Chestnut Grove Cemetery; Baxter D., born April 28, 1894, died March 14, 1953, buried Chestnut Grove Cemetery; Maud Statter, wife of James Clarence Jones; Dorothy C., wife of Hobert Jones; Jessie F., born 1902, died young, buried Duncan Cemetery on Short Creek; and Sam Russell, born April 18, 1904, died June 25, 1963, buried Duncan Cemetery. Russell married Effie Duncan, who was born June 17, 1903, died April 23, 1976. Their children: Jimmy, Fred Elton, and Ruth E. Johnston. By wife Mary Stults, children were: Ollie H., born May 6, 1909, died Dec. 9, 1929, buried Chestnut Grove Cemetery, and Vestie Johnston, who married a Qualls.

JOLLIFF, William (Billy) Martin (D.O.B. 8-6-47, D.O.D. 5-9-92) and Dannie Webb Qualls. Billy and Dannie were married Feb. 5, 1971, and to this union was born one son, William Daniel Jolliff (D.O.B. 3-4-73). Dannie and Daniel now reside in the Brush Creek Community of Perry County.

(Left to right) Daniel and Dannie Jolliff.

Dannie, born in Hohenwald, Jan. 8, 1948, is the daughter of Waco Melvin (D.O.B. 10-18-24) and Ina Webb Duncan Qualls (D.O.B. 12-11-25) who were married March 6, 1943.

William (Billy) was the youngest child born to William Franklin (D.O.B. 10-6-?, D.O.D. 10-6-79?) buried in Hot Springs, AR, and Geraldine Martin Jolliff (D.O.B. and D.O.D. unknown) buried in Flint, MI. William (Billy) has a half-brother, William (Buddy) Franklin Jolliff II, in Gulfport, MS; half-sister, Aliene Jolliff Williams, in Temple, TX; brother, Michael Jolliff in Clio, MI; and a sister, Kathleen Jolliff Lobdell, in Montrose, MI.

Billy was a 1966 graduate of PCHS, a Vietnam veteran and a truck driver with various companies most of his adult life.

Dannie was a 1966 graduate of PCHS. She worked in garment plants and as a nurses aid at Perry County Hospital. Helping people in hospitals was an enjoyable experience for her.

In 1983 Dannie and her sister, Barbara Jackson, started babysitting at her house in Linden until Oct. 15, 1984, when they opened the first licensed day care in Linden, which is called J & J Day Care Center. This was located in the building where Tiny Tot is now located. in 1988 Dannie moved to a new building which is located two-tenths of a mile off Hwy. 13 South on Marsh Creek Road. After back surgery in July 1990, Dannie sold J & J Day Care to Brenda Davis Whitehead, who was an employee of J & J. Dannie is still employed at J & J and has enjoyed working the past 10 years with all the children that have ever been enrolled at J & J. To over half the children of Perry County, she is known as "Aunt Dee," which she will always cherish as long as she lives.

William Daniel Jolliff (D.O.B. 3-4-73) is a 1991 graduate of PCHS and has been employed with Pat's Inc. of Linden since graduation. Daniel enjoys outdoor sports such as boating, swimming, and car racing. He is presently dating Gwen Mercer of Linden.

JAMES ARTHUR JONES – Pauline Greer. James Arthur Jones (1922-1979) was the only son of Nancy Aldridge (1902-1942) and Grady Jones (-1924) He married Pauline Greer, Ilsley, KY, in 1943. Four children are Nancy Hall, Sheila Bruce, Robert Jones and Kelly Jones. There are 10 grandchildren and great-grandchildren.

Robert, Pauline (wife of Arthur Jones), Sheila Bruce and Nancy Hall.

Arthur served in the U.S. Army during W.W.II. He received a medical discharge and returned to live in Ilsley, KY, (near Dawson Spring) for the rest of his life and is buried there. He worked in various jobs in the coal mines, acquiring "black lung" disease, which was a contributing factor to his early death. Pauline, children and grandchildren all reside in the area of Madisonville, KY.

Arthur's half-sisters are Helen Faye Halbrooks Greeson, Rosa Lee Halbrooks Johnson, and Ruby Halbrooks Hodges. Arthur's paternal relatives (Jones) lived in the Ilsley, KY, area, but were originally from the Perry County area. They are related to the Barbers, also. Grady Jones, Arthur's father, died of flu or pneumonia (1924) and was buried in Russellville, AL, when Arthur was two years old. Arthur and his mother, Nancy Aldridge Jones, returned to live with the James Aldridges and she taught school at "Frog Pond"; and later at Bethel, staying with the Barney Duncans. There she met and married Fred Halbrooks (1901-1953, buried at Bethel), son of Robert M. and Mollie DePriest Halbrooks. Arthur's family lived in Bethel, DePriest Bend, Cypress Creek, Coon Creek and Linden. He lived some of the time with his grandparents, Tim Jones and Elma Brewer in Kentucky. Great-grandparents were Tim and Martha Barber Jones. Arthur's mother, Nancy (Nannie) Aldridge Jones Halbrooks, died of a stroke Dec. 26, 1942, at age 40. She is buried at Bethel.

Arthur joined the CCC prior to joining the U.S. Army. It was funds earned from this service that he sent his mother to help pay for building a house in Linden (Mill St. Newtown). In his early years, he became close friends with his maternal cousins, Jim and Andrew Crosby and his maternal family (James Aldridge). He was an avid fisherman and loved music, particularly the guitar.

See references on: Aldridge, Halbrooks, half-sisters – Rosa Lee Halbrooks Johnson, Helen Halbrooks Greeson, and Ruby Halbrooks Hodges.

ADAM AND BYRON KELLY FAMILY, Adam Newton Kelly was born to Alfred and Laura Kunkel Kelly on Aug. 12, 1901, at lower Cypress Creek in Perry County, one of five sons and seven daughters (Vera, Eva, Lena, Adam, Fred, Frank, Mary, Martha, Jim, John, Sue, Nellie).

Adam is survived by his beloved wife, Byron, of 63 years, whom he married on April 5, 1930, at Columbia, TN. Byron was born Byron Augusta Bell to Charles and Winnie Coble Bell on Jan. 6, 1910, at Tom's Creek in Perry County, one of four daughters and five sons, one of which was her twin brother (Leonard, Fernie, Brown, Roy, Vera, Mary, Louise, Byron, Bernard).

Their three children are Adam Newton Jr., born April 14, 1931; Peggy Ann, born Oct. 16, 1932; and Charles Alfred, born Dec. 30, 1935, all of which were born in Howard County, IN. There are eight grandchildren (one of which is deceased) and two great-grandchildren.

Adam began employment in the steel industry in West Virginia and Ohio. Following their marriage, Byron joined Adam in Kokomo, IN, where Adam completed a 36-year career with the steel industry. During a portion of that time, they found rewarding pleasure in ownership of a farm in Bunker Hill, IN. In addition to caring for their children and the home, Byron worked as a Sunbeam Appliance demonstrator in various Indiana cities.

Subsequent to Adam's retirement from Continental Steel Corporation in Kokomo, IN, they purchased a truck/camper and joined a Camper Club which included members from four midwestern states: Illinois, Indiana, Michigan and Ohio. They traveled in all of the United States and Mexico. In between tending to their farm during growing seasons, they spent their winters in Florida.

Following residence in Indiana for 43 years, they sold their farm and returned to Linden, TN, while continuing to spend some winters in Florida. In addition to serving as Senior Citizens' Director, Adam served on the Election Commission for more than 15 years until health forced him to quit in 1992. He subsequently passed away March 19, 1993, just prior to his and Byron's 63rd Wedding Anniversary that would have occurred April 5, 1993. Adam is laid to rest in the Kirk Memorial Cemetery in Linden where he will one day be joined by his beloved wife, Byron.

Both of their sons retired from Chrysler Corporation and reside in southwest Florida. Their daughter resides in Charleston, SC, and is employed by the Southern Bell Telephone Company. One grandchild, Michele Kelly Bixler, and two great-grandchildren, Nicholas and Elizabeth Bixler, reside in Kokomo, IN. Another grandchild, Debbie Kelly, resides in Southwest Florida. Three grandchildren, Jamie, Charles and Jenifer Kelly, reside in St. Louis, MO, and two, Stephen and Catherine Glover, reside in Charleston, SC. The remaining grandchild, Sheri Kelly is deceased and laid to rest at Bunker Hill, IN.

JOSEPH KELLEY, came from Virginia and settled in Perry County about 1821. The family doesn't know who his wife was. He died between 1850 and 1860.

The Joseph Kelley Family.

His son, Joseph Kelley, first married Jane and they had six children. Jane died and Joseph married Martha Elizabeth Kirk Mitchell, daughter of Peter Akin Kirk and Elizabeth Locke. Martha's first husband, James J. Mitchell, died in Virginia. It was in 1862 during the Civil War. Joseph and Martha had four children: Joseph, Ellen, Jefferson Davis (Jeff), and Martha. It was said that when Joseph was an old man that he liked to help his son Jeff on his farm. He would drive the mules and wagon all day while Jeff and his kids would pick corn. Joseph died in 1878 and Martha in 1925. They were buried in the Bee Creek cemetery.

Jeff Kelley married three times. First to Mary Ella Fergerson, daughter of John Thomas Fergerson and Mary Mariah Bates. Their children were Willie, Lillie, Bertha, John Robert and Letha. Mary died in childbirth in 1909. Jeff then married Willie Bell Holder. She died in about 10 months after their marriage and their daughter, Fannie Bell Kelley, died in about two months and was buried with her mother. Jeff married Laurie Hickerson. They had six children: Leonard, Viola, Mary Lucy, Gracie, Ollie and Dollie Kelley. It was said that Jeff Kelley's word was his bond and he did business with a hand shake. He died in 1921.

Robert Kelley married Ida Mae Lomax,

daughter of Robert Lomax and Mary Richardson, in 1920. Their children are Clemmie, Clenard, Ruby, Rada, Irene and Helton. All were born in Perry County. Robert farmed and during the Depression the Kelley family never lacked for food and clothing. Robert got up before daylight and cut crossties and worked his farm till dark. Ida, Clemmie and Clenard would pick and shell peanuts to sell for what they couldn't grow in their garden. The family lived in Perry County until 1943 when they moved to Clifton in Wayne County. Robert Kelley is a well-respected man in Clifton. He was mayor in 1974 and in 1978 he fulfilled a lifelong dream when he went to Israel and Rome. In 1982 he lost his beloved wife. Robert was still an active man at the Senior Citizen Center in Clifton. He was Citizen of the Month in April 1985. In 1978 he married Lucille Moore and moved to Linden.

Rada Kelley, youngest daughter of Robert and Ida, married James Rolf Brashier in 1947. James was the son of Annie Hamilton and Thomas Edward Brashier. Their children were Johnnie, Donna and Ricky Brashier. Johnnie was born in Wayne County and Donna and Ricky in Hardin County. The Brashiers moved to Gibson County in 1961 and have made it their home since. Donna's daughter Amy married Jonathan Murphree and they have two children, Ashley and Dylan Murphree.

KIDD FAMILY, Samuel H. and Lena Jo Horner Kidd live on Lick Creek in Perry County on the family farm of Lena Jo Kidd. The farm has been in the Horner family since 1852. Lena Jo is the only child of William Leonard and Aucie Allen Horner, both deceased April 23, 1970. Leonard Horner was born July 9, 1903, the only child of Jesse James and Ida E. Patterson Horner.

Lena Jo and Samuel H. Kidd.

Aucie Allen Horner was born June 10, 1903, the oldest of eight children born to Alonzo Clinton and Cora Jane Marshall Allen of Marsh Creek.

Jesse James Horner was born March 19, 1877, son of William Sparks Horner and Ann Jane Coleman Horner. Ida E. Patterson was born Aug. 29, 1885, daughter of William Robert and Dixie Ann "Patterson" Patterson of Lick Creek.

William Sparks Horner was born Aug. 17, 1850, the son of Jesse and (Polly) Patterson Horner. Jesse Horner was born March 15, 1816, the son of John and Sarah Sparks Horner who were married Oct. 1, 1814. Jesse Horner gave the land for the oldest church in the county known now as Lick Creek Baptist Church (formerly known as Union Primitive Baptist Church).

Samuel Hunter Kidd was born Oct. 31, 1935, the only child of Mary Hunter Kidd and Samuel Scott Kidd of Clarksville, TN. Mary Hunter Kidd was born Aug. 22, 1902, in Clarksville, TN, and died March 5, 1993. Samuel Scott Kidd was born Jan. 1, 1905, in New Albany, MS. He died June 1, 1987. Mr. Kidd came to Clarksville with the Civilian Conservation Corps. Samuel Hunter Kidd served in the United States Coast Guard from 1956-1960.

Sam and Lena Jo Kidd married April 15, 1961, and have one son, Scott William Kidd, born Jan. 28, 1967. Scott served in the Navy during Desert Storm. He married Nancy Fay Sharp of Hohenwald, TN, on April 6, 1991.

KILPATRICKS, The Kilpatricks of 1850 Perry County all appear related. John W. Kilpatrick (45, born South Carolina) and James M. Kilpatrick (40) were sons of James Miller Kilpatrick (born c. 1781) who died in Maury County before 1850. In 1852 his son, Andrew B. was appointed administrator of his estate. Other sons were Enos Simpson Kilpatrick (born 1806) and William Allen Kilpatrick (born 1815, Buncombe County, NC) (latter in Copiah County, NC, in 1850).

Also in 1850 Perry County were A. B. (Alfred Burton) Kilpatrick (30), John Kilpatrick (26) and Joshua W. Kilpatrick (23), believed younger sons of William Kilpatrick (born c. 1767), oldest brother of James Miller Kilpatrick, both of whom had early come to Maury County. They were sons of James Kilpatrick Jr., of 1800 Pendleton District, SC, living next to oldest son William. James Jr. is also listed in 1790 and 1810 Rutherford County, NC. The 1810 Buncombe County, NC, census shows James (Miller) Kilpatrick (with four sons) along with Andrew, Joseph and William (Wilson) Kilpatrick, all believed to be his uncles. Two 1807 Pendleton District, SC, deeds (William's and James Miller Kilpatrick's) and two Buncombe County, NC, deeds (1811 Andrew Kilpatrick's and 1816 another James Kilpatrick's – son of Joseph) give us James Miller Kilpatrick's middle name. In 1807 William sold land to "James M. Kilpatrick" and a week later "James Miller Kilpatrick" sold that land (Deeds filed Anderson County, SC, book L). The Buncombe County deeds, in Book H, show James M. or James Miller Kilpatrick witnessed or proved these deeds.

Also in 1850 Perry County was Andrew Kilpatrick (75) (of above 1811 deed) and his wife Martha (74) living with son-in-law Allen Barber. Earlier, Andrew was in 1820 and 1830 Hickman County, TN – and 1840 Wayne County, TN, near William.

A 1915 letter from a John Kilpatrick of Houston, AR, advised that William Kilpatrick had come from North Carolina (sic-apparently from Pendleton District, SC) to Maury County and settled on dry fork of Cathey's Creek. He gave William's children as Samuel White, James M., Thomas, Joshua, Frank, Burton, and Harriet, and advised Samuel had sons John and one living (in 1915) in Christoval, TX. In 1970 descendants of the Texas son, Dr. William Thadeous Kilpatrick, advised William's children were Samuel Watson, James M., Thos., Frank, A. B., Joshua, and Harriett. Research shows William also had older children – Peggy and Benjamin Miller, plus Lucinda who married 1834 Anderson Pogue.

In 1850 Giles County, TN, Samuel W. Kilpatrick, physician, had five children, including William T. (11), and John G. (1). Dr. Samuel W. died before 1860 when his widow Martha was living in Perry County with children, Rufus R. (13), John G. (11), and Franklin M. Note the older William Kilpatrick's daughter, Harriet (19), was living with Dr. Samuel W.'s family in 1850. In 1850, William's sons, Benjamin M. and James M., were in Madison County, TN. It appears understandable that Samuel W.'s sons, John and William T., would not be aware of all of William's children.

KILPATRICK – COOPER, William Allen Kilpatrick, a farmer born Oct. 8, 1843, died Nov. 2, 1874. He was the son of Enos Simpson (1806-1867) and Martha McCorpen (1809-1874). William is buried at Dabbs Cemetery, Rock House Creek, Perry County, TN.

William Allen Kilpatrick and Mary Melvina Cooper Kilpatrick.

He was a Civil War veteran, Confederate soldier, a private in C Company, 2nd Cavalry BN. Married Mary Melvinia Cooper Jan. 8, 1863. She was born Jan. 13, 1846. William died at age 31, leaving five children.

Mary Ellen Lewis was born Nov. 25, 1863. Married Derring John Lewis. Two children – Veca Melvinia and Derring John Lewis Jr.

William (Bill), born Feb. 12, 1868, died June 15, 1952. Married Joshie Elizabeth Halbrook. Five children: William Harrison (Hart), Melvinia, Julie Mae, Robert Marshall (Bob) and Allen Brice (see biography on Kilpatrick-Halbrook).

James Samuel was born Aug. 25, 1869, died March 22, 1870.

John was born Dec. 31, 1870, died March 13, 1971. Married Lillie Mae Catron. Eight children: Clarence Thomas, Mary Atlas, William Allen (Will), Isaac (Ike), Claude, G. M. (Garner), Edward (Ned), and Andrew (Andy).

Eliza Alice Lamar was born Dec. 25, 1872, died March 29, 1953. Married James Thomas Lamar. Nine children: Clara Elizabeth Irving, Mary Cornelia, Nealie Lamar, Johnnie Whitfield Lamar, James Russell, Flossie Beatrice, twin boys died, and William Thomas.

Amelia Velena (Betty) was born Feb. 16, 1875, died Oct. 29, 1959. Married Matthew McClain – 12 children: William Thomas, Johnnie Melvinia, John Turley, Felix Martin, Capitola Black, Gladis Cathrine, Alice Kennedy, Madolia, Lavonia, Matthew Elizabeth, Martha, and Jessie Reba.

William went away to war leaving five children, age range of two years to 11 years. Amelia Velena was born three months after her father's death. His health grew bad and was dismissed from the army. Started home following the rising and setting of the sun. Traveled by foot at night and in the daytime, he would hide in fence corners from the enemy. Winter was coming and he came to a small farm house. An old man and an old lady lived there and had lost their son in the line of duty. They took William Allen in and nursed him back to health. He stayed all winter there, and by spring he was feeling better. He felt that he should stay and help with the crop and so he did. When the crops were all planted in early summer, he started home again from where he thought was Chambridge, MS, finally reaching Perry County. His health was deteriorating again and continually grew worse and finally dying with consumption.

Mary Melvinia, Bill and Mary Ellen continued to help on the Dr. I. N. Black farm. She also took over the Shoe Cobbler business. After all the children were grown, Mary Melvinia married Judge Thomas Broomfield Whitwell on Nov. 4, 1891. Both are buried at McClain Cemetery in Lewis County in Mt. Joy Community. Mary Melvinia was the daughter of William McAdams Cooper, 1823-1862, and Eliza Tombs. *Submitted by great-granddaughter Joy Kilpatrick Gordon.*

KILPATRICK – GRINDER, Allen Brice Kilpatrick, born Dec. 31, 1911, Sugar Hill Hollow, Perry County, passed away March 18, 1985, buried O. A. Kirk Cemetery. Brice was the youngest of five children born to William (Bill) and Joshie Elizabeth Halbrooks (See Kilpatrick – Halbrooks). As a young boy, Brice, his brothers and father did sharecropping on the Dr. I. N. Black farm. Brice has two brothers and two sisters: William Harrison (Hart), Martha Melvina, Julia Mae, and Robert Marshall (Bob) (See Kilpatrick – Halbrooks). In the 1940s and '50s, Brice farmed, did timber work and county road work. Brice retired from Tennessee Department of Transportation in Perry County.

Emma Jane (Grinder) Kilpatrick and Brice Kilpatrick.

July 19, 1931, Brice married Emma Jane Grinder, born Jan. 20, 1910, passed away Oct. 30, 1982. Emma was a factory employee and housewife. She is also buried at O. A. Kirk Cemetery in Perry County. The daughter of Noah Theodore and Mary Jane Ary Grinder. Noah, born Nov. 11, 1875, died Jan. 12, 1924. Mary Jane, born Jan. 10, 1881, died Nov. 19, 1954. Emma is seventh of 13 children (See Grinder – Ary).

Brice and Emma have four children: (1) Troy Wesson, DuPont foreman, born Feb. 16, 1934, married May 7, 1955 to Shirley June Cotham, born Dec. 19, 1936, residing now in Old Hickory, TN. Two children: Mark Wesson, attorney, born March 23, 1960, married July 9, 1988 to Dawn Hill, one son, Ryan Wesson, born Dec. 18, 1991; and Paula Elaine, recreational therapist, born Nov. 30, 1969, married May 28, 1991 to Rex Miller.

Troy W. was inducted into the U.S. Army in November 1956. Served two years active duty, spending 18 months in Germany. He was assigned to the division, 12th Infantry Battalion.

(2) Loy Elene, homemaker, born Feb. 4, 1936, married 1966, Donnie Harold Qualls, born June 19, 1931. Three daughters: Donna Elaine, educator, born Nov. 7, 1967, married Aug. 12, 1989, Robert John Erisman III, one son Robert John (R. J.) Erisman II, born Feb. 20, 1993. Julia Jane, educator, born Sept. 19, 1969, married Michael Wayne Thomasson. Rhonda Jo, educator, born Oct. 6, 1972.

(3) Roy Douglas, cabinet and chair maker, born Aug. 29, 1938, married Aug. 9, 1958, Judy Wade, born Nov. 5, 1939. Two daughters: Karen Lynn, Registered Nurse, born Oct. 14, 1965. Kelly Ann, Occupational Therapist, born Dec. 3, 1968.

(4) Thelma Joy, bank employee, born Oct. 12, 1942, married Nov. 11, 1961, Billy Joe Gordon, born Dec. 7, 1935. Two daughters: Emily Denise, educator, born April 10, 1965, married Aug. 1, 1986, Michael Scott Blackwell, born Sept. 1, 1963, live on Coon Creek. One daughter, Kristin Eve Blackwell, born Oct. 7, 1988. Dana Jo, educator, born Sept. 12, 1966, married Sept. 5, 1987, Gregory Allen Roberts, born July 10, 1967, live on the Dr. I. N. Black farm. *Submitted by daughters, Loy Qualls and Joy Gordon.*

KILPATRICK – HALBROOK, William Allen (Bill) Kilpatrick, born Feb. 12, 1868, died June 15, 1952. Buried on Rock House Creek, Dabbs Cemetery in Perry County.

William (Bill) and Joshie (Halbrook) Kilpatrick

The son of William Allen, born 1843, died 1874, buried on Rock House Creek at Dabbs Cemetery, Perry County. William's (Bill) mother was Mary Melvinia Cooper, born 1846, died 1938. She is buried at the McClain Cemetery in Lewis County, Mt. Joy Community.

On Aug. 20, 1889, William (Bill) married Joshie Elizabeth Halbrook, buried at Dabb's Cemetery, Perry County, born June 18, 1870, died June 10, 1944. Joshie is the daughter of Ethelbert and Martha Edwards Halbrook (see biography of Halbrook – Edwards). William (Bill) farmed all his life for Dr. I. N. Black on Sugar Hill Farm. His father died at a very early age, leaving several small children. Bill was only six years old and the oldest little boy. He had to help his mother all he could to provide for the smaller ones. Bill's brothers and sisters were Mary Ellen; James Samuel, died as an infant; John; Eliza Alice; Amelia Velena (Betty) (see biography on Kilpatrick – Cooper). Joshie had two sisters and three brothers – George A. (Ann) Halbrook, Gwee Halbrook, Doshie Halbrook Marlin, Robert (Bob) Halbrook, Emily Jane Halbrook Anderson (see Halbrook – Edwards biography).

William (Bill) and Joshie had five children: William Harrison (Hart), born July 17, 1890, died Aug. 14, 1980. Buried on Hurricane Creek. Married Pearl Holt, one daughter Vera McLemore Hickerson; Martha Melvina, born Dec. 27, 1893, died March 18, 1967. Married Frank Hensley. Both are buried in Lewis County, Downey Cemetery. Children are: Marie Sharp, Robert, Ross, Raymond, Willard, and Ruby Webb; Julia Mae, born April 5, 1900, died Oct. 27, 1946. Married Tom Dunn. Both are buried at Bethel Cemetery, Perry County. Children are: Jake, Martha Cotton, Velma Harder, Inez Jackson, Jim, and Joe; Robert Marshall (Bob) Kilpatrick, born Oct. 20, 1902, died January 1985. Married Willie Belle Stinnet. Both are buried in Lewis County at the Bacus Cemetery. Five children: Odell Conner in Missouri, Jewell Conner in Lewis County, Roy Kilpatrick and Bill Kilpatrick in Lewis County, and Clyde Kilpatrick in Missouri; Allen Brice Kilpatrick, born Dec. 31, 1911, died March 18, 1985. Married Emma Jane Grinder. Both are buried at Dr. O. A. Kirk Cemetery. Four children: Troy Wesson, Loy Elene Qualls, Roy Douglas, Thelma Joy Gordon. *Submitted by granddaughter Joy Kilpatrick Gordon.*

KILPATRICK – WADE, Roy Douglas Kilpatrick was born Aug. 29, 1938 in Perry County at Sugar Hill, the son of Brice and Emma Grinder Kilpatrick. Brice Kilpatrick was born Dec. 31, 1911 and Emma Kilpatrick was born Jan. 20, 1910.

Roy and Judy Kilpatrick and daughters Karen Lynn and Kelly Ann.

Roy married Aug. 9, 1958 to Judy Wade, born Nov. 5, 1939 at Brush Creek, daughter of Tom and Lorene Trull Wade. Tom Wade was born May 20, 1912. Lorene Trull Wade was born Feb. 18, 1916. Roy and Judy have two daughters, Karen Lynn Kilpatrick, born Oct. 14, 1965 and Kelly Ann Kilpatrick, born Dec. 3, 1968. Roy owns and operates his own business and a former Circuit Court Clerk of 16 years. Judy Wade Kilpatrick has worked at Perry Memorial Hospital since August 1964. Karen Lynn Kilpatrick is a Registered Nurse and owns and operates her own dance studio. Kelly Ann Kilpatrick works as an Occupational Therapist.

ENOS SIMPSON KILPATRICK,
Enos was born March 4, 1806, in North Carolina. It is thought that Enos was the second son of James Miller Kilpatrick and Elizabeth Watson. James and Elizabeth were married in Rutherford County, NC, on Nov. 10, 1803. The family left Buncombe County, NC, around 1820 and went to Maury County, TN, with James' brother, William, and other close friends of this Kilpatrick family.

The first documented fact regarding Enos in Maury County was his marriage to Martha McCorpen on Feb. 19, 1830. Martha was born in 1809 in Kentucky.

Enos was a blacksmith whose smithy was in the town of Columbia. Between 1835 and 1838 he paid taxes on three lots in Columbia. In 1837 Enos executed a Deed of Trust to Americus Bradshaw and Alexander McKey, both of Maury County in which he pledged the contents of his smithy and much of his personal belongings. This was apparently collateral for a loan or for a previous debt that had gone unpaid.

Enos was listed in the 1840 Maury County census and the 1850 Giles County census. His occupation: blacksmith.

Between 1850 and 1857, Enos moved his family, with the exception of his oldest child, John Franklin Kilpatrick, to Perry County, where they settled on the head waters of Rock House Creek. In the 1860 census he was listed in Perry County. His occupation: farmer.

In 1857, in Perry County, Enos again got himself in a bit of financial trouble. John Watson Kilpatrick (believed to be Enos' older brother) was appointed the executor of the estate of Johnathan Reynolds. Enos owed Johnathan Reynolds $146.43 when Johnathan died. Acting on behalf of the estate, John W. Kilpatrick had to sue Enos for the amount due. A judgment was recovered in court and the county constable was sent to collect the money from Enos. Enos was not to be found. He had moved his family and all their personal belongings out of Perry County. A public sale of his 360 acres was ordered. The high bidder was John W. Kilpatrick ($172.05). Enos was given two years to redeem his land and two years to the day, Enos came forward and paid his debt plus six percent interest to John W. Kilpatrick.

Enos died in Perry County on June 11, 1867, leaving an estate consisting of personal property and about 360 acres of land. The division of the estate was handled by his son, John F. Kilpatrick.

Enos' wife Martha, died in Perry County on Jan. 14, 1874.

Children of Enos and Martha Kilpatrick: John Franklin, 1831-1907, married (1) Teressa Inman, (2) Mary Morrow, (3) Malvina Durham; James A., born 1832; Elizabeth Jane, 1834-1869; Mary Ann, born 1836, married Daniel Barber; Martha Francis, 1838-1882, married Samual Toombs; Cyntha A., 1840-1921, married James Hollabaugh; William A., 1843-1874, married Mary Cooper; Somina C., born 1845, married William Keeling; Susan L., 1847-1870; Nancy L. Eliza, born 1850. *Submitted by Marvin E. Kilpatrick, great-great-grandson of Enos S. Kilpatrick.*

JIM KILPATRICK,
Willodean and Jim live on the farm in DePriest Bend that her great-great-grandfather, Randell Depriest, lived on. Randell was born in North Carolina in 1789. He received a grant in 1810 for some land on the head of Cane Creek. He started a house and for some reason he had to go back to North Carolina. When he returned, someone had finished the house and was living in it. He later moved to a farm in DePriest Bend, and became one of the first settlers of that section of Perry County. Randell willed some of his children land except a son named John, who he willed his slaves and when they freed that left him without anything.

William Harrison DePriest, Emaline (Harder) Depriest, and their granddaughter, Montie Depriest.

William Harrison DePriest, Randell's son and Willodean's great-great-grandfather, was born on May 29, 1831. On April 5, 1849, he married Emaline Harder. They had five sons: Fayette, Joe, Gus, Legrand, and Willodean's great-grandfather Lonnie DePriest.

William Harrison DePriest died on the farm in DePriest Bend on March 1, 1917. William Harrison had always lived with a few hundred yards of his father's Randel DePriest's old homeplace. William Harrison DePriest served in the Confederate army during the War Between the States and was severely wounded at Thompson's Station, Williamson County. His obituary describes him as a man who lived a sober, upright and industrious life and accumulated a large amount of real estate. On April 4, 1917, only one month and four days after William Harrison died, his wife Emaline died at her home in DePriest Bend. Her obituary says her death was due to pneumonia and the great shock of the death of her husband.

Lonnie DePriest, Willodean's great-grandfather, and William Harrison's son and Randell DePriest's grandson, also lived on the old homeplace in DePriest Bend. He married Geraldine Dickerson. Their children were Joe, Randolph, May, Ada, Montie, Lottie, Nettie, Vivan, Dewey and Willodean's grandfather Ernie DePriest.

Lonnie DePriest died at the age of 75 on Nov. 17, 1936. He fell from the barn loft and injured his side. He was thought to be recovering but developed pneumonia causing his death. His wife, Geraldine, had died on May 3, 1930.

Willodean's grandfather, Ernie DePriest, married Cora Walker in 1921. They had one daughter, Clora Lee. Clora Lee married William Asbury. They had two daughters, Willodean and Wanda Jean. Willodean married Jimmy Kilpatrick and they have two sons, Kevin Stewart and Jamie Lynn Kilpatrick. Kevin married Lisa Creasy in 1989. Jamie married Andrea Jackson in 1992. Kevin and Lisa have two daughters, Courtney Dawn and Alexander Paige Kilpatrick. They also live on the old homeplace making their children Courtney and Paige the eighth generation to live there. The rock wall that is in front and back of the house came from the chimneys of the old original house.

JOHN CHEATHAM KIMBLE,
born Aug. 11, 1881, died May 22, 1953, married Mary Ann Talley, born July 12, 1886, died Nov. 17, 1954, on April 13, 1901, in Linden, TN. They had three daughters and four sons.

Bertie Lee, born 1903, died 1978, married Charles D. Ary, born 1902, died 1971 of Flatwoods, TN. Mary Ethel, who married Bynum Cotham of Linden, TN, was an elementary and high school teacher and also Supervisor of Instruction for the Perry County School System. Ollie Franklin, born 1906, died 1966, married Annie Akers, born 1906 of Hohenwald, TN. They had one son, Bobby Franklin, born June 22, 1940, died Aug. 19, 1990. Osby, born May 18, 1910, died May 15, 1965, married Izle Moore, born Sept. 11, 1915, died Jan. 11, 1990. Johnnie Pearl, born Feb. 9, 1913, died Jan. 11, 1992, was unmarried. She was an elementary and high school teacher and also Supervisor of Instruction for the Perry County School System. Jesse Daniel married Mary Jane Bates. Their children are Joan and Jimmy. Paul Mayhugh, died 199?, married Normay Brookins. Their children are Letty, Mark, Matt, Penny, Jennifer, and John.

O. A. KIMBLE,
whose parents were John C. Kimble and Mary Ann Talley and Ella Izle Moore whose parents were Albert Arnold Moore and Julia Edna Moore were married in Linden, TN, Sept. 11, 1935. They were both life-long residents of Perry County. Mrs. Kimble died Jan. 11, 1990 having been a widow for many years. Although she received very little education herself, she always encouraged and expected her children to do well in school. She was a gifted seamstress and enjoyed embroidery and quilt making. During the last few years of her life, she enjoyed attending the annual American Quilt Society Show in Paducah, KY, with her daughters.

All the children in the family are graduates of PCHS. Alice Ruth, an elementary school teacher in Pinellas County, FL, and a graduate of Austin Peay State University, Clarksville, TN, married Richard James Eshelman, son of Foster and Mina Eshelman of Rochester, NY. They have three children: Richard Jay, Donna Lee and Tiny Allyson and live in Clearwater, FL. Mary Nell, an elementary school teacher, married Rick Smith. They have one son, Timothy A., and live in Linden, TN. John Allen is a retired employee of *The Perry Countian* which in years past was the local weekly newspaper. He is a member of the First Christian Church, Linden, TN, and a resident of Linden, TN. Patsy Lee, an elementary school teacher, married Baxter V. (Jack) Haston, died June 13, 1987. He grew up in Beardstown, TN, and was the son of Thelma and Jack Haston. He was an elementary school teacher and principal in Todd County, KY. Both he and Patsy were graduated from APSU. Their children are Gregory Lee and Jennifer Elaine, and the family lives in Trenton, KY. Frank O'Neil died Dec. 30, 1978, married the former Marla Wildman of Linden, TN, who had three sons. Their son is Shawn O'Neil Kimble of Kuttawa, KY. Julia (Judy) Margaret, a graduate of APSU and an employee of JC Penney, married James Richard Ussery, son of Sterling Harris Ussery and Missouri Agnes Hudgins. Richard served in the U.S. Navy during the Vietnam Era from 1967-72 aboard the aircraft carrier *USS John F. Kennedy*. Judy and Richard live in Hopkinsville, KY, and have one son, Michael Alan. William Moore, an employee of the U.S. Postal Service and also the Dana Corporation, married the former Robbie Miller. They live in Linden, TN. David Samuel, an employee of Bates Fabricating of Lobelville, TN, married the former Laquita Bradley. She has one son, Joe Ben Bolin. Their children are Kathleen and David, and the family lives in Linden, TN.

WILLIAM MOORE KIMBLE, and Robbie (Miller) Kimble were married July 5, 1979. William is mentioned elsewhere in this book. Robbie was born on Eagle Creek in Wayne County, the daughter of Homer Miller and Agnes (Shaw) Miller. Homer's father was Jess Miller and his mother was Alice (Walker) Miller. Agnes (Shaw) Miller's father was Cicero Shaw and her mother was Lula (Alley) Shaw. Lula's parents were Fred and Ann Pamela Alley. All these ancestors were born, lived and buried on Eagle Creek, with the older ones being some of the original settlers of this area, living on lands from original government grants.

Robbie has three children from previous marriages: a daughter Kathy Ann (Barber) Ayers, two sons Donald Wayne and Billy Gene Sharp. Robbie had one brother, Brodie Miller, who married Nell (Barber) Miller; they have three children Dale Miller, Linda (Miller) Tinin, Brenda (Miller) Strickland. Brodie, died December 1992 and Nell died January 1994.

Robbie has two sisters: Ann (Miller) Dunn is married to Joe Dunn. She has three children from a previous marriage, Johnny Whitt, Jimmy Whitt, and Jackie Ann (Whitt) Qualls. Joe and Ann have one daughter Tammy Jo Dunn. Judy (Miller) Bell has two sons: Paul Edward Bell, Terry Lynn Bell, and one daughter, Adrian Michelle Bell.

KIMBLE/KIMBEL, William born in Scotland came to this country in 1774 and settled in Alabama, where he followed his trade as a brick mason.

His son Franklin H. Kimbel was born in Alabama in 1799. He prepared for the profession of medicine there and came to Tennessee as a young man, locating first in Wayne County and then moving to Perry County where he continued his medical career until his death in 1864. He was a member of the state legislature in 1851-52 and again in 1855-56. He was clerk of the circuit court in Perry County during the 1840s and in 1860 was county court clerk. He was a Democrat.

In 1840 in Perry County, Franklin married Eliza King who was born in Cheatham County, TN, in 1813. Eliza died in 1883 in Perry County. They had six children: Robert Alexander, Benjamin F., Elizabeth (died in infancy), James Wiley and Jon Nathaniel who were twins, and Sims Allen.

On June 21, 1873, James Wiley, born 1848, died May 4, 1908, married Sarah E. Evans whose parents were Davy Evans and Sally Tucker. James and Sarah's children were: Wiley, Ben, David, Jane, Sims, and John C. Kimble who married Mary Ann Talley. Mary Ann Talley's parents were Carroll Coleman Talley, born 1831, died March 12, 1912 and Mary Jane LaRue/Lerrue, born April 15, 1852 or 53(?), died March 13, 1925, who were married Sept. 21, 1876. Mary Jane LaRue's parents were Mary Pauline Breechan/Breecheen and James LaRue. Carroll C. Talley's parents were Allen Talley and Nancy Tucker.

KING FAMILY, William Clyde (Bill) and Essie Frances Broadway King live in the Bend of the River Community (also called Culp's Chapel) in Perry County, TN. Bill was born in Decatur County, July 21, 1923, to John and Molly Smith King. He has four sisters: Gladys Sims, Allie Mae Sims, Edna Hendon and Ruby King. He had two brothers, James and Curry King, both deceased. As a young man Bill and his friends often crossed the Tennessee River to Perry County in a flat-bottomed boat. On one of these trips to Perry County, Bill and Essie Broadway began dating and later were married in Corinth, MS, on Dec. 24, 1947. They lived a short time in Decatur County and Hughes, AR, but moved back to Perry County in 1950.

William Clyde (Bill) King in 1951.

Essie and Bill have three daughters: Billie Frances (Davis), born Nov. 18, 1948; Barbara Jean (Williams), born Aug. 16, 1950; and Peggy Helen (Smotherman, born Jan. 20, 1953. They also have three granddaughters. Billie married William Clyde Davis Jr. (deceased) of Wayne County and their daughter, Gina Michelle Davis, was born Dec. 8, 1966. Peggy married Jerry Lynn (Pete) Smotherman (deceased) of Wayne County. Their daughter, Tara Lynnette Smotherman, was born June 7, 1971. Barbara married Charles Williams of Stewart County and their daughter, Lisa Ann Williams, was born Jan. 8, 1974. Finally, a boy was born in the family – Gina Davis married Jerry Lancaster of Decatur County and their son, William Collin Lancaster, was born on March 7, 1989.

Essie, a native Perry Countian, grew up on the same farm where they now live. She was born Dec. 5, 1926 to Grady Randle Broadway and Eula Smith Broadway. Essie has one sister Virginia Lee (Richardson) and they were the only grandchildren of Willie J. and Alla J. Thompson Broadway. Grady Broadway was born Sept. 16, 1904, on Cedar Creek. Grady's paternal grandparents were Alex and Sarah Lomax Broadway. His maternal grandparents were Amos and Jane Roberts Thompson. Eula Smith Broadway was born Oct. 26, 1907, to Ruben J. and Addie DePriest Smith of Marsh Creek. Eula's maternal grandparents were Henry Houston and Dora Elizabeth Beasley DePriest. Her paternal grandparents were Luther (Bud) and Betty Hughes Smith.

As a young couple Grady and Eula moved to the Bend of the River. Grady was a farmer and bought the John Denton farm. He and Eula ran a general store that was the "social center" of the Bend. Folks came there to get groceries, learn news, or play dominoes. The store once served as post office and elections were held there for years. Although Grady's father was a Republican, Grady became a Democrat. Bill was also a Democrat and all of Essie and Bill's children and grandchildren followed the family tradition and are Democrats. Grady and Eula were members of Mt. Auburn Methodist Church where Grady served as song leader. Their children, grandchildren and great-grandchildren are also Methodists.

The Kings enjoy gardening and country life in general. Bill instilled the love of sports in his children. They taught their children to love God, their family, their neighbors, and this land. They are proud they lived in Perry County.

ALEXANDER KING, born 1815, died before 1900, most likely Perry County. It is possible he is buried in the Cude Cemetery, Beardstown. His mother was Rebecca, who had married second a Dodson and Alexander had half-Dodson siblings. I believe Rebecca King Dodson is buried in the Cude Cemetery. Alex married early 1840s, probably Hickman County, to Rebecca T. Sharp, daughter of William and Elinor Sharp. It is thought that Elinor was daughter of Elijah Mayfield. Rebecca Sharp was born February 1826 in what is now present day Lewis County in the area of Newburg. She died after 1900 and I assume buried in the Cude Cemetery. They had three children survive infancy: 1) Indiana King, born Dec. 15, 1845, Lewis County, died Dec. 6, 1915, Lobelville, buried Leeper Cemetery. She was the third wife of Andrew C. Cude. 2) Abner W. King, born 1848, married, Perry County, April 10, 1869, Millie A. Meacham. 3) Joshua B. King, known as "Pony," born Sept. 3, 1852, died Aug. 21, 1915, Perry County, buried Cude Cemetery. He married March 12, 1871, Perry County, Martha Jane Baars.

Abner King's wife, Millie Meacham, born 1852. By 1880, they had four children: 1) Elizabeth King, born 1870. 2) Rebecca King, born 1871. 3) William A. King, born 1873. 4) James King, born 1878. Apparently this family moved from Perry County. Pony King's wife, Jane Baars, born Nov. 20, 1848, died July 26, 1936, buried Cude Cemetery. She was daughter of

George and Lena Baars. Their children: 1) George King, born Nov. 5, 1874, died March 9, 1956, buried Cude Cemetery. He married Feb. 17, 1895, Perry County, Sarah L. Gilmer, who was born Oct. 8, 1872, died April 8, 1952. They had Amon, Herman, Eddie, Annie, Gertrude, and Alexander. 2) Indiana King, born July 1876, died 1943, buried Ledbetter Cemetery, wife of Robert T. Ledbetter. He was born Aug. 30, 1874, died July 21, 1935, and had married first Docie Frances Young. Children of Robert and "Dena," were Sam, Myrtle, Norma and Patry Lee. 3) Harriett King, born 1877. 4) Rebecca King, born August 1880, died 1957, buried Cude Cemetery. She married Aug. 9, 1901, Perry County, John Caswell Lomax as his second wife. They had several children, but believe all died in infancy. 5) William B. King, born Sept. 18, 1881, Perry County, died Nov. 21, 1960, Westside DePriest Cemetery. He married Aug. 17, 1902, Perry County, Roffie Lorene DePriest. Children are Amber and Albert Leo. 6) W. Abner King, born Dec. 12, 1884 near Beardstown, died March 18, 1969, buried Cude Cemetery. He married April 15, 1911, Perry County, M. Addie Harris. Addie was born June 12, 1889, died Sept. 4, 1965. Their children: Claude, Mattie Pearl, Beryl A., and Mildred Louise. 7) Norma King, born Aug. 8, 1885, died Sept. 2, 1893, buried Cude Cemetery. 8) Mattie King, born July 5, 1889, per marker, closer to 1886 per census, died May 2, 1970, buried Cude Cemetery. Her marriage, Perry County, Sept. 28, 1914, J. Hugh Warren. He was born June 14, 1887, died Nov. 6, 1966, son of Fate Warren and Amanda Brown. One daughter, Louise Warren, born 1917.

BYRON CLYDE KING, and Mary Lee Bromley were married Dec. 5, 1909, in Flatwoods, TN. Clyde was the son of Joseph Allison and Izora Braxton Kittrell King. Mary was the daughter of James Akin and Eliza Elmira Goodman Bromley. They were educated at the school of Flatwoods. Clyde later went to a business school in Nashville where he studied bookkeeping.

Byron Clyde King and wife Mary Lee Bromley King.

They lived around Flatwoods for several years where he farmed for a living. Their first children were born while they lived there: Byron, Jan. 19, 1911, and James Allison, Feb. 26, 1916.

They moved to Coon Creek around 1924 where he farmed for his step father-in-law, Alvin Ross Warren. Here twin daughters were born May 26, 1924. They named them Lois and Louise and they lived a very short time. Another daughter, Mary Jo, was born Oct. 28, 1926.

In 1929, Clyde got a job as bookkeeper for Kittrell Chevrolet at Centerville, TN. The family moved there, Byron finished high school there in 1930, and James in 1934. Mary Jo finished grade school there in 1941.

Clyde left Kittrell's in 1936 and established King Motor Company, where he sold Plymouth and DeSoto cars for four years. After selling the dealership they moved back to Perry County, where he ran a saw mill. They built a home on Brush Creek, Hwy. 100. Mary Jo entered high school and graduated in 1945.

All the family were members of the Church of Christ, and Clyde helped to build the church building in Linden by sawing the lumber supplied by Andrew Vaughn. Many members helped.

Mary died Aug. 16, 1965, age 75, and Clyde followed her on Feb. 4, 1967, age 82. They are buried in the Warren Cemetery on Coon Creek.

Their daughter Byron now lives in the homeplace after retiring from teaching in Hickman County schools for many years. Her adopted daughter, Marie, with her husband Thomas Erwin and son Jeffery Carroll, also live on the place.

James was a veteran of World War II, received a Purple Heart for wounds received in battle in France. He was in the 6th Armored Battallion. He married Betty Lee Beasley, March 19, 1947 in Corinth, MS. James was a rural mail carrier in Perry County for 24 years. They have four daughters: Allyson, Carolyn, Janice and Joanne. James died Dec. 14, 1983, and is buried in Kirk Cemetery at Linden.

Mary Jo married Tom Beasley. They have two children, Barbara and Jeffery.

JOSEPH ALLISON KING and Izora Braxton Kittrell were married in Lewis County on Feb. 20, 1881. Joseph was born Feb. 16, 1863, in Freestone County, TX, the son of Hugh Bryson Venable and Margaret Ann Choat or Clements King, the granddaughter of Arthur Choat of Wayne County. After the parents both died in 1857, Joseph, a brother and a sister were brought to Wayne County to their Aunt Violet and her husband Andrew Williams. They grew up on Green River and went to school there. Joseph was known as a great fiddle player.

Joseph Allison King and Izora Braxton Kittrell King.

Izora was born March 16, 1862, in Maury or Perry County, the daughter of Benjamin C. and Martha Jane Dowdy Kittrell. Benjamin's family lived in Sumner County and Maury County, then moved to Farmer's Valley, Perry County before 1860. Martha Jane's family was from Coon Creek.

Joseph and Izora lived on Rock House Creek for several years, then moved near Flatwoods, where he farmed. They were members of the Church of Christ.

Their children were: Hugh Blanche, died young; Joseph Braxton (Brack), married Mollie Phillips; Byron Clyde, married Mary Bromley; Benjamin Davis, married Birdie Bromley; Martha Ann and Verna Mae both died young; Mortie Kittrell, married Brown Armstrong; John Hunter King.

John Hunter attended school in Flatwoods, and on to Freed Hardeman College, where he graduated in 1919. He joined the U.S. Navy and served one tour, was on the *USS Tennessee* when it was commissioned. After he came out of the Navy, he accepted a job at the new Woolworth store in Nashville. Very shortly after, he died in 1924 at the age of 23.

Joseph died Sept. 4, 1907, and was buried in the Kittrell Cemetery at Farmer's Valley. After his death, Izora moved into Flatwoods. She kept boarders, many of them students at the school nearby. At one time she was a school teacher, ran a store, and later the switchboard operator at Flatwoods.

Her daughter, Mortie, and family lived in the house with her. Brown later bought the house, which is known as the Armstrong house. Brown and Mortie had four children: Joe, Sylvia, Lorraine, and Robert (Bob). Bob now owns the place, built a new home and lives there with his wife, the former Allene Warner of Lobelville.

Izora died Dec. 21, 1941, at Flatwoods, two weeks after the Japanese attack on Pearl harbor, her life spanning some historic times. Her father was at the Battle of Shiloh, a few weeks before she was born. She was over two years old before he saw her. She had been named Julia by her mother, but he changed her name to Izora Braxton; Braxton was for Gen. Braxton Bragg. She was buried beside her husband in the Kittrell Cemetery at Farmer's Valley.

ROBERT THOMAS KING, came from his native Hardin County down the Tennessee River to Perry County in 1892, where he married Mary Dixie Isabelle Tucker, Dec. 18, 1892. He was one of four orphans left by Thomas Rex King (1836-1876) and Sarah Elizabeth McLaren King (1839-1875).

R. T. and Dixie (Tucker) King.

Thomas Rex King, a Confederate officer, was in the Battle of Shiloh and numerous other major Civil War encounters in Tennessee and Georgia, suffering from wounds and disease during his over four years of service. Sarah Elizabeth McLaren was great-granddaughter of Capt. (later Major) Daniel McLaren, a cavalryman in the South Carolina militia during the Revolution. His wife was Mary Stephenson.

R. T. was the grandson of Edmund King (1790-1852) and Nancy Emerson King (ca. 1800-ca. 1836) and the great-grandson of John King (1758-1842) a Revolutionary War soldier, who survived the bitter winter at Valley Forge as a private soldier in The Commander-In-Chief's Guard, a body of mostly Virginia troops assigned to attend Gen. George Washington's person and property. John King, native of Louisa County, VA, migrated to South Carolina at war's end. There he married Sarah LeMaster (1774-1845), originally from Amherst County, VA. (Walter King, one of John's many siblings, moved to East Tennessee where he married Nancy Sevier, youngest daughter of Gen/Gov. John Sevier and his first wife, Sarah Hawkins. Austin Augustus King, a son of Walter and Nancy S. King, was the governor of Missouri around 1850. At least three of John King's brothers were soldiers in the Revolution.)

Mary Dixie Tucker King (1870-1950) was the daughter of Dickson Tucker (1835-1912) and his second wife, Mary Elizabeth Edwards (1840-1920), daughter of Andrew Jackson Edwards (1819-1908) and his first wife, Ann Sanders (ca. 1823-ca. 1879). Dixie's great-grandfather was John P. Tucker (1752-ca. 1845), a Revolutionary soldier from Halifax County, VA, who fought in the Battle of Yorktown. Another of her great-grandfathers, Andrew Edwards, served in the Revolution from Virginia.

R. T. King had two sisters and one brother: Nancy (1862-), never married; George Randolph (1867-1945) married Sarah Theresa Shull; and Cynthia May (1870-1957) married Benjamin F. Copeland (1870-1945). The George King family migrated to Arkansas, while the Copelands moved farther west of Oklahoma.

R. T. and Dixie King had nine children: (1) Lena (Leona) Elizabeth (born and died 1893); (2) James Atlas (1894-1966), married Madalene McFall (1889-1958), no issue; (3) Clara Lee (1886-1980) married Webb Alfred Godwin (1892-1965); (4) Eulah Belle (1899-1979) married Carl Leslie Westbrook (1899-1975); (5) Thomas Rex (1901-1905); (6) Tommie Elizabeth (1903-1950) married Dorris E. Moore (1889-1971), no issue; (7) Robert Elmer (1906-1985) married first Elsie Ferguson (born 1908), divorced, no issue, and second Stella Mae Roberts (born 1916); (8) William Emery (1908-1987) married Willie Louise Betes (born 1911); and (9) Mary Eve (1910-1979) married Joseph Leonard Jackson (1904-1972), no issue.

R. T. and Dixie King's grandchildren are: Mary Dixie Godwin (born 1925) married first Orvie W. Dabbs, divorced, and second Philip J. Weeks; Webb A. Godwin Jr. (born 1929) married Bess Vandergriff; Sarah Dene Westbrook (born 1920) married John George Lyon Jr. (1918-1971), divorced; Robbye Lee Westbrook (born 1922) married first Charles H. Jones Jr. (born ?), divorced, and second James Arnold Welch (1929-1993), divorced; Jack King Westbrook, (born 1923) married Willie Mae Matthews (born 1923); Marcia Ann King (born 1955), married Willie Ronnie Holder (born 1945); and Patricia Ann King (born 1942) married Fred J. Michon (born 1936).

Great-grandchildren of R. T. and Dixie King are: Barbara Joyce Dabbs, married Edward D. Morgan Jr., and Tamara Lynn Weeks; Janet W. Lyon, married first James N. Clemeau (1940-1984) and second J. L. Driver, Sarah Ann Lyon, John G. Lyon III, married Judith Wortham, and Jean Elizabeth Lyon, married William Dale Markie; Haven Lee Westbrook, married Michael Len Jenkins, and Matthew King Westbrook, married Patricia Harju, divorced; and Stephanie Rene' Michon. *Submitted by Robbye Lee Westbrook, granddaughter.*

JOE KINGTON FAMILY, The Kingstons, with their son, Joe IV, moved to Red Bank Creek from the Nashville area in 1987. They are glad to be out of the city.

Joe Kington Family: Logan (front), Sharon, Joe III, and Joe IV.

Joe IV was named after his great-grandfather. This first Joe Kington moved west as a child in a covered wagon. As an adult, he moved to Huntington, WV, and operated a coal mine there. His son, Joe Jr., married Helen Jenkins. During WWII, Joe and Helen worked at Los Alamos, and later Oak Ridge, where Joe III was born. The Kington ancestors are Welsh.

The Roberson family is of Scottish descent; the name was originally spelled Robertson. The Robersons have lived in Bledsoe County, TN, since receiving a Revolutionary War land grant there. Sharon is fifth of the eight children of Peter C. and Nova Bickford Roberson. The Bickfords operated a grist mill at Cane Creek Falls in Bledsoe County before the land became part of Falls Creek Falls State Park. Sharon grew up on the family dairy farm near Pikeville that was the childhood home of her father's brother, Sam Roberson of Perry County.

Logan Roe was added to the family in 1990. He was named for his great-uncle, Roe Roberson, who, in turn, was named for his great-uncle, Hezekiah Monroe Roberson, a Confederate cavalryman. He was also named for the family's former neighbor and substitute grandfather, Logan Scruggs. Mr. Scruggs was the fifth son born in a two-story log cabin on Pin Hook Road, near the present Starwood amphitheater, around 1906. Logan was the last name of the Scruggs' family doctor. Mr. Scruggs was named in his honor.

Before moving to Perry County, Joe Kington worked in telecommunications, and then enjoyed 10 years in architectural woodwork production.

The Kington family likes gardening, camping, reading, hunting and fishing.

EULA VICTORIA KIRK, born 1904, attended Freed-Hardeman College and Austin Peay University. She taught school and worked with the Perry County school system until retiring.

She married Clint Greer and they had one daughter, Marion Ruth Greer. She later married Austin Dabbs. Marion Ruth Greer married Clyde Turnbow. They have three children: Janet Rose Turnbow, married Ralph Copeland, two children – Shelly Copeland and Shane Copeland, one grandson, Justin Copeland; James Robert Turnbow, married Rosemary Godwin, one child – Holly Beth Turnbow; and Thomas Glenn Turnbow.

EVELYN RUTH KIRK, (1920-1973), daughter Nesby Kirk. Attended public school in Perry County and then attended U.T. at Martin, TN. Taught school in Perry County before working for the FBI in Washington. She married Ed Townsend and moved to Henry County during the 1940s. They had five children: Kirk Townsend and Cynthia are deceased; Janice Townsend lived in LA, married to Thomas Fowler; Judy Townsend married David Varner, lives in Kentucky, teaches in Henry County, two children – Cindy and Amy Varner; Tom Eddie Townsend is an optometrist and practices in Henry County, married Melanie Bivens.

HARRY THOMAS (SONNY) KIRK, was born in 1924 and reared in Flatwoods. Educated in Perry County schools, he later attended David Lipscomb College and Freed-Hardeman College before volunteering in the U.S. Navy. He served three years as Pharmacist Mate during WWII. Returning to Tennessee, he joined the staff of McDonald Funeral Home in Hohenwald. Moving to Linden Aug. 21, 1952, where he managed the funeral home until his death Aug. 21, 1985. His wife, Dot, continued working there following his death.

Harry Thomas (Sonny) Kirk

He was married to Dorothy Jean Baker (1926), daughter of John Levi Baker and Lena Adelle Downey of Hohenwald. Three children were born to this family.

Michael Thomas Kirk (1946), married to Miriam Jane Duncan (1947), is lieutenant colonel in the U.S. Air Force. They have two children – Michael Thomas Kirk Jr. (1971) and Amanda Jane Kirk (1975).

Dr. Anthony Wayne (Tony) Kirk (1950), married to Deborah Lee Matthews (1950), is chairman of the Physical Education Department at Freed-Hardeman University. Matthew Thomas Kirk (1978) and Andrea Lee Kirk (1982) are their children.

Karen Jean Kirk (1954), married to Danny

Lee Dauksch (1953), is bookkeeper for the Pinckneyville Medical Center in Pinckneyville, IL. Their children are Audree Leigh Dauksch (1975) and Kirk Berton Dauksch (1978).

All are active members of the Church of Christ.

NESBY THOMAS KIRK, (1889-1977), son of William Akin Kirk, taught school in Perry County a number of years in the early 1900s. Served in the U.S. Army during the first World War. Served as a rural mail carrier from 1920-1955. He married Nanny Lou Beasley (1900-1968), daughter of William Berry Beasley and Nancy Shelton.

They had three children: 1) Evelyn Ruth Kirk, 1920-1973, married Ed Townsend. 2) Harry Thomas Kirk, 1924-1985, married Dorothy Baker. 3) William Hoyt Kirk, 1928, married Bettye Doyle.

William Hoyt Kirk was reared in Perry County, Flatwoods Community. He attended public school in Perry County and later attended David Lipscomb College and Peabody College. He served almost four years in the U.S. Navy during the Korean War.

Started his teaching and coaching career in 1958. He taught and coached at Freed-Hardeman University from 1963-1994.

He had preached for the Church of Christ in Perry County at Brush Creek and Linden since 1969. He married Bettye Lou Doyle, daughter of Pleas Ethan Doyle and Martha Irene Lomax. They have one daughter, Patricia Ann Kirk, married Anthony Haston. Patricia (Patti) has one son, Kirk Anthony Haston. She has taught in Perry County since 1974. She is the fourth generation of teachers. She is a Level III teacher in the state of Tennessee.

OBE ATHA KIRK, son of William Akin (Bill) Kirk and Victoria W. Kirk, was born Feb. 22, 1885, on the Ledbetter farm in Perry County, TN. He attended public schools in both Linden and Flatwoods and graduated about 1905. He taught school on Hurricane Creek in 1905 and taught on Sinking Creek in 1906. In 1908 he borrowed some money and went to Nashville to enter school. He and William Earl Boyce of Flatwoods entered the University of Nashville Medical School and Miss Mary Boyce, sister to William Earl, went with them to keep house for the boys while they studied medicine. She was a severe taskmaster and made both of them study hard enough to finish medical school. The University of Nashville Medical School was taken over by the University of Tennessee and both Kirk and Boyce graduated from the University of Tennessee Medical School and were granted a Doctor of Medicine Degree on May 7, 1912.

He married Lockie Rankin Graves, daughter of Tom Graves and Mary E. Cotton Graves, on Sept. 1, 1912. Dr. Kirk started practicing medicine on Cedar Creek about 1910, as a medical student, and practiced there until moving to Flatwoods in early 1913. He bought a horse and buggy, but rode the horse most of the time. There were few roads even for a buggy in Perry County.

Thomas Atha Kirk was born Feb. 11, 1915, in Flatwoods, and William Clark Kirk was born Oct. 29, 1917. In December 1921 the family made a moved to Linden. It took all day for the move with three wagons and mule teams to move the furniture. By this time Dr. Kirk had bought a Model A Ford but continued to ride a horse until 1926 or 27. Shortly after moving to Linden, Dr. Kirk was appointed County Health Officer and served in that capacity until his death in 1955.

Dr. Obe Atha Kirk and wife Lochie Graves Kirk with children, Thomas Atha (left) and William Clark Kirk.

During the Depression in the early 1930s, money was very scarce in Perry County. Dr. Kirk took hay, corn, vegetables, hams or even wild game as payment for medical bills. He never refused medical treatment for anyone, regardless of what they could or would pay. He had a very hearty appetite and enjoyed good homecooked food. He probably ate at least one meal or more with most every family in Perry County.

Lockie Graves Kirk was diagnosed with cancer of the breast in 1931 and died of cancer on March 23, 1934. She is buried in the Flatwoods Cemetery.

Dr. Kirk then married Nancy Estalee Hankins Trull in August 1935. Estalee died May 8, 1992, and is buried beside Dr. Kirk in the Kirk Cemetery in Linden, TN.

When World War II broke out in Europe and Selective Service became law, Dr. Kirk was appointed Medical Advisor for Local Board No. 72. He served in this capacity through World War II and until his death in 1955. Doing physicals on everybody that went through Board No. 72, as a volunteer, he was awarded the Citizens Medal for Patriotism by President Truman in 1948. Also a citation by Gov. Prentice Cooper of Tennessee and another award by President Eisenhower in 1955 after his death.

After a very memorable "Dr. Kirk" Day on May 30, 1953, he died suddenly on March 30, 1955, and was the first person buried in the Dr. O. A. Kirk Memorial Cemetery in Linden, TN.

THOMAS ATHA KIRK, (1915-1974), son of Dr. O. A. Kirk and Lockie Graves Kirk, born Feb. 11, 1915, in Flatwoods, TN.

Education: Graduated Linden High School in 1931; Bachelor of Arts, Vanderbilt University in 1936, ATO Fraternity. Masters Degree from George Peabody College in 1950.

Military Service: January 1943 to September 1945, Weather Observer in U.S. Army Air Force.

Married: Frances Quinn, daughter of Judge Pat Quinn and Marie Baker Quinn on May 10, 1945.

Children: 1) William Quinn Kirk, born March 30, 1946. Education: West End High School, 1964; B.S., University of Tennessee, Knoxville, 1972; MBA, University of Tennessee, Knoxville, 1984; Military Service: U.S. Army Aviation 1966-1970, helicopter pilot; Married: Karen Lee King, June 22, 1991; Children: Savannah Lee Kirk, Nov. 24, 1991 and Katherine Camille Kirk, May 3, 1994. 2) Marie Kirk, born Dec. 17, 1949. Education: West End High School, 1967; Dennison University, 1971; Masters S.E., Peabody College, 1972; J.D., University of Washington, 1981. Practice of Law and Fieldenkries Therapy, Freeland, WA.

Thomas Atha Kirk died May 28, 1974, and is buried in the Pat Quinn plot of Grandview Cemetery, Maryville, TN.

WILLIAM AKIN KIRK, was born Feb. 18, 1859, in Perry County. He was the son of James Akin Kirk and Lucinda Tennessee Grimmett. Lucinda Grimmett was the granddaughter of Dozier/Josiah Grimmett who served in the Virginia Militia in Capt. Swinfield Hill's Company during the American Revolution. James Akin Kirk and Lucinda G. Kirk are buried in Bethel Cemetery, Perry County, TN.

(Left to right) Obe Atha Kirk, William Akin Kirk, Nesby Thomas Kirk, Victoria Whitwell Kirk, baby, Elsie May Kirk and Osbie Ervin Kirk. Ca. 1895.

William Akin (Bill) Kirk lived in the Beech Creek – Tennessee River area of Perry County and told that he heard the guns from the Battle of Shiloh. Bill Kirk married Victoria Augeline Whitwell (daughter of Thomas and Melissa Ward Whitwell) on Feb. 5, 1884. The family moved to Troy, TN, about 1890, but returned to Perry County in 1895. He lived in various parts of Perry County for the remainder of his life. He taught school in the county when he was a young man. He also served as a member of the County Court of Perry County, being a magistrate for his district. He was often referred to as "Squire Kirk" and said that he never had one of his decisions reversed by the Supreme Court. He also served as a County Judge and as a school board member. He gave unselfishly of his time to the interest of the public.

The children of Bill Kirk and Victoria Kirk were as follows: Obie Atha Kirk, born Feb. 22, 1885 in Perry County, died March 30, 1955 in Linden, TN; Osbie Ervin Kirk, born Feb. 16, 1887 in Perry County, died March 29, 1959 in Baltimore, MD; Nesbie Thomas Kirk, born Sept. 3, 1889 in Perry County, died March 24, 1977 in Linden, TN; Gertie Claris Kirk, born Oct. 6, 1892 in Obion County, died July 10, 1893 in Obion County; Elsie May Kirk, born May 17, 1894 in Obion County, died Oct. 31, 1895 in Obion County; William Claude Kirk, born Feb. 10, 1898 in Perry County, died July 10, 1986 in Warren, OH; Lexie Elmer Kirk, born Sept. 14,

1901 in Perry County, died Jan. 31, 1984 in Waynesboro, TN; and Eula Victoria Kirk, born April 1, 1904 in Perry County.

Victoria Whitwell Kirk died June 8, 1936 and is buried in Bethel Cemetery, Perry County, TN.

William Akin (Bill) Kirk died Feb. 4, 1947, and is also buried in Bethel Cemetery.

WILLIAM CLARK KIRK,
son of Dr. O. A. Kirk and Lockie Graves Kirk, born Oct. 29, 1917, Flatwoods, TN.

William Clark Kirk and his wife, Virginia with children Susan and Jason.

Education: Linden High School, 1935; David Lipscomb College, 1937; U.T.N., 1954-1956.

Military Service: July 1943 to April 1946, Combat Engineer for U.S. Army; 1947-1966 Tennessee Army National Guard, Retired Major Medical Service Corps, Tennessee ARNG, Jan. 1, 1966.

Married: Virginia Sue Blevins, daughter of Garrett Anderson Blevins and Lurla Christian Blevins, Nov. 27, 1959. Their children: 1) Susan Clarke Kirk, born Nov. 10, 1965; Education: Perry County High School, 1984, and B.S., Freed Hardeman University, 1988. Lives in Nashville, TN. 2) Jason Obe Kirk, born Oct. 9, 1968. Education: Perry County High School, 1987. Military: U.S. Air Force 1988 to present, Sr. A., U.S. Air Force, McGuire AFB, New Jersey.

William Clark Kirk and wife, Sue, reside in Linden, TN.

WILLIAM CLAUDE KIRK,
1898-1986. Married June Harder. Their children: 1) Noah Claude Kirk, married Margaret Whittaker; 2) Gene Akin Kirk; 3) Betty June Kirk, married Joseph Germans. Their five children: Greg Germans; Gary Germans; Lisa Germans who married Mitchell Milone, two children Mominic Milone and Kirk Milone; Gene Germans; and Lori Germans.

BENJAMIN CAESAR KITTRELL,
and Martha Jane Dowdy were married November 1860 in Perry County. Benjamin was the son of George and Elizabeth Hunter Rutherford Kittrell. George was with Andrew Jackson at the Battle of New Orleans. Elizabeth was the daughter of James and Elizabeth Cartwright Rutherford. James was at the Battle of Yorktown at the end of the Revolutionary War. Elizabeth Cartwright was the daughter of Robert Cartwright, who brought his family down the Cumberland River with the Donelson flotilla to settle near Nashville. They arrived April 24, 1780. Robert signed the Cumberland Compact in May 1780.

Benjamin Caesar and Martha Jane (Dowdy) Kittrell

Benjamin's family lived near Hampshire in Maury County. They were farmers and later moved to Perry County and settled at Farmer's Valley about 1848. They were here when the Civil War broke out. Benjamin and two younger brothers volunteered, Benjamin on July 9, 1861. He served in Co. 1, 6th Tennessee Confederacy. He was at Shiloh, then when the Confederates left Corinth, MS, he was in the rear guard and was captured. After being sent to Alton, IL, to prison camp, he was exchanged Sept. 9, 1862. He served until the end of the war and paroled in North Carolina, May 1865 and returned home.

He bought the family farm at Farmer's Valley and settled down there with Martha Jane and Izora, their daughter born while he was gone. He was a justice of the peace in 1873. He and Martha Jane were members of the Church of Christ.

Martha Jane was born Nov. 24, 1845, the daughter of Jordan and Mary Barber Dowdy from Coon Creek, who were married Feb. 1, 1843. Her grandparents were Thomas and Fannie Hinson Dowdy and Allen and Martha Kilpatrick Barber, who came from North Carolina and settled early on Coon Creek.

After Jordan's death in 1851, Mary married Alvin Warren, Sept. 5, 1857. They each had five children, then five were born to them. Each had 10 children, but the total was 15.

Benjamin and Martha Jane had 12 children: Izora Braxton, Mortimer Breece, M. Cicily, Benjamin Roscoe, George Hunter, Lulu Gregg, Mattie Blanche, James R., William Lamar, Dorothea Whitney and Simon Trigg Kittrell. Maxie and James died young.

Benjamin died Oct. 4, 1890, and Martha Jane died March 29, 1913. Both are buried at the Kittrell Cemetery, Farmer's Valley.

LAFFERTY AND THOMPSON,
Thomas Pleas Lafferty was born in Perry County, TN, on Dec. 25, 1872 to Cordelia Ann (Edwards) and Malachi Lafferty. Tom's mother died when he was very young.

Malachi Lafferty remarried a third time after Ann's death. Tom had one full sister, Lillie Ann, a half-sister Martha Emily (from Mal's first wife), and two half-brothers, Charles A. and Jackson M. (by Mal's third wife). While still a teen, Tom went to Missouri and stayed with his uncle, Bill Lafferty.

However, because of the Mal's ill health in the 1890s, Tom returned to Tennessee to care for his father who had lost his third wife to death also.

Forrest P. Lafferty and Ruth Dowdy Lafferty

Eli Vise, Tom's first cousin, decided that it was time for Tom to take a wife and introduced Tom to his sister-in-law, Ethel (Thompson) Jeter, a young widow with a small daughter. In November of 1897, Tom married Ethel Leona Thompson Jeter.

Ethel (1881-1971) was the daughter of James Andrew Pitts Thompson (1847-1912) and his wife Sarah (Sally) Culp (1855-1888). Ethel's grandparents were Charles Washington (1810-1895) and Sarah (Dodson) (1810-1889) Thompson and W. Neely and Julia Culp.

Both the Thompson and the Culp families had lived in the area of the Culp's Chapel Methodist Church (later known as Mount Auburn). Charles Washington Thompson was a trustee of the church and the family was very faithful to it. Ethel's father, J. A. P. Thompson was a Sunday School teacher, and her grandmother Sarah was known for her hospitality to ministers and her Christian example. Both Charles Washington and Sarah Thompson are buried in the cemetery behind the church as is Sarah's father, Fortunatus Dodson.

Family tradition says that Neely Culp provided some of his slaves to help build Culp's Chapel Church. Neely was the grandson of Henry Culp and related to the many Culp families in the area. As the church was named Culp's Chapel, it appears that several members of the various Culp families were active and contributing members. The wedding of Sarah Culp to James A. P. Thompson took place in the church on Aug. 27, 1872.

James and Sarah lived in Wayne/Perry County and had three children while there: Charlie, Lillian, and Julia. Sometime in 1878/1879 they started to Missouri where some of the Thompson relatives had gone. In attempting to cross a large river their wagon overturned and all their possessions were lost. They turned back and settled in Obion County, TN. There three additional children were born: Ethel, Oscar, and John Wesley. Charlie, Julia, and John Wesley died in childhood. Sarah Culp Thompson died in 1888 and Ethel returned to Perry County to live with her Thompson grandparents.

Following their marriage, Tom and Ethel lived in Perry County on the Lafferty family farm looking after Tom's father, Malachi, until his death about 1900/1901. In 1911 they moved to Decatur County living there until 1925 when they returned to the family farm which Tom had not sold. They remained there until Tom was no longer able to farm and sold out and moved into town (Clifton) where they lived until Tom's death in 1955.

Tom and Ethel's children were: Gladys Oreen, born 1900, married first Fieldon Lacey, second Lewis Tate; Dallas Ann, born 1903, married Farris Brawley; Lela Winfred, born 1905, married William E. Baker; Forrest Paul, born 1908, married Ruth Irene Dowdy; James Thomas, born 1911, married Sophia Smith; Clara Mae, born 1914, married George E. Sewell; Frank Thompson, born 1920, married first Lorrayne Hinson, second Margie, third Nina Wiles.

Forrest Lafferty was a member of the graduating class of the new Perry County High School in Linden in 1929. He began his teaching career in Perry County that fall at Culp's School where he remained for three years.

On Dec. 19, 1931, Forrest married Ruth Irene Dowdy of Clifton, TN, who was also a teacher. Ruth was the daughter of Rosa Lee (Boggs) and Nathan Turnbo Dowdy.

Forrest and Ruth continued their teaching careers in one and two teacher rural schools in Perry County. During the years from 1931 to 1943 they taught at Culp's School, Tom's Creek, Marsh Creek, White Oak, Brush Creek and Lego. Jobs were scarce during the Depression and teachers were often paid in "scrip," meaning they had to wait for the money or find someone to change it to cash almost always discounting it. However, both of them always said that in those days they were happy to have a job as so many were without work.

The school year was only eight months at that time as children were needed to help on the farms. Teachers did more than just teach. In these rural schools, the teacher also built the fire in the wood stove to provide heat, drew and carried water from the well and maintained the school building. Usually the school consisted of one room with all grades together. The only "teaching aid" was a blackboard and a limited number of textbooks. Most of the children walked to school and everyone brought their "lunch pail" which often contained biscuits and sorghum molasses.

While in Perry County, Forrest and Ruth had a son who died a few hours after his birth on Jan 18, 1939. He is buried at Culp's Chapel Cemetery. Then on Feb. 10, 1940, their only daughter, Patsy Ruth was born.

In 1943 with World War II in progress, Forrest took a job with TVA and they left Perry County.

In 1947, both Forrest and Ruth returned to teaching at Frank Hughes High School in Clifton. Some years later Forrest returned to the Perry County school system as principal at Lobelville High School for two years. In the fall of 1958 both Forrest and Ruth accepted teaching positions in Memphis. With Ruth as an elementary teacher and Forrest as guidance counselor and later high school principal, they continued in the Shelby County School System until their retirement in 1971.

Returning to Clifton in retirement, Forrest and Ruth kept their Perry County ties with participation in the Perry County Retired Teachers Association. Both maintained their life-long interest in education.

Ruth Dowdy Lafferty died May 29, 1984. Forrest died June 29, 1991. They are buried at the Clifton City Cemetery. *Compiled and submitted by Patsy Lafferty Flowers*

LANCASTER–HOUSTON, Benjamin Lancaster, born about 1783 in Edgecombe County, NC, and wife, Sarah Harriet Whitfield (born about 1785 in Virginia) came from North Carolina through Willamson County and settled on Beaver Dam Creek in Hickman County area in early 1800. Descendants of this family live in Perry, Hickman, Decatur, and surrounding counties. Benjamin, a minister, wife Sarah, and son, Gabriel, were listed in membership of Coon Creek Primitive Baptist Church in Perry County in 1849. Benjamin and Sarah had at least six children. Known sons were: John, born 1805, who married Rachel Harder; David L., born 1807, married Parmelia Davidson; William, born 1808, married Mary Ann (Polly) Davidson; and Gabriel, born 1813, who married Martha Cotham, also had a second wife, Nancy Sarah Horner Whitwell, daughter of John Horner Jr. John and Gabriel were both ministers.

David L., (born 1807) who settled in Decatur County, married Parmelia Davidson (born 1805) of Williamson County, and had Harvey (born 1829), Jesse Johnson (born 1831), William F. (born 1833), Evaline (born 1835), Benjamin M. (born 1836), David A. (born 1840) and John G. (born 1841). David, Parmelia, and his second wife, Cynthia Duck, are buried in the Gardner-Wylie Cemetery in Decatur County. David and Cynthia had children Sarah Bathsheba (born 1854) and Dr. Gabriel Scott Lancaster (born 1858).

William F. (born 1833, died 1899), son of David L. (1807), married Eliza Jane Houston (born 1847, died 1933). Their children were Lorenzo Lafayette (born 1872), Luana L. (born 1876), Mary B. (born 1879), George (born 1882), and Arthur J. (born 1891).

Lorenzo Lafayette (Fate) married Mary (Mollie) Houston (born 1880, died 1946), daughter of Mary Myracle and Felix Houston (born 1853, died 1940). Felix was the son of Jefferson Perry Houston (born 1822) and Jane Lofton (born 1820). Jefferson Perry was the son of John L. Houston, a native of Indiana who settled in Decatur County about 1818, and Jane Graham (born about 1800), daughter of John Graham (born about 1760 in Scotland). Known children of John Graham and wife Sarah were Charles, Elizabeth, Jane, Sarah, Robert Crawford, and Mary (Polly) Graham. John L. Houston and Jane Graham's children were Johanna, Jefferson Perry, John Graham, Sara Jane, Laverna Ann, Eliza, Martha Ann, Jasper Newton, and Samuel Madison Houston.

Fate Lancaster and Mollie Houston's children were: Bertha (born 1903) who married Rufus Mayes; William Tillman (born 1906), married Clara Duck; Lena (born 1910), married Nealie Woods; Opal (born 1914), married Edgar Hays; and Wilma Mae (born 1920), married William Franklin Graves. All five children, mother and father, and grandparents are buried in the Mt. Tabor Cemetery in Decatur County. Children of Wilma Mae Lancaster and William F. Graves were: Yvonne, Wilda, Joe Nell, James Larry, Patricia, and Marcia Graves.

BENJAMIN LANCASTER SR., from Edgecombe County, NC, will dated Sept. 24, 1793. Names of children: Benjamin, Robert, Elijah Lancaster, a son Levi Boyet, also names of Thomas Boyet, with son Benjamin Boyet. Other names in will: Jacob and Thomas Boyet. Signers of the will were Thomas and Samuel Merritt. Buyers at sale of estate: Robert Sr., Robert Jr., Henry, Hartwell, Elijah Lancaster.

Benjamin Lancaster II, little is known about this Benjamin. He was a slave holder in Humphreys County, TN, 1820-1830. Known children so far, are (1) Benjamin Marion Lancaster, born 1783, married Sarah Harriet Whitfield. (2) The Rev. David Lancaster, born 1782, died March 26, 1860, married Nancy Redford, Feb. 21, 1807, Williamson County, TN. His children were: John, Nancy, Angeline, Samuel, William D., Martha, Lucy, Mary. (3) Polly Lancaster, married Owen Williams.

Benjamin Lancaster III, raised his family around Hickman and Perry County, TN. He was Primitive Baptist preacher, as was some of his sons. (Source: *Spences History of Hickman County, TN.*) Benjamin, 1783-1859, married Sarah Harriet Whitfield, 1785-1860. They are more than likely buried on Lick Creek, Perry County, TN, where their home was located. They had a large family – six sons and two daughters. Five sons have been identified.

(1) John Lancaster, (Feb. 13, 1806 – December 19, 1852), married Rachel Harder (born 1804), daughter of John and Delila Harder. They had nine children: Deliah Catherine, born 1827; William Henry, born 1829; James David, born 1831; Sarah H., born 1833; Pleasant Gaberial, born 1835; Joel Marion, born 1837; Mary M., born 1839; Louisa, born 1841; and John F., born 1843.

(2) Col. David S. Lancaster, (Jan. 14, 1807 – 1891), married Permelia Davidson, (1805-1852), daughter of Daniel Davidson. They had nine children: Harvey L. W., Dec. 3, 1829 – March 17, 1890; Jesse Johnson Parish, 1831-1898; John G., 1841-Oct. 17, 1912; James David Andrew, 1841-April 24, 1867, shot and killed, Hickman County, TN; William F. (Bill), 1833-1899; Benjamin N., September 1836-1901; Sarah Bathsheba, 1854; Gaberiel Scott, February 1858-1908; Elvira Evaline, 1835.

(3) Gaberial Andrew Lancaster, 1813, married first Martha Cotham (1819-1860), daughter of Isaac and Sarah (DePriest) Cotham. They had 12 children: Rhoda C., 1837; John Andrew, 1839-October 1889; William Henry, March 20, 1884-April 26, 1914; Eleanor, 1840; Harvey N. (Harry), 1842; Julina C. 1845; Sarah Elizabeth, 1847; Mary A., 1849; Elizabeth J., 1851; Martha Ann Priscilla, 1853; Cordelia P., 1857; Naomi W., 1859; Gaberial Andrew, married (1860), second Nancy Sarah (Horner) Whitwell (1826-Nov. 7, 1910), daughter of John and Sally (Sparks) Horner Jr. They had three children: Jemina Adelaid, Dec. 31, 1862-March 14, 1947; Harriet, 1863; and J. Frances, 1865.

(4) Elijah Hicks Lancaster, Oct. 6, 1809-March 8, 1882, married Jane Johnson. They had eight children: Alex; Lydia; Benjamin; Christine; Paralee Isabel, Oct. 15, 1849-April 17, 1867; Alice; Lonnie; and Thomas.

(5) William B. and Sarah Harriet (Whitfield) Lancaster. Further information.

(6) Unknown female born (1815-1820).
(7) Unknown male born (1820-1825).
(8) Unknown female born 1820-1825).
Submitted by Nancy Lancaster Mathews

CALVIN ANDREW LANCASTER,
(April 8, 1872-September 1950), son of David Andrew and Milly (Barber) Lancaster. He married Sept. 27, 1894, to Nancy Lee Hinson, (May 14, 1866-Feb. 26, 1939) daughter of James P. and Bettye Elizabeth (Jame) Hinson. Calvin spent his life as a Church of Christ preacher. They raised a large family.

(1) Ollye Dora (Sept. 17, 1895-February 1974), married Williard Parker Riley, son of Joseph Alvin and Nancy (Warren) Riley. Children: Edward Leeroy (May 7, 1916), married Florence Espravink; Habert Lee Sr. (March 4, 1919), married Clara Dell Shephard; Obie Lee (Feb. 5, 1921), married first Nell Sheppard, second Bee Lee Hennings; Willard Parker Jr. (Aug. 9, 1925), married Edith Myrtle Bryan; Calvin (June 11, 1928), married Sherry; Betty Ann (July 20, 1934), married Melvin Carl Owen; Ima Dean (May 14, 1931), married first Mr. Sheppard, second Stanley Ozug.

(2) George McKinley (June 27, 1897-Oct. 3, 1972), married first Mary Estalee Fain, (March 1, 1902-Feb. 9, 1937), daughter of John Bristol and Willis Inez (Bishop) Fain. They had children: (A) Percy Olson (Sept. 21, 1928), married first Nov. 1, 1947, Bonnie Lou Staggs, had issues James Percy, Nancy Lou Lancaster, (Mathews), Shirley Marie, Linda Fay, Roy Phillip. Percy O. married second Dorothy (Collins) Lawson. (B) Mary Ellen, (June 9, 1930), married Vernon Scott. They had issues Grady Lee, Robert Leeroy, Raymond Thomas, Lynn Thomas. George McKinley married second Carrie Pearl Scott, (Jan. 1, 1914), daughter of Barley and Sarah (Auburn) Scott. They had a child, Lawrence George (July 22, 1949), married July 11, 1964 to Kathey Victoria Martin. They had children, Lawrence McKinley, Regina Gail. George and Carrie adopted her nephew James Thomas (Scott) (March 15, 1941).

(3) Ardellar (May 13, 1899-May 20, 1975), married June 29, 1913, to Jesse Lee James Sr. (1894-1972) son of Bebb and Cora Lee (Mays) James. They had children (A) Verna D. (Aug. 15, 1914), married James Henry Garrison. (B) Estelle (Nov. 18, 1915-December 1964), married Cleon Shults. (C) Lee Carter, (Nov. 13, 1917), married Edith Josephine Whitehead. (D) Paul Etau, (Dec. 9, 1919), married Erma Dean McCearren. (E) Nancy Lee (Feb. 19, 1921), married James Leemore Cotham. (F) Jesse Lee Jr. (Jan. 11, 1924), married Martha Jane Whitehead. (G) Dewey Roosevelt (April 4, 1926), married Betty Jane Sisco. (H) Lillian Jauneita (April 9, 1930), married first Edward Banks, second Charlie Carroll. (I) Billy Joel (Dec. 21, 1932), married first Jane Brewer, second Dorris Marie Ayers. (J) Bobby Lee Osco, (May 24, 1934), married Betty Jo Brewer. (K) Jerry Lee Williams (June 30, 1939), married first Jo-Anne Talley, second Shirley Tibbs. (L) Larry Roy Eugene (Jan. 21, 1943), married Patsy Joy Grimes. (M) Jimmy Springer (Jan. 14, 1947), married Norma Dorris DeVore.

(4) Grady Stevenson (June 13, 1900-March 3, 1975), married March 1, 1926 to Mildred Ella Vasbinder, (Feb. 23, 1907-Sept. 27, 1961) daughter of William and Esther Ella (Born) Vasbinder. They had children: (A) Robert Dean (Dec. 4, 1926), married Dorris Lorraine Coffman, (B) Vivian Ella (Nov. 5, 1927), married James Harold Graham, (C) Jo-Ann (July 25, 1931), married Walter Croft Bagnell, (D) Sara Kay (July 19, 1940), married William John Trethewey.

(5) Dewey Roosevelt (Nov. 30, 1903-Jan. 27, 1975), first unknown in Michigan. Been said he has a son, but unknown. Second, Ann Knudson from Michigan, also had a brother, Joe.

(6) Ester Lucille (May 11, 1905-Aug. 5, 1986), married King David Rawdon (March 1, 1903-Jan. 15, 1972), son of William Levi and R. Mindy Elizabeth (UNK.) Rawdon. They had children: (A) Reba Jewel (Nov. 12, 1923), married Jesse Clyde Oliver. (B) Neva Ruel (Sept. 2, 1925), first Clarence Lopp, second Willard Clark, (C) Lema June (Dec. 13, 1926), married Raymond Patton, (D) adopted David Wayne (March 7, 1959).

(7) Herman Andrew (June 14, 1909-Sept. 4, 1910), died infancy, buried with grandparents David and Milley Lancaster, Goeforth Cemetery, Slippery, Lewis County, TN. *Submitted by Nancy Lancaster Mathews*

DAVID ANDREW LANCASTER,
(May 6, 1833-September 1892), son of William B. and Mary Ann (Polly) Davidson Lancaster. Married Mary Melinda (Millie) Barber (April 25, 1831-Oct. 18, 1909), daughter of Long John E. and Sarah (Hinson) Barber. They are buried on their property, Goeforth Cemetery, Slippery, Lewis County, TN. They had seven children:

(1) Dorinda Allice, (Sept. 10, 1854), married Perry County, TN, to W. F. Prewitt. No further information. This family lived in Arkansas.

(2) Frances Paralee (Jan. 3, 1857-March 30, 1942), married first Thomas J. Dukes. They had two children: (A) George Marion (D-1956), married Winnie Jane. Their children were Rudolph, Randolph, Raymond, Jessie (F), Lessie (F), Bessie, Irene. (B) Ella, married James Monroe Duncan. Their children: Fannie Mae, Billy Rae (twins), Hershal Marion, Carlos Rueben, Lynville, Florine. Frances Paralee (Lancaster) Dukes then married Rueben Whitwell. They had these children: (C) Minnie Belinda (July 1881), (D) William Harry (Aug. 27, 1884-July 25-1950), (E), Donnie Lee (Nov. 27, 1887), (F) Jessie Lillian (Oct. 29, 1890-May 15, 1963), (G) Nettie May (Feb. 14, 1894-Dec. 10, 1974), (H) Ettie Ola (May 21, 1897), (I) Elsie Leora (March 29, 1903).

(3) Levisy Louise (Dana) (Aug. 3, 1858), married W. T. Hinson, Perry County, TN. Nothing further known.

(4) Juley A. (Feb. 15, 1862). Nothing further known.

(5) John William, (July 11, 1866-May 14, 1936), married May 26, 1887, to Amanda Allice Hinson, (Nov. 29, 1872-March 12, 1949). Their children: (A) Minnie Inez (July 25, 1888-Jan. 4, 1889), (B) Charles David (Jan. 10, 1890-April 16, 1965), married Nov. 6, 1910, Perry County, TN, Emma Bell Dotson (Aug. 28, 1891-Sept. 28, 1977), (C) Leslie Howard (Feb. 24, 1893-Oct. 24, 1959), married June 25, 1916, Perry County, TN, Willie Baker (June 29, 1892-March 23, 1976), (D) James Everett (March 5, 1897-March 31, 1939), married Jan. 14, 1917 to Cora Brandon (1899-May 12, 1972), (E) Jesse Hobson (Jan. 16, 1900-March 27, 1952), married March 5, 1921 to Pearl Curtis (Oct. 16, 1900-Nov. 6, 1982), (F) George Winfred (Aug. 10, 1902-Dec. 17, 1902), (G) Era Beatress (Oct. 11, 1904-still living), married April 19, 1924, to Charlie Brown Johnson (Feb. 22, 1906-Feb. 19, 1951), (H) Mattie Lou (Sept. 21, 1907-Jan. 14, 1983), married Oct. 8, 1926, to Thomas Taylor Hastings (Sept. 17, 1903-Oct. 16, 1959), (I) Martha Pauline (March 7, 1910-still living), married Oct. 18, 1927, to William Thedie Cook (March 3, 1898-July 6, 1965).

(6) James David (June 25, 1868-April 3, 1942), married July 2, 1894, Perry County, TN, to Sarah Ellen (Wing), Webster) (Jan. 14, 1866-Nov. 19, 1938), daughter of Calvin and Mary (Westbrook) Wing. She had a child by first husband – Mary Elizabeth Webster (January 1889), married Herman E. Gordon. (A) Edith Pearl Lancaster, (March 27, 1896-Dec. 22, 1984), married Jan. 5, 1920, to Alvin Booker Riley, (Feb. 19, 1883-Feb. 28, 1936). (B) Walter A. (July 15, 1899-July 21, 1917), never married. (C) Myrtle R. (December 1901), married first Adney Bonds, second Mr. Dalton. (D) Twin Leslie (Nov. 1, 1903-Nov. 18, 1937), married Stella Gordon. (E) Twin Jessie (Nov. 1, 1903, died six weeks old).

(7) Calvin Andrew (April 8, 1872-Sept. 30, 1950), married Sept. 27, 1894, to Nancy Lee Hinson, (May 14, 1866-Feb. 26, 1939), daughter of James P. and Bettye Elizabeth (James) Hinson. Further information. *Submitted by Nancy Lancaster Mathews*

WILLIAM B. LANCASTER,
son of Benjamin Marion and Sarah Harriet (Whitfield) Lancaster, born 1808, died before Sept. 9, 1891. Married daughter of Daniel and Polly (Miller) Davidson Jr. Miss Mary Ann (Polly) Davidson was born 1813. They reared a large family in and around Perry County, TN.

(1) David Andrew Lancaster, (May 6, 1822-September 1892) married around 1853 to Mary Melinda (Millie) Barber, (April 25, 1831-Oct. 18, 1909) daughter of Long John E. and Sarah (Hinson) Barber. (Further information)

(2) Lucinda Lancaster, died around 1877, married Johnathan Duncan (1834), son of John and Mary (Lynch) Duncan. Their children: (A) Mary Elizabeth (1853), married Nov. 6, 1879, to James H. Simmons. (B) Martha C. (1861), married John H. Harper. (C) William Henry (June 2, 1855-May 19, 1918), married July 18, 1883 to Saphronia Adaline Hinson. (D) John Riley (1860), married to Sarah Elizabeth Skelton. (E) Thomas Marion, (Jan. 9, 1865-Aug. 1, 1907), married Sept. 26, 1886), to Margaret Saphronia Hinson. (F) Jennie Eveline, a twin, (March 10, 1868-Aug. 29, 1947) married Nov. 9, 1882 to George Whitfield Skelton Jr. (G) James Monroe (March 10, 1868), a twin, married Ella Dukes (went by Whitwell name).

(3) Deliaha Mae Lancaster, married Richard James Quillen. They had a son, Wesley Quillen, married Ruth Jane Baker.

(4) Mary Katherine Lancaster, (Sept. 5, 1840-July 27, 1921), married March 31, 1858, to John Andrew Carroll, son of Andrew Sterling and Nancy Anne (Kelly) Carroll. They had children: (A) Mary Ann (June 5, 1859-Jan. 27, 1945),

a twin, married John Bell DeVore. (B) Eliza Campbell (June 5, 1859, a twin, died infant). (C) William Andrew (May 31, 1861-July 19, 1939), married Nancy Jane Pace. (D) John Frank Sr. (Oct. 5, 1863-June 16, 1937), married Margarett Johnston. (E) Elizabeth (Jan. 3, 1872-1970), married James P. Mathis. (F) Isabella (June 30, 1868-Dec. 12, 1937), married William Hardy Warren. (G) Ada (March 27, 1874-1907), married Thomas Grimes.

(5) Leeroy W. Lancaster, (1844-Feb. 4, 1912), married first Mary, second Martha. Known children: (A) Mary Louella Elizabeth, (April 5, 1874), married Herman Britt Talley. (B) Paralee (born 1860), married Aug. 23, 1891 to James Skelton. (C) Livona Elzada (Jan. 1871-1903), married Wyatt H. Hinson. (D) Lancaster, female. (E) Lancaster, male.

(6) Sarah Elizabeth Lancaster, married Nov. 20, 1869 to James Poole Talley, son of Allen and Ferila (Hensley) Talley. They had children: (A) Orpha Virginia Ann, married Dec. 24, 1890, John David Rivers. (B) Sarah Harriett (1873), married Oct. 3, 1896 to Robert Lee Hensley. (C) Samuel Houston (Jan. 6, 1874-May 17, 1949), never married. (D) James Elisha (March 1879), never married.

(7) John Monroe Lancaster (October 1847), married Sarah Elizabeth Talley (1848), daughter of Allen and Ferila (Hensley) Talley. They had children: (A) Elizabeth (1868), married Mr. Kincaid. (B) John William (1873). (C) Jesse W. (January 1876), married Roxie F. (D) Margaret C. (1878). (E) Mary Maude (June 27, 1880-Oct. 19, 1949), married Bud Graves. (F) Martha M. (July 1882). (G) Lou, a female, (1887), married Mr. Rowdon.

(8) James Marion Lancaster, (1852), married Lusa (Nettie Lynch?). They had a child, Coy Lancaster Sr.

(9) Thomas J. Lancaster, (1853), nothing further.

(10) Rachel E. Lancaster (1855).

(11) Jessie B. Lancaster, married Nov. 30, 1874, to L. C. Dean.

(12) Wesley V. Wright Lancaster, (June 16, 1856-May 10, 1948), married Ada Vandiver.

(13) A. J. Lancaster, married Burnice Lewis.

Submitted by Nancy Lancaster Mathews

ELKANAH A. LAND, first saw the light of day in Hickman County, TN, on March 28, 1827. He was the son of Cooper B. and Hannah Anderson Land. He was one of 11 children. Elkanah was born in poverty and reared with very meager means of livelihood. On June 6, 1844, Elkanah married Nancy Barber, daughter of Elida and Jane Dowdy Barbara. Elkanah leased a small tract of land and cleared it of all the timber, the winter after he married. His young wife helped him in the forest during the daytime and ran the spinning wheel at night, weaving all the cloth needed for their clothing. They learned the valuable lessons of honest toil and frugal living.

They had four children: William R. (Dec. 7, 1846 – May 12, 1897), Mary F. (March 9, 1851), Elizabeth Jane (June 29, 1856), Nancy H. (Donna) (Jan. 29, 1856), W. R. married Sarah C. Beasley (Oct. 27, 1867), Mary R., married R. H. Godwin (April 4, 1866), Elizabeth Jane, married Cullen S. Vick (Sept. 3, 1868) and Nancy H. married Tommie Downey (Oct. 27, 1870).

Elkanah Land and wife Nancy gave little attention to the spiritual side of their nature at first. Brother Johnston was preaching on Beaver Dam Creek in Hickman County. Here Elkanah and wife heard him, became interested and before the meeting closed, both were baptized into Christ. In 1862 Bro. Land became a minister in the Church of Christ. He was very active in the little congregation at Beaver Dam. It was not long until his zeal for Christ and knowledge of his truth were recognized and his services in great demand. He held many debates, he feared no man and was well armed with the truth.

E. A. and Nancy Barber Land

In Nov. 1880, Bro. Land made a trip to Arkansas riding horseback. He held meetings in Russellville and Chickalah, also Buffton. The meeting at Buffton resulted in 25 new additions to the church. Bro. Land's preaching was confined in the most part to Hickman, Perry, Wayne, Lewis, Humphreys, Benton, Lawrence, Hardin, and Maury counties in Tennessee. He preached some in Mississippi, Kentucky and Alabama. His travels were all horseback. It has been estimated that he baptized about 2,000 people into Christ.

Goodspeed's History of Tennessee reports that Elkanah A. Land was the leader of a small group of Perry Countians in the Confederacy in the Civil War. He was with a group at Fort Donelson about the time it was captured. In 1844, Elkanah and wife came into possession of a 600-acre farm on Brush Creek in Perry County. He farmed his land and ran shop until 1862 when he began to devote all his time to spreading of the gospel. The churches throughout many counties and states still feel the influence of the life of this great man of God.

Nancy Barber Land passed away Dec. 31, 1907, and is buried "On the Hill" on Brush Creek, where the old school/church building used to be.

Elkanah Land died at Hohenwald, TN, April 17, 1915, at the age of 88 years and nine days. He was buried in the cemetery by his beloved wife. At his request, Bro. H. N. Mann of Riverside Church of Christ, conducted the funeral services and gave exhortations to this brethren and sisters to live faithful to the Lord. These counties mentioned have never known a better or greater man than that of Elkanah A. Land.

LAND, William R., was born Dec. 4, 1846, the son of Elkanah Anderson and Nancy Barber Land. Little is known of his youth.

William married Sarah Mayberry Beasley, the widow of Fielding W. Beasley. She had three Beasley children: Frances (Monk) married Robert Tucker and died soon thereafter; Louisa (Mize) married Elijah Warren, Brush Creek, she was his second wife; and Peter Alexander, married Mary Barber. Their descendants live in western Perry County, near the river.

William and Sarah Mayberry Land

William and Sarah lived on Brush Creek, where he farmed. His father was a preacher of the Church of Christ, and it has been said that William preached some at Brush Creek.

They had three children: John Land, married Magdalene Warren, after her death he married Eva Cude Bastin; Elizabeth, married Robert Lacher; George T., married Leanna E. Warren.

William died May 9, 1897 and is buried on Church House Hill on Brush Creek. His tombstone states: "A devoted Christian and honest man lies buried here."

Sarah's death date is unknown, as she has no tombstone. The 1900 census has her birth year as 1840. She probably outlived William.

Their younger son, George T. Land, was born Aug. 12, 1879, on Brush Creek. He married Leanna Warren, born Jan. 15, 1876, the daughter of Elijah and Sarah Frances Tucker Warren, also on Brush Creek. Their children were Augusta and Lila. Augusta married Jack Beasley, and Lila married Harris Kittrell.

They lived on Brush Creek in the W. R. Land house, where George farmed and raised cattle. Later they moved to Linden where they lived when he died. He fell dead in the courthouse Sept. 12, 1933, and is buried in the Warren Cemetery on Brush Creek.

Leanna went back to Brush Creek. Her daughter Lila and Harris Kittrell lived with her until Lila's death in 1958. She then stayed with her granddaughter, Betty King and her husband James. She died April 1963 and is buried beside George in the Warren Cemetery.

WILLIAM W. LANE, (1839-1862), volunteered in the Confederate Army in 1861 at the outbreak of the war. He left behind his wife, Polly Lomax Lane, and their three children on a tenant farm on the Buffalo River. He died in Arkansas in 1862 of yellow fever and is buried in the Little Rock Confederate Cemetery (near to downtown). His particular grave is unknown but old records of the cemetery show his interment.

The oldest of William's three children was James Haywood Lane (1857-1935) who was only four when his father went off to the war. Times must have been very hard for the Lane children but James grew up to be a good farmer. In 1885 James married Martha Jane Barham (1858-1931), the daughter of Balaam (1838-1917) and Henritta Barber Barham (1837-1891). Balaam had also served in Confederate service having ridden with the 10th Tennessee Cavalry organized by Bedford Forrest when operating behind Union lines in Tennessee in 1862.

James Haywood and Martha Jane Barham Lane

While living on the Buffalo River farm, James and Martha Jane's children, Dena Arlillian, Mary Henrietta, Bonnie Elizabeth, William Thomas and Martha Berthalee attended the old Frog Pond School across the Buffalo River from their farm. James and Martha Jane would paddle them back and forth across the river each day in a canoe. In about 1907, James and Martha Jane moved their brood to Cane Creek on the Perry-Hickman line in the area of the old Enon Primitive Baptist church where they were members. Their hard work paid off and in time they owned 250 acres and a fine home built of poplar lumber that still stands near the caves on Cane Creek.

Dena (1886-1934) married Miles Olen Murray (1885-1960) and their children were Lola May (1913-89), Robert Lane (1915-81), Willie Barham (1917), Walter Haywood (1920-44) and Martha Louise (1922). Willie and Walter both joined the Navy during W.W.II. Walter died when his destroyer went down in the English Channel but Willie came home safely and spent many years in the Navy.

Mary (1888-1949) married William Lee Curl (1886-1967). Their children are Grace Lane (1916-1972), Mattie Virginia (1919-1950), Myrtle Pearl (1921), Mary Lee (1924), William Russell (1927), twins Annie May (1933) and Andrew Ray (1933) and Minnie Sue (1935).

Bonnie (1890-1963) married James Earl Hinson (1892-1975). Their children were James Howard (1915-1994), Mabel Edna (1919) and Sophia Mae (1922).

William Thomas (1893-1966) married Cora May Cotton (1901-1983). Their children are Dimple Rue (1924) and Myrtle Loudean (1927).

Martha Berthalee (1896-1979) married Carlos Rushin Cude (1895-1966), son of John Bell Cude (mentioned again in this book). Their children are Eva Pauline (1919-1994), Lila Pearl (1922), twins Ralph Lane (1924-1978) and Ruby Lee (1924) and Dorothy Ann (1931).

LARUE, The LaRue (Leroux) family first arrived in New York in 1680 from France by way of Holland. They were French Huguenots fleeing to America for religious freedom. They were prosperous pioneer land owners in Virginia and Kentucky before coming to Tennessee. Isaac Jr. (1757) and Bethia LaRue settled on grant land in Bedford County, TN, 1806.

Their son John (1788), married Clara Hardin. They were land owners in Bedford and Lincoln counties owning 42 slaves when the slaves were freed in 1865. John and Clara had 10 children one of whom was James Madison.

Dick and Anna LaRue

James (1822), married Mary (Polly) Brecheene. To this union were born nine children: Frances, Levi, John, Josiah, Isaac, William, Mary Jane, Milton and Albert. James was granted land in Bedford County which he farmed until the Civil War. He and two sons, Josiah and Levi served in the Civil War. James, private Co. E 27th Regiment, Tennessee Infantry, was wounded in the leg, captured, taken prisoner and spent time in Rock Island, IL, prison. After the war they moved to Lawrence County, then to Lewis County and his senior years were spent in Perry County. He is buried in Starbuck Cemetery, Perry County, TN.

James' grandson, J. H. Richard (Dick) LaRue (1874-1958), was of the next generation to maintain roots in Perry County. Dick was the son of Isaac and Catherine Fain LaRue. He married Rose Anna Harper, born 1874, daughter of Marcus and Helen Fain Harper. They moved to Perry County about 1912 and bought a farm in the Grapevine Hollow, Bethel Community, where the airport is now located. He was a farmer, carpenter, and Primitive Baptist. They had eight children: Ann, Walter, Roxie, Mary, Pauline, Irene, Leslie and Mildred. The two surviving children are Leslie and Mildred.

Ann married James M. (Tobe) Clifton. They had eight children who were born and raised in Perry County. Walter (1897-1973) was a farmer, master Mason and served as deacon in the First Christian Church in Linden, TN. He and Addie Clifton LaRue lived in the Grapevine Hollow where they raised eight daughters. Addie is presently living on their farm in the Hollow.

Mary married Jim Clifton and had five children before she died in 1938. Pauline married Bob Marlin, they divorced and she married Bill Hinson. She and Bill had three boys. After his death she married Dick Weems and had a daughter.

Two of Dick and Rose Anna LaRue's daughters moved to Kentucky: Mrs. Eathern (Roxie) Skellions, and Mrs. Rupert (Irene) Miller. Roxie had four children and Irene had two children by her first husband, Carl Churchwell.

Leslie (1914) and Maudie Broadway LaRue currently live in the Bethel Community. Leslie is a master Mason and lay leader of the Bethel United Methodist Church and retired Genesco employee. Maudie and Leslie raised three daughters.

Mildred married Wilburn Broadway and moved to Cedar Creek in 1943. They had one daughter. Mildred continues to live on Cedar Creek enjoying her retirement and her work in the Cedar Grove United Methodist Church.

LARUE/BARBER, Walter LaRue and Addie Clifton married in 1917. Walter and Addie had eight children: Lois Hazel (Ms. Richard Kimbel), Lola Mae (Ms. Jesse Barber), Nancy Florene (Bobbie) (Ms. James Broadway), Ruby Jewel (Ms. George Kelley), Dorothy Faye (Ms. Jesse Smith), Donna Joyce (Ms. Gus Dabbs), Betty Wanda (Ms. Melvin Morgan), Linda Helen (Ms. Barney Doyle). They reared their eight daughters in the Grapevine Hollow in Perry County, TN. Lola Mae, second child of Walter and Addie, was born April 18, 1920.

Ernest and Josephine with children Velma and Allie Mae Barber

While Lola was growing up in the Grapevine Hollow, a young man named Jesse was growing up on Cedar Creek, near the iron furnace.

John Henry Barber married Martha Catherine Gladden and had four children: Ernest Berry, Monroe, Meeks, and Harriett.

Walter and Addie Clifton LaRue with their eight daughters, at the family home Walter built for them in the Grapevine Hollow in 1931. From left to right: Lois Hazel, Lola Mae, Nancy Florene (Bobbie), Ruby Jewell, Dorothy Faye, Donna Joyce, Betty Wanda, and Linda Helen. Walter and Addie are seated. Photo taken in 1953.

Ernest Berry Barber married Josephine Stephens and had three children: Velma (Ms. John Fultz), Allie Mae (Ms. Peters), and Jesse Henry. Josephine died a short time later and Ernest remarried.

Jesse Henry Barber (Aug. 21, 1922) was the youngest child of Ernest Berry Barber (1898) and Josephine Stephens of Morgan City, MS. Jesse and Lola Mae (1920-1993) married Dec. 7, 1940, they followed work to surrounding areas but finally settled and made their home in the Grapevine Hollow. Jesse worked in the woods for many years as a logger while Lola cared for their four children: Jesse Henry Jr., Kenneth Paul, Gloria Jean (Ms. Bill Green), and Betty Lou (Ms. Wayne Hamm).

Kenneth Paul Barber (Oct. 15, 1944) married Betty Jewell Hester (1944). Ken and Betty graduated from Linden High on May 5, 1962. Ken left to serve in the U.S. Navy, May 12, 1962. In June, Betty started school at George Peabody College for Teachers. Ken and Betty renewed their relationship via mail and were eventually married June 7, 1964. While Ken was aboard *USS Grand Canyon*, stationed in Newport, RI, their son Kenneth Paul Jr. was born. Ken's tour of duty came to an end Feb. 2, 1966. The family of three moved back to Tennessee, making their home in Nashville, TN. Ken attended the University of Tennessee in Nashville, receiving a Masters Degree in Public Administration in 1974. While living in Nashville, two daughters were born, Pamela Jewell and Jacquelyn LaRue. Ken and Betty moved to Perry County making their home on the Gussie Goblet Farm in 1975.

Kenneth Paul Barber Jr., oldest child of Ken and Betty, was born in June of 1965. He married Kimberly Renea Qualls in June of 1984. Paul, Renea, and their two children, Kenneth Paul Barber III and Stephen Mykl, now reside in Smyrna, TN.

Jacquelyn LaRue Barber (May 8, 1971), third child of Ken and Betty, graduated valedictorian of the 1989 class of Perry County High. Jacque completed a Bachelor of Science Degree, majoring in accounting from the University of Tennessee in Martin in May of 1993. Following graduation, Jacque moved to Bellevue, TN. She is presently employed as a staff accountant for Dempsey, Wilson and Co., in Brentwood, TN.

ROBERT AND ANN LASTER, live in Flatwoods in Perry County. Ann is the daughter of Richard and Opal Keeling Graham of Perry County. Robert is the great-great-grandson of Benjamin Casesar and Martha Jane Dowdy Kittrell. Benjamin was born Feb. 24, 1832, and died Oct. 4, 1890. Martha was born Nov. 24, 1845, and died March 29, 1913. They are buried in the Kittrell Cemetery near Farmers Valley, which is still in the family. Their daughter, Izora Braxton (March 16, 1862-Dec. 21, 1941) married Joseph Allison King (Feb. 16, 1855-Sept. 4, 1907). Their daughter, Mortimer (Mortie) Kittrell (March 20, 1895-Feb. 27, 1976), married Horner Brown Armstrong (March 27, 1895-March 22, 1979). Their children were Joe Brown, Sylvia, Lorraine, and Robert.

Sylvia Armstrong (Oct. 18, 1917-Aug. 11, 1968) on June 15, 1938 married Walter Herman Laster (Nov. 17, 1914-Aug. 8, 1988). Their children were Thomas (Sept. 9, 1939), Joe (March 17, 1941), and Robert (Bobby) (May 10, 1942).

Robert Laster married Ann Graham on Feb. 22, 1964. Their children are Roger Dale (adopted) (March 24, 1962), Melissa (Nov. 10, 1968), and Todd (Feb. 9, 1977).

MICHAEL PRENTICE LAWRENCE, was born the eldest of four children on Oct. 18, 1951, to Ira Herbert and Dorothy (Wilsdorf) Lawrence. Michael was educated in the Perry County School System and attended Hohenwald Vocational School after graduation in 1969. Michael began employment with Perry Farmers Co-Op in 1972 and is currently employed with this firm at the present time.

Ginger Lawrence Bell, Connie Lawrence, Michael, and Mitchell (front).

Michael married Connie (Hinson) of Hohenwald (Lewis County), TN, in 1973, and they have two children, Ginger Michelle (Bell) and Mitchell Royce, who both still live in Perry County.

Michael's paternal grandparents are the late Ira Acres and Beulah (Patterson) Lawrence, both of whom are interred in the Lawrence Family Cemetery on Owl Hollow prong of Tom's Creek in Pineview.

Michael's maternal grandparents are the late Roy Prentice and Amie (Trull) Wilsdorf. Roy Prentice is interred in the Smith Memorial Cemetery on Tom's Creek in Pineview. Amie is still living at her home in Pineview, in the Haven Hills Community.

Michael's maternal great-grandparents are the late Robert Henry and Ethel (Cotham) Wilsdorf, formerly of Pineview Community, both of whom are interred in the Pineview Cemetery on Tom's Creek in Pineview.

Michael's paternal great-grandparents are the late Miles L. Lawrence and Elizabeth Louisa (Bab) (Bell) Lawrence, formerly of the Pineview Community, both of whom are interred in the Bell-Robertson Cemetery.

Michael's maternal great-great-grandparents are the late Elmer Lewis and Mary (Smith) Wilsdorf formerly of the Pineview Community, both of whom are interred in the Coble Cemetery on King's Branch prong of Tom's Creek in Pineview.

Ira Herbert, Michael's father, was employed most of his life as a heavy equipment operator with several different construction companies, but in his latter years was employed with Lewis Products Co. in Hohenwald (Lewis County), TN. He passed away in 1981 at his home in Pineview and is interred in the Smith Memorial Cemetery on Tom's Creek in Pineview.

Dorothy (Wilsdorf), Michael's mother, was employed in her early years as a secretary with the Perry County A.S.C.S. office and also Perry Farmers Co-Op, but in her latter years, before retirement, was employed with Johnson Controls Inc. of Linden as a production employee. Dorothy still lives in her home in Pineview in the Haven Hills Community.

Roy Prentice, Michael's maternal grandfather, was employed most of his life as the manager of Perry Farmers Co-Op in Linden, and continued as a part-time employee after his retirement. He passed away in St. Thomas Hospital in Nashville, TN, in 1980.

Amie (Trull), Michael's maternal grandmother, was employed in her early years as a production employee with Washington D.C. Inc. in Linden, but in her latter years, before retirement, was employed with the Perry County School System as a cook at Pineview School.

Ira Acres, Michael's paternal grandfather, was employed most of his life as a farmer, but was employed part-time as a heavy equipment operator with Perry County Highway Department. He passed away in 1973.

Beulah (Patterson), Michael's paternal grandmother, spent her life as a homemaker and mother of 10 children, also she did odd jobs, such as sewing for her family and friends in the Pineview Community. She passed away in 1973.

Elmer Lewis, Michael's maternal great-great-grandfather, came to Perry County from Saxony, Germany in 1855. He was employed as a farmer in his early years, but in his latter years, was employed as a tanner with a big tanyard in the Wilsdorf Hollow prong of Tom's Creek in Pineview. He passed away at an early age in 1882.

Mary (Smith), Michael's maternal great-great-grandmother, came to Perry County from the state of Virginia with father, Charles Gotthardt, who established the first tannery in Perry County. She spent most of her life as a mother and a homemaker to nine children, five of whom only reached adulthood. She passed away in 1923 after living her latter years with her youngest son, Robert Henry and his family.

Miles L., Michael's paternal great-grandfather, served as a Confederate soldier during the Civil War, but the rest of his life was unknown to this writer.

Elizabeth Louisa (Babe) Bell, Michael's paternal great-grandmother, came to Perry County with her parents, John and Ester (McDaniel) Bell. It was said how she attained her nickname (Babe) was because she would carry one of her younger brothers or sisters on her hip when they were very young. (Babe) married Miles Lawrence on or about Jan. 30, 1873, and they had two children, Ira Acres and Molly. Molly married J. C. Mosher in 1924, of which very little is known other than he was a very good furniture maker, and a part-time preacher. *Submitted by Michael P. Lawrence*

LEDBETTER, According to the will of Henry Ledbetter, Brunswick County, VA, dated Sept. 23, 1749, he and his wife Edith (Williamson) Ledbetter had four children: Elizabeth (Ledbetter) Walton, Charles, Henry, and Drury Ledbetter.

Col. Drury Ledbetter, American Revolutionary War soldier, was born about 1734, Brunswick County, VA, and died about 1799 in Greensboro, Wilkes County, GA. He married Winifred, daughter of Sampson and Elizabeth (Chamberlain) Lanier about 1760. One of their 11 children was Rowland Ledbetter.

Rowland Ledbetter was born about 1764, probably in Brunswick County, VA, and died Sept. 2, 1842, in Madison County, TN. He married before 1787 to Sarah, daughter of Stephen and Mary Vaughn of Chesterfield County, SC. Children of Rowland and Sarah: Nancy, born

1787, married William Wilkins; Henry, (1789-1859), married Ann Phillips; Jesse, (1791-1855), married first Sallie Little and second Betsy Bowman; Wesson, (1793-1872), married first Nancy Wade and second Sarah Kimble; Rebecca, born 1795, married James Powell; Betsy, born 1797, married James Haislip, died Marshall County, TN; Henrietta, born 1799, died before 1860, married Laban Haislip; Isaac, born 1801, married first Sallie Acuff, second Martha Haynes, and third Emma Smith. Died in Perry County, TN; Katherine (1803-1835), married James McMullen; James Johnston, (1807-1865), married Jane Wade; William Riley, born 1810, died at age 23, married Eliza Meesy.

Henry Ledbetter, son of Rowland and Sarah, was born Oct. 28, 1789 in Robeson County, NC, and died May 12, 1859 in Perry County, TN. He married Ann Phillips in March 1812 in Anson County, NC. They emigrated to Lincoln County, TN (now Marshall) in 1818, then to Richland Creek in 1830, and finally to Perry County, TN, in 1837. Henry and Ann Ledbetter were the parents of 12 children: Matilda (1814-1878), married William Porter and moved to Delassus, St. Francois County, MO; Docia (1815-1851), never married; Susan, born in 1816, married Frank Baird and moved to Missouri; Betsy (1818-1887), married Samuel Young on April 10, 1837; James Pinkney, born 1820, married Mary Steel. Methodist minister and lawyer, lived in Perry County, TN.; Rueben Phillips (1822-1881), married Nancy Weems. Born in Marshall County, TN. Lived in Perry County, TN, then Delassus, St. Francois County, MO, with other family members for about two years, but moved back to Perry County, TN, in failing health where he died; Greene (1823-1901), married Lizzie Terry in 1844. He was a farmer in Perry County, TN; Manervia, born in 1824, married George Young and lived all her life in Perry County, TN; John (1825-1899), married Lizzie Tate in 1866; Sallie (1827-1871), married Abner Smith in 1864; Sophia (1829-1863), married Abner Smith, died in Perry County, TN; Henry McKendre (1830-1913), married Mary Vaughn in 1851. Lived all his life in Perry County, TN, as a farmer. He was also elected to the state senate in 1889.

LEDBETTER, One of the more prominent Perry Countians of the late 1800s and early 1900s was the Rev. H. McKendree Ledbetter, who lived on Lick Creek. When he died in 1916, it was written, "the county has lost one of its best loved and leading citizens, but his influence for good is not dead."

H. McKendree Ledbetter with wife (first or second) and granddaughter, Anna Sparks in mid 1890s.

The Ledbetter family is said to have sprung from three Irish brothers that emigrated to America and settled in Virginia and North Carolina about the year 1730. Rowland Ledbetter, who had been born in Virginia in 1764, moved first to North Carolina and then on to Lincoln County, TN, with his wife, Sarah, about 1811. Among their 11 children was Henry Ledbetter, born 1789.

After moving with his family to Tennessee, Henry returned to North Carolina briefly in 1812 to marry Ann Philips. Henry and Ann moved to Perry County in the early part of 1837. Their 12 children were mostly prosperous farmers, with two sons serving in the Tennessee State Legislature.

One of those two sons was H. McKendree Ledbetter. Born on Dec. 18, 1830, in Lincoln County, TN, McKendree was seven years old when he moved with his family to Lick Creek in Perry County. With no local schools, McKendree and his siblings were taught at home and it was later said that "he was a man of strong intellect." In 1852, he married Mary E. Vaughan, who had been born in 1833. They had 10 children, including twins Matilda and Minerva, born in 1869.

Like his brother Reuben Phillips Ledbetter, who had moved to Maury County around 1865 and was elected to the Tennessee State Legislature about 1867, McKendree was active in politics. He was elected to the Tennessee State Senate as a Republican in 1886, representing Perry, Hardin, Lawrence and Wayne counties. In the Senate, he was particularly well known as a zealous champion of the temperance cause. In 1892, he was ordained as a minister in the Methodist Episcopal Church (his brother James Pinkney also served as a Methodist minister).

McKendree was to have a son-in-law and grandson who also served in the Tennessee State Legislature. One of his twins, Minerva, married Jesse Sparks of Lick Crick, who served in the State House in 1909. Minerva and Jesse's son, Kent, also served in the State House in 1923.

After Mary Vaughan Ledbetter died in 1895, McKendree was remarried in 1897 to Nancy Shannon, who survived him at his death in 1916. At the time of his death, McKendree had 24 grandchildren, 34 great-grandchildren, and one great-great-grandchild. Among his many descendants was Kent Cartrite, a rancher in Sunray, TX. Kent is descended from McKendree and Mary's daughter Mary Ledbetter Hunt.

LEDBETTER, Lawrence A. was born on Big Spring creek in Perry County on Nov. 15, 1933. After his graduation from Linden's Perry County High School in 1953, he moved to Nashville where he still lives. On May 5, 1956, he married Velma Holt, the daughter of Jonie and Thelma Mercer Holt. Velma was born June 24, 1935, on Hurricane Creek and graduated from Lobelville High School in 1956. Lawrence and Velma have a son and daughter. Ricky Allen Ledbetter is married to the former Lori Hope. They have a son, Nicholas Allen, and live in New Port Richey, FL. Dara Lynn and her husband Dwayne Williams have a daughter, Laura Shannon, and live in White House, TN.

Lawrence has done extensive research on the Ledbetter family genealogy and is a charter member of the Perry County Historical Society. His lineal ancestors in Perry County are:

Father. James Allen Ledbetter. Born April 17, 1890. Died Jan. 18, 1976. His wife, Laura Sue Hunt, born April 8, 1902. Died Aug. 23, 1991.

Lawrence and Velma Ledbetter in 1954.

Grandfather. Abram Harwell (Dick) Ledbetter. Born June 15, 1865. Died Nov. 23, 1940. His wife, Matilda Catherine Ledbetter, born Jan. 30, 1866. Died Oct. 16, 1947.

Great-grandfather. Coleman Harwell Ledbetter. Born Feb. 6, 1844. Died Oct. 21, 1927. His wife, Docia Ann Ledbetter, born Dec. 10, 1845. Died April 24, 1928.

Great-great-grandfather. Abram Harwell (Bud) Ledbetter. Born about 1825 in Tennessee. His wife's name was Anne.

Great-great-great-grandfather. Wesson Ledbetter. Born March 1793 in Anson County, NC. Came to Perry County in 1836. Died about 1872. His wife, Sarah Kimble. *Submitted by Lawrence A. Ledbetter.*

RUEBEN PHILLIPS LEDBETTER, son Henry and Ann (Phillips) Ledbetter was born Jan. 21, 1822 in Marshall County, TN. On March 4, 1847, Rueben was married to Nancy Weems in Perry County, TN. In 1865, they emigrated to Maury County, TN, where Rueben became a farmer. He was elected to the Tennessee legislature about 1867. Later, they moved to Williamson County, TN, for three years before moving to Delassus, St. Francois County, MO, early in 1880. He returned to Perry County, TN, in 1881, for health reasons, and died there on Nov. 8, 1881. Family records state he was buried at the family burying ground with his parents. They are buried in the Young Cemetery outside of Pineview, TN. Rueben and Nancy were the parents of nine children, all born in Perry County, TN, except for their last child, Mary, born in Maury County, TN.

1) Hartwell Brown (Feb. 6, 1848-Nov. 18, 1925). After law school at Lebanon, TN, he emigrated to Farmington, St. Francois County, MO, where he practiced law and married Georgiana Williams on Dec. 23, 1884.

2) Nancy Ann (Sept. 4, 1849-April 8, 1880). Married John Kinzer on Sept. 18, 1867, Maury County, TN; lived there for nine years before moving to Delassus, St. Francois County, MO, where she died.

3) Robert Payne born on March 12, 1852. Farmed in Tennessee, Missouri, and Kentucky before returning to Perry County, TN, where he married Mary Ann Ledbetter on Sept. 21, 1891.

4) Mattie Manervia, born Jan. 25, 1854. Moved to Maury County, TN, with her family; married there to James Bunch on Oct. 21, 1875.

5) John Adams (Oct. 19, 1856-June 26, 1858) twin brother of Henry Clay, died of whooping cough.

6) Henry Clay, born Oct. 19, 1856. Moved to Williamson County at age 20 where he married Allie May McKinley on Jan. 28, 1880. Farmed in Tennessee, Missouri, and Kentucky. His first wife died and he married Mary Eloise Wilson of Williamson County, TN, on April 12, 1899. They lived in Robertson County, TN.

7) Clara Webster (Feb. 22, 1859-March 26, 1932) moved to Maury and Williamson County, TN, before emigrating to Delassus, St. Francois County, MO, in 1880, where she married Francis Marion Hastings on April 24, 1881. Four grown children: Francis Kossuth (1887-1946); Grace Hastings Lashley (1892-1971); August Dewitt (1895-1940); George Lee (born 1899).

8) Sallie Elizabeth, born Dec. 2, 1861; lived in Maury and Williamson County, TN. Married Rufus C. Tucker in Williamson County, Jan. 17, 1878. Emigrated to Farmington, St. Francois County, MO, where Rufus was a lawyer and judge.

9) Mary Ganaway Hamilton, born Dec. 2, 1865; married Felix D. Robertson on Jan. 2, 1880, in Williamson County, TN. Lived in Missouri, Tennessee, and Texas before settling in Arkansas where Felix died in 1904. There are many descendants of Rueben and Nancy (Weems) Ledbetter still residing in St. Francois County, MO.

LEE-ROGERS, Morris Donald Lee was born April 2, 1920, in Lobelville, TN, to Hansom Albert Lee and Maggie Ethel Sweatt. They lived mostly on Lagoon in Perry County. He attended school in Lobelville. He entered the service in June 1941 and served as a sergeant in the U.S. Army until September 1945. He fought in World War II. He married Mary Rue Rogers on Aug. 1, 1942, in Corinth, MS. Mary Rue was the daughter of John Louis Rogers and Cora Qualls. She was born Nov. 16, 1923, in Linden, TN. She attended school in Linden, Perry County, TN.

Morris Donald Lee and wife Mary Rue Rogers Lee in 1957.

Morris and Mary Rue lived mostly in Perry County. He worked some in Michigan during the '50s at the automobile plants as there weren't very many jobs here. They lived several years in Mud Spring Hollow in Lobelville, TN. Their children attended school there. He worked cutting and hauling timber, farming and drove the school bus. He died in his home on Nov. 17, 1964.

Mary Rue worked in factories, restaurants and at the hospital before her retirement. She now lives on Shelton St. in Linden, TN. They had six children together: Jesse Morris Lee, June 9, 1943; Teddy Gene Lee, Oct. 21, 1946; Betty Joyce Lee Culp, Sept. 11, 1949; Karen Fay Lee Gilley, Oct. 14, 1952; Nathan Louis Lee, July 18, 1956; Troy Lynn Lee, Nov. 3, 1961.

The family continues to grow. Mary Rue now has 17 grandchildren, and nine great-grandchildren and another one due in July.

LEE-SWEATT, Hansom Albert Lee married Maggie Ethel Sweatt in Lobelville, TN. They had 11 children together: Clyde Douglas, Ollie L. Whitehead, Mary Lou L. Myatt, Eunice Pearl L. Andrews, Morris Donald, H. B. (Henry Benjamin), Raymond, Rudolph, Eliza Bell L. Bandy, James Randel, and John Madison.

They lived most of their lives on Lagoon in Perry County, TN. He worked in the wood cutting timber. She was busy raising a garden trying to feed so many. He died in 1953. She lived until February 1980. They are buried at the Curry Cemetery in Lobelville near their home. They had a large family and their children have carried on the tradition. Their grandchildren number 34.

AARON LEWIS FAMILY, It is generally accepted that the Lewis family is of Welsh descent. Early Lewises from North Carolina were among the first settlers in Perry County. George Lewis came to Tennessee through the Cumberland Gap and settled in the Yellow Creek District of Dickson County.

George served for a time as the overseer of a road construction project in the Yellow Creek District. George had a son, Aaron, born July 14, 1794, died Feb. 17, 1848. Other children? Both George and Aaron frequently served as jurors during county court sessions in Dickson County.

Aaron married Polly Ann Dickson, born 1792, died May 16, 1866. No documented "proof" has been located which establishes Polly as James Dickson's daughter, but there was a close association between the Lewises and the Dicksons. Additionally, Aaron and Polly had a son named James Dickson Lewis.

When Perry County was organized, the group met at the home of James Dickson in the Lick Creek Community on the first Monday of January 1820. Aaron Lewis was elected the first county trustee. He was a veteran of the War of 1812. He was buried on a hill at the lower end of what was known in 1930 as the John Myatt farm on Lick Creek. To the union of Aaron and Polly, 10 children were born: (A) James Wilson, born April 18, 1817; (B) Elizabeth A., born Sept. 5, 1818, died 1867; (C) William Kennedy, born May 3, 1820, died March 23, 1892, buried Starbuck (old Lewis) Cemetery, Cypress Creek Community in Perry County. He was born in Dickson County, TN, moved to Perry County and farmed along Cypress Creek. During the Civil War, he served as a Confederate in the 42nd Regiment of Tennessee Infantry. He married Susana J. (Janie) Coleman, (born 1829, Hickman County, TN) in 1844. They had four children: Abner, married Martha Owen; Jim, married Minnie Dickson; Walker, married Jennie Goblet; and Franklin.

(D) John Tipton, born May 17, 1822, married Ann (maiden name unknown), lived in the Pineview Community. They had three children: William Russel, Nancy Harriet, and unknown daughter.

(E) Sanice, born April 16, 1824, died in infancy.

(F) James Dickson Lewis, born July 3, 1825, died May 21, 1891. Married Elizabeth Lavina (Betsy) Coleman, born Sept. 18, 1830, died Nov. 21, 1886. Betsy was the daughter of Abner Coleman and Mary Polly Sparks and the sister of Janie Coleman. They lived in the Deer Creek Community near Pineview. James Dickson Lewis was a farmer and blacksmith and is buried in the Starbuck Cemetery. They had eight children: 1) Mary Jane, born March 8, 1851, died Jan. 31, 1915, married William Tom Weems. 2) W. R. (Billy), born Oct. 27, 1853, married Josephine Brady. 3) John Aaron, born Sept. 9, 1856, married Laura Francis Weems, born Jan. 26, 1870, died March 27, 1931. She was the daughter of Walton Weems and Jane Bully. 4) John D., born Nov. 24, 1861. 5) G. R. (George), born Feb. 20, 1859, married Malinda Turnbo. 6) Christian, born April 9, 1866. 7) Martha (Mattie) Hale, born April 18, 1869, died June 8, 1908, married W. B. (Will) Ledbetter. 8) Susan Forrest, born May 17, 1874, married Ed Coleman.

(G) Maragret, born Sept. 5, 1829.

(H) Mary Harriet, born Feb. 17, 1830, died March 28, 187?.

(I) Coleman, born about 1833, married Mary Mays. They had three children: Coleman Jr., born 1863, died 1937, married Jeannie Dickson, born 1872, died 1940; James, married Maggie Patterson; Mattie, married Pleas Horner.

(J) George, born 1834, died of TB.

CECIL VIRGIL LEWIS, (Great-grandson of Aaron and Polly Lewis) Cecil Virgil Lewis was the sixth of seven children born to the union of John Aaron and Laura F. Weems Lewis. His date of birth was Nov. 23, 1905 on Spring Creek, Perry County. Early years were spent farming. He died Nov. 12, 1980.

Cecil married Emma Lauis Horner Howard who was born Oct. 1, 1907, also in Perry County. She was one of three children born to Jesse and Emma Heath Horner. Lauis, Martha and Cecil were each adopted by different families in the area following the death of their parents. Lauis was reared by Benjamin R. and Florence Howard. Lauis died Jan. 25, 1974.

Four children were born to Cecil and Lauis:

1) Florence Francis, born Sept. 26, 1927, in Spring Hill, TN. She married Hugh Cearley who was born Sept. 30, 1921, and died Jan. 24, 1994. They had one child, Phillip Denton, born Aug. 9, 1957, who married Betty Galloway, born March 9, 1956, on Aug. 3, 1978.

2) Robert Virgil (Buddy), born Aug. 24, 1929, in Spring Hill, TN, and died June 16, 1992. He served in the Korean War in the U.S. Navy. Upon returning from the Navy, he married Nell Hinson, born Aug. 27, 1933. They had one son, Dennis Lane, born Nov. 19, 1956.

3) John Howard (Tony), born Aug. 8, 1933, in Perry County and married Freida June Whitwell, born June 1, 1935. Freida was the daughter of Kent Franklin and Evelyn Duncan Whitwell. This family is documented elsewhere in this volume.

4) Freddie Gene Lewis, born July 6, 1938, on Cypress Creek, married Wardie Mercer, born Jan. 7, 1938, daughter of Hershal and Dorothy Mercer of Perry County. They were married Aug. 24, 1957. They have two sons: 1) Roger Dale, born Feb. 27, 1959, married Rosa Blaylock, born March 9, 1961. They have two daughters, Keely, born July 3, 1984 and Rachel, born Sept. 30, 1988. 2) Nick Anthony, born June 1, 1964, married Julie Burkett, born Dec. 26, 1964. They have two children, Cara, born Aug. 20, 1987 and Burk, born Aug. 28, 1990.

EDWARD ALLEN LEWIS, (Great-grandson of Aaron and Polly Lewis), Edward Allen (Ed) Lewis, born Oct. 19, 1899, died Oct. 11, 1979, was the son of John Aaron Lewis and Laura Francis Weems Lewis. He married Edna C. French, born may 27, 1904, died May 5, 1993, daughter of William Thomas French and James Ada Shepard French. They had one son, John William Lewis.

Ed was a farmer and also bought and sold cedar posts. He sold the posts that were used to erect a fence around Davy Crockett's mother's grave in West Tennessee. In the 1960s Ed and Edna owned and operated Lewis' Cafe on Hwy. 100 in the Cypress Creek Community. They continued in this business until they retired.

Their son, John William Lewis, born April 11, 1922, died Nov. 17, 1968, married Irene Tillman, born Aug. 1, 1922. She is the daughter of Jesse Lee Tillman and Mallie Jane (Sallie) Patterson Tillman. John William was the owner and operator of Lewis' Garage at the corner of Main and Mill Streets in Linden until his death, at the age of 46, in 1968. Irene worked at various garment factories in both Perry and Decatur counties, at Fox Furniture Company in Linden and at Johnson Control's Linden Products Division from which she retired in about 1988. John William and Irene have two children:

A) Ronald Boyce (Ronnie) Lewis, born Dec. 19, 1946, married Barbara Jo Wharton, born 1950, on July 5, 1968. She is the daughter of the Rev. Yancy and Faye Wharton. Ronnie and Barbara have one daughter, Telesa D'Shan Lewis, and divorced in 1971: 1) Telesa D'Shan Lewis, born March 15, 1970, married Michael Dillenger. They lived in California and have one son: Chase Michael Dillenger, born Feb. 28, 1990. Michael also has a daughter, Shanoah, born 1988, who lives with them. Ronnie later married Virginia Ward (Ginny) Martin, born Sept. 11, 1952, on June 8, 1974. She is the daughter of Edmond Duke (Bud) Martin and Marion Ward of Jackson, TN. Ronnie and Ginny have two daughters: Rebecca Ann Lewis, born Sept. 30, 1976; and Sara Lynn Lewis, born Aug. 22, 1980. Ronnie is a pharmacist and partner in the Super D Drug Store chain. Ronnie and Ginny live in Germantown, TN, and own and operate two Subway restaurants.

B) Sherry Lynn Lewis, born July 10, 1950, married George Allen Lineberry, born Aug. 22, 1944. He is the son of Robert Irvin Lineberry and Grace Pauline Bunch Lineberry of the Whiteoak Creek Community. They live in Huntsville, AL, where George is an engineer at the U.S. Army Missile Command and Sherry is a cosmetologist and the owner and operator of Sherry's Beauty Shop. They have three children: Amanda Lynette, born June 9, 1970; George Allen Jr. (Allen), born April 27, 1971; and Aimee Lavonne, born July 29, 1979.

JOHN AARON LEWIS, born Sept. 9, 1856, died 1928, is the son of James Dickson Lewis, born July 3, 1825, and Elizabeth Lavina (Betsy) Coleman, born Sept. 18, 1830. He married Laura Francis Weems, born Jan. 26, 1870, died March 27, 1931. She is the daughter of Walton Weems and Jane Bully. They have seven children:

(A) Mary Magruder, born Dec. 9, 1888, married Dick Weems. They have four children: 1) Aubry, never married; 2) Harold, married Susie Clifton. They have four children: Harley, Magruder Ann, Bruce and Annette. 3) Dean, married Grace Hamm, no children. 4) Otis, married Frankie Lee. They had three children: Janice Gail, Randy and Robbie Dean.

(B) Jesse Walton (Jess), born Oct. 23, 1891, married Calvin (Cal) Barber. They have four children: 1) Herman, married Hazel Strickland. They have five children: Archie, David, Paul and twins Jean and Jean. 2) Lucille, married ? Hickerson. They had two children: Leonard and Arnold. 3) Thurman, married ? 4) Louise, married ?

(C) Lena Vermont, born Sept. 17, 1894, died Dec. 15, 1968, married Wess Gabbard. One son, John Pershing (J. P.) who never married.

(D) Fred Augustus, born March 9, 1897, died Dec. 26, 1920, married Dixie Beasley. One daughter: Venice, married ? Birdsong. They had three children: Jerry, Barbara and Donnie.

(E) Edward Allen (Ed), born Oct. 19, 1899, died Oct. 11, 1979, married Edna C. French, born May 27, 1904, died May 5, 1993. Listed separately in this volume.

(F) Cecil Virgil, born Nov. 23, 1905, died Nov. 12, 1980, married Emma Lauis Horner, born Oct. 1, 1907, died Jan. 25, 1974. Listed separately in this volume.

(G) Lois, born 1908, died 1931, married Joe Starbuck. One daughter, Mary Neal, who married ? Sadler. They have three children: Joseph Mark, Rebecca Rhea and Suzanne Marie.

JOHN HOWARD LEWIS, (Tony), born Aug. 8, 1933, one of four children of late Cecil Virgil Lewis and Lauis Horner Howard, adopted daughter of Benjamin R. and Florence Howard. John (Tony) married on Sept. 17, 1954 to Freida Jane Whitwell, born June 1, 1935, daughter of Kent and Evelyn Duncan Whitwell.

John and Freida, both natives of Perry County, now reside on lower Cypress Creek near the Tennessee River where they reared their three children. John and Freida are rich in their faith in God, have been blessed with their loving children and grandsons. John served three years, 1951-54, in the U.S. Navy in the Korean War. Freida's occupation – housewife and N.A. for 10 years. John, a great lover of hunting and fishing (descendant of pioneer John Lewis). Freida, a lover of reading and writing, inherited from Ramey grandmother, Mercy L. Ramey Duncan.

Jill, born Oct. 14, 1956, married James Terry Duke on May 1, 1978. Terry was born Dec. 8, 1954. They reside in Decatur County. Jill has two sons: Jacob Lewis Duke, born Nov. 23, 1982, and James Seth Duke, born Jan. 25, 1985. Jill's occupation is R.N. manager out-patient D.C.G.H., graduate of Baptist Nursing School.

Rose Ann Moore, born April 13, 1959, married Timothy Albert Holt on May 29, 1977, divorced. Married Lynn Ray Moore on Dec. 18, 1987, born April 15, 1960. Rose's occupation is office manager over placement of foster children in Jackson, TN. Went two years college at A.P.S.U.

Johnny Whit, born Nov. 2, 1962, married Irene Moore Ward on Jan. 8, 1993, born Nov. 19, 1953. He is a graduate of A.P.S.U. Assistant manager U.S. Fish and Wildlife Refuge in New Johnsonville, TN. Resides in Perry County. *Submitted by Johnny Whit Lewis*

LEWIS, Martha Sue (Lewis) Barber, born 1931, the daughter of Clint Atlas Lewis and Sally Augusta (Qualls) Lewis. Their two children, Jo Theo (Lewis) Mathis, Martha Sue (Lewis) Barber. The granddaughter of Joe T. Lewis, was born 1875 and Izora (Barber) Lewis born 1870. Joe T. was a farmer, logger and lumber hauler with team and wagon Hohenwald, TN. My father, Clint A. Lewis, born in 1901, farmed and hauled lumber with team and wagon, later a truck, to Hohenwald, TN. My and Jo's great-grandfather, James K. P. Lewis, born in 1847 in Kentucky, great-grandmother Louisa was born in 1850 in Tennessee. James K. P. logged with a team of oxen, in his day. Ken and Martha Sue have some of the ox shoes. They were found in the hollow in back of their home on Coon Creek. They have found five half of the shoes. My father, Clint Atlas Lewis, died at home in 1933 with appendicitis when I, Martha Sue, was two years old.

Augusta and Clint Lewis

I, Martha Sue Lewis, married Kenneth H. Barber in 1948. We have four children: 1) Lema Lou (Barber) Malkowski, born Sept. 28, 1949, husband Donald Malkowski, born March 25, 1948. They married June 22, 1968, and they have three children: David Scott, born Dec. 10, 1968; LaDonna Sue, born Dec. 17, 1969; Robert Donald, born May 4, 1971. They live in Clarksville, TN. Lema Lou works at Ford Glass Plant in Nashville, TN. 2) Kenneth Deone Barber, born Sept. 2, 1954. Deceased at birth and is buried in Qualls Cemetery, Brush Creek. 3) Ramonia Sue (Barber) Sanders, born Aug. 10, 1955 in Detroit, MI. Married James Douglas Sanders, born June 28, 1952. They married June 8, 1974. They have two sons, Adam who was born Oct. 13, 1977, and Noah who was born Aug. 9, 1984. Ramonia is a nurse. She worked several years for Dr. Turner and is now working for Perry Home Health. 4) Kenneth H. Barber Jr., born June 23, 1957, in Detroit, MI. He married Kathy (Stump) Barber. They had one son, Jason, born June 23, 1982. He is now married to

Sherley (Highman) Barber and has four step-sons – Shane, Shadd, Shawn and Shasten Highman. Kenneth Jr. spent 10 years in U.S. Air Force as crew chief, now employed with CCA Correctional Center at Clifton, TN, as a guard.

Kenneth and Martha Sue were married Sept. 25, 1948, at Corinth, MS, in the courthouse, still standing today. They were married by Howard Plaxico, J.P. They went to Detroit on July 15, 1950, spent 10 years there. My husband worked as a mechanic. They then moved to Waynesboro, TN on July 17, 1960. He worked there as mechanic for Barnett Motor Co., one year while building our present home in Perry County on Coon Creek. Then worked as mechanic and sawmill operator until present time. I, Martha Sue Barber, worked at Washington garment plant and Linden Products, until 1979, where I injured my hand and now I am a housekeeper.

I lost my father at two years old and my mother raised my sister and me alone. She was a widow the rest of her life. She was 88 years old at her death, Aug. 13, 1992. She was the daughter of Wilburn and Nannie (Barber) Qualls. She had one sister, Maudie (Qualls) Parnell. Gusta (Qualls) Lewis was buried in the Qualls Cemetery by her husband on Brush Creek, 1992. She was born and raised on Brush Creek. Clint and Gusta Lewis had five grandchildren and seven great-grandchildren. Besides Kenneth and Martha's children, Joe Theo Mathis and Floyd W. Mathis married Aug. 8, 1942, in Corinth, MS, by Johnnie Jobe, J.P. They had one son, Bert Lewis Mathis, a Church of Christ preacher, born Dec. 17, 1945. He married Judy (Barber) Mathis, born Sept. 9, 1947. They have two children, Robert Lewis Mathis, born May 8, 1970; Jerry Elizabeth, born Sept. 25, 1975. They all live in Hickman County.

My father, Clint Atlas Lewis had two brothers – John L. Lewis, born 1896, and Frank Lewis, born 1898. John L. Lewis married Eve (Shelton) Lewis. Frank married Maggie (Qualls) Lewis. Johnnie and Eve had three children: Alice, Mary Ruth, and Hershel. Frank and Maggie had two children: Ima Jane and Joe Henry. Joe T. Lewis has one brother, James Carroll Lewis, born in 1879. His wife, Etta (Gladden) Lewis, born in 1883.

They married on Aug. 8, 1902, Bond Book. They have seven children: Mary, born 1905; Leonard, born 1907; Strazzy, born 1909; Jim, born 1912; Fannie, born 1915; Marie, born 1917; Etheal, born 1919. They lived in Trenton, TN. This information is from census of Perry County and to the best of my knowledge. *Submitted by Martha Sue Barber*

WILLIAM WALKER LEWIS,

son of William Kennedy and Jane Coleman Lewis, documented elsewhere in the volume, born July 15, 1864, married to Eugenia Margaret Gobelet. Eugenia (Genia) taught school and was a seamstress. Walker farmed, was a merchant and worked at a spoke factory in Jackson, TN. To this union was born nine girls.

1) Ola Ann, born on Cypress Creek, an LPN married to James Swan Williams. Two children: (A) Clara Ann, married to W. T. Brewer with two children: William Thomas Brewer III and Geneva Ann Brewer. (B) Lucy Jane, married to Harold Holland Hawks with six children: Harold Holland, married to Mary Ann Flowers and to Donna Belton; Catherine Lynn, married to James Gaylon Johnson; James Walter, married to Valerie Henry and Patti Bryers; Mark William, married to Anne Sanford Hooper; Labina Lee, married to James Farrar Maxwell; and Patricia Ann, married to Jeffrey Watkins and John Herron McLemore.

2) Ima Sue, born in Hohenwald, TN, teacher, married to Ernest Terry Barnes, one child: Eugenia Alley, married to Clifford Oneal Longmire, one child – Terry Lee who married Cindy Hogan.

3) Hazel Elizabeth, homemaker, married to Gaylord Wilshire Humphries, seven children: (A) Margaret Elizabeth, married to Billy Balentine and Harold Adams, four children: Elizabeth Anne Balentine, married Norman A. Robe; Margaret Elaine Adams, married Allen G. Hardy; Sarah Katherine Adams, married Robert Ray Eepley; Harriet Eugenia Adams, married Tommy Cecil Carter Jr. (B) Mary Wilodean, married to James W. Woods, three children: Constance Dean, married Terry William Bredgman; James W. Woods Jr., married to Georgia; Cynthia Lee. (C) Gaylord W., married to Bernice Elderburg, two children: Pamela Jean, married to Wayne Victor Vail; Gaylord Dietrick; (D) Douglas Daniel, married Eleanor Oliver, one child: Debria, married Frederick D. Blackburn. (E) Labina, married Hansell Edwin Doster, two sons: Edwin Gaylord and Gilbert Clay. (F) Helen Elizabeth, married Robert T. Cowart, five children: Robbie Dianne, married Shelton S. McCord Jr.; Brenda Gail, married Berton Josh Thomas; Glen Michael; Robert Darell; Lisa Brigetta. (G) Lewis Adair, married Evelyn Roach, two children: Terresa Sheryl and Sherlia Denice.

4) Nora Lee, deceased.

5) Labina Clair, an LPN, married Albertus Outlaw, no children.

6) Mary Augustus, teacher, married John David Roberts, one son: John David Jr., married Barbara Ann Veter, one child – Matthew John.

(7) William Margaret, married Duncan Berry Temple, one child: Susan Gayle, married James D. Cruzen, and to Kenneth Dewayne Cook, one child: Brian Duncan Cruzen.

LINEBARGER/LINEBERRY,

Perry Linebarger (age 60+) first appeared in the Tennessee census records in 1830 in Wayne County. Ages of males in the household of Peter match the ages of Tobias and Henry Linebarger who were first listed as heads of households in 1840 and 1850 respectively. This appears to discredit the stories told about Tobias and Henry being the first two Linebargers to come to this area. The name may have been either Lineberger or Leinberger.

Tobias, born 1810, died 1873-79, and Henry, born 1820, died Dec. 27, 1866, married sisters, Nancy, born 1821, died 1870-73, and Winnie Whellus (Wheelas? Wheelar? Wheeler?), born 1830, died Aug. 7, 1891. Census records indicate that the husbands were born in North Carolina, but the wives were born in Tennessee. Both couples initially lived in Wayne County in the Flatwoods area. Henry and Winnie later moved to Perry County, still in the Flatwoods area. The families' names first appeared as Lineberry in the 1870 census.

Children of Tobias and Nancy (birth dates are taken from census records and are approximate) are: Peter Jasper, born 1837; James Allen, born 1840; Mary Jane, born 1842; John, born 1844; Rebecca A., born 1846; Elizabeth, born 1848 (died as infant); Thomas B., born 1852; Samuel Houston, born 1855; David H., born 1857; Isaac Wheelar**, born 1859; Emily, born 1862.

Henry and Winnie's children are: Elizabeth Jane, born Dec. 16, 1847, died ?; Charley, born Feb. 18, 1850, died 1921; Isaac Wheelus**, born Jan. 5, 1852, died July 30, 1940; William RoAnn (Rowan?), born Oct. 25, 1853, died Dec. 1, 1928; Mary Ann, born Sept. 17, 1855, died October 1857; Henry Martin, born Jan. 10, 1857, died October 1857; Phebe Malinda, born Aug. 10, 1859, died Dec. 21, 1940; Jefferson Davis, born Oct. 6, 1862, died Jan. 24, 1941; Mary Parlee, born Nov. 15, 1864, died March 1865; Henry Allen, born Sept. 11, 1866, died Jan. 22, 1950, married Oct. 26, 1890 to Florence Levona Evans, born Nov. 29, 1875, died June 25, 1962, of the White Oak Creek Community in 1890. Florence was the daughter of James W. Evans and Sara Davidson.

**Note: *It seems unlikely that brothers (Tobias and Henry) would each name a son (double first cousins) Isaac Wheelas, yet both appear in census records. Henry's Isaac was born in 1852; Tobias' Isaac in 1859.*

Henry Allen and Florence lived on what maps show today as the Lineberry Fork of White Oak Creek, and became known as "Uncle Bud" and "Aunt Florence." To this marriage was born 12 children with 11 living to adulthood. Those 11 were:

(A) Ora Myrtle, born July 2, 1820?, died 1891, married first Jeff Keeling and second Amos Culp. Children: Willard Keeling, Myrtle Culp, Levona Culp, Elzona Culp, A. C. Culp.

(B) Esley Bradford, born March 26, 1893, married Minnie Lee Richardson. Children: Andrew, Mary Love, W. H. (Bache), Arlis, Ira, Mildred Jean.

(C) Carrie Elizabeth (Bess), born April 30, 1895, married Oscar (Red) Warren. Children: James, Audrey, Guy, Edsel.

(D) Jimmie Parthenia, born Aug. 17, 1897, married Robert Alvin (Tip) Inman, Children: Willie, P. J., Vernell, Viola, Johnny.

(E) John Dee, born June 21, 1899, married Vera Gladys Engler. Children: Gary Darrel, Ronald Allen (Buck), Donna Lee, Jackie Doran.

(F) Robert Irvin, born Dec. 24, 1901, died April 25, 1990, married Grace Pauline Bunch, born Dec. 6, 1912, died March 4, 1993. Children: George Allen Lineberry, Bobby Irvin Lineberry.

(G) Winnie Ethel, born Feb. 22, 1904, married Grady Issac Wheat. Children: Wilma, Reva, Roberta, Douglas Eugene, Vera Dee, Johnny Wayne.

(H) Nina Lee, born July 27, 1907, married Elvis Warren. Children: Edith, R. D., Wilford.

(I) Henry Vernon, born April 6, 1910, never married.

(J) Eldora (L. Dora), born July 15, 1913, married Atlas Skellion.

(K) Opal Louise, born Nov. 21, 1916, married Hillard Wilson Bunch. Children: Norma Faye, Linda Kay. *Submitted by George A. Lineberry Sr.*

IRVIN AND GRACE LINEBERRY,

Robert Irvin Lineberry, born Dec. 24, 1901, died April 25, 1990, is the son of Henry Allen Lineberry, born Sept. 11, 1866, died Jan. 22, 1950, and Florence Levona Evans, born Nov. 29, 1875, died June 25, 1962. He and Grace Pauline Bunch, born Dec. 6, 1912, died March 4, 1993, were married April 8, 1936. She is the daughter of George LeRoy Bunch, born Aug. 8, 1890, died March 22, 1963, and Nora Steele, born Oct. 4, 1894, died 1948/49.

Irvin and Grace were both from the White Oak Creek Community in Perry County. They settled in the community where he farmed, worked at sawmills and later sharecropped with George S. Sewell; she taught school in the county elementary schools. In early 1944 they moved to Ypsilanti, MI, near Detroit. Irvin worked at Ford's Willow Run airplane plant, and their first child was born during the 15-month stay in Ypsilanti. They returned to the White Oak Creek Community in the Spring of 1945.

In 1948 they bought a small farm and grocery store from Moncy Denton Clifton. Irvin farmed and operated the store until 1979; Grace was the postmaster of the Peters Landing Post Office from 1948 until it closed in 1956 or 1957. She then taught school at Lobelville, Lego and Cedar Creek elementary schools until her retirement. They have two sons, George Allen, born Aug. 22, 1944 and Bobby Irvin Lineberry, born Sept. 20, 1951.

George Allen married Sherry Lynn Lewis, born July 10, 1950, on Dec. 14, 1968. She is the daughter of John William Lewis and Irene Tillman Lewis.

Upon graduation from college (Tennessee Technological University) in 1967, George Allen moved to Huntsville, AL. He was employed first by the National Aeronautics and Space Administration's (NASA) Marshall Space Flight Center and from 1968 until the present by the U.S. Army Missile Command, also located at Huntsville.

George and Sherry's children are: Amanda Lynette, born June 9, 1970; George Allen Jr. (Allen), born April 27, 1971; and Aimee Lavonne, born July 29, 1979.

Bobby Irvin married Carolyn Jean Weatherly Coble, born March 17, 1949, on Oct. 20, 1978. She is the daughter of Ewell Brown Weatherly and Estell Loggins Weatherly. In 1980, Bobby and Carolyn moved to Huntsville where Bobby, also a graduate of Tennessee Technological University, too is employed by the U.S. Army Missile Command.

Sherry and Carolyn, both cosmetologists, built, owned and operated The Beauty Hut until family demands required more time at home. Later they each operated Sherry's Beauty Shop and Carolyn's Beauty Shop which were located at /in their respective homes. Bobby and Carolyn's children are: (1) Regina Mae Coble Lineberry, born June 20, 1968, married Carl Glenn (Glenn) Peacock, born Sept. 21, 1969. They have two children: Brandon Glenn, born April 8, 1991, and Britanny Mason, born Oct. 21, 1992. (2) Sebrina Dale Coble Lineberry, born Nov. 20, 1970, married Ronald Eugene (Ronnie) Smith, born March 16, 1969. They have one son, Ronnie Kason, born Feb. 2, 1993. *Submitted by George A. (Allen) Lineberry Jr.*

JOHN DEE LINEBERRY,

born June 21, 1899, died Jan. 27, 1980, is the son of Henry Allen Lineberry, born Sept. 11, 1866, died Jan. 22, 1950, and Florence Levona Evans, born Nov. 20, 1875, died June 25, 1962.

John grew up in the White Oak Creek Community in Perry County where he worked at sawmills and taught school. In approximately 1928, he moved to Ohio where he met Vera Gladys Engler, born March 11, 1899, died March 27, 1992 and they were married on April 27, 1929. John worked for the American Sheet & Tin Plate Company and beautiful Tuscora Park located in New Philadelphia. After the steel company closed, John went to Akron, OH, and became a machinist in the Wheel & Brake Division of Goodyear Aircraft. Vera stayed home most of the time, however, sewed and cleaned house for others to supplement their income. They have one daughter and three sons: Donna Lee Lineberry, born Oct. 24, 1929; Ronald Allen Lineberry, born March 4, 1931; Gary Darrell Lineberry, born Nov. 5, 1932; and Jackie Doran Lineberry, born April 9, 1935.

Donna Lee married Henry Lloyd Muehlhoffer, born Feb. 15, 1926, died May 27, 1974, on Sept. 13, 1947. They had no children. Henry served two years in the U.S. Navy during W.W.II and then worked for a hardwood flooring company until he decided to become a barber. Donna was a secretary for the Timken Company until retirement in 1990.

Ronald Allen (Buck) married Janet Ferguson Lineberry, born Oct. 11, 1958, on June 25, 1977. They have no children. Ronald and his first wife, Carolyn Sue Casteel, have two children. (1) Daughter, Rondee Lou Lineberry, born Nov. 26, 1956, married Mark Kappler, born Dec. 19, 1954, on Aug. 5, 1976 and they have three children: Angela, born March 7, 1977, Able, born July 31, 1981 and Aaron born June 3, 1983. (2) Son, Michael Allen Lineberry, born Aug. 7, 1953, married Karen Correll (divorced). They have a son, Michael, born May 3, 1977.

Ronald (Buck) served in the U.S. Army during the Korean conflict and is a machinist for The Timken Company.

Gary Darrell married Evelyn Sheets Lineberry, born June 29, 1936, on Nov. 3, 1956, and they have one daughter. (1) Kathy Sue Lineberry, born May 13, 1957, married Steven Barry, born Sept. 6, 1957, died Sept. 26, 1986. They have two children: Steven, born Sept. 18, 1988, and Emily, born March 23, 1991.

Gary served four years in the U.S. Air Force and has recently retired from a tool supply company where he was service parts manager.

Jackie Doran (Jack) married Jean Collinsworth, born April 24, 1942, died Feb. 16, 1985, on Sept. 19, 1961. They have two sons and one daughter. (1) Jackie Doran Lineberry Jr., born Oct. 30, 1962, married Dena Adkins, born Nov. 4, 1968, May 22, 1986. They have three children: Aliesha Rae, born Oct. 7, 1986; Deanna Jean, born Oct. 27, 1987; Devin Joshua, born Sept. 10, 1991. (2) John Gary Lineberry, born June 23, 1967. (3) Stacey Lynne Lineberry, born March 2, 1971.

Jack served four years in the U.S. Army and has recently retired from Goodyear Air Craft where he worked in the Mail Delivery Department.

LOMAX,

Samuel Lomax was born in 1762 and died in Perry County in 1833. He married Temperance Bugg, daughter of John and Elizabeth Bugg. He helped explore and settle the area known as Hickman County and named some of the creeks in the area. He and Temperance had nine children, their first being John Lomax.

(Left to right) Elsie, Ida, Robert Allen, Mary and Bertha Lomax.

John Lomax first married Elizabeth Horner and they had six children. She died in about 1825 in Beardstown. Next he married Phoebe Hufstedler, daughter of Jacob Hufstedler. They had seven children, Joseph, Samuel, Nancy, John, Thomas R., Elizabeth and Sarah Lomax. In 1851 John and Phoebe left Tennessee to settle in Dunklin County, MO. John had built a raft of pumpkin ash and when the spring floods came he and his family climbed aboard and floated down the Tennessee, Ohio and Mississippi rivers to Missouri. His grandson, Bobby Lomax, said they had some hollow logs on the raft for protection from bad weather and to store supplies. John died in 1854 and Phoebe in 1959 in Dunklin County, MO.

Joseph Lomax married Sarah Elizabeth Horner, daughter of Jesse Horner and Mourning Denton. They had 13 children. Years later Ida Lomax Kelley never tired of telling and showing her grandchildren the muzzle loading gun that her grandpap Joseph Lomax had hid from the Yankees during the Civil War. He hid it in the rocks around his homeplace.

Robert Allen Lomax was the youngest son of Joseph and Sarah Lomax, born in 1873 in Cedar Creek in Perry County. He married Mary Adaline Richardson, daughter of John Thomas Richardson and Sarah June Atkisson. He had only three daughters that lived, Bertha Lee, Ida Mae, and Cora Elsie Lomax. Ida always went to the field with her father because she liked to be outside instead of in the house all the time. He called her Pete.

Ida Mae Lomax married Robert Kelley in 1920. Robert was the son of Jefferson Davis Kelley and Mary Ferguson. They had five children, Clemmie, Clenard, Ruby, Rada, and Helton Kelley. Ida was much loved by all of her children and grandchildren. She loved all flowers and her grandchildren used to swear she could stick a dead twig in the ground and it would grow. She made beautiful quilts and loved to crochet. She died in 1982 and was buried in Clifton in Wayne County.

LOMAX,

Samuel Lomax, 1762-1833, born in England, served in the Revolutionary War, War of 1812 and was a farmer. He lived in Georgia,

Williamson County, Hickman County, and Perry County, TN.

Bertha, Ida and Elsie Lomax

Samuel, circa 1778, married Temperance Bugg, 1765-after 1820, (daughter of John and Elizabeth Bugg). Their children were: John, Josiah, Mary, Sarah, Elizabeth, William, James, Temperance, Nancy and Thomas.

John, 1785-1856, married first, Elizabeth Horner, 1781-1810, (daughter of John Sr. and Elizabeth Russell Horner). Their children were: William, Russell, Andrew, James, Wilburn and Anna.

John married second, Phoebe Hufstedler, 1808-1859. Their children were: Joseph, Samuel, infant Lomax, Nancy J. (Nannie), John (Red), Thomas R., Elizabeth, and Sarah.

John was a stonemason. Just after 1850 John and Phoebe dug out a log and went down the Tennessee, Ohio and Mississippi Rivers to Dunklin County, MO, and lived there the rest of their lives.

Joseph, 1827-1900, a farmer, married Sarah Elizabeth Horner, 1830-1905, (daughter of Jesse and Mourning Denton Horner). They were married 54 years and had 12 children. Their children were: Martha Ann, William Andrew, Nancy Caroline, John William, James Samuel (Bud), Thomas Andrew, Mourning Elizabeth, Joseph Russell, Sarah Catherine, Phoebe Jane, Mary Lee, and Robert Allen.

Robert Allen Lomax, 1893-1957, a farmer and musician, married 1892, Mary Adaline Richardson, 1872-1956, (daughter of John and Sarah Jane Adkisson Richardson). Their children were: Sara Isabella, boy unnamed, Bertha Lee, Robert E. Lee, Ida Mae, Cora Elsie.

Bertha Lee, 1898-1988, married 1913, John Henry Harder, 1893-1959, (son of Frank Willis and Mary Lee Bates Harder). Their children were: Floyd Allen, 1913, married Norma Jack Morris; Hollis, 1920, married Kathleen Pauline Broadaway; Mary Edith, 1923, married John W. Hime; William Franklin, 1925-1985, married Velma Matilda Dunn; Sarah Helen, 1931-1951, married Hillard L. Mackin.

Mary Edith married 1941, John Wesley Hime, a farmer, (son of William and Ira French Hime). Their children are: Dorothy Helen, 1942, married 1963 Larry Wylie, 1940, (son of R. L. and Oma Lee Polsgrove Wylie). Children: Mary Michelle, 1968, married 1992 Douglas Spicer Roth (son of Charles and Georgia Roth), and John Robert, 1971; Johnnie Lee, 1944, married 1972 John Powell Cloar, 1938, (son of Wallace and Sylvia Turner Cloar). Child – Laura Lee, 1976; William Thomas, 1947, married 1968 Mary Ann Roberts, (daughter of John Walter and Arleane McCrutcheon Roberts). Children – John David, 1973, and Mary Elizabeth, 1978.

Ida May, 1903-1982, married Robert Kelly. Their children are: Clemmie, Clinnard, Ruby, Rada, and Helton.

Cora Elsie, 1907-1993, married Lewis Davis. Their child is Mavis.

LONG, Augusta Catherine (Gussie) DePriest Powers is the great-great-great-granddaughter of Hugh Widdom Long who sailed with five brothers from New South Wales to North Carolina around 1775. They were of Scotch-Irish descent.

Albert Long, age 8; Evaline, age 77; and Elnora Long, age 12. Photo taken in 1911.

His son, Hugh Washington Long, was born in Rutherford County, NC, in 1799 and married Martha Burnett of Petersburg, VA, born 1799.

They moved to Perry County in 1831, and bought 265 acres of land, reared their family in what is today Decatur County. She died Sept. 12, 1865. He died Nov. 2, 1865.

Their son, Henry Hugh Long, born 1834, was the seventh of 12 children. He married Augusta Evaline Simmons, daughter of Benjamin and Louisa Young Simmons. She was born in 1834.

They settled on Deer Creek in Perry County. They owned 468 acres of land. He was a staunch Republican and they were Missionary Baptists.

He was a captain in the Union Army during the Civil War and served under Gen. A. N. Haney. They had four children: Sarah, James N., Frances, and John W. He died in 1896 and she died in 1919. They are buried in Bible Hill Cemetery.

John W. Long, born 1869-1912, married Catherine (Kitt) Blackburn, born 1869-1905. They had eight children: Watson, Ervie, and Dora died in infancy, Howser, McKinley, Andrew, Albert, and Elnora lived and reared families.

Elnora Long, 1899-1981, married Fred DePriest, 1895-1974. They raised seven children: Augusta Catherine (Gussie), Joseph R. (Buck), Mavis, Pauline, Vernon, Franklin, and Ruth.

Gussie, born 1917, married Earl Powers, 1920-1953.

Joseph R. (Buck), 1921-1993, married Julia Dabbs, born Nov. 16, 1926. He was a veteran of WWII.

Mavis, 1924-1989, married C. D. McKinney, 1924-199?, who is buried in Ohio. They had two children: Marsha, born 1949, and Debra, born 1953.

Pauline's history is in this book.

Vernon DePriest, born 1930, married Joan Sedlacek, born 1944. They had three children: Tammy 1966, Tracy 1967, and Timothy 1976. Vernon is a veteran of the Korean War. They live in Michigan.

Franklin, born march 1939, married Linda Edwards, born 1938, and they have two children: Sandra, born 1962, and Cynthia, born 1964. He lives with third wife, Ella, in North Carolina. He served 26 years in the U.S. Navy.

Ruth DePriest, born 1942, married Bobby Hinson and they had three children: Renee, Michelle, and Angela. She married second, Lt. Col. Ted Outlaw, USAF, in 1972. He was a widower with three children: Mike, Julia, and Mark. He adopted her three. They have a son, Evart, born in 1977. They live in Texas.

ETHEL LOUISE LONG, born 1917, in Perry County married Robert Philip Spencer Sept. 4, 1933. He was born in Decatur County, in 1912. One son, Robert Long Spencer, was born Sept. 13, 1934. Louise is the great-great-great-granddaughter of Hugh Widdom Long. He and five of his brothers sailed from New South Wales to North Carolina in 1775. He was buried in North Carolina. Father of Hugh Washington Long, born in Rutherford County, NC, 1799, married Martha Burnett of Petersburg, VA, born 1799. They moved to Perry County in 1831 and purchased 265 acres of land in what is now Decatur County, but was then Perry County. He died in 1849 and his wife died in 1865.

Their son, Capt. Henry Hugh Long, born 1834, Perry County was seventh of 12 children and spent his life on a farm. He learned the tanner's trade but abandoned it after serving his

(Left to right) Robert and Linda Spencer and son, Bobby; Mr. and Mrs. Idlet Long; Susan Spencer (front); and Mr. and Mrs. R. P. Spencer in 1966.

apprenticeship. He married Evaline Simmons in 1854. She was born in 1834 and was the daughter of Benjamin and Louisa (Young) Simmons. He died in 1896 and his wife died in 1919.

Our subject served in the Federal Army in the Second Tennessee Cavalry under Col. Haney after the general surrendered, he was mustered out in 1865 in Nashville. First elected sheriff of Perry County after the war and served from 1868-1870. He was a staunch republican conservative liberal reasoner in politics and Mason. He and his wife were Missionary Baptist. They had four children: Sarah, Frances, John and James Nathaniel (Jim), (1858-1926). He married Sarah Lou Blackburn in 1882. She was born in 1858 and died in 1930. She was the daughter of Augusta and Rebecca (Carter) Blackburn. They had five children; Henry Hugh (1884-1946), married Hattie Coble. Their children were Mabel, Homer, Lexie, Clyde and Elsie, Johnny James (1886-1971). He married Ada Lancaster. Their children were James William (Billy), Leslie and Mary Lou.

Isaac Idlet (1890-1971) married Mae Spencer (1897-1988) in 1916. Their daughter was Louise.

Ethel Elizabeth (1892-1951), married Clyde Smith. At his death she married Dorsey Carnell. Bethel Berry (twin/1892-1893). Louise's grandfather was James N. (Jim) Long was a prayerful man. He prayed daily and nightly and daddy Idlet was a jovial and compassionate. They were Republicans, Masons, Baptist and farmers. They, along with their wives, are buried in the Denson's Landing cemetery.

Robert's Long Spencer's children and grandchildren make the ninth generation. *Submitted by Mrs. Louise Long Spencer*

LONG-CLOYD, Pauline DePriest Cotham Cloyd is the granddaughter of John W. and Catherine Blackburn Long. The third daughter of Fred and Elnora Long DePriest was born in 1926. She married John W. Cotham 1945. He was the son of Jim and Susie Strickland Cotham. Their son, John W. Cotham Jr., was born Oct. 19, 1946.

Zachary Dill, five, and Taylor Dill, six months, children of Ricky and Amber Dill.

She married second, Malcum Cloyd, son of Ernest and Irene Cloyd, Feb. 1954. They had two children: Sheilah, born Nov. 1, 1955, and Ronald, born Sept. 17, 1957. Malcum died March 7, 1977 and is buried in O. A. Kirk Cemetery.

John W. Cotham Jr. married Betty Jane Daniel, daughter of Jack and June Roberts Daniel on Jan. 1, 1967. They had two children: Amber, born June 18, 1968, and Craig, born April 13, 1971.

Amber Cotham married Ricky Dill, son of Herbert Jr. and Glenda Mercer Dill on June 28, 1986. Their two sons are: Zachary, born Aug. 16, 1988, and Taylor, born June 22, 1993.

Zachary and Taylor are ninth generation of the Long family beginning with Hugh Widdom Long.

Sheilah Cloyd married Johnny Hester, son of Jack and Mary Hester. Their son, Jeremiah was born Sept. 28, 1973. Jeremiah is in the U.S. Army stationed in Panama.

Sheilah married second, Terry Miller, in 1983. They have two sons: Terry Jr. (T.J.) born Aug. 7, 1984 and Joel, born Aug. 29, 1986. They live in Oklahoma.

Ronald Cloyd, born Sept. 17, 1957, married Janet Tompkins in August 1977 and they have three children: Amity, born Dec. 3, 1979; Julia, born Sept. 28, 1983; and Mary Ann, born Aug. 8, 1987.

GEORGE LOVELESS, father of Pryor Lee Loveless, was born in Caswell County, NC, about 1788. In December of 1823 he moved with three children: Pryor Lee, Lucy (Smithson) and Peter R. Loveless to Tennessee. George made his home in Gray's Bend, Hickman County, a few miles from Centerville. George erected a mill along Indian Creek. He married Nancy Morgan of North Carolina. Other children of George and Nancy were Sibba (Bates) and Sarah J./Sally (Hickman).

Clayton, Don, Iva Sue, and Dera May Loveless.

Pryor Lee Loveless, born June 16, 1820, died April 24, 1867. Pryor married Mahley Caroline George, born 1821, died Sept. 13, 1862. Pryor Lee was a gunsmith and had 13 children: Melissa Elizabeth, born June 13, 1842, married William Mayberry; Stiza Caroline, born July 19, 1843, married William Crawford; Mary Johnson, born Dec. 15, 1844, married William Ship; Martha Atlantic, born Oct. 13, 1846, married Everett Easley; Loretta Crispen, born Jan. 17, 1850, married Hezekiah Hickman; Sarah Peterson, born April 30, 1848, died Dec. 15, 1854; Venella Jane, born Feb. 13, 1852, married Alvin Tate; William Jackson, born Sept. 21, 1854, married Margaret Ship; Pricilla Emaline, born Nov. 15, 1856, married Willis Brown; Ford George, born Oct. 31, 1858, married Dora Burns; Pryor Hezekiah, born Sept. 7, 1861 and Mahaley Easter, born Sept. 7, 1861, twins died day of birth; and John M., Sept. 13, 1862, died Sept. 3, 1865.

Several of Pryor's children moved to Perry County. William Jackson Loveless moved to Lobelville where he raised his family and ran the "Loveless Hotel" for many years.

Ford George Loveless was a farmer and lived outside of Lobelville near Cane Creek on what was called "Burns Hill." Ford married Dora Burns, born March 12, 1870. Dora was the daughter of John W. Burns and Tabitha Greer of Perry County. Ford and Dora had seven children: John Lee, born February 1886, moved to Arizona, was a state representative and mayor of Chandler, AZ, for many years, died in Arizona; Lloyd E., born November 1888, died as a child; Ross B., born August 1890, died as a child; Clayton Howard, born March 1893, died in Texas; Don A., born April 1896, died as a child; Dera May, born Jan. 6, 1899, married Gaydon Carrol DePriest; Iva Sue, born Aug. 26, 1902, married Luther Ray Burns (had three sons: Frank, Ralph and John Andrew).

Dera May Loveless married Graydon Carrol DePriest, son of William Samuel DePriest and Nancy Ethel Burns. Graydon was a farmer and later owned DePriest's Grocery Store at DePriest's Bend. They had one daughter, Helen Sue, born Aug. 22, 1922. Dera contracted tuberculosis and they moved to Chander, AZ, hoping the climate would improve her health. Dera died Feb. 23, 1927 in Arizona and is buried in DePriest Bend Cemetery. Graydon later married a widow, Lillie Baars DePriest who had two children, Frank and Laverne. Graydon and Lillie had one child together, Carrol (Bud) DePriest.

Helen Sue DePriest married James Horace Kee, son of Walter Berry Kee and Jenny E. Moore of Camden, TN. Helen and Horace had four children: James Richard Kee, Linda Sue (Vaughan), Barbara Jean (Dunham), and Betty Ann (Birdwell).

LYNCH, Arron/Orron born 1805, and Sarah/Sally (Johnson) Lynch, born 1811, were married in Davidson County, TN, on Oct. 1, 1832. They moved to Perry County, on Cane Creek, some time after the births of their first two sons. The rest of their children were born in Perry County: James M., born 1836, died 1909, married Malinda Edwards; John, born 1838, married Frances (Fanny); Sarah A., born 1840, died 1922, married John Adams McClearen; David D., born 1843, died 1923, married Sarah J. Skelton. David served as a private in the Confederate army, 1864 to 1865, C. Company, 4th Regiment, Infantry. Wounded in the leg while fighting for "The Cause." Mary Elizabeth, born 1845, was deaf and dumb; Joseph, born 1850, married Rebecca Baucum; Emaline, born 1852; Malinda, born 1855, married Nicholas V. Spears; Thomas J., born 1860, married first to Martha Josephine (Josie) Shepard, second to Francis (Frankie) Campbell.

Most of the brothers and sisters moved to Hickman County, at Farmers Exchange. John and his wife remained in Perry County, as did his mother and father.

John and Frances (Fanny) had the following children: John Jr., born 1858/59, died before 1860; Lonnie, born 1861; Alexander L., born Nov. 12, 1865, on Tom's Creek, died Feb. 12, 1922, in Missouri. He married Nov. 30, 1884 – divorced May 1893, Mary Ann (Molly) Horner, born Aug. 8, 1869, in Perry County, died

Nov. 20, 1942, in Lewis County. Molly was the daughter of Pleasant and Nancy Ann Woods also of Perry County; George W., born 1866; Samuel E., born 1867; William E., born 1874.

Johnny (Popa Joe) Osco and Ethel (Mama Lynch) in May 1958.

Alex and Molly had the following children born in Perry County: Johnie Osco (Poppa Joe), born Nov. 17, 1886, on Tom's Creek, died Nov. 2, 1968, in Lewis County, married Oct. 31, 1910, Ethel Lee Ghist (Mamma Lynch), born Jan. 24, 1892, died Oct. 22, 1961. Ethel was the daughter of Rufus Benjamin and Mozella (Goodman) Ghist; William Otto, born 1888, died 1969, married S. Lover Brown; Nettie, born Dec. 8, 1891, married Jim Jackson; Nora, born 1893, died young; Claude, born 1897, died young.

Johnie Osco and Ethel had nine children: Mable Geneva, born Aug. 22, 1911, in Hickman County, married Shirrel O'Guin; Johnie Osco Jr., born March 13, 1913, in Perry County, died July 3, 1939, Lewis County; Elbert J., born March 1, 1915, in Perry County, married Lois O'Guin. Edith Mae, born 1917, died 1982, in Indiana, married Leonard Ellis Pace; Lena Lillian, born 1919, died 1968, married George E. (Dick) Prince; G. N., born July 25, 1921, in Lewis County, married Nov. 23, 1946, Nora Roberta Pace, daughter of Henry Claude and Virginia Marie (Spears) Pace; Myrtle Evelyn, born 1923, died 1983, married J. C. Devore; Glyne Alline, born June 4, 1925, married Benjamin Ellis Mullins; Robert Howell, born Jan. 17, 1928, married Lois Peevahouse.

G. N. and Nora Roberta Pace Lynch have four children: Garry Don, born March 21, 1948, Lewis County, TN; Danny Earl, born Nov. 21, 1949, Lewis County, married Ellen Laginess, May 28, 1977, in Ecorse, MI; Barbara Elaine, born Oct. 8, 1951, in Trenton, MI; Shelia Jean, born July 29, 1953, Lewis County, married Terry Hampton, May 4, 1974, in Ecorse, MI.

Danny and Ellen have two children: Danny Earl II, born March 24, 1981, in Wayne County, MI; Katie Marie, born March 17, 1986, in Wayne County, MI.

Shelia and Terry have two children: Bryan Young Hampton, born Nov. 27, 1975, in Wayne County, MI; Sherry Elaine Hampton, born Oct. 23, 1978, in Wayne County, MI.

MARRS, The Marrs claim Scotch descent. The first of the name came to Virginia from Scotland in 1690. The Marrs families played quite a part in the wars that ensued over the years from the time of their arrival. Thomas Marrs, the only son of the first arrival in Virginia, was at Braddock's defeat in 1755, serving under Colonel George Washington. John Marrs, grandson of Thomas Marrs, served as Ensign in Capt. Dulin's Company in the War of 1812. Robert Marrs served under Commodore Perry on the coast of Africa, later participated in the Mexican War, and fired the first shot in the Naval attack on Vera Cruz. James Marrs served with the Militia Infantry, Nashville, TN, actually participating in the Creek War of 1813-1814, a sub conflict of the War of 1812.

George Washington Marrs

James and Sarah Marrs were listed in the 1830 census for Perry County. James was born in Virginia and Sarah was born in North Carolina. Records indicate they settled around Rockhouse in Perry County, having purchased land for one cent an acre, before moving to the Lobelville area. They were possibly some of the first settlers around Lobelville since the creek flowing from Tennessee Gas Pipeline into Buffalo River was named Marrs Creek. Generally creeks, hollows and certain landmarks were named after the first settlers in an area. Land records indicated they owned this land reaching to the Qualls Bend area on Buffalo River, and also land on Russells Creek at Marrs Hollow.

Elizabeth Cockrell Marrs and James Francis Marrs

Joseph Marrs, son of James and Sarah, fought in the Mexican War. He served in Co. K, 3rd Regt Tenn Inf, and died at Encero, Mexico, June 1848, age 28 years.

James and Sarah's children listed in the 1850 census of Lobelville were Hugh (born 1830), Armistead (born 1828), George W. (born 1832), James (born 1835), John J. (born 1837) and Sarah (born 1840). There were three other children born prior to this date, but are unknown at this time.

This family was a typical Southern family of Celtic origin. The type of culture brought here by these early settlers produced a people that were very hardy, liked practical jokes, loved music, liked to tell stories, but were somewhat arrogant, hard drinking and loved to fight. This probably explains why so many of the Marrs family were heavy drinkers of liquor. It might also explain why the Southern people were so quick to go to war.

At the outbreak of the Civil War, George W. and John J. Marrs enrolled in Co. F, 53rd Infantry Regiment, CSA, as did a lot of the residents around Lobelville and Perry County.

George was shot through the shoulder sometime in 1863 by statement of Dr. J. E. Bates of Lobelville.

Legend has it that one of the Marrs remaining at home during the Civil War mined and sold lead, somewhere on Russells Creek. Statements were made by local people that said he would not let anyone go with him to pick up the lead, and most say that no one has found it to this day. Saltpetre, used for making gun powder, was taken from the Jay Bird Hollow Cave, located in the same area.

Out of this family, Hugh N. (great, great grandfather of John L. Marrs) married Louisa Fielder of Hickman County. They had eight children, named Sarah, James, Claiborn, Louisa, Tennessee Polk, Ida, Samuel and Iantha (nickname Earl). Sarah married James Jackson (1876), James married Polly, Tennessee Polk married John "Dutch" Bates (1887), Iantha Earl married Sam W. Bates (1885), Ida married William Gray (1885) and Claiborn (great grandfather of John L. Marrs) married Mary Elizabeth Skipworth (1879). Iantha Earl's second marriage was to Monroe Morrison (1900).

Claiborn and wife Elizabeth Skipworth had four children, named Samuel (Sweeter), Carrie Lamar, Nellie and James Francis (grandfather of John L. Marrs). Samuel married Elizabeth Dailey, Carrie married Ben Greer, Nellie married William Dailey and James Francis married Sarah Elizabeth Cockrell.

James Francis and Elizabeth had two children, named Casey and Guy (father of John L. Marrs). Casey married Adron Cunningham in 1933 and they had one child named Greta. Guy married Lorene Heath in 1933 and they had two children named John L. and Betty Jo.

Betty Jo married J. N. Long in 1957 and their children are Dennis, Jill and Jna. Dennis married Shelia Johnson and their children are Josh and Casey. Jna married Jimmy Jackson and they have one daughter named Kala. Jill married Robert Bailey and they have one son named Jackson.

John L. married Marie Stanfield in 1957 and their three children are John Keith, Nina and Chad. John Keith married Lavonda Adkins and their children are John, Matthew and Brian. Nina married Greg Monroe and they have one son named Grant. Chad is 15 and is a freshman at Perry County High School.

Guy Marrs owned and operated a sawmill from about 1950, mostly around Perry County. He stayed in this business until he died at age 56 in 1967. It seems that once sawdust gets in your blood, you need not try to get it out. After 20 years as Postmaster of Lobelville, John L. never lost interest in the lumber business, and still continues the business today with his family.

The grandchildren of Betty Jo Long and John L. Marrs make up the eighth generation of this family history.

MARSHALL, William Raymond Ernest Marshall, born Aug. 2, 1906 the son of William T. and Myrtle Alexander Marshall. Raymond, the eldest of nine children, married Katie Maude Hensley, the youngest of eight children, born Aug. 10, 1910 to Porter and Harriet Hensley. Raymond and Maude Marshall made their home in the Pineview Community, where Raymond, better known as W. R., owned and operated a sawmill. This way of life eventually influenced three of the Marshall sons to follow into the family sawmill business.

W. R. and Maude Marshall had ten children, six boys and four girls:

Oscar Ray Marshall, born Oct. 22, 1926, sawmill owner and logger, married Margie Imogene Depriest. They have two sons, Ronnie Keith Marshall and Michael Norman Marshall.

Beulah Irene Marshall, born March 15, 1929 homemaker and wife, married Robert H. Depriest. They have two daughters, Barbara Joyce Depriest and Beverly Sue Depriest.

Willie Sue Marshall, born Feb. 11, 1933 store clerk and tax assessor clerk, married Billy W. Ramey. They have two children, Teresa Diane Ramey and Randy Michael Ramey.

Wiley Edwin Marshall, born April 9, 1936, Perry County Highway Department employee, married Barbara Faye Polan. They have two daughters, Traci Marianne Marshall and Terry Michelle Marshall.

Alton Issiac Marshall, born Feb. 11, 1941, sawmill owner and logger, married Janet Culp Rainey. Alton has two daughters, Christy Lane Marshall and Desta Beth Marshall, and two stepdaughters, Sonya Lynn Rainey and Michelle Leigh Rainey.

Troy Kirk Marshall, born Feb. 22, 1943, sawmill owner and logger, married Martha Lou Dedrick. They have one daughter, Tammy Renae Marshall.

Jeanette Jean Marshall, born Aug. 31, 1944, nurse, married Jesse Willard Warren. They have one son, Stephen Lynn Warren.

Johnie Wayne Marshall, born April 2, 1947, Hohenwald Vocational School Teacher, married Joyce Ann Stephens. They have one daughter, Ellen Annette Marshall.

Ricky Hal Marshall, born Oct. 21, 1949, Perry County Schools-Teacher, married Carla Ann Hinson. They have two daughters, Amber Rae Marshall and Brandi Ann Marshall.

Deborah Kay Marshall, born June 21, 1955, homemaker and wife, married Kerry Dewane Westbrooks. They have three daughters, Dianna Michelle Westbrooks, Kathryn Aline Westbrooks and Kara Delayne Westbrooks.

W. R. and Maude Marshall were active members of the Tom's Creek Baptist Church in Pineview. High priorities for the Marshall family were church and educational endeavors. W. R. and Maude encouraged and insisted that their children better themselves through education and community involvement.

W. R. loved the outdoors and spent many hours hunting and fishing. He was an avid outdoors man and shared this love with his sons and daughters. The Marshall family also shared a love for sports. Several of the children participated in two or more sports in school.

W. R. and Maude were also musically talented, each being able to play several instruments (banjo, guitar, mandolin, harmonica, juce, dulcimer and zither).

This musical heritage was handed down to the children. A gospel group, the Pineview Gospel Singers, is composed of the children, grandchildren and their spouses.

A strong family bond is still quite evident with all 10 children living in the Pineview Community.

Katie Maude Marshall died July 11, 1975. W. R. Marshall died Dec. 9, 1978. They are buried in the Pineview Cemetery. Their legacy lives on through the lives of their 10 children, 20 grandchildren and 11 great grandchildren.

BARTLEY MATHIS, sometimes shown as Bartlett Mathis, was born 1825, probably in Hickman County. He was the son of Cornelius D. and Lucinda Mathis of Hickman County, near Aetna. His wife, Minerva, was born 1818. They lived in Hickman County until moving to Perry County, by 1880. At least five children were born to them: Joseph Mathis (born 1847) nothing known about him; Martha Jane Mathis (1849-Jan. 25, 1928, Maury County); Pleasant J. Mathis (born 1852); Albert L. Mathis (born 1855); and John F. Mathis (born 1857). The last child is probably John Frank Mathis of Hickman County.

Other children of Cornelius D. Mathis were Joseph of Hickman and Wayne Counties, Elbert W. Mathis and James Bluford Mathis, both of Perry County, David Mathis of Hickman and Weakley Counties, George Washington Mathis of Hickman County, Mary Mathis, wife of Green G. Sharp of Hickman County, and Catherine Mathis, wife of Roaden/Rawdon/Rhoden, most likely of Perry County. *Submitted by Merle Stevens.*

ELBERT W. MATHIS, born 1833, son of Cornelius D. Mathis and Lucinda, who may have been an Anderson. Oftentimes the name appears as Mathews in the old records. Elbert was listed on the 1860 and 1870 Perry County census with wife, Linda, born 1842, and the following children: Mary F. (born 1860); Lucinda P. (born 1862); William E. (born 1866) and Louisa T. (born 1868). No further records are known on this family. *Submitted by Merle Stevens.*

JAMES BLUFORD MATHIS, born 1836, probably Hickman County, son of Cornelius D. and Lucinda Mathis. He may have been married once before moving to Perry County. He died in Perry County before 1894. About 1860 in Perry County, he married Mary E. Dabbs (born 1845, still living in 1920). After Bluford died, she married, Nov. 29, 1894 Perry County to William J. Wilson, (born 1837).

Mary indicates she had 11 children born to her, all born in Perry County, nine are known: 1) James Wilson Mathis (Oct. 1862-about 1940, Marsh Creek), buried Roberts Cemetery. He married Dec. 29, 1887, Perry County, to Josie Wilson; 2) Sarah Elizabeth Mathis (Feb. 22, 1863, Marsh Creek- Jan. 16, 1955, Cedar Creek) buried Roberts Cemetery. She married Milton Green Tomerlin Dec. 21, 1882, Marsh Creek; 3) Thomas S. Mathis (born March 1866) married Martha Hughes on Oct. 6, 1892 in Perry County; 4) Joseph Mathis (born 1867) probably died as a young boy; 5) Josephine Louise Mathis (born Oct. 1869) probably buried Church Grove Cemetery, Dyer County. She married James H. Evans Aug. 14, 1887 in Perry County; 6) Fannie Mathis (Dec. 18, 1872, Perry County-May 27, 1929) buried Craig Cemetery, Cedar Creek. She married William R. Paschall June 7, 1888 in Perry County; 7) Willie Mathis (born 1875); 8) Robert L. Mathis (born Sept. 1877, Marsh Creek) died in West Tennessee. He married Martha Ella Richardson Aug. 25, 1895 in Perry County; 9) Etta Mathis (born 1886) may have died 1925, buried in Roberts Cemetery. She married G. Monroe Hardin May 8, 1909 in Perry County.

James Wilson Mathis married Josie Wilson, born 1872. Josie married second Charlie Little, buried Roberts Cemetery. Children of James and Josie: 1) Will H. Mathis (1889-1949) buried Robert Cemetery. He married Cora Kidd Sept. 1, 1908 in Perry County. She was born 1893, daughter of Peter Kidd and Fannie Mackin, died July 24, 1976. Their children, Hazel, Garland, Carrie, Dollie and Mary; 2) Robert Albert Mathis (1890, Perry County-Nov. 14, 1968) buried Woods-Treadwell Cemetery. He married Martha Treadwell (1891-1929) Dec. 15, 1911 in Perry County. Children: Floyd, Maudie, Lillian, Lee Dell and William; 3) Benjamin Mathis (July 9, 1892, Perry County-April 26, 1958) buried Milan, TN. He married first to Lizzie Ann Phillips (Sept. 16, 1889-Nov. 9, 1908) and had two sons, James F. and Joe Carlos. Benjamin married second to Mary Francis Oliver and had three children; 4) Minnie E. Mathis (born 1895, Perry County) lived in Milan, TN. She married George E. Comer Dec. 24, 1916 in Perry County. He was born in 1891 the son of Nathaniel and Jane Comer. Known children are Georgia L., Effie Jane, Doris and James; 5) Mark M. Mathis (June 24, 1897, Perry County-May 13, 1971, Parsons) buried Roberts Cemetery. He married Dena Lee Grooms (Jan. 14, 1902-Sept. 24, 1976) on Jan. 7, 1917 in Perry County. Six children: Edith Murl, Mittie Pearl, Dorothy Mae, Loula Genevie, Robert Earl and Shirley Nell.

JESSE MANUEL MATHIS, better known as "Whig" (March 20, 1844, Lewis County-March 10, 1919, Perry County) is buried in Cook Cemetery on Cane Creek. His marker reflects a birth year of 1853, but this is wrong. His parents were John Mathis and Martha Henrietta Hinson. He was a Confederate soldier in the Civil War. Whig married twice, first to Rosie Ann Hudson who died July 12, 1894, buried Cook Cemetery. His second marriage, Oct. 14, 1894, Perry County to Mrs. Alice Dunn (born Dec. 1875).

She had a daughter, Carlie Dunn, who married Arthur Rochelle. His children by both marriages: 1) Dona Mathis (Aug. 27, 1865-Feb. 17, 1939) buried Cook Cemetery. She married J. Newton Chandler June 5, 1880 in Perry County; 2) Houston Mathis, thought to be born 1875; 3) Brantley Jones Mathis (Aug. 29, 1877-June 5, 1937) buried Totty's Bend, Hickman County; 4) believe a Louisa or Eliza Mathis; 5) Lee Mathis; 6) possibly a Betty Mathis; 7) Hurkey J. Mathis (Feb. 18, 1880-Aug. 26, 1908) buried Cook Cemetery; 8) Charles A. Mathis (1882-1960, Oklahoma; 9) John Douglas Mathis (1885-1964, Trenton, TN); 10) Martha O. Mathis (Oct. 12, 1888-June 13, 1934) buried Warren Cemetery, Perry County. She married Asbury Warren Dec.

31, 1913 in Hickman County; 11) Dee Mathis, born 1895; 12) Reuben Mathis, born 1897; 13) Ollie Mathis, born 1899; 14) Ida Mathis, born 1900; 15) Mammie Pearl Mathis (July 5, 1904-Feb. 7, 1930) buried Betty Bastin Cemetery, Lewis County, wife of Arthur James Talley; 16) Arlin Mathis married Mattie Qualls Feb. 28, 1915, Perry County.

Most of the census for this family is missing and a lot of the data is unsure. *Submitted by Merle Stevens.*

ROBERT L. MATHIS, son of James Bluford Mathis and Mary Dabbs, married Martha Ella Richardson. She was born Sept. 1880, Marsh Creek. They had seven known children, possibly others: 1) Emma L. Mathis, born April 1897; 2) Ollie W. Mathis (July 6, 1899-July 28, 1901) buried Roberts Cemetery; 3) Homer W. Mathis, born 1903; 4) Gertrude J. Mathis, born 1905; 5) Beulah B. Mathis, born 1907; 6) Robert Freddie Mathis, born either Jan. 28 or Aug. 4, 1909, Marsh Creek; 7) Martha Mathis, born Jan. 3, 1912, Marsh Creek. *Submitted by Merle Stevens.*

THOMAS S. MATHIS, married Martha Hughes (born 1868). They had several children that died as infants. Some of their children: 1) Granville L. Mathis (Nov. 3, 1893-April 24, 1959) buried Roberts Cemetery. He married Luda Duncan. It is assumed this is the Luda Mathis buried in Craig Cemetery (Jan. 23, 1890-Nov. 8, 1966); 2) Minnie Mathis, born 1896, married Newt Smith Aug. 20, 1916 in Perry County. She may have lived in Arkansas. Their first child, Dora Lucille Smith (April 17, 1917, Perry County-May 2, 1917, Perry County) buried Craig Cemetery; 3) Mary L. Mathis, born 1898, had died by 1910; 4) Viola Mathis, born March 23, 1904, married Albert Grooms (June 11, 1889-Aug. 16, 1961) buried Roberts Cemetery. *Submitted by Merle Stevens.*

BILLY RALPH McCAIG, and Betty Dabbs McCaig were born in Perry County, living most of their lives on Crooked Creek. Ralph is a veteran of the US Navy, serving four years aboard the *USS Rich* and *USS Coats*. He toured many foreign countries, also serving at Norfolk, VA, Millington Naval Base and Key West, FL, where he received his Honorable Discharge May 11, 1955.

Betty and Ralph McCaig

Ralph worked several years on tow boats and with the Corrections Dept. of Turney Center, Only, TN. Betty worked in the garment industry 15 years and has been with Johnson Controls Inc. for 18 years.

Ralph, born March 8, 1931, is the son of Lester and Nellie Spencer McCaig. His parents are buried near the homeplace on Crooked Creek. Ralph has four sisters, Linda, Katherine, Jean and Gayle; he has one brother, Ewell. Two brothers, Hillard and Franklin, are deceased.

Betty is the daughter of Robert Samuel and Flora Kirk Dabbs. She was born Jan. 30, 1935. Her parents are buried at Northern Cemetery on Crooked Creek. Betty has six brothers: Rex, Sam Jr., Nolan, Olan, Billy and Reid; she has five sisters: Robert, Reida, Bonnie, Julia and Kyra. All 12 children are still living. Five of the boys are veterans.

Ralph and Betty have three children: Pat E., born March 23, 1951; B. Gaye, born July 19, 1953; Ralph Jr., born Aug. 11, 1956.

Pat graduated 1969, Perry County High School, then attended UT Martin, receiving a BS degree. She married Jackie Hanes Sept. 4, 1970 while they were students. Jackie received BS and Masters degrees, plus several extra hours.

Pat and Jackie have three children: B.J., born July 20, 1978; Jae Anne, born Dec. 9, 1979; Amy Lee, born March 15, 1982. They live in Adolphus, KY and teach in Sumner County School System.

Gaye graduated 1971 Perry County High, then attended UT Martin, receiving an Associates degree. She enjoys writing poetry, traveling and helping others. She is a secretary living in Nashville, TN.

Ralph Jr. attended Perry County schools, then graduated 1974 Macon County High School, Lafayette, TN. He married Donna Marrs in 1978. They have two children, Chad Lindsey, born Oct. 18, 1978, and Matthew Drake, born March 30, 1987. Ralph Jr. is a Correctional Officer at Turney Center, Only, TN. Donna works with the school system. They live in Waverly, TN.

DOSSIE EWELL McCAIG, was born Dec. 11, 1929, near Lobelville in Perry County, TN. He was the oldest of eight children born to Paul Lester and Nellie Spencer McCaig. He attended Perry County schools, graduating from Lobelville High School in 1949. After graduation he enlisted in the U.S. Navy, serving as aircraft engine mechanic.

Ewell and Mildred McCaig, March 1, 1992.

May 9, 1953, after returning from service, Ewell married Mildred Hopper, daughter of Clyde and Fannie Hopper, of Decaturville, TN, and granddaughter of C.N. and Mary Elizabeth Holder Hudson.

Ewell followed aircraft work for many years, living in Nashville, TN and Birmingham, AL. While in Nashville, Mildred was employed with National Life and Accident Insurance Company.

While in Birmingham, a son, Ronnie Dale McCaig, was born in 1956. Before leaving Birmingham, Ewell attended auto body and fender repair school.

After returning to Tennessee he worked as auto body and fender repairman while living at Lexington and Hohenwald. Mildred re-entered the work force, working at Henry I. Seigel Co. at Hohenwald for several years.

Early in 1968 Ewell became employed with Consolidated Aluminum Company, of New Johnsonville, as General Maintenance Mechanic. In mid summer the family moved to Waverly, and Mildred began work at Lobelville Garment, which later became Red Kap Industries. She worked there for many years until the plant closed, then began working for Johnson Controls of Linden.

After Consolidated Aluminum Co. closed, Ewell was employed with the Tennessee Department of Correction as correction officer at M.T.R.C. at Nashville, and Turney Center, at Only before retiring in June, 1993.

Their son, Ronnie, married Jo Ann Gonzales of Houston, TX. They have three children: Spencer Adam, Dustin Allan and Nina Marie, who are now living in Houston.

Ewell and Mildred have a home on Crooked Creek, near Lobelville, on a portion of the McCaig homeplace.

PAUL LESTER McCAIG, was born in Perry County near Lobelville, Dec. 18, 1904, the seventh child of William T. and Lee Ella Bugg McCaig. He had brothers, William Clyde, Walter and Long, and sisters, Hattie, Florence, Grace, Bertia and an infant sister who died at birth or shortly after.

Lester and Nell McCaig

His grandparents were William H. and Mary McCaig. Evidence points to the fact that William B. and Susan McCaig were the parents of William H. McCaig, these being the great grandparents of Lester McCaig. All were born in Perry County. It is believed that the first McCaigs to settle in Perry County were from Scotland.

Many of the family left Perry County and settled in and around Dyer County in West Tennessee. Some moved to Arkansas, Alabama, Texas and other parts of the country.

Jan. 3, 1929, Lester McCaig married Nellie Spencer, daughter of Doss and Fannie Loggins Spencer. They had four sons and four daughters: Ewell married Mildred Hopper; Ralph married

Betty Fay Dabbs; Franklin died in 1953; Hillard died in 1940; Linda married Curtis Rogers; Katherine first married Larry Edwards, second to John Trull; Jean married James Clark; Gayle married Ronald Aydelot. There were 15 grandchildren.

They lived most of their life on a farm in the Crooked Creek community. Lester made a living for his family farming, raising peanuts, corn, hay and cattle. He operated a peanut picker for the farmers throughout the area. Living near the Tennessee River, he also dug mussel shells, and worked for TVA, clearing along the banks of the river before Kentucky Lake was formed. Like many Perry Countians, he also worked periodically in Detroit in the automobile industry to supplement the family income. In later years he worked with the Perry County Highway Department.

Nellie, a very quiet, soft spoken, hardworking lady, was a faithful Christian who was devoted to her family. She raised a strawberry crop for many years. This supplemented the family income. She also continued working on the farm and raising cattle until her death.

Lester died March 22, 1982; Nellie died Dec. 21, 1991. Both are buried at the Crooked Creek Cemetery near the family homeplace.

McCOLLUM-DEPRIEST, James K. Polk "Jim" McCollum, son of John McCollum, married Mary Amanda DePriest-McCollum. During their short marriage, they had four children before "Jim" died in an unfortunate fatal accident at his home. On Dec. 26, 1878, "Jim" went out to the wood pile to get a back log for the fireplace. The ground was covered with ice and sleet. "Jim" had put the large log on his shoulder and proceeded toward the house when he slipped on the ice and fell. The large log fell and hit him on the side of his head as he fell. The incident broke his neck and he died instantly.

Jim and Mary Amanda's children were: 1) Sarah Priscilla Jane (Aug. 28, 1868-Oct. 17, 1946) married Wyatt Cowart; 2) Emma April 27, 1870-March 5, 1965) married Alex P. Poole Jr. (See Rains-Poole Families); 3) John Leander "Johnnie Lee" (July 6, 1872-March 10, 1952) married Margaretta "Maggie" McCandless. She was raised by John Golong and Mattie (Walker) Rains family (See Rains-Poole Families); 4) Mary Amanda Lucretia "Mollie" (April 5, 1878-Jan. 5, 1950) married first John Baird and second Foster Spencer. "Jim" and Amanda (DePriest) McCollum are buried in the Red Bank Cemetery as is also his father John McCollum, who died Oct. 12, 1877 on Terrapin Creek in Perry County NW of Lobelville. *Submitted by Oden and Ruby (McCollum) Fowler.*

JOHN McCOLLUM, (1813 Davidson Co.-1877 Perry Co.) was the youngest son of Levi and Margaret (Patton) McCollum. The McCollum brothers (Levi, Thrasher and John) had come from Guilford, NC to the Nashville area in the 1790s and settled at Vaughan's Gap a few miles SW of Nashville in Davidson County, TN. The three aforementioned brothers are listed several times in Davidson County, TN Court Minutes 1799-1803.

John McCollum and Susannah "Susan" Carothers McCollum circa 1870.

Levi McCollum Sr. (May 2, 1770 NC-Aug. 26, 1821 Hi Co.) settled near Vaughan's Gap, Davidson County, TN and thereafter relocated to Hickman County and purchased 100 acres on Beaverdam Creek of the Duck River for $500 on Dec. 15, 1819. Levi McCollum Sr. married Margaret (Patton) circa 1795 and their children were: 1) Thomas born 1795, married Lucretia; 2) William Patton born 1796; 3) Mary "Polly" born 1800, married William N. Barham Sept. 4, 1817, Davidson County; 4) Levi Jr. (Sept. 10, 1801-Nov. 17, 1866) married Elizabeth; 5) James E. born 1803, married Rebecca Murphee; 6) Jane born 1805, married Egbert A. Meadows; 7) Henry born 1807, married Elizabeth; 8) Hulah born 1809, married Wm Sutton; 9) Patton (1811-Jan. 1835) married Sarah P.; 10) John (Nov. 23, 1813-Oct. 12, 1877 P Co.) married Susannah "Susan" Carothers Aug. 8, 1839, Hi. County, TN. "Susan" Carothers was the daughter of Andrew and Catherine (Howell) Carothers, who came to Hickman County from Franklin County, GA circa 1810.

John and "Susan" (Carothers) McCollum lived with his widowed mother, Margaret (Patton) McCollum after Levi Sr. died at the age of 51 years. Margaret Patton McCollum (1772 NC-Jan. 18, 1851 Hi. Co. TN) died at the age of 79 years. In March of 1855, Margaret Patton McCollum's son, James E. McCollum and his son-in-law, J.D. Easley did bring suit and won a judgment against John McCollum et al for division and settlement of the Margaret Patton-McCollum estate. On March 7, 1855, the "old homeplace" was sold to settle the court case. It was soon after mid 1855 that the John McCollum bought a tract on Terrapin Creek in Perry County, which was a few miles NW of Lobelville. John died in 1877 and was buried in the Red Bank Cemetery near Terrapin Creek, Perry County.

After the death of John McCollum, their son, Andrew J. McCollum, brought his mother to their home in Doniphan, Ripley County, MO. There she lived until her death on Jan. 9, 1879. She is buried in the Oak Ridge Cemetery at Doniphan. The children of John and Susan (Carothers) McCollum were: 1) William Patton (Sept. 26, 1841-Dec. 20, 1912, nr. Rutherford, Gibson Co. TN) married Mary Dotson Aug. 7, 1866; 2) Andrew J. (Sept. 23, 1842-Jan. 25, 1929) married first Alice Harrinton March 4, 1866 and second Emma Borth Nov. 27, 1879. A.J. and Emma (Borth) McCollum are buried in Athkins, Ark. Cemetery; 3) Thomas J. (July 6, 1844-June 16, 1908) married Martha Jane Morris. They are buried in the Salem Methodist Church Cemetery nr. Rutherford, TN; 4) James K. Polk (Jan. 25, 1847-Dec. 26, 1878) married Mary Amanda DePriest March 31, 1867. They are buried in the Red Bank Cemetery nr. Terrapin Creek. (See JKP McCollum history); 5) Mary Elizabeth (Nov. 10, 1848-circa 1905) married George W. Ashley Sept. 18, 1865. They are buried in the Bakerville Cemetery, Hu, Co.; 6) Levi Cass (Jan. 9, 1851-Dec. 28, 1852); and Margaret Catherine (Nov. 9, 1855, Terrapin Crk. P Co.-Aug. 23, 1910) married William Monroe Stewart Jan. 4, 1871, P Co., TN. They are buried in the Stewart Family Plot, Towles Cemetery, three miles so. of Doniphan, MO. (See Stewart Monroe history.) *Submitted by Morris Monroe Stewart.*

MCDONALD, The McDonalds are Scotch Irish who came to California then on to other states. George McDonald, born about 1774, died 1850, married Mary Yearn (1812-1919).

Elsie and Fred Tucker

George and Mary McDonald came to Tennessee from Virginia in a covered wagon drawn by oxen. One ox died, so they didn't go on, but settled in the hills of Tennessee.

George and Mary McDonald had nine children. One was William M. born in Virginia in 1849, and died in 1919. William (Bill) McDonald married Henrietta Clementine (Tina) Barber (1853-1901), part Cherokee Indian. They had eight children: one was Lurah Mae (1895-1969).

Lurah Mae married L.B. (Barney) Duncan. They had two daughters: Elsie (Duncan) Tucker and Lena Lorene Duncan (1917-1919). Lena is buried in Qualls Cemetery (Copeland).

Elsie married Fred Tucker, and they had two daughters. Helen Tucker Southall has two sons: Ronnie and Mike. Ronnie has two sons: Tucker and Duncan Southall. Clara Tucker Lynn has one son, Mitchell B. Tucker Sr. and one grandson, Mitchell Jr.

ANN "HOMER" KITTRELL McDONALD,

a slave in Maury County, where she was purchased as an infant by the George Kittrell family around 1838. According to family lore, Ann's weight was 10 pounds when she was purchased at auction in Columbia; her selling price, $100 in gold.

Mrs. Conna J. McDonald Craig; granddaughter of "Ann Homer."

In 1855, Ann came with the Kittrells to Perry County to continue her tenure of servitude in Farmer's Valley. Two years, perhaps, after her arrival, she married (jumped the broom with) James "Jim Homer" McDonald, a slave from the Homer McDonald estate, located between Farmer's Valley and Flatwoods. Thus, explained the agnomen "Ann Homer". When the war was over and they had been granted their freedom, a religious ceremony was performed.

From a previous marriage, Jim McDonald's children were: John, Dudley, Bud, Martha Liz (Boppie), Frank and Leanna. The children born of the union with Ann Kittrell were: Isaac, Wiley, Bryce, Louis, Dock, Thomas, Ophelia and Mary Addie.

After the war, as was often the case, when slaves maintained good rapport with their masters, Ann and Jim continued to work on their respective Home Estates. Then, in 1873, Rufus Kittrell, youngest son of George Washington Kittrell, conveyed by deed to Ann McDonald, a homestead of her own. Her little cabin, modest and serene, on its plot of approximately three acres, stood for years on the trail that became known eventually as the Ann Homer Ridge. There, Ann McDonald lived, from the time of her departure from the "Big House" until she died, and was buried nearby in 1923.

On May 8, 1884, Ann McDonald's son, Isaac, was united in marriage to Jane Fisher of Perryville. It was in Perryville that Jane and Isaac came eventually to make their home. Jane Fisher's parents were Isabel and John Bell Fisher. In addition to Jane, there were three older daughters: Adeline, Mary and Florence, and three sons: Isham, Henry Clay and John. Jane's sister, Florence, was married to Isaac's brother, Frank.

Isaac and Jane McDonald's children were: Ethel Pearl, Feb. 14, 1885; Alvin Louis, 1888; James Edward Erbie, Aug. 11, 1890; Nyla Mae, 1884; Conna Jewel, Dec. 15, 1890; and Willie Homer, April 11, 1906.

Pearl McDonald married Granville Garrett in 1902. Their children were: McDonald, May 17, 1903; Lawrence Angleo, March 1, 1905; Granville Hugh Kirston, March 10, 1907; George Landon, June 3, 1910; and John Wilson Kerry, Aug. 8, 1913.

Pearl McDonald Garrett died in April 1914. Alvin Louis McDonald died in 1894. Nyla Mae McDonald died in 1896. Homer McDonald died of drowning in 1941. Erbie McDonald died in 1946. Jane Fisher McDonald died May 28, 1934. Her date of birth was Oct. 13, 1866. Isaac McDonald died March 3, 1940. His date of birth was Aug. 26, 1858.

Conna Jewel, youngest daughter of Jane and Isaac, and granddaughter of Ann Homer, was married to Newt Craig of Perry County in 1926. Conna and Newt Craig's children include: Helen Gwen, May 20, 1927; Newt Craig Jr., May 3, 1929; McDonald, April 11, 1931; Ray Eugene, Nov. 23, 1933; Carolyn Virginia, Jan. 25, 1936; Roy Lynn, March 30, 1938; and Reba Jane, July 4, 1941.

To complete Ann McDonald's story, the writer has relied heavily upon oral history, as related to her since early childhood, by her mother, Conna J. Craig; Conna, who had received it herself through the years from her doting father, Isaac; especially in that she so resembled his beloved mother, Ann. The writer also has talked, at length of late, with descendants of the Kittrell family. Their recounting of the saga, she often finds, amazingly concurs with her own.

It will endure, it is hoped, as a tribute to Ann McDonald's memory. *Lovingly submitted by her great granddaughter, Helen Craig Smith.*

EMELINE COLE KING McDONALD,

born 1841 Lawrence County, TN, daughter of William Cole and Mary Nixon Cole, married first Cheatham King as his second wife. Born to them was one son, John W. King, born ca. 1863, and one daughter, Sarah Catherine Cheatham King, born Jan. 18, 1867, after the death of her father, Cheatham King.

Emeline Cole King McDonald; b. 1841 Lawrence Co. TN.

Cheatham King lived on Buffalo River, Perry County, TN where he ran a mill and "still." He was also part owner of a small farm. He died late 1866. He was first married to Martha ?. They had: John born ca. 1844; Elizabeth born 1846; Elbert born 1853; Marida (m) born 1858. Emeline King with her two children were living with her father, William Cole, and his second wife, Mary S., in 1870 in Perry County, TN. Siblings of Emeline Cole were: John, her twin; Mary Catherine born 1843; Sarah J. born 1845; Margaret A. born 1847; Nancy E. born 1850; Leroy born 1857; one half: Louisa born 1866; Alice H. born 1868; Rebecca born 1870; Emeline Cole King married second to William McDonald, a Methodist minister, on Jan. 7, 1875 Perry County, TN. Their children were: Pheoby born 1876; Isaac born 1878; Thomas born 1880; and Mindia born Aug. 25, 1884.

Emeline died March 7, 1920 at the home of her daughter, Mindia McCasland, wife of Irvin S. McCasland. Mindia died March 8, 1920, one day after her mother. Both died with the flu and were laid out on the same bed. Mindia left nine children: Edgar Allen born 1901; Wm. Paul born 1903; Melrose Irvin born 1905; Earl Sylvester born 1906; Annie Elizabeth born 1906; Albert Sydney born 1910; Andy Ervin born 1913; Berta Marie born 1916; and Alice Elma born 1919, a small baby at her mother's death and whom her grandmother Emeline had named.

Sarah Catherine Cheatham King married John Young Warrington Sept. 13, 1883 in Hardin County, TN. Children: Rosa Etta born 1884; Elizabeth Vesta born 1890; Mary Fannie born 1892; Elmer Allen born 1896; Grace Priscilla born 1899; John Carlos born 1901; John Y. died 1902. Sarah married second Wm. H. Geans. She died Feb. 22, 1941.

Thomas McDonald married Lena ?. Children: Aubry, Marie and Alberta.

Isaac McDonald lived in Arkansas.

Pheby McDonald married James Dedrick, lived on Cedar Creek, Perry County, TN. Children: Emmy married Brown; Annie married Stamps; Bill died because of a tumor of the brain.

BOBBY ARNOLD AND BARBARA LEE McGEE FAMILY,

James Hugh McGee, the first born son of Elijah Allen and Nancy Jane Grimes McGee, married Cynthia Caroline Wiley in 1880. Their 10 children were all born in Perry County. The third child, Johnnie Andrew McGee, was born Feb. 2, 1885, probably on Beech Creek in Perry County.

The McGee Family. Back (left to right): Barbara and Bobby McGee. Front (left to right): Blair, Brooke, Oville and Arnold McGee.

When he was about 12 years old, Johnnie left home and began working for other people and it is believed that he first worked for a Richardson family on Cedar Creek.

When Johnnie Andrew was 24, he married Cora Asile Lomax, the daughter of Jesse and Jenny Frances Churchwell Lomax, and moved to the Cedar Creek Community. While living there, Johnnie and Cora had two children, Thelma Kathleen (June 3, 1910) and Jesse Earl (June 3, 1912).

After they moved to the Jim King Hollow in the Bethel Community, they had another child, Johnnie Arnold (June 15, 1915).

They moved again to the Joe Dabbs Hollow in the Bethel Community and had the last two of their five children, Golden Andrew (April 30, 1917) and Lolamae Sene (Oct. 24, 1918).

The house they lived in burned and the whole family moved first to Sugar Hill and then to the Bernard Duncan Farm just east of Linden.

Johnnie Andrew got his first pair of mules and began sharecropping for himself in about 1915. They finally purchased a home of their own in 1944 and Johnnie retired from farming. Cora died Dec. 24, 1944 and Johnnie continued to live in the home until his death on April 19, 1956.

Johnnie and Cora's son, Johnnie Arnold, married Docia Oville Tate, the daughter of William Escar and Pearl Ledbetter Tate, on May 21, 1939. They moved to the Escar Tate family farm, living with Oville's mother Pearl. Their son, Bobby Arnold McGee, was born June 9, 1945 at the King Daughters Hospital in Columbia.

Arnold farmed until 1955 when he also began working as a carpenter and plumber, and Oville taught school.

In 1965 they moved to Nashville and both worked there with Metro Nashville Schools (she in teaching and he in plumbing maintenance) until they retired in 1980 and returned to Perry County.

Bobby attended college at Vanderbilt University and obtained a B.A. in 1971 after returning from a four year tour of duty with the U.S. Air Force Security Service.

On June 12, 1979, while attending Law School at the University of Tennessee, Bobby married Barbara Sue Lee, the daughter of Raymond and Nellie Lee.

Bobby is an attorney in Linden and Barbara teaches at Perry County High School Their two daughters, Brooke Alayna (May 12, 1982) and Blair Alysse (Dec. 15, 1986), live with them on Lick Creek.

Brooke and Blair will probably be full of the "Blarney" since both of their paternal lines (Tate and McGee) have Irish ancestry.

JOHN ANDERSON McGEE, (1834-1918) and Caroline Vickers McGee (1842-1902). John A. McGee was a Methodist minister.

The McGee Family. Standing: Etta. Seated (left to right): Jessie W., Mitchell, Shofner and Jim.

To this union was born: Thomas Mitchell McGee (1877-1950). He came to Perry County, Linden, TN from Dover, TN, Stewart County. He owned and operated a blacksmith shop and grist mill in Linden, TN until 1950.

Thomas Mitchell McGee married Etta Margaret Beasley Feb. 5, 1909. She was a seamstress. To this union three children were born. Thomas Shofner McGee (1910-1987) attended Middle Tennessee State Teachers College at Murfreesboro, TN. He served with the United States Navy during World War II in the South Pacific Theatre. He was employed with the Federal Government for 38 years in the Postal Service. He retired in 1973 from the Nashville Post Office, Nashville, TN. He was a member of the International Checker Hall of Fame in Petal, MS. He married Daisy Allen in 1940. She was a homemaker. To this union two sons were born.

Thomas Allen McGee born 1946 is an engineer.

Patrick Mitchell McGee born 1949 is an engineer. Married Marilyn Elizabeth Arnold in 1973. She is a school teacher. To this union two daughters were born, Meredith Anne McGee, born 1978, and Lauren Elizabeth McGee, born 1980.

James Kent McGee (1911-1989) was employed by the Atomic Energy Commission at Oak Ridge, TN, Paducah, KY, Colorado Springs, CO was an engineer. He retired from the State of Tennessee Highway Department at Nashville, TN. He served in the United States Army during World War II in the European Theatre. He married Rob Strickland in 1939. She is a teacher and Guidance Counselor with the Davidson County School System. They had one son, Robert Stephen McGee, born 1954. He is an Engineer in the Planning Department.

Jessie Woodrow McGee, born 1914, married Edward V. Averett (1907-1971) in 1932. He was a rural mail carrier. To this union two sons were born: Thomas Edward Averett, born 1933. He worked at Dupont and married Earline Hinson Mercer Sept. 3, 1962. Earline was born 1934. To this union one daughter was born, April Averett, April 18, 1967.

Jimmy Joel Averett, born 1936, is employed at Tennessee Department of Transportation. He married Maybelle Arnold 1955. Maybelle was born 1935. To this union two sons were born: Jimmy Arnold Averett, stillborn in 1968, and Joel Edward Averett born 1971. Maybelle was employed at Linden Apparel.

ROBERT WILLIAM McGOWAN, and Grace Ellen Fossey McGowan purchased 100 acres on Cotton Branch from Herschel Mercer in 1965. In 1967, they built a cabin on the banks of Cotton Branch, and in 1981, electric power was brought from Rockhouse Creek Road and a permanent home was built on the cabin site. Robert and Ellen moved into their new home in October 1981.

Robert retired from Memphis State University in 1980. He was Professor of Biology from 1949 to 1980. During this period, he received the Distinguished Teacher Award; Distinguished Alumni Award, Lambuth University; State President of the Tennessee Ornithological Society; Fellow, Tennessee Academy of Science. Prior to joining the MSU faculty, Robert was Naturalist with the Tennessee Department of Conservation. He served in the European Theater in WW II.

Robert was born in Paris, Henry County, TN, June 5, 1922, son of Robert William McGowan and Mary Elizabeth Thompson McGowan. Robert has one brother, Joel Hugh McGowan of Paris, TN. Robert has written a weekly commentary column for several years for *The Buffalo River Review.*

Ellen was born in Memphis, TN Sept. 9, 1924, only daughter of Elisabeth Jarrell Fossey of Humboldt, TN and Dr. Herbert Fossey of London, England and Memphis, TN.

Ellen lived several years in Chicago and in Humboldt. She received a M.A. Degree from Memphis State University and continued studies at the Memphis Art Academy. Ellen taught music at the American Conservatory of music, Chicago, and at Lambuth University. Ellen taught for several years in the Memphis and Shelby County Public School System.

Ellen and Robert have two children:

Ellen Elizabeth (Beth) McGowan, born 1949, presently employed with Federal Express Corporation, Memphis, TN. Beth received a M.A. Degree from Memphis State. She has two daughters, Laura Ellen Smith and Rachel Lane Smith, both recent graduates of Lambuth University, Jackson, TN. Both presently reside in Memphis.

Robert (Rob) William McGowan III, born 1947, served in Vietnam during the Vietnam War. He received a B.A. Degree from Memphis State University and a Master of Fine Arts Degree from Cranbrook Art Institute in Bloomfield Hills, MI. Robert and his wife, Peggy Mahoney McGowan live in Memphis but own a weekend cottage on acreage joining the McGowan property on Cotton Branch. They plan to retire in Perry County. Peggy won an Emmy Award for her camera work on the Johnny Carson Show in Hollywood, CA.

McLEMORE-BATES, Mary Louise McLemore Bates was born Aug. 1, 1942 in Linden, the daughter of Vera Elizabeth Kilpatrick McLemore Hickerson and the late Millard Fraley McLemore. She now lives in Lobelville and has two children: a daughter, Adriane Leigh Bates Medlock, born Dec. 16, 1967, married to Van Duane Medlock Sept. 11, 1993; and a son, Jason Elisha Bates, born Feb. 24, 1976. Both of her children live in Lobelville. Mary Louise has one sister, Marjorie Faye McLemore Weatherly, born Sept. 20, 1937 in Linden and married to Jack Turner Weatherly, born Oct. 2, 1931 in Lobelville. They have three children: a son, David Mac Weatherly married to Janice Denise Dowdy Weatherly. They have three daughters - Amanda Denise Weatherly, Andrea Leigh Weatherly and Alecia Eve Weatherly; a daughter, Jennifer Lynn Weatherly Zemer married to Gerald Michael Zemer, who has a son, Calvin Gerald Zemer; and another daughter, Amy Louise Weatherly Risner married to Billy Risner.

Louise McLemore Bates

Millard Fraley McLemore was born on July 5, 1909 in Flatwoods, the son of Thomas Hurt McLemore and Molly Fraley McLemore. They had another son, Alton L. McLemore, married to Mae Graves McLemore. They had two children, Doris Nell McLemore Clay and Alton L. McLemore Jr. Thomas Hurt McLemore was the son of Richard Morris McLemore (1851-1924) and Ella B. Chappell McLemore (1856-1902) daughter of Tom Chappell. Richard Morris McLemore was the son of James Henry McLemore (1826-1905) and Sarah (Sallie) Ann Whitaker McLemore (1828-1909). The McLemore's and Whitaker's moved to Flatwoods from Halifax County, NC. Molly Fraley McLemore was the daughter of Willis Saul Fraley and Jocie Weaver Fraley, sister of Jenny Fraley Culp and Nannie Fraley Culp. Millard Fraley McLemore's mother died when he was a child and Thomas Hurt McLemore married Bessie Turnbow and they had three more children: a daughter, Frankie Gail McLemore Love married Sam Love. Mother of Doris and Beverly; a son, Charles C. McLemore married Joyce Cooper McLemore. Father of Thomas H. McLemore and Carol Ann McLemore Barnette; and another daughter, Waweida (Buddie) who never married.

Vera Elizabeth Kilpatrick McLemore Hickerson was born on Aug. 10, 1913 in Linden. She is the daughter of William Harrison Hart Kilpatrick (1890-1980) and Mary Pearl Holt Kilpatrick (1896-1944). Hart was the son of William (Bill) Alen Kilpatrick (1868-1952) and Josie E. Halbrooks Kilpatrick. Bill was the son of William Alen Kilpatrick (1843-1874) and Mary Melvina Cooper Kilpatrick Whitwell. William Alen served in the Civil War. Josie E. Halbrooks Kilpatrick was the daughter of Thelbert Halbrooks and Martha Edwards Halbrooks. Mary Pearl Holt Kilpatrick was the daughter of Albert Lenley Holt and Docia Louise Epley Holt. Albert was the son of Mitch Holt and Elizabeth Holt. Docia Louise was the daughter of Jasper Epley. Vera Elizabeth Hickerson is now married to Elmer Hickerson, they live in Lobelville, TN.

JERRY ALLEN McMINN, and Vicky Jane Qualls McMinn are residents of Brush Creek, having moved here from Ripley, MS in June 1994. Jerry Allen McMinn (Nov. 25, 1940) is the son of Elder Carman Allen McMinn (July 12, 1916-June 1, 1990) and Ludie Elizabeth Woods McMinn (Aug. 20, 1923) of Milan, TN. After graduating from Medina High School, Jerry attended West Tennessee Business College, Lambuth College, Austin Peay State University and Memphis State where he earned his BS in History in 1965 and an MA in Geography in 1968. He was ordained as a Primitive Baptist Elder in 1966 and has pastored churches in Tennessee, Arkansas, Ohio and Mississippi.

Elder Jerry A. McMinn married Nancy Lee Rower of Findlay, OH on Jan. 1, 1971. To this union two children were born: Sarah Elizabeth on June 2, 1972 and Phillip David on April 23, 1976. Nancy McMinn departed this life on March 24, 1993.

Vicky Jane Qualls McMinn (Jan. 13, 1955) is the daughter of Elder Waco Melvin Qualls (Oct. 18, 1924) and Ina Webb Duncan Qualls (Dec. 11, 1925). She is a native Perry Countian and a 1973 graduate of Perry County High School. After graduating summa cum laude from Middle Tennessee State University in 1977 with a BA in English and Spanish, "Miss Vicky" taught for ten years at PCHS. She and Elder Jerry A. McMinn were married on June 11, 1988, and she moved to Ripley, MS, where he was living and pastoring Pine Hill Primitive Baptist Church. They lived there for six years, during which time many visits and phone calls were made back and forth to Brush Creek.

Front row (left to right): Jerry McMinn and Vicky McMinn. Back row (left to right): Sarah McMinn Pannell and Phillip McMinn.

Sarah graduated from Ripley High School in 1990. She and Kenneth Ray "Ken" Pannell were married at Pine Hill on Jan. 25, 1991 and currently reside in the Pine Grove community, east of Ripley. Sarah received her Associate Degree in Nursing from Northeast MS Community College in May 1993 and is employed as RN at Tippah County Hospital.

Phillip graduated from Ripley High in 1994 and will report for National Guard basic training in August.

MEALER, A genealogy search of the Mealer family of Perry County has never been sought by the Mealer descendants that now reside in Perry County. What little information that is known has been handed down by second and third generation descendants of this family.

Around the late 1800s and early 1900s, this family resided in Beardstown. They moved from Williamson County and settled near the Cane Creek bridge around Beardstown on their eventual move to West Tennessee (Obion County). Will Mealer was a carpenter and Methodist preacher living in Beardstown and was known to build houses along the buffalo River area near the bridge crossing to Cane Creek. He married to Emer Robertson or Robinson and they were the parents of five children: Willie, Bertha Mealer Warren, Fred, Marvin and Cola Mealer. His wife died and Will Mealer preached her funeral. She is buried (unmarked) in the Beardstown Cemetery. Will Mealer then married Lillie Potts and moved to Obion County in West Tennessee. Will Mealer's young bride bore him two more sons, Elbridge and Hillard Mealer.

Fred, Marvin and Cola Mealer all moved to Chicago, IL during or about the great depression years. Fred died while living in Chicago and is buried there. Marvin later returned to West Tennessee and his children and grandchildren reside there. Cola Mealer was married to Era Warren and they were the parents of four children. One daughter lives in California and the other children and grandchildren live in the Chicago area. Cola and Era Mealer are buried in the cemetery on the hill on Brush Creek (the old Church of Christ site).

Bertha Mealer Warren was married to Johnny Warren. They lived on Brush Creek until their deaths and are both buried in the Warren Cemetery on Brush Creek. Their children include Charles Warren, who resides in Perry County and a daughter, Grace Hankins who lives in Hohenwald. One son drowned in Brush Creek in the 1950s; a son, Elmo, no information; another daughter, Thelma, married Jim Hudson.

WILLIE MEALER, (1894-1951) was married to Lula Southern (1896-1970). She was from Williamson County. They were the parents of nine children: Louella, Lucille, Rueben, Louise, Maie, Sue, Ola, Eula and Zula (twins). Willie and Lula Mealer are both buried in the Beech Grove Cemetery in Hickman County.

Louella Mealer Wood was married to Oscar Wood and has lived in Perry County all her life. She now resides in Linden. Her children are Nell Wood Graves, Bill and Donnie Wood.

Lucille Mealer Armstrong (1915-1980) was married to Clarence Armstrong and lived in Gleason, TN at the time of her death. She and her husband are buried in the Williams Cemetery at Pleasantville, TN. They were the parents of four children: Alton, Magalene Staggs, Briany Wilbanks and Wylie Armstrong.

Rueben Mealer is married to Evon Pace and lives in Jackson, TN. Their children are Faye M. Bundage, Fairlyon M. Hill, Lynn and Ricky Mealer.

Louise Mealer Duncan is married to Ralph Duncan and lives in Hohenwald, TN. Their children are Polly Lampley, June Duncan and Pat Garrett.

Maie Mealer Mullins is married to Smith Mullins and lives in Linden, TN after spending many years in Detroit, MI. Her first husband, Thelbert Halbrooks, was killed in an auto accident in 1955. He is buried in the Beech Grove Cemetery. They were the parents of two sons, Leon and Ray Halbrooks.

Sue Mealer Parnell (1926-1969) was married to Edward Parnell Jr. and lived in Nashville and Bowling Green, KY at the time of her death. She is buried in the Woodlawn Cemetery in Nashville. Their children include, Joann and James Alvin Parnell.

Ola W. (Bill) Mealer is married to Matilda Knight and lives in Nashville, TN. Their children include, Karen and William Mealer.

Eula Mealer Cross is married to Edward Cross and lives in Pleasantville, TN. Their children are Bonita C. Grimes and Steven Cross.

Zula Mealer Qualls is married to Walter Qualls and lives on Sinking Creek in Perry County. Their children are Joyce, Ann and Donna Qualls.

Elbridge and Hillard Mealer were thought to have lived in West Tennessee. Lillie Potts Mealer died in the 1980s.

MERCER-SHARP, Edd Walter Mercer and Lillie Young Sharp were married on Feb. 18, 1917. They lived most of their married lives in the southeastern portion of Perry County, with the exception of a few years they lived in Gibson County. Walter was a farmer and a logger all of his life. He came to Perry County as a young child with his parents, grandparents, aunts and uncles, brothers and sisters in a covered wagon train bringing all their possessions, including a sawmill. They all came from the area of Leitchfield, KY where his great grandfather and great grandmother lived. Lillie was raised in the area near the Wayne, Lewis and Perry County lines, primarily in southeastern Perry.

Edd Walter Mercer Family. Front row (left to right): Dewey, Lillie, Walter, Larry. Back row (left to right): Joe, Arlie, Bertha, Obie, Mary Lou, Ray and Robert; Johnny not pictured.

They had 10 children: Bertha Mae Mercer (born Aug. 15, 1919) who married Herbert Blankenship and had three children; Joe Ivey Mercer (born Oct. 14, 1921) who married Olene Hickerson and had three children; Obie Mercer (born April 18, 1924) who married Bernice Hickerson and had four children; Ray Mercer (born Sept. 15, 1926) who married Marie Trull and had five children; Mary Lou Mercer (born May 25, 1929) who married Dennis Aaron Hendrix and had three children; James Arlie Mercer (Aug. 10, 1931-Dec. 22, 1984) who married Inez McCalister with no issue; Johnny Mercer (born Nov. 27, 1933) who married Velma Rae Anderson and had two children; Robert Mercer (May 18, 1936-Jan. 13, 1962) never married; Dewey Mercer (born Aug. 25, 1938) who married Aleta Bates and had three children; and Larry Wayne Mercer (born July 9, 1941) who married Shirley Ann Rainey and had three children.

Walter's great grandfather was John Mercer who married Rose Ann Bradley. One of their sons was Samuel Comer Mercer (Dec. 11, 1853-Aug. 12, 1915) who married Nancy Ellen Decker (March 2, 1854-Nov. 15, 1931) and had nine children. The oldest son was John Allen Mercer (Dec. 10, 1873-Dec. 23, 1951) who married Mary Frances Wilson (April 28, 1875-Jan. 1, 1906) and had eight children. They were: Jess Thomas Mercer (April 1, 1893-1965); Rebecca Emaline Mercer (March 27, 1894-Aug. 10, 1978); Nancy Jane Mercer (Nov. 8, 1896-April 1, 1897); Edd Walter Mercer (Dec. 8, 1897-July 5, 1971); Luther Willard Mercer (March 26, 1899-March 30, 1982); Eugene Mercer (Oct. 8, 1901-July 17, 1986); John Irvin Mercer (April 4, 1904-Aug. 3, 1974); and Evans Mercer (Jan. 5, 1905-April 1905).

After Mary Francis Wilson died, John Allen married Nora Ada Hickerson and had five more children. They were: Rose Lillian Mercer (born May 4, 1907); Thelma Aslee Mercer (born Feb. 16, 1910); Samuel Hershel Mercer (Feb. 11, 1915-June 7, 1989); Leslie Carl Mercer (May 1, 1921-Feb. 17, 1974); and Carmie Mae Mercer (born Feb. 24, 1924).

Lillie Young Sharp was the daughter of John Franklin Sharp and Lucinda Junetta Tatum. They had five children who died in infancy plus the following: Mary Jane Sharp (born June 22, 1888); George Washington Sharp (born Jan. 30, 1890); Nancy Edna Sharp (born Nov. 2, 1893); John Sharp (born April 5, 1897); Sally Sharp; Lillie Young Sharp (March 14, 1898-March 18, 1994); Suzie Ann Sharp (Sept. 8, 1900-May 12, 1991); Pearl Sharp; Richard Marvin Sharp (born Feb. 22, 1906); Brown Sharp (born April 25, 1908); Whit Sharp (born March 18, 1909); and Bud Sharp (Jan. 13, 1913-Jan. 18, 1975). John Franklin's parents were Samuel Miles Sharp and Hulda Odom. Lucinda's parents were Joshuah Y. Tatum and Nancy Hickerson.

JOSEPH M. MIDDLETON AND SALLY McDONALD, Joseph M. Middleton was born in Perry County Jan. 22, 1868 and died Jan. 3, 1955. He was a farmer. His father, Greenberry Middleton, came to Tennessee from South Carolina. Greenberry Middleton served in Company A 3rd Tennessee Volunteers during the Mexican War 1846-1848. He died in 1870. He married Martha Tracy (1830-1918). To this union six children were born: Victoria Middleton, Dora Middleton, Grant Middleton, Donie Middleton, Asalee Middleton and Joseph M. Middleton.

Joseph M. Middleton married Sally McDonald (1873-1945) in 1891. To this union six children were born: Bertha Leona Middleton (1893-1969); William Waco Middleton (1894-1923); Nora Thornton Middleton (1896-1900); Grady Middleton (1889-1938); Claude Leroy Middleton (1903-1983); Floyd McDonald Middleton (1905-1927).

Bertha L. Middleton married George Carroll Allen in 1911. To this union four children were born: Jessie Maurine Allen (born 1914); Joseph Elgia Allen (1919-1972); Daisy L. Allen (born 1922); Sally F. Allen (born 1929).

Jessie Maurine Allen was an Educator in Perry County School System from 1936-1977.

Joseph Elgia Allen married Bonnye White in 1945. He was a salesman.

Daisy L. Allen married Thomas Shofner McGee in 1940. To this union two sons were born: Thomas Allen McGee (born 1946) an engineer, and Patrick Mitchell McGee (born 1949) an engineer.

Patrick Mitchell McGee married Marilyn E. Arnold in 1973. To this union two daughters were born: Meredith Anne McGee (born 1978) and Lauren Elizabeth McGee (born 1980). Marilyn E. Arnold is a school teacher.

Sally F. Allen married Giles T. Webb in 1971. She attended Union University, Jackson, TN and majored in business administration.

William Waco Middleton served in the United States Army during World War I.

Grady Middleton married Alma B. Hines in 1923. To this union one son was born, Loyde Mayo Middleton (born 1925) married Sarah Louise Locke in 1951. He was a Methodist minister. They both served as missionaries in Bolivia, S.A. To this union two children were born: James Ernest Middleton (born 1953) and Patty Louise Middleton (born 1957).

James Ernest Middleton married Dr. Lynne Wilcox July 10, 1976. To this union two children were born: Martin Middleton (born 1984) and Jennifer Middleton (born 1988).

Dr. Patty Louise Middleton is a medical doctor in North Carolina.

MONROE, By 1880 Samuel B. Monroe, his four sons and one daughter had moved from Lauderdale County, AL to Perry County, settling in the area between Spring Creek and Lick Creek near the Tennessee River. Samuel B. Monroe's Scotch Irish parents had emigrated from the Ulster District of Ireland and settled in North Carolina where he was born in 1811. Samuel B. Monroe was a skilled carpenter and mechanic. These skills were instilled in and passed on to sons, grandsons and great grandsons. Samuel B. had six children by his first wife, Mary (surname unknown): Rueben H.; Pugh Huston; Mary Ann; Josephine; Neill R.; and Martha F. The 1880 census showed Samuel B. living with his second wife, the former Mrs. Winney Cranford and their infant son, James. Samuel B. was 69.

Samuel B.'s oldest son, Rueben H., married Martha Cannon, daughter of John Cannon. They had four children: William Samuel, Dempsey, Rueben T. and Lizzie. William Samuel Monroe married Docia Ester Young. The 1880 census listed them and three daughters: Bessie, Hessie and Willie M. They later moved to Arkansas.

Rueben T. Monroe married Eliza Bell. They had three children: Ola M., who married Oscar Dickson; a son, Ernest Jack; and another daughter, Dotias. Billy Monroe who now lives in Parsons, TN, is a descendent of Ernest Jack Monroe. Rueben T. later married Florence Young Howard. Eliza and Rueben T. are buried in Hopewell Cemetery.

The Monroe Family

Mary Ann Monroe married William Raby in Lauderdale County, AL and in 1880 Mary Ann was living with her nephew Rueben T. Monroe in Perry County.

In 1880 Samuel B. Monroe's son, Neill, was living in Perry County with his second wife, Julia A. Young; four stepdaughters and two sons, two year old, Benjamin, and three month old, R.J. Docia Ester, one of Neill's stepdaughters, married William Samuel Monroe and stepdaughter, Florence's second husband was Rueben T. Monroe. Neill was a peanut farmer and also served as Sheriff of Perry County about 1880. By 1890 Neill and Julia had sold their properties and moved to Ohio County, KY. Part of these properties are now a part of Mousetail Landing State Park.

Clarence B.'s son, Pugh Huston Monroe, married Martha Hays in Lauderdale County, AL and had three children: Samuel Sims, Lizzie and Louis. Pugh Huston served in the 9th and 35th Alabama Infantry Regiments in the Civil War. After Martha Hays death, Pugh Huston married Sara G. Hunt. They had two daughters, Florence and Pearl. Sometime prior to 1880, Pugh Huston and his family joined his father and brothers in Perry County. Clarence B., Pugh Huston and Martha Cannon Monroe are buried in Hunt Cemetery. Pugh Huston's son, Samuel Sims Monroe, married Josephine Marie Gotthardt in 1885 at the home of her grandfather, Matthew James Dickson, on Lick Creek Road. Samuel Sims worked at the Gotthardt Tannery on the Tennessee River at the mouth of Lick Creek. They moved to Louisville, KY and later to Arkansas. Samuel Sims was a blacksmith, carpenter, tanner and miller before heeding the call to preach the Gospel. The last 15 years of his life he was an evangelist preacher organizing churches for the Church of God.

Known descendants of the Monroe family live in Tennessee, Arkansas, Mississippi, Arizona, California, Illinois, Kentucky, Louisiana, Oregon, Texas, Wisconsin and Missouri. *Submitted by Guy E. Monroe.*

MOORE-CULP, Ross Moore (born 1825) married Eunus Whitson. Their son John G. (March 14, 1849-Aug. 29, 1891, Perry Co.) married Julina Groom (1852-1929) on Feb. 12, 1870. John and Julina are both buried in Moore Cemetery.

Roy and Iris Culp

John G. and Julina had a son, John Wesley Bradford Moore (July 17, 1889-Feb. 13, 1969). He married Myrtle Kimble (Feb. 24, 1887-Nov. 18, 1969) on Feb. 4, 1912. Their daughter, Iris, was born April 13, 1917 in Perry County on Swindle Road. She married Roy Lionell Culp (May 23, 1921-Oct. 31, 1993) on Feb. 26, 1941 and had three children. Roy is buried in Wood-Treadwell Cemetery.

Children of Roy and Iris are:

John Thomas Culp (born Dec. 23, 1941) married Betty Joyce Lee Culp (born Sept. 11, 1949) on Dec. 22, 1967. Their children: Tammy Lynette Culp Cunningham (born Sept. 19, 1969) married Robin Brent Cunningham (born July 11, 1965) on March 23, 1989. Children - Joshua Evan Cunningham (born Dec. 11, 1990; Trudy Gail Culp (born Oct. 28, 1972) married Bobby Dwain Hinson (born June 8, 1971) on Dec. 16, 1992; and Corey Lee Culp (born June 4, 1978).

Mary Carolyn Culp (born Oct. 12, 1943) married first George Edward Tangerstrom. Their children: Paula Sue Tangerstrom Williams (born July 30, 1967) married Eddie Williams. Children - Amber Leigh Williams (born Dec. 6, 1986) and Jonathan Cole Williams (born Aug. 12, 1988); George Edward (Bubba) Tangerstrom (born July 11, 1968); and Amanda Louise Tangerstrom (born Sept. 19, 1971). Carolyn's second husband was Danny Christie.

Dwight Paul Culp (born Aug. 27, 1945) married first wife, Jean Inman Culp and had a child, Wanda Evon Culp Raimey (born March 29, 1968) married Randy Michael Raimey (born Sept. 13, 1954) in August 1990; Dwight Paul Culp married second to Judy Ryder Culp and had a child, Wendy Culp (born Jan. 19, 1976); Dwight Paul Culp married third to Sheila Kay Reynolds Johnston Erranton (born June 15, 1961) on June 15, 1990. Sheila's children: Corey Dale Erranton (born June 26, 1980) and Carrie Beth Erranton (born April 30, 1984).

MOORE-GURLEY, Malinda Lee Moore (daughter of Hershel and Bessie) and Robert Lee Gurley, born Feb. 17, 1940, (son of Loyd and Offie Jane Dunavan) were married Dec. 30, 1962 by Elder T.L. Webb Jr. in his home on Culpepper Street, Milan, TN. They lived in Atwood with his parents until Dec. 1963. They moved near Milan and their oldest daughter, Susan Denise was born May 25, 1966, at the City of Milan Hospital.

Tabitha Gurley

In August 1966, they purchased their first home with 44 acres of Carroll County land. The Gurleys moved in October to their home near Atwood. They bought the second farm of 42 acres and built a new home in 1970. Their second daughter, Tabitha Lee, was born April 26, 1975 in City of Milan Hospital.

Malinda was employed by International Telephone and Telegraph of Milan. The company offered her a transfer in October 1978. The Gurleys transferred with ITT to Johnson City in December. They lived just outside Jonesborough, the oldest town in Tennessee for six years, returning to Atwood Dec. 13, 1984.

Robert has been employed in housekeeping at the City of Milan Hospital since March 1988. Malinda has been employed as a printed circuit technician by Consulting Engineering Company Inc. since November 1989.

Susan married Christopher Wayne Prichard, born Aug. 27, 1963 (oldest son of Wayne and Carolyn) of McLemoresville, TN on Jan. 6, 1989. Their children are: Caitlin Suzanne, born April 8, 1990 in City of Milan Hospital, Milan, TN and Courtney Belle, born May 18, 1993 in Key West, FL. They lived in Key West from June 1990 until June 1993, and now live in Jacksonville, FL. Chris is an aircraft mechanic in the United States Navy stationed on the *U.S.S. Washington*, aircraft carrier.

Tabitha lives with her parents in Atwood and she is preparing to continue her education after her graduation from West Carroll. *Submitted by Susan Prichard.*

ANITA FAYE MOORE, was born Oct. 19, 1957 to Rogers and Ollie Mae Ellison Moore. She had one sister, Lydia Joy born 1951. She was born in Linden, TN and lived in the Bethel community until she left home for college. After attending Columbia State college for two years, she graduated from CHS UT in Memphis with a degree in Pharmacy in 1979.

Ollie Belle Magee Harder, age 16.

She married Jim Worden 1983 from Knoxville, TN. They moved to Greenville, NC. They were divorced in 1988. She continues living there, working for Hollowells Drug Stores.

Anita became interested in family history at an early age. She received information from her family including distant cousins that were descendants of the Bunch family. Opal Bunch Evans and Don Richardson were very informative.

Anderson Bunch (1788-1867) was the first of the Bunch family to come to Cedar Creek, Perry County. He had four girls and eight boys. His grave is a crypt built of fieldstone with the initials A.B. carved on the top slab. It is located in the family cemetery on Cedar Creek. Several of his family are buried in this cemetery.

Anita Moore is the great granddaughter of Ollie Belle Magee Harder, who is the great granddaughter of Anderson Bunch. His son, John, was father of Martha Ann who married Elishia Bailey Magee. Their children were: Sallie Mary (July 4, 1882-Sept. 19, 1944) married John

Thomas Turner (1880-1944); John Lewis (1884-); Ollie Belle (Feb. 8, 1886-Oct. 23, 1975) married Prince William Harder (1881-1945); Willie Thomas (1887-1940) married Mary Holder (1890-1966); Nancy Carrie (1888-1911) married John Ferguson (1883-1975); Eddie Lee (1903-1908).

Ollie Belle Magee Harder was known as "Mom Belle" by her family and friends. She had a lively personality. She loved her family, enjoyed reading and especially loved all the different flowers she had growing in her yard. Her great granddaughter, Anita Faye, shares many of her characteristics.

ARNOLD ONEIL MOORE, son of Arnold and Edna Moore, was born March 12, 1927 on Swindle Creek, a branch of Cedar Creek in Perry County, TN. He attended Cedar Creek Elementary School and finished two years of high school at Cedar Creek. He was drafted into service at age 18 and after World War II, he worked at restaurant and truck driving jobs.

Arnold Oneil Moore and Grace Marie Duncan Moore, married April 29, 1950.

He married Grace Marie Duncan April 29, 1950, daughter of Claude and Ora Lynch Duncan of Hohenwald, TN. They had children: Gary Oneil 1954; Lynda Schummer; Barbara Ann 1957-1964; David Mitchell 1962; Candy Hessler; and Rickey Claude 1964.

Arnold Oneil and Grace Moore left Tennessee for work in Michigan in 1950. Grace died 1980 and is buried in Swiss Cemetery in Hohenwald, TN. Arnold continued living in Michigan until his retirement in 1982, then he returned to Tennessee. His second marriage was to Ollie Mae Ellison Moore in 1981. They live on the farm in Bethel Community where she has lived since 1950.

He has enjoyed raising cattle and hogs, farming, gardening, hunting, fishing and entertaining his family. He is "Pa" to his children and six grandchildren. He has two stepdaughters, Joy Moore Pitts and Anita Moore. He has two stepgrandchildren.

BRADFORD ALONZO MOORE, and Stella Ann Bunch Moore had two children: Fount Kendrick Moore, Dec. 25, 1917, and Holly Abner Moore, Dec. 18, 1921.

Holly Moore married Nola Mae Peace, born May 21, 1931, on Oct. 6, 1947. They have three children: Sandra Ann Moore, May 4, 1950; Randy Keith Moore, April 30, 1954; and Mary Lisa Moore, born Nov. 21, 1962.

Sandra married Greg Johnston on Jan. 3, 1975. Greg was born March 20, 1947. They have a daughter, Holly Ray Johnston, born Feb. 25, 1981.

Randy Moore married Sammy Gail Richardson on April 22, 1978. Gail was born Sept. 24, 1957. They have two sons: Eric Keith, born Oct. 20, 1981, and Blake Hunter Moore, born May 10, 1990.

Mary Lisa Moore married James "Tim" Marlin on July 26, 1986. Tim was born July 5, 1963. Lisa and Tim are expecting their first child in October.

DONNA RAE MOORE, was born Sept. 30, 1948 in Chadron, NE to John Wilburn Moore and Loretta Laura Horton Moore. She lived in Nebraska, Tennessee, South Dakota and Colorado. She married first to Merlin Eugene Elliott on March 29, 1969 in Boulder, CO and had one child, James "Jim/Jimmy" Lee Elliott, born Oct. 16, 1967, Boulder, CO. Donna married second to Russell Louis Skinner on Dec. 15, 1979 in Aurora, CO.

Donna Rae

Donna graduated from Fairview High School in Boulder, CO in 1966 and took a job at the new K-Mart working for them 13 1/2 years at two different stores. She married Merlin Eugene Elliott in Boulder, CO. They loved camping, hiking and rebuilding antique cars. Merlin started Jim sanding car fenders and other parts that he couldn't hurt when he was about three years old. Jim loved working with "Pa" and learned the pride that came with finishing a beautiful car. He enjoyed the money he received when the car was sold. Merlin would always give him $200 in $5.00 bills, which Jimmy said made him feel richer. They moved to Englewood, CO in March 1976. Donna still worked for K-Mart but at a different store in management and Merlin was General Manager for a plastics company until they were sold. He then found the job of his dreams, getting paid for rebuilding antique cars. Jimmy was in the second grade, he loved scouting, soccer, biking, baseball, riding his motor bike and driving his mom crazy with practical jokes he would pull on them and friends. Merlin passed away Jan. 16, 1978 at the age of 30.

Donna then married Russell Louis Skinner Dec. 15, 1979 in Aurora, CO and moved into his home outside Castle Rock. They raised cows, turkeys, dogs and cats and helped Dad with the haying each summer. They bought some equipment to make his life and theirs a little easier. This included a 1952 Reo Fire Truck fully equipped. Dad used the generator and water pump on the truck to irrigate his fields. They loved spending the weekends at Dad's and antique hunting on the way down and back home. While there, they would always have a friendly family poker game, kids included, that lasted all night or until the pennies and nickels ran out, and Dad would get out the old guitar every once in a while.

James Lee Elliott (son of Donna) Donna and husband, Russell Skinner

They moved to Kiowa, CO in 1989 where Russ works as an insurance salesman for Farm Bureau. He has been agent of the year several times and in 1993 he earned two out of three Agent of the Year honors. Donna has worked for Woerner Engineering as Personnel, Payroll and bookkeeper for the last 13 years.

They love to snow ski, collect antique hobnail glassware, Hummels and misc, "what ever we like". Donna's genealogy area has grown continually and currently there are almost 12,000 names of connected family members computerized. Donna tries to add family stories as she can, but just computerizing the names and dates has kept her pretty busy.

Russ and Donna became grandparents of a beautiful little boy Nov. 6, 1993. Brandon Scott Elliott was born to James Lee and Jodie Lynn Jackson Elliott at Yokouska, Japan Naval Base. Russ and Donna were there when he was born and spent three weeks with them. *Submitted by Donna Rae Skinner.*

GARRETT HOBART MOORE, (1899-1979), was the son of Issac Bradford Moore and Mary Ophelia Richardson Moore. He was the grandson of James Ross and Eunice Whitson Moore, also William "Billy" and Amanda Bunch Richardson. He was named for the Vice President under President William McKinley.

Wilma Moore and Garrett Hobart

In the year 1918, he married Lydia Mae Graham. She was the daughter of Jackson Mason and Ella Jane Moore Graham. To this union was born one son, Rogers Oneil Moore, in 1925. Lydia died in 1928 leaving her husband and her young son. Hobart's second marriage was to Wilma Coleman in 1932. She was a devoted wife, loving mother, hard worker and a great homemaker.

Hobart loved farming, especially with the mules and plow. He liked the old way best. He raised cattle and hogs until he became disabled in later life.

He lived in Perry County, Cedar Creek community, on the farm near his birth place. He is buried with his parents and relatives in Harder Cemetery near his farm.

His son, Rogers Oneil Moore, married Ollie Mae Ellison in 1947. They moved from Cedar Creek to Bethel Community in Perry County on the Buffalo River. With the help of his Grandpa Graham, they bought the Sam Polk farm. Rogers farmed and hauled agricultural lime to Perry, Gibson and Lewis County farmers. He died June 1971 and was buried in Harder Cemetery.

Rogers and Ollie Mae Moore had two daughters; Lydia Joy, 1951, and Anita Faye, 1957.

Lydia Joy married Joe Anthony Pitts of Wayne County 1973. They have two children: Jane Anna, 1973, and Jason Anthony, 1976.

Anita Faye married Jim Worden of Knoxville, TN 1983 and divorced in 1988. *Submitted by Joy Pitts.*

HERSHEL ROBERT MOORE,

second son of Rob and Belle, born Oct. 10, 1910, married Bessie Bell Smith (oldest daughter of John and Bertha) on Jan. 20, 1933. Squire "Brat" Moore officiated in his home. They lived on Cedar Creek for a year; in 1934 they moved to Gibson County near Rob Moore. Their first child, Walton Hershel, was born Aug. 31, 1934.

In 1936 they moved back to Cedar Creek and lived on the Smith Farm and then moved to the William and Minnie Bunch's farm in 1937. In 1938 they returned to the Brazil, TN Community. In 1939 they moved with Robert Moore to Lynn Point Community. Their daughter, Malinda Lee, was born Dec. 3, 1941.

The Hershel Moore family moved to Van Dyke, MI in April 1946, where Hershel worked on the assembly line at Chevrolet Gear and Axle, Detroit, and then in shipping receiving at Ford Motor Company, Mound Road Division, Ryan, MI. Walton graduated from Lincoln High School, 1952.

In June 1952, the Moores returned to Gibson County, TN. They bought a grocery store outside of Milan, TN. Malinda graduated from Milan High School, 1959.

Walton married Mary Ann Hayes, born May 10, 1937 (daughter of Guy and Erna) on Sept. 10, 1955 in Corinth, MS.

Hershel, Bessie and Malinda moved into a new home in the Lynn Point Community in Oct. 1962. Malinda married Robert Lee Gurley, born Feb. 17, 1940, (son of Loyd and Offie Jane) on Dec. 30, 1962, in the home of Eld. T.L. and Sister Edith Webb. Eld. Webb performed the service.

After the births of five grandchildren and 20 happy years, Hershel and Bessie built a new home in Linden, TN, Nov. 1982. They moved to Brooklyn Ave., Linden. They lived there until her death June 29, 1992, after a four year battle with cancer. She was buried July 1, 1992 in the Harder Cemetery, Cedar Creek. *Submitted by Malinda Gurley.*

HILLARD AND MATTIE MOORE,

Hillard and Mattie's two children are Mavis Chloe, born Dec. 16, 1933 and James Hillard, born Feb. 13, 1948. Chloe attended the New Cedar Creek School built ca 1925 for the first four grades. They had moved to Decaturville, TN where she graduated from high school. While attending Decaturville High School, she met and later married Calvin Wesley "Pete" Lacy. After he graduated high school, he served from 1952-1956 in the U.S. Navy. They were married Sept. 17, 1956 in Corinth, MS. They have no children.

James Hillard Moore and Family in 1987.

They continued their education by attending Middle TN State Univ. where they prepared for teaching careers. Chloe taught at Eagleville High School 1957-1959. They moved to Walled Lake, MI 1959 and taught school, Pete taught 5th grade and Chloe was Librarian. After returning to Tennessee, Pete taught at Turney Correction Center 1973-1981.

In March 1976, Chloe changed her profession to Bookkeeper for Perry Farmers Co-op and Pete, Linden City Recorder 1986.

They live on their portion of property inherited from Hillard and Mattie; referred to as the McCurdy Hollow.

Pete's parents are Jess Milton (Feb. 4, 1897-Aug. 14, 1969) married Dec. 16, 1917 and Bessie Elnor Moody (Nov. 3, 1895-May 31, 1957, buried at Mt. Lebanon Cemetery). Pete is the youngest of three boys, J.B. (May 15, 1924-July 7, 1993) buried at Mt. Lebanon Cemetery, and William Charlie (born Jan. 31, 1928).

James Hillard married Wanda Kaye Pevahouse (born Jan. 1, 1949), daughter of Celia and Carnis; married Aug. 24, 1968 by Nolan Young. They attended Cedar Creek School built ca 1955; graduated Perry County High School 1966. To further their studies, they attended Hohenwald Vocational School, Kaye studied Lab Technician and James, Welding and Maintenance. James served ca two years in the U. S. Army, 1968; worked at Parsons Vulcan Mat'ls, Hohenwald Dana Corp, now employed at Linden Graham Lumber Company. Also, like his forefathers, James has been interested in farming and caring for hogs and cattle on his farm which was the homeplace of John and Ella Broadway, his grandparents. Kaye has worked at Perry County Hospital and is now employed at Angelica Uniform Corp.

They have two children, James Brian, born Jan. 30, 1971, and Heather Renee, born Aug. 6, 1977. After Brian graduated from high school, he continued his studies as Emergency Medical Technician and worked with Life-Tech Ambulance Service ca two years; is now employed at Clifton Correctional Corp. of America. Heather is a junior at Perry County High School and after graduation, she plans to continue her studies to become an Elementary School Teacher.

Kaye's parents were Therial Carnis (Jan. 29, 1921-Jan. 20, 1965) married Feb. 10, 1940 and Celia Asilee Bridges (Aug. 19, 1922-Jan. 28, 1983). They are buried at Wood-Treadwell Cemetery. Her stepfather is Eli Robert "Bobby" Cook, born April 23, 1923, married Aug. 30, 1968.

JAMES MOORE AND JESSE MOORE,

were brothers. James Moore was born about 1765 in Virginia. His wife, Elizabeth, was born about 1766 in North Carolina. Elizabeth was the daughter of Abraham Denton Sr. They were parents of at least four children: 1) Ann, born 1793, married Caswell Swindle and lived at the Arnold Moore farm on Swindle Creek; 2) Elijah married Jane Holder; 3) Mary married Isaac Horner; and 4) Garrett, born between 1800-1816.

Bratt and Mary Moore

Elijah and Jane had the following children: 1) James Ross Moore born about 1825; 2) Garrett Littleberry "Dick" born 1822, married Deliah Akins and were parents of Henry Moore; 3) Loucinda, born 1820, married Henry Grooms and were parents of Clint, Ross and Alfred Grooms; 4) Elizabeth, born 1828, married Elihue Pevahouse and were parents of Jess, John and Liz Pevahouse; 5) John G., born about 1824, married Nomida Whitson and were parents of Johnny Moore.

Elijah, father of the above children, died young and Jane married John Tracy, who was a widower with several children. John and Jane had Isaac, Martha, Sally and Joseph.

Ross Moore, oldest child of Elijah and Jane, married Eunice Whitson, daughter of Harrison Whitson and wife, Ludia Tracy-Lydia was daughter of John Tracy and his first wife. Ross and Eunice had the following children: 1) John married Julia Grooms, daughter of Henry and Lucinda Grooms; 2) James "Jimmy" married Martha Jane Wiley and was father of Ennis and Eason; 3) Isaac Bradford "Brat" married Mary Richardson. I. B. was born 1865, died 1948, and Mary was born 1868, died 1946.

I.B. and Mary had five children: 1) Edna (1889-1974) married Arnold Moore (1892-1974); 2) William Ross Moore (1893-1974) married Gertie Broadway (1899-1972); 3) B. Alozo "Taft" Moore (1894-1974) married Stella Bunch (1895-1983); 4) G. Hobert "Hobe" Moore (1898-1979). His second wife was Wilma Coleman, born 1911; 5) J. Abb Moore (1903-1972) married Cressie E. Lomax (1904-1986). *Submitted by William R. Moore Jr.*

JAMES ABNER MOORE, (Aug. 6, 1903-Oct. 20, 1972) and Cressie E. Lomax (Aug. 14, 1904-Dec. 17, 1986) were married Jan. 1923. There were three children: Nella B. Moore, Inez Moore and Faye Moore.

Nella B. Moore (born Nov. 15, 1923) and Bob Horner (Sept. 16, 1916-Sept. 1, 1978) were married Nov. 1946. There were three children: David, Nancy and Mark Horner.

David Horner (born Nov. 5, 1947) married Divonne Dabbs (born April 22, 1956). Their three children are: Justin Horner (born July 25, 1976), Tessa Horner (born Feb. 13, 1981) and Leigha Horner (born July 24, 1985).

Nancy Horner (born April 29, 1950) married Larry A. Warren (born Jan. 4, 1948) and they have two children: Cayce Warren (born Dec. 31, 1975) and Blake Warren (born Jan. 22, 1980).

Mark Horner (born Nov. 21, 1957) married Sharon Tatum (born Feb. 6, 1960). They have two children: Jared Horner (born May 1, 1989) and Colby Horner (born Dec. 5, 1991).

Inez Moore, second daughter of James Abner Moore (born Sept. 16, 1926) and Wilford Hamm (Nov. 22, 1923-June 11, 1993) were married Feb. 1, 1947. They had one child, W.C. Hamm (born Dec. 21, 1954). He married Sherri Webb (born Jan. 28, 1963) and they have two children, twins: Hayden Hamm and Haley Hamm (both born Jan. 28, 1994).

Faye Moore (born April 7, 1929), third daughter of James Abner Moore, married John Arthur Jones (May 9, 1932-June 16, 1981). There were three children: Artie Jones (born Dec. 15, 1955) who married Robbie Steward (born June 2, 1957) and have two children, Brent Jones (born Sept. 9, 1983) and Brittany Jones (born April 9, 1985); Michelle Jones (born April 27, 1962); and Jamie Jones (born Sept. 18, 1970).

JAMES HENRY MONROE MOORE, was born Nov. 12, 1870, the son of John G. and Julina Grooms Moore. He married M.E. (Lizzie) Thompson (born Sept. 21, 1873) on July 27, 1892. Monroe and Lizzie had four children: Arnold (Sept. 17, 1893); Bertrude (Jan. 7, 1895); Robert Allen (Dec. 27, 1899); and Riley (Sept. 18, 1906). Monroe owned and operated a blacksmith shop, operated a gristmill, and ran a steam sawmill on Cedar Creek. He also made caskets and Mrs. Lizzie lined them. After Mrs. Lizzie died on April 11, 1944, Monroe married Ella Thompson Broadway (born Sept. 10, 1878) on Nov. 21, 1944. Monroe died Jan. 7, 1952.

Monroe and Lizzie Moore

Robert Allen Moore married Minnie Gertrude Richardson (born April 14, 1900) on Oct. 7, 1917. They had two sons: Hollis Osteen (Jan. 12, 1921) and Osco Brown (Jan. 9, 1923). Minnie died Feb. 1, 1953. Allen married Aulma Richardson and they owned and operated Moore's Grocery near their home on Cedar Creek.

Osco married Syble Broadway (born Aug. 27, 1924) on Aug. 16, 1941. They have three children: Joyce (April 4, 1943), Billy (Jan. 25, 1948) and Tommy (Jan. 29, 1956). Osco died May 8, 1983. Joyce married Kenneth Garrison (born March 16, 1943) on Sept. 28, 1962. They have two children: Sharon (Feb. 11, 1964) and Brent (Aug. 12, 1972). Sharon married Tim Bastin (born Dec. 9, 1959) on Nov. 24, 1982 and they have three daughters: Ciji (Jan. 3, 1984), Jena (Jan. 23, 1989) and Macy (March 6, 1991). Billy married Melissa Conder on Sept. 1, 1992. Tommy married Becky Patterson on June 4, 1988 and they have two children: Rachel (Feb. 6, 1982) and Mason (Jan. 28, 1991).

Osteen married Margaret Broadway (born Jan. 21, 1924) on Feb. 22, 1941. They have two daughters: Jane (Sept. 29, 1941) and Carol Ann (Dec. 11, 1944). Jane was married to Wayne Stutts and they had two children: Todd (Feb. 12, 1963) and Karen (Oct. 29, 1960). Todd married Gwen Bowman on Nov. 12, 1988 and they have one child, Nicole Marie (May 22, 1991). Karen married Frank Ittel on March 7, 1987. Carol married Larry Summar (born Oct. 28, 1942) on July 16, 1965 and they have two children: Bart (Sept. 10, 1969) and Carrie (April 30, 1973). Bart married Rachel Hall Oct. 3, 1992. Carrie is engaged to marry Jason Pettus on May 14, 1993. *Submitted by Joyce Moore Garrison.*

JOHN CURTIS MOORE, was born May 10, 1947 in Hohenwald, TN, son of John Wilburn Moore and Loretta Laura Horton. John lived in Nebraska, Tennessee, South Dakota, Colorado and Oregon.

John Curtis Moore

John married first to Wanda Marie Mills Aug. 31, 1967, Rushville, NE and had two children: John Preston Moore, born June 22, 1968, and Angela Mae Moore, born Nov. 30, 1969. John married second to Jana Crawford Dec. 1, 1972, Boulder, CO and had two children: Christopher John Moore, born June 10, 1974, and Jamie Rae Moore, born May 19, 1976.

John was the oldest of four children. He loved to ride motorcycles from the time he was very little, he got the bug from his dad who had a Harley Davidson that he would go for rides on all the time. When John was 15, his mother bought him a motorcycle so that he could have a paper route to earn money. Two days after getting the cycle he was hit by a hit and run drunk driver. He was lucky to be alive as he was injured very seriously and almost lost his leg and arm. After school John moved to Chadron to be near his father. He met and married Wanda Mills and they had two children, John and Angela. This marriage ended in divorce.

John enlisted in the Army Feb. 26, 1971. After basic training, he was sent to Red Stone Arsenal, AL for training. While marching one day, the drill sergeant saw him limping and asked what was wrong. John told him that the steel plate in his leg bothered him in cold weather. He was sent to the hospital for x-rays and immediately discharged and told he should have never been accepted for active duty. John then moved back to Colorado where he met and married Jana. They lived in Colorado for a while then moved to Nebraska. In 1976 John was working as a security guard for an electronics company. Jana and Christopher were in Colorado visiting her parents. John drove to Colorado to pick them up and while there he received a call that the pipes on the mobile home had frozen and burst. He left to go back to take care of the trailer and was killed when he ran into a bridge. Jana was then six months pregnant with their second child, who was born 2 1/2 months after Johns death. John was buried at Fort Logan National Cemetery in Denver, CO.

John's first wife, Wanda, remarried and allowed her husband to adopt the children after John's death. The children as of 1981, had still not been told that they were adopted and who their real father was.

Jana also remarried and had a little girl, before that marriage also ended in divorce. The boys, Christopher and Jamie have grown up to be very nice looking boys.

JOHN WILBURN "WEB" MOORE, son of Albert Arnold Moore and Julia Edna Moore, was born Dec. 26, 1923 at the family home near Linden, TN. John married Loretta Laura Horton Sept. 6, 1946 in Chadron, NE and had four children: John Curtis, born May 10, 1947, Hohenwald, TN; Donna Rae, born Sept. 30, 1948, Chadron, NE; and Larry Dean and Terry Wayne, born July 8, 1954, Chadron, NE.

John Curtis and Donna Rae Moore, children of John Wilburn Moore.

John grew up on the family farm near Linden, TN. He was inducted into the Army Oct. 20, 1945 and was eventually stationed at Fort Robinson, Nebraska (now a museum) working as a Vet Technician taking care of the mules and other animals. He was also a dog trainer. It was while he was stationed there that he met and married Loretta Laura Horton. They stayed in

Nebraska until John was discharged Jan. 18, 1947, moving to Tennessee just in time for the birth of their first child, John Curtis. On the move again back to Nebraska just before the birth of daughter, Donna Rae. They stayed only as short time before returning to Tennessee again. John helped his dad work the farm for about two years before heading back to Nebraska where John worked for a roofing company. He applied and was hired at the Black Hills Army Ordnance Depot, also known as Igloo, SD. He received many safe worker and safe semi driver awards over the years. The family lived there when the twins, Terry and Larry were born. The kids all started school at Igloo. They had many good times and had a lot of things to keep them busy.

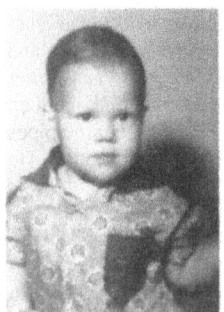 

Larry Dean and Terry Wayne Moore, children of John Wilburn Moore.

John came home later than usual one night as he had been helping fight a forest fire on the Depot property. The family ate dinner, John and Donna went to do their homework. John and the twins were watching TV and Loretta was doing dishes, she reached into the lunch pail and took out the Thermos to wash it, then reached in for the silverware, screaming, she threw a small ball over her shoulder across the room, where Donna setting at the table caught the ball and started laughing as her father about doubled into laughing. The cute little fur ball was a baby cottontail rabbit that John had found under a pallet of bombs that morning. John would always bring rabbits home to Donna who had about a dozen that she had raised, for pets and to sell to the Army. John always loved animals, fishing with the kids on the weekends, hunting for gold and uranium in the black hills of South Dakota, where he had several mining claims, farming and his Harley Davidson motorcycle.

John Wilburn Moore, son of Albert and Julia Moore.

The family lived at Igloo until Donna graduated from the eighth grade. They then moved to Nebraska for a year. Loretta then took the children to Colorado and John stayed in Nebraska. John had several jobs driving delivery trucks cross country but he missed farming and animals. He finally bought some land in Nebraska and raised a few cows, pigs, chickens and his pet bronze turkey, "Tom". He later moved to LaJunta, CO where he bought a piece of land along the Arkansas River, taking his pet turkey in a specially made cage. This turkey became the best watch dog. Always setting atop the chicken shed and protecting the house. No one knows what happened to "Tom" but he disappeared one night without a sign.

John's separation from Loretta had lasted many years and finally ended in divorce in 1976. The kids were separated from John for several years but when they were old enough to find him they never lost track again. At his passing July 21, 1990, he had three living children and 11 grandchildren and a new addition in November 1993, a great grandson he always wanted, but didn't live to see.

John died at the Veterans Hospital in Denver, CO of lung cancer, which he had been fighting for the last few years. He had lived in LaJuanta, CO for several years and would come by bus to Castle Rock where Donna or Larry would meet him and drive him on up to Denver for his doctor appointments. He had given up truck driving and farming as his health was getting bad.

His children were with him at the hospital his last days. He was slipping in and out of coma so the chaplain had been requested. He passed away only a few hours later. He was buried July 25, 1990 at the Fort Logan National Cemetery in Denver, CO with full military honors. His oldest son, John Curtis is also buried at Fort Logan National Cemetery.

JULIA EDNA MOORE, (1889-1974) was the daughter of Issac Bradford and Mary Ophelia Moore. She was granddaughter of James Ross and Eunice Whitson Moore and William "Billy" Richardson and Amanda Bunch Richardson.

Albert Arnold and Julia Edna Moore

Julia Edna Moore married Albert Arnold Moore, son of Monroe and Lizzie Thompson Moore in 1911.

To this union were born four daughters and three sons, one son died at four years of age. Mary Hazel 1913 married Cecil Carter. Ella Izel 1915 married Osby Kimble. Della Olivia 1916 married William Ferd Groom. Julia Irene 1919 married Floyd Pephin. Bradford Wayne 1921 died 1925. John Wilburn 1923 married Loretta Horton. Arnold Oneil 1927 married Grace Duncan.

Arnold and Edna Moore moved from Cedar Creek community to Swindle Creek in 1920. The farm was bought by Issac Bradford Moore from Robert Thompson and was deeded to Edna Moore at his death. At the death of Edna and Arnold, which was one month apart in 1974, each child was deeded a portion of the farm.

They worked hard on the farm. Edna was noted for "good cooking" and feeding her family and friends. Arnold enjoyed farming, especially working in the woods, hauling logs and ties with teams of mules.

They lived on Swindle Creek until their deaths. They were buried in the Moore Cemetery on Swindle Creek. *Submitted by Arnold Oneil Moore.*

LARRY DEAN MOORE, twin son of John Wilburn Moore and Loretta Laura Moore, was born July 8, 1954 in Chadron, NE. He lived in South Dakota, Nebraska and Colorado. Larry married Paula Lynn (Elliott) Fauth on July 24, 1976 in Mitchell, NE and had three children: Abby Leigh born Feb. 9, 1979; Jarred Dean born Dec. 3, 1980; and Maggie Lynn born Feb. 23, 1986.

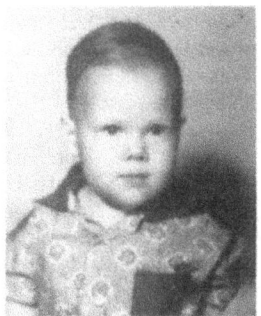

Larry Dean Moore

Larry completed 11th grade in Boulder, CO.

Larry met Paula while living in Nebraska. They were married July 24, 1976 and moved to Kearney where Paula attended college. This is where Abby was born. After Paula graduated, they moved back to Mitchell where the family lived when Jarred and Maggie were born. Paula was a manager for Ken's pizza and Larry worked for Banner Drilling, as a driller in Kansas, Wyoming, Nebraska and Colorado drilling oil wells. The family then moved to Colorado in 1989. Larry took a job working for Denver Brick, for several years as a fireman, and Paula found a job with Wal-Mart and is now in the Assistant Manager Trainee Program. Then in 1992, Larry took a job with Wal-Mart as Shipping and Receiving Manager. Larry also has a paper route that he travels every morning thru the area south and west of Castle Rock delivering the Denver Post each morning before reporting to his job at Wal-Mart.

Abby is in the 9th grade at Douglas County High School. She likes math, choir and has gone to three different school camps. She likes to ride horses, read, go to 4-H with her dog, boys, music and color guard. The group goes to competitions, performs at football games and their color guard team took fourth at state this year. Abby starting playing the violin when she was 10, but has switched to the Chello which was her first choice anyway.

Jarred is in the 7th grade at Douglas County

Junior High. He likes to snow board, play baseball, football, ride his bike, inner tubing on the Platte River and riding 4-wheels with Uncle Oneil.

Larry, Abby, Paula, Jarred and Maggie

Maggie is in the 2nd grade at Castle Rock elementary learning how to read and do math. She likes playing with nintendo, barbie dolls, swimming, horse back riding and going to grandma's. Maggie has had open heart surgery and is doing quite well.

The family likes to go on picnics, panning for gold in local streams, and vacations to Tennessee when schedules permit.

ROBERT ROSS MOORE, second son of John and Juliana Groom, born Dec. 14, 1875, and Malinda Belle (daughter of Billy and Mandy Bunch Richardson) born Nov. 27, 1877, were married Oct. 4, 1896 by John Madison Broadway. They had two sons, Wesley Hillard, born Nov. 13, 1907, and Hershel Robert, born Oct. 10, 1910.

1931, Tilda and Robert Moore.

In the summer of 1916, Hershel developed crossed-eyes or double vision. Albert Grooms and Rob took him to Columbia, TN to see and eye specialist, their way of travel was by horse and buggy. The first night was spent with the Tom Conner family in Lewis County; the second night they stayed with the Tom Smith family in Maury County. The third day they went on into Columbia and saw the doctor. He prescribed medicine to correct the problem rather than glasses. The return trip was two days on the road with nights at the Smiths and Conners. Hershel still does not wear glasses at the age of 83.

During the winter of 1917-18, Enos Moore and Rob Moore went rabbit hunting with sticks. The snow was so deep the rabbits couldn't run. The men would see the rabbits breath thru breathing holes, poke the sticks in and make the rabbits jump out. They would then knock them in the head. Early hunting on Cedar Creek. Robert (Rob) and his brother, Monroe, were blacksmiths and also ran a gristmill to make corn meal.

Belle Moore died April 26, 1929, she is buried at the Bunch Cemetery, Cedar Creek. On Oct. 23, 1929, Rob married Cora Grooms. She died of typhoid fever Aug. 15, 1930 and was buried at the Bunch Cemetery. (1897-1930) daughter of Chesley Groom.

Rob told his sons if one of them would marry and bring in a cook that he would not remarry. Neither Hillard nor Hershel seemed ready to marry. So Feb. 28, 1931, Rob married Tilda (Moore) Pevahouse, born Feb. 8, 1882, daughter of Johnny Moore, widow of Jess Pevahouse. She had one living daughter, Cressie.

Rob and Tilda moved to Gibson County, between Frog Jump and Brazil, TN in Dec. 1932. They moved to Lynn Point Community, between Rutherford and Bradford in Dec. 1939. In 1958 they moved to Milan near Hershel and Bessie Moore where Rob Moore died Oct. 29, 1961. He was buried at Bunch Cemetery, Cedar Creek, between his first wives. Mrs. Tilda Moore moved to Michigan to live with her daughter, Cressie Barnhill until her death Feb. 18, 1969. She is buried at Bethel Cemetery, Bethel, Perry County. *Submitted by Hershel Moore.*

TERRY WAYNE MOORE, twin son of John Wilburn Moore and Loretta Laura Moore, was born July 8, 1954 in Chadron, NE. He lived in South Dakota, Nebraska and Colorado. He married first to Pamela Hockman Jan. 6, 1975 in Boulder, CO and had two children: Shane Anthony Moore, born Jan. 31, 1976, and Heather Jo Moore, born Nov. 29, 1977. Terry married second to Kerri Renee Neilson on Nov. 19, 1981 and had John Curtis Moore, born Feb. 12, 1982.

Terry Wayne Moore

Terry completed school in Boulder, CO. He joined the Navy and was stationed at Groten, CT submarine base. Terry married Pam and took her with him. After leaving the Navy, they moved to Nebraska to be near Terry's brothers and father. This marriage ended in divorce.

Terry then met and married Kerri and had one son, John Curtis, that was named after Terry's older brother that died in 1976. This marriage also ended in divorce.

Terry has worked at the Oklahoma prison as a computer operator for about a year, he then moved back to Nebraska and worked for the Platte Valley bank as the computer systems supervisor until the bank was sold. He then worked at different jobs before going to Grand Island, Nebraska Law Enforcement School. This got him a job working for the Scottsbluff County Sheriff's office as the jailer, and he just recently transferred to the juvenile department working with kids.

Terry has always been a good mechanic and you can usually find him in the garage working on something. His oldest son, Shane, who now lives with him, has also become a pretty good mechanic. His daughter, Heather, lives with her mother not too far from Terry and Shane.

WALTON HERSHEL MOORE, (son of Hershel and Bessie), born Aug. 31, 1934, married Mary Ann Hayes (daughter of Guy and Erna Hayes), born May 10, 1937 in Corinth, MS, on Sept. 10, 1955. They lived outside of Milan when their first son, Anthony "Tony" Walton was born July 20, 1957, in Milan Hospital. They moved to Dell Street in Milan before their second son, Russell Glenn, was born Sept. 5, 1958 in Milan Hospital. Their family was completed by the birth of their daughter, Sarah Ann, on Dec. 26, 1962.

Tony and Linda Moore and children, Nicole Lindsay and Matt.

Walton went to work for the National Guard as a full time employee in 1963.

They moved to their new home in April 1968, it is located on Christmasville Road outside of Trenton.

He retired in Oct. 1992, after 40 years as a Guardsman and 29 years as a full time Guardsman.

Anthony "Tony" Walton Moore married Linda Louise Martin, born Dec. 9, 1956, in Trenton First Baptist Church Sept. 22, 1978. They lived in Milan for a couple of years and then moved to the family house at Lynn Point. Their son, William Matthew, was born Aug. 2, 1984, in City of Milan Hospital. They moved to Trenton where Tony opened his own business, Modern Medical Care. Their daughter, Lindsay Nicole, was born June 29, 1991 in Jackson. Linda and Tony are both licensed practical nurses.

Russell Glenn (Speedy) went to Jamaica with the Peace Corps for two years in 1983. He returned home in early 1985. He was married to Robin Matthews Sept. 22, 1988 at her home outside Trenton, by Squire Josephine Jackson. Because of a freak automobile accident, Russell was killed April 11, 1990. He is buried at White Rose Cemetery, Gibson, TN.

Sarah Ann "Sam" married Donald Anthony Hardwick, born June 21, 1961, on April 19, 1985 in Humboldt, TN. They have lived in Jackson, Selmer and South Fulton, TN; Fulton, KY; Myrtle Beach, SC; and now live in Wilson, NC.

Meagan Learray was born March 23, 1987

at Jackson, TN. Walton Russell was born Jan. 17, 1991 in Jackson, while they were living in South Fulton. Don is the manager of the Wal-Mart Discount Store in Wilson, NC. *Submitted by Walton Moore.*

WESLEY HILLARD MOORE, first son of Rob and Belle, born Nov. 13, 1907 on Cedar Creek, Perry County. He attended the Old Cedar Creek School built approx. 1880, located on the hill above where now stands the Old Sutton Primitive Baptist Church. He graduated from 10th grade there. At that time, that was as far as students could go to school, unless one went to Linden. Since the mode of transportation was by horse and buggy and the gravel roads not kept in very good condition; having to leave home to rent rooms in Linden; not many students finished high school. At the age of 22, Hillard almost died of typhoid fever.

Hillard and Herschel Moore

Hillard helped his father and uncles with their blacksmith shop and grist-mill, farming and caring for the animals. His greatest interest was in husbandry and he continued this line of work throughout his life in taking the best of care of his pigs and cattle on his farm.

On July 31, 1932, Hillard married Mattie Odle Broadway, (daughter of John and Ella); they were married by Squire "Brat" Moore on Cedar Creek.

Mattie finished 10th grade at Cedar Creek School and moved to Linden to finish high school. She and Eleanor Smith rented or "Boarded Out" rooms their first year at the home of Glenn and Maude Wood (Sarah Breeding's parents); their second year they rented rooms from Joe and Bernadine Hufstedler until their graduation in 1930. Mattie continued her education to become a school teacher.

After living in different counties - Perry, Gibson, Decatur, they moved back to Perry County, when they bought out the heirs after Ella Broadway's death in 1957.

Hillard died March 16, 1976 and Mattie died Dec. 11, 1983. They are buried at the Broadway Cemetery on Cedar Creek, Perry County.

WILLIAM ROSS MOORE, (1893-1974) and Gertie Broadway Moore (1899-1972) had four children: 1) J. Willard Moore (1917-1976) married Norma Ledbetter, born 1931. They had three children: Tom Moore, born 1954, married Cathy Tice, born 1952 and they had Caleb, born 1981, and Brooks, born 1984; Brenda Moore, born 1959, married Leslie "Buster" Dabbs, born 1958, and they had Autumn, born 1986; Terry Moore, born 1964.

2) William Ross Moore Jr. married Helen Whitwell on Feb. 4, 1948 and they had three children: Alice Marie (April 1, 1949), Mary Jane (Dec. 31, 1950) and Joe Thomas (Oct. 2, 1952).

Marie married Jimmie Howard (March 9, 1949-Nov. 7, 1992) on Dec. 12, 1970. They had Kelley Lynn Howard (Jan. 20, 1973) and James Heath Howard (Aug. 17, 1978).

Mary Jane married Dennis McDaniel on Dec. 14, 1969 and they had Lana Deniece (Nov. 1971-May 2, 1990), Denny McDaniel (Dec. 16, 1972) and Darrin Ross (April 19, 1980).

Joe Thomas married Barbara Phillips Oct. 1969 and Millissa Rogers Oct. 1985. His children were: Tammy Sherree Moore (born April 28, 1970) married Chad Eric Richardson in June 1989 and they had a son, Cain Eric (Oct. 17, 1989-April 15, 1993); Christa R. Moore (born June 25, 1973) married Jimmy M. Brown in April 1991 and they have Caja Brown, born July 3, 1992; Joe Brandon, born Jan. 24, 1977; and Zachary Batton Moore, born Feb. 3, 1986.

3) Johnnie Bratt Moore, third child of Ross and Gertie (June 29, 1921) married Neva Graham (Sept. 14, 1928) on May 9, 1947. They had two children: Barbara Jean Moore (Nov. 15, 1948) and Jimmy Neal Moore (Aug. 16, 1952). Jimmy married Cathy Bates (June 22, 1952) on Sept. 11, 1970 and later divorced. They had one child, Camilla Dawn Moore (Sept. 2, 1971).

4) James Kenneth Moore, fourth child of Ross and Gertie, was born in 1924 and died in 1931. *Submitted by Marie Moore Howard.*

KATHRYN NEWTON, Niles and Kathryn Newton Wheeler live in Willard, OH. Kathryn is the great-great granddaughter of John Newton.

*John Newton was a native of North Carolina where he was a farmer and stockman. He had a large family. Three of them were *Charles, Jesse, and John. *John's family migrated to Perry County, TN, in the early 1800s and settled on Lick Creek about 1818.

*Charles Newton born Feb. 16, 1810, died Feb. 16, 1881 grew up in Perry County. Charles married Susan Whitehead born Oct. 11, 1813, died June 11, 1881. Charles served four years in the Confederate Army. He was a farmer, Democrat, a member of the Primitive Baptist Church also had a liberal education and taught school in the area where he lived. In 1844 the family moved to Missouri and moved to Hot Springs County, AR, in 1854. In 1869 the family migrated to Denton County, TX. The trip took about two weeks by covered wagon. When they made this trip Charles was 59 and Susan was 56 years of age.

The children of Charles and Susan were: John Whitehead, James Lewis, Richard Monroe, William Lenier, George Washington, Martha Ann, Charles Peyton, Mary Jane, Sarah Elizabeth, *Reuben Pickett, Sir Isaac, Ellen Adeline, and Corey Pettigrew.

Charles and Susan are buried in the Tyson Cemetery near Sanger, TX. John (father of Charles) is buried on the Sir Isaac farm which is now under water from the Ray Roberts Lake.

*Reuben Pickett Newton born Jan. 9, 1849, died July 9, 1917 was born in Denton County, TX, and he married Laura Meeks Burleson on Easter Sunday April 16, 1876. Laura was the daughter of Bennett Mustgrove Burleson and her mother was Matilda M. Lowrey. Reuben and Laura moved to Clay County, TX, in the late 1800s and settled on a large tract of land. At first they lived in a log cabin and about 1900 they built a large house. He was a rancher and interested in education which resulted in three of his children becoming school teachers. He died on the Newton Ranch in Clay County. Laura was born in Sanger, TX, March 21, 1855, and died Sept. 6, 1941, in Wichita Falls, TX. Both of them are buried in the cemetery at Antelope, TX.

The children of Reuben and Laura were: Roxie Lena, Mary Ellen, Estella Belle, Mildred Effie, *Emory Charles, and Mattie Ruby.

*Emory Charles Newton born Dec. 15, 1886, died Aug. 24, 1954, was born in Denton County. He was a rancher and farmer. He was schooled to be a teacher and was always interested in education. He lived most of his life on the Newton Ranch. He married Alma Dawdy on Jan. 26, 1913. Alma born July 15, 1896, died Feb. 16, 1968. Alma was the daughter of Benton Blithe and her mother was Margaret Jane Dansby. Both of them are buried in the cemetery at Antelope, TX, in the area where they both spent most of their lives.

The children of Emory Charles and Alma were: Winifred Roxie, Reuben Benton, Emory Charles, Laura Marie, *Alma Kathryn, and Robert Prescott.

Alma Kathryn born Aug. 31, 1922, married Niles Wheeler on Oct. 29, 1945. The children of Niles and Kathryn are: Clinton Charles and Edith Karen.

NIX, In the early 1800s, William Nix I and his wife, Burnett, brought their family from North Carolina and settled in the Roans Creek area. Several years later, the family migrated to Texas. They left behind their oldest son, Carroll, to gather the crops and settle the family business. He was to follow his father and family to Texas at a later date.

John H. and Bettie Ann (Horner) Nix. Circa 1920.

During this time, Carroll taught a "subscription" school as well as farmed. While traveling the area to solicit pupils for his school, he visited the Young family on Lick Creek and met their daughter, Elizabeth. Carroll and Elizabeth were soon married. He spent the rest of his life in Perry County, never joining his family in Texas. He is buried in the Pineview Cemetery as are many of his descendants.

Carroll fought in the Civil War and was taken prisoner of Union forces at the Battle of Vicksburg.

Carroll and Elizabeth had one daughter, Lizzie, who married a Mr. Burnett. Elizabeth died quite young. Carroll then married Priscilla Putman. They had four children: Martha, Safronia, Tom, and John Henry.

Martha married Paul Mederis. Safronia married Richard Tubbs. Tom Nix married Della Tate and they reared their family on Roans Creek and Toms Creek. Their children were Ray, Carroll, Wilbur, and Priscilla. Before her marriage Priscilla taught in Perry County schools. Wilbur continues to live in Perry County near Britts Landing.

John Henry Nix married Bettie Ann Horner in 1876. She was the daughter of John Valentine and Elizabeth Dilworth Patterson Horner. John and Bettie lived on Lick Creek, and their ten children (including two sets of twins) were born there. Four of the children died in early childhood: Cornelius, Franklin, Bobby, and Lucious. The other children were Walter, Claude, Betsy, twins Zack and Zeb, and Lucille, the twin of Lucious. From about 1910 to 1925 Claude, Betsy, and Lucille each taught some years in Perry County schools.

Walter married Lula Patterson and spent most of his adult life in Humphreys County. Betsy married R.A. Kelton of Rutherford County, and Lucille married Bell Hunter of Cheatham County.

Zack Niz married Sadie Madden. They had three daughters, two of whom live in the Pope Community on Cypress Creek. They are Elizabeth (Mrs. Jack) Sutherland and Nell (Mrs. C.W.) Briley. The third daughter, Sue is now deceased. She was married to Watt French, and several of their children live in the county.

Zeb married Hazel Beasley. They had one son, Johnny, and all are now deceased.

Around 1910, Claude Nix moved his father, mother, and unmarried brothers and sisters from Lick Creek to Pope on Cypress Creek. They lived there until 1938 when the family moved to Linden. Claude was married to Lorene Stewart in 1925. She had come from Crockett County to teach school on Cypress Creek. Claude and Lorene had one daughter, Patty. In 1944, she was married to Troy Carrington and they live in West Memphis, AR. *Submitted by Patty Nix (Mrs. Troy) Carrington*

WILLIAM ALFRED O'GUIN, 1914 came from Sulphur Creek in Hickman County to work at Goodman/Starbuck sawmill on Lost Creek in 1937. Here he met and married Sarah "Sallie" Dickson Shelton, 1907-1988. To this union were born Sarah Katherine 1937 who married Gerald J. Herzog in 1959; William Howard 1944 who married Betty L. Trull in 1967; Ronald Thomas 1947 who married Lottie M. Campbell in 1969; and Jean Laverne 1949 who married David Wayne Qualls in 1968.

Alfred is the son of Sidney Thomas O'Guin, 1880-1965 and Callie Narcisse Beasley, 1883-1954 both from Hickman County who are buried in Chessor Cemetery in Hickman County. He is the grandson of John Lafayette O'Guin 1858-1935 and Mollie Chandler 1865-1924 and Mark Beasley and Mattie Lewis all from Hickman County.

John Lafayette O'Guin was the son of Thomas O'Guin and Mary Bates. Thomas served in Civil War Co. "F" 42 Tennessee Infantry. Thomas O'Guin father Tyler O'Guin came to this country from Ireland and settled in Perry County on Tom's Creek.

Alfred and Sallie O'Guin.

Mollie Chandler was the daughter of John Chandler who died in the Civil War and Adeline Loftus 1842-1924. Adeline is buried in Chessor Cemetery, Hickman County.

Sallie is the daughter of Milton Clarence Dickson 1878-1918, and Sara Mandy Odella "Della" Marshall 1883-1918 who are both buried in Bible Hill cemetery in Perry County.

Della Marshall is the daughter of Kelly S. "Bud" Marshall 1864-1944 and Margaret Barnett 1861-1929.

Alfred O'Guin married Mary Dee Cook in 1989 and are now living on MockinBird Lane in Centerville.

D. ALLEN O'GUIN, born 1861, died 1898, buried in Danielsburg cemetery. He and Dora Sharp had three children, all born Tom's Creek. 1) Verda Lillian O'Guin, born Feb.14, 1892, died Jan. 20, 1981, buried Danielsburg cemetery. She married Aug.. 11, 1919, Perry County, to John Daniel Curl. He born July 31, 1881, Perry County, died Sept. 20, 1957, Pineview, son of John Curl and Addie Vaughan. One son, John Andrew Curl. 2) Fount McKinley O'Guin, born December 1894, died Jan. 8, 1979, buried Danielsburg cemetery. He married Sept. 27, 1914, Perry County, Connie Mae Luckett. She born Jan. 7, 1891, died May 23, 1986, buried Danielsburg cemetery, daughter of Jesse Luckett and Margaret Moore. Their children, Myrtle, David A., Connie Pearl, Ruth, and Joe O'Guin. 3)Ila Oda O'Guin, born March 8, 1896, one mile below Pineview cemetery died Sept. 23, 1985, Linden, buried Pineview cemetery. She married March 26, 1920, DePriest Bend, Marion Osby Cotton. He was born Jan. 4, 1889, died Oct. 23, 1960, buried Pineview cemetery. He had married first, Venus Horner in 1913. He and Oda had three children, twins Hilda and Helen Cotton born and died 1923 and Garvis Lunn Cotton.

After Allen O'Guin died, Dora married Jarrett Nathaniel Baars, born 1853, died 1922, buried Beardstown cemetery. His parents were George and Lena Baars and he had married first, Sarah E. Cude, 1872. He and Dora had five, possibly six, children. 1) Velera Pearl Baars, born Jan. 13, 1905, married Jan. 1, 1922, Fred Cotham Wilsdorf. Fred born May 31, 1902, Perry County, son of Henry Wilsdorf and Ethel Marie Cotham, died Oct. 18, 1986, buried Pineview cemetery. Their children, Laverne; Fred C.,Jr.; Charles Lindy; and Doris Wilsdorf. 2)Sue Elizabeth Baars, born May 14, 1907, Beardstown, died Feb. 3, 1907, buried Pineview cemetery. Her husband, William Nathan Horner, born 1898, died 1948, son of Jessie Wilson Horner and Emma Daniels. Children of Sue; Dan, Nova, Norma, and Gary. 3) Nathaniel Baars died as an infant, buried on Buffalo River near Beardstown. 4) Mollie Baars, born May 5, 1910, per Perry County birth records. She must have died as an infant unless this is Nathaniel. 5)Willie Baars, born July 10, 1912, died Jan. 7, 1977, buried Danielsburg cemetery. His wife, Nancy, daughter of Robert Aldridge, born Feb. 8, 1909. They had two daughters, Sylvia and Rita. 6) Lena Baars, born Jan 26, 1915, married June 1, 1935, Virgil Fred Carlton. He born June 27, 1906, Perry County, died Sept. 22, 1983, buried Pineview cemetery. His parents, William Carlton and Beulah Rainey. Their children, Billy N., Johnny, and Carolyn.

HARDY O'GUIN, (circa 1755-1774-after 1840) came to Perry County after the 1810 census, where he is identified in Anson County, NC, and in 1800, Robeson County, NC. Between 1810 and 1812, Hardy migrates with his family into the Roans Creek area of Perry County. He is listed in the 1812 Humphreys County tax returns in Captain Simpson's County militia unit but no deeds in Humphreys County are credited to him. Placing Hardy on Roans Creek in 1812 would place the O'Guin family some 20 miles out on the frontier and below the Duck river boundary. During 1813 both counties of Hickman and Humphreys petitioned the State of Tennessee, General Assembly to fund a company of militia rangers to protect the area from savages. The area below the Duck river in what would become Perry, Maury, and other counties was not to be opened until after 1818 Treaty signed by Andrew Jackson and Issac Shelby with the Chicasaw Indian nation. In the 1820 census, Hardy O'Guin and family are listed in Humphreys County. The county lines of Perry were in continuous change and remained that way well into the 1850s. Only two deeds have been attributed to Hardy and it is assumed that Hardy lived and remained on Roans creek until his death after 1840. On May 11, 1824, Hardy has his deed entered into the Entry Book No. 1 pp. for 50 acres. With the threat of land speculators jumping claim on registered land, the Tennessee General Assembly on Nov. 24, 1824, authorized occupants to have preference to register land. Hardy registers his 50 acre on Roans creek as a homesteader for 12 1/2 cents an acre. Hardy marked his property corners with "H O G." Hardy's son Tyler purchased a 5 0 acre tract on the July 26, 1826, paid 1 cent and branded his property corners with "T O G." The property was located on the North side of Roans creek and the north prong of said creek and east of Moses Nix's 50 acres. In the 1830 census, Hardy and wife have ten children living with them and Hardy's family could have been as large as 13 or 14 children since several children had reached maturity, married, and had families living close by. Hardy is identified in the 1820 (Humphreys), 1830 (Perry), 1840 (Perry), Hardy's 50 acres and a later purchased tract of 25 acres are sold form by his heirs on Aug 7, 1854. In this deed, Tiler (Tyler), Solomon O'Guin and Sarah O'Guin sell

227

to James O'Guin for $15.00 interest in two tract, district 4 on Roans creek-east side of Tennessee river. First tract of 50 acres, second tract of 25 acres. Corners are identified as marked "H O G."

There is one other reference of Hardy's residence in a deed of 1854 when J. W. Daniel sells a 100 acre tract to W. J. Daniel. In this deed description the following is stated "beginning in the hills between Crooked creek and Roans creek, the part of said tract sold lies beginning the old Hardy O'Guin place on Roans creek.

Hardy didn't seem to hobnob in the county seat of Perryville. He wasn't one of the signers to the county petition for state charter. His son Tyler did sign the petition and as did another son Daniel, who lived on the Buffalo river. There was some resentment by the residents of Perry County who lived east of the Tennessee river (petition for county division1826) and the expense "traveling long distance" and of crossing the ferry run by John Reeves circa 1829 to reach Perryville for the April term of court. For some reason unknown, Hardy was called for the Circuit Court of Law and Equity jury duty for the years 1826, 1827, and 1828. On the first Monday of April 1827, Hardy didn't appear for jury duty and the Sheriff was sent to bring him in. Hardy was fined $25.00 which was equivalent at 12 1/2 cents an acre to a 200 acre farm! Hardy didn't hesitate the next year of 1828.

Hardy died sometime after 1840 and lies with his first and second wives on Roans Creek, at a location near the Pineview road and Roans Creek. This cemetery unknown. *Submitted by Larry D. Stewart.*

JOHN "JACK" O'GUIN, (circa 1829, Perry County-after 1900) eldest son of Taylor (Tyler) O'Guin. Jack's parents were Tyler O'Guin and mother unknown. This family consisted of John "Jack" as the eldest, (2) Francis M. born 1829, (3) James born 1831 (4) Margaret born 1833, (5) Thomas born 1835, (6) Patrick born 1838, (7) Elizabeth born 1839 (8) Mary born 1842 (9) William born 1844. Tyler's wife died circa 1844 and Tyler married an Agness born circa 1829 Tyler and Agness had the following children. (10) Minny P. born 1849 (11) Gemima J. born 1850 (12) Peter D. born 1852 (13) Samuel H. born 1854 (14) David T. born 1856 (15) George W. born 1856 and (16) Sarah E. born 1859.

Jack's grandfather, Hardy and father, Tyler O'Guin came from Anson County, NC, to Perry County between 1810-1812 and settled on Roans Creek, just west of Lobelville. Jack's father, Tyler was a signer to the county charter to the State Assembly for the creation of Perry County in 1819. (See O'Guin, Hardy history).

About 1850, John "Jack" married Nancy M. Daniel (circa 1833 Perry County to March 30, 1909) Jack and Nancy raised a family of 9 children in District 4, Perry County in the Roan and Crooked creek area. Their children were: (1) Sarah Elizabeth (1852-1930) m. 1869 P. Co. Thomas Lindley Stewart (See Stewart, Tom history) (2) James W. born 1855 (3) William F. born 1858 (4) Mary M. born 1859 (5) David A. born 1863 (6) Henry A. born 1864 (7) Riley Commodore born 1867 (8) Commodore S. born August 1871 (9) Ida V. born November 1878.

The O'Guin families appear to have lived a life of moderation, never wanting more than they could use and apparently never taking sides during the Civil War conflict which raged across the Perry, Hickman, and Humphreys county areas in more of an inter-county feud than a war of nations. In the 1850 agriculture census, John "Jack" at 21 years of age work with his father Tyler farming their 50 acre tract. This family is listed with 45 acres of improved land out of a total of 65 acres that they owned. Their farm livestock and produce is listed as follows: 2 horses, 2 milk cows, 4 cattle, 2 sheep, and 20 swine. The Tyler O'Guin family is noted with production of wheat, Indian corn, oats, Irish potatoes, and sweet potatoes. The family also produced 50 lb. of butter. In the 1860 agriculture census, it appears that John "Jack" is farming 24 improve acres of 100 and is noted with livestock and agriculture production 3 horses, 1 milk cow, 2 oxen, 2 cattle, 15 sheep, and 14 swine. John "Jack" is shown with a production of wheat, Indian corn (200 bushels,) wool, sweet potatoes, and 50 lbs. of butter. The Tyler family is farming 45 improved acres of 400 acres. Their livestock and produce is identified as follows: 2 horses, 1 milk cow, 3 cattle, 6 sheep, and 9 swine. The family is noted with production of Indian corn (400 bushels), wool, Irish potatoes, and 100 lbs. of butter.

John "Jack" O'Guin dies sometime after the 1900 census and possibly as late as 1905 when he is shown with the Tom Stewart family as a bearded elderly gentleman with his wife Nancy (see photo, Stewart, Tom history). Nancy M. Daniel-O'Guin is listed in the Perry County death records. She is identified on March 30, 1909, at the age of 76 years, Tom's Creek and with A.L. Daniel as her physician. Jack and Nancy are buried in the Danielsburg cemetery just east of Pineview on the Tom's Creek road approaching Lobelville.

WILLIAM HOWARD O'GUIN and Betty Trull O'Guin were born in Perry County. Howard in Lobelville, Lost Creek, 1944. Betty in Linden, Chestnut Grove, 1946. They were married at Chestnut Grove Church of Christ in 1967. To this union were born Dana Renea O'Guin in 1971 and Jonathan Howard O'Guin in 1976.

Howard and Betty O'Guin

Howard is the son of William Alfred O'Guin 1914 from Sulphur Creek near Coble in Hickman County and Sarah "Sallie" Dickson Shelton, 1907-1988 born on Deer Creek, Perry County and buried in Chessor Cemetery, Hickman County. He is the grandson of Sidney Thomas O'Guin, 1880-1965, and Callie Narcisse Beasley, 1883-1954, both from Hickman County and buried in Chessor Cemetery; and Milton Clarence Dickson 1878-1918 and Sarah Mandy Odella "Della" Marshall, 1883-1918 buried in Bible Hill Cemetery in Perry County.

Betty is the daughter of Sam Andrew Trull, 1920-1984, from Perry County and Dorthie Estelle Riley, 1920-1967, from Wayne County, both buried in Chestnut Grove Cemetery. She is the granddaughter of Silas Wesley Trull, 1891-1967, and Sally Matt Berry 1893-1981, from Perry County and E.C. Riley and Mollie Graham from Wayne County.

Howard, Betty, and family reside on Highway 13 South where they have lived for the past 23 years.

ONLY OWENS, English lord, emigrated to Philadelphia, PA, in 1676 with his wife, five children, and their families.

James Only Owens, son of Only, was married in England and brought his family to America. Peter Owens, James son, was married in Maryland in 1743 to Elizabeth Dorman. Their children were: Only (1745), Joshua (1746), Mary (1749), Sophia (1751), Samuel (1752), and Elizabeth (1754).

Only Owens (1745) married Sarah Layfield. They migrated to Orange County, NC. Their children were: Nancy, Elizabeth, Belitha, Lear, Lavinia, Samuel, John, and Thomas.

Belitha and his brother, Samuel, migrated to Tennessee in about 1806. Belitha settled in the "Squeeze Bottom" area of the Buffalo community in Humphreys County. He married three times: 1) Mary Ennis, 2) Elizabeth Roberts, and 3) Rebecca Pierce. His children were: John (1804), Only (1806), Zadock (1807), Jesse (1812), Smallwood (1814), and Fuqua (1841). Fuqua was reared by his half-brother Smallwood and Mary Penn Owens. He was a veteran of the Civil War. Belitha died in 1842 and is buried in the Owens Cemetery by his first wife. The cemetery is located in Humphreys County in the Buffalo Community.

Jessie Owens, son of Belitha, married Ethalinda Parham and had the following children: Stephen (1836), James (1838), Matilda (1840), Pernina (1842), Dennis (1844), Larbourn (1847), Silas (1849), and Susan (1855). They lived in the 8th District of Perry County for many years. Many of the children moved to Gibson County where Ethalinda died in 1895. Jesse died in 1900 and is buried in Humphreys County.

Smallwood Owens married Jarva (?). They had two children who died young as did their mother. Smallwood then married a widow, Mary Penn Laxton who had a son, James P. Laxton. Smallwood and Mary had ten children: Nancy (1848), Amenda (1850), Richard (1852), George Riley (1854), Katura Ann (1856), Camantha Alice (1859), David Wilson (1861), Andrew Johnson (1864), Ella (1865), and Jesse Thomas (1861). Mary Penn was the daughter of John Penn who was an early settler of Perry County. John Penn and seven of their eight children migrated to Arkansas in 1852, leaving Mary in Tennessee.

Katura Ann married William F. Gray of Perry County, and after her death, he married her sister, Ella. They are buried in the Gray Cemetery with some of their children.

George Riley married Martha Melvina Murphree, daughter of Levi and Hannah Sparks Murphree of Hickman County and they had two children: David Monroe (1880) and Mary Pearl (1882).

David Monroe Owens married Ellen Olivia Pinkerton (1885-1960) daughter of John Cooper Pinkerton and Mary Elizabeth Horner Pinkerton of Perry County. Their children were: Mildred May (1905), Edward Clinton (1916-1978), and John Riley (1919-1968).

Mildred May married Arthur D. Bowen and had two sons: Clint Owens Bowen (1925), and William Levi Bowen (1927).

Clint Owens Bowen married first Ellen Marie Hickman, and after her death, he married Mary Stewart. They had three children: John Stewart Bowen (1962), Mary Elizabeth Bowen (1963), and Robert Lee Bowen (1964). *Submitted by Mary Bowen.*

PACE, William Edmond, born March 16, 1870, Perry County, died Jan. 18, 1947, Lewis County, son of William and Sarah Ann (Grimes) Pace. He married Roberta E. "Birtie" Register, born March 12, 1873, died Aug. 8, 1926, daughter of Thomas B. and Vienna O. (Griffin) Register, of Hickman County. William and "Birtie" had the following children: Clara Bell, born 1897, died 1903; Henry Claude, born March 5, 1900, Tom's Creek, died Nov. 4, 1976, Lewis County. He married Dec. 25, 1928, Virginia M. Spears, born June 11, 1909, daughter of Sidney M. and Nora (Murphree) Spears; Clyde Thomas, born 1901, Tom's Creek; Larremore Leon, born 1902; Clifford Curtis, born 1904, died 1950. He was hit by a truck while crossing the street in Taylor, MI; Carmen Register, born 1906, died 1977, married Grace Churchville; Leonard Ellis, born 1909, died 1969, married Edith Mae Lynch daughter of Johnnie Osco and Ethel L. (Ghist) Lynch.

Left to right: Will Pace, Birtie Pace, Claude Pace, Leon Pace, Clifford Pace, Carmen Pace, and Ellis Pace.

Henry Claude and Virginia Pace have three children: Nora Roberts, born May 29, 1930, Lewis County, married Nov. 23, 1946, to G.N. Lynch, born July 25, 1921, son of Johnie Osco and Ethel L. (Ghist) Lynch; Melba Jean, born April 10, 1934, Lewis County, TN, died May 27, 1980, Rockwood, TN, married Clyde Ashbrook, Oct. 21, 1951; Claude Sidney, born Jan 17, 1937, Lewis County.

Nora Roberta and G.N. Lynch have four children: Garry Don, born March 21,1948, Lewis County, TN; Danny Earl, born Nov. 21, 1949, Lewis County, married May 28, 1977, to Ellen Laginess, born May 5, 1955, daughter of Howard and Catherine (Barber) Laginess, of Michigan; Barbara Elaine, born Oct. 8, 1951, Trenton, MI; Shelia Jean, born July 29, 1953, Lewis County, TN, married May 4, 1974, to Terry Hampton, born Sept 23, 1949, son of Ercell and Joanna (Jones) Hampton, of Kentucky.

Melba and Clyde Ashbrook have one son: James Curtis born March 1954, Lewis County, TN, married Claudia Griffith.

Danny and Ellen Lynch have two children: Danny Earl II, born March 24, 1981, Wayne County, MI; Katie Marie, born March 17, 1986, Wayne County, MI.

Shelia and Terry Hampton have two children: Bryan Young, born Nov, 27, 1975, Wayne County, MI; Sherry Elaine, born Oct. 23, 1978, Wayne County, MI. Children:

Curtis and Claudia Ashbrook have one daughter: Mellissa Ann, born June 1975, Rockwood, TN.

PAFFORD-CRAIG Nolen Pafford and Fleta (Craig) Pafford were united in marriage on June 24, 1922. Nolen was born May 31, 1900. He was the son of Oscar Neal Pafford and Julia (Totty) Pafford. His father, Oscar Neal, was son of David and Delphis (Herndon) Pafford of Benton County, TN.

Fleta (Craig) Pafford was the daughter of Wyly Black Craig and Ida (Marshall) Craig. She was born Aug. 24, 1904. Fleta's father and mother came to Benton County from Perry County, TN, where they were married. They settled in the Beaverdam community in the tenth civil district.

To Nolen and Fleta (Craig) Pafford were born three sons, Aubrey, Gordon, and Wyly Ray Pafford.

Nolan's mother, Julia, passed away when the children of Nolen and Fleta were very young. Nolen and Fleta continued to live with Nolen's father, Oscar. Fleta was a very young loving daughter-in-law, taking wonderful care of Julia during her illness. After her death she cared for Mr. Oscar as she called him, as if he was her own father. Fleta was very strong in her convictions of the teachings of the Bible. She was a faithful member of Beaverdam Church of Christ. They also attended Chestnut Hill Church.

Fleta and Nolen's sons have contributed much to Benton County by public service. Aubrey served with the U.S. Marines in Korea for six years. He also served 28 years as policeman and Chief of Police. Gordon served 27 years as County Court Clerk, his widow, Jane, holds this office at the present time having been appointed to same upon Gordon's death in 1993.

Fleta (Craig) Pafford died Jan. 26, 1972, Nolen died on July 5, 1972, their sons Aubrey died on Dec. 21, 1987, and Gordon in 1993.

Fleta's father, Wyly Black Craig, born July 13, 1878, in Tennessee and was the son of Eliazar Hardeman Craig born Feb. 29, 1836, and Margaret Greer who was born 1836 and died Sept. 20, 1884, leaving a husband and twelve children. (Two died very young).

Eliazar Hardeman Craig then second married Nancy Elizabeth Trull, born March 17, 1857, who died May 13, 1922. They had five children.

Eliazar Hardeman Craig was the son of Andrew Craig II born 1787 and his second wife, Martha Dupuy (Hardeman) Craig. Andrew was the son of Andrew David Craig, (mainly known as David Craig) who was born in Washington County, VA.

Andrew Craig II died in Williamson County, TN, May 27, 1863 and Martha D. (Hardeman) Craig born March 16, 1803, died March 12, 1864. Their three children were: Eliazar Hardeman Craig, Andrew David Craig III, and Sarah (Craig) Berry. Several of this family are buried in the Chestnut Grove Cemetery, Linden, Perry County, TN. *Prepared by Hazel Craig. Submitted by Jane Pafford.*

ARCHA PARNELL The Cook Cemetery located on Cane Creek near the Old Enon Church had a square fence enclosing four graves. They are Archa Parnell 1837-1887, Sally Wall Parnell 1843-1887, and Molly Parnell 1862-1883, John R. Parnell, 1869-1887.

Son, granddaughter, and great granddaughter of Archa and Sally Parnell. E.H. Parnell, Lessie Parnell Warren, and great granddaughter Edna Parnell Cotton.

Little is known of Archa Parnell's early life. It can be stated with reasonable certainty that he was a sickly hunchback child with a sore leg. He had an Irish Brogue that may indicate a recent arrival from Ireland or acquisition of his speech from his parents.

In the 1850 census of Humphreys County, there was a Henry, age 80, who lived on Blue Creek. HIs wife was 42 years of age. Both are listed as having been born in North Carolina. In this household lived Archephus, age 13. The writing was indistinct, could have been 18 or 13, if it were 13 then, this would place the birth of Archephus in 1837 which is the birth of our Archa.

Archa lived in the household of David Rice Harris sometime after the census of 1850 until his marriage sometime in the late 1861. It was during this time that Archa because of his infirmities, became a trucker rather than a farmer. He hauled freight between the Beardstown stores and Nashville via Leepers Fork and Hillsboro which is on the Natchez Trace.

Archa started working with Mr. Egbert Haywood Shepard and lived on his farm in the house on the right hand side of the road going up Cane Creek. Presumably all the children were born in this house on the Shepard farm.

As with all pioneer families, life was hard and short for most people and the Parnell's were no exception. Sally Walls Parnell was 19 when her first child was born, and 33 years old when her seventh child was born. She was dead two years later, leaving a sickly hunchbacked husband age 41 and seven children: Molly (16); Samuel (12), Robert (10), E.H. (8), Clara (6), Elizabeth (4), and Egbert Haywood (2). They continued to live in the small house on the Shepard property.

Arch married Tinnie Saunders from Wayne

County sometime in 1879. The first child of this family was Donna, born 1880. A second child Fannie was born in 1883.

The family broke up when the second wife was unable to handle the problems of two infants and five Parnell children. John had died of measles in 1887, and Mollie died 1883. By this time, Sam Parnell had married Julia Duncan, this young couple reared little Egbert together with their own children. Mr. Moore in Centerville took Elizabeth, a teacher in Beardstown by the name of DePriest took Clara, and Mr. and Mrs. E.H. Shepard took E.H. "Dick" to live in their house.

Fannie Parnell Arnold and her mother Tina Saunders Parnell are buried in the Riverside Cemetery near Hohenwald, TN. Donna Parnell Lynch is buried in Salem Cemetery in Wayne County.

ARCHIE RALPH PARNELL, was the fifth child born to Samuel Thomas and Julia Ann Duncan Parnell on Nov. 1, 1897, on the Duncan Farm in the community of Brush Creek in Perry County. His only formal education he obtained at the Brush Creek Elementary School. In the same community of Brush Creek lived a young lady that he attended school with, dated, and married. Her name was Maudie Parlee Qualls, born Nov. 9, 1900. She was the daughter of Wilburn and Nannie Barber Qualls. Ralph and Maudie were married Aug. 19, 1917.

Ralph and Maudie were the parents of seven children: Shelby, Leonard, Irma, Howard, Hayes, Jack, and Clint.

Willard Shelby was born July 21, 1918. On Sept. 10, 1938, he married Lorene Craig, daughter of Charlie and Laura Craig. They had three children: Boyd (Nov. 13, 1941), Faye (Aug. 20, 1946), and Kyle (Sept. 24, 1950). Shelby died Sept. 24, 1984, at the age of 66 and is buried in the Dr. O.A. Kirk Memorial Cemetery.

Leonard Thomas was born Feb. 17, 1920. On June 26, 1948, he married Allene O'Guin, daughter of George and Rhoda O'Guin. They had two children: Carlton (Feb. 2, 1950-1952) and Kathryn (Oct. 25, 1955). Leonard died June 22, 1986, at the age of 66 and is buried in Qualls Cemetery on Brush Creek.

Irma Lee was born March 17, 1922. She married Lee Jackson, son of Frances Jackson in April of 1940. Lee died in May 1954 and is buried in Qualls Cemetery.

Howard Kirk was born Oct. 26, 1925, and died Dec. 4, 1925. Howard is buried in Qualls Cemetery.

Earl Hayes was born Jan. 23, 1927. On Feb. 4, 1950, he married Jessie O'Guin, daughter of George and Rhoda O'Guin. They had two children: Carolyn (Dec. 14, 1950) and Dale (Sept. 29, 1952).

Jack Wilburn was born March 18, 1929. On Dec. 11, 1948, he married Ola Victoria Qualls, daughter of Wiley and Birdie Qualls. They had two children: Bobby (Dec. 29, 1954) and Rickie (July 28, 1959). After Olav passed away in 1988, Jack later married Wanda Williams. Jack died June 19, 1993, at the age of 64 and is buried in the Qualls Cemetery.

Clint Edward was born Dec. 23, 1940. On Aug. 9, 1963, he married Judith Cook, daughter of Archie and Jeanne Cook. They had two children: Rhonda (Feb. 16, 1971) and Jeffrey (Jan. 4, 1973).

Ralph and Maudie were married for 65 years and during that time they lived in the community of Brush Creek on the Qualls farm. They were active members of Brush Creek Church of Christ.

Ralph's livelihood was farming. He grew such things as peanuts, hay, and corn; and raised chickens, cattle, and hogs. Besides being a farmer, Ralph also during the non-farming season worked odd jobs such as logging and cutting timber. He also helped do masonry work on the Brush Creek and Coon Creek bridges.

On March 29, 1983, Maudie died at the age of 82. Ralph died on Sept. 2, 1984, at the age of 86. Both are buried in the Qualls family cemetery on Brush Creek. At present they are survived by three children, Irma, Hayes, and Clint; ten grandchildren and thirteen great-grandchildren. *Submitted by Rhonda Parnell Gibbs, granddaughter.*

EDWARD A. PARNELL, SR., was born to Sam T. and Julia Ann Parnell on May 8, 1895, on the Duncan Farm on Brush Creek in Perry County. He attended elementary school at Brush Creek and high school at Dickson where he was a star football player. It was there he met and courted Lucy Young. They were married on Dec. 15, 1917. They both received their Teacher's Certificates at Dickson. After their marriage they moved back to Perry County. There Ed began to teach school until he was drafted into the Army on Sept. 17, 1918. Lucy took over the school while he was in the Army. He was discharged on Dec. 8, 1918, and returned to Brush Creek to become a farmer for the remainder of his life.

Ed and Lucy Parnell

Ed and Lucy had their first son, Sam Lanier, on Jan. 30, 1920, on Brush Creek. Then they moved to the Godwin Farm on the Buffalo River, where their second son, Edward A., Jr., was born on Feb. 19, 1924. Soon after they moved to Coon Creed and lived there until 1933. Ed then bought the Barber Farm on Cane Creek where he farmed, hauled logs to the sawmill and worked on road building and repairs.

He was a very hard-working man during the years in Perry County. Besides farming every year, he got a job as an oiler on a crane when they built Highway 100. This was a good job, and he made very good money during this time. However, he would not give up his farm life to follow the construction business, so he stayed on the farm. He raised a garden each year to feed the family. He planted corn to feed the stock and to make meal for cornbread. He planted wheat to sell and to make flour for biscuits, cookies, and cakes. That he loved very much.

In 1948, Ed sold the farm on Cane Creek and bought the Wilson Farm on Cranor Road in Murfreesboro. The family moved there in November of that year. There he farmed the place and worked with a home builder helping to build houses as long as he was able to do the work.

Ed and Lucy were very active in the work of the Church of Christ wherever they lived. Most of the time, when a preacher came to preach at their congregation, he spent the nights with them. Ed taught a Bible class for a number of years and led singing when they needed him.

Ed Parnell, Sr., died on July 9, 1988, at the home on Cranor Road. He was buried in Roselawn Memorial Gardens in Murfreesboro. He was survived by his wife, Lucy, sons Sam and Ed, Jr., three grandchildren and six great-grandchildren.

EGBERT HAYWOOD PARNELL, Archa (1837-1887) and Sallie Walls Parnell (1843-1878) had seven children: Molly, Samuel, John Robert, Ezekiel Hercules (Dick), Clara, Elizabeth, and Egbert Haywood.

Egbert and Elizabeth Barber Parnell.

Egbert (1876-1955) was born in Perry County the seventh child of Archa and Sallie. Egbert went to live with Sam and Julia Parnell at the age of eleven after the death of his parents.

Egbert married Sarah Elizabeth Barber (1877-1962). They farmed in Pleasantville, TN, before moving to Lewis County. They had five children: Myrtle Hinson (1898-1981), Mattie Edwards (1900-1988), Willie O'Guin (1901-1988), Wymer (1905-1926), and Grady (1910).

Egbert was a brave and caring man on many occasions. Once when he was on a mission of mercy on a horse, he had the horse knocked from under him by a truck and he miraculously survived.

Egbert's integrity was without equal. Once he walked two miles to a store in Pleasantville to return seven cents the storekeeper had overpaid him. He raised pear and apple trees so therefore he had such fruit to share. He would never let a man or animal go hungry.

Myrtle married John C. Hinson. They farmed on lower Cane Creek until retiring and moving to Linden. They had five sons.

B.E. (Red) (1918-1993) married Anna Mae Conger (1915-1983) and lived in Linden except when Red was serving in a tank battalion during World War II. They had two sons: Johnny and Sammy.

Harold (1920-1986) married Mavous Warren (1922-1993). They lived much of their lives in Perry County before moving to Humphreys County. They had two daughters: Patricia Buchanan and Kathy Cunningham. Harold served in the Pacific during World War II.

Leland (1921-) married Martha Haynes (1925-). They lived in Perry County for a short time before moving to Hickman County. They have two children: Susan Kihlmire and Richard. Leland served in France in an engineering battallion during World War II.

Larry (1923-) married Marion Trautman (1930-). Larry worked with Transcontinental Gas Pipeline Corp. for 35 years, living in four states in the south before moving to Perry County in 1982 to retire. They have two children: Debbie Bradley and Larry, Jr.

Charles (1928-) married Helen Dill (1932). They have spent their married life in Hamilton County. They have a son, Mark. Charles spent time in the Army during the Korean War.

Mattie (1900-1988) married Ernest Edwards (1899-1985). They resided in Hickman County for a time before moving to Lewis County. Ernest was County Tax Assessor for many years. They had five sons:

Leonard Carlton (1920-) married Bessie Spears (1923). They reside in Lewis County. They have three children: Linda Boyle, Sharon Swan, and Ricky Carlton.

Bernard (1922-) married Eunice Parks. They reside in Williamson County. Bernard has two sons: Doran and David.

James Max (1929-) married Carma Potts (1927-). They resided many years in Ohio before moving to Lewis County. Max has a daughter: Sherri Graver.

Billy Kenneth (1935-) married Martha Anderson (1932-). They reside in Lewis County. They have two children: Susan Davis and Kenneth.

Bobby Kirk (1935-) married Linda Hickerson (1938-). They reside in Lewis County. They have two sons: Stephen Kirk and Gregory Earl.

Willie married Herman O'Guin (1909-1979). They resided in Pleasantville for many years before moving to Maury County. They had no children.

Grady (1910-) married Ila Peach (1903-1991). They resided in Perry County before moving to Maury County. He was a mechanic by trade. They had a daughter: Ruth and an infant son who died at birth.

Wymer (1905-1926) resided with his parents until his death.

EZEKIEL HERCULES PARNELL
and Nancy Elemeda Vick were married Dec. 20, 1891. E.H. was the son of Archa and Sally Walls Parnell, Nancy Elemeda Vick was the daughter of Cullen S. Vick and Elizabeth Jane Land Vick.

Meda's parents, the Cullen Vicks, built a small house near their large home on Brush Creek for the young couple to begin housekeeping. E.H. "Dick" was farmer, also worked in timber and did paralegal work for attorneys while Meda kept the house, and cared for the family.

A little baby boy named Arthur D. Parnell was born to the couple on June 29, 1893. On Dec. 15, 1894, another little boy came along, named Charlie Devine. The third child was a baby girl given the name, Ethel Lou Della, born Aug. 16, 1897.

E. H. Parnell and Meda Vick Parnell with their five children: Arthur, Charlie, Alma Parnell Tucker, Ethel Parnell Barham, and Lessie Parnell Warren.

Sometime later Dick and Meda decided to leave Brush Creek. They rented the Jack Taylor Farm on Highway 13 near Linden. A little girl, Alma Elizabeth, came to bless this home on May 29, 1899. Later another little girl, Lessie Reed, was born June 10, 1901. Dick and Meda decided to buy the Taylor farm, was deeded Feb. 25, 1905. The Parnells continued to live there until Jan 28, 1907, when they decided to move further down Highway 13 to a farm owned by Jim Aldridge, near Scaggs Bluff. The Parnell family continued to live here until their death.

In 1928, the large two story house burned, very little was saved. Dick Parnell had Chestnut logs cut from the farm. Will McClanahan Construction Co. of Centerville built the log house in 1929. It is still there, the present owners are Murry and Rosita Stribling.

May 1935, Meda Parnell suffered a stroke, she was completely paralyzed on the left side. In October 1935, Mr. and Mrs. Parnell sold the farm to daughter Ethel and Tommy Barham and daughter, Pauline for them to move there and care for Grandmother Meda. Meda suffered a second stroke in December 1935 and passed away. She was buried in the family cemetery on the Brush Creek Hill near her parents and grandparents. Dick lived until Nov. 26, 1958, and was buried by his beloved wife.

Arthur married Gussie Barham (June 21, 1892). They had two girls, Edna Elmeda, and Hilda. Arthur died March 23, 1952, and Gussie died June 2, 1970. They are buried in Mt. Zion Cemetery in Henry County.

Charlie married Effie Burns (Dec. 30, 1893-Dec. 22, 1971). Charlie died Sept. 6, 1982. They had two sons, Frank Burns and Fred Carter. Charlie and Effie are buried in Downey Cemetery near Hohenwald, TN.

Ethel married George Thomas Barham (April 15, 1894-July 30, 1982). Ethel died Feb. 7, 1981. They are buried in Barham Family Cemetery. They were parents of one daughter, Pauline.

Alma married William H. Tucker (March 8, 1888-Nov. 10, 1978). Alma died Nov. 16,1 991. They are buried in Vaughan-Tucker Cemetery. They were parents of one son, Dr. William H. Tucker.

Lessie married Gola Warren (Dec. 5, 1900-Jan 9, 1992). Lessie died April 6, 1972. They had three girls: Laverne, Julia, and Ruby Jo.

LENIER PARNELL
Samuel Lenier Parnell, son of Edward Alvin Parnell and Lucy Young Parnell was born on Brush Creek in Perry County Jan. 30, 1920.

Samuel Lenier Parnell in 1943.

Lenier was married to Naomi Bernice Hinson, daughter of William Eddington Hinson and Mattie Cleo Elkins Hinson, in Centerville, TN, Sept. 21, 1946. To this union were born two children. William Edward Parnell, born June 21, 1949, died June 21, 1949, and is buried in Evergreen Cemetery, Murfreesboro, TN; Samuel Lenier Parnell, Jr., born April 1, 1952, in Murfreesboro, TN.

Samuel Lenier Parnell, Jr., married Sara Ann Roberson March 23, 1974, in Memphis, TN. To this union were born two children, Samuel Lenier Parnell III, born Sept. 21, 1980, and James Andrew Parnell born Aug. 9, 1983, in Knoxville, TN.

Lenier Parnell attended and graduated from Chestnut Grove Elementary School the spring of 1933. He was employed that summer as a water boy, for a construction company building highway 100 bridge across Coon Creek.

He attended and graduated from Bethel Junior High School Farmers Exchange, TN, on Cane Creek in 1936, and Hickman County High School, Centerville, TN, in 1938. That summer he was accepted by the National Youth Administration and assigned to a group building an addition to Perry County High School, Linden, TN.

The fall of 1938 the N.Y.A. approved, among others the transfer of Lenier Parnell from Cane Creek; M.H. Warren, Brush Creek, and Caruthers Cotham, Linden, to Austin Peay State Normal School Clarksville, TN. They were assigned to the school Maintenance Department and became roommates at Rob Hall. The N.Y.A. required each student to work 100 hours per month. For which they received room, board, tuition, books, and $13.00 per month. Lenier served a hitch with, Troop K 109 Cavlary, Tennessee National Guard, 1938-1941.

Dec. 7, 1941, found Lenier at the University of Tennessee Knoxville classified "One C." He returned to Perry County "One A," and was inducted into the U.S. Army March 10,1942.

His military odyssey included among others, stopovers at Ft. Overthrope, GA; Camp Polk, LA; Ft. Knox, KY; Camp Young, CA; Oregon State College; Fort Lewis, WA, (assigned to 14th Field Artillery Observation Battalion for duration); Camp Shank's, NY (Poe); England; Utah Beach, France, (Gen. G.S. Patton Commanding);

through southern France to Bliesbruck; Luxemburg; Aachen, Germany, (Battle of Bulge, Dec. 2, 1944-Feb. 7, 1945); Magdeburg, Germany, May 8, 1945; Discharged Oct. 31, 1945, Camp Atturburg, IN.

Encouraged by his wife Naomi, he returned to school and received a B.S. degree, Austin Peay State University 1948 and a M.A. from George Peabody College, 1949, in Industrial Education.

Lenier was employed by the Murfreesboro Practical Trades School, teaching shop math, wood shops, drafting, and blue print reading, 1949-1951. Base Civil Engineers Stewart AFB, Project Engineer, Planner, Surveyor, OJT instructor, 1953-1970. Rutherford County Planning Director 1970-1980. An active member of the Church of Christ, he with his wife Naomi are at home in Rutherford County.

SAM PARNELL, Samuel Thomas Parnell, son of Archa Parnell, was born Feb. 2, 1866, near the mouth of Cane Creek in Perry County. He married Julia Duncan, born March 27, 1864, daughter of Willis Duncan in Perry County. To this union were born six children: Robert, Walter, Will, Edward, Ralph, and Lattice.

Samuel Thomas Parnell and wife Julia Duncan Parnell.

Samuel Lenier Parnell was born Jan. 30, 1920, in a small house beside Brush Creek on the Duncan farm in Perry County. When Grandfather Sam purchased a 750 acre farm from a Timber Company, on Coon Creek in Perry County, my Father Ed Parnell moved into the Duncan home for a short time. I was four years old when we moved into a house on the side of a hill overlooking Grandfather Sam's home.

On Coon Creek, when I could see my cousins playing in yard, it was down to Grandmother's house. All the stories will never be told of the fun we had as we made use of the yard, spring orchard, barns, gardens, and an abandoned log house. A fist full of Grandmother Julie's cookies more than made up for the assigned chores she found for us.

In the late 1920's, there were fifteen families living on the Farm. The Farm was almost a self-supporting unit, with a few of the adults going to the cities for winter work.

The Farm Operation consisted of a blacksmith shop, saw mill; custom hay bailing; peanut picking; and wheat threshing; growing corn; cotton; wheat; hay; cattle; sheep; hogs; gardens; and orchards. Mules and horses furnished the source of power for cultivating the fields. The saw mill was powered by a wood fired steam engine. A steam traction engine was used to power the peanut picker and the wheat thresher.

When not working the fields the men and boys were busy splitting chestnut logs into rails (a no-fence law required that the crops and pastture be fenced), cutting timber, hauling logs to the mill to be sawed into lumber and railroad ties. Products produced on the farm were hauled to Centerville, Hohenwald, and the Tennessee River by wood, steel rimmed wheeled wagons. Suitable land was cleared and made ready for cultivating.

Grandfather Sam was a firm believer in education. Provisions were made for the children to attend Chestnut Grove Elementary School. He later gave a tract on which Perry County built the Parnell School.

Corn and wheat were sent to the mill for grinding into meal and flour. The mills were powered by water or one lung gas engines. The miller was paid in money or tollage.

The Farm furnished fruits and vegetables, fresh dried and canned; meats, fresh, cured, and canned. The Watkins' man came by to provide over the counter drugs suitable for man and beast.

Members of the Church of Christ, Grandfather died Feb. 4, 1935, and is buried beside his beloved wife Julia who died June 26, 1948, in the Chestnut Grove Cemetery in Perry County. *Submitted by Samuel L. Parnell.*

WALTER THOMAS PARNELL, was the second child born to Sam T. and Julia Duncan Parnell on March 9, 1890. Walter married Mamie Lila Culp in November 1910. Mamie Culp Parnell was born May 10, 1887.

Walter Thomas and wife, Mamie Lila Culp Parnell.

Walter and Mamie were the parents of three children. James Palmer, born Dec. 17, 1911. James Palmer married Lucille Wade November 1935. James Palmer and Lucille had two children, James Parnell born Aug. 17, 1942 and Linda, born Nov. 23, 1945. James is married and has two daughters. Linda is married and has one daughter.

The second child of Walter and Mamie was Lucretia Parnell, who was born Jan. 10, 1917. She finished high school in 1937, later married Arthur Marmo II. He died in 1974 and Lucretia has married again and lives in Chicago, IL. She had no children by either husband, her second husband in Harold Konatske.

The third and last child born to Walter and Mamie was Clovis Dewey Parnell. He was born April 29, 1926. Clovis married Betty Jo Hinson of Lewis County on Aug. 15, 1947. They had one child Teresa Jo Parnell, who was born June 25, 1948. Teresa graduated from college and became a teacher in Gulfport, MS. She married Wallace Gentry Long III of Nashville. Teresa and Wallace have two sons: Wallace Gentry Long IV, born Oct. 8, 1972, and Jason Parnell Long, born Jan. 3, 1975. They both are in college at Mississippi State University.

Betty Jo Parnell passed away Jan. 2, 1994, and is buried in the Dr. Kirk Memorial Cemetery. Before her death, she served as secretary for her husband, Sessions Judge Clovis Parnell.

Walter and Mamie lived in Perry County all their married life. Mamie died April 9, 1960, and Walter died Feb. 6, 1961. They are buried in Chestnut Grove cemetery.

WILLIAM HUBERT PARNELL, was born May 6, 1892, on Brush Creek to Samuel and Julia D. Parnell. The family soon moved to a farm on Coon Creek where Will grew up. He served in the Army in Europe during World War I and, after being discharged, returned to the family farm.

Will Parnell on left.

On Aug. 17, 1920, Will married Lorene Daniel at her home in Beardstown; at first, they lived with his parents and he raised cotton as a sharecropper. They had two children: Glen Daniel, born March 12, 1922; and Julia Ruth, born June 5, 1927.

Sometime after Glen's birth, they moved to Beardstown where Will and his father-in-law, Commodore Daniel, operated a general merchandise store until Commodore's death in 1937. Will then began driving a school bus to Linden where he also bought a shoe and harness shop. In 1940, he was named Assistant Conservation Officer, and for many years he was an agent for Modern Woodman of America Insurance.

Lorene died Aug. 24, 1940, following a short bout of pneumonia and was buried in Chestnut Grove Cemetery near Linden.

In 1945 Will moved to Linden. In 1948 he married Vera O'Guin; they divorced after a few years. In 1964 he married Mary Lee Jackson and they were together until he died on Jan. 29, 1968. He was buried beside Lorene at Chestnut Grove.

Glen and Julia both attended Beardstown Elementary and Perry County High School. Near the end of his senior year, Glen tested positive for tuberculosis. After graduating, he went to Colorado Springs for treatment, and returned to Tennessee in 1945 as an apprentice undertaker in Knoxville. While there, he was hired as a reservations manager by Delta Airlines. He stayed with Delta until his death on Sept. 12, 1981. He and his family had lived in Houston, TX, since 1953.

Glen was married Jan. 10, 1953, to Verla Johnson in Lincoln, NE. They had one child,

Kristin Lorene, born Nov. 15, 1961. Kristin married Tom Caine, and they have two children, Sean Patrick, born May 15, 1988, and Kelsey Lorene, born Sept. 13, 1991. Verla died July 11, 1993, and was buried alongside Glen in Forest Park Cemetery in Houston.

Julia graduated from Middle Tennessee State College in 1949 and worked as a recreation director on a tobacco farm in Connecticut, then for the City Recreation Department of Tampa, FL. In Tampa, she met Rollie Whitworth; they married Oct. 14, 1950. They have two children: Glenda Louise, born in Tampa Dec. 1, 1951; and Richard Wayne, born Aug. 11, 1956, in England.

As a military family, they lived in many places before Rollie retired at his last duty station, Offutt AFB, in Bellevue, NE. Julia taught life science in the Bellevue Public Schools for eighteen years and retired in 1987. They continue to live in Bellevue.

Glenda married Ricky James Chappell, and they had two sons, Ricky, Jr., born Jan. 27, 1969, and Kenneth Wayne, born May 23, 1978. Ricky presently resides in Nashville. Kenneth lives with his mother and her new husband, Mark LaFlamme, in Bellevue.

Richard married Debbie Saunders and is stepfather to her sons Sean Eric and Kevin Shay. They also live in Bellevue.

PASCHALL, The first Pascal came from Rowen, France, to England to escape religious persecution in the first half of the 16th century. He or his immediate descendants then anglicized the name by adding another "l" (Pascall). Later on they added the "h" (Paschall).

Mike Paschall Family. Front row: Caldonia, Ashby, Mike. Back Row: Ada, Lula, and Cleveland.

In 1720 two brothers, John and William Paschall came to Baltimore, MD, from England. There they separated, John going to Delaware and William going to North Carolina.

William died ca. 1774 in Bute County, NC. Wife Reliance, second wife Tabitha. Their children: Samuel, John, Isiah, William, Elisha, James, Dennis, Thomas, Sarah, Dianna, Rachel, Ruth, and Reliance.

Thomas born ca. 1775 died 1821. He was a Revolutionary War soldier, married Charity. Their children: Thomas, William, Nancy, John, Henry, Elizabeth, Michael Wood, Sr., Robert, Mary, Martha, and Bushaby.

Michael Wood born 1787 died after 1850 married Elizabeth Wood. Their children: William, Michael Wood, Jr., Thomas, John C., Anderson, James, and Mary.

John Christmas (my great grandfather) born 1820 Warren County, NC, married Penelope Laughter, 1843. Their children: Edward and Francis. They came and settled in Maury County, TN, (Cathey's Creek) ca. 1851. Illness struck the family the first winter and his wife and son Francis died. He then married Sarah Tolly in Lewis County, TN, 1853. Their children: Mary Elizabeth 1854-1929 married John Tom Marshall; Nancy Caldonis 1857 married Andrew Jackson Love 1876; John W. 1858-1907 married Nannie Anderson; Michael Henry 1865-1944 married Caldonia Elizabeth Kirk; Frank Jonathan 1867-1918 married Sara Alice Flowers, William Richard 1869-1917 married Fannie Matthews; James M. 1874 married Miss Roberts.

Michael Henry (my grandfather) married Caldonia Elizabeth Kirk 1884. Mike (as he was called) came to Perry County, TN, in 1880 and lived for awhile with his brother John on Cedar Creek. Mike ran a grist mill first in Lobelville, TN, then at Rise Mill in Linden, TN. He served as Tax Assessor, Bond 1907-1919. Elected Sheriff 1921 and served two terms. He then owned a cabinet shop on Mill Street where the Senior Citizens Building is now located. Children of Mike and Caldonia: Elmer Cleveland 1884-1958 married Ida Bunch 1907, Mr. second time Sarah Kimble; Ada Florence (my mother) 1886-1964 married Thomas Blain Tucker 1902; Lula Lee 1889-1991 married O.T. Craig; Almer 1891-1896; Ashby Osborn 1893-1974 married Lucille Haggard, second wife Lorene Morris.

Ada Florence and Thomas Blain Tucker had ten children: Fred 1903-1909; Clara Emogene 1905 married Ray O'Guin; Glady Onedia 1907-1986 married Jack Young; Lula Rubena 1910 married Joe Dabbs; Tom Paschall 1914 married Mary Evelyn Orr; Verna Elmore 1917 married Elvin (Ebb) Stutts; Willie Ray 1920 married Chole Warren; Linda Ruth 1922 married John Elliott; Michael Henry (M. H.) 1928 married Betty Faye O'Guin; Loretta Jane 1932 married George Osborn.

Tom Paschall and Evelyn Tucker born in Marshall County, TN, (Bear Creek Community) married 1936 and have two children: Barbara Ann and Lynda Lee.

Barbara born 1940 Linden, Perry County, TN, married Kenneth Whittle and live in Mt. Juliet, TN. They have three children: Amanda Kay, Rachel Wilkes, and Nathan Wayne.

Lynda born 1942 Linden, Perry County, TN, married Richard Smith and live in Alexandria, VA. They have one daughter, Jennifer Amie. *Submitted by Tom Paschall and Evelyn Tucker.*

WILLIAM R. PASCHALL "Bill," born Sept. 13, 1869, Maury County, died Dec. 28, 1917, Perry County, buried Craig cemetery on Cedar Creek. His wife, Fannie Mathis was daughter of James Bluford Mathis and Mary Dabbs. Bill and Fannie had several children 1) Robert F. Paschall, born 1889, died 1939, buried Craig cemetery. He married Ila Tucker, she born 1902, died 1969, daughter of Robert and Mollie Tucker. After Robert died, she married Isaac Pope. Children Alva Mae, William R., and Winfred Howard. 2)William A. Paschall, born 1893. 3)Cora Lee Paschall, born June 18, 1898, died Dec. 26, 1919, Perry County, buried Craig cemetery. She married June 4, 1916, Perry County, E. Denton. 4) Kate Paschall, born Oct. 20, 1903, Perry County, died Nov. 11, 1918, Perry County, buried Roberts cemetery. She probably died from complications from childbirth. She married Nov. 18, 1917, Perry County, Iverson Wiley. A daughter was born to them, Nov. 3, 1918, Perry County, died Nov. 4, 1918, Perry County. 5) John B. P Paschall, born 1906. 6)Jessie Paschall born 1908, married Wes Wheat. 7)Hessie Paschall, born Dec. 16, 1909, Perry County, married Blu Wheat. 8) possibly a child, Woodrow Paschall, born Nov. 2, 1912, died June 20, 1915, buried Craig cemetery.

PATTERSON, A grave marker in Pineview Cemetery near Tom's Creek reads, "A Sinner Saved by Grace If Saved At All." It is the requested epitaph of Thomas Dickson Patterson whose sins were small by current standards.

Left to right: Micah Reed Patterson Roth (seated), Dana Patterson Roth, Robert Alan Patterson, Kyndra Patterson Roth, and Hubert H. Patterson, Jr.

T.D. Patterson and Aurora Rixena Patterson raised a large family of five sons and three daughters. Two additional sons died at young ages. He farmed on Tom's Creek and ran a country store nearby. More a leader than a driver he exhorted the boys by the words, "Let's get it done, boys."

H. H. and Pearl Donnell Patterson on their 50th wedding anniversary in 1967.

His father, Jesse Harvey Patterson, born around 1830 in Perry County was killed at the Battle of Murfreesboro on Stones River in Tennessee. A Lieutenant, in the CSA his name appears on a group memorial in Evergreen cemetery. He was married to Mary Ann Dickson, daughter of William "Canady" Dickson. Their children William born Jan. 28, 1856, in Perry County, and Thomas D. (above) was born, June 17, 1860. Jesse Harvey Patterson was the son of Robert Carson Patterson.

Myrtle Estelle Patterson, born Nov. 16, 1882, was the first child of Thomas D. and Aurora, married Joseph Bandy of Nashville, TN, died Dec. 9, 1965.

Ernest Wright Patterson, born Dec. 9, 1884, became a coal mine operator in Overton and Fentress counties of Tennessee, died on Oct. 15, 1945. His wife, Lera Harris died Nov. 23, 1980. Their child, Catherine, graduated from UCLA and recently retired as a bank vice-president in Nashville, TN.

Left to right: E. W. Patterson, Lee Patterson, Jewell Patterson, Hubert Patterson, and Burris Patterson. Taken circa 1940 at Dickson, TN.

Ephram Lee Patterson, born Feb. 21, 1887, was a merchant and undertaker in Perry County died April 13, 1949. He was married to Flossie Lee Pope who died Jan. 31, 1971.

Bernie Patterson, born Aug. 3, 1889, died Jan. 31, 1897.

Jewell Enlow Patterson, born March 16, 1892, went to Florida during the booming twenties and made a career with Florida Power and Light Company. His wife, Edna shared his love of fishing and the outdoor life around south Florida.

Hubert Hugo Patterson, born March 4, 1894, followed his brother E.W., to the coal fields of middle Tennessee and became the commissary operator of Patterson Brother's operating several mines in the Wilder-Davidson area. The events of the 1930's, strikes, depression, and eventual closure of most of the operations is chronicled in the TV documentary organized by Dr. Homer D. Kemp of Tennessee Tech in 1985. H. H. Patterson later moved to Livingston, TN, becoming an alderman, church deacon, and merchant.

He married his high school sweetheart, Pearl Donnell Patterson and two children, Hubert H., Jr., and Gloria were born on Jan. 16, 1921, and Jan. 7, 1922, respectively. Of these more later. Pearl won awards for her letters to the editors of Nashville papers. Returning to school she was awarded a BS in English in 1950 from Tennessee Polytechnic Institute.

Dewey Bliss Patterson, born Oct. 13, 1898, died Dec. 13, 1912.

Burrus Brush Patterson, born Jan. 27, 1901, became an actor and later moved to Miami, FL, where he worked for Pan American Airlines and enjoyed his hobby of Ham Radio, making friends world wide. He died Nov. 15, 1972. His stage name was Kenneth Wayne.

Flossie Lucille Patterson, born Oct. 1, 1903, lived in Detroit, MI, most of her working life. She had many friends in boating and horse racing circles. Her 16mm films recorded events there and in Dickson during family reunions. In the north she used the name Jacquelyn and was married to Alton Miller. Died April 7, 1970.

Tillie Mai Patterson, born Dec. 10, 1907, is living in Lakeland, FL. A Tennessee resident for most of her life, she served as house matron at UT Martin for a number of years. She married Leslie Brooks Elinor who died Dec. 22, 1977. Her daughter Nancy obtained a Ph.D. in Education and is employed in the Vero Beach, FL, school system. Her daughter, Marinessa is a world class Bridge Tournament player. Her son, Thomas Curtis Elinor, "Buddy," operates an automobile dealership in Haines City, FL.

Tillie "Babe," was born with musical talent and still whacks a mean syncopated piano beat for senior affairs in Lakeland.

H. H. Patterson, Jr., born Jan 16, 1921, gradauted from Tennessee Tech and served in the Navy as a Lt. (jg) in World War II. He was later employed by Sandia Labs, a contractor to the Atomic Energy Commission. He is married to the former Hilda G. Spivey who has received numerous Red Cross awards as a Water Safety instructor. Now living in Los Lunas, NM, they are active in the Experimental Aircraft Association's Young Eagles Program. The Association aims to introduce one million young people, ages eight to 17, to flight by 2003, the one hundred year anniversary of the Wright Brother's triumph at Kitty Hawk. Their three children Bob, Tom and Dana Roth live in Albuquerque. Daughter Dana and husband John Roth have two children, Kyndra and Micah.

Gloria Patterson Lakin now living in Ocala, FL, has four children. Three, Charles Thomas, Peggy Sue, and Patsy Ruth are employed as teachers in the Ocala school system. Margie Lakin Budd was Ph.D. in Multimedia Studies and is employed in Washington, DC. Gloria's husband who died in 1991 was a graduate in physics at the MS level and was employed in various branches of governmental service devoted to aerial and submarine warfare.

Gloria is a gifted musician who can play several instruments and currently plays piano for social gatherings.

WILLIAM PATTERSON, and Margaret Mayfield Branch were the parents of Robert C. Patterson. Jesse Harvey Patterson was a son of Robert C. Patterson and Malinda W. Carson. Jesse Harvey was married to Polly Ann Dickson. He was killed in 1862 in the Battle of Stones River in Murfreesboro, TN. Jesse Harvey and Malinda Carson had two sons William Robert Patterson born Jan. 31, 1856, died April 25, 1928, married May 11, 1879, to Dixie Ann Patterson born Feb. 12, 1863, died Feb. 18, 1898. Second marriage July 23, 1903, to Edna McKnight born July 26, 1882, died July 2. 1910. The second son, Thomas Dickson Patterson, born Jan 17, 1860, died Dec. 7, 1932, married to Aurora Rixena Patterson. Dixie Ann and Rixena, daughters of William and Sallie Nix Patterson married Patterson brothers. William Robert Patterson's children are Ida Ethel Patterson (Horner) born Aug. 29, 1880, died Jan 24, 1905, Clyde W. Patterson (Humphreys) born Feb. 1, 1882, died Jan. 6, 1949, Jesse Harvey Patterson born March 21, 1884, died Nov. 17, 1938, Egbert Patterson born Sept. 24, 1888, died Feb. 20, 1929, Ralph Patterson born Oct. 21, 1891, died July 9, 1955, Herbert Patterson born May 4, 1894, died April 30, 1949, and Leta Andra Patterson (Bradshaw) born Sept. 26, 1905, died Dec. 21, 1992 (Mother-Edna McKnight).

W. R. Patterson and some of his children.

Herbert Patterson married June 25, 1925, Mary Bell, daughter of Charlie Herman Bell and Winnie Hibernie Coble. Herbert and Mary Patterson had one son, Herbert Edwin, born May 23, 1930, married July 20, 1949, to Dorothy Jean Rainey, born Jan. 13, 1932, daughter of Earl William and Sophronia Denton Rainey. The children of Edwin Patterson and Dorothy Rainey Patterson are:

Donna Kay Patterson born Nov. 16, 1952, married June 19, 1983, to Thomas Edwin Lee. Their children are Elizabeth Patterson Lee born Oct. 24, 1986, and Lawson Edwin Lee born Nov. 5, 1993. Donna Patterson Lee has a B.S. and M.Ed. degree from Middle Tennessee State University in Murfreesboro, TN, where she was a member of Kappa Delta Sorority. Donna teaches Home Economics at Dickson County High School in Dickson, TN, where she lives with husband Tommy Lee, who is supervisor of Special Education in Dickson County. Tommy has a B.S. and M.A. degree plus 45 hours from Austin Peay State University in Clarksville, TN, where he was a member of Pi Kappa Alpha Fraternity and Kappa Delta Pi Honorary Society.

Herbert Edwin Patterson, Jr., born May 5, 1955, married Oct. 8, 1983, to Dalyn Brenda Chittenden. They have one daughter, Rachael Lynn Patterson, born May 5, 1993. Bert attended Middle Tennessee State University in Murfreesboro, TN. He is self-employed in the family business, Pat's Inc. in Linden, TN. Bert and Dalyn own and operate Buffalo River Motel in Linden. Dalyn received a Laboratory Technician License in 1983 from Cumberland School of Medical Technology in Cookeville, TN. She is a licensed Insurance Agent and has her own agency in Linden with Shelter Insurance Company.

William Earl Patterson born Aug. 2, 1960, has a B.S. degree from Middle Tennessee State University in Murfreesboro, TN, where he was also a member of Kappa Alpha Fraternity. He is a licensed Real Estate Agent. Bill is self-employed in the family business, Pat's Inc., in Columbia, TN, where he lives.

Jean Alyne Patterson born Sept. 26, 1974, is a third year student at Middle Tennessee State University in Murfreesboro, TN.

The Patterson children's grandmother, Mary Bell Patterson, also furthered her education in graduate school at Middle Tennessee Normal School in Murfreesboro, TN (now MTSU). Herbert Patterson, their grandfather continued his education at Savanah Institute in Savanah, TN.

The Patterson children and their parents are all members of the Christian Church in Linden, TN.

W. P. AND ELIZABETH S. PATTERSON

William P. Patterson, son of English born parents, in Ohio Aug. 5, 1843. Lived in Illinois, but crossed the Mississippi River to enlist with Co. I 6th Regiment of Iowa Infantry Volunteers on July 17, 1861, and was discharged Jan. 1, 1864. Having been shot in the right side and damaged the lobe of his lung, he was making his way home when he got to Perry County. Here he worked for Lewis Wilsdorf in his tan yard, meeting Elizabeth Wilsdorf born April 17, 1856, won her hand in marriage and married her May 9, 1870.

Front row: Lizzie Patterson, Aunt Daisy, Grandpa Patterson, Aunt Annie, and Uncle Ed. Back row: Laura (Edna's mother), John, and Robert "Rob."

They were the parents of seven children, Mary Annie, June 7, 1872-June 9, 1942, married Clem Dyer, Sept. 15, 1889, they had five children: Fred, Dec. 10, 1897-Nov. 3, 1936, married to Roxie Skelton Sept. 17, 1916. Guy, May 14, 1892-Jan 7, 1931, married Freda Hunt May 23, 1910. Ollie Mai, Oct. 23, 1895-July 22, 1933 married Charles T. Gilbert Oct. 18, 1914. Charlie, Sept. 30, 1908-July 10, 1972 married Bess Byrd, Nov. 27, 1926.

Second child Laura Elizabeth, Feb. 25, 1874-Jan. 26, 1929, married Samuel Morton Bell, Dec. 26, 1902, their children were: Edna Mae, Nov. 12, 1903-May 24, 1993, married Bob Barham Dec. 11, 1923, and Laura Lorane, Aug. 14, 1909-November 1990, and married Joe M. Starbuck.

Third William Edward, Feb. 22, 1877-March 11, 1923, married Emma Strickland, they had two sons John W., 1903-1981 married first to Linda Poore and second to Hazel Gibson, Ralph Edward, Jan. 21, 1991-March 25, 1970, never married.

Fourth is Robert Lewis, Dec. 7, 1879-1950 married Bradie Lee Deere, no children,

Daisy Victoria, Oct. 14, 1883-1964 married to William Bell, Dec. 13, 1902, their children are Roy W. married Bessie M. Bell, Pauline B. married John W. Horner.

Sixth child was John Eliva, May 16, 1892-Dec. 7, 1966, married November 1913 to Mamie Cotton to this union were two daughters Mable Louise and Ruberta Patterson.

The last child was a girl named Hannah J., Jan 29, 1889-July 6, 1889. And so ends the W. P. Patterson lineage and hope there are other brothers to W. P. to carry this lineage on. There is a story about Mr. Patterson not being able to return to visit with his family until later years and the settling of the estate. Edna Barham had a silver spoon that was part of the estate, and was kept until 1940s. W. P. and his wife, William E., Robert L., Daisy, John, and Hannah are all buried in the Pineview Cemetery.

W. P. AND ELIZABETH PATTERSON

William P. Patterson, son of English born parents, in Ohio Aug. 5, 1843. They moved from Ohio to Illinois at some point, and William crossed over into Iowa to enlist with the Iowa troops July 17, 1861, and served with the 16th Regiment of Iowa Infantry, received his discharge July 21, 1865. Having been shot in the right side and damaged the lobe of his lung, he was making his way home when he reached Perry County. Here he went to work for Lewis Wildsdorf in his tan yard. Here he met Elizabeth Wilsdorf, Lewis' daughter, born April 17, 1856, and became her husband May 9, 1870. They were parents of seven children.

John E. Patterson

1. Mary Annie, June 7, 1872-June 9, 1942. Annie married Clem Dyer and they had four children. 1. Guy, May 14, 1892-Jan. 7, 1931, married Freda Hunt. Children: Carl, Carter, and Hunt. 2. Ollie Mai, Oct. 23, 1895-July 22, 1933, married Charles T. Gilbert. Children: Grace, Mary, Helen, Melba, and Katherine. 3. Fred, Dec. 10, 1897-Nov. 3, 1936, married Roxie Skelton. Children: Billy and Georgia. 4. Charlie, Sept. 30, 1908-July 10, 1972, married Bess Byrd, November 1926. Children: Betty and Margaret.

Mamie Cotton Patterson

2. Laura Elizabeth, Feb. 25, 1874-Jan. 26, 1929, married Samual M. Bell. They had two daughters. 1. Edna Mae, Nov. 12, 1903-May 27, 1993, married Bob Barham Dec. 11, 1923. Two daughters: Melvis and Margie. 2. Laura Lorane, Aug. 14, 1909-November 1990, married Joe Starbuck March 10,1928. Daughter, Betty.

3. William Edward, Feb. 22, 1877-March 11, 1923, married Emma Strickland. They had two sons. 1. John W. Patterson, 1903-1981, first married Linda Poore then Hazel Gibson. One daughter, Betty. 2. Ralph Edward, Jan. 21, 1911-March 25, 1970, never married.

4. Robert Lewis, Dec. 7, 1879-1950, married Bradie Deere, no children.

5. Diasy Victoria, Oct. 14, 1883-1964, married William N. Bell Dec. 13, 1902. They had two children. 1. Pauline, Oct. 4, 1904-Dec. 6, 1988, married John W. Horner, no children. 2. Roy W. Bell, Dec. 11, 1914, living, married Bessie Bell. Son, Tommy married Penny Goff.

6. John E. Patterson, May 16, 1892-Dec. 7, 1966, married Mamie Cotton November 1913. They had two daughters. 1. Mabel, Aug. 7, 1914-living. 2. Ruberta, Jan. 22, 1919-living, married Hugh Nickell, Sept. 4, 1937. They had three children. 1. Johnnie Rue Nickell, Nov. 5, 1940. 2. Charles B. Nickell, March 21, 1946, married Sherry Akra. They adopted two children, David and Amy. 3. Kenneth Nickell, March 20, 1947, single.

Johnnie Rue married Brian M. Hersey in 1964 and one year later in 1965 a son, Brian M. Hersey, Jr., was born. Later Johnnie and Brian were divorced and in 1974 Johnnie married Carver England. They had twins. William Colbert England (Billy), Sept. 8, 1976. Kristol Michelle (Krissy), Sept. 8, 1976.

7. Hannah Julinia, Jan. 29, 1889-July 6, 1889. This is the end of the W. P. Patterson line as there are no males to carry the name in Tennessee. *Compiled by Mabel Patterson and Roy Bell.*

PATTERSON-DEPRIEST, Alice Patterson, born Oct. 31, 1896, is the daughter of James Washington Patterson and Margaret Melvina Kunkel. She was married to Obed Bray DePriest Dec. 25, 1924. Alice and Obed had three children: Fay, Jim, and John. Fay married Stanton Smithson and they had six children: Joe, Sue, Hal, Lyn, Jyl, and Kay. Jim married Ruby Jo Barham and had two children, Janet and Brenda. John married Irene Duff; they had no children. John's second marriage was to Donna Barnes and they had one son, Jim, and he adopted her son, Patrick.

Obed was the son of Pleasant W. and Anna Scott. His brothers and sisters were: Leonard, who married Annie McClanahan and had two sons, Glenn and Charles, and six children by his second marriage to Vera Morris; Fred married Elnora Long; Mattie married Everett Belisle; Mavis married Elmer Bandy; Gradie married Minnie Woodford; Jack married Annie Grimes; Scott, Fernie, and Nellie Fay died single.

Obed was born Nov. 7, 1891, and died Sept. 12, 1957. He received a degree in Law from Cumberland University, served a term in State Legislature, and was a rural mail carrier for 39 years. Since his death his wife, Alice, has lived alone, and is now 97 years old. Alice has been a member of the Methodist Church since 1916, member of United Methodist Women, retired school teacher, Charter Member of Home Demonstration Club with a 100% attendance record for over 50 years, and still enjoys sewing, crafts, and reading.

Alice is a descendant of the Patterson and Kunkel families. *Submitted by John DePriest.*

PATTERSON-GRAVES, Rex and Wilda Patterson have lived on Cypress Creek in Perry County for the past thirty years. They married in 1959, and have two children, Mark and David (born 1961) and Melody Ann (born 1964), and are members of Tom's Creek Baptist Church. Rex, (born 1937), a native of Perry County, graduated from the University of Tennessee at Martin in 1960, and has worked for the State of Tennessee for 33 years. He is an environmentalist with the Health Department. Wilda is a former bank employee. Their son, Mark, who also graduated from U.T.M. in 1984, married Annette Rose and they have on daughter, Elizabeth Anne, born Aug. 7, 1990. Mark works for the State of Tennessee, Finance Department as a computer specialist, and Annette is a librarian in the Williamson County school system. They live in Fairview, TN. Melody Ann married David Steinquest. They have one son, Ethan David, born May 17, 1994. Melody is a graduate of Austin Peay State University and is a teacher in the Montgomery County school system. David is a music teacher at A.P.S.U. They live in Clarksville, TN.

Wilda Faye (born 1940) in the daughter of William Franklin Graves and Wilma Mae Lancaster of Decatur County. William is the son of James Franklin Graves and Bertha Yarbro, and Wilma was the daughter of Lorenzo Lafayette (Fate) Lancaster and Mary (Mollie) Houston.

Rex's parents were Howell and Nettie Jane Roberts Patterson of Pineview. Howell (1889-1957) was the son of James Washington Patterson (born 1859) and Margaret Melvina Kunkel (born 1865). He had two sisters, Alice and Alta. James Washington's father was Robert Harrison (born 1838) son of Robert Carson born 1789 in Virginia, son of William Patterson. Four generations, Robert C., Robert H., James Washington, and Howell are all buried in the Pineview Cemetery on Tom's Creek.

Howell served in World War I and was a rural mail carrier from the Densons Landing Post Office from 1940 to 1945. He was a life long farmer in the Tom's Creek community, where he and Nettie were born and raised. Howell and Nettie were active members of Toms Creek Baptist Church.

Nettie Jane Roberts' (1902-1972) parents were Polly Ann Baker and John Peter Roberts, Sr. Polly Ann's mother and father were John Sails Baker and Nancy M. Ledbetter. John Peter Roberts was the son of William A. Roberts and Martha A. Barnett.

PATTERSON-KUNKEL, William Patterson, born in Virginia in 1750 died in Williamson County, TN, in 1816. He married Margaret Branch (1762-1839) in 1784. They had eight children: William, John, Robert Carson, James, Elizabeth, Mary, Carson, and Thomas Carson.

Robert Carson born in North Carolina (1789-1873) married Malinda Carson (1800-1850) in 1817 in Bedford County, TN. They settled on Toms Creek in Perry County and are buried in the Pineview Cemetery. Their children were: William (born 1818), among the first, if not the first child born in Perry County; Mary Polly (born 1822); Martha Ann (born 1826); Elizabeth Dilworth (born 1827); Jesse Harvey (born 1830); Sara Myra (born 1833); Margaret (born 1836); Robert Harrison (born 1838); Carson W. (born 1841); and Ruth (born 1843).

Robert Carson and Malinda's son Robert Harrison (1838-1914) married Mary Ellen Blackburn (1835-1889) in 1856, the daughter of Leroy Blackburn of Bedford County. Robert H. enlisted in the Confederate Army and served in Company C, Tenth Regiment of the Tennessee Cavalry from 1862 to 1865, and was a prisoner of war the last year. Robert Harrison and Mary Ellen had six children: Robert L. (born 1856), James Washington (born 1859), Malinda Ellen (born 1861), David C. (born 1866), Emma J. (born 1869), and William L. (born 1873. He and his second wife, Margaret Tipton Lewis, married in 1891 an and had one daughter, Beulah, born in 1895.

James Washington (1859-1931) married Mosella Daniel in 1881 and had one son, Walter (1882-1964). After her death he married Margaret Melvina Kunkel (1865-1956) in 1886 and had Howell (born 1889), Lela Alta (born 1894), and Mary Alice (born 1896).

Hartman Kunkel, born in Bavarian, Germany, came to United States on the ship, Vesta, and landed in New Orleans in 1845. His children, Peter, Mag'd, Casper, Marie, John Adam, and Margaret were with him. John Adam, husband of Martha Hufstedler (1840-1919) was born 1828 in Germany and died 1908. He enlisted in the Confederate Army in 1861, and served in Company I of the 24th Regiment Tennessee Infantry, and engaged in the Battle of Shiloh in 1862. John Adam and his wife, Martha, are buried in Kunkel Cemetery on Cypress Creek.

John Adam and Martha's children were: Margaret Melvina (born 1865), who married James Washington Patterson; John Adam, Jr. (born 1868); Emma Jane (born 1871); Laura Frances (born 1873); James Franklin (born 1875); George W. Bliss (born 1881); and Albert Donelson (1884). This was Martha Hufstedler's second marriage. She was married in 1859 to John Holbrooks Pope and they had one daughter, Nancy E. Pope.

The Hufstedler family begins with Jacob Hufstedler, who came from Germany with wife, Susannah, and settled in North Carolina, South Carolina, and then Tennessee. Their son, Jacob, (1785-1860) and wife Alcey Moore, had John, David, Joseph Freeman, James Henry, Elizabeth, Pinckney, Samuel Moore, Susannah, and Alcey.

James Henry Hufstedler (1813-1873) married Elizabeth Elder Salmon (1818-1893) and had twelve children: Mary Jane, Alsey, John Wesley, Martha (wife of John Adam Kunkel), Nancy, Samuel Moore, James Clay, Jacob F., Margaret, William Henry, and George Washington. *Submitted by Alice DePriest.*

Standing, left to right: Alfred and Laura Kelly; Jim and Emma Kunkel; John Kunkel, Howell Patterson, Margaret and James Washington (Jim) Patterson. Front row: Walter Patterson, Alice Horner, John Adam and Martha Kunkel, and Albert Kunkel. (about 1893)

First row, left to right: Howell, Walter, Clifford, Lula, Ida, and Effie Patterson; Second row: James Washington and Margaret (Kunkel) Patterson and baby, Alta; Robert Harrison and Margaret Tipton (Lewis) Patterson; Sally Patterson; Robert L. and Martha (Rushton) Patterson; Back row: Emma Patterson; David Carson and Margaret (Poore) Patterson, with Mabel; William L. and Margaret (Horner) Patterson; Tom, Clem, and Byrd Patterson. (about 1894)

PATTON-HUNT, John V. Patton was born in Tennessee on June 11, 1859, to John F. and Elizabeth Patton. John V.'s grandmother was a full-blooded Creek Indian. He farmed on Cane Creek and married Sarah Lucinda Hunt on Nov. 10, 1879. She was born in 1863 and raised in Perry County. To this union were born nine children.

Sarah L. Hunt Patton at 80 years old in 1943. (1863-1947)

Elmer Patton (1882-1955) married Mamie P. Primm (1882-1957); Selmer Patton married Al Rilely; Ollie Patton married V. V. Matlock; Ova Patton married Dump Crabb; Bud, Delmer, and a baby girl died young. Pollie Patton married Isaac Paul Primm. She was the last surviving child of John and Sarah's, born April 1, 1894, and died Oct. 29, 1988. Alma Patton, born July 16, 1904, died April 3, 1979, married Ida Rowena Little April 17, 1929.

John V. had seven sisters and one brother. Francis Patton, born 1837 in Tennessee; Mary Patton, born 1839 in Tennessee; Nancy Patton, born Nov. 24, 1845, in Perry County, TN, died Aug. 7, 1889, married William Franklin Oakley, Sr., in January 1886 in Perry County; Susannah Patton, born 1847, in Tennessee, married S. L. McCage on Jan 6, 1866; Sarah Patton, born Sept. 2, 1852, in Tennessee, married John Craig Oct. 22, 1874; Etta Patton, born Dec. 9, 1861, d. in 1923, married Joe Byrd, Feb. 15, 1878. His brother Thomas H. Patton, born 1849 in Tennessee, married Martha Brown, March 14, 1872.

John and Sarah moved from Perry County to Eagle Creek in Benton County about 1890. He died in 1936 and she in 1947. They are buried in Byrds Hill Cemetery on Eagle Creek in Benton County.

Children of Elmer and Mamie Patton: Rye-deceased, Mamie Lou married Fred Faulkner, Ollie Ann married D. M. Chappell.

Children of Al and Selmer Riley: Hattie married Paul Bates, Albert married Pauline Edwards, they divorced and he married Geraldine White, Lettie married Robert Dunn, Fred married Charlene Berry, Stella married J. C. Rogers, Nelson married Eula Mae Hutchinson.

Children of Isaac and Pollie Primm: Clyde married Stella Price, Emease married Hugh Haskins, Wilson married Verna Daley, Olian married Reba Howe, Evelyn married Gordon Livingston, Lois married Jack Cripe, Paul married Jean Kelly, Louis married Beth.

Children of Vollie and Ollie Matlock: John W. married Beulah Witherspoon, Thomas L. married Lavern Cannady, Cindy married Dean Golden, Clifford married Marjorie Sherwood, Stella-never married.

Ova married Dump Crabb. They had no children.

Children of Alma and Rowena Patton: James-killed in action, Korea July 3, 1952, Johnny married Reba Smith, David married Nell Kelly, Earl married JoAnn Haskins, now divorced.

PEERCY-HESTER, John Pearcy born in Devon, England, in 1737 married Ann Spencer (1738) and had eleven children. John ran away from home to serve on the high seas for ten years, before settling in America. May 3, 1779, John received from Thomas Jefferson, the Governor of Virginia, a land grant of 185 acres.

Frelan and Mary Peercy Family

James Pearcy (May 4, 1763) was born in Buckingham County, VA, the third child of John and Ann. James married Elizabeth "Betsy" Smelser/Smeltzer. James was drafted a short time before the Battle of Guilford of the Revolutionary War. According to Wayne County, KY, Marriages and Vital Records 1801-1860, he claimed compensation for eight months of service.

William Pearcy (1790) was born in Beford County, VA, and married Senah (Cenia) Clatcher in 1813.

Mark A. Pearcy (April 6, 1814) son of William and Senah, married Sarah Hix of Tennessee.

Frelan Piercy (Feb. 6, 1855) son of Mark and Sarah, was born in Wayne County, KY, married Mary "Polly" Privett, and had eight children.

Richard (Dick) Piercy (Sept. 20, 1873) son of Frelan and Polly, met and married Ida Lou Smith (1879) while working in Kentucky for her father Samuel Smith. Richard and Ida Lou and their ten children moved to Nashville, TN, in 1920.

Sophia Jewell Piercy, eighth child of Richard and Ida Lou, was born Feb. 9, 1915, and married John Tate Hester (1916) of Lobelville, TN. Sophia (1915-1991) was a devout Methodist and dedicated teacher, serving the profession for thirty years. Sophia and John T. had three children: Betty Jewell (Ms. Kenneth P. Barber), Johnnia Ruth (Ms. Paul Cherry Elliott), and William Thomas.

Betty Jewell Hester (April 9, 1944) married her high school sweetheart Kenneth Paul Barber on June 7, 1964. Betty and Ken had three children; Kenneth Paul, Jr., Pamela Jewell (Ms. James A. Bunch), and Jacquelyn LaRue. Betty and Ken moved to the Gussie Goblet farm on Marsh Creek in Linden, TN, in August of 1975. Ken is currently President of Sequoyah Administrative Services and spends the remainder of his time caring for the 115 acres on Marsh Creek. Betty, her children now grown, follows in the footsteps of her mother. She is a substitute teacher for the Perry County school system.

Pamela Jewell Barber (Sept. 13, 1969) married James A. Bunch on Dec. 21, 1991. James A. Bunch is the youngest child of Dennis L. and Mary Alice Bunch of Wingo, KY. Pamela is a graduate of Perry County High (1987) and Tony a graduate of Graves County High School in Kentucky (1987). The two graduated from the University of Tennessee at Martin in May of 1991. They now make their home in Nashville where Tony is an accountant for Central Parking System and Pamela is a marketing assistant for the Baptist Sunday School Board.

PEGRAM-BURNETTE-BELL, George William Pegram was born in Dinwiddie County, VA, the oldest child and son of George Scott and Francis Taylor Pegram. He came to Davidson County, TN, (now Cheatham County) with his parents prior to 1823, as George Scott purchased 730 and 1/4 acres of land there April 18, 1823. George Scott owned 1988 acres in Davidson County at one time. The town of Pegram received its name from George Scott and his brother William. George William had brothers and sisters as follows: Thomas Isles born ca 1805. Roger P. born Feb. 6, 1806. Sally born ca 1808. Patsey born ca 1809. Glenn born ca 1813. Edward born ca 1816. John Peter born April 6, 1818.

George W. married (1) Sally or Sarah L. Burnette, daughter of Leonard and — Burnette Oct. 3, 1826, in Davidson County, TN. Children: Caroline born 1830 married E. N. Bell. Louisa born 1833 married James Thornton. Sally or Sarah born 1840 married Heath ? Georgianne born 1841 married Frank Sutton. James Thomas born 1846 married Nancy Lunn.

After acquiring several hundred acres of land, he built a log house in Pegram, TN, near the present home of Paul and Joyce Anderson. These buildings along with the Pegram Cemetery were torn away when Insterstate 40 was being built.

Sally died in 1846 at the age of 41, being born June 9, 1805. She was buried near the home and her stone is one of the two still intact after excavations for the highway. It reads:

Sarah L. Pegram, born 6-9-1805, departed this life on 9-19-1846 in the 41st year of her age.

Another stone reads:

Sallie - Pegram, born August 1, d. February 2, 1829.

This is believed to be one of her children who died young.

George W. then married (2) Mary (Polly) Bell, slightly older than his oldest daughter, and moved to Perry County, TN, before 1853. He received a land grant of 250 acres Sept. 9, 1853, in Perry County and eventually became owner of several hundred more acres on Tom's Creek. Their children: William Malibar born 1849 married Amanda Sharp. Jane born 1851 married Alex Heath. Adeline born 1860 married ____. John Henry born 1864 married ____.

Adeline and John Henry were minors at the time the estate was settled.

Mary (Polly) died July 17, 1876, and George W. died prior to Sept. 16, 1876, (same year) as that was the date of the settling of the estate. The following is a list of the heirs:

Sarah Heath, Thomas, Jane Heath, John Henry, Jasper Thornton (grandson) son of Louisa (deceased), Caroline Bell, William Malibar, Adeline Pegram, and Georgianne Sutton.

George W. and Mary are both buried in Perry County.

Caroline Pegram born 1830 married Eldridge Newsom Bell. Their children: John H.

born 1852 married Mary Robertson. William Green born 1853 married Mary Jane Coble. Mary Bell born 1855 married Dock Cagle. E. N. Bell, Jr., born 1856 married Sarah O'Guin. George Washington born 1860 married Manerva Robertson. Anna Jane born 1861 married John W. Claiborne. James Thomas born 1863 married Mollie Ayers. Elisabeth Louisa born 1865 married William David Cantrell. Charles H. born 1867 married Hibernia Coble. Henry Harrison born 1869 married Ida L. Fuller. Montgomery born 1873 married Minnie Pirtle.

Caroline and Eldridge Newsom are buried in Perry County.

CRESSIE PEVAHOUSE, step-daughter of Rob Moore (parents were Jess and Tilda—they are buried at Bethel Cemetery).

To further her education Cressie went to Paducah, KY. While attending school, she met and married C. L. Barnhill. After they married, he went into the United States Army. When he returned from service, he became a Missionary Baptist Minister. They lived on a farm in Paducah, KY, while rearing their children:

C. L. Barnhill born Dec. 6, 1918, married Cressie Pevahouse Barnhill on Sept. 28, 1940. She was born Dec. 13, 1915. They had five children:

1. Reba Mae born Sept. 10, 1941, married Joe Moyers. They had six children: Jay, Robin, Jeff, Reba Fay, and Jon Racheal.

2. Mary Ann born April 13, 1943, married Charles Draffes. They had three children: Christon Ann, Phil, and Mike.

3. Linda Lee, born April 14, 1946, and was not married.

4. Linda Lee's twin brother Leon Barnhill also born April 14, 1946, and married Wendy Garuis. They had three children: Kelley, Morgan, and Jorden.

5. Larry Barnhill born Sept. 25, 1947, married Carol Hugehson. They had two daughters: Sarah and Rebecca. *Compiled by Reba Mae Moyers.*

PAUL E. PEVAHOUSE, born 1909 was the son of Elihue and Ida Gentry Pevahouse. He was married in 1933 to Cora Alice Anderson, daughter of Andy Carrol and Kathryn Haynes Anderson. They had three boys: James Edwin, Clyde Eugene, and Gary Wayne. They lived in the Bethel Community. He died 1975 and is buried in the Bethel Cemetery.

Edwin, Paul, Cora Alice, Eugene, and Gary.

James Edwin Pevahouse, born 1935 married Eva Dean Grooms in 1954 following their divorce, he married Lera Mae Warren in 1973 and had one son, James Edwin, Jr. (1974) who married Ingrid Parnell in 1993. James Edwin graduated from Perry County High School in 1953 and works for Johnson Control in Linden, TN.

Clyde Eugene Pevahouse born 1936 graduated from Perry County High School in 1955 and worked as a sale clerk at Turnbow's Cash Store in Linden for 34 years. He is a member of the United Methodist Church at Flatwoods, TN, where he now resides. He was married to Dorothy Graves Hickerson, daughter of Clyde H. and Weda Treadwell Graves in 1976. Dorothy had previously been married to Billy Ralph Hickerson and had two sons: Michael Ralph Hickerson (1964) and Kyle Gilbert Hickerson (1964).

Michael Ralph married Terri Summers and they had one son, Jonathan Michael Hickerson. Following their divorce, he married Sheila Baker Pope who had two children by a previous marriage: Clayton Pope and Cassie Pope.

Kyle Gilbert Hickerson married to Janice Skelton in 1990 and they have one daughter Kayla Brooke Hickerson, born 1992.

Gary Wayne Pevahouse (1944) married Janet Louise Cantrell in 1964. They had two daughters: Cynthia Alice and Susan Renea'. He has worked for Tennessee Gas Pipeline for 24 years. He now resides at Portland, TN.

Cynthia Alice married Denny Joel Chandler in 1964 and they had two daughters, Megan Brooke Chandler, Ashlan Nicole Chandler, and one stepson, Jonathan Chandler.

Susan Renea' Pevahouse (1968) graduated from MTSU, and teaches first grade in Lobelville Elementary School.

Susan married, Barton Keith Greenway of Perryville, TN, on July 8, 1994.

WANDA KAYE PEVAHOUSE, born Jan, 1, 1949, at Lewis County Hospital in Hohenwald, TN. Kaye was raised in Perry County on Cedar Creek, where she attended Cedar Creek Elementary and Perry County High School and one year at High Forest Laboratory School in Hohenwald, TN.

Celia and Carnis Pevahouse

On Aug. 24, 1968, she married James Hillard Moore born Feb. 13, 1948. James left in November 1968 for Military Service, where he served two years; one of which was spent in Vietnam.

James and Kaye had two children; James Brian Moore born Jan. 30, 1971, at Perry County Hospital, Linden, TN. Brian graduated Perry County High School 1989; attended one year at Columbia State in Columbia, TN. Brian went to Jackson State College in Jackson, TN, where he became an E.M.T. He worked 1 1/2 years for Perry County Ambulance Service. Brian now works for C.C.A. at Clifton, TN.

Heather Renee Moore born Aug. 6, 1977, at Decatur County Hospital in Decatur County. Heather is finishing her junior year at Perry County High School.

Kaye's parents were Therial Carnis Pevahouse born Jan. 29, 1921; d. Jan. 25, 1965, and Celia Aslee Bridges born Aug. 19, 1922; d. Jan. 28, 1983. They were married Feb. 10, 1940, by Josh Broadway. Carnis served in the Army for two years; when he returned home, he was a self-employed truck driver. Celia was a housewife. Both are buried in the Woods-Treadwell Cemetery.

Kayes maternal grandparents: George Daniel Bridges born 1890 married May 15, 1910, d. Sept. 15, 1965. Married by Rev. S. J. Treadwell. Martha Ann, Bertha, Elizabeth, Jane, Inman, Bridges born Sept. 13, 1888, d. July 20, 1958. They are buried in the Woods-Treadwell Cemetery.

Carnis's parents were John Wesley born March 6, 1899; d. Aug. 31, 1931; married Feb. 8, 1892 and Lilly Mae Grooms born Sept. 23, 1903; d. Nov. 2, 1941. They had three other children: Eldon, Eva, and Dorothy. They lived on Swindle Creek. John and Lilly were buried in Bethel Cemetery along with Eva and Dorothy. Eldon was buried at Woods-Treadwell Cemetery. Carnis also had two half brothers, Loral and Bufford Boyd.

During the Battle of Shiloh, people living on Swindle Creek could hear the boom of cannons and people living near the Tennessee River could see smoke come down the river like puffs of clouds.

Jess Pevahouse born Feb.14, 1862; d. Oct. 14, 1928. His first marriage was to Martha Swindle. They married July 8, 1882. They lived on Swindle Creek. Martha died shortly after their marriage. On Feb. 28, 1884, Jess' second marriage was to Linda Wilson. Linda was an only child of John and Ann Wilson. Jess and Linda had seven children: Lila, Eliza, Lula, Minnie, Ida, Cora, and Wesley. Jess' third marriage was to Tilda Moore. They had three children: Effie, died at the age of 16; Brownie, who lived only a few days, and Cressie. Cressie married C. L. Barnhill.

Jess' parents were Robert Elihue and Elizabeth A. Moore. Elihue was in the military in the Civil War when he took sick while serving in Nashville, TN. His wife rode a horse from Perry County to Nashville and stayed with him until his death. She returned to Perry County to raise her family of seven children: John, Jess, Elihue, Eliza, Mandy, Linda, Jane, and LeRoy.

Elihue's father was Daniel Pevahouse born ca 1808 in Kentucky. Later in life, he moved to Perry County on Swindle Creek where he was a farmer.

DAVID P. POOLE, was born Dec. 27, 1893, and died July 24, 1983. He married Ms. Florence Daily. They had no children and were residents of Lobelville. David was the second of three children born to James K. Polk McCollum and Amanda DePriest (See McCollum, JKP history). David was the grandson of Alex Thomas P. Poole and Julie Ann Rains-Poole-Roberts (See Rains-Poole Families history).

David P. Poole

David related a story to the author of this article, of the origins of the P. Poole family name. The surname in England was "Pettypool." Upon arrival to the Americas, the "Pettypool" ancestors shortened the name to P'Poole and hence the frequency of "P" in many Poole names. David was the custodian of the old Rains Notebook, letters, and photos until his death in 1983. The old Rains Notebook was placed in the Tennessee State Archives at Nashville along with some Confederate money and other artifacts of the family. *Submitted by Oden and Ruby (McCollum) Fowler.*

LEMUEL MICAJAH POPE, was born Dec. 4, 1829, in Hickman County, TN, the son of James Andrew and Nancy Halbrooks Pope. He moved to Perry County about 1854 and on Jan. 15, 1857, married Martha Ann Horner, daughter of Jesse and Mary Peterson Horner, who was born Nov. 26, 1839. Three children were born: Adeline, 1858; James Robert, 1859; William Cornelius born Nov. 2, 1861. Lemuel, a gunsmith, enlisted in Co. C, 10th Tennessee Cavalry, CSA, and died while a prisoner of the Union Army in Illinois, on Sept. 28, 1863. Martha Ann Pope then married William Bussell, but she died on May 9, 1866, leaving the three small children to be raised by their maternal grandmother, Mary Patterson Horner Sparks and their step grandfather, Jesse Sparks, Jr.

Lemuel Micajah Pope

William Cornelius Pope, the youngest child of Lemuel and Martha, married Mary Frances Cooper, born Nov. 7, 1861, on June 17, 1883, in Hickman County. Five children were born of this marriage: Jurettie, born and died 1884; Josie born 1886 and died 1887; Jesse David born April 25, 1888; Myrtle born 1890 and Flossie born 1892. William "Billy" Pope was a Primitive Baptist "preacher" and owned and operated a combination general store and post office at Pope, TN, a community named for his father, Lemuel and uncle, James Pope. Family tradition states that "Billy" Pope performed more marriage ceremonies and baptisms than any other minister in the county. Billy Pope died in 1936, following his wife's death in 1932.

Jesse David, the only son of Billy and Mary Frances Pope, graduated from Branham and Hughes Academy at Spring Hill, TN, in 1912, after which he taught grades 1 through 8 at the Starbuck school on Cypress Creek. One of his pupils, Frances Ruth Ayers, born Aug. 5, 1898, the daughter of E.J. and Ethel Starbuck Ayers, became his wife on May 4, 1918. In 1913, Jesse began work as a bookkeeper at First National Bank in Linden, and continued there until 1923. In 1923, Jesse and Ruth moved back to Pope, TN, where he operated the store and post office owned by his father. In 1929, they moved back to Linden and purchased a dry goods store and were active in this business until the closing in 1978. He was elected President of First National Bank on Linden in 1935 and continued in that capacity until his death on Oct. 10, 1984.

Three children were born to Jesse and Ruth Pope: an infant who died at birth; Don Ayers, who married Virginia Duncan and had three children, Jerry, David, and Joel; Jessie Ruth, who married Billy Tiller and had no children.

The Pope family first came to Tennessee around 1806, when John Pope came from North Carolina and purchased land in Williamson County. A son, Cary Pope, moved first to Hickman then to Wayne County. A son of Cary's, James Andrew, remained in Hickman County and he and his wife, Nancy Halbrooks Pope, had 14 children, one of whom was Lemuel Micajah Pope, the first Pope to move to Perry County.

RICHARD AND ELIZABETH HINSON POPLIN, Richard Poplin was born ca 1799, North Carolina of English ancestry. He married in Guilford County, NC, in 1825 to Elizabeth Hinson (born ca 1804), daughter of John "Short Johnny" Hinson. In 1830, Richard and Elizabeth, along with other members of their families, emigrated to Hickman County, TN, where they purchased an occupant claim on Brushy Fork of Beaverdam Creek from Daniel Lancaster. Here they raised their family of eight children: 1)John Poplin (1826-1905) married No. 1 Marcy Deaton; No. 2 Mary Ann Mahala Breece; No. 3 Mrs. Minerva Jane Hinson Curry (1848-1933), daughter of Elijah Lazarus Hinson and Evaline Davidson. Minerva Jane was John's second cousin. 2)Lazarus Poplin (born ca 1828, NC), married Permelia ?; they went "West" in 1857. 3)Keziah Poplin (born ca 1830); 4)Nancy Poplin (born ca 1833); 5)Cordelia Poplin (born ca 1838, TN), married James P. Hinson; 6)Aaron Poplin (born ca 1839, TN, died in Civil War), married Rhoda J. Hensley (daughter of John A. Hensley and Eliza Jane Crowell). 7)Myrick Poplin (born ca 1842, died in Civil War); 8)Ruth Ann Poplin (born ca 1848). No further knowledge of Lazarus, Keziah, Nancy, or Ruth Ann.

In 1853, John Poplin purchased 436 acres on Coon Creek, in Perry County, from John E. Barber. In April of 1854, John sold this property to father, Richard. Richard and Elizabeth lived there the rest of their lives and both are buried in unmarked graves at the head of Coon Creek, probably in the Poplin Hollow Cemetery. Elizabeth died sometime between the 1870 and 1880 census. Richard sold his 436 acres in May of 1877 to brothers, Newton Jasper and James Harvey Hinson. Richard Poplin died sometime between 1877 and 1880.

John Poplin 1826-1905

The writer is a great, great granddaughter of Richard and Elizabeth Hinson Poplin, through their son, John, and his second wife, Mary Ann Mahala Breece Poplin.

Other families with whom this family has strong ties are Barber, Mathis, Hensley, Quillen, Breece, Qualls, Davidson, Duncan, Loveless...to name a few. *Submitted by Helene Myers Hamm.*

PORTIA-ROBERTSON-BELL, Nathaniel Robertson born 1802 in South Carolina, died before 1870 wife Matilda born 1812, died before 1870, came to Tennessee with his mother, Delilah, born 1780 death date unknown. Nathaniel and Matilda had William C., Sept. 11, 1828-Feb. 23, 1890, married Carolina Adaline Portia in 1850. She was born Sept. 30, 1828, to Joseph and Victoria Pavout Portia and died Sept. 28, 1900. They came from France to Evansville, IN, then to Roans Creek, then to Toms Creek. Here she married W. C. Robertson, they were the parents of eight girls, Matilda June 1, 1852-? married to George Lynch. Sarah Adeline Feb. 26, 1855-Dec. 3, 1936, married Charles Bell Sept. 6, 1872. Minerva Victoria 1860-? married William George Bell Oct. 1, 1877. Eliza A. Jan. 22, 1866-June 1, 1943, married Joe Horner. Leona Sept. 8, 1871-July 4, 1927 married William Lee (Billy) Horner. Melinda March 10, 1870-? married Henry Ledbetter.

Sam M. and Laura E. (Patterson) Bell

Sarah married Charles H. Bell son of John and Esther McDanial Bell. Charles and Sarah lived all their lives on Toms Creek and are buried in the Bell-Robertson cemetery. Their children are Samuel M. June 12, 1873-Oct. 27, 1933, married Laura Patterson Dec. 26, 1902; twins Mary Jane and Martha Jean, Mary 18 Aug. 1874 July 12, 1909 married Francis M. Thorton, Feb.

11, 1900, Martha died Dec. 22, 1874. Edward E. March 20, 1879-Sept. 8, 1964 married Vera Elise Shepard Dec. 26, 1908. Ida Rue July 19, 1892, July 25, 1980 married Emmett Lafeyette Cotham. Sam and Laura Bell were the parents of Edna Mae Nov. 12, 1903-May 27, 1993, married Bob Barham Dec. 11, 1923. Laura Lorene Aug. 12, 1909-November 1990 married to Joe M. Starbuck, all of these are buried in Swiss cemetery. Edna and Bob have two girls, Melvis Virginia Dec. 18, 1929 and married Leroy Staggs, June 1, 1949 in Kentucky. They have three children Sandra Kay June 9, 1960, married Jeff Cameron and have Bret, Dec. 9, 1986. Gary Lee Oct. 9, 1963, his daughter is Jerica Jan. 13, 1987. Stephen Barham Staggs Feb. 16, 1965. Other daughter of Bob and Edna is Marjorie Ann Sept. 23, 1935, married Naymond D. Graves Aug. 22, 1958, they have three children Barbara April 13, 1959-April 14, 1959, Melissa Jean, Jan. 9, 1961 married Tim Carroll Jan 21, 1977, and divorced Feb. 12, 1984, then married Jeffery Scott Raymer March 8, 1922. Anthony Lee Nov. 8, 1963 and is unmarried at this time.

Melissa and Tim have three children Sabrina Lynn Sept. 8, 1977, Katrina Gwen, Feb. 1, 1979, and Brandon Wade Carroll March 23, 1983.

ASBERRY QUALLS, son of Richard and Margurite Kilpatrick was born Sept. 1, 1866, at the Dowdy Place on Coon Creek in Perry County, TN. He was left without a mother at the age of three and without a father at the age of ten. He grew up under the hand of his grandfather and stepmother. At the age of 21 he married Mary Baucom who had come from Missouri two years earlier. They were married on Nov. 20, 1877. They spent most of their remaining time on Brush Creek in Perry County, TN. Nine children were born to them.

Mary Baucom Qualls and Asberry Qualls

1. Margaret Cora Q. Rogers born 1888-1942. 2. Leona April 29, 1891-Oct. 27, 1891. 3. Henry Qualls 1892-1976. 4. Jess Qualls 1895-1976. 5. Dixie Qualls Laxton 1898-1944. 6. Robert Qualls 1901-1980. 7. Roy P. Qualls 1904-1920. 8. Richard E. Qualls 1906. 9. Ottis A. Qualls 1913-1993.

A. B. Qualls and Mary lived together for 65 years until his death on Dec. 22, 1952. He was 86 years old. Mary lived 13 years after his death. She died on Nov. 4, 1965. Her knowledge of the family and her remarkable memory has made possible most of the information given back to the first Qualls in this part of the country. She was 94 years old at the time of her death and her memory was good until the end.

Mary was the daughter of Aaron Baucom and Lucinda Qualls.

BOBBY JOE AND EVA (TATE) QUALLS, Bobby Joe, born 1941, and Eva (Tate) Qualls, born 1942, live in the Coon Creek Community in Perry County.

Bobby Joe and Eva (Tate) Qualls

Eva is the daughter of the late James E. Tate, born 1917, and Estelle (Lineberry) Tate, born 1919, of Perry County. James E. was the son of William Spence Tate, born 1892, and Cora (Walker) Tate, born 1896, of Perry County. William Spence was the son of John T. Tate, born 1855, and Dora (Corder) Tate, born 1872, of Perry County. John Tommy was the son of Aaron Tate and Jane (Childress) Tate of Perry County, birth dates unknown. Aaron originally came from Ireland.

Estelle (Lineberry) Tate was the daughter of Elvis Lineberry, born 1891, and Nora (Howell) Lineberry, born 1891. Elvis was one of the well-digging Lineberrys. Elvis Lineberry was the son of Sam Lineberry, born 1856, and Mary Ann (Williams) Lineberry, born 1865, of Wayne County. Sam was the son of Tobif Lineberry who originally came from Germany. He married a Wheeler but her name is not known at this time.

Bobby Joe is the son of Leonard Brown Qualls, born 1918, and Maybelle (Jackson) Qualls, born 1921, of Perry County. Maybelle is the daughter of the late Stanley (Dock) Jackson, born 1900 and Freddie (Gregory) Jackson, born 1900. Stanley Dock was the son of Nathaniel Natt Jackson, born 1848. Freddie is the daughter of the late William Edward Gregory, born 1869, and Estelle (Voss) Gregory, born 1873, of Perry County. William Edward was the son of James B. Gregory, born 1834, and Martha (Cayce) Gregory, born 1840. Martha (Cayce) Gregory was the daughter of John Cayce, born 1810, and Rebecca (Morris) Cayce, born 1811, of Hickman County. John Cayce was the son of Joshua and Peggy (Sharp) Cayce who were married in 1812. Birth records of Peggy and Joshua are not available. Peggy (Sharp) Cayce was the daughter of John Sharp who died in the 1820s. It is believed that John and his family came from Hickman County.

Leonard B. Qualls is the son of the late William, born 1892, and Mollie (Sharp) Qualls, born 1892, of Perry County. William is the son of Joe B. Qualls, born 1868, and Ezora (Warren) Qualls, born 1870, of Perry County. Joe B. is the son of Riley Qualls, born 1828, and Smithy (Hilburn) Qualls, died 1919. Riley was the son of Isham Qualls, born 1785, and Elizabeth (Baucom) Qualls, born 1794. Isham came from Ireland in 1803. He came to North Carolina and in 1805 he enlisted in the Army. He fought in the war of 1812 and it is believed he accompanied General Andrew Jackson to New Orleans in 1814. On his way back from New Orleans, it is believed he stopped off in Perry County where he met his wife Elizabeth Baucom. They lived mostly in the Coon Creek/Brush Creek area except for a trip back to North Carolina. Most of the Qualls families in this area are descendants of Isham and Elizabeth (Baucom) Qualls.

Both Bobby Joe and Eva Qualls graduated from Linden High School in 1959 and 1960 respectively. Immediately after graduation, Bobby enlisted in the U. S. Navy. One year later after Eva graduated, they were married on Sept. 22, 1960. They moved to Norfolk, VA, where Bobby was stationed in the Navy. While in Virginia, they had a son, Bobby Michael Qualls, born 1963. Bobby remained in the Navy and retired from active duty in 1978 as a Chief Petty Officer at Mt. Clemens, MI.

During his Navy career, Bobby was stationed at San Diego, CA; Olathe, KS; Norfolk, VA; Brooklyn, NY; Norfolk, VA (second time); and Mt. Clemens, MI, where he retired from active duty at the Naval Air Facility.

While Bobby was in the Navy, Eva pursued her career in sales and bookkeeping.

After Bobby's retirement from the Navy in July 1978, the couple moved back to Perry County with their son Bobby Michael. They make their home in the Coon Creek Community on the southern edge of the Qualls family farm.

Bobby and Eva have one granddaughter, Brandi Michelle Qualls, born 1981. Bobby Michael is married to Wendy (Gilbert) Qualls, born 1965, of Hickman County.

Bobby and Eva are employed in Perry and Decatur County and are active in the Church at Brush Creek.

QUALLS, On June 10, 1850, a petition for the division of the property left to the widow Qualls "now Lady Lane" (or Ione), and her children, was filed in Perry County. The petition spoke of her oldest son who lived on Buffalo River. This is the first location we can find of our ancestor David E. Qualls.

David E. Qualls was born in Tennessee on Sept. 9, 1819. He was listed in the 1850 Perry County Census with his wife Mary, age 30, and a daughter, Elizabeth, age 5. He was listed in deed records in Perry County, as he bought and sold many parcels of land, either by himself or in partnership with W. I. Davidson or R. D. Alexander.

In 1860, in the David Qualls household, besides his wife Mary, are Jane Nichols and her two children and a 65 year old Elizabeth Wood. Their connection to David are unknown, although, we believe Elizabeth was his mother-in-law. Living next door, was his daughter, Elizabeth and her husband, John Rodgers.

David and his daughter had both lost their spouses by 1870, and were in the same house again, along with Elizabeth and John's children, Tennie Byrd and Henry Green Rodgers, and Elizabeth's new husband, William Edward Davidson. William Edward was the son of Sousannah Alexander and step-son of W. I. Davidson. They later had two children of their own, Will and Molly.

On Jan. 2, 1872, David Qualls married Mary E. Rosson, daughter of Stephen Rosson. Mary helped David raise both of his grandchildren.

The burial places of John Rodgers, Mary Wood Qualls, and William Edward and Elizabeth Davidson are unknown. David Qualls died Oct. 18, 1883, and is buried at the Davidson Cemetery at the Qualls bend in Lobelville. Mary Rosson Qualls married John Nicholson and moved to Lewis County at the turn of the century. *Submitted by Jo Ann Lawson and Marsha Essary.*

DONNIE QUALLS AND LOY K. QUALLS

have lived in Perry County all of their lives. Loy is the daughter of the late Brice and Emma Grinder Kilpatrick. One of two children, Donnie was born to the late Lando and Addie Harper Qualls. Donnie served in the Korean War and returned to gain his B.S. degree at M.T.S.U. He taught school 12-14 years in the public schools of Perry County, served as principal on the elementary level, and as counselor at P.C.H.S. for four years. Donnie worked 16-17 years with First State Bank of Linden as an Assistant Cashier, was elected to two consecutive terms as Perry County Judge/Executive where he served until retirement. Loy worked with the garment industry several years. After our children were in school she returned to work in food service at P.C.H.S. retiring as manager.

To this union three daughters were born. Donna E. Erisman married Robert John Erisman II. To this union was born a son, Robert John Erisman III. Donna received her B.S. degree at A.P.S.U. and Masters Degree at Trevecca College. Presently she teaches sixth grade in the Perry County School system.

Julia married Michael Thomasson of Hickman County. She received her Bachelor of Science in Business Administration degree at Freed-Hardeman College. She also received her Master Degree at F.H.U. in Education. Presently Julia teaches in the Hickman County School System.

Rhonda is not yet married. She received her Bachelor of Science in Special Education at Austin Peay State University. She is presently working towards her Masters of Special Education also from Austin Peay State University. She plans to teach children with special needs.

Isham Qualls was born in Ireland around 1785. He came to the new world and settled in North Carolina at 20 years of age. He fought in the war of 1812 and served with Andrew Jackson at New Orleans in 1814.

On his return from New Orleans he married Elizabeth Baucum. They lived on Brush Creek. To this union nine children were born.

Riley Qualls, one of the nine was born Feb. 13, 1828. The sixth child of Isham and Elizabeth was the father of most of the Qualls family in this area. Most of the others moved to Missouri, Arkansas, and Texas.

Riley married Smithy Hilburn and lived at the old house place. (Now the Donnie Qualls place.) After a short stay in Texas they returned to the old home place and had seven boys.

Joe B. Qualls the seventh boy married Ezora Warren Qualls and to this union eight children were born. Joe B. lived to a ripe old age on the old home place and died on March 15, 1956.

Space does not permit a more in-depth discussion of all descendants. I will be happy to share what I have with others.

EDDIE THOMAS QUALLS, (born July 21, 1957) and Kerrie Ann Kurty (born Feb. 14, 1956) now live on the land where Eddie's Grandfather Waco and Grandmother Lillie Qualls lived in the Brush Creek Community.

Eddie's parents are Waco Melvin (born Oct. 18, 1924) and Ina Webb Duncan Qualls (born Dec. 11, 1925). They reside in the Brush Creek Community of Perry County.

The Eddie Thomas Qualls family.

Kerrie's parents are Eugene (born June 15, 1934) and Jean Kurty (born Sept. 2, 1934). They reside in Hohenwald, TN.

Eddie graduated in 1975 from Perry County High School. He is presently employed at Certified Industries in Hohenwald, TN, where he has been for the last five years.

Kerrie graduated in 1974 from Sacred Heart in Bloomfield, MI. She was owner and operator of Hohenwald Cleaners for two and a half years. She now cares for foster children in her home.

Eddie and Kerrie were married on the front porch of his parents home on April 22, 1989. Kerrie had four children: Lonnie Eugene, born July 17, 1976, Shaun Jeffrey born Dec. 28, 1978, (his twin brother died at birth), Kyle Wayne born Sept. 11, 1980, and Dustin Alan born Nov. 30, 1982. Their father is Jeff Matthews; he now resides in Michigan.

Eddie and Kerrie are expecting their first child around the end of October 1994. Eddie's three sisters, Dannie, Vicky, Barbara, and brother, Ronnie, along with Kerrie's brother Dan Kurty are hoping and praying for a healthy baby.

HENRY ATLAS QUALLS, was born July 4, 1913, the son of Jess and Dora Qualls. Jess was the son of A. B. (Berry) and Mary Qualls. A. B. was the son of Richard, the son of Riley, the son of Isam Qualls. Isam was born in Ireland about the year 1780, and came to America in the early 1800s.

Pearl and Henry Atlas Qualls

Atlas was the oldest of three children. His brother, Elmo, died at a very young age, about seven. His sister, Melba, married Elmer Rodgers. They had one daughter, Ann.

Atlas' father was a share-cropper and timber cutter. He lived on George Land's farm near the mouth of Brush Creek. Atlas grew up there and graduated from high school in 1932.

In August of 1934, Annie Pearl Edwards came with her parents, Oscar and Cetah Edwards, from Burlison, TX, to visit her maternal grandparents, Robert and Smithy (Bob and Pitt) Aldridge. Soon afterwards she decided not to return to Texas. Atlas and Pearl were married Oct. 27, 1934.

Atlas and Pearl built a small house on his dad's place. Their first son, Amos Eugene, was born Dec. 1, 1935. By this time Atlas had begun to build a small wood-working shop as he had had experience helping both of his grandfathers in their shops. They built chairs, cabinets, wagon wheels, and both had grist mills. Then, on Feb. 4, 1939, Jerry Franklin was born.

They continued to live in their small house for some time and attended the Lower Brush Creek Church of Christ until they moved to Chestnut Grove.

Atlas and Pearl bought an acre of land on top of the hill at the intersection of highway 100 and Short Creek Road in 1946. There they built a woodworking shop and a home where they still live. On Oct. 18, 1948, Henrietta Joy was born. All three of their children received their grade and high school education in Perry County.

Eugene graduated from UT at Knoxville with a degree in chemistry. He married Ann Alexander and they have on daughter, Michelle.

Jerry graduated from medical school at UT in Memphis. He married Lorene Carson and they have seven children: Michael, Daniel, Rachel, Jeremy, Matthew, Laurel, and Caroline.

Joy attended Draughon's College in Nashville. She married Paul Klutts and they have two sons, Steven and Thomas. *Submitted by Atlas Qualls.*

ISHAM QUALLS, was born around 1785 and lived in Ireland with two half sisters. Leaving his kin behind he crossed the Atlantic between 1803 and 1805 and settled into North Carolina. He entered the army to fight in the War of 1812. On his way back from New Orleans he stopped in Tennessee where he met and married his wife, Elizabeth Baucom.

Wiley and Birdie Qualls and son on his graduation day from Perry County High School.

Elizabeth was born on April 5, 1794, on Brush Creek. The Rich Warren farm is where a lot of Elizabeth's relatives including Elizabeth were raised.

Isham and Elizabeth lived mostly on Coon Creek and some on lower Brush Creek. When they decided to move back to North Carolina they only had seven children. They stayed in Coffee County, TN, for about a year before ending up in North Carolina. In about three years they moved back to lower Brush Creek where they both died of old age. Isham is buried in a Coon Creek cemetery and Elizabeth is in the Qualls Cemetery on Brush Creek.

Isham and Elizabeth Qualls had nine children: Moses, Sally Bryson, Tom Matt, Mary Ann Murray, Lucinda Baucom, Riley, Hubbard, Patsy Ethridge, and Isham.

The sixth child, Riley Qualls, has the most descendants in this area. Riley was born Feb. 13, 1828, and married Smithy Hilburn in 1846. Also like his parents his residence was also lower Brush Creek. He died Nov. 6, 1890, and Smithy died in 1919.

Riley and Smithy raised seven boys: Richard, William T., Henry, Dock, John O., Z. R. "Buddy," and Joe B. Qualls.

Joe B. was born Feb. 1, 1868, and died on March 5, 1955. He married Ezora Warren on July 15, 1888. She was born July 1, 1870. A lot of their children's names will be recognized because almost all of them raised their families here. They had a large family, too. A total of nine children: Leora Wesbrooks, William, Lula McAlister, Doctor Wiley Qualls, Thomas Waco, Lonzo T., Emma Qualls, Gennievee Bates, and Lando Qualls.

Doctor Wiley Qualls born Jan. 8, 1895, married Birdie Victoria Duncan on Nov. 7, 1921. Birdie was born March 29, 1904, and died Sept. 4, 1966. Doctor Wiley died Oct. 23, 1981. He mainly worked on the farm and some at a sawmill. They raised seven children: Edward, Elva Qualls, Charles, Ola V. Parnell, Doctor Wiley, Jo Nell Barber, and Glenn Qualls.

Edward Qualls was the only one who doesn't have descendants. He was killed while he was a teenager. He was riding a bicycle on Highway 100 when he was struck by a vehicle.

Glenn Webster Qualls, born April 24, 1945, married Rachel Ann Barber on Oct. 20, 1965, lived in Hohenwald for awhile till she joined Glenn in Lawton, OK, where they had their first daughter, Kimberly Renea. Renea, born Oct. 4, 1966, married Kenneth Paul Barber, Jr., on June 30, 1984. Paul was born June 10, 1965, and is an accountant. Renea is a housewife, mother of two, and cake decorator. They have two sons: Kenneth Paul Barber III, born Aug. 24, 1988, and Stephen Mykl born April 23, 1992. They live in Smyrna, TN.

Glenn and Rachel's second daughter, Misty Dawn, was born Dec. 6, 1973. Misty has not married yet. She lived in Hermitage, TN, and is going to school at Draughon's Junior College to become a Legal Assistant. *Submitted by Renea Barber.*

QUALLS, Ronnie Melvin and Deborah "Debbie" Dean Mathis reside in the Marsh Creek Community. Debbie was born in Leavittsburg, OH, on April 12, 1954, and moved to Perry County, TN, when she was five years old. Ronnie was born Jan. 19, 1953, in Hohenwald, TN, but has lived his entire life in Perry County.

The Ronnie Melvin Qualls family. Left to right: Alan, Daron, Ronnie, Quinn, and Debbie Qualls.

Ronnie Melvin is the son of Waco Melvin (born Oct. 18, 1924) and Ina Webb Duncan Qualls (born Dec. 11, 1925).

Deborah "Debbie" Dean Mathis is the daughter of Edith Murl (born June 29, 1919, died April 30, 1973) and Mae Loudean Richardson Mathis (born Oct. 13, 1917, died July 28, 1990). Debbie also has four brothers, Jerry Mathis, Milton Mathis both of Parsons, TN, Garney Mathis of Linden, and Ricky Mathis of Cedartown, GA.

Ronnie and Debbie were married on April 12, 1974, by the late Elder O. L. Newton of Hohenwald, TN. The service took place at the Brush Creek Primitive Baptist Church of Perry County. To this union were born three children: Daron Levi Feb. 28, 1982, Alan Lee Dec. 12, 1984, and Debralea Quinn Qualls Oct. 3, 1986.

Ronnie and Debbie and their three children have lived on Marsh Creek for the last twelve years of their life, and are anticipating moving to the Cypress Creek community on Highway 412 west.

Ronnie is a 1980 graduate of National Hardwood Lumber Inspection School of Memphis, TN. He worked for ten years as supervisor and manager of a wholesale lumber yard and sawmill operations in Camden, TN. While in Camden, Ronnie was also a part time employee of Rowland Realty where he was in real estate sales and appraisal. After being transferred to Hohenwald, TN, he has been manager of a wholesale hardwood concentration yard and sawmill operation for the past four years. He is also presently in partners with his nephew Daniel Jolliff in a lumber manufacturing business known as Wright Branch Hardwood in Perry County.

Debbie is a 1972 Perry County High School graduate. After graduation she was employed at Linden Products what is now known as Johnson Control Inc., until their first child was born. After that big event, she became a full time house wife and mother to two other children.

WACO QUALLS, Waco "Melvin" and Ina Webb Duncan live on Brush Creek in Perry County. Melvin and Ina, now known as Pa and Granny, have five children, five grandchildren, and six step-grandchildren.

Melvin is the son of Thomas "Waco" (born Dec. 17, 1900, died Jan. 28, 1978) and Lillie Jane Hinson Qualls (born March 19, 1903, died Nov. 7, 1993).

Ina is the daughter of Webster Calvin Duncan (born Nov. 29, 1885, died Jan. 14, 1956) and Jeanette Norman (born March 15, 1887, died Jan 5, 1937) who resided on Upper Brush Creek.

Melvin was born Oct. 18, 1924. Ina was born Dec. 11, 1925. Melvin at the age of 18 and Ina at the age of 17 traveled to Cornith, MS, where they were married, along with Elva and J. C. Qualls, in a double ceremony on March 6, 1943.

Front, left to right: Ina and Melvin Qualls. Back row: Dannie Jolliff, Ronnie Qualls, Barbara Jackson, Eddie Qualls, and Vicky McMinn.

On Jan. 8, 1948, Melvin and Ina were the proud parents of their first of five children, Dannie Webb Qualls. Dannie married Feb. 5, 1971, to William "Billy" Martin Jolliff (born Aug. 6, 1947, died May 9, 1992). From this union was born one son William "Daniel" Jolliff March 4, 1973. Dannie and Daniel now live on Brush Creek.

On Jan. 19, 1953, came their second born Ronnie Melvin Qualls. On April 12, 1974, Ronnie married Deborah "Debbie" Dean Mathis born April 12, 1954. From this union three children: Daron Levi Feb. 28, 1982, Alan Lee Dec. 12, 1984, Debralea "Quinn" Oct. 3, 1986. They now reside in the Marsh Creek Community.

Their third child was born on Jan. 13, 1955, Vicky Jane. Vicky and Jerry Allen McMinn were married on June 11, 1988. Vicky also acquired two children Sara Elizabeth born June 2, 1972, and Phillp David born April 23, 1976; their mother Nancy Rover McMinn died in 1983. Sarah was married Jan. 25, 1991, to Kenneth Pannell; they reside Booneville, MS. Jerry and Vicky reside in Ripley, MS, but will be moving to Brush Creek Community of Perry County.

About two years later on July 21, 1957, was born the second son and fourth child Eddie Thomas. Eddie was married April 22, 1989, to Karen Ann "Kerrie" Kurty Matthews born Feb. 14, 1956. Kerrie had four boys before they married: Lonnie Eugene b born Jan. 17, 1976, Shaun Jeffrey born Dec. 28, 1978, his twin brother died at birth, Kyle Wayne born Sept. 11, 1980, and Dustin Alan born Nov. 30, 1982. They now reside in the Brush Creek Community.

Sept. 5, 1959, came the last child to this union Barbara Kay. She married Ricky Dale Jackson born May 5, 1956, of Linden on July 2, 1978. They have one son Ricky "Brian" Dale born Sept. 19, 1980. They live about two miles south of Linden at the corner of Highway 13S and Highway 128.

Elder Melvin Qualls was ordained as a Primitive Baptist minister in 1963 and has served as pastor of Brush Creek Primitive Church for almost 30 years. Ina has been a mother to many others in addition to her own five and a homemaker, except for a few years working at Zemer Engineering in Flatwoods along with her husband.

WALTER KIRK QUALLS, and Zula (Mealer) Qualls live on Sinking Creek in the south side of Perry County. Walter has lived there many years moving there when he was young from Brush Creek, and they have the following children: Joyce, Patrica, and Donna.

Walter's father, Eli Thomas Qualls had first married Maude Cooper and they had the following children: Doctor Cooper, Percy Scott, George, and Helen. After Maude died, Eli Thomas married Martha Jane Barber and had the following children: Walter Kirk and Nancy Elise Qualls.

Eli Thomas was the son of Doctor Wiley and Nancy (Duncan) Qualls and they had the following children: Molly, Eli Thomas, Elijah, and Rily B. Qualls.

Doctor Wiley Qualls was the son of Riley and Smith (Hilburn) Qualls, they had the following children: Richard H., William Thomas, James Henry, Doctor Wily, John D., Ziby R., and Joseph B.

Riley Qualls was the son of Isham and Elizabeth (Baucom) Qualls, they had the following children: Moses, Sarah, Thomas Matthew, Mary Ann, Lucinda, Rily, Hubbard, Isham, Jr., Martha.

Isham Qualls the ancestor of the many Qualls of Perry County was born in Spartenburg County, SC, 1785. He was a true man of the great frontier had the spirit of adventure. He made the trip to the new land of Kentucky and while there the War of 1812 began. Isham then went in Indiana and enlisted in the U. S. Army for five years. He was sent to Lake Superior.

After the war he returned to Tennessee and settled for a time in Warren County and while there he met Elizabeth Baucom and they married. Then Isham and Elizabeth settled in Perry County, but Isham was compelled to go to Texas and remained there for seven years. Then Isham and Elizabeth returned to Perry County where they lived out the remainder of their lives.

Nancy Duncan the wife of Rily Qualls was the daughter of Elijah and Nancy (Morgan) Duncan, Sr., and they had the following children: William, Mary, Willis, Elijah Je. (Toad), Pleasent, Soloman, Sarah, Eli, and Nancy.

Elijah Duncan, Jr., was born in Indiana about 1807 and came to Perry County as a child, his father was possibly Abraham Duncan.

Nancy Morgan wife of Elijah Duncan, Sr., was the daughter of James and Tabitha Morgan.

RAINEY HOTEL, When considering the history of Perry County, the Rainey Hotel provides one of the most familiar memories. William B. Rainey (Jan. 23, 1862-June 15, 1923) and Emma Taylor Rainey (Aug. 4, 1868-Feb. 23, 1962), proprietors of the Rainey Hotel, married and reared twelve children: Cecil, Ben, Tom, Curgus, Earl, Elmer, Earlean, Mary, Ila, Belva, Lois, and Verna. Built during the Civil War period, the hotel served Linden until the late 1970s when it was destroyed by fire.

During the fifty plus years that Emma resided at the hotel, she and her family provided food and shelter for travelers from all over the USA. At her death in 1962, Emma Rainey had 37 grandchildren, 65 great grandchildren, and 6 great-great grandchildren.

After Emma's death, her son Curgus and his wife Jeanetta operated the Rainey Hotel. Their children, Brenda and Larry, were raised there and helped in the garden, which produced the fresh vegetables the Raineys served their guests.

The Rainey Hotel

Also, Curgus worked as an electrician. During the Depression years, Curgus left Linden and received his electrical training in Detroit, and used it to train workers in Russia, at the atomic energy plant in Oak Ridge, and to install many of the first electric lights in Perry County. When Curgus died in 1962, Jeanetta ran the hotel until it burned down in the late 1970s.

Curgus and Jeanetta Rainey.

Church and family values played an important role in Rainey history. The Rainey children spent time on the banks of the Buffalo River swimming, fishing, and eating catfish and homemade desserts. Although time and distance have spread the Rainey family, a small group still meets yearly on Memorial Day weekend at the family cemetery.

Today, the Rainey family contributes to the economic livelihood of Perry County in various ways from the family farm to the health profession and to industries like the cable company and the local Piggly Wiggly. The following is an abbreviated list of Rainey descendants. An * indicates a Perry County resident.

1. Cecil Rainey and Bess Tinnin: *Jim/two children. *Mary Dean and Edward Trull/Janie, Jimmy, Rose Ann, and Bill.

2. Ben Rainey and Gertie Prichard: Stella and Bill Hogue. Louise. *Watt and Lorene/Jimmy Dan and Wayne. *Leonard and Charlotte/Shirley and Jerry. *William and Opal/Tony and Barbara.

3. Tom Rainey and Rushe Morgan (Baltimore, MD): Myrtle and Ebb Skelton. Jack and Margaret/two girls. Kent and Novella/four children. *Bill and Emma/three children. *Bobbie/two children.

4. Curgus Rainey and *Jeanetta Denton: Brenda and Harvey Stringer/Shawn and Susan/Bolivar, TN Larry/Nashville, TN.

5. Earl Rainey and *Fronia Denton: *Dorothy Jean and Edwin Patterson/Donna, Bill, Burt, Gennie Lynn "Buddy" Alton Rainey. *Edna Earl and Fred Dickerson/Diana. *Joe. *Jimmy. Dale.

6. and 7. Elmer and Earlean Rainey died young.

8. Mary Rainey and Grady Shelton: Brown/two children. Lynn/five children. Jack/five children. *Bobbie and Fred Parnell. Mildred and Rye Aaron/two children. *Nadene and S. B. Tatum/two children. Betty and "Soup" Depriest/three children.

9. Ila Rainey and Nick Dowdy (Union City, TN): Margaret and Rembert Woodroof/three children/Nashville, TN. Irma and Odell Cutler. Jean/four children. Bille/two children.

10. Belva Rainey and Harold Bastin: *Billy/three children.

11. *Lois Rainey and Joe Sanford.

12. Verna Rainey and Gilbert Messick (Baltimore, MD): Carolyn/three children. Marilyn and Earl Hess/three children. Gilbert, Jr. (the first) died as a baby. Gilbert Jr. (the second) and Scarlett/three children.

Submitted by Brenda Joyce Stringer and children Shain and Susan.

RAINEY-TRULL, MaryDean Rainey was born Dec. 6, 1926, in Linden, TN, to William Cecil and Bess Tinin Rainey. She graduated from Linden High School in 1944 and then attended Nashville Business College. She worked at Linden Apparel for many years and then Johnson Control until her retirement in 1989.

Edward Trull and Mary Dean Rainey Trull, 1943.

Edward Allen Trull was born Aug. 22, 1925, in Perry County to Nancy Estalee Hankins and John B. Trull. He attended Perry County Schools. He joined the Navy in 1944 at the age of 18 and served his country in World War II aboard the U.S.S. Marblehead. He went to work for the State Highway Department in the 1970s and retired in June of 1990.

Mary Dean and Edward were married March 5, 1945, in Franklin, KY. Four children were born to this union; Glenda Jane (born Dec. 21, 1946), James Edward (Jimmy-born Feb. 5, 1949), Rose Ann (born Aug. 17, 1953), and William (Bill-born Aug. 13, 1967).

Jane married Clenus Denton in May 1964 and three children were born to this union, Regina (born May 2, 1965), Jeff (born Nov. 8, 1966) and Marcy (born March 28, 1971), and six grandchildren, Brandi Michelle Qualls, Chaz and Trey Edwards, Dustin and Donovan Denton, and Kerri Lane Miller.

Jimmy never married and remains at home with his parents.

Rose Ann married Don A. Deere from Lexington, TN, and two sons were born to this union, Brandon Michael (born Feb. 2, 1974) and Justin Brent (born Feb. 7, 1978).

Bill married Carol Clark of Lobelville, TN, and a daughter, Shayna Brooke (born Dec. 5, 1986) was born to this union.

Mary Dean and Edward are members of The Linden Church of Christ and reside at 121 Flower St. in Linden, TN.

RAINS-POOLE, John Golong Rains of upper Perry County near the Bone Springs Cemetery on old Highway 13 between Buffalo and Lobelville, is descended from Captain John Rains, Sr., of Davidson County, TN. Captain Rains was a noted Indian fighter, who made many sojourns with his Mero District militia and scouting parties in the late 1790s and early 1800s, into the (Hickman and Perry counties) frontier areas south of the Duck River which were Chickasaw Indian lands until 1818. Captain Rains came from Virginia to middle Tennessee where he was married to Christina Rains. Christina died March 17, 1826. Captain Rains died March 26, 1834, at the age of 96 years. Their known children are as follows: (1)Elizabeth, who married a Dunn. She died Nov. 11, 1832. (2) William, who died July 27, 1837. (3) Virginia, who died June 12, 1846 (4) Nancy, who married a Boyd. She died Sept. 2, 1858, at the age of 68 years and is buried at the Parson Whiteside's Church, four miles southeast of Nashville. (5) Jonathan H. Rains married Hannah Hinkle on Sept. 20, 1831, near Fayetteville, Lincoln County, TN. She was the daughter of Captain Joseph Hinkle, Esq.

Alex P. Poole family circa 1895. Julie Ann Rains (back row right).

Jonathan H. and Hannah Hinkle-Rains had nine children as follows: (1) Sarah born Jan. 25, 1833, (2) Christina born Feb. 17, 1835 (3) Mary born Oct. 11, 1836 (4) Julie Ann (Feb. 25, 1838-Nov. 19, 1924). Julie Ann married Alex Thomas P. Poole. At his death (1864), Julie Ann married Frank Roberts. (5) J. H. Rains, Jr., born Feb. 3, 1841 (6) John Golong (Oct. 6, 1844-Nov. 29, 1935). John married Mattie Walker, daughter of John and Elizabeth Walker of Hickman County. (7) Virginia Jane born July 7, 1845 (8) Malvina born Oct. 4, 1845, near Nashville (9) Josephine born Oct. 14, 1848, near Smith's Sulphur Springs, Williamson County, TN.

Julie Ann Rains' marriage to Alex Thomas P. Poole (Sept. 23, 1824-Sept. 29, 1864) produced a son, Alex P. Poole, Jr. (Jan. 28, 1864-July 5, 1931). A story which has come down through the family of Alex T.'s tragic death was related by his great grandson David P. Poole (1893-1983). "In that year of 1864, Alex T. Poole and two neighbors were at his home making sorghum molasses when a Yankee scouting party rode up. The two neighbors ran for cover but Alex T. Poole claimed that he wasn't doing anything wrong and wasn't going to run. The Yankees claimed that Alex T. was harboring bushwackers and a Southern Sympathizer. Without hesitation, the Yankees shot him dead on the spot." Alex T. P. Poole is buried in the Ladd cemetery, on Peeler Branch, Humphreys County. John Golong Rains and his sister Julie Ann Rains-Poole-Roberts are buried in the Bone Springs Cemetery as also the Alex P. Poole family members.

Alex P. Poole, Jr. (Jan. 28, 1864-July 5, 1931) married Emma E McCollum (April 20, 1870-March 5, 1965). Emma E. was the daughter of James K. Polk "Jim" and Mary Amanda DePriest of Perry County. Alex and Emma E. had three children: (1) Mattie Lee (Dec. 28, 1891-June 9, 1926) (2) David P. Poole (Dec. 27, 1893-July 24, 1983). David married Florence Daily (3) Long P. (Nov. 10, 1903-June 18, 1927).
Submitted by Oden and Ruby McCollum.

NANCY GRAHAM RAINS, (born July 10, 1760, North Carolina, died Sept. 4, 1855, age 95, Decatur County, TN, married March 2, 1787, Randolph County, NC, Anthony Rains, Revolutionary War Veteran, born Oct. 13, 1757, Caroline County, VA, died March 25, 1837, age 79, Randolph County, NC) moved to Perry County, TN, on Arms Creek in what is now known as the Beacon community of Decatur County.

According to her granddaughter's diary, on "Sunday morning, September the 9th, 1838 one hour by sun," the recently widowed Nancy and several mostly-related families started out in covered wagons pulled by oxen from the Brush Grove Creek area of the old Hillsborough District in the northeast corner of Randolph County, NC.

On a narrow mountain pass while crossing the Blue Ridge Mountains, the wagon train met an oncoming wagon. The wagon had to be taken apart then put back together after all the covered wagons had passed. During the trip, 23 days spent traveling, a pet banty chicken would jump out to get a drink whenever the wagons stopped to water the oxen. The banty would jump back in when his wagon started rolling.

The travelers crossed the Tennessee River at Perryville by ferry at sunrise on Oct. 9, 1838. The last day of their journey, they camped on a cedar hill coming out of the town of Flat, or Parsons Flat as it was called later.

Other people in the caravan, most with families, included: John and Rebekah Rains Hays, John Gain, Hale Aldridge from Deep River, John McDaniel, Sookie Wilson, Thomas and Mary "Polly" Rains Phillips, Harmon and Jane Rains Bray, John J. and Nancy Rains Rosson, George and Jane Lineberry and daughters.

Family legends remind us of the hardships early settlers faced. There were no trains and only a few badly maintained roads. People either walked or went everywhere on horseback. Most roads were no more than Indian or animal paths. Indians in the area were said to be peaceful, however, bears, wild boars, and large cats killed unfortunate ones. Shotgun shells were scarce so white men used bows and arrows, too.

Women made soap from grease and ashes which somehow made clothes white. So many died of childbirth complications, dried cow teats were used for baby bottles. Cutting wood for cooking and heating and carrying water from creeks and springs took their toll.

"Uncle Muddy Hays had arthritis of the back so bad, his long white beard touched his knees. When he died, his family tacked string across his chest and legs to straighten him out in the coffin. It was summer and he swelled. While his funeral was being preached, the string broke and he sat up. The nickels fell off and his eyes bulged open and away we went! Me and my sister jumped out the window and run and run and run and run. It was eight o'clock than night before we got back home," as the legend was told.

It is thought that Nancy Graham Rains, sister of John Graham who died shortly after being elected to the state legislature, moved to Perry County to join her eldest son, John Anthony Rains.

John A. Rains left Warren County, TN, and settled in the territory west of the Tennessee River in 1819. In November of 1821, when the territory became part of Perry County, John was elected the first Register of Deeds. Perry County was divided in November of 1845 when the land west of the Tennessee River formed Decatur County. John was again elected Register, serving in that capacity from 1821 until his death in 1848.

Other early pioneers who lived in that part of Perry County from which Decatur County was formed: Rev. Lawrence L. and Jane Cox Myracle, Rev. L. M. Steed, Jacob Myracle, Gideon and Sarah Long Duke, John and Sarah Burton Graham, James Sanders and Frances Jones Frizzell, William Davis, Moses Arms, Kinchin Ivy, Benjamin Ivy, and Aaron Hammer.
Submitted by Shelia Douglas.

LOUIE RAMEY, Patrick Hughes, born about 1830 in Ireland, stowed away on a ship to America when he was 12 years old. Little is known about his early years. He married twice, first to Malinda, then to Louisa Weeks. Patrick had children: 1) Elizabeth (Dec. 29, 1857-Sept. 5, 1903) married Luther V. Smith; 2)Malissa (1871-1949) married Hugh B. Ward; 3) Sophrinia A. (1876) married Henry Perason; 4) Martha A. (1877) married Thomas Mathis on Oct. 6, 1892; 5)"Sally" (1879) married S. D. Groom on March 8, 1893; 6) "Cubby" married Joe Marvin and they lived in Mississippi; 7) Charlie, the only son, never married. He drowned in the Tennessee River near Denson's Landing. he was buried without the family's knowledge. Then they heard of his death, dug him up to make a positive identification, then reburied him at the same place.

Malissa Hughes (1871-1949(married Hugh B. Ward on Nov. 3, 1903, in Perry County. They had Martha Pearl, Grady Lee, Claude, and Ancil.

Martha Pearl (Sept. 6, 1904) married Louie Ramey. They slipped off early on Monday morning, Dec. 2, 1929, to Cow Hollow where Joe

Thompson married them. Joe's wife served as witness.

Grady Lee (Jan. 28, 1908) married Mary Stevens on Dec. 23, 1939. They live on Marsh Creek.

Claude (June 12, 1911) married Pearl McCuiston in September 1949 in Perry County. They now live in Parsons, TN.

Ansil (Aug. 3, 1916) married first Brownie Stevens, (sister of Mary Stevens who married his brother, Grady Lee) and second, Shirley Woods. He died Aug. 12, 1951, and was buried in Roberts Cemetery on March Creek.

George Ramey and wife, Mattie Vivian Meredith, were both born and raised at Grand Rivers, KY, near Paducah. They had the following children: Louie; Guy, who married first a Hickerson and second, Gertrude; John, married Gladys Whitwell in 1925; Henrietta, married Thus Duncan; Captola, married Walker Denton in 1911 and separated in 1927; and Mercy, married Ollie Duncan.

George died young and, in 1913, Mattie Vivian moved with her children to Perry County where George's brother, Bob Ramey and wife Henrietta, had migrated several years earlier. One child, Henrietta, who had married Thus Duncan, elected to remain in Kentucky.

Louie Eugene, born Nov. 18, 1884, had married Lillian Duncan, daughter of John Duncan, in Kentucky, and they had the following children: Ervin and Cecil (twins), Eugene, Christine, Hugh, George, Lewis, Douglas, Willodean (Averett), and Melvin (twins). Another set of twins died at birth. Lillian died on March 12, 1928, of pneumonia, soon after the birth of Willodean and Melvin. She was buried in the Craig Cemetery on Cedar Creek.

In 1929, Louie married Martha Pearl Ward, daughter of Hugh B. and Malissa Hughes Ward. They had the following children: 1) Rosa D. (April 21, 1931) died at the age of three of pneumonia, 2) Lois (March 4, 1933) married Riley Warren, 3) Mickey (Oct. 16, 1935) married Oscar Hemby, 4) Jack (Oct. 4, 1937) married first Cola Young and second Peggy Anderson, 5) Bob (March 29, 1940) married Christine Lomax, 6) David, and 7) Paul (March 24, 1949) died as a result of an automobile accident on Nov. 21, 1976, and was buried in Roberts Cemetery on Marsh Creek.

David (April 30, 1943) son of Louie and Pearl Ramey married first Peggie Ward. They had two children: 1) Ginger (June 2, 1964) married Tim Hill and 2) Nicholas (May 26, 1968) married Shannan Potts on June 16, 1990. Ginger and Tim have three children: 1) Seth (June 10, 1986), 2) Sara (Feb. 22, 1988), and 3) Rachel (Nov. 21, 1989). Nick and Shannan have on child, William David (March 7, 1994). David Ward Ramey married second June Defoe of Lewis County on May 1, 1993.

JOSEPH JOHN RANDEL,

wife Ann, and eleven children were Quakers. They lived in many states. Perhaps it was because of religious persecution or just trying to find a desirable place to live and farm. They were first recorded living in the Bush River area of South Carolina.

Joseph and Ann died in Preble County, OH. Their son, Moses (1776-1860s) was as well-traveled as his parents. He, his wife Rebecca (1769-1860s), and children lived in South Carolina, Georgia, Kentucky, Indiana, and Perry County, TN. They were parents of six children. During the time the Randels lived in Spencer County, IN, they changed from Quakers to Baptist. Because of the disease "milk fever," they left Indiana for Tennessee. Moses and Rebecca's oldest son, Amos (1799-1882), was born in Georgia. He married Rebecca Finn (1798-1867), in Sumner County, TN, in 1817 and lived there a few years. Their second child was born in Indiana. By 1820 Moses and his family and Amos and Rebecca and their two daughters were on Rockhouse Creek, Perry County. In 1823, Amos received a land grant on the upper part of Cedar Creek. He remained there the rest of his life.

Rebecca Ann Randel Thompson, born June 2, 1830, died Dec. 26, 1912.

Amos and Rebecca had eight children. The oldest, Polly (1818-early 1900s), married James Kelley. They raised a large family in Missouri and lived to celebrate their sixtieth wedding anniversary. Nancy C. (1820-1914) married William Horner. They had ten children. They lived on the Amos Randel homeplace (Cedar Creek). Some of their descendants are living there at the present. James C. (1822-1847) married Marie Wells and had one daughter. William Riley (1825-1900) married Caroline Comstock and had ten children. They moved to Missouri and then to Kansas and raised their family there. John W. (1828) drowned in the creek when young. Rebecca Ann (1830-1912) married Robert Wiley Thompson. They had ten children. Amos J. (1832) died 1840-50. Nathaniel (Nacy) (1834) died 1846.

Rebecca Finn Randel was hung by "bush whackers" during the Civl War. She was able to touch her toe to the ground and prevented her neck from being broken. A family servant hid in the bushes and cut her down as soon as the "bush whackers" left. She never fully recovered and died a few years later.

Moses and Rebecca Randel, and Amos and Rebecca Finn Randel have many, many direct descendants in Perry County today, but not one bears the name of Randel. *Submitted by Beverly Thompson Hardison and Patricia Hardison Long.*

RAY-COTTON,

Charlotte Irene Cotton born Dec. 28, 1911, to Irvin Robert and Savannah Graves Cotton in Perry County. She was married to Arthur Franklin Ray son of John F. and Lou Ella Dixon Ray. Reverend Charles S. Parker performed the wedding ceremony in her father's home on Rockhouse Creek in Perry County Dec. 25, 1936. Arthur was first married to Myrtle Bell. They had two children.

Charlotte and Arthur's children:

1. John Hedge Ray (step-son of Charlotte). He was born July 14, 1928. June 7, 1959, John H. and Janet LeCompte were married in the Lutheran Church in Jennerstown, PA. Children of John H. and Janet Ray: 1. John Arthur born Feb. 7, 1960. 2. Rebecca Ann Ray born Dec. 28, 1965, was married June 1976 to Cooper Williams in Henry Fords Church in Greenfield Village in Dearborn, MI. John H. served in the U.S. Army, Goosebay, Labrador 1945-1948.

2. Joe Dixon Ray (step-son of Charlotte) was born May 8, 1931, in Wayne County. He married Patsy Ruth Johnson, Aug. 19, 1952, in a civil ceremony in Cornith, MS. Children of Joe D. and Patsy Ruth Ray: 1. Vicki Jo Ray born Dec. 9, 1954. She married Chris Richard in 1976, in First Methodist Church in Belleville, MI. Children of Chris and Vicki Jo Richard: 1. Joey Johnson born July 30, 1986. 2. Caitlin Ann born Dec. 8, 1989. 2. Alisa Ann Ray, born Jan. 25, 1962, in Belleville, MI. Joe Dixon Ray served in U. S. Marine Corps 1952-1955.

3. Harold Cotton Ray, born May 22, 1940, in Wayne County on Green River. He was the last child in our "Cotton Family" to be born at home. Harold Cotton Ray and Judith Ann Rebman were married June 22, 1963, in the Sacred Heart Church in Memphis. Children of Harold Cotton and Judy Ray: 1. Arthur Franklin Ray II, born Oct. 16, 1963. Arthur Franklin Ray

Family of Charlotte Cotton and Arthur Ray, Sept. 4, 1965, First United Methodist Church. Wedding of Charlotte Marie Ray and Robert Eugene Davis, Jr. Left to right: Harold Cotton Ray, Judy Ray (baby) Arthur Franklin Ray II, Charlotte Ray, Charlotte Marie Davis, Arthur Franklin Ray, Janet Ray, John H. Ray, Pat Ray, Joe D. Ray, and Vicki Jo Ray. Alisa Ray-flower girl. Johnny Ray-ring bearer.

II and Janet Martin were married Dec. 28, 1991, in the First Methodist Church in Huntsville, Al. 2. Geoffrey Michael born March 28, 1967. 3. Christian Morley born July 28, 1969. Captain Harold Cotton Ray served in U. S. Air Force, 56 Medical Squadron, Scott Air Base, IL, 1963-1969.

4. Charlotte Marie, the only daughter of Charlotte and Arthur Ray was born Sept. 25, 1943, in Lawrenceburg. She died Nov. 30, 1981, from a massive heart attack. She is buried in Graves Cemetery. Charlotte Marie and Robert E. Davis, Jr., were married Sept. 4, 1965, in the First United Methodist Church in Hohenwald, TN. Children of Charlotte Marie and Robert E. Davis, Jr.: 1. Robert Cotton Davis born Jan. 15, 1968. 2. Emily Marie Davis born Aug. 18, 1970. Robert Eugene Davis, Jr., served in the United States Army 1962-1966.

5. Arthur Claire Ray born June 27, 1945, and died July 2, 1945. He is buried in Graves Cemetery in Perry County. Mrs. Charlotte Ray taught 36 years in the Tennessee Public School System and one year in California. She is now retired and lives in Hohenwald. *Submitted by Charlotte Cotton Ray.*

JOHN RAY, born 1870, was living in Perry County, 1900 census. His wife, Cynthia Ann Davis, born 1874, daughter of John Riley Davis, Jr., and Elizabeth C. Mathis. John and Cynthia married Aug. 31, 1890, in Wayne County. In 1900 they had three children: Oscar, born 1893; Walter, born 1895; and Bessie, born 1898.

WILLIAM AND SARAH (DAILY) RICE, William Rice, the son of Thomas and Biddie (Decker) Rice married Sarah Daily, the daughter of Wesley and Sucky (Mitchell) Daily. They lived near Lobelville in Perry County, TN. Their children were James, Betsy, Elijah, William, Mary, Sally, Nancy, Susan, and Emily Rice.

Mary Rice married David Jackson Blackwell, the son of Jesse and Sarah (Wilkins) Blackwell Jan. 20, 1842, at Lobelville. They lived in Perry County until around 1870 when they moved to Hickman County. *Submitted by Donna Clyde Arms, granddaughter of William Jesse and Susan Malinda (Wilkins) Blackwell, daughter of James Clyde and Arles (Blackwell) Wright.*

ADMIRAL AND IRENE TURNER RICHARDSON live at Rt. 1 Decaturville, Decatur County, TN.

Irene is the daughter of Charlie and Sarah Lou Evans Turner.

Admiral was born on Cedar Creek in Perry County. He is the great-grandson of John Thomas and Sarah Jane Adkinson Richardson.

John, born 1839 died 1930 on Cedar Creek in Perry County, was the son of John W. and Mary Horner Richardson.

John W. and Mary were married March 5, 1818, at Beardstown in Perry County, TN. They had 14 children: Annie born 1821, Sarah born 1822, Calvin born 1824, William Alfred born 1827, Joseph born 1829, Jemimia (Minnie) born 1832, Elizabeth born 1834, Issac born 1836, Mary Jane and John T. (twins) born 1839, Nancy born 1840, Martha and Melinda (twins) born 1843, and Katherine born 1848.

John W. was born near Augusta, GA, in 1776. Moved to Cedar Creek, Perry County, TN, about 1800. Joined Andrew Jackson militia as a mounted gunman in 1811 and fought at the battle of New Orleans. He was discharged April 27, 1815. He received a land grant of 80 acres in Perry County in 1855, another 80 acres 1871. He got a pension in 1870 at the age of 94 years, died 1879 at the age of 102 years 8 months 5 days. His wife, Mary Horner Richardson got his pension, died 1880.

John T. born 1839 married Sarah Jane Adkinson, marriage date unavailable, died 1930. They had eight children: George Lewis born 1862 married first Josephine Hamm. married second Sarah Ann Pigg Inman (Sissy), Sarah Ann born 1865 married Joseph Russell Lomax, James M. born 1866 married Phebe Jane Lomax, William H. born 1868 married Arkie Delphia Hinson, Mary Adaline born 1871 married Robert Allen Lomax, Joseph W. born 1873 married Minnie Peace, Robert and Malissia (twins) born about 1880.

James M. married Phebe Jane Lomax 1895 died 1940. They had four children: John Wesley born 1886 married Ida May Shelton, James Robert (Thomps) born 1889 married first Minnie Evans, married second Bertha Lee Inman Hudson, William Alvin born 1892 married Mary Belle Inman, Sarah Lee born 1894 died 1895.

John Wesley married Ida May Shelton 1907. They had four children: Elmer Brown born 1909 married Rena Adams died 1941. Admiral born 1911 married Irene Turner, Johnny Clyde born 1915 married Lola Stafford died 1984, Myrtle born 1920, married Loyd Inman.

James Robert (Thomps) married first Minnie Evans. They had two children: James Allen born 1911 or 1912 died in infancy, Gracie born 1913 married Earnest Hagan, married second Bertha Lee Inman Hudson 1917. They had five children: Roberta Louise born 1918 married Johnny Kenamore died 1952, Ruby born 1920 married Robert (Rob) Dedrick, Clovis born 1923 married Wilton Mackin. Hazel born 1925 married Dee Burcham, Odean born 1927 died in infancy. One step-daughter Bonnie Hudson born 1916 married Hillard Ward.

William Alvin married Mary Belle Inman 1908. They had five children: Ida Lee born 1909 married Tobe Hickerson, William Jackson (Bill) born 1913 married Cletus Grinder; he was wounded in World War II during the invasion of Luzon, Pearlie Mae born 1916 died 1933, Ollie Dee born 1920 married Opal Graham; he was killed in World War II, June 6, 1944, D-Day in Germany, Mamie Gertrude born 1923 married Marvin Dedrick.

DON AND DOROTHY RICHARDSON, live on Cedar Creek in Perry County. Dorothy is the daughter of Fred and Eva Battles Ray of Wayne County, TN. Don is the great-grandson of William "Billy" and Amanda Louanne Bunch Richardson. William "Billy" Richardson was born in 1841, died 1885, on Cedar Creek in Perry County. He was the son of Benjamin and Jemima "Mima" Horner Richardson. Benjamin Richardson, whose parents are unknown, was born near Augusta, GA, in the late 1700s. He came with his brothers, John, William, and Joseph to Hickman County, TN, about 1807. Benjamin, his brother John, and their brothers-in-law, William and Isaac Horner, came to Cedar Creek about 1825.

William "Billy" Richardson

John Richardson's wife was Mary "Polly" Horner, sister of "Mima," William and Isaac Horner. John and "Polly" were married March 5, 1818, at Beardstown, TN, by Squire James Yates.

Known by the immediate family, but not yet found in official documents, is the fact that "Mima" and Polly's parents were John and Elizabeth Russell Horner. John's father was William Horner. Elizabeth Russell's parents were George and Elizabeth Bean Russell, pioneers who settled in East Tennessee long before it became a state in 1796. William Bean, a brother of Elizabeth Bean Russell, and his wife Lydia Russell, a sister to George Russell, are recorded in most Tennessee histories as being the first permanent white settlers in Tennessee.

Benjamin and Mima Richardson had eight children. They were: Mary Ann "Polly," born 1830, married Bill Peace. Jane "Jency," born 1832, married first to John Denton, second to Andy Lomax. John, born 1836, died young. Martha, born 1839, married Thomas Horner. William "Billy," born 1841. Russell, born 1846, married Mattie Delf. Wyatt, born 1849, married Mary Hodo. Nancy, born 1851, married Joseph "Little Joe" Richardson.

"Mima" Richardson died in 1853 and is buried in the Harder Cemetery on Cedar Creek. Benjamin later married a widow, Lottie Adkisson, and they had two children, Sara "Jube" and Adaline.

William "Billy" served in the Civil War and was wounded at the Battle of Shiloh. After the war, in 1866, he was married to Amanda "Mandy" Bunch, daughter of Thomas and Jane Wiley Bunch of Cedar Creek.

Billy and Mandy had seven children. They were: Mima Jane "Babe," married Elijah A. "Eck" Cotham. Mary Ophelia, married I. B. "Brat" Moore. Nancy Elizabeth "Lizzie," died young. Alonza L., married Tennessee "Tin" Mayberry. Samuel Clinton married Josie Bunch. Malinda Belle, married Rob Moore. Elisha Alexander "Alex," married Frances "Fannie" Bunch.

Alex, born 1881, died 1953, and "Fannie," born 1881, died 1917, were married in 1906 and had the following children: Elise, born 1907. William David "Willie," 1909-1974. Elvis Andrew "Taft," 1910-1928. Izel, born 1914, married Joe B. Magee. Mary "Dolly," 1916-1939, married Kermit Hickerson.

William David "Willie" married Ida Broadway, born 1915, daughter of Robert Dixon

"Dixie" and Mallie Duncan Broadway, in 1932, and had three children: Don, born 1933, married Dorothy Ray. Frances, born 1935, first married Jack Richardson, second to R. T. Groom. Lyle, born 1940, married Dixie Burcham Tucker. *Submitted by Don and Dorothy Richardson.*

GENE AND HELEN RICHARDSON,
Gene Harold Richardson born May 3, 1924, son of Pleas L. and Flora Dotson Richardson. He has two brothers and three sisters, James Andrew, Tom Young, Christine, Florine, and Lillian. His grandparents were Joseph (Little Joe) and Nancy Richardson.

Family of Gene and Helen Richardson, left to right: Paulette, Helen, Gene, Jacky, and Ricky, Sept. 9, 1986.

Gene spent three years in the Navy, after being discharged and World War II was over he married Helen Marie Young born June 2, 1925, daughter of Jack and Gladys O. Tucker Young.

Gene and Helen were in the theater business from 1946-1962. Living in Elizabethtown, KY, for several years, moved back to Tennessee in 1962 where they now live and Gene is retired. Helen is working with South Central Human Resource Agency where she has been for the past 26 years.

They have three children and seven grandchildren. Larry Gene (Ricky) born July 14, 1948, married Allyson King and they have three children, Kristin, Kerry, and Jonathan. Paulette born May 31, 1954, married Dennis Wayne White. They have two children, Christopher DeWayne and Richard Keith. Jacky Enoch born Feb. 4, 1966, married Sandy Grooms. They have two children, Daniel Ryan and William Alec.

RICHARDSON-EVANS,
George Lewis Richardson married Josey Hamm and they had four sons: Joseph Will, Ed, Robert, and Grade Richardson. This marriage ended in the death of Josey. George married Sara Ann Pigg Inman whose husband had also died. Sara and her husband John Inman had one son, Alvin and four daughters, Hester, Addie, Ida, and Ada Inman.

After George and Sara married they had four children of their own: Fred, Claude, Lonnie, and Odis Richardson. Lonnie is the sole survivor.

James (Jim) Evans and Daisy Belle Walker were married. To that union five children were born: Jessie Belle, Wesley, Henry, A. B., and Sallie. Sallie was never married as she died a teenager and Wesley never married. Henry married Carrie Willie Riley and A. B. married Opal Bunch. A. B. and Opal had one son, Howard. Howard's wife is Cynthia and they have three sons: Matthew, Brian, and Steven. Howard and family live in Greensboro, NC.

Claude Richardson and Jessie Belle Evans were married. Then after Claude's death Jessie married Lonnie Richardson. They had three children, Malton, Margaret, and David. Jessie Belle Evans Richardson passed away Jan. 17, 1994.

Malton married Shirley Reynolds of Franklin, TN, and they have one son, Dee Richardson. Dee is married to Angie Flippers of Franklin where they all now reside.

Margaret married Gerald Monroe, son of W. G. and Margaret Monroe. They have one son, Greg and one daughter, Melanie. Greg married Nina Marrs, daughter of John L. and Marie Marrs and they have one son, Grant. Melanie married Richard McEndree, son of Lewis and Gwen McEndree. Margaret and Gerald's marriage ended in divorce. She then married Bill Hobdy of Camden, TN. This marriage ended in death. She later married Herbert Dill, Sr.

David married Diana Hufstedler, who is the daughter of Clovis Hufstedler and Elizabeth Byrd Hufstelder of Linden, TN. They have one daughter, Patricia Jean (P. J.) and a son David Jarrod Richardson. They had another infant son, Alanson Jacob, born Oct. 19, 1979, and died Oct. 29, 1979.

Most of the Richardson-Evans descendants were raised in the Short Creek, Cedar Creek, and White Oak Communities.

JAMES EDWARD RICHARDSON,
and Norma Doyle Richardson live in Lobelville, Perry County, where James is serving his second term as Mayor. Norma is the daughter of Johnson E. and Effie Rodgers Doyle who were life-long residents of Perry County. James is the son of William Hobert "Hobe" and Sallie Matt Culp Richardson. "Hobe" was born March 28, 1903, died Sept. 30, 1975, and is buried in the Culp Family Cemetery on White Oak Creek, Perry County. He was one of six children born to Alonzo and Tennie Mayberry Richardson; the great-grandson of Benjamin (whose parents are unknown) and Jemima "Mima" Horner Richardson.

Alonzo was born June 21, 1872, died March 18, 1944, and was married Oct. 24, 1891, to Tennessee "Tennie" Mayberry born March 9, 1874, died Nov. 15, 1935, and both are buried in the Bunch Cemetery on Cedar Creek, Perry County. Their children were: Etta Lee born 1894, died 1952, married Arnold Lomax; Cora Bell born 1897, married Henry Bunch first. Oscar Davis second; Minnie G. born 1900, died 1953, married Alan Moore; William Hobert born 1903, died 1975, married Sallie Matt Culp; Claude B. born 1906, died 1978, married Nina Delphia Harder; Clovis born 1913, died ?, married Ruth Shelton. Hobert and Sallie Matt were married approximately 1922, making their home first on White Oak Creek, Perry County. Their farm was a gift from Sallie Matt's parents, Amos W. and Katie Kittrell Culp. The following children were: Bernis Amos, born November 1923 on White Oak Creek, married Hazel Louise Bledsoe born May 1929; Ernest Lonzo "Pete" born January 1926 at Peter's Landing, died April 1993, buried in the Culp Family Cemetery, married to Dorothy Irene Link born August 1932 in Jonesboro, AR; William Hobert, Jr (W. H.), born October 1928, died January 1985, buried in Benton, AR, was first married to Iva Nell Skelton, Wayne County, TN, then married in 1954 to Ruby Vernell Hathcock, born June 1932 in Caney, AR; James Edward, born January 1932 on Cedar Creek, Perry County, married February 1952 to Norma Sue Doyle, born October 1933 in Beardstown, Perry County; Ray, born March 1945 in Nashville, TN, married November 1962 to Patricia Lou Morris, born September 1945 in Linden, Perry County.

Interesting to note that all five sons served in the U. S. military. Bernis, Ernest "Pete" and W. H. all served in the U. S. Navy during World War II. Ray served in the U. S. Air Force.

James Edward retired from the U. S. Army, 1948-1969, having served in the Korean War and with his final tour of duty at Ft. McPherson, GA. At this facility two children were born David Darryl in 1953 and Gloria Gayle in 1955. His one grandchild is Christina Nichole Iannarelli, born 1978.

RICHARDSON-HORNER,
John Richardson born 1776 Augusta, GA, died Aug. 19, 1879. He was a Gunsman for Andrew Jackson Military as Mounted Gunsman 1814, fought Battle of New Orleans. He was a tall 7 ft. dark complexion man. Wife Mary Polly Horner born Sept. 15, 1802, died Sept. 5, 1880. They had 14 children including two sets of twins. Their age at marriage was 42 and 16 and they married in Beardstown, TN. He was 72 when the last child was born.

Lonnie and Jessie Belle Richardson.

Norma and Edward Richardson, August 1986.

Ruth and Kennie Horner.

Annie Richardson, born April 18, 1821, died Cedar Creek. Sarah or Sallie Richardson born Oct. 24, 1822, died Aug. 19, 1900. Calvin Richardson born Aug. 3, 1824, died Aug. 16, 1902. William Alford Richardson born July 13, 1827, died Feb. 11, 1897. Joseph Richardson born Feb. 8, 1829, died May 30, 1892. Jemima (Minnie) Richardson born Feb. 9, 1832, died ? Elizabeth Richardson born Feb. 9, 1834, died ? Issac Richardson born May 6, 1836, died ? (Mary Jane Richardson) born March 7, 1838, died May 14, 1910. (John Lewis Richardson) born March 7, 1838, died Jan. 6, 1930. Nancy Richardson born June 13, 1840, died ? (Martha Richardson) born Oct. 28, 1843, died July 5, 1922. (Melinda Richardson) born Oct. 28, 1843, died young. Katherine Richardson born Jan. 18, 1848, died ? John (Johnnie) Lewis Richardson born March 7, 1838, died Jan. 6, 1930 married Sarah Jane Adkinson born Feb. 4, 1844, died Oct. 10, 1901 (?) buried on Swindle Creek Cemetery.

Children: George Richardson born June 10, 1860, died Oct. 5, 1959. Will Richardson, born June 20, 1868, died Jan. 28, 1961. Sarah Anna Richardson born 1865, died 1953. James W. Richardson born Sept. 12, 1866, died Jan. 31, 1940. Mary Lee Richardson Lomax born June 23, 1871, died May 3, 1956. Lissie Richardson Horner born after 1872, died winter 1918. Joe Richardson, born _____, died _____. Infant, born _____, died _____. Lissie Richardson Horner married John Carroll Horner 1898 exact date ?

Children: Olie Horner born 1899, died 1902. Taft Horner born July 7, 1911, married Ocie Carter, No. 2 Lucille Waters. Betty Horner born Feb. 11, 1930, died Nov. 2, 1932. Tennie (Kennie) Lee Horner born July 5, 1917, married Amanda Ruth Ward, born Nov. 30, 1922, No. 2 Eva Wilson Horner born Oct. 16, 1916. Joe Larson Horner born March 1, 1941, still born. William Parlie Horner daughter born May 31, 1943, still born. Mary Paulette Horner Burcham born Aug. 29, 1944, married Sept. 7, 1965. Franklin Dee Burcham born July 1, 1942. April Burcham born April 3, 1966. Franklin Dee Burcham, Jr. born Feb. 12, 1969. Amanda Lee Burcham born June 7, 1974. Freddie Ruth Horner daughter born July 13, 1947, still born. Patsy June Horner Hinson born Jan. 4, 1951, married Willie B. Hinson, born Dec. 11, 1946, married March 14, 1969. Robby B. Hinson born Nov. 13, 1969, married Shirley Flippo July 3, 1993. Christopher Lee Hinson born Nov. 30, 1974. *Submitted by Patsy Horner Hinson.*

JOHN W. RICHARDSON, (born Dec. 24, 1776), near Augusta, GA, came to Tennessee, Perry County with his brother, Benjamin. John married Mary (Polly) Horner March 5, 1817, at Beardstown, TN.

They had fourteen children: Annie (born April 18, 1821), Sarah or Sallie (born Oct. 24, 1822), (died Aug. 19, 1900). Calvin (born Aug. 3, 1824), (died Aug. 16, 1902). William Alford (born July 13, 1827), (died Feb. 11, 1897). Joseph (born Feb. 8, 1829), (died May 30, 1892). Jimima Minnie (born Feb. 9, 1832). Elizabeth (born Feb. 9, 1934). Issac (Ike) (born May 6, 1836). A set of twins: Mary Jane and John L. (Johnnie) (born March 7, 1839). She died May 14, 1910, and he died Jan. 6, 1930. Nancy (born June 13, 1840). A second set of twins: Martha and Malinda (born Oct. 28, 1843). Martha died July 5, 1922, and Malinda died young. Katherine (born Jan. 18, 1848).

John W. died Aug. 19, 1879, and Polly died Sept. 5, 1880.

John L. (Johnnie) went across the Tennessee River to Decatur County and brought back his wife, Sarah Jane Adkison (born Feb. 4, 1844). They had eight children. George was born June 10, 1860, and died Oct. 5, 1959. Sarah Ann was born in 1865, and died in 1953, she was married to Russ Lomax. James W. was born Sept. 12, 1866, and died Jan. 31, 1940. William Henry (Will) was born June 20, 1868, married Arkie Hinson on April 1, 1894, and died Jan. 28, 1961. Mary Lee was born June 23, 1871, and died May 3, 1956; she was married to Bobby Lomax. A set of twins Liss R. and Robert were born. She lived to have two sons, Taft and Kenny Horner. Robert was stillborn. The baby was Joe. *Submitted by Riley Richardson.*

JOHNNIE RICHARDSON, was born Jan. 6, 1830, and married Sarah Jane Adkins (date unknown). They had one son, James M., who was born Sept. 12, 1866. James married Phebee Jane Lomax Aug. 30, 1885. James and Phebee had four children. The first, born July 12, 1886, was John Wesley. John Wesley married Ida Mae Shelton Sept. 12, 1907. Second, was James Robert, who was born Sept. 16, 1889. He married Bertha Inman June 24, 1917. James and Phebee had one daughter, Sarah Lee, born Jan. 10, 1894, and died July 27, 1895. William Alvin Richardson was born to James and Phebee Feb. 16, 1892. William married Mary Belle Inman Oct. 11, 1908. William died Feb. 11, 1964, and Mary Belle died Aug. 2, 1974. William and Mary Belle had five children:

Mr. and Mrs. William Alvin Richardson.

The oldest, Ida Lee, was born July 12, 1909, and married Henry Tobe Hickerson on Feb. 27, 1938. Tobe and Ida had one child, Mary Ann, born Sept. 9, 1939, and died June 15, 1958. She drowned during a boating accident.

Second was William Jackson (Bill). Bill was born Aug. 16, 1913. He married Cletus Grinder on April 30, 1945. Bill was wounded in World War II on Feb. 7, 1945 during the Invasion of Luzon. Bill and Cletus had four children. Wanda Jo born May 19, 1950. Wanda married Tom Cook. Tom and Wanda had one child, Cory Drew, who was born April 28, 1985. Raymond Dee was born to Bill and Cletus Jan. 26, 1948, and died Dec. 13, 1957. Judy Kay was born Aug. 18, 1953. She married Lynn Thomason on Aug. 24, 1974. Judy and Lynn had three children: Ansley Marie born Dec. 1, 1977, Jeffrey Lynn born Aug. 31, 1979, and Ryan Lyndon born May 19, 1985. Ricky Lee was born Feb. 17, 1960, and married Kim Hovis on Sept. 14, 1991.

The third child born to William and Mary Belle was Pearlie Mae. Pearlie was born Oct. 15, 1916, and died Nov. 15, 1933.

Ollie Dee was born April 28, 1920. Ollie married Opal Graham Oct. 11, 1943, and was killed in World War II June 6, 1944—D-Day in Germany.

Mamie Gertrude was born to William and Mary Belle on Feb. 14, 1923. Mamie married Marvin Horace Dedrick April 14, 1938. Marvin and Mamie had two daughters. The oldest, Katie Sue, born Dec. 5, 1941, married Raymond Samuel Polan, Jr. Katie and Jr. had one son, Michael Ray. They divorced and Katie married Jesse Morris Lee Dec. 16, 1967. Mike, Katie's son, married Tina Lou Dabbs June 26, 1980. They had two children. Mitchell Ryan born Oct. 19, 1981, and Courtnie Charisse born June 22, 1986. Martha Lou was born to Marvin and Mamie March 20, 1947. Martha married Troy Kirk Marshall May 5, 1967. Troy and Martha had two children. A son, who was stillborn March 26, 1969, and a daughter, Tammy Renea, born April 24, 1972. Tammy married James Mickeal Wood (Mike) Feb. 19, 1993. Mike was born Oct.4, 1966.

RUBEN RICHARDSON, Max R. and Louise Richardson Ivey lived in Perry County, TN, from 1978-1991 but owned land and cabin on Cypress Creek since 1966. We now live in Cordova, TN, Shelby County.

The Ruben Richardson Family.

The source of my information on the Richardson family was passed from generation to generation starting with William Richardson who according to family members was a Revolutionary War soldier. He was born in North Carolina and moved to Wilks County, GA. His wife's name is unknown. Their son John was born in 1776. The family moved to Vernon, TN, old 'county' seat of Hickman County in the 'early' eighteen hundreds. John enlisted in the army there in the company of Captain Thomas Porter in the Regiment of Tennessee Mounted Gunmen and fought in the War of 1812. After the battle of New Orleans, he was honorably discharged at Nashville April 27, 1815. He later received two land grants in Perry County. He married Mary Horner of Beardstown, TN, March 5, 1818. She was the daughter of John Horner and Elizabeth Russell Horner. They had fourteen children including two sets of twins and reared them all except two to adulthood. They lived on Cedar Creek until they were very old then went to live with their son Joseph on Cypress Creek. They are buried in the John Richardson Cemetery on Cypress Creek. John was born the year our Declaration of Independence was signed, fought under General Andrew Jackson in the battle of New Orleans, and lived under 19 Presidents from George Washington to Rutherford Hayes. He lived 103 years, Mary 78. Their children were Anna married Andrew Lomax-Sarah married Thompson Grooms-Calvin married Sarah Tinnin-William married Jane Childress-Jemima married John Tinnin-Elizabeth died at fourteen-Issac married Samantha Ward-Jane-married first Horner Denton, second Darb Lomax-John Thomas, twin to Mary Jane, married Sarah Atkinson-Nancy married Grooms-Martha, twin to Melinda, married John Lomax-Melinda died at eight years-Catherine married William Griffin.

My grandfather Ruben, whose parents were Issac and Samantha, married Martha Richardson and lived in Perry County until 1917. While living there Ruben owned a saw mill and worked as a carpenter. He helped to build several houses. They moved to West Tennessee when my father, Leslie, was seventeen. There he met and married my mother, Otis Evans, daughter of James and Josephine Mathis Evans also of Perry County.

Max and I met and married in Dyer County, TN. His grandparents are Mr. and Mrs. Amon Ivey of Decatur County, TN, and Mr. and Mrs. Ezra Hughes of McNairy County, TN. His parents are Murry and Ava Hughes Ivey.

The picture I am sending to be included in this part of the book is of my grandfather Ruben's family. My father is the little boy in the sailor suit. He died at age 88. *Submitted by Louise Ivey.*

TOM Y. RICHARDSON,

(born March 7, 1911) and Lota M. Tucker (born July 10, 1914) were married March 21, 1936. Tom was employed by the State of Tennessee, Correction Department, as Director for Records for 26 years. Lota was a teacher in Perry County, Humphreys County, and Davidson County for 29 years. They both retired to the good life in 1976.

Tom and Lota Richardson.

They had two sons: Tommy Bruce (born April 2, 1937). He married Peggy A. Weatherly of Camden and they had three children-Michael Bruce, Brian Patrick, and Elizabeth Ann: Robert Eric (born Dec. 3, 1943). He married Ginger Key of Gallatin.

Tom was the son of Pleas Richardson (1876-1948) and Flora Dodson (1878-1960). She was the granddaughter of Dickson Tucker and Mary Elizabeth Edwards and Andrew Berry and Lou Rainey.

WILLIAM ALFRED RICHARDSON-JOSEPH ANDREW "LITTLE JOE" RICHARDSON,

William Alfred Richardson born July 13, 1827, died May 20, 1892, and married Martha Jane Childress. He was the fourth child of John and Mary Horner Richardson. He owned a grocery store on Cedar Creek. They are Watt French's great grandparents. Joseph Andrew "Little Joe" Richardson born Aug. 28, 1853, died May 1, 1923, married his second cousin.

Joseph Andrew "Little Joe" and Nancy "Nan" Richardson, mother and father of Lou Richardson French.

Nancy "Nan" Richardson born Oct. 12, 1851, died March 10, 1944, are Watt's grandparents. They are buried in the Starbuck Cemetery on Cypress Creek. Their children: Billy married Mary Harder, Pleas married Lillian, Delphia married Marion Starbuck; Lou married Hart French; and Dora married Tom Epley.

WILLIAM "WILL" HENRY RICHARDSON,

(born June 20, 1868), son of "Johnny" L. and Sarah Jane Adkinsen; and Arkie Delphia (born Oct. 12, 1874), daughter of Larkin and "Mollie" Hinson were married April 1, 1894.

The Will Richardson Family, June 1953. Standing: Bertha, Dewey, Coy, Ernie, Riley, Delphia, Eddie and Della. Seated: Will and Arkie.

They were the parents of nine children. Mary Ellen Bertha Lee (born Dec. 16, 1894), married Dec. 24, 1913, to John Thomas Smith. They had six children. Emma Bessie (born Dec. 23, 1897); married Jessie Lineberry and they had two children: Loda and Alene. Sue died Feb. 20, 1920. Dewey Lee (born Aug. 24, 1900), married Ila Broadway and they had three children, Clyde, Jack, and Moncie. Ila died Dec. 8, 1946. Dewey married Zula McDonald, Sept.. 1, 1950. He died Oct. 20, 1973. Coy Elmer (born Dec. 29, 1903), married Annalize Ward Dec. 25, 1925. They had one child, Lois. Coy died Jan. 1, 1984. Riley Elvin (born Nov. 3, 1905), married Etta Brown Harder (born July 31, 1907), they had a daughter, Lovie Radine. Eddie Clay (born Oct. 11, 1908), married Bonnie Keeling and they had three girls: Oda, Helen, and Dean, and one son, Ralph. Erne Eli (born April 6, 1911), wed Etta Inman and had three children, Imogene, Maxine, and Sammy. Delphia Dollie (born Nov. 26, 1913), wed Floyd Broadway on Oct. 18, 1935. Their three children are Ted, Peggy, and Danny. Floyd died Jan. 11, 1963. Delphia married Gid Merriman on Nov. 7, 1969. He died in 1972. Ida Della (born May 3, 1917), married Kermit Hickerson Sept.. 13, 1940. They have one daughter, Linda (born April 29, 1943).

They also took their two grandchildren, Loda and Alene Lineberry into their home due to the death of their mother.

Arkie died Feb. 4, 1958. Will died Jan. 28, 1961. They were buried at Harder Cemetery. *Submitted by L. B. Smith.*

RICHARDSON-GRINDER,

William Jackson Richardson was born Aug. 16, 1913. On Aug. 30, 1945, he was married to Norma Cletus Grinder Richardson, born Nov. 28, 1920. This union had four children.

Raymond D. Richardson, born Jan. 26, 1948, deceased.

Cletus and Bill Richardson, 40th wedding anniversary.

Wanda Jo Richardson, born May 19, 1950. On Oct. 23, 1982, she was married to Tom Cooke. They have one son, Corey Drew born April 28, 1985. They reside at Hixon, TN.

Judy Kay Richardson, born Aug. 18, 1953. Judy was married to Jeffrey Lynn Thomason Aug. 24, 1974. Three children: Ansley Marie born Dec. 1, 1977; Jeffrey Lynn, Jr., born Aug. 31, 1979; and Ryan Lyndon born Mary 19, 1985. They reside at Clarksville, TN.

Ricky Lee Richardson, born Feb. 17, 1960. He resides at Harvest, AL.

William Jackson's father was William Alvin Richardson. Born Feb. 16, 1892, died Feb. 11, 1964. Mother was Mary Bell Inman. Born Nov. 23, 1886, died Aug. 2, 1974. Both are buried at the Harder Cemetery on Cedar Creek.

Norma Cletus Grinder Richardson's father was Noah Theodore Grinder. Born Nov. 11, 1875, died Jan. 12, 1924. Mother was Mary Jane Ary, born Jan. 10, 1881, died Nov. 19, 1954. Both are buried at the Ary Cemetery, Sinking Creek.

William Jackson Richardson was inducted into World War II, Jan. 14, 1942. Was wounded Feb. 7, 1945, in the Phillippines—received a Purple Heart, was discharged Sept. 1, 1945.

TENNESSE ROPER RICKETTS,

born April 10, 1879, died Dec. 13, 1941, is buried in

Swiss Cemetery, Hohenwald. He was son of William L. Ricketts and Nancy Ledora Montague. He married Henrietta "Etta" Boyce, daughter of Samuel Miles Boyce and Harriett Elzada Sisco. Their children were: (1) Frank Ricketts, born 1898, died World War I, Nov. 2, 1918, near Brest, France; (2) Kate Ricketts, born Oct. 4, 1900, died June 19, 1982, wife of Porter Gray; (3) Mary Maude Ricketts, married James Russell Brown; (4) Earl Ricketts, married a Hickerson; (5) Claude A. Ricketts; (6) Herbert S. Ricketts.

Left to right: Frank, Tennessee Roper (father), Kate, Henrietta Boyce, and Mauel Ricketts.

Roper Ricketts married again after Etta died. He married Mrs. Sallie Sisco, June 3, 1917, in Perry County.

DAVID AND LINDA RILEY, Alvin David Riley born Feb. 28, 1946, and Linda Jane Duncan born Oct. 19, 1945, were married Sept.. 2, 1967, in Hohenwald, TN. They have two children Regina Lynne born May 29, 1969, who was married on Aug. 10, 1991, to Robert Gene Brewer born June 25, 1970. Alvin David Riley, Jr., born Jan. 12, 1971, who was married on July 16, 1993, to Ernestine Sharp born May 7, 1968. They have one son William Edward, born Aug. 3, 1993.

David is the son of Ira Alts Riley born Oct. 12, 1902, Sept.. 18, 1982, and Martha (Dollie) Hickerson Poore Riley born Oct. 19, 1907, June 10, 1978. David was the grandson of Alvin Booker and Minnie Whitwell Riley. And David Leroy born 1865-1931 and Landora Hickerson born 1874-1944.

Linda is the daughter of Robert Edward Duncan born Feb. 6, 1908, Nov. 9, 1993, and Myra Doyle Duncan born Oct. 13, 1911. She was the granddaughter of Webster Calvin born Nov. 24, 1885, Jan. 14, 1956, and Jeanette Norman Duncan born Feb. 14, 1887, Jan. 14, 1956. And William Jefferson and Jennie Johnson Doyle.

ELLPHAZ RILEY, came from Ireland to South Carolina in the late 1700s. He moved to Logan County, KY, then later traveled south and eventually settled on Beech Creek in Wayne County, TN, around 1818.

His great-grandson, William Calvin Riley, farmer/schoolteacher (May 29, 1854-May 16, 1897) married Adeline Warren (Feb. 15, 1859-March 14, 1946). They lived at Slink Shoals along the Buffalo River, and later moved to the Carter Place on Little Opossum Creek, Flat Woods. Both are buried in the Carter/Riley Cemetery, Perry County.

William and Adeline had eight children: Cicily, Dora (Phillips), Jeanie (Phillips), Alice (Downey), Myrtle, May (Porter), Sallie (Holt), and Elvis.

Riley's children, left to right: Sue, Paul, Wylodean, James, Ruth, Iva, and Willie.

Evis Calvin Riley, farmer/World War I veteran, U.S. Army (Jan. 15, 1897-Nov. 25, 1976) married Izorah Grinder (Oct. 13, 1898-May 1, 1952) on April 6, 1919. They lived at the Carter Place are buried in the Carter/Riley Cemetery.

Izorah (Grinder) Riley was the daughter of Theodore and Mary Jane (Ary) Grinder, who are buried in the Ary Cemetery on Sinking Creek in Perry County. Theodore and Mary Jane had thirteen children: Izorah, Molly (Carter), Sadie Mae (Tatum), Zell, Loyd, Ab, Emma (Kilpatrick), Opel (Garner), Wesson, Osborne, Sue (Hamm), Cletus (Richardson), and Clint.

Elvis and Izorah Riley had eight children: Willie, Iva, Ruth, James, Joe Lee, Wylodean, Paul, and Sue.

Willie, World War II veteran, U.S. Coast Guard (April 10, 1920-Sept. 15, 1976) married Mary Helen Epley. Children: David, Danny, Jeanette, and Elizabeth.

Iva married Johnny Fibelkorn. Children: Carolyn, Linda, and Freddie.

Ruth married James Shearon. Children: Edward, Faye, and Wayne.

James married Westell Burgess. Children: Randall and Darlene.

Joe Lee: June 26, 1930-June 1, 1931.

Wylodean married James McCormack. Children: Kent, Kay, Kevin, and Cliff.

Paul married Magdalene Danley. Children: Kevin, Lori, and Kerry.

Sue married Melvin Jones. Children: Phil and Terry.

MARY CRITTENDEN PATTERSON RITCHIE, (Crittie), was born on Blue Creek in Humphreys County, TN, near Waverly on May 11, 1906, to William Valentine Patterson and Margaret Lockett. She grew up in McEwen with her two younger brothers, William Lockett Patterson and Ezra Russell Patterson who was named for his grandfather. (Mary Crittenden was named for her maternal grandmother.) After teaching in Tennessee and Kentucky prior to graduating from Western Kentucky Teacher's College (now Western Kentucky University), she subsequently taught in Biloxi, MS, before moving to Lillybrook, WV, where she met her husband George Dewey Ritchie. They had two children, Roger Lowell (deceased) and Martha Ruth, born May 4, 1945, who is married to James Louis Klemm.

Mary Crittenden Patterson Ritchie, 1986.

Although Mary P. Ritchie was born in Humphreys County, her family ties are strong in Perry County. Her father, William Valentine Patterson, was born May 8, 1874, on Tom's Creek. He was the fourth of ten children born to Ezra Russell Patterson (1846-1924) and Martha Malinda Horner (1845-1921), his first cousin. W.V. Patterson died July 7, 1925, at the Paris, TN, home of his sister Laura (Mrs. David C. Cooper) while en route home from a Texas trip to visit his sisters Elnora (Mrs. Andrew Cude) and Cora (Mrs. John A. Knuckle). He also had sisters Josephine (Mrs. Robt. Rushton) and Eva (Mrs. Joel Poore) and brothers, Jesse, Robert, Eddie, Foster, and Ray. W.V. Patterson is buried in Pineview Cemetery, Tom's Creek, but his drawing of the Patterson "Tree" genealogy chart lives on.

Ezra Russell Patterson, the grandfather of our subject, was the son of William Patterson (1818-1865) and Sarah Mayfield Branch (1819-1852). Ezra's wife, Martha Malinda Horner, was the daughter of John Valentine Horner (1824-1913) and Elizabeth Dilworth Patterson (1827-1892). Elizabeth D. Patterson and William Patterson were both children of Robert Carson Patterson (1789-1873), son of William Patterson and Margaret Branch, and his wife Malinda W. Carson (1800-1850), early settlers of Perry County. All of the above are buried in Pineview Cemetery, as are John Valentine Horner's parents, John and Sarah Horner.

Mary Patterson Ritchie retired from teaching school in 1970 and continues to be quite active in church groups and quilting. *Submitted by Martha Ruth Ritchie Klemm.*

ROBERT REID AND MARY HENRIETTA CRAWFORD ROACH moved to Perry County in 1958. R. R. Roach began work as Agricultural Extension Agent Jan. 1, 1958, and retired January 1990. The family moved from Bowling Green, KY, where Reid had served as Assistant Extension Agent in 4-H Club Work. He had previously worked in Leitchfield, KY, and as Vocational Agriculture Teacher at Irvine County High School after graduating from the University of Kentucky with a M.S. degree. He had a B.S. degree from Tennessee Polytechnic Institute and served in the U.S. Coast Guard in the Pacific Theater during World War II. Previously he worked in Michigan at Auto and Tire Plants.

Reid was born in Clay County, the son of Albert Curtis Roach and Venus Valeria Dulworth Roach, who reared 12 children and were forced from their Willow Grove (Clay County) home by the construction of the Dale Hollow Dam. This family with the younger children moved to Algood, TN. Several family members are buried in the Algood Cemetery.

Robert Reid Roach, 1958.

Reid and Mary Henrietta Crawford Roach were married in 1953 at the old Algood Church of Christ building. She is the daughter of Herman Fowler and Rosa Chalus Bowers Crawford, who moved from Windle to Algood, TN. The Crawfords had one other daughter who died as a baby. Several family members are buried at Okolona Cemetery in Overton County.

Brenda Marie Roach, daughter of R. R. and Henrietta, was born in Bowling Green, KY, in 1955. Jerry Wayne Roach, son of R. R. and Henrietta was born in 1957 in Bowling Green, KY. A son Terry E., twin to Jerry Wayne, died the day he was born.

Brenda Roach married Jackie Dale Byrd at Beardstown Church of Christ in 1977. Craig Ryan Byrd was born in 1978, Bridgett Rose Byrd was born in 1983 and died shortly after birth. Timothy Brent Byrd was born in 1988. This family lives on Highway 13 in Beardstown Community.

Jerry Wayne Roach, son of Reid and Henrietta, married Vivian Denise Stracner in 1980 at Mt. Zion Church of Christ near Savannah, TN. Their son, Jeffery Wayne Roach, was born in 1983 and son, Clayton Tyler Roach was born in 1989. Jerry's family lives on Cane Creek on a farm previously owned by Fred Long, earlier by Wesley Duncan and earlier by the Edwards Family. A family cemetery is located on this farm on the banks of Cane Creek.

SAM ROBERSON, My branch of the family was not known in Perry County until I moved here in 1977, but they were prominent in Tennessee history. James Robertson, my great-great-great grandfather, was born about 1737, and served in an expedition against the French and Indians in 1756. He was in the second Virginia regiment Bunker Hill.

His son William, my great-great grandfather, fought at Kings Mountain. Then the Cherokee ceded the lower Sequatchie Valley to the whites, he moved into Bledsoe County and took up land under Revolutionary War land grants.

William's son James, my great-grandfather, was a prominent citizen of Bledsoe County. He served as a colonel in the state militia at the Battle of New Orleans, and the Creek Wars. He built Belle View, one of the first brick houses in Bledsoe County. The place burned in the early 1900s and no trace remains.

His son James, my grandfather, was born in 1816. He grew up next door to the Cherokee and spoke the language fluently. When the tribe was banished to Oklahoma, the chiefs asked to speak with him. According to legend, they asked has advice on whether to fight or submit. He counseled submission. They could fight, he said, but they could not win, and would only be exterminated. Like most of his neighbors, he taught the tribe got a raw deal.

Grandpa married late. He freed his slaves and gave them a choice of $500 in cash or 40 acres and a mule. Several chose the land, and three of these were living until I was about twelve. After the war ended, a young Yankee schoolmarm was brought down to teach in the valley. Old J. M. moved right in and married her. Selina Kendall was 19. Grandpa was near 60.

In the next twenty years they raised ten children. My father, James Howard, was the fourth child, born 1872. He married Myrtle Barnett, second daughter of a country doctor, in 1899. They moved to Cuba after the Spanish-American War, but soon returned to Pikeville. They, too, raised ten children, same gender and in the same order as Grandpa's. I was the eighth child and sixth son of the union.

I grew up in Pikeville, joined the Navy at 19, and was at Pearl Harbor when the Japanese bombing took place. I served in the Aleutians, the South Pacific, and Central Pacific campaigns. I left the Navy in 1946, went to Alaska, where I lived and worked for 30 years. My first wife, the former Eileen Schmer, died in Seward in 1972. I bought a motor home and became a gypsy freelance writer, wandering wherever the four winds took me, writing travel and hunting stories for a living. Each fall, I ran back up the Alcan to work the bear hunting season as a professional guide.

In 1977, I tired of wandering, bought a place on Red Bank and settled in. In 1985, I married Annie F. Ward, of Eufaula, AL. We built a log house on the place, which we call Goober Gulch, and here we plan to stay.

ROBERTS-BAKER, Peter Roberts, Sr., was born 1812 in North Carolina. He was married to Permelia Cunningham, born 1816, in Virginia. They came to Tennessee from North Carolina in a covered wagon. On the way his father left to pick up supplies and was never heard from again. Peter and Permelia had eight children: James, William A., Susan, Sleaney, Sarah Ann, Paralee, and Peter Harris Roberts, Jr. Peter, Sr., died in 1887, and Permelia died in 1905. They are buried in the Roberts Cemetery on Tom's Creek.

William A. Roberts (1842-1932) married Martha Barnett (1846-1932). She was the daughter of Jeremiah Barnett, Sr., (born 1812) of Virginia and Amanda Hogwood (born 1823). William and Martha's children were: John Peter, Sr.; Alonzo M.; James A. (Jimmy); W. T. (Tommy); Lee; and Mattie. William A. was the last surviving Civil War veteran in Perry County.

John Peter Roberts, Sr., was born 1872 and died 1953. He was married to Polly Ann Baker (1877-1924) daughter of John Sails Baker (born 1839) and Nancy Malinda Taylor Ledbetter (born 1846). Nancy was the daughter of Rev. James Johnson Ledbetter an Jane Wade. Rev. Ledbetter was the son of Roland Ledbetter of Virginia, and Sara Vaughn of South Carolina. John Sails and Nancy Malinda had eleven children: Polly Ann, Issac Thomas, Jane, John, Johnson Lafayette, Elbert, Martha, Nettie, Estelle, Molly, and Doshia. John Peter Roberts and Polly Ann Baker's children were: Nettie Jane (1902-1972) who married Howell Patterson (born 1889); Clyde Ellis (1907-1986) married but had no children; and Reed Ernest (1910-1978) who married Myrtle O'Guin, daughter of Fount M. and Connie Luckett O'Guin. Reed and Myrtle had one son, Larry, born 1944. Larry married Diane Bolton of Williamson County.

ROBERTS-BELL, Henry Herman and Ella Bell Roberts lived most of their married lives on their farm on Lick Creek in Perry County. Herman's parents were James Newel Roberts (1854-1918) and Eliza Jane Esslinger Roberts (1854-1918). They moved from Houston County to Perry County about the year 1900 with their six children: (sons) Charlie; Lennon (Len)-wife, Lizze Cook; Herman-wife, Ella Bell; (daughters) Leora (Lee)-husband, John Bell; Maggie-husbands (1) Gunter (2) Lee Downey; Eva-husband, Alf Trull, went to California, died and buried there. Herman's parents were buried in Standling Rock Cemetery.

Herman and Ella Bell Roberts.

The family's work in timber and love for the beautiful countryside, natural resources, and lovely people led them to settle in Perry County.

Ella's parents were Joseph N. Bell (1847-1901) and Matilda C. Robertson Bell (1852-1921), all were born in Perry County. Her parents were buried in the Bell Robertson Cemetery on Toms Creek. Surviving children born to them: Robert-wife, Maggie Wilkes; John-wife, Leora (Lee) Roberts (five children); Joe-wife Lela Johnson (six children); Boyd-wife, Matilda Smith (five children); Loyd-wife, Martha Cook (one child); Jasper-wife, Lena Tate (two children); daughters-Malenda-husband, James Beakley (five children); Victoria-husband, John Wilkes (four children); Della-husband, Will Sharp (no children); Ella-husband, Herman Roberts (10 children).

Henry Herman Roberts and Ella Bell Roberts were married in her home on Toms Creek on Dec. 5, 1905. He was born May 3, 1884, died Jan. 12, 1959. She was born Dec. 23, 1886, died Feb. 12, 1972. Both buried in Kirk Memorial Cemetery.

To Ella and Herman Roberts the following named children were born: Irene Camele Roberts (1906-1924) buried Standing Rock Cemetery; Ira Herman (1908-1993) buried Kirk Memorial Cemetery; Lucille Roberts Moore (1909); Carlos Edwards 1911-1990, buried Detroit, MI; Infant son, (1913-1913 (3 days old)), buried Standing Rock Cemetery; Stella Roberts King

(1916); Ella Pearl Roberts Ward (1917); Gladys Lorraine Wilsdorf (1919-1977), buried Kirk Memorial Cemetery; Lillian Inez Roberts Howard (1924); Priscilla Ilene (1927-1929) buried Standing Rock Cemetery.

Deceased sons-in-law; Elmer King (1906-1986), Riley Moore, Clark Hartford, Joe Wagley, and Ray Howard. Deceased daughters-in-law: Gladys Ledbetter Roberts, Viola Lofton Roberts, and Anna Rose Roberts.

ROBERTS-GORDON, Gregory Allen Roberts from Shelby County was born on July 10, 1967, married Dana Jo Gordon, born Sept. 12, 1966, on Saturday, Sept.. 5, 1987, at Linden United Methodist Church. Greg's father is Billy Joe Roberts, born Sept. 18, 1939, son of Albert Roberts, born April 14, 1895, and died June 19, 1958. His mother was Emma Roberts, born Oct. 7, 1901, and died Feb. 3, 1981. Greg's mother is Dorothy Morris Roberts from Shelby County, born Feb. 2, 1940, is the daughter of Dorothy Freeman, born April 24, 1919, an died Jan. 5, 1988.

Greg and Dana G. Roberts, January 1990.

Dana's father is Billy Joe Gordon from Hickman County, born Dec. 7, 1935, son of James Elbert Gordon, born Dec. 7, 1897, and died Jan. 23, 1977. His mother is Willie Lee Poore Gordon born Oct. 3, 1903, and died Dec. 9, 1990. Dana's mother is Joy Kilpatrick Gordon born Oct. 12, 1942, daughter of Allen Brice Kilpatrick born Dec. 31, 1911, and died March 18, 1985, and Emma Jane Grinder Kilpatrick born Jan. 20, 1910, and died Oct. 30, 1983.

Greg's brother is Gary Joe Roberts of Nesbit, MS. Gary's wife is Tracy Hopkins Roberts. They have two children: Jessica Blair Roberts and Michael Daniel Roberts.

Dana's sister is Emily Denise Gordon Blackwell wife of Micheal Scott Blackwell. They have one daughter: Kristin Eve Blackwell.

Greg and Dana reside on the Dr. I. N. Black farm in the Sugar Hill Community. Greg is a maintenance worker and Dana is a Kindergarten teacher for the Perry County School System.

JOHN PRESLEY ROBERTS, (Jan. 7, 1889- Aug 29, 1979) is the son of Peter Harris Roberts (Feb. 21,1858- Aug. 28, 1927) and Eliza Minerva Barnett Roberts (Aug 22, 1858-April 17, 1979). John married Lela Ann Warren (May 6, 1903- April 15, 1991) May 21, 1922. They bought the Petty/Ledbetter house in Linden, and made this their home. The lot on which the house was located was at one time the location of the first town-school, called the Old Academy School.

The John and Lela Roberts Family.

John P. Roberts taught school at Denson's Landing; Veteran in World War I; and a rural mail carrier from 1920-Feb. 1, 1958. He retired with 38 years of service. During the years, he always found time for his love for singing in the church, playing the piano, and instrumental music. He organized a brass band in the late 1920s, made up of 20-40 members. Due to the growing interest in the band, men from Dickson, Hohenwald, and other towns joined the Linden Concert Band. They had the honor of playing at the dedication of the Alvin C. York Bridge over the Tennessee River near Perryville, July 4, 1930; Cotton Carnival at Memphis in 1932; War Memorial Building in Nashville; and at the opening of the new high school gymnasium in Linden, 1944.

Lela Ann Warren attended school at Sugar Hill and Farmer's Valley, walking about two miles each way. Later attended school at Frank Hughes College at Clifton. She was at Clifton when the Tennessee River froze over in 1918.

John and Lela had ten children. They are: (1) Garry Presley (Feb. 16, 1923-Feb. 4, 1994) married Frances Allen (Nov. 9, 1925- May 24, 1987) April 10, 1945. Children: Margaret Gail (born July 17, 1947) married Charles Larry Wilson (born Feb. 4, 1946) Aug. 24, 1968. Children: Courtney Gail (born Oct. 11, 1971) and Anessa Leigh (born June 21, 1974). Gail and Larry divorced 1975. Gail married Michael T. McClester (born Nov. 20, 1946) May 29, 1982. Rachel Cheryl (born Jan. 6, 1951) married Charles R. Grizzle (born March 8, 1948) June 6, 1970. Children: Trina Page (born Sept.. 24, 1971) and Amanda Michele (born April 28, 1978). Stephanie Lee (born July 14, 1954) married David McIntyre Daniel (born Nov. 24, 1954) June 4, 1977. Son Justin Mark Daniel (born April 1, 1981).

(2) James Gola (May 9, 1925- Aug. 22, 1946) killed in a car wreck one week after returning home from military service.

(3) Lela June (born Nov. 28, 1926) married Jack Sparks Daniel (Dec. 12, 1920- Sept. 23, 1962) Feb. 22, 1947. He was killed in an airplane crash. Children: (1) Betty Jane (born April 9, 1948) married John W. Cotham (born Oct. 19, 1946) Jan. 1, 1967. Children: Amber Michele (born Jan. 18, 1968) married Rick Dill (born Aug. 6, 1963) June 28, 1986. Children: Zachary Daniel (born Aug. 16, 1988) and Taylor Evan (born June 22, 1993). (2) James Roberts (born Sept.. 1, 1952). (3) Glenn David (born May 26, 1960) married Jennifer Wilson (born June 26, 1963) June 29, 1985. Son: Matthew Robert (born May 23, 1989). June Daniel married Josiah (Joe) Tooley, Sept. 10, 1979.

(4) Dorothy Jane (born Feb. 1, 1928) married William A. Edwards (July 3, 1929-Nov. 2, 1987) Nov. 26, 1953. Children: (1) Richard William (born May 8, 1956) married Gloria Greer, April 10, 1993. (2) Mary Ann (born Nov. 23, 1957) married Roy Stewart (born June 20, 1952) Feb. 17, 1979. Mary Ann and Roy's children are Jonathan Wade (born Jan. 24, 1980), Stacee Leigh (born Aug. 5, 1982), Joshua Edward (born April 19, 1988), and Jeffrey Mark (born June 17, 1989). (3) Andrew Joseph (born Jan. 1, 1962).

(5) Harris Carrol (born June 30, 1933) married Sammie L. Savage (born June 28, 1941) March 24, 1961. Daughter: Kimberly Carol (born Feb. 12, 1972).

(6) Bobby Clark, (born May 20, 1935) married Dorothy Ward (born July 7, 1942) Nov. 4, 1961. Children: Tonya Lynn (born Feb. 15, 1972) and David Houston (born Aug. 20, 1977).

(7) Sue Ann (born April 16, 1938).

(8) Billy Frank (born May 30, 1939, married Suzanne Odle (born June 24, 1949) June 10, 1967. Children: Mark Presley (born Dec. 28, 1967) and Audrey Sue (born March 16, 1970).

(9) Carolyn Videlle (born April 22, 1943) married Charles Edwin Cotham (born Nov. 11, 1943) Dec. 30, 1961. Children: Jeffrey Charles (July 9, 1962-May 11, 1988); Katrina Carol (born April 13, 1964) married Charles T. Campbell (born Nov. 22, 1959) Aug. 27, 1988-Son: Jeffrey Charles (Chase) (born June 25, 1992); Anissa Cheryl (born March 20, 1968) married David E. Burns (born March 12, 1967) March 16, 1991-son: Jordan Isaac (born June 11, 1993).

(10) Sammy Kirk (born April 6, 1946) married Sherry Ary (born Aug. 13, 1952) Aug. 20, 1970. Son: James Brett (born July 23, 1971) married Amy Lynn Wiseman (born Sept.. 1971) Aug. 7, 1993.

ROBERTSON-HORNER, Joe Pleas Horner Dec. 27, 1864-Feb. 6, 1940, married Jan. 10, 1883, to Eliza Adeline Robertson Jan. 22, 1866-June 1, 1943. Eliza was the daughter of W. C. Robertson in another section. She and Joe were the parents of several children as follows; Emma D. June 1, 1884-Oct. 12, 1947, and married to Ivison Barber; Ida Nov. 22, 1885-May 11, 1929, married Dec. 29, 1907, to Joel T. Banks; William Arthur, May 10, 1888-Jan. 12, 1964, married first to Iva B. Moore, second to Nettie A. Moore; Osa Lee, Nov. 12, 1889-April 20, 1973, married first to Nevia Daniel, second Lucy Duncan; George Odis, Dec. 12, 1891-Aug. 13, 1974, married first to Bessie Danial, second to Louise O'Guin; Hershel, Nov. 22, 1898-April 14, 1984, married to Grace Whitwell, Ercell Jan 3, 1900-Jan. 26, 1981, married first to Plummer Duncan, second to Tom Cagle and third to Dee Cunningham; Gladys Feb. 24, 1902-Oct. 23, 1982 married Aug. 4, 1918, to Eddie Carroll; Celeste March 7, 1904-Oct. 30, 1937, married to Leroy Brown; Mattie Dec. 14, 1906, still alive married to Hershel Revo Chessor. Most of these children and their spouses are buried in Horner Cemetery in Hickman County.

Our subject is William Arthur who married Nettie A. Moore. Their children are Arthur, who married Mattie Lou Mathis, Ota or Ocie W., married Marietta Jenkins; Elsie, married a Bates; Ralph Harding, married Beatrice Chandler; Geneva, married Ezra King; and Joe Lawrence, married Gladys Park Sept. 4, 1948.

Joe Lawrence and Gladys are the parents of four children, Kenneth Ray March 7, 1952, married Cynthia Ann Perry, their children Stacy Marie Feb. 6, 1976, and Emily Kay Dec. 13, 1983, second wife Beverly Lovett Rosh; Mary Elaine Aug. 10, 1954, married Harry L. Newcomb, child Alice Virginia, Feb. 16, 1985, Roger Allen Nov. 22, 1958, married Deborah Lee Henry their child is Caroline Glynn Nov. 8, 1985. Joe and Gladys make their home in Columbia, TN, as does his children. They are members of the Methodist Church and are very active in the work of the church.

GREENBERRY RODEN, born 1771, Chester County, SC, fought in War of 1812, listed as resident of Dickson County, TN. 1820 Census of Wayne County listed him, wife, three boys, and three girls. Part of the family had lived in a cave on Rockhouse Creek for three years before building a cabin. They were in southern Perry County and in the area of later established Ary Cemetery. No records have been found to show names of wife and children, except one.

Green B. Rhoden, born 1805, Tennessee listed on 1830-40-50 Census with Catherine, born 1810, North Carolina. He bought and sold land in Perry County. Six of his eight sons fought in the Civil War. Three for the South and three for the North.

Green B. Rhoden and Catherine possibly had twelve children as Margaret, born 1828, was not on the 1830 Census but was on the 1840-50 Census. Catherine, born 1858, on the 1860 Census possibly daughter of Mary Ann and John Dudley Keeling.

John, born October 1829, married (1) Mary Hulabaugh (Hollabaugh), (2) Cynthia Killpatrick. On 1900 Census, Oregon County, MO, with son John Levi and wife, Louisa L. John Levi and Louisa L. on 1910 Census of Lincoln County, OK.

Franklin, born March 1831, married Margaret Ary, born 1831. 1900 Census of Oregon County, MO, has Frank, age 69, and a widower. His eight children were born in Arkansas and Tennessee.

Alexander, born May 16, 1832, married Margaret Jane Turnbow, born Jan. 23, 1832. Married Feb. 15, 1854. Eight children. John Turnbow lived in Lewis County so 1854 must have been Alexander's move from Perry County. Alexander's oldest son, George Thomas, born April 8, 1855, Lewis County, married Luranie Jane Sims, born March 1, 1857, in Lewis County. Their children were born there and just before 1900 they moved to Tarrent County, TX.

George, born 1834, married Mary Ann _____, born 1842. They had five children and lived in Perry County, 1860 Census and in Wayne County, 1870 Census, Greenberry (18), son of Green B. and Catherine was listed in this household, 1870.

Mary Ann, born Aug. 16, 1836, married John Dudley Keeling in 1854. 1900 Census listed them in Oregon County, MO. They had eleven children.

William, born 1838, married Nancy C. Kennedy, born 1840. They had six children, 1870 Census listed them living in Perry County.

Levi, born 1840, married Caroline _____, Levi was married twice and had five children.

Louisa, born Dec. 6, 1843, married James LuAllen and went to Oregon County, MO.

Mahala, born 1846, married John Whitehead, March 15, 1866.

Margaret, born 1850-no information.

Greenberry, born 1853, Oregon County, MO.

James T., born September 1855, married Milla A. Sharp. They had seven children in Tennessee and he was in Oregon County, MO, in 1900.

This is one family that grew up in Perry County, TN, and perhaps has descendants in all states of these United States of America.

Ways Family Name spelled: 1619-Roughton, Rawton. 1660-Wroughton, Rotten. 1690-Rodin, Rhodin 1700-Roden, Rodden, 1800-Rowton, 1830-50, Rawton, Rhoden, Roaden, Roden, Rowden.

RODGERS-ROGERS, Sara Jane (Barber) Rodgers 1856-1944. George Thomas Rodgers 1856-1939. George Thomas Rodgers and wife Sara Jane (Barber) Rodgers both were born in 1856. His father's name was James or Jim Rodgers. George Thomas lived to be almost 84 years old. He worked as sawmill operator, made chairs and other items of wood. The above picture shows only a thumb left on his right hand. It was told that he got them cut off at the sawmill. He also farmed some. At one time they owned a farm on Coon Creek. They are buried on a hill over-looking Coon Creek in Perry County. Also buried in this cemetery is Billy Tom Warren, Jr., son of Billy Tom and Kitty Ruth (Rodgers) Warren. Kitty is the granddaughter of George and Sara Rodgers.

Sara Jane and George Thomas Rogers

It was told that Sara Jane Rodgers sold a feather bed and bought a tombstone for her husband, George, and that when she died a similar stone was bought for her. The farm that George Thomas Rodgers owned was purchased in 1901 from J. B. Qualls as recorded in deed book at courthouse in Linden, TN. It was located and bordered on Coon Creek. In 1913 he deeded this farm to all six of his sons. Listed below are the names of his sons in the order that they were born. John Lewis Rodgers 1877, W. Robert Rodgers 1878, George (Cap) David Rodgers 1881, Jim Rodgers 1884, Thomas Jefferson Rodgers 1886, and Dick Rodgers 1890. It is told that there was a daughter named Lula Mae that died at an early age (born Dec. 12, 1892).

On April 13, 1931, the farm was sold to Irvin Shelton for $458.33. $253.59 went back to their father George Thomas, $166.66 to S. T. Parnell to satisfy their part of a $200.00 note that he held against the six Rodgers brothers. $38.07 went to pay land taxes for the years of 1929 and 1930. John Lewis Rodgers and wife are buried in the Qualls Cemetery on Brush Creek in Perry County. Also buried there is Dick Rodgers and wife, and W. Robert Rodgers. W. Robert Rodgers (Rob) was first buried with his father George Thomas Rodgers on Coon Creek, and was later moved to the Qualls Cemetery. Jim Rodgers is buried on Brush Creek at the Warren Cemetery where the old Brush Creek Church of Christ building used to be on the hill. George (Cap) Rodgers is buried in the Warren Cemetery on Cane Creek. Thomas Jefferson Rodgers and wife are buried in the Flatwoods Cemetery at Flatwoods, TN.

RODGERS-ROGERS, John Lewis Rodgers was born in 1877. His wife Margrette was born in 1888. They were married on Aug. 24, 1905, and their first son was born on Aug. 20, 1906. John Lewis Rodgers was the oldest of seven children born to George Thomas and Sara Jane Rodgers. Cora Margrette Rodgers was the daughter of Berry and Mary Qualls. She had brothers named Otis, Richard, Robert, Roy, Henry, Jess, and sisters named Dixie and Leona Qualls.

Emmett and Agnes Rogers

Listed below are the sons and daughters of John Lewis and Margrette Rodgers. Eddie Atlas Rodgers Aug. 20, 1906, Effie Willie Mat Rodgers Doyle March 2, 1908, Maggie Mable Rodgers Gregory Nov. 12, 1909, Walter Berry Rodgers Nov. 20, 1911, Emmett Elee Rodgers March 10, 1914, Jessee James Rodgers March 3, 1918, Kitty Ruth Rodgers Warren Nov. 11, 1920, Mary Rue Rodgers Lee Nov. 16, 1923, and Sara Sue Rodgers Coble July 31, 1928. Their father John Lewis Rodgers was a farmer and sawmill worker. He died 1939. Cora Margrette died in 1942.

Emmett Elee Rogers born March 10, 1914, Agnes Mae Mathis Rogers born March 1, 1921, Emmett Elee Rogers and Agnes Mae Rogers were married May 31, 1941, in Perry County, by Brother C. N. Hudson. They were married by the side of the road near Beardstown. Agnes Rogers is the daughter of Albert and Gertrude Marrs Mathis of Lobelville. She had brothers named John, Roy, Frank, Murphy, Ralph, and sisters named Willie and Lois Helen. Emmett Rogers farmed most of his life on the Vaughan farm at Scaggs Bluff just north of Linden, putting in long hours and hard work. He also dropped the "D" from the Rodgers name spelling it "Rogers." They had one son. He is Roy Lee Rogers, born Aug. 26, 1942.

RODGERS, Lillian Rodgers Barber born 1909 was married to George Floyd Barber born 1905. She was the great-granddaughter of James Rodgers born 1824 and Nancy Rodgers born 1822 in Tennessee, occupation was farming. Their children, Mary Jane born 1850, G. A. born 1853, George Thomas born 1855, Filix born 1861. All children were born in Tennessee. Filix later went to Texas. George Thomas born 1855 and Sarah Jane Barber Rodgers born 1856 were grandparents of Lillian Rodgers Barber. George Thomas, was a farmer and sawmill operator and a sawyer, when they had large chestnut and poplar logs. He preached at a church near my son's Kenneth H. Barber house and on the hill at Clay Campbell place on Coon Creek Church of Christ.

Lillian Rodgers Barber and George Floyd Barber.

My great-grand daddy, James Rodgers and my husband's, Floyd's Barber grand-daddy bought a pair of iron gray mules together in 1869 to be partners in corn crop. They mortgaged a peanut crop they had already had made across creek in front of W. T. Barber's house on Coon Creek where my son Kenneth H. Barber lives today; purchased mules from James Copland for $125.00 and he lived up the creek above W. T. Barbers about two miles on the south side of the creek. The same side as W. T. Barbers house. James Rodgers was down creek about two miles on same side.

Mr. Joseph Trull lived up the creek about one mile above W. T. Barber. Al Trull, Joseph's son, married his neighbor's daughter, Molly Barber, was W. T. Barber's daughter. Sarah Barber married George Thomas Rodgers; she was the daughter of W. T. Barber. George Thomas Rodgers was the son of James Rodgers. Floyd Barber was grandson of William Thomas Barber and Elender P. McClaster Barber. My father, George David "Cap" Rodgers was born, Oct. 18, 1881, and died April 29, 1948.

Mother Cora Alma Warren Rodgers was born Feb. 4, 1886, died Nov. 7, 1953. She was the daughter of William H. "Billy" Warren and Serena Catherine "Dowdy" Warren. My brothers are Clyde Rodgers born 1902, George Floyd Rodgers "Doug" born 1904. Sisters are Flora Rodgers Qualls born 1907. I Lillian was born 1909. Lucille Rodgers Harper was born 1911. Clyde Rodgers married Pauline French 1924. Doug Rodgers married Gertrude Chandler 1922. Flora Rodgers married Dayton Qualls in 1928. Lillian Rodgers married Floyd Barber in 1928. Lucille Rodgers married Pat Harper 1931. Lillian Rodgers Barber is the great-great-granddaughter of Eligah and Lotty Warren. Eligah was born Feb. 22, 1799, in North Carolina.

My grand-daddy George Thomas Rodgers and Sarah Jane Barber Rodgers children are John, Rob, Cap, Jim, Brooch, Dick, and Lula Rodgers. And Lillian Rodgers Barber and Floyd Barber's children are: Hildred, born July 9, 1929, married to Martha Sue Lewis, married Sept. 25, 1948. Helen, born March 19, 1932, married to Hansel Qualls, married March 19, 1949. Hassel, born Sept. 23, 1935, married to Isabel Downey, married July 9, 1957. Hazel, born Feb. 5, 1938, first husband Paul Davis married 1955, second husband Ben Boswell. Hershel, born May 4, 1940, first wife Barbara Pitts married 1964. Hubert, born Feb. 13, 1944, married to Bertha Adams Phillips, married 1974. Huron, born Sept. 15, 1949, single, lives at home with mother.

All of my great ancestors came from North Carolina on both Rodgers and Warren side.

This information was obtained from the Perry Census and to the best of my knowledge. *Submitted by Lillian Rodgers Barber.*

ROY LEE ROGERS, Aug. 26, 1942, and Maxine Faye (Morris) Rogers June 3, 1943, on Friday June 9, 1961, Miss Faye Morris daughter of Mr. and Mrs. James Morris of Linden became the bride of Mr. Roy Lee Rogers son of Mr. and Mrs. Emmett Rogers of Linden. The marriage vows were read by Judge J. A. Vaughan. Mrs. Rogers is a graduate of Linden High School class of 1961 and Mr. Rogers graduated in 1960.

Roy Lee Rogers and Maxine Faye Morris Rogers on their wedding day.

There were three boys born to this marriage which lasted for 27 years until her death June 12, 1988, from Leukemia. Listed below are their names and birth dates.

Michael Lee Rogers May 14, 1963, Gary Wayne Rogers July 21, 1966, Christopher Scott Rogers March 19, 1971.

Christopher Scott Rogers and Vivian Valerie Kilpatrick were married June 9, 1990. Valerie is the daughter of Wayne and Shelby Kilpatrick.

Gary Wayne Rogers and Shelly Rae Knoblock were married July 18, 1992. Shelly is the daughter of Richard and Donna Knoblock. A baby is expected to be born to them at the time of this writing.

Michael Lee Rogers and Melissa Gaye Dedrick were married Aug. 2, 1985. Melissa is the daughter of Andrew and Lockie Dedrick who live on Cedar Creek. Melissa has two brothers, Wayne and Lannie Dedrick. To this marriage two children are born at present. They are Joshua Cain Rogers born Sept. 19, 1988, and Caitlin Faye Rogers born Sept. 8, 1991. Caitlin Faye was named after her grandmother Faye.

ARTHUR JOHN HENRY RUSSELL, born at Beardstown, Nov. 13, 1914, attended school at Beardstown and Pineview. He married Pauline Hudson, Oct. 1, 1936. She was born Aug. 25, 1916, on Brush Creek, and attended Beardstown and Linden schools.

Pauline and Arthur Russell (holding Ray); (middle) Foy and Mary Russell.

Their children were: Jackie Foy, born Feb. 23, 1938, died of cancer June 1975, married Janie Smith in 1959; they had daughters, Vicky Renee who married Carl Barber in 1980, and had daughters, Brandi Dawn, and Kristen; Foy's other daughter is Tammy Denise, who married Larry Howell. She is an RN. Mary Edith Russell, born Feb. 7, 1942, married Earl H. Leegan in 1960, and had two sons: Earl, Jr., and Russell Keith. Earl, Jr., married Jamie Mizell in 1981, and had Kirsten Marie, Oct. 25, 1989. Russell Keith, born Feb. 1, 1965, married Melissa Page, and has sons, Jesse, born Aug. 4, 1990, and Cody, born Aug. 15, 1992.

Arthur Ray Russell born Nov. 22, 1944, married Brenda Marshall, and they have a daughter Gwendolyn Kay, born Sept. 2, 1963. Ray worked as operator of T.V.A. steam plant several years in New Johnsonville, then in Texas, Wyoming, and Kansas.

Arthur John's parents were Andrew Jackson (Jack), born July 19, 1880, in Humphreys County, and Maggie Barham of Perry County; she was the daughter of Will and Harriet Sharp Barham. Jack died in June 1923, and Maggie died in 1946. Jack and Maggie had four children. The oldest, Floyd (1905-1972) married Bonnie Twomey. He was seventeen when his daddy died, and took over the farming and caring for the family with Arthur's help. Beulah Mae (1909-1994) married Lee F. Aldridge. Arthur John (1909-1990) was a farmer, and later janitor at the hospital and health center in Linden. Delilah (1922-) married Jesse Byrd.

Arthur John's great-grandparents were John Henry and Josie Little Russell; his great-great grandparents were William and Agnes Russell who came to Tennessee from Kentucky in 1800. His great-great-great grandfather was George Russell who married Elizabeth Bean, daughter of William Bean, first white child born in Tennessee. He was captain at Kings Mountain under John Sevier, and was killed by Indians while hunting in 1796. His skeleton was found years later.

Arthur John's maternal grandparents were Isaac and Leonna Kelly Sharp, and his great-great grandparents were Edward and Tabitha Mayfield Sharp. Most of these ancestors were farmers.

BERRY SANDERS, my great-grandfather was born July 12, 1813, in Hickman County, TN, and died Feb. 20, 1885. He lived near Vernon, TN, in Hickman County. Proof of his parentage has not been found, but at the time four Sanders families were living in Hickman County, TN. Willie (Wiley), Alfred M., and Benjamin Sanders, it is probable that these were all brothers, and likely one of them was the father of Berry Sanders. Berry was born just 30 years after General Washington discharged his army on April 19, 1783. Many veterans came across the mountains of North Carolina and Virginia to receive land grants.

Verna (holding James Otis), Jess, James (holding Hazel Aline Sanders), and Ruby L. Sanders (standing).

Berry Sanders first married a woman by the name of Betty Tibbs. She bore him a son, Wiley McDonald Sanders. After Betty Tibbs died, Berry married Naomi Williams, daughter of Ibbie Williams of Whitfield, TN. After his marriage, he moved with his family to Perry County, TN, where he worked as a blacksmith, around Beardstown, TN (Pinhook Hollow Community). Berry and Naomi had nine children. By his first wife was born only one child. Wiley McDonald Sanders. Gilbert W. Sanders, Nov. 4, 1847. James S. Sanders (my grandfather), May 11, 1849. Sophronia E. Sanders, March 14, 1851. J. Robert Giles Sanders, Sept. 20, 1853. Malinda Sander, Jan. 25, 1855. William E. Sanders, June 18, 1857. Carroll Green Sanders, May 14, 1858. Thomas R. Sanders, Feb. 22, 1863. Mary Ann Josephine, Nov. 10, 1866.

The third son of Berry was my grandfather, James S. Sanders, who married Martha DePriest. He was born on May 11, 1848, in Hickman County. He was married to Martha DePriest on Dec. 5, 1878. Martha DePriest was the daughter of Milton DePriest. They had two sons, John Albert and James Elmer, and twins who died as babies. He died Feb. 8, 1897, and is buried in DePriest Bend cemetery, in Perry County.

Grandmother Martha was born Jan. 16, 1857, and died Feb. 11, 1923. Also buried in the DePriest Bend cemetery. My Uncle John Albert was born July 24, 1881, in DePriest Bend. He was married to Jennie DePriest, daughter of Gus DePriest. Albert died March 30, 1911. He is buried in DePriest Bend cemetery. One daughter, Ora May was born on Oct. 21, 1900. My father, James Elmer, was born Aug. 24, 1883 in DePriest Bend. At the age of 17, he married Ellen Bates. They had three children: Ray, Roy, and Ruby. Their mother died and is buried in DePriest Bend cemetery. James Elmer then married my mother, Verna Bishop on Sept. 24, 1917. They had three children: Jess Willard, Hazel Allene, and James Otis. The first son, Jess (me) was born Sept. 20, 1918. Hazel was born August 1920. Otis was born April 19, 1922.

Jess married Evelyn Dowdy on Jan. 8, 1941, in Davidson County, TN. Jess and Evelyn have three children. Jessie Linda Sanders Terrell, born Dec. 31, 1942. Linda has two children: Scott Blackwell and Kim Terrell. Willard D. Sanders was born Dec. 20, 1946. He married Donna Gunselman, and they have three children: Heather, Holly, and Heidi Sanders. James Douglas Sanders was born June 28, 1952. He married Ramona Barber and they have two children; Adam and Noah Sanders.

The Sanders Family Genealogy is compiled in a book which is in the Perry County Library, in Linden, TN. The book is entitled "Across These Hills," which was compiled and published by Mrs. Jessie Moore of Route 1 Box 333, Harrisburg, IL, 62946. She is the daughter of Winnie Sanders Ellis, and a granddaughter of Thomas Alex Sanders and great-granddaughter of Willey McDonald Sanders and a great-great-granddaughter of Berry Sanders. To her and Dorthy Hudson, whose grandmother was Jospehine Sanders; we are grateful for their long and hard work in compiling all the information presented here. Mr. Jess Sanders-Rt.#3 Box 195-Linden, TN, 37096 (Perry County-Coon Creek Community).

JESS AND EVELYN DOWDY SANDERS, were reared in Perry County, TN. In 1964 they moved from Nashville, back to the Dowdy family farm on Coon Creek in Perry County. Evelyn is the daughter of the late Sidney Douglas and Eve Tucker Dowdy. Evelyn is the great-great-granddaughter of Thomas Dowdy. Thomas Dowdy was born in Pittsboro, NC, in 1745. He was one of the first settlers of Perry County. His wife, Rebecca Sarah, was born in Currituck County, NC. They received a 2800 acre land grant in Perry County from the government. The property was from the current Sanders Farm on Coon Creek to the head of Poplin Hollow.

Jordan Allen Dowdy and Family

Allen Jourden, Jr., was Evelyn's great grandfather. He was married to Mary Barber. They had five children. He died when a slave put a poison weed in his coffee. Mary managed the 2800 farm for five years then married a widower named Alvin Warren of Brush Creek, in Perry County. He had five children from a previous marriage and together they had five, making a total of 15 children in their family.

Evelyn's grandfather on her father's side was Allen Jourden Dowdy. He married Marthie Nemigle Berry on Feb. 9, 1870. They had twelve children, now deceased, and many grand and great grandchildren. Evelyn's grandfather on her mother's side was Dr. W. B. Tucker. He married Louisa Jane Beasley. They had five children who are all now deceased. They were Samuel Tildon who died at 18 months, James Thompson, Maude, Eve, and William Homer. Thompson married Mamie Coble of Centerville, Hickman County, TN. They had two children: James and Billy, now deceased. Maude married Oscar Baars. He was a school principal that drowned on the way to school while trying to cross a rain swollen Buffalo River in a boat. They had three children: Mary, Myrtle, and Sarah. Eve married Sidney Douglas Dowdy (Tom). They had four children: Tom (deceased), Evelyn, Forrest Winder, and Max (deceased). Homer married Alma Parnell. They had one child; William Homer, Jr. William Homer is a doctor and lives in Mobile, AL.

Dr. W.B. Tucker and Family

Evelyn pays tribute to her grandfather, the late Dr. W. B. Tucker, one of Perry County's great citizens. He practiced medicine in Perry and Lewis counties for many years. He drove a buggy over muddy roads and crossed over rain swollen streams to bring comfort to the ones who were sick. He was a courageous man who always thought of others first. He is buried in the Vaughn/Godwin Cemetery overlooking the old Tucker home place on the Buffalo River. He has five grandchildren: Myrtle Baars Phillips, of Nashville, TN; Dr. William H. Tucker, of Mobile, AL; Evelyn Dowdy Sanders, of Linden, TN; F. Winder Dowdy, of Linden, TN; and Billy Tucker, deceased, of Nashville, TN.

Jess and Evelyn have three children: Jessie Linda, Willard Dowdy, and James Douglas. Jessie Linda Terrell, was first married to Michael Gordon Blackwell and they had one child, Michael Scott Blackwell. Her second marriage was to the late Jack Terrell and they had one child, Kimberly Dawn Terrell. Both children live in Linden, TN. Willard Dowdy Sanders, married Donna Marie Gunselman. They have three children: Heather Nicolle, Holly Michelle, and Heidi Noelle. The family lives in Old Hickory, TN. James Douglas Sanders, married Ramona Barber and they have two children: Adam Douglas and Noah James. The family lives in Linden, TN. Jess and Evelyn have one great-great granddaughter, Kristin Eve Blackwell. She is the child of Scott and Denise Blackwell also living in Linden, TN.

ORA MAY SANDERS, was born Oct. 21, 1900, the only child of Albert and Jennie DePriest Sanders. Her father died when she was eleven years old.

Ora Sanders

"Miss Ora" was a teacher for a brief time, but is most remembered for her work in the banks at Lobelville. In June of 1972 she had worked fifty years in the bank, but did not retire until Dec. 31, 1977.

In addition to her work, she efficiently managed her family farm in DePriest Bend. It was not unusual to see her in boots and old clothes, walking the fields with her dog, checking the crops and the creek.

She gardened, and was a good cook and hostess. She enjoyed having friends and family visit her in the brick house she had built on the farm.

This attractive woman with her pretty white hair, sparkling brown eyes, and sharp wit, enjoyed travel, having had her first plane (to Texas) after she was well in years. Another great thrill for her was going backstage and meeting bandleader Lawrence Welk after his performance in Nashville.

June 8, 1981, she died in the hospital in Linden after a long illness. She was buried beside her father in DePriest Bend Cemetery.

SAVAGE-BEASLEY, James Harold Savage-born October 1896, died October 1978. Buried in Kirk Cemetery, Linden. He was in the first class to graduate from Linden High School. He attended Vanderbilt University and drafted into the army, but was rejected because he had tuberculosis. He went to Texas for the cure and where he was employed by the railroad for six years before returning to Perry County to manage the family business.

Harold and Lottie Savage

March 1929, he married Lottie Veal Beasley-born June 1904, died March 1983. Buried in Kirk Cemetery, Linden. Education: Flatwood School and Hohenwald High School graduate. Received Teacher's certificate from Murfreesboro Sate Teachers College; taught at Little Swan, Chestnut Grove, and Linden. She was Worthy Matron in Eastern Star.

During the beginning of their courtship, since he could not drive, a friend, Wilburn Taylor, drove him to call on her. Needless to say, he soon learned to drive.

Occupations: Merchants of Best Way Grocery chain and John Deere Dealership, cattle and row crop farmer, lumber man, and he served fourteen years as City Alderman (1952-1965). They were active in Linden Church of Christ. They raised two children. James Cathey Savage married Barbara Poindexter, and Shirley Ann Savage married Douglass Lewis.

SAVAGE-CULP, Martha Alice Savage was born in Linden Aug. 31, 1911, the daughter of James Cathey and Alice Kennedy Savage. Alice was one of the ten children born to Mr. and Mrs. Savage (eight boys and two girls). She attended Linden Grade School and had perfect attendance for five consecutive years graduating from Perry County High School in 1929, salutatorian of her class, played basketball on the high school team in the eighth grade and four years in high school. She became a member of First Christian Church at age 12 and is now one of the oldest active members having been a member for seventy-two years; having taught the Youth Sunday School class for 20 years.

She attended Middle Tennessee State Teachers' College in Murfreesboro. She received a scholarship to Murfreesboro to play basketball there. She was the first person in Perry County to receive such. After attending College she taught two one-teacher schools. The teaching equipment at that time consisted of a broom, a box of chalk, two erasers, a water bucket, a dipper, and a register. School books were not furnished by the state. The other 29 years were taught at Linden Elementary School, where she coached the girls' basketball team 20 years. She taught seventh grade and also eighth grade English. She retired in 1965 just before the schools were integrated.

On Dec. 25, 1936, Alice married Leonard Oakley Culp, the son of Frank Brown and Molly Fraley Culp, Leonard's mother died when he was an infant. He was reared by his maternal grandparents. Leonard attended school at Rockhouse School through the tenth grade, then came to Linden and graduated from Perry County High School in 1930. He played basketball on the high school team. This team went to the State Tournament in Knoxville in 1930, did not win the championship trophy but did win the sportsmanship trophy. He was a member of the First Christian Church in Linden. He was in the lumber business with his father for a few years, then had a lumber business of his own, working in Perry, Wayne, and Madison counties. He worked several years in Kentucky, was forced to retire in 1972 because of arthritis conditions. He was killed in a traffic accident on Highway 100 in Dickson County on Dec. 6, 1974, buried in Kirk Cemetery in Linden.

Alice's brother Joe Frank Savage has made his home with her for fifty years after the death of his mother in 1944. Alice Culp and Joe Frank Savage are the only survivors of James Cathey and Alice Kennedy Savage (1994). *Submitted by Alice Savage Culp.*

SAVAGE-ELDER, Jo Lynn Savage was born Sept. 10, 1955, at Vanderbilt Hospital, Nashville, TN. Her parents, James Cathey and Kitty Estes Savage carried her home to Linden, TN. Jo Lynn attended schools in Linden, Waverly, and Lexington before graduating from Clarksville High School. She attended Shelby State Community College and Memphis State University. She has been employed by Delta Airlines as a flight attendant since 1985.

On Feb. 14, 1991, Jo Lynn married Thomas Patrick Elder in Arlington, TX. Pat was born April 15, 1956, in Fort Worth, TX, the son of Thomas Julian and Loine Standley Elder of Arlington. He graduated from Arlington High School and from the University of Texas at Arlington with a Master's degree in Civil Engineering. For twelve years he was with the Army Corps of Engineers. In 1991 he became an engineer for the city of Arlington.

Jo Lynn and Pat are the parents of Cayce Colleen Elder, born Jan. 7, 1993, at Arlington Memorial Hospital. They make their home in Mansfield, TX. *Submitted by Kitty E. Savage.*

SAVAGE-LEWIS, Shirley Anne Savage Lewis was born in Linden, TN, in November 1935. Her parents' ancestry was English and Scot-Irish. She attended school in Linden then went to the University of Tennessee at Martin, TN, where she met her future husband, Granville Douglass Lewis.

Left to right: Douglass, Laurie, Shirley, and Doug Lewis.

Granville Douglass was born in Bolivar, TN, in August 1934. His father, Marion Hollis Lewis was descended from the Welsh and the English. His mother, Susan Alton Douglass, English and Scottish. At the age of six, Douglass's parents moved to Lexington, TN, where his mother taught Home Economics in the Lexington High School and his father worked for the L&N Railroad and farmed the family's small farm west of town. After graduation from Lexington High School, Douglass attended Vanderbilt University for one year before transferring to the University of Tennessee at Martin, TN, where he met his future wife, Shirley Savage. Douglass first studied agriculture before deciding to study for the ordained ministry.*

Both Douglas Lewis and Shirley Savage finished their Bachelor of Science degrees at the University of Tennessee at Knoxville, in July 1957 and were married in the First Christian Church in Linden, TN, in August 1957. That hot, humid Sunday afternoon was a busy day for a town the size of Linden. In addition to their wedding in the First Christian Church at 4 o'clock, two funerals were also held that afternoon in Linden, one at 2 o'clock in the Christian Church and the other at 4 o'clock in the Methodist Church. Some of the groom's relatives who traveled quite a distance had a disabled daughter. After managing to get their daughter in her wheelchair inside the Methodist Church, they realized they were attending a funeral instead of the wedding. Arriving early at the Christian Church, a friend of the bride and groom remarked that he was there in time to see one good man rolled horizontally out of the Church and another good man (the groom) escorted vertically into the Church.

From 1957 to 1960 while Douglas was studying for a Bachelor of Divinity degree at Vanderbilt Divinity School in Nashville, TN, Shirley supported the two of them by teaching in a Nashville elementary school. In 1969, they traveled to Germany for one year where Douglass attended the University of Hamburg. In the fall of 1961, they moved to Durham, NC, where Douglass studied for and received in 1966 his Ph.D. in religion at Duke University. Again Shirley supported them financially by teaching for the first two years they were there. Their daughter, Laura Kent Lewis, was born at Duke University Hospital in January 1964. In the fall of that same year, the family moved to Athens, TN, where Douglass served as chaplain and professor of religion at Tennessee Wesleyan College from 1964 to 1967. Their son, Granville Douglass Lewis, Jr., was born in Athens, TN, in September 1965. In 1967 the family moved to Chicago, IL, where Douglas served on the staff of the National Council of Churches and later began an institute on ministry development. During this time, Shirley taught in the Chicago inner city schools and Laura and Doug attended Oscar Meyer Elementary School.

In 1974 the family moved to West Hartford, CT, where Douglass was on the faculty at Hartford Seminary and Shirley taught in the high school in the Hartford inner city. During this time Shirley studied at Trinity College, Hartford, where she received a Masters of Arts degree in American Studies in May 1982. In 1982, Douglass was chosen as president of Wesley Theological Seminary in Washington, DC, where he continues to serve.

Laura finished high school at William H. Hall High in West Hartford, CT. She received a Bachelor of Arts degree from Drew University in Madison, NJ, in 1986, and a Masters of Business Administration from the American University in Washington, DC, in 1990. She presently lives in Washington, DC, and works for Booz, Allen, and Hamilton, Inc., a management consulting firm.

Douglass, Jr., graduated from The Emmerson Preparatory School in Washington, DC, in 1984. He received a Bachelors of Science from Elon College in Elon, NC, in 1990. He presently lives and works in Rockville, MD, where he is a sales manager for The Sport and Health Club.

*It may be noted that Miss Savage had always declared that she would never marry a "preacher" or a farmer. Mr. Lewis is an ordained clergy member of the United Methodist Church and his free time is spent digging in his garden.

SAVAGE-POINDEXTER, James Cathey Savage born January 1931, died April 1991. Buried Kirk Cemetery, Linden. Education: Linden High School 1950, and the John W. McClure School of the National Hardwood Lumber Association, Memphis, 1955. U. S. Navy for four years (1950-1954) served as Admiral's driver. Employment: Bruce Lumber Company and Whitson Lumber Company in Nashville.

Left to right: Mark, Stephen, Barbara, Patrick, and Jim Savage.

September 1956, married Barbara Eudora Poindexter born January 1932. Education: Shiloh High School, 1949; Memphis School of Commerce, 1951. Employment: Memphis, Light, Gas, and Water; Nashville Electric Service.

1959-They came to Perry County to operate a restaurant (Greyhound Grill). Other occupations: Personnel Manager at Linden Apparel Corp., and merchant; cattle and row crop farmer, lumber man, merchant, and Postmaster for 29 years. They had three sons:

Markus Harold Savage born September 1957. Education: Perry County High School, 1976, and Hohenwald Vocational School, 1981.

Stephen Blair Savage born January 1960. Education: Perry County High School, 1978, attended Middle Tennessee State University.

Patrick Jon Savage born May 1964, died December 1988. Buried in Kirk Cemetery, Linden. Education: Perry County High School, 1982, University of Tennessee, Martin.

They were all cattle and row crop farmers and merchants. The family is and was active in First Christian Church, Linden.

SAVAGE-SCHNEIDER, Barbara Anne Savage and her husband, James Henry Schneider, live in The Woodlands, TX, with their daughter, Anne Michelle Schneider. Barbara's family is from Perry County. She is the daughter of James Cathey, Jr., and Kitty Estes Savage. Barbara lived with her maternal grandparents, Frank and Lillian Potter Estes, for one year and started school at Linden Elementary School. Her first grade teacher was Miss Bertha Westbrooks. She returned to Linden with her parents when she entered the sixth grade. Her favorite memory is playing basketball with Aunt Alice (Alice Savage Culp) as her coach. Many happy memories are associated with visits to Linden over the holidays and summer vacations, and the opportunities to visit with her Savage and Estes relatives. Barbara is proud to have 33 aunts and uncles, most of whom were reared in Perry County. She also has 39 first cousins.

James Henry and Barbara Anne Savage Schneider with daughter Anne Michelle Schneider.

Barbara was born Feb. 12, 1951, at Vanderbilt Hospital in Nashville. She graduated from Clarksville High School in 1969, Clarksville, TN, and holds a B.S. degree from Memphis State University, and a Master's degree in Geology from the University of Tennessee, Knoxville. She worked as a geologist for Chevron Oil Corporation for 12 years and now owns a travel agency in The Woodlands. Her husband is a native Texan, born April 11, 1955, in Sinton, TX, the son of Joe Henry and Iona Williams Schneider of Poteet, TX. A graduate of Texas A & I University in Kingsville, James is an independent consulting engineer in the oil industry. Their daughter, Anne Michelle Schneider is a 6th grade student at Collins Intermediate School. She plays clarinet and soccer and is an excellent student. *Submitted by Kitty E. Savage.*

ALICE KENNEDY SAVAGE, The maternal ancestry of the Linden Savage family goes back to the ancestral home on the islands of Colonsay and Oronsay off the western coast of Scotland. In 1493, the Cathey family, members of the Macfie Clan, were driven from the islands to Galloway and Carrick in the lowlands of Scotland when the land was taken by the Scottish Crown. Between 1611-1618, the Catheys migrated to Ulster, North Ireland, when powerful landlords confiscated their lands. Mary Cathie Gillis, of Glasgow, Scotland, wrote: "The process was aided by the English Crown persecution, killing, and banishment of many who would not deny their Presbyterian beliefs... The Catheys took to Ireland and to America their religion, their firm belief in a good education, and the character to work hard and prosper..." The Catheys remained in Ireland 90-100 years before migrating to America.

Back row: Lynn, Cassie, Harold, and Henry. Front row: Horace, James, Mr. Savage, Tom Kent, Mrs. Savage, Joe Frank, Sam, and Alice. ca. 1917.

John Cathey, born in Ulster, Ireland, came with his family to Lancaster County, PA, where he died in 1742/43. His son, Alexander Cathey, born 1707, Ulster, Ireland, married Mary Elizabeth Pinkney, and after his father's death, they travelled down the Great Wagon Road, stopping briefly in Augusta County, VA, with other family members. Their son, John Cathey, was probably born there in 1744/45, before they continued their journey to Rowan County, NC. Alexander Cathey died in 1766 and is buried in the Thyatira (Old Cathey Meeting House) Cemetery, Rowan County. The late Alice Kennedy Savage was descended from two of Alexander's sons: John and William, who both came to Maury County, TN, in the early 1800s.

John Cathey, son of Alexander, died 1824 in Maury County, TN, married Mary Erwin of Rowan County, NC. Their daughter, Elizabeth, married Alexander Kennedy in Rowan County in 1788. In 1797 John Cathey purchased land in Tennessee Territory (now Sumner County) and moved his family westward. His daughter, Elizabeth and her husband, Alexander, died about 1805 in Sumner County, leaving five orphaned children. Andrew Kennedy, the father of Alexander, took the youngest child, George Alexander Kennedy to Maury County.

William Cathey, John's brother, was born 1747, Rowan County, NC, married Alice Hagan. He served as a major in the Revolutionary War, and for his services received several land grants. One, a grant for 4000 acres on the south side of Duck River, was in the present day Maury County, TN. Cathey's Creek was named for this early settler. William Cathey's son, Alexander Cathey married Nancy Sanders. Their daughter, Elizabeth Cathey married her second cousin, George Alexander Kennedy. George A. Kennedy and his wife both died at Hampshire, TN. The youngest of their ten children was John Henry Kennedy, born Nov. 13, 1847, Maury County; died Feb. 4, 1936, who was twice married and the father of eleven children. His first marriage was to Josephine Bonaparte Noles, daughter of Eliza Bateman and Allen J. Noles. The fourth of their five daughters was Alice Olivia Kennedy (1875-1944) who married James Cathey Savage, Sr.

Much of the above data came from Boyt Henderson Cathey's 1993 book, *Cathey Family History and Genealogy, Vol. I*. Submitted by Kitty E. Savage.

FRANK KENNEDY SAVAGE, was born April 17, 1949 (Easter Sunday), in Nashville, TN, the son of James Cathey and Kitty Estes Savage. The family lived in Waverly, TN, when he was born, but much of his early childhood was spent in Perry County. Frank attended schools in Linden, Waverly, and Lexington. He graduated from Clarksville High School and Austin Peay State University.

On Aug. 13, 1973, he married Elizabeth Anne Kading, born Aug. 29, 1954, daughter of Leroy and Dixie Hubbard Kading of Wilmington, DE. Her mother's family, the Hubbards, lived in Lawrence County, TN. She attended Austin Peay State University, graduated from East Carolina University at Greensville, NC, and received a Master's degree from Vanderbilt.

Frank Kennedy and Liz Savage with son Jesse Kennedy Savage.

Frank is an engineer with the Rheem Corporation in Montgomery, AL, and Liz teaches elementary school there. They are the parents of two chlidren: Jesse Kennedy Savage, born Dec. 3, 1982, Kinston, NC; and Sarah Elizabeth Savage, born June 23, 1989, Gallatin, TN.

HENRY KENNEDY SAVAGE, was the third child of the ten children of James Cathey and Alice Kennedy Savage. He was born Feb. 5, 1901, in Linden, TN. He spent his early childhood working on his Dad's farm northeast of Linden. He attended elementary school in Linden and then went to Huntington, TN, to finish high school.

Henry K. Savage

Henry was very active in sports, mostly basketball. He came to Nashville and attended Falls Business College. While in Nashville he met Mary A. Hickson in 1926. They were married at Hobsons Chapel Methodist Church Feb. 27, 1927. At this time he was employed by the Tennessee Central Railroad as a traffic clerk.

On Jan. 29, 1928, Henry and Mary had their only child, Henry Hickson. In March of that year he started to work at DuPont in Old Hickory, TN. He worked in the Traffic Department, Rayon Division, then transferred to the Film Department in 1952 as Traffic Supervisor, remaining there until his retirement Dec. 31, 1963. After his retirement he became interested in refinishing antique round oak tables. He made many winter vacation trips to Fort Meyers, FL, where he was the No. 1 fisherman on the beach pier. He would catch 50 or more trout per day. He still remained active in all DuPont retirement parties and was well known by all the Nashville railroads and trucking agencies.

He was always a very supportive neighbor in his East Nashville community. He was an executor to several families of DuPont retirees. He enjoyed going to several coffee clubs a day. His favorite coffee spot was Mallards restaurant of Madison, TN. He was an expert at figuring out income taxes—down to the penny. He had a photographic memory for all financial purchases he had made during his lifetime.

During his later years he would visit his wife, Mary, at her nursing home every day. He was always helping other members of the nursing home. He enjoyed genealogy in his final years, visiting cemeteries at Shady Grove, TN, and Kettle Mills, and his mother's father, John Henry Kennedy buried at the Cathey cemetery near Hamshire, TN. He attended the Savage reunion every May for many years. Henry died Dec. 25, 1992, and is buried at the Spring Hill Cemetery in northeast Nashville. His wife, Mary, is in a nursing home in Franklin, TN. Survivors include his sister, Alice Culp; brother, Joe Frank Savage; son, Henry Hickson Savage; granddaughters, Phyllis S. Booth, Gail S. Hollister; great-grandsons, Jeffery Booth, Bennett Hollister, and Jonah Kennedy Hollister.

JAMES C. SAVAGE, SR., The known paternal ancestry of the James Cathey Savage, Sr., family of Linden, TN, begins with Robert Savage, who died in Surry County, VA, in 1698. Robert had two sons, Charles and Loveless, the latter being the direct ancestor. Loveless died in 1728, Surry County, leaving two sons, Robert and Loveless, Jr. Loveless, Jr., was the father of four sons: Robert, Charles, Loveless, III, and (?) John. The late Tom Kent Savage did extensive research on his paternal lines, but was unable to document whether Robert or Loveless, III, was the father of Robert, who died in Edgecombe County, NC, in 1797. Robert married his first cousin, Rhoda, the daughter of Charles Savage, and they were the parents of two daughters and one son, William Savage.

Standing, left to right: Alice, Tom Kent, Sam, Henry, Joe Frank, (seated), Harold; surviving children of James Cathey and Alice Kennedy Savage in 1978.

William Savage served in the War of 1812 under the command of Captain David Barnes, Regiment of North Carolina Militia. On Jan. 7, 1813, in Tarboro, Edgecombe County, NC, William Savage married Penelope Grimes, the daughter of John Culpepper and Martha Howell Grimes. John C. Grimes was the son of Thomas and Chloe Llewellyn Grimes. Martha Howell was the daughter of Jethro Howell. The Howell family donated the land for the town of Tarboro. After the death of her husband, Martha Howell Grimes came to Hickman County, TN, with her two sons, John W. and James Grimes, and her daughter, Penelope Grimes Savage.

The 1820 Census lists William Savage in

Maury County, TN, and by 1825, he owned land in Hickman County on Dunlap Creek. William Savage died Oct. 17, 1849; Penelope died after 1870. They are buried in the Stand Cemetery in unmarked graves next to their son, Perkins Savage. William and Penelope Grimes Savage were the parents of: Asa, Julia, John, Perkins, Churchwell, Jesse James, Martha, Temperance, Elizabeth, and the twins, Alabama and Indiana, who died young.

Jesse James Savage, born July 1, 1827, was twice married. In 1857, he married Elizabeth Catherine Region (died 1862) and they had two daughters: Mary E. (1857-1878) and Lenora Jane (1859-1938) who married William Charter Nichols.

On June 15, 1863, Jesse James Savage married Frances Catherine Delk Wiley, the daughter of Jacob Benton and Annie Crowell Delk. She was the widow of Robert Wiley with whom she had one son, John T. Wiley, who married Molly Delk. Catherine Delk Savage was born Nov. 13, 1834/6; died Feb. 19, 1891. Jesse James Savage died Jan. 22, 1899. They are buried in the Delk Cemetery in Maury County. Their children: Sam Will Savage (1864-1931) married Anna Farris; Docia A. Savage (1866-1933) married John T. Wiley; James Cathey Savage (1868-1926) married Alice Olivia Kennedy; Jesse Joshua Savage (1871-1937) married Martha Weatherly; May Savage (1882-1950) married George Sharp of Perry County. (They are buried at Flatwoods, Perry County.)

George Savage (1875-1891) never married, and Lucy (born and died 1877). *Submitted by Kitty E. Savage.*

JAMES CATHEY SAVAGE, SR. was born in Maury County, TN, April 11, 1868, the son of Jesse James and Catherine Delk Savage. He married Jan. 14, 1896, Alice Olivia Kennedy, the daughter of John Henry and Josephine Noles Kennedy of Maury County.

Alice Kennedy and James Cathey Savage

In 1898, in partnership with John T. Wiley, he opened a general store in Farmer's Valley near Flatwoods. In 1899, Mr. and Mrs. Savage moved to Linden with their two small children. Mr. Savage operated a store in Linden until the mid-twenties when ill health forced him to retire. Harold, his eldest son, returned from Texas to manage the family store. Mr. Savage was an extensive landowner, and frequently traveled over the county buying peanuts and other produce. He served as vice-president of the National Bank in Linden, and his son, Henry, told of his father receiving sheets of U. S. paper currency which had to be cut into bills. As part of his bank duties, Mr. Savage had to sign each bill. Mr. Savage died July 1, 1926.

Mrs. Savage, born Oct. 10, 1875, Maury County, taught school at Hurricane Mills in Humphreys County before marriage. She died June 4, 1944. Mr. and Mrs. Savage are buried in the Kittrell Cemetery (Isom Church) in Maury County.

The Savage family has always been active in the First Christian Church.

Their children:

James Harold Steve, born Oct. 12, 1896, Love's Branch, Maury County.; died Oct. 19, 1978; married March 24, 1929, Lottie Viel Beasley (1904-two children).

Josephine Catherine (Cassie) Savage, born July 26, 1898, Cathey's Creek, Maury County; died Oct. 23, 1970, Gracey, KY; married Jan. 29, 1918, Robert Daniel Lewis (1883-1959). They are buried in the Pace Cemetery, Tom's Creek, TN. Three sons.

Henry Kennedy Savage, born Feb. 5, 1901, Linden; died Dec. 25, 1992, Nashville; married Feb. 27, 1927, Mary Adelaide Hickson (born 1904). Henry is buried in Nashville. One son.

Lynn Shous Savage, born March 4, 1903, Linden; died Dec. 3, 1934; buried Kittrell Cemetery, Maury County. Never married.

Horace Hart (Cop) Savage, born June 27, 1905, Linden; died May 11, 1977, Parsons, TN; buried Decatur County, TN; m(1) Mildred Hazel Hufstedler Warren; (2) Gertrude Hopkins Hayes. No children.

James Cathey Savage, Jr., born Oct. 12, 1907, Linden; died April 21, 1971, Clarksville, TN; married March 26, 1945, Mary Elizabeth (Kitty) Estes (born 1928). Six children.

Sam Benton Savage, born Sept. 5, 1909, Linden; died Jan. 30, 1984; married July 10, 1937, Louise Agnes Gladden (1917-1982). Three children.

Martha Alice Savage, born Aug. 31, 1911, Linden; married Dec. 25, 1936, Leonard Oakley Culp (1908-1974). No children.

Tom Kent Savage, born March 30, 1913, Linden; died Feb. 26, 1993, Clarksville, TN; married Dec. 18, 1941, Mary Emma Harder (1921-1979). Five daughters.

Joe Frank Savage, born Jan. 13, 1916, Linden. Never married.

Harold, James, Sam, and Tom Kent are buried in the Dr. O. Λ. Kirk Memorial Cemetery, Linden. Alice Savage Culp and Joe Frank Savage are the only surviving children of James Cathey and Alice Kennedy Savage. *Submitted by Kitty E. Savage.*

JAMES CATHEY SAVAGE, JR., the son of James Cathey and Alice Kennedy Savage was born, Linden, TN, on Oct. 12, 1907. He attended the Linden schools, but after the high school in Linden burned, he went to Hampshire, TN, where he lived with his cousin, George Savage, until he graduated from Hampshire High School. He attended Middle Tennessee State Teacher's College at Murfreesboro, and taught in the Perry County school system for several years. During the Depression years, the county funds were depleted and the county issued warrants in lieu of checks. The teachers could hold the warrants until funds became available, or they could go to the "money sharks," some of who charged one-third the value of the warrant for cashing it. James taught in rural schools where he had to build fires, carry water from a spring, and sweep the schoolhouse. He served as principal of the Linden Elementary School where he also taught 8th grade English.

James Cathey, Jr. and Kitty Estes Savage

During the war years, James helped tend the family farm, and on March 26, 1945, he married Mary Elizabeth (Kitty) Estes in Booneville, MS. Kitty, the daughter of Frank and Lillian Potter Estes of Linden, was born Aug. 5, 1928, in Waverly, TN. They were living in Oak Ridge, TN, in 1945 when the Atomic bombs were dropped and Japan surrendered. They returned to Linden, and a few months later, James entered the lumber manufacturing business. He operated a mill for Moss Tie Company in Waverly, TN, and later owned his own mill. He worked as a cross-tie inspector, and after graduating from National Hardwood Lumber School in Memphis, he worked as a lumber inspector in southern Kentucky. He died April 21, 1971, in Clarksville, TN, and is buried in the Dr. O. A. Kirk Memorial Cemetery in Linden.

Kitty Estes Savage, a graduate of Linden High School, grew up in Obion, TN, where she attended school until her tenth grade year when her family moved to Linden. She is a graduate of Austin Peay State University. She taught in the Montgomery County school system for twenty-seven years. She retired in 1993 and lives in Clarksville where she enjoys her hobbies of family research and crafting.

Children:

James Cathey Savage, III, born June 26, 1947 (See James C. Savage, III)

Frank Kennedy Savage, born April 17, 1949 (See Frank K. Savage)

Barbara Anne Savage, born Feb. 12, 1951 (See James H. Schneider)

Jo Lynn Savage, born Sept. 10, 1955 (See Thomas Patrick Elder)

Robert Estes Savage, born Oct. 4, 1956, Nashville, TN; married Janice Lanon Cooke; Medically Retired, U. S. Army; lives Nashville, TN; two children: Robert Shane Savage, born July 27, 1977, and Desiree Savage, born July 10, 1978.

John Alan Savage, born Nov. 30, 1958, Nashville, TN; computer consultant; graduate of Clarksville High School 1976, Nashville Tech 1979, attended Tennessee Tech, Cookesville. Divorced; one daughter, Erika Lee Savage, born Dec. 4, 1979. *Submitted by Kitty E. Savage.*

JAMES CATHEY SAVAGE, III was born June 26, 1947, Nashville, TN; the eldest son of

James Cathey Savage, Jr. and Kitty Estes Savage. He spent his early school years in Linden under the tutelage of Mrs. Lorene Nix (kindergarten) and Miss Bertha Westbrook (1st grade). He attended schools in Waverly, Lexington, and Linden before graduating with honors from Clarksville High School in 1965. After graduating from Austin Peay State University, he joined the army and served in Vietnam with the 75th Rangers, 1st Division.

Jim and Clara Savage

In 1973, after completing his Juris Doctorate at Memphis State University, he reentered active duty as a judge advocate prosecutor and defense counsel in Germany and Georgia. He has served as an Air Force, Army, and VA attorney. He is the recipient of the Bronze Star, CIB, and numerous other military awards.

Jim has advanced degrees in law from John Marshall School of Law, Georgetown University Law Center, and a M.S. in Criminal Justice from Troy State University. He has taught numerous classes in government contracts, real estate, and law as an adjunct professor at the law school and university level. He is admitted to the Bars of Tennessee, District of Columbia, Maryland, and several Federal courts including the U. S. Supreme Court.

Jim met Clara Parra when she was a Doctor of Education candidate at Harvard University. Clara, a native of Cumeral, Columbia, is the daughter of Josephine Parra and the late Antonio Parra. She graduated from the Cundinamarca (State) High School and from the National University of Columbia where she was valedictorian of both graduating classes. She did graduate work at Javerina University and the Pan American Federation of Medical Schools. She received both a Master's degree and a Doctorate from Harvard. After graduation, she continued her affiliation with Harvard as an Administrative Fellow in the Graduate School of Education. Dr. Savage is currently an international fund-raising instructor/consultant with Wellesley College Vice-President for Development.

In 1986, Jim and Clara married in Panama City, Panama. They are the parents of six year-old James Cathey Savage, IV, and four year-old Anthony Joseph Savage. Jim is also the father of Sean Patrick (13) and Catriona Sarah (8), from a 1975 marriage in Dublin, Ireland.

Since 1986, Jim has served as Chief Counsel for the U. S. Army Research Laboratory, Watertown, MA. He is an Army Reserve Lieutenant Colonel and currently serves as Massachusetts State President and National Judge Advocate for the Reserve Officers Association. He has been named American Legion's "Outstanding Citizen of Massachusetts," and has been honored with Exceptional Professional Achievement and Excellence in Government awards by the Boston Federal Executive Board. He is listed in several current Marquis's *Who's Who*...

The Savage family of Burlington, MA, are active church members, and Jim serves on the United Church Board for World Missions.

Regardless of where Jim lives or travels, Perry County will always be "HOME."

JOHN M. SCROGGINS,

came from Ireland and settled in Perry County, TN. He and his wife Mary had several children. One of their offspring was Hiram Hightower Scroggins. Hiram Hightower was born in 1823, legend has it that he was very small at birth, but grew up to be very, very tall. Hi (nicknamed) was six feet seven inches. He married Mary Jane McAllister. In January of 1855 their daughter Sarah Ann was born.

They were residing in Perry County when the war between the states began. Hiram enlisted on Nov. 6, 1862. He was in Company B, 10th Tennessee Cavalry under Colonel N. N. Cox at Linden, TN. He was paid $24.00 for the use of his horse. The 10th being under the command of General Nathan Bedford Forrest.

Hiram was wounded in the left hip, while on a raid chasing Union General Wolford, near Cleveland, TN. He later returned to duty. During the retreat from Chickamaga on Nov. 17, 1863, he was captured by men under the command of Union General George E. Thomas. He was sent to Louisville, KY, prison and then on to the newly opened federal prison at Rock Island, IL. Just how long Hiram stayed in prison is not known, for the next we hear of him, he is back farming in Perry County. His service records indicate that he probably escaped. He is listed as deserting the federal prison. Hiram applied for a Confederate pension from the state of Tennessee in 1902.

Sarah Ann Scroggins married William Alonzo Fuller in Perry County on Dec. 31, 1876. All ten of their children were born there. Mary Elizabeth (Mollie), William Harrison, Alice, Nancy Ann, Burness Tilda, Johnny B., Jesse L., Osbra Waco Levi (Dick), Idella Isabella, and Hiety Susie Deaner.

In 1903 Burness Tilda Fuller married Millard Wilburn Neisler, at Chester County, TN. All the Fuller and Neisler families moved to Pinson, Madison County, TN. On Jan. 8, 1904, Roy William Neisler was born. He could recall (as a child) the crop failures and the families loading their total goods onto flat bed railroad cars at the Artision Springs (Highway 45) and moving to Gibson County. The Fullers settled on one side of highway 104 and the Neislers on Bluff Road.

Roy W. Neisler married Dixie V. Roberts on Sept. 16, 1926, at Dyersburg Courthouse. During 1928 he arrived in Flint, MI, and went to work for Chevrolet Mfg. Four children were born in Michigan: Shirley J., Nov. 26, 1935; Gerald Wayne, Feb. 28, 1941; Dwight David, June 21, 1946; and Randy Gwen, Nov. 22, 1954.

Shirley, Dwight, and Randy continue to live in Flint, MI, while Gerald resides in Anaheim, CA. *Submitted by Shirley J. Neisler Cole.*

CARL L. SEBELIUS,

and Judy Millen Sebelius first came to Perry County in 1965 looking for a place near water as a weekend and vacation retreat from their very busy schedules. They found New Era landing and enjoyed the retreat for several years as renters. Once the property was for sale, they immediately bought it from Harold and Juanita Boyd in 1969. The property previously had been owned by the James R. Moore family and served as their home and farm and eventually became a fishing camp until the Boyds bought it.

Carl L., Jr., and Judy Millen Sebelius

The Sebelius daughters have considered the land a place to learn about the outdoors and to enjoy hunting and fishing with their parents. As they have grown older, they have found New Era to be their weekend retreat and vacation land. Ann Sebelius Hale lives in Jackson, MS, with her husband Kevin V. Hale who also has enjoyed many days on the Tennessee River. Carl and Judy's youngest daughter, Carolyn, who is training to be a teacher at UT at Knoxville, TN, finds New Era an excellent training ground for her job and a place to relax.

Carl Louis Sebelius, Jr., is the son of Carl Louis Sebelius and Lucille Soper Sebelius. He was born in Nashville, TN. The Sebelius family lived in Nashville, TN, and Geneva, Switzerland, where he finished high school. He returned to Nashville to attend Vanderbilt University. Upon finishing college in 1961, Carl, Jr., married and moved to Memphis, TN, where he attended UT College of Dentistry and remained to teach at his alma mater. Judy Millen Sebeluis is the daughter of Ernest Hall Millen and Morraine Wallis Millen.

Judy was born in Springfield, MO, lived in Alabama. She finished high school in Lewisburg, TN, Marshall County. She finished nursing school in Nashville, TN, and moved to Memphis, TN, as Carl's bride. They both love middle Tennessee and the Tennessee River, and there is no better place to enjoy both than at their home in Perry County.

ANDREW DANIEL SHARP,

son of John V. Sharp, married Sarah Ellen Sisco, daughter of John Thomas Sisco.

Their children, (1) Ethel Sharp, 1889-1931, married James Monroe Hickerson; (2) William Arnel Sharp 1891-1980; (3) Bertha Alice Sharp, born 1894; (4) Grady L. Sharp, born 1897; (5) Marvin Robert Sharp, 1900-1954; (6) Sewell Treadway Sharp, 1902-1931; (7) Eunice B. Sharp, 1904-1932; (8) Nesby W. Sharp, born 1906; (9) Alford Harvey Sharp, born 1910. All but the last two were born in

The Andrew Sharp family, ca. 1912 (front), Alford; (middle), Andrew (seated), Eunice, Sewell, and Nesby; (back), Grady, Arnel, Bertha, and Marvin.

Perry County. Then the family moved to Marshall County, OK.

EDWARD SHARP, born Jan. 17, 1787, Kentucky, possibly Shelby or Jefferson County, died Feb. 14, 1866, Perry County. I believe he is buried in the Sharp cemetery, Sharp Hollow, east of Beardstown. He was most likely son of old John Sharp, an early settler of Tennessee.

The Sharp Homeplace in Sharp Hollow, east of Beardstown.

He married April 28, 1810, Shelby County, KY, Tabitha A. Mayfield aka Dorcas. She was born June 2, 1791, South Carolina, died Oct. 24, 1876, Sharp Hollow at the home of her son Isaac, Perry County, buried Sharp cemetery, no marker. Her father Elijah Mayfield was a Revolutionary War soldier. Nine children were recorded in the Bible record, but at least four others were born according to early census records.. The nine that lived to maturity 1) Mariah Sharp, born May 23, 1811, married James Campbell. 2) William Sharp, born Sept. 20, 1912, nothing known about him. 3) George F. Sharp, born May 27, 1815, died 1864, near the Lewis-Maury County line, buried Hensley cemetery, Lewis County, which no longer exist. He married July 8, 1836, Maury County, Elizabeth Hensley. 4) Mary Ann Sharp, born Jan. 27, 1817, was wife of a Beakley or Blakley, probably Perry County. 5) John A. Sharp, born Nov. 6, 1818, moved to Arkansas. 6) Uraith Catherine Sharp, born Nov. 7, 1820, died April 28, 1856, buried Harder cemetery, Rock House Creek. She was the first wife of Edmond Harder. 7) Isaac Haudie Sharp, born Aug. 13, 1822, died February 1891, Sharp Hollow, buried Sharp cemetery. He married first Aug. 10, 1843, Maury County, Leonna Kelley and second to Mary Jones Barham. 8) Elizabeth Jane Sharp, born April 19, 1828, died Dec. 11, 1857, Perry County. She married Dec. 2, 1846, Dr. Joseph Gaytard Smith, his first wife. 9) James Mountable Sharp, born Sept. 30, 1830, died Jan. 19, 1908, buried Palestine cemetery, Lewis County. He married March 25, 1852, Sarah Clayton, daughter of John and Nancy Clayton. *Submitted by Merle Stevens.*

GEORGE F. SHARP, son of Edward and Tabitha Sharp, married Elizabeth Hensley. She was born 1819, died Perry County and is buried on a creek near Linden per a descendant. Elizabeth was a sister to the twins, Enoch Hickman and Abraham Thomas Hensley of Lewis County. In the mid 1840s the Sharp family moved to Arkansas, but returned to Tennessee after a few years. The known children were 1) Fountain Elliott Pitts Sharp, born 1839, died Feb. 4, 1865, at Camp Chase, OH, as a POW in the Civil War. 2) Jasper M. Sharp, born either 1844 or 1845, Arkansas. It is possible he was a twin, if so, born Oct. 31, 1845. Jasper died January 1883, Franklin County, TX. He married June 3, 1869, Perry County, Susan Elizabeth Barham. 3) Newton Asbury Sharp, born Oct. 31, 1845, Arkansas, died Jan. 25, 1907, Birmingham, AL. He married 1866 Nancy Ellen Hulme, daughter of Isaac Newton Hulme and Nancy Jane Clayton. 4) Nancy A. Sharp, born Jan. 5, 1849, died Aug. 16, 1908, Lake County, TN. She married first Thomas Jefferson Edwards and second Willis C. Clayton. 5) Sarah A. Sharp, born 1856. 6) Ursley A. Sharp, born 1859, probably died in Arkansas. She married first July 30, 1876, Perry County, William Stokes and second Sherred Watson. 7) George Sharp, born 1862, lived Oklahoma. Ursley Sharp's husband William Stokes was born 1856. I assume he died and she married Mr. Watson. Her children were Robert, Lula, and Tom Stokes and Mary and Ona Watson.

MARTIN V. SHARP, born 1834, son of William Anderson Sharp and Agnes Hensley, married Mary C. Smith, July 15, 1855. Per census they had seven children. 1) Mary A. Sharp, born 1856, married Jan. 25, 1880, Perry County, William M. Cox. 2) Amanda Sharp, born 1859, married Jasper F. Cox, Feb. 27, 1881, Perry County. 3) Millie A. Sharp, born 1863, married Dec. 29, 1881, Sinking Creek, Milton Brown Dabbs. 4) Nettie L. Sharp, born 1866, married Pleasant William Whitwell, Aug. 5, 1884, Perry County. 5) Luvenia C. Sharp, born 1869. 6) Attie U. Sharp, born 1874. 7) Sidney L. Sharp, born 1877. *Submitted by Merle Stevens.*

JAMES SHARP, born 1799, Kentucky, came to Perry County in the 1830s. He may have been son of John Sharp, an early settler of the area. On Aug. 17, 1820, Maury County, James married Eliza Mayfield, daughter of Samuel Mayfield and Zuridicy Rhoades. She was born 1804, Kentucky and died in the 1860s, Perry County. James died in the 1850s, Perry County. From early census records, they had at least eleven children. I have record of 7. 1) Elizabeth Sharp, wife of William Hickerson. 2) James Calvin Sharp, born 1831, died between 1876 and 1880, Madison County, AR. He married twice, first wife Mary Lucas of Perry County. 3) Mary Sharp who married Millington E. DePriest. 4) Dicy Sharp, probably Zuridicy, wife of William A. Tolle. 5) John F. Sharp, born 1838, nothing further known about him. 6) Samuel Miles Sharp. 7) William A. Sharp. Dicy Sharp, wife of William Tolle, was born September 1836, died early 1900s in Texas. William A. Tolle, born 1830, probably in Hickman County, son of Jonathan Tolle, died 1888, Perry County. William and Dicy had ten children. 1) Eliza Jane Tolle, born 1855, married Dec. 1, 1874, Perry County, her first cousin once removed, Shadric Monroe Mayfield, son of John Mayfield and Susan Lewis. 2) Martha J. Tolle, born 1859. 3) John William Tolle, born 1860, married Perry County, Martha Adaline Graves, daughter of Isaac Lee Graves and Parthena Ledbetter. 4) George Franklin Tolle, born 1862, first married Dorothy Clementine Clayton of Lewis County, daughter of George M. Clayton and Frances Caroline Sharp. 5) Josephine A. Tolle, born 1865, married Feb. 24, 1892, Perry County to William S. Bartley. 6) Alice V. Tolle, born 1867, married Perry County, Jan. 5, 1896, William M. Tatum, son of Joshua Tatum and Nancy Hickerson. Alice died soon after in Perry County. 7) Priscilla Angeline "Molly" Tolle, born 1869, Perry County, married John Moses Cooper, Jr. as his second wife. He was son of John Cooper, Sr., and Mary Ann Parker. 8) Felix Whitman Tolle, born 1871, married Isadora Frazier. 9) Nancy Ellen Tolle, born 1873, married Nov. 29, 1893, Perry County, to Robert N. Frazier. 10) Samuel Mack Tolle, born 1879, married Sarah Elizabeth Cooper, daughter of his brother-in-law, John Moses Cooper, Jr. and first wife, Sirvilla Angeline Sharp. This family, with the exception of daughter Alice, moved to Texas/Oklahoma late 1890s.

William A. Sharp, son of James and Eliza, born 1847, died after 1870, in either Perry County or Maury County. His wife, Nancy Odom, born 1848, was still living Maury County, in 1910. She was daughter of John Odom and Lydia Vincent. William and Nancy had five known children. 1) Mary P. born 1868. 2) James C., born 1869, died 1919, Maury County, married Ida Boshears. 3) Martha E. born 1870. 4) Elizabeth born 1872. 5) J. F. born 1874. Many descendants of James and Eliza Sharp still live in Perry County. *Submitted by Merle Stevens.*

JAMES SHARP, born 1835, son of Samuel Sharp and Millie Mayfield, died Oct. 29, 1863, in the Civil War. His wife, Ellen J. Aydelott, born Nov. 17, 1839, daughter of Abner Finely Aydelott and Martha A. Peery of Hickman County.

George W. and Ellen Rawdon

After James died, Ellen moved with her three children to Perry County. She died Oct. 20, 1894, Dallas County, TX. Their children were 1) Fletcher Marcenus Sharp, born August 1859, died 1944, Dallas County, TX. He married Oct. 23, 1879, Perry County, Sarah Alcy Rawdon, daughter of George W. Rawdon and Mary Ann Graves. 2) John S. Sharp, born November 1861, died 1917, Gibson County. He married Sept. 8, 1881, Hurricane Creek, to Mary P. Rawdon. 3) Millie Ann Sharp, born Dec. 10, 1863, died Jan. 1, 1952, New Mexico. She married Jan. 4, 1880, Perry County to James Thomas Rawdon. Ellen J. Aydelott Sharp married second, George W. Rawdon, a widower, Sept. 8, 1872, Perry County. George W. was born July 23, 1834, died Sept. 2, 1896, Dallas County, TX. He had children by both wives. *Submitted by Merle Stevens.*

JAMES CALVIN SHARP, son of William Hickerson and Elizabeth Sharp, married Mary Rhoden. Mary was born May 9, 1856, Tennessee and died Dec. 30, 1923, Cedar Hill, TX. They had twelve children. I have information on eight. 1) John M. Hickerson, born Nov. 4, 1872, Perry County, died Jan. 7, 1920, Perry County, buried Ary Cemetery. He married 1893, Perry County, Carrie Sanford/Turnbow. She was born 1875, Perry County, died 1939, buried Ary Cemetery. They had at least one son, Elihugh Hickerson, born Oct. 20, 1902, Perry County, died Nov. 16, 1923, Perry County, buried Ary Cemetery. James Monroe Hickerson, born 1877, died 1922, buried Ary Cemetery. In 1904, Perry County, he married Ethel Sharp, daughter of Andrew Daniel Sharp and Sarah Ellen Sisco. Ethel born 1889, Perry County, died 1931, Oklahoma. 3) Henry W. Hickerson, born July 1879. 4) Laura Ann Hickerson, born Dec. 11, 1881, Flatwoods died Dec. 1, 1949, Flatwoods buried Ary Cemetery. She married 1895 Flatwoods, to John Vinson Hickerson. He was born June 30, 1872, Flatwoods, died Sept. 1, 1934, Flatwoods, buried Ary Cemetery, son of Samuel Hickerson and Sarah Lucinda Dabbs. John and Laura parents of eight children, Samuel Thomas, Robert L., Henry, David H., Bessie Elizabeth, James Allen, Hessie Mary, and Cleo Edgar. 5) Pat Hickerson, born 1883, married and reared a family in Texas. 6) Ed Hickerson, born March 8, 1886, died Jan. 19, 1953, Texas. 7) Flay Lee Hickerson, born Aug. 20, 1889, Flatwoods, died Dec. 17, 1963. He, too, married and reared a family in Texas. 8) Cloe Hickerson, born Feb. 2, 1893, died Oct. 3, 1984, married Jack Moore and lived Texas.

An update on children of John and Carrie Hickerson, per 1920 census, they had sons Kyle B. Hickerson, born 1911, died 1965, buried Ary Cemetery and Richard Hickerson. Kyle Black Hickerson, married Beulas Mae Sanders, she born 1912, Perry County, died April 28, 1988, buried Ary Cemetery. *Submitted by Merle Stevens.*

JASPER M. SHARP, son of George F. Sharp and Elizabeth Hensley, married Susan Elizabeth Barham. She was born Jan. 20, 1850, Perry County, died Feb. 27, 1919, Perry County, buried Wilburn Cemetery. Her parents were Allen Barham and Margaret J. Sheppard. The Sharps moved to Texas about 1882, Jasper became ill and died, Susan brought her children back to Perry County to be near family. They had seven children. 1) Margaret Addie Sharp, born March 1870, died Oct. 17, 1952, buried Bell-Robertson Cemetery. She married Jan. 3, 1889, Perry County, to Alvin M. Cotton. 2) Fountain Elliot Pitts Sharp, born October 1871, died 1935, buried Pineview Cemetery. He married Dec. 9, 1894, Perry County, Martha C. Baars. 3) John William Sharp, born January 1874, died 1951, buried Pineview Cemetery. He married, March 6, 1899, Perry County, to Della Bell. 4) Dora Elizabeth Sharp, born March 27, 1876, Perry County, died Dec. 2, 1924, Tom's Creek, buried Danielsburg Cemetery. She married first March 8, 1891, Perry County, D. Allen O'Guin. Jarret Nathaniel Baars was her second husband. They married Jan. 25, 1903, Perry County. 5) Lula Sharp, born December 1879, Perry County, married May 3, 1906, Perry County, Henry Dan Beakley. He was born 1877, Perry County, and they moved to Arkansas. 6) Newton Washington Sharp, born April 18, 1882, Franklin County, TX. He was nine months old when his father died and the family returned to Tennessee. Newt died May 19, 1961, buried Pineview Cemetery. His wife, Vira Elizabeth Talley, born March 9, 1891, Beardstown, died Nov. 19, 1968, buried Pineview Cemetery.

Alvin M. Cotton born 1862, died 1928, buried Bell-Robertson Cemetery. He and Addie Sharp had four children. 1) Mamie Jane Cotton, born 1889, died 1974, buried Pineview Cemtery. She married Nov. 8, 1913, Tom's Creek, John E. Patterson. He was born 1892, died Dec. 7, 1966, son of William H. Patterson and Lizzie Wilsdorf. They had two daughters, Mable who married Glenn DePriest and Roberta, wife of Hugh Nickell. 2) Myrtle Cotton, born 1891, died 1967, buried Danielsburg Cemetery. She married Aug. 17, 1913, Perry County, Henry Elmer Bell. He was born 1889, died 1961. One daughter, Gladys May Bell Marress. 3) Roger L. Cotton, born 1898, died 1979, buried Danielsburg Cemetery. His wife, Mary Lee Bates, born 1902, died 1967. Two sons, Van Otis and James. 4) Cora Mae Cotton, born Sept. 29, 1901, Perry County, died June 4, 1983, Birmingham, AL, buried Kirk Cemetery. She married, Nov. 24, 1922, William Thomas Lane. He was born Feb. 17, 1893, Perry County, son of James Haywood Lane and Martha Jane Barham, died Feb. 7, 1966. Two daughters, Dimple Rue married Edward Clint Coble and Myrtle Loudean, married Hale Brown Vick.

JOHN SHARP, born 1811, died late 1880 or early 1881, is buried on Sinking Creek, location unknown. He was son of Nehemiah Sharp and Milly Clayton. John married Jan. 24, 1833, Maury County, Elizabeth Vincent. She was born 1814, daughter of George Vincent, Jr., and Hulda Littleton. She died in the early 1879s, buried Sinking Creek. John and Elizabeth had eleven or twelve children. Their daughters were Malinda, Hulda, Sarah, and Milly, none of which married. Their sons were George, John V., Nehemiah, William, James, Willis, Charles Mack, and possibly Wiley. George died as a young man and Charles as a young boy. Assume both are buried on Sinking Creek per family. Malinda died 1853, Hulda died 1879, Sarah died 1876, and Milly died 1882. The other sons married and had families.

Nehemiah Sharp, born 1839, died about 1870 as results from injuries received during the Civil War a few years before. His wife, Martha Hickerson married a Flowers afterwards and moved to Oregon County, MO.

William Sharp, born May 10, 1844, Perry County, died Jan. 15, 1919, Lewis County, married twice. First to Liddy Sims and second to Sarah Josephine Vincent.

Levi Sharp, a descendent of John Sharp.

James Sharp, born May 10, 1844, Hardin County, TN. His wife, Sarah Elizabeth Christine Hickerson, daughter of John D. Hickerson and Nancy Treece. She was born 1849, Perry County, died 1931, Hardin County. Sarah had married first, I. G. Rooden, 1866, Perry County.

Willis Sharp, born Sept. 16, 1853, died April 3, 1951, Lewis County. He married Paralee Kizar Whiteside.

I have a picture of a Levi Sharp. He is a descendent of John Sharp, but there were more than one Levi. I do not know who this one is. *Submitted by Merle Stevens.*

JOHN B. SHARP, son of John V. Sharp and Mary Jane Fraley, married Margaret L. Rhoden. The Rhoden name can be spelled many different ways. She was born about 1861. After John B. died, she married, Wayne County, a widower, John R. Davis. They had one son, John Davis, who lived in Michigan.

James Sharp, son of John and Elizabeth Sharp.

The Sharps had several children. (1) Mary Ann Sharp, born 1879, married May 22, 1895, in Perry County Samuel Riley. He was born in 1875, and their children by 1910 were Ashley, Thomas R., Fred C., and William A. Riley. (2) Ada Sharp, born 1885, died Jan. 2, 1974, married William Tatum. (3) Wiliam Levi Sharp, born July 21, 1888, Perry County, died Nov. 1, 1970. He married first Anna Evans, Jan. 9, 1910, Perry County. She was born 1896, Perry County, daughter of James H. Evans and Josephine Louise Mathis. Anna died in1917; their children, William, John Earl, Cecile Otis, Irene, and Robert Lyle Sharp. William Levi Sharp married again and had children; one was Bailey Sharp. (4) Addie Sharp, born 1892, died 1971, and buried in Wayne County Memory Gardens, married Dec. 21, 1913, Cisero A. Wilson, Wayne County. (5) It is possible that Lula J. Sharp, born 1883, was a daughter. I believe this Lula married Dec. 23, 1900, Luther Phillips, Wayne County.

JOHN FRANKLIN SHARP, born on Sinking Creek, died July 29, 1918, Linden. He and his wife, Lucinda J. Tatum, were first cousins once removed. Lucinda was the daughter of Joshua Y. Tatum and Nancy E. Hickerson. I believe 16 children were born to this union. I have the names of most. 1) Mary Jane Sharp, born June 2, 1888, died Dec. 6, 1962, buried Flatwoods Cemetery, wife of John DeWhitt Tatum. He was born March 4, 1885, died Nov. 21, 1938, parents of Lenny D., Mary Estalee, Claude Isaac, Richard, John D. Jr., Josephine, Woodrow, and Della J. 2) George Washington Sharp, born January 1890, buried Ary Cemetery. His wife, Ethel Moon died Aug. 6, 1989. Their children, Ester, Jack, Osby, John T., and Earl Brandon. 3) Nancy Edna Sharp, born Nov. 2, 1891, Perry County, died Jan. 5, 1962, buried Ary Cemetery. She married June 25, 1916, E. Johnson Whitehead, he born July 21, 1890, died Feb. 25, 1926. Edna had at least one son, Bailey Sharp. 4) Sarah Mae Sharp, born Nov. 25, 1895, Perry County, died Jan. 23, 1978, Hohenwald, buried Banks Cemetery, wife of Jay Hugh Whitehead. He born 1894, died 1946. Their children were Edith Clarice, Arthur, Ernest, Miles, Hershel, Jr., and J. T. 5) John Sharp, born April 5, 1897, Sinking Creek, died Dec. 8, 1985, buried Ary Cemetery. His wife was Etta Mae Simpson, born Oct. 9, 1905, died Nov. 2, 1967. They had seven children, with two sons dying as infants. 6) Lillie Y. Sharp, born March 14, 1898, buried Kirk Cemetery. She married Feb. 18, 1917, Perry County, Ed Walter Mercer. He born Dec. 8, 1897, died July 5, 1971, son of John Allen Mercer and Mary Wilson. Their children, Bertha, Mary, Joe, Obie, Ray, James Arlie, Dewey, and Larry Mercer. 7) Susan Anne "Susie" Sharp, born Sept. 8, 1900, Perry County, died May 12, 1991, buried Ary Cemetery. She married March 11, 1917, Perry County, Luther Willard Mercer, son of John Allen Mercer and Mary Wilson. He born March 26, 1899, Perry County, died April 30, 1982, buried Ary Cemetery. They had Clyde, Ralph, Esther, Dorothy, Kathy, Ann, Audrey Faye, Betty, and probably Fred Franklin Mercer. 8) Sadie Pearl Sharp, born 1903, died January 1972, married Aug. 29, 1918, Wayne County to John Whitehead. They had Buddy Melvin, Julia, Dorothy, Johnnie Pearl, Juanita, Mildred, and Billy Whitehead. 9) male twin Sharp to Pearl, born and died 1903. 10) Richard Marvin Sharp, born Feb. 22, 1906, died Oct. 4, 1974, buried Ary Cemetery. His children William, Malcolm, Glenn, and Betty. 11) Brown Sharp born 1908, married Melba Westbrooks. She born 1921, daughter of Pete Westbrooks and Dale Dabbs. Melba died Feb. 20, 1981, buried Kirk Cemetery. They were parents of Era Nell, Evelyn, Dorothy, Helen, Willie Mae, John, and Billy Sharp. 12) Whitfield Sharp, born Dec. 20, 1909, died June 1, 1985, buried Ary Cemetery, served in World War II. 13) Bud Sharp, born 1913, died Jan. 18, 1975, buried Kirk Cemetery. His wife, Bessie Mae Hendrix, born 1924, daughter of Charlie Hendrix and Bessie Ann Brooks. Their children, an infant son buried Ary Cemetery, Roy, Eddi, Ruby, Kathy, Reba, Rita, Sylvia, Rhonda, and Gail Sharp. *Submitted by Merle Stevens.*

JOHN V. SHARP, called Jack, was born 1835, Lewis County, which was Hickman County at the time. He died November 1879, Perry County and is possibly buried on what was the Willis S. Sharp farm, Sinking Creek.

Mary Jane Fraley Sharp

He was son of John Sharp and Elizabeth Vincent. I suspect his middle name was Vincent. Jack was in the Civil War as a Confederate. He married in Perry County, 1856, to Mary Jane Fraley, daughter of John Fraley and Francis Kaisinger. She was born 1839, Perry County, died 1924, Perry County, buried Sharp Cemetery. There are no markers in this cemetery. Jack and Mary Jane had nine children. (1) John B. Sharp born 1857, died before 1896. He married March 21, 1878, Perry County, Margaret L. Rhoden. (2) George W. Sharp, born 1858, Sinking Creek, married Oct. 9, 1881, Rockhouse Creek, Margaret Henrietta Grinder. She was born 1861, Rockhouse Creek, daughter of Robert Grinder and Polly Ann Ledbetter. They had five children, none survived infancy. (3) Levi Sharp, born Jan. 3, 1860, died Jan. 7, 1948, Joplin, MO. He married Oct. 28, 1883, Perry County, Frances Suzannah Selph. They lived Perry County until early 1900s, moved to Arkansas and then to Missouri. (4) Mary J. Sharp, born 1862, died 1873. (5) William Sharp, born 1864, died West Tennessee. He married Jan. 12, 1888, Perry County, Sarah Jane Tatum. (6) Andrew Daniel Sharp, born Aug. 21, 1866, near Flatwoods, died Sept. 8, 1943, Oklahoma. He married Dec. 25, 1887, Flatwoods, Sarah Ellen Sisco. She was born Jan. 25, 1868, Flatwoods, died June 10, 1911, Oklahoma, daughter of John Thomas Sisco and Mary Etta Sharp. (7) Samuel Sharp, born 1868, died early 1900s, buried Sharp Cemetery on Sinking Creek. His wife, Martha Comelia Ann Pope, born 1871, died 1936. (8) Nehemiah Sharp, born 1870, nothing else known. (9) Willis S. Sharp, born May 25, 1871, Perry County, died Dec. 19, 1927, at home on Sinking Creek, buried family cemetery. He married Dec. 22, 1889, Perry County, Mary Elizabeth Tatum. *Submitted by Merle Stevens.*

ISAAC HAUDIE SHARP, born 1822, son of Edward and Tabitha Sharp, married as his second wife, Mary Jones Barham. Mary was born 1848, died 1913, Little River County, AR, daughter of Allen Barham and Margaret J. Sheppard. After Haudie died, Mary married Jan. 18, 1898, Perry County, William Curl. Mary and Haudi had three daughters, Martha Ann and two infants. Both infants are buried Sharp Cemetery, Sharp Hollow, Perry County.

Mary J. Barham Sharp

Martha Ann Sharp, born June 1, 1865, Sharp Hollow, died March 7, 1935, Plainview, TX. She married Nov. 29, 1883, Perry County, William Thomas Aldridge. He was born Dec. 25, 1861, Perry County, son of William Nelson Aldridge and Elizabeth Newton, died Dec. 4, 1921, Little River County, AR. Eight children born, all in Sharp Hollow. (1) Genevia Elizabeth Aldridge, born Sept. 27, 1884, died Sept. 29, 1916, buried DePriest Bend Cemetery. She married 1899, Perry County, Jess Lee DePriest. (2) John Austin Aldridge, born Aug. 4, 1886, died May 15, 1941, Lake Village, AR. He married April 12, 1907, Perry County, Mary Ellen Langley, daughter of Joseph Langley and Augusta Curl. (3) Isaac Nelson Aldridge, born July 9, 1889, died Dec. 21, 1970, LaGrange, AR, husband of Katie Johnson. (4) Henry Fulton Aldridge, born Feb. 26, 1891, died Sept. 16, 1908, Marmaduke, AR. (5) Naomi Estalee Aldridge, born Jan. 21, 1895, died Oct. 4, 1987, Abilene, TX, wife of Homer Basil Mason. (6) Thomas Milford Aldridge, born April 1897, died Jan. 14, 1960, Little Rock, AR. (7) Theatus Allen Aldridge, born Jan. 23, 1900, died Dec. 16, 1915, Little River County, AR. (8) Tussey Comodore Aldridge, born April 14, 1903, died Dec. 13, 1991, Abilene, TX.

Only Genevia Aldridge DePriest stayed in Perry County. Her husband, Lee DePriest, born March 17, 1878, died Aug. 2, 1944, buried DePriest Bend Cemetery, son of Pleasant DePriest and Sarah J. Fuller. They had five children (1) William Jesse DePriest, born Aug. 3, 1900, died Dec. 5, 1957, buried DePriest Bend Cemetery, married Betty Bates. (2) Zula DePriest, born Nov. 5, 1902, died Dec. 17, 1972, buried DePriest Bend Cemetery. She married Wesley Duncan. (3) Lindsey DePriest, born April 24, 1904, died 1980, Virginia. He married first Cynthia White and second Viola Johnson. (4) Donald Austin DePriest, born Aug. 25, 1906, died July 6, 1966, buried DePriest Bend Cemetery. He married Mrs. Thelma Boren Brown. (5) Tom Milton DePriest, born April 5, 1914, married Roxie Kelly. *Submitted by Merle Stevens.*

ISOM HAUDIE SHARP, son of Edward Sharp and Tabitha Mayfield, was a Confederate soldier. His first wife, Leonna Kelley, born 1825, daughter of Thomas Kelley and probably Malinda Howell.

John D. Sharp, son of Isom Sharp.

Haudie and Leonna had six children. 1) Sarah Sharp, born 1848, died Feb. 2, 1929, DePriest Bend, buried Sharp Cemetery, Sharp Hollow. She never married. 2) John D. Sharp, born 1851, died May 1883, Sharp Hollow, buried Sharp Cemetery. He married Oct. 25, 1877, Perry County, Martha H. Barham. She was born 1856, daughter of Allen Barham and Margaret J. Sheppard. She possibly died in Mississippi at an "old soldiers home for widows." They had two children, Ona D. Sharp, born Aug. 8, 1878, died Oct. 24, 1883, and Auston Sharp, born Aug. 17, 1882, died Jan. 21, 1883, both died Sharp Hollow and buried there. The widow Martha, married second, 1896, Augustus Patry and third 1901, William H. Patton. 3) Harriett Sharp, born 1853, buried Sharp Cemetery. She married Oct. 6, 1879, Perry County, William Thomas Barham. 4) Caldonia Sharp, born 1855. 5) Elizabeth Sharp, born 1856, died Feb. 2, 1885, White County, AR. She married George Carroll, 1882. They had two daughters, America Carroll died age 19, about 1895, buried Sharp Cemetery and Hattie Carroll, born January 1884, Arkansas, died about 1904, Texas. Hattie married Jan. 14, 1899, Perry County, George Albert Baars. He was born 1877, died 1951, buried DePriest Bend Cemetery, son of Jarrett Nathaniel Baars and Sarah E. Cude. After Hattie's death, he married Sept. 14, 1914, Perry County, Jennie DePriest Sanders. The Baars had two children, infant daughter Baars and Lillie M. Baars. Lillie, born Aug. 7, 1901, married first Aug. 25, 1917, Perry County, Roy DePriest, two children, Frank and Laverne. Then she married Graydon Carroll DePriest, Dec. 26, 1931, one son, Graydon Carroll, Jr. 6) Catherine Sharp, born 1859, died young.

NEWT AND VIRA TALLEY SHARP

had ten children, all born Densons L Landing. 1) Jasper Sharp, born 1907, died age five, buried Wilburn Cemetery. 2) William Sharp died as an infant, buried on Buffalo River. 3) Mary Sharp, born November 1909, died February 1910, Densons Landing, buried on Buffalo River. 4) Dora C. Sharp, born Sept. 6, 1911, died May 25, 1972, buried Pineview Cemetery. She married James Bernice Jones. 5) John E. Sharp, born April 21, 1913, died April 21, 1920, Perry County, buried near Beardstown on Buffalo River. 6) Paul Henry Sharp, born Feb. 15, 1917, married Dec. 23, 1939, Linden to Norma E. Bell. 7) Opal C. Sharp, born 1918, married a Leeper. 8) Geneice Sharp is Mrs. Lewis. 9) Pearl Sharp, born Aug. 31. 1923, died July 14, 1980, buried Kirk Cemetery. She married Albert H. Coleman. 10) Bessie Mae Sharp, born Feb. 3, 1926, died March 20, 1992, Jackson, buried Kirk Cemetery. She first married a Higdon and second James W. Allen.

In Perry County birth records, there is a Reely Sharp, male, born July 4, 1910, father Hunter Sharp, born Texas and mother Vera Sharp, born Perry County. This could be Newt Sharp and Vira Talley.

SAMUEL SHARP, born 1869, son of John V. Sharp and Mary Jane Fraley, married Martha Cornelia Ann Pope. Their children (1) Ethel Sharp, born 1891, died 1965, buried Chestunt Grove Cemetery, Coon Creek. She married Jan. 28, 1912, Perry County, Laz Albert Inman. He was born 1888, died 1945. (2) Maggie Sharp, born 1896, died 1934, buried Napier Cemetery, Lewis County. She married March 12, 1922, Wayne County, Everett Skelton. (3) Myrtle Sharp, born Aug. 27, 1899, Flatwoods, died April 16, 1994, buried in Downey Cemetery, Lewis County. She married Aug. 6, 1916, Wayne County, Enoch L. Whitehead. (4) Ollie Sharp, born about 1904, died 1992, married Wayne County, Oct. 16, 1923, Agnes Poag. (5) Osbie Sharp, born May 9, 1905, died Feb. 22, 1946, buried Wayne County. He married Nov. 24, 1928, Wayne County, Neva Dean Luna.

SAMUEL MILES SHARP, was born in Perry County in 1841, the son of James Sharp and Eliza Mayfield. He died in 1912 and is buried in Flatwoods, TN. He served in the Civil War and was the father of two children by his first marriage to Hulda Odom; John Sharp, who married Lucinda Tatum, and Eliza Jane Sharp, who married John Treadwell. Samuel Sharp later married Elizabeth Boyce Garner who was born in 1841 and died in 1927.

Left to right: Ernest and Elam Sharp.

Elizabeth Boyce was previously married to John Garner who lost his life in the Civil War. The children of John Garner and Elizabeth Boyce were Molly Garner, who married Taylor Graves; John Garner, who married Cord Grinder; and Martha Garner, who married William Harder.

Not much is known of the ancestry of Samuel Miles Sharp. He had a sister Mary, who married John R. DePriest. The children of Samuel Sharp and Elizabeth Boyce Garner Garner were:

James (Jim) Sharp who married Rowena Shelton. Their children are Thomas H. Sharp and Catherine Sharp married Holly Godwin.

George Sharp who married May Savage Their children were Miles, James, Cassie, and Leora, who died at a young age.

Samuel Theodore (Bud) Sharp who was born in April 1870 and died April 1939. He was married to Delphia Graves who was born in March 1881 and died in February 1972. Both are buried in Flatwoods, TN. S. T. (Bud) Sharp was postmaster, farmer, and operator of a general merchandise store in Flatwoods.

The "Bud" and Delphia Sharp family, left to right: Kenneth, "Bud" (holding Mary), Delphia (holding Wilson), and Kola.

The children of S. T. (Bud) Sharp and Delphia Graves were:

Kenneth Sharp, 1904-1966, married Sarah Ann Kelly, who died in 1991. Their children are James Kelly, Carry, and Robert Keith.

Kola Sharp, 1906-1982, married Ann O'Donnell, who died in 1964. Their children are Donald and David.

Mary Sharp, 1910-1992, married Tom Godwin. Their children are Mary Ann and Tom Godwin, Jr.

Wilson Sharp, 1912-1976, married Sue Anderson. Their children are Suzanne and Judy Elsie..

Walton Sharp, 1916-1985, married Christine Vaughn. Their children are Carolyn, Bill, and Rebecca.

Ernest Sharp, 1918, married Lucille Dodson. He served in the United States Air Force from May 1942 until December 1945. They are parents of two children, Jean E. and John F.

Elam Sharp, 1920-1988, married Norma Blankenship. He served in the United States Navy during World War II. Their children are Debra Kay (deceased), Steven, and Gary.

S. T. (Bud) Sharp and Delphia Graves also were parents of three children; Lloyd, Ruth, and Marqurite, who died in infancy.

WILLIAM "BILL" SHARP, son of John V. Sharp and Mary Jane Fraley, married Sarah Jane Tatum, daughter of Joshua Y. Tatum and Nancy E. Hickerson. Jane was born Feb. 15, 1872, died Dec. 18, 1956, Coon Creek, buried Chestnut Grove Cemetery.

Their children: (1) John Willis Sharp, born Nov. 9, 1888, died Oct. 13, 1965, buried Chestnut Grove Cemetery. He married Martha Ann "Mattie" Hickerson, born Oct. 9, 1892, died Oct. 17, 1983, daughter of Martin Hickerson and Emily J. Inman.

(2) Mary R. "Mollie" Sharp, born Nov. 27, 1892, died June 13, 1970, buried Qualls Cemetery on Brush Creek. She married Sept. 4, 1910, Perry County, William Riley Qualls. He was born April 10, 1892, son of Joe B. Qualls and Ezora Warren, died Oct. 23, 1973.

(3) Dovie M. Sharp, born July 10, 1895, died Feb. 4, 1979, buried Chestnut Grove Cem-

etery. On Sept. 3, 1911, Perry County, she married James Henry Qualls, born Aug. 24, 1892, died Jan. 31, 1976.

(4) Brown Sharp, born March 21, 1901, died June 20, 1970, buried Church Grove Cemetery, Dyer County.

(5) Duffy Sharp, born 1903, wife of Henry Qualls.

(6) Dale Sharp, born July 17, 1909, died Oct. 26, 1970, buried Church Grove Cemetery; she was wife of Thad Phillips.

WILLIS S. SHARP, son of John V. Sharp and Mary Jane Fraley. His wife, Mary Elizabeth Tatum, was born June 27, 1868, Perry County, died March 24, 1936, near Flatwoods, buried Sharp Cemetery, Sinking Creek. Her parents were Joshua Y. Tatum and Nancy E. Hickerson.

Back: Mattie and Emma. Front: Willis (father), Lillian, Lizzie (Tatum), and Ashley Sharp.

They had nine children, all born at home place on Sinking Creek. (1) Emma Ella Sharp, born Jan.2,1891, died Nov. 12, 1978, Weakley County. She married Jan. 17, 1909, Sinking Creek,Riley B. Ary. He was born 1883 Perry County, died Feb. 10, 1971.

(2) Martha Elizabeth Sharp, born Dec. 12, 1892. Married Mar. 12, 1911, Sinking Creek, William Lee Tatum. He was born Dec. 25, 1891, died June 17, 1961, buried Wayne County.

(3) Mary Lillian Sharp, born Sept. 26, 1895, died Sept. 5, 1985, buried Swiss Cemetery, Hohenwald. She married Nov. 16, 1913, Sinking Creek, Olan Dabbs, son of Rufus Walker Dabbs and Rebecca Cicily Smith.

(4) Ashley Sharp, born 1898, died age three, Sinking Creek, buried Sharp Cemetery.

(5) Infant daughter, buried Sharp Cemetery.

(6) Mayhugh Sharp, born Aug. 5. 1902, died Jan. 21, 1976, buried Kirk Cemetery. He married Dec. 14, 1924, near Flatwoods, Anna May Garner, daughter of John Will Garner and Cordelia Grinder.

(7) Jenny Ann Sharp, born April 9, 1905, died Oct. 20, 1920, Sinking Creek, buried Sharp Cemetery.

(8) Jasper Owen Sharp, born July 12, 1908, died Feb. 16, 1979, buried Swiss Cemetery. He married Feb. 11, 1934, Sarah Marie Hensley, daughter of Frank Hensley and Melvina Kilpatrick.

(9) William Leslie Sharp, born Sept. 26, 1911, died Sept. 24, 1951, Dyersburg, TN. He married Sept. 27, 1931, Perry County, Eva Pearl Hickerson, daughter of William Nathan Hickerson and Cordonia F. Duncan.

SHEPARD, It is not known for sure the name of our first Shepard ancestor, but in 1623 there were three Shepards listed in Virginia who had come from England to Virginia. One by the name of Robert Shepard, which we feel quite sure is our family line, whose wife was Jessica Hubbard. They lived and died in Gloucester, though exact dates of birth, marriage, and death are unknown. They had at least one son, Samuel, and a daughter who married a Burrell.

Samuel Shepard I married Mary Kavanough in Gloucester, VA, where their children were born and lived. They are as follows: Elizabeth, Samuel II, Robert born about 1732, James, and William Shepard.

Robert Shepard born about 1732, married in 1758 to Elizabeth Blackstone, born about 1737. Their children were: William (1759), died during the American Revolution; Samuel III, born June 3, 1762, in Goochland County, VA, served in the American Revolution. Other children were Thomas born Nov. 15, 1766, Elizabeth born April 9, 1769, Benjamin born Jan. 6, 1771, Mildred born July 18, 1773, and Frances, birth date unknown.

Samuel Shepard III enlisted in the American Revolution from Goochland County, VA, and returned there after the war ended. On Dec. 2, 1790, he married Jenny Guill at Prince Edward County, VA. Their children were as follows: William (Sept. 19, 1791), Samuel M. (1794), Robert (1797), John (1800), Martha (1803), James N. (1806), and Mary (birth date unknown).

About 1812, Samuel III with his family moved to Wilson County, TN, where he died on Dec. 3, 1837.

William Shepard's birth date, Sept. 19, 1791, was recorded in the old Shepard family Bible. Family records show that he was married Sept. 12, 1813, to Jane Price Brightwell. Jane was born Feb. 27, 1793, in Virginia. They soon returned to Wilson County, TN, where William's parents had moved about 1812. Their children are as follows:

1) Louisa was born Jan. 8, 1815. She married Armstead D. Lain. Their children were Haywood B. Lain, born Oct. 1, 1835, in Perry County; Malinda A. Lain, born Feb. 14, 1834, in Perry County; William W. Lain born on April 4, 1838, in Perry County; Martha Ann Lain born March 29, 1839; Samuel R. Lain, born July 14, 1841; Lucy J. Lain born March 1, 1844; Douglas Lain (birth date unknown); Susan Lain born April 14, 1851. Family records indicate that other children, Mary, Floyd, Thomas, and Franklin died young.

2) Elizabeth was born 1816, died 1817.

3) Malinda Ann born Dec. 24, 1817, married Thomas B. Whitwell.

4) Samuel Russell, born Oct. 13, 1820, in Wilson County, TN, married first Malinda (maiden name unknown) in Perry County. He left Perry County after death of his wife, going to Huntsville, AR, and then to Texas in 1863. His second marriage was to Sarah A. Thruston in 1866, daughter of Atreet Thruston of Versailles, MO, and Sarah A. Gradick Thruston. They had five children all born in Mt. Pleasant, TX. Sarah died May 12, 1876. Samuel Russell was in merchandise and cotton brokerage business until 1880. On May 26, 1880 he married his third wife, Millie Sanders, and took his family to Cook County, TX, and from there to Tenton County, Texas, where he died March 16, 1885, and is buried in the Shepard Cemetery at Bolivar.

5) Egbert Haywood was born Oct. 13, 1825, in Wilson County. His father, William, moved from Wilson County to Perry County in 1829 where he lived on Cane Creek and farmed until his death. He is buried in Shepard Cemetery on Cane Creek, as is his wife, Jane.

EGBERT HAYWOOD SHEPARD, was born Oct. 13, 1825, in Wilson County, TN, son of William Shepard (born September 19, 1791) and Jane Price Britwell Shepard (born Feb. 27, 1793) and grandson of Samuel Shepard III and Jennie Guill Shepard. He was the great grandson of Robert and Elizabeth Blackstone Shepard, the great great grandson of Samuel I and Mary Kavannaugh Shepard, and the great great great grandson of Robert and Jessica Hubbard Shepard. Robert and Jessica lived and died in Gloucester, VA.

Front row; Malcom, Willie, Thelma, Willie Ray, and Fannie Burns, Bertha Shepard Simpson, Ola, and Sylvia Burns. Back Row: Gilbert and Addie Shepard, Josiah (Buddy) and Jane Shepard. William Haywood (Billy) and Hartie Shepard.

Egbert Shepard married Naomi (Nanny) Wilburn in 1843. She was born Nov. 17, 1827, daughter of John Wilburn of Perry County. He located on an 1100 acre farm near the junction of Buffalo River and Cane Creek in 1849. In 1862 he enlisted in the 10th Tennessee Confederate Cavalry and served until captured. He was a merchant for many years at Beardstown. He gave by deed in 1893 the land which the Beardstown Church of Christ now stands. He and family were all members of the Church of Christ.

Egbert and Nanny were parents of the following children: John (1855), Josiah Baker

(1855) married Nancy Jane Edwards, Thomas, Sallie married John Thomas Edwards, Nancy married Sam Cude, and Donnie.

After the death of his wife on Sept. 17, 1878, he married Mary Jane Smith on Nov. 17, 1881. Two children were born to them; namely, Samuel Clinton Shepard and Era Elizabeth Shepard. Egbert died March 20, 1904. He and both wives are buried in the Shepard-Edwards Cemetery on Cane Creek.

Josiah Baker Shepard was born 1855 in Perry County, TN, son of Egbert Haywood and Naomi Wilburn Shepard. His wife was Nancy Jane Edwards, born 1855, daughter of William Hodge Edwards and Nancy Wilburn Shepard. Their children were: Hartie Wilson Shepard (1833-1959), Francia Elmora Shepard (1884-1957) married Willie Arthur Burns, Bertha Pearl Shepard (1885-1978) married Amon King, Ola Mae Shepard (1887-1969) married George Simpson Burns, Gilbert Jerome (1887-1957) married Addie Rebecca Alexander, William Haywood (1893-1947) married Byron Maye DePriest. She had one sister, Vera Byrd, and two brothers, Iru and Carter DePriest.

Josiah Baker Shepard died Nov. 8, 1929. Nancy Jane Edwards Shepard died March 26, 1936, and are both buried in the Cane Creek (Shepard) Cemetery, as well as all other members of family with the exception of Francia and Ola Mae who are buried in the Burns Cemetery at Beardstown.

These families are all members of the Church of Christ.

JAMES WILLIAM SHEPARD, was born June 26, 1834, the son of Robert Shepard and Susan Guill Shepard. (See Robert Shepard Family) His grandchildren confirm that he was called "Jimmy." He died Jan. 26, 1874, and is most probably buried in the Old Wilburn Cemetery. About 1860 he married Martha Jane Wiggs also of Perry County (See William M. Wiggs Family). At the time of his death he left Martha Jane Wiggs Shepard an expectant mother with five young children. Their six children were:

1) Jimmy M. Shepard, born Oct. 4, 1861, died 1893, married Rebecca Blackburn. They were the parents of: Uren, Myrtle Eunice, and Willie Shepard. Myrtle Eunice Shepard born Sept. 29, 1886, died Dec. 21, 1986, at age 100, Centerville, TN. In 1902 she married John Richard Pinkerton. As Jimmy and Rebecca Shepard both died young, their children were partially raised by their uncle Rufus Shepard and his mother Martha Jane Wiggs Shepard. Willie died in Arkansas as a very young man.

2) Mary Elizabeth Shepard, born Jan. 3, 1865, died Sept. 6, 1925, married John Bell Cude (See Cude Family). She was the victim of a tragic train wreck in Obion County, which also claimed five other members of her family. The Sept. 11, 1925, *Linden Times* describes this accident.

3) William A. Shepard, born Jan. 1, 1867, died Dec. 6, 1888; went to Missouri to help build a railroad.

4) John Robert Shepard, born Feb. 25, 1869; died Oct. 18, 1961, East Point, GA; buried Oakmont Cemetery, Hickman County, TN. Robert Shepard married Nannie Wilkes, Aug. 11, 1894. They were the parents of Raymond Shepard, born Oct. 21, 1896, died Oct. 15, 1969, married Mary Ella Crabtree; Mattie Shepard, born July 8, 1897, died 1960, married Oliver Walker Sawyer, Dec. 16, 1916, Hickman County; Mary Lottie Shepard, born Aug. 5, 1901, married Revo Jones McClanahan, Aug. 23, 1923, Hickman County; Eva Hortense Shepard, born Sept. 14, 1904, died Jan. 4, 1988, married Tom Miller; and Walter Batten Shepard, born March 11, 1909, died 1973, married Bertha Duncan.

5) Odella Shepard, born May 17, 1872, died Aug. 11, 1894, never married.

6) Rufus Thomas Shepard, born Aug. 18, 1874, died Feb. 27, 1961, Centerville, TN, born Oakmont Cemetery, Shipps Bend. Rufus married first Annie Laura Deason, July 11, 1895, Perry County. She was born Jan. 22, 1879, the daughter of Charlie Pinkney Deason and Ida Jameson Deason; the granddaughter of Elijah R. Deason and Cynthia Sue Cooper Deason and Joshua S. Jameson and Martha Jane Blanton Jameson. Neither of these families had Perry County connections that have been determined. However, Elijah R. Deason is buried at the Old Beardstown Cemetery. He was a known Methodist minister, physician, schoolteacher, musician, and magician.

Rufus Shepard and Annie Laurie Deason were the parents of Vera Luray Shepard, married William M. McClanahan; Claude Eric Shepard, married first Suzie Weatherspoon, second Grace Davis; Clive Aubrey Shepard, married Amy Weatherspoon; Wilma Lee Shepard, married William Howard Witherspoon; and James Charlie Shepard, married Julia Marie Byers. The stories of these families are found in the history of Hickman County, TN.

After the death of Annie Laura Deason, Rufus Shepard married Martha Jane Dotson, Florence Crowell Shands, Margaret Ethel Shepard McKay, and Eva Patterson Bell, who outlived Rufus by several years. By his marriage to Florence Crowell Shands, there was an additional daughter, Martha Laverne Shepard, who married Hardie Lee Askins. Martha Shepard Askins spent many years in Michigan, but now resides in Dickson, TN.

Little of the life of "Jimmy" Shepard is known. He may have served the Confederacy for a time with Co. C, 10th Tennessee Cavalry. Family tradition handed down through grandson Charlie Shepard says that Jimmy Shepard "wanted nothing to do with that war." Martha Jane Wiggs Shepard lived to a ripe old age and is well spoken of by all who knew her. *Submitted by Gail Shepard Tomlinson.*

ROBERT SHEPARD, In 1849 Robert Shepard (born ca 1795, Price Edward County, VA) was issued a West Tennessee Land Grant of 107 acres in Perry County on the Buffalo River. He was the son of Samuel Shepard and Jane Guill Shepard who had come to Wilson County, TN, about 1810. Samuel's parents were Robert Shepard and Elizabeth Blackstone Shepard of Goochland County, VA, whose family has been reconstructed from the Douglas Register; marriages of Prince Edward County, VA; estate settlement of Robert Shepard in Goochland County, VA; and the Revolutionary War Application of Samuel Shepard of Wilson County, TN.

On June 6, 1822, Robert Shepard married Susan Guill in Wilson County, TN. Susan died Dec. 20, 1879, and is buried in the Old Wilborn Cemetery off Highway 13. A headstone exists, though it is lying on the ground. It is not known when Robert Shepard died, probably sometime after 1880. Jane Guill's and Susan Guill's parents have not been established. There were several Guill families in Wilson County that may be traced in the future.

Robert Shepard's brother, William, and his wife Jane Price Britewell, had settled in Perry County around 1825. William's line established itself more firmly in the county, as he was the father of Egbert Haywood Shepard, prominent in the Cane Creek area.

Robert and Susan Shepard farmed and were the parents of five known children.

1. Margaret Jane Shepard, born May 27, 1827, died Oct. 22, 1904; first married a Sharp, second married Allen Z. Barham; buried Brush Creek. They had several children. Margaret Jane Shepard Barham was deeded the land grant property in March 1879 with both Robert and Susan signing.

2. Mary Elizabeth, born ca 1831.

3. James William Shepard, born June 26, 1834, died Jan. 26, 1874, probably in Perry County. He married ca 1860 Martha Jane Wiggs also of Perry County (See William M. Wiggs story), and they were the parents of six children. (See James William Shepard Family story)

4. Sarah Shepard, born about 1839.

5. Susan C. Shepard, born about 1849.

What is known of Robert Shepard in a more personal way comes from *Linden Times*, Thursday, May 13, 1880, pg. 1, FROM BEARDSTOWN: "We have a very old man living in our district. Old Uncle Bob Shepard, as he is commonly called, will, if he lives, soon celebrate his 84th birthday. He was born in the old State of Virginia, and immigrated to Wilson County, in this State, but remained there only a short time when he moved to Davidson County, and lived on an adjoining farm to General Jackson. He has spent many hours in conversation with "Old Hickory." He remembers the death of the father of our country well, and only lived a short distance from him at that time. Uncle Bob is enjoying splendid health at present, and can walk two miles almost as quick as anyone. He talks of going to Texas this fall. Until two years ago he never failed to work in the crop and make a regular hand." *Submitted by Gail Shepard Tomlinson.*

WILLIAM HAYWOOD "BILLY" SHEPARD, was born March 21, 1893, in Perry County, TN, son of Josiah Baker Shepard and Nancy Jane Edwards Shepard. He married Byron Maye DePriest. She was born Aug. 15, 1905, Perry County, TN, the daughter of Albert DePriest and Sallie Matt Ridings DePriest. William was a merchant and farmer, and served in World War I, 163rd Infantry, 41st Division.

Their children were: Virginia Janice Shepard, born June 28, 1924, married Joseph Byrd Carmical; Carrie Nell Shepard, born Feb. 11, 1927, married James Edward DePriest; Billy Shepard, Jr. was born May 1, 1929, married Martha Irene DePriest.

William Haywood Shepard died Aug. 29, 1947, and Bryon DePriest Shepard died Sept. 26, 1963. Both are buried in the Shepard-

Edwards Cemetery on Cane Creek. This family were all members of the Church of Christ.

William Haywood (Billy) Shepard

Billy Shepard, Jr., was born May 1, 1929, in Perry County, TN. On Dec. 30, 1949, Billy, Jr., married Martha Irene DePriest, daughter of Jesse and Betty DePriest. She was born March 30, 1930. Billy served in the U.S. Army for some time until he became disabled. He and Martha Irene lived in Nashville most of his adult life where he worked at the Ford Glass Plant.

They had two children: Lesa Ann Shepard, born Sept. 30, 1955. On Aug. 10, 1987, she married David Guy Conner. He was born Jan. 21, 1953, and died in 1989. Their only child was Jason William Conner, born Sept. 11, 1989; Bill Allen Shepard, born April 14, 1962, married Sandra Barnes, born Dec. 20, 1958. They have two children; Amanda Shepard was born Feb. 8, 1980, and Bill Allen Shepard, Jr., was born Nov. 16, 1985. There are two step-children, Carol Barnes born July 22, 1975, and Shannon Barnes born Nov. 25, 1976.

Billy Shepard, Jr. died Oct. 13, 1976. He is buried in Harpeth Hills Gardens. Martha Irene continues to live in Nashville, TN.

SIMMONS-PEEBLES,
James Henry Simmons, born Jan. 12, 1855, near Hickman/Perry County line, TN, died Jan. 28, 1916, in Benton County, TN. James Henry is buried in Byrd's Hill Cemetery according to his death certificate. Byrd's Hill is now known as Eagle Creek Baptist Church Cemetery. He was the son of Levi Simmonds born in North Carolina and Rebecca Phillips probably also born in North Carolina who lived many years in Perry County, TN.

Ann Peebles, granddaughter of Delphia (Simmons) Peebles, May 1958.

A daughter of James Henry Simmons was Delphia Simmons born in Perry County, TN, on July 9, 1886, and died Dec. 29, 1968, in Benton County. Delphia Simmons married James Wesley Peebles who was born 1885 and died December 1927.

The only son of James Wesley Peebles and Delphia (Simmons) Peebles was Jacob Henry Peebles who was born Aug. 4, 1924, in Benton County and died Oct. 2, 1980. On Oct. 12, 1945, Jacob Henry married Mavis Marie Arnold who was born Oct. 1, 1924. Mavis is the daughter of Charlie Allen Arnold, born Sept. 1, 1902, died Sept. 18, 1976, and Lenora Bell Jordan who was born Jan. 13, 1906, she being the daughter of Leander Green Jordan who was born March 11, 1867, dying Feb. 4, 1945, and Martha Louise Presson, born Feb. 5, 1866, dying Aug. 6, 1956. They are buried in Cowell's Chapel Cemetery, Benton County.

Jacob Henry (Jake) Peebles and Mavis (Arnold) Peebles had one daughter, Winona Ann Peebles, born June 22, 1946. Ann Peebles married James Hillsmon Ford, born April 25, 1945. Their issue: (1) Regina Ann Ford born Oct. 18, 1966, married Jerry McGuire. Regina and Jerry's issue is: Allison Payge McGuire who was born June 21, 1989. (2) Dana Leigh Ford, born March 21, 1970.

Jacob Henry (Jake) Peebles was a Mason, was employed with the Benton County Electric System for 33 years. *Submitted by Mavis Arnold Peebles.*

JOHN THOMAS SISCO,
born June 6, 1848, died April 11, 1930, buried Sisco Cemetery, Lewis County. He was the son of William Sisco and Mary Ann Campbell and the grandson of James Campbell and Mariah Sharp.

Mary Etta Sharp Sisco

His wife, Mary Etta Sharp, born Nov. 5, 1848, Hickman County, daughter of John Sharp and Margaret Jane Whiteside, died Dec. 3, 1908, Perry County. The story I was told, was that John buried his wife near his home, which was somewhere on Sinking Creek. He then moved to another place on Sinking Creek and moved her grave with him. Today, her marker stands vigil over a one grave cemetery I called the Lone Sisco Cemetery, between the Ary and Graves cemeteries. Her marker is very descriptive. On May 20, 1909, Perry County, John married again, to the widow Mrs. Nannie C. Paschall. Later, John moved again, but this time left the first wife buried where she was. John and Mary Etta had four children live past infancy. 1) Sarah Ellen Sisco, born Jan. 25, 1868, Perry County, died June 10, 1911, Oklahoma, wife of Andrew Daniel Sharp. 2) William A. Sisco, born July 2, 1870, died Feb. 21, 1927, buried Swiss Cemetery, Lewis County. He married April 19, 1891, Perry County, Mollie Estalee Smith, daughter of Simeon Smith and Elizabeth Cayce. 3) Henry Sisco, born May 3, 1877, died May 26, 1923, buried Yorkville, TN. He married Aug. 3, 1900, Perry County, Addie Richardson. 4) Jacob Andrew Sisco, born on April 21, 1888, Sinking Creek, died May 13, 1920, buried Centerville, TN. His wife was Bessie Maud Arnold.

JAMES LLOYD SLOAN,
was born Jan. 17, 1841, on Waldens Ridges, Rhea County, TN. His father was James B. Sloan of Irish descent and he came to Tennessee from New York. His mother was Mary A. Sterrit of Scotch descent and lived in Virginia when they married.

James Lloyd Sloan and Alice Imogene (Ledbetter) Sloan.

James Lloyd was the youngest of 12 children. His father died when he was seven and soon the family moved to Nashville. A year later, they moved to Virginia (about 1849) where James learned the printers trade. The family moved back to Nashville in 1854 where he learned the molders trade.

When the Civil War broke out, he enlisted in Company D, 11th Tennessee. He was Orderly Sgt. of his company, declining the Captaincy, he was made 2nd Lieutenant. After serving two years, his services were demanded by the Confederate government in manufacturing munitions.

James met and married Sarah Wills Corbett Jan. 8, 1862, while stationed with his regiment at Cumberland Gap in Tennessee. After the war, James studied law and was admitted to the bar while living in Centerville, TN. He then moved to Linden in 1869 where he lived until his death Aug. 26, 1906.

He was very active in community affairs, helping to build the First Methodist Church where a room of the church was dedicated to him and called Sloan's Chapel. He was an active Mason in the Linden Lodge #210. In 1904, James was chosen Grand Master of Masonic Order for the State of Tennessee.

James and Sarah had five children: 1) Fannie married and moved to Ft. Worth, TX; 2) Leon W. settled in Virden, IL; 3) James P. settled in Memphis, TN; 4) Walter N. lived in Linden for a few years and then moved to Memphis; 5) Lloyd Henderson "Chester" (Feb. 7, 1867-June 17, 1945) was born in Centerville and married Alice Jones (November 1866-May 5, 1947) of Maury County, TN.

Chester and Alice had two sons: 1) Lloyd Wood Sloan (March 29, 1889-Sept. 29, 1942) State Veterinarian of Paris, TN. He married Willie Lee Hickerson and they had a son, James Lloyd Sloan (Aug. 31, 1912-March 22, 1979). James

Lloyd lived in Linden all his life. He was appointed County Veterinarian in 1960. He married Alice Imogene Ledbetter, daughter of Alonzo B. Ledbetter (Jan. 27, 1873-Oct. 30, 1951) and Beulah Culp Ledbetter (April 24, 1889-Feb. 4, 1981). Alonzo's parents were John Nelson Ledbetter and Sarah Alice Johnson. John Nelson's father was Green Ledbetter. Beulah Culp's parents were Robert Culp and Mary Virginia Chappell. 2) Lyle B. Sloan (Nov. 7, 1892-March 3, 1926). Lyle played professional baseball as a left-handed pitcher for the Washington Senators and played with the St. Louis Cardinals 1916 and 1917. He had to give it up because of bad health. He served as deputy clerk in Linden for eight years before his death at age 32.

James Lloyd and Imogene had three children: James Lloyd Sloan (Jan. 7, 1933) of Kingston Springs, TN, Eddie Lee (Aug. 3, 1934), and Charles Terrence (Oct. 14, 1939).

SMITH, Frederick N. (Rick) and Mary N. Kimble were married in 1968 at Aldersgate Methodist Church in Largo, FL. They have one son Timothy A. (Tim) who was born in 1970 in Orlando, FL. They now live in Linden, TN.

Rick's family was from Indiana moving to Florida when he was a young child and then moving back to Indiana in the 1970s. He is retired from the U. S. Navy and is now owner of Rick's Refrigeration. He is a member of the Perry County Veterans Association.

Mary Smith is currently librarian at Linden Elementary/Middle School. She is a graduate of PCHS, Austin Peay State University at Clarksville, TN and Tennessee State University at Nashville, TN. She is a member of the Tennessee Association of School Librarians, the National Quilters Society, and the American Quilt Association.

Timothy A. Smith is a graduate of PCHS. He served in the U. S. Navy from 1990-92 during Operation Desert Storm aboard the helicopter carrier USS Tripoli. He was stationed first in Kuwait (Persian Gulf) and later in San Diego, CA. He is presently employed with Johnson Controls in Linden, TN.

JAMES MARION SMITH, married Minor Mitchell and they lived in the lower end of Perry County near the Humphreys County line. We don't know any of the relatives of James Marion or where they were buried or lived. He was known to have a step-brother named Edgar and a sister. Minor Mitchell was reared by the Rains family and had a brother, Jack Mitchell. Without further searching, we can't name other relatives or even her parents.

J. Marion was born Oct. 27, 1876, and departed this life April 13, 1949. Minor Mitchell Smith was born July 4, 1877, and passed on Sept. 1, 1966. She died at the home of her daughter, Oddie McCaig, on Crooked Creek in Perry County. Marion, Minor, and son Leslie Smith, born Aug. 23, 1909, and died Oct. 23, 1909, all rest in the Bone Cemetery, located close to their home place.

Their children consisted of James Leonard (Lynn or Bulger) Smith who married Grace Spencer of Red Bank. They had two sons and two daughters. Dempsey married Sue DePriest Coffey and they had two children. Reuben married Mary Jo Doyle and they had three sons: Jeff, Phillip, and Johnny, and three grandchildren. Velma Smith Parnell had two children, Gary and Diane, and is presently married to Bob Walters. They have two grandchildren. Janie Russell was married to Foy Russell, son of Arthur and Pauline, and before he passed away with cancer, they had Vicky and Tammy, and Janie has two grandchildren.

Marion and Minor had two daughters: Earlie, who is married to Jack Ambs and lives in Linden, Oddie McCaig who married Long "Skinner" McCaig (deceased) and had sons: Paul, Glen "Corky" (deceased), and Jim McCaig. Ray Smith was married to Annie Pearl Clark and they had seven boys and three girls. Ray and wife are deceased. Woodrow "Tut" Smith lived in Linden and was married to Mildred Walker of Lobelville. They had a son, Billy, killed on pipeline construction and a daughter Barbara who lives in Jackson, TN. *Submitted by Mrs. Reubin W. Smith.*

SMITH, Lee Garry and Billie Nell Bryson Smith live on Marsh Creek. Billie, born May 29, 1933, is the daughter of Barney Lee and Julia Mae Hufstedler Bryson. They had a son and daughter, both dead and are buried at the Alberson Cemetery on Hurricane Creek. Barney Lee Bryson was born Dec. 2, 1895, and died Aug. 26, 1987, buried at Sutton Cemetery on Marsh Creek. His wife, Julia Mae Hufstedler, was born Dec. 30, 1901, and died April 8, 1993, and buried at Suton Cemetery on Marsh Creek.

Lee Garry Smith, Jr.

Lee and Billie have one son, Lee Garry Smith, Jr., born April 11, 1966. He is married to Rhonda Sue Goodson and they live in Centerville, TN.

Barney Lee Bryson's parents were George Washington Bryson and Nancy Kilpatrick Bryson. They are buried at the Alberson Cemetery on Hurricane Creek. Their children were in order of birth: James Plummer, Oscar Wiley, (died in World War I), Barney Lee, Nora Grace, and Margaret Izora.

George W. Bryson's parents were Columbus and Margaret Bryson. Nancy Kilpatrick's father was Joshua Kilpatrick. Julia Mae Hufstedler's parents were Newton Carroll Hufstedler and Sara Mahala Wilson Hufstedler. They are buried at the Union Methodist Church Cemetery in the Lane View community near Trenton, TN. Their children were, in order of birth: Chesley Rubin (died in infancy and buried at Bethel Cemetery south of Linden, TN) Julia Mae, Johnnie Matt, Joe Kendrick, Martha Jane, Ida Lucretia, and Sara Newton.

Sara Mahala Wilson's parents were Joe Wilson and Nancy Julia Randle Wilson. Nancy Julia's mother was Mahala Randle.

Newton Carroll Hufstedler's parents were John Kendrick Hufstedler and Angeline Ward. John Pinkney Hufstedler's mother was Martha Whitwell. John Kendrick Hufstedler's mother was Jane Randle and his father was John Pinkney Hufstedler. They are buried in Pinkney's Tomb in Perry County, TN.

Lee Gary Smith was born May 5, 1922, the son of Robet Carroll and Ida Elizabeth DePriest Smith. Robert Carroll Smith was born Oct. 14, 1883, and died Dec. 24, 1958, buried at Sutton Cemetery on Marsh Creek. His wife, Ida Elizabeth DePriest, was born Nov. 19, 1885, and died Aug. 6, 1973, with burial at the Sutton Cemetery on Marsh Creek. Their children were, in order of birth: Beulah, Guy Washington, Robert Clarence, Woodrow Wilson, Marie, Mahala Louise, Mary Bess, Lee Garry, Marjorie Elizabeth, and Nelle Eunice.

Robert Carroll Smith's parent's were George Washington and Margie Smith Smith. Their chidlren were: Robert Carroll, Newt, Nannie, Lewis, and Emma.

Ida DePriest's parents were Houston DePriest and Dora Beasley DePriest. Their chidlren were: Thurman, Henry, Brown, Homer, Lura, Addie, and Ida (twins).

George Smith's father was Jessie Smith, who moved to Perry County from Maury County.

Dora Beasley DePriest's parents were Beverly and Caroline Miller Beasley who moved to Perry County from Hickman County. *Compiled by Lee G. and Billy Nell Smith.*

SMITH, Pineview is distinguished by three of its citizens, Nonnie Smith Presson, Bulow Smith, and their niece, Virginia Clayborne, who compose *The Perry County Music Makers.*

Nonnie, Bulow, and Virginia made music of a rare and special quality—the old traditional string band music.

Nonnie used as her main instrument a large, custom-built zither, which gave a haunting harmony to traditional and folk songs along with Nonnie's own compositions; in fact, Nonnie was probably the only person in the county who played the zither in old-time string band style.

When Nonnie was eight years of age, her father, James A. Smith, a music teacher and author, visited a friend, Henry Wilsdorf, of German descent, who gave him a small zither; On his way home to his humble cabin he learned to strum the instrument and shortly thereafter, Nonnie began to play it, too.

At the age of 12, Nonnie composed two songs: "Trail of the Lonesome Pines" and "Fishing Birds Return," Nonnie had already been playing the harp with her mother, Mary, at the age of three.

Nonnie wore out four conventional zithers before she became acquainted with Grady Moore, a famous guitarist from Nashville, who designed a large zither with 54 strings to replace the Austrian zither with 32 strings, which produced a softer sound and different pitches.

In 1930, Nonnie and Bulow were broadcasting their music on radio at Knoxville, TN, and also on WTNT and WSIX in Nashville, TN.

By the late thirties, their music was out on Vocalion Records and they later joined the traveling, tent show Bisbees Comedians, and performed along with Rod and Boob Brasfield, the famous comedians from Lewis County, TN.

Over the years after they had stopped traveling on the road and performing, Dr. Charles Wolfe, a professor at MTSU, began searching for Nonnie and Bulow, in the early seventies, while teaching a class, he asked if anyone had heard of The Perry County Music Makers, and a student, Ronnie Hinson, raised his hand and said, "I know them." Then through his sister, Roberta O'Guin, the band was rediscovered.

Then Dr. Wolfe contacted his friend, Dr. Steve Davis, a professor at Austin Peay University, and they traveled to Pineview, interviewed the band members, and in 1974 they agreed to cut some new albums on Davis Unlimited Records.

Dr. Wofle sent one of the albums to the Smithsonian Institute and shortly thereafter the three member band was invited to perform at the institution.

The Perry County Music Makers were flown to Washington, D.C., on July 6, 1976, to perform on the Mall at the invitation of the Smithsonian Institute to celebrate the Bicentennial of the United States, before hundreds of people, and while they were there many of their albums sold. The group returned to Pineview on July 12, 1976.

Dr. Davis said, "I want all of the songs and music by Nonnie Smith Presson I can get because her unique ability of playing the zither will live long after her." *Compiled by Roy W. Bell, Michael Lawrence, Mabel Patterson, Amie Wilsdorf, and Roberta O'Guin.*

Nonnie and Bulow's home.

JOHN THOMAS SMITH, In the 1780s, John Thomas Smith and his Wales bride arrived in America and settled on Swan Creek in Maury County. Their children were as follows: Simeon Smith (1823-1903), Jesse Smith, Lee Smith, Robert Smith, George Smith, Manda Smith, Mollie Smith, Ida Smith, and Elizabeth Smith. Of these children, Simeon Smith liked to hunt. He became friends with the Indians, who used a hunting trail that led from Swan Creek in Maury County to Sinking Creek (in Perry County) where the Toll Hollow is located. At that time, the Indians, who were Cherokee, lived in wigwams.

John Thomas Smith

James Arnette came to America from Armenia in the 1700s. He settled on Sinking Creek in the Toll Hollow area in the early 1800s. He fell in love and married a Cherokee woman from that area. They had a daughter named Frances (born 1824, died 1910) who married Jonathan Toll. They (the Tolls) had a daughter also named Frances who married Simeon Smith. Their children were John Smith, Robert Smith, George Smith, Margie Smith, Clementine Smith, Luther Valentine Smith, and George Washington Smith (twins).

Luther Valentine Smith (born Sept. 23, 1854, died 1914) married Betty Elizabeth Hughes (born Feb. 29, 1856, died Sept. 5, 1903). Their children were Samuel Smith who married Lizzie; Carroll Smith who married Jane Kimble; Ruben Smith who married Addie DePriest; Liza Smith who married Roy Palmer; John Thomas Smith; and Charles Smith who died in France in 1918 serving his country during World War I.

John Thomas Smith (Nov. 23, 1889, died June 23, 1987) married Bertha Lee Richardson (born Dec. 16, 1894) in Dec. 23, 1913. They lived near Kellys Landing on the Tennessee River. Later they purchased the John Denton farm on Upper Cedar Creek where Bertha Lee Smith lives today. She will be 100 years old on Dec. 16, 1994. Their children are Bessie Bell Smith (May 13, 1915) married Herschell Moore, Zula Lee Smith (Aug. 1, 1918) married Frank Horner, Luther Brown Smith (March 16, 1929), Jessie William Smith June 19, 1923) married Dorothy Larue, Billy Carlos Smith (July 24, 1926) married Rena Faye Ward, Nellie Darlos Smith (July 11, 1932) married James Howell.

Luther Brown Smith married Lydia Amanda Broadway on June 18, 1941. To this union, the following children were born: Tex Nelson Smith (April 4, 1942), Shirley Violet Smith (June 23, 1949), and Michael Brown Smith (Sept. 25, 1955).

Tex Nelson Smith married Patsy Warren (June 23, 1948) on June 17, 1968, in Cairo, IL. Their children are Gabriel Nelson Smith (Oct. 19, 1974) and Mary Ann Smith (March 31, 1980). Gabriel became an Eagle Scout on Feb. 19, 1993. He now attends college at MTSU, Murfreesboro, TN.

Tex and Patsy Warren Smith own Smith's Pharmacy located on Mill Street, Linden, TN. Their business has been in operation since Feb. 9, 1976.

Shirley Violet Smith married Stanley Tucker July 19, 1968. They had one son, Robert Nelson Tucker, born June 22, 1970. Stanley Tucker died May 22, 1977. Shirley Tucker married Harry Mathenia April 25, 1980. They have one daughter, Amanda Mathenia born May 13, 1981.

Michael Brown Smith married Gail Hobbs June 25, 1980.

JOHN THOMAS SMITH, born Nov. 23, 1889; son of Luther Valentine and Elizabeth; and Bertha Lee, born Dec. 16, 1894; daughter of Will and Arkie Richardson; were married Dec. 23, 1913, by I. B. "Brat" Moore.

John Smith Family, 1949. Bessie, Jessie, Bertha. Luther Brown, Darlos, Zula, Carlos, and John Smith.

John and Bertha had six children: Bessie Bell (born May 13, 1916) married Hershel Robert Moore on Jan. 20, 1933. Zula Lee (born Aug. 1, 1918) married Frank Porter Horner on Oct. 10, 1936. Luther Brown (born March 16, 1920) married Lydia Violet Broadway on June 23, 1941. Jessie William (born June 29, 1923) married Dorothy Faye Larue on June 28, 1945. Billie Carlos (born July 26, 1926) wed Rena Fae Ward. Nellie Darlos (born July 11, 1932) wed James Edward Howell Nov. 3, 1948.

John and Bertha united with the Primitive Baptist Church, Simmons Meeting House, Cedar Creek together and were baptized Oct. 28, 1923, by Elder W. C. Pope.

They lived their entire lives on Cedar Creek. They were blessed with 19 healthy grandchildren; 35 great grandchildren; 10 great-great grandchildren and still counting.

Their marriage of 73 years six months came to an end with the death of "Captain" John, June 23, 1986. He was buried in Harder Cemetery.

"Miss" Bertha or Mama as she is known still lives in the family home at the young age of 99. *Submitted by Bertha Lee Smith.*

JOSEPH GAYTARD SMITH, a physician, born Feb. 25, 1825, died June 27, 1891, Hopkins County, TX. He married three times, most likely all in Perry County. His first wife, Elizabeth Jane Sharp, daughter of Edward Sharp and Tabitha Mayfield, died 1857. They had five children. 1) James E. Smith, born Feb. 18, 1848, died Oct. 31, 1866, Perry County. 2) Helena Artemesia Smith, born Nov. 28, 1849, died Oct. 23, 1923,

Hopkins County, TX. She married April 15, 1870, Perry County, John W. Randel. He was born Aug. 13, 1849, died Dec. 6, 1932, Texas. His mother was Mary Mathis Randel. 3) Mary Elizabeth Smith, born Feb. 23, 1852, Perry County, died Jan. 2, 1929, Hopkins County, TX. She married June 25, 1868, Perry County, George Washington Taylor. He born Dec. 13, 1848, died Aug. 2, 1910, Texas. 4) George Madison Smith, born Nov. 29, 1853, died April 5, 1923, Texas. 5) Harriet R. Smith, born Dec. 28, 1855, died March 15, 1913, Texas. This family moved to Texas early 1870s.

Dr. Smith's second wife, was also an Elizabeth Sharp. I believe she was the daughter of Samuel Sharp and Millie Mayfield of Hickman County and a double first cousin of his first wife, Elizabeth Jane. They married April 18, 1858, and she died Oct. 19, 1860, Perry County, leaving one daughter, Sarah Elizabeth Smith. Sarah was known as Betty and was born April 29, 1859, married William James Tarrant of Lewis County and they moved to Texas. Joseph G. Smith's third wife, Nancy G. Shepard of Perry County. Nancy was born Aug. 8, 1838, died in Texas Feb. 15, 1925. Children were born to this marriage.

SIMEON SMITH, born De.c 3, 1831, died March 5, 1918, buried Swiss Cemetery, Hohenwald. He was son of Wiley Smith and Ann Stringfellow, reportedly of Indian descent. Simeon married Oct. 12, 1854, probably Hickman County, Frances Elizabeth Cayce. Elizabeth was born March 6, 1837, died June 12, 1924, at the home of her daughter, Victoria Tatum on Sinking Creek, buried Swiss Cemetery. She was daughter of John and Rebecca Cayce. Of 14 children born, two lived in Perry County, several of the others lived here off and on. Victoria Smith, born March 7, 1870, died Nov. 18, 1951, Sinking Creek, buried Dabbs Cemetery on Little Rock House Creek. She married March 1, 1891, Perry County, Elisha Black Tatum. Tack Tatum, as he was called, born March 30, 1872, died Feb. 1, 1951, buried Dabbs Cemetery. His father, Sublet A. Tatum, is also buried there. They had three sons. 1) W. Lee Tatum, born 1892. 2) Loyd S. Tatum, born May 1, 1895, died Aug. 16, 1967, buried Ary Cemetery. He married Feb. 8, 1914, Perry County, Delphia Bromley. Their children, James Black, Dorothy, and Delores. 3) Cayce Tatum, may be spelled differently, born 1901.

Rufus Walker Dabbs, born Oct. 7, 1873, Perry County, son of Joseph Dabbs and Jincy Angeline Randel, died 1945, buried Dabbs Cemetery. In Perry County, June 18, 1893, he married Rebecca Cicily Smith, daughter of Simeon and Elizabeth. Cicily born Feb. 29, 1876, Lewis County, died April 13, 1951, buried Dabbs Cemetery. Their 12 children were all probably born Perry County. 1) Olan A. Dabbs, born July 39, 1894, died Dec. 24, 1974, buried Swiss Cemetery, Hohenwald. He married Nov. 16, 1913, Perry County, Mary Lillian Sharp. 2) Oma Victoria Dabbs, born Dec. 23, 1895, died Dec. 8, 1968, buried Hickerson Cemetery, Hurricane Creek. She married July 29, 1912, Perry County, Jadie Hickerson. 3) Onis Hilmer Dabbs, born Jan. 30, 1898, died May 16, 1959, buried Swiss Cemetery, husband of Mattie J. Hickerson. 4) Nancy Smith Dabbs, born Aug. 23, 1899, died Sept. 12, 1971, buried Swiss Cemetery, he married Lee DePriest, Dec. 13, 1924, Sinking Creek. 5) Maggie Dale Dabbs, born Aug. 24, 1901, died Oct. 12, 1951, buried Dabbs Cemetery. She married March 17, 1918, Perry County, Pete Westbrooks. 6) female infant Dabbs, born and died April 4, 1903, buried Dabbs Cemetery. 7) Austin Glenn Dabbs, born Oct. 14, 1904, died April 24, 1980, buried Kirk Cemetery. His wife, Eula Kirk. 8) Rufus Thelma Dabbs, born Dec. 26, 1907, died Sept. 22, 1977, buried Downey Cemetery, Lewis County. Thelma married John W. Ford. 9) Foy Ehoarth Dabbs, born Oct. 7, 1909, per WPA Bible records and Oct. 1 per Perry County birth records. 10) Joe Simeon Dabbs, born May 29, 1912, per WPA Bible records and May 15 per Perry County birth records. 11) Ina Lee Dabbs, born May 25, 1914, died July 20, 1926, buried Swiss Cemetery. 12) Alton Dabbs. *Submitted by Merle Stevens.*

PINKNEY L. SMOTHERS, (1839-1904) was born and grew up in North Carolina, where he was trained as a masterbuilder/architect. It is believed that Pinkney came to West Tennessee as a Confederate soldier in the "war of northern aggression." After the war he resumed working in his chosen profession (masterbuilder/architect). About 1867 Pinkney was commissioned to design and supervise the construction of the (then) new Perry County Courthouse in Linden. His design of that courthouse was in the North Carolina/Virginia Piedmont tradition.

Pinkney L. Smothers and Perry County's second courthouse, which Pinkney designed and constructed.

While working on the courthouse, Pinkney met and fell in love with a Perry County girl named Marie Etta Trantham (1852-1913). They were married on Dec. 29, 1870, by G. L. Pearson. They had a total of ten children, however, only three survived to adulthood: Annie L. Smothers Pierce (1871-1913), Alice L. Smothers (1889-1918), and Robert Carl Smothers (1893-1927).

After completing the new courthouse, Pinkney went on designing and building other residential, commercial, and public buildings in and around Linden. Among these was an inn (an early hotel and dining room), which he and his family lived in and operated. It was built on property near the new courthouse, which Pinkney purchased from Thomas French in 1874. At that time (the late 1800s and early 1900s) there were few good roads in Perry County and a trip to Linden from even relatively nearby communities in the county, was a full day's journey. Consequently, when the county court was in session the members of the court from outlying communities stayed at Pinkney and Marie Etta's inn.

Around 1880, Pinkney was disabled in a construction accident and was unable to function as a masterbuilder. After that, he and the family expanded their business in Linden to include a livery stable and a general store, built on property Pinkney purchased from J. C. and A. M. Taylor in 1880.

Pinkney, Marie Etta, Annie, Alice, and Carl are buried in the cemetery at the Chestnut Grove Church of Christ near Linden.

Pinkney and Marie Etta had two grandsons: Fount T. Smothers (1893-1967) and Pink (ney?) Smothers (1919-1971). Fount fought in France in World War I in the 114th Field Artillery, a unit completely composed of volunteers from West Tennessee, under Maj. Gordon Browning (of Milan). When Maj. Browning ran for governor, Fount helped manage his campaign and served in his administration. That election broke "Boss" Crump's political stranglehold on Tennessee. Fount later represented Davidson County in the state legislature. Fount had two children: Katherine Smothers Douglas, of New Orleans, LA, and Fount T. Smothers (Jr.), A.I.A., of Thompson Station, TN; six grandchildren and five great grandchidren. Pink became a circus performer and later operated his own circus. He had one child: Shirley Smothers of New Orleans, LA. Without realizing he was following in his great grandfather's footsteps, Fount (Jr.) studied architecture, became an architect and served as Professor of Architecture and Director of the School of Architecture at both Ohio University and Louisiana State University.

SPARKS-EDWARDS, When Bess Edwards left Perry County in 1898, her family was headed to west Tennessee by covered wagon and train. It wasn't that far by modern standards, but at the time it was quite a distance and Bess had no way of knowing if she would ever return. But return she would, to the country where her family had lived since the mid-1800s.

Bess Edwards Sparks and daughter Elizabeth, about 1916.

The Edwards had come to America from Wales, settling first in Virginia in the early 1700s. David L. Edwards, whose father, Andrew, was a veteran of the Revolutionary War, was the first in the line to move to Tennessee, settling in Hickman County. David, himself, was a veteran of the War of 1812. It was his grandson, William Hodge Edwards who was first known to move to Perry County.

William was born in Hickman County, but was living in Perry County with his first wife, Nancy Wilburn, by at least 1854. They had seven children before Nancy died near the end of the War Between the States. William later married Mary Agnes Wollard, and they had three children, including Samuel David (Sam) who was born near Beardstown in 1868.

In 1889, Sam Edwards married Eula Beard, who had been born at Beardstown in 1871 (Eula's father, Wiley Beard, was a member of the family from which Beardstown received its name, and a veteran of the Confederate Army who was wounded at the Battle of Shiloh.). To Sam and Eula were born four children before they made their move to west Tennessee: William Otis, Wiley Enloe, Bess (born in 1892), and Mary Pauline. Two more children were born after the move: Elva and Samuel Thomas.

When Bess did return to Perry County, it was to be a teacher. She lived with her first cousin Eugenia Beard Dodson and her husband, Ashley Dodson. While living with the Dodsons, Bess met a young lawyer/farmer/newspaperman, J. Kent Sparks. They were married on Dec. 18, 1913, and spent most of the rest of their lives on the Sparks family's farms on Lick Creek. Bess and Kent's first child was Elizabeth Sparks, born in Linden in 1914. Elizabeth married Willie Henry Hudson, of Perry County, in 1940; they had one child Ann Elizabeth. Ann has two children from her marriage to Reed Westbrook of Perry County—Brian Reed and Michael Hudson. Willie passed away in 1963 and Elizabeth died in 1984.

Bess and Kent's second child, Jessie Eugenia, was born in Linden in 1929. She was married to David D. Walker, also of Perry County. They had two daughters: Elizabeth (Beth) Sparks and Sara (Sally) Kent. Beth is married to William Daniel (Bill) Steinert and has two children, Eugene (Gene) Samuel Cantrell, III (from an earlier marriage) and Sara Elizabeth Steinert. Sally married Donald Keith Lemonds from Memphis. Jessie passed away in March of 1994.

An active member of the Lick Creek and Linden communities, Bess was particularly involved in her church, First Christian, and was known as an accomplished seamstress and flower gardener. She passed away in Linden in 1973, and is buried with her husband, who died in 1966, at Kirk Memorial Cemetery.

SPARKS, If his great-great-grandfather, Matthew Sparks, hadn't been killed by Creek Indians in 1793, J. Kent Sparks might very well have grown up in Georgia instead of Perry County. After Matthew's death, his large family scattered, with his widow and three of their sons settling in Hickman County, TN, around 1810.

The Sparks family had been in the New World since at least 1607, listed as land owners as early as 1636. About 1750, Matthew moved with his wife Sarah to North Carolina from Maryland. They had a large family—13 children—with the older boys serving in the Revolution. Following the war, most of the family moved to Georgia, building "Sparks Fort" as protection against the Creeks. Matthew left the fort one morning to hunt turkey; that's when he was killed.

Kent Sparks, about 1920.

Jesse Sparks was one of Matthew's sons who settled in Hickman County, along with his wife, Elizabeth. They had ten children, including Jesse, Jr., who married Mary Patterson, and lived on Lick Creek in Perry County, along with his sister, Ann, who never married. (Jesse Sr. went on to remarry and have seven more children!) Jesse, Jr., was a slave-owner who, by the time of the War Between the States, had freed his three slaves. He was too old to fight in the war, and was rumored to have buried his money on his land. Tradition says that a group of marauders threatened to hang Jesse if he didn't reveal the location of his money, but Ann and the freed slaves created such a commotion shouting and banging on pans that the men moved on. Jesse, Jr. and Mary had but one son, Jesse born in 1860. In 1887, he married Minerva Ledbetter (born in 1869), daughter of prominent Perry Countian, Reverend H. McKendree Ledbetter, who served in the Tennessee State Senate. Jesse continued to farm his family's lands on Lick Creek, but was also involved in banking and served in the Tennessee State House. Minerva and Jesse had two children, Kent, born in 1888 and Amma, born in 1890. Amma would attend Ward's Seminary in Nashville and marry D. E. Starbuck in 1909. She died in 1920 during the birth of their second child, who was raised by his grandmother, Minerva Sparks, and named Jesse (Buddy) Sparks III. Buddy attended Athens College in Alabama and farmed with his Uncle Kent, spending most of his life on Lick Creek.

Kent graduated from Branham and Hughes Military Academy and Cumberland Law School. He returned to Perry County to practice law and serve as postmaster and newspaper editor. During this time he met a new school teacher, Bess Edwards; they were married in 1913. Their children Elizabeth and Jessie Eugenia grew up to be teachers as well—Elizabeth taught in Perry County for 38 years.

After his father died, Kent returned to his first love—farming and farmed on Lick Creek for the rest of his life. He also followed his father and grandfather into politics, serving one term in the Tennessee State House and 36 years on the Perry County Court. His granddaughters Elizabeth and Sara Walker (from Jessie's marriage to David Walker of Perry County) have also been involved in politics, working for members of the United States Senate. Kent was active in the Methodist Church and the Farm Bureau, and was a 50-year Mason. He passed away in 1966, followed by his wife Bess in 1973. They are both buried in Kirk Cemetery.

ROBERT LONG SPENCER, born Sept. 13, 1934, in Perry County, son of Robert Phillip and Louise Long Spencer married Linda Faye Coble, born June 1, 1940 in Lobelville, daughter of Albert William "Bear" and Helen Marrs Coble were married Dec. 19, 1955, they had five children.

Robert L. and Linda Spencer with their children: Bobby, Susan, and Billy.

Robert Keith "Bobby" born Oct. 8, 1956. He had three sons; Keith, born Aug. 22, 1977; Kevin, born Jan. 17, 1982; and Kaleb, born Oct. 8, 1987. Sandra Kaye and Sheryl Faye, twins were born Sept. 14, 1957, and lived seven hours.

Helen Louise, born July 1, 1958, was stillborn. Susan Lynn, born Oct. 7, 1960. She had two daughters and one son: Heather Lynn Lineberry, born Aug. 5, 1977; Jennifer Renee Lineberry, born Nov. 17, 1980; and Phillip Thomas Hickerson, born March 9, 1990.

W. R. (Bob) and Johnnie Spencer.

William Phillip "Billy" born July 23, 1973. Robert is the great great grandson of Thomas Sharpe Spencer, born in Humphreys County. His father was Thomas Sharpe Spencer II, born in Humphreys County (1844-1910), married Ella Branch (1850-1931). He volunteered in the Civil War at age 16. Being too young to serve as a soldier, he served as aide to the troops. They had 11 children. Thomas Sharpe III, Margaret, Marvin, George, Carrie, Paul, Arthur, Ruth, and two died in infancy.

Robert's grandparents were William Robert "Bob" (March 26, 1880-1965) and Johnnie Pearl McAlister (1885-1979), both were born in Decatur County and married in 1905. Her parents were John W. and Sarah Anderson McAlister. They had ten children.

John Thomas married Cordie Sims; Sarah Alice, married Eddie Usry. Their children were Ray and Dorothy. Margaret Irene married O. E. Baugus. Their children were Billy Jo and Betty; Robert Phillip married Louise Long. Their son was Robert Long Spencer; Prince Ivey married Ronald Bawcum. Their children were James Robert and Thomas; William George had no children; King David married Evonne Wheeler. Their children were Joy, Aaron, and Bryan; Bernice Earline married James Martin. Their child was Gerald Dean. After James Martin's death, she married Roy Garber; Myrtle Laverne married Earl Odle; Frances Lunell married Charles Dodd. Their child was Deborah. France' second marriage was to Myron Culpper. Their children were David, Betty, and Terry.

Robert's grandfather was Robert "Bob," who was a farmer and timber man. His father was Philip "Tip" who worked as a cross tie inspector for the Koppers Company and later supervisor. All were members of the Church of Christ and Democrats.

Descendant of "Big Foot" Thomas Sharpe Spencer, an early settler from North Carolina, who first settled in the area of Castilian Springs, TN. He is documented in the histories of Summer and Davidson counties. He was ambushed and killed by Indians while crossing the Cumberland Plateau on his way back to North Carolina. *Submitted by Robert Long Spencer.*

JOHN ROBERT STAFFORD, was born and raised in Madison County, Jackson, TN. At the age of 24, he met Deborah Jan Clifton who was born and raised in Perry County, near Flatwoods, TN. They were married Nov. 2, 1974, and moved to Perry County the following year. Jan's father, George Aaron Clifton, owned a farm in the southern part of the county, on Farmers Valley Road. John and Jan purchased a mobile home and lived on the farm near her parents the first ten years of their marriage.

John and Jan Stafford have two daughters; Deborah Jean, born Feb. 20, 1976, and Rhonda Kay, born Feb. 20, 1980.

When John and Jan moved to Perry County, he started working at a local automotive plant, Linden Products, which is now called Johnson Controls. At present, Johnny has worked with this company for 20 years.

In 1986, the Cliftons deeded a portion of land a short distance from where John and Jan had lived for them to build a house. They still live in their house on the Clifton Farm.

DANIEL STARBUCK, born March 9, 1799, in Guildford County, NC, came to Perry County around 1823 and purchased land on Cypress Creek. He had married Elizabeth Beeson on Aug. 22, 1822, and soon after moved to Tennessee. Their three children Austin, born Aug. 21, 1823, died October 1823, Erastus, born Oct. 8, 1824, and Darius born June 5, 1826, and was the first person to be buried in a marked grave in the Sutton Cemetery. After the death of Elizabeth, Daniel married Nancy Shelton on March 10, 1831, and this couple had 11 children.

In 1852, Daniel, a carpenter and farmer, moved his family to Missouri where he died on Sept. 28, 1870.

The elder son, Erastus, stayed in Perry County and on Dec. 6, 1847, married Mary Ann Burcham, born May 22, 1828, the daughter of William and Mary Garrett Burcham. The couple had six children: William born 1848, Daniel born July 26, 1850, Elizabeth born 1853, Thomas born 1855, Darius born 1858, and Mary born 1861. Erastus, a farmer, enlisted in Company E, 6th Regiment of Tennessee Cavalry on September 18 at Bethel, TN. He died on Jan. 8, 1863, at Bolivar, TN.

Daniel Starbuck

Daniel Starbuck, who was named for his grandfather, married Eugenia Journey, the daughter of Fielding and Sarah Harris Journey, on Sept. 11, 1879. Eugenia, born May 18, 1858, whose mother died when she was very young, was raised by her maternal grandfather, David Rice Harris, who gave the land for the establishment of the town of Linden.

The children of Daniel and Eugenia Starbuck were: Ethel Elizabeth, born July 14, 1880, Mary Addie, born 1882, Bessie Rilda born 1884, Johnnie McCall, born 1886, Samuel Hawkins, born 1888, Daniel Eugene, born 1891, and Martha Lena born 1895. Daniel was a farmer, lumberman and served as president of the Perry County Bank. Eugenia Starbuck died July 29, 1901, and Daniel died May 12, 1906.

Ethel Elizabeth Starbuck, the oldest child, married E. J. Ayers born Nov. 9, 1872. The couple married on Oct. 25, 1887, at the family home on Cypress Creek. E. J. Ayers, the son of W. H. and Nancy McMillon, was a farmer and lumberman who moved to Perry County from Giles County, as a young man. To Ethel and E. J. Ayers, the following children were born: Frances Ruth, birth date Aug. 5, 1898; Daniel Earl, birth date Jan. 6, 1900, died Oct. 3, 1902; James Paul, birth date Jan. 7, 1905, died Aug. 14, 1968; Lena Ethel, birth date Aug. 22, 1907, died April 9, 1994; Dick Donald, birth date Dec. 30, 1912, died Dec. 25, 1993.

Ruth Ayers married Jesse David Pope on May 5, 1918, and had three children: an infant who died at birth, Don Ayers, who married Virginia Duncan, and Jessie Ruth, who married Billy Tiller.

Paul Ayers married Wilma Jennings Durham and had the following children: James Wesley, Jo Ann, and Billy Ralph, a son by Wilma's former marriage.

Ethel married Jack Wilburn and had one child, Jean. Dick married Kathleen Wyatt and had no children.

The Starbuck line of Perry County descended from Edward Starbuck, who settled on Nantucket Island about 1659. The land purchased by Daniel Starbuck when he came to Perry County in 1823 remains in the family to the present time.

JACOB THEODORE STAYROOK, (1911-) married Ione Carmichael (1912-1974) moved to Perry County in 1962 from Lewis County. They built a home and a commercial business on Crooked Creek known as Crooked Creek Marina. They operated this business until 1971 at which time they built another home on Toms Creek near Britts Landing. Ione attended the Methodist Church in Lobelville during this time. After Ione's death Jake moved to the head of Crooked Creek and then away from Perry County.

Jake's people are from Pennsylvania where distant cousins still belong to the Mennonite Church. Jake's genealogy can be found in *The Hertzler-Hartzler Family* by Silas Hertzler, 1952. The Stayrook family is also reference in *Mifflin County Amish and Mennonite Story 1791-1991* by S. Duane Kauffman. Jake's distant cousin, S. Ruth Stayrook has brought her tree forward from Nicholas Stayrook (1842-1903) and Mary Plank (1843-1906) to present. She has published *Family Record of Nicholas Stayrook and Mary (Plank) Stayrook and their Descendants*, 1970. Nicholas was a brother of Jacob, grandfather of Jake who lived in Perry County.

Ione (Carmichael) Stayrook was from Alabama. She was orphaned at a young age and was partly raised by an aunt and uncle by the last name of McFerson in Lawrence County, TN, but she moved back to Birmingham before reaching adulthood. Ione and her youngest brother James Albert Carmichael (1916-1976) are buried at Northern Cemetery on Crooked Creek. Albert lived in the Crooked Creek community for several years after retiring with 30 years service in the U. S. Air Force.

The son of Ione and Jake is James Theodore (1942-) married Christine (Raymer) (1943-) from Lewis County. James had completed school and left home before his parents came to Perry County. James and Christine lived several places in Perry County before making their home on Cane Creek. They resided there for 13 plus years at which time James was transferred by Tenneco to Kentucky.

The eldest son of James and Christine is James Thomas (1961-). He was born at Perry County Hospital in Linden. Tommy attended Perry County schools and graduated from Perry County High School in 1980. He completed Auto Diesel School in Nashville and now operates "Tommy's Market and Tire Center, Inc." in Lyles, TN. Tommy married Lisa A. Westbrooks (1963) from DePriest Bend. They have one child, Melissa Dawn (1993-).

The younger son of James and Christine is Michael Anthony (1967-). Michael graduated from Perry County High School in 1985 and obtained his B.S. Degree from Tennessee Technological University in Cookeville in 1991. Michael is currently employed by Yamakaya in Portland, TN.

The daughter of Ione and Jake is Ione Elizabeth (Stayrook) DePriest (1945-) married John Vernon DePriest (1945-). Elizabeth was Valedictorian of the last class to graduate from Lobelville High School in 1963. She graduated with honors from Baptist Hospital School of Nursing in Nashville in 1966. She became a Certified Occupational Health Nurse in 1981 and obtained a S.S. Degree from St. Francis University, Joliet, IL, in 1990. She became a Certified Case Manager in 1993. Elizabeth has been employed by Oscar Meyer Foods in Goodlettsville, TN, for 20 plus years.

Elizabeth and John have two children, Reneé and William. See also DePriest, John Vernon.

STEELE, The Steeles came from England and settled in North Carolina near the state line of Virginia. When the first settlers came to settle in Tennessee the family of Abraham Steele, who married Nancy McDaniel, started a home in Tennessee in Blount County, near Old Waters Mill which is near Hubbard Station, now erected. They came from Buncombe County, NC (Asheville) sometime after 1830.

Gus Allen Steele and Bobbie Tatum Steele, 1990.

To this union was born John Wesley Steele (nickname "Bouncer") (Sept. 9, 1821 to July 4, 1896), who married Elizabeth Hedrick (May 5, 1829 to April 15, 1903) of Monroe County, TN. From this union came Marady Franklin Steele (nickname "Bud") (Oct. 18, 1856 to Sept. 6, 1918), wife Martha Moser Steele (1855-1884). To this union was born Gus Columbus Steele (Feb. 26, 1875 to July 29, 1931). He married Loy Melson Steele (Oct. 5, 1873 to April 18, 1947) of Blount County. From this union came Lesley Auston Steele, (June 14, 1902) who married Medley Allen Stiles Steele (Oct. 27, 1899 to July 13, 1935). Her parents were Dr. Allen Fletcher Stiles, M.D. (March 12, 1879 to Dec. 29, 1932) Estalee Walker Stiles (Oct. 6, 1877 to June 26, 1952) of Robinsville, NC. The only child born to this union was Gus Allen Steele (March 27, 1932) in Robinsville, NC.

Marady Franklin Steele (Bud), and Martha Moser Steele, late 1800s.

After the death of Gus Steele's mother (1935) he moved to Blount County, TN, where he lived with his grandmother Loy Melson Steele. He attended Lanier Elementary and High School, and lettered in football and baseball. After graduation from high school he was employed with the State of Tennessee as a Trooper for the Department of Safety. In 1958 he was transferred to Perry County. In 1984 he retired after 30 years of service with the Department. In 1964 he married the former Bobbie Jane Tatum who was born and reared on Sinking Creek in Perry County. After graduation from Linden High School where she lettered in basketball, she was employed by First State Bank in Linden, TN, where she is presently employed. Her grandparents—Lev and Elizabeth Anderson Tatum and Theodore and Mary Jane Ary Grinder.

Front row: Gus Columbus Steele, Lesley Auston Steele and Myrtle Meloy Steele; Second Row: Addie Belle Steele, Lillian Steele, Elmer Walker, Grace Lee Walker, and Eulice Steele. Photo taken at the old Spring House, 1910.

Gus and Bobbie live at 108 Riverside Drive, Linden, TN. No children to this union. *Submitted by Bobbie T. Steele.*

CALVIN ASHLEY STEPHENS, was born Feb. 15, 1892, at Brush Creek, Perry County. He died April 25, 1946, and is buried in the Stephens Cemetery on Brush Creek. Married first to Mary Marshlean McCalister, born Sept. 16, 1887, died Nov. 9, 1913, buried in Stephens Cemetery. Marshlean has one child Nancy Lucille Stephens born July 2, 1913, married John Smith. Ashley married secondly to Mamie Elizabeth James born Jan. 22, 1899, died March 26, 1932. Their children were: (1) John William Sanders Stephens born Oct. 29, 1915, married March 19, 1938, to Bessie Adell Wood born Jan. 14, 1922. She died Sept. 25, 1979, and is buried in Stephens Cemetery. (2) Noah Raymond Hardy Stephens born Jan. 31, 1917, died Feb. 14, 1918. (3) Sallie Juretta Isabel Stephens born Nov. 22, 1918, married Cliford McDonald. (4) James David Stephens born Aug. 8, 1920, married Lorene Jones. (5) Julie Janie Marshlean Stephens born June 1, 1922, married Woodrow Hensley. (6) J. B. Stephens born Feb. 14, 1924, married Ludene Reeves. (7) Ezra Ray Stephens born March 6, 1926, married Mable Hinson. (8) Nettie May Estell Stephens born Dec. 8, 1927, married Merner McClearen. (9) Zula Viola Stephens born Jan. 3, 1930, married George Branum. Ashley Stephens married the third time to Nora Jane Goforth, born Aug. 12, 1909, died Oct. 19, 1968. Their children were: (1) Ola Mae Stephens born Oct. 5, 1934, married Ray Ward. (2) Sarah Fredia Irene Stephens born July 10, 1938, married Ray Talley. (3) Jimmie Riley Ruffin Stephens born March 16, 1942, died July 1, 1971, married Ludene Whitworth born Aug. 21, 1944. (4) Horace Wayne Stephens born Aug. 3, 1946, married Margaret Spears.

A picture of the old Stephens house. It was later moved and used as a barn.

In the olden days, the main income to support this large family came from farming and making wood chairs with only White Oak splits as bottoms, Hickory rounds and backs with Maple posts front and back. Ahsley made these Maple chairs for 24 years with the price being $1.00 per chair. The largest amount he ever received was #25.00 for a set of six chairs.

Formerly known as Stephens Town, the Stephens farm and cemetery passed into the hands of Calvin Ashley Stephens and now to Ahsley's son John W. Stephens. He swears that he is going to hang on to it as long as he lives. John W. Stephens, who lives in Linden, TN, said that he had the occasion to take apart the family home which was a log cabin and move it across Brush Creek to use as a barn. There was a school in Stephens Town. Ollie Qualls was the first teacher to our memory around 1923. She was Clay Qualls' daughter.

John William Stephens married Bessie Adell Wood on March 19, 1938, died Sept. 25, 1979, born to this marriage were three daughters: (1) Mamie Sue Stephens DePriest, (2) Bessie Louise Stephens Duncan, (3) Joyce Ann Stephens Marshall, three granddaughters, three grandsons, three great grandsons, and two great granddaughters. John W. Stephens and Wilma Coleman Moore were married April 3, 1981.

STEPHENS, Essie Stephens Pinegar heard much about Perry County during her early years from her parents, James Jasper and Serena Catherine Stephens. In 1979, she went to see for herself what Perry County was like and why the Stephenses put down roots there.

James Jasper Stephens and Serena Catherine Stephens with children: Sparlin, Evert and Dealie, 1906

She learned that James Calvin Stephens, born 1802, and Mary Manier, born 1806, with their six children came from Caswell County, NC and settled on Brush Creek in 1847. The land is still owned by Stephenses, including the Stephens Cemetery. There James and his descendants lay, some in unmarked graves.

At this time, Mary's father is unknown and her mother was Nancy B. Her grandmother was Mary Fonvielle Green. They were French and lived in Warren County, NC.

Nothing is known about Caroline, Silly M. and Amanda, daughters of James and Mary. A story about James K. Polk said he walked into the woods and was never seen again. Mary Margaret married Columbus Bryson. Many of their descendants live in Perry County.

Essie descended from Ruffin Sanders, who married Nancy Ann Barber, daughter of Allen and Martha Kilpatrick Barber. Martha's parents, Andrew and Martha Kilpatrick, came to Perry County about 1820.

Out of Ruffin and Nancy's 11 children, five grew to adulthood. The three youngest were Andrew Taylor, John Alex and Samuel Ruffin. The two oldest, James Allen and Joseph Calvin, were Essie's direct ancestors.

James, born 1853, and Eliza McDonald, born 1840, married in 1872. Her parents, George and Mary Yearn McDonald were Irish. James farmed and was a licensed doctor. They had three daughters, Mary Anner, Nancy Jane and Serena Catherine, mother of Essie.

Joseph Calvin, born 1856, married in 1877 to Rachel Evaline Hinson, born 1857. Her parents were Elijah and Evaline Davidson Hinson, Scotch-Irish and German. Out of ten children, two daughters, Frances and Margaret, and then six sons, James Jasper, Lee, Arch, Siah, Milton and Egbert lived to adulthood. Sarrah and Macklin died in infancy. James Jasper was Essie's father.

James Jasper and Serena Catherine, first cousins, married in 1898. Their first four children, Sparlin, Nancy, Evert and Dealie were born in Linden. Nancy died when two months old.

Like earlier Stephenses, they moved West— West Tennessee! Here Freeman, Fritz L., Woodrow, Essie and Henry were born. Between Freeman and Fritz L. was Clyde, who was born in Missouri.

In 1927, James along with Catherine and their children, except Evert who was married, moved to Arkansas. There he farmed and was a merchant, as he had been in Tennessee. They reared their children in White County where they all married, except Dealie. She married in Missouri.

Essie, a true Stephens, moved west also, to Porterville, CA. She has a daughter and two sons to whom have passed the stories of the early days of Perry County. When Essie and her daughter, Millie visited Perry County, they were profoundly affected by the thought of being able to walk where their ancestors had trod and drink from the spring where they had drunk. The wild roses blooming in the fence row, the beauty and tranquillity of the Brush Creek area helped them to see why the Stephenses put down roots in Perry County.

STEPHENS (STEVENS), John J. Stephens settled in the Third Civil District of Perry County, in 1877. He was born in Fayette County, TN on May 15, 1842. He and a twin sister, Thursday Rebecca, were the youngest children of John Haywood and Frances McCulley Stephens. His grandfather, William, moved the family from Johnston County, NC in 1830, where the Stephens family had resided since 1741 and were cotton planters.

John J. Stephens and Mattie V. Denton Hickerson

John J. Stephens and two older brothers fought for the South during the Civil War. All three survived, but John J. was wounded twice. After the war, he returned to Fayette County and married Cordelia Tatum. They had two sons, Thomas William Stephens, Nov. 15, 1866 (his line spells it "Stevens"), and G.G. (Garra) Stephens, Sept. 18, 1868. Cordelia died Jan. 19, 1876 during childbirth and Garra died June 25, 1877. They are buried at Mt. Pleasant Cemetery in Hickory Withe, TN.

John J. and son, Thomas, moved to Perry County shortly after his younger son's death. In 1878 he married Phalisie Ann Coleman, daughter of Abner Coleman, ex-sheriff and commissioner of Perry County. They had three children: William Forrest (Nov. 11, 1879), Mary Cordelia (1884) and Charles Coleman (Aug. 12, 1890).

John J. Stephens' children married and had children as follows. Thomas W. married Annie Quarles and sired Essie, Jack, Ike, Guy, Joe, Newt, Creola, Billy, Mary and Brownie Stevens. Tom Stevens died Aug. 22, 1942, and is buried in Bethel Methodist Church Cemetery in Perry County.

William F. Stephens married Kitty Viola Grimes, and sired John H., George L. and Kittie Mae Stephens. Will Stephens died Aug. 17, 1945, and is buried in the Mineral Springs Cemetery, in Howard County, AR.

Mary Cordelia Stephens married Andrew Polk Denton. Their children were Eula Mae, Lessie, Arka D., Joe V., Jeanetta P. Mary Love and Mattie V. Delia died in 1964, and is buried in the Denton Cemetery on Cedar Creek.

Charles Coleman Stephens married Georgie Pearl Grimes, and sired one daughter, Eugenia. Charles Stephens died June 23, 1962 and is buried in the Mineral Springs Cemetery.

John J. Stephens died Feb. 23, 1938, at age 95. He is buried in the Bethel Methodist Church Cemetery in Perry County. His tombstone indicates he served in the 8th Regt. Tennessee Inf. during the Civil War. Actually, he began the war in C Co. of 38th Regt. Tennessee Inf. which was raised in Fayette County, just prior to the battle of Shiloh. This regiment was mistakenly called the 8th throughout the war. On July 15, 1863, he and an older brother joined B Co. of the 16 Tennessee Cavalry. He finished the war in the cavalry under Gen. Forrest. He was wounded twice and carried a minie' ball embedded in his leg to his grave

MERLE STEVENS, I was born March 8, 1945, Abilene, TX. My maternal great grandparents, John Morris and Priscilla Angeline Sharp moved to Texas in the mid 1880s. For the most part, my direct lines lived Swan Creek, Hickman County. I have had relatives live in Perry County, since the 1830s. Other family members have been in and out of Perry County as well. My second great grandfather, Green G. Sharp, married his third wife in Perry County, Sept. 17, 1896, Virginia Catherine Freeman. His son, John T. "Tobe" Sharp, born 1865, Hickman County, per family, "moved west". I suspect this is the Tobe Sharp who married Aug. 30, 1885, Perry County, Eliza Armstrong. A brother, George Washington Sharp lived briefly in Perry County. Another brother, William Sharp, married 1848 a Perry County girl, Catherine DePriest. A nephew, Willis Monroe Sharp lived Perry County before moving to Gibson County.

Adults: Green Garner and wife, Sarah Barham, and her mother, Margaret Shephard Barham. Children: (not in order) Arthur, Edd, Hattie and Roxie Garner.

An uncle, Elias Greenville Clayton and family were in Perry County, 1880, before moving to Texas. A cousin, Matthew Clayton, son of John Clayton, lived in Perry County, 1870s.

Other cousins to live in Perry County, Nehemiah Vincent and wife, Lucinda Pugh, 1860. James C. Sharp and wife, Sophie Caroline Churchwell, 1850, before moving to Arkansas. Levi Sharp, died Civil War, his widow, Mary Jane Thompson, married second, Oct. 17, 1871, Perry County, Dr. Joseph Evans Martin. Three of Levi Sharp's children married in Perry County, before moving to Obion County.

More cousins to live in Perry County from time to time. James Spencer Sisco, married 1869, Perry County, Sarah Elizabeth Sharp. Alonzo Leonidas Sisco married 1887, Perry County, Sallie Marvin.

Others, Margaret Fedelia Smith married Pitts Brashear Graves, Dec. 24, 1891, Perry County. There are others as well.

For years I have researched these families. I am sure I have made mistakes. A lot of my information comes from others and their mistakes become mine. There are still a lot of lost relatives as well.

I will be more than happy to share what I have. My address in 1707 3rd, Brownwood, TX 76801 and should be for a long time, unless I win the Texas LOTTO.

The picture with my story, Garner and Barham, is not related to me. I copied the picture in Abilene, TX from a Perry County cousin and wanted to share it. Submitted by Merle Stevens.

AARON JAMES "DOCK" STEWART,

was the second son and the sixth child of Sampson and Beadie Prater-Stewart (See STEWART, Sampson history). "Dock" was born in April 1847 on Tumbling Creek in Humphreys County. By 1845, Dock's father, Sampson sold off his tract of land and had purchased from his uncle Lindley Box, a 270 acre farm on Garner's Creek in Dickson County, just over the Humphreys-Dickson line and a short distance north of the Hickman County line where he and his family are found in the 1850 census. When Beadie died in 1854, Sampson sold his farm and relocated with his four sons: Abraham B. "Abe" (1845-1863), Aaron James "Dock" (1847-1913), Thomas Lindley "Tom" (1850-1923) and William Monroe (1852-1906) to Mississippi where his brother Abraham had moved to in 1838. Sampson's daughters, Catherine "Kitty" b. 1836, Mary A. (1838-1881), Martha Jane "Janie" (1840-1890) and Sarah "Puss" (1842-1899) had married by this time and remained in the Perry and Humphreys County area. In 1858, Sampson purchased a 270 acre farm in Tippah County, MS. Sampson followed his step-father's lead and had all four of sons names placed on the title. During the War Between the States, Sampson's sons, Abraham and Dock joined Confederate forces. Abraham B. "Abe" (1845-1863), joined the First Mississippi Partisan Rangers (Mounted Cavalry), while Aaron James "Dock" (1847-1913) as a 14 year old boy joins the 41st Tennessee Infantry Company C. Abe was mortally wounded in the Battle at Wyatte, MS on Oct. 13, 1863 while serving with the First Mississippi Partisan Rangers. He was brought home where he died and was buried on the family farm. Aaron James "Dock" (1847-1913) while with 41st Tn. Inf. Co. C. at the battle of Fort Donelson (1862), was captured, interned at Camp Butler, near Springfield, IL and held there until the Cartel of prisoner exchange, where Dock was released at Vicksburg, MS (Sept. 23, 1863).

By the late 1860s, Sampson was forced to lose his farm to taxes and financial burdens. Sampson and his four sons return to the Perry County area after a ten year absence. Dock came to live with his sisters, who were living in the Perry County area. There he met Parthena Baker. Dock and Parthena were married March 4, 1868, Perry County. In the 1870 census, Aaron James "Dock" had married Parthena Baker (1850-1923) and they were living next to her parents Ezekial and Nancy Blackwell-Baker. Sometime after 1880, Dock and Parthena moved their family to the Humphreys County area near Bakerville, in an area known as "Chalk Hollow." Dock is noted in the Bakerville Review paper in the early 1900s for his hunting and taking many a plump turkey. Dock farmed in this area all his life and is thought to have died in January of 1913. Dock is buried in the Fowlkes Cemetery at Bakerville. His son, George F. Stewart, is the only family member known buried with him and is placed beside him. Dock's grave which was unmarked until 1986, when a Veterans CSA marker was obtained and placed on the grave by Monroe Stewart of Monroe, LA. John Edmison. Mrs. Parthena Baker-Stewart's final years were spent with her daughter, Anna Elizabeth (Mrs. John Edmison). Parthena is buried in the Mt. Zion Cemetery near Woodland Mills, TN.

Dock and Parthena raised a family of ten children: (1) Joseph E. "Joe," born Feb. 7, 1869, P. Co. - Dec. 31, 1947, married Mollie A. Owens, July 26, 1890. (2) Martha Jane "Mattie," Oct. 4, 1871-Nov. 2, 1947, married Charles D. Moseley, Oct. 4, 1903. (3) Mary Louise "Boodie," March 9, 1877-Sept. 25, 1946, married Rufus "Rufe" Burcham, May 27, 1903. (4) William Thomas "Will," Dec. 6, 1878-Nov. 11, 1960, married first Sophia Wherry; second Hettie Ann Conatser. (5) George F., June 14, 1880-June 20, 1908. (6) John Dee "Dee," Jan. 24, 1883 - March 22, 1962, married Ada Younger, Dec. 27, 1904, daughter of John "Jack" and Paralee Thornton-Younger, (7) Nancy Mabelle "Mabel," March 30, 1884-March 12, 1945, married Ed Shaver, Feb. 12, 1901. (8) James Elmer, April 7, 1887 - Dec. 9, 1969, married first Velma; second Claytie Ingram. (9) Emma Sade, January 1890, married Wes Merrell. (10) Anna Elizabeth "Annie," June 7, 1892-Oct. 29, 1980, married John Ether Edmison.

Dock's son, John Dee Stewart moved to Obion County in 1913. There John Dee spent his entire life as a farmer and died in the home of his son, Clifford Stewart, of the Fremont Community near Union City. John Dee and his wife, Ada, died June 24, 1949, are buried in the Fremont Cemetery near Union City.

Clifford Stewart, Sept. 19, 1904-Sept. 11, 1981, was the only child of Dee and Ada Stewart. Clifford married Feb. 22, 1930, Alma Robinson, died April 11, 1982. Clifford and Alma were members of the Fremont Church of Christ where they are buried.

Bobby Glenn Stewart, born Aug. 30, 1937, is the only child of Clifford and Alma Robinson-Stewart and grew up in the Dixie Community near Union City, where he graduated from the Dixie High School. He graduated from the Freed-Hardeman College, David Lipscomb College, George Peabody College and Murray State University. Bobby is a minister of the Church of Christ as well as a school teacher. Bobby has been a minister since 1955 and has taught for 34 years in the Fulton County schools. Bobby married Evonne Brewer, daughter of Doyle and Gladys Brewer. Bobby and Evonne reside in Troy, TN. *Submitted by Bobby Stewart, Troy, Tennessee.*

DORSEY B. THOMAS "DOSS" STEWART,

(Dec. 23, 1876, P Co. District 8-Oct. 20, 1940, Buffalo, Hu. Co.) was the fourth child of ten born to Thomas Lindley "Tom" and Sarah Jane Elizabeth O'Guin-Stewart (See Stewart, Tom history). Shortly after Doss's birth, the family moved from District 8, Perry County to the Buffalo, Humphreys County area. By 1899, the family was reported in the Bakersville Review as moving from the Robert's Creek area to Pruitt Springs area, just north of the Perry County line. In Feb. of 1899, Doss married Martha Elizabeth "Mattie" Shaw (Oct. 1882 - June 3, 1936), daughter of Robert and Sallie Murry-Shaw. The couple was married at the bride's home. On Oct. 9, 1903, the Bakerville Review reported Doss and Mollie living at Grassy Branch near Buffalo, TN.

Martha Elizabeth "Mattie" Shaw Stewart with children: Claytie, Buddie and daughter Earlie. Photograph circa 1905. Also Dorsey B. Thomas "Doss" Stewart. Photograph circa 1920s.

Doss and Mollie raised a family of eight children with seven reaching maturity. Their children are as follows: (1) Earlie B. 1901, married Tom Merideth. (2) Claytie born Sept. 1903. (3) Buddie Clayton married Mary Merideth. (4) Etta born 1907, married Bud Warren. (5) Hillman born July 1910, married La Verne Vaughn of Kentucky. (6) John Walter "Whiz" born Sept. 11, 1912, married Jewell Warren, buried James Cemetery, Buffalo, TN. (7) Elton (Oct. 19, 1914-1929) (8) Henry born Nov. 30, 1922, married May 26, 1945 Lorraine Dyer.

Claytie Stewart remembers the family's kerosene burning refrigerator. This refrigerator was purchased sometime during the 1940s and replaced an old ice storage box. Ice was hard to come by as it had to be brought from town (Waverly). Claytie also remembers that sliced loaf bread was a special commodity which was only purchased on special occasions such as the annual foot washing services which was a three day event at the Primitive Baptist Church, Buf-

Parthena Baker-Stewart and Nancy Maybell Stewart-Shaver, circa 1915; and John "Dee" Stewart, son of Aaron James "Dock" Stewart.

falo, TN. "Store Bought Sliced Bread" had to be ordered in advance from the local general store in Buffalo. People from outside the area, who were attending the "Foot Washing Services" were brought to the local homes of the church members and had dinner. Claytie remembers that the children had to wait last as sometime there wasn't much food left.

Doss and Mattie are buried in the Bone Springs Cemetery, Old Hwy 13, just south of Pruitt Springs and north of the Perry County Line.

ELISHA STEWART, (1795, VA-circa 1825, P Co. TN) and his brother, Bartholomew Grayson Stewart (Jan. 5, 1786, VA-April 29, 1849, Ma. Co., TN) came to Perry County sometime in 1819 and prior to the 1820 census. Their residence in Perry County is unknown as no deeds are recorded until 1823 when the General Assembly of the state of Tennessee passed a law allowing homestead recognition and allowed the residents of the property that they resided on to pay 12 1/2 cents per acre. (See Stewart, William Sr. history.)

Elisha Stewart married (circa 1815, Hi. Co., TN) Mary "Polly" Box, daughter of Abraham Box and Catherine Lindley-Box of Tumbling Creek, Humphreys County. Their marriage produced four sons: (1) Abraham B. (1815, Hi. Co. - 1863, Tp. Co., MS) married Elizabeth Evins (Dickson County). (2) Sampson (1818, Hi. Co.-circa 1883 P Co.) married Beadie Prater (Dickson County), daughter of John and Ailey Prater. (3) Lindley (1820-1888) married Betty Sanders; second Eliza Beasley (both marriages produced 22 children). (4) Robert Elisha, born 1825, married Huldah C. Hobbs. By 1825 Elisha had deceased and his widow Mary "Polly" Box-Stewart moved the family back to Hickman County on Garner's Creek near her father-in-law, William Stewart Sr. After 1830, Mary "Polly" Box-Stewart married her second husband, William Spicer. On Nov. 17, 1838, William Spicer, of Humphreys County distributed to his wife Mary (Box-Stewart) Spicer, Abraham Stewart, Sampson Stewart, Lindley Stewart and Robert Stewart tracts of land along Tumbling Creek, Humphreys County, TN.

Lindley remained in Humphreys County until his death while brothers Abraham (1843-157 acres), Robert E. (1856-50 acres) and Sampson Stewart (1858-270 acres) ventured to Tippah County, MS. After the Civil War in the late 1860s, Sampson lost his farm to taxes and declining finances forced him and his sons, Arron James "Dock" (1847-1913), Thomas Lindley "Tom" (1850-1923) and William Monroe (1852-1906) to return to the Perry County area to live with sisters Sarah "Puss" Stewart-Smith (1842-1899), Mary Jane Stewart-Crowell (1840-1890) and Mary Ann Stewart-Baker (1838-1881). (See Stewart, Sampson history.)

Then Elisha came with his father to Hickman County, where his father, William Stewart Sr. (1756, VA-1833, Ma. Co., TN) had purchased (Oct. 1809) 200 acres on Garner's Creek from Robert Weakley, Speaker of the House of Representatives, State of Tennessee and land speculator. The year 1809 on Garner's Creek was the last year noted for Indian raids into the Hickman County area. Elisha and his brothers B. G. Stewart, Andrew and William Jr. are noted (Sept. 11, 1812) as petitioners of the 36th Regiment & 6th Brigade of the Tennessee Militia requesting the General Assembly of the State of Tennessee, allow them to wear their own uniforms (homespun).

Elisha's father, William Stewart Sr. (1756, VA-1833, Ma. Co., TN) was a revolutionary war veteran as noted in an application for a pension (Rev. War Pension #S-39097) in Madison County (1825). (See Stewart, William Sr. histories.) Submitted by Morris Monroe Stewart, 111 Masonic St., Monroe, LA.

HAROLD ELTON "JACK" STEWART, (1917) and Virginia Ellen Igleheart (1922) presently are retired and reside in Hermitage, TN and Clearwater, FL. They resided (1955-1988) in Mt. Juliet, TN at the "Clear View" farm where Jack operated his real estate business and developed the first subdivision in the area known as The Clearview Estates. Jack and Virginia have two children Larry Douglas (1947) and Shirley Ann (1950) who have given them a total of eight granddaughters and one great grandson. Larry is married (1986) to Harriet Weglarz-Stewart, daughter of Stanley Valentine Weglarz and Marilyn Terese Szymkowski. They reside at the old homeplace in Mt. Juliet, where they are keeping herd on five girls; Marie Celeste (1979), Amanda Lenore (1986), Laura Elizabeth (1988), Emily Virginia (1990) and Claire Noel (1991). Additionally, Larry has one daughter by a previous marriage, Vanessa Ann (1971), who is married (1991) to Mr. Geoffrey Bridge (1953), son of William Richard Bridge and Alta Louise Payne-Bridge. They have one child, Zachary Evan (1992) and are expecting another in July 1994. Geof and Vanessa Bridge reside with their family in Selma, TN.

Jack and Virginia Stewart Family and Grandchildren. Back Row: Harold E. "Jack," Virginia E., Larry D., Harriet, Shirley and Allan. Front Row: Claire, Kerry, Amanda, Emily, Erin, Marie and Laura.

Shirley is married to Mr. Allan Gardner Scully (1947), son of Ross Harold and Lois Virginia Gardner-Scully. They have two daughters, Keri Ann (1976) and Erin Valerie (1979). They presently reside in Hockessin, DE, which is outside of Wilmington, DE. Jack and Virginia Ellen (Igleheart) have been married 50 years this past January 15. They were married in Evansville, IN in 1944 while he was a welder at the Evansville Ship Yards building L.S.T. Troop landing crafts and Virginia was a riveter at the airplane factory. Virginia had come to Evansville from Owensboro, KY where she and her mother had resided since moving from their farm at Panther, KY. Virginia's parents were Columbus Edgar "Ed" Igleheart (1873-1937) and Amanda Frances Igleheart (1881-1970).

Jack can trace his roots to Perry County which date back to the founding of the county in 1819. Jack's father's side, Carl Elton Stewart Sr. (1895-1953), of the family goes back to Jack's great grandfather, Elisha Stewart (1794, VA-circa 1825, P Co.), and his brother Barthomew G. Stewart (1786, VA-1840, Ma. Co.), came into the county as it was opening after the Chickasaw Treaty of 1818 negotiated by Andrew Jackson and Isaac Shelby in Franklin, TN. (See Stewart, Elisha history.) Jack's grandfather, Thomas Lindley "Tom" (1850-1923), and great grandfather, Sampson Stewart (1818-circa 1883) returned to Perry County from northern Mississippi after the Civil War to reside with Tom's sisters, who had married and resided in the county. (See Stewart, Thomas L. history.) On Dec. 13, 1869, Thomas Lindley "Tom" Stewart married Sarah Elizabeth O'Guin (1852-1930), daughter of John "Jack" O'Guin (1827-after 1900) and Nancy M. Daniel (circa 1833-1909). (See O'Guin, John history.) Jack's great great grand and great great great grandfathers, Tyler and father, Hardy O'Guin came into Perry County from Anson County, NC after 1810. Tyler and his brother Daniel O'Guin were signers to the Perry County petition to the State of Tennessee for recognition as a county on Sept. 23, 1819. (See O'Guin, Hardy history.)

Jack's mother's, Katie Pearl Vickery (1898-1988) family goes back to the 1860s, when his great grandfather Jonathan Vickery (1815-after 1870) and great grandmother Elizabeth Smith Vickery (born 1819) moved to the Crooked Creek area of Perry County, where four of 14 children were born. (See Vickery, Jonathan history.)

Perry County has played a sufficient role in the development of the Stewart-O'Guin-Vickery clans as this short narrative proudly exhibits. *Submitted by Larry D. Stewart, Mt. Juliet, TN.*

MARY ETTA "MOLLIE" STEWART, (Feb. 4, 1880-Jan. 20, 1943) was the fifth child of Thomas L. and Sarah J. Elizabeth O'Guin-Stewart. (See Stewart, Tom history.) She was married three times but had no children.

Molly Etta "Mollie" Stewart-Batton and Dr. James A. Batton along with James A. Batton Jr. and May Agnes Ruston-Batton.

Mollie was married on Jan. 26, 1898 to her first husband, Dr. J. A. Batton, the father of J. Arthur Batton from his first wife Katie Miller, who had died in 1898. Dr. Batton, a physician of Humphreys and Hickman counties was born Jan. 21, 1857 and died at Coble, TN on June 24, 1919.

After Dr. Batton died on June 24, 1919, Mollie married Belfield F. Thompson. He was born July 8, 1854 and died July 25, 1928. After Mr. Thompson died, Mollie married George W. Chessor. Dr. J. A. Batton, Mollie Stewart and Belfield Thompson are buried in the Walker Cemetery near Coble, TN. Mollie Stewart's grave is between the two. Mollie Stewart Batton Thompson was caring for her father, Thomas L. Stewart, when he died Aug. 13, 1923 at Coble.

In the accompany photograph are Mollie and Dr. Batton (standing) and James Arthur (June 11, 1886-July 26, 1934) and his wife, Mrs. May Agnes Ruston-Batton. Jesse Arthur Batton attended the Centerville Training School. He later lived at Coble over a period of years, during which time he married Miss May Rushton of the Coble Community. He later became a prominent successful automobile concern in both Lobelville and Linden, in which he was actively engaged on the day of his death. He died at the age of 48 of a heart attack. James Arthur is buried in the Sulphur Creek Cemetery near Coble. *Submitted by Monroe Stewart, Monroe, LA.*

MORRIS MONROE STEWART, (Bud) the second son and third child of Thomas James Stewart and Margaret Beulah Fraizer-Stewart. (See Stewart, Thomas James history.) Bud was born Sept. 2, 1915 in Flat River, MO. He graduated from the University of Missouri where he was a starter on the varsity basketball team, in June of 1937. That same year, he and his high school sweetheart, Virginia were married on Aug. 1, 1937. This arrangement has worked quite well over the years with Bud and Virginia celebrating their 57th anniversary this August. Bud and Virginia have two daughters: Sarah Margaret born March 23, 1939 and Marilyn Morris born Dec. 30, 1951. Sara Margaret is a teacher and organist for her Methodist Church in Houston, TX. Sarah Margaret and her husband, Melvin Ballard, a native of Arkansas, have three children; Thomas Stewart Ballard born Sept. 28, 1967, Fredonna Elizabeth born April 27, 1971, and Margaret Catherine, who is named for her great great grandmother Margaret Catherine McCollum-Stewart. (See Stewart, Monroe history.) Bud and Virginia are very proud of their grandchildren and their achievements. Thomas Stewart Ballard is currently enrolled at the Brooklyn School of Music in New York, NY. His musical studies are in Operatic Tenor vocals. Fredonna Elizabeth has graduated from high school and has capitalized on her dancing studies. Fredonna Elizabeth has finished her first year with the Tulsa Ballet Company in Tulsa, OK. She also does costume design. Margaret Catherine is a senior in high school and wants to pursue her ambition of being an astronaut following graduation.

Bud's interest in family genealogy has truly brought wonderment in his search for his family roots which started with his grandfather, William Monroe Stewart's marriage (1871) to Margaret Catherine McCollum on Terrapin Creek just west of Lobelville. From these beginnings on Terrapin Creek to the Musical Halls of New York and a Professional Ballerina has surely celebrated Bud as "Grandson of a Share Cropper and a grandfather of a Ballerina and Tenor."

Marilyn Morris, a graduate of Sam Houston State University, Huntsville, TX; has lived for the past 18 years in Houston, TX. She has recently moved to Monroe, LA, where she works as an executive secretary.

Bud and Virginia Stewart

After Bud's graduation from college, he worked for Swift & Co., Ralston Purina, Farmington, MO State Hospital #4 and served a hitch in the Navy during WW II. Bud worked for the USDA for 20 years until his retirement in 1980. Bud and Virginia have resided in Monroe, LA for the past 18 years. Bud has continued to keep himself active through his work at the River Oaks School, family genealogy and as a southwest regional officer, national membership chairman and genealogist with the Clan Stewart Society of America. Virginia runs a "tight ship," and is an excellent cook and homemaker. In her spare time when not supporting Monroe in his endeavors, Virginia pursues her interest as a quilting artist. Bud and Virginia's network of friends span's throughout the southeastern states, which they had developed through Bud's genealogy work. Among Bud's many genealogy "finds," he is proudest of his locating and acquiring from an heir, the complete publication of the Clan Stewart Magazine which was published for 20 years by one of the outstanding genealogists. Bud acquired this collection and it is now a part of the Clan Stewart Society of America's collection. *Submitted by Mrs. Virginia Murdick-Stewart.*

SAMPSON STEWART, (1818 HI. Co.-circa 1883 P. Co.) was the second of eight children born to Elisha Stewart (1794-1825) and Mary "Polly" Box (1798-circa 1863). (See Stewart, Elisha history.) At the time of his father's death, he and his family had been living in Perry County since 1819 when the territory was opened as a result of the Chickasaw Treaty of 1818 signed by Andrew Jackson and Isaac Shelby in Franklin, TN (Oct. 19, 1818). His mother moved the family back to Hickman County to live near his grandfather, William Stewart Sr. (See Stewart, William Sr. history.) During the late 1820s, William Sr. and his son Andrew C. and their families relocated to Madison County to follow BG Stewart. Sometime after 1830, Mary "Polly" Box-Stewart married a William Spicer (1789 NC-before 1860). William Spicer relocated the family to the Tumbling Creek area, Hu. Co. On Feb. 11, 1835 Hi. Co., Sampson married Beadie Prater (1819-1854 Di. Co.), daughter of John and Ailey Prater. On Nov. 17, 1838, William Spicer, of Humphreys County distributed to his wife Mary (Box-Stewart) Spicer, Abraham Stewart, Sampson Stewart, Lindley Stewart and Robert Stewart tracts of land along Tumbling Creek, Humphreys County, TN. By 1845, Sampson sold off his tract of land and had purchased from his uncle, Lindley Box, a 270 acre farm on Garner's Creek in Dickson, County where he and his family are found in the 1850 census. Beadie and Sampson have the following children: (1) Catherine "Kitty" born 1836, married James Batton born 1810. (2) Mary A. (1838-1881) married John E. Baker born 1832. (3) Martha Jane "Janie" (1840-1890) married James Farley Crowell. (4) Sarah "Puss" (1842-1899) married first Joseph J. Smith, second Bill Daily. (5) Abraham B. "Abe" (1845-1863), Abe was mortally wounded in the battle at Wyatte, MS on Oct. 13, 1863 while serving with the First Miss. Partisan Rangers. He was brought home where he died and was buried on the family farm. (6) Aaron James "Dock"(1847-1913) married Parthena Baker. Dock fought as a boy with the 41st Tn. Inf. Co. C. at the battle of Fort Donelson (1862), was captured, interned and exchanged at Vicksburg, MS, Sept. 23, 1863. (7) Thomas Lindley "Tom" (1850-1923) married (1869 P. Co.) Sarah Elizabeth O'Guin (1852-1930). (8) William Monroe (1852-1906) married (1871 P. Co.) Margaret Catherine McCollum (1855-1910).

When Beadie died in 1854, Sampson sold his farm and relocated with his four sons to Mississippi where his brother Abraham had moved to in 1838. Sampson's daughters had married by this time and remained in the Perry and Humphreys County area. In 1858, Sampson purchased a 270 acre farm in Tippah County, MS. Sampson follows his step-father's lead and has all four of sons names placed on the title. At the conclusion of the Civil War, Sampson was faced with the severe conditions and destruction that the northern Mississippi area has suffered. By the late 1860s, Sampson is forced to lose his farm to taxes and financial burdens. Sampson and his four sons return to the Perry County area after a ten year absence. In the 1870 census, Aaron James "Dock" has married (1868 Hu. Co.) Parthena Baker (1850-1923) and they are living next to her parents Ezekial and Nancy Blackwell-Baker. Thomas Lindley "Tom" is found living with the John and Nancy O'Guin family and are listed as newlyweds. William Monroe is found living with the John E. and Mary A. Sanford family. In the 1880 census, Sampson is found living with his aunt Providence Claiborne in Perry County.

Sampson is remembered by a grandson, Walter Oscar Stewart, who stated "that around 1881, Sampson traveled from Perry County in a two wheel cart to visit his son William Monroe and family, who lived at that time in Rutherford, Gibson County. Upon his return to Perry County, Sampson died." *Submitted by Thomas James Stewart Jr.*

THOMAS JAMES STEWART SR., (Oct. 24, 1873-Oct. 9, 1951) was the second child born to William Monroe and Margaret Catherine McCollum-Stewart on Terrapin Creek, Perry County. (See STEWART, William Monroe history.) During 1877-1878, he moved with his family to Rutherford, Gibson County and lived with the James Farley and Martha Jane Stewart-

Crowell family. His father worked as a mason's helper to James Farley Crowell, who was a mason. In 1883, the family relocated to Ripley County, MO near Doniphan on Dudley Creek. It was just prior to this move, grandfather, Sampson Stewart, came to visit the family for the last time as he would die later that year (1881). The family's move to Missouri was not without hardships. William Monroe's share crop that season wasn't successful and the family was forced to go to Arkansas and pick cotton to raise funds to see them through the winter. Thomas James took odd jobs to help out with expenses, as well as work required on their farm. One year Thomas rode the mail until winter and had to quit due to lack of clothing. Little by little Thomas James picked up an education. In 1890 "Tommy" landed his first teaching job at the ripe age of 17. He taught at a one room school at the Well Creek area, nine miles northwest of Dolphin, MO. During his summer vacations, "Tommy" would take teaching courses at Cape Girardeau, MO. He finally finished and received an A.B. degree at the age of 35. In 1910, he received a position at Sikeston, MO. While attending at Southeast Missouri State Teachers College at Cape Girardeau, "Tommy" met Margaret Beulah Frazier and they were married Aug. 23, 1911. He next received a position as principal at Flat River. "T. J." spend the next 37 years at Flat River. In 1947, he retired and was honored by the Flat River High School Alumni with a Scholarship fund developed in his name.

Thomas James Stewart Sr. and Margaret Beulah Frazier, married August 23, 1911. Photo circa 1911.

"T. J." and Margaret Beulah raised six children: (1) Mary Catherine Stewart - born at Flat River, MO, Dec. 19, 1912 and died Jan. 14, 1913. She is buried at Towles Cemetery. (2) Thomas James Stewart Jr. was born Oct. 18, 1913 at Flat River, MO, married Mary Catherine Peterson Oct. 20, 1937 at St. George's Church, St. Louis, MO. She was born Jan. 25, 1915. (3) Morris Monroe Stewart was born Sept. 2, 1915 at Flat River, MO, married Virginia May Murdick Aug. 1, 1937 at First Presbyterian Church, Flat River, MO. She was born Nov. 30, 1916. (4) Fraizer McVale Stewart was born Sept. 2, 1915 at Flat River, MO, married Carolyn Sue Hunt on June 28, 1941 at Denver, CO. She was born Feb. 12. (5) Walter Harry Stewart was born Oct. 22, 1920 at Flat River, MO, married Elma St. John Ballou on Aug. 25, 1968 at First Presbyterian Church, Carbondale, IL. She was born Jan. 21. (6) Lee Anne Alice Stewart was born July 13, 1924 at Flat River, MO, married Ermal Eden Spitzmiller on Jan. 28, 1950 at First Presbyterian Church, Flat River, MO. He was born May 29. *Submitted by Morris Monroe Stewart.*

THOMAS LINDLEY STEWART,

(Tom), (Jan. 29, 1850-Aug. 13, 1923) was born on Garner's Creek, Dickson County. His parents were Sampson and Beadie Prater-Stewart. (See Stewart, Sampson history.) In 1854, Tom moved with his father to Tippah County, MS and worked a farm there for the next 15 years. Tom was too young (10 years old) to serve in the Civil War. His two older brothers, Abraham and Aaron, served the south with Abraham being killed. After the loss of their farm in the mid to late 1860s, Tom with his father and brothers returned to the Perry County area to live with his older sisters, who had remained in the area. On Dec. 13, 1869, W. L. Daniel M. G. married Tom and Sarah Jane Elizabeth O'Guin (Aug. 31, 1852-Oct. 26, 1930), daughter of John "Jack" (circa 1827 - after 1900 P. Co.) and Nancy M. Daniel-O'Guin (circa 1833 - 1909 Tom's Creek, P. Co.). The couple is identified in the 1870 census as newlyweds and are living with her parents on Roans Creek, Perry County. Tom and Sarah were blessed with 10 children: (1) William Allen "Wid" (1870-1918) married (1892) Dora L. Mitchell. (2) Nancy Josephine (1872-1948) married Jesse Fuqua "Jesse" Merideth. (3) John Wilson "John" (1874-1923) married (1894) Mary Jane "Mollie" Sterling. (4) Dorsey B. Thomas "Doss" (1876-1940) married (1899) Martha Elizabeth "Mattie" Shaw. (5) Mary Etta "Mollie" (1880-1943) married (1899) first Dr. James Batton, second Belfried Thompson, third George Chessor. (6) James Andrew "Andy" (1883-1979) married first Stella Pruett, second Annie Lee Morrison. (7) Minnie Lee (1885-1955) married Sterling Mause Canada. (8) Lillie May (1889-1921) married (1909) William Wiley Terry. (9) Robert A. (1893-1893) (10) Carl Elton Sr. (1895-1953) married (1915) first Katie Pearl Vickery (1898-1988), second Ruth Bingham (Snowden?).

Tom farmed in Perry County. He noted on the tax lists from 1875 through 1878 as leasing 350 acres in District 8. By the 1880 census, Tom had moved his family to District 4, Humphreys County in Buffalo area. On Dec. 28, 1899, the Bakerville Review reported that Tom was moving from the Roberts Creek area to Pruitt Springs area. The family continued to live in this area in what Mary D. Merideth-Perry remembers as a double saddle bag log cabin. She related a story of one Christmas eve that she and her parents, Jesse Fuqua Merideth and Nancy Josephine Stewart-Merideth, spent with her grandparents at this house. "Grandmother had fixed a quilt pallet on the floor in front of the fireplace where the grandchildren would sleep. She remembers that her grandfather, Tom slept on the floor with them while grandmother slept in the bed in the same room. Her parents slept in the loft above. She remembered that dried pumpkin rinds and other dried items hung around the fireplace."

Tom and Sarah lived with various children during their later years. Both are buried in the Bone Springs Cemetery, Old Hwy 13, on the Perry - Humphreys County line. *Submitted by Larry D. Stewart, Mt. Juliet, TN.*

WILLIAM STEWART SR.,

(1756 VA - 1833 Ma. Co., TN) while not documented as ever living in Perry County, did have many descendants who came to make Perry County their home. William Sr. is first documented in Tennessee when he purchased (Oct. 1809) 200 acres on Garner's Creek from Robert Weakley, Speaker of the House of Representative, State of Tennessee and land speculator. Actual Indian raids continued in the area with the last noted Indian raid occurring on Garner's Creek in 1809. The Hickman County petitioners continued identifying to the Tennessee State Assembly the threat of Indian raids and requesting funding of the militia as late as 1812.

William Sr. is believed to have come into Tennessee as early as the 1790s as there is some indication there were family ties with the Weakly, Drake and Maulding families which resided in the Robertson and northern Davidson County area. It is believed that William Sr., his wife Mary (1757 VA.-Oct. 10, 1822 Hi. Co., TN), and four of their eventual nine children came overland from the Whythe, VA area. William Sr. and Mary raised a family of nine children which consisted of (1) William Jr. (1783 VA-1818 Hi. Co.) married Judith born 1785. (2) Bartholomew Grayson (1786 VA-1840 Ma. Co.) married 1809 Robertson Co., Sarah "Sally" Maulding (1791 VA-1858 Ma. Co.), daughter of Capt. Richard

Thomas Lindley "Tom" and Sarah Elizabeth O'Guin-Stewart family. Known individuals: Carl Elton Stewart Sr., 1895-1956 (Back row with banjo); John "Jack" O'Guin, 1827-after 1900 (Bearded man); Nancy M. Daniel-O'Guin, 1833-1909 (Front of "Jack"); Sarah Elizabeth O'Guin-Stewart, 1852-1930 (Beside Nancy/mother); Thomas Lindley "Tom" Stewart, 1850-1923 (Behind Sarah); James Andrew "Andy" Stewart, 1883-1979 (Front row right end); and Dorsey B. Thomas "Doss" Stewart, 1876-1940 (Front row left end).

Maulding of Maulding Station, Robertson Co., TN. (3) Andrew C. (1788 VA-1878 MS) married (Hickman Co.) Hannah Carothers (1791 GA-1861 Sh. Co.). (4) Elias born circa 1790 VA. (5) Elisha (1794 VA-circa 1825 P Co.) married Mary "Polly" Box (1798 SC-circa 1863 Hu. Co.). (6) Mary "Polly" born circa 1796, married Joisah Hanna. (7) Nancy born circa 1806, married Jesse M. Hanna. (8) Markus born 1805, married Susan. (9) Markus born 1808.

B. G. Stewart distinguished himself in Hickman County where he was the first register (1807), District Surveyor (1809) and Colonel (1812) Hickman Co. Milita. Upon the relocation of the county seat from Vernon to Centerville, the Stewarts decided sell out (1819) and relocate west.

Elisha and his brothers B G Stewart, Andrew and William Jr. are noted (Sept. 11, 1812) as petitioners of the 36th Regiment & 6th Brigade of the Tennessee Militia requesting the general Assembly of the State of Tennessee, allow them to wear their own uniforms (Homespun).

Prior to the 1820 census, Elisha and Bartholomew G. had relocated to Perry County. Elisha and his family remained in Perry County until his death (circa 1825) and later relocate back to Hickman County (Stewart, Elisha history). Bartholomew G. Stewart left Perry County and was instrumental in the development of Madison County, where he was the 9th District Surveyor, a County Commissioner, Justice of the Peace and was a signer to the county petition for the State of Tennessee General Assembly for recognition of the County of Madison (Oct. 10, 1821).

By the mid to late 1820s, Andrew C. and the Hanna families relocated to Madison County. Andrew C. distinguished himself in the development of Spring Creek Academy (north of Jackson) and is on the county board of education. Jesse M Hanna is county sheriff (1825). In 1851, Andrew C. Stewart relocated his family to Shelby County north of Memphis. In 1878 at Andrew C.'s death, his obituary is featured on the front page of the Memphis Daily Appeal. Andrew C. and his wife Hannah are buried in the Elmwood Cemetery, Memphis, TN.

William Sr. relocated with other members of his family in the late 1820s to Madison County, where B G Stewart had preceded them. William Sr. had at this time reached his late sixties and lived out the remainder of his years with his daughter, Nancy, and her husband, Jesse M. Hanna.

William Stewart Sr. (1756 VA - 1833 Ma. Co., TN) was a revolutionary war veteran as noted in an application for a pension in Madison County (1825).

Upon his death on Dec. 12, 1833, his obituary appeared in the National Banner and Nashville Daily Advertiser, Friday, Dec. 27, 1833.

WILLIAM MONROE STEWART, (Oct. 10, 1852 - Dec. 29, 1906) was the youngest son and the 8th child of Sampson and Beadie Prater-Stewart. (See Stewart, Sampson history.) "Dock" was born on Garner's Creek in Dickson County, just over the Humphreys-Dickson line and a short distance north of the Hickman County line. When Monroe's mother, Beadie died in 1854, Sampson sold his farm and relocated with his four sons: Abraham B. "Abe" (1845-1863), Aaron James "Dock" (1847-1913), Thomas Lindley "Tom" (1850-1923) and William Monroe (1852-1906) to Mississippi where Sampson's brother, Abraham had moved to in 1838.

William Monroe and Margaret Catherine McCollum Stewart. Married January 1871 in Perry County, Tennessee. Photo circa 1893. Children are: (Back row) Dora Ethel, Emma Jame, Lulu May (Front row) Mary Myrtle and Minnie Lee Stewart.

Monroe's older sisters: Catherine "Kitty" born 1836, Mary A. (1838-1881), Martha Jane "Janie" (1840-1890) and Sarah "Puss" (1842-1899) had married by this time and remained in the Perry and Humphreys County area. In 1858, Monroe was a six year old boy when his father and older brothers moved to Tippah County, MS to farm a 270 acre tract that Sampson had purchased. During the War Between the States, Monroe's brothers Abraham B. "Abe" (1845-1863), joined the First Mississippi Partisan Rangers (Mounted Cavalry), while Aaron James "Dock" (1847-1913) as a 14 year old boy joined the 41st Tennessee Infantry Company "C." Abe was mortally wounded in the battle at Wyatte, MS on Oct. 13, 1863 while serving with the First Miss. Partisan Rangers. He was brought home where he died and was buried on the family farm. Aaron James "Dock" (1847-1913) while with the 41st Tn. Inf. Co. C. at the battle of Fort Donelson (1862), was captured, interned at Camp Butler, near Springfield, IL and held there until the Cartel of prisoner exchange, where Dock was released at Vicksburg, MS (Sept. 23, 1863). By the late 1860s, the family's fortunes turned for the worse and the farm was lost to taxes and financial burdens. Monroe, then approximately 18 years old, left the Tippah County area with his father and three brothers and returned to the Perry County area after a ten year absence. Monroe came to live with his sister and family (Mr. and Mrs. J. Farley Crowell) in the 8th District of Perry County. There Monroe met and married (Jan. 4, 1871) Margaret Catherine McCollum, daughter of John and Susan Carothers-McCollum. (See McCollum, John history.) Monroe and Margaret started their family on Terrapin Creek hollow, just west of Lobelville and raised a family of 10 children: (1) William Andrew (May 21, 1872-1872) (2) Thomas James "Tommy" (Oct. 24, 1873-Oct. 9, 1951) married Margaret Beulah Fraizer, Aug. 23, 1911. (See Stewart, Thomas James history.) (3) Alice Isabelle born April 16, 1875, married Edd Lee Lacy, Sept. 25, 1892. (4) Walter Oscar born Sept. 25, 1892, married Elizabeth Melvenia Booker, July 15, 1906. (5) Dora Ethel born Jan. 24, 1880, married James Anderson McClaren, Aug. 15, 1897. (6) Lulu May born Feb. 15, 1881, married Joseph A. Showman, April 19, 1900. (7) Emma Jame, born Oct. 24, 1883, married Dr. J.A. Atkisson, April 19, 1900. (8) Mary Myrtle, born Oct. 1885. (9) Minnie Lee born Jan. 1892.

About 1875, Monroe and Margaret Catherine moved their family to Ripley County, MO to live near Margaret's uncle Andy McCollum, who would become an influential person of the county. "Uncle Andy" served 20 years as circuit clerk and was elected for two terms as the Ripley County representative to the Missouri Legislature. A short time later Monroe moved his family back to the Lobelville area. About 1877-1878, the family moved to Gibson County and lived near James Farley Crowell and his sister, Martha Jane Stewart-Crowell. By 1883, the family relocated to Ripley, MO near Doniphan on Dudley Creek Towles Community. Times were hard and trying for farmers trying to make a living sharecropping. Monroe Stewart's son "Tommy" remembers one such drought which forced the family to move to Success, AR to pick cotton that fall. By Christmas, the family had saved $100 and were able to move back to Ripley, MO. By the Autumn of 1891, the family was back on its feet and Monroe and Margaret's son "Tommy" was working as a construction laborer to help support the family's finances. Between seasons, the children were sent to school. "Tommy" went on to achieve a college education in eight years of alternating teaching and working. (See Stewart, Thomas James history.) Monroe died Dec. 29, 1906 and Margaret Catherine died Aug. 23, 1910. They are buried in the Towles Cemetery, Doniphan, Ripley County, MO. *Submitted by Thomas James Stewart Jr., Titusville, FL.*

LYDIA GRAHAM STORY, (1806-1853) was married to Bennett Story about 1821 in Tennessee, possibly Perry County or Warren County. They had 11 children according to the censuses: 1830 Tipton County, TN; 1840 Perry County, TN; and 1850 Cass County, TX next door to her brother, Charles Graham. In 1848 they moved to Cass County and settled next door to Sarah Graham Bowman Graves. Bennett Story mentioned in Navarro County, TX records with other Storys.

Liddie was born in 1806 in North Carolina, probably Randolph County, to John and Sarah Graham. Lydia d. in March 1853 in Cass County, TX.

Bennett B. Story was probably the son of Senith and Samuel Story Sr. and probably the grandson of Elizabeth Speed and Daniel Story. It is believed that Bennett's siblings were Samuel Jr., Jesse, Henry J. and Nancy Hill Story. Henry J. married M. E. Glass in 1817 Tennessee, 15 children; Samuel Jr. was married to Nancy Titus who later married Adam Self and found in the 1850 Fannin County, TX census; Nancy Hill Story was the second wife of Lydia's brother, Robert Crawford Graham. After Lydia died, Bennett remarried Mrs. Eliza Fitzhugh on Aug. 9, 1855 in Cass County. Bennett Story, born 1801 in North Carolina and d. 1864 in Cass County, TX.

Nine of Liddie and Bennett Story's children were: Edward W., 1822-1891 Cass County and married C. A. in Tennessee on June 11, 1846, then Emily Jane, had at least seven children; James W., born 1825 and married Lusanna/Verancy; probably Ben; Calvin C., 1833-1859; Robert B., 1835-1862; Mary Ann, born 1838 and married Judson Vaughn, had at least nine children; Martha Jane, born 1843 and married Robert Guess; Asenith "Cenny" born 1848 and married Joseph Milsap, had at least eight children; Zachariah T., born 1851 and married Martha Jane (maybe Moore), had at least two children.

Cass County Will Book, dated Dec. 10, 1874, lists Lydia Story's family and mentions her farm next door to Wiley Graves.

Lydia's son, Edward W. Story, and his wife deeded on June 30, 1848 to Cass County for $50 the 50 acres to be used for a more centrally located county seat, although it was not moved from Jefferson until 1852. Lydia's brother-in-law, Major Jeremiah Preston Wood, suggested that they name the new county seat "Linden" after the 1847 vote to relocate the county seat to a more central site.

STRICKLAND, Stephen Strickland was born May 23, 1786 in the territory west of the river Ohio. It was the western part of Pennsylvania at that time. He was in Tennessee in 1803 and signed the petition of the general assembly to create a new county later named Stewart.

John Monroe and Agnes Ann Barnett Strickland

In about 1808 he married Sarah Medlock, or Matlock. She had a brother Ned and sister Molly, who married Smith Choate.

Stephen and Elihu fought in the 1812 Indian War. In 1815 Stephen and Elihu signed a deed for Jones Mercer in Humphreys County, TN. It is not known who Elihu was, but he was thought to be Stephen's brother or father.

In 1819 Stephen signed the petition for a new county which was Perry, with his three sons who were about four, eight and nine years old. Stephen received several grants of land in Perry County, one of which his descendants live on today. Stephen and Sarah had eight children.

Luke was born 1810 and died 1853 in Dade County, MO. He married Delila Woods in Trigg County, KY. His wife and family moved to Springtown, TX after his death.

Elizabeth was born Jan. 16, 1813. Nothing is known of her.

Jonathon was born Oct. 13, 1811, married Sarah Ann Woods in Trigg County, KY; later moved to Dade County, MO. He stayed there till the 1880s, then moved to Parker County, TX. He died in 1879 in Azel, TX.

Benjamin was born Oct. 14, 1815 and married his cousin, Eleanor Medlock. They left Tennessee in the 1860s going to Hunt County, TX.

Thomas was born Nov. 3, 1817 and married Elizabeth Garrett in Arkansas. He was in Hunt County, TX in the 1840s and received a grant of land there. There is a Strickland graveyard there where all are buried south of Greenville named Edda Lake.

Martha was born Jan. 25, 1822 and married Smith Choate, son of Milton Choate. They stayed in Perry County, TN. A few of their children went to Parker and Wise counties in Texas.

Polly Ann was born Feb. 5, 1825 or 27, and married Lemmie Tate. One of their children, Alvin, was born 1851, gave his family in the Goodspeeds Book written in 1886.

Stephen Downs, born Dec. 3, 1824, remained a bachelor. He stayed with his father and died in the 1870s.

Stephen Strickland's first wife died about 1830. He married the second time to Elizabeth "Betsy" Thomas, the daughter of Cordy Thomas. Their children are as follows:

Sarah Ann, born Jan. 4, 1838, married John S. Stringer, according to family history.

Cassandra, born May 13, 1840, married James Tanner; married a second time to Tob Wilson.

Susan Ann was born July 19, 1842 and married John Greer. John died in 1869 after serving in the Civil War, leaving her with two sons, Stephen and Andrew.

John Monroe Strickland was born Dec. 4, 1844 and died Feb. 23, 1923. He married Agnes Ann Barnett, who was born Dec. 1849 and died April 25, 1928. She was the daughter of Jerry Barnett and Amanda Hogwood.

John Monroe fought in the Civil War for the Confederacy in the 10th Cavalry in 1862. In 1863 he was with Major Cox. In 1864 John was a prisoner in Morristown, TN. He refused to sign the oath for the Federals and told them he wanted to go home.

Louisa Ann, born Oct. 30, 1847, married J. D. Barnett of Arkansas and a second time to John Epperson.

Stephen Strickland died about 1861 and his second wife Betsy died around 1900. John Monroe Strickland was the great grandfather of Jimmy D. Strickland. He was blind in 1922 when one of his grandsons was born, but he held him and said he was a fine boy.

John M. and Agness had eight children. Thomas M., Mandy, John Breckinridge, Susie C., Doshie, Martha and Grover Cornelius born Jan. 12, 1885. He married Jessie Virginia Halbrooks. She was the daughter of Robert and Molly DePriest.

Their children were Jewel, Robert, Nina, James Paul, Walter J. Mack and Verna Sue.

Mack Strickland was born April 30, 1921 and married Gladys Evans Broadway, who was born April 6, 1918 and died Jan. 29, 1979. She was the daughter of Elbert and Lexie Tomblin. Their children are Jimmy, Bobby, Tommy and Janis.

Jimmy Strickland was born April 30, 1942 on his father's birthday, also the birthday of his great great grandfather, Alex Broadway, who was born April 30, 1841.

Jimmy married Glenna C. Duff in Mobile, AL. Her father, Glen Duff, was from Roane County, TN. Her mother was Cecelia Godwin from Escambia County, AL. They have two sons, Neal and Joshua.

This doesn't end the story, as the families will continue on forever. Apologies are made to anyone who was left out or any mistakes made, but everyone could not be put in. Special thanks go out to the many people who helped with this work, and especially those who had kept some of the work from years ago that was done by them. *Submitted by Jimmy D. Strickland.*

SUMMERS, George Thomas and Mary Josephine Tate Summers (Jo) moved from Memphis to Perry County in the summer of 1975 with their three children, Terri Lynn, born July 28, 1965, George Thomas II, born March 28, 1967 and Susan Michelle, born Nov. 22, 1969. They had traveled through Perry County many times to go canoeing on the Buffalo River, and finally decided to escape city life to live in Lobelville. They lived in what was known as the "John Argo" place on 7th Avenue. The children loved living there. They quickly made new friends and enjoyed the pleasures of rural living, such as swimming in Cane Creek, fishing or playing in the barn.

In the summer of 1981, the family moved to Flatwoods and operated the Flatwoods Grocery, which was across from Ary's Grocery in downtown Flatwoods. Susan and Terri were very much opposed to this idea, and vowed they would rather stay in Lobelville by themselves than to move. But, once they got settled in Flatwoods, they decided it was a fine place to live as well.

While living in Flatwoods, Terri met and married Michael Ralph Hickerson in May of 1983. They lived in the home of Ms. Connie Webster, which at one time was a hotel. The couple then moved to the Bethel Community in Linden. It was while living there that their son, Jonathan Michael was born on Aug. 12, 1985. They later divorced. Terri then married Kevin Allen Spry in July 1989. They have one daughter, Brittany Leigh, born Aug. 6, 1991. They live in Linden.

Susan graduated from Perry County High School as did her older brother and sister. Only, she continued her education by attending Columbia State Community College. While still in college and working too, she married Bill Carroll, whom she had dated since high school. They moved to Hohenwald. Susan graduated from Columbia State with a degree in accounting. The couple had one daughter, Ashley Nicole, born July 17, 1991, before divorcing in 1993.

Growing up, George was a typical boy, always into mischief. He especially liked to tease the girls at school, or his sisters, it didn't matter. Terri was usually the target since he and Susan were "buddies." But, as they got older, Susan and her friends got their share as well.

Of all the children, it was George that loved Flatwoods the most. He never tired of going to the river. Swimming, fishing, canoeing or camping, he loved them all. It was also in the river that he lost his life. He was drowned while canoeing in August of 1990. One can't help but wonder how he would react to having two cute nieces and a handsome nephew around to aggravate, or how they would gang up on him! Jonathan can barely remember his Uncle George now. But one of the things he tells about him is how George would try to scare him with a Halloween mask, and how he wishes he were here now to take him fishing.

SUTTON, From a hill, high on a tree-covered hillside, frigid water cascades over limestone boulders from the cave overlooking a tract of land that once embraced the tanyard of James R. Sutton, a person descended from a long line of Suttons who specialized in "tanning" hides for conversion into leather.

James R. Sutton Family

Mary Elizabeth Dickson, a widow with two sons, Addison and Matthew C., married James Renick Sutton on July 4, 1878, on Lick Creek, Perry County, TN, at the home of the bride's parents, Mary Elizabeth and Matthew Canidy Dickson. After the ceremony, the couple mounted horses and traveled to the Sutton Farm on Marsh Creek.

James R. Sutton was a tanner by trade, an occupation that had been handed down to him for generations. He became noted for his generosity by employing any young man he judged deserving to work in his tan-yard. Once a year, he would take the hides to St. Louis for sale. While there, he would buy a year's supply of staple groceries as well as other household necessities. Also, the clothing he would bring to the family reflected care and excellent judgment in his selections.

James R. gave his son, Fred, a sizable tract of land adjoining the family farm. After a few years, he had a disagreement with his mother over a drinking problem and left Perry County, never to return. Daughters, Minnie and Lydia, attended Union University at Jackson, TN, but Lydia died while in her teens. Minnie married Alec Hufstedler, who farmed at the Sutton homeplace for a few years, then the couple moved to Memphis, where Alex trained to become a dentist. Dr. Hufstedler practiced his profession in Linden, Obion and Union City, TN, for an extended number of years.

Sarah Elizabeth "Sallie" became a teacher and met Nicholas Neely Norton, also a teacher. Consequently, they were married on Oct. 22, 1905. After Sallie's death on Sept. 10, 1912, Nicholas continued teaching and advancing his education, which included a Masters Degree from George Peabody College and graduate work at the University of Chicago. With a B.S. Degree from Middle Tennessee State Teachers College, his daughter, Mary Norton Bell, taught in the elementary schools of Perry County for 40 years. His daughter, Thelma, held responsible positions with the Louisville and Nashville Railroad (now CSX) for 28 years.

JOSHUA SUTTON, who died in Perry County in the 1850s, was born in Virginia, a son of Jonas and Sarah Sutton. The family moved to Lincoln County, KY, and Joshua was married to Mary Ratikin on July 30, 1807, in Pulaski County, KY. They moved to Bedford County, TN, and Mary died there on May 27, 1830. Their children were Sally, Jonas, Joseph Ratikin, Uriah, John A., Levi and James R.

Joshua was later married to Margaret Vickory. Her death date is not known but their children were Joshua Jr., Micajah, William and Jerusha.

During Joshua's lifetime he and his son, Levi had purchased 1,112 acres in Perry County, said to be in the Tom's Creek area. On June 23, 1857, Levi bought from Joshua's heirs their interest in the land with the widow's dower being reserved.

JAMES SWAFFORD, was born in Germany in the early 1700s. He walked across France, England, Ireland into "Wales" a part of "The British Isles." James' father was also named James. While working in Wales, he fell in love with a Wales girl and married. He raised a family of 14 children. He owned a ranch with a shop for repairing tools, raised cattle, goats and poultry of many different kinds.

Darcy, Jerry and Perry Swafford, 1993.

His third child was James III. When James III became of age he went over into Ireland and worked. He fell in love with an Irish girl named Renny Howard and they were married in a church wedding. This James was born about 1745.

James and his bride came to America along with the Quakers and lived in the Quaker settlement for several years. During this, he and his wife had five or six children. About 1776, James III and his wife had raised 14 children. James III served in the Revolutionary War for seven years. After some years he moved down the coast line and seem to settle in North Carolina, when North Carolina and Tennessee were one state. John Swafford, one of James III's children, married Mary Fields, a North Carolina girl, in 1795. By 1818, he and his wife raised 14 children. William L. Swafford, one of John's children, married Nancy Craig and moved to Decatur County in 1857. He enlisted in the third regiment of West TN Cavalry, Union Army and served from June to October. At which time the regiment was captured and put in prison. He escaped and returned home. One of William's sons, also named William, married Margaret Roarh in January of 1853 and to them were born 14 children. They are listed a Mary Ann, John L., Joseph Asberry, Judy C., James W., Maggie J., Amerela, Louisa. A., Sarah C., Isaac D., Henry T., Thomas A., Horace M. and an unknown infant died at birth.

William, our family's great grandparent was leading the Republican party in the Decatur County area around the Parson area. He is mentioned in Goodspeed's History of Tennessee PP 893. He served as magistrate and leading education services from 1876-1882. He fought for better schools and education. He and Margaret were Missionary Baptist and set a good example for their children.

One of William's sons, Joe Asberry Swafford married two sisters; the second after the first sister had died. His first wife was Judy Bussell in 1880. On the birth of their first child Maud, Judy died. He and the child stayed with the Bussell family and he later married Vinnia Bussell. Their union produced the following children: Claudia (1883), Ellis Bud (1885), William (1890), Joseph G. (1899) and Dave (1901).

Joe G. Swafford (1899-1960) married Elena Smith (1905) in 1931. In 1931, they lived in Perry County. Joe Asberry Swafford (1931-1973) married twice. His first wife was a Dottie Shephard in 1955. They raised three boys, Dale, Johnny and Jerry. They all live in Richmond Hill, GA. In 1960, Joe's second marriage was to Johnny Belsha. They have three children, Dorsey, Perry and Myra.

SANDRA GRINDER SWANSON, was born on Cedar Creek in Perry County in 1941. Her family lived on the Tennessee River where her grandfather, Earl Lamar Harder operated a store until the depression forced him out of business. They moved to Wayne County when the Tennessee Valley Authority bought the land to expand the dam system that brought electricity to the rural area. She grew up in Wayne County. She married Murray L. Swanson Jr. of Mound, MN. They live in Evanston, IL with their two children, Meredith and Christopher.

Sandra has four brothers. Nolan Harder Grinder married Barbara Sieber and has three children, Kimberly, Kevin and Angela. Gailand Osburn Grinder married Patsy Wade and has one child, Amelia who is married to Jeff Kuehn. They have one child, Victor. John Wayne Grinder is married to Sharon and has one son, Brian. Terry Webb Grinder married Sue Cotham and has one child, Alexandrea.

Sandra is connected to many of the families who settled in Perry County in the early 1800s. Her father is Ary Osburn Grinder and her mother is Nettie Hazel Harder. On her father's side, her grandparents were Noah Theodore Grinder and Mary Jane Ary. Her great grandparents were William Henry Grinder, Sarah Jane Ledbetter, William Henry Ary, and Mary Jane Warren. Family tradition suggests that the Grinders are related to Robert Grinder, the man who owned the Natchez Trace Inn where Meriwether Lewis died. William Henry Ary fought for the South in the Civil War in the 9th Cavalry. Later he donated the land where the Ary Cemetery on Sinking Creek is located. He and his wife, Mary Jane Warren are buried there as well as Noah Theadore Grinder and Mary Jane Ary. William Henry Grinder and Sarah Jane Ledbetter are buried on Rockhouse Creek.

On her mother's side, Sandra's grandparents were Earl Lamar Harder and Minnie Elizabeth Bunch. They are buried in the Harder Cemetery on Cedar Creek. Her great grandparents were William Henry Harder, Sarah Atlantic Anderson, George Thomas Bunch and Martha Emily Kelley. Her great-great grandparents were Jeremiah Harder, Harriet Young, John Anderson, Elizabeth Whitwell, George Dabney Bunch, Mary Elizabeth Denton, Joe E. Kelley and Martha Kirk. William Henry Harder and George Dabney Bunch both fought in the Civil War for the South. William Henry Harder was a Captain who was wounded at Shiloh, captured by Northern soldiers, and sent to Camp Douglas in Chicago where he was held prisoner. Later, he was exchanged and went back to his unit. He served in several capacities in spite of his wounds and was with Lee when he surrendered at Appomattox. Typewritten copies of a book he wrote about his experiences circulate in the family, and there is a copy of this book at the Perry County Library.

Sandra enjoys her visits back to Perry County. She hopes to learn more about her family, become reacquainted with relatives she already knows and to meet many more cousins as she does research. *Submitted by Sandra Swanson.*

JOE BURNS SWEENEY, was born Feb. 13, 1930 in the Beardstown Community of Perry County. He is married to the former Ruby Jean Culp who was born Dec. 22, 1932 in Lobelville. They were married on Nov. 23, 1951 and have three children, who are: Stella Jo, born in 1954 and married to David "Dave" Rhodes. They have two sons David Bryant and Mitchell Bartlett Rhodes.

Joe Burns and Ruby Culp Sweeney, December 1951.

Timothy Culp, born in 1957 and married to Donna W. Wisdom. They have two sons Cayce Wisdom and Clay Culp Sweeney.

Donna Ann, born in 1958 and married to Charlie Carroll. They have one son, Stephen Tyler Carroll. Joe's wife, Ruby is the daughter of Hershel Clarence and Maggie Reeves Culp. Joe is the great-grandson of Milton Abercromby Sweeney born in 1853 who was the 13th of 17 children born to Charlie and Sally H. Sweeney of Williamson County and his wife Mary Juan Burns Sweeney born in 1857, the daughter of Jesse Burns and Nancy Sarah Fitzgerald. After coming to Perry County in the late 1800s, Abercromby and Juan lived in the Beardstown Community until his death in 1934. Their children were Lulu born in 1875, Jesse Edward born in 1877 and Biney born in 1880. Lulu Sweeney married Henry Burns and they had six children: Effie, Gusta, Ashley, Hollye, Elred and Boyd Burns. Jesse married Addie Twoomey, daughter of I. J. and Savannah Twoomey. Addie's mother died at an early age and she was raised by Carroll Burns and his wife Betty Black Burns. Jesse and Addie had three children, Myrtle born in 1903, married Charles Daniel and they had three children Hazel, Nell and Betty Faye. Cayce Carroll born in 1906, married Thelma Louise Burns and they are the parents of Joe Burns and Bobby Carroll Sweeney. Mary Helen born in 1922, was never married.

Joe's mother, Thelma Louise Burns Sweeney was the daughter of William Arthur "Willie" Burns born in 1881 and Francia Elnora Shepard born in 1884 and the granddaughter of Joseph Clinton Burns and Sally Craig Burns. Thelma's maternal grandparents were J. B. and Nancy Jane Edwards Shepard. Willie and Fannie's other children were Malcolm born in 1908, Willie Ray born in 1914, Randel born in 1917 and Mary Francis born in 1920. Joe's brother, Bobby Carroll grew up in Perry County but in recent years has lived in Channelview, TX. He is married to the former Jonnie Barnette and they have six children: Randy, Keith, Mary Kimberly, Mark, Mike and Doug Sweeney. Joe retired in 1986 after 37 years of service with Tennessee Gas Pipeline Co. He also served on the Perry County Quarterly Court, on the Perry County Board of Education and two years in the U.S. Army's 7th Infantry Division during the Korean War. Joe and Ruby are members of the Lobelville United Methodist Church.

HAZEL CHAPPELL SWINEY, born March 31, 1914, Flatwoods Community, Perry County, TN, married Earl Swiney Dec. 28, 1940. He was born May 8, 1910 in Alcorn County, MS, to John & Minnie Swiney; died Jan. 19, 1993 in Springfield, IL. Her parents were Nimrod Henry Clay Chappell and Rosetta Mae Chappell. She has one brother, Jessie Albert Chappell, and six sisters, Mable, Helen, Della Mae, Sarah, Minnie Lee and Laney Rebecca. Hazel Chappell Swiney resides in Springfield, IL, having moved there from Perry County in Sept. 1983. The following summary was submitted by her.

Hazel Chappell Swiney and Earl Swiney

I was told that my grandfather, Jesse Chappell, on my father's side of the family was a noble and honorable man. His parents brought him to this country during slavery times. He was married twice; had 14 children by his first wife, to whom was unknown to us, perhaps they were separated, bought and sold as slaves. He met my grandmother, Louise Smith, and married her the second marriage. They had 14 children together. They were owned by the Master Square Chappell of Flatwoods, TN. Mr. Square Chappell gave them a home on his farm to employ his family. He was good to them considering those days; at least they were all together and were not sold and separated. My father told us kids that they lived in a log cabin with a stick and dirt chimney, and a dirt floor. I remember father saying rattlesnakes came up into the house out of the dirt floor sometimes.

My grandfather in those days often fought duels, and he never lost a fight.

My grandmother Louise was a quiet and modest person.

My grandfather Alexander, on my mother's side of the family died when my mother was only 12 years of age, and my grandmother Candis was left with 10 kids to raise.

My mother, Rosetta Mae, was one of the elder children at home at the time. She took over and lent a helping hand until she got married to my father, Nimrod Chappell, in the year of 1913, at the age of 18. There were eight of us children. Three of my sisters died at an early age. We have had our share of ups and downs, but God was with us. We were brought up in a religious household. I remember father telling the family of an incident that happened to him once during the year of World War I. He had to make a trip to Clifton, TN on business. He was driving his horse and buggy along the countryside and out of nowhere he barely escaped being killed by a hand grenade. The white man fled into the woods. Father drove away in a hurry. My father was not a fearful man but almost always he carried a concealed weapon for protection on trips. Prayer and faith kept him going.

When my grandfather, Jesse Chappell's Master Square John Chappell took ill on his death bed, he asked that my grandfather Jesse come and pray by his bedside. Grandfather took Mr. Square John Chappell at his word and went and humbly prayed for his recovery, unfortunately he passed away. Perhaps shortly after Mr. Square John Chappell's death the slaves were all set free and grandfather was on his own to live where he chose. So he moved off Mr. Chappell's farm and built a house sufficient for his family.

This is the story of the Chappell family as I know it. Our family acquired the name Chappell from the Master Square John Chappell.

ARNOLD AND OVILLE TATE/ McGEE, Aaron Tate, born in Ireland 1827, came to America with his family when very young. The family's first home was in one of the Carolinas. In the early 1840s the family moved to Perry County and settled in a hollow about five miles south of Linden, now known as Tate Hollow. At the approximate age of 18, Aaron married Jane Childress who was 12 years old at the time of their wedding.

Aaron and Jane remained on the family farm and reared their children - Andrew, Thomas, Limuel and Rebecca Ann. Jane died in 1901 and Aaron died in 1910. They were buried in the Bethel Cemetery.

May 4, 1882, Limuel married Sallie Ann Westbrooks, daughter of Thomas and Anairy Hamm Westbrooks of Short Creek Community.

Limuel and Sallie became parents of five children - William Escar, Elonzo Limuel, Egbert

Jackson and Jessie Sula. Limuel contracted typhoid fever July 1901 and died from its effects. His youngest child, Jessie Sula, was one year old and the oldest, Escar, was 18. Escar became the father figure in the home, taking the responsibility of helping his mother rear the younger children.

Oville and Arnold McGee with son Bobby.

It became necessary for Escar to seek other employment to supplement income from the family farm. In the fall of 1902 he found work in Memphis as a street car conductor and worked there for 11 years. Soon after returning to Perry County he bought a small farm on Short Creek about one mile east of Linden.

After building a new home on the farm, he married Pearl Ledbetter, oldest daughter of R. T. and Docia Frances Young Ledbetter on May 3, 1918. They had two children, Docia Oville (Jan. 15, 1919) and Frances Ann (June 15, 1925).

In December 1932, Escar's common cold developed into double pneumonia. Within a week he died and was buried in Bethel Cemetery. Pearl, Oville and Frances continued to live on the farm.

In 1936, after becoming the first Tate to graduate from high school, Oville entered M.T.S.U. and received a lifetime teaching certificate in 1938. She returned to Perry County and began her 42 year teaching career in a one teacher school on Lower Hurricane Creek.

Johnnie Andrew and Cora Lomax McGee's son, Johnnie Arnold, married Oville on May 21, 1939. Their only child, Bobby Arnold McGee, was born June 9, 1945.

On June 12, 1979 while attending Law School at U.T. Knoxville, Bobby married Barbara Lee, daughter of Raymond and Nellie Hinson Lee. Their daughters, Brooke Alayna born May 12, 1982 and Blair Alysse born Dec. 15, 1986, live with them on Lick Creek on the farm previously owned by Thomas Young, Bobby's great great grandfather.

Oville continued her education and was granted two degrees: B.S. from M.T.S.U. at Murfreesboro and M.S. from George Peabody College of Vanderbilt University at Nashville.

Oville taught school. Arnold farmed and did construction work. They moved from Short Creek to Nashville in 1965. After retiring from Metro Nashville Davidson County Schools in 1980, they returned to Short Creek.

In August 1946, Frances Ann received a B.S. Degree from M.T.S.U. and married Lester Hogancamp, son of Bruce and Sadie Hodges Hogancamp of Marshalltown, IA. He was discharged from the Army and they made their home in Iowa where their only child, Randy Allen, was born Nov. 10, 1948.

Randy's marriage to Nancy Zink, 1971, resulted in two children: Nathan Allen, Sept. 21, 1976, and Amanda Elise, Sept. 10, 1980.

Pearl Tate died Feb. 20, 1988 and was buried in Bethel Cemetery.

JESSIE GRAY TATE AND JUNE DOWLAND TATE,

were married Aug. 21, 1943 in Lake City, AR. They lived in Union City, TN, Brownsville, TX and Greenwood, MS where Jesse G. Tate was Flight Instructor in the Army Air Force, discharged in October 1945. They moved back to Perry County to the farm at Lobelville where Jesse was born April 21, 1921. Jesse is the son of Charles Lemual Tate and Mildred Gray Tate, had one sister Mary Tate Bonner, born May 14, 1923. Charles Lemual Tate was the youngest son of Lemual Tate and Martha Flowers Tate. Mildred Gray Tate was the only child of Jesse Frank Gray and Nellie Burns Gray. Jesse Frank Gray died when Mildred was very young and Nellie Gray married J. C. Edwards. Mr. Edwards bought this farm in Oct. 1, 1879 from Elias Horner and wife, Mary Horner. At the death of Nellie Gray Edwards, this farm passed to Mildred Gray Tate. At her death, the farm was divided between Jesse G. Tate and June D. Tate and Mary Tate Bonner and S. V. Bonner.

Nathaniel Tate Zeitlin and Anna Tate Zeitlin, children of Janice Tate and Manuel Zeitlin, grandchildren of Jesse G. Tate and June Dowland Tate.

June Dowland Tate was born Dec. 2, 1924 to Vernon W. Dowland and Lucy Tilghman Dowland at Kenton, TN, Gibson County. June Dowland had one sister, Joy Dowland Gray. Vernon W. Dowland was the son of Henry Dowland and Ethel Irene Horner Dowland. She was the daughter of Elias Horner and Mary Horner and moved from Lobelville, Perry County, TN when she was four years old. This was sometime near the sale of the farm to Mr. T. C. Edwards. Lucy Tilghman Dowland was the youngest daughter of Benjamin H. Tilghman and Fannie Henry Tilghman.

Jesse and June Tate have one daughter, Janice, born March 3, 1946. She is married to Manual Zeitlin. They have two children, Anna Tate Zeitlin, born Jan. 5, 1987 and Nathaniel Tate Zeitlin, born Aug. 15, 1988. Janice Tate had one brother, Jon Dowland Tate, born Nov. 9, 1951, died Dec. 12, 1971. Manuel, Janice, Anna and Nate reside in Nashville, TN where Manuel is an Architect.

The farm where June and Jesse Tate reside was sold by June's great grandfather Elias Horner to my step grandfather, T. C. (Clem) Edwards Oct. 1879. It has been in our family about 120 years. *Submitted by Jesse G. Tate.*

TATUM-GRINDER,

George Black Tatum (Nov. 19, 1899-May 19, 1979). Parents Lev Tatum and Elizabeth Anderson Tatum. George was the youngest of eight children born to this union. Brothers: Matt Tatum, Irvin Tatum, Valentine Tatum and Oscar Tatum. Sisters: Fannie Tatum Turner, Martha Tatum Goodman Loveless and Polly Tatum Cooper. After the death of Elizabeth, Lev married Ada Curry Tatum. Children born to that union were: Pete Tatum, Nath Tatum, Alf Tatum, Elmer Tatum, Edith Tatum Crowell, Alma Tatum Dailey, Wilton Tatum Whitehead and Jessie Tatum.

Mr. & Mrs. George Tatum

Sadie Mae Grinder Tatum (Jan. 2, 1903-Sept. 9, 1961). Parents Noah Theodore Grinder (Nov. 11, 1875-Jan. 12, 1924) and Mary Jane Ary Grinder (Jan. 10, 1881-Nov. 19, 1954). Sadie was one of 13 children born to this union. Brothers: Abner Warren (A.W.) Grinder, Loyd Jessroe Grinder, William Zellnah (Zell) Grinder, Wesson Ledbetter Grinder, Ary Osburn Grinder and Theodore Clint Grinder. Sisters: Izorah Grinder Riley, Mollie Grinder Harder, Emma Jane Grinder Kilpatrick, Virginia Sue Grinder Hamm, Orbit Opal Grinder Garner and Norma Cletus Grinder Richardson.

Sadie's mother, Mary Jane Grinder, was left a widow at a young age with 13 children and had an extremely hard time rearing them. At that time, no aid of any kind was available. Her parents, William Ary (Aug. 7, 1840-April 20, 1924) and Mary Jane Warren Ary (Dec. 18, 1846-Jan. 11, 1922), owned several hundred acres of land on upper Sinking Creek and were faring well. When they were in their last years, they decided to give their eight children their inheritance and see how they used it. It is thought the amount was $1,500.00 each. Mary Jane Grinder bought a few acres of land with a house and barn. The house was in a low area and the creek was a constant threat. Once it got up so much that it ran through the hall of the house and the family had to wade out the back way and spend the night in the barn. After this, she moved to the upper part of her land, and with the help of her older children, built the house were she was living at the time of her death.

George and Sadie were married Dec. 26, 1920 by Esquire William (Bill) Kirk, in the front yard of the Kirk home on Sinking Creek, in Perry County. At the time of their deaths, they owned the Kirk place (purchased in 1943) where they were married. The farm is still in the Tatum family. Five children were born to this union.

Noah Carl Tatum (Sept. 26, 1922) is retired from the School System of Lewis County, Hohenwald, TN, where he served as Supervisor of Schools. He is serving as a Supply Minister for the Methodist Church at this time. He married Louise Grimes Tatum of Hohenwald, TN where they reside. Their children are: Garry Wayne Tatum, Marsha Ann Tatum Johnston and David Michael Tatum.

Samuel Black Tatum (S.B.) (Nov. 11, 1924) is retired from Meriwether-Lewis Electric Cooperative, Linden, TN. He is married to Nadean Shelton Tatum from Linden, TN where they reside. Their children are: Sammy Dale Tatum and Sharon Dean Tatum Horner.

Elizabeth Jane Tatum (June 24, 1928-Oct. 10, 1930).

Harold Ary Tatum (Dec. 24, 1930) is retired from the Military (U.S. Air Force). He is married to Faye Hodges Tatum from Ludowici, GA where they reside. Their children are: Rhonda Faye Tatum Hahn and Pamela Elaine Tatum McCullough.

Bobbie Jane Tatum Steele (Aug. 15, 1933) employed by First State Bank, Linden, TN. Married to Gus Allen Steele, formerly of Maryville, Blount County, TN. He retired from the Department of Safety-Tennessee State Trooper in 1984 after 30 years of service with the Department. They reside in Linden, TN. No children born to this union.

George and Sadie were proud of their three sons that served their country during times of wars. Carl and S. B. served during World War II and Harold served during the Korean War. *Submitted by Bobbie Tatum Steele.*

TATUM, The Tatum Family of Perry County is directly descended from John Tatum and Mary Wright Tatum. John Tatum was born in 1762 in Spotsylvania County, VA. He and Mary Wright (born 1765, Granville County, NC) were married Oct. 20, 1783. He died Aug. 3, 1824 and is buried, along with his wife Mary, in Dickson Union Cemetery on Old Charlotte Pike in Dickson, TN.

John Tatum was a Revolutionary Soldier, and is listed on monument in Dickson County Courthouse in Charlotte, TN. He was a member of the Dickson County Court, having served as a magistrate for several years. He is listed on many court documents in the State Archives.

The Tatum Family who settled in Perry County is comprised of descendants of George Washington Tatum and Parthenia Murrell. George Washington Tatum (born Oct. 22, 1802) was the eighth of 13 children born to John and Mary Wright Tatum. They came into Perry County as a westward gravitation from Dickson County (which at the time became parts of both Hickman and Perry counties respectively).

We are the primary descendants of Sublett Allen Tatum (born Oct. 22, 1839), who was the fifth of nine children born to the union of Parthenia Murrell and George Washington Tatum.

LEVEN HILLMAN TATUM, the third child of Sublett A. and Margaret A. Tatum, married Mary Elizabeth Anderson (born May 28, 1868). To this marriage was born Irvin (1885-1948); William Madison (Dec. 15, 1887-July 13, 1975); Oscar (June 26, 1890-Feb. 6, 1959); Sarah Francis "Fannie" (May 23, 1893-July 2, 1977); Polly (June 26, 1894-Jan. 4, 1977);

Martha (1896-July 15, 1974); Val (1898-1950); George (Nov. 18, 1899-May 19, 1979). The first wife of Leven Hillman died Jan. 10, 1902.

Leven Hillman Tatum, March 19, 1864 to January 10, 1925.

Leven Hillman Tatum was married a second time to Lila Ada McCurry (born Feb. 22, 1888). To this marriage was born Alma (Jan. 15, 1904-Dec. 25, 1976); Woodrow Pete (Feb. 20, 1907-May 20, 1973); Alf (Sept. 22, 1909 - now living in Lewis County); Nathan Allen (June 26, 1912-Feb. 2, 1989); Edith (March 17, 1915 - now living in Lewis County); Elmer (May 16, 1918 - now living in Memphis, TN); Wilton (Feb. 22, 1921 - now living in Lewis County); and Jessie (April 3, 1924-May 29, 1956). Leven Hillman died Jan. 10, 1925 and is buried in the Dabb's Cemetery along side his first wife, Mary Elizabeth. The second wife of Leven Hillman died March 15, 1968 and is buried in the Flatwoods Cemetery.

Nathan Allen, the fourth child of Leven and Ada Tatum, was married Sept. 21, 1935 to Laura Adkins (born May 12, 1917). To this marriage was born Jack Bedford Tatum (born Nov. 16, 1936). He now lives on the head waters of Sinking Creek with his wife, Barbara Jane Loveless Tatum (born July 16, 1940). They were united in marriage Feb. 23, 1958. To this marriage was born Jeffery Scott (born Sept. 28, 1962) and Beverly Jane (born April 18, 1976).

Nathan and Laura also had a daughter, Mary Francis Tatum (born May 30, 1938). She now lives in Ramer, TN with her husband, Charles Hollie. To this marriage were born Mark and Sherrie Hollie.

TATUM-SHELTON, Samuel Black "S.B." Tatum and Verna Nadean Shelton Tatum reside in Linden. They were married Oct. 18, 1952.

S. B. Tatum's parents were George Black and Sadie Mae Grinder Tatum of the Sinking Creek Community. Nadean's parents were Mary Elizabeth Rainey and Grady Shelton of Linden.

S. B. was the second born of four children: Noah "Carl," Samuel Black, Elizabeth Jane, Harold Ary and Bobbie Jane Tatum. All are still alive, except for Elizabeth Jane, who died as a young girl. Carl lives in Hohenwald, TN, Harold lives in Ludowici, GA and Bobbie Jane lives in Linden.

Nadean was the sixth born of eight children: Mildred Opal, Ralph Lynn, Mary Laverne, Brown, Grady Jack, Verna Nadean, Bobbie Jo and Betty. Nadean, Bobbie Jo and Betty are the only survivors, they reside in Linden, TN.

S. B. was born Nov. 11, 1924 on Sinking Creek. At the age of 18 was drafted into World War II. He served his country on the *USS Anthony*, a destroyer #DD515, squadron 24 of task force 58.

Samuel Black "S.B." and Verna Nadean Shelton Tatum with their two children, Sammy Tatum and Sharon Tatum Horner.

After the war he returned to Linden in 1945, and worked in construction. Later he went to barber school and worked as a barber before finally going to work for Meriwether Lewis Electric cooperative for 35 years.

Nadean was born March 29, 1930. She graduated from Perry County High in 1949 and started working for Linden Apparel. Through the years she has been a housewife, mother and worked with the Head Start program.

As stated earlier, these two were joined in holy matrimony on Oct. 18, 1952. From this union were born two children: Sammy Dale and Sharon Dean Tatum.

Sammy was born Dec. 20, 1954. He graduated from Perry County High in 1972. He received a degree in nursing at the University of Tennessee at Martin, TN in 1981.

At this time he is a registered nurse in the emergency department at Williamson Medical Center in Franklin, TN.

Sammy is married to Phyllis Ann Canterbury Tatum. They were married April 12, 1986, and live in Franklin, TN. At this time they have no children.

Phyllis is a licensed Esthetician in Nashville at Illusions Day Spa. She is the daughter of Mary Hazel Hargrove Canterbury and the late Okey Athel Canterbury Jr. of Nashville, TN. Phyllis has one sibling, James O. Canterbury, who lives in Maderia Beach, FL.

Sharon Dean Tatum Horner was born Feb. 6, 1960. She graduated from Perry County High in 1978, and has since been employed with First State Bank in Linden. Sharon is married to Robert Mark Horner. They became one on Dec. 19, 1986. Mark is an employee of the Perry County Highway Department. They have two children: Jared Mark Horner born May 1, 1989, and Colby Tatum Horner born Dec. 5, 1991.

SUBLETT TATUM, was born on Swan Creek in a hollow called Tatum Branch in Hickman County. Sublett worked at the sawmills in Tatum Branch. He then married (March 26, 1858) Margaret Ann Miller (born March 25, 1840), the daughter of Dave Miller and Josephine Anderson. Sublett and Margaret's first child was Mary Francis (born Jan. 18, 1860). Sub served in the Civil War Co. 1 24 UNF from Hickman County. Sublett and his family moved in 1864 to the head waters of Rockhouse Creek and

Carter Hollow, a part of Cotton Branch. Sublett bought a track of land on Rockhouse Creek and then sold it. In 1884 Sublett invested in 1/3 interest in the Jack Tatum farm on the head waters of Sinking Creek. Mary Francis married George Washington Tucker. Sublett and Margaret's other children were Josiah George Allen (born Dec. 18, 1861 d. at age nineteen). He is buried in the backyard of Dr. Black's place at Sugar Hill in Perry County. The other children of Sublett and Margaret were born on the head waters of Rockhouse Creek. Leven Hillman was born March 19, 1864. Sarah Caroline was born Jan. 9, 1866 and was married to Lawrence Graves. Martha Ann was born March 16, 1868 and died in May of 1869, she is buried at Dabb's Cemetery on Rockhouse Creek. Theodore Joseph was born March 23, 1870.

Sublett A. Tatum, 1839 to 1908.

Elisa Black "Tack" (born March 30, 1872) was married March 1, 1891 to Mary Victoria Smith (born May 10, 1870). They lived on the head waters of Sinking Creek. To this marriage were born Lee, Lloyd and Cazzy Tatum. Tack bought a farm and moved on further down Sinking Creek. They lived there until his death, Feb. 1, 1951. Thomas Dickerson (born Jan. 20, 1875) married Ellen Boyce and to this marriage were born Barnet, Jack, John, Maria and Hattie. Julia Parthenia (Feb. 13, 1877-Nov. 1886) is buried at the Dabb's Cemetery. The wife of Sublett A. Tatum died June 21, 1897 and is buried along side her daughter in Dabb's Cemetery. Sublett A. Tatum died Feb. 18, 1908. He served as a Confederate soldier, and his grave is marked in Dabb's Cemetery on Rockhouse Creek in Perry County with a white marble marker. His second wife, Mary Jane Phillips Tatum, was a recipient of a Confederate widow's pension as is stated in the war records at the Tennessee National Guard Archive in Nashville, TN.

JERRY TAYLOR, born Jan. 8, 1928 in Henderson County, TN, is the great great grandson of William Taylor and Mary Bridwell. William and Mary moved from South Carolina to Dickson County, TN about 1808. They were the parents of 11 children including, Mary born 1804, Margaret born 1806, Jane born 1808, Jessie born 1816, George born 1819, Elizabeth born 1820 and Andrew Jackson born 1825. Jessie married Elizabeth Wood and after her death, married Mary A. Ledbetter in 1885. Jessie and Mary are buried in the Taylor Cemetery near Linden.

Andrew Jackson Taylor was in Perry County by 1845. He married Tempe and they had five children. William born 1846, married Mary; George born 1849, married Mollie Beasley; Andrew Jackson born 1853, married Rosanna "Rosie" Meacheam; Joe born 1855, married Reansa Beard; and Martha Amelia born 1860, married William "Billy" Crosby. After Tempe's death, Andrew married Elizabeth Bingham Meacheam, the mother of "Rosie." Andrew and Elizabeth were the parents of seven children, Thomas Franklin "Tom" born 1863, married Alice Morgan; Ella born 1865, married Jim Beasley; Theodosia Emmaline "Emma" born 1868, married Joe Raney; Sarah A. "Sally" born 1870, married Wm. H. Young; Robert born 1873, d. 1895; Sam A. born 1876, d. 1955; Lula E. born 1881, married Joseph Parks. Andrew Jackson Sr. and his children, William, Joe and Emma are buried in the Rainey Cemetery in Perry County. Sally is buried in the Young Cemetery, and Martha is buried in the Simmons Cemetery in Perry County.

Jerry and Louise Taylor

Andrew Jackson Taylor Jr. and Rosie were the parents of eight children all born in Perry County, Mary born 1876, married George Pritchard; Obed born 1878, married Susan Craig; Andrew Garfield born July 22, 1880, married first, Merton Houston, second, Maud Morgan, third, Rhoda Bradfield, and 4th, Elizabeth Sanders; Joe Ashley born 1883, married first, Beulah Anderson and second Cora Rogers; Norma Tempe born 1886, married O. T. Craig; Minnie Elizabeth born 1889, d. 1912; Clyde Thomas born 1891, married Mary Clyde Laster; and Lloyd Franklin born 1896, married Rennie Hendrix. Andrew and Rosie moved their family to Henderson County, TN about 1900.

Andrew Garfield Taylor and Merton Houston had one daughter Lena born 1904, married Robert Dodd. Andrew and Maud had three children, Myrtle born 1907, married Rupert Prichard; Joseph Morgan born 1913, married Vernice Howard; and Cara Maud born 1914, married Clyde Waugh. Andrew and Rhoda had four sons, Alf Daniel born 1921, married Mattie Turnbo; Bob Peay born 1922, married Christine McLin; Ted born 1924, married Sue Northern; and Jerry born 1928, married Louise Bizzell.

Jerry Taylor married Louise Bizzell on June 1, 1947. After living in Pemiscott County, MO and Peoria, IL for many years. Jerry and Louise now live in Memphis, TN. They have three children, Judy born 1948, married John Miller; Debra born 1953; and Michael Andrew born 1961, married Debra Parks. Judy and John have two sons, John Christopher "Chris" born 1976 and Steven Lee born 1980. They reside in Memphis, TN. Debra resides in Memphis, TN. Mike and Debra are the parents of a daughter, Monica born in 1987 and a son, Craig born 1991. They live in Norcross, GA.

VIOLET MAY (COTTON) THOMPSON, daughter of Irvin and Savannah (Graves) Cotton, was born Aug. 14, 1902 in Perry County. She was married April 5, 1930 to Paul Oakley Thompson, son of George Orr and Martha Jane (Porter) Thompson. Paul was born May 10, 1906 in Florence, AL, died April 22, 1979 and is buried in Graves Cemetery.

Paul E. Thompson and Doris June Thompson on their wedding day.

Children of Paul O. and Violet (Cotton) Thompson:

Paul Edwin Thompson, born April 20, 1932 in Perry County, was married Aug. 24, 1956 to Doris June Holt, daughter of Clint and Lillian Rose (Mercer) Holt. June was born June 4, 1936 in Perry County. Children of Paul Edwin and June (Holt) Thompson: 1.) Mike Thompson, born Sept. 30, 1957 in Lewis County, was married Dec. 28, 1985 to Lorie Brown. Their children: Grant Thompson, born July 16, 1960 in Maury County and Morgan Thompson, born Nov. 30, 1989 in Maury County; 2.) Paris Thompson, born July 26, 1960 in Shelby County, was married July 5, 1986 to Judy Shipp. One child: Coleman Thompson, born Aug. 6, 1991 in Maury County; 3.) Jeffery Thompson, born and died March 19, 1964 in Dickson County and buried in Swiss Cemetery, Hohenwald; 4.) David Thompson, born Oct. 10, 1965 in Lawrence County, was married July 7, 1990 to Sandra Tharp. One child: Shelby Thompson, born June 16, 1991 in Maury County; 5.) John Thompson, born and died Nov. 27, 1967 in Hardin County, buried in Campground Cemetery, Pinhook Road in Hardin County.

Marjorie Thompson, born Nov. 6, 1934 in Perry County, was married June 20, 1958 to Tommy Lee Bates, son of Everett and Tommie Ruth (Black) Bates. One child: Kimberly Bates, born March 15, 1968 in Williamson County.

THOMPSON, The first written record of William Thompson, 1776-1869, was his marriage in 1820 in Maury County, to Sarah Wiley, 1800-1873, (daughter of Robert and Sarah Wiley). It is known William had relatives in Hickman County, TN.

After William and Sarah's marriage, they bought a farm on Sinking Creek, Perry County. Later they bought 4,000 acres on the Tennessee River. It was known as Thompson's Landing, now known as New Era. Their nine children were: Thomas married Eliza; Juliana Craig married William Pace; Robert Wiley married, 1846,

Rebecca Ann Randle (daughter of Amos and Rebecca Finn Randle); William Jr.; Amanda married Rufus Martin; Mary Jane married, first, Levi Sharpe, and second Dr. Joseph Marvin; Rufus K.; John W.; Augustus A. Tragedy struck the Thompsons during the Civil War. William, John, Rufus and Augustus joined the Confederate Army. William and John died early in the war. Rufus and Augustus died in Union prison camps.

Joe and Martha Thompson, 1923.

Robert Wiley, 1826-1885, and Rebecca Ann Thompson's, 1830-1912, children were: Amanda married Dr. Joseph Marvin; Amos married Jane Roberts; Sarah Malone married Bill Harder; William married Ida Guthrie; Martha; John Wesley married Elvira Richardson; Joseph Yarbro married Martha Murphy; Robert Allen married Dovie Vise; Melinda Ella married John Broadaway.

Joseph (Joe) Yarbro Thompson, 1868-1961, married first in 1887 Alice Lee Kirk, 1870-1895, (daughter of James Akin and Lucinda Grimmit Kirk). Joe and Alice's five children were: Asbury; a son, died in infancy; Bessie Lee married first Newton Denton - three children, married second Isom Turnbow - eight children, married third, R. E. Austin; Dossie J. married Mary Kimble - 11 children; Commodore Perry married Guyeulla Denton - 12 children.

Joe married second, 1896, Martha Elizabeth Murphy, daughter of Milton and Delilah Gilbert Murphy. Their children were: Clora Mae married James McNally; Beulos Rebecca Ann Melinda married Ernest Roscoe Broadaway - children, Roscoe McNally and Kathleen Pauline; Fred McMillian married Lona Bunch - one son, Benton McMillian; Billy Webb married Doris Crane - children, James Webb and Charles Roscoe; Amos Gassaway Brown married Lou Marlow; Pauline married first Lee Weems - one son, Bobby Frank, married second Jim Freeman - one son, Billy Joe, married third Calvin Holcomb; Golden Garner married, 1937, Sara Edna Midgett. Joe married, 1928, third Ruth Holder Lomax and fourth, 1941, Annie Roberts Denton. Joe was a farmer, Primitive Baptist Minister and Sheriff of Perry County.

Golden Garner, 1912-1988, and Sara Edna Midgett, 1916-1989, (daughter of Edgar and Era Douglass Midgett) were the parents of: Patricia Faye, 1939, and Beverly Ann, 1941.

Patricia Faye married first, 1956, Thomas Porter Curtis Jr. Their children are Thomas Porter III, 1957; Charles Michael, 1959; and Golden Thompson, 1968. Thomas Porter III married Jody Butler - children Thomas Porter IV, 1985, and Steven Michael, 1988. Patricia married second Thomas Wayne Long.

Beverly Ann married, 1959, Wallace Eugene Hardison. Their children are: Wallace Eugene II, 1962, and Sarah Ann, 1965.

Golden was an electrician for DuPont. He organized the Long Hollow Jamboree and played the ukulele. *Submitted by Patricia Thompson Long and Beverly Thompson Haridson.*

TILLER, William Floyd and Margaret Patterson Tiller moved to Perry County from Hickman County, TN in 1948, with their four children. Upon moving to Linden, Floyd established Tiller Furniture and worked there until his death March 10, 1951. Family members continue to operate the business.

The early Tiller family was in Virginia in the late 1700s, then moved to Alabama in the early 1800s and William Baker Tiller, a Civil War veteran, the grandfather of Floyd, moved to Lincoln County around the end of the war. Some families connected to the Tiller line include Mullins, Andrews, Mitchell and Loving.

Margaret Patterson Tiller was born in Moore County, TN, the daughter of Lonnie Lee and Gertrude Wiseman Patterson. Her maternal grandparents were Tom and Sara Bean Wiseman. The Beans were early settlers in Franklin County, TN and trace their ancestry to William Bean, born in 1730 in Scotland and died in South Carolina in 1794. Margaret Tiller's paternal great grandfather, Logan Madison Patterson, served with the Confederacy as a Lieutenant of Co. G 44th Tenn. Infantry and was killed during the Battle of Shiloh. His father, William Patterson, born 1793, married Rachel Clendening, the granddaughter of Colonel Anthony Bledsoe, Indian fighter, who died July 20, 1788 at Bledsoe's Fort, in Sumner County, TN, following an Indian attack. Other families connected to the Patterson family include Sherrill and Grigsby to John Grigsby, Revolutionary War soldier, born 1728 in Virginia and died 1794; the Garrison family to Arthur Garrison, Revolutionary War soldier.

The children of Floyd and Margaret are: Bettye who married Jim Tucker and their children are Pam, Lisa and Ted; Billy, who married Jessie Ruth Pope, no children; Bobby who married Marijon Young and their children are Felecia, Kristi and Brian; Joe Mac married Elizabeth Howell and their child is Najie.

TININ-BRUCE, John Thomas Tinin, a teacher and lawyer, was the son of John McNairy and Jemimah Richardson Tinin. He was born Sept. 26, 1856 in Perry County, TN. He attended school at Linden Academy and Bethel College in McKenzie, TN.

John Thomas Tinin and Mary Bruce Tinin with granddaughter Mary Dean Rainey, 1927.

Mary Palestine Bruce, a teacher, was the daughter of Silas and Keziah Leathers Bruce. She was born Dec. 19, 1858 in Dickson County, TN.

John Thomas and Mary Palestine met in Dickson, TN and were married Dec. 25, 1885. Sometime after they were married they moved to Decaturville, TN and taught school. Then they moved to Galatia, IL so John Thomas could attend law school. After completing this course, they returned to Decaturville and lived about three years. Then they moved to Linden and bought a home. John Thomas opened a law office and Mary gave up teaching to be a mother and homemaker. They had nine children Geanie C., Chester Bruce, Carrie, Jesse Ewell (twin to Bess) (these all died as infants and are buried at Culps Chapel), Tom A. (Sept. 26, 1889-March 18, 1969), Willie E. (July 25, 1892-Nov. 15, 1974), Aaron Stanley (Oct. 19, 1893-July 31, 1979), Bessie Jewell (Oct. 1, 1896-June 3, 1980) and Loudine (June 16, 1900-Nov. 1984).

Tom, a bachelor, worked for the Linden Post Office and was bookkeeper for Ray O'Guin Truck Lines. Stanley became a Pharmacist and married Parnell Derrick. He owned a drug store in Lawrenceburg, TN. They had two children, Stanley Jr. and Mary Jo. Willie E. was a teacher. She married Bennett B. Wilson and they had three children, Bennett B. Wilson Jr. (Dick), John Bruce and Mary Emily. Bess, a teacher, married William Cecil Rainey and they had two children, James Cecil and Mary Dean. Loudine also was a teacher. She married Wade Lamb and they had two children, John Thomas and Mary Wadine.

John Thomas and Mary remained at this

Grandchildren of John and Mary Tinin, July 1934: (Left to Right) Mary Wadine Lamb, John Thomas Lamb, Mary Dean Rainey, Stanley Tinin Jr., Mary Emily Wilson, Mary Jo Tinin, John Bruce Wilson, James Cecil Rainey and Bennett B. Wilson Jr.

homeplace and enjoyed their children and grandchildren until their deaths.

John T. died March 30, 1936 and Mary Palestine died March 7, 1941. They are buried at Culps Cemetery near Clifton, TN.

TININ-RAINEY, Bessie Jewell Tinin was born Oct. 1, 1896 in Galatia, IL to John Thomas and Mary Bruce Tinin. She was educated in Perry County and West Tennessee Normal School in Memphis, TN. She taught her first school at age 16 in Rogersville, TN. She also taught school in Perry County on Brush Creek and Sinking Creek before her marriage to William Cecil Rainey.

Bess and Cecil Rainey in the summer of 1953 leaving on a trip to Florida.

William Cecil Rainey was born Aug. 5, 1891 in Perry County, TN. He was the son of William B. and Emma Taylor Rainey of Perry County. He was a farmer and livestock dealer and also worked for McDonald Funeral Home for many years.

Mary Dean Rainey and Jim Rainey, 1940.

Bess and Cecil were married Jan. 21, 1921 in Linden, TN. Four children were born to this union, two daughters (died at birth), a son, James Cecil (Jim - born May 3, 1925) and a daughter, Mary Dean (born Dec. 6, 1926)

Jim married Nima Mae Mathes in January of 1956 and two children were born to this union, Gordon Thomas Rainey (born Jan. 26, 1957) and Resia Beth (born Aug. 5, 1960).

Mary Dean married Edward Allen Trull March 5, 1945 and four children were born to this union, Jane (born Dec. 31, 1946), Jimmy (born Feb. 5, 1949), RoseAnn (born Aug. 17, 1953) and Bill (born Aug. 13, 1967).

Cecil died June 2, 1956 and Bess died June 3, 1980. They are buried in the Rainey Cemetery in Linden, TN.

TININ-RICHARDSON, John McNairy Tinin, a farmer, was born March 9, 1831 in McNairy County, TN. He married Jemimah Richardson, born April 25, 1832, in Perry County, TN. They lived in a log cabin on Cedar Creek and raised eight children. They were John Thomas, Jimmie, Charlie, Jess, Will, Martha Jane, Melissa and Julia. John McNairy died March 5, 1899 and is buried at Culp's Cemetery. Jemimah died Jan. 28, 1905 and is buried at Culp's Cemetery.

TOM A. TININ, son of John Thomas and Mary Palestine Bruce Tinin, was born in Decaturville, TN, Sept. 26, 1889 on his father's birthday. Tom was a bachelor and remained at the homeplace in Linden until his death March 18, 1967.

Tom A. Tinin, 1963.

He worked for the post office and Ray O'Guin Truck Lines. He was a collector of Indian Artifacts and was known to have had one of the best collections in the South. He was approached by a representative from the Smithsonian Institute in Washington, DC one time wanting to buy his collections for the museum, but he wouldn't sell it. Tom could be seen most every day driving his A-model Ford out to someone's farm and freshly plowed fields to hunt "Indian Rocks." He had all his artifacts displayed in a room of his home and enjoyed showing them to anyone that wanted to look. He also took pride in the fact that he never dug an Indian grave, everything he had, he found on top of the ground, or it was given to him by farmers who found things in their fields when they were plowing.

Tom, a Methodist, was also known for his beautiful tenor voice and sang in the choir. He's buried in the Dr. O. A. Kirk Cemetery.

MILTON GREEN TOMERLIN, born May 30, 1859, Giles County, died March 9, 1935 in West Tennessee. He married Sarah Elizabeth Mathis, daughter of James Bluford Mathis and Mary E. Dabbs. They had six children, all born at Cedar Creek. 1) James Walter Tomerlin, born Sept. 21, 1883, died March 11, 1964, Giles County, buried there in Maplewood Cemetery. His wife Lillie May Dickey, born Dec. 3, 1888, died July 5, 1969. Children Hessie, Carl, J. L., Hazel, Elizabeth, Earl and another girl. 2) Alice Florence Tomerlin, born April 2, 1885, died July 6, 1984, buried Roberts Cemetery. Her husband, Samuel Washington Hardin, born Nov. 5, 1882, died April 9, 1959, buried Roberts Cemetery. He had been married once before and had a son, Ernest. Ernest died young, buried Roberts Cemetery. Children of Samuel and Alice are an infant buried Roberts Cemetery, Leslie Brown, Pauline, Ray Hassle and Leonard Hollis. 3) John Franklin Tomerlin, born Dec. 29, 1888, married Aug. 31, 1912, Flatwoods to Gertrude Bunch. She was born April 9, 1897, Perry County, died June 10, 1983, buried Milan, TN, daughter of Howard Bunch and Rachel Horner. Four children, Durward Maxwell, Velma Lucille, Joy Marie and Mary Jean. 4) William Albert Tomerlin, born Dec. 27, 1890, lived Belles, TN. His children, Mildred, Cecil, Elois, Edith and possibly others. 5) Mary Hilda Tomerlin, born Sept. 13, 1893, married a Knight and had children. 6) Minnie Belle Tomerlin, born Jan. 13, 1897, married Tom Dabbs and had Alton and Harold Dean Dabbs.

GARNER McCONNICO TOOMBS (TOMBS), born 1804, was the seventh child of Edmund Toombs and his wife Sabra. Garner was named for the Reverend Garner McConnico who came to Williamson County, TN in 1799 from Richmond County, VA - Lunenberg Parish. The Toombs family moved with the Reverend McConnico and were members of his Big Harpeth Baptist Church located three miles from Franklin, TN.

Edmund Toombs bought land in Maury County, TN, Oct. 1, 1820 and can be found on the 1820 Maury County census with five males and three females enumerated. One of those males was Garner Toombs.

Garner Toombs was listed in the 1830 Maury County, TN census, the 1850 Lewis County, TN census and in the 1860 Perry County, TN census.

Children of Garner Toombs and his wife Sabra were: William Y. Toombs 1824; Louisa Elizabeth Toombs 1824-1901, married Wm. Cooper; Edmund Toombs 1829, married Lydia Sims; Lucinda A. Toombs 1831, married Joseph Smith; Allen H. Toombs 1832; Sarah A. Toombs 1837; D. S. Samuel Toombs 1840-1883, married Martha Francis Kilpatrick.

It is believed but undocumented, that D. S. Samuel Toombs and Martha Francis Kilpatrick were married on Jan. 9, 1861 in Perry County, TN. Martha Kilpatrick was the daughter of Enos Simpson Kilpatrick and Martha McCorpen Kilpatrick who resided in Perry County, TN between 1850 and 1867 on the head waters of Rock House Creek.

The 1860 Perry County, TN Census indicates that the Garner Toombs family and the Enos S. Kilpatrick families lived in close proximity. The Toombs family was enumerated on page 48 dwelling number 312, while the Kilpatrick family was on page 49 dwelling number 318.

Thus the family connection to Perry County, TN is made through the Toombs (Tombs) and Kilpatrick families.

Prepared by Mrs. Roger Bonnie Bassetti, wife of the great great great grandson of Garner Toombs and Enos Simpson Kilpatrick.

TREADWELL-HINSON, Defo Treadwell and Martha Louise Hinson, have deep roots in Perry County. They migrated to Gibson County, at Trenton the year of 1942.

Martha Louise Hinson, born on Coon Creek of Perry County, is the daughter of Luther Hinson and Ophelia Hinson. Luther Hinson is the son of William Hinson and Martha Hinson. William Hinson is the son of Dr. Hugh Hinson and Sarah Duncan. Dr. Hugh Hinson is the son of Jordan

Hinson and Rachel Hufstedler. Ophelia Hinson is the daughter of John Forrest Hinson and Minnie Hensley. John Forrest Hinson is the son of Jordon Hinson and Sarah McDonald. Martha Hinson is the daughter of Newton Jasper Hinson and Sarah Skelton.

Defo and Martha Louise Hinson Treadwell

Defo Treadwell, born on Rockhouse Creek of Perry County, is the son of George Treadwell and Lillian Barber. George Treadwell is the son of Daniel Treadwell and Mary Harder. Daniel Treadwell is the son of George Treadwell and Catherine Hassell. Lillian Barber is the daughter of William Franklin Barber and Annie Qualls. William Franklin Barber is the son of Daniel Barber and Mary Ann Kilpatrick. Daniel Barber is the son of Allen Barber and Martha Kilpatrick. Mary Harder is the daughter of Edmond Harder and Catherine Sharp. Annie Qualls is the daughter of Jordon Qualls and Josephine Vickrey.

Defo and Martha Louise went to school in Perry County. He went to school on Hurricane Creek and she went to school on Coon Creek.

On March 1943, he received his World War II draft notice from Perry County. He reported to the draft board at Linden with a group of young men that were to report at Ft. Oglethorpe, GA. He had a choice of the U.S. Army or U.S. Navy, and he entered into the U.S. Navy for a period of duration plus six months, with time in Europe and the Pacific. He was discharged at Memphis Naval Station on the 8th of January, 1946. He met Martha Louise Hinson about a year later, and they married on Dec. 23, 1948. Their first daughter, Patricia was born Aug. 11, 1950. She and her husband Jimmy Higdon have one son, Justin Higdon born Aug. 15, 1978. Their second daughter, Emily was born April 11, 1961. She and her husband, John Swain have one daughter, Teresa Swaim, born Dec. 14, 1988.

Defo went back to school in 1958 and took Business Administration and again in 1961 he took a job with a Farm Equipment Dealer in Milan, TN as an Accountant and Parts Manager for 23 years before retiring.

Martha Louise, a homemaker during all these years, and Defo are enjoying retirement here at Trenton at the present time. *Submitted by Defo Treadwell.*

TRULL-DENTON, Glenda Jane Trull was born Dec. 31, 1946 in Nashville, TN. She is the daughter of Mary Dean Rainey and Edward Allen Trull. She graduated from Perry County High School in 1964. She worked at Linden Apparel for many years before going to work for First State Bank where she has been employed for the past 11 years.

Jane Denton, Regina Denton Edwards, Marcia Denton Miller, Jeff Denton and Clenus Denton, July 1, 1989.

Clenus Roe Denton was born Aug. 22, 1943 in Perry County, TN. He is the son of Margrette McAfee and Leslie Brown Denton. He graduated from Linden High School in 1963. He worked for Linden Apparel as a machine mechanic until the plant closed. He now works for Henry I. Siegel Co. in Hohenwald, TN.

Jane and Clinty were married May 29, 1964 in Linden, TN. They have three children, Regina (b May 2, 1965), Jeffrey Scott (b Nov. 8, 1966) and Marcia Leah (b March 28, 1971).

Regina is married to Rick Edwards of Hohenwald and they have three children Brandi Michelle Qualls (b Oct. 10, 1981), Chaz Carlton (b April 8, 1990) and Trey Denton Edwards (b Aug. 31, 1992). Regina works for Robinson Mfg. Co. and Rick works for Bates Fabricating in Lobelville.

Jeff married Stephanie Warren of Clifton, TN. They have two sons, Dustin Scott (b Oct. 7, 1989) and Donovan Ross (b Feb. 1, 1994) Denton. Jeff works for Linden Automatic Tool and Stephanie works for Johnson Control.

Marcy is married to Jimmy Miller of Hohenwald and they have one daughter, Kerri Lane Miller (b Sept. 4, 1990). Marcy works for The Bank of Perry County and Jimmy works for the Dana Corp. in Hohenwald.

TRULL-HANKINS, John B. Trull was born Sept. 26, 1896 in Perry County, TN. He was the son of William Allen and Martha Elizabeth Barber Trull. He was a farmer and worked on the John Godwin Farm on Coon Creek for many years.

Johnny and Estalee Hankins Trull, 1922.

Nancy Estalee Hankins was born Jan. 13, 1906 in Lewis County. She was the daughter of Henry Edward and Minnie Jane Hankins of Lewis County.

Johnny and Estalee were married July 30, 1922 by J. A. Land in Linden, TN. To this union were born two sons, Obe Atha (April 23, 1923-July 30, 1986) and Edward Allen (born Aug. 22, 1925).

Atha married Bonnie Ruth Campbell Aug. 29, 1950. To this union were born three children, Marguerita Laurell (born July 22, 1951), Judith Lynn (born Nov. 6, 1953) and John Robert (born April 26, 1960).

Rita (Ms. Garry O'Guin) had two children, Patrick Ryan (born Jan. 18, 1976) and Reagan Lynn (born May 20, 1978). Judy (Mrs. Billy Alley) had three children, Morgan Breanna (born Sept. 14, 1979), Skyelar Brittany (born Dec. 11, 1983), and Summer Lindsey (born Aug. 4, 1988). Robbie had two sons, Joshua Caleb (born Sept. 22, 1980) and Robert Corey (born Nov. 29, 1985).

Edward married Mary Dean Rainey March 5, 1945. To this union were born four children, Glenda Jane (born Dec. 31, 1946), James Edward (Jimmy-born Feb. 5, 1949), Rose Ann (born Aug. 17, 1953) and William Allen (Bill-born Aug. 13, 1967).

Jane (Ms. Clinty Denton) had three children, Regina (born May 2, 1965), Jeffrey Scott (born Nov. 8, 1966) and Marcia Leah (Marcy-born March 28, 1971), and six grandchildren, Brandi Michelle Qualls, Chaz & Trey Edwards, Dustin and Donovan Denton, and Kerri Lane Miller.

Jimmy Trull never married.

Rose Ann (Mrs. Don Deere) had two sons, Brandon Michael (born Feb. 2, 1974) and Justin Brent (born Feb. 7, 1978). They live in Lexington, TN.

Bill has one daughter, Shayna Brooke (Dec. 5, 1986).

Johnny died May 30, 1974 and is buried in the New Trull Cemetery on Coon Creek. Estalee died May 8, 1992 and is buried at the Dr. O. A. Kirk Cemetery in Linden, TN. Atha Trull died July 30, 1986 and is buried in the Dr. O. A. Kirk Cemetery in Linden.

TRULL-ROBERTSON, Walter Trull was born Dec. 1, 1926 in Perry County, TN, the son of A. R. Trull who was born April 7, 1890 and Della Warren Trull who was born Dec. 1, 1906. On April 20, 1946, Walter married Mary Frances Robertson who was born Jan. 20, 1927 in Benton County, TN.

A. R. (Dick) Trull

The issue of Walter and Mary Frances (Robertson) Trull is as follows:

Jerry Trull born March 15, 1947, married Donna Florence April 13, 1967 and there are two children: Cara Trull (1968-1984) and buried in the Liberty Methodist Cemetery, Camden and Caycie Born October 1982.

Terry Trull, a twin to Jerry, born March 15, 1947, married Charlotte Jordon Aug. 1969 and there are three children: Bryan, born Aug. 1970; Mandy, born Jan. 1981; and Matt, born Jan. 1983.

Kay (Trull) Peach Horton born Oct. 3, 1950, first married Jimmy Peach in 1969. They had two children: Tim Peach, born March 1970 and Christopher Scott Peach, born June 1971 and died in an automobile accident November 1993. Chris is buried in Eastview Cemetery, Benton County, TN. Kay married second Lynn Horton in 1986 and has one stepson, Jeremy Horton, 16 years old.

All of the Trull and Horton families live in and around the Camden area in Benton County. *Submitted by Donna and Jerry Trull.*

TRULL-WARREN, A. Renauld (Dick) Trull), born 1890 in Perry County, TN married Della Warren in 1919.

Alf Trull with wife and son.

The known siblings of Dick Trull, to our knowledge, are:

Alf Trull, born Perry County, TN, moved to Chicago, IL. Made his home there, died and was buried in Illinois.

Jenny Trull, a sister, born in Perry County. She also moved to Chicago, IL, married a Mr. Mealer.

Ginny Trull, a sister, born in Perry County, married Jess Trull. In later years Jenny Mealer and Ginny Trull moved to Milan, TN.

Baxter Trull, also born in 1890 died in 1944. His wife, we think was Virgie, born 1898 and died in 1988. They are buried in the Chestnut Grove Cemetery, Perry County near Linden, TN.

B. Trull, born 1874 and died in 1961, wife was Alma, born 1891, died 1988.

C. B. Trull lived in Hohenwald, TN, married and died in Lewis County.

A. R. (Dick) Trull and Della (Warren) Trull lost an infant son, James Henry Trull, born Aug. 1923 and died Sept. 1923, buried at Beardstown, TN in De Priest Bend Cemetery. After A. R. Trull died, Della married Hershal Hardin. They had one child, Betty (Hardin) Sorrall.

It is believed that Salathiel Trull was the father of A. R. (Dick) Trull and his siblings, however it has not been proven. *Prepared by Hazel Craig and submitted by the Walter Trull Family.*

J. HOWARD TRULL, (born April 4, 1929) and Sue Culp Trull (born March 15, 1929) live on the old Barnabas Beasley farm formerly owned by his grandfather, Samuel T. Parnell and later by his parents Jesse and Lattis Parnell Trull on Coon Creek in Perry County. Sue is the daughter of Tom and Nora Lineberry Culp. Howard's great grandfather, Joseph Trull was born in North Carolina in 1805. It is thought that Joseph settled in Perry County around 1840. He died in 1870. His youngest son, William Allen, born in 1861, married Martha Elizabeth (Mollie) Barber in 1881. Mollie was the daughter of William T. and Ellender McCallister Barber. To this union were born Fanetty (Netty), Doss, William (Bill), Sarah (Sally) Jesse, John (Johnny) and Osby.

Mr. & Mrs. Jess Trull, 1979.

In 1921, Jesse Trull married Lattis Parnell, the daughter of Samuel Thomas and Julia Duncan Parnell. Julia was the daughter of Willis and Mary (Polly) Warren Duncan and Samuel Thomas was the son of Archa and Sally Walls Parnell.

To this union were born Mary Loudean and Julius Howard. Loudean married Elijah Warren in 1938; Howard married Sue Culp in 1947 after they both graduated from Perry County High School. Sue's grandparents were William Buck and Mary Elizabeth Denton Culp, and David and Mary Lee Howell Lineberry.

Howard and Sue have four children: Tommye Gale (died in infancy), David, Julia and Allen.

David Trull received an AA degree from Freed-Hardeman College in 1969 and received a B.S. degree from the University of Tennessee in 1971. He has taught vocational agriculture at Perry County High School since 1971. He is married to the former Connie Dauksch and they have two children, J. B. and Buck.

Julia Trull received a B.S. degree from Freed-Hardeman University in 1982 and a Pharm. D. degree in pharmacy in 1986. Julia is presently employed by Vanderbilt University Hospital, Nashville, TN. She is married to Jimmy Hinson and they have one son, Jay.

Allen Trull received a B.S. degree from Freed-Hardeman University in 1987 and is currently teaching Biology and Chemistry at Lewis County High School, Hohenwald, TN. He is married to the former Cynthia Carden and they have two children, Joshua and Haylee Rae.

In 1945, Jesse and Lattis Trull purchased the Beasley farm from the remaining heirs of S. T. Parnell and he and Lattis lived in the old farm house until Jesse's death in 1988.

Howard and Sue erected a new home on the farm in 1948 and Howard farmed for seven years. Realizing his need for further education, he entered Freed-Hardeman College in 1954. After receiving an AA. degree from Freed-Hardeman College in 1956, a B.S. degree from Middle Tennessee State University in 1957 and a M.A. degree from George Peabody College in 1958, he returned to Freed-Hardeman to teach in the Biology department. He took a leave of absence from teaching in 1967 and completed the Ph.D. degree in Biology in 1969 at the University of Mississippi. He has been a member of the faculty of Freed-Hardeman University for 36 years, while commuting from his home in Perry County. Sue operates a day care center for preschool children in their home on Coon Creek.

Both David and Allen Trull built new homes on the Trull farm and now reside there with their families,

SALETHEAL TRULL, (Oct. 13, 1837-May 1926) was married to Phoebe Jane French (1840-1928). He was a Civil War veteran in the Union Army, a private in F company of the 2nd Tennessee Cavalry. Both are buried at Qualls Cemetery. There were nine children born to them. They were: James Henry Trull (1855-1920) whose wife was named Ann; Nancy Elizabeth Trull (1856-1886) who married Hardiman Craig; Thomas Allan Trull (1860-1941) who married Sally Ophelia Berry; Martha Trull (1862-Feb. 5, 1936); John Trull (1866-1944) who married Ruby Shelton; Jessie Taylor (1869-1942); Jennie Trull (July 5, 1872-Aug. 4, 1896); Maggie Trull (1874-1946) who married William Clay Barber; and Nettie Trull.

Thomas Allan Trull listed above was married to Sally Ophelia Trull (1861-1929). Sally was the daughter of Benjamin Basil Berry (born 1825) and Sarah Craig (born 1837). They had six children who were: Colonel Wilkins (Wix) Trull (1887-1981); Ben Trull (1889-1972); Wes Trull (1891-1967); Sarah Trull (born 1894); America Trull (d. 1956); and Mike Trull (1900-1940).

Wix Trull married Hattie Jackson (1861-1936) on June 22, 1907 at Beardstown Community. They had 12 children who were:

Minnie May Trull (April 22, 1908-April 17, 1966) who married Ed Berry and had one son, James Kyle Berry. After Ed Berry died, Minnie married Clarence Tucker, but had no children; Mamie Pearl Trull (born Dec. 21, 1909) married Carl Ruff Depriest and had three sons. They were Charles Reed, Edward Earl and Roy David Depriest; Mary Lucille Trull (Nov. 15, 1915-Jan. 26, 1916) died as an infant; Inez Ruth Trull (Jan. 26, 1919-Oct. 1993) had two sons, Robert Wayne and Billy Don Trull. She later married Ralph Graves, but they divorced later; Sally Ellen Trull (Jan. 27, 1920-Feb. 3, 1991) married Carl Qualls. She had two children, Larry Robert and Linda; Tom Natt Trull (March 4, 1922-Dec. 1992) married Mary Dan Westbrooks. They had two sons, Bobby Harvey and Lennie, and two daughters, Tommie Elizabeth and Deborah; Bessie Marie Trull (Dec. 26, 1924-Dec. 4, 1978) married Charles Nolan with one son, Charles Edward Nolan. She later married Earl Smith; Hessie Maude was a twin to Bessie and she married Richard Hunnicut with one son, Billy Joe Hunnicut. They divorced and she married Ross Broadway and had three children, Jerry Wayne, Mary June and Jeff; Robert Obie Trull (Jan. 21, 1929-Feb. 1976) married Nella Graves Monroe in 1956, but divorced in 1959. Addia Mavis Trull (March 15, 1931-May 1932); Nellie Faye Trull (born Feb. 11, 1934) married Robert Aldridge and had four children, Edward Leon, Gary Eugene, Rheda Faye and Rebecca Ann.

The youngest, Hattie Lee Trull (born Aug. 2, 1936) married Arlis Lineberry (born July 10, 1928) in September 1956 and had three children. Particia Carol (born July 20, 1958) married Jacky Graham (born Jan. 27, 1956) and had two children, Brandi (born March 3, 1979) and Mandi (born March 16, 1981). Alan Lynn (born March 18, 1962) married Kay Walker. The third child was Billy Lee Lineberry. *Submitted by Hattie Lineberry.*

TRULL, The very earliest Trull ancestor living in Perry County, that we can trace, is: Salathiel Trull born in 1837 and died in 1926. His wife was Phoebe Jane Trull, born in 1840.

Their issue: Jennie Trull who was born July 5, 1861 and died 1931.

Other possible issue: J. H. Trull born 1855, died 1920, who married Ann (last name unknown), born 1861, died 1931. Jessie Taylor Trull born 1869 and died in 1942. He was married to Martha A. Trull who was born March 17, 1860 and died Feb. 5, 1936. John O. Trull was born 1866 and died 1944. *Submitted by Walter Trull Family.*

ANDREW (ANDY) HARLAN TUCKER, and Elecia S. Carney Tucker currently live at 110 Polk Street in Linden. The house is the former home of Woodrow Culp.

Andrew and Elecia Tucker

Andrew was born May 24, 1964 to Billy F. and Sue Gilbert Tucker in Linden. He is the grandson of Frank and Vera Tucker and Douglas and Earlie Riley Gilbert. He graduated from Perry County High School and went to Freed-Hardeman College in Henderson, TN for two years. He then attended Hohenwald State Area Vocational-Technical School for two years. After working for G.E. Corp. in Columbia, TN for a year, he moved to Murfreesboro, TN and worked for Whirlpool Corp. in Lavergne for the next three years. While in Murfreesboro he met Elecia in the summer of 1987.

Elecia Sue Carney was born Feb. 9, 1966 in Louisville, KY. Her father is Bro. John "Jack" Vernon Carney Jr., born Aug. 17, 1937 to John Vernon and Mary Clair Hunt Carney of Nashville. Elecia's mother is Carrie Lee Jones born April 12, 1940 in Washington, DC to George Ira and Emily Wiggington Jones. Elecia's parents currently live in Shelbyville, TN.

Elecia, although born in Kentucky, had lived in Louisville, Greensboro, NC, Kingsport, Nashville, Wartrace and Shelbyville, TN by the time she was 12 when her family settled in Bell Buckle, TN for the next 16 years. After graduating from Cascade High School, she attended Tennessee Tech in Cookeville for one year, then East Tennessee State University for a year and a half. After leaving school, she was a manager for a McDonald's in Nashville for a year and then managed Deli Junctions in Nashville and Murfreesboro for one and a half years. She then moved back home and was a Telemarketing Sales Representative for National Pen in Shelbyville where she met Andy.

Married on June 18, 1988, they lived in Murfreesboro until a job opportunity for Andy came open at Johnson Control in Linden. In Feb. 1990, they moved to Linden with the intention of staying permanently and raising their family there.

Their daughter, Jacey Adara, was born July 17, 1991 and son, Jacob Andrew, on April 8, 1993. Andy is currently employed by Bates Manufacturing in Lobelville, TN as a Manager of Process Engineering and Elecia is staying home being a housewife and mother.

BILLY F. AND SUE TUCKER, Billy Tucker (born Sept. 5, 1930) and Margaret Sue Gilbert (born Nov. 26, 1937) were married Aug. 24, 1957. They have three children, Kenneth Douglas (born June 20, 1958) who married Janice Evans, Cynthia Sue (born July 6, 1961) who married James Anderson Jr. and Andrew Harlan (born May 24, 1964) who married Elecia Sue Carney.

Billy and Sue Tucker

Sue is the daughter of John Douglas Gilbert (born April 15, 1906) and Earlie Riley (born Jan. 17, 1911). She is the granddaughter of Jake Riley and Ida Mathis and William Dee Gilbert and Mollie Diveney.

Billy is the great-great-great grandson of John P. Tucker who served in the Virginia Line, Continental Army during the Revolutionary War. After the war, he came to Hickman County and lived there until his death and is buried in Hickman County. Billy is the great-great grandson of Joseph Tucker (born 1785) and Sarah McMillan. Joseph served with Andrew Jackson in the War of 1812 and after the war came to what was then Hickman County. He settled and claimed land along the Buffalo River and extended his claims up Short Creek. He signed the original petition of Sept. 22, 1819 asking that this area be granted status as Perry County. Joseph, his wife and some of his children are buried on the Duncan farm overlooking Buffalo River.

Billy is the great grandson of Dickson Tucker (born March 15, 1835) and Mary Elizabeth Edwards (born Oct. 18, 1840). Dickson served in the 2nd Tennessee MTD Inf. during the Civil War as a scout. At that time, his home was the Tucker farm on Short Creek and he and his wife, along with some of his children, are buried on that farm.

Billy is the grandson of William Issac Harrison Tucker (born March 8, 1877) and Ethel Lee Berry. Ethel Berry is the daughter of Andrew Berry and Lou Rainey.

Billy is the son of Andrew Franklin Tucker (born April 23, 1905) and Vera Jane Cotham (born Oct. 4, 1906). Vera is the daughter of Issac Jesse Cotham (born May 29, 1879) and Alice A. Hufstedler (born Nov. 4, 1881).

Military service seems to be a part of the Tucker lifestyle. James, Billy's brother, was in the U.S. Navy during World War II and Billy was in the U.S. Navy during the Korean War.

FRANK & VERA TUCKER, Andrew Franklin Tucker born April 23, 1905 and Vera Jane Cotham born Oct. 4, 1906 were married June 8, 1926. They had two sons, James O. and Billy F. Frank is the son of William I. and Ethel Lee Berry Tucker. Vera is the great-great granddaughter of Issac Cotham and Sarah DePriest.

Frank and Vera Tucker

She is the great granddaughter of John Cotham born September 1808 and Eliza Sanders born 1812. John and Eliza's children were America born 1834, married a Dotts; John M. born September 1837, married to Hahulda DePriest born 1851, daughter of Issac DePriest born 1815 and Phoebe Sisco born 1818; Richard Fane born Aug. 7, 1844 and Tennessee A. Twomey born July 11, 1845. They were Vera's grandparents. Susan Sanders Cotham born June 19, 1847, married William A. McClearen born February 1846. Richard and Tennie's children were James D. born Nov. 15, 1866, married Ida H.; Thomas D. born March 31, 1868, married Nannie Ellison born February 1870; Ida I. Cotham born Oct. 8, 1869, married Joe Edwards, born Dec. 2, 1864; John M. born July 28, 1873, married Sallie Harriet born Sept. 27, 1870 and Myrtle E. Carson born May 11, 1887; Ada N. Cotham born June 7, 1882, married Manford Rea; Issac Jesse born May 29, 1879, married Annie Alice Hufstedler born Nov. 4, 1881. I. J. and Annie are Vera's mother and father. They were married Sept. 16, 1900. Their other children were Bynum born May 5, 1903, married Byron Whitwell born Jan. 26, 1905 and Ethel Kimble born March 29, 1908; Richard F. born March 28, 1909, married Mahala L. Smith born

June 23, 1917; John P. born Aug. 7, 1911, married Mary Louise Bass born April 25, 1915; Clopton T. born March 8, 1914, married Thelma Broadway born Aug. 2, 1922 and Alice Kilpatrick born March 5, 1936; Willie Carothers born Feb. 2, 1917, married Mulice Harberson and Jesse Glynn born Feb. 15, 1921, married Velma Blose born Aug. 23, 1922. The last three boys were in the service during WW II. Clopton in the U.S. Navy, Carothers in the Army Air Force, a pilot who was killed in Europe early in the war, Glynn was a pilot in the Naval Air Force. Annie A. Hufstedler Cotham was the daughter of James Henry Hufstedler and Eudoxia A. Rasbury.

TUCKER-DUNCAN, Ann Randel Jackson Ogilive and son Mitchell Jackson of Kentucky came to Perry County to visit with their family for one year. They returned to Kentucky and died soon thereafter. Mitchell came back and lived the rest of his life among family. Mitchell is buried in the Duncan Cemetery on Short Creek. The family consisted of Ann Randel Jackson Ogilive, Mollie Jackson Hinson, married Eli Larkin from England. Ida Marze Hinson married James Solomon Duncan. L. B. (Barney) Ducan married Lurah Mai McDonald. Elsie Ducan married Fred Tucker. Helen Tucker married William Southall. Their children were Ronnie and Michael. Ronnie Southall married Genia Coston from Arkansas. Their children were Tucker and Duncan Southall. Clara Tucker married Mr. Lynn. Their child is Mitchell Bradford Tucker Sr. (Mitch). He married Chris and their son is Mitchell Bradford Tucker Jr.

E.L. & Mollie Hinson on their 60th wedding anniversary.

A story which has come down through the family starts on the Dec. 1, 1862 in Linden under the leadership of B. G. Rickman and W. H. Cude, where 106 men were organized with Rickman as captain. W. H. Cude as 1st Lt., J.R. Land as 2nd Lt., E.H. Shepherd as 3rd Lt., W.H. Edwards as 1st Sgt., Carroll Beasley as 2nd Sgt. and E.L. Hinson as 3rd Sgt.

They went into camp on the Cane Creek at the Bethel Church near what was then called Shelton Town, west from there to Ash Wood between Mt. Pleasant and Columbia where they divided a short time. There they were ordered to report to N. B. Forest.

The Yankees encamped at Franklin came out to about them and they met at Thompson's station for their first engagement. Third Sgt. E.L. Hinson's report of this battle states that they captured 2,500 infantry men. "We fought on the ground and the Yankees said we were the first infantry men they ever saw wearing spurs." Mr. Hinson was on his hands and knees when something passed over his head. He looked up and turned around when he saw his colonel falling. He had been shot in the stomach with a minnie ball. The top of Mr. Hinson's hat was burned all across.

Eli Larkin (Lark) Hinson, son of Ida Hinson Duncan was a Primitive Baptist Minister and sheriff of Perry County for a number of years.

JAMES O. (JIM) AND BETTYE TILLER TUCKER, Jim and Bettye have lived on Riverside Drive in Linden for 34 years. Jim is the son of Andrew Franklin (Frank) and Vera Cotham Tucker. Bettye is the daughter of Floyd W. and Margaret P. Tiller. Jim and Betty's children are Pamela Jean, Lisa Elaine and Ted Alan Tucker.

James and Betty Tucker

Jim is a descendant of early settlers of Perry County, Joseph Tucker and Pinkney Hufstedler.

Jim represents State Farm Insurance Company and has represented them for 36 years. His offices are located in Linden and Centerville, TN. Betty has supported Jim in his business interest as well as rearing their children. Jim is also a partner in Tiller Furniture Company located in Linden which opened for business in 1948 and has operated continuously since.

Jim has been active in the promotion and advancement of Perry County. Jim served on the Linden Board of Alderman for 12 years, president of the Buffalo River Country Club during its incorporation, committee for locating Mousetail Landing State Park (named the Park), made the first aerial survey of the park location. Jim also picked the site for the Perry County airport and served as the airport manager for several years. Jim is also a licensed pilot and aircraft owner.

JOSEPH TUCKER was the grandfather of George W. Tucker with Robert P. and Leander Tucker being the father and mother.

George Washington Tucker (June 30, 1844-May 18, 1927). On Sept. 29, 1878 George married Mary Frances Tatum (Jan. 18, 1860-July 30, 1945).

Mary Frances' (Fanny) parents were Sublette and Peggy Ann (Miller) Tatum.

George and Fanny had one son, Robert Allen Tucker (July 24, 1879-1976). He was married to Michal Jane (Jenny) Campbell (May 17, 1878-Dec. 21, 1944).

Robert and Jenny had four children, one died at birth April 13, 1904. There was one daughter Myrtle Lizzie (Tucker) Halbrooks, (Nov. 14, 1901-Oct. 24, 1979). Myrtle married Dorsey Dewey (Jack) Halbrooks (Oct. 23, 1899-June 5, 1958) Dec. 21, 1922.

George Washington Tucker and Mary Frances Tatum Tucker.

Myrtle and Jack had four children, Dorsey Virginia Weaver, Irma Dean Lineberry, Robert Hiram, Jackie Ruth Byrd.

There were two sons born to this union Guy George Tucker (Jan. 22, 1906-March 12, 1993). Guy married Carmenette June 4, 1933. Carmenette was born Oct. 1, 1914. To this union one son was born, Stanley Guy Tucker (1947-1977). Stanley had one son, Robert Nelson Tucker.

Fred Hiram Tucker (Jan. 14, 1909-May 21, 1964) married Elsie Duncan, born Nov. 17, 1913, on April 23, 1931. To this union three children were born. Helen Mae (Tucker) Southall, Clara Winifred (Tucker) Lynn and James Ronald Tucker, born and died 1949.

Helen T. Southall has two sons, William Ronald and Michael Albert Southall. Ronnie has two sons, Tucker Glen and William Duncan Southall.

Clara Tucker Lynn has one son, Mitchell Bradford Tucker Sr. Mitchell has one son, Mitchell Bradford Tucker Jr.

The Tuckers were a large family, homesteading land in Perry County, TN part of which is now owned by Thomas and Alice Duncan, children of Bernard and Bonnie (DePriest) Duncan.

George and Mary Frances are buried on this farm. A lifetime deed was made to the effect of a burial plot for them.

At the time it was homesteaded it was known as cane brake. Over the years by many people the land was cleared and is now being used as row crops and pastures.

George Tucker was about 18 years of age and was plowing in the bottom that is now under the bridge just outside of Linden on 412 East, he was shot at during the Civil War.

Fred Tucker, son of Robert and Jenny was about three years of age, his mother had made him a new apron dress, was all cleaned up and out to play. Fred was very unhappy about the dress, he took a nail and punched holes in his dress. Needless to say no more apron dresses.

Fred taught school for five months in the fall of 1928 after he graduated. He wasn't very happy teaching, he quit and started farming with his father and brother. He continued to farm until his death.

KENNETH DOUGLAS TUCKER, (born June 30, 1958) and Janice Lee Evans (born Feb.

15, 1962) were married June 7, 1985 in Murfreesboro where both were attending M.T.S.U.

Kenny, Christopher and Blake Tucker

Kenny was born in Nashville, TN but spent most of his childhood in Perry County and attended school at Perry County High. He attended Freed-Hardeman College and Middle Tennessee State University. He is the son of Billy and Sue Tucker, the grandson of Frank and Vera Tucker and Douglas and Earlie Riley Gilbert.

Janice is the daughter of Robert Evans (born Dec. 1, 1941) and Sally Lynn Karpus (born May 31, 1943). Robert's father was Carl Evans Sr. and his mother was Frenzie McFarland, the daughter of Earnest McFarland and Mattie Edgin.

Sally is the daughter of Antone Karpus (born March 22, 1913) and Minnie Huissen (born May 31, 1920). She is the granddaughter of Joseph Karpus and Ann Waitek, who came to America from Lithuania and Adrian Huissan and Elizabeth Vreeke who came to American from Holland.

Kenny and Janice have two sons, Christopher Andrew (born March 26, 1987) and Blake Alexander (born June 1, 1990).

JOHN LOCKE VAUGHAN, William Vaughan was born in Virginia but came to Williamson County, TN, where he married Melissa Craig. They moved to Marshall County, MS, and William became a plantation overseer. Around 1848 or 1849 he moved his family to Perry County and continued to farm until his death in 1865. His wife, Melissa Craig Vaughan died around 1850.

A son, John Locke Vaughan (1847-1914), of William and Melissa Vaughan, was in the harness maker's trade in Williamson County, TN for five years and farmed there for five more years. In 1875 he began farming in Perry County, TN. In 1880 he bought his home farm, which consisted of 500 acres of land on Buffalo River. On this farm is the Vaughan-Tucker-Godwin family cemetery. John Locke Vaughan married Martha Ann Stewart of Decatur County, TN, on Sept. 26, 1877. To this union five children were born: Myrtle Estelle, Minnie Adelle, Sallie M., John William and Andrew Thomas.

Myrtle Estelle (1878-1962) married Samuel F. Polk (1870-1953). Myrtle was a school teacher who taught in Oklahoma and in Perry County, TN.

Minnie Adelle (1880-1956) married Commodore Perry Godwin (1875-1919). To this marriage three children were born: John William, Thomas Stuart (Stewart) and Ruth Godwin. John William (1906-1979) married Mary Elizabeth Kelly and they had two daughters — Mary Jean (1933) who died in infancy and Martha Ruth Godwin Edwards (1937) who still resides in Perry County and is a Perry County High School teacher.

John Locke and Martha Ann Stewart Vaughan and children. Standing: Sarah, Minnie, Myrtle. Kneeling: John and Andrew.

Thomas Stuart (Stewart) Godwin (1910-1968) married Mary Elizabeth Sharp (1910-1992) and they had two children—Mary Anne (1933) and Thomas Stuart Godwin Jr. (1939). At this time, Mary Anne Godwin Perdue lives in Selmer, TN, and Tom Godwin Jr. is in Knoxville, TN.

Ruth (born 1914), a retired school teacher, still resides in Linden, TN.

Sarah M. Vaughan (1883-1902) died at the age of 19 while attending college in Nashville, TN.

John William Vaughan (1886-1946) married Kittie Bates (1893-1958). They had two children—John Andrew (1913-1973) and Christine V. Sharp (born 1916), a retired teacher who still resides at the family home five miles north of Linden.

Andrew Thomas Vaughan (1888-1957) married Rue Bone (1895-1953) and they had two sons: Thomas (1915-1931) and William Locke (Billy) (1921-1945). Thomas died when he was a junior in high school. Billy died during World War II. He was a tail gunner returning from his first mission in 1945 and was gunned down. He was buried in St. Louis, MO.

JAMES OWEN VICKERY, (Jan. 13, 1850 TN - Sept. 5, 1907 Hu. Co., TN) came to Perry County with his father, Jonathan Vickery (See VICKERY, Jonathan history) prior to the 1860 census from Williamson County, TN. James Owen married his first wife Margaret Baker in Humphreys County on June 22, 1877. By the 1880 census, James Owen is listed as a widower and lives in the Buffalo area, District 4, Humphreys County. There were no children identified from this marriage. In the 1880 census, James Owen's close neighbor is a Mary A. Neblett (1835 Mt. Co.-Aug. 4, 1890 Hu. Co.), TN school teacher, daughter of Thomas Neblett (1805 TN-after 1860), who had come from Montgomery County area with his cousin, Sterling Mc. Neblett (Caulk Bottom, Hu. Co.) and settled (450 acres - 1854) in the Squeeze Bottom area on the Buffalo River and south of present day Buffalo, TN. James Owen apparently met and courted Mary A. Neblett's daughter, Nannie Lenore Neblett-McDonough (Sept. 13, 1861 Hu. Co. - Dec. 2, 1928 Dav. Co.). Nannie had recently divorced and apparently had come with her daughter, "Lillie," to live with her mother. Nannie L. and James Owen were wed on Sept. 5, 1886.

Back Row: Carl Eldridge and Katie Pearl. Seated: William Henry "Will," Nannie Lenora Neblette-Vickery, Dorsey Franklin. Standing: Robert Clay, Bruce, Lucy, Ollie Lura. Inset: James Owen Vickery.

In the 1880 census, Nannie Lenore Neblett is listed as a boarder living with the O. P. Rossible, (machinist) family at Pinewood, Hi. Co. Nannie L. (19 years old) is working in the "Pinewood" Cotton Mill (1848-1910) which was operated by Mr. Sam Lowry Graham (1812-1892) in Pinewood, Hickman Co., TN. This mill produced spun and woven cotton rope and unbleached fine-quality cotton sheeting. Mr. Graham operated his mill and maintained a village for his workers. He did not tolerate bad influences in his village and reportedly paid the N.C. and St. L. Railroad $10,000 to route its line and miss Pinewood by three miles thus keeping undesirables out. Later that year, Nannie L. married James T.E. McDonough on Oct. 25, 1880 in Dickson, Di. Co. From this marriage, Sallie Endra "Lillie" McDonough (Aug 5, 1881 - Dec. 2, 1956 Nashville, TN married Dave Bass) was their only child and the marriage ended shortly thereafter with James T. reportedly leaving for Arkansas.

James O. and Nannie L. raised a family of 13 children as follows: (1) Dorsey Franklin (Sept. 13, 1887 - Feb. 16, 1928, Union City, TN) married Carrey Brown (2) William Henry "Will" (July 4, 1890-April 12, 1958, Memphis, TN) (3) Mary Lee "Lou" (Nov. 3, 1891 - Oct. 19, 1892, Buffalo, TN) (4) Loulie (Aug. 9, 1893 - Oct. 17, 1939, Nashville, TN) (5) Owen (July 7, 1895 - July 7, 1895, Buffalo, TN) (6) Carl Eldridge (July 28, 1896 - Aug. 24, 1972, Nashville, TN) married first to a Newby and second unknown (7) Katie Pearl (Nov. 13, 1898 - Sept. 12, 1988, Nashville, TN) married May 14, 1915 to Carl Elton Stewart Sr. (See Stewart, Harold E. history) (8) Robert Clay (Feb. 4, 1901 - Jan. 26, 1964) married Winnie Midget (9) James David "Jim" (Dec. 9, 1902 - July 23, 1903, Buffalo, TN) (10) Lucy (Oct. 30, 1903, twin, - July 18, 1978, Nashville, TN) married Leslie Ingram (11) Bruce (Oct. 30, 1903, twin, - Feb. 23, 1994, Nashville, TN) married Dec. 1, 1929 Mattielynn Vickery (12) Ollie Lura (Oct. 30, 1903 - Dec.

26, 1985, Monroe, LA) married George G. Shaver.

With James Owen's death in 1907, Nannie struggled with a family of 13 children. At James Owen's death the three eldest sons, Dorsey (20 yrs/1907), William (17 yrs/1907) and Carl (11 yrs/1907) were old enough to hire out to local farmers and to "share a crop" but there were obstacles to overcome. Dorsey and William had been born deaf and Nannie L. from this remote area of Humphreys County sent the boys on alternating years to the Deaf School at Knoxville through the 1900s. All members of the Vickery family learned "To Sign" and communicate with their eldest brothers. Dorsey "Doss" would later go to Waverly High School where he played tackle on the varsity football team. Nannie L. with the help of neighbors, made ends meet. The family lived on the Lindley Ship farm on Shipp's Bend in Buffalo, TN. Reportedly, Nannie L. earned money for her family as a midwife and a local photographer. She purchased a Kodak "Browie" pat. 1916 which she took to local ball games and to churches meetings and took pictures of individuals which she sold for 10 cents a piece. These photographs have become, in some cases, the only known photographs ever made of these individuals and surviving today.

James Owen, Nannie Lenore, James David (Jim D), Mary Lee, Owen Vickery rest in a family cemetery on a sloped hillside on the farm Nannie Lenore Neblett's grandfather, Thomas Neblett purchased in 1854. Periwinkle has been planted in this cemetery and now radiates for 50 yards in every direction just as their descendants have radiated in every direction and profession from their Perry County roots.

JONATHAN VICKERY, (1815 TN-after 1880 P. Co., TN) brought his family to Perry County, 4th district (Crooked Creek area?) sometime prior to the 1860 census. In 1861, Jonathan is noted on the tax records of Perry County. In the 1870 census, Jonathan states that "he work on farm." By the 1880 census, Jonathan lists his occupation as minister (Methodist) at the age of 67 years. In a 1831 petition to the Tennessee General Assembly, petitioners on Crooked Creek, Perry County requested funds and a 10 acre tract to erect a Methodist Episcopal Church. It could be deduced that Jonathan could have been the minister of that church in 1880. Jonathan and Elizabeth Smith-Vickery were married Feb. 13, 1839 in Williamson County. By the 1840 census, Jonathan is listed in Bedford County. In 1850, Jonathan and his family are listed in Williamson County. In 1860 census, Jonathan had moved to Perry County. With Jonathan and his family moving every 10 years to a new county, it could be deduced that Jonathan was in fact a minister prior to the 1870 census. There are no land deeds attributed to Jonathan Vickery in Williamson, Bedford or Perry County, while a Thomas Vickery, who entered the county at about that time, relationship unknown, purchased several acreage's. With an occupation that required frequent changes of assignment, it could be speculated that he leased land or had a share crop arrangement rather than having to despose of any land ownership for his next assignment.

Robert Clay, Bruce, Nannie Lenora Neblette Vickery and Dorsey Franklin Vickery.

Jonathan's lineage is unclear. Jonathan identifies that he is born in Tennessee and is the possible son of one of three Vickory brothers, who came into Bedford County prior to the 1820 census. In the 1810 census of North Carolina, John, Absolum and Richard are shown living in Randolph County. By the 1820 census, all three are missing from the North Carolina census but appear in Bedford County, TN.

Jonathan and Elizabeth Smith-Vickery had 14 children to live to maturity as follows: (1) John, born 1840, married 1866 Perry County, Roseanne M. Birk (2) Isaac W., born 1842 (3) Nancy A., born 1843, married 1873 Perry County, D.J. Fitzgerald (4) Sarah Jane, born 1846 (5) Mary, born 1847 (6) Priseilla, born 1849, married 1866 Perry County, James Baucan (7) James Owen (1850-1907) married first (1877 Hu. Co.) Margaret Baker, second (1886 Hu. Co.) Nannie Lenore Neblett (1861-1928) (See Vickery, James O. history) (8) Abaslum, born 1851, married Altha Tippett (9) Margaret, born 1852, married Plebes Clayburn 910) Hester A., born 1854, married (1880 Perry Co.) William Goodman (11) Amy L., born 1857, married (1872 Perry Co.) D.R. Pollard (12) Annenta Caroline (1860-1933) married (1877 Perry Co.) James B. Cantrell (13) Mira Emmaline, born 1860, married (1879 Perry Co.) W.H. Fitzgerald (14) King, born 1862.

The accompanying photograph represents a time honored profession which was followed by Jonathan, his son James Owen Vickery and by James' son, Dorsey Franklin Vickery. Also shown are James Owen Vickery's wife, Nannie Lenore Neblett-Vickery and two other sons, Robert Clay and Bruce Vickery.

CHARLES E. WADE, and his wife, Martha, came from Giles County sometime after 1850. They lived just outside of Linden, TN in 1860 and he earned a living as a tanner and carver. Charles was born ca: 1814 somewhere in Tennessee. He married Martha ca: 1836. They had seven children together.

James T. Wade - born ca: 1837.

Frank George Wade - born ca: 1841.

William Malcom Wade (Oct. 29, 1843-May 26, 1894) In Sept. 1862, at Bethel, TN, Malcom enlisted in the 6th regiment of the Tennessee Cavalry commanded by Captain Webb and was discharged in July 1865 at Puluski, TN. William Malcom married Eliza Ann Cooper of Benton County on Nov. 29, 1866. They also had seven children: Mary Ann Wade (March 21, 1868-1969) married Simon Graves on Jan. 10, 1890; Charles Fletcher Wade (March 12, 1869-Oct. 13, 1961) married Idelia Garner on March 3, 1889; William Henry Wade (Oct. 20, 1870-Nov. 22, 1954) married Mary Etta Gill on Dec. 24, 1896; Rufus Franklin Wade (July 16, 1872-Oct. 5, 1964) married Elizabeth Garner on June 1, 1897; James Farris Wade (Jan. 10, 1874-1956) married Florence Cox on Nov. 15, 1895; Robert Malcom Wade (March 29, 1876-April 9, 1961) married Julia Ann Vaughn June 6, 1904; Martin B. Wade (Oct. 24, 1878-Oct. 7, 1882); Martha Ann Jelica Wade (March 17, 1881-April 14, 1968) married Rev. John Clinton Ross on March 17, 1901; and Isaac Derryberry Wade (Jan. 5, 1884-March 26, 1964) married Lura R. Graves.

Howard, Arthur and Richard Wade

Rufus Demarkus Wade (Aug. 5, 1845-April 3, 1924) On Feb. 1, 1864, Rufus enlisted in the 6th Tenn. Cavalry, the same as his older brother. He was discharged on July 26, 1865 at Pulaski, TN. He returned to Perry County and married Mary Ann Arnold "Polly" on March 5, 1868. They also had seven children: James Martin Wade (Oct. 2, 1870-Jan. 1, 1940) married Matilda Jane Ledbetter in 1889; Albert Clarence Wade (Jan. 14, 1872-Feb. 17, 1923) married Katherine Ann Bethel; William Irvin Wade (Feb. 10, 1874-Oct. 20, 1928) married Francis E. Goodman on Feb. 25, 1894; Carra Cordelia Wade (Nov. 3, 1876-before 1900); Bettie Izora Wade (March 13, 1878-Oct. 14, 1932) married Oliver Clinton Childers; Mary Etta Wade (Oct. 13, 1881-?) married J.E. Branton; and Rufus Henry Wade (April 29, 1883-before 1900).

Mary F. Wade - born 1849.

Amon D. Wade - born 1853.

Henry F. Wade (Nov. 23, 1855-Sept. 15, 1922) married Mollie Baker and they had five children: John Edward Wade (Feb. 28, 1882-March 28, 1957) married Ruby Gleason on Sept. 16, 1903; Jeanie Wade married Sessler; Maude Wade married Leffet; Jessie Wade married Harris L. Seibert; and Gilbert Wade died May 5, ? in Arizona.

WADE-TRULL, Tom Norris Wade was born May 20, 1912 in Perry County, Chestnut Grove Community, the son of John Berry Wade and Arah Barham Wade. John Berry Wade was born May 18, 1886, Arah Barham Wade was born Sept. 21, 1890.

Tom married Lorene Trull Wade, born Feb. 18, 1916, daughter of Clem Hardiman Scelathal Daniel Trull (Hoss) born Feb. 6, 1887 and Sallie Mattie Warren born Aug. 14, 1893. Tom and Lorene have three children: Don Norris Wade born Oct. 16, 1936, Judy Wade Kilpatrick born Nov. 5, 1939 and Sue Ann Wade French born Nov. 27, 1947.

Don married March 26, 1960 to Sara Don Gibson of Parsons, TN, born Aug. 29, 1941. They have two sons, Berry Don Wade born May 23, 1964 and Jeffrey Don Wade born April 7, 1968. They make their home in Franklin, TN. Berry Don married Ann Swell from Memphis, TN. They have one daughter, Katy Lynn Wade, born March 18, 1993.

Tom and Lorene Wade at their 50th Wedding Anniversary.

Judy Wade Kilpatrick married Roy Douglas Kilpatrick Aug. 9, 1958. They have two daughters Karen Lynn Kilpatrick born Oct. 14, 1965 and Kelly Ann Kilpatrick born Dec. 3, 1968.

Sue Ann Wade French married Jimmy French. They have one daughter, Shonda Ann French born Aug. 5, 1975.

WALKER-MALIN, Gus Walker died in Perry County, TN in 1892. He was married to Mary Jane Dennison in Perry County. After Gus' death and burial there, Mary Jane (Dennison) Walker and her sons, William Andrew, Edward Hicks, Grover Cleveland and Robert Purcell, along with daughter, Mary Ethel, moved from Perry County to Benton County in 1905. Mary Jane's elderly mother, Mary Jane Dennison, accompanied them also. They settled in the Sugar Tree section.

In 1909, the family moved from Sugar Tree, TN to the Beaverdam community in the 10th civil district. They invested in about 1,000 acres of land. The Walker family gave of their land to build the Pembroke School, helped with the construction and their children attended school there. Their land was divided between the children, including the son-in-law.

When TVA built the reservoir, only two sections escaped the flooding, that being land owned by William Walker and the son-in-law, Ray Spence, married to Mary Ethel.

Son, Edward Hicks Walker, married Turney Mae Bivens. Their issue: Hazel, Edward Hicks, Robert, Nell, Pauline, Kenneth, Margaret Westell and Carolyn J.

Margaret Westell, born Dec. 6, 1928 in Benton County, TN, married Bennie Wayne Malin, born June 10, 1926 in Benton County. He was the son of Benjamin Rodger Malin and Velia (Crosnoe) Malin.

Benny Wayne Malin had a heart transplant at the V.A. Hospital in Richmond, VA about seven years ago in 1987. He died in the fall of 1993 from cancer, probably a result of the many medications he had to take since the transplant.

He and Westell have lived and made their home in the Detroit area since shortly after their marriage and his discharge from the service in the mid 1940s. They have spent most of their vacations over the years visiting back home in Tennessee with their families. They had two children in Michigan. A son, Jerry Wayne Malin, and a daughter, Rita Ann Malin.

JOHN THOMAS WALKER, the first Walker in Perry County, TN, was born in North Carolina in 1854. His mother died in childbirth; his father left to fight in the War Between the States and was never heard from again.

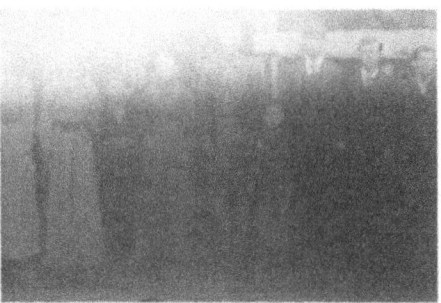

John Walker Family

In 1870, John left North Carolina, heading west with a horse, a dog and a shotgun. He stopped first in East Tennessee, working for two or three years before heading west again. His second stop was in Nashville, where he worked three more years and bought two more horses. While in Nashville, he met Jessie Albright — They were married and headed west again. This time they stopped in Perry County where they bought 1,240 acres of land adjoining White Oak Creek and built a log cabin. This land is still owned by their son Henry's boys - Jim, Frank and Henry Jr.

John and Jessie Walker had eight children: Ross, William, Henry, Pleas, George, Daisy, Eva and Elizabeth. John died in 1918 and was buried on Walker's Hill, overlooking White Oak Creek. Jessie passed away in 1926 and was also buried on Walker's Hill.

Ross Walker was seven feet tall - of such immense stature that word would go out when he was in Linden and people would gather just to see him. He bought the Peter's Landing store and made quite a name for himself in business and also owned a lot of farm land. The store was stocked with groceries, farm equipment and building supplies and received all its shipments by way of the Tennessee River. It was also a Post Office and Ross Walker put in one of the early community telephone systems. Ross bought all kinds of crops including cotton, corn, peanuts, eggs and chickens, and had a grist mill for grinding corn meal. As the store was open seven days a week, Ross's brother, Henry worked there as well.

William Walker moved to Athens, TX and never returned to Perry County. Pleas Walker moved to nearby Humphreys County, TN. Daisy and Elizabeth married and lived close to their parents in Perry County. Eva never married, living on her family's land her entire life.

George Walker was a farmer who worked six days a week, but on Sunday he would only feed and care for the sheep, hogs, cattle and work stock - no other work was done on the Sabbath. His nickname was "the Major," and though he was always quiet, people would come from all around seeking his advice. He married Zenober Jane Middleton and they had nine children, with one girl dying at birth. The four other girls - Moncie Kilpatrick, Jessie Waters, Golden Halford and Pauline Holder - are all now over 65 years of age and living within a short distance of the George Walker farm. Golden still has her parents' farm.

There were also four boys - John, David, Charlie and Jody - who between them had 70 years of military service. David and Charlie worked their way through college and law school. Charlie has practiced law in nearby Lexington, TN for 40 years, and his two sons, Ken and Richard, are practicing with him at this time. David is retired and living in Ripley, TN. John and Jody are deceased.

Jane Middleton Walker passed away in 1973; George Walker died in 1976. They are both buried in the Culp's Chapel Cemetery.

JOHN W. WALKER, along with his wife Catherine and children came to Perry County before 1830 from probably Rockingham, NC. He bought land on both sides of the Tennessee River, Morgans Creek and Crooked Creek. They made their home on Morgans Creek, what now is Decatur County. There, he and Catherine raised and educated their family. John was a farmer and dry good merchant.

John W. Walker (ca. 1800-1880), was born in Virginia, married Catherine (ca. 1798-died after 1850 census). She was also born in Virginia. They had the following children.

James S. (ca 1824-1885) married first Ellen ? (ca. 1837-1874). They lived in the 9th Dist. Decatur Co. Known children: Frankie (ca. 1861), Valeria (ca. 1863), Mary P. (ca. 1866), William (ca. 1872) and Lonia (ca. 1874). Ellen probably died after her last child. Then James married July 29, 1875 to Emeline Roden (ca. 1840-?). They had one known child, Jillie (ca. 1877).

William B. (1826-1897), married first Mary ? (ca. 1826-1853). They had one child Gus A. (1853-1896), married Maria Jane Denson (1853-1918). (See Denson) After Mary died William married Sarah Ann Raney (1826-1904). They lived in the 4th Dist. Perry Co., and had the following children: Almira (1854-1893); Virginia C. (1856-?); Adam B. (1858-1913); and Sara M. (1860-1881).

David (ca. 1828-?) Little is known about David. After the 1850 census, he can no longer be found. He was listed as being 22.

Robert S. (1830-ca. 1872) married Rebecca J. ? (ca. 1847 - ?). They had two children, John W. (ca. 1869-?) and Dorsey Robert (ca. 1873-?) and lived in the 5th Dist. Decatur Co. When Robert died, Rebecca married in 1875 to Joseph H. Thomas.

Diana (ca. 1836-1881) married John W. Clifft (ca. 1832-after 1900). They lived in the 5th Dist. Decatur Co., and had the following children: William R. (1862-?) married Rachel C. Baker 1862; John F. (ca. 1864); Emmerson E. (1865-?) married Nora J. Thomas; Sister (ca. 1868); C.G. (1874) married M. Frances Gibson 1877; George W. (1875-1960) married Emma M. Baker (1880-1903). After Diana died, John married in 1883 to H. E. Baker. Children by second marriage are: Belva A. (1884) married first Joseph L. Thomas, second Tilden Gibson; Mary

T. (1886) married A. C. Moore; Edith V. (1892); and Zachariah (1890).

Mary Ann (1835-1892) married John F. Wood (1832-1895). They had no children. Both are buried at Wood Cemetery, Decatur County in the back yard of Mr. Canada. There is just one monument. John was in business with his father-in-law, Walker and Wood. They had a warehouse on Brodies Landing.

March A. (ca. 1840) nothing else is known. *Submitted by David and Diane Walker.*

WILLIAM B. WALKER, was born in Tennessee, probably Perry County, to John and Catherine Walker. He lived in the 4th Dist. on Crooked Creek, where he raised his family. Billy, as he was known, was said to be a good provider for his family. He farmed and lived on the land his father owned and left him after he died. He was a man of many trades like so many were. His main source of income was from raising peanuts and the sale of timber. He would sell cross ties to the Railroad. Billy was half owner in a Sorgham Mill. He belonged to the Masonic Lodge.

William B. Walker (1826-1897) married Mary ? (ca. 1826-1850+). They had one son, Gus A. After Mary died, William married Sarah Ann (Sally) Raney (1826-1904). They had four children. Most of whom are buried at Crooked Creek Cemetery.

Gus A. (1853-1896) married Maria Jane Denson (1853-1918) (See Denson). They lived in the 4th Dist. Children: William A. (1874-1956) married Lula Baker (1881-1963); Edward Hicks (1878-1935) married Turney Bivens (1891-?); Mary Ethel (1881-1960) married Roy L. Spence (1883-1955); Grover Cleveland (1884-1964) married Hallie McAuley (1893-1975); Robert Purcell (1892-1957) never married.

Almira (Alley) (1854-1893) married James William Chance (ca. 1850-1890). They lived in the first Dist. Children: William Walker (1874-?); James William (1875-?); Robert Hercules (1878-1962); Sarah E. (1881-?); Victoria (1888-?) married Alex Lynch. Most of the Chance family moved to Humphreys County.

Virginia C. (Jennie) (1856) married J. Perry Coble (1856-?). They lived in the 4th and 6th Dist. Children: Virginia C. (1879-?) married George M. Dukes; Sallie (1880-?); Emma Dora (1884-1887); Bessie (1886-?); Sadie (1888-?); G.W. (1889-1890); Mattie (1892-?); Bernard (1893-?); Bernice (1894-?); Ruth (1896-?).

Adam B. (1858-1913) married Niecy Elizabeth Cottrell (1866-1954). They lived in the second Dist. Children: William W. (1884-?) married Elsie Pirtle; Arthur E. (1887-1919) married Emma M. Hill (1890-1986); Fannie Mai (1890-?) married first Ed Daniels, 2d Roy Keyser; John Weaver (1892-1976) married Cora Ethel Phebus (1893-1970); Leffler Barnett (1896-1974) married Annie A. Loggins (1902-1990).

Sara M. (1860-1881) married James W. Ridens. They had one known child W.H. (ca. 1879). Sara died young and is buried in Crooked Creek Cemetery. *Submitted by David and Diane Walker.*

WALKER-DENSON, Gus A. Walker, 1853-1896, was born on Morgan's Creek, Decatur County to William B. and Mary Walker. They had moved to the 4th Dist. on Crooked Creek where William B. was farming the land his father owned and later purchased more. Gus would soon encounter a young lady living a few houses away, Maria Jane Denson (1853-1918). They were married June 8, 1872 by T.J. Haney, J.P. Perry County. Gus, a farmer by trade, was a good father and provider for his family. They lived in the 4th Dist. also and had the following children.

William A., 1874-1956, married 1900 Lula Baker, 1881-1963, daughter of John and Mary Jane Myatt Baker. Their children: Ralph Andrew 1901-1908; Guy Andrew 1903-1989; Clay 1908-1993; Gus 1912-1975; Mary Jane 1914-.

Edward Hicks, 1878-1934, married 1912 Turney Bivens, 1891-. Children: Hazel 1913-1981; Edward Hicks Jr. 1916-1959; Robert Woodrow 1918-1961; Nell 1921-1978; Pauline 1924-; Kenneth L. 1926-1965; Margrett Westelle 1928-; Carolyn Jean 1931-.

Mary Ethel, 1881-1960, married 1903 Roy L. Spence, 1883-1955, son of John T. and Mary Elizabeth Odle Spence. Children: Martin West (Adopted).

Grover Cleveland, 1884-1960, married 1915 Hallie McAuley, 1893-1975. Children: Blondell 1916-1994; Ralph Hilman 1918-, married 1945 Audrey B. Herrin 1919-1967; Naomi Estelle 1923-1991; Jesse D. (Tuff) 1925-1993; H.C. (Pid) 1927-.

Robert Purcell (Bob) 1892-1957, never married.

After Gus died, William, his oldest son, gave bond and was granted Guardian of his minor brothers and sisters. About 1905, they all moved to Sugar Tree. In 1907, they sold their inheritance they received from their grandfather William B. Walker to their Uncle Adam B. (Bud) Walker. Around 1908, Jannie along with her children and son-in-law, Roy Spence, traveled by steam boat and moved to the 10th Dist. at Beaver Dam, Benton County where they bought 1,000 acres of land.

By 1910, Jannie, 55, was living with her son, William and wife Lula, along with the other children. In April, Jannie's mother had died. Her last request was to be taken back to Denson's Landing to be buried with her husband. The grandsons did so by taking her across the Tennessee River on a skiff, which was a terrifying experience. The family decided to be buried in Chalkhill Cemetery, Benton County.

In 1914, the four Walker brothers along with their sister and her husband, Roy Spence, gave nine acres of land to build Pembroke School. Grover's daughter, Blondell and William's daughter-in-law, Geraldine were two of the many School Teachers at this school.

The rest is history. There are many Walker descendants still living in Benton County. Submitted by David and Diane Walker.

NORMA WALLS, lives on Cedar Creek, Perry County. She is the granddaughter of Irving and Isabell (second wife) Anderson Walls. First wife and children's names are unknown, except one daughter, Sallie, born in the 1870s. They were originally from Kentucky, Irving, a timber worker, moved to follow work. Date unknown when they moved to Tennessee. Isabell died in 1895 at Danville, TN.

Robert Walls in March, 1918.

Irving and Isabell had three children: Ora, Jim, Robert (Bob). Ora married Tom Paschall, and they had seven children: Alma Sanders, Grover Paschall, Dorothy Arkus, Tommy Walls, William Paschall, Maggie Stanfill and Inez Vastbinder. The Paschall family moved to Wrigley, TN around 1930. Jim worked on a boat and drowned in the Mississippi River, leaving no descendants. Robert (Jan. 10, 1895-April 11, 1968), lived with Bob and Sukey Anderson, Isabell's brother, until he was six years old. Irving remarried during this time; his wife's and step-children's names are unknown.

The Walls family moved to Cedar Creek in the early 1900s. Irving and family moved to Missouri during World War I. He is buried there.

Robert was drafted in 1918 in the Army, and served overseas (Pvt. 42 Co, Trans Corps) during WW I. He married Altha Campbell (Jan. 23, 1895-Sept. 18, 1977) March 10, 1929, by Squire I. B. Moore. She was the daughter of Asa (Ace) (April 22, 1874-Feb. 22, 1948) Campbell.

Altha had one brother, Clarence (Nov. 21, 1893-Oct. 23, 1918) in Brest France, (Pvt. Co A, 19th Reg. Div. A). He married Cliffie Ward. They had one child, Beatrice Campbell, who married Calvin Arnold. They live in Troy, TN, and have one child, James Calvin Arnold Jr.

Altha had one sister, Beatrice (Bertie), (July 26, 1899-July 11, 1980). She married Will Dabbs. They had one child, Oneal (Oct. 23, 1928-July 7, 1988).

Altha's grandparents were Willis and Nancy Kelly Campbell, and James (1826-1900) and Amanda Peace (1848-1933) Ward. Her great grandparents were Miram Campbell, Bill and Polly Richardson Peace and, Rubin and Sallie Smith Ward.

Robert and Altha had three children: Irene (July 13, 1931-May 23, 1935), Edward (Aug. 12, 1933-May 20, 1935) and Norma, born Oct. 19, 1936.

BILLY AND BETTY WARD, are natives of Perry County and have lived here all their lives, except the four years Billy lived in Gilbertsville, KY, as a child.

Betty Jo Hickerson Ward was born June 21, 1935, in the Bethel community, the daughter of Kyle Black Hickerson and Beulas Mae

Sanders. She has a sister, Dorothy Jean Simmons, and a brother, the late Billy Ralph Hickerson. She has one niece, Jackie Skelton, two nephews, Michael Ralph Hickerson and Kyle Gilbert Hickerson, one grand-niece, Kayla Brooke Hickerson, and one grand-nephew, Michael Jonathan Hickerson. She married Billy Douglas Ward on Dec. 26, 1973, in Linden, TN.

Billy and Betty Ward

Her grandparents were William (Bud) Sanders and Ann Kimble and John Hickerson and Carrie Turnbow. Her great-grandparents were Ervin Sanders and Betty Tanner and James Calvin Hickerson and Mary Rhoden.

Betty's parents and grandparents and several other relatives are buried in the Ary Cemetery on Sinking Creek. Betty is a member of the First Baptist Church of Linden.

Billy Douglas Ward is the son of Richard Ward and Tola Peace. Richard was born in 1911 and died in 1986, while Tola was born in 1912 and died in 1981. They were married Dec. 23, 1932 by Squire I. B. "Brat" Moore at the Old Hobert Moore Place. They are buried in the Peace Ward Cemetery behind the old home place on Cedar Creek, along with Tola's parents and both of their grandparents.

Billy was born Dec. 3, 1933 and lived on Cedar Creek until May 1940, when they moved to Gilbertsville, KY, where Richard went to work building on Kentucky Dam. They lived there until June 1944, when they moved back to Cedar Creek.

Billy loves sports of all kinds, with deer hunting as his all time favorite. At the end of his present term, he will have served 28 years as alderman in the Town of Linden. Billy is a deacon in First Baptist Church in Linden.

Billy first married Verna Sue Strickland, daughter of Neal Strickland and Jessie Halbrooks, on April 28, 1952, in Corinth, MS. They had a daughter, Vivian Elaine Ward, born Nov. 12, 1957, in Linden, TN. She married Horace Edward Warren II, son of Horace Edward Warren Sr., and Peggy Wildman, on March 13, 1976. They have two children, Erin Leigh, born July 8, 1983, in Nashville, TN, and William Clay, born Dec. 28, 1990 in Oxford, MS. They are currently living in Oak Ridge, TN. Billy's first marriage eventually ended in divorce in March 1973. He later married Betty Jo Hickerson on Dec. 26, 1973, in Linden, TN.

With the help of Kaye Moore's Pevahouse history, Don Richardson's family history, and most of all, a special thanks to John B. Lomax for information from his book, Samuel Lomax and his descendants, Billy was able to trace his grandparents back to the twelfth generation, some of which were born before 1700 or shortly thereafter.

The grandparents are as follows:

Fifth Generation - Riley Peace and Ida Pevahouse and George B. Ward; Lizzie Richardson.

G. B. Ward was one of the three original board members when the Cedar Creek School District was formed and built the high school in 1926.

Sixth Generation - James (Jim) Ward and Amanda (Mandy) Peace; John W. Richardson and Sallie Broadway; Tom Peace and Mary Lomax; Jess Pevahouse and Linda Wilson.

Seventh Generation - Bill Peace and Mary Ann Richardson; Elihue Pevahouse and Elizabeth Moore; John Wilson and Ann Moore; John W. Lomax and Martha Richardson.

Eighth Generation - Benjamin Richardson and Jemima Horner; Andrew Lomax and Annie Richardson; Paschall Broadway and Sallie C. Broadway; Daniel Pevahouse, William Lomax and Mourning Denton.

Ninth Generation - John Horner Sr. and Elizabeth Russell; John Richardson and Mary Horner; John Lomax and Elizabeth Horner; Samuel Denton and Eunice Conger.

Tenth Generation - William Horner and Elizabeth Alred; George Russell and Elizabeth Bean; Samuel Lomax and Temperance Bugg; John Horner and Elizabeth Russell.

The Russell and Bean families are recorded in most Tennessee histories as being the first permanent white settlers in Tennessee. This was in East Tennessee, long before it became a state in 1796.

Eleventh Generation - George Horner Sr. (born c. 1725); John T. Alred Jr. and Margaret Chaney; John Bugg and Elizabeth Bugg (born c. 1730); Joseph Lomax and Margaret Lomax.

Twelfth Generation - John Horner (born c. 1696); John T. Alred Sr.

JAMES ARTHUR "BOSS" WARD,

(1881-1927) married Clara E. Richardson (1893-1980) in 1908. Their children: Leonard, James, Hillard, Loyd, Lillian, Edith, Gussie, Ruth and Martha (1925-1936).

After the death of James Arthur, Clara married Grady Richardson and had children: Jimmy Frank (1934-1940) and Grady Jr.

Leonard Ward (1910-1980) married 1) Willie Kelley (1915-1932) and had one child who died at birth. Leonard married 2) Cressie Cotham and had son, Billy. After Leonard and Cressie divorced, he married Elsie Inman and had children: Christine, Norma and Jerry Donald Ward.

James Hillard married Bonnie Hudson and they had children: Rena Fay, Boyce, Joe and Ralph Ward.

Loyd married Maggie Burcham and had two children, Peggy Ann and Johnny Wayne Ward. They had a foster son, Anthony Jackson "Tony" Peterson.

Lillian married Abb Grinder and had children: Betty June and Billy Ward Grinder.

Edith Ward married Wess Ward and had children: Johann and Thomas Ward. Thomas Ward is the present Sheriff of Perry County.

Gussie married Elvis Inman and had daughter, Willidean Inman.

Ruth married Kennie Horner and had two children: Paulette and Patsy Horner.

Grady Richardson Jr. married Christine Trull and had children: Barbara Ann, Karon and Garry Richardson.

JAMES H. WARD,

(Sept. 4, 1826-May 1900) was married on April 27, 1873 to Amanda Jane Peace. They had nine children: Sarah A., William T., Mary "Polly," Mima E., Martha E., James A. "Boss," Nannie Jane, George Brown and Robert J. Ward.

George and Lizzie Ward

Sarah A. "Sallie" (April 22, 1874-Feb. 27, 1948) married Asa Campbell (Dec. 12, 1960-July 4, 1936).

William T. (Nov. 16, 1875-July 1945) married Mary Ludy Broadway (Oct. 7, 1874-Aug. 22, 1951).

Mary "Polly" (Dec. 25, 1876-July 23, 1950) married Henry W. Broadway (May 18, 1867-Feb. 27, 1940).

Mima E. born April 5, 1878 died young.

The Ward family in September 1900. Front row: Colonel Henry Polly (holding baby Myrtle), Amanda, Ludie (holding baby Grady) and Bill. Standing: Robert, George, Sam, Martha, Boss, Nanny and Bob.

Martha E. (Aug. 14, 1879-Nov. 11, 1902) married on June 20, 1901 to Samuel A. Broadway (Feb. 14, 1880-Oct. 10, 1957).

James A. (March 16, 1881-April 8, 1927) married on Feb. 19, 1908 to Clara E. Richardson (June 15, 1893-Jan. 3, 1980).

Nannie Jane (Jan. 19, 1883-Feb. 27, 1951) married on Sept. 17, 1905 to Robert T. Broadway (Dec. 8, 1881-May 8, 1926).

George Brown (Dec. 17, 1885-Jan. 9, 1950) married on Feb. 16, 1908 to Lizzie W. Richardson (March 11, 1894). Their children were: Richard H. (Oct. 25, 1911-Aug. 6, 1986) who married Tola M. Peace (Aug. 7, 1912-June 1981) on Dec. 23, 1932; Nettie L. (Dec. 13, 1913); Gertie M. (Feb. 12, 1916) who married James Ernie Peace (May 8, 1916) on April 26, 1935; Fred E. (Nov. 17, 1917) who married Ruth Coleman (June 27, 1924) on March 4, 1948; George Brownie (Feb. 18, 1920-May 7, 1982) who married Ruth June Kihu (June 21, 1919) on July 28, 1946; Jettie Opal (Nov. 13, 1921) who married Arther L. Clifton (Dec. 8, 1910) on March 17, 1944; William Ray (May 7, 1931) married Ollie Mae Stephens on Sept. 22, 1951.

Robert J. (Nov. 24, 1887-Jan. 11, 1951) married Minnie Pevahouse (1892-April 21, 1917) on Jan. 7, 1910.

NATHAN WARD SR., was born in Virginia about 1770 and died about 1856 in Perry County, TN. He moved to Perry County with his family and a brother, William, about 1818. He lived in the Buckfork area on Marsh Creek. He had three sons: Reubin, William and Nathan Jr.

Reubin was born about 1849 on Cedar Creek, Perry County. He married Sarah (?) about 1822 and they had 11 children.

Their third son, James H. Ward (1826-1900) married Amanda Peace on April 23, 1873. She was the daughter of William Zachery Peace and Mary Ann Richardson. They lived on Cedar Creek, Perry County, TN and had seven children.

Their fourth child, James Arthur (March 16, 1881-April 8, 1927) married February 19, 1908 to Clara Edith Richardson (June 15, 1893-Jan. 5, 1980). They had eight children: Leonard Brown, James Hillard, Lillian Alma, Flora Edith, Gussie, Lloyd, Ruth and Martha.

In 1928, Clara married Grady Richardson and had two sons, Grady and Jimmy Frank, and a daughter, Flora Edith (Jan. 30, 1916-June 24, 1976) who married Thomas Wesley "Wess" Ward (June 5, 1911-Sept. 10, 1970) on Dec. 2, 1939. They lived on Marsh Creek, Perry County, TN, and had three children: JoAnn, Janet Edith (stillborn) and Thomas Ward.

Jo Ann (Jan. 17, 1942) was married on July 26, 1958 to Paul Dewayne Carroll. They had three children: 1) Rhonda (March 11, 1959) married Dec. 17, 1976 to Tom Edd Young; they have one son, Thomas Matthew (Jan. 28, 1991; 2) Steve Carroll (March 19, 1961; and 3) Jimmy Ward Carroll (April 11, 1964). Jimmy was married twice and has a daughter, Chloe Miranda Carroll (March 7, 1992).

WILLIAM WARD, born 1800 in Kentucky, died about 1850, married around 1826 to Rutha, born 1801 in Tennessee. They lived on Marsh Creek, Perry County, TN near the Tennessee River. They were listed in the 1830-1850 censuses of Perry County. They had 11 children. Their fifth son, Wesley, born Nov. 15, 1832 on marsh Creek, died Feb. 10, 1910, married first Evaline DePriest about 1855. They had two sons, William H. and John Lewis. She died during the Civil War. Wesley was a private in F Co. 2nd M.I. Tenn. which stayed in Perry County. Then around 1866, he married Mary Louanne Wiley; they had two children, George Erving and Rutha Ward. Mary Louanne first married a Samuel Denton and had one child. He died during the Civil War. Mary Louanne died about 1882, then Wesley married Julia Ann Ferguson, May 11, 1884, in Decatur County. They had one son, Walter F. Ward, born Feb. 20, 1885, and died March 25, 1919.

Back row: Flora Edith and Wess. Front row: Thomas and Jo Ann Ward.

Wesley was mentioned in a court record in 1858 as an heir by descent of Nathan Ward Sr. in which he and his brother and sister got one-fifth part of land of Nathan Ward Sr.

George Ward, born March 3, 1867, died April 3, 1918, married first Martha Green. They had three daughters, Ida, Olivie and Cliffie. Martha died in 1899 and their daughters were sent to three of their uncles on her side.

Nov. 3, 1900, George married Sally Tomblin, born Dec. 25, 1878, died Nov. 1, 1948 on Marsh Creek. They had eight children: Rex, Fred, John, Ann, Ernest, Thomas Wesley (Wess), Roger and Bertha.

Thomas Wesley (Wess) Ward, born June 5, 1911, died Sept 20, 1970, married Dec. 2, 1939 to Flora Edith Ward, born Jan. 30, 1916, died June 24, 1976 in Perry County. They had three children, Jo Ann, Janet Edith (who was stillborn) and Thomas Ward, born July 14, 1956. He married Rendia Howell, born July 14, 1956. They were married Dec. 26, 1979, and have one son, Wess Frelon Ward, born June 30, 1981.

WARREN-CHESSOR-CURRY, Martha Belle Warren born June 4, 1925 on Cane Creek, Perry County, TN. Her mother and dad were Myrta Estalee Hinson and Lloyd McKinley Warren. She was born Feb. 15, 1903, died March 15, 1989. He was born March 8, 1900. They married Dec. 1, 1917. Both are buried in Kirk Cemetery in Linden, TN. Martha had four sisters and two brothers. Elsie Carroll born 1918, married W. B. Cates, married second W. B. Hogan; Chloe Lazell born 1920, married Willie Ray Tucker, died Feb. 10, 1984; Mavous Marie born 1922, married Harold Hinson, died Sept. 14, 1993; Claudia Charmain born 1927, married Dean Weatherspoon (divorced); Lloyd (Budo) born 1933, married Carolyn Sofge; Jerry Granville born March 1939, married Patricia Brown.

Martha Chessor Curry

Martha married Ralph Carson Chessor June 27, 1945. They had four children - Carson Wayne born Aug. 7, 1946, Joey Michael born Aug. 26, 1951, Gerry Anthony born Jan. 16, 1953 and Angela Dawn born Jan. 24, 1966.

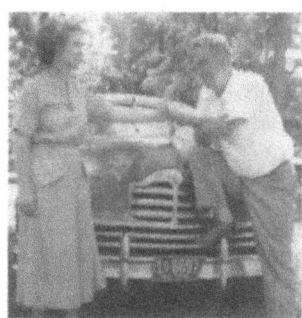

Lloyd and Myrta Warren

Carson married Ruth Ann Heffner May 1, 1965, two children, Jeffrey Wayne born Aug. 3, 1966 and Wendy Dianne born March 19, 1970. Carson married second Carol Bostic. Jeff married Marie Baron May 1992, Wendy married Doug Brown May 1993. Joey married Gail Louise Lydon April 1973, they have two children James Michael born July 7, 1976 and Jodie Elizabeth born Jan. 26, 1982. Gerry Anthony married Carolyn Patricia Kincaid, they have two children, Matthew Warren born Aug. 7, 1976 and Chelsea Leigh born Sept. 19, 1982 in Germany. Chelsea lost almost all of her left foot in a lawnmower accident.

Angela Dawn married Jon Daniel July 17, 1987. They have a son, Jason, born Jan. 16, 1990.

Martha's grandparents were Jonathan Harvey Hinson and Callie Barber Hinson, born April 17, 1877, died July 8, 1968, she was born Nov. 23, 1883, died Oct. 23, 1908, buried in Cook Cemetery on Cane Creek. They married Aug. 3, 1899. Jonathan Harvey married second Martha Jane Hickerson. He was a Primitive Baptist minister.

William Hartie and Isabell Carroll Warren, born Nov. 8, 1876, died June 15, 1957. She was born June 30, 1868, died Dec. 12, 1937. They had three children - Claude, Elta and Lloyd. Claude and his family were killed in a train wreck at Rives, TN in 1925, except a son who was 18 months old at the time. They are buried in Warren Cemetery on Cane Creek.

Ralph Carson Chessor died Jan. 7, 1987, buried in Memory Gardens, Centerville, TN. He was a World War II veteran, served in the 115th

F.A. from 1939 to 1945. Active in combat in France and Germany, was stationed in England.

Martha married John Frank Curry March 14, 1988. His birthday Aug. 16, 1922. A veteran of World War II, he served in England in the Air Force. Martha has one stepdaughter, Shiela Niece, born March 6, 1953. She married Edward Niece born July 7, 1952. They have two children Brandi born Aug. 23, 1973 and Morgan born Aug. 14, 1984. Brandi married Jeff Coble; they have a son Chase Lane Coble born June 10, 1993.

Martha and John Frank live in Lobelville, well and happy as of April 27, 1994.

Martha is a member of the Primitive Baptist Church of Christ, baptized in December 1945. Her mother and sisters and a brother are members. She is an artist, was the originator of the artist Guild in Hickman County, also the first President and helped to establish the Maury County Artist Guild. Her work hangs in numerous homes across the United States. *Submitted by Martha Curry.*

WARREN-DOWDY Thelma Virginia Warren Hugueley is now living in Hughes, AR. She is the daughter of William (Billy) Elijah Warren and Mary Elizabeth (Lizzie) Dowdy. They were both born in Perry County.

Billy was the oldest child of Joseph Allen Warren and Mary (Polly) Tate and was born Dec. 22, 1866 near Lobelville, TN. Lizzie was the oldest child of Allen Jordan Dowdy and Martha Nemigie Berry and was born Oct. 3, 1871 near Linden, TN.

Billy and Lizzie were married on May 23, 1889 at the Dowdy farm, after Lizzie had cooked a wedding meal for about 100 guests. Billy farmed with his father until 1916, when they moved to Bogoto in Dyer County. In 1919, they moved to a farm outside Kenton in Gibson County. Billy died Dec. 18, 1926.

Their 11 children are: Mary Nemigie married Joe Washburn; William Henry married Lillian Curry; Fanny Ophelia married Jessie Lee Brown; Katie Nancy Jane died of a seizure at 23, never married; Mytle Lee died at 16 months; Verdie Lou married Rob Taylor; Thelma Virginia married Elmer Hugueley; Elma Lucy died at 3 months; Dalton Allen married Qua Norman; Joe died at birth; Robert Clayton married Anna Littleton. All were born in Perry County.

Lizzie died in Thelma's home in East Gary, IN July 4, 1952. Billy and Lizzie are buried in North Union Cemetery in Gibson County, TN.

Thelma was born Feb. 23, 1905 in Perry County. She married Elmer Marion Hugueley Jan. 8, 1924 in Gibson County. Elmer was born April 21, 1905 and died Sept. 30, 1982 in West Memphis, AR. He is buried in Crittenden Memorial Park in Crittenden County, AR.

Thelma and Elmer had eight children: Marion Charles died at 3 days; Cora Elizabeth married Albert Glen Warren; Irene Jenise married Forrest Jackson Dunlap; Betty Lou married James Milton Rose; Shirley Mae married Jack Tietge; Jo Ann died at 16 years; Virginia died at birth; Elmer Ray married Linda Faye Ford.

Elmer and Thelma have 11 grandchildren, 27 great grandchildren and one great great grandchild.

Thelma is the descendent of four Perry County families, Warren-Tate-Dowdy-Berry. She inherited some very good genes. *Submitted by Jenise Hugueley Dunlap, daughter of Thelma.*

WARREN-PARNELL, James Cassitey Hannica (Jim) Warren was born Feb. 11, 1870. In 1890, Perry County, TN, he married Clara Adeline Parnell. Clara was born Dec. 17, 1875 and died Oct. 24, 1944. They had seven children:

Ova Mai Warren, married Gilbert Leslie Hardin on March 8, 1908 and they had six children, James Grady, Riley Leslie, Edward Hershel, Raymond Earl, Elsie Marie and Elizabeth Lorene.

Marion Hercules Warren married Annie Andrews and they had two children Effie and Earlene.

Alice Warren, married J. B. (Cooch) French on Jan. 4, 1919 and they had four children, Jessie, Bill, Jack and Fred.

John Warren died during World War I.

Boss Warren, married Geretta Horner and they had two children, Elmer Ray Warren and Boss Warren Jr.

Charlie Warren, born June 26, 1904, married Edna Westbrook on Oct. 5, 1924. They had 13 children. (Please see Warren-Westbrook History.)

Della Warren, born Dec. 1, 1906, married A. R. Trull. They had four girls and 3 sons. *Submitted by Mary Trull.*

WARREN-WESTBROOKS, Charles Warren, born June 26, 1904, son of J. C. Warren and Clara Adeline (Parnell) Warren of Perry County, TN, married Edna Westbrooks on Oct. 5, 1924 and their children are as follows: James Earl Warren, born Sept. 7, 1925, married Jolly Lynch; Egbert Vonell (Pat) Warren, born Jan. 21, 1927, married Irene Flowers; Opal Ludene (Dene) Warren, born Oct. 15, 1928, married Alfred Weatherly; Nell Warren, born Oct. 19, 1930, married Herchel Townsend; Elizabeth Ruth (Buster) Warren, born June 4, 1932, married Ralph Douglas; Ralph Edward Warren, born Feb. 28, 1934, never married; J. D. Warren, born March 21, 1936, died Feb. 10, 1975, married in St. Louis, MO to Erna; Charlie Robert (Bud) Warren, born April 14, 1938 and died Jan. 10, 1990; Howard Wayne Warren, born March 6, 1940 and died Jan. 7, 1942, married Sue Troutt; Larry Hermon Warren, born April 5, 1942, married Linda Jones; Danny Ray Warren, born March 6, 1944, married Murriel Roland; Gary Lynn Warren, born Aug. 12, 1948, married Elizabeth Perry.

Charlie Warren died April 15, 1976. Edna (Westbrooks) Warren died Jan. 28, 1980. Edna was the daughter of John and Dosha Westbrooks of Perry County, TN. *Submitted by Walter Trull.*

ANDERSON W. WARREN, The following genealogy of the Anderson W. Warren family was obtained by his son, Neil O. Warren, who was born Feb. 28, 1911 in Perry County near Lobelville. Neil lives in Old Hickory and obtained the information from the 1850, 1860 and 1870 Perry County Census stored at the State Library at Nashville.

Anderson Warren's grandfather, Elijah (Sobby) Warren, born Feb. 22, 1799 near Shad Creek, NC, moved to Perry County in the early 1800s and his family was: Elijah Warren, wife Gathasa (Gatsy), children, Elijah, Rachel, Joseph Allen, Milton, Mary J. and Andrew (Andy). He was listed as a farmer and hatter.

The Anderson W. Warren Family. Left to right: Mattie Pearl Warren (on father's lap), Anderson W. Warren (father), Julie Dorton Warren (mother), Grayce Mai Warren and Neil Olen Warren.

One of Elijah's (Sobby) sons, Joseph Allen Warren, was born June 6, 1843 and died in 1928. He was listed in the 1850 census as age seven, and in the 1860 census as age 18. He served in the Civil War, 1861-1865. He married Mary Polly Tate, born Jan. 9, 1847 and died March 16, 1910. Their family included children: William E. (Billy), Joseph, Michie, Anderson W., Alice, Harvill, Dennis, Martha Jane and Donie.

One of Joseph Allen Warren and Mary Polly Tate Warren's children, Anderson, was born July 4, 1881 and died March 4, 1941 on his farm near Waverly. Anderson was born on Lost Creek where he grew up as a young man and walked eight miles a day to and from Lobelville to school. He continued to pursue his education and became a teacher, having taught in Perry County on Lost Creek, Bone Springs, Border Springs and Lobelville.

Anderson married Julia Dorton Dec. 25, 1901. Julia was born March 15, 1882 and died July 1, 1962. They lived near Lobelville and in Lobelville. Their family included Neil Olen, Grayce Mai and Mattie Pearl.

While teaching in Lobelville, Anderson accepted a position in the Nashville post office in 1913. Grayce was born there Oct. 29, 1913. She married Robert Ferguson in 1930. They had three children, Bobby Ferguson, Angeline Goodwin and Bonnie Stockman. Robert died in 1989.

The Anderson Warren family moved to Waverly in August 1916 as a rural carrier. Anderson was a prominent man of Humphreys County becoming postmaster Jan. 1, 1922. He was a school board member for several years. Mattie Pearl was born there Nov. 21, 1916. She married Layton Ridings in 1937. She taught school in Humphreys County 37 years before dying Sept. 20, 1972. Layton died in 1982.

Neil married Agnes Miller Batton Dec. 25, 1931. To this marriage was born Beverly Joy Warren Stokely, who taught school 30 years, 21 years at the DuPont school. Beverly has three sons, Jimmy, Andy and Billy. Agnes taught school 32 years, 27 years at DuPont school in Old Hickory. Neil worked for the Post Office Department 43 years at Waverly, Old Hickory and retired as Manager, Labor-Management Relations for the Memphis Region June 1971.

Since Anderson W. Warren's mother was a

Tate before her marriage, his family branches off into the Tate, Ledbetter and Gilmer families.

WARREN, Bernard and Sally Warren lived on Brush Creek in Perry County. Bernard was one of four children born to Elijah and Sarah Tucker Warren. Bernard was born Aug. 16, 1881. He was a farmer most of his life. He also owned a grocery store at one time. He taught singing at Brush Creek Church of Christ, where he was a member. He also led singing there. He died Aug. 22, 1955 and was buried on Brush Creek at the family cemetery near his home.

Sara, Bernard, Gola and Ferd Warren

Sally Harriet was one of four children born to Joe and Elizabeth Craig Beasley, May 19, 1883. She was a homemaker and a "good" seamstress. She sewed for her family and neighbors as well. She died Jan. 13, 1934 and was buried beside her husband.

Bernard and Sally had four children, Gola Ray, born Dec. 6, 1900 and died Jan. 1992; Ferd Burkett, born Dec. 5, 1907 and died 1993; Joe Elijah, born March 7, 1911 and died Dec. 13, 1929; and Sara Elizabeth, born April 13, 1921.

Gola Ray married Lessie Parnell. They had three children. Laverne Reed, born June 19, 1921; Julia Elizabeth, born Oct. 26, 1927; and Ruby Jo, born May 15, 1930.

Ferd Burkett married Lorene Toland. They had four children: Nell, born Nov. 1929; Jim, born June 1932 (deceased): Joe and Paul.

Sara Elizabeth married Stanley McDonald Curry Sept. 21, 1946. Stanley was born May 30, 1914. They have two children, Donald Wayne, born July 6, 1948 and Dana Beth, born July 10, 1955. Don married Carol Ann Elliott. They have three children: Donald Mark, born Oct. 4, 1972; Matthew Elliott, born Nov. 24, 1977; and Melinda Beth, born Nov. 18, 1978. Dana married James Claude Neelley on Dec. 14, 1974. They have three children: James Ryan, born Aug. 12, 1980; Curry Beth, born April 24, 1983; and Joseph Blake, born Feb. 1, 1987.

WILLIAM "BILLY" WARREN AND CATHERINE DOWDY WARREN, "I know not what the truth may be, so, I tell the story as was told to me."

The early known history of the Warren family began in the state of North Carolina with the birth of Elijah Warren Sr. on Jan. 22, 1799. As a young man, Elijah married Gathasa "Gatsy" Barber on Sept. 17, 1820. The couple migrated to Middle Tennessee and eventually settled on Hurricane Creek in Perry County. Elijah and Gatsy reared a family of 10 children. Elijah Sr. died Aug. 22, 1877 at the age of 78 years.

Elijah's oldest son, Alvin Warren, was born Sept. 17, 1821. He grew up in the Coon Creek Community of Perry County, and reared a large family on a farm in that community. He was married twice. His first wife, Serena Hilburn, died Oct. 23, 1856. He later married Mrs. Mary Barber Dowdy, widow of Jordon Dowdy, who died Sept. 9, 1852. Jordon Dowdy was poisoned by one of his slaves who put Black Eyed Susan weed in his coffee. It is said that Jordon whipped the slave woman for hitting his wife. The slave was found guilty, and was sold for $1,000 and her ten-month-old baby was sold to a southern cotton king for $500.

W.H. "Billy" Warren and Cathy Dowdy Warren

Mary Barber Dowdy Warren was actually Alvin's step-mother's sister. Alvin was four years younger than his step-mother. There was a large family. Alvin had children by his first wife, Serena Hilburn, and Mrs. Dowdy had children whose father was Jordon Dowdy.

The oldest of Alvin's children was William Hardy (Billy) Warren, who was born Dec. 5, 1846. He married Serena Catherine Dowdy, his step-sister, on Feb. 10, 1866. To this union 14 children were born. Billy and Cathy lived their early years of married life on a farm in the Coon Creek Community of Perry County. Their four oldest children, Jan, Eloria, Leona and Elta, died in early childhood, and are buried in a cemetery on upper Coon Creek.

About the year 1900, Billy and Cathy bought a farm of 200 acres, more or less, on Lower Cane Creek from Buddy Shepherd for the sum of $975.00. The family all worked on the farm, pooled their resources and bought more land. The old two-story house that was built by Buddy Shepherd still is maintained, and is nearing 100 years of age. The farm and house are now (1994) owned by his grandson, Charles M. Warren Jr. of Clarksville, TN.

Billy died Sept. 6, 1921 of heart failure at the age of 76. Cathy preceded him in death July 15, 1921 at the age of 71 from an unknown cause. Before his death, Billy selected a knoll on the farm for a family cemetery which overlooks the beautiful valley of Cane Creek. A three-foot rock wall surrounds this plot, and is known as the Warren Family Cemetery.

Billy and Cathy provided in their will that each of the four sons, Asberry, Ashley, Hardy and Charles would inherit a farm - each valued at $2,000. The six daughters, Ezora, Ada, Ida, Alma, Miggie and Lottye, married husbands who owned farms. They were given $2,000 in money instead of a farm.

Lula who died in early adulthood, was the first to be buried in the Warren Family Cemetery in 1906.

Records reveal at the date of this publication that only ten grandchildren of Billy and Cathy Warren survive. There are as follows: Myrtle Warren Roberts, Linden, TN; Mae Warren Holt, Linden, TN; Cathy Warren Cotton, Hohenwald, TN; Flora Rogers Hudson, Charlotte, TN; Lillian Rogers Barber, Linden, TN; Lucille Rogers Harper, Linden, TN; Walton O. Warren, McKenzie, TN; Charles M. Warren Jr., Clarksville, TN; Theda Edwards Long, Linden, TN; and Catherine Edwards Leeper, Tupelo, MS.

CLARENCE WARREN, born 1880, son of Burr Warren and Amelia Morris. He married Louisa Williams, born 1880, daughter of George W. and Susan J. Williams. They were living in Perry County in 1900 and 1910. Per 1910 census, they had six children: John Warren, born 1901; Eva, born 1904; Annie, born 1905; Susie, born 1906; Arthur, born 1907; Elva, born 1909.

WARREN, Pictured are Fred Warren and Ina Harder Warren. They were married Nov. 8, 1941, had two daughters (Freddie and Linda), and have been life long residents of the Rockhouse Creek Community of Perry County.

Fred and Ina Harder Warren

Fred was the son of Al Warren and Rowena Hufstedler Warren. He was one of three boys and two girls. Fred's brothers and sisters were Alga, Willard, Walton and Ruth. Fred was a WW II veteran and member of the local chapter of the Disabled American Veterans. Most of his years in the work force were spent as a carpenter. He assisted in building many of the homes in Perry County up until 1978. After his retirement, he spent many hours building wood crafts, some of which have been displayed for public view of his work. Fred once served as a County Magistrate and was an employee of the County Highway Department prior to becoming a carpenter. He attended the Primitive Baptist Church. His hobbies were fishing and hunting.

Ina was the daughter of Robert Lee Harder and Leora Hinson Harder. She was one of nine children, brothers being Carlus, Wilburn, Bryan, Clifford, Leonard; sisters being Eugenia, Ila and Mary Jewel. Ina was a devoted housewife and later worked as a nurse's aide. Her hobbies include sewing, crocheting and gardening. Ina is a member of the Warren Methodist church.

At the time of this writing, Fred is deceased (1986), as well as one brother, Willard. Ina currently lives in the family home on Rockhouse Creek. Both daughters are married, and Ina has three grandchildren, Brent and Stacey Hinson, and John H. White, IV. Ina currently has one sister living (Ila) and she continues to be actively involved in things she enjoys.

GOLA RAY WARREN, the oldest son of C. B. and Sally Beasley Warren. He was born in Perry County and died Jan. 9, 1992 in the Perry County Nursing Home. He was buried in the Gola Warren Cemetery. He taught singing school in his younger years and was the song leader and Elder at the Lobelville Church of Christ for many years.

Gola Ray Warren Family

He married his childhood sweetheart Sept. 19, 1919. His wife, Lessie Reed Parnell (1901-1975) was the daughter of E. H. and Meda Vick Parnell. They lived in the Burns Hill community about 50 years where my father farmed and drove a school bus. They had three daughters: Laverne Reed Curry (June 19, 1921), Julia Elizabeth Patterson (Oct. 26, 1927) and Ruby Jo Weatherly (May 15, 1930). Our father remarried to Era Mealer, Oct. 1975. She died in a Nursing Home in Chicago in 1992. She is buried on Brush Creek Hill.

JAMES FRANKLIN WARREN (July 22, 1858-Sept. 11, 1953) is the son of Alvin Warren (born Sept. 17, 1821) and Mary "Polly" Barber Dowdy (May 1, 1821-July 21, 1901) married Sept. 5, 1857. His grandfather, Elijah Warren Sr. (born July 22, 1877) migrated to Perry County from north Carolina. It is thought that Franklin's grandmother is Mary Campbell.

Frank and Tennie Warren Family

Franklin Warren married Tennessee Missouri (Tennie) Tucker (March 15, 1860-Oct. 9, 1932). Tennie is the daughter of Dickson Tucker and Betty Campbell. Franklin and Tennie were married Jan. 1879. To this union, eight children were born.

Franklin and "Tennie" lived on Coon Creek in Perry County until they moved to a farm at the mouth of Hurricane Creek, now known as the Ledbetter farm. The cost of the farm was $6,500.00. The Warrens, thinking they could not pay for the farm, moved to Rockhouse Creek, and bought the old Randel farm from Dr. J. P. Dabbs at the mouth of Rockhouse Creek on Buffalo River. Later Franklin bought adjoining farms once owned by Pinckney Hufstedler; the Wrights; the Kings; The Kittrells; and later all this was bought by Carroll Warren. Franklin Warren later bought another tract of land known as the John Bastin farm. This farm later became the Farry Warren farm. A farm east of the main farm was purchased by Al Warren in the later years.

Franklin and "Tennie" Warren's children are as follows: Henry Agnes (Oct. 19, 1879-Sept. 11, 1953) married George D. Whitwell. Their children are George Dewey (July 26, 1898-Oct. 12, 1978); Walton Thomas (Sept. 26, 1900-March 11, 1955); Gladys Adalee (Sept. 24, 1902-1981); Byron Maybelle (Jan. 26, 1905-May 4, 1948); Kent Franklin (Oct. 11, 1908-Feb. 28, 1964); William Carroll (June 1, 1911-Feb. 28, 1913); Eva Millesia (born March 25, 1915).

Carroll Nix (Oct. 22, 1881-Nov. 6, 1962) married Minnie Jane Hufstedler (April 29, 1878-July 4, 1976) married Sept. 9, 1900. Their children are Lela Anne (May 6, 1903-April 15, 1991); James Gola (Feb. 14, 1905-March 7, 1988); Minnie Sue (born April 22, 1910); Videlle Eudoxie (born July 14, 1913).

Odella Walton (May 20, 1883-Oct. 27, 1966) married Brantley Whitwell. Their children are Willie Larlene (born May 27, 1906); Clyde Claimon (born Oct. 13, 1910); Wilton Elvie (born May 9, 1914); Wilma Jack (born June 12, 1918); Joe Thomas (born Jan. 7, 1921).

Mary Elizabeth (Betty) (Jan. 10, 1885-May 17, 1904) married Welsey Tharp (born Dec. 1881).

Alvin (Dec. 1, 1887-April 2, 1962) married Mattie Rowena Hufstedler (Jan. 12, 1895-Nov. 4, 1976) married July 23, 1911. Their children are Alga Lucille (born Aug. 11, 1912); Fred Olga (March 19, 1914-Oct. 13, 1986); Jess Willard (Dec. 27, 1915-Aug. 8, 1980); Walton Olythus (born Sept. 8, 1926); Mattie Ruth (born May 24, 1930).

Ethel Dickson (May 15, 1890-July 2, 1971) married John Thomas Tharp (March 24, 1886-Feb. 27, 1971). Children: Thelma Tennessee (born May 18, 1909). Second marriage - Chesley Barber (d. July 20, 1957). No children.

Farry Franklin (March 4, 1894-Sept. 24, 1976) married Lona Gertude Grinder (Feb. 20, 1895-Feb. 1979) married Sept. 1913; J. F. Warren (Oct. 16, 1915-Oct. 21, 1989).

Chesley Oscar (Sept. 12, 1896-Oct. 27, 1977) married Alma Richardson (Oct. 9, 1895-April 23, 1987) married June 17, 1916. Children: Chesley Floyd (July 7, 1917-May 6, 1990).

Franklin Warren selected a beautiful hill near his home for a family cemetery. His wife, Tennie, was the first to be buried there. He, three sons and their wives, one daughter and others are now buried in the Warren Cemetery.

Four Warren brothers, Carroll, Alvin, Farry and Chesley lived on Buffalo River - Rockhouse Creek farms until their death. Only two of the Warren children still live on their father's farm - Videlle W. Dabbs and Mattie Ruth Warren. There is one granddaughter - Dorthy W. Lomax.

JESS WILLARD WARREN, and Eleanor Mae York were married Feb. 8, 1941 in Perry County. They lived most of their married life on Rockhouse Creek, on the farm known as the Cotton place, in Perry County.

Jess Willard Warren (known by all as Willard) is the son of Alvin (Al) Warren and Rowena Hufstedler Warren. He was born Dec. 27, 1915 in Perry County. Willard's parents lived their entire life in Perry County, mostly on Rockhouse Creek. Willard had two brothers, Fred O. and Walton O. Warren. He had two sisters, Algie L. and Ruth M. Warren.

Eleanor is the daughter of Allen Y. York and Nannie Bennett York. She was born Aug. 28, 1921 in Lewis County. Eleanor had four brothers, Edward L., Monroe F., Claude L. and Alvin C. York. Alvin was killed in action in World War II. Eleanor's father, Allen York, was born in Campbell County, TN. He came to Lewis County when he was a young man. Eleanor's parents lived most of their married life in Lewis County, TN and are buried in Kittrell Cemetery on Big Swan Creek in Lewis County, TN.

Willard's parents are buried in Warren Cemetery on Rockhouse Creek in Perry County.

Willard and Eleanor had two sons: Jess Willard Warren Jr. (born Nov. 20, 1942) and Larry Alvin Warren (born Jan. 4, 1949). Jess Willard married Jeanette Jean Marshall Dec. 10, 1964 in Perry County. Jean's parents are Raymond and Maude Marshall of Perry County. Jess and Jean have one son, Stephen Lynn Warren (born Jan. 29, 1967); Larry Alvin married Nancy Carol Horner June 1, 1968 in Perry County. Nancy's parents are Bob Horner and Nell Moore Horner. Larry and Nancy have two children, Cayce Gwenn Warren (born Dec. 31, 1975) and Zachary Blake Warren (born Jan. 22, 1980).

Jess Willard Warren Sr. died Aug. 8, 1980 and was laid to rest in Warren Cemetery on Rockhouse Creek, Perry County.

Eleanor was remarried to Ira Roberts Oct. 4, 1985. Ira died March 11, 1993 and was buried in Kirk Cemetery, Linden, TN.

WILLIAM CAREY WEBB AND MARTHA ANN DODSON WEBB, William Carey Webb was born in Perry County 1840. This family originated in North Carolina, then to Tennessee. William C. Webb married Martha Ann Dodson. William C. Webb was sheriff in Perry County and collected the revenue in 12 counties. To this union the following children were born: Dr. Emma Webb married Dr. Brown Godwin; Allen Webb married Ruth; Ennis Webb married Ila Tubbs; Waco Webb married Latitia Vaughan; Lena Webb married Mack Craig; Atlas Webb married Bonnie O'Neal April 29, 1906; Larrimore Webb, born April 25, 1885, married Maude Harris May 20, 1909. To this union were born four sons. Ned Webb born Nov. 26, 1912; William Carey Webb born July 21, 1917; Giles T. Webb born Sept. 25, 1921; Joe L. Webb born July 9, 1923. Larrimore was Circuit Court Clerk and substitute mail carrier in Perry County. He died Dec. 3, 1949. His wife, Maude, was a homemaker. She died Nov. 23, 1972. Ned Webb died Nov. 16, 1936, and William C. Webb married

Grace Gobelet June 13, 1937. One child born, Ted Webb March 3, 1938. Ted Webb married Betty Barker Oct. 6, 1956. They had one son Ronald born Aug. 11, 1957. He married Laura Layne. They had two daughters: Chrystal born Jan. 3, 1986 and Rachel born Aug. 6, 1989.

Larrimore Webb - April 25, 1885 to Dec. 3, 1949

William C. Webb married second, Tommye Edwards in 1960. William C. Webb died in 1968, Tommye died in 1990.

G. T. Webb married Dorothy Clifton 1947. One child born, Emily Jean, Feb. 28, 1949. Dorothy Webb died 1969. G. T. Webb married Sally F. Allen 1971. G. T. Webb died 1983.

Joe L. Webb married Mary Lancaster 1947, their children: Steve Webb born Oct. 30, 1948 and Cathy Webb born June 12, 1950. Steve married Linda Cower, one daughter born, Martha Jo Jan. 23, 1976, married second time to Catherine McDowell. Cathy married Danny Lindsey. They had one son, Stephen born Dec. 13, 1970. Danny Lindsey died 1992.

G. T., Billy and Joe (brothers) served in the U.S. Navy during World War II. They were on the same ship, the *U.S.S. Wyoming* in the Atlantic Zone. They went on different ships. Joe went to South America and then to the Pacific on patrol craft. Billy went to the invasion in North Africa, on the *U.S.S. KA Thomas Stone,* and *U.S.S. Tuscaloosa Hummingbird* at York town, VA and Guantanomo Bay, Cuba. Billy retired with 20 years service. G. T. went to the Air Craft Bennington in the Mediterranean, *U.S.S. Huntington, U.S.S. President Adams, U.S.S. Wyoming, U.S.S. Mountrail, U.S.S. Timbalier, U.S.S. Ticonderoga and U.S.S. Reckbridge.* G. T. retired with 20 years of service.

WEBB, The name of Webb is of Anglo-Saxon origin. It is derived from the occupation of weavers. Genealogists trace the family back to Dorsetshire, England. An early ancestor, a Henry Webbe (born 1570) was knighted and given a Coat-of-arms. The emigrant ancestor was William Webb who settled in Virginia between 1640-1650. His son, Giles, fathered four sons: James, being in the House of Burgesses (1658, 59, 60). A later descendent, another James, was a bondsman, sheriff and a signer of the Stamp Act (1765). Research has proven a Webb-Daniel Boone relationship.

Several Webbs served as officers in the Revolutionary War, one being Commissary John Webb of North Carolina, from whom the Perry County Webbs are descended. Records show that John Webb owned property in Perry County in 1823. He had six children: one being, John Love Webb, father of William Carey Webb. W.C. (1840-1909) attended the Commercial College in St. Louis and was in the mercantile business there for a short while prior to the Civil War. He was a vast land owner; had slaves but freed them before the war. He became a captain for the 6th Tennessee Federal Cavalry. History records show he and his regiment captured a Colonel Frierson, over 50 of his men, contraband of war, and burned the courthouse in Linden. After the war, those who were bitter enemies became friends again; bitterness forgiven and forgotten. In 1867, he became Collector of Revenue for the 6th Congressional District, an area of 12 counties. He served as sheriff at one time. W.C. erected a gristmill and sawmill on the Buffalo River in 1872. W.C. deeded much of his property to the county for the construction of Linden School (now the site of the Buffalo River Apartments) and the A.M.E. Church. In 1880, the county purchased a farm from John L. Webb and W. C. that was later used for "paupers," it was actually called "the poor house." William Carey was elected Chancellor Clerk of the Court in 1883.

W.C. Webb

William Carey married Martha Ann Dodson and had five sons, two daughters: Allen, Waco, Atlas, Larrimore, Ennis, Emma and Lena. N.B. Hardeman, President of Freed-Hardeman, performed the wedding ceremony (in his home) for Atlas Webb and Bonnie Daisy O'Neal of Henderson, April 29, 1906. Atlas became a farmer, served as tax assessor in the 20s. He was elected sheriff in the 20s, 30s and again in the 40s. He was an ardent fox hunter in the area and an avid supporter of baseball and basketball.

Atlas and Bonnie had five children: O'Neal, Juanita, John Love, Matthew and Norville Kyle. O'Neal (Teak) never married, Juanita married Jack Bates, John Love (Luke) married Lorene Conder; six children: Ned, Joyce, Holly, Bonnie Mae, Cheryl, Gil. Matthew (Pat) married Nancy Colley of Amarillo; two children: Colley Pat and Pam. Norville Kyle (Sonny) married Mable Hopper of Jackson; three children: Larry Joe, Gene and Mike. "Teak" lived in Jackson, TN, died in 1959. Juanita and "Luke" reside in Linden. "Pat" died in 1972; his family lives in Texas. "Sonny" moved to California in 1948, but since 1953 he and his family have lived in Scottsdale, AZ.

WEBSTER, Arthur Glen and Eula Mae DePriest Webster were married Aug. 3, 1947 in Corinth, MS. Eula was the daughter of Homer and Leota (Dabbs) DePriest, and was born on Buck Fork of Marsh Creek and has five brothers; Bates, Roy, John, Paul and Frank; five sisters: Ruth, Alta, Dorothy, Betty and Loudean.

Arthur Glen and Eula Mae DePriest Webster

Glen moved to Perry County Jan. 4, 1935 with his parents, Arthur Hollis and Connie Mae (Morris) Webster, and brother, Charles Edward. Glen was born Aug. 24, 1929 in Gibson County, TN and Charles was born Feb. 7, 1933. Charles married Johnnie Mae Bromley on April 18, 1950, and they have two children: Randall Edward, Nov. 19, 1953 and Twila Mae, Oct. 11, 1959.

Connie Mae was born in Gibson County, TN, April 22, 1911. Arthur Hollis was born on Little Beech Creek in Wayne County, TN, Feb. 12, 1911. He moved to Gibson County with his parents, Johnie LeRoy and Lillie Mae (Steele) Webster in wagons. Arthur Hollis and Connie Mae married Aug. 4, 1928, in Trenton, TN and went to Reel Foot Lake with his brother, Claude and wife, Matha, on their wedding day.

Glen and Eula attended public schools in Perry County, where Glen graduated from high school in 1947 and Eula completed the 10th grade. They had three children, Michael Glenn, born June 26, 1949 in Hohenwald, TN (Boyce's Clinic); died July 19, 1949 in Dyersburg, TN, and was buried in the Flatwoods Cemetery. Glenda Paulette was born Oct. 19, 1950 in Dyersburg, TN, married Jimmy Trent in Dec. 1968 at Oakhaven UMC, in Shelby County; they had one son, Michael Anthony, born July 10, 1970. Paulette died Oct. 26, 1990 and as buried in the Flatwoods Cemetery.

Steven Anthony was born March 11, 1955 in Dyersburg, TN; graduated from Oakhaven School, Memphis and served in the U.S. Air Force four years. He married Patti Jean Christian March 26, 1991 at Oakhaven UMC by Rev. Roseberry. They have one daughter, Samantha Jean, born Dec. 21, 1993 at Baptist East Hospital in Memphis, TN.

Glen's youngest brother, Jerry Wayne, was born on Cedar Creek Sept. 6, 1945 and the whole family moved to Flatwoods Sept. 22, 1947. Jerry married Dexter Faye Franks at Flatwoods UMC March 11, 1966, by Rev. Troy Bunch. They have two daughters, Christy Remea, Nov. 11, 1969, and LuCindy Robin, Nov. 1, 1973.

Eula Mae Webster died Dec. 27, 1993 and is buried in the Flatwoods Cemetery. Glen lives in Flatwoods most of the time.

JOHNNIE LEEROY WEBSTER, was born March 1, 1877, married Lillie Mae Steele, born Feb. 16, 1880, wed Aug. 1896. They had four sons: Willie Homer, born Dec. 11, 1898; Claude Leegrant, born Nov. 7, 1905; Arthur Hollis, born Feb. 12, 1911; and a son, born Aug. 2, 1897, but died Aug. 3 or 4. One daughter, Fannie Estalee, born June 14, 1901. Johnnie and Lillie Mae were born in Wayne County, TN. He was the son of John Clayborn (Bud) Webster and Amanda (Mandy) Pevahouse Webster. Lillie Mae was the daughter of Joshua Alexander Steele, born March 15, 1834; died Dec. 9, 1902; and Lucinda Emaline Malissa (Grimes) Steele, born Sept. 11, 1849; died Oct. 7, 1896. They were married Aug. 31, 1874.

Johnnie Lee Roy Webster and Lillie M. Steele Webster

Johnnie and Lillie Mae lived on Little Beech Creek in Wayne County, TN and were farmers.

Willie Homer married Winnie Davis Harder Feb. 10, 1918, in Wayne County, TN. They had three daughters and one son: Dorothy Louise, born Jan. 22, 1919; Nettie Viola, born Jan. 13, 1921; Mary Lillie, born March 13, 1927, died July 17, 1979; and Franklin Homer Lee, born April 1, 1937, died June 20, 1937.

Fannie Estalee married John Wesley Graham Feb. 9, 1919. They had two sons and two daughters: Roy Mason, born July 9, 1920; Robert Max, born Aug. 26, 1936, died Oct. 13, 1982; Neva Merle, born Sept. 14, 1928; Reba Nell, born March 21, 1932.

Claude Leegrant married Lillie Matha Dismuke Dec. 21, 1924. They had five sons and four daughters. Claude Leegrant Jr., born Sept. 1, 1927; Jack Bruce, born Oct. 19, 1936; Billie Rogers, born June 9, 1940, died Sept. 28, 1940; Larry Grant, born Feb. 12, 1948; Raymon, born Dec. 26, 1952; Clara Fay, born Sept. 24, 1931; Lottie Mae, born Feb. 2, 1942; Alice Marie, born Nov. 11, 1945; Peggy Ann, born Jan. 23, 1951.

Arthur Hollis married Connie Mae Morris Aug. 4, 1928. They had three sons: Arthur Glen, born Aug. 24, 1929; Charles Edward, born Feb. 7, 1933; and Jerry Wayne, born Sept. 6, 1945. Johnnie and Lillie Mae moved from Wayne County to Gibson County, then back to middle Tennessee, to Perry County where they settled in the Cedar Creek Community. This move was made in covered wagons and their cattle were driven both ways. Most of their children eventually followed them back to Perry County to live. Johnnie and Lillie Mae are buried in the Culp Cemetery on Beech Creek.

JERRY WAYNE WEBSTER, born Sept. 6, 1945, son of Arthur Hollis and Connie Mae Morris Webster, married Dexter Faye Franks, born Aug. 30, 1945; daughter of Jimmie and Lessie Irene Holt Franks. They were married in Perry County, TN at Chappell Memorial UMC; Flatwoods Community, by Rev. Troy Bunch on March 11, 1966.

Jerry and Dexter have two daughters, Christy Remea, born Nov. 11, 1969, and LuCindy Robin, born Nov. 1, 1973. Christy married Randell Steven Nichols from Columbia, TN, May 26, 1990. They have one daughter, Holly Catherine, born Nov. 14, 1991.

Jerry Webster Family

Jerry has two brothers, Arthur Glen, born Aug. 24, 1929 and Charles Edward, born Feb. 7, 1933. Jerry was born while his parents lived in the Cedar Creek community in Perry County. In 1947, the family moved to the Flatwoods community, where Jerry, Dexter and LuCindy still reside. His father, Arthur Hollis, born Feb. 12, 1911, in Northern Wayne County, TN; in the Little Beech Creek community. Jerry's mother, Connie Mae Morris Webster, born April 22, 1911, in Gibson County, TN, in the Neboville community.

Dexter has one sister, Shirley Mae Franks Kelley, born May 27, 1940, Selmer, TN; three brothers, E.J., born Feb. 19, 1935, Newark, OH; Willard Gene, born Sept. 21, 1937; and William Earl, born June 3, 1942, Flatwoods, TN. Her father, Jimmie, was born Dec. 12, 1912, Wayne County, TN; parents were Ernis and Bessie Middleton Franks. Dexter's mother was born on Beech Creek, in Wayne County, TN on Dec. 30, 1918. Parents were Jimmie and Minnie Turnbow Holt.

JOHN WEEMS, and his wife, Nancy Wilkins bought their first piece of land in Perry County in 1821. They moved here from Dickson County, TN. Their family eventually settled on the land that is presently Mouse Tail Landing State Park.

Nancy Wilkins was born in Virginia on May 16, 1781. John was born in South Carolina on Dec. 12, 1778. Their oldest children were born in Georgia as early as 1807. They were in Dickson County, TN by 1814.

John served as a private in the TN State Militia during the Creek Indian Wars in Capt. Cuthbert Hudson's Co. He served from Sept. 28, 1814 to March 28, 1815. This qualified him as a veteran of the War of 1812.

John and Nancy probably lived in Franklin County, GA after their marriage where their children were born. Richard was born ca 1807, daughter Nancy ca 1810 and it is believed, a son, John R. was born in 1811. The ones born in Dickson County were Walton, born in 1814, Wilkins in 1816, James T. in 1818, Clara ca 1820 and Augustus in 1821. Betsy was born ca 1828 in Perry County.

The Cumberland Presbyterian Church was formed in Dickson County in 1810 and the family probably became members when they lived there. Several of the sons were Masons when they became adults.

John apparently farmed for a living because he bought several pieces of property in Perry County. He served as a Justice of the Peace for several years.

This Weems family almost always spelled their name Wims until around the 1850s when they began to use the spelling Weems, except for the descendants of Wilkins Wims who all seem to have kept the original spelling.

John died on June 5, 1861 and Nancy on April 7, 1867. They are buried in the Weems Cemetery near the State Park.

Richard married Nancy Ann Tatom and eventually moved to Arkansas. He may have died in Denton, TX.

John R. does not show up on most peoples information of this family, but he seems to fit in too well to ignore. He and James T. moved into Texas in the early 1850s and their families' lives always seemed to be intertwined. Some of their children married each other. John married Mary Ann Oliver and James T. married Elizabeth (Betty) Bunch. John is buried in Williamson County, TX as the other three are buried in San Saba County, TX.

Walton married Mary Jane Bulley and is buried in the Weems Cemetery in Perry County.

Wilkins was in Texas by 1846. He married Elizabeth Chambers there. After her death, he married her sister, Mary. He is buried in Northeast Texas.

Augustus married Susan Tatum and they are buried next to John and Nancy in the Weems Cemetery.

Nancy married a Mr. Ledbetter. Clara married a Mr. Taber and Betsy married a Wm. Smith.

WESTBROOK, The family Coat of Arms was issued prior to 1700. It is Red and Gold. It has a shield with a leopard's face and an embowed leg clad in armour.

Front row left to right: Earl B. and Aline Hinson Westbrooks. Back row left to right: Children: Deborah Kay, Kerry Dwane and Lisa Ann.

The family was a very powerful wine merchant family based in London. They were accepted at court by the royal families, because of the very fine wines they imported.

Harriet Westbrook married Percy Shelly (the romantic English Poet). Her heart was broken when she found out that he was living with Mary Shelly (who wrote the original Frankenstein). So Harriet committed suicide by jumping off the London Bridge and drowning herself. At this time, the family had a falling out and parted company. The ones who left, went to Ireland.

The Westbrook family lived outside of London in a country house that had several hundred rooms. The house is now a museum of Decorative Arts. In the families collection is a doll house that is (second only to the Tate Baby House) so detailed it has sterling silver flatware in the dining room for 24 place settings.

A Col. Thomas Westbrook founded Westbrook, Maine. There is also a Westbrook, CT.

Sometime later, the family moved to North Carolina. They were supposed to have had a very large plantation in Alabama sometime during the 1920s. One of our family members married Mr. Wynne at Castallian Springs, TN. They lived in Wynnewood until their deaths around 1973. Wynnewood is now a state-owned museum. Portraits of these relatives hang in one of the bedrooms today.

Turner Westbrooks, born Southampton County, VA, married Temperance Dunn, born about 1800 in Georgia, about 1822. Their children: Thomas Newton (April 28, 1823) married Anni Ary Ham on Sept. 13, 1843; Huldah born (1824) married William Hill Sept. 27, 1849; Mary E. (1825) married Calvin Wing Oct. 12, 1844; (all the above married in Davidson County, TN) Benjamin L. (1827) married Mary E. Tucker Sept. 27, 1849; Samuel C. (Dec. 24, 1829) married 1) Louisa Tucker (1850) 2) Eliza Inman (Oct. 23, 1848-Feb. 5, 1899); Georgie Hardiman (March 3, 1876-1960), father of Grand Ole Opry star, Cousin Wilbur Wesbrooks (1939-1948), married 1) Rebecca Candra Johnson Nov. 1, 1896, 2) Maggie Finley; James Lewis (1879) married Della Johnson Dec. 30, 1896; Loradie (1883-1940) married John E. Warren Jan. 25, 1903; Barney B. (1886-1945) married Leora Understand Qualls (1889-1955) on Oct. 21, 1906; Elzada (1889) married Denis Barber on June 16, 1906.

Barney was a huge man, six feet tall and weighed 350 pounds. He was a farmer and merchant, running "Qualls and Wesbrooks" grocery and general store with his father-in-law, Joe B. Qualls. Barney's children: Homer B., Henry T., "Cootie," Chesley Lee.

Homer B. (April 29, 1908-Aug. 28, 1955) married Docie Armada Kelly (April 16, 1905-Feb. 16, 1950) on March 6, 1927. Their children were Earl B. and Alonzo Burnice. Earl B. was born Dec. 18, 1927 in Perry County, TN. He married Aline Hinson on March 24, 1950. He served Occupational Forces, 6th Div. in Korea 1946-47. His children: Deborah Kay, Kerry Dwane and Lisa Ann.

Deborah (June 10, 1951) married Jimmy Hardin March 19, 1994, adopted Deborah's son Matthew Lynn, March 21, 1994. Matthew was born March 6, 1989.

Kerry (Aug. 31, 1954) married Deborah Kay "Marshall" Denton on March 17, 1976. Children: 1) Dianna Machelle "Denton" (July 10, 1974) Maury County, TN adopted by Kerry; married Bryan Keller Aug. 22, 1993, one child, Kelsey Jade, born March 29, 1994 in Davidson County, TN. 2) Kathryn Aline was born Feb. 13 1978 in Davidson County, TN. 3) Kara Dalayne was born Dec. 26, 1979 in Davidson County.

Lisa Ann (Dec. 23, 1963) married James Thomas "Tommy" Stayrook on Dec. 4, 1983. They have one child, Melissa Dawn, born June 13, 1993 in Davidson County, TN.

Alonzo Burnice Westbrooks (June 16, 1940) married Linda Marilyn Richardson on June 29, 1967.

THOMAS NEWTON WESTBROOK,

arrived in Davidson County about 1820 to join his brother, Samuel H., who had preceded him and had served in the West Tennessee Mounted Militia in the War of 1812. They were sons of Samuel Westbrook Jr., a lieutenant in the Southampton Co., Virginia, militia during the Revolutionary War. Samuel Jr. married to Hannah Turner, was five generations removed from James Westbrooks, the headright in Virginia in 1650.

Thomas Newton and Anni Ary Ham Westbrook

Samuel H. Westbrook married Lidia West in 1814, and Turner married Temperance Dunn in 1822, both in Davidson County. They migrated to Sangamon County, IL, in 1823 in the company of the Thomas Ridley Westbrook family, whose exact relationship to Samuel and Turner has not been established.

Apparently Turner died in Illinois and Temperance returned to Davidson County where she appears in the 1840 census with nine children, presumable all born in Illinois. They were: Thomas Newton (1823-1897) married Anni Ary Ham (1825-1900) in Davidson County; Huldah (1824-?) married William Hill; Mary E. (1825-?) married Calvin Wing; Benjamin L. (1827-1870) married Mary Emmaline Tucker (1821-1901). (She was the widow of William Halbrook); Samuel C. (1829-?) married first Louisa Tucker (1831-1870) and married second Eliza A. Inman; Sarah Jane (1831-1907) married William Mack Tucker (1825/26 - ca 1859) (he had been married previously); Louisa (1834-?); and possible Joseph C. (1832-?) married first Clarissa ?, and second Saphronia C. Tanner (1848/49-?); and William (1836-?) married Ruth ?. (The placement of Joseph and William in this family is based on circumstantial evidence and is not documented.)

Thomas, Benjamin, Samuel, Sarah J. and Louisa moved to Perry County with their mother prior to 1849, the year of Benjamin's marriage to Mary E. Tucker. The Westbrook and Tucker families were very close. The four Tuckers mentioned above were children of Joseph and Sarah M. Tucker, and another daughter, Nancy Ann, married James A. Westbrook, second son of Thomas N. and Anni A. Westbrook. (Dickson Tucker, a brother, is said to have observed, "If it weren't for the Westbrook men, half the Tucker women would be old maids!") Joseph Tucker, the father, was the son of John P. Tucker, Halifax County, VA, whose Revolutionary War service included the battle of Yorktown. John P. died in Hickman County.

Thomas N. and Anni A. Westbrook's children were: Samuel H. (1844-1926) married first Mary E. Rushing (?-1873) and second Frances I. McMurry (?-1926); James A. (1847-1926) married first Nancy Ann Tucker (ca 1845-1877) and second Virginia America Bulla (1863-1935); Hulda Frances (1848-1910) married Benjamin Franklin Campbell (1851-1931) (he married first Nancy J. Qualls); John Lewis Westbrook (1852-1912) married Lucinda Jennie Childress (1853-1921); William Thomas (1856-1915) married Frances F. Grace; Henry W. (1859-ca 1869); Sally Ann (1863-1944) married W. Lemuel Tate (1869-1901); Charles Winfred (1866-1945) married first Minnie Viola Brinn (1866-1942) and second Nanye Shepherd (1866-1942); and Doss (Dorse) Addison (1871-1960) married first Harriett Inman (?-1894) and second Lelia Ada Perry (1876-1959).

Thomas N. and Anni Ary (sometimes "Annira") Westbrook, John L. and Lucinda J. Westbrook, W. Lemuel and Sally W. Tate, and Charles W., Minnie B. and Nanye S. Westbrook all are buried in Bethel Cemetery in Linden, as are numerous other later descendants of Thomas N. and Anni A. Ham Westbrook. Submitted by Jack K. Westbrook, great, great grandson).

WALTER LAFAYETTE WESTBROOK SR.,

(1871-1938) married Cora Ezra Hufstedler (1869-1959) in Perry County March 1, 1894. Cora was the only child of John Kendrick Hufstedler (1848-1919) and his first wife, Mahuldah Ann Whitwell (1851-1871). John was the oldest child of Pinkney Hufstedler (1814-1895) and Louisa Jane Randle (1831-1923) and Mahuldah was the only child of Thomas B. Whitwell (1816-1886) and Harriett Shepard (1817-1876), his first wife.

Back row left to right: Perry, Lois, Bertha and Carl. Front row: Walter Jr., Walter Sr., Ralph, Pinkney and Cora Hufstedler Westbrook.

Walter Westbrook was the first child of John Lewis Westbrook (1852-1912), fourth child of Thomas Newton and Anni Ary Ham Westbrook. John was born in Perry County, where he married Lucinda Jennie Childress (1853-1931) Dec. 10, 1870. Her parents were William A. Childress (1826-1891) and Adeline Manerva Randle (1830-1911).

John Lewis and Jennie Childress Westbrook's other children were: Docia Ann (1875-1918) married Commodore J. Doyle (1871-1953); Willie Newton (1877-1933) married Sally Frances Horner Turnbow (1878-1950); Arthur Harvey (1879-1956) married first Annie Wright and second Creola Stevens (born 1908); James Samuel (1882-1965) married Cora Alma Rawdon (1886-1960); Charley Clyde (1888-

1974) married Myrtle Pope (1890-1973); and Troy Frank (1899-1967) married Pearl M. Conder (1900-?).

Descendants of Walter L. and Cora H. Westbrook are: Bertha Gertrude (1895-1978); Grady Patterson (1897-1898); Carl Leslie (1899-1975) married Eulah Belle King; Perry Ernest (1902-1979) married Mary Vera Finney (born 1912); Lois Earline (born 1904) married James Paul Bell (1903-1943); Ralph Edward (1906-1939) married Sammie Bates (born 1914); Walter L. Jr. (1909-1981) married Mary Louise Daniel (1912-1990); John Pinkney (1912-1989) married first Charlotte Auralie Glavin (1918-1962), second Josephine Irma Adreozzi Volante (1911-1975), divorced, and third Edith May Davis Dorsa (born 1919).

Carl L. and Eulah King Westbrook were the parents of: (1) Sarah Dene (born 1920) married John George Lyon Jr. (1918-1971), divorced, parents of Janet Westbrook (born 1945) married first James Norton Clemeau (1940-1984) and second J. L. Driver (born 1941) (Janet adopted Angela Joy Linton in 1986); Sarah Ann (born 1949); John George III (born 1953) married Judith Wortham (born 1955) and they have James Robert (born 1989); and Jean Elizabeth (born 1956) married William Dale Markie (born 1954); (2) Robbye Lee (born 1922) married first Charles H. Jones Jr. (born 1915), divorced, and second James Arnold Welch (1929-1993), divorced; and (3) Jack King (born 1923) married Willie Mae Matthews (born 1923) whose children, both adopted, are Haven Lee (born 1959) married Michael Len Jenkins (born 1952) and Matthew King (born 1961) married Patricia Harju (born ca 1961), divorced; and (4) James Edwin (born & d. 1928).

Perry E. and Vera F. Westbrook had two daughters: (1) Cora Viera (born 1934) married John Eugene Burney Jr. (born 1930) and they had Mary Ann (born 1963) married Hiram Chism Allen IV (born 1963) and John Eugene III (born 1966) married Laura Elizabeth Thorn (born 1965); and (2) Perry Ann (born 1943) married Gerald M. Cox (born 1943). Their children are David Arthur (born 1967) married Juanita Evonne Nelson (born 1966) and Philip Wayne (born 1971).

Mary Paul (born 1929) is the only child of James P. and Lois W. Bell.

Walter L. Jr. and Louise Daniel Westbrook had two sons: (1) Larry LaFay (born 1932) married Ruth Janiel Smith (born 1934) and their children are Larry Neil (born 1955) married Candy Carolyn Yancey (born ca 1956); Jerry Randall (born 1959); and Stephen Perry (born 1962). (2) Jerry Daniel (born 1936) married Nancy Anne Jones (born 1940). Their children are Wendy Louise (born 1962) married first Michael W. Keaton (born 1957), divorced, second Frederick A. Friton (born 1964), divorced, and third Timothy Kinkead (born 1959); Jill Ann (born 1965) married Brian Neil Fall (born ca 1964), divorced; and Nancy Danielle (born 1971).

John Pinkney and Auralin Glavin Westbrook had the following children: (1) Karen Diane (born 1940) married first Fred Walter Schuyler (born 1939), divorced, and second Ernie Brown; (2) Eric Adair (1944-1980) married first Katherine Juanita Wion, divorced, and second Sue Davia Berson (born 1944); (3) Ian Vincent (born 1949) married first Pamela Lee Richman (born 1950), divorced, second Mary Ruth Saltsman (born 1953), divorced, and third Kim Powell; and (4) Kevin Charles (born 1950) married first Diana Lynn Whitten, divorced, and second Jane Christine Davis. *Submitted by Sarah Dene Westbrook Lyon, granddaughter.*

GEORGE DIBBRELL WHITWELL,

was born on Hurricane Creek to Thomas and Melissa. He came into this world on Dec. 25, 1868, with good Democrat blood flowing in his veins and a strong fighting nature that kept him active for 85 years. He died Oct. 10, 1953.

He met the daughter of Franklin Warren and decided to court her, a courtship to which her family highly objected. But, true love prevailed and he married Agnes Warren Feb. 24, 1894. Henry Agnes Warren (Oct. 19, 1879-Sept. 11, 1953).

They settled on a 400 acre farm on Marsh Creek, Perry County, TN. Their home was built in 1873 by the previous owner, Wiley Roberts. (Dibbler) fathered seven children, births and marriages as follows: Rev. Dr. Dewey Whitwell (July 26, 1898-Oct. 12, 1978) married Nellie Lee Wall on Oct. 11, 1921. Had one daughter, Wanda Bradford. Walton Thomas (Sept. 26, 1900-March 11, 1955) married Elise Anderson on Dec. 17, 1927, one daughter, Peggy Mabry. They divorced, he later married Aline Petway. Gladys Adalee (Sept. 24, 1902-1981) married John Ramey Oct. 10, 1925, three children: Mildred Hudson, Nelson and Billy Whit. Byron Mable (Jan. 26, 1905-May 4, 1948) married Bynum Cotham Dec. 25, 1925, four children: Margaret Landers, Dean Anderson, Doris Parnell and James. Kent Franklin (Oct. 11, 1907-Feb. 28, 1964) married Evelyn Duncan Dec. 25, 1926, nine children listed separately under Kent Whitwell. William Carroll (June 1, 1911-Nov. 1, 1913. Eva Melissa (born March 25, 1915) married John C. Westbrooks March 10, 1935, div., later married Tom Petty, one son: Jack Norman Westbrooks.

JOHN RANDEL WHITWELL,

born Feb. 17, 1856, Perry County, son of Elijah Houston Whitwell and Jincy Angeline Randel, died Oct. 3, 1938, MS. He married July 19, 1876, Perry County, Permelia Adeline Campbell, born Dec. 20, 1858, Hickman County, died May 28, 1925, MS. She was daughter of Edward Campbell and Margaret Elizabeth Nance. Their children, all born in Perry County. 1) Edward Elijah Whitwell (Jan. 14, 1882-Feb. 21, 1940, MS) 2) Mattie Ether Whitwell (Dec. 17, 1883-Feb. 21, 1951, TX) 3) Oscar Whitwell, born 1885, died young, Perry County. 4) Noah Leonard Whitwell (Sept. 5, 1888-March 9, 1952, TX) 5) Minnie Mae Whitwell (Aug. 16, 1891-Sept. 3, 1953, TX) 6) Bertha L. Whitwell (March 17, 1897-Dec. 19, 1985, CA) 7) Elbert Moncie Whitwell, born April 1, 1899, was living in Oklahoma. *Submitted by Merle Stevens.*

KENT FRANKLIN WHITWELL,

(Oct. 11, 1907-Feb. 28, 1964) lived in Perry County his lifetime. The son of George and Agnes, he met and married Mattie Evelyn Duncan Dec. 25, 1926. Evelyn (Sept. 26, 1912-June 30, 1965) was the daughter of William Ollie Duncan (Jan. 10, 1882-Feb. 11, 1953) and Mercy Lora Ramey, born ?, d. age 25, both of Lyon County, KY.

After Ollie's wife died he brought two young daughters to live in Perry County, Cedar Creek. His daughter Evelyn married Kent Whitwell and Beatrice married Grady A. Ward, descendant of Martha Whitwell Ward.

Kent and Evelyn lived on a 260 acre farm, located on Marsh Creek and reared their children there. Kent was a mischievous person who loved his neighbors so much he would stop his work to visit, laugh and joke with them. Evelyn, also a good neighbor and Christian soldier, they parented nine children: Arden Earl (Nov. 28, 1927-Dec. 27, 1954) married Shirley Woods Ward Sept. 10, 1953, one son, Gregory Neil (born Dec. 17, 1954). Helen Vivian (born Nov. 26, 1929) married W. R. Moore Jr. Feb. 4, 1948, three children, Marie Howard, Jane McDaniel and Joe. Freida June (born June 1, 1935) married John Howard Lewis Sept. 17, 1954, three children, Jill Duke, Rose Ann Moore and Johnny Whit. Emily Fay (born Feb. 17, 1938) married Alton Marlin 1956, J. D. Powers 1960, John Washam 1966 and Cleon Wooley 1969, has one adopted daughter, Carla Duck. Rita Gail (born March 6, 1942) married Paul Pearcy Jan. 8, 1960, four children, Kenneth, Randell, Vicki Rainey and Van. Linda May (June 29, 1945-July 12, 1989) married Larry Dixon Dec. 2, 1962, div. Thomas Loggins July 29, 1967. Andy Kent (born Oct. 17, 1947) married Carolyn Cruse, div., two children, Kent Mitchell and Misty Gaye.

WHITWELL, Brothers Thomas and Robert Whitwell immigrated to Virginia from England, date not known. Thomas came from Virginia to Kentucky on his horse through the Cumberland Gap over 200 years ago. He settled in Barron County, KY. Robert came later to Kentucky and moved to Lafayette County, MS.

Thomas (May 10, 1774-Nov. 9, 1846) married Mary Sheperd on May 5, 1798. Mary died on July 26, 1838. They bore 11 children, one being Baptist Reverend Pleasant Whitwell (July 29, 1803-Dec. 20, 1875). He married Margaret Anderson (1801-July 1877). Both were natives of Barron County, KY. They and their parents were early immigrants to Tennessee, coming to Hickman County in 1823. They were married in Hickman County and came to Perry County in 1837, where he remained as a farmer.

He entered the Ministry of Primitive Baptist Church and in his day was one of the strongest believers and exhorters of that faith in this county. He was a Democrat in political belief and served as first clerk of Perry County Court for eight years.

A son of his, Thomas Bromfield (Aug. 23, 1826-Dec. 25, 1901) married Nov. 25, 1847 to Melissa C. Ward (Nov. 2, 1828-Oct. 6, 1890. They had a family of ten children.

Thomas fought with the Confederacy in the War Between the States, under the command of General George Dibbrell. He returned home after four years to help feed his family. In 1870, he was elected judge of Perry County for three terms of eight years each. In 1879, he bought 1,200 acres of land on Hurricane Creek.

His children are as follows: Mary Elizabeth (Nov. 18, 1848-July 3, 1887) married George

Sheffield on Feb. 12, 1872; William Carroll (Dec. 13, 1850- Dec. 18, 1918) married Ella Watson, div. Nov. 14, 1876; Martha Jane (March 5, 1853-Aug. 4, 1902) married Chesley Sutton on Oct. 29, 1872; Thomas Palmer (May 24, 1855-Oct. 7, 1892) married Mary C. Starbuck on Dec. 30, 1874, div. Later married Virginia Pace on Oct. 9, 1876; Margaret Josephine (Feb. 8, 1858-?) married Edward Murphy on May 27, 1877 and Callie Graves on Oct. 23, 1887; Andrew Jackson (Aug. 3, 1860-June 12, 1897) married Permalie Kirk on Dec. 22, 1885; Sara Alice (Jan. 19, 1863-late 1940s) married Newton Dotson; Victoria Angeline (Feb. 28, 1866-Jan. 8 1936) married William Kirk; George Dibbrell (Dec. 25, 1868-Oct. 10, 1953) married Agnes Warren; Pleasant Lee (March 4, 1873-Oct. 15, 1914) married Maggie Voss. *Submitted by Freida Whitwell Lewis.*

WILLIAM & ABIGAIL ALLEN WIGGS,

William M. Wiggs, born NC Aug. 14, 1806, died Jan. 22, 1859, probably in Perry County. He had lived a great deal of his life in Williamson County, being counted there in the census of 1830, 1840 and 1850. He is likely the son of John Wiggs and Obedience "Biddy" Wiggs whose marriage apparently dissolved just before 1830. Biddy Wiggs is found a close neighbor to her children the remainder of her life. John Wiggs is thought to be the one who married Catherine Hood, Lawrence County, 1836. John is possibly a son of Henry Wiggs, born in Scotland, who settled in Wayne County, NC. Henry's will indicates two unnamed sons.

Martha Jane Wiggs Shepard - 1842 to 1922

Sept. 10, 1824, Williamson County, William Wiggs married Abigail "Abbey" Allen, born NC, Feb. 28, 1801; the daughter of George Allen and Abigail Cooper Johnston Allen.

George Allen was the son of Capt. Charles Allen (Revolutionary War Patriot) and Nancy Ann Vincent of Warren County, NC. This Allen line can be traced to the 1600s in Old Rappahannock County, VA.

William and Abigail farmed and moved into Perry County between 1850 and 1860. Abigail Allen Wiggs is found in the 1860 census as a widow with five of her eight children living at home. She died Dec. 12, 1868.

Their known children are:

Green Wiggs (June 25, 1829-Feb. 23, 1894) married Elizabeth Jane Wade Johnson about 1863. She is the subject of an obituary, *Perry County News* April 18, 1913. There was apparently an earlier marriage for Green Wiggs in the 1850s. He is buried at Chestnut Grove as is Jane Wade Wiggs.

Rebecca Abigail Wiggs, born about 1831, married June 26, 1850 to Braxton J. Wall, Williamson County.

William James Wiggs, born about 1833, married a Nancy and then a Sarah, probably sisters. They may have been Campbells. Sarah may have been Green Wiggs' first wife. William James Wiggs was a Confederate Soldier in Company H, 10th Tennessee Cavalry.

William James Wiggs and wife, Nancy, were the parents of William S. Wiggs, Green Wiggs II, Thomas Henry Wiggs & Abigail Wiggs. The child of his second marriage to Sarah J. (Campbell?) Wiggs was Sarah R. Wiggs.

William S. Wiggs married Nancy Carolyn Goodwin; their children were James William Wiggs, Andrew Houston Wiggs and Simeon Archibald Wiggs.

James William Wiggs married Lou Ethel Hinson; their children were: Martha May Wiggs, married Newt Arnold; Iva Jane Wiggs, married William Lewis; Ora Bell Wiggs, married Robert Lane Murray; and Andy Earl Wiggs, married Dorothy Mae Mathis.

Mary Ann Wiggs, born about 1836; first married an Adams, then John Wilburn of Perry County, a medical doctor. Several of the Shepard and Wiggs family are believed to be buried in the Old Wilburn Cemetery in the field just west of the present George Cotton home, Hwy 13 N.

Benjamin Rufus Wiggs (July 12, 1837-May 11, 1894, Commerce, Hunt Co., TX); interred Mt. Zion Cemetery. He first married Martha A. Lain, Aug. 23, 1860, Perry County; and second Martha Ann Clayton, May 2, 1872, Perry County. Much is known of this family.

Nancy Henry Wiggs (Sept. 9, 1839-Jan. 22, 1928, Sanger, TX) Jan. 10, 1861 she married Samuel Russell Lain, Perry County. This family is also well documented.

Martha Jane Wiggs (April 6, 1842-May 4, 1922, Lobelville) About 1860 she married James William Shepard, son of Robert and Susan Guill Shepard. (See James William Shepard Family) They had six children, Jimmie M., Mary Elizabeth, William A., John Robert, Odella and Rufus Thomas.

Martha Jane Wiggs Shepard's photo accompanies this story. This great lady was left a widow at age 32 with five children. The sixth child, Rufus, was born eight months after the death of his father in 1874. For the remainder of her life, Martha Wiggs Shepard lived with her children and helped them raise their children. She was especially helpful to Rufus after the death of Annie Laura Deason Shepard, and was influential in the lives of their five children. Grandchildren, Charlie Shepard and Wilma Shepard Witherspoon concurred that, "if ever there was a saint on earth, it was Grandma Shepard." Penniless and dependent, she was known as a diplomat with a great sense of when to speak and when not to speak. She died in 1922 in Lobelville while living with her daughter, Mary Elizabeth Shepard Cude, on Cane Creek.

George J. Wiggs, born about 1846. *Submitted by Gail Shepard Tomlinson.*

ALEXANDER F. WILEY,

(born 1790), son of Robert and Sarah Wiley of South Carolina, moved to Middle Tennessee in the early 1800s along with his six brothers and three sisters. He served in the War of 1812, married Sally Farris in 1822 (Maury County), died 1859, and buried in the Harder Cemetery, Perry County. Alexander and Sally were the parents of: Robert (born 1825), Malinda (1827), Sarah (1830), Mary Louann (1832), Caleb (1835), Martha (1836), John (1843) and William Robert (Bill) Wiley (born 1846, Perry County, died 1877).

James Alexander Wiley and Alice Permelia Bunch Wiley with their son James Ross Wiley and their granddaughter Anna Laura McClain.

William Robert Wiley married Mary Charlotte (Lottie) Graves (born 1845, Decatur County, died 1928). Their children were: Caleb; Garrett L. (Babe) (born 1875) 1894 married Bernice Grooms; Robert; James (Jim) Alexander, born 1871 Perry County, died 1940 Gibson County.

James Alexander Wiley, a Perry County farmer, and Alice Permelia Bunch (born 1873 Perry County, died 1955 Gibson County) were married 1893 in Perry County. Their children, all born in Perry County, were: Thomas Kay (Tom) (1894-1968, Weakley Co.); Lillie Mable (1897-1974, Gibson Co.); and James Ross Wiley (1904-1992, Gibson Co.)

Thomas Kay Wiley married first to Johnnie McClain. Their children, all born in Gibson County, were: Cecil May, Alice Virginia, Russel Guy, Alfred Allen and Lowell Ludlow. Tom married his second wife, Virgie Elizabeth Flowers in 1929. Their children were: Dessie Remel, Geneva, Eva, Dollie Mae, Sue Alice, Gerald Ray, Lillie Grace, Francis Kay, Louise, Carol Lee, Linda Darnell and Martha Ann.

Lillie Mable Wiley married James Henry McClain. Their children, all born in Gibson County, were: Anna Laura, James Coy and David Paul.

James Ross Wiley and Rausy Somers (1905, Dyer Co.-1982, Gibson Co.) were married 1923 in Gibson County. Their children, all born in Gibson County, were: James Ewin (1924-1984, Gibson Co.); Beulah Mae (born 1926); Harold Edward (1927); William Robert (1930); Martha Jean (1935) and Shirley Ann Wiley (1937).

James Ewin Wiley married Albeta Webb in 1942. Their children were Wanda (born 1942); Ronnie (1945-1989, Gibson Co.); and Roy (1949).

Beulah Mae Wiley married Harman (Bud) James in 1942. Their children were: John Wayne (1942); Harman Ross (1944); Lindell Dale (1951-1980, Obion Co.); and Tommy Gale (1957).

Harold (Bill) Edward Wiley married Barbara Lovell in 1948. Their children were: Andre (1949), Katana (1951), Gina (1954), Andrea (1961) and Yelena (1971).

William (Bob) Wiley married Betty Rumbly in 1949. Their children were: Charlotte (1950), Janice (1953) and Paula (1954).

Martha Jean Wiley married Ted Terry Tucker in 1953. Their children were: Theda Terry (1954), Mark Torin (1956) and Timothy Theil (1959).

Shirley Ann Wiley married George Edward Parish (born 1935) in 1955. They had one child, Jerry Lynn Parish (1957). *Submitted by Jerry Lynn Parish, Nashville, TN.*

CLEMENT AND JOMIMMA "JAN" BAUGUS WILKINS, According to Spence's History of Hickman County, TN, Clement and Clarissa (Decker) Wilkins moved from Franklin County, GA to Yellow Creek, Dickson County, around 1798, then to Hickman County. Their families secured land grants in Hickman, Perry and Humphreys Counties. One son, Richard, married Susan Epperson. Their children were Thomas, Clement, John, James, Nancy, Susan, Melenda and Lucinda.

Clement Wilkins and four children: (Inset) Clement Wilkins. Front: Martha, Susan Malinda. Back: "Tobe" and Sophia.

Clement, born 1824, married Jomimma "Jan" Baugus, born 1833, the daughter of Jeremiah and Nancy Baugus. Their children were Martha, Susan Malinda, John, Thomas, Margaret, Nancy C., Nina and Sophia. They were living in Hickman County in 1850. 1860 Perry County Census lists Jeremiah 61 years old from Georgia and Nancy 56 from South Carolina.

Susan Malinda Wilkins, born 1852, married William Jesse Blackwell, son of Jackson and Mary (Rice) Blackwell in 1872 Only, Hickman County. Their children were B. Varden, J. Memol, Donna S., Cuba O., Lloyd B. and Arles B. He and his family moved to the Texas Panhandle around 1888. Arles was three years old. Susan, died in Clarendon and William Jesse, died in Amarillo. They are both buried in Odd Fellow Cemetery, Clarendon, Donley County, TX.

According to Perry County records 1871-1877, the property of Jeremiah Baugus, deceased, was auctioned and his son, G.W. Baugus was the high bidder. He paid the other heirs in installments. Surviving heirs were G.W. Baugus, Elizabeth Loggins, (formerly Elizabeth Cuff), M.J. and Jefferson Baugus.

Elizabeth Loggins, deceased, left surviving her William and Thomas J. Loggins and Lewis Cuff.

M.J. Wilkins, deceased, left surviving her Martha E., Susan M., John R., Nancy C., Thomas J., M.J. (Gemima Jane) "Nina" and Sophia E. Wilkins. M.J. would be Jomimma "Jan."

Clement Wilkins was guardian of William Baugus, minor heir of Thomas Logan, deceased.

Clement Wilkins was also guardian of Martha E., Susan M., John R., Nancy C., Thomas J.J., Gemima Jane and Sophia E. Wilkins, heirs of Clement Wilkins and grandchildren of Jeremiah Baugus, deceased. Settlement, October 1874, shows Malinda Blackwell (she married in 1872).

Clement married Betsy Wilkins Sept. 3, 1872, and according to 1880 Census, they were living in Hickman County and Nina, 17, and Sophia E., 10, were living with them.

G.W. Wilkins married Emily ? (1860 Census) and H.J. Wilkins Jan. 16, 1893; Nancy C. married J.A. Warren Aug. 30, 1896; John R. married Sarah Murphey Jan. 14, 1875; Susan M. married William Jesse Blackwell 1872; Martha E. married John King Dec. 20, 1875; Nina (Gemima Jane) married Gilbert Maxwell Feb. 5, 1873. *Submitted by Donna Clyde Arms, granddaughter of William Jesse and Susan Malinda Wilkins Blackwell. Daughter of James Clyde and Arles B. Blackwell Wright.*

JENCY JANE WILLIAMS-WILLIAMSON, (1823-1901) Jency Jane Williams Graham said in the 1850 Cass County, TX census that she was born in 1823 Indiana while the 1860 Grayson County, TX census showed her born 1823 in Tennessee.

Jency Jane Williams Graham (1823 to 1901).

Jency Jane Williams/Williamson married about 1841 to Tillman Williamson "T.W." Graham, born 1817 in Nunnelly, Hickman County, TN to Charles Graham and possibly the daughter of Jesse Williamson/Williams of Hickman County. In July 1838, T.W. bought 77 acres from Smith Criddle and William B. Murphree. In April 1847, from Texas T.W. sold one-third undivided interest of 77 acres lying on the Davidison County line on the waters of the Big Harpeth River on the Dickson County line to Smith Criddle. T.W.'s lawyer was James Newton Bowman. The two-thirds of undivided interest of the 77 acres may have been part of an inheritance from T.W.'s mother to him and his two sisters.

One Joseph N. Williams/Williamson of Warren County, TN served from Sept. 20, 1814 until April 20, 1815 in the War of 1812 in Company C under Captain Asahel Raines Infantry, second Reg. Tenn Militia. T.W.'s grandfather, John Graham, had a sister named Nancy Rains of Randolph County, NC and Perry County, TN, wife of Anthony Rains, a Rev. War veteran.

One Parthenia Williams, born 1822 TN and head of the household, lived two doors from both Charles Graham and Robert Crawford Graham in the 1850 Cass County, TX census. Her two children were born in Texas: Albert, born 1844 and Sarah, born 1845. Parthenia may have been a sister-in-law to Jency Jane Williams Graham. T.W. and Jency Jane Graham's children were: Charles Granville, 1843 Perry County-1930 Carter County, OK, and married Mary Savage; James Perry, Nov. 1844 Cass County, TX - 1920 Stephens County, OK, and married Dorothy Elizabeth Ireland; John Rayburn, Dec. 15, 1845 - April 17, 1917 ?Stephens County, OK, and married Annie Keys; Rosa Abeen, March 4, 1846 - July 22, 1879 Cooke County, TX, and married Dewitt C. Simpson; Tillman Williamson "Tip," Aug. 9, 1849-Nov. 30, 1907 Stephens County, OK, and married Elizabeth West Wood; Robert D., Nov. 1850-after 1910 Grady County, OK, and married Victory Pickett then Mary Ellen (Cox) Pounds; James Holcombe, Dec. 22, 1852 - Feb. 3, 1909 Grady County, and married Sarah Thompson; Thomas Marion, Aug. 1854-May 9, 1939 Garvin County, OK, and married Sophia Lee (a Chickasaw) then Nannie Bell (Herndon) Bowles; Mary Charlotte Belle Zora "Belle," July 18, 1856 Whitesboro, Grayson County, TX-Aug. 25, 1929 Tarrant County, TX, and married Reuben Thompson; Sarah Emma Camilla, Feb. 15, 1858 and married Clayburn Edward Crouch; William Benjamin, Feb. 18, 1860-Oct. 15, 1945, and married Heneritta Lavilla Thompson.

ELMER LEWIS WILSDORF, was born in Saxony, Germany July 21, 1825. He came to the United States around 1850 and after a few stops settled in Perry County, TN in what is known until this day as the Wilsdorf Hollow on Tom's Creek a few miles south of Pineview. There he farmed, owned and operated a tannery. His great-great grandson, Benno Wilsdorf, owns part of the same farm today (1994). Elmer Lewis married Mary Ann Smith who lived on Lick Creek in 1852. She lived with her mother, Elizabeth, and stepfather, Charles Gotthardt. She was born in Virginia, Aug. 20, 1932. Lewis and Mary were the parents of nine children, four of which died in infancy, Matilda Anne, George William, Oscar and Edward. Five of their nine children lived to adulthood, Elizabeth, Mary, Laura, John and Robert Henry.

Mary Ann Smith Wilsdorf

During the Civil War, Elmer Lewis was hanged for his money which he had buried in two different places. His wife told them (night riders) where half of the money was buried to they cut him down before he died. The 1860 Census listed his personal property and real estate value at $7,500.00.

Elmer Lewis died Aug. 25, 1882 at the age

of 57 years. Mary Ann died Dec. 17, 1923 at age 91 years. They and their four children who died in infancy are buried in the Coble Cemetery on the South Prong of Tom's Creek.

Their children, grandchildren, great-grandchildren and their spouses:

Elizabeth Wilsdorf married William Patterson. They had six children: (1) Mary Annie Patterson married Clem Dyer. They had four children - Fred Dyer married Roxie Skelton, Ollie Dyer married Thomas Gilbert, Guy Dyer married Freda Hunt and Charley Dyer married Bessie Byrd; (2) Laura Patterson married Sam Bell. They had two children - Edna Bell married Bob Barham and Lorene Bell married Joe Starbuck; (3) Robert Patterson married Bradie Deere. They had no children; (4) Edward Patterson married Emma Strickland. They had two children - John Patterson married Linda Poore and Ralph Patterson never married; (5) John Patterson married Mamie Cotton. They had two children - Mabel Patterson married Glenn DePriest and Roberta Patterson married Hugh Nickell; (6) Daisy Patterson married William Bell. They had two children - Pauline Bell married John Horner and Roy Bell married Bessie Bell.

Mary Jane Wilsdorf married James O'Guin. They had five children: (1) Elmer O'Guin married Ruby. They had five children - Elmer O'Guin Jr., Hugh O'Guin, Theda O'Guin, Roberta O'Guin and Dean O'Guin; (2) Lula O'Guin married Patterson; (3) Gladys O'Guin; (4) Will O'Guin; (5) John O'Guin.

Laura Wilsdorf married John Pitts. They had eight children: William Pitts, John E. Pitts, Jesse Pitts, Henry Pitts, Robert Pitts, Thomas Pitts, Maude (Bobo) and Mae (Parden).

John Wilsdorf married Kate Augustia Hunt. They had three children: John Wilsdorf Jr., Charles Wilsdorf and Sue Augusta Wilsdorf (Robinson).

Henry Wilsdorf married Ethel Cotham. They had eight children: (1) Lewis Wilsdorf (he died young); (2) Fred Wilsdorf married Velera Baars. They had four children - Fred Wilsdorf Jr. married Dorothy Jo Hinson, Laverne Wilsdorf married Leslie Brewer, Lindy Wilsdorf married Mildred Lineberry and Doris Wilsdorf married Clyde Long; (3) Roy Wilsdorf married Amie Trull. They had two children - Dorothy Mae Wilsdorf married Herbert Lawrence and James Wilsdorf, divorced; (4) Lucille Wilsdorf married Jesse Trull. They had four children - Max Trull married Laura Olson, Miles Edward Trull married Willow Dean Brewer, George Hadley Trull married Jean Alexander and Charles Lee Trull married Gladys Tinnell; (5) Nell Wilsdorf married Walter Hopkins. They had one child, Marie Hopkins married Cecil Johnson; (6) Bessie Wilsdorf married Claude Dodson. They had one child, Dan Dodson married Lanelle Boehms; (7) Juanita Wilsdorf married Carlos Cude. They had no children; (8) Rudy Wilsdorf married Lorene Roberts. They had two children - Mark Wilsdorf married Lenjoy Moore and Dale Wilsdorf, not married. *Submitted by Fred C. Wilsdorf Jr.*

FREELINHUYSON WOOD, (1845-1910) was married in 1866 to Nancy Ellen Nance who was born in Maury County. Freelinhuyson and Nancy Nance were the parents of seven children: William N., John L., Elbert, Melvin, Florence, James Lafayette (Jimmy) and Etta. Nancy Ellen Nance Wood died about 1887. Freelinhuyson then married her sister, Juliett Nance Burleson. They were the parents of one child, Sarah Wood Brewer. Freelinhuyson later moved to Lawrence County, TN and died shortly thereafter and was buried near Summertown.

James Lafayette Wood and Mary Ellen Wood

William N. Wood and John L. Wood lived in Maury County, TN. Elbert Wood lived in Obion, TN and is buried in the Obion City Cemetery. Melvin F. Wood was a drifter and lived near Mt. Pleasant, TN. He is buried in Mt. Pleasant. Florence Wood Wyrick lived until her death in Alabama. She is buried in Alabama. Etta Wood Buie lived in Linden, TN. (She was the mother of Ruthie (Willie) Anderson, who resides in Perry County.) Etta and her husband, Ewell Buie, are buried in the Linden Cemetery. Sarah Wood was married to Herman Brewer and lived in Lexington, TN at the time of her death. She and her husband are buried in the Bethel Cemetery. Sarah Wood Brewer was a half-sister to Jimmy L. and Mary Ellen Burleson Wood.

James Lafayette Wood, the sixth child of Freelinhuyson and Nancy Nance, was born June 10, 1882. He married Mary Ellen Burleson in 1904. She was the daughter of Juliett Nance Burleson and Robert Burleson from Barnesville. James (Jimmy) worked at various public works during his lifetime. He moved his family to Short Creek in Perry County in the early 1920s. James Lafayette Wood died on March 24, 1940. He is buried in the Bethel Cemetery. Mary Ellen Burleson Wood died July 7, 1970 and is buried beside her husband in the Bethel Cemetery.

James L. (Jimmy) Wood and Mary Ellen Wood were the parents of nine children: Oscar, Arthur, Adell and R.T. Wood, four of the children (Homer, Alfred, Ruby and Rosetta) died before reaching one year of age from whooping cough and other related illnesses, Willie died at age five from membranous croup. He is buried in Hohenwald.

JEREMIAH M. WOOD, was born March 4, 1804 in Greenville District, SC to West and Nancy (Smith) Wood. He moved with his family to Tennessee.

He married before 1828 in Perry County, TN to Mary Graham, daughter of John and Sarah (Bunten) Graham. Mary was born March 10, 1810 in Warren County, TN.

They were the parents of eight sons as follows: John West, 1828-1900; William M., 1830; Hiram H., 1832-1911; Bailey B., 1833; Martin Van Buren, 1835; Jeremiah Preston, 1839-1873; James Knox Polk, 1844-1917; and an unknown son.

Jeremiah moved his family in the 1840s to Cass County, TX. He named the town of Linden, TX for his hometown of Linden, TN. Linden is the county seat for Cass County.

Jeremiah died on Aug. 10, 1870 and Mary died on March 19, 1895. They are buried in the Center Grove Cemetery (it was known as Graham Graveyard when they were buried there).

John West and Hiram Wood moved to Hunt County, TX in the 1860s. John moved to Stephenville, TX about 1890. Bailey moved to Indian Territory (Oklahoma). Jeremiah Preston and James K. P. stayed in Cass County, TX. *Submitted by Sue Wood.*

JAMES LAFAYETTE WOOD, son of Freelinghuyson Wood and Nancy Ellen Nance, born June 10, 1882 in Lewis County, TN. Married on March 2, 1903 to Mary Ellen Burlison born Feb. 29, 1880. James suffered a stroke and died March 24, 1940. Mary Ellen died July 8, 1970. Both are buried in the Bethel Cemetery. Born to this marriage four children:

Children of James L. and Mary Ellen Wood: Oscar, Arthur, Adell and R.T.

James Oscar Wood, born July 10, 1904, married Emer Luella Mealer, Dec. 30, 1928. Luella was born Jan. 23, 1912. Oscar died July 26, 1978, buried in Bethel Cemetery in Linden, TN. Born to this marriage: Era Nell Wood, James William "Billy" Wood and Donnie Gene Wood.

Robert Arthur "Fatty" Wood, born Dec. 31, 1908, married July 28, 1928, to Gladys Mahan, born July 14, 1913. "Fatty" died April 28, 1968, buried in the Bethel Cemetery in Perry County. Born to this marriage: Lorene Wood, Mary Dean Wood, Robert "Bobbie" Wood and Jimmy Lee Wood.

Roy Thomas "R.T." Wood, born Feb. 12, 1924 in Perry County, TN, married Sept. 19, 1942 to Sarah Maude Trull. "R.T." died Nov. 1, 1987. Maude died Feb. 17, 1993. Both are buried in Bethel Cemetery, Linden, TN. Born to this marriage: Linda Faye Wood, Glenda Gaye Wood, Tommie Delores Wood, James Michael Wood, Gloria Jean Wood and Mary Ellen Wood.

Bessie Adell Wood, born Jan. 14, 1922 in Perry County, TN, married John William Stephens on March 19, 1938 in Linden, TN. Died Sept. 25, 1979, and buried in Stephens Cemetery on Brush Creek. Born to this marriage three daughters:

Mamie Sue Stephens, born March 6, 1939 in Perry County, TN, married Fulton Ray DePriest July 4, 1958. Born to this marriage two children: Nancy Lynne DePriest born March 6,

1960, married Gary Mark Bentley Sept. 4, 1982. They have one son, Phillip Mark Bentley born Sept. 17, 1990; David Ray DePriest born Aug. 18, 1964, married Kellye Ruth Attkisson July 4, 1987. They have one daughter, Jessica Rae DePriest born Oct. 22, 1993.

Bessie Louise Duncan born Jan. 24, 1942 in Perry County, TN, married Hollis Ray Duncan on Dec. 24, 1960. Born to this marriage were two sons and a daughter: Timothy Ray Duncan born Jan. 20, 1963, married Susan Renee Davis July 23, 1982. Born to this marriage one daughter, Tiffany Suzanne Duncan, Nov. 7, 1983. This marriage ended in divorce. On March 4, 1989, he married Stephanie Jones. This marriage ended in divorce. On Feb. 26, 1993, Timothy Ray Duncan and Debbie Himes Crum were married; Tony Randall Duncan born June 7, 1966, married Tammy Sue Burgess on June 21, 1985, the children born to this marriage are Troy Ravis Duncan born April 27, 1990, Travor Stephens Duncan born Aug. 6, 1993, Trena Louise Duncan born April 28, 1978.

Joyce Ann Stephens born Oct. 26, 1947 in Perry County, TN, married Johnie Wayne Marshall on March 23, 1967. Born to this marriage was one daughter, Ellen Annette Marshall born Dec. 2, 1972.

JAMES OSCAR WOOD, (1904-1978) lived on Sinking Creek and Cane Creek. He farmed and worked at sawmills most of his life. He married Louella Mealer Wood in 1928. Their children are Nell Wood Graves, Bill and Donnie Wood. Their grandchildren include: Dianne Graves Eakin, Brenda Graves King, Jeffrey Graves, Vickie Wood Simmons, J. Michael Wood, D. Brian Wood, Leanne Wood Smith and Jonathan N. Wood. Oscar Wood is buried in the Bethel Cemetery.

Louella Mealer Wood and Oscar Wood

Robert Arthur Wood (1908-1968) lived in Linden and worked at sawmills most of his life. He married Gladys Mahan Wood in 1928. Their children are Lorene Wood, Dean Wood McCullough, Bobby and Jimmy Wood. Their grandchildren include: Robbie McCullough, Kathy McCullough Harkins, Debbie Wood, Bobby Wood Jr. (1963-1974), Terry, Scott, Eric and Allison Wood. Arthur Wood is buried in the Bethel Cemetery.

Adell Wood Stephens (1922-1979) lived on Brush Creek and in Linden, TN in 1938. She married Johnny Stephens in 1938. Their children are Mamie Sue Stephens DePriest, Louise Stephens Duncan and Joyce Stephens Marshall. Their grandchildren include: Lynn and David DePriest, Tim, Tony and Trena Duncan and Ellen Marshall. Adell Stephens is buried in the Stephens Cemetery of Brush Creek.

Roy Thomas (R.T.) Wood (1924-1987), a veteran of World War II, lived in Linden and Detroit, MI most of his lived and worked at GMC. He was married to Sarah Maude Trull Wood (1925-1993). Their children are Fay Wood Cooper, Glenda Wood Smith, Tommie Wood Justice Vaughnn, Gloria Wood McKenzie, Mary Wood Crumby and James Michael Wood. Their grandchildren include: Gwen Cooper, Tommy Smith, Sarah and Leslie Justice, Alicia Berger, James, Jason, Jessie, Justin and Shannon Wood, Chanel and Joseph McKenzie, Tony Jr., Jonathan, Sheena and Lindsey Crumby. R.T. and Maude Wood are buried in the Bethel Cemetery.

WEST WOOD, was born about 1784 in South Carolina of unknown parentage. On April 28, 1803 in Greenville District, SC, he married Nancy Smith.

They had moved to Tennessee by 1812 as West Wood was a sergeant in Captain Michael Molton's Troop of Cavalry of the Tennessee Volunteers at that time. They were part of John Coffee's Regiment. He served off and on until 1814. He was living in Dickson County, TN when he joined.

West was the first Sheriff of Perry County, TN, serving from 1820 to 1828. In 1821 he had 160 acres of land surveyed on Cedar Creek.

West and Nancy were the parents of at least eight children. The names of four of these are: Jeremiah M., born March 4, 1804; Elizabeth, who married Jesse Taylor; William; and Nancy H.

They moved to what is now Cass County, TX in the 1840s with the families of Jeremiah and Nancy. William moved to Kentucky and on to Illinois. Later he moved to Hunt County, TX. Elizabeth and Jesse Taylor stayed in Perry County. Nancy married William Ledbetter and later James R. Davis.

West Wood filed for Bounty Land in 1850 for his military service, but died before it was awarded. He died Nov. 3, 1852. Nancy reapplied for the Bounty Land and received it on June 6, 1856. *Submitted by Sue Wood.*

WOOD, A recent study of the Wood family was traced 20 generations to William Wood who was married to Juliana (last name unknown). In 1318, they bought the estate known as Beckenham Kent, near Coulsdon, England. He became Sir William Att Wood and was a Captain of the King's Guard. In the fourth generation, John Wood was the son of Peter Atte Wood Jr. He was called to Parliament in 1459 as de Wodes. He built Sanderstead Court, while holding Coulsdon Manor under a 20 year lease. In 1530, Denes Wood made her will and called her late husband John Attwood of Sanderstead, signing as Dene Attwood, and mentions her daughter Agnes and four sons, the first as John and the third as Nicholas. Nicholas Wood was an officer of the Queen and Sergeant of the Queen's carriages. Harmon Wood, the grandson of Nicholas Wood, left England and came to Boston, MA. John Wood, a brother to Harmon, left County Surrey, England and came to Plymouth Colony in America in the year 1635 on the ship, Matthew. John had married Joan Coleson of St. Martins, England.

Thomas Wood, son of John Wood, lived in Bristol County, MA. He was a surveyor. He and his wife, Rebecca, had seven children. The children and grandchildren of this generation began to move and settle all over the state of Massachusetts and Connecticut.

Daniel Wood, a great-grandson of Thomas Wood, was born Feb. 27, 1750 in Cheshire, MA. He was married to Rebecca Ingalls, who was born in 1752. Daniel and his brother, Nathan, both served in the War of the Revolution on the side of the Colonists and both were engaged in the Battle of Bennington. Daniel and Rebecca Ingalls Wood had nine children. The youngest child was Elisha Wood.

Elisha Wood was born in 1787. He was married to Elsea Bourne and they resided in Cheshire, MA. Elisha Wood died Oct. 6, 1849. Elsea Bourne Wood died March 3, 1858. They were the parents of ten children. The seventh child was Luther Wood. Luther Wood was born in 1805 and moved from Massachusetts and settled on public lands in Lewis County, TN in 1844.

WILLIAM WOOD, was born ca. 1820 in Perry County to West and Nancy Smith Wood. William fathered ten known children, five of them being born in Tennessee, one in Arkansas and three in Illinois. By his first wife, name un-

Andrew Jackson Wood Family in 1918.

known, William had four children: Martha Jane, married William Peach Clayton; Mary M.; James Monroe, married Ervina Isabell Tolar; and Robert G., married Elizabeth Taylor in Perry County.

Martha Jane (1844-1880 in Bandera, KY) and William P. had seven children: Elizabeth Peach; Lydia Annie Mary, married John Nesbitt and Ira Goodwin; Libbie Gertrude; Charles Peach, married Alice Adelle Tuttle; Emma Francis; Mattie, married William Parker and Charles Balcom; and Katie, married Sam Thompson.

James Monroe (1852-1938, Dallas, TX) and Ervina Isabell were parents of six children: William, born 1879, died young; Jess L., married Liza Sharp; Betty Dallas, married Howard A. Sharp; Ida Mae, married Dan S. Bragg; George F., born 1895; and James Robert "Bob," married Alma Hardin.

Betty and Howard had ten children: Lonnie, married Audie Byrd; Lela Velma Minnie, married Cecil C. Bearden; Ellen Ovilian, married Viola Allen; H. B. married Francil Allen; Woody Robert, married Lula Vee Key; Enoch Arden; and Thomas.

Robert G. (1854-1941, Tampa, FL) and Elizabeth had four children: Arthur Blaine, married Agnes O'Neil; Oscar Turner, married Cora Victoria Shaw; Fred Jesse, married Vida M. Robertson; and Laura Ethel, married Carl Gamon Sims.

Oscar Thomas and Cora had eight children: Rose; Virginia, married William D. Moorhead; Robert Oscar; James Edward; Charles William; John Richard; Elinor, married Lester Gilbert; and Catherine, married Lewis Greer.

William Wood's second marriage was to Sarah Ann Onstott, ca. 1856. Six children were born to them: Julia Ann, married to Alfred M. Lackey and William A. Story; John Wesley, married Savannah Murray; Sarah Matilda "Sallie," married John Franklin Fulfer; Andrew Jackson "Jack," married Senith Louella "Ella" Watson; Samuel Hunt; and Benjamin F.

Following the death of William in Hunt County in December 1885, Sarah Ann moved to Craighead County, AR, where she married Hiram Gregg in 1887. She died there ca. 1888.

Julia Ann (1858-1892, Pemiscot County, MO) and William had five children: Robert Lee, married Julia S. Coram; Birdie Lee, married first to Charles L. Ledbetter, second to Theodore Hedges and third to John Henry Fulfer; William Arnett, married first to Uriah Hall and second to Mattie Goodman; Ruth Estelle, married Alfonso Kinkaid; and Rosa Alma, married Charles Lee Thompson.

Robert L. and Julia S. had two children: Nellie May and Della Lee, married James T. Whitehouse.

Birdie Lee and Charles L. had two children: Burton, who died in infancy, and Edward Harmon, married Edna Lee Erwin. Birdie Lee and Theodore had four children: Raymond; Clova; Freeman; and Flora Bell, married William Hubert Barker. Birdie Lee and John Henry had two children: Sherman, married Marie Reeder, and Lovetta, married Robert Jennings Hall.

John Wesley (1860-1931, Soper, OK) and Savannah were parents of six children: Thomas Wesley, married Alma E. Rogers and Geraldine; Charles Lofton, married Bonnie Rogers; Moody, married Lonnie Cross; Verna Bell, married Ernest M. Futrell; Willie, married Poley Loper; and Noel Preston, married Mattie Era Crowder.

Sarah M. "Sallie" (1863-1907, Hunt County, TX) and John F. had six children: John Wesley, married Lula Laura Smith; Samuel Harvey, married Mertie Cynthia Wilkins; Ella Addye, married Luther White; Pearl, married John L. Lovelace; Luther Franklin, married Alma (?) and Stella M. Rumfield; and Ima Richelou, married Lyle Alton Stoddard.

Andrew Jackson "Jack" (1864-1918, Hunt County, TX) and Senith Louella "Ella" (1872-1938, Hunt County, TX) were parents of 14 children: George Franklin, married Mattie Velma Dean; William Lawrence, married Lois Pope; Martha Annie, married Luther Clayton Pope; Henry Elbert, married Eliza May Webb; Berry A., married Sarah A. "Sadie" Evans; Claude Jack, married Velma Harris; Montie Russell, married Bertha Irene Woodard; Bob, married first to Mattie Hutcheson and second to Louise Mason; Lelia Gracie, married James Loised Hewitt; Grady Wheeler, died as an infant; Nellie Myrtle, married Melvin Smalley and Pete Miller; A.J. "Pete," married Bessie Bennett; Lou Ella, died in infancy; and Edwin Burlon (1916-1931).

George F. and Mattie Velma had three children: Laura Juanita, married Fred Horace Hollon; Claude Cedel, married Angie Fleming; and Joe Donald, killed in auto accident in 1938.

William Lawrence and Lois had five children: James, died in infancy; Louie Leon, married Maudine Cloninger; Thelma Bernice, married first H.C. McWhorter, second to Fulton Teel; Helen Franes, married Eldred England and Henry Walker; and Dorothy Nell, married Joseph H. Morgan.

Martha Annie and Luther Clayton had four children: Lawrence Hubert, married Millie Sue Miller; Almeta, married J.B. Hill; Imogene "Jane," married Burl Wayne "Buddy" Heath; and Tommie Joe, married Max Wayne Dunn.

Henry Elbert and Eliza May had three children: Willard Rayburn, married Marion Jones; Dorothy Marie, married Kenneth Earl Moore; and Bill Ray, married Terry Alene Brookshire.

Berry A. and Sarah A., "Sadie" had six children: Walter Preston, married Pearl Myrtice Owens; Andrew Jackson "Jack," married Ruby Johnson; Tressie Lee, married Clifford C. McFadden; Susie Mae, married Jimmy Teel and James Frank Castle; Berry A. Jr., married Mary Nell Martin and Betty Ruth Merrell; and Jo Marie, married Curtis Ray Winton.

Claude Jack and Velma had seven children: Claude Jack, Jr.; Nellie Pearl, married Burl P. Adams and Donald N. Smith; Frances, married Robert Stephens, Ernest Ruth and Billy Wayne Boyd; Eulace C. "Woody," married Lorene I. Paschall, Else Glendora Willis and Marie Hornick; Dorothy Vivian, married (?) Dorrough and (?) Hernandez; Ray Raymond, married Anna Volker; and Yvonne Alfa, married Ronnie Frederick Brandon.

Montie Russell and Bertha Irene had three children: Edward, married Betty Rice and Ruth Zona; Montie Ray, married Sandra Coppinger and Deborah Michelle Reiber; and Linda Marie, married Travis Lee Owens.

Bob and Mattie had one son, Weldon Dean.

Bob and Louise had twin sons: Charles Robert, married Judy Lynn Baker and James Rodney, died in infancy.

Lelia Gracie and James Loised had three children: Mildred Frances, married Gene Oren Vance and Edwin Thomas Williams; Bobbye Joyce, married William Thomas Richardson and Thomas Alton Davis; and Anna Blanche, married Joe P. Moore Sr. and Robert B. Camp; and James Ray.

Nellie Myrtle and Melvin had two children: Melva Jean, married Ernest B. Waters and Roy Lee, married Barbara A. Robertson.

A.J. "Pete" and Bessie had one daughter, Mary Lou, who married Charles A. Needham. *Submitted by Dorothy Marie Wood Moore.*

WORLEY-WARD, Edd Worley and Lucy Worley Kelley of Houser Creek had four children: Ann, Irma, Lelna and Doris.

Irma married Arthur Coates of Centerville, TN and they had four children: Andy, Nicky, Phil and Glenda.

Zelna married Clarence Harris.

Doris married Glendine Worley and they have one son, Mike.

Ann married Rex Ward who died Feb. 21, 1974. He was the son of George and Sally Ward who lived on Cedar Creek. Ann and Rex had two children: Russ and Cliffie who were born in Lobelville at Dr. Salhany's Clinic.

Russ married first, Cindy Landers, and had a daughter, Hannah Ward. He married second, Carolyn Skelton and had a son, Jabee. Carolyn had a daughter, Holly, by a previous marriage.

Cliffie married James Parsons and had one son, Chris James Parson. She married second, in 1993, Manuel Bunch, who had two children by his first wife, Lola Hinson Bunch. Their names are Mark and Joel. Manuel is the son of Daniel and Pauline Bridges Bunch. Daniel Bunch died in 1985. Manuel was raised on White Oak Creek and at present, they live in his grandparents house on White Oak Creek.

JACK YOUNG, (May 7, 1901-Feb. 26, 1984) married Gladys Oneita Tucker Sept. 1924. Jack was the son of William H. and Sallie Taylor Young. He had three sisters and three brothers, Lillie Mae, Mary, Sallie Matt, Clifford, Bob and Joe. Gladys was the daughter of Thomas Blaine and Ada Paschall Tucker. She had five sisters Clara O'Quin, Rubena Dabbs, Verna Stutts, Ruth Elliot and Loretta Osborne. Four brothers, Tom T., Willie Ray and M.H.

Jack and Gladys Young and daughter, Helen Richardson in 1974.

Jack and Gladys had two children Helen

Marie (June 2, 1925) and Paul Dempsey (Sept. 19, 1927) who died at age of 26 on May 24, 1953.

Jack was a barber but retired as a mail carrier. He built one of the first Barber shops in Linden, the family moved into the back quarters and made that their home in 1928. In September of 1930, their dreams were shattered when one side of the Town of Linden burned and they lost their home and business. In the year of 1932 he rebuilt and started over again.

Helen married Gene Richardson, son of Pleas and Flora Dotson Richardson, and they have three children, Larry Gene (Ricky), Paulette and Jacky.

Paul Dempsey married Beatrice Robinson and had one daughter Marla Kay Young, born Dec. 15, 1948.

Jack, Gladys and Paul are buried at Kirk Cemetery in Linden.

YOUNG, H.M. Ledbetter was born in Lincoln County, TN, Dec. 18, 1830, the youngest of a large family. His parents were Henry and Anna (Phillips) Ledbetter. He later acquired a large farm. At 21, he married Mary E. Vaughn, daughter of William Vaughn. Children were: Sarah, who married T.G. Young; Susan married A.E. Goblet; Mary married S.H. Hunt; Henry N.; Martha; Minerva; and Cora Bell. Their mother was born in Williamson County.

Children of T.G. and Sarah Young were: Mollie, who married Jim Starbuck and had children, William, Henry, Joe, Allie, Lillie and Sarah; Allie, married John Simmons (no children); Bess (single); Cora married Bob Young (no children); Robert married Kyle French. Their children were Florine, Sarah and Thomas Eugene; J. Clyde (born 1892) married Lela Alta Patterson (born 1894) in 1921. Alta was the daughter of James W. and Margaret Kunkel Patterson. Clyde died in 1972 and Alta in 1974, both at the age of 80.

Clyde and Alta Young had two children: Mary Pauline (born 1925) married Roy Miller, and Lela Ruth (born 1936) married Glyn Broome. Both daughters live in Clarksville, TN.

Pauline and Roy's sons are: David Stuart (1953) married Rebecca Renfro. Their children are Matthew, Joshua and Lindsay; and Roy Stephen (1955) married Linda Harper and had two children, Susan and Laura.

Ruth and Glyn's children are: Glynda who married Bob Krantz and had Alan and Whitney; Lynn married Mary Obe and had Caitlin; and Dina married Dick Wilkins and had Danielle and Dianna. *Submitted by Pauline Miller, Clarksville, TN.*

1929-30 Linden Team. Front row, L to R: Carmon Dickson, (Lomax), Lilly Hugh Anderson (Ickle), Sammy Bates (Westbrooks), Kitty Bates, Julia DePriest ad Fronia Denton (Rainey). Back row, L to R: Trinkle Shelton - Coach, Madelyn Hufstedler (Shelton), Lota Tucker (Richardson), Thelma Ferguson, Lammon - Assistant Coach.

INDEX

— A —
ACREE, Larry 41
ADAMS, Hodge 12
ADKINS, Geneva L. 59
ALBERSON, Moses 64
ALDRIDGE, Harley 60, James Allen 64
ALEXANDER, 119, Honey 20, Lamar 20
ALLEN, Flossie Esther 64, Joseph 41, Joseph Henry 64, Maurine 65
ALLEY, Judith T. 59
ANDERSON JR., James M. 67
ANDERSON, 65, 164, Andy Carroll 65, Bessie Louise 66, Bonnie Halbrooks 66, Dorothy Dean 67, James Black (J.B.) 67, James Robert (Bob) 67, John 12, Robert D. 16, 17, Sam 16, Samuel T. 67, Solomon Pete 68, William Earl (Bill) 68, W.J. 47, William Thomas 68
ARMSTRONG, Fount 18
ARY, 69, 162, Alf 55, Charles D. Sr 16, Helen 59, 69, Keith 55, 69, Ottie Lee 18
ARY-WARREN, 69
ASHTON, 69, 70, Mike 19
ASHTON-BATES, 69
ASHTON-BROWN, 70
ATKINS, Samuel 12
AUSTIN, J.B. 36
AVERETT, Lolamae 20
AYERS, 70, Dick 38, 55, E.J. 38
AYERS-WYATT, 70

— B —
BAARS, Daniel 70
BAARS-MAYER, 70
BAKER, 71, 251, Larkin 14, Lois R. 59, William N. 16
BANDY, Dr. Jimison 71
BANKS, G.M. 40
BARBER, 203, Abraham 12, Allen 71, 12, Betty 20, Brownie Sue 72, Jerrie 36, Kenneth H. 72, Nancy Caroline 72, Rodger I. 72
BARCOFCY, A.O. 20, Mattie 20
BARHAM, 73, George Thomas (Tommy) 73, Balaam 74, George Wesley 74, Hartwell 14, Josiah 74, Thomas N. 74, William Thomas 74
BARNETT SR., Jeremiah 75
BARNETT, Amanda 41, D.A. 41, John W. 41, Sarah Ann 41, William Ransom 41
BASIN, Annie 20
BASS, Kenny 36, W.H. 17
BASTIAN, Josiah 20
BATES, 69, 77, 217, Andrew Jackson 75, Armada James Lily Hunt (Madie) 75, Dillard Hunt 76, Dora Caldonia Jim 30, John R. 76, John Redner 77, John Will 44, Judith A. 59, Lew Ellen 64, Moses 14
BATES-HINSON, 77
BATES-HUNT, 77
BATES-RILEY, 77
BATES-WARREN, 78
BATTON, Arthur 78
BAUCOM, Aaron 79, Moses 20
BAUGUS, Jommima (Jan) 306, R.A. 44
BEARD, Edythe 38, Orby 38, W.E. 20, Wiley B.
BEASLEY, 256, Bob 79, Dora Elizabeth 79, Flora 79, Betty 80, Gloria Ghayle 80, J.B. 46, J.C. 55, 80, Martha 80, J.M. 38, 80, J.P. 46, Jeffrey T. 80, Joel Gooch 81, John Allen (Jack) 81, John 8, Littleberry 81, Martha Elizabeth Craig 81, Tom Alva 81
BEATTY, Thomas S. 17
BELL, 82, 97, 237, 239, 251, Charles H. 82, Eldridge Newsom 83, John 83, R.T. 41, Tommy W. 59, Willie Green 82
BELL-PATTERSON, 82
BELL-ROBERTSON, 82
BERRY, Claude Teaney 83, Elizabeth 20, Joseph G. 17
BIFFLE, J.J. 17
BIRD/BYRD, 84
BIRDSONG-WILLIAMS, 84
BISHOP, Pamela C. 59
BLACK, James (J.B.) 67
BLACKWELL, Mary (Rice) 84, Denise 59, 85, Michael Scott 85
BLAKEMORE, Connie L. 59
BOWEN, Mary 5, 6,
BOWEN, 85
BOWIE, James 17
BOWMAN, James Newton 85
BOYCE JR., Lt. William Earl 87
BOYCE, Albert Erasmus 86, Robert Clair 86, Sam 19, Samuel Claud 86, Samuel Miles 86, William Earl 19, 86, 87, Virginia Bromley 87, William H. 87
BOYD, Elsie Carrie Harder Ellison 88, Frances 88, Stanley 88, T.M. 41
BRADFIELD, W.A. 36
BRADLEY, Jill DePriest 88
BRADSHAW, Les 54, Leta 54
BRAKE, Elsie 89, Lonnie 89
BRASHEAR, T. M. 10, 11, 14,
BRASHER, Tammy A. 59
BREEDING, Edward 89, E.S. 38, Sara 89
BRIDGES, Joseph Brown 89
BRILEY, Joshua 12, 90, Nancy (Howell) 90
BRITT, Eula 40, William O. 10, 12
BROADAWAY, 90, Ernel 41, Paschal 90,
BROADWAY, 91, Dixie 92, Jeff 92, Joyce Labelle 92, Norma 92, Paschal 93, Sarah 93
BROMLEY, Charles 18, Evelyn Nell 93, James Akin 94, Minerva Goodman 94, R.C. 19, William Ewing 94
BROMLEY-DESANTIS, 93
BROOKS, Deems 39
BROWN, 70, H.M. 14, James H. 14, Joseph 10, 12, Milton 11
BRUCE, 286
BUNCH, Howard 94, Joseph 95
BUNDY, Sam 40
BUNTEN/BENTON/BRUTON/NEWTON, Sarah 95
BURCHAM, 96, Levi 95
BURCHAM-WARD, 96
BURNETTE, 237
BURNS, David Edward 96, George 96, George Simpson 97, Joseph Cayce (Joe) 97, J.W. 36, Nick 60
BUSSELL, C.C. 41, J. Pope 41
BUTLER, J.R. 44, J.Y. 41
BYRD, Frances Elizabeth 64, George W. 36

— C —
CAGLE, Gil 48, Ginger C. 59, Ginger Graham 48
CAMPBELL, Jim 15, Thomas 10
CANTRELL, 97
CANTRELL-BELL, 97
CARMICAL, Jimmy Terry 98, Joseph Byrd 98
CARRINGTON, Carline 41, Patty Nix 37
CARROLL, Susan M. 19, William Edward (Edd) 98, William (Will) T. 99
CARTER, Brownlow 40, Flossie 40, Floyd 40, Ila 40, Jack 56
CATES, 99, 107, Joshua 12
CATRON, Bud 40, Dolly 40
CHANDLER, Tyre, 99, William 17

CHAPPELL, Clovis Gillham, 100
CHERRY, Myron 36
CHESSOR, 297
CHILDRESS, Jesse 12, John, 100
CHURCHWELL, Ray 56
CLARK, Edgar 36, Homer 47, John R. 41
CLIFTON, 100, Larry L. 59, Tobe, 100
CLIFTON-CROSSNO, 100
CLOYD, 211
COBLE, 101, Adam, 101, Henry, 101, James John William, 102, Jesse, 102, John R. 16, William Henry, 102
COBLE-ESTES, 101
COBLE-HOWELL, 101
COLE, F.A. 47
COLEMAN, 103
COLLINS, Artie 36, Willard 39
COMBS, 143
CONDER, William Morgan 103
CONDRA, Jesse 39
COOPER JR., John Moses 104
COOPER, 192, Elizabeth Ann 104, Jacob Daniel 104, John M. 104, J.G. 41, J.W. 20, Robert Cross 104, Thomas Spencer 105
CORLEW, W.C. 18
COTHAM, Janie H. 59
COTHAM-SMITH, 105
COTTON, 105, 245, Alvin M. 105, Bruce 47, Donald Bruce 105, Irvin Robert 106, Jarad 106, Marvin Eunice 106, Paris 107, Whitney 107, Willie Lee 107
COX, Nicholas N. 16
CRAFTON, 108
CRAIG, 229, A.D. 14, Adelaine 40, Ashley 40, Black 40, Brown 109, Helen 110, Mack 36, Mack Wayne 39, McDonald 110, Nathan 40, O.T. 111, Robert Hardeman 111, Tapp 112, Nancy Ethel 143
CRAIG-CRAFTON-HARDEMAN, 108
CRAIG-DENTON, 108
CRAIG-FARRAR, 108
CRAIG-GREER-TRULL, 109
CRAIG-HORNER, 109
CRAIG/CRAGG, 107
CRAIG/CRAGG-CATES, 107
CROCKETT, David 10
CROSBY, 112, Bill 8, Mary L. 59
CROSSNO, 100
CRUDUP, Robert 14
CRUSE, Mary B. 59
CUDE, Andrew C. 113, Homer 12, John Bell 113, William Hodge 113
CULP, 113, 114, 220, 256, J.H. 17
CULP JR., Woodrow (Woody) Willis 116
CULP SR., Woodrow Willis 115

CULP, 220, 256, Allen 115, Frank Brown (Pete) 115, Gary 55, Sheila D. 59, Tom 55, Woodrow 38
CULP-GILMER, 114
CULP-LEE, 114
CULP-SMITH, 114
CULP/GILMER, 113
CURL-WARREN, 116
CURL-WATSON, 116
CURRY, 180, 297, Mattie Louise Tate 63

— D —
DABBS, Billy R. 56, Brenda A. 59, Buster 41, John P. 116, Leslie O. 59, Nat 12, Ottis James 117
DAILY, Sarah 246
DANIEL, 117, Clyde A. 62, Homer 36, J.B. 14, Jack 44, Jim 38, Mary 38, Woodson 118
DAVIDSON-ALEXANDER, 119
DAVIDSON-HESTER, 119
DEADRICK, 120
DEAVER, 119
DEERE, James Yuther (Jim) 120
DEFORD, Drisden 17
DELZELL, Bobby 37
DENSON, 295
DENSON, James 121
DENT, D.W. 40
DENTON, 108, 121, 288, Mary Sam 56, Samuel 12, 122
DENTON-WILEY-WARD, 121
DEPRIEST, 122, 123, 132, 215, 235, Ada 63, Albert 63, Bell 40, Byron Shepard 63, Barney 8, Beulah 123, Celia Carolyn 32, Claude 60, Danny Shepard 123, Dora Deane 32, Dora Elizabeth Beasley 32, Ellen 41, Ernie 63, Frances Lorraine 32, Henry Houston 32, Ira 63, James Edward 124, Jessie Thurman 32, John Thurman 32, 124, John Vernon 125, Ione Elizabeth 125, Mary Elizabeth 32, May 63, Millington E. 125, 126, Pleasant Whitfield 61, 126, Randolph 126, 127, Randolph (Randal) 127, Sally Matt Ridings 63, Samuel Rudolph 127, Thomas Newton 127, Trent 55, W.H. 36, William Harrison 128, William Henry 128, William Jesse (Jess) 128, Betty Jane Bates 128, William Samuel 129
DESANTIS, 93
DICKSON, 129
DICKSON-KIMBLE, 129
DILL, Margaret A. 59
DIXON, James 10, 12, 14, Joseph 12

DODSON, 130, C.B. 14, Elizabeth K. 55, Fannie 130, James M. 14, Martha Ann 300
DOTSON, J.M. 11, Pearl 20
DOWDLE, Don 16
DOWDY, 298, Thomas 12
DOYLE, Bessie Lee Johnson 131, Ira W. 130, Jennie Sharon D. 59, Johnson E. 131, Lou 20, William Jefferson 131
DUNCAN, 291, Eli 8, Mrs. Fred 20
DUFF-LEEPER, 132
DUNCAN SR., Elijah Thomas 134
DUNCAN, 132, Edgar James 133, Edith 135, Elijah 133, James Pleasant (Pete) 134, L.B. 53, Vernon 135, W.T. 38,
DUNCAN-DEPRIEST, 132
DUNCAN-SHANNON, 132

— E —
EASLEY, Edward W. 14, John 14
EASTEP, Berry 48
EDMONSON, W.E. 37
EDWARDS, 135, 167, 270, Aaron Burr (Burrell) 137, Adda Mae Westbrooks 137, Claude Clement 137, Clem 60, James D. 137, J.T. 36, 47, James Morton 137, Jean 56, John T. 137, L.E. 36, Martha R. 59, Paul 41, Thomas 138, T.W. 14, W.A. 14, W.J. 36
EDWARDS-TUCKER, 136
ELDER, 256
ELLIOTT, 173, James Lee 138
ELKINS, Garland 39
EPLEY, Ray 50, Robert 139
ERISMAN, Donna Q. 59
ESTES, 101, 139, Abraham 139, Chester Franklin (Frank) 37, 140, John 140, John Marshall 141, Lillian Potter 141, William Robert (Bob) 141
EVANS, 142, 247, F.T. 41, James H. 142, Thomas 12
EZELL, Chester R. 59, LaDon K. 59

— F —
FAGAN-FERGUSON, 142
FARRAR, 108, 143
FARRAR/PIERCY/HESTER, 143
FERGUSON, 142, 143, Daniel Reed 143, George 144, Henry Jefferson 144, Nancy Ethel Craig 143, Neal H. 44
FERGUSON-COMBS, 143
FESMIRE, Linda A. 59
FITZGARLY, Nancy 41
FLOWERS, Elmus 41, William J. 14
FLOWERS/TATE, 144
FLUTY, Rex A. 145

FORTNER, Vicky L. 59
FRALEY, Jacob 12
FRALEY-HOLLABAUGH, 145
FRANKS, E.M. 41, Sue A. 20
FRENCH, Watt 145, William Hart 146

— G —

GARDNER, Claude 36
GARNER, 146, Opal 20
GARRETT, 172
GEAN, Penick 41
GHOLSTON, A. 11
GIBSON, Austin 41, Ottis 56
GILMER, 113, 114, Albert 63, John Samuel 146, Kate Leota Morrison 146, William H. 147, Sarah 147
GILMORE, Ralph 36
GLADDEN, Lillie 20, Myrtle 20
GLASS, G.W. 41
GOBELET SR., Marian Adolph 147, Marion Adolph Gobelet Sr. 147
GODWIN, Brown 36, John 38, John W. 55, J.W. 41, Miko C. 59, R.H. 47, R.H. Jr. 38, Thomas Stuart 148, Tom 55, William G. 148
GODWIN-SHARP, 148
GORDON, 252, Linda K. 59
GORDON-KILPATRICK, 149
GOTTHARDT, John 40, 149, Carl Frederick 149
GRAHAM, 150, Allen Henry 48, 150, Alvin John Wesley 151, Charles 14, 151, Charles Gibbs 152, Granville 152, Jack Denton 48, Jackson M. 152, Joan 48, John 153, John Wesley 48, Richard 153, Robert Crawford 153, Sherry Lee 48, Tennessee Texas (Mary) 153, Tillman Williamson 154, Tommy 44, Tommy Lee 48
GRAHAM-RAYBURN, 150
GRAVES JR., Elijah Thomas 156
GRAVES SR., Elijah Thomas 156
GRAVES, 154, 235, Andy Cook 155, Arthur Anson 155, Charlie 155, Henry Lee (Jack) 157, Ida Mae 157, Isaac 158, Joseph Lee 158, J.I. 46, Lawrence 158, Mattie Ann 159, Osbie Brown (Tick) 159, Ransom 159, Robert Webster (Rob) 160, Ronnie 48, Sarah Graham Bowman 160, Thomas Flavy 161
GRAY, R.H. 53
GREER, 109
GREESON, 167
GREGORY, James B. 161, Jim 8
GREGORY-VOSS, 161
GRIFFIN, Oswald 10, 12
GRIMES, Boyce 18, Dick 33, Glenn 18, 19, 55, Glenn Springer 161, Marie 19, Marie Boyce 161

GRINDER, 193, 249, 283, Ary Osburn 163
GRINDER-ARY, 162
GRINDER-LEDBETTER, 163
GRINDER-THARP, 163
GROOM, Alfred Wintry 164, Madie 164, Altie Bertha 164, Wallace 164, Wallace Denton 165
GROOM-ANDERSON, 164
GROOMS, William Jasper 165
GROOMS-PRICE, 165
GURLEY, 220
GUTHRIE, Robert A.

— H —

HAGGARD, C.L. 41, Martin 44
HALBROOK, 193
HALBROOK-EDWARDS, 167
HALBROOKS, 166, Robert M. 167
HALBROOKS-GREESON, 167
HALL, W.C. 36, 39
HAMM, Audrey 18, Ezra A., 168, Ross 18
HAND, Hugh B. 14
HANKINS, 288
HARDEMAN, 108, N.B. 39
HARDER, 168, 169, Edmond 170, Edmund Green 170, John Nicholas 170, John W. 16, William H. 16
HARDER-RAGSDALL, 170
HARDISON, William L. 48
HARMON, Jacob 10, 12, O.A. 15
HARPER, Wiley V. 171, Willie Pat 171, Lucille Rodgers 171
HARRIS, David 10, 11, 61, G.L. 11, Jean 171, Ralph 171, Thomas 53, 55
HARRISON, Johnny 38, Pamela 38
HARVEY, Jesse 54
HAYES, A.G. 41
HEADY, 172
HEATH, 172
HEDGES, John 41
HEINRICH, Lena Graham 48
HENDRIX-GARRETT, 172
HENDRIX-MERCER, 173
HERNDON, Jackie 38, Lindsey 38
HERRON, J.B. 17
HESTER, 119, 143, 173, 237, Ida Lorina Tate 63, John 173, Sophia 173
HESTER, 143
HESTER-ELLIOTT, 173
HICKERSON, 174, Dianne Dee 51, Fred Lee 50, Jake 50, John 174, Marion D. 175, Thirl 175, Vivian 175, William 175, William Jefferson 175
HICKERSON-LEDBETTER, 174
HICKS, Olan 39
HILDENBRANDT, Norma 20

HILL, Charles W. 41, John 36, Wm. M. 41
HINSON, 77, 176, 178, 287, Billy E. 59, E.I. 8, Elizabeth 239, George, 176, 177, Hollis 56, Johnny 177, Johnathan Harvey 20, 177, Linda 59, 177, Newton Jasper 20, N.J. 60
HINSON-INGRUM, 176
HITT, Lorraine DePriest 32
HODGE, Wm. 12
HOGAN, David 12
HOLCOMB, Donna L. 59
HOLDER, Wallace 55, Walton 55
HOLLABAUGH, 145, 178, George 12
HOLLADAY, Bert 57
HOLLAND, Tom 39
HOLMES, William 10, 12
HOLT, 179, Kenneth 36
HOOLIGAN, Jerry 12
HOOPER, Enoch 10, 12
HOOTON, 179
HORNER, 109, 179, 180, 247, 252, Daniel 56, 180, Dixie 54, Egbert 54, Frank P. 180, Gary 56, Herbert 54, Hollis Roma 181, Ida Ethal 54, Jemima Russell 181, J.V. 54, Jesse James 54, Pleasant 182, Ralph 54, Thomas L. (Boss) 182, Thomas Oren 183, William 183, William Buck 183, William Lee (Billy) 184
HORNER-CURRY, 180
HORNER-MOORE, 180
HOTEL, Rainey 243
HOUSELL, Bess 40
HOUSTON, 200, John L. 10, 12, Sam 10
HOWARD, 184, Benjamin R. 59, J.M. 55, Lisa A. 59, Marie M. 59
HOWELL, 101, 184, Roy Robert 185
HUDGINS, O.E. 39
HUDSON, 185, C.N. 36, 39, 185, Dorotha 5, 6
HUFSTEDLER, 186, Catherine M. 59, Jacob 12, Louise Jane Randel 2, Pinkney 2, Samuel Boyd 186
HULME, I.N. 14
HUMM 10
HUMPHREYS, Clyde 54, Will 54
HUNT, 77, 236, E.C. 36, Joel Monroe 187, J.M. 46
HUNTER, Waymon 40

— I —

INGRUM, 176
INMAN, Ezekeil 187, Marshall Allen 188

— J —

JACKSON, 188, 189, Andrew 10, David 84, Jean 20, Stonewall 17
JAMES, B.B. 36, 39, William 189

313

JARMON, William 10
JOHNSON, 190, Eugene 36, Jennie Bessie Lee 131, Ennis 189, Maie 189,
JOHNSTON, James Albert 190
JOLIFF, 190
JONES, 191, M.S. 47, R.E. 47
JORDAN, James R. 13
JOURNEY, 84
JOYNER, N.L. 41

— K —

KELLEY, James 14, Joseph 12, 191
KELLY, Adam 191, Byron 191
KENNAMORE, Willard 56
KIDD, 192
KILPATRICK, 149, 192, Enos Simpson 194, Jessie 20, Jim 194
KILPATRICK-COOPER, 192
KILPATRICK-GRINDER, 193
KILPATRICK-HALBROOK, 193
KILPATRICK-WADE, 193
KIMBAL, R.A. 47
KIMBLE, 129, 194, F.H. 14, O.A., 194, R.A. 14, William Moore 195, Mary N. 268,
KIMBLE/KIMBEL, 195
KIMBRO, F.C. 36
KING, 195, 196, Clyde 39, Mary Jo 81, Alexander 195, Byron Clyde 196, Robert Thomas 196, W.L. 41
KINGTON, Joe 197
KINSER, James H. 14
KIRK, Atha 33, Clark 33, Claude 33, Ethel 40, Eula Victoria 197, Evelyn Ruth 197, Frances Quinn 33, Harry Thomas (Sonny) 197, Hoyt 39, Izora 18, Lexie 33, Marie 33, Nesby Thomas 18, 198, Obie Atha 15, 33, 198, Thomas Atha 198, William Akin 198, William Clark 199, William Claude 199, William Quinn 33
KITTRELL, Benjamin Caesar 199, M.B. 47
KUNKEL, 236

— L —

LACY, Chloe 55
LAFFERTY-THOMPSON, 199
LANCASTER SR., Benjamin 200
LANCASTER, Calvin Andrew 201, David Andrew 201, J.J. 36, Nettie Alexander 63, U.J. 44, William B. 201
LANCASTER-HOUSTON, 200
LAND, 202, Elkanah A. 39
LANE, William W. 202
LARUE, 203
LARUE/BARBER, 203
LASTER, 204

LAWRENCE, 204, Dorothy W. 55, Jill E. 59, Michael 55, Robert 41
LAWS, Ernest 36
LAYTON, Wallace 39
LEDBETTER, 163, 174, 204, 205, H.N. 47, J.O. 38, J.P. 14, Rueben Phillips 205
LEE, 114
LEE-ROGERS, 206
LEE-SWEATT, 206
LEEPER, 132, Green D. 20, John 14
LEWIS, 207, 256, Aaron 10, 12, Bertie 41, Jane 56, Robert Daniel (R.D.) 118, Cassie Savage 118, Aaron 206, Cecil Virgil 206, Edward Allen 207, James H. 17, Jimmy 8, John Aaron 207, John Howard 207, J.W. 14, William Walker 208, W.H. 17
LINEBARGER, 208
LINEBARGER/LINEBERRY, 208
LINEBERRY, 208, Irvin 209, Grace 209, John Dee 209
LIPSCOMB, David 36
LIVENGOOD, Anita R. 59
LIVERMAN, Clint 31, 56
LOGGINS, Jane H. 59
LOMAX, 209, James 12, Thomas 14, 20
LONG, 210, Ethel Louise 210, Evaline (Simmons) 41, Henry H. 14
LONG-CLOYD, 211
LOVELESS, George 211
LUSK, Elmer 36
LYNCH, 211
LYNN, O.J. 37

— M —

MACKIN, Lynda 16, 59, Randy 16
MADDEN, Stanley 37
MALIN, 294
MARLIN, Grady 39, Lisa M. 59
MARRS, 212, Guy 34, John L. 34
MARSHALL, 213, Ray 56, Rickey H. 59
MARTIN, James 15
MASSEY, John 20
MATHIS, Bartley 213, Elbert W. 213, James Bluford 213, Jesse Manuel 213, Robert L. 214, Thomas S. 214
MATTHEWS, Elbert 12
MAXWELL, William S. 14
MAY, Glenda James 19
MAYER, 70
McCAIG, Billy Ralph 214, Dossie Ewell 214, Paul Lester 214
MCCLISH, H.W. 36
McCOLLUM, 215, John 215
McCOLLUM-DEPRIEST, 215
MCCORKLE, Jahue 41

McDONALD, 215, Ann (Homer) Kittrell 216, Emeline Cole King 216, Sally 219
MCDONOUGH, James Lee 36
McGEE, Bobby Arnold 216, Barbara Lee 59, 216, John Anderson 217, Arnold 282, Oville Tate 282, Jessie Gray 283, June Dowland 283,
McGOWAN, Robert William 217
McLEMORE-BATES, 217
MCMINN, Jerry Allen, 218
MEADOWS, W.W. 46
MEALER, 218, Willie 218
MEDARIS, B.W. 41
MERCER, 173, 218, Anne E. 59, Cynthia L. 59, Dewey 59, Jerry 36, Natham 56
MERCER-SHARP, 218
MIDDLETON, Joseph M. 219
MILLER, Menjou 40
MILLS, Paul C. 36
MONROE, 219
MOORE, 180, 220, Anita Faye 220, Arnold ONeil 221, Deborah K. 59, Donna Rae 221, Garrett Hobart 221, Bradford Alonzo 221, Hershel Robert 222, Hillard 222, Mattie 222, James 222, Jesse 222, James Abner 223, James Henry Monroe 223, John Curtis 223, John Wilburn (Web) 223, J.T. 41, Riley 39, W.A. 55, Julia Edna 224, Larry Dean 224, Robert Ross 225, Terry Wayne 225, Walton Hershel 225, Wesley Hillard 226, Wm. C. 14, William Ross 226
MOORE-CULP, 220
MOORE-GURLEY, 220
MOTON, Ben 40
MORRIS, Andy 40, Nick 40, R. Wayne 59
MORRISON, Kate Leota 146
MURPHY, L.B. 15, Mark 10, 12

— N —

NEELEY, S.L. 11, 15
NEWSOM, Green B. 10, 12
NEWSOME, E.J. 41
NEWTON, Kathryn 226
NIX, 226, Claude 37, E.C. 41, J.H., 8, Mary M. 41
NORTH, Ira 39
NORTON, John W. 47
NUNNERY, A.U. 41

— O —

ODLE, Ed 40, George 40, Nettie 40, Sister 40
O'GUIN, D. Allen 227, F.M. 41, Hardy 227, John (Jack) 228, Robert 56,

William Alfred 227, William Howard 228
OWENS, Only 8, 228

— P —

PACE, 229
PAFFORD, 229
PAFFORD-CRAIG, 229
Parker, Elba 41 **PARNELL SR.,** Edward A. 230
PARNELL, 230, 298, Archa 229, Archie Clovis 56, Dorothy Rainey 54, Edwin 54, Ethel Lou Della 73, Ralph 230, Robert Haywood 231, Lenier 231, Sam 232, Walter Thomas 232, William Hubert 232,
PASCHALL, 233, William R. (Bill), 233
PATTERSON, 82, 233, 234, 235, 236, W.P. 235, Elizabeth S. 235, Herbert Edwin 54, Howell 41, Lula 30, Mary Bell 54, Ralph 44, Rex 41, Robert 12, T.D. 47, William 12, William Earl 54, William Robert 54
PATTERSON-DEPRIEST, 235
PATTERSON-GRAVES, 235
PATTERSON-KUNKEL, 236
PATTON-HUNT, 236
PEARSON, C.L. 8, 16, 38, George W. 47
PEEBLES, 267
PEERCY, 237
PEERCY-HESTER, 237
PEERCY/PIERCY, 143
PEGRAM, 237
PEGRAM-BURNETTE-BELL, 237
PENIX, Sarah 41
PENKLEY, L.M. 41
PERRY, Jack 38, Mary 38
PETTIGREW, James A. 16
PEVAHOUSE, 238, Austin 56, Bob 41, Cressie 238, Dorothy Lee 159, Leslie 40, Ray 40, Rosie 40
PHILLIPS, Tamra R. 59
PIERCY, 143
PLUNKETT, Joe 45, Mary Lou 20, Peggy 45, Tony 20
POINDEXTER, 257
POLK, James K. 10
POOLE, 238, 244, A.P. 44
POPE, 239, Don 38, 47, J.D. 47, 53
POPLIN, Richard 239, Elizabeth Hinson 239
PORTIA, 239
PORTIA-ROBERTSON-BELL, 239
POTTS, William 41, William N. 59
PRICE, 165
PRINCE, Miles 14
PULLEN, John E. 46
PUTNAM, Margaret 37

— Q —

QUALLS, 240, 241, 242, Lucinda 79, Asberry 240, Billie 55, Bobby Joe 240, Dovie 20, Eva (Tate) 240, Eddie Thomas 241, Ellen 20, Henry Atlas 241, Patricia A. 59, Waco 242, Walter Kirk 243
QUALLS-TRULL, 243
QUINN, Martha 41

— R —

RAGSDALL, 170
RAINEY HOTEL, 243
RAINEY, 243, 287, Edna Earle 50, Tommy 48
RAINEY-TRULL, 243
RAINS, John A. 10, 12, 14, Nancy Graham 244
RAINS-POOLE, 244
RAMEY, David 58, Louie 244, Peggy 58, Tola 37,
RANDAL, Nancy 12, Harvey 20, Louise Jane 2, Malinda Mahalia Markham 2, Nathaniel Moses 2
RANDEL, William H. 104, Joseph John 245
RAWDON, Maria V. 59
RAY, John 246, Martin 36
RAY-COTTON, 245
RAYBURN, 150
REEVES, Joyce D. 59
RHODES, Carrie 40, David 56, David R. 59, J.W. 55, Revis 40, Tavy Rodger 64
RHUL, Bill 36
RICE, William 246, Sarah (Daily) 246
RICHARDSON, 246, 247, 287, Cletus 20, Don 246, Dorothy 246, Gene 247, Helen 247, James Edward 247, John W. 248, Johnnie 248, Loretta G. 59, Norma 56, P.L. 38, Ruben 248, Tom Y. 249, W.J. 46, William (Will) Henry 249, William Alfred 249, Joseph Andrew (Little Joe) 249
RICHARDSON-EVANS, 247
RICHARDSON-GRINDER, 249
RICHARDSON-HORNER, 247
RICKETTS, Tennesse Roper 249
RICKMAN, B.G. 14, 17
RIGGS, Bob 36
RILEY, 77, David 250, Linda 250, Ellphaz 250
RITCHIE, Mary Crittenden Patterson 250
RITTER, Terry C. 59
ROACH, 250, Denise S. 59
ROBERSON, Sam 251
ROBERTS, Dana G. 59, Eliza (Barnett) 41, John Presley 41, 252, Johnny 37, Martha A. (Barnett) 41, P.M. 41, R.R. 40, W.A. 41, W.M. 46
ROBERTS-BAKER, 251
ROBERTS-BELL, 251
ROBERTS-GORDON, 252
ROBERTSON, 82, 239, 252, 288
ROBERTSON-HORNER, 252
ROBINSON, Brown 40, Ella 40, Jessie 40, Pauline 40
RODEN, Greenberry, 253
RODGERS, 253, 254, Effie 130
RODGERS-ROGERS, 253
ROGERS, 206, 253, Chris 55, Paul 36, Roland, C.P. 39, Roy Lee 254
ROSE, Dave 38, Dottie 38
RUHL, Bill 39
RUSHTON, H.R. 46
RUSSELL, Arthur John Henry 254
RUTLEDGE, Frank 38

— S —

SAIN, Harold 39
SALMON, James 12
SANDERS, Berry 255, Jess 255, Evelyn Dowdy 255, Ora May 255
SAVAGE III, James Cathey 259
SAVAGE JR., James Cathey 259
SAVAGE SR., James C. 258, James Cathey 259
SAVAGE, 256, 257, Alice Kennedy 257, Frank Kennedy 258, Henry Kennedy 258, J.C. 38
SAVAGE-BEASLEY, 256
SAVAGE-CULP, 256
SAVAGE-ELDER, 256
SAVAGE-LEWIS, 256
SAVAGE-POINDEXTER, 257
SAVAGE-SCHNEIDER, 257
SCHNEIDER, 257
SCHOFIELD, John N. 17
SCOTT, James 12
SCROGGINS, John M. 260
SEBELIUS, Carl L. 260
SHANNON, 132
SHARP, 148, 218, 264, Andrew Daniel 260, Alma 40, Edward 261, George F. 261, Martin V. 261, James 261, James Calvin 262, Jasper M. 262, John 262, John B. 262, John Franklin 263, John V. 263, Isaac Handie 263, Isom Haudie 263, Newt 264, Vira Talley 264, R.M. 17, Samuel 264, Samuel Miles 264, S.T. 18, William (Bill) 264, Willis S. 265
SHELTON, 284, Irvine 38, 47, 55
SHEPARD, 265, 36, Egbert Haywood 265, E.H. 36, James William 266, Robert 266, William Haywood (Billy) 266

SHOUSE, M.R. 41
SHY, J. Lewis 16
SIMMONS, Faye 48, James 11, Thomas 14
SIMMONS-PEEBLES, 267
SIMMS, T.W. 46
SIMS, T.W. 46
SISCO, John Thomas 267
SKELTON, Carmack 36, Felix 19, Terry 55
SLATTEN, W. Bruce 59
SLOAN, James Lloyd 16, 38, 267
SMITH, 105, 114, 268, Alex 40, Bernard 40, Cora 40, Harrison 40, Mary, 118, James Marion 268, J.E. 46, John 40, John Thomas 269, Joseph Gaytard 269, Kitty 40, L.B. 55, Mary K. 59, Pearl 40, Simeon 270, Son 40, Warren 14
SMOTHERS, Pinkney L. 270
SMOTHERMAN, Peggy 48
SOUTHALL, Mike 55, Ronny 55
SPARKS, 270, 271, Jesse 47, J. Kent 16, 55
SPARKS-EDWARDS, 270
SPENCER, 271
STAFFORD, John Robert 272
STANLEY, John 12
STARBUCK, Daniel 46, 272
STARK, H.C. 37
STAYROOK, Jacob Theodore 272
STEELE, 273, Gus 5, 6, 47
STEPHENS (STEVENS), 274
STEPHENS, 273, 274, Calvin Ashley 273
STEVENS, 274, Elisha S. 17, Jack 33, Merle 274
STEWART SR., Thomas James 277, William 278
STEWART, Aaron James (Dock) 275, Dorsey B. Thomas (Doss) 275, Elisha 276, Harold Elton (Jack) 276, Mary Etta (Mollie) 276, Milus 38, Morris Monroe 276, Sampson 276, Thomas Lindley 278, William Monroe 279
STORY, C.R. 41, Lydia Graham 279
STRICKLAND, 280, Jewel 37, Lavon 40
STRINGER, Hulon 33
SUMMERS, 280
SURATT, Celia Erwin 32, James Anderson 32, Mary Bess 32
SUTTON, 280, James A. 62, James B. 13, Joshua 281
SWAFFORD, James 281
SWANSON, Sandra Grinder 281
SWEATT, 206
SWEENEY, Joe Burns 282
SWINEY, Hazel Chappell 281

— T —
TANNER, E.E. 41, Wiley 12
TATE, 144, 282, Jessie Gray 44, 283, June Dowland 283
TATUM, 283, 284, John 8, Leven Hillman 284, Sublett 284
TATUM-GRINDER, 283
TATUM-SHELTON, 284
TAYLOR, Dick 40, Jerry 285, Jesse 14, John W. 17, William N. 14
THARP, 163
THOMAS, Charles 38, George 40, Pamela 38, Rederick 40, Ressley 40, R.N. 14, Rosie 40, Roy 40
THOMISON, Anita L. 59
THOMPSON, 199, 285, Brice 16, Violet May (Cotton) 285, W.R. 8
THORNTON, J.A. 36
TIDWELL, Paul H. 53
TILLER, 286
TININ, Tom A. 287
TININ-BRUCE, 286
TININ-RAINEY, 287
TININ-RICHARDSON, 287
TODD, David P. 17, George R.C. 17
TOMERLIN, Milton Green 287
TOOMBS (TOMBS), Garner McConnico 287
TOTTY, James 36
TRACY, John 12
TREADWELL-HINSON, 287
TRIMBLE, Harold 36
TRULL, 109, 243, 289, 290, 293, David 55, 56, 59, J. Howard 36, 39, 289, Saletheal, 289, Sallie Matt 20
TRULL-DENTON, 288
TRULL-HANKINS, 288
TRULL-ROBERTSON, 288
TRULL-WARREN, 289
TUBBS, M.A. 47
TUCKER, 136, 291, Andrew (Andy) 290, Bettye Tiller 291, Billy F. 4, 5, 6, 290, Ethel 20, Frank 290, Glenn 20, Grace 20, G.W. 38, Harlan 290, James O. (Jim) 13, 291, Joseph 12, Kenneth Douglas 291, M.H. 36, Nona 20, Sue 290, Vera 20, 290,
TUCKER-DUCAN, 291
TURNBOW, Godwin 47, Mattie 39, Rosemary E. 59
TURNER, Gordon 36, 57, John 16, Jon K. 59, Mollie Goblet 16
TWILLA, Clara Dell Dudley Bates 63, John H. 44

— V —
VAN DYKE, Frank 39
VAUGHAN, John Locke 292, Sherman B. 59
VAUGHN, A.T. 39, Katie 40

VICKERY, James Owen 292, Jonathan 293
VOSS, 161

— W —
WADE, 193, Charles E. 293, Lorene 20
WADE-TRULL, 293
WAGGONER, Lewis C. 14
WALKER, Alene 38, D. Ellis 36, John Thomas 294, John W. 294, Rupert 38, William B. 295
WALKER-DENSON, 295
WALKER-MALIN, 294
WALLS, Norma 295
WARD SR., Nathan 297
WARD, 96, 121, Billy 295, Betty 295, James Arthur (Boss) 296, James H. 296, Nathan 12, Rendia H. 59, Thomas 56, William 12, 297
WARD, 309
WARREN, 69, 78, 116, 289, 299, 300, Anderson W. 298, Catherine Dowdy 299, Clarence 299, C.N. 47, Gola Ray 300, Jack 38, Jess Willard 41, 300, J.R. 56, Larry A. 59, Loy 37, Mary DePriest 32, Nancy 59, William (Billy) 299,
WARREN-CHESSOR-CURRY, 297
WARREN-DOWDY, 298
WARREN-PARNELL, 298
WARREN-WESTBROOKS, 298
WATSON, 116
WEATHERLY, David 16
WEBB, 301, Gil 59, John 12, John L. 11, 38, 47, Melinda G. 59, Martha Ann Dodson 300, 301, William Carey 14, 17, 300, W.C. 38, 40, 46
WEBSTER, 301, A.H. 18, Dexter 19, Johnnie Leeroy 301, Jerry 19, Jerry Wayne 302
WEEMS, John 12, 302
WELCH, Nicholas 12
WESTBROOK SR., Walter Lafayette 303
WESTBROOK, 302, Thomas Newton 303
WESTBROOKS, 298, Adda Mae 137
WHARTON, Osborne 41, Yancey 41
WHITAKER, J.C. 8
WHITEWELL, Josephine H. 2
WHITFIELD, S.D.H. 17
WHITWELL, 304, Dewey 32, George Dibbrell 304, John Randel 304, 47, Kent Franklin 304, Thomas 8, 46, Willis H. 17,
WIGGS, A.W. 16, Abigail Allen 305, J.W. 38, 47, William 305, W.J. 47
WILDER, Jacquelyn G. 59, Steven D. 59
WILEY, 121, Alexander F. 305

WILKINS, B.C. 36, Clement 306, James 12, Jomimma (Jan) Baugus 306
WILLIAMS, 84, Michele M. 59, Traci H. 59
WILLIAMS-WILLIAMSON, Jency Jane 306
WILSDORF, Elmer Lewis 306, Roy P. 55
WOOD, 308, 309, Ben 41, 59, Ernest 41 Freelinhuyson 307, Jeremiah H. 307, James Lafayette 307, James Oscar 308, West 10, 12, 308, William 308
WORLEY, 309
WORLEY-WARD, 309
WYATT, 70

— Y —

YARBRO, Billy R. 59
YARBROUGH, Joe 36
YATES, James 10, 12
YORK, Anita 38, J.W. 41, Tim 38
YOUNG, 309, Clifford 37, H.J. 14, Jack, 309, John 12, Louise 20,

Perry County Auto Company, left to right: Arthur Batton, owner; "Chigger" Long, child; unidentified; George Lancaster; Clabe Warren, 1922.

Family Tree

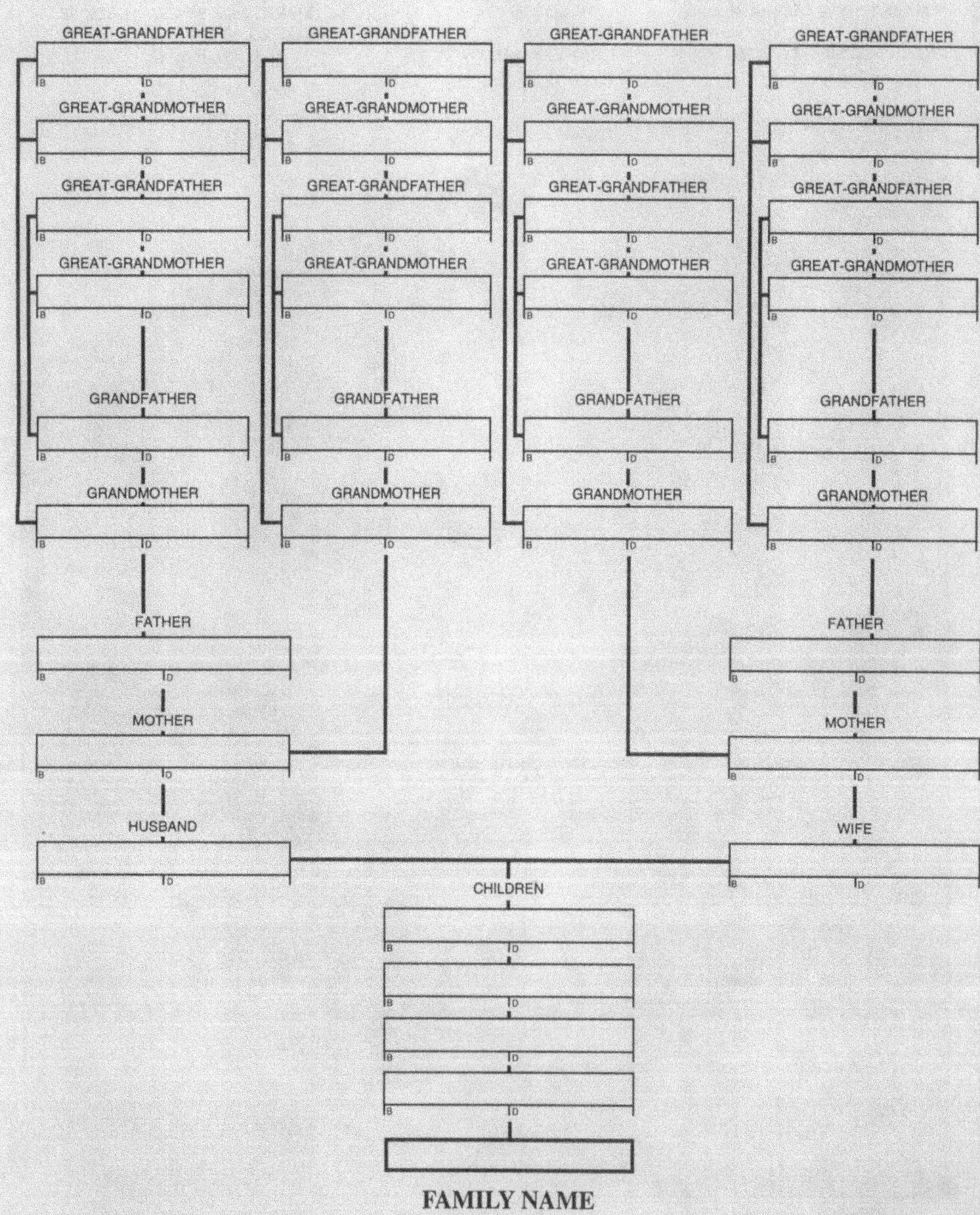

FAMILY NAME

Family Record

NAME	BIRTH		DEATH	
	Date	Place	Date	Place

Family Record

NAME	BIRTH		DEATH	
	Date	Place	Date	Place